CHRISTGAU'S RECORD GUIDE: THE '80S

ALSO BY ROBERT CHRISTGAU

ANY OLD WAY YOU CHOOSE IT

ROCK ALBUMS OF THE '70S: A CRITICAL GUIDE

CHRISTGAU'S
RECORD GUIDE:

〜〜〜〜〜〜〜〜〜〜〜〜〜〜〜〜〜〜

THE '80s

ROBERT CHRISTGAU

PANTHEON BOOKS
NEW YORK

Christgau, Robert.
    Christgau's record guide: the '80s / by Robert
Christgau.
    p. cm.
    ISBN 0-679-73015-X
    1. Sound recordings—Reviews. 2. Rock music—Discography.
I. Title. II. Title: Record guide.
ML156.9.C533 1990
016.78242166'0266—dc20   90-52512
                                              MN

Book Design by Maura Fadden Rosenthal
Manufactured in the United States of America
First Edition

FOR NINA · · · · · I'm done, wanna go to the park?

CONTENTS

ACKNOWLEDGMENTS

Because I've never abandoned the unethical practice of soliciting musical opinions from friends and acquaintances and then incorporating the niftier ones into my work, more than the usual countless number of people contributed to this book. And the publicists who have sent me background material and answered factual questions about albums reviewed in this book number in the hundreds. But M. Mark, Kit Rachlis, and Doug Simmons, my editors at *The Village Voice,* have all improved my reviewing in more specific ways. And for continuing conversational stimulation I must single out my friends and colleagues Greil Marcus, Roger Trilling, Georgia Christgau, Steve Levi, John Piccarella, John Rockwell, Nelson George, Vince Aletti, Simon Frith, Greg Tate, John Morthland, Poobah Emeritus Tom Carson, Steve Anderson, Stanley Crouch, Deborah Frost, Barry Michael Cooper, Joe Levy, Robert Sietsema, and Marshall Berman. In the '80s I was affluent enough to leave my filing and schlepping to underemployed smart people who ended up contributing to my intellectual weal as well: Robert Baskett, David Mikics, Steve Anderson, Holly Fairbank, the great Jeff Salamon, Julian Dibbell (who we'll meet again), yeoman collater and fact-checker David Schweitzer, Emily Marcus, and Margaret Logan. Robert Cohen of Manhattan's Finyl Vinyl (East Coast source for classic American music; in California try Alameda's Downhome) provided invaluable advice on the rock library. And lots of folks lent me records (many of which I have now home-taped, heh-heh): Vince Aletti, Brian Chin, Georgia Christgau, Sebastian Dangerfield, Randall Grass, Tom Hull and His Amazing Database, Ben Mapp, Greil Marcus, Jon Pareles, John Piccarella, Kit Rachlis, Ira Robbins (professional courtesy beyond the call of professional responsibility), John Rockwell, Doug Simmons, and Tom Smucker. Finally, Geoffrey Stokes lent me records and advice last time and got left out of that book, so here he is now.

I consulted hundreds of books in a decade's writing, but a few deserve special mention. Joel Whitburn's *Billboard* guides—especially *Top Pop Albums* and *The Billboard Book of Top 40 Hits*—are invaluable sources for anybody who still thinks pop music ought to be popular. Ronnie Graham's

Da Capo Guide to Contemporary African Music is every Afropop fan's bible. And Ira Robbins's *New Trouser Press Record Guide* is competition to be proud of and nervous about. Ira and I have always had serious critical differences, but I depended on his fanatical accuracy in dozens if not hundreds of cases and occasionally used his and his collaborators' reviews to jumpstart one of my own.

This book was originally planned with Pantheon's Wendy Goldwyn, who passed it on to Wendy Wolf when she decided to change careers. And Wendy Wolf saw it through to the end—even after she had resigned from Pantheon, she made time from the turmoil of her own life to provide both practical and editorial advice. At Pantheon, Frances Jalet-Miller, Patra McSharry, and copy chief extraordinaire Ed Cohen were also generous with their attention. Marisa Brunetti and Lesley Oelsner made permissions less onerous than they might have been; Terri Hinte and Bob Merlis dropped in some good words; and Leslie Berman went out and got the damn things. And from start to finish, my agent Bob Cornfield was there when I needed him, as usual.

But two people with the same last name deserve the biggest thanks. As the project began, I was paying Julian Dibbell chickenfeed to collate the *Village Voice* columns the book was based on. By the time it ended, no one except me had put more thought into it. He copy-edited the entire manuscript, but he also functioned as a de facto text editor, working deep into many nights to clean up my obscurities without homogenizing my style. As for Julian's Aunt Carola, she's my wife. Like many mamas, she doesn't have as much time for music as she once did. But she knows what I need from her, and whenever she observed me flagging, on the book or one of the hundred-plus columns that went into it, she would gird herself up and offer what I treasure: her opinion. Carola and I collaborate monthly in *Video Review,* and on occasion I've borrowed words and sentences from that work as if they were my own. I plan to crib from her like crazy until she writes more criticism herself. I can't lose—either I get her going or I look like a wise guy.

INTRODUCTION

DECADE

Let's wrap it up, OK?

The '80s were above all a time of international corporatization, as one major after another gave it up to media moguls in Europe and Japan. By 1990, only two of the six dominant American record companies were head-quartered in the U.S. Bizzers acted locally while thinking globally in re audiences/markets (will it sell in Germany? Australia? Venezuela? Indonesia now that we've sunk the pirates? the U.S.S.R.?) and artists/suppliers (world music was a concept whose geoeconomic time had come). After a feisty start, independent labels accepted farm-team status that could lead to killings with the bigs. Cross-promotional hoohah became the rule—the soundtrack album, the sponsored tour, the golden-oldie commercial, the T-shirt franchise, the video as song ad and pay-for-play programming and commodity fetish. Record executives became less impresarios than arbitragers, speculating in abstract bundles of rights whose physical characteristics meant little or nothing to them. Rock was mere music no longer. It was reconceived as intellectual property, as a form of capital itself.

The '80s were when stars replaced artists as bearers of significance. The '70s had yielded their honorable quota of Van Morrisons and Randy Newmans and Patti Smiths and John Prines, all of whom were still around, as were new variants like Blood Ulmer and Laurie Anderson and the Mekons and Kid Creole. Those are only my nominees, however; yours are different. Nobody blinked when break-even commercial nonentities like Morrison and Newman were ranked with the Stones and Stevie Wonder among the crucial rockers of the '70s. But in the '80s the only list that computed was pure megaplatinum—Prince and Bruce and U2 and Michael Jackson and Madonna, with maybe a few million-selling status symbols like Sting, Talking Heads, R.E.M., or Public Enemy (sorry, not Elvis Costello) tacked on for appearance's sake. When art is intellectual property, image and aura subsume aesthetic substance, whatever exactly that is. When art is capital, sales interface with aesthetic quality—*Thriller*'s numbers are part of its experience.

The '80s were when '70s fragmentation became a way of life. The "adult contemporary" market flashed its charge cards as the teen audience became more distinct than at any time since the Beatles. Even within a domestic market that counted for so much smaller a piece of the whole burrito, enormous new subsets arose, from rap's slouch-strutting B-boys to the affluently spiritual ex-bohemians of new age. Tiny subsets got serviced, too—by hardcore crazies and lesbian singer-songwriters and disco recidivists and jazzbo eclectics and shit-rockers and Christians and a dozen varieties of messenger from the African diaspora. The metal and country audiences split at previously invisible seams; folk music came back. Leading the semipopular parade as it exploited an unpaid army of interns was college radio, a growth industry designed to expose American college dropouts with day jobs, hungry hopefuls from enterprising Britannia, and other marginal pros who'd made a cult for themselves. Behind every subset were small-time entrepreneurs with vision; when and if profits mounted, these visionaries were reimbursed for their foresight by somebody with better distribution. The system worked so equitably that sometimes a subset would end up with some sense of itself, and sometimes a visionary would have money in the bank when the dealing stopped.

The '80s were when rock became less and more political. After the Clash faltered, white musicians who considered popularity a good thing left revolution to the Tracy Chapmans and Public Enemys to come. But with a few dismaying exceptions (Neil Young, Paul Westerberg, Joan Jett) and a few predictable ones (Johnny Ramone, John Anderson, Duran Duran), rock-and-rollers had no use for the reactionary chiefs of state pollsters said their demographic supported (pollsters also discovered that clubgoers constituted America's most electorally apathetic subculture). In the U.K. Paul Weller worked to revive Labour, in the U.S. Bruce Springsteen turned union benefactor, and from Amnesty International to the Prince's Trust, charity/cause records/concerts/tours signified varying admixtures of rock resistance and rock responsibility. The socially conscious lyric didn't displace the love song, but politics became a sexy pop topic; by a strange coincidence, rampant reactionaries and responsible liberals united in a censorship drive at around the same time. Dylan was big in Tiananmen Square. Ad hoc groups of democratic socialists (and secret reactionaries, just like in the '60s) sang "Imagine" and "Give Peace a Chance" all over Eastern Europe.

The '80s took rock sexuality and rock sexism over the top. Where Bono and Springsteen epitomized sensitive macho—not primarily sex symbols, they were free to flaunt their heterosexual normality—Prince and Michael Jackson were gender-unspecific and proud. One kinky, the other neuter, they did less than nothing to ease the suspicion that straight, potent black males remained unacceptable fantasy figures in mainstream America. Not that kink could go all the way—it was fashionably unshaven George Michael, not drag queen Boy George, who packed lasting squeal appeal, and it was a Prince song about Nikki jacking off that inspired Mrs. Sen. Gore to found the PMRC. Soon glam-metal studs with hair down to here were taking pseudoblues woman-bashing to ugly new extremes of backlash, and presumably straight, presumably potent rappers were rendering their instinctive radicalism half-useless with street misogyny that made Blackie Lawless sound like a game-show host. As a historical corrective, the late '80s ushered in the folkie postmadonna—often punky or dykey, always autonomous, sometimes even funny. The '80s were also good to women with axes, hard-rock bimbos, and sexually assertive females who called their own shots. Cyndi Lauper got away with a song about Cyndi jacking off. Madonna got into trouble giving head to a saint.

The '80s were a time of renewed racial turmoil after ten-plus years of polite resegregation. As they began, AOR was 99 percent white, and Ray Parker Jr., who later created the decade's preeminent kiddie anthem, couldn't get on pop radio because he was "too r&b"; as they ended, AOR was 98 percent white, and the Beastie Boys, who earlier created the decade's best-selling rap album, couldn't get on "urban" radio because they had "no street credibility." In between came the "Beat It" video, *Purple Rain, Yo! MTV Raps,* Professor Griff, Living Colour vs. Guns N' Roses, and race-baiting comedians who entered to "Whipping Post" the way white-and-proud rock bands entered to "Also Sprach Zarathustra."

Technology changed everything in the '80s. Cable brought us MTV and the triumph of the image. Synthesizers inflected the sounds that remained. Sampling revolutionized rock and roll's proprietary relationship to its own history. Cassettes made private music portable—and public. Compact discs inflated profitability as they faded into the background of busy lives.

The '80s were contradictory. The '80s were incomprehensible. The '80s weren't as much fun as they should have been.

MUSIC PROCESSING

That was rock in the '80s, all right. But for better or worse, this isn't a book about rock in the '80s. It's a book about rock records—rock albums—in the '80s, and the '80s have taught us (hammered home the old truth, really) that records don't equal rock and roll. Which doesn't mean, unfortunately, that a book about the records of the '80s is immune to the aforementioned complications. There's no way any decent critic can respond to records without bumping up against every one of them now and then. But there's also no way a mere record reviewer can address them systematically. If this guide isn't fun, I should go into another line of work. But for sure it's always partial and often contradictory. And though I don't believe it's incomprehensible, I'd never claim it was comprehensive.

Every month I write capsule reviews of 20 albums and arrange them alphabetically by artist into a *Village Voice* column called the Consumer Guide. Those columns are the basis of this book. Mostly I cover "rock," but I've felt free to wander ever since falling for Terry Riley's *A Rainbow in Curved Air* in 1970, and in the '80s, with categories crumbling all around me, I wandered plenty: in addition to "accessible" "downtown" "classical" items, relevant (note fudge-word) jazz, and hard-edged or crossover-prone country, all of which I'd been paying some heed since the middle '70s, I dipped early and often into the international musics that trickled and then flowed my way. But by no means did my tastes prove catholic or impartial—they wouldn't be tastes if they were. I've never really gotten salsa, and to this day the only Caribbean or Latin American music I know well is reggae, although albums from Trinidad and Cuba and the Antilles and Haiti and Brazil and Argentina and Colombia and Chile and El Salvador have won my heart. And though China and Algeria and various European countries are represented, you'll hardly notice them amid the dozens upon dozens of records from sub-Saharan Africa, which for me proved the decade's great untapped pop mine.

About three-quarters of the nearly three thousand reviews appear pretty much as originally written. Those that don't fall into five categories: stuff I missed, stuff I botched, best-ofs, EPs, and 1980 (which is when I was crushing out the '70s book). To add contemporaneity and give myself a head start, I've tried to base new and rewritten reviews on scraps and exegeses from my other writing of the time—the Guide's Additional Consumer News appendix, longer *Voice* reviews and essays, regular work for *Playboy* and *Video Review*—but even so some five hundred are previously unpublished down to the last phrase.

So is almost everything in the back, divided once again into Subjects for Further Research (substantial artists meriting a paragraph of general comment), Distinctions Not Cost-Effective (minor or over-the-hill artists good for a one-liner), and Meltdown (bad artists worthy of opprobrium). I've also provided a brief glossary, cross-referenced the compilations and soundtracks that proved such quintessential '80s forms, and compiled a list called New Wave, two hundred postpunk bands and individuals whose hype, word-of-mouth, or good first impression induced me to give their LPs or EPs at least two (usually three or more) complete plays. To me this list seemed a symptom of the age. Some of these artists are well-regarded, others utterly obscure. Many toward the top gave me pleasure, a few toward the bottom made me mad. But in my opinion, not one wound up deserving more space than it took to spell their, his, or her name right.

Such calls are even more subjective than most critical judgments: picking twenty albums a month from the plethora of competent-plus professional and semiprofessional releases kept getting harder as the '80s proceeded. I worried constantly that I should give people one more try, but in a hundred individual instances the overproduction of self-expression made that impossible. So I did what I could to weigh the two decisive general criteria, importance and quality. Importance divided into cultural impact (commercial or occasionally just sociopolitical reach, with added panache preferred), subcultural acclaim (especially from rock criticism's producers and consumers, but also from alternative radio and dance DJs), and past performance (increasingly problematic as more and more artists truck on into middle age). Quality boiled down to my grading system. Consumer Guide reviews end with grades that in theory run from A+ down to E−, though grades below C− have always been rare and in the '80s virtually disappeared—I'd be surprised if there are more than three dozen in the book. The '70s edition offered an amusing table defining each grade, but this time I'd like to lay them out less schematically. I'd like to tell you about B+ records.

In school, B+ is a good grade—almost any student will settle for the near-excellence it implies. It's a compliment in the Consumer Guide too. No record gets a B+ unless half its tracks provide notable satisfaction; few get a B+ unless at some point I want to hear the thing when it's not on and I'm still enjoying it after five or so plays. B+ is my cutoff point—it's what I listen for. Any B+ record I find I write about. And I come up with a lot of them. B+ is the most common grade in this book—the mode, as statisticians say. It's also the median—as many records are B+ or above as B+ or below. In fact, B+'s are so numerous that at least 60 percent of the records reviewed herein get a B+ or better. This means I must not be such a contrary bastard, even if I have a funny way of handing out compliments—complaining about stuff that could be better or isn't as good as it's said to be. And it also means that close to two-thirds of the records I write about give me a charge. But before you get too jealous, recall that New Wave list, then ponder the thousand or so bands that didn't make the two-play cut—with "new wave" accounting for a third of my listening at most. More labels than I can count have me on their lists, and when I don't get something I phone or write away, occasionally even seek out imports and indie product retail. For more than twenty years, my worklife has been structured around an unromantically systematic weeding-out process. I'm a music processor.

Once upon a time I tried to listen to everything I got, but these days I divide the loot into a few items I hope to get to forthwith, many I'll try to play sooner or later, and even more that I stockpile lest my trend-seeking colleagues or the all-knowing public latch onto something I took for a piece of shit. Whenever I'm home I stack records on my elderly BIC record changer (pardon the vinyl fetishism for now—I'll get to cassettes and CDs in due time), usually from a special pile of 100–150 records under active consideration, often with something as yet unheard slipped in. As I go about my business I notice details and conduct a semiconscious sort. Most of the six records remain in current-play, but a few get shifted closer to limbo, or out into the reference collection, or into the heap awaiting my next visit to the warehouse, or onto the discard pile. And every once in a while I get a bead on something and write it up, although usually that phase takes more planning.

I try to play things that one way or another suit my mood, but only rarely while I'm working will I play a record solely because I feel like hearing it. If rock criticism wasn't such a good job—if I didn't enjoy my work—I wouldn't be able to do it at all, because I'd no longer be any kind of fan, and thus would have no feeling for the fans I write for. But it is a job, and one of my qualifications is that I don't bore easy. My chief complaint is that I don't have more time for the good stuff.

Forget B+'s. I've replayed a lot of B+'s over the past year, just to make sure I hadn't overrated anything, and most of them sounded fine. But unless duty calls or a visitor makes a request, chances are I'll never find the opportunity to listen to them again. And even if we climb up to A level, the bulk is overwhelming. An A— is a record with at least one intensely enjoyable or rewarding side, plus extra goodies when you turn it over. An A has two such sides, very convenient with the new prestige longform rendering the whole concept of the side obsolete. And an A+ is a record you want to play over and over—essentially, a record you never get tired of. In the '80s most A+'s were granted retrospectively, either to A records like Sign "O" the Times and Born in the U.S.A., which always sounded really great when I had occasion to play them again, or—and this is the big one—to A records like Omona Wapi and In a Special Way, which I actually wanted to play over and over once I was done writing about them.

I hope this strikes most of my readers as strange. I hope they're not just collectors or compulsive consumers—I hope they return often to the records they like best. But consider the numbers. In the '70s, I found more than 500 A-level albums; in the '80s, the figure was up 35 percent, to over 650. There's no such thing as speed listening, so at a modest estimated mean length of forty minutes it would take some 220 hours to get through every '80s A. Once. That's five-and-a-half forty-hour weeks, nine twelve-hour-a-day weekends. It would be work—pleasure as work, more fun than my job and probably yours, but work nevertheless. This little piece of strange-but-true plays right into the theory of my colleague Simon Frith, who's fond of saying that the '80s turned leisure into responsibility—thus rendering it, let me add, contradictory and incomprehensible and sometimes not-fun. Even as a culture of supposed surfeit was transformed into a culture of supposed scarcity, option overload continued to fuck with our minds.

POSTPUNK-POSTDISCO FUSION

In 1980, when I brought forth a comparable book about the '70s, I was untroubled by such dark thoughts. Taking for granted the theoretically depressing themes of fragmentation and the semipopular whilst thumbing my nose at '60s crybabyism, I argued that the '70s were when the music had come into its own: only *after* countercultural upheaval could individual musicians buck rationalization's conformist tide to create oeuvres and one-shots of spunk and substance in the belly of the pop beast. It helped that I got off on the '70s more than most rock and roll lifers—I thought Steely Dan and Lynyrd Skynyrd were great bands then, and I still do—and it also helped that the future looked bright. Just like some '70s-haters, I felt as if the punk insurrection had been designed to my specifications, unpredictability included. For all its antihippie rhetoric, punk meant to make something of a not dissimilar cultural upheaval, only without the '60s' icky, and fatal, softheadedness.

From this vantage I can see that my confidence was bolstered by a consensus more sustaining than what I got out of Monterey or Woodstock or Chicago '68 or the Mobilization or any number of excellent Grateful Dead concerts. The core of this consensus was colleagues and correspondents of shared yet far-flung musical enthusiasms, its body and soul the cohort that materialized at any number of punk-etc. gigs. On the one hand, an inferred community of music-lovers cum discophiles; on the other, a lived-in community of music-lovers cum night people. Predicated here on a shitload of discrete sound-objects whose aesthetic was so legible you could build a canon around it, there on a burgeoningly inchoate scene that didn't shrivel up and die when the Sex Pistols quit on us. Predicated here on the biz, there on bohemia.

For anybody who loved punk, 1980 was an exciting time, because punk's flakstorm, christened postpunk in the twinkling of a convolution, was still raging. Just like real revolutionary movements, punk was at its best before the world got it down, but that doesn't mean its diffusion into strictly musical issues was a perversion—a view now promulgated by true believers as well as dilettantes who've gone on to better things. Maybe John Rotten-Lydon hated rock and roll, but we loved the stuff—and we were sure we understood it better than the keepers of the pop machine. However reduced our spiritual ambitions, the growing legions of postpunk fans and postpunk musicians were fighting all kinds of battles as the decade began—for airplay, for venues, for viable business structures. And by any reasonable standard we won those battles. Commercial radio is as reactionary as ever, but the college variety gets more music to more people than Tom Donahue ever dreamed. The painfully nurtured alternative club circuit is now so taken for granted that every breach in its integrity is bewailed as an attack on the natural order. And though the Record Industry Association of America didn't know it, there were more records available to the dedicated fan in the '80s than in the glut years of the middle '70s—certainly more of spunk if not substance. No one can know how many more only because no one sees all of them, not with the engine of production a profusion of sporadically distributed independent and import labels, many very specialized or local, for whom a run of five thousand spells hit.

In some sense these labels are still the biz, obviously. But it's just as obvious that they aren't the same biz we assumed in postpunk's early days. Even though we meant to retool the pop machine, we still depended on it to belch out major music—*Rumours* and *Rust Never Sleeps* and *Dancer With Bruised Knees,* Roxy Music and Chic and Donna Summer. Though intergenerational aesthetic comprehension was already eroding, the banal notion that the biz was the root of all banality was not yet an article of faith, because the biz was still where records came from. Young CBGBites may not have thought *Rumours* was a better album than *Talking Heads 77,* or *Some Girls* a better album than *This Year's Model,* but at least they recognized all four as competing aesthetic objects—accepted the terms of the comparison. So when in early 1979 I asked the gods of history for a fusion of the two great subcultural musics of the '70s, the smart punk then establishing a commercial beachhead and the dumb disco then sopping up venture capital, my petition was regarded as misguided, but not preposterous by definition.

I'll say. All over the place, in the biz and bohemia and then unknown scenes between, that's exactly what happened. Soon it became clear that punk wasn't just an attitude with the lineaments of a movement—it was also a rhythm onto which partisans projected an attitude. Simple and unswinging, fast to frenetic, what John Piccarella dubbed the "forcebeat" moved bodies in a way the Allman Brothers—to choose the archetypal boogie band (and with two drummers, too)—did not. And of course, so did a disco pulse that whatever its polyrhythmic gestalt could also be pretty simple—a disco pulse that at its most mechanical consisted of a kickdrum booming away

130 times a minute. It wasn't at all preposterous to put them together into "DOR" (for dance-oriented rock), and soon punk types were hotfooting something slightly more elegant than the pogo. So even as the biz withdrew its support from a disco subculture it had smothered half to death, it began investing in various dancy punk offshoots from England that eventually produced not just such fringe phenomena as industrial and acid house, but the so-called New Pop and the so-called Second British Invasion.

Except for a short-lived New York white-funk tendency, DOR action was sporadic among U.S. bands, who soon adopted a broad orthodoxy—the guitar-oriented garage aesthetic. But with a few hints from transplanted Jamaicans (a crucial Britpunk inspiration, too), kids in Harlem and the South Bronx had already put their own version of punk attitude in effect. Aggressively minimalist, rejecting the pop status quo and stripping music down to what they liked, the early rappers responded to pretty much the same sense of simultaneous surfeit and constriction that their white counterparts downtown couldn't stand, and in pretty much the same way. The big difference was that they didn't have the luxury of regarding their music as a way out—instead, they tried to make it a way in. And though it took years—live rap began around the same time as live punk, but the first rap record wasn't released until 1979, and not until 1984 were there rap albums in any quantity—that's what it became.

As I write, many pop savants are arguing that disco ended up changing rock and roll more than punk, but this theory is just a provocative way of deflating conventional wisdom. Disco sure didn't change *rock* more than punk did—rock as opposed to rock and roll, the artistically self-conscious music that made the critical analysis of rock and roll inevitable. Long ago I defined "rock" as "all music deriving primarily from the energy and influence of the Beatles—and maybe Bob Dylan, and maybe you should stick pretensions in there someplace." Now I would have to add, "only that stuff has gotten old, so these days I spend most of my time on music deriving primarily from the energy and influence of the Sex Pistols—and maybe Talking Heads, and maybe you should stick, er, postpretensions in there someplace." Because insofar as rock and roll is an object of critical scrutiny—and you'd best believe this tome is full of crit—the '80s belonged to postpunk.

Though punk's program failed on both sides of the Atlantic, its adherents made up in commitment what they lacked in numbers, setting off a countertradition of deep-to-compulsive change. As producers, they founded the alternative biz and infiltrated all aspects of the established biz; as consumers, they supported a retail network designed to adapt. They seized college radio and helped define import-oriented disco record pools. They were among the first white people to take rap seriously or to think rap was fun; they identified with styles from foreign lands. In old fart mode, postpunk zealots proved even more self-righteous than diehard hippies, howling with rage when anyone pointed out that hip hop was taking on the world while indie rock ate its own tail. And there had always been a disco version of all this alternative action—often the original version. But at its best postpunk was open in a way disco wasn't: CBGBites got into Chic more readily than Fun House regulars got into the Ramones, and liked African dance music more than most dancers. And because indie-rockers weren't so hungry for a way in, their independence was more principled. When parental-warning stickers became an issue, for instance, dance labels favored accommodating censorship forces. Rock indies resisted.

Good for them—they had right on their side. But note that the rock labels had less to lose by not compromising—except perhaps for a few metal specialists, they had little interest in or hope of reaching the kind of audience serviced by the chain stores and rack jobbers demanding the warnings. Having learned to make their margin by selling to the converted in specialty shops, indie rock had given up on what's construed as the "mass" audience. And by and large the product reflected this—even when it was really good (as opposed to pretty good, which was far more common), it had no reach. Dance/rap music, on the other hand, was something of a national sensation by decade's end, and while it would be foolish to go on about the nobility of its manufacturers—profit was without doubt their first consideration—it would be cynical to dismiss their aesthetic principles, or to deny that their music did as much as indie rock to keep its audience alive and kicking, maybe even thinking. It wasn't only money they'd be sacrificing if they were banned from the malls. It was impact. They liked having impact. Who wouldn't?

THE MEANING OF ROCK

That's one of the many questions this book will glance off without answering. It has everything to do with rock and roll but much less to do with the record reviewing that for more than twenty years has been the cornerstone of my criticism. To the extent that most artists' careers can be understood in terms of their musical output, and that as far as history is concerned this output will consist of record albums, the method still makes sense. But with Madonna a legitimate contender for rock hero of the decade, its limitations are definitely showing. I've always been relentless about consistency. Sure the lead cuts are great, I'd scoff, but can you name anything else on the record? To many discerning consumers, however, consistency is now at best a bonus—they want three good songs. The '80s were terrible for singles sales, but only in metal, rap, and new age (and rarely there) did albums go platinum without a promotional boost from a "hit" single. MTV is a singles medium, as is "adult contemporary" radio; even AOR devotes the contemporary portion of its programming to putative singles. Not counting dance DJs—who kept the single alive with twelve-inches but would groove to anything, the odd LP track included—the album's only significant new outlet was college radio.

Nor would I swear any longer to the ultimate importance of individual artists' recording careers—of oeuvres and one-shots that as often as not emanate from safely outside the belly of the pop beast. Without doubt there's a sense in which rock criticism's subject has always been a cultural organism that doesn't generate fixed meanings—whose meanings are defined not just by artists (even collectively), but by "noncreative" workers in the distribution network and, crucially, by fans who convert product to their own uses. And while it's philistine to pretend that the music has no formal attractions of its own, that it doesn't produce works that impinge unaided upon those who know the language, it's evasive if not effete to make too much of the microcosm those works create.

Basically, this dilemma was the ground of the "rockism" debate that raged through the U.K. music press in the early '80s. Rockism wasn't just liking Yes and the Allman Brothers—it was liking *London Calling*. It was taking the music seriously, investing any belief at all not just in its self-sufficiency, which is always worth challenging, but in its capacity to change lives or express truth. One result of this debate was that as the '80s ended, the hippest and most fruitful rockcrit fashion pumped functional pop that fetishizes its own status as aural construct over rock that just goes ahead and *means*. This schema was convenient in a couple of ways. For one thing, the blanker music is the more you can project on it—the more listeners, especially professional interpreters, can bend it to their own whimsies, fantasies, needs. And rarely has it been noted how blatantly the rockism debate that produced the fashion favored the growing nationalism/anti-Americanism of U.K. taste.

I mean, really—British rock has always been "pop." Irony, distance, and the pose have been its secret since the Beatles and the Stones, partly because that's the European way and partly because rock wasn't originally British music—having absorbed it secondhand, Brits who made too much of their authenticity generally looked like fools. This polarity was reversed briefly around 1976—American punk was an unabashed art pose, while the British variant carried the banner of class struggle. But when the Sex Pistols failed to usher in the millennium, lifelong skeptics who'd let their guard down for a historical moment vowed that they wouldn't get fooled again. Ergo, Rock Against Rockism.

For all the hybrids and exceptions, American rock really is more sincere, even today. Or anyway, American rockers *act* more sincere—they're so uncomfortable with the performer's role that they strive to minimize it. Often their modus operandi is a conscious, and rather joyless, fakery. But sometimes—and here's where the schema becomes a lie—they end up inhabiting amazing simulations of their real selves, whatever exactly those are. The early '80s proved an especially rich time for this aesthetic, especially in L.A., where singer-songwriter sincerity had been perfected a decade before. So roots-conscious postpunk Amerindies X, Los Lobos, and the Blasters, together with two Twin Cities bands, the virtuosically post-hardcore Hüsker Dü and the roots/junk-inflected quasihardcore Replacements, were spearheading a U.S. rockism revival just as the New Pop was dwarfing a U.K. indie scene symbolized by Joy Division–styled gloom merchants.

Antirockism had no way of accounting for these bands, and now in effect claims that they never happened. After all, who did they reach? Sloppy American college boys and similar pretentious punters—not real people (or classy ones, either). I'm exaggerating, of course, although I do recall a U.K. Los Lobos review that took offense at their flannel-covered bellies. And certainly it's true that Amerindie garage orthodoxy, which is at least as narrow-minded as any more wittingly trendy musical ethos, seems close to the end of its rope. But *Wild Gift* and *How Will the Wolf Survive?* and *Hard Line* and *Metal Circus* and *Let It Be* remain. They impinged on me then, and they impinge on me now—I know, because I replayed every one while making this a book I can vouch for. For me, they hold up, stand the test of time, reveal new shades of meaning—all that stuff good art was supposed to do back in the modernist era. Rock lives.

Presumably, this comes as no news to my core readership. If the Consumer Guide has a typical consumer, he's a sloppy college boy or similar pretentious punter, and he treasures at least a couple of the albums just named. But that doesn't mean he knows exactly why, and especially since one nice thing about the past ten years is how elastic that "similar" has proven to be—my favorite fan letter of the decade was written by a thirty-seven-year-old black woman with an Italian surname and a newfound thirst for classic country music, and I hear from lots of postpunks who've kept the faith in his or her own fashion—I feel obliged to put the aesthetic in general terms before moving on to the exceptions that have made antirockism fruitful and necessary. Because the embarrassing truth is that the rock meaningfulness in which all the great Amerindie bands traffic is in the end a matter of words.

The canard that rock critics only care about words has a history so long that around the dawning of James Taylor there was a smidgen of truth to it. But the most genteel songpoetry shill always knew he or she was in it for the song, not the poetry, and since punk, critics no less than songwriters have been acutely aware of music and especially musicians. The '80s were replete with singer-songwriters who refused to stop there. The Replacements' Paul Westerberg (who's been keeping an ear on Bob Mould and Exene Cervenka since Hüsker Dü and X broke up) exemplifies the auteur quote unquote who prefers the expressive discipline and limitations of a band; so does John Cougar Mellencamp. Sting, that pompous ass, exemplifies the opposite (and so does Bob Mould, though Exene is hanging in there). Though the bands critics like best are rarely virtuosic, they generate their own unmistakable *sounds:* X and Hüsker Dü and the Smiths and Talking Heads and countless lesser entities can be ID'd without vocals inside of eight bars. Yet nobody would be interested in these bands without vocals.

This isn't just because the vocalists are essential and usually dominant musically—it's because the lyrics they articulate (or slur) make the music mean. They specify it, sharpen its bite. And at whatever level of change-your-life, cognitive dissonance, sound example, comforting half-truth, or craven banality, meaning—or anyway, the show of meaning—is something audiences still expect from popular music. So from garage to garret to private studio to pop factory, from Big Black to Red Crayola to Al Green to Milli Vanilli, we're inundated with well-made songs—well-made not because they revitalize the European concert tradition with jazzy harmonic apercus, as polite little well-made songs are supposed to, but because they yoke sense and/or nonsense to sound and/or noise, often aided by a hook sending in mnemonic reinforcements. Original genius as highbrows define it isn't the point—that's one reason pop truth feels social. Hard-felt expressive lyrics as well as cynically crafted manipulative ones resuscitate clichés, and the basic compositional strategy is recycle and cut-and-paste, if not in the melody then in the arrangement, which as rhythm rises to the top is where the music lives.

One reason the '80s were so disquieting for rock-and-rollers, though, is that this perceptual process has gotten less reliable. Even the best songs don't always impact the way they used to. That's partly just fragmentation as a way of life—the sense that you share a song with an audience is another reason pop truth feels social. But it's also because there are so many great songs. Time was, only a few adepts and the occasional lucky duck knew how to bring one off, but remember, when Leiber & Stoller were coming up people wondered when some superman would finally high-jump seven feet. Now the high school record—by a kid from Athens, Georgia, of all places— is seven-six, and well-made rock and roll songs are commonplace, one more instance of the industrialized world's endemic cultural overproduction.

This means there's a sense in which the whole rockism debate was a response to overproduction—that in a much more vulgar way than was immediately apparent it was yet another chapter in the cycle of feverish excitement and premature boredom that has ruled Britannia's pop taste since the teddy boys. Nevertheless, the crisis is real, augmented by the formal exhaustion that becomes inevitable when thousands of skilled crafts-people poke around the same parameters at the same time. Granted that theories of formal exhaustion are too tautological to explain much, and that the right artist in the right place at the right time can make them look ridiculous—who would have believed that Neil Young would make one of 1989's best albums out of the same materials he'd been messing with for twenty-one years and throwing away for eight or nine? Of course there'll still be high-impact songs created as I've described above, in "rock" and sometimes in "pop" too. Utilizing the traditional verbal language of rock and roll, with its gauche blank patches and unliterary colloquial logic and sudden flashes of axiomatic plainspeech, some of them will impinge on our collective life, and many of them will affect individual lives. Many albums full of such songs are recommended in this book. But the fact remains that the game has changed—even sloppy college boys know there has to be something else out there. And there is.

MUSIC GAP

Between 1980 and 1990, rock evolved drastically, meaningfully, essentially, and crucially—though not self-sufficiently—as music. Mere music. Most of the innovators ignored the melodic and harmonic details that fascinate trained music critics, and while art-rock types made their contributions, it was along the meld lines of punk-disco fusion that the most telling changes appeared. As quasi-organ keyb, the synthesizer, a plaything of dance wimps before arena bands and pop factories took it up, transformed the timbral identity of a music that's always been more about sound than notes—pop partisan Stephen Holden believes such archetypes as Boy George and Madonna even sing like synthesizers. And in its epochal sampler form, the synthesizer both epitomized and undermined rock's reduction to capital. On the dire side, studio schlockmeisters learned to construct full arrangements from taped libraries of licks and beats, so that musicians became extraneous even in "band" music, and some believe rappers and dance DIY-ers were even worse—that by sampling hooks whole from old hits and flops they cannibalized history, robbing the past of more than they could possibly give the future. I say their claim-jumps were righteous and past due. Rap sampling was postmodernism without the fuss, traditionalism giving traditionalists the finger. It was the people taking control of technology, joining a pop battle that began when rogue entrepreneurs discovered that Edison's phonograph wasn't a dictaphone. It won't be the whole future. But it's here to stay.

And the synthesizer wasn't even the big story, because the '80s were a rhythm decade like no decade since the '50s—a decade of drummers as well as drum programmers, disco over the edge, funk grooves motorvating the most piddly PoMo and New Pop and CHR, B-boys and -girls who talked more musically than their churchified counterparts sang. It was the decade that appreciated Charlie Watts and made James Brown its Elvis. Maybe attitude was the secret of punk, maybe Tommy Ramone was; the secret of postpunk was rhythm, young drummers coming out of nowhere by the hundreds. Only it turned out they weren't good enough, for if anything was killing indie rock by decade's end, it was the death-rattle of the solid four and its fancier variants—or else the inability of its practitioners to come up with a message, attitude, chord change, or whatever as interesting as a decent dancebeat. Less slyly offhand than Paul Westerberg or Chuck Berry, the vain, nasty, prolix eloquence of street-rhyme tradition was something new in rock and roll, but to comprehend rap you had to parse its groove. Put the muscular funk of the Sugarhill Gang up against the herky-jerk hither-and-yon of De La Soul and you'll learn plenty about their respective lyrics—and more. And the information will be direct and accessible like Steely Dan's chords never were.

Unfortunately, this isn't to say many children of the '50s—or the '60s, or maybe even the '70s—are capable of absorbing it. The famous generation gap still looms and lurks, with those who first rallied against its inequities now on the other side, where they continue to pursue their own interests—and continue to take shit, though not for the same reasons. The worst thing an L.A. hardcore kid could call you before the invention of the yuppie was "boomer," meaning baby-boomer, meaning a member of what that horrible old fart Peter Townshend once dubbed "My Generation." My generation has been over thirty for fifteen or twenty years now, and while it isn't quite as set in its ways as its predecessors—the mystique of lifelong growth isn't altogether a bad thing—it trusts itself a lot more than it trusts rap.

And though I suppose this self-regard is healthy, as they say, I wish it were less predictable. When punk arose at least there was a split, with forever-young hippie stalwarts enthusiastically participating or observing. But for the vast majority of boomers rap is pure Other, and a great many postpunks aren't too fond of it either. Just as the demands of punk rhythm reinforced simple ageist complacency and paranoia in alienating my contemporaries from the Ramones and the Sex Pistols, so the radical music of rap, reducing melody all the way down to hook and sometimes dispensing with that, turns off both big-chillskis and postpunk zealots. Once again there's a strong ideological element: rap's gangsterish connections and black-power in-your-face are meant to scare the fainthearted just as punk rage and alienation were. But rap's synthesis of attitude and sensibility is so complex and contradiction-ridden that it's usually simplistic (and self-serving) to blame its rejection in this or that arena solely on race. Class animus from above is a more reliable constant, and the turnoff potential of rap's piggish sexual politics shouldn't be pooh-poohed. But age would seem an even more telling factor, with purely musical affinity crucial. Many aging rock-and-rollers just can't get with its new rhythmic language—the language of many of the decade's best albums.

Complicating this question further is the spread of what's usually called world music, though with Europhile and Afrophile factions increasingly distinct, world beat is the more evocative term. In the U.S., world beat is not kid stuff. Its enthusiasts are decidedly thirtyish, and insofar as they're attracted to the dance rhythms of black Africa and its diaspora, they're responding—and responding rhythmically—to the same dissatisfaction with foursquare rock and roll songcraft that's made rap so attractive to young whites. The difference is that where rap is aggressively disjoint, world-beat rhythms are suffused with spiritual confidence; they seem whole in a historical moment out of conceptual control. Sure some world-beat fans are chronic tourists who prefer their black folks exotic and out of sight, but more prefer their entertainers all grown up rather than mannish boys—or stuck in the petulantly middle-aged permanent adolescence of so many rock stars, aging punks most definitely included. Call it the yin half of a rhythm decade that could certainly use a little. I'm happiest on both sides myself.

Rock and roll's '80s were multifarious in the extreme. Ornette's acolytes made smarter jazz-rock than Miles's; folkies in and out of the closet explored roots that included folkiedom itself; the classically trained didn't seem so culturally deprived; and Brian Eno married Roger Williams and named the baby George Winston, who discovered a grassroots demand for the aural escape of new age. There were good country albums and good blues albums and vault finds from all manner of titans, notably Jimi Hendrix; occasionally some dinosaur would peek out of his cave and make a record that proved he wasn't extinct, though that didn't happen nearly as often as the papers said it did. But rap and related dance musics, world beat, and what I've broadly designated postpunk were the vital movements. They'll continue vital, too—including postpunk, which is too big to just disappear. Sloppy college boys will have plenty to do with their ears for the foreseeable future. And they don't have to be the only ones. Really, boomers—I know the children cut into your loud time something fierce, but there's an awful lot new to hear for those with the will and spirit to listen. There is no need to forswear the pleasures of your youth, or to bog down in de facto nostalgia. That's one thing this book is for.

CANONS AND LISTENING LISTS

In the A lists way in back you will find representatives of all the afore-mentioned strains and others besides, listed by year in an order of preference as exact as fond memory and available replay time could make it. If you've read this far, I hope you've managed to infer the sensibility if not exactly the criteria that went into those lists. But it's only polite to try and lay it out. I am a rock-and-roller—my attraction to 90 per cent of the pop and semipop I like was set in motion by Chuck Berry thirty-five years ago. So I go for a lyric that says something, with some wit would be nice. And I like a good beat. (Next time you play Chuck Berry, who isn't ordinarily regarded as the rhythmic equal of Jerry Lee Lewis or Panama Francis, concentrate on his beat for a while. He smokes.) Overproduction having rendered these cultural commodities too easy to come by, my standards have been sharpened. Unlike the change addicts of indieland, I've been in the game long enough to know the difference between novel and new, and I'm not such a knee-jerk progressive that I believe new is always better. But I'm obviously not a golden-ager, either. There was popular music in the '50s and '60s and now the '70s (as well as the '20s and '30s and '40s) that retains an irreducible and unduplicatable magic. But anybody who thinks that kind of magic disappeared in the '80s understands neither history nor Parlia-ment-Funkadelic. (The Sex Pistols, maybe. Not the Ramones.)

In case it needs saying, I am who I am: a white male born into the Queens lower-middle class in 1942, my left politics and B.A. in English chosen rather than thrust upon me. Except to note that my daughter's tastes in entertainment cut into my listening time, I admit to no hardening of the tympanum. Sure I enjoy special rapport with my contemporaries, but I also know when they're full of shit, which is usually. In fact, I'd argue that twenty-year-olds have a harder time recognizing a mediocre Lou Reed record than I have recognizing a mediocre Replacements record. Youth comes with the musical territory, and by now my eternal attraction to the theme is so disinterested that all youth music partakes of sociology and the field report. To me, Thelonious Monster, Michelle Shocked, L.L. Cool J, and the Pet Shop Boys are all kids working out their identities, and in each case I get off tuning in.

Not that I think disinterest renders my judgments somehow objective. They have authority, sure—I'm knowledgeable and hard to con, and over the years many readers have found my tastes as well as my analyses useful. But if knowledge doesn't keep pace with production its usefulness diminishes, and in the '80s that wasn't just a tall order, it was physically impossible. I have little doubt that hidden away on that New Wave list (down some from the top, where I've listened hard enough to be certain of what isn't there as well as what is) are artists who could give me a thrill, tell me something I don't know. But I'm almost as sure that I can live my life happily without learning their secrets. Within the bounds of my tastes— which tend to exclude metal and "hard rock," romantic and Romantic slow stuff, folk music both authentic and secondhand, demijazz because it's half-assed and the real thing because it doesn't fit conceptually, and all manner of salable schlock—I haven't missed much domestically released English-language rock, a term I define very broadly. I've kept track of country and blues and taken my pick of more far-flung styles, with serious hiatuses indicated in the Subjects for Further Research section. But where in the '70s it was possible for me to imagine that a Consumer Guide compendium could be the basis of a canon, that's no longer how things are structured.

Because if on the one hand megaplatinum is what signifies, on the other the '80s were a time in which every quiddity of taste was worked for profit. For better and worse, it put the whole notion of a legible aesthetic behind it. I've made what I call postpunk (New Wave when I'm feeling sarcastic) the artistic center of the decade—well over a third of my A's are in the category. Yet the average college radio honcho would consider me hopelessly narrow and ill-informed. From hardcore to metal to garage grunge to neopsychedelic to art-damaged English dance music to sensitive singer-songwriters (again!), intelligent young people live for whole subgenres I could care less about. Similarly with the dance chart, chock full every week of records I'll never hear in my living room and would barely notice in a disco. The crux of world beat, meanwhile, is misprision—the ignorant reinterpretation to which outsiders like myself subject all transplanted culture.

I do persist. I believe my albums have something to give me and something to tell me—that they're a way of pleasure and a way of knowing. With not just critical authority but any presumption of shared musical experience as dead as Janis and Jimi, my grades are still designed to quantify aesthetic substance, whatever exactly that is. Against the Amerindie expressionists, so ignorant they believe any "alternative" is superior by definition, and the pop postmodernists, so cool they recognize no meaning but flux, I posit a relative permanence. But a canon? What do you take me for?

Don't answer that. Just believe me when I tell you I want this book to be regarded as one man's—all right, one critic's—listening list. An entertaining one for sure. Full of ideas too. Maybe even providing a fragmented overview for an unwhole time, no more partial than the newfangled rhythms us old guys have such trouble grabbing onto. And very useful, I swear—since more than half these records have given me major pleasure and/or minor insight at least once in the past ten years, anyone who likes rock and roll should be able to find fifty if not five hundred personally worthwhile titles herein. But in the end, it's just music processing, a job I get off on.

HOW TO USE THIS BOOK

This guide is arranged alphabetically by individuals' last name (Styrene, B., Petty), title (Captain, Mr., DJ), or nickname (Kid, Biz, L.L.) and groups' first word (Cocteau, They, Orchestra). Alphabetization proceeds as if spaces and punctuation weren't there, with English-language articles ignored; foreign-language articles are treated as words, numbers and abbreviations as if spelled out. Artist names will vary slightly when their billing does—I respect the record as text, compensating as sanely as possible for internal inconsistencies (which usually means following the label rather than the cover art). Drastic anomalies (Lucinda Williams was just Lucinda on her 1980 album) are cross-referenced, as are collaborations that might get lost in the shuffle. Nearly 150 compilations and soundtracks are interspersed alphabetically by title through the text and indexed in the appendix.

As I've explained, completeness was impossible in the '80s, and maybe inappropriate too. I've located every U.S.-released rock B+ I could, including cassettes and twelve-inch EPs. But I'm sure I've missed dozens, maybe hundreds, and in the various rock-related styles, not to mention the other genres that tickle my sensibility—especially those available only as imports, where my forays are sporadic—my breadth of coverage is even less reliable. I've tried to trace the outlines of recording careers, but a good many listings stop short in the middle, or begin and end with a single review. If I admire one record by an artist, especially a rock-and-roller, I almost certainly know the surrounding work, so figure when I skip something that I consider it disappointing in a boring way. It's common for a group to hit it right once, often on a debut album, and then sink into drought, confusion, compromise, or self-imitation, and there are only so many times you can say that before your readers wonder why you're bothering.

Why I choose to say it about some records and not others is often somewhat arbitrary, though critical hyperbole or unwarranted chart action do get me going. Similarly, while I've been diligent about B+'s, I've been negligent about B's—competent records with a few striking cuts on them. Most of the records I don't review—by artists on the New Wave list, for instance—are probably a little worse, in the B− or C+ range, where moderately clever, hard-working, and original people make music that sounds OK and rarely if ever catches you short. But some would no doubt turn out to be B's if I gave them my full attention for a play. I just don't have the time. I've learned from doing the job with newsworthy artists that distinguishing a B from a B− from a C+ is the most soul-wearying aspect of music processing, and I'm not mad enough to pursue it; often the B's I do write about are albums I want to like more, because they're conceptually worthy or have a couple of gems on them. So it's conceivable that I missed a thousand B's in the '80s. No one will ever know, or care—including me.

Each artist's entries are arranged chronologically, in order of U.S. appearance. Dates reflect actual year of original release (which sometimes differs from the pub date on the jacket), although especially with imports I sometimes reviewed the record much later. (Three important late-'79 U.K. releases that never found a U.S. record company—Pere Ubu's *New Picnic Time,* the Sex Pistols' *Great Rock'n'Roll Swindle,* and *The Raincoats*—are snuck in as 1980 albums, which in the U.S. they should have been.) I've noted whatever label I originally encountered a record on, with significant subsequent changes (not intracorporate logo switches or imports gone domestic) reported in brackets at the end of the review. I haven't caught them all, I'm sure—there's a lot of product being dealt these days. And while I've tried to note significant CD/cassette-only bonus cuts, I've definitely missed a lot of those.

I'm no vinyl fetishist and no audiophile. If anything, I prefer CD sound, although the upfront percussion of early digital remixes was irritating, and if CDs prove as durable as their manufacturers claim, which I doubt, I'll be grateful—it's depressing to pull a prized title out of its cardboard jacket and find the music obscured by surface noise. Nevertheless, there's something about CDs that's always bothered me: they only have one side, so unless you program your CD player, which most don't, you consume a whole album at once. This may be the way God planned it, but it's inhuman: except in the flush of rapt concentration or first acquaintance (or when enjoying an illicit C-90), the typical vinyl or cassette owner has always used albums one seventeen-to-twenty-three-minute, four-to-six-song side at a time. Crucial perceptual habits have grown up around this time frame, which is based partly on vinyl's physical limits and partly, I suspect, on an attention span bound up in the mysteries of the industrialized sensorium, but in the CD era it's disappearing. Song lengths over five minutes and album lengths over fifty are now common, and even worse, these already puffed-up albums are generally wolfed down, well, two sides at a time.

I'm sorry, that's the way I hear things even if it means my whole approach to reviewing is obsolete. The side isn't dead yet—although cassettes are fragile and clumsy, they're cheap, and they continue to outsell CDs. But as a commercial proposition, especially for the relatively affluent consumers who buy records in quantity (and record guides to advise them), digital is taking over, and with it whole new vistas in perceptual organization and product availability.

The disappearance of vinyl was engineered by bizzers who liked CD profit margins—once you own the equipment, they cost less than vinyl to manufacture, and they let you repackage (and resell) your bundles of rights. But each repackage has a start-up cost, and as vinyl is deleted, which is now a runaway phenomenon, the accountants will be figuring out what titles justify digital remastering—from their point of view, of course. It's my practice to respect the "work" anyway: I've never felt obliged to figure out which album is in print and which isn't. But especially with uncommercial artists on major labels—sometimes artists who in their minor-label manifestation are profit-makers—the prospects of finding some of the older titles on my A lists are grim. And since repackaging is a very literal concept—first two sides at a sitting, then bonus tracks to sucker in vinyl-owners, finally recompiled oeuvres—I can't guarantee that the CD version of an album would hit even me the way I describe it. Most of the time the difference won't be that great, especially if you invest in a CD player that's easy to program. But with individually compiled Personics-style tapes (digital, of course) in the middle-distance offing, the '80s may be the last decade for which an album guide makes a whole lot of sense.

In the short run, used record stores will do big business. And sometimes I imagine that vinyl isn't really going to disappear—that it will simply become a specialty item, marketed by mail or in boutiques by visionary entrepreneurs who begin by buying tons of cutouts and end up investing in discarded pressing equipment and obtaining vinyl-only rights to quiddity-tickling music the majors don't have time for. Insofar as my '50s and '60s self expects a social dimension of rock and roll, this will be highly unsatisfactory, but it will also be better than nothing. For social dimension I'll have to settle for the next Madonna, Prince, Springsteen, or Kool Moe Dee, who I'm sure will keep me occupied. That pop machine really is good for something. Only you know what? I'm not so sure I understand it better than its keepers anymore.

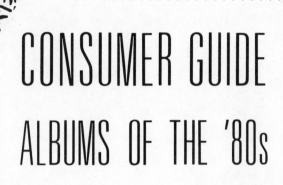

CONSUMER GUIDE

ALBUMS OF THE '80s

Gregory Abbott: *Shake You Down* (Columbia '86). The title single is a deceptively slight slow burn, a come-on so unassuming you don't notice you're being seduced until after you've slipped into something more comfortable, and most of the album works the same subliminally hooky con—harmless until it whispers "gotcha," it's a model of consumer calculation. The persona is green-eyed handsome man with the wherewithal to support his fine tastes and yours. The songs are tuneful ditties with Bacharach/Bell chords and harmonies. And the singing is generic Spinners—growling or crooning or letting his falsetto do the talking, Abbott has learned to make the most of the edgy strain that's his unavoidable vocal trademark. There's something all too '80s about his bid to create a great love man without a great voice—if in 1971 Bill Withers was a toilet installer expressing his higher self and in 1978 Ray Parker Jr. was a bizwise craftsman selling his irrepressible formal exuberance, then in 1987 Abbott is a brokerage grunt looking to maximize his profitability. But by reinventing a black pop of modest means, he takes a first step toward returning that great crossover in the sky to the people. Wouldn't it be nice if somebody else took another one? **B+**

ABC: *The Lexicon of Love* (Mercury '82). Since Bowie and Ferry sold surface in disguise back when they were supposedly saving rock and roll, I don't worry about this tribute band's lack of depth. Martin Fry's candid camp and ad-man phrasing don't fully justify his histrionic flights, but they do give him room to be clever, which is clearly his calling—some of these synthetic funk rhythms make me laugh out loud, and he's an ace jingle writer. "If that's the trash aesthetic I suggest that we forget it"? Not when your throwaways include bon mots like "looking for the girl who meets supply with demand." Original grade: B plus. **A—**

ABC: *Beauty Stab* (Mercury '83). I don't get these complaints that Martin Fry has abandoned his shallow but ingratiating popcraft for a brave/pretentious but/and ill-advised stab at social significance. Except for "The Look of Love," a supercatchy fluke that apparently confused people, instant hooks weren't how the first album worked either, and his shallowness was always more apparent than real. As with the debut, give this one five spins and you'll remember every track, with "She's vegetarian except when it comes to sex" your first but not last aha. Whether you'll enjoy it all as much is another matter—there's a slight loss of verve. But that was then and this is now. **A—**

ABC: *How To Be a Zillionaire* (Mercury '85). The look of the Mark I ABC fooled Anglophobes into dismissing the music as fashion-plated pandering even though it was as politically suggestive as Anglophile heroes get. So don't let the look of the Mark II ABC fool you into hoping the music is outrageous, or even campy. Sure

"Be Near You" is catchier than anything on *Beauty Stab,* but when Martin Fry is on his game the hooks that make ABC sell coexist with the glossy electrofunk and dense wordplay that make (or made) them sparkle. As a great romantic he's just trying for a comeback.   **B—**

Paula Abdul: *Straight Up* (Virgin '88). If Debbie Gibson already has platinum imitators, there's more to the world than is dreamt of in Madonna's philosophy. This unthreateningly dusky disco-dolly-next-door plays the field romantic-metaphorwise, with a weakness for can't-help-myself. She's less imitator than imitation, short on tokens of self-creation—her only writing credit is the only time she threatens to play around.   **C**

Dele Abiodun: *Adawa Super Sound* (Shanachie '85). Sunny Adé aside, this is the best-conceived juju album ever released in the U.S. One half is specialty items to engage the untrained ear—dub here, funk there, out harmonies somewhere else, all integrated unobtrusively into the basic weave. The other half is tipico medley, like on a real African juju album, which oddly enough is the first time that self-evident ploy has ever been tried out on the American public.   **A—**

Dele Abiodun: *It's Time for Juju Music* (Super Adawa import '85). Juju strikes some as an odd place to have begun selling Africa to white people—subtle, discursive, hard to dance to. But in Nigeria it's just pop music. The funk and pop fusions claimed for this old-timer, who toured the U.K. way back in 1974, still sound more like shadings to me, but he's absorbed Martin Meissonnier's (not Sunny Adé's) production philosophy. In its tuneful construction and clean, hot mix, this item recalls *Synchro-System,* only it has a ruminative side that's very Nigeria-specific. Maybe that makes him ingenuous. Or maybe it means he knows his market.   **A—**

Colonel Abrams: *Colonel Abrams* (MCA '86). With Eurodisco orgymaster Cerrone and Ameridisco worker-bee Sam Dees augmenting Anglodisco scenemaker Rich-ard Burgess in the coproducer's slot, you-know-what revival is obviously on tap. Ah well, it could be lots worse, and it probably will be—I hope not with this artist, a likable fella whose Teddy Pendergrass impression has its social function. Though speaking of soul, I wonder why the only ladyfriend he makes me care about is eight years old tops.   **B**

The Accelerators: *Leave My Heart* (Dolphin '83). Even on generic rockabilly Gerald Duncan has a way with words, pinning down the thwarted lust that's always added nervous energy to the style. "Two Girls in Love" is as fine a lesbians-from-the-outside song as the Amazing Rhythm Aces' "Emma-Jean," and "Regina" brings "Brother Louie" down home. Duncan comes up with hooks half the time, too. But his singing is so mild and his band so contained that only the most striking material lifts off. Just our luck that in an age of interesting bands with nothing to say an interesting songwriter doesn't put quite enough into the music.   **B**

AC/DC: *Back in Black* (Atlantic '80). Replacing Aerosmith as primitives of choice among admirers of heavy machinery, these Aussies are a little too archetypal for my tastes. Angus Young does come up with killer riffs, though not as consistently as a refined person like myself might hope, and fresh recruit Brian Johnson sings like there's a cattle prod at his scrotum, just the thing for fans who can't decide whether their newfound testosterone is agony or ecstasy. AC/DC can't decide either— "Shoot To Thrill," "Given [sic] the Dog a Bone," and "Let Me Put My Love Into You" all concern the unimaginative sexual acts you'd imagine, and "What Do You Do for Money Honey" has a more limited set of answers than the average secretary would prefer. My sister's glad they don't write fantasy and science fiction, and if you're female you're free to share her relief. Brothers are more deeply implicated in these matters.   **B—**

AC/DC: *Dirty Deeds Done Cheap* (Atlantic '81). A 1976 Australian LP released in the wake of their ascension to the U.S. top ten, this is where those of us who weren't paying attention meet the blokelike croak of the legendary Bon Scott, asphyxiated by his own vomit shortly after *Highway to Hell* broke them Stateside. Now I understand why they say Brian Johnson has a great voice—he's got about about three times the range and wattage, the bloke as fantasy-fiction demigod. But those who prefer Scott's charm have a point. Like Ian Hunter or Roger Chapman though without their panache, he has fun being a dirty young man—he almost slavers through "Ain't No Fun Waiting Round To Be a Millionaire," and "Big Balls" is fully outrageous in its class hostility. Needless to say, sexual hostility—disguised as fun, of course—is more his speed.   **C+**

AC/DC: *For Those About To Rock We Salute You* (Atlantic '81). Brian Johnson takes over, defining an anthemic grandiosity more suitable to their precious-metal status than Bon Scott's old-fashioned raunch. Also dumber. "Let's Get It Up" is a limited sentiment in any case. But I'd appreciate some indication that Johnson knows the difference between his dick and the light tower.   **C**

AC/DC: *Who Made Who* (Atlantic '86). The soundtrack to Stephen King's *Maximum Overdrive* is no best-of, not with Bon Scott shafted (the tired "Ride On") and two of the three new songs instrumentals. Still, one instrumental is showtime, the title tune is really a tune, "Hell's Bells" will give Christians fits, and sexual metaphors are kept to a minimum. I wish their only great work of art, the drum-hooked fucksong "You Shook Me All Night Long," wasn't buried on side one the way it's buried on *Back in Black*. But this is their most presentable collection nevertheless.   **B**

AC/DC: *Blow Up Your Video* (Atlantic '88). The brutal truth is that sexism has never kept a great rock-and-roller down—from Muddy to Lemmy, lots of dynamite music has objectified women in objectionable ways. But rotely is not among those ways. I mean, these guys have never known how to throw a party. Sure their costumery is good for a laugh, but Brian Johnson shrieks too much, which gets positively painful as he grows hoarse with the encroaching years, and they've always

been stingy with their famous killer riffs. Their reunion with Vanda & Young no more signals their renewed determination to make good albums than Elton John's reunion with Bernie Taupin. It signals commercial panic, and unlike Elton they're unlikely to reverse their downward sales path over the long haul. I eagerly await their retirement and the dynamite best-of I trust will prove subsequent upon it.   **C+**

Adam and the Ants: *Kings of the Wild Frontier* (Epic '80). This isn't rock and roll, sez here—it's "sexmusic," a/k/a "antmusic," heralding Arapaho (Apache) (Kiowa) (pirate) warrior ideals as a futuristic reaction against Brit-punk nihilism. The scam has whole subcultures working for it in England, but here it's the sex and the music that'll determine whether Adam is David Bowie or Marc Bolan (or Gary Glitter). The sex is your basic line-drawings-of-spike-heels stuff, redolent of Sex, the haberdashery once owned by Adam's ex-manager. The music, needless to say, is rock and roll, a clever pop-punk amalgam boasting two drummers, lots of chanting, and numerous B-movie hooks. Especially given Adam's art-school vocals, I find that the hooks grate, but that may just mean that when it comes to futuristic warriors I prefer Sandinistas.   **B**

Bryan Adams: *Reckless* (A&M '85). The megabuck stops here. Maybe I'll let Bruce Springsteen teach me how to hear John Cougar Mellencamp, but damned if I'm going to let John Cougar Mellencamp teach me how to hear Bryan Adams. From antipunkdiscowave strut to *Flashdance* homage, he's a generic American hunk, only whiter because he's Canadian. Where Sammy Hagar flaunts his anticommunism and Don Henley flaunts his mouth, Adams flaunts nothing more and nothing less than his young reliable bod. Like all the above-mentioned good and bad he shares a mysterious nostalgia for the recent past with a lot of people who aren't half dead yet, at least chronologically. And more than any of them he has real problems relaxing, which puts him square in the soul-as-will-and-idea tradition of Lou Gramm, Pat

Boone, Sophie Tucker, and so many others.   **C—**

Bryan Adams: *Into the Fire* (A&M '87). It's got to be deliberate, the voice of the common man or some such. Nevertheless, making all allowances—overlooking quotes/references ("eight miles high"), universals ("the rent is due"), attempted wordplay ("a table for one and a broken heart to go"), and simple idioms ("count me in," "white flag," "heaven knows," "it's up to you")—I count an astonishing fifty-six full-fledged clichés on what's supposed to be a significance move, from "caught in the crossfire" in the first line to "the worst is over" in the third-to-last. And while "Only the Strong Survive," the biggest offender with twelve, steamrollers across despite it all, neither Don Henley soul nor emergent social conscience justify the dumbness density. I know the salt of the earth is the shape of things to come, but these words of wisdom are beyond the pale.   **C+**

King Sunny Adé: *The Message* (Sunny Alade import '81). All I know about Adé is that he's the (or a) king of Nigerian juju. His voice is gentle, his rhythm insinuating and very poly, his guitar graceful and faintly Hawaiian. Also, he comes up with good hooks—"Ma J'Aiye Oni" was on my interior jukebox for weeks. I play this a lot, and even at that don't think it matches the one with the orange cover that I lost at Charing Cross six weeks ago. When I went back to buy a second copy at Stern's, 126 Tottenham Court Road, London WI, I was told I'd never see it again and advised to plunk down another six quid for this substitute. I'm glad I did, but anyone who knows where I can find the one with the orange cover please advise.   **A**

King Sunny Adé and His African Beats: *Juju Music* (Mango '82). *The Message,* the unavailable-in-the-U.S. Nigerian LP that precedes this made-for-export overview conceptually, actually comes closer to pop—it's brighter, edgier, more tuneful. The music here is all flowing undulation; even the experimental synthesizer interjections, while recalling the startling syndrums of great disco, seem somehow rubberized, springing suddenly outward and then receding back into the slipstream. It's almost as if Chris Blackwell, aware that it was absurd to think AOR, aimed instead for a kind of ambient folk music that would unite amateur ethnologists, Byrne-Eno new-wavers, reggae fans, and hip dentists, just for starters. But never fear—not only do these confident, magical, surpassingly gentle polyrhythms obviate the organic and the electronic, the local and universal, they also make hash of distinctions between background and foreground. I can imagine somebody not loving Sunny Adé; I can't imagine somebody disliking him. Original grade: A plus.   **A—**

King Sunny Adé and His African Beats: *Ajoo* (Makossa '83). Since his import-if-you-can-find-it *The Message* is still my favorite Adé, not to mention my first, I thought it wise to check out the *five* LPs Adé released in Nigeria between Mango albums. They sounded pretty good, but since "universal language" is as parochial a concept as any other one-world idealism, I wasn't too surprised to discover limits to my appetite for a conservative, consciously recycled music I half understand. Makossa, a Brooklyn label which has manufactured and distributed African records since 1967, has now released this Nigerian Adé in a cleaner, brighter pressing. I know several neoconnoisseurs who consider *Ajoo* his best since the first Nigerian Adé *they* heard, *Check "E";* I'd say second-best since *The Message* (the first shipment of which arrived in the States warped) because I prefer *Bobby,* featuring an elegiacally lyrical side called "Late Olabinjo Benson." One indication of *Ajoo*'s quality is that Adé recut "Ewele" and "Tolongo" (as well as *Maa Jo*'s title tune) for *Synchro System,* but that's not necessarily a consumer plus. "Gbeyogbeyo," however, would make Vangelis turn green if he weren't so badly discolored already. **A—**

King Sunny Adé and His African Beats: *Synchro System* (Mango '83). Top-billed keyboard player Martin Meissonnier has definite ideas about how to produce his client for the non-African market. By emphasizing discrete melodies and heating up the mix, he variegates Adé's flow, which is how art works in the U.S.A. Since the impact of overviews like *Juju Music* is un-repeatable, the switch came none too soon. This more conventionally unified album may not seem quite as arresting as the debut, but that's mainly because it arrived second. There's no clearer way to hear the talking drums and choral singing that make juju music what it is.   **A—**

King Sunny Adé and His African Beats: *Aura* (Island '84). Three albums into this world-class popmeister's American career, his U.S. debut begins to seem like the com-promise purists claimed it was—not be-cause it's too American, but because it's not American enough. Now when I want something subtly polypercussive I'll choose one of his Nigerian LPs rather than *Juju Music.* And when I want a heavier, hookier groove I'll pull out *Synchro Sys-tem*—or more likely, this one. With Mar-tin Meissonnier back behind the glass and Stevie Wonder's earthbound harmonica on native ground, it's every bit as consistent as *The Message* and—by (Afro-) Ameri-can standards—considerably more propul-sive. At times it's even obvious, regular. Next time I assume they'll go all out for a dance-chart hit. And I can't wait to hear it.   **A**

King Sunny Adé: *Return of the Juju King* (Mercury import CD '88). Shortly after he split with Island, Adé also split with the African Beats, which may be why this fifty-five-minute compilation from three recent Nigerian LPs never generates that familiar aura. Could also be the weak-ness of digital remixers for percussion. Talking drum fans'll love it.   **B+**

King Sunny Adé and His African Beats: *Live Live Juju* (Rykodisc '88). Like so many live albums, it promises the real deal and then reduces an event that once en-gaged five or more senses to an aural ab-straction. Worse, the percussive bias of both recording method and performance concept undercuts the momentum of the ensemble groove. Ruined by the Fallacy of the Drum Solo, in quadruplicate.   **B—**

Aerosmith: *Greatest Hits* (Columbia '80). I could quibble with side two, which doesn't conceal their sudden decline the way it might have, but the *Sgt. Pepper* "Come Together" is a keeper, and except

for the Anglophile "Kings and Queens" the post-*Rocks* tracks do create a context for themselves. Side one is the great Amer-ican "hard-rock" band sounding more relaxed and bluesy than the one that made *Rocks*—because originally it was relaxa-tion that made their white blues so Ameri-can. Such revelations are what best-ofs are for.   **A—**

Aerosmith: *Done With Mirrors* (Geffen '85). Their knack for the basic song and small interest in guitar-hero costume drama always made them hard rock that deserved the name, not to mention an American band. Still, with almost a decade of bad records collective and solo behind them, there was no reason to expect a thing from this touching reunion. And against all odds the old farts light one up: if you can stand the crunch, you'll find more get-up-and-go on the first side than on any dozen random neogarage EPs.   **B+**

Aerosmith: *Classics Live II* (Columbia '87). Six of eight tracks on Corporate Re-venge II were cut New Year's Eve 1984, a money gig for sure, and every one was at least eight years old at the time; a seventh previewed a song soon to appear on their Geffen debut—but recorded, heh heh, while they were still under CBS jurisdic-tion. And what we get is some of the toughest and least indulgent live metal ever vinylized, not quite *Greatest Hits* (four dupes) but way beyond *Live Bootleg* or Corporate Revenge I. Professional-ism—who can predict it?   **B+**

Aerosmith: *Permanent Vacation* (Geffen '87). Don't let the twelve tracks, blues moves, or ace Beatle cover mislead you. Horns here and here and here plus mello-tron there and there plus song doctors all over the place add up to running out of gas again already.   **C+**

Aerosmith: *Gems* (Columbia '88). Any-body who doubts they made a great album once (and only once) should check the title and then explain why buried gems from *Rocks* lead both sides of their second best-of. Because *Rock*'s openers got used up the first time is why.   **B**

Aerosmith: *Pump* (Geffen '89). If fried brains is your idea of a rock dream, the first side will do the job at least as good as whatever raging slab is also your idea of a rock dream. For five songs, everything loud and acrid about them just keeps on coming—not even tune doctors can stave off the juggernaut. Of course, their idea of a rock dream is also the traditional "Young Lust" and "Love in an Elevator"—OK as far as it goes, but I could do with more "Janie's Got a Gun," in which an abused teenager offs her dad.   **B+**

African Acoustic Vol. 2: Kenya Dry . . . (Original Music '88). "Dry" is what Africans call acoustic guitar, and for the first side, which samples tribal languages before homing in on Swahili, this collection of '50s rarities sounds like a sweetly typical folk-song collection—just happens to be out of Africa is all. But as the B progressed through catchy little guitar tunes and relaxed harmony groups I got a more specific vibe, and when the notes adduced African heroes Jimmie Rodgers and Jim Reeves I decided I was right. Fans of string bands, bluegrass, and other old-time country music: if you find polyrhythms daunting, boring, or whatever, this could be your way in.   **B+**

African Connection Vol. I: Zaire Choc! (Celluloid import cassette/CD '88). Assembled by the biggest and sharpest manufacturer-distributor of an African style perfected in Europe, this is the showcase the slick, deep, joyously cosmopolitan, unselfconsciously commercial body-music the Paris-Kinshasa connection was waiting for. Contrasting vocal hooks, quicksilver guitar figures, and negotiable rhythm changes are orchestrated with a skill that evokes a great dancefloor DJ working the crowd for an hour-long peak. For sure it's more than a quality disco compilation: selections don't just hang together, they stand out, with Sam Mangwana, 4 Etoiles, and Papa Wemba some of the famous hard-to-finds featured. The secret, though, is in the selection and the flow—bet the compiler did literally do time on the Paris club scene, testing every track in the crucible of Saturday night.   **A+**

African Connection Vol. II: West Africa (Celluloid import cassette/CD '88). Since Senegambia and its Islamic environs nurture solo expressive practices more indi-vidualistic (more "Western"?) (more "soulful"?) than those of the Congo, these pop moves by Salif Keita, Youssou N'Dour, and Parisian pets Toure Kunda might not mesh all that well with Alpha Blondy and epigones' Afro-reggae grooves even if they were snazzier. Quite educational, moderately entertaining.   **B+**

African Connexion: *African Connexion* (Oval import EP '84). On the patois "bright side," this half-black, half-white London septet generates the kind of Afrolift that makes highlife seem like a generic description, with guitar and saxophone confidently inauthentic as they wheel free. The English-language "dark side" has the bite of good protest reggae—but not the depth of groove.   **B+**

African Head Charge: *Off the Beaten Track* (On-U Sound import '86). Hoping against hope that it's some fucking place, I occasionally find myself suspecting that cut-up and dub are where the semipop action is. Enthusiasm, iconoclasm, and willingness to live in the present make it the avant alternative to neoclassicism—aware of the weight of history and the unavoidability of received materials, but also aware that past glories have been and gone. Then I listen to Curlew or Fats Comet or *Mute Beat* or Version X and go back to my four-four. Thing is, the semipop action ought to be more than metaphorical; rock bricolage is too cerebral and reggae subtract-a-track too spacy to work that body. Although in my casual experience Adrian Sherwood's vast output combines both problems, this fourth album by one of his array of studio-only projects adds minimelodies galore and a shifting but reliable bass-and-drum pulse—Jamaica steeped in field recordings and heavy machinery—to the usual panorama of depth charges, funny noises, exotic rips, and spoken words. Kind of like Augustus Pablo if Pablo weren't so pastoral, and so pop.   **A—**

African Image: *African Image* (Gramavision '83). Brutally honest right down to the name, the label promotes South African pop pros Thomas Mkhize and Glynn Storm as "more structured and somewhat less dense than Adé's highlife [sic] style," praising their "state-of-the-art production values, modern instrumentation, and pronounced rock, jazz, and pop influences." In short, decorative exoticism, a touch slick, with pleasing Zulu chant melodies and a trap drummer who'd fit in on Carson. I like every one of its six cuts. And love none of them.   **B**

African Music (Vertigo import '83). It took the Dutch to assemble a decent compilation of Nigerian highlife, the r&b-ish horn-and-guitar music that came over from Kenya with founding father E.T. Mensah in the '50s. Less brassily arranged than Congolese rumba, these four-minute classics from the style's masters skip all over the past decade-plus yet mesh as gentle pop epiphanies for untrained ears. Many feature sax solos almost as laggardly as the gritty, half-conversational singing exemplified by patriarch Dr. Victor Olaiya. Both elements pulling against effervescent guitar hooks and the lift of multiple drums in indigenous patterns I couldn't begin to specify, with the pleasingly received guitar solos occupying a middle ground where the music resolves. Though such generalizations don't hint at the reggae side trips and rock steals and best-selling vocals also present, they do sum up the music's sky-above-mud-below tension—an animistic charge that doesn't demand a literal belief in anybody's or anything's soul.   **A**

The African Typic Collection (Virgin '89). Annotator-cocompiler Jumbo Vanrenen's latest Afrodisco sampler showcases the Caribbean-Camerounian rhythm—designated "makassi," and don't ask me to tell you more or recognize it on the dance floor—that was the making of Sam Fan Thomas, who has his name on three of the six cuts and his fingers in two others. As the owner of one Thomas LP, I hereby certify that this one is more catchy, infectious, and all the other meaningful things Afrodisco samplers should be. It closes corny with a "Peter Gabriel inspired" (oh dear) Mandela tribute, opens fresh with an acoustic-guitar-based mesh of African dances. In between, relentless genericism does its number.   **A—**

Age of Chance: *Crush Collision* (Virgin EP '87). These troublemakers top their agitpop with covers of "Disco Inferno" (name that tune) and "Kiss" ("You got to know how to talk / If you want to impress me / And it would help if you know how to walk . . ."). Their "sonic metal disco" aims to reintroduce the Human League to the Gang of Four, and who knows—if they can achieve world revolution, maybe I can overcome my Phil Oakey problem.   **A—**

Age of Chance: *One Thousand Years of Trouble* (Virgin '87). At their strongest these Leeds lads have the postsituationist aggro down. Slogans like "Take It!" and "Don't Get Mad . . . Get Even!" are presented literally, yelled over loud funk beats that combined with their wall of noise makes them white rap the way Led Zep were white blues. Advocating insurrection ain't planning revolution, but it ain't surrender either.   **B+**

A-Ha: *Hunting High and Low* (Warner Bros. '85). Quite aware that I don't qualify as a pubescent female, I tried to be understanding. It's not their fault they're blond, after all—they're Norwegian. But though they'd clearly have been better off raised closer to the blues—in Wales, say—the gutturals of fellow Scandinavians from Gasolin' to the Nomads suggest that their precious Yes-gone-Europop accents are chosen freely. Over music they probably exerted less control.   **C—**

Mahmoud Ahmed: *Ere Mela Mela* (Crammed Discs import '86). Because taste leads to knowledge, I enjoy fair familiarity with the West African music that's second cousin to rock and roll and none with its distant relatives in North Africa and the Middle East. But where knowledge ends, taste rules. Ahmed is a singer of unmistakable authority, and maybe an album of the "many standards" he's contributed to "modern Ethiopian music" would expand my horizons. Or maybe this is that album—I don't know. I do know that soon I lose the charge I get from the lead cuts, generated less by the "strange, almost Indonesian-sounding scales" of the vocals than by the two-sax horn section, which (maybe because it utilizes those scales) could be Afro-*Brilliant Corners* or ill-tempered synthesizer or avant-garde blues. For tastes that run to the Master Musicians of Jujouka and Om Kalsoum, he may be Elvis.   **B+**

The Alarm: *Declaration* (I.R.S. '84). Oh, I know who they *sound like*—that Mick-cum-Joe front man, those football choruses, the militant *strum* of it all. Brings a tear to the eye, yes it does. But the whatchacallum, the Clash, wrote whatchacallum—*songs!* And does anybody know what these boys are declaring *for?*   **C+**

The Alarm: *Change* (I.R.S. '89). Breaking on through, they sounded a lot like the Clash. College radio staples, they sound a lot like U2. Ain't artistic evolution somethin'?   **C**

Ali & Tam's Avec l'Orchestre Malo: *Ali & Tam's Avec l'Orchestre Malo* (Planisphere import '86). Kinshasa professors folkify and jazzify Zairean pop, thus defeating soukous's relentless professionalism—textures more acoustic, solos more personal, rhythms more relaxed. Contemporary and traditional, catchy and sweet—tries to improve on modernity rather than escape from it.   **B+**

Terry Allen & the Panhandle Mystery Band: *Smokin the Dummy* (Fate '80). *Juarez,* this sculptor-painter cum singer-songwriter's 1975 debut, was pretentiously half-assed mock mythopoeia; *Lubbock (on Everything),* his 1979 double, was genuwine laugh-a-minute highbrow-lowbrow. This time Allen's satire is a little thinner, and he undercuts his more sincere songs by playing them for comedy, the only vocal trick he knows. "Texas Tears," "The Night Cafe," and "Redbird"—plus some funny ones—are recommended to sideman Joe Ely, whose band has always mystified the Panhandle.   **B**

Dave Alvin: *Romeo's Escape* (Epic '87). Alvin's hoarse timbre, bellowing passion, and approximate pitch call up other songwriter front men—such dubious predecessors as John Prine and Guy Clark, who at least can claim to sound like themselves. Nevertheless, he's a born songwriter—guitarist, too. The country demos and Blasters covers hold their own. The X cover is why he moved on.   **B+**

Phil Alvin: *Un "Sung Stories"* (Slash '86). He loves a good lyric, and if he can't write them or order them up, he has only to ransack his record collection for oldies that are just strange enough. Mixing country blues with Cab Calloway, Peetie Wheatstraw's murderous "Gangster's Blues" with a supremely mournful country song called "Collins Cave," he goes for narrative and gets it. The arrangements range from very spare to orchestral, and never mind Tower of Power—Alvin goes to Sun Ra when he wants Ellingtonia, Dirty Dozen when he wants polyphony. The only exception to all this smart stuff is a perfectly OK "Daddy Rollin' Stone." I hope it breaks AOR, I bet it won't, and I wish he didn't have to bother.   **A−**

Amaphisi / Uthwalofu Namakentshane: *City Shoes, Rural Blues* (Kijima import '88). Showcasing two deserving mbaqanga acts, both fond of squeezeboxes. Good. But as an American who's listened to more mbaqanga than 99 percent of those who've heard any at all, I shouldn't have to strain to distinguish between the one described as spearheading a "revitalization of traditional Zulu music" and the one said to be "zulu jive's fastest rising group." Hint: the latter shares a family tree with the Soul Brothers, so bear down on the harmonies.   **B**

Les Ambassadeurs: *Les Ambassadeurs* (Rounder '84). Though it's billed as "dance music from West Africa" (these folkie labels, anything for a buck), what you notice is more for the ears than the feet—the emotional range of Mali tenor Salif Keita, a far more stirring singer than the renowned Rochereau, and the way Kante Manfila's guitar anchors synth here and horns there. Gorgeous. And if you wonder what Keita's emoting about, read the notes. He doesn't much like war, prefers past leaders to present, hopes the poor man's prayers will be answered but que sera sera, praises not just cops but also informers for combating the drug scourge, and passionately opposes the newfangled practice of men marrying women older than themselves. Oh well.   **A—**

Arto Lindsay/Ambitious Lovers: *Envy* (Editions EG '84). Shifting abruptly from funk to skronk to varying intensities of Brazilian pop, this may seem scattered to some, but I find its coherence riveting. I suppose what holds it together is Arto's persona—really more a sensibility, post-modernist humor coexisting with humanistic lyricism, which is articulated rhythmically but also in singing that ranges from lock-ma crazee to wittingly sweet and unaffected. In this context both his fake-gibberish verbal-vocalese and his surprisingly detailed atonal strums (not his lyrics) sound like translations from the Portuguese. And "Let's Be Adult" deserves heavy rotation in every disco from here to Rio.   **A**

Ambitious Lovers: *Greed* (Virgin '88). Guess the title's because this is more commercial than *Envy*, which I guess Arto called that because he was insecure about playing funk and samba. Well, he's not insecure any more. With Peter Scherer melding Brazil and the Black Rock Coalition into a spectrum of astonishing bands, he's sitting on top of one of the sharpest, coolest, bestest funk or samba records ever made—funk as light and samba as pop as the Michaels McDonald or Franks could hope for, only all fused and fucked with. Moments of guitar anarchy (from Vernon Reid or Bill Frisell when chops are called for, from Arto when Arto is) add a New York edge to the tropico hedonism, and there's a consciously childlike playfulness to Arto's vocal technique that's a hemisphere away from the sun-dazed romantic insouciance of his Lusophone mentors. Which certainly isn't to say he lacks insouciance—the bespectacled sometime skronkmaster is as sexy as George Michael when he wants to be, which on these post-postmodern love songs he does. Wonder what *Lust* will sound like.   **A**

John Anderson: *John Anderson* (Warner Bros. '80). The songs fade on side two, but not since Hank Williams Jr. fell off his mountain and Gary Stewart fell off his bar-

stool has anybody put so much vocal muscle into unadorned hard stuff. Convincer: Buddy Spicher's fiddle break on the definitive "She Just Started Liking Cheatin' Songs."   **B+**

John Anderson: *2* (Warner Bros. '81). In the right's first flush of power, as Nashville nostalgia merges revoltingly with El Lay schlock, Anderson's modest regard for the verities becomes not just a virtue but a treasure. Unlike, let us say, Eddie Rabbitt, he knows the difference between traditionalism and conformism, sentiment and bathos, makin' love and makin' out, fiddles and strings; he has the guts to attack "the power of the almighty dollar."   **A—**

John Anderson: *I Just Came Home To Count the Memories* (Warner Bros. '81). He's smart, he's honest, but what makes him a country comer is the edge on his husky baritone, too indistinct and decorative to be called a vibrato or even a burr. His instinctively sentimental reading of "Don't Think Twice" establishes the limits of baritone, smarts, and honesty all at once, and I spent enough time pondering whether this was worth a B plus to conclude that I'd have known in a jiffy if I was as familiar with the Frizzell and Delmore covers as I am with the Dylan. Which should tell you what kind of B plus it's worth. This kind: **B**

John Anderson: *Wild and Blue* (Warner Bros. '82). Anderson is Ricky Skaggs without Jesus—his voice lowdown rather than angelic, his roots in the honky tonks rather than the mountains, his album wild and blue, a sexier way to say (and sing) highways and heartaches. But his gift for ballads is still a little soft, which means he comes up a touch short on the ones you know and can't quite turn filler into the staff of life.   **B+**

John Anderson: *All the People Are Talkin'* (Warner Bros. '83). Anderson's slur manages to suggest comedy, sex, and rock and roll successively and sometimes simultaneously, and his fifth album in three years is his finest yet—the first to surround great hits with uniformly high-grade filler. Or maybe it's the first to make the filler sound hitbound—his defiant "Haunted House" surprised Warners by stiffing before his defiant "Black Sheep" took off.

Suggested follow-ups: the hapfully plaintive "Look What Followed Me Home" and the undefiant public service announcement, "Let Somebody Else Drive." Time: 28:40.   **A**−

John Anderson: *Eye of the Hurricane* (Warner Bros. '84). In which Anderson exercises his rights as a major country star and does nothing but show off the reason he's a major country star—his tonsils. As distinguished from, say, labelmate Gary Morris, he's blessed not just with a great instrument but with what'll pass for a great natural instrument—its intensity seems completely informal and rarely even hints at mannerism. I prefer him a little less doleful for sure. But I respect his rights.   **B+**

John Anderson: *Greatest Hits* (Warner Bros. '84). Except maybe for Ricky Skaggs, this folksy eccentric sings fewer embarrassing songs than anyone in country music. Unlike Skaggs, he plays at innocence rather than striving for it, which is why there always seems to be something comic bubbling under the eager warmth of his voice. And as you soon learn from lyrics like "Black Sheep" and "Swingin'," he's unlike Skaggs in another way as well: he's not a moralistic tight-ass.   **A**

John Anderson: *Tokyo, Oklahoma* (Warner Bros. '85). Anderson loves a good lyric the way David Johansen loves a good lyric, the way Willie Nelson loves a good tune—and he loves a good tune, too. With "Twelve Bar Blues" and "A Little Rock 'n' Roll and Some Country Blues" defeating their billing and the title tune crossing "Fujiyama Mama" and "Promised Land," this is the rock and roll album I was afraid he'd never make—he's allowed three slow songs, especially when one is as sad as "Down in Tennessee."   **A**−

John Anderson: *Countrified* (Warner Bros. '86). What's made him the decade's premier country star artistically has been his disinclination to act like one—he's never climbed on the Nashville assembly line like Skaggs and Strait and so many smaller fry. Until now. He goes for George's intensity rather than Merle's hang-loose, but he won't convince you he thought these songs were special, and

though this may mean the truth is still in him, don't bet on it—not after he yanked the difficult-to-program album he's got in the can. And just in case country radio isn't mollified, he provides a gratuitous cover of Merle's "Fightin' Side of Me." In the Vietnam era jingoistic trash at least made sense on its own neurotic terms. Who's he gonna beat up on in 1986? CISPES? Alexander Cockburn?   **B**−

John Anderson: *Blue Skies Again* (MCA '88). First side's generic Jawn: sunny title tune for a new label, "Duet of the Polyester Poets" with a new labelmate, and a song his wife worked on, which is the only reason I can forgive its country wet dream of a hook: "Every night you make my day." Second side's brilliant: titles like "His and Hers" and "Lying in Her Arms" are taken as far as they can go. Wonder if Jawn knows the difference anymore.   **B+**

John Anderson: *10* (MCA '88). The noncommittal title says a lot—about professionalism, about product. Not so much compromised as off his game, he kicks in with two winners and finishes off with a triumphant trope: "There's a light at the end of the tunnel / And for once it ain't a fast moving train." In between he goes all mushy about God, love, children, born-to-losers, and the working man.   **B**−

Laurie Anderson: *Big Science* (Warner Bros. '82). Like protest singers, novelty artists put too much strain on the words. Anderson's performance, as they say, is richer and subtler than Si Kahn's or John Prine's. But her music is more, as they say, minimal, which diminishes replay potential. Don't get me wrong—she achieves moments of humor so exquisite (timing and timbre of the pilot's chuckles on "From the Air," for instance) that I just have to hear them again, and when I do I enjoy the rest. But while Anderson's alienated patriotic (and romantic) affection is clearly her own invention, it's just as clearly a variant on your basic boho Americanism (and sexuality)—a variant that adds only a voice, not words, by which I mean ideas. Richard Pryor she ain't.   **A**−

Laurie Anderson: *Mister Heartbreak* (Warner Bros. '84). It should come as no surprise that art-rock is what this art-world heroine is up to, at least on record. And though for sheer wordcraft I'll still take Dave Alvin or August Darnell, as art-rock lyricists go she's top-class—compare Fripp & Co., or collaborator Peter Gabriel. Given how often art-rock projects are sunk by literary malfeasance, not to mention Anderson's fundamentally verbal shtick, she'd better be. And given how often art-rock projects are sunk by silly music, it's a good thing too that this putative violinist-composer has accrued so much studiocraft, utilizing sometime co-producer Bill Laswell not so much to pin down a groove as to perfect the kind of coloristic electronic effects semiexperimentalists like to fool around with. As a result, the aural content is as suggestive as the lyrics, with a sensuality and sonic panache Anderson the narrator has no trouble living up to. For art-rock, rich stuff. **A—**

Laurie Anderson: *United States Live* (Warner Bros. '84). Taking a deep breath, I dutifully put on side one the moment the box arrived and to my surprise raced through the rest almost consecutively. Then I was able to jump around—which I have, just about daily, ever since. This is partly a function of sheer quantity—hard to get tired of four-and-a-half hours of fairly good anything very fast. Maybe after playing all ten sides five times minimum I should have a favorite, and it's true a few jokes have paled. But even though the live set is more conceptual comedy à la *Big Science* than rockish breakthrough like *Mister Heartbreak,* the composer-turned-performance-artist's three years as a nominal pop star have done something for her. Words carry this aural document, but minimal (if not minimalist) accompaniment and arrangement (and of course performance) assure that their movement is always musical. And if the meanings could be more pointed, Anderson is hardly the first major artist to leave the driving to us. **A**

Laurie Anderson: *Home of the Brave* (Warner Bros. '86). Multimedia ain't omnimedia, and if she ever gets to do a movie again I hope she hires Jonathan Demme or at least Julien Temple. A credible groove ain't a compelling groove, and I'm inclined to blame the auteur rather than Nile Rodgers, Jimmy Bralower, or even Adrian Belew. But this soundtrack establishes her as a dynamite entertainer nevertheless. Her timing and intonation are so slick that even when she says something strange you catch yourself taking it for granted. Most of her material is perfectly comprehensible to anybody with a working knowledge of lower Manhattan. And if you're thinking this is faint praise, stop condescending—she's got more to say than 98 percent of the plodders, stumblers, and lurchers whose chief aim in life is keeping their avant-garde credentials in order.   **A—**

Laurie Anderson: *Strange Angels* (Warner Bros. '89). Anderson feels powerless, a speck of dust at the speed of light, and these are the bleakest songs she's ever written. Positing progress as the force that prevents history from righting itself, she looks the death of nature in its prosthetic eye and sees the devil coming a lot sooner than, for instance, equal pay for women, which she calculates is due along about 3888. But she also feels connected to the pop firmament, often constructing her lyrics like a human sampler, and this is her most mellifluous music ever. She's taken voice lessons to match the tunes she's writing, and hired sidepeople—notably *Graceland* bassist Bakithi Khumalo, whose fretless flow unifies the four lithest tracks—who she knows will add a savvy, sensual sheen to her most cerebral constructs. Some find these pop moves a mark of compromise; I find them pleasingly complex. A soothing glimpse of the end of the world.   **A**

The Angry Samoans: *Inside My Brain* (Bad Trip EP '80). Like so many of their coscenemakers, these dorks cultivate race and sex shock; one of them has had unkind words for his "adopted Jew parents," and the band's abuse of a "pathetic male queer" is now on record. But these six foreshortened songs, self-destructing in under ten minutes total, sum up the only hardcore punks to put the social distortion they yell about on the map. Sure a lot of what's inside their brains started somewhere else, but that's where it ended up, and by copping to their part—even their "new generation" anthem-if-you-want-to-call-it-that is called "Right Side of My Brain"—they give themselves a shot at beating it, by whatever means necessary. They're solipsistic enough to claim the gone girlfriend in "You Stupid Asshole" no longer exists, and fair enough to add that they're stupid assholes themselves. And they insult Rodney Bingenheimer, which must be why skinheads think they go too far. If Carly Simon can make great rock and roll, why not them? **A**

The Angry Samoans: *Back From Samoa* (Bad Trip EP '82). An LP in format and perceived weight, a seventeen-minute EP in real-time length, this is the most offensive record I've ever liked, and damn near perfect if superannuated hardcore with metal hooks could be your meat. Todd Homer is good enough to half convince me he's as demented as he sounds, and I don't mean in a cute way—I pity anyone (especially any female) who has to treat him like a human. "They Saved Hitler's Cock" is the most brutal and ludicrous of these fourteen frags, "Homo-sexual" ("I'm like you") and "Ballad of Jerry Curlan" ("drinks toilet water takes it up the ass butt-fucks his dog") the scariest. All of 'em are catchy. And almost every one gives me a laugh. **A**

The Angry Samoans: *Yesterday Started Tomorrow* (PVC EP '87). In which they snarl as hookily as ever through a pop phase signaled by an average song length of 2:02 and the occasional appearance of the word "love" (as in "Somebody To Love," which you know is a cover only when you check the credits). Mental illness per se, sometimes caused by lost "love," is now their explicit subject, to such an extent that though inwardness was their great virtue in hardcore's halcyon days, here I could stand a little unwonted aggression. Maturity strikes again. **B+**

Angry Samoans: *Gimme Samoa: 31 Garbage-Pit Hits* (PVC CD '87). There's something heart-warmingly perverse about turning these proud piggos into yuppie fodder, and after all, how many other major '80s bands could fit their entire recorded output onto one pricy piece of plastic-coated aluminum five inches in diameter? Including even a few outtakes—the same ones that pad PVC's rerelease of *Inside My Brain* into something collectors might respring for, and I must admit they're growing on me. Some disparage the Samoans as incipient Dead Milkmen, which isn't such a terrible insult and also misses how disturbing they were—Rodney Bingenheimer wasn't their only enemy. In fact, maybe they still are disturbing—maybe that analysis is a pornography-is-boring move, an attempt to trivialize the threatening. Always a reluctant fan, I find that their bad attitudes reinforce each other played back to back in this format: hard, catchy, unashamed straight-teen-male hostility so funny that there's no denying the educational value of its self-knowledge, though maybe more for observers than participants. In very short, a punk touchstone. **A**

Angry Samoans: *STP Not LSD* (PVC '88). Their material is still pretty surefire, but it's also pretty scattershot, because in 1988 they're reduced to a joke band—there's no scene worth outraging any more, as the bands that try it prove. Better folk-rock acid casualties and recycled recycled Sabbath than B.A.L.L. parodying Bangla Desh or Rapeman beating somebody else's meat. **B+**

Angst: *Angst* (Happy Squid EP '83). No, not San Francisco's answer to Bauhaus—just forthrightly country-tinged postpunk songs about astronauts, kicking heroin, sucking the president's cock, and other sensible subjects. **B**

Angst: *Lite Life* (SST '85). These three guys are smart enough to know they have a problem—they can't sing. They're also smart enough not to let that stop them. After declining the Most Inappropriate Cowpunk Band Name Lariat Twirl and qualifying for the Eklekticism Rools Speed Trials, they enter the Music Machine Memorial Songwriting Contest and do all right—you'd swear "Just To Please You" (or was it "Never Going To Apologize"?) was the track that caught you humming on *Pebbles VI*. **B**

Adam Ant: *Friend or Foe* (Epic '82). Telescoping into a year and a half the kind of career that used to take a decade, Adam fires his group, hires some horns, and tops off his meretricious, confidently catchy hit debut and his meretricious, arrogantly bombastic flop follow-up with some ruminations on life's little ups and downs. The first surprise is that four of these are arrogantly catchy. The second surprise is that all four dwell—allusively in the title tune—on Adam's status as victim-of-the-press, a theme that was death to rock and roll in a less self-conscious age. Still has trouble with real life, though, which is probably why the rest bombs.   **B**—

Anthrax: *I'm the Man* (Island EP '87). Title tune's supposed to be the great Beasties rip, and it is, though the jokes wear thin pretty quick. Band's supposed to be smart metal, which given their Queens roots and "Hava Negillah" rip probably just means they're Jewish.   **B**—

Anti-Choc: *Anti-Choc* (Stern's Africa import '88). Though the latest Zaiko Langa Langa spin-off is advertised as roughing up slow old-fashioned rumba and hyping up fast newfangled kwassa kwassa, I find the trad harmonies homy and the quick-fingered picking hypnotic. Soothing at any speed. Also danceable.   **B+**

Anti-Nowhere League: *Anti-Nowhere League* (Faulty Products EP '82). "And I drunk that / And I drunk this / And I spewed up on a pint of piss / So what?" barely suggests the delicious flavor of the cheerful, scabrous, utterly lumpish banned-in-Britain B side to their laff-riot remake of Ralph McTell's "Streets of London." Unfortunately, the U.S. release is extended half to death by heavy-punk originals yclept "I hate . . . People" and "Let's Break the Law." Be grateful they got lucky twice.   **B+**

Any Trouble: *Where Are All Nice Girls?* (Stiff '80). In which Clive Gregson attempts to answer the burning new-wave question: what would Elvis Costello be like if he weren't an obscurantist? And convinces no one that Joe Jackson is the right answer.   **C+**

Apollonia 6: *Apollonia 6* (Warner Bros. '84). In which our heroine fucks the principal, opens up for her pretty boy, sings quite a bit, and talks cute rather than dirty. The tracks are more than serviceable Starr Company issue; the formula is less than kicky shock.   **B**—

Joey Arias: *Arias on Holiday* (Flaming Pie EP '87). Billie Holiday impressions—including Madonna's "Holiday"—by a flaming Ann Magnuson crony, and guess what: *they don't come off campy*. If the very idea makes male heterosexual jazz fans vomit, they've got their own bag.   **B**

Joan Armatrading: *Me Myself I* (A&M '80). The perennially unclassifiable London West Indian meets Instant Records' Barry Gottehrer for her punchiest and most attractive album—she even comes close to laughing a couple of times. The title tune is to narcissism as "Brown Sugar" is to racism—she doesn't prettify it, but she doesn't forswear its pleasures, either. Suggesting to this white male heterosexual that unclassifiable may be a polite way to say unreachable—and that unreachable may be why even songs as well-realized as these wouldn't take that extra pop leap if Gottehrer weren't motorvating them.   **B+**

Joan Armatrading: *Walk Under Ladders* (A&M '81). Where Barry Gottehrer is attracted to Blondie and the Go-Go's, Steve Lillywhite's meal tickets are U2 and the Psychedelic Furs. And in a singer-songwriter whose large voice creates a grandiose impression that does less than nothing for her terse habits of speech, the switch from one to the other is the wrong kind of big deal.   **B**—

Joan Armatrading: *The Key* (A&M '83). Folkies manqué to the contrary, it's not hard rock she's unsuited for, a point she drives home on the side-openers, which are as nasty as this album gets both musically and emotionally, and also as rousing. What she's unsuited for is pop—the way Steve Lillywhite's hooks lockstep with her alto singsong on "The Key," "Drop the

Pilot," and "The Game of Love" makes the friendly sentiments expressed therein seem mechanical. And since she's always been a tough broad, maybe they are.   **B**

Joan Armatrading: *Track Record* (A&M '83). This convenient best-of goes light on her best and biggest album, *Me Myself I,* dividing neatly between Steve Lillywhite new wave, which means the drums are loud, and Glyn Johns rock, which means she gets to be loud under her own power. She's a little long-winded, but that's mostly because she puts so much thought into her relationships, which in turn is because she puts so much feeling into them; this is one of those rare pop stars who's invariably serious but never pompous, which is why she isn't a bigger star. The best-of format puts her seriousness in musical perspective—makes it seem almost beautiful sometimes.   **A—**

Joan Armatrading: *The Shouting Stage* (A&M '88). Some faithful decry the bows to pop fashion from lounge to CHR, others hear her fulfilling her destiny. Haven't her fans learned after all these years that beyond raw tunecraft her music is irrelevant? With that proud, brawny voice, she's incapable of pop ingratiation—anything she does is her, and most folks are always gonna think she's weird. P.S.: This time the tunecraft's about average.   **B**

Steve Arrington's Hall of Fame: *I* (Atlantic '83). Funk vocals are so cartoon-defined you'd figure the bassist to end up with the real band after the split. But it must have been Arrington's parts of Slave's collective compositions that made them stick. Here he proposes nothing less than to modulate the nasalities, glottal constrictions, and Mel Blanc raunch of Ohio playing into an emotionally integrated—soulful, as the expression goes—singing style. Funnier lyrics would make this task easier. Likewise funnier bass parts.   **B+**

Steve Arrington's Hall of Fame: *Positive Power* (Atlantic '84). Arrington's bass does pop now, but whether you really get his funk depends on how well you connect with the way he turns the style's loony-toon vocals into pear-shaped tones. Me, I jump only for the synthesized-kalimba

hook of "Young and Ready," and he chants that one.   **B**

Steve Arrington: *Dancin' in the Key of Life* (Atlantic '85). Unless you count Amy Grant, pop doesn't get more explicitly Christian—not only does the back cover thank Jesus Christ rather than the usual God, but the record invites us to convert. Granted, Arrington's a Jesse Jackson–type Christian—remembers that petroleum is still a finite resource, takes pains to acknowledge the right to choose in a song where the abortion isn't done. But his positivity theology doesn't sell the music any more than some other ideology would. The music sells the theology, and augments it: for the first time he's making like a songwriter, designing hooks for his vital rhythms and mellifluous vocal cartoons. The title track lives up to its dreams of Stevie, both songs about babies are choice, and it all comes together with the goofy yet spiritual scat coda to "Stand With Me" (which means stand up for Jesus, children).   **A—**

Steve Arrington: *The Jammin' National Anthem* (Atlantic '86). Here we come up against the perils of Christianity as a political matrix in black music (and life). I don't doubt the goodness of Arrington's heart any more than I do his Stevie-cum-Bootsy vocal and rhythmic dexterity. But last time he was brimming with charity and full of fun, where now the anxiety that besets anyone who sticks to "old-fashioned" values in a time of upheaval erodes his tolerance. So he sounds a little frightened—of gays, of teen violence, of a "new age" that won't look like his dreams no matter how many anthems he writes. He misses Martin Luther King a lot. So do we all.   **B**

Artists United Against Apartheid: *Sun City* (Manhattan '85). Each side closes with a well-meaning failure: "Revolutionary Situation"'s collage of indistinct South African voices over Keith LeBlanc humdrum is an object lesson in political correctness that might have made a collectible B, and Bono's country blues is simply ignorant. And now, with my sorehead credentials in order, I'll add that Gil Scott-Heron's superrap is as astute and moving rhythmically as it is ideologically and that Peter Gabriel's largely instrumental "No More Apartheid" is a worthy successor to "Biko." What's more, each side begins with the title tune, which can grow on you in a big way, although I don't think its failure to break pop is cause for special indignation—had the programmers cooperated, it would have been a case of politics (and hype) overcoming musical taste as much as the opposite. So it goes. As a cultural materialist, I admire Little Steven's strategy anyway—with his medium-saturation outreach, he's preaching to *potential* faithful, which is always the idea. Sometimes raising consciousness does as much good as raising money. Which can be forwarded to the Africa Fund, 198 Broadway, NYC 10038.   **A—**

The Art of Noise: *(Who's Afraid of?) The Art of Noise* (Island '84). There's no denying that this concatenation of musical-instrument imitations and collapsing new sound effects generates considerable episodic interest and the occasional groove. But only "Close (To the Edit)" sustains much jam, and "Beat Box" goes on so long it ends up insulting the memory of "Rapture" and *Duck Rock* both. What some people won't dance to nowadays.   **B**

The Art of Noise: *In Visible Silence* (Chrysalis '86). Not only do they sacrifice meaning to sensation, they happily exploit ersatz meaning as a sensation-heightening device. So fine, don't trust them. Only since when is music supposed to be trustworthy? Just note that deprived of genius Trevor Horn these mad studio pros have to go with what they know, subjecting their sound-effects music to hook and beat when no grandiose electronic joke comes to mind. And good—not since the glory days of the Penguin Cafe have instrumentalists confounded the arty and the trivial and had fun at the same time.   **A—**

The Art of Noise: *In No Sense? Nonsense!* (Chrysalis '87). First dislocated electrohop, then zap-pow disco, now shards of soundtrack—genteel yodels and heavenly choruses and string quartets, "Crusoe" and "A Day at the Races" and

"Dragnet" (the "real" one). And for their next trick, postmodernist Muzak so funny you'll forget to laugh.   **B—**

Ashford & Simpson: *A Musical Affair* (Warner Bros. '80). "Love Don't Make It Right," the big (black-radio) hit, is A-grade filler, just like "I Ain't Asking for Your Love": moderately catchy, moderately wise. "Happy Endings," the follow-up, is filler filler, just like the follow-up follow-up "Get Out Your Handkerchief": token ironies aside, both titles are self-explanatory. "We'll Meet Again" is their assault on Broadway.   **C+**

Ashford & Simpson: *Solid* (Capitol '84). Hooked by their most confident and attractive single since 1978's "Is It Still Good to Ya" (and maybe since whenever), this never rises nearly so high again, but the nontitle side especially is a return to the consistency of *So So Satisfied* and *Stay Free.* Which is to say that these world-class songwriters have made themselves another groove album. But not to suggest the pertinent contradiction: the groove is a flow, the flow hips and hops.   **B+**

Ashford & Simpson: *Real Love* (Capitol '86). If I gave points for attitude, I'd up this a notch for fidelity to formula: Nick and Val wrote it, Nick and Val sang it, Nick and Val produced it, and they hope you like it too, Mr. Crossover Gatekeeper. But not even "Nobody Walks in L.A.," which makes good on its title but is too quirky and local for a single, takes it on home. So while they go four for eight overall—one-two-three on the first side, lead cut on the second—only their many fans will care.   **B**

Robert Ashley: *Perfect Lives (Private Parts): The Bar* (Lovely '80). Ashley's previous recorded excursion into pulse-plus-words quasi-rock was appealingly hypnotic, but I thought it inauspicious that when I heard and saw this piece live early in 1980 I had a hard time staying awake. No such omens with the album, which is like a state-of-the-art update of the Velvets' "Murder Mystery." One improvement is that you can follow the words, which offer both hook phrases ("We don't serve fine wines in half-pints buddy") and literary satisfaction (dialogue/confrontation between white common-sense-materialist bartender and black cocktail pianist of mystical mien). Also gratifying is the ironic poppish context Ashley finds for the avant-MOR blandouts of such Soho luminaries as producer-arranger Peter Gordon and keyboardist-arranger "Blue" Gene Tyranny. Time: 27:51.   **A**

Asia: *Asia* (Geffen '82). The art-rock Foreigner is a find—rare that a big new group is bad enough to sink your teeth into any more. John Wetton and Steve Howe added excitement to contexts as pretentious as King Crimson and Yes, but this is just pompous—schlock in the grand manner, with synthesizers John Williams would love. And after listening to two lyrics about why they like their girlfriends, three about "surviving," and four about why they don't like their girlfriends, I'm ready for brain salad surgery. Inspirational Verse: "So many lines/You've heard them all/A lie in every one/From men who never understand your personality." **C−**

Rick Astley: *Whenever You Need Somebody* (RCA '87). Launching his career with seed money from Thatcher's Enterprise Allowance Scheme, Astley graduated from singer-bandleader to tape op and tea boy at Stock Aitken Waterman, where he ripened for a year before donning a full set of SAW hooks and emerging as beefcake juicier than Adam Faith, Marty Wilde, or Johnny Wadd. And that's according to the notes—it's the image he wants to project. Musically he's a throwback to such long-forgotten rockaballad singers as Don Rondo, with more muscle and less sweetness or swing. Blame him on Northern Soul, its attraction to Afro-America finally revealed as I-am-somebody for nobodies with a master plan.   **D+**

Aswad: *Live and Direct* (Mango '84). These black Brits' considerable commercial success in their non-Ethiopian homeland guarantees no more than any other band's commercial success; though they're avowedly more roots, their songs for lovers ("Your Recipe") and rhythmic extensions ("Soca Rumba") are as serviceably undistinguished as those of Third World, a commercially successful band indeed. And I'm sure they could have made their U.S. introductions more winningly than with a year's dub album followed by a live job. Inspirational Intro: "You know what live and direct mean? It mean live and direct."   **C+**

Aswad: *Crucial Tracks* (Mango '89). Where their opposite numbers in Steel Pulse yoke reggae militance to rock aggression, they soften reggae hope with pop salesmanship. Singing sweeter and smarmier than Gregory Isaacs if not Billy Ocean, Brinsley Forde doesn't lend much force to lyrics like "Set Them Free" and "Back to Africa." Nor does their obvious eagerness to insert cutesy hooks do much for their aura of righteousness. Like so many black pop best-ofs, this one showcases beautiful music—I dig their dabs of dub. But if Lionel Richie came up with a liberal lie on the order of "Give a Little Love"—"Only we can make it better / Only if we try"—reggae fans would cry Babylon from here to Nostrand Avenue.   **B−**

Sweet Pea Atkinson: *Don't Walk Away* (Island '82). Was (Not Was) repay Atkinson for his vocal chores by producing a solo debut, and spare us D. Was's bug-eyed late-capitalist existential cynicism in the bargain. Trouper that he is, Atkinson will sing any nonsense they hand him, but he obviously finds his truth in Dionne Warwick, the Tymes, General Johnson, and Eddie Rabbitt, and I'll go along with that. Meanwhile, the Was Bros. have learned enough about Linn drums to provide the kind of bug-eyed late-capitalist existential displacement that lends realism to orders like "dig deep, don't be nice" and "dance or die."   **A−**

Attack of the Killer B's (Warner Bros. '83). Non-LP B sides are odd tracks out by definition, and while most of these would blend attractively if unobtrusively into albums by their respective auteurs, their proximity is strictly packaging. It's revealing that compiler Bob Merlis has stretched his concept around four ringers, including the German version of "Shock the Monkey," which opens side two for the excellent reason that unlike most of its fellow prisoners it's got a killer hook. Not that any rock-and-roller won't want to hear the Marshall Crenshaw and Gang of Four and T-Bone Burnett rarities included, and that collectors won't covet the rest. But I thought collectors already had them.   **B**

Attitude: *Pump the Nation* (Atlantic '83). Produced by the System, a/k/a Mic Murphy and David Frank, they got the juice— all three of these young people possess more mellifluous voices than Murphy, and more singing technique as well. But they don't have as much personality—Murphy's synth-compatible vocal style is far more idiosyncratic and engaging than their postsoulfulness. And in the great artist-producer tradition, Murphy & Frank give up two great conceits for the singles and save the rest for themselves.   **B**

Au Pairs: *Playing with a Different Sex* (Human import '81). For months I struggled to get with the commendable postpunk feminism and accessible quasifunk rock and roll of this gender-balanced quartet, and for months I failed. Only in person did I notice that gender symbol Lesley Woods had about as much to say now as Grace Slick did in 1967—more than you'd predict and less than you'd hope—and that on the whole they sounded like a bored Gang of Four. Dozed off during the climactic "It's Obvious." Which I found rousing anyway. Ditto for the album when I got home.   **B+**

Au Pairs: *Sense and Sensuality* (Roadrunner import '82). The renown of this sorry punk-funk gone pop-jazz is as depressing as anything in the annals of Anglophilia. Lesley Woods's line on free love is as priggish as the rest of her leftism and her separate-but-equal rhythm section couldn't make the earth move if one of them played tractor. Don't blame me for the metaphor, either—it's Lesley's, by way of famed protofeminist E. Hemingway, which proves that she's either open-minded or just plain dumb. Not since the Stranglers has a Brit group sexed it up so unconvincingly.   **C**

Avengers: *Avengers* (CD '83). These fourteen cuts constitute the recorded output of a late-'70s San Fran punk band best remembered for "We Are the One," the finest U.S. indie single of 1977, and a 1979 Steve Jones–produced EP. The notes extol their "breakthrough—however brief— into a vision of life expressing firsthand passion and revolt," but to me Penelope Houston sounds like a valley girl with too much attitude. If her "We are not Jesus (Christ!) / We are not fascist (pigs!) / We are not capitalist (industrialists!) / We are not communists" confounded cant on the single, over the long haul her antipolitical railing, lapsed-Catholic obsessions, and assertions of self-sufficiency protest too much. And I wish she knew she was singing flat.   **B**

Aztec Camera: *High Land, Hard Rain* (Sire '83). At first I did the obvious thing and pigeonholed this as high-grade pop— richer and truer than Haircut 100 or even the dB's or the Bongos and ultimately feckless anyhow. Now I think it's more like U2 with songs (which is all U2 needs). For sheer composition—not just good tunes, but good tunes that swoop and chime and give you goosebumps—Roddy Frame's only current competition is Marshall Crenshaw, and unlike Crenshaw he never makes you smell retro. His wordcraft is worthy of someone who admires Keats, his wordplay worthy of someone admired by Elvis C.; he sings and arranges with a rousing lyricism that melds militance and the love of life. These are songs in which sweet retreat can't be permanent, in which idealism is buffeted but unbowed—songs of that rare kind of innocence that has survived hard experience. So far, anyway—Frame is still very young. How unusual it is these days for youth to add resonance to what used to be teen music. Original grade: A.   **A−**

Aztec Camera: *Oblivious* (Sire EP '83). Remixing the signature cut from their best (first) album and adding three old B sides that beat the filler off its Knopflerized follow-up, this is cultbound nevertheless: too slight and loose for anybody but converts and mamas to love, or buy. Cf. their new B side, "Jump," which is slight and loose for the ages—Roddy Frame's loaded Eddie Van Halen parody is one of the great art statements in the history of inept guitar. If only some ombudsman at Warners would tack it on here.   **B**

Aztec Camera: *Knife* (Sire '84). Given the putrefaction potential of the straightforwardly literary romanticism Roddy Frame affects, it's amazing he did so brilliantly with it even once. In fact, it's fairly amazing that second time out he gets away with it three songs' worth—three songs whose verbal lyricism sharpens the consistently winsome music, which is the kind of unlikely feat critics expect of straightforwardly literary types. Silly though it seems, Frame may be right to worry that his youth is passing at twenty-one, unless you want to blame the five merely winsome songs on producer Mark Knopfler, who probably thought "Here lies the essence of my peers" a deep line and certainly cheered "Knife" on to nine minutes.   **B+**

Aztec Camera: *Love* (Sire '87). Not only is this Roddy Frame's solo debut in disguise, it's the worst kind of solo debut, replete with electronic everything and hacks/pros like Marcus Miller and Tommy LiPuma. Yet even after three straight slow ones on side two, the kid is putting over his own style of hit-factory romance the way he once put over his own style of schoolboy verse. The voice still gives off that sincere ache. And strummed or picked, the guitar lifts off every time.   **A—**

Eric B. & Rakim: *Paid in Full* (4th & B'way '87). Rakim raps quick and clean and almost quiet about the business at hand, which is moving the crowd. Eric B.'s grooves approach a classic swing on nothing but scratch and sampled percussion, with touches of horn or whistle deep in the mix. If you spent your life listening to people brag, sometimes without opening their mouths, you'd overrate the new crew too. **B**

Eric B. & Rakim: *Follow the Leader* (Uni '88). Ahh, sampling—it'll turn a minimalist into a melodist every time. If like me you've found their Brownian motion grooveful but a touch austere, maybe you'll get hooked by the obscure Arabian-nights snatches (first a snatch of the snatch, then finally completion), or the girls (speeded-up guys?) singing (this can't be—beatmasters please advise) "You're so stupid, you're so rough." Or the symphonic intro. Or maybe Rakim's ever-increasing words-per-minute ratio—the man loves language like a young Bob D. Beatmaster's P.S.: It's the fucking Eagles, speeded up, singing "You're so smooth, the world's so rough." **A—**

Babyface: *Tender Lover* (Solar '89). Though Teddy Riley got the credit, the streetwise sweets of new-jack love man Bobby Brown were mostly this producer's doing, and for his star turn he dispenses with the new jack—comes packaged as the title concept, with no prerogatives and not too many fast ones to spoil the fantasy. I mean, after he gets home from work, fantasy enough in the age of structural unemployment, he promises to cook dinner too. This would have serious attractions as a corrective to the sexist fantasies of hip hop if there was any reason to think neo-B-boys would listen. But it's my guess they'll just take "Whip Appeal" literally and figure the guy for a bondage freak. **B**

Back to the Beach (Columbia '87). Stevie Ray Vaughan's "Pipeline"? Herbie Hancock's "Wipe Out"? Dave Edmunds's "Wooly Bully"? Pee-wee Herman's "Surfin' Bird"? This soundtrack opens up undreamed vistas of recontextualization, then shuts them down. Unlike Los Lobos claiming Ritchie Valens, the participants find no deep cultural resonance in the ancient texts, and unlike French, Frith, Kaiser & Thompson romping over "Surfin' U.S.A.," they get no kick out of destroying them, either. All they manage is trademarked modernizations consonant with the CHR fodder Mark Goldenberg shovels Aimee Mann and executive culprit David Kahne pours all over Marti Jones. The only winning cuts—and by me this includes even Pee-wee's—come from dodos too simple to aim for anything harder than fun fun fun: Eddie Money, Frankie Avalon, and Annette Funicello. **C+**

Bad Brains: *Bad Brains* (ROIR cassette '82). Turn a fusion band into hardcore propheteers and you end up with fast heavy metal. The best kind for damn sure, especially since they turn their rage into Positive Mental Attitude. I like it fine. But great punks give up more than a salubrious blur. [Later on Relativity.]   **B+**

Bad Brains: *Rock for Light* (PVC '83). Mediocre hardcore you can ignore, especially if you live in an area where they dig up the street a lot; hardcore of a certain quality you love or hate. More than ex-fusioneer Dr. Know on "gits," it's the distinctive if not exactly authoritative blackboard-screechy "throat" of H.R. that provides the quality here, and I like it, kind of. Though this repeats five tunes from their ROIR cassette, it's definitive by virtue of its Ric Ocasek production and vinyl audio. You know what to do.   **B+**

Bad Brains: *I Against I* (SST '84). As a reggae band, they were a hardcore band with a change-up; as a metal band, they're a hardcore band with a great windup and no follow-through. The small problem is H.R.'s lyrics, which he's still smart enough to blur with the speed and attitude that make the lead and title cut their strongest song since "Pay to Cum." The big problem is Dr. Know, who's got a hundred Hendrix moves and no killer riffs.   **B−**

Bad Brains: *Quickness* (Caroline '89). For H.R. this precedent-setting band has devolved into a money gig—he feels more comfortable juicing his Afro-universalist utterances with the reggae-inflected world-rock of his solo records and his alternate group Human Rights. And though the title tune claims to jam the disco with acid rock and hardcore rather than hip hop/go go/bebop, the shit sure sounds like metal to me. Sure sounds like Dr. Know, too—on his own H.R. is only a bore, but in this context his male chauvinist arrogance comes through loud if not clear.   **C+**

Bad Company: *10 From 6* (Atlantic '85). Recollected in a best-of's serviceably tuneful tranquility, their gut-crunch is smarter and more laid-back than anyone cares to notice, its deterioration less striking than its formal fortitude. Their tales of priapism and peripatesis avoid posture because they are posture, lean and mean as a clean machine. Would all "hard rock" were so austere. Pure as punk, in their way.   **B+**

Bad Religion: *How Could Hell Be Any Worse?* (Epitaph '82). Greg Griffin's vocals fall into a naturally musical off-key drone that make him sound at times like a mullah in mourning, which is appropriate—he's not as arrogant about his nihilism as most hardcore kids. On the other hand, he's not as funny about it as the best ones, either.   **B**

Bad Religion: *Into the Future* (Epitaph '83). Like a less musicianly version of the departed TSOL, this promising L.A. hardcore outfit has moved on to slower-tempo, organ-drenched hard rock that resembles nothing so much as late Hawkwind. Some may call it caterwaul, but I find myself moved by its anthemic ambition—and achievement. Conceptual clincher: the way they surround the dystopian-gothic tales and images—the kind of stuff that comes naturally to committed teenagers who know they're growing up but don't know they like it—with "It's Only Over . . ." and ". . . When You Give Up."   **A−**

Bad Religion: *Suffer* (Epitaph '88). This comeback is hailed as a hardcore milestone, probably because it's coherent. Relatively sane as their bitter analysis is—and I mean relative to both hardcore despair and mainstream complacency—it sounds a little pat. As if they're already a little slow for speedrock and don't want to upset the apple cart.   **B**

Bad Religion: *No Conviction* (Epitaph '89). Like a good rapper, Greg Graffin is once again singing his own tune—no matter how the three chords play themselves out on the (probably nonexistent, but never mind) lead sheet, the natural drone of his voice adds a music of its own. And he's still finding naive new truths in disillusioned hardcore truisms. "Culture was the seed of proliferation but it has gotten melded into an inharmonic whole" is bad writing; so's "Prescience was not lacking and the present was not all." Yet propelled by the drone and the three chords, they clobber you with the life-probe that's always been rock and roll's secret, excuse, or reason for being.   **B+**

Philip Bailey: *Chinese Wall* (Columbia '84). Pretty convoluted: great falsetto of great drummer-led black pop band seeks solo identity, turns for production aid (and duet on single) to drummer who's led great (i.e., best-selling) white art-rock band back into money by ripping off (appropriating?) black rhythms and vocals. Funny thing is: though Phil Collins plays a little louder than Maurice White, he's got almost as many chops and may even sing better. Even at that, for Vegas-gone-to-heaven I'll take Earth, Wind & Fire over Phil & Phil. But I'll certainly take Phil & Phil over Genesis for lush/sensuous/zippy soundtrack.   **B+**

Anita Baker: *The Songstress* (Beverly Glen '83). In a time when the only black people with the guts to go for the soul are Mississippi recidivists and moldy oldies, this L.A. sophisticate has the audacity to pretend she can make pop music out of the shit. The violin and woodwind touches hark back to when soul had something to sell out with, the jazzy guitar comps look forward to when it'll storm the big rooms, the funky bottom bespeaks commitment, the hooky songwriting bespeaks smarts, and the voice sings.   **B+**

Anita Baker: *Rapture* (Elektra '86). Having listened far more than natural inclination dictated, I've become actively annoyed with this vocal watershed. From its strong lounge-jazz beat to its conscious avoidance of distracting lyrical detail, it's all husky, burnished mood, the fulfillment of the quiet-storm format black radio devised to lure staider customers away from white-bread temptations like soft rock and easy listening. God knows it's more soulful, and sexier, too, but that's all it is—a reification of the human voice as vehicle of an expression purer than expression ever ought to be.   **B−**

Anita Baker: *Giving You the Best That I Got* (Elektra '88). Where five years ago Baker was a soul singer who honored the traditional soul audience's lounge leanings, now she's an arena-lounge singer manufacturing generalized intimacy for 26-to-45s. Rid of funky minor-label producer-songwriter Patrick Moten, she composed two tracks for *Rapture* and worked on a third. Here she's down to two collaborations as the credits edge toward El Lay—if Britten-Lyle and the Perris have anted up, can Carole Bayer Sager and Toto be far behind? She's not a total loss yet—despite the universal lyrics and inflated choruses, three tracks make something of her established standards. But unless she suffers reverses I wouldn't wish on Frank Sinatra, she'll never risk an interesting album again.   **C+**

Marcia Ball: *Soulful Dress* (Rounder '84). Most of the new rash of soul folk, survivors and revivalists both, do little or nothing to redefine the values they hold dear, but this reformed country singer avoids any hint of neocon nostalgia. With her rolling bayou backbeat, her standards you never heard before, her habit of belting the man she's loyal to, and the moleskin burr that textures her every line, she has the makings of a downhome Bonnie Raitt. Just in time.   **B+**

Afrika Bambaataa & Soulsonic Force: *Planet Rock—The Album* (Tommy Boy '86). In retrospect, the sheer dumb catchiness of the Kraftwerk hook sweetens one's love-feh relationship with the title tune, and the way "Lookin' for the Perfect Beat" digests, funkifies, and elaborates the winning earnestness of "Planet Rock" 's technofuturism was electrohop's transcendent moment. With the ambitious but unconvincing "Renegades of Funk" filling out side one, you'd figure this for a convenient way to store two classics. But though side two does skip both Bam-Brown's "Unity" and Bam-Rotten's "World Destruction" (because neither bear the Soulsonic Force name, I suppose), two of the previously unreleased tracks are anything but filler. And while one features Melle Mel/ Doug Wimbish and the other Trouble Funk, nobody ever said Bam doesn't need help, least of all Bam—there isn't a more public-spirited natural leader on the frenetically competitive rap scene. Which is probably why his groups avoid the male-bonded braggadocio that supplies so much of rap's emotional energy.   **A**—

Afrika Bambaataa and Family: *Beware (The Funk Is Everywhere)* (Tommy Boy '86). Selected producers cut Bam's electro leanings with the prescribed heavy guitars, and musically this tops the UTFO albums, say. But neither leader nor followers give up the rhythms or reasons of a ranking MC, and I'm grieved to report that only "Kick Out the Jams" overcomes the formlessness of personality his detractors have always charged him with—it's got Bill Laswell all over it.   **B**

Afrika Bambaataa and Family: *The Light* (Capitol '88). No kind of sellout, not even a mishmash, just a great DJ trying to reproduce the anything-funky ambience of his parties, go go to reggae to disco to rap. Unfortunately, the ability to hear still ain't the ability to create. On the John Robie–coproduced disco side, "Reckless" (UB40 with dance hook) and "Something He Can Feel" (Nona Hendryx and Boy George back from limbo together for the first time) are pretty great; so's "World Racial War" (Professor Griff please copy) on the Bill Laswell–coproduced funk side. None of them saves the party from approaching mishmash.   **B**

Bananarama: *The Greatest Hits Collection* (London '88). London postfeminists who appropriate girl-group epiphenomena *affectlessly,* to signify inauthenticity, they fare better with odious Stock Aitken Waterman synthpop than with the shallow Swain & Jolley synthsoul they started out with—where Leee Johns sounded dreamy wafting through that detached mix, these lucky lasses just seemed untouchably dreamlike. It's some kind of camp achievement that like the totally plastic singles group they play at being, they're equal to their most "meaningful" early material nevertheless, and some kind of camp limitation that their rilly greatest hits are "Venus" and "Na Na Hey Hey Kiss Him Goodbye." I know, the Dixie Cups didn't have any discernible identity either. But they could sing.   **B**+

Bangles: *Bangles* (Faulty Products EP '82). They have more Beatles in them than Fanny and the Go-Go's combined, but nothing in the songs tells you why they bother or keeps you so busy you don't have time to wonder. It's almost as if the not quite soulful rubber harmonies are ends in themselves—as if these women can't get past their own craft because craft comes so hard to them.   **B**

Bangles: *All Over the Place* (Columbia '84). Definitely reduces the nostalgia-cum-nausea factor that it's women who execute these familiar heart-stopping harmonies, and thank God there's not a trace of Liverpool or even Britannia in the accents. But the value of these songs isn't merely negative—they're thoroughly realized in both the writing and playing. Though the style is as derivative and even retro as on EP, they don't seem to be dabbling any more. Maybe they project such confidence because they know exactly what they want to say: don't fuck me over.   **A**—

Bangles: *Different Light* (Columbia '86). Right, they're maturing into a less derivative pop synthesis, as if that means shit these days. Like the Raspberries before them, they're brilliant when they emulate the Beatles and mature popsters when they don't. And for what it's worth, the four most striking tunes here are the four nonoriginals—every one, for what it's worth, written by a guy.   **B**

Bangles: *Everything* (Columbia '88). No no no, last time wasn't serious, that was just PR—you didn't buy that *Rubber Soul* malarkey, did you? This time, though—this time they're serious. They wrote all the songs themselves. Got two about suicide, one about a complicated girl, a historical thing about glitter, and eight, well, love songs. But serious love songs—"Lately I dream that I'm in your arms," "I'll do anything you want me to," "All I ever really want is you." Really.   **B**—

Lester Bangs and the Delinquents: *Jook Savages on the Brazos* (Live Wire '81). This gets over on music—Velvets meet Voidoids in Austin. But anybody who thinks the music isn't Lester should check out the Delinquents' adequate-at-best surf-punk LP—he gets great ideas out of his band, just the way he did on "Let It Blurt" with the already great Robert Quine. The singing is adequate-at-worst (his drawl no longer recalls Eric Bloom), and the lyrics celebrate one man's victory over nihilism with suitably disengaged enthusiasm.   **B+**

Lester Bangs: See also "Birdland" With Lester Bangs

Tommy Bankhead and the Blues Eldora-dos: *Tommy Bankhead and the Blues Eldorados* (Deep Morgan '85). After thirty-five years as a professional, Bankhead is as authentic as blues gets and his first album sounds that way. I can even hear the harp-only prison song as a set-opener. I can even imagine checking out this hunch at some East St. Louis joint next time I'm out that way.   **B**

Ronnie Barron: *Blues Delicacies, Vol. One* (Vivid Sound import '80). The erst-while Reverend Ether, who worked as Paul Butterfield's sideman after declining Dr. John's shingle, here adds a respectfully raunchy collection of standards to the modest store of first-rate New Orleans rock and roll LPs. This is no *Wild Tchoupitoulas* or *Fats Domino* or *Crawfish Fiesta*, but it sure holds its own against Mac Rebennack's *Gumbo* or Lee Dorsey's *Yes We Can.* A minor delight for the afi-cionado and a revelation for the unini-tiated. Problem is, it'll cost you 15 bucks as a Japanese import, if you can find it. Rounder, Alligator, Flying Fish—help! Warners—oh never mind.   **A−**

Lou Ann Barton: *Old Enough* (Asylum '82). She's got a fine little instrument, like a nubile Bonnie Bramlett—the drawl pure cracker, the pitch and rhythm deep blue. But what she's selling with it is tractability. For Glenn Frey she poses as a flapper in the age of *Deep Throat,* for Jerry Wexler she sings good old songs in good old Mus-cle Shoals. Sincerely in both cases I'm sure, which makes things worse.   **C+**

Rob Base: *The Incredible Base* (Profile '89). Still trying to prove that "It Takes Two" had something to do with *him,* not just Lynn Collins and James Brown and

the gods of mixology, he swings half these ten cuts on a real funky concept. Hard, hard, the boy is hard—at the very least "The Incredible Base" and "Turn It Out (Go Base)" and "Get Up and Have a Good Time" and "If You Really Want To Party" are worthy follow-ups to one of the greatest singles ever, which is enough. And "Ain't Nothing Like the Real Thing," a slow one with a mean streak that gives its moral some bite, is the best in show. I bet he can't follow it up.   **B+**

Basement 5: *1965–1980* (Antilles '81). *Second Edition* fans take note: Every time I hear ex-PiL drummer Richard Dudanski and reggae-pro guitarist J.R. hit their groove, I think maybe *The Flowers of Ro-mance* was just a dream I had. The lyrics are stupidly militant at times—England's problem isn't "female rule," it's Thatcher's rule, and not even that—but when things get this boom-boom-boom I can ignore the words if need be.   **B+**

Toni Basil: *Word of Mouth* (Chrysalis '82). The only woman ever to offer to take it up the ass on top 40 radio (close your eyes and really concentrate on "Mickey" if you don't believe me) tops that trick by making four words out of "Don't want no-body" and then playing the double nega-tive both ways. If like me you think it's kind of neat for a bizzer who's pushing 40 (helped out on *The TAMI Show* in 1965) to come on as a dirty teen dream, you'll enjoy the cunning of her modestly futuris-tic El Lay pop-rock. But if like me you've never fathomed the appeal of (David Essex's) "Rock On" and treasure other versions of "Be Stiff" and "Little Red Book," you won't mistake her for Blondie or Nick Lowe.   **B+**

Batman (Warner Bros. '89). Packaging this as a soundtrack is as ridiculous as complain-ing that there's only six minutes of Prince in the movie, because the movie it's de-signed for exists only in Prince's head—his six minutes of soul are a distraction from Tim Burton's nostalgic ominoso futurism, which Danny Elfman's otherwise useless score expertly evokes. "The Future" is Prince's most visionary piece since "When

Doves Cry," and as aural objects, all the others are more than passable. Yet they are designed for a movie, and all of them—especially the received "Partyman" and the subpoignant "Vicki Waiting"—cry out for the focus of Prince's unrealized alternate version. Hence, what "Batdance" deconstructs is mainly itself.   **B+**

Stiv Bators: *Disconnected* (Bomp '80). The power-pop accoutrements are audible through Greg Shaw's cruddy production. But because it soft-pedals Stiv's unfortunate but well-inhabited persona—even the signature "Evil Boy" is kinda winsome—the record lacks tension, not to mention a reason to exist.   **B**

The Bats: *Daddy's Highway* (Communion '89). These New Zealanders are wimps if not simps. Robert Scott's reedy if not weedy quaver cries out for Kaye Woodward to chime in, and the one-foot-at-a-time folk-rock pulse can get pretty lame. But their jangly modesty is touching and smart—they understand the formal and historical limitations of their chosen style. And even though only one of their homely metaphors—" . . . there'll be a morning sky/Bringing you some peace tonight"—unites words and music into a pop moment, the atmosphere sustains.   **B+**

The BBC: *Dutch* (Emotional EP '83). Denizens of the Pennsylvania night, these sauerkraut lovers also love MTV, because in Sauerkrautland MTV is another place to get music—music that offers an excuse to do the Dutch, a dance funkier and funnier than you'd figure.   **B**

The Beach Boys: *Rarities* (Capitol '83). Half alternate takes, half vault finds—notably two *Wild Honey* rejects, one of them Bruce Johnston's friendly "With a Little Help from My Friends"—this beats most of their '70s output, no doubt because it's from the '60s, and serves as a reminder of what an oddball *entity* they were when Brian was still functional. Next in the series: Glen Campbell.   **B+**

The Beach Boys: *The Beach Boys* (Caribou '85). Would you get excited if the Four Lads released a comeback album with Boy George and Stevie Wonder songs on it? Bet they still harmonize pretty good, too. **C**

Beastie Boys: *Rock Hard/Party's Gettin' Rough/Beastie Groove/Instrumental* (Def Jam EP '84). With their boomy beats and big guitar, can these white boys rap the rap? "I can play the drums." "I can play guitar." "Not just B-boys we're real rock stars." Uh-oh. "Rock and roll rhythms are raunchy and raucous / I'm from Manhattan you're from Secaucus." Well, maybe. "I'm a man who needs no introduction / Got a big tool of reproduction." Very funny.   **B+**

The Beastie Boys: *Licensed To Ill* (Def Jam '86). The wisecracking arrogance of this record is the only rock and roll attitude that means diddley right now. With the mainstream claimed by sincere craftspeople and the great tradition of Elvis Presley, Esquerita, Creedence Clearwater Revival, the Sex Pistols, and Madonna sucked into a cultural vacuum by nitwit anarchists and bohemian sourpusses, three white jerkoffs and their crazed producer are set to go platinum-plus with "black" music that's radically original, childishly simple, hard to play, and accessible to anybody with two ears and an ass. Drinking, robbing, rhyming, and pillaging, busting open your locker and breaking your glasses, the Beasties don't just thumb their noses at redeeming social importance—they pull out their jammies and shoot it in the cookie puss. If you don't like the joke, you might as well put your money where your funnybone is and send a check to the PMRC. Original grade: A.   **A+**

Beastie Boys: *Paul's Boutique* (Capitol '89). One reason nobody knew what they'd do for an encore is that *Licensed To Ill* redefined rap as music: it was avant-garde rap and pop metal, foregrounding riffs and attitude any hedonist could love while eliminating wack solos and dumb-ass posturing. Jam-packed, frenetic, stark, the sequel isn't as user-friendly. But give it three plays and half a j's worth of concentration and its high-speed volubility and riffs from nowhere will amaze and delight you. It's an absolutely unpretentious and unsententious affirmation of cultural diversity, of where they came from and where they went from there. They drop names from Cézanne to Jelly Roll Morton to Sadaharu Oh, sample the Funky Four Plus One (twice), Johnny Cash, Charlie Daniels, Public Enemy, the Wailers, Eek-a-Mouse (I think), Jean Knight, and Ricky Skaggs (I think) just as tags—for music there are countless funk and metal (and other) artists I can't ID even when I recognize them. And they make clear that they're not about to burn out on their vaunted vices— not cheeba, not pussy, certainly not fame. The Beasties are still bad—they get laid, they do drugs, they break laws, they laze around. But they know the difference between bad and evil. Crack and cocaine and woman-beaters and stickup kids get theirs; one song goes out to a homeless rockabilly wino, another ends, "Racism is schism on the serious tip." Here's hoping other bad boys take these bad boys seriously.   **A**

The Beat Farmers: *Tales of the New West* (Rhino '85). Like so many roots bands, they write good songs and cover better ones—even in a nonpurist movement, Velvets-to-Springsteen-to-Spoonful is a broad-minded parlay. And like so many roots bands, their singers aren't sharp enough to bring it together—can't understand the difference between having fun, making fun, and being funny before mixing them up, can't at least be soulful instead of something vaguer, like "genuine." Original grade: B plus.   **B**
The Beat Farmers: *Van Go* (Curb '86). Except for the deadpan "Gun Sale at the Church" and maybe the Johnny Cash impressions, their country-rock is now proudly generic. In a world of lame concepts this approach is jake with me, and if their sharpest song originated with Neil Young, well, they didn't write the flattest one either.   **B**

Beat Happening: *Jamboree* (Rough Trade '88). As with any pop band, catchy tunelets aren't enough: what the tunelets say, how they sound, and what how they sound says also matter. Some find the calculated simplicity and semiunrehearsed spontaneity recombinant, the unadorned lyricism and rude guitar doubly tonic. I find the adolescence recalled cum childhood re-

visited doubly coy and the neoprimitivist shtick a tired bohemian fantasy. Catchy, though.   **B−**

The Beatles: *Rarities* (Capitol '80). The Brit version made sense, because lots of Beatle songs are unavailable on U.K. LP. In the U.S. the group's been cannibalized more efficiently—not counting the curious two-second *Sgt. Pepper* outgroove, only five of fourteen songs here are unknown to owners of their Capitol album catalogue. Two early Lennon-McCartneys, the assured close-harmony "Misery" and the fragile quavery "There's a Place," are very much worth your acquaintance. "Sie Liebt Dich" is fun, "You Know My Name (Look Up My Number)" is a goof, and "The Inner Light" is a B side—George's B side. Except for "Across the Universe," which Phil Spector did not improve, not one of the nine alternate versions differs from the original by more than a whit. The U.K. *Please Please Me* includes "Misery" and "There's a Place." I regard it as a superior investment.   **C+**

Beat Street (Atlantic '84). I wish Grandmaster Melle Mel hadn't bothered with the plot summary (I also wish he'd stop saying "Huh!" all the time), and I wish Jake Holmes hadn't bothered with the "love theme" (he can do the sequel, *Bleecker Street*). But executive producer Arthur Baker (with the help of executive producer Harry Belafonte, I'm sure) has done his best to drown the dreck in electrohop, with Bambaataa and the System fashioning gratifyingly sharp tracks. In addition, Rubén Blades proves that romance isn't dead, just Jake Holmes. And Sharrock returns. Original grade: B plus   **B**
Beat Street Volume 2 (Atlantic '84). The other half of what might be a great single disc. Jazzy Jay's scratching captures the movie's virtues a lot more eloquently than Melle Mel's words, Tina B divas all over Jenny Burton, and the two novelty raps tell you their producer knows something even if he is David Belafonte.   **B**

Francis Bebey: *Akwaaba* (Original Music '84). On the recordings of Paul Berliner and elsewhere I've always found the African thumb piano—mbira, kalimba, sanza—overly delicate, fragile as a music box. These experimental compositions, by a Camerounian musicologist who calls on a wide range of supplementary African instruments and techniques, are lithe and lovely. And when Bebey breaks into his subguttural chest voice you won't know whether to gasp or giggle.   **B+**

Jeff Beck: *Flash* (Epic '85). With his customary focus, loyalty, and consistency of taste, the mercurial guitarist plumbs a "new" idea copped from such innovators as Foreigner and Duran Duran—funk-metal fusion. Pitting Rod Stewart (on a convincing if utterly context-free "People Get Ready") and Arthur Baker (out to produce Foreigner and Duran Duran and apt to do a damn good job of it) against Wet Willie's vocalist and Cactus's drummer, he nevertheless turns in the best LP of his pathologically spotty career by countenancing Nile Rodgers's production on five tracks. So what do we have here? We have half a good Nile Rodgers album, more or less.   **B**

Walter Becker / Donald Fagen: *The Early Years* (PVC '85). Eternally faithful to early Dan, I hoped to descry the lineaments of unspoiled genius in these 1968-1971 demos, but all I got was demos. Between Fagen's scratch vocals and three grooveless drummers who sound relieved to remember their parts, these are songs casting about for a form—that is, for Gary Katz, whose smooth swing suited them far better than the bare bones Kenny Vance resorts to. Worth salvaging: "Don't Let Me In," in which they turn their collegiate cynicism on themselves for once.   **C**

David Behrman: *Leapday Night* (Lovely Music '87). The problem with semipopular minimalism, new age, snooze music, whatever, isn't its quietude—nothing wrong with a record that lowers your pulse rate if that's what you're up for. But its acolytes aren't on very friendly terms with their brains—when their music isn't just stupid, it pampers the vaguer emotions. Behr-

man's a poetic intellectual, a post-Cagean electronic composer whose moods and textures are generous enough for semipop—or for sentimentality, some "rigorous" academic rivals might sniff, as if they'd know. These computerized synth pieces interact with live violin on "Interspecies Smalltalk," live trumpet on "Leapday Night." The former is like Behrman's *On the Other Ocean/Figure in a Clearing* with spontaneity built in, the latter like Miles's "Yesternow" or "Shhh/Peaceful" on a floppy. Bye, Michael Hedges. Pack it in, Durutti Column.   **A−**

Harry Belafonte: *Paradise in Gazankulu* (EMI-Manhattan '88). Anybody who thought Paul Simon was jiving about political lyrics should check this socially conscious malapropism by Miriam Makeba's ex. Banned from South Africa himself, Belafonte sent arranger Richard Cummings and lyricist Jake Holmes in to lay down tracks with Makgona Tsohle, Brenda Fassie, even the Soul Brothers (who turned Simon down), and both representatives made a mess with the boss's full approval—Makgona Tsohle play cream cheese, the Zulu word for power turns into a woman's name, and the interracial love duet with Jennifer Warnes is no less saccharine for being punishable by death. Yet the Obed Ngobeni–backed title song is a triumph—a tremendously hot piece of assimilationist mbaqanga that conveys apartheid's insanity and mbaqanga's joy-pain in English ironic enough to get past the the SABC. Did I say Simon wasn't jiving?   **C+**

The Bellamy Brothers: *Greatest Hits* (Warner Bros. '82). Shameless, hooky, and slick, their country is about as pure as Mike Curb, who signed them, but if you can resist "If I Said You Had a Beautiful Body Would You Hold It Against Me" you don't eat fried food, and I say the hell with you. Nonpuritans are directed to "Get into Reggae Cowboy," which I'm glad I never heard on the radio because it might have palled there—in controlled doses it's the equal of "Lovers Live Longer" and "Redneck Girl."   **B+**

The Bellamy Brothers: *Strong Weakness* (Elektra '83). The problem with the lesser songs of these country slickers isn't that they're too dumb—it's that they're not dumb enough. I love their harmonies, but I prefer to keep their minds at a safe distance.   **B**

The Bellamy Brothers: *Greatest Hits Volume Two* (Curb '86). Whatever its pretensions, all country music offers the same primary reward: tuneful variations on the verities of the ordinary. These harmonizing eclectics sometimes outdo themselves. The rueful, nostalgic "Old Hippie" is Nashville's own "Born in the U.S.A."— "He ain't tryin' to change nobody / He's just tryin' to adjust"—and "Lie to You for Your Love" is a generic paradox that puts their strong weakness for ass-man smarm in perspective. Climax: "I Love Her Mind"—because her mind controls her body, naturally.   **B+**

The Bellamy Brothers: *Greatest Hits Volume III* (MCA '89). As they paunch out, they're passable humorists in "Hillbilly Hell" and fascinating sociologists-cum-chroniclers in "Rebels Without a Clue" and "Kids of the Baby Boom." But their harmonies have never had that fraternal magic, a failing that renders their maturing love songs inoperable.   **B−**

Pat Benatar: *In the Heat of the Night* (Chrysalis '80). Where some "eclectic" rock and rollers brim with sheer experimental joy, Benatar is sodden with try-anything-once ambition. From showbiz "hard rock" ("Heartbreaker") to big-beat "cabaret" ("Don't Let It Show") to received "futurism" ("My Clone Sleeps Alone") to fake-Blondie "Eurodisco" ("We Live for Love") she shows about as much aesthetic principle as Don Kirshner. Though she does have a better voice than Kirshner.   **C+**

Pat Benatar: *Best Shots* (Chrysalis '89). Does anyone remember anymore that she was originally a "cabaret" act? Does anyone remember anymore that early on she was sold as "new wave"? Cher without innocence, chutzpah, acting ability, or "Gypsys, Tramps, and Thieves," she finally semiretired to family life. This best-of is her artistic legacy. I'm sure she's a good mom—pretty sure, anyway.   **C**

Berlin: *Pleasure Victim* (Geffen '83). Although my tastes in porn don't run to designer whips, Terri Nunn's sex-object impersonation on the cunningly entitled "Sex (I'm a . . .)" generates a mild buzz. But that's the only good part—the rest is flimsy synth-pop sans even a flash of pink, unless songs about the Metro make you wet your pants. Time 27:07.   **C+**

Sandra Bernhard: *I'm Your Woman* (Mercury '85). Marianne Faithfull's survivor and Grace Jones's dominatrix both went up against Barry Reynolds's austere mechanics from strength, and better men wrote their best songs—John Lennon, Iggy Pop, Shel Silverstein, Melvin Van Peebles. The music here is Reynolds's ballgame, and if Bernhard's compulsively slippery irony is strength, I'm a great artist. I assume she gets to certain under-30 women because they find the twin escapes of dominance and submission wickedly seductive, and trust they're far enough from her fantasy star-world to take her as a metaphor for what's most oppressed and/or neurotic in themselves. I assume guys think she's more fun than reading the personals.   **C+**

Sandra Bernhard: *Without You I'm Nothing* (Enigma '89). If Laurie Anderson's a musician, so's this conceptualist. Her band includes Ivan Julian and Adele Bertei, and she needs 'em: she credits composers on eleven of twelve cuts, including the boite medley (thank God for cabaret, it lets you stay in New York and enjoy your co-op), the Prince cover (for Sheila E., Apollonia, Vanity, Wendy, and Lisa), and "The Women of Rock 'n' Roll" (the story of her magic night with Stevie Nicks, who hasn't called in six months).   **B+**

Chuck Berry: *Hail! Hail! Rock 'n' Roll* (MCA '87). This wasn't the great Chuck Berry concert if only because his voice is half shot—all those cracks don't ruin the fun, but they don't expose unexpected nuances in it either. Though Julian Lennon and Linda Ronstadt are less obtrusive when you can't see them trying to look like they belong, most of the cameos are still only adequate-to-embarrassing; the sole triumph is Eric Clapton's "Wee Wee Hours," with a typically miraculous solo from the omnipresent Johnnie Johnson. And so what? It's still the best live album the man ever made. I mean, what do you want?   **B+**

Best of House Music (Profile '88). Rough and unmediated house may be more fun than Euro-abstraction for sure, but it's for-dancers-only with a vengeance—formally, it's almost as exclusionary as hardcore. Thoughtfully sorted onto diva, sleaze, jack-your-body, and jack-of-all-nations sides, these cuts earn a permanent spot in my reference collection rather than my heart or my somatic memory. Even Marshall Jefferson's "Rock Your Body" and Moonfou's "Shut Up" disintegrate into breaks designed exclusively for the communal intoxication of the steamy floor. I don't get out enough, but I know what jacks my body when I do.   **B**

Best of Studio One (Heartbeat '83). Never an aficionado of medium-tempo vocal groups, second-level soul men, or for that matter '60s reggae, I don't find this loving first-U.S.-release compilation of Coxsone Dodd tracks especially transcendent. "Oh Mr. D.C." and "Row Fisherman Row" are the finest Sugar Minott and Wailing Souls ever to come my way, and the Termites' "My Last Love" is a sure shot ina one-shot style. But the Heptones ain't the Mighty Diamonds, Dennis Brown ain't Perry Como, and Alton Ellis ain't Tyrone Davis, a second-level soul man if ever there was one. And so it goes.   **B+**

Beverly Hills Cop (MCA '85). Highlights: Patti LaBelle contained, Harold Faltermeyer kisses Herbie Hancock's ass, the System rocks and rolls again, Shalamar writes to order (buy the 12-inch). Redundancy: the Pointer Sisters (buy the album—theirs—if you must). Lowlights: Junior, Rockie Robbins. Lowlifes: Danny Elfman (formerly of Oingo Boingo), Glenn Frey (formerly of the Eagles).   **B−**

The B-52's: *Wild Planet* (Warner Bros. '80). I keep waiting for number two to come through on the dance floor the way the debut did, but "Party out of Bounds" and "Quiche Lorraine" are expert entertainments at best and the wacko parochialism of "Private Idaho" is a positive annoyance. Only on "Devil in My Car" and "Give Me Back My Man" do they exploit the potential for meaning—cosmic and emotional, respectively—that accrues to the world's greatest new-wave kiddie-novelty disco-punk band.   **B+**

The B-52's: *Party Mix* (Warner Bros. '81). Six remixes, three from album two on side one and vice versa. Its implicit equation of party and disco offends old new-wavers, but at EP list for half an hour's music the extravagance is recommended. Hyped sound doesn't hurt this music, the stretches revolve around breaks or sound effects silly enough to belong, and two of the remakes are condensations. Fess up—wouldn't you love to own a "Dance This Mess Around" that begins "I'm not no limburger"?   **A−**

The B-52's: *Mesopotamia* (Warner Bros. '82). For a while I was afraid they were going to get encrusted in their own snot, but they really are an ordinary dance band from Athens, Georgia, which turns out to be no ordinary thing. David Byrne isn't the secret, just the secret ingredient—one more semipopulist with his own bag of tricks, like fellow ingredient Ralph Carney except his bag's bigger. A "party" record that never invokes that pooped word, this six-cut mini lists for $5.98, as good a deal as onion dip.   **A−**

The B-52's: *Whammy!* (Warner Bros. '83). Though they still pick up some great ideas at interplanetary garage sales, their celebration of the pop mess-around is getting earthier. "Whammy Kiss" and "Butterbean" do actually concern sex and food, respectively, while "Legal Tender" and "Queen of Las Vegas" show off a healthy respect for money—that is, a disrespectful attraction to its alluring usefulness. "Song for a Future Generation" is a completely affectionate, completely undeluded look at the doomed, hopeful, cheerfully insincere dreams and schemes of the kids who dance to B-52's songs. And the Yoko One tribute is for real.   **A—**

The B-52's: *Bouncing Off the Satellites* (Warner Bros. '86). Sorry, but my fond belief in Kate & Cindy as postmodern girl duo has just gone the way of my fond hopes for Joan and Chrissie as rock and roll future. Except for the postfeminist "Housework," they contribute watercolors posing as Kenny Scharfs—not only don't "Summer of Love" and "She Brakes for Rainbows" redeem anybody's '60s retro, they don't even take off on it. So Fred's abrasive camp saves the day, and talk about satiric justice—he gets off a credible nudist anthem, a credible psychedelic fantasy, and (get this) a credible ecology song in the process.   **B+**

B-52's: *Cosmic Thing* (Reprise '89). AIDS having robbed them of their most essential musician, this is an almost touchingly brave attempt to dance away from the edge of ecocatastrophe. Earthquakes, tidal waves, bushfires, waste dumps, toxic fog, maybe even that Chrysler big as a whale are counterposed to and in theory renewed by positive natural forces—junebugs, spaceships, cosmic vibes, an expanding universe, poor rebellious kids having innocent fun. They're trying to be seriously silly, and they're right to believe serious silliness is a healer. But between Ricky Wilson's guitar and the permanent defeat his loss doesn't merely signify, they can't quite bring it off. It's enough to make a grown man cry.   **B**

The Bhundu Boys: *Shabini* (Discafrique import '86). The toast of London last time I checked, these Zimbabweans are suspiciously cuddly in their folk-pop naiveté. But their guitars tickle exactly where Thomas Mapfumo's kick, and in the title tune and elsewhere the folk-pop naiveté of their melodies could tempt you to trust even that portion of humanity that swears by *The Face*. [Later on Hannibal.]   **B+**

Bhundu Boys: *True Jit* (Mango '88). In the end, their made-in-U.K. breakthrough attempt is a catchy, unconventional pop record—not only is the song for war-dead children about kids they knew, but you can be sure it doesn't suggest the war was unnecessary. But that's all it is. Ingratiation

is so ingrained in these former freedom fighters that they're almost swallowed by former Sade producer Robin Millar, who goes for pan-Africana with quasi-Zairean horns and transforms subtle cross-rhythms into upfront hooks. Rewriting "Skokiaan" as "Happy Birthday" because they know "Happy happy Africa" won't wash anymore, structuring "Rugare" ("work hard and reap the fruits of your labour") around schlocko synth chords and bridges that go nowhere, they're victims of crossover, compromising and accommodating when they should be expanding and appropriating. And they're still not half-bad.   **B+**

Bhundu Boys: *Tsvimbodzemoto: Sticks of Fire* (Hannibal '88). Though you can understand why the soaring interplay of the Bhundus' postchimurenga is classified as a soukous variant, it's folkier in basic approach and rockier in basic instrumentation, as comes clear on their Zimbabwe-recorded second album. Though the sound is thinner than FM technocrats might decree, it suits the band's peculiarly Zimbabwean polyrhythms, in which guitars and keybs take over lines indigenous to the thumb piano. Anyway, it's not so thin you're gonna notice as you fly around the ceiling. Congenital lead-asses start with side two.   **A—**

Big Audio Dynamite: *This Is Big Audio Dynamite* (Columbia '85). Because he sang both their pop hits, Mick was always slotted as the Clash's loverboy, but that was just his vocal cross to bear—he was really the intellectual, which is why he now specializes in what the handout calls "humor particularly irony." Though "A Party" and "The Bottom Line" are wordy enough for Ellen Foley, their anger would surface instantly if Joe were spitting them out. He might even make something of the Nippophobic "Sony" and the loverboy's lament "Stone Thames." But as it is, only "$E = MC^2$," laid down across cosmic keyb chords, lives up to Jones's goofily internationalist spirit.   **B—**

Big Audio Dynamite: *Megatop Phoenix* (Columbia '89). Forward-looking of Mick to devote himself to interracial rock-the-house. But strip away the samples and give the lyrics the respect they deserve and you're left with a mild voice over beats so dinky only college radio could dance to them. Plus a sweet pop song that isn't called "Feelings" because that title's taken.   **C+**

Big Black: *Racer-X* (Homestead EP '84). First two tracks are power packed if conventionally anarchic neo–no-wave hostility, though the guitar barrage keeps building. Second side is music to play loud when you feel like going out and stealing a pneumatic drill. Climax is a trash-compacted version of "The Big Payback"— James Brown, white-rage style.   **A−**

Big Black: *Atomizer* (Homestead '86). Though they don't want you to know it, these hateful little twerps are sensitive souls—they're moved to make this godawful racket by the godawful pain of the world, which they learn about reading everything from textbooks to bondage mags. This is the brutal guitar machine thousands of lonely adolescent cowards have heard in their heads. Its creators deserve credit for finding each other and making their obsession real. But not for anything else.   **B+**

Big Black: *The Hammer Party* (Homestead '86). One side the 1983 Ruthless EP *Lungs,* the other the 1984 Ruthless EP *Bulldozer,* and if you think Steve Albini is less than profound now, here's where you shore up your belief in progress. "Steelworker" presages "Deep Six" 's gothic fantasies about the working class (or is it just guys with muscles?). "Pigeons" is a cute bit about an oppressed teenager whose mom makes him kill feathered rodents. Beyond that it's sound and fury.   **B**

Big Black: *Songs About Fucking* (Touch and Go '87). Anybody who thinks rock and roll is alive and well in the infinite variety of its garage-boy permutations had better figure out how these Hitler Youth rejects could crush the competition and hang up their spikes simultaneously. No matter what well-meaning rockers think of Steve Albini's supremacist lies, they lie themselves if they dismiss what he does with electric guitars—that killdozer sound culminates if not finishes off whole genera-

tions of punk and metal. In this farewell version it gains just enough clarity and momentum to make its inhumanity ineluctable, and the absence of lyrics that betray Albini's roots in yellow journalism reinforces an illusion of depth—these are hateful and sometimes hackneyed, sure, but never sucker fare like "Jordan, Minnesota."   **A−**

Big Boys: *Lullabies Help the Brain Grow* (Moment '83). If this exemplary hardcore unit can't quite break their LP into the general-interest zone, I begin to wonder whether the new punks are ever going to reach anyone with a full head of hair. The Big Boys are far from monolithic, cutting the blur with ballad tempos and funk rhythms and even horns. Randy Turner's mock my-voice-is-changing squeal has an old (white) blues singer's authority. And their unmistakable heart in no way softens the ranting fury that's the signature of the style. But without a guitar ace (Bad Brains) or a songwriter (Descendents) or both (Black Flag), they cross over only at their best—about six cuts out of fourteen here, including the two slowest.   **B**

Big Brother and the Holding Company: *Cheaper Thrills* (Made To Last '84). Postpunks should forget Janis Joplin and dig this: just because they practiced in their own $300-a-month Marin commune doesn't mean they weren't a garage band. A classic garage band, in fact, and they played out a lot. That's one reason this low-fi one-night-only live-in-1966 tape overcomes the expected flaws to give forth more raunch than most singles catalogues. Janis Joplin is the other.   **B+**

Big Country: *The Crossing* (Mercury '83). With its bagpipe guitars and Celtic blues lines, Stuart Adamson's Skids-U2 hybrid avoids any hint of rock purism. Although "Chance" is the only fully realized song here, the rest sound good from a distance. But I wish Adamson didn't sing like Colonel Bryan Bowie and, even worse, write like Bishop Kahlil Masefield. Regaled with martial rhythms, I always feel safer knowing exactly what the war's about.   **B**

Big Country: *Peace in Our Time* (Reprise '88). Five years ago these fools parlayed a video, some guitar harmonics, and the oppression of Scotland into comparisons with future band-of-the-decade titleholders U2. A stiff, an EP, and a negotiation later, they're ready to settle for something simple in platinum on a rival label. Social consciousness or no ("Time for Leaving" actually explains why a U.K. laborer is emigrating), they're just pros with pretensions this time around. Which suits the rival label just fine. **C**

Big Youth: *Progress* (Negusa Nagast import '80). To the sexy singsong, colorful patois, and spacy tracks of Jamaican toasting, Manley Buchanan adds something like unalloyed joy—he looks and often sounds like the happiest man on earth. It's not just ganja, either—if ganja could do that, Peter Tosh would *be* the happiest man on earth. Somehow Youth embodies everything most benign about Rastafarianism—even when he's berating Babylon, which is often, he's unsectarian about it, suffused with humanitarian compassion for all victims of wickedness, Babylonians included. His most songful album is full of suffering and violence, yet its fundamental mood is one of gentle transport, the spiritual certainty of the born prophet. And for a sample of heaven ganja-style, it closes off with two sweet dubs. **A−**

Big Youth: *Rock Holy* (Negusa Nagast import '80). Seeing Youth live gave me new insight into why they call it toasting—he's a toastmaster, a Rastafarian George Jessel, complete with carry-a-tune crooning, name-dropping tributes, and shuffle-off-to-Babylon stage routines. All of which were wonderful—the enthusiasm was that unmediated. His evolution into a roots Mr. Entertainment has changed his records, which now include songs. Not great songs, either, as I would say. But "Get On Up" is a great chant, "Bang Dibo" a great goof, "Many Moods of Big Youth" a great mélange, "We Can Work It Out" a great cover (by anybody). And he outsings Kurtis Blow. **B+**

Big Youth: *Some Great Big Youth* (Heartbeat '81). Youth's first official U.S. release after a dubwise decade of JA stardom features the five best cuts from 1981's *Rock Holy* and two good ones from 1980's *Progress,* which may be his idea of progress but isn't mine. Like countless rockers before him, Youth is proud of his hard-won evolution from make-do genius to able pro. Me, I'd rather hear him chant over exotic brass and sistren than almost-sing almost-songs with or (as in this case) without them. **B+**

Big Youth: *Live at Reggae Sunsplash* (Sunsplash '84). Like most live toasting LPs, this tends to wander. The band intro is as irrelevant as most, tracks sometimes just fade out, and there are few recognizable songs. But the two you're sure to notice—"Hit the Road Jack" and "Every Nigger Is a Star"—are the best introduction on record to the militantly entertaining visionary optimism of the most untranslatable of the great reggae artists. And the show as a whole sums up his loopy, unselfconscious moral confidence like nothing else. **B+**

Big Youth: *A Luta Continua* (Heartbeat '85). First side's the usual homiletics—broad-minded as ever, musicianly rather than dubwise, and nothing his fans need to know. But on side two he gets mad, savoring the phrase "shit-eating grin" on "K.K.K." and livelying up the tenacious militance of the title track with Afrobeat horns. This is what college radio ought to be for. **B**

"Birdland" With Lester Bangs: *"Birdland" With Lester Bangs* (Add On '86). Since I knew Lester, I don't entirely trust my moderate delight with this nine-cut, twenty-six-minute demo, recorded one day in 1979 with the future Rattlers, soon to kick him out (as Lester told the tale) because he was "too fat." But since Lester was a genius, I have to mention that it's manifestly more confident than 1981's perfectly acceptable *Jook Savages on the Brazos,* with which it shares four songs, preserved for posterity a second time after the singer had the opportunity to develop some mannerisms. He was better off relying on force of personality—musically he always had the instincts, and words were no problem.   **B+**

Elvin Bishop: *Big Fun* (Alligator '89). Where his pint-sized labelmates give themselves hernias rocking the house, the bluesman-turned-hayseed tells some jokes and takes it easy. If you don't believe not getting riled is a spiritual thing with him, pay his guitar some mind.   **B+**

Biz Markie: *Goin' Off* (Cold Chillin' '88). Except for the timeless "Pickin' Boogers," not one of the class clown's hits has the life of "This Is Something for the Radio," which sounds like it was tossed off late one night on ludes: "We just talkin' over this beat, I don't know what the hell we're doin' . . ." If you love "Vapors" and all those songs with Biz's name in the title but not the credits, figure I'm nitpicking. If come to think of it you don't, wonder yet again how long a street genre can survive high intensity commodification.   **B**

Clint Black: *Killin' Time* (RCA '89). He's got good looks, fondly crafted songs, and a trenchant if anonymous voice, subtle even for Nashville neotraditional. Buoyantly in love on "Straight From the Factory," he quickly follows with as gracious a breakup song as you could hope to hear. Yet though she may have left him "A Better Man," he's not together enough to live without her. So for the rest of the album he spends a lot of time in bars—every one subtly and trenchantly evoked, of course. Original grade: B+.   **A−**

Black Britain: *Obvious* (Virgin '87). After six more years of Thatcher and the dawning of electrohop, it's as if Linx had laminated the soft edges of its prophetic premeditated funk to a flash, beatwise sheen. Both vocals and politics are more strident, pausing for love only to flog the jezebel whose lust for diamonds ends in the murder of an innocent jeweler by an innocent (sez they) black Briton. Though it is obvious, it scores points, zapping unguarded rhythm sensors like a sharpshooter in a video arcade. Here's hoping it grows in wisdom.   **B+**

Black Flag: *Jealous Again* (SST EP '80). Black Flag are committed to rage, not in itself—I don't believe their "I've got something personal against you" even though I know it's true—but as a musical principle. Five songs, seven minutes, as arty as no wave, with a comparable relationship to punk precedents, which for L.A. are basic Brit. The sound is extreme and unique, all forced rhythm and guitar blur with no ingratiating distractions—no humor, irony, hooks, or (God knows) melody. Well, maybe irony.   **B**

Black Flag: *Damaged* (SST '81). Although the B side drags more painfully than I bet was intended, this is powerful stuff. Gregg Ginn is the greatest noise guitarist since Johnny Thunders, new vocalist Henry Rollins can snarl along any tortured contour they serve up, and "Rise Above," "Six Pack," and the uproarious "TV Party" prove they can write songs as well as gnash fragments. Inspirational Verse: "I wanna live / I wish I was dead." [CD version includes *Jealous Again*.]   **A−**

Black Flag: *Everything Went Black* (SST '82). Stuck in legal limbo, they resort to historic alternate-take arcana featuring the three screamers who passed through the band before Henry Rollins took possession—except for side four, which is filled with radio ads for Flag gigs. These are still collector-only, I suppose. But as punk-era Firesign Theatre, worth going out and flattering a geek with a skateboard to hear.   **B**

Black Flag: *My War* (SST '84). Depleted by the kind of corporate strife I thought these guys were too cynical to fall for (which may be why they did), Henry Rollins's adrenalin gives out. The consequent depression is so monumental that even Greg Ginn succumbs, adding only one classic to his catalogue of noise solos ("The Swinging Man") and grinding out braindamaged cousins of luded power chords behind the three dirges that waste side two. But things do start off manically enough, with the title tune (refrain: "You're one of them") and five minutes of Henry explaining why he smiles so much (which I never noticed).   **B−**

Black Flag: *Slip It In* (SST '84). "Slip It In" is by somebody who learned about sex from movies. "Black Coffee" carries this antidrug thing too far. "Wound Up" could be tighter. "Rat's Eyes" cries out in agony for Sabbath's chops. "Obliteration" is an ace accompanist's solo turn. "The Bars" isn't about prison—or saloons. "My Ghetto" is an outtake from the rant side of *Damaged.* "You're Not Evil" is right on.   **C+**

Black Flag: *Who's Got the 10¹/₂?* (SST '86). *My War, Slip It In,* the *Live '84* tape, the instrumental sides, Henry's poetry readings—it was all too much, the excess production of bohemian businessmen ready to shove any old shit up the wazoos of their presold believers. So I hardly heard the 1985 studio LPs *Loose Nut* and *In My Head,* which prove their sharpest since *Damaged,* with *Loose Nut* especially showing off Greg Ginn's fangs as lyricist and riffmaster. The demented acceleration and guitar squiggles of this live date improve most of the hottest songs from the '85 albums. And while introducing the band members by cock size may protest their belated obsession with sex too much, I can't complain when the answer to the title question is Kira, who plays bass so stalwartly she deserves all the credit she can get.   **A−**

Black Flag: *Wasted Again* (SST '88). As even they may realize eventually, they never were much of an art band—just such a good rock and roll band you'd sit still for their bullshit. Despite the uneven pre-*Damaged* tracks, this beer-party compilation sums up their contribution to Western civilization quite neatly. In retrospect, their rampaging anomie seems pitilessly self-critical. They always knew their fun was fucked; they even knew it wasn't all that much fun. But that didn't fool them into concluding it was no fun at all, much less bad or something.   **A**

J. Blackfoot: *City Slicker* (Sound Town '83). "The Way of the City" and "Street Child" and "Where Is Love" and the not-quite-dumb-enough "One of Those Parties" don't sound like a country boy's response to the city—they sound like an unreconstructed soul journeyman giving weary moderns everywhere cheap sobs and snickers they might pay for. But as an un-

even soul album this scores around 50-50. "The Way of the City" is on the up side for its Memphis–New Orleans fusion, one of the few marks of musical development. In the old days soul men usually left tunes as lightly ebullient as "All Because of What You Did to Me" to the gals, so that's progress. And the title rap actually does sound like a country boy's response to the city. Inspirational Verse: "Get the sweetnin' out of gingerbread and never break the crust."   **B**

Black Havana (Capitol '89). Not a real house compilation, my sources say, and good—bet stay-at-homes enjoy these Kenny Ortiz commissions more than the authentic stuff on Republic, DJ International, FFRR, Great Jones. It's funkier and more tropical than the club norm—bearing down on salsa, dancehall, rap—without eschewing surefire house machinations. For once the trancy breaks and cries in the night— "Throw 'Em the Chicken," "Like This Like That," the drugged, distorted "Do It Steady"—are as haunting as they're supposed to be. And the way each side breaks into cool, lush escape music is pure coconut milk.   **A−**

Black Stalin: *You Ask for It* (Kalico '84). Heir to the voluble wit of calypso tradition, Leroy Calliste is droller than any Jamaican Rasta you can think of whether he's being dragged kicking and jamming into soca clichés or talking back to a vocoder that won't shut up about "better days are coming." With its Cuban horns and displaced steel drums, the music has its own witty take on the tradition. And if I don't understand every topical reference, maybe it's just as well—any kind of Rasta going on about "corruption" can get me laughing out the other side of my mouth pretty quick.   **B+**

Black Star Liner: Reggae From Africa (Heartbeat '83). Because the great African groove is airborne where the Jamaican is of the earth, bass-and-drums on this seven-artist, eight-cut compilation do little more than follow standard patterns, and the chantlike tunes remind you how much Jamaican melodies owe to English hymns and nursery rhymes. But that's in no way to suggest that this music isn't captivating on its own terms. The vocals bear the same yearning relationship to their more stylized Jamaican inspirations that Jamaican vocals do to the showier models of U.S. soul: the need to reach out to the black diaspora has rarely been more palpable. And the lyrics, all in English, explain some whys and wherefores. Original grade: A minus.   **B+**

Black Uhuru: *Sinsemilla* (Mango '80). With Sly Dunbar and Robbie Shakespeare drumming up your basic buzz and Ansel Collins's slyly dissonant piano flourishes catching the occasional fire, this sexually integrated Jamaican trio get up on music alone. But only the pan-Africanist theme songs "World Is Africa" and "No Loafing" get all the way over. Must reflect the special enthusiasms of the integrationist among them, who happens to be Babylonian born and raised.   **B+**

Black Uhuru: *Red* (Mango '81). Believe me, Michael Rose isn't trying to fill anybody's shoes—he'd probably rather not wear shoes. The ululation and ragged sense of line are pure country, like Jamaican field hollers; lots of times the songs don't even rhyme. But "Youth of Eglington" lets you know right off that this is a country boy who reads the papers, and with Rose pouring forth and Sly and Robbie rolling that rockers riddim, you don't really care that it never gets any better.   **A−**

Black Uhuru: *Tear It Up—Live* (Mango '82). Third album's awful soon for a live one, you might think, and then notice that only one of the eight titles is on *Red* or *Sinsemilla.* That's because six of them can be found—in clearer, denser, trickier, scarier, *longer* versions—on 1979's *Showcase,* available as a Joe Gibbs import. "Abortion" is anti, natch, and Jah knows where they can stick it, but you'd never guess from these remakes how effective it and all Uhuru's early songs can be. Here in Babylon we call this kind of thing a scam.   **C−**

Black Uhuru: *Chill Out* (Island '82). This hasn't made itself felt the way *Red* did for fairly marginal reasons, hype/timing not least among them—the need for a new

Marley becomes less urgent as the self-evident truth that there ain't gonna be one is absorbed. The musical margin is about urgency as well—not the quality of the riffs and riddims but rather the relative elegance, and detachment, of their execution. In a music of margins, such fine distinctions encompass worlds of woe that high-tech pros like Sly and Robbie abandon at their peril.   **B+**

Black Uhuru: *Anthem* (Island '84). Uhuru's three U.S. releases after *Red* were so disappointing that I ignored this when it came out in England late last year, but I understand why those who didn't resent the dub/disco effects now mixed into "What Is Life?" and "Botanical Roots" and "Try It." All the songs are so strong and catchy and righteous—so anthemic—that it seems perverse to distract from them in any way. But they're also so strong they stand up to the treatment. The plus on the U.S. version is the cover—Rufus's "Somebody's Watching You" was an interesting choice competently rendered, while Steve Van Zandt's "Solidarity" is a very interesting choice that turns wishful thinking into dream come true.   **A**

Black Uhuru: *Brutal* (RAS '86). Junior Reid joins the group ululating in much the way Michael Rose did before he developed into a singer, and the big loss is even more crucial: politics, some rudimentary specificity. But up against the run of ridmic rhetoricians, they do fine. Both Reid and Duckie Simpson have a knack for rhetoric, and while Sly and Robbie should have pushed Simpson's "Reggae With Me" out on the dancefloor where it belongs, this is their most pyrotechnic production yet—they've brought Babylon back home.   **B+**

Black Uhuru: *Positive* (RAS '87). Sly and Robbie won't knock you out, but on Uhuru's best records they never do—given the right songs and performances, all they have to do is make them righter. Junior Reid is now a raspy soul wailer in command, which not so paradoxically gives Duckie Simpson and Puma Jones more room to express themselves, and harmonize too. And while the bootstrap capitalism of the title tune is more Babylonian than the self-made Reid knows, "Pain" and "Dry Weather House" and Simpson's climactic "I Create" place blame with a negativity nonbelievers can relate to.   **A—**

Rubén Blades: *Maestra Vida: Primera Parte* (Fania '80). Willie Colon's vocalist has created a salsa album so artistically ambitious that it brooks no comparison—a music drama complete with synopsis and recorded dialogue that purports to sum up half a century of NuYorican struggle. As a non–Spanish-speaker with access to a privately provided trot, I'm impressed with his reach, his grasp, and his acting ability, but as a veteran of rock opera I feel constrained to note that these things rarely work as planned even when the audience knows the language. Since I'm no salsa expert, I can only observe that both the studied casualness of the production style—songs over backtalk, impromptu-sounding chorus—and the musical-comedy overture seem more effective dramatically than musically. Still, the context helps makes salsa accessible to the nonexpert. And it's possible Blades isn't just smarter than the Neon Philharmonic—he could be smarter than, gosh, Pete Townshend himself.   **B**

Rubén Blades: *Maestra Vida: Segunda Parte* (Fania '80). On a major label, this would have been disc two of a double-LP, relieving us of another overture. But the rock world rarely produces a song as physically beautiful (or solicitously observed) as "Carmelo, Después (El Viejo DaSilva)." Too many violins and not enough clave. But his heart and his head are in the right place.   **B**

Rubén Blades y Seis del Solar: *Buscando America* (Elektra '84). The claim that only racism and lousy promotion denied Blades's *Maestra Vida* diptych the attention this major label debut has received is half truism and half one-upping guff. Nor do I miss the horns that helped make *Siembra,* his most renowned Willie Colon collaboration, an international phenomenon. The seven-man rhythm section he sings with here encourages conversational intimacy and renders irrelevant the high romanticism classic soneros drown in and Blades doesn't have the voice for. It also accents the narrative details which Blades the writer provides in such abundance. Nor must you know Spanish (or follow the crib sheet) to enjoy his rhythmic, melodic, and dramatic subtleties—they're right there in the music. Which vagues out only once—behind the pious generalities of the eight-minute title track.   **A—**

Rubén Blades y Seis del Solar: *Escenas* (Elektra '85). From loud syndrums to choked-up harmonies to generalized lyric, the Linda Ronstadt duet points up the risk Blades runs of falling into a modernist version of salsa's romantic overstatement. But the risk has a payback—whether he's synthing up *la melodía* or cataloguing international freedom fighters, his ability to skip along the shores of schlock without ruining his best pair of shoes helps distinguish him from middlebrow popularizers. It might even be what makes "The Song of the End of the World" a gleeful blowout rather than some stupid satire.   **A—**

Rubén Blades y Seis del Solar: *Agua de Luna* (Elektra '87). Establishing his progressive credentials and his rock credentials simultaneously, Blades commits two progressive rock errors, relying on synthesizers for texture and literature for aesthetic complexity. It's a measure of his gift and his freedom from pretension that between his supple voice and even suppler groove he induces you to listen to the damn synths—and that the words sound (and translate) like they make sense until you bear down line by line. As I bet García Márquez knows, this kind of compression isn't realistic or magical, much less both. It's an impressionistic code.   **B**

Rubén Blades: *Nothing but the Truth* (Elektra '88). Although familiarity has tempered my dismay, my first response to Blades's assault on Anglophonia was embarrassment—just what WEA needed, another Jackson Browne album. Admittedly, it's a pretty good Jackson Browne album, with various class acts (Uncle Lou, Elvis C., Sting, and studio luminaries) pitching in for their (and my) favorite Hispanic liberal. When I'm feeling corny I'm moved by the AIDS song, the homeless song, and the barrio song. And except for Sting's contribution, I'm impressed by the rest—literate lyrics about feckless idealism, feckless love, and Latin America are never easy to come by. But that doesn't mean they're easy to bring off, and deprived of Seis del Solar's rolling undercurrents Blades is forced to serve them up straight, a skill he hasn't practiced like he has his English. Not that practice would make perfect—cf. Jackson Browne.   **B**

Rubèn Blades y Son del Solar: *Antecedente* (Elektra '88). Coming off a failed literary album and a failed rock album, Blades augments a revamped, renamed Seis del Solar with salsa trombones and begets a dance album for the people of Panama. Which kind of leaves his friends from non-Latino cultures in the lurch—is this the "real" salsa record of our crossover dreams? Beats me. The (translated) lyrics are intelligently romantic (with an Indian smuggler smuggled in), and after the usual unusual effort, I can report that the tunes are solid, the grooves Latino, and the vocals proof of a major pop intelligence—he's revamped the floridity of an entire tradition in the image of his own physical limitations. Can you dance to it? Better than me, I'm sure.   **B+**

The Blasters: *American Music* (Rollin' Rock '80). One of two bands cited as proof that L.A. punks aren't just bigots with mohawks (the other, the Go-Go's, has—gulp!—girls in it), these rock and rollers don't quite fit their rockabilly revivalist pigeonhole. Where the average Whitecat is so pencil-necked he can hardly hold up an acoustic bass, they have muscles, and where the average Rockin' Ronnie Weiser signing is a barely literate has-been who never really was, they have brains and potential. Or so songs like "Barn Burning" and, believe it or not, "American Music" lead one to believe. They do get that chickenshit Scotty Moore guitar sound right, though. With Ronnie at the boards, they don't have much choice.   **B+**

The Blasters: *The Blasters* (Slash '81). Ex–Canned Heat piano man Gene Taylor and a horn section anchored by New Orleans's own Mr. Lee Allen wreck that neobilly image, as do the three reempowered remakes from their debut. Neobilly's just an excuse that lets them play blues—plus r&b, country, New Orleans, all the unfash-

ionable vernaculars they love—to a young and hungry audience in a recharged dramatic context. If the originals work better than the covers, that's partly because Phil Alvin's expressive moan does sound pinched sometimes, so even when you don't know the source recording (which you probably don't), you can imagine it fuller. And it's partly because Dave Alvin is a songwriter with John Fogerty's bead on the wound-tight good times of America's tough white underbelly.   **A−**

The Blasters: *Over There: Live at the Venue, London* (Slash EP '82). If you want to give the EP a bad name, stick to bands like Devo and the Chartbusters. These guys are too good for a quickie, but though the songs they choose are classic, they cover them only adequately.   **B**

The Blasters: *Non Fiction* (Slash '83). "Train whistle cries / lost on its own track" could be half a haiku for Hank Williams should these American traditionalists ever turn Japanese, and if "Leaving" is worthy of George Jones, "Bus Station" and "It Must Be Love" pick up where Tom T. Hall left off. None of which is code for countrybilly—this is r&b Jerry Lee could be proud of. It's just that Dave Alvin writes with an objective colloquial intensity that fits the straight-ahead dedication of his cross-racial and -generational band the way James Taylor's ingrown whimsy suited the laid-backs he hung with. In other words, Dave might qualify as the last great singer-songwriter if only he was a singer. And brother Phil is. Original grade: A minus.   **A**

The Blasters: *Hard Line* (Slash '85). *Non Fiction* imagined a world in which the American music the Blasters love remained the common tongue of ordinary guys, guys whose connection to their cultural history helped them understand where they were—not in control, but at least conscious. The follow-up attempts to reach those ordinary guys with producers and stereo and more drums and no horns and a John Cougar Mellencamp song, and also with the kind of fancy stuff that comes naturally—accordion here, acoustic version there, Jordanaires all over the place, and the Jubilee Train Singers on a fiercely joyous remake of "Samson and Delilah," which with its ancient threat to tear this building down is good reason not to fret about philosophical retreat. As are "Dark Night," about a race murder, and "Common Man," about some president or other, their two most pointedly political tracks ever. What's softened is the bite of the writing—where *Non Fiction* nailed specifics (plastic seats, repentant husband wiping ashes off the bed), here Dave Alvin settles (or works) for a level of generalization suitable to pop. Guess he's decided that sometimes ordinary guys don't want things spelled out so fine. He may be right.   **A**

Blondie: *Autoamerican* (Chrysalis '80). It's odd at best that the two hits and the two high points are the two songs predicated on black sources—the resourceful reggae cover "The Tide Is High" and the genius rap rip "Rapture" (which stands, let me assure my fellow Flash fans, as the funniest, fondest joke she ever told on herself). Elsewhere power pop turns power cabaret and *Sgt. Pepper* turns white album, only without Lennon-McCartney, or even McCartney. Debbie sings better all the time, but a better singer than she'll ever be couldn't save "T-Birds," or "Faces." They got what they wanted and now what? Original grade: B plus.   **B−**

Blondie: *The Best of Blondie* (Chrysalis '81). This could convince the unwary listener that they're the great mindless pop band they pose as—songs from all over the place cohere as if they were created only to get on the radio. Nor is this impression discouraged by the tactful Mike Chapman remixes that bring three early efforts into the new wave age. But go back to *Parallel Lines,* or the first side of *Plastic Letters,* and recall how an art band makes songs cohere—it creates them to go on a record. If they also get on the radio, that means the scam worked.   **A−**

Blondie: *The Hunter* (Chrysalis '82). I've feuded for years with moralists who accused the band of abandoning a lowbrow purity they never claimed in the first place, but this is a lousy record by any standard—the pop, the eclectic, even the arty. That Debbie is writing all the lyrics is only symptomatic—the tragedy is that of an ab-

sorptive, synthetic talent trying to find its essence, a doomed project that's doubly disorienting because she's canny enough not to believe in "self-expression" per se. Instead she gallumphs about in search of referents, referents she seemed to locate naturally back when she could walk the Bowery without a disguise.   **C**

Blondie: See also Debbie Harry/Blondie

Alpha Blondy: *Apartheid Is Nazism* (Shanachie '87). Reggae from a multilingual Ivory Coast star who puts message up front, this probably wouldn't get over on words even if you understood Mandingue or Dioula—in French and English, the politics are naive and toothless. As usual in West African pop, the voice is too mild, and as usual in West African reggae, the rhythm section is too buoyant. But glancing off such dance tunes as "Idjidja" and "Kiti" and, yes, "Come Back Jesus" (not to mention the base-covering "Sébé Allah Yé"), the singing completes an eloquently transatlantic groove—Afropop dread, a fast-flowing stream whose depth can't be fathomed. This achievement is also very West African.   **B+**

Alpha Blondy and the Wailers: *Jerusalem* (Shanachie '88). There's something suspect about this ex-Manhattanite turned part-time Parisian and his multilingual Islamic reggae from Abidjan—he's a third-world marketer's dream even if he's marketing himself. But at worst he puts out a finer grade of generic Wailers than Rita's ever going to front, and three cuts sound like acts of genius rather than strokes of luck: the otherwise Francophone "Kalachnikov Love," whatever that means (and I want to know); "Jerusalem," slipping with a sly presumption of innocence from basic English to pidgin Hebrew, pidgin Arabic, and pidgin French; and "Travailler C'Est Trop Dur," which breaks his loping skank into a pretty gallop. After all, there's something suspect about Prince, too.   **B+**

Alpha Blondy: *Cocody Rock!!!* (Shanachie '88). Released Stateside more than four years after it was recorded, this proves he's subject to the usual concepts of stylistic development—likable hit-plus-filler that sounds crude after what followed.   **B−**

Alpha Blondy: *The Prophets* (Capitol '89). Praying that he's Bob Marley, the U.S. major bites. And gets a professional reggae album with the drums too loud, sliding gradually from felt convention to grooveful genre work. Most remarkable thing about it is the dedication to "the planet Earth" and various oddly spelled principals in the battle for Israel.   **B**

Alpha Blondy: *Revolution* (Shanachie '89). Finally the great weird one he had in him. Its seven cuts include a chanson in Dioula, a crude, endearingly right-on crossover bid called "Rock and Roll Remedy," and the Solar System vamping for ten minutes behind a speech by Côte d'Ivoire's 84-year-old president Félix Houphouët-Boigny, a Francophile bourgeois as unrevolutionary as any head of state in Africa. Wish my French was up to what the Old Man is saying; wish my Dioula was up to what the songs about bleeding and elections are saying. I do know that the lead love song ends up in a mental hospital, because it's in English.   **A—**

Blotto: *I Wanna Be a Lifeguard* (Performance '87). One of indie rock's greatest failure stories, they burst upon us in 1980 with the title tune, a novelty number at least as hilarious as "Snoopy vs. the Red Baron" (which couldn't have cracked commercial radio in the boring commercial '80s either, I bet). Here they compile a best-of from their DIY EPs/LPs for a slightly larger DIY concern—they would have been happy to sign with a major, but not for shit money, no sir. In among the mildly amusing and hopelessly unfunny you'll find the definitive top-40 bar-band parody "(We Are) The Nowtones." The metal parody they don't have the chops for.   **C+**

Kurtis Blow: *Kurtis Blow* (Mercury '80). Ramones fans will claim his first-beat sledgehammer is monotonous; I enjoy its simplicity just like I do the Ramones'. Not as much, I admit—"All I Want in the World (Is To Find That Girl)" would be a retarded change of pace even if Kurtis talked it, and he doesn't. But though it bodes ill for both his rhythms and his politics, the bare competence of his Bachman-Turner Overdrive cover has special charm, and his hit metapun is a true breakthrough.   **B+**

Kurtis Blow: *Deuce* (Mercury '81). It's hard to believe six different social observers collaborated on these raps—"Take It to the Bridge," the throwaway boast, is more meaningful than "Starlife," the wishful single—and Kurtis's natural singsong makes me grind my teeth. But the light, spare, clean, catchy, inauthentic funk rings my bell—every cut, every time.   **B+**

Kurtis Blow: *Tough* (Mercury '82). The title track breaks out more breaks, "Baby, You've Got to Go" makes the most of its bad sexual politics, and the rhythm tributes are rhythmic enough. But even on a five-song mini his speech rhythms wear as thin as his singing, which he still hopes is his future.   **B**

Kurtis Blow: *Party Time?* (Mercury '83). If Kurtis's strongest album has a problem, it's Kurtis, who despite his quick lips and habit of command doesn't sound entirely at home with all this lovingly streetified social-awareness-you-can-dance-to. But who ever said rap was about words? The muscular funk that powered the sound systems when Kurtis was coming up combines with the digitalia that shakes the B-boxes now and some well-placed hook riffs to get him through the hyperconscious patches. Time 27:35. List: $5.98.   **A—**

Kurtis Blow: *Ego Trip* (Mercury '84). After declaring for revolution, always a good move, Kurtis slips in a sidelong "to the next phase," and he's clearly trying to get there. But unlike his cut buddies in Run-D.M.C., he's a little too headlong to make much music out of the shifts and starts of spare synths, and his political rhymes don't evince the acuteness of observation and fellow feeling one values in a revolutionary.   **B—**

Kurtis Blow: *America* (Mercury '85). Blow's pop credibility soared when he finally got one of his precious femme choruses on the radio, ruining the otherwise serviceable "Basketball" rap. There's nothing quite so intrusive here, and Blow's singing has come up some—in fact, he's now just what the world needed, another serviceable funk loverboy. Fortunately, he can still talk that talk, and his reunion with Davy DMX makes a lot of noise.   **B**

Blow-Up: *Easy Knowledge* (Polar '84). Six out of eight songs on this half-hour-plus "EP" get to the heart of smart teen disillusion, which is as much as I ever expect of the L.A.-spawned nuevo-*Nuggets* approach. The Standells cover sounds like Dylan and states Blow-Up's credo, which in the great smart-teen tradition comes perilously close to making a fashion statement about not conforming to style. Of course they look up to Steve Wynn and Dan Stuart—they're young in L.A. Jim Carroll takes imagination.   **A—**

Sugar Blue: *Cross Roads* (Europa '81). You may remember his harmonica from "Miss You" (or if you're lucky Johnny Shines's *Too Wet To Plow*), but if you figured he could sing at all you didn't guess his voice would be as rich and mellifluous as his harp, more King Pleasure than Little Walter. Nor would you have predicted an existential blues in the style of Mark-Almond. Original grade: A minus.   **B**

Blue Angel: *Blue Angel* (Polydor '80). There's a lyric sheet for some reason, and God knows the colorized cover cultivates a look, but the selling point of this uptown power pop is Cyndi Lauper's cute, zaftig voice—the songs all feature little toon-tricks designed to show off its swoops and swells. Try the band feature, a '50s cover that goes "Wo, wo, cut out," and the auto-biographical '50s tribute, "Late."   **C+**

The Bluebells: *The Bluebells* (Sire EP '83). Leading up to a stirring chorus and going out on a rousing coda (more stirring and rousing on the London import 12-inch, I must report), "Cath" is one of those pop strokes that'll show up on anthologies with "Turning Japanese" and "Starry Eyes" in 2001. Brendan Behan's "Patriots Game" shoulda been a Dylan song. "Everybody's Somebody's Fool" ain't bad. Original grade: B plus.   **B**

Arthur Blythe: *Da-Da* (Columbia '86). Blythe is a major musician and except for one piece of dinky funk this passes pleasantly enough, but its conceptual confusion epitomizes jazz's commercial impasse. Not only does Blythe play safe every which way, but there's no logic to his successes. You wouldn't figure the synthed-up ballad from Brazilian pop romantic Djavan to generate more atmosphere than the readings from Coltrane and Roland Hanna. Or Kelvyn Bell to provide the album's liveliest moment on the other funk attempt. Or the neat remake of "Odessa" to generate respectable heat up against the wild one on 1979's *Lenox Avenue Breakdown,* back when there was reason to hope Black Arthur would beat this shit.   **B**

BoDeans: *Love and Hope and Sex and Dreams* (Slash '86). Leading off, "She's a Runaway" is a pleasant shock: he abused her, she shot him. Enough to make you imagine they embrace postroots to advance if not subvert it. Whereupon they get down catchy wimmin songs that could have been written and forgotten twenty years ago, though "Misery" is recommended to George Strait.   **B—**

Bohannon: *Alive* (Phase II '81). Indifferent to concepts like "content" and "originality," this casual dance-hit rip cycles (and recycles) about three basic riffs and some raucous yowsah-yowsah into an album that divides into irresistibly inspired A side and delightfully tossed-off B as surely as any New Orleans novelty or rockabilly romp. If you're tired of getting your rhythmic jollies from well-meaning art students, give this natural Afro-American a try. Original grade: A minus.   **B+**

Gary U.S. Bonds: *Dedication* (EMI America '81). This is impressive and good-hearted. Not only did B. Springsteen get a record deal for the rock and roller whose oldies have been topping B.'s show since whenever, he got him a hit. Featuring the voice of none other than B. Springsteen, who comes more naturally to these impressive, good-hearted, new B. Springsteen songs (as well as the Dylan and Browne and Lennon-McCartney oldies) than the rock and roller. For one thing, B. has more soul.   **C+**

The Bongos: *Drums Along the Hudson* (PVC '82). Although these casually lapidary popsongs sounded slight as singles, they gain authority laid down seven or eight to a side. But for all their jumpy originality they're still slight, and Richard Barone's lyrics are so oblique you have to wonder what his angle is. Growing up isn't *that* confusing—or that personal.   **B+**

Bongwater: *Double Bummer* (Shimmy-Disc '88). The whole two-record set teeters on the edge of in-joke, avant-bullshit, and not-for-profit self-indulgence. But where the found tape documentaries w/neoexpressionist noodling are exactly as interesting as their sources (surreal pre-Watergate Nixon, the standard radio evangelist), Ann Magnuson's rock dreams and Chinese "Dazed and Confused" and Monkees cover and straight satirical Tuli Kupferberg chantey have the unjudgmental plasticity of the best camp. Can't quite claim she's worth the price of admission—a talent to watch, say.   **B**

Bon Jovi: *Slippery When Wet* (Mercury '86). Sure seven million teenagers can be wrong, but their assent is not without a certain documentary satisfaction. Yes, it proves that youth rebellion is toothless enough to simulate and market. But who the hell thought youth was dangerous in the current vacuum? Would you have preferred the band market patriotism? And are you really immune to "Livin' on a Prayer"?   **B−**

Bon Jovi: *New Jersey* (Mercury '88). I see three ways to take the transparently pseudo Springsteenian sincerity of Jon's bid to improve his artistic reputation and his platinum multiple at the same time. You could lie back and enjoy its giant hooks, identifying with the masses all the while. You could cheer its de facto deconstruction of rock "authenticity." Or you could blow lunch. As someone who learned to love "Livin' on a Prayer" in heavy rotation at a swimming pool, I reserve the right to choose option one upon

suitable stimulus from somebody else's radio. Now pass the bucket.   **C+**

The Boogie Boys: *City Life* (Capitol '85). "Here is proof that rapp is music," only don't worry, it isn't as bad as that. Just another electrofunk-based albumm from B-boys stale before their time. They spin off some unlikely rhymes—"bank accounts" and "name's pronounced," fresh indeed—and a great many insults that boil down to "you don't smell good." And for better or worse, they never emanate more charm than when they sing a sad it-ain't-me-babe called "Runnin' From Your Love." Original grade: B.   **B−**

Boogie Down Productions: *Criminal Minded* (B Boy '87). Though one's moralistic quibbles do recede as history demonstrates how much worse things can get and how little music has to do with it, KRS-One's talk of fucking virgins and blowing brains out will never make him my B-boy of the first resort. I could do without the turf war, too—from the Lower East Side, not to mention Kingston or Kinshasa (or Podunk), Queens and the South Bronx are both def enough. But his mind is complex and exemplary—he's sharp and articulate, his idealism more than a gang-code and his confusion profound. And Scott LaRock was a genius. Sampling blues metal as well as James Brown, spinning grooves to toast by, blind-siding the beat with grunts and telephones and dim backtalk, he was spare and rich simultaneously. Music will miss him more than Jaco Pastorius and Will Shatter put together.   **B+**

Boogie Down Productions: *By All Means Necessary* (Jive '88). Deprived of the great murdered beatmaster Scott LaRock, KRS-One is reduced to a stark minimalism that matches his mood: still brandishing his piece on the cover, he's as serious as Jesse inside, occasionally pretentious but never full of himself. He criticizes the self-proclaimed kings of a scene too democratic to support royalty and the self-proclaimed godfathers of a scene too young to have an old school, identifies tribalism as the white man's game, and comes out strong for peace through strength. Only "Jimmy" is much fun, and

"Jimmy" is a condom commercial. But at his best—"Stop the Violence," which might conceivably catch black radio in a community-spirited moment of weakness—he's as complex and cold-eyed as the kings themselves, with two extras: he's not middle-class and he's on a mission.   **B+**

Boogie Down Productions: *GhettoMusic: The Blueprint of Hip Hop* (Jive '89). KRS-One isn't just serious, he aspires to sainthood, and tough noogs if you think that makes him "boring" or "pretentious" or any of that racist, anti-intellectual cant—he comes so close that the whole of the record is greater than the minimalism of its blueprint stylee. Austerely sampled or all the way live, the music per se is almost hookless and swingless. But the dubwise skank of his natural groove carries his rhymes when the rhymes don't capture the consciousness like a good hook should. Though I wish he didn't feel compelled to argue what color Moses was, his fundamental conceit—a peace harder than violence—is visionary. And when he takes no shit from the police, I say amen.   **B+**

James Booker: *New Orleans Piano Wizard: Live!* (Rounder '81). Booker's legendary prestidigitation put me off at first—this is the most ornate piano style ever to escape New Orleans, and I prefer my boogie sans soupcons of Chopin and Tatum. Eventually, though, his arpeggios, harmonies, and insidious timing create an irresistible roller coaster effect—I even started to groove with the dips and slides of his singing. Believe me, "On the Sunny Side of the Street" was never like this before and will never be the same again.   **A−**

James Booker: *Classified* (Rounder '83). This is palpably more strident. The Longhair medley just isn't as sly and delicate as it should be, and in general there's too much reliance on the left hand, with the consequent loss of dynamic subtlety compounded by a klutzy drum mix. But except on his unintentional travesty of "King of the Road," Booker's forthright way with songs like "All Around the World" and "Lawdy Miss Clawdy" and even "Hound Dog" has a barroom feel missing from the live disc. And the glorious schmaltz of "Swedish Rhapsody" was intended by an artist with a passion for camp.   **B+**

The Boomtown Rats: *Greatest Hits* (Columbia '87). A decade ago, Bob Geldof had a bright idea: he pretended to be a punk. Since then he's thought mostly about shouldering his world-historical mission, and though that hasn't precluded more bright ideas, none of them has involved his music.   **B−**

Duke Bootee: *Bust Me Out* (Mercury '84). Yes indeed, the man can sing, though given that he made his name as a musician and writer I'm equally gratified he can rap. Competently in both cases. The difference comes in what he sings or raps. The songs are standard funk fare, the raps his most pointed and bent since "The Message." And Doug Wimbish and crew make escape from Sugarhill sound like freedom now.   **B+**

Bootsy: See Bootsy Collins.

Boston: *Third Stage* (MCA '86). Never again can us wiseasses call it corporate rock without thinking twice. Whatever possessed Tom Scholz to spend seven years perfecting this apparently unoccupied articulation of an art-metal thought extinct years ago, it wasn't megaplatinum ambition. He's more like the Archbishop of Latter-Day Arena Rock, perfecting majestic guitar sounds and angelic vocals for hockey-rink cathedrals the world over—and also, since he's patently reluctant to venture from his studio retreat, elegiac melodies suitable to a radio ministry. If he seems more hobbyist than artist, more Trekkie than Blind Boy Grunt, that's no reason to get snobbish. And no reason to listen, either.   **C**

Boulevard of Broken Dreams: *It's the Talk of the Town and Other Sad Songs* (Hannibal '89). In which sixteen Netherlanders pay pomo tribute to near-tragic pop like "I Cover the Waterfront," "I Get Along Without You Very Well," and "A Cottage for Sale." About half the songs (the earliest from 1927, the latest from

1949) are new to me, and if I'd grown up with the originals, I might find the conceptual distancing a distortion, even a sacrilege. But at this late date it's their salvation. The four vocalists, who betray just enough accent to remind you where they're coming from, honor the era's well-enunciated conventions with care, and Roland Brunt's jazzy sax undercuts the violins without patting itself on the chops. If they were French they'd overdo the camp or the sincerity, but the Dutch have the mercantilist knack of respecting a culture for its natural resources. In fact, at this remove they probably understand it better than we do.   **A**—

Jean-Paul Bourelly: *Jungle Cowboy* (JMT import '87). Though there could be more flesh on the voice and more sass in the lyrics, Johnny Watson (with shades of Mose Allison, and, well, Blood Ulmer) isn't such a bad vocal model for a guitar player who wants to better himself. Nice Memphis Slim cover, too. And mostly, nice guitar-based jazz-rock, intense and funky, with sidemen from both sides of the synthesis and not a whiff of "fusion"—the kind of small gift that suggests the genre is still good for bigger ones.   **B+**

David Bowie: *Scary Monsters* (RCA Victor '80). No concepts, no stylistic excursions, no avant collaborations—this songbook may be the most conventional album he's ever put his name on. Vocally it can be hard to take—if "Teenage Wildlife" parodies his chanteur mode on purpose the joke's not worth the pain, and if you think Tom Verlaine can't sing, check out "Kingdom Come"—though anyone vaguely interested has already made peace with that. Lyrically it's too facile as usual, though the one about Major Tom's jones gets me every time. And musically, it apotheosizes his checkered past, bringing you up short with a tune you'd forgotten you remembered or a sonic that scrunches your shoulders or a beat that keeps you on your feet when your coccyx is moaning sit down.   **B+**

David Bowie: *Let's Dance* (EMI America '83). Anyone who wants Dave's $17 million fling to flop doesn't understand how little good motives have to do with good rock and roll. Rodgers & Bowie are a rich combo in the ways that count as well as the ways that don't, and this stays up throughout, though its perfunctory professional surface does make one wonder whether Bowie-the-thespian really cares much about pop music these days. "Modern Love" is the only interesting new song, the remakes are pleasantly pointless, and rarely has such a lithe rhythm player been harnessed to such a flat groove. Which don't mean the world won't dance to it.   **B**

David Bowie: *Tonight* (EMI America '84). What makes Bowie a worthy entertainer is his pretensions, his masks, the way he simulates meaning. He has no special gift for convincing emotions or good tunes—when he works at being "merely" functional he's merely dull, or worse. With Nile Rodgers gone, the dance potential of the second album of his professional phase is negligible, and he's favoring the tired usages that have been the downfall of an entire generation of English twits. In this setting, not even Leiber-Stoller's long-neglected "I Keep Forgetting" makes much of an impression.   **C**

David Bowie: *Never Let Me Down* (EMI America '87). Maybe he's lost touch so completely that he's reduced to cannibalizing himself just when the market dictates the most drastic image shift of his chameleon career. But maybe this is just his way of melding two au courant concepts, Springsteenian rock and multiproducer crossover. After all, why pay good money to outsiders when your own trunk of disguises is there for the rummaging? Of course, crossover artistes can generally sing. When Bowie wants to play the vocalist, he still puts on a bad Anthony Newley imitation.   **C+**

David Bowie: See Tin Machine

Bow Wow Wow: *Your Cassette Pet* (EMI import cassette '80). Only two great songs on this eight-selection shorty—all the rest is Antmusic. It's certainly true, though, that Adam's old backup boys display a lot more verve and cheek and high good humor than the new ones. Not only that, "Sexy Eiffel Towers" and the sly, loving, brazen "Louis Quatorze" almost justify Malcolm McLaren's dubious project of inventing a sex life for his fourteen-year-old Galatea.   **B+**

Bow Wow Wow: *See Jungle! See Jungle! Go Join Your Gang Yeah! City All Over, Go Ape Crazy* (RCA Victor '81). You don't play Afrobeats with a surf band's chops—what makes real African music captivating is a tonal range so subtle it creates little hooks among the polyrhythms. Yet a lot of this transcends its own klutziness. M. McLaren's propagandistic conceits are so outrageous they're comical, especially in a little samba called "Hello, Hello Daddy (I'll Sacrifice You)" ("Eat the heart of my kith and kin! / That's what I'm interested in!"). And the good-legged adolescent grace and vivacity of the wondrous Annabella touch my heart every time she opens her mouth.   **B+**

Bow Wow Wow: *The Last of the Mohicans* (RCA Victor EP '82). This Kenny Laguna–produced attempt to convince the record company that Annabella is Joan Jett opens with a cover of the Strangeloves' "I Want Candy" that isn't as pointless as one might wish—Annabella being female, the oral metaphors instantly evoke toffee-on-a-stick, and don't think Malc doesn't know it. There's also the nubile "Louis Quatorze," remade in what would be record time for anybody but Malc. And three more sexual fantasies, the most outrageous (and sexiest) of which concerns a consensual gang bang. Unfortunately, Annabella's Debbie Harry impression on that one doesn't convince me she's of age.   **B**

Bow Wow Wow: *I Want Candy* (RCA Victor '82). Ever the creative marketer, Malcolm McLaren bestows upon the world a compilation comprising the dubious if sexy *Last of the Mohicans,* a throwaway instrumental, and four cuts—good, though not top-notch—from the band's still estimable debut LP for this label. Which is preferred unless you don't own "Louis Quatorze" in one of its proliferating versions, and maybe even if you do.   **B−**

Bowwowwow: *Twelve Original Recordings* (Capitol '82). Ever the creative marketer, Malcolm McLaren sticks the purportedly never-to-be-vinylized *Your*

Cassette Pet together with almost everything else his latest victims recorded for EMI. Docked the max for lying.   **E**

Bow Wow Wow: *When the Going Gets Tough, the Tough Get Going* (RCA Victor '83). Mike Chapman adds few if any hooks and Annabella Lwin shockingly little verve to their pattering Afrobeats. None of Malcolm McLaren's pubescent-sex fantasies was half as dumb or exploitative as "Aphrodisiac." And though I'm glad they're expressing themselves, only the glorious "Rikki Dee" ("I work at the WC") tells me any teenage news I hadn't guessed.   **C+**

Boyoyo Boys: *Back in Town* (Rounder '87). The lead voice of the band that changed Paul Simon's life isn't a voice, it's a rather thin and monotonous alto saxophone, devoid of vibrato or growl—though if the unidentified player had the personality of, say Oliver Lake, he'd still be overmatched by any of dozens of South African singers you can hear. Ain't all that much going on below, either. Take it one cut at a time.   **B**

Bobby Braddock: *Hardpore Cornography* (RCA Victor EP '83). In which the Nashville cynic conceives his own tribute quickie, this one chockablock with Homer & Jethro homages. What a demo—Don & Phil are already fans of "The Elderly Brothers," and that punny George Jones imitator Elvis Costello will eat up "I Lobster but Never Flounder." But who can measure "Dolly Parton's Hits"?   **B+**

Ruby Braff: *Very Sinatra* (Finesse '82). At fifty-five, cornetist Braff has eleven years on the object of his veneration, but that's not why he adores melody so much more effectively than Frank these days. It's that in the end he's just as devoted to craft and a lot more modest about it; he has less talent, I suppose, but more taste. And it's taste above all that enables one to make a convincing case for the ersatz elegance of traditional pop.   **A−**

Billy Bragg: *Brewing Up With Billy Bragg* (CD '84). Nice lad, always votes Labour, means well with the girls. So why does he subtitle this modest collection of songs-with-electric-guitar "a puckish satire on contemporary mores"? Some believe he's wiser than he knows. I suspect he's not as smart as he thinks he is. [Later available as part of Elektra's *Back to Basics* compilation.]   **B**—

Billy Bragg: *Talking to the Taxman About Poetry* (Elektra '86). How could one deny such a fine young man, especially with his harsh guitar and gratifying piano or trumpet reflecting his Clashy lineage when one thinks about it? That depends on how much one resents having to think about it. The lyrics are another matter—they're made to be thought about. Only soon one realizes that the politics, his forte if not his raison d'être, are surprisingly clunky. And that when it comes to the cons and pros of getting married he never misses a trick.   **B**+

Billy Bragg: *Help Save the Youth of America: Live and Dubious* (Elektra EP '88). It isn't music that makes Bragg so much fun live, so I'm not surprised that the songs are as flat here as in their studio versions—especially since some of them are studio versions. And live fun feeds on context, so I'm not surprised either that the stage patter translates poorly—especially since Bragg takes the task of translation so literally that he provides the Russian version of his remarks on the Moscow-recorded title tune. The video will no doubt feature somebody signing.   **B**—

Billy Bragg: *Workers Playtime* (Elektra '88). He's got a way with a tune and even some money. So maybe it's time to wonder why he has such big problems. Why are women always rejecting him? And why are the people always rejecting him? Not completely, of course—he's a modest success. But in both arenas he falls far short of his putative expectations, and I smell a reason in the barely concealed sob he can't get rid of. From unjust justice all the way to hopeless love, the catch in the throat is kind of seductive—until it starts to make you sick. This is the voice of a man who expects defeat—not only does he feel born to lose, but he doesn't have what it takes to throw a good wake. So why should the working class follow him to the crossroads? Why should Mary?   **B**

The Brains: *The Brains* (Mercury '80). From Steve Lillywhite's loud-with-portent upscale of the perfect "Money Changes Everything" to two atrocious Alfredo Villar songs that would fit fine on a Queen album, their magnified shortcomings are an object lesson in major label meets new wave—the compromises undermine art and commerce simultaneously. Fortunately, Tom Gray's gray matter prevails—life has blessed him with a college education and proximity to the Sex Pistols' U.S. debut. Unlike the power-pop boys, he's seen down to the woman underneath his girls, and just because he plays organ doesn't mean he can't punch it up. Lost rock and rollers in a provincial capital, the Brains are the real Iron City Houserockers—forward-looking yet tradition-drenched entertainment.   **A**—

The Brains: *Electronic Eden* (Mercury '81). Put in enough time with this one and despite its dull initial impact every track will give up a hook—a dull hook, perhaps, but in these brite days there's a kind of satisfaction in that. The problem is that the hooks don't connect to much—when the most memorable lyric on the follow-up is about how that guy has got her hypnotized, you begin to wonder just what money has changed, and how.   **B**

Glenn Branca: *The Ascension* (99 '81). Okay, so he makes hot "experimental" ("serious") ("classical") ("new") music. What we wanna know is whether it's cool rock and roll ("rock"). Not by me. It's great sonically, with ringing overtones that remind me of a carillon or the Byrds, but the beat's overstated and the sense of structure (i.e. climax) mired in nineteenth-century corn. This can be endearing in Pete Townshend or Bruce Springsteen (maybe even opera), but it sounds weak-minded in an artist of such otherwise austere means.   **B.**

Dollar Brand: *African Marketplace* (Elektra '80). More than any other jazz musician I know of, the South African pianist doesn't just honor and evoke popular traditions, he redefines them, injecting his Ellingtonian structures with r&b-based urban dance rhythms and strange (to us) tribal voicings. As often as not his band projects a crudely gorgeous songfulness most unjazzlike in its simplicity—folklike tunes repeat obligingly, ostinatos just don't quit. Take the synthesis for the patriotism of an exile who believes in the wisdom of his people and his land and refuses to indulge his alienation from both.   **A—**

Dollar Brand: See also Abdullah Ibrahim

Brazil Classics 1: Beleza Tropical (Sire '89). I have to tip my hat to any record that can induce me to dig rockpoets Caetano Veloso (four tracks) and Milton Nascimento (two), both of whom I've resisted (uneasily, but with increasing vehemence) for a decade. But in fact my pleasure is more like grudging respect or bemused enjoyment—I admire the Arto Lindsay–translated lyrics, hum along in unguarded moments. Fact is, every certified auteur on this unexceptionable compilation could support a fetching best-of. Fact also is, the only ones I'm sure I'd dig would be by Gilberto Gil (three), an old fave, and Jorge Ben (two), whom David Byrne has sold me on.   **B+**

The Breakfast Club (A&M '85). Disco domo emeritus Keith Forsey is the great spirit behind this consumer fraud. He even wrote the Simple Minds hit, which in a rare moment of aesthetic perspicuity they've disowned, as well as utterly negligible songs for such artistes as Elizabeth Daily, Karla DeVito, and Wang Chung. Plus one, two, three, four instrumentals.   **D—**

Breakin' (Polydor '84). Only students of secondhand black need sample this de facto El Lay hip hop sampler. Ollie and Jerry's title hit can be purchased separately, as can Carol Lynn Townes's "99½" should that strike your fancy. And you'll never notice side two until "Ain't Nobody"—not when Chaka starts singing, but when the keyboard intro comes on. I mean, El Lay hip hop is nothing *but* keyboard intros.   **B—**

Breaking Circus: *The Very Long Fuse* (Homestead EP '85). A guitar band with drum machine, as Chicago as Big Black or industrial dance music. Or maybe Big Black *is* industrial dance music. Well, this isn't—it's hard-edged rock and roll, more like Australia's Celibate Rifles than Britannia's identically configured Three Johns. In standard postpunk mode, the appeal is sound not sense—the good lyrics come in snatches at best. But the sound would never have caught my ear without the completely realized "(Knife in the) Marathon," a dark tale of Olympic racism, or terrorism, or simple skulduggery. **B+**

Edie Brickell & New Bohemians: *Shooting Rubberbands at the Stars* (Geffen '88). Her Suzanne Vega voice is jazzed up with glowing slips and slides that recall Jo Mama's long-forgotten Abigale Haness. Her well-named boys are nuevohippies with chops, also like Jo Mama, a braver band they probably never heard of. Her lyrics are escapist as a matter of conviction—"Don't let me get too deep," she implores, as if she could if she tried. I await the Jo Mama CD.   **B—**

The Bridge: A Tribute to Neil Young (Caroline '89). The boho life certainly is rife with irony—having started out as punks, various avant-garagists find themselves paying respects to Johnny Rotten's favorite hippie. Less ironic is that Young and Rotten got rich and they didn't, which is partly the times, but also partly because they have less to say. They parody, they imitate, they cover, sometimes two or three at once, not because they're complex but because they've never figured out what they're doing. In contrast, Victoria Williams and Henry Kaiser, who started out as music nuts, seize their good songs. And Sonic Youth, who may get rich yet, seize a catchy piece of junk.   **B**

Bronski Beat: *The Age of Consent* (MCA '84). Good politics don't have to be this monochromatic, and neither do albums with two good singles on them. Problem's pretty simple—the narrow dynamic range that afflicts so many falsettos, even those with impeccable reasons for singing like women. And before you call me per-snickety, swear you wouldn't rather hear Donna Summer's "I Feel Love."   **C+**

Bobby Brown: *Don't Be Cruel* (MCA '88). It's the eternal fast one/slow one problem—when he states his prerogatives and tries to make the world dance he's irresistible, when he masks his motives and tries to make the tenderoni moan he's an obvious con. But he earns his prerogatives: the internal rhymes and voice-electrobeat patterning of the title track are so tricky they're hooky. And since I've never been much of an expert on tenderoni, I'm willing to suspend judgment on the half that leaves me unmoved.   **B+**

Bobby Brown: *Dance! . . . Ya Know It!* (MCA '89). Disco postmodernists say there's no such thing as a song any more—only versions. Talk about the triumph of theory. Proof that they're full of it can be found on Brown's *Don't Be Cruel,* where the song versions of five of these nine dance-remixes-cum-consumer-frauds can be found.   **C**

Charles Brown: *One More for the Road* (Blue Side '87). This long overdue piece of record-making hits you with its craft and taste. Of course, you think. Brown's powers are undimmed since he topped the charts as a lounge singer forty years ago, so why shouldn't he sound just as fine in the studio today? And he does. With Billy Butler on guitar, his combo is at least as choice as the Three Blazers, and he has forty years of lounge classics to draw on—"One for My Baby," "I Miss You So," "Who Will the Next Fool Be," all right. There's only one problem: Brown is no Nat King Cole. His voice slips into the lugubrious so reflexively that at times you suspect clutch problems with the master reel, and it could just be that he's best appreciated over a highball—or else, like so many chart-toppers before him, in three-minute doses.   **B+**

Clarence Gatemouth Brown: *Alright Again!* (Rounder '81). Texans, Jesus—give them a black man in a cowboy hat and they won't stop jawing about the wide open spaces until they fall off the barstool.

And what is this thing they have for blues brass in platoons? I mean, Bobby Bland can sing over, under, and around that shit, but this old pro obviously hasn't bulled his way past a tenor sax in twenty years. Still packs a fairly sharp guitar, I grant you, and he can make you listen up with that violin of his. But he's fronting some very unswinging white boys, and his idea of contemporary is the stock-market woes of small businessmen.   **C+**

James Brown: *People* (Polydor '80). Anybody who thinks his first Brad Shapiro album was mechanical should get a load of what a real assembly line sounds like. *Original Disco Man* was a labor of vanity, and when it didn't hype his career the way he'd been told it would JB went back on automatic. Shapiro & Co. respond in kind.
   C+

James Brown: *James Brown . . . Live: Hot on the One* (Polydor '80). Hard to believe almost ten years have passed since JB had the wherewithal to release a live double—not the new tunes, which he mostly skips for old stuff, but the commercial credibility. Hard to believe this one's so different—busier, relying on band and backup rather than the acuity of Brown's singing. Hard to believe it's so alive—until you play the damn thing, which only slackens to make room for the latest edition of "Man's World."   **B+**

James Brown: *Nonstop!* (Polydor '81). Titles like "Popcorn 80's," "Love 80's," "Super Bull/Super Bad," "I Go Crazy," signal a contract-fulfilling rehash, but this time he's rehashing the right stuff in the right way—the horn charts and rhythm arrangements are as tricky and on the one as in any newfangled funk you want to name. Most of the sweet ache has disappeared from "I Go Crazy" since 1960, and I'm not going to claim that the successfully renegotiated tempo makes up for it. But it is a consolation.   **B+**

James Brown: *Bring It On* (Augusta Sound '83). The fast side is honorable and dispensable—great title riff plus filler, nothing anyone who owns some early-'70s JB is likely to need or even want, though neophytes will dance to it now. The slow side comprises the three strongest covers

Brown's released since he stuck a classic "Kansas City" onto *Everybody's Doin' the Hustle* in 1975. He still approaches high notes with the caution of someone who's hoarse as indelibly as he's black and proud, but he's emoting like he wants you to believe "Tennessee Waltz" and "For Your Precious Love," and in between comes "The Right Time," which isn't really slow at all and features a Brownette who approaches any kind of note as if she owns it. Time: 28:45.   **B+**

James Brown: *Gravity* (Scotti Brothers '86). Not a James Brown album—a James Brown–influenced Dan Hartman record, with James Brown on vocals. Unlike Brad Shapiro, who manufactured good music this way in 1979, Hartman takes his humdrum copyrights and urges the great one to go for the expressiveness he hasn't commanded in over a decade rather than the rhythm he'll take to his grave. Don't believe me—just compare any of Polydor's most recent compilations: *James Brown's Funky People* (featuring Lyn Collins, Fred Wesley, Maceo Parker, and James Brown), *Dead on the Heavy Funk 74–76* (salvaging a total of zero good LPs), or *In the Jungle Groove* (long-promised, worth-waiting-for, full-length, '69–'71 dance classics). Hartman would love every one.   **C+**

James Brown: *I'm Real* (Scotti Brothers '88). Fact is, he hasn't known what to do with his reality, originality, genius, and so forth since the mid-'70s, when disco took the bump out of the JB funk that made modern dance music possible. Though after years of floundering he figured out the new groove, Brad Shapiro still had to show him the ins and outs of its glitz; now that young dance musicians have reacted back to JB funk, cramming and twisting its bottom while running poesy across the top, he needs Full Force (who like Shapiro aren't true genre insiders, just pros who can take the genre to the bridge) to hip him to its lore. The raps and hooks are nothing special. But whether it's live or Memorex, the dense hostility of the drum attack is both fresh and in the tradition—his tradition.   **B**

James Brown: *Motherlode* (Polydor '88). Damned if I noticed "People Get Up and Drive Your Funky Soul" on the *Slaughter's Big Rip-Off* soundtrack, but for nine minutes it climaxes the instrumentals and vamps on side two of this revelatory-as-usual Chris White vault job, hopping along on some swinging souly-funk genre cusp of its own—not "Sex Machine," but in the same worth-the-price-of-admission league. The spare, curlicued "Untitled Instrumental" is more like jazzy-funk, the rest just JB playing rough and getting loose in the halcyon early '70s. Which come to think of it is also worth the price of admission.   **A–**

James Brown & Friends: *Soul Session Live* (Scotti Brothers '89). Beyond Aretha, forget the cameo attractions—Billy Vera (wan), Joe Cocker (rough), and Robert Palmer (compared by JB to Elvis, Otis, and Jackie, and don't you sometimes wish he was just as far out of the way?). Also, the band's not improving, and even at that it's sharper than his voice, which you probably figured and which does in his umpteenth de facto best-of once and for all. Is this what he's showing his parole officer? Poor guy.   **C**

Julie Brown: *Goddess in Progress* (Rhino EP '84). Never one to turn up my nose at a cheap laugh, I'm delighted to report that like the notorious "Homecoming Queen's Got a Gun," "I Like 'Em Big and Stupid" ("What kind of guy does a lot for me? / Superman with a lobotomy") and "Cause I'm a Blond" ("Being chosen this month's Miss August was a compliment I'll remember for as long as I can") go after their targets with a fine lack of discrimination. Elsewhere on the EP Julie makes love, or at least it, with a space invader (She: "That sure is a big piece of machinery you've got!" He: "I made it myself") and fights a clubland hangover. Music's catchier than a jeans jingle, too. Original grade: B plus.   **A–**

Jackson Browne: *Hold Out* (Asylum '80). Never hep to his jive, I'm less than shocked by the generalized sentimentality disillusioned admirers descry within these hallowed tracks, though the one about the late great Lowell George (think it's him, any other El Lay rocker die recently?) is un-

usually rank. I grant that the sincere vocals and rising organ chords do make my
heart swell in spite of itself once in a while.
But I wonder whether the lost kids (i.e.,
Lost Kids) in "Boulevard" wear mohawks, and whether JB will ever find it in
himself to sing to them. Inspirational Line:
"That girl was sane."   **C+**

Jackson Browne: *Lawyers in Love* (Asylum '83). A satire on, celebration of, and
lament for the upper-middle classmates an
Orange County liberal knows like he
knows his neighbor's backyard, the title
song is a coup: poignant, droll, political
about his own experience rather than some
victim's. And dat's dat. Anticlimax: the
yearningly Springsteenian—get this title—
"For a Rocker."   **C+**

Jackson Browne: *Lives in the Balance*
(Asylum '86). These antiwar songs give
him plenty in common with Holly Near—
he even puts nueva canción musicians on
the title track. While Browne goes in for
higher octane folk-rock, I'll pass on the
remixes if you don't mind. The difference
is that Browne shouldn't be doing this—
however goody-goody his fans or political
his recent rep, he's a pop star who's
stretching his audience and endangering
his market share merely by making such a
statement in 1986. And he's thought hard
getting here—not only does his way with
words render these lyrics somewhat deeper
than Holly Near's, but his moralistic put-
downs have that edge of righteous anger
nobody's yet found the formula for. Original grade: B plus.   **B**

Jackson Browne: *World in Motion* (Elektra '89). May he remain a protest singer in
perpetuity, and not just because I wish his
love songs were history. But n.b.: the two
standouts are "My Personal Revenge," a
pledge of forgiveness by Sandinista hard-
liner Tomás Borge, and Little Steven's—
yes, Little Steven's, his stock always
improves when he doesn't sing—"I Am a
Patriot." You think the secret flaw of the
archetypal singer-songwriter might be
songwriting?   **B**

B.T. Express: *Greatest Hits* (Columbia
'80). All ye need know of the Average
Black Band, with their straight-ahead
"Old Gold" tricked/tripped up in the
remix to mesh with "Future Gold" that's
worth its weight only in the minds of suckers for a glitzy prospectus. Original grade:
A minus.   **B**

Lindsey Buckingham: *Law and Order*
(Asylum '81). This fluent, affluent rumina-
tion on the price of sin and the wages of
success really isn't how they do it in L.A.
anymore, which must be why I had such a
hassle getting a handle on it. Moral signposts are provided by the covers: rock and
roll "It Was I" (love is painful), pop "September Song" (and the most precious thing
there is), country "A Satisfied Mind" (so
be thankful for what you've got). Now if
only Lindsey didn't spend so much time
flexing his archness, all this might be per-
ceptible to the naked ear.   **B+**

Harold Budd/Brian Eno: *The   Pearl*
(Editions EG '84). Budd's previous work
with the avant-pop sound-environments
king was a mite tacky—he tended to signify spirituality with wordless vocal choruses that reminded me of the Anita Kerr
Singers, though I'm sure they boasted a
prouder lineage. These ten pieces are more
circumspect and detailed, and while they
do slip into decoration they're the most
intellectually gratifying (and emotionally
engaging) music Eno's put his name on
since his first Jon Hassell LP. Finally he
succeeds in making soporific an honor-
ific.   **A—**

Harold Budd: *Abandoned Cities* (Cantril
'84). This phonographic record of a gallery
installation called *Image-Bearing Light*
moves slowly but not glacially. Sounds like
chords on a color organ played back at
16-r.p.m.—stark yet soothing. Recommended to seekers after low-down ambience.   **B+**

Harold Budd: *The White Arcades* (Opal
'88). Long before Brian Eno hyped ambient, there was the less pretentious term
background music, and you can be sure our
brave new age will goop up the margin
between the two. At his most austere, Eno's
old buddy Budd is hyperromantic, and this
isn't exactly austere—with the proper in-
ducement (hypnosis, or a large bribe), he
might even call it a sellout. Weak-minded-
ness passing itself off as spirituality—it's

what new agers seek in classical music. Budd's angle is to eliminate any vestige of difficulty from the concept.   **C+**

Bebe Buell: *Covers Girl* (Rhino EP '81). Everybody's (everyman's?) (everystar's?) favorite girlfriend gets production from Rick Derringer and Ric Ocasek on material originating with Love, Tom Petty, Iggy Pop, and—the biggest winner, no doubt because it's the biggest obscurity— the Nightcrawlers, whose "Little Black Egg" went local in L.A. circa 1967. Those who complain about the size of her voice would probably do the same about her tits. I say she sings with a courtesan's confidence and intend a compliment. Original grade: A minus.   **B+**

Solomon Burke: *Soul Alive!* (Rounder '84). With the "Bishop of Soul" backed by Brenda Bergman's Realtones, this live double from America's premier folkie label looks like an irrelevance, but the D.C. audience signifies otherwise. Burke's singing has lost subtlety rather than power, and since all but two of the twenty-four songs he sets his voice to are relegated to medleys, his readings of specific lyrics aren't the issue so much as the preacherly context he creates for them—the way his monologues connect musically acute texts like "If You Need Me" and "Hold What You've Got" and "Down in the Valley" and "Gotta Get You Off of My Mind" to the facts of love in a world where women sign their own welfare checks.   **B+**

Solomon Burke: *A Change Is Gonna Come* (Rounder '86). With his fondness for the grand gesture, I just knew Burke was going to build the hushed title cut to a crescendo, but instead of trivializing the song with a false resolution he maintains its tension for seven minutes. That's the triumph, but the same level of taste prevails— this is a modern soul album that engages the material at hand instead of pimping for reactionaries. And with contributions from the likes of Paul Kelly and Jimmy Lewis, the material is worth engaging.   **B+**

T-Bone Burnett: *Truth Decay* (Takoma '80). Having put the omega on smarmy Alpha Bandmate Steve Soles (who does

show up in the credits, but not—unlike the ever-adroit David Mansfield—as a band member), Burnett produces the best Christian record of 1980 for John Fahey's Buddhist blues label. Of course, you could also call it the best rockabilly record of 1980— something has happened to rockabilly since Sam Phillips talked Jerry Lee into defaming the Pentecost. And since Burnett is equally comfortable with the (divine) "power of love" and a (fleshly) "love that's hot," maybe something's happened to Christianity, too.   **A−**

T-Bone Burnett: *Trap Door* (Warner Bros. EP '82). Gosh, I guess he wasn't really rockabilly after all. "Hold On Tight" is El Lay at its best, and it's hard to imagine Jerry Lee himself covering "Diamonds Are a Girl's Best Friend" with more purpose or panache. Not that this is altogether unproblematic—as catchy and incisive as the originals are, as casually as they're delivered, not one jumps off the record with the unassuming confidence of the cover's pure pop. This is an artist who can't shake his own self-consciousness. That's why he came on rockabilly.   **A−**

T-Bone Burnett: *Proof Through the Night* (Warner Bros. '83). Since I've never measured America's decline by the willingness of its female citizens to take their clothes off, some of Burnett's allegories fail to touch me as I know they should. But I'm a sucker for a humble man with a proud guitar.   **B+**

T Bone Burnett: *T Bone Burnett* (Dot '86). Burnett's foray into straight country is right purty, but it could stand to get a little bent. Abjuring strings, backup choruses, trap sets, puns, and sales potential, it takes the neo out of neotraditionalism, and though I smiled when T Bone bought his baby "clothes of rayon," I was disturbed to realize that even his synthetics are ensconced in the past.   **B+**

T-Bone Burnett: *The Talking Animals* (Columbia '88). Hate to let the cat out of the bag, but this guy is pretentious. He's not dumb, not incapable, not even charmless (incredible shaggy dog story at the close). And country change-of-pace aside, his parables and exhortations have gotten more pointless with every record. Help him, Jesus.   **B−**

Burning Spear: *Social Living* (Burning Spear import '80). Less militant and archetypal than *Marcus Garvey,* this nevertheless lives up to a wonderful title and wonderful title song. In its sinuous vocalizations and giving groove, its single and unison horns, the music is all charity and cooperation—it's why Winston Rodney is preaching "Social living is the best." And yea though he droppeth the names of European countries in "Civilize Reggae," it's reggae and not Europe that's doing the civilizing.   **A−**

Burning Spear: *Hail H.I.M.* (Burning Spear import '80). Strange to hear it come down to material in a singer so infused with the spirit. But what I remember is what I don't remember—the difference between the first three songs, "African Teacher" and "African Postman," and "Cry Blood Africans," except that the last one has crying in it. Maybe it's the well-known positivity problem, because when he's angry he comes across: Columbus was a "damn blasted liar" indeed.   **B**

Burning Spear: *Farover* (Heartbeat '82). Ever more delicate backup horns subsume ever more docile backup vocals as his unearthly outcries grow more coaxing, less admonitory. But the end is the same: Winston Rodney is so synchronic that in 1982 he gives up pretty much the same trancy buzz as in 1976. He's just less excited about it.   **B+**

Burning Spear: *Reggae Greats: Burning Spear* (Mango '84). Spear's back-to-Africa wail can enthrall Babylonians with no particular interest in reggae, though it's probably too out for dabblers who consider their Marley and UB40 albums exotic. He's a left-field classic, like Hound Dog Taylor or Jimmy Rogers in blues. Unfortunately, this compilation, devised solely to take its place in Island's new Reggae Greats series, invites hair-splitting. The 1976 debut *Marcus Garvey* is more of a piece, which matters with a prophet of autohypnosis like Rodney; the 1979 compilation *Harder Than the Best* configures eight of the same tracks more gracefully. Scout around for both before putting money down on this substitute. But don't be afraid to settle.   **A−**

Burning Spear: *People of the World* (Slash '86). Like many angry young men before him, Winston Rodney has mellowed with the gathering years and assets. And like many angry young men before him, he's surrendered some edge. Innate musicality plus the right cushy production will sometimes benefit victims of this syndrome, and here he finds the formula, keyed to a horn section that happens to comprise three American women. So all hail unity and the honorable disc-race.   **B+**

Burning Spear: *Mistress Music* (Slash '88). This kicks off with one of Spear's strongest and strangest songs—"Tell the Children," which rather than inculcating them with doctrine informs them she's their mother but Spear's not their father. What's the mystical symbolism, one wonders. Answer: there is none. With the third song called "Woman I Love You" and the fifth all "Girl I love you," I guess this is just music for his mistress—or to be precise, mistresses.   **B**

Burning Spear: *Live in Paris* (Slash '89). Where once Winston Rodney was Spear, here Spear is Rodney's since disbanded band. Thrills and chills come from brass belles and caustic guitar and chameleon keybs, while Rodney's indistinguishable exhortations provide essential atmosphere—a physically compelling aural environment. Kind of like the rhythm section.   **B+**

Charlie Burton and the Cut-Outs: *Is That Charlie Burton or What?!?!* (Wild '82). Burton's only competition among nouveau rockabilly composers is the Blasters' Dave Alvin, and like almost anyone with a knack for song form in 1982 he's flexible. In fact, his only remaining link to pure rockabilly is a fondness for novelty numbers like the factual "Rabies Shots" and the utterly heretical "Breathe for Me, Presley!," and in the end his sense of humor is his limitation. In rock and roll of any kind you have to sing better than Robert Klein.   **B+**

Charlie Burton and the Hiccups: *I Heard That* (Wild '86). The Hiccups make with good old guitar, bass, and drums while

Charlie fakes some rockabilly up front, and when it works it's quite catchy in an utterly received sort of way. The conservatism isn't annoying or boring because although Charlie loves this music—listen to "One Man's Trash"—he doesn't give a damn for roots or form. He just wants to write some songs. I'm not sorry he doesn't share my liberal respect for Vietnam and world hunger, and when he diddleybops through his parents' coronaries I know why. Inspirational Verse: "Water's thick, but blood is thicker / Daddy (Mommy) had a bum, bum ticker."   **B+**

Bus Boys: *Minimum Wage Rock & Roll* (Arista '80). They climax with their own "Respect," which climaxes "If you don't like rock 'n' roll music you can kiss my ass." And they mean it, man, though their idea of rock 'n' roll—AOR guitar breaks, rhythms less funky than Jeff Porcaro's or Don Christensen's, harmonies that owe the Beach Boys and Steely Dan—is too uncool to break through the prejudices of the hipsters prone to cheer five blacks and a Chicano for putting it out. Sometimes they aim too straight for the charts, but when they play their existential joke—speaking up for dishwashers and shoeshine boys, for blacks who think immigrants are destroying the neighborhood and blacks who win one for the coach and blacks who join the Klan so they can join a band—I say cool. Inspirational Verse: "Bet you never heard music like this by spades."   **B+**

The Bus Boys: *American Worker* (Arista '82). At first I was no more impressed by this professional black arena-rock than I am by, say, professional lesbian folk-rock. Less, actually—bombast is annoying. But in the end I was disarmed by their audacity, esprit, and sheer versatility—not many arena-rockers are comfortable simulating funk, reggae, and surf music—and won over by the songs themselves, every one informed by the kind of middle-American compassion you might expect from a black band with enough soul to hope to touch the arena-rock masses.   **B+**

Kate Bush: *The Dreaming* (EMI America '82). The most impressive Fripp/Gabriel-style art-rock album of the postpunk refulgence makes lines like "I love life" and "Some say knowledge is something that you never have" say something. Part of the reason is that Bush is flaky enough to seek the higher plane in "a hired plane," although as you might expect the resulting analysis often crumbles under scrutiny. It also helps that the emotional range of her singing sometimes approaches its physical range, although when it doesn't you'd best duck. But the revelation is the dense, demanding music, which gets the folk exoticism of current art-rock fashion out of mandolins and uillean pipes and didgeridoos rather than clumsy polyrhythms, and goes for pop outreach with hooks rather than clumsy polyrhythms.   **B+**

Kate Bush: *Hounds of Love* (EMI America '85). Just as her music says she hopes everyone does, I respect and like this woman. Though it's tempting to slot her with Laura Nyro, you never get the sense she's a fool—she's more circa-*Hejira* Joni Mitchell. Her best songs can't match their best, but sonically she's magnificent, outstripping her art-rock mentors, and it would be churlish to deny her to audiophiles and/or young women seeking independent role models. Nevertheless, to be a Romantic with a capital R in 1986 is to be a Victorian like Tennyson, who provides Bush her epigraph. It is deliberately to cultivate a sensibility whose time you know perfectly well has passed.   **B**

Kate Bush: *The Whole Story* (EMI America '86). This extravagantly brainy spiritual sexpot was made for the Fairlight synthesizer, and her beautifully crafted best-of proves it. Even the best of the old U.K. hits she strews among the tokens of her American breakthrough, 1980's "Army Dreamers," lives and dies with its lyric. But as she learns to manipulate her electronic orchestra, which took a while (cf. 1980's "Breathing"), the songs turn into compositions, so that if the unfettered emotionalism of "Hounds of Love," say, isn't your cup of tea, you're still rooting for her as she takes off her shoes and throws them in the lake. And then there's "Running Up That Hill," a woman's orgasm in 4:58.   **A—**

Kate Bush: *The Sensual World* (Columbia '89). The longing for contact and obliteration are themes grand enough to support a little grandiosity, and because she's smarter than the average art-rocker, she brings something worth telling to them—even something worth "expressing." She knows herself better, too; typical that her roots move is Trio Bulgarka rather than some Afro-source having nothing to do with who she is. Just wish she convinced me that the Trio Bulgarka had more to do with who I am. The title song could give Henry James a boner. The one where her beloved turns into Hitler is art-rock.   **B**

Bush Tetras: *Better Late Than Never* (ROIR cassette '89). With Pat Place slash-sliding away and Cynthia Sley OK to be in the same room with, the postliberated axewomen of Emma Goldman's (Zelda Fitzgerald's?) version of the Contortions were an up on chutzpah alone. A pioneering rhythm-and-paranoia band, their "Too Many Creeps" / "Snakes Crawl" / "You Taste Like the Tropics" summed up the Lower East Side circa 1980. But in their quest for that tropical flavor, the authors of "You Can't Be Funky" showed their true chops. At fifteen songs this is virtually their entire studio output. Wound too tight, it soon wears thin.   **B—**

Mzikayifani Buthelezi: *Fashion Maswedi* (Rounder '88). A traditionally raised country Zulu, he sings like he's calling cattle or berating his six wives while his brother saws away on concertina or violin and groups of wives and male underlings muscle up to the mike. Pretty raw even for mbaqanga, and pretty repetitive, too—Jo'burg rhythm pros provide the now-familiar four-four. But familiarity doesn't flatten the overall intensity—instead, Buthelezi's wail demonstrates its character. If someone had bothered to pick and choose from his one hundred-plus titles instead of rereleasing an old album, he might end up more than a strange name in a catalogue.   **B+**

Butthole Surfers: *Butthole Surfers* (Alternative Tentacles EP '83). Unlike most horror-show hardcore, their tales from the crypt eschew the reassuring glow of celluloid, yet they don't smudge like pulp, either. For openers a guy comes on and shrieks, "There's a time to fuck and a time to crave / But the shah sleeps in Lee Harvey's grave." Then there's a lot of guitar noise. More axioms: "Jimi Hendrix makes love to Marilyn's remains," "I smoke Elvis Presley's [ed.: not Costello's?] toenails when I want to get high," etc. More guitar noise. As nihilist grossout goes, pretty neat and impossible by definition to sustain. Yet sustain it they do, not because necro-copro is such a powerful idea, but because the guitar noise crests and roils like a river of shit—because, though I hate to put it this way, there are actually songs down there. Rarely has such demented caterwaul reached vinyl in recognizable form.   **A—**

Butthole Surfers: *Live Pcppep* (Alternative Tentacles EP '84). At first I detected an emotional power signifying something more than an arty posthardcore band whose outrageousness was truly original. But soon I noticed that one of the three new songs—striking statistic in a band whose recorded output comprises two longish EPs—was a noise interlude. So now I'm wondering whether they mightn't be an original posthardcore band whose outrageousness is truly arty, or whose emotional power is truly a fake. Oh well—at least they'll evolve toward big-beat no wave (performance art?) rather than heavy metal. Original grade: A minus.   **B**

Butthole Surfers: *Psychic . . . Powerless . . . Another Man's Sac* (Touch and Go '85). Truly repulsive music imposes the most stringent of aesthetic standards—who wants to listen if it's just good? So while I'm sort of impressed by the (relative) accessibility of their first full-length LP—guitar that might actually win over some wayward metal freak seeking X-rated thrills—I must report that only "Lady Sniff," punctuated by perfectly timed gobs, pukes, farts, belches, and Mexican radio, lives up to "The Shah Sleeps in Lee Harvey's Grave."   **B+**

Butthole Surfers: *Rembrandt Pussyhorse* (Touch & Go '86). I respect these guys, really—their dedication to dementia is a rare and wondrous thing. But their claque's idea of accessibility is Iron Butterfly on bad acid digging deconstruction, yet another version of the touching avant-garde truism which holds that the proper study of incoherence is incoherent. Upped a notch or two for concept, attitude, hype, bullshit, somewhere in there. **B**—

Buzzcocks: *A Different Kind of Tension* (I.R.S. '80). I suppose people call them a pop band because they still write about love, but that they say "I can't love you" rather than the usual does make a difference. Not in profundity—one sentiment is as banal as the other—but in a mood that suits a sound as bright and abrasive as new steel wool. Pete Shelley articulates his truisms with insight as well as flair, especially in "You Say You Don't Love Me" and "I Believe." My favorite, though, is Steve Diggle's "You Know You Can't Help It," about sex, which I'm happy to report he likes—although he does observe that "love makes war." Hey, does it? **B**+

Buzzcocks: *Lest We Forget* (ROIR cassette '88). A nineteen-cut compilation recorded at seven U.S. gigs in '79 and '80, long after Howard Devoto had gone his foolish way, this is half *Singles Going Steady,* only with the opposite effect—instead of proving how tight and commercial they are, it proves how raw and punky they were. Which combination is definitely no contradiction—in fact, it establishes their classic status once and for all. You'll miss "Orgasm Addict" and "Everybody's Happy Nowadays." But you won't need them. **A**—

David Byrne: *Songs From the Broadway Production of "The Catherine Wheel"* (Sire '81). Byrne's take on the rhythms of Africa is even more perilous for imitators than Coltrane's on the mysteries of the Orient, but this surprisingly apt translation-to-disc of his Twyla Tharp score proves his patent is worth the plastic it's imprinted on. The magic's all in Byrne's synthesis of the way drums talk and the way Americans talk—middle Americans, not Afro-Americans. Beset by contingencies they can't make sense of, his protagonists twist from one side to the other, yet somehow emerge from the end of the tunnel with their wills intact. Must have to do with that unnatural rhythm. **A**—

David Byrne: *Music for The Knee Plays* (ECM '85). I didn't trust my instant attraction to these obviously derivative occasional pieces until I looked at the label and realized that five of the twelve originated with "Trade/Arr. by." There's no tune like an old tune, and if this music really was "inspired by the Dirty Dozen Brass Band," then I think Byrne's fusion of New Orleans horn voicings with Soho-avant calm is more satisfying than theirs with bebop and funk. I also think his words do Robert Wilson proud and then some. **A**—

David Byrne: *Songs From True Stories* (Sire '86). It isn't all as archly mawkish as the rearranged dreamsongs from his group's worst album. Pretentiously dinky is more the prevailing mood—a soundtrack only, like so many arty soundtracks before it. One where Byrne, Meredith Monk, the Kronos Quartet, and some locals who couldn't have known what they were getting into do for Texas what Byrne & Eno did for Africa. **C**+

David Byrne: *Rei Momo* (Luaka Bop/Sire '89). Byrne respects and understands distance, an essential faculty in world-beat projects, and his increasingly sinuous singing should make this Latin synthesis a natural. The lyrics are explicitly social without sacrificing the nervous literacy of his established voice. He picks good musicians and provides proper arrangements. And the result is a respectful, highly intelligent dud. Irritating though the muscular masculinity of sonero tradition may be, any doubts as to why it's there are dispelled by Byrne's inability to wrap his weedy chops around salsa that's too tasteful by half. And I'm beginning to suspect he writes *rock* lyrics—words that can only impact loud, grating, and straight-ahead. **C**+

J.J. Cale: *Special Edition* (Mercury '84). When he came up, Cale seemed one more carrier of the laid-back contagion, but fifteen years later, with the contagion dispersed into the adult-contemporary ether and its carriers in hock up to their souls, you have to respect him for the principled bluesman he's proven to be. Principled, but distinctly minor—only convinced narcoleptics want the complete set. The rest of us will be happy to stop at this compilation, though we'd be happier if it didn't pass up "Call Me the Breeze" and "I Got the Same Old Blues" for more up-to-date entries. **B+**

Calling Rastafari (Nighthawk '82). Produced in three days by a Jewish wheeler-dealer from St. Louis, this fundamentalist compilation—roots reggae as a music of militant religious homily—has an irresistible integrity. Its simple determination matches its singsong melodies and solid rhythms, and the singing is crucial: Culture's Joseph Hill hasn't sounded so impassioned since *Two Sevens Clash,* the Gladiators' Albert Griffiths outgroans Marley on "Small Axe," and the Itals' Keith Porter does "Herbs Pirate" so nice you'll settle for owning it twice. **A—**

Cameo: *Cameosis* (Chocolate City '80). "Shake your pants, I like the way they dance / Shake your pants for action and romance," goes the biggest hit on their big-

gest album, which gets these disco-funk careerists' thematic daring just right. I'm waiting for the follow-up: "Shake your ass, I like its heft and mass / Shake your ass, oh no, that sounds too crass." **C**

Cameo: *Feel Me* (Chocolate City '80). Incredibly, or do I mean accidentally, their sixth album in four years on the production line is a discernible improvement, and not because the hits (or lyric sheet) are necessary. It's all groove and sound: drummer/leader shows off like bosses do, Moog man's old-fashioned Walter Carlos gurgles fit da funk like they ruined der Bach, and the slow ones are down to two, one a bow to the Spinners. **B—**

Cameo: *Alligator Woman* (Chocolate City '82). Funkateers think this is "new wave" not just because the title hit sounds like the B-52's but because secret virtuoso Larry Blackmon keeps the groove stripped down and off balance. Unfortunately, the hooks are few, the humor is forced, and the ballads suck. For theoreticians mostly. **B**

Cameo: *Style* (Atlanta Artists '83). It never peaks, which means it'll never be as hot a party record as the A side of *Alligator Woman,* but this on-the-one cartoon (cf. Slave's *Showtime*) is an all-round showcase for syndrum natural Larry Blackmon, funk's most underutilized resource. Keyb man Charles Singleton does smart stuff with the slow stuff by covering "Can't Help Falling in Love" and making something of the atmospheric "Interlude (Serenity)." Maybe next time they'll only abandon their God-given tempo to sex it up heavy like on "Slow Movin'." **B+**

Cameo: *Word Up* (Atlanta Artists '86). Larry Blackmon's a funny drummer, and I wouldn't say albums are something he just gets away with. But Vince Aletti named his column "The Single Life" after Blackmon's last significant effort for a reason. So buy the twelve-inch. And if you want more, wait for the best-of his current masterpiece makes inevitable. **B**

Camper Van Beethoven: *Telephone Free Landslide Victory* (Independent Project '85). Some believe "Take the Skinheads Bowling" makes these pranksters a one-joke band, but there are loads of jokes in that song alone, most of which they don't bother to tell—for instance, do you bowl with the skinheads or with the skinheads' heads? So count them a seventeen-joke band, one for each cut, including instrumentals. If only Brave Combo could relax like this, the world might yet dance (and fall all over itself) to world dance music. Existential indecision lives. **A—**

Camper Van Beethoven: *II & III* (Pitch a Tent '86). I was annoyed by all the instrumentals at first—Balkan folk dances as psychedelic cowpunk, a mite *précieux,* don'cha think? Not really, and plenty catchy in the end regardless. There are too many lyrics aimed at the foibles of acquaintances and potential fans as well. And every last one is a hoot in their dryly absurdist manner. **A—**

Camper Van Beethoven: *Camper Van Beethoven* (Pitch-a-Tent '86). Without benefit of a "Skinheads" or a "Bad Trip," this is the most convincing of the three very good albums they've dashed off in a year and a half—sixteen tracks, eclectic in a panfolkrock mode that now seems unselfconscious if not inevitable, even the instrumentals equipped with words of one sort or another sometimes. Their stance is bemused when it's not just spaced out, and their "Interstellar Overdrive" is too conceptual for my tastes. But I reserve the right to read good politics into the likes of "Joe Stalin's Cadillac" (is LBJ's Cadillac is Somoza's Cadillac is General Pinochet's

Cadillac is my Cadillac I'd like to drive it off a bridge has anyone seen the bridge). So far their productivity seems proof against the desperate indulgences that can overcome talented bands with dodgy commercial prospects. They're an encouraging aberration in a bad time. I wish them a tour bus w/driver that never lets them down. **A**

Camper Van Beethoven: *Vampire Can Mating Oven* (Pitch-a-Tent EP '87). At first I thought they'd tossed off some makeshift DIY to convince major money they were still prolific, but the deadpan positivity of these six cuts is no throwaway (I hope). Thwarted love, meaningless love, ice cream, never go back, instrumental breakdown, all distinguished by the calm acceptance of fate that marks their brilliant cover of "Photograph" as unmistakably as it marks Ringo Starr's brilliant original. **A—**

Camper Van Beethoven: *Our Beloved Revolutionary Sweetheart* (Virgin '88). Suddenly these postmodern postfolkie weirdos are transformed into, of all things, a rock band—sans chops. And unfortunately, chops are an issue: both the one-dimensional matter-of-factness of the vocal concept and the time-keeping worldbeat-by-numbers of the rhythmic philosophy stick out of Dennis Herring's honest AOR production, which messes up the band's balance even though it leaves everything but the mix untouched. Beneath this disorienting surface the message continues its evolution toward postanomie, and it would be a kick to hear "Life Is Grand," say, on the radio. Not AOR, though—college radio, where the nay-sayers it's aimed at call the shots. **B+**

Camper Van Beethoven: *Key Lime Pie* (Virgin '89). After an instrumental establishes the band's voice, out march four amazing songs—two literal, two associative, all smart, ambitious, eccentric, eloquent, unassuming, compassionate, and cognizant of history. Music's a more forceful version of their by now homy-sounding bouzouki-rock, and when the country-rock guitar hook snakes professionally out of the associative "Sweet Hearts" it makes sense somehow. But on an album they call "bittersweet"—"not gloomy, but moody" —those four songs are pretty much it. "Pictures of Matchstick Men" smirks cheerfully at hippie nostalgia, and "All Her Favorite Fruit" is all those good adjectives. But both are swamped by music that's not gloomy, not moody, just lugubrious; the big drumbeats evoke nothing so much as the gong at a Chinese funeral. They knew better back when skinhead jokes were funny.   **B+**

Captain Beefheart and the Magic Band: *Doc at the Radar Station* (Virgin '80). Beefheart is an utter original if not some kind of genius, but that doesn't make him the greatest artist ever to rock down the pike—his unreconstructed ecoprimitive eccentricity impairs his aesthetic as well as his commercial reach. Only don't tell grizzled punks now discovering the boho past, or avantish rockcrits who waited patiently through the cleansing storm for musicianship to come round again. In synch with the historical moment for once, Beefheart offers up his most uncompromised album since *Trout Mask Replica* in 1969—never before have his nerve-wracking harmonies and sainted-spastic rhythms been captured in such brutal living color. Me, I've always enjoyed his compromises, which tend to be crazier than normal people's wildest dreams, and wish he'd saved some of his melodic secrets for the second side. **A−**

Captain Beefheart and the Magic Band: *Ice Cream for Crow* (Virgin/Epic '82). Two cuts have no lyrics, one has no music, and guess which your humble wordslinger prefers. Ornette or no Ornette, the Captain's sprung Delta atonality still provides surprising and irreducible satisfactions, but his poetry repeats itself more than his ideas warrant. Any surrealist ecologist who preaches the same sermon every time out is sure to provoke hostile questions from us concrete-jungle types.   **A−**

Irene Cara: *What a Feelin'* (Geffen '83). I know voice lessons are a must if you want to get to the Oscars, and believe me, I prefer this woman to most of her white exemplars. But I wish she'd gotten her training in church rather than at Performing Arts.

And would suggest that a creative writing teacher couldn't possibly hurt.   **C+**

Belinda Carlisle: *Belinda* (I.R.S. '86). At least Jane Wiedlin's solo was a well-meaning failure. This one's pure El Lay, vacuous would-be CHR with chief songwriter Charlotte Coffey spelled by numerous ringers. The best you can say about the best of these songs—namely, "Band of Gold"—is that you've heard it before; the best you can say about the rest is that once in a while you think you have.   **C**

Don Carlos and Gold: *Raving Tonight* (RAS '83). Like so many dread heartthrobs, this long-ago Black Uhuru cofounder loves Jah more than Woman, which whatever its limits sure beats hating Woman. In the hallowed reggae tradition, the melodies all seem to have been written by the same gifted five-year-old, who wins gold stars only for "Music Crave" and "Spread Out." But his way of taking off from a simple refrain gives reggae's religious impulse a musical dimension this unbeliever can feel in his soul, or whatever it is.   **B**

Don Carlos: *Just a Passing Change* (RAS '84). Although Carlos isn't as consistent as ranking romeo Gregory Isaacs, his peaks—the title tune, in which he glimpses Selassie's ghost from behind modest dub and haunting horns, and "I Just Can't Stop," in which he flees Babylon till the break of dawn—bliss out the way true spiritual pop should. They lift the gracefully ordinary tunes way up even if three generically anonymous closers drag side two back down.   **B+**

Paul Carrack: *Suburban Voodoo* (Epic '82). These songs are catchy and apt ("Don't want no washed-up dishes softsoaping me," eh?), and unlike his pop mentors in Squeeze (he was on board for *East Side Story*) and Noise To Go (bandmate Nick Lowe produced and helped compose), Carrack seems to Mean It—he's soulful in the manner of somebody like Allan Clarke (of the Hollies, how could you forget?). In fact, I bet his sincerity is the envy of his compulsively ironic co-workers. Unfortunately, it leaves me wondering whether he's a little simple-minded or a minor con man.   **B**

Paul Carrack: *The Carrack Collection* (Chrysalis '88). Compiling hits by Ace, Squeeze, Carlene Carter, and Mike and the Mechanics, all sung by the featured attraction, who recently earned the right to sell out under his own name. Nice songs, but in this context they reveal themselves as more fungible than anyone but Carrack's solicitor would prefer. Always wondered why his catchy Nick Lowe–style album, here mined for filler, never made an impression.   **B**

Joe "King" Carrasco and the Crowns: *Joe "King" Carrasco and the Crowns* (Hannibal '80). Genuine punk Tex-Mex, Sir Doug meets Them meets the Shadows of Knight meets Sam the Sham, and the only problem is that the Ramones thought of it first: toons stripped down to their hooks, with Kris Cummings's friendly Farfisa doodles replacing Johnny's monomaniacal strum and echoes of polka and norteño in the jerky propulsion of the thing. Minimalism with roots, kind of— the irony in these calls to fun is a lot sweeter, a lot surer of its ground, than New Yorkers commonly get away with.   **A−**

Joe "King" Carrasco & the Crowns: *Synapse Gap (Mundo Total)* (MCA '82). A man of simple beliefs, I count as good any album comprising twelve unprepossessing tunes I can hum after half a dozen plays, and my cheer increases when half of them pique my simple aesthetic sense. I hear Joe "King" is overreaching—defying the three-minute rule, polymultitracking, gimmicking around. But as far as I'm concerned nothing drags, nothing protrudes, and the Zorba solo and reggae number could come off a Sam the Sham album. In short, the main reason I prefer the debut is that it came first.   **A−**

Joe "King" Carrasco and the Crowns: *Party Weekend* (MCA '83). Even when he was nervoused out Joe King always used to be fun because what kept him going was high spirits—at worst, a little extra adrenalin. Now he sounds as hyper and overextended as Richard Gottehrer's

production. Good parties are such fragile things.   **B**

Joe "King" Carrasco and the Crowns: *Tales From the Crypt* (ROIR cassette '84). Seven numbers previewed on these "basement tapes 1979" made the Crowns' Billy Altman–produced debut, and though some claim the demos have more spirit, nobody's ever accused Altman of slick. Not that I'm accusing these of sloppy, but on songs alone I'll take the vinyl whenever a turntable is available.   **B**

Joe "King" Carrasco and the Crowns: *Bordertown* (Big Beat import '84). Problem with King's pared-down Tex-Mex party-up has always been that it leaves him nowhere to go—got away with baroque jokes for an elpee, but when he tried to pop it up he schlocked it up. Yet now he comes bursting out of his dead end with his spunkiest music ever, and the secret—I didn't believe it either—is politics. "Who Buy the Guns?" ("That kill the nuns yeah yeah") and "Cucaracha Taco" ("When they drop el bomb on everyone") are only the most successful experiments on an album that manages to be silly/cautionary and harmless/seditious as well as hedonistic/humanistic and stoopid/smart.   **A−**

Joe King Carrasco y las Coronas: *Bandido Rock* (Rounder '87). That a "dumb" purveyor of Farfisa retro should transform his Chicano joke into anti-imperialist militance didn't flabbergast smart hedonism fans—only that he then produced effective anti-imperialist songs in his hedonistic silly-detail mode. And that he fails to do the same with slogans and a "better" band comes as no surprise at all.   **B−**

The Jim Carroll Band: *Catholic Boy* (Atco '80). Two big differences between Jim and Patti—Patti has no jump shot and Jim's a boy. Hence the title, I know, 'cept women get away with this kind of fringe/decadent hero/survivor myth/boast better than men—it's fresher for them, not such a line. Face it, Jim's a phony—a moral weakling who's been charming suckers ever since he ran away from home. And if that's not the end of it, well, charming suckers takes talent—a lot easier to get by tending bar. He's got a great eye, a great memory, great connections. He knows how to put himself across. And he wrote "People Who Died." **B+**

The Jim Carroll Band: *Dry Dreams* (Atco '82). Last time he was a poseur maudit who had something to say about excess and its excesses because he stuck to bohemia and kept things literal. This time a title song about his subconscious presages lines like "Flamingo blood melts down her lips." Call him pretentious, versifier—how about decadent? Any way you cut it, "People Who Died" was a one-shot. **C+**

Carry On Oi! (Secret import '81). I don't claim to get all the words, but between bands like the Partisans and Red Alert and Garry Bushell's compassionate fictionalized notes I think this compilation gives the lie to the liberal Nazi-baiting the style's subjected to. And the way one band after another emits virtually indistinguishable bellows of jolly rage is mutually reinforcing—gives you the sense that all that enthusiasm adds up to a movement. But the songs really are pretty hard to tell apart. And the recitations and pub-sing laffs that tie it all together wear thin even faster than most concept moves. **B**

The Cars: *Panorama* (Elektra '80). The problem's not immersion in formula. The problem's not exhaustion of formula. The problem's boredom with formula. This is longer, slower, and denser as well as older, with lyrics that skirt social commentary and music that essays textural pretension. Its peaks are "Touch and Go" and "Up and Down." Savor the rhythm of those phrases, Ric, and grow no more. **B−**

The Cars: *Shake It Up* (Elektra '81). They've always cultivated a dark side— girls make boys want to end it all even after the boys have grown up. They've always basked in the shadow of Roxy Music, too. But they've never been so stylishly nightmarish—except for the title cut, even the fast ones don't aim for fun. Gary Numan—everywhere you turn these days, Gary Numan is sitting with the lights out, staring off into space. **B**

The Cars: *Heartbeat City* (Elektra '84). With hooks recurring as predictably as zebras on a carousel or heartbeats in a city, the glossy approach the Cars invented has made this the best year for pure pop in damn near twenty, and it's only fair that they should return so confidently to form. They still don't have much to say and they're still pretty arch about it, but that's no reason for anybody to get unduly bothered, and neither is Greg Hawkes's Fairlight. **B+**

The Cars: *Greatest Hits* (Elektra '85). In retrospect, it seems fairly incredible that this was once the stuff of cause célèbre— that the battle was joined over pop product so sleekly affectless. But of course, once upon a time affectlessness was progress; once upon a time a pop fan couldn't count on the radio to push his or her buttons. Those for whom struggle is all will claim that the sparer and supposedly fresher debut remains definitive, but they're just hyping their own dashed hopes. Fleet, efficient, essentially meaningless, this is the Cars' gift to history—seven seamless years of it. **A−**

Carlene Carter: *Musical Shapes* (Warner Bros. '80). Touted as the next Marshall Chapman since she surfaced in 1978, Mother Maybelle's most famous granddaughter and Nick Lowe's most famous wife comes up with enough nasty, compassionate songs to make believers out of Marshall's followers, all seven hundred of 'em. Dave Edmunds cameos as a chow-sucking trucker, Nick has the synth to light up "Ring of Fire," and Carlene has the balls for "They got the balls and I got the bat." But she can't muster the insouciance one would expect from the Mary Magdalene of Cool. **B**

Peter Case: *Peter Case* (Geffen '87). Case's problem is that he's a born actor who won't cop to it. Folkies have always enacted authenticity, and great ones from Dylan to Roches have role-played with a vengeance. But by pretending that his songs are about "sin and salvation" rather than the more problematic "America," Case evades challenges to his new homespun persona—supposedly, sin and salvation are everybody's heritage. And hence he's no more convincing now than he was when he led a group named after the Beatles' sneakers.   **B**

Johnny Cash: *Rockabilly Blues* (Columbia '80). Merely by copping to the magic concept "rockabilly," Cash can kick up comeback talk. And comparison with his rockabilly rockabilly for Sun (where he was always the countriest) establishes that by the standards of an ordinary mortal he's a better singer now—more flexible physically, more expressive emotionally. But the technique is a cover for what's lost, probably forever—stolid depth as immovable presence. Same goes for the arrangements—defiantly understated for Nashville, they're customized rock-country up against the austerities of the Tennessee Two. In other words, an honorable country album with some pretty good songs on it.   **B−**

Johnny Cash: *Columbia Records 1958–1986* (Columbia '87). Turns out he was always a folkie, a damn good one despite such lovable pop trifles as "A Boy Named Sue" and its decade-late follow-up "The Baron." The whole first side was recorded in his first seven months with the label; in fact, three of the five tracks were cut and wrapped on August 13, 1958. By contrast, exactly one selection was busy being born between February '71 and March '79, the country trifle "One Piece at a Time," and while I'd substitute its assembly-line companion piece "Oney" for Nick Lowe's December '79 "Without Love" (which has more assembly line in it than anyone's letting on), that gets the trajectory of his career about right. Lately he's righted himself some, but it's the ageless stuff he's best at—John Henry and Ira Hayes, "Orange Blossom Special" and "Ghost Riders in the Sky," and let us not forget "Highway Patrolman," which proves Bruce Springsteen is Woody Guthrie if anything ever did.   **A−**

Johnny Cash: *Johnny Cash Is Coming to Town* (Mercury '87). I'd have let his contract lapse too—the pathetic *Class of '55* proved he was a has-been, huzzahs and all. But he was holding a few in reserve, like definitive Elvis Costello and Guy Clark, overdue James Talley and (why did nobody ever think of this?) Ernie Ford, and

the song-factory prizes any Nashvillean with a mind to can turn up: "The Night Hank Williams Came to Town," a hit, and "Heavy Metal (Don't Mean Rock and Roll to Me)," recommended to Mikhail Gorbachev for Goskino's next tractor movie. And then there are the two originals, which convince me he's still a has-been.   **B+**

Johnny Cash/Jerry Lee Lewis/Carl Perkins: *The Survivors* (Columbia '82). Survivors of what, pray tell. Oh—of whom. We get it. We know you all were trying, too—especially Big Jawn, whose concert it was. So we regret to inform you that you sound dissipated anyway, which has an odd effect on the gospel tunes and makes for the most magnificently thrown-away "Whole Lotta Shakin'" of Jerry Lee's intensely nonchalant career.   **B−**

Rosanne Cash: *Seven Year Ache* (Columbia '81). It's a tribute to persistence of something-or-other that somebody should still be getting decent music out of the sterile studio-rock formula. What that something-or-other might be is perhaps indicated by the identity of the somebody, who is a second-generation pro rather than a punk revoloo.   **B+**

Rosanne Cash: *Somewhere in the Stars* (Columbia '82). That "Third Rate Romance" is the least impressive thing here is proof enough of Cash's continuing growth—"Third Rate Romance" is damn near impossible to ruin, and she doesn't come close. But since I was never much of a Ronstadtian myself, I can't quite make the leap from admiring the assured warmth and easy precision of Linda's de facto successor to inviting her over.   **B+**

Rosanne Cash: *Rhythm and Romance* (Columbia '85). Nobody's going to mistake this one for a country record, not with Waddy Wachtel's hooks bobbing by like bull's eyes in a shooting gallery. But it's not just another compulsorily catchy stab at immortality either. Cash may have her eye on MTV, but she's a child of Nashville nevertheless—when she cheats she knows it's wrong even if she's got a right, and when she sings she hurts.   **A−**

Rosanne Cash: *King's Record Shop* (Columbia '87). If I can't claim to find any special hope in this record, I'll settle for pleasure. The catchiness of Rodney Crowell's production would seem manipulative behind a shallower singer, but Cash—like fellow roots renegades Tina Turner and the Nevilles—has the stuff to imbue the arrangements with some self. It's perverse to complain about the programmatic "Rosie Strike Back"—a hard-hitting pop song for battered wives is a wondrous thing by definition. And her romances are truer than most. **A—**

Rosanne Cash: *Hits 1979–1989* (Columbia '89). "Seven Year Ache," "Hold On," and "I Don't Know Why You Don't Want Me" announce themselves as classics every time. They're classic country, classic pop, classic Rosanne, and though she's the decade's premier interpretive singer, she wrote them all. Their only competition is a Tom Petty tune, which suggests something about her musical affinities. But I miss "Rosie Strike Back" and "The Real Me"—from a nonpop, non-country, non–Tom Petty vantage the rest of these perfectly enjoyable selections seem half a touch too cute, languid, soft. And fairly depict the decade's premier interpretive singer nonetheless. **A—**

The Celibate Rifles: *Quintessentially Yours* (What Goes On '85). All right, they do lash out with a nice, nasty buzz—reminds me of those long-lost speed boys the Vibrators. But no pretenders who take most of their 1985 Yank debut from their 1983 Aussie debut and none of it from the follow-up are getting any rock and roll future awards from me. **B+**

Exene Cervenka: *Old Wives' Tales* (Rhino '89). Always a notebook-toter, she goes for the roots and poetry you'd expect—in other words, folk-rock. Her protest-tinged sincerity cries out for jolts of junk guitar. But sisterly tales like "She Wanted" and "White Trash Wife" detail the natural feminist sympathies rock and roll floozies—who God knows have plenty to do just protecting their asses —rarely have time for. Pray for the X versions. **B**

Champaign: *How About Us* (Columbia '81). The exquisitely churchy harmonies take us back to the halcyon days of soul, but the material takes us back to the Doobie Brothers, or is it Christopher Cross? Golden voices and hearts of mush. **B—**

Champaign: *Modern Heart* (Columbia '83). This clean, middle-American pop-funk's commitment to quality is so modest that its "concept" may well be *not* to stand out. So it takes forever to penetrate. But where most merely professional tunesmiths get irritating with prolonged exposure, Champaign start to glow—modestly, of course. **B+**

James Chance and the Contortions: *Live in New York* (ROIR cassette '81). Boy, has this shit dated—it's worn as thin as the sidemen's professionalism and James's embouchure. And the titles go beyond petty candor into keep-your-self-to-yourself-please—a "White Cannibal" with "Money To Burn" and (give this boy a benefit) "Sophisticated Cancer"? Sure it's nice to hear "King Heroin" covered with so much soul. But when he opens with "I Feel Good, I Got You" he's lying three ways. **B—**

Change: *The Glow of Love* (Warner Bros./RFC '80). "New and true and gay," this gold album confirms disco's continuing autonomy as a market and as a style. From the Rodgers-&-Edwards rip of "A Lover's Holiday" to the good ole Giorgio Moroder of "The End," here's the complete bag of tricks. Luther Vandross's best Teddy Pendergrass impression doesn't redeem the militantly escapist lyrics and probably isn't meant to. But "It's a Girl's Affair," sung by Jocelyn Shaw, is a softcore treat—and spell that "Girls' " on your next printing, please. **B+**

Change: *Miracles* (Atlantic '81). Where their debut took off from its moments of raunch, this is pure fantasy fare—the you-can-work-it-out advisories "Hold Tight," "Your Move," and "Stop for Love" never get down (to details), and "On Top," "Heaven of My Life," "Paradise," and "Miracles" aren't exactly realistic (note titles). But what a terrific fantasy—so bright and casual and full of life. The hip punch of Mauro Malavasi's keyboards puts the dream in motion, and Diva Gray's lithe, modest vocals bring it to bed.   **B+**

Marshall Chapman: *Take It On Home* (Rounder '82). Having failed to connect as a rip-roaring rock-and-roller, she now fails to connect as a Nashville gal. Except on two cuts, that is—"Bizzy Bizzy Bizzy" and "Booze in Your Blood," both of which sound pissed off. Hear me, Marshall? I said *pissed off.*   **C+**

Marshall Chapman: *Dirty Linen* (Tall Girl cassette/Line import '87). So finally she gives up, living modestly if that off songwriting royalties, and after four or five years self-produces a ten-buck, ten-song tape that gets vinylized in West Germany, the disposable-income capital of the world. Naturally it's her best record by a mile and a half, because she's not trying to prove anything—just putting her songs on the table in front of the perfect little rock and roll groove of her no-name band. The singing is relaxed and aware, the writing sharpest when it means to cut a little, as on "Bad Debt" (rhymes with "You haven't taken out the garbage yet") and "Betty's Bein' Bad" ("She's not mad / She's just gettin' even / Betty's bein' bad / It's her way of leavin' "). May she glorify her Pignose amp forever.   **A—**

Tracy Chapman: *Tracy Chapman* (Elektra '88). "Fast Car" is so far-seeing, "Mountains o' Things" so necessary, that it's doubly annoying when she puts her name on begged questions like "Why" and "Talkin' Bout a Revolution." Maybe I should be heartened and so forth that Intelligent Young People are once again pushing naive left-folkie truisms, but she's too good for such condescension—even sings like a natural. Get real, girl.   **B+**

Tracy Chapman: *Crossroads* (Elektra '89). I like her best here when she's most objectionable—keying her politics to the anachronistic locution "government relief," making her lover commit first, identifying evil with white people. She's still too solemn, but at least she's not too tasteful, and how else do you describe a musician who gives the impression of singing solo with acoustic guitar while deploying five or six musicians a track? As a musician who gets over on her voice, that's how.   **B**

Cheap Trick: *One on One* (Epic '82). Yeah, I'd written them off too—until I heard "If You Want My Love" once and immediately made it twice, after which it went on automatic replay in my head for forty-eight hours. The most eloquently eclectic Beatle tribute ever recorded, it sets the tone of this one-of-a-kind arena-rock band's raw, ersatz tug of war, and though Rick Nielsen's Lennonesque tunes and Robin Zander's McCartneyesque screams do grate (and not against each other), I'll take it cut for cut over Paul's sweet, authentic one. Inspirational Sex Rant: "I wanna live in your body." Original grade B plus.   **B**

Cheap Trick: *Lap of Luxury* (Epic '88). Having floundered imitating themselves, they come back imitating Journey. Or is that Richard Marx? Billy Squier?   **C**

Clifton Chenier: *I'm Here!* (Alligator '82). Especially in a rhythmically conservative style like zydeco, it's rare that a band can carry an album, but that's the story here. First record I've ever heard hot enough to convince me that all those wild tales about the accordion man weren't so much pepper sauce. Just too bad it happened after he began to lose his strength.   **B**

Chequered Past: *Chequered Past* (EMI America '84). Breeding tells, right? So cross Steve Jones (ex-Pistol), Tony Sales (ex-Ig), Nigel Harrison (ex-Blondie), and Clem Burke (ditto), each sired by a great band, and what do you get? Fast heavy metal, of course, a little too classy for satanism or even blatant sexism, but who cares when what we get from the Nietzsche Sales reads on the cover is "Only the Strong (Will Survive)" in "A World Gone Wild." The secret, as in most bands great and ghastly, is the man with the concept: singer and songwriter Michael Des Barres (ex-Silverhead), whose "daddy was an aristocrat," and who's been ruining rock and roll in a vain attempt to prove that that makes him special for close to a decade. Breeding tells.   **C—**

Neneh Cherry: *Raw Like Sushi* (Virgin '89). Daughter of a Swedish artist and an African percussionist, stepdaughter of Don Cherry and the London scene, she's a twenty-four-year bohemian, a socially responsible hedonist, a sexy two-time mom—and a relief from bimbo macho and exchangeable female dance phenoms. Slogan: "I know where I'm goin' and where I'm comin' from." Alternative: "If you're gonna do it, you've got to do it right." And oh yeah: "I came already." The music doesn't quite rock one's house. But it's far more beatwise than the Brit norm, and she can sing/talk that song/rap. Bohos who sell—the most interesting kind.   **A**−

The Chesterfield Kings: *Here Come the Chesterfield Kings* (Mirror '83). If you're going to live in the past, you might as well go whole hog like Greg Prevost, who in the great blues purist tradition performs only covers—of titles no one but other garage-band collectors has ever heard. The upshot is a seamless archive of quaint adolescent macho, definitive yet utterly negligible protohippie songs rendered by a band whose claim to expertise is the mastery of a dozen marginally distinct varieties of crudity.   **B**+

Chic: *Real People* (Atlantic '80). As on Sister Sledge's follow-up, Rodgers & Edwards have run out of sure shots—no "Good Times" here. But *Risque* was more than "Good Times," and this beats *Risque.* Jumpy, scintillating rhythms fuse with elegantly abrasive textures for a funk that's not light but sharp. Plus postchic words that go with the attention-grabbing heat and invention of Nile Rodgers's postrock guitar. Original grade: A minus.   **A**

Chic: *Take It Off* (Atlantic '81). Despite their best efforts, this projected dancefloor comeback is a lot less songful than *Real People.* Almost as artful, though. The telegraphic precision of the lyrics, the wary solicitousness of the singing, and the spare, nervous overload of the rhythms all bespeak a black-bourgeois modernism that is of a city most blacks don't even dream about—that alien power center where even the best times seem to go sour.   **A**−

Chic: *Tongue in Chic* (Atlantic '82). This is their groove album. Maybe their throwaway album as well, yet I enjoy it fine, because I get from Chic what devotees of Memphis soul used to get from Booker T. & the M.G.'s. Which group you prefer is partly a matter of which rhythms feel like life to you, of course, so I'll add that like New York these are pretty swift. I'll also add that their in-concert theme song makes me wonder what the live album might be like.   **A**−

Chic: *Believer* (Atlantic '83). Although you'd figure the collaboration would suffer after both Nile and Nard started coming up with good albums of their own, the damage is amazingly slight. The title track, a true song of faith ("Stand back-to-back, believer / Meet head-to-head / Fight toe-to-toe, believer / Dance cheek-to-cheek"), achieves the tough-minded positivity the rest of the album aims for. The true song of praise that comes next is every bit as believable. And the rest is blessing enough in this negative time.   **B**+

The Chills: *Brave Words* (Homestead '88). Like the Go-Betweens, these sexually integrated New Zealanders give the impression that they could write about anything they wanted—they choose love as a subject out of formal tact, because it's appropriate to the genre. Though they have more tunes than most—more tunes than the early Go-Betweens—what makes them stick is Martin Phillips's cracked, straining, nervous delivery, fit to break down with the next cliche (not too many formal tacticians write songs called "Rain" anymore). Side two isn't as catchy, but shows off a few other options—one song opposes settling down, another is pro. Bet they take a while making up their minds.   **A**−

The Chills: *The Lost EP* (Homestead EP '88). Recorded '84–'85, two years before *Brave Words,* and it sounds it. First side you wonder why the songs aren't quite there—maybe it's you. Second side crumples the quandary with "Whole Weird World" ("Nearly there . . . nearly," they claim) and the four-part (suite?) "Dream by Dream." Neither title is sufficiently ironic. Not juvenilia—they'd already been around four or five years. But only New Zealanders would guess.   **B−**

The Chills: *Kaleidoscope World* (Homestead '89). "Eight Songs From Eight Members From Eight Phases of the Chills!" announces this '82–'84 singles comp, extensively annotated for the collectors it's aimed at. And unlike the mid-period *Lost EP*—next they'll construct an album from work tapes by Martin Phillips's pre-Chills Same—it doesn't bog down in horizon-stretching. These are simple pop songs by young people who are proud they can play them. They're slight, but they have the spirit. Best in show: the meaningless "Satin Doll," which Phillips wrote when he was seventeen—presumably for the Same. Time: 28:04.   **B+**

Alex Chilton: *Like Flies on Sherbert* (Peabody '80). Right, this bag of wrecked covers and discarded originals is, what's it say here, "self-indulgent." If Keith Richards or Rat Scabies were to dare such a thing, I'd throw it in the garbage myself. But that don't take nothing away from "Baron of Love, Pt. II"—the opening cut, in which composer Ross Johnson raves distractedly about sex and gore. Or the line about nipples in "Rock Hard." A very bright music nut who knows from the inside how much craziness goes into the most normal-seeming product (he did front the Box Tops, remember), this longtime advertisement for self-abuse doesn't prove craziness is universal. Just makes you forget that things most certainly wouldn't be more fun if it was. [Later available as Line import.]   **B**

Alex Chilton: *Bach's Bottom* (Line import '81). These 1975 tracks, the best already released on Chilton's long-gone Ork EP, are about as Memphis as a garbage strike. Not only does anarchic equal chaotic equal sloppy equal a mess, but soulful equals spontaneous equals off-the-cuff equals a mess. None of which is to deny that he knows how to mess around.   **B+**

Alex Chilton: *Feudalist Tarts* (Big Time EP '85). After ten years of falling-down flakedom only a cultist could love or even appreciate, Chilton looks around and straightens up. The bottlenecked "Lost My Job" comes close to such beacons of his lost decade as "Bangkok" and "Take Me Home and Make Me Like It." The precocious Memphis soul singer and the prescient American pop eccentric both get their chops into the Carla Thomas and Slim Harpo covers. And when he slips into Willie Turbinton's amazing "Thank You John"—that name is upper-cased and lower-cased simultaneously—he remembers that it isn't only too-much-too-soon white boys who get twisted around in this world.   **A−**

Alex Chilton: *No Sex / Under Class / Wild Kingdom* (Big Time EP '86). Too blocked or tuckered out (from what?) to put a whole album together, the inventor of power pop follows *Feudalist Tarts* onto the brutalist charts with yet another award-winning shortie. A's an AIDS song: "Can't get it on or even get high / Come on baby, fuck me and die." Lead B points out that he's not "a rich musician." And while the finale's title promises a summing up, instead it's a real B, with throwaway guitar solo rendering it almost as long as the other two combined. Really does deserve a side all to itself. EPs sure do help you get away with stuff.   **B+**

Alex Chilton: *High Priest* (Big Time '87). Chilton had a chance to lead his little flock back onto the paths of righteousness. In a microcosm where nobody can tell good pop junk from utter shit anymore, his first four cuts are a refresher course: one Slim Harpo let get away, a callow Goffin-King throwaway, his own tasteless Buddhist joke, and "Volare." Each the real thing, each different, each undreamed by the Fanzine Filosofy. But after that he lets things slide, from a straight (for him) declaration of love to a Lowell Fulson boogie to covers the Fleshtones could think of. These are parlous times, Alex. Sloppy's getting harder to bring off, and cute ain't enough.   **B+**

Stella Chiweshe: *Ambuya?* (GlobeStyle import '87). A woman in a man's domain, "Zimbabwe's queen of the mbira" here reorchestrates an instrument so delicate most Westerners hear it as a toy or sound effect. Neither innovation makes her a rebel, just a Shona revisionist adapting conventional wisdom to transcultural reality: by replacing the customary shakers with a band—another woman's mbira, two marimbas, and unobtrusive bass-and-traps for world-dance accents—she takes a gentle music out of the village without downplaying where it's coming from. I hear courage and tradition in her kind, playful, nasal-to-breathy singing, but not sexual brass, which distinguishes her instantly from other African women intrepid enough to run their own musical shows. [Later on Schanachie.]   **A**−

Chops: *Chops* (Atlantic '84). The great playing here isn't by Chops, four horn players harmonizing smarmily behind a singing keyb man designated Funki. The stars are Sugarhill escapees Doug Wimbish, Dennis Chambers, and Keith LeBlanc, who put more power, personality, and invention (and chops) into bass, drums, and more drums than the supposed front men do into their supposed front instruments. But who can't make the front men disappear.   **C**+

Christmas Rap (Profile '87). First side's rap in the spirit of the season, full of good cheer and unabashedly materialistic from Mrs. McDaniel's macaroni-and-cheese and King Sun-D Moet's realism to all the name-brand shit in Ghetto Santa's bag before it gets stolen—Gucci and Jaguar, Barbie Doll and G. I. Joe, not to mention the gold and the diamonds and the pearls, not to mention the butler and the limo and the chauffeur. Second side's hip hop copping to the season, with the Disco 4's bass-and-jingle-balls and the Showboys' cutups fronting for tales and boasts that aren't sucker, just snooze. Pop fans will settle for the Run-D.M.C. on *A Very Special Christmas*. Rap fans will prefer it to the Surf M.C.'s album, which said M.C.'s suggest you ask Santa for. Modesty wouldn't get them anywhere either.   **B**+

A Christmas Record (ZE import '81). Most of this oddly ambitious nine-song anthology seems a little off, but that suits its odd ambition, which is seeking the spirit in an audience turned off by seasonal shtick.

Was (Not Was) and Alan Vega take on involuntary and semivoluntary poverty, the Waitresses aim for the singles bars, and Davitt Sigerson should by all rights be earning royalties up there with Irving Berlin—or at least Torme-Wells, or Davis-Onorati-Simeone.   **B**+

CH 3:   *Ch 3* (Posh Boy EP '81). There's a Clashlike fierceness here that other L.A. hardcore boys only put themselves out of joint for. This is probably due to the Clashlike tunes. Derivative, manic, angry, fun.   **B**+

CH3:   *Fear of Life* (Posh Boy '82). They're too neat—too pop, too heavy metal, too defined—for hardcore purists, but these hooks come the way I like them: one recitative/mechanical handclap/girl response/sound of breaking glass per hyperdriven two-minute song. Too bad they didn't cop more of the EP (say "Mannequin" and "I Got a Gun" in addition to "Manzanar"), thus stretching this specially priced but suspiciously unclocked album to customary hardcore length. Approximate time: 22:30. Original grade: A minus.   **B**+

The Church: *Remote Luxury* (Warner Bros. '84). I see these Aussies as the wimp Del Fuegos—musically they wind up just where they want and epistemologically they go next to nowhere. All right, so the songs are quite pretty in a modernized early-Faces/late-Zombies kind of way—more consistently so than the '60s competition (which gives them a leg up on the Fuegos, who like the macho boys they are take on the Stones). I even get the point: the sweet, melancholy alienation the band cultivates is an attractive alternative to the crass pragmatism and/or self-righteous nihilism of their contemporaries. But where my own fave formalists the Shoes are honest enough to focus their lyrics on the very limited social milieu essential to the nurture of such alternatives, these guys evade specifics via metaphor and have the presumption to reproduce their hazy poetry on the inner sleeve. Which may help explain why the music sometimes almost drifts away.   **B**

The Church: *Starfish* (Arista '88). Anybody who can't hear this album's pretty textures and expert hooksmanship has problems with his or her central nervous system. I mean, facts are facts. But tastes are open to dispute, and anybody who gets off on its lulling rhythms and obscure lyrics has his or hers stuck in the '60s and up his or her ass respectively.   **B**

Ciccone Youth: *The Whitey Album* (Enigma/Blast First '89). "Into the Groovey" you should know. "Burnin' Up" you shouldn't, 'cause this one's "the original demo on four-track cassette," and also 'cause it sucks. "Addicted to Love" was cut live to a canned backing track in a record-your-own-single booth and will make my top ten if they deign to release it as a single. The rest is funny mixes, found girl talk, beats from a band not noted for same, and other remembrances of their avant-bullshit roots. Why don't they take this stuff to John Cage? I want to be sure I get course credit.   **C**

Circle Jerks: *Group Sex* (Frontier EP '80). Like the Angry Samoans, although not as clearly or catchily, these slammers double-time metal riffs behind the rants, yielding such indelible plaints as "Deny Everything" ("I'm being framed"), "Paid Vacation" ("It's Afghanistan!"), and "Group Sex" (sensitive reading from the personals plus screaming title chorus). If you think L.A. punk rage is laughable, here's its antithesis—laffs.   **B+**

Circle Jerks: *Wild in the Streets* (Faulty Products '82). Having concluded that *Group Sex* was one of the cutest little hardcore tantrums extant, I waited for this earsore to kick in and blamed length when it didn't. But the real reason is that boring old professional problem, material. As Tom Paxton could tell them, political commentary is no substitute for good tunes, even when your best are rarely more than three notes long. And if the whine is your natural voice you're better off complaining about teenomie anyway. Time: 25:17.   **C+**

Eric Clapton: *Just One Night* (RSO '80). Who needs another live double? A master guitarist whose studio albums have been cited for unfair trade practices by Sominex, that's who. All your AM and FM faves plus, served hot, raw, or both.   **B+**

Eric Clapton: *Money and Cigarettes* (Duck/Warner Bros. '83). The groove is as inspired as this crack band of blues 'n' boogie pros can make it—when Cooder, Lee, Dunn & Hawkins play their hearts out, mere professionalism (also mere boogie) gets left behind, and Clapton's guitar hasn't rung so crisp and clear since *Layla.* The drawback is that the music is the message, everything Clapton boasts he ("still") has "left to say" on "Ain't Going Down," his only notable new song. If blues power were my idea of God, I might feel a transcendent presence even so. But blues power in itself isn't even my idea of a foxhole.   **B+**

Eric Clapton: *Behind the Sun* (Duck '85). Eric was never the nonsinger he was wont to declare himself in retiring moments, but his vocal gift only made sense when laidback was commercial. On this album he isn't retiring—he's looking for work. So he resorts to none other than Phil Collins, once his Brit-rock opposite but now just a fellow "survivor" (and how). For several reasons, including market fashion, Collins mixes the drums very high. This induces Eric to, um, *project* in accordance with market fashion. Sad. And also bad.   **C−**

Eric Clapton: *Journeyman* (Duck/Reprise '89). What did you expect him to call it—*Hack? Layla* and *461 Ocean Boulevard* were clearly flukes: he has no record-making knack. So he farms out the songs, sings them competently enough, and marks them with his guitar. Which sounds kind of like Mark Knopfler's.   **B−**

Guy Clark: *The South Coast of Texas* (Warner Bros. '81). Clark is hardly the last surviving singer-songwriter, but so much of the competition has gotten into rock auteurism or pop demos that those who miss the old ways pay him more mind than they used to. This is his best since 1975's aptly titled *Old No. 1.* The "Rita Ballou" lets us know he's singing easier, and turns like "her breath's as sweet as chewing gum" and "the road to good intentions / Is paved with the fools that I've been" remind us of his vernacular knack. But only on "New Cut Road," real bluegrass canonfodder, does the music add meaning as well as tangibility. Which is why the competition is into rock auteurism and pop demos.   **B**

Guy Clark: *Greatest Hits* (RCA Victor '83). My, here's a useful item—replaces three whole tracks from the just-this-minute-deleted *Old No. 1,* two of them bittersweet love-and-sex songs, with three newer Texas-mythos numbers. Very conceptual, but not exactly an improvement, and I even like two of the new ones: "Broken Hearted People," which is also a bittersweet love-and-sex song, and "Texas Cookin'." I also miss the bittersweet love-and-sex song "Instant Coffee Blues" very much. Maybe Texas-mythos types understand food better than outlaws—the man has written well about home-grown tomatoes.   **B+**

The Clash: *London Calling* (Epic '80). Here's where they start showing off. If "Lost in the Supermarket," for instance, is just another alienated-consumption song, it leaps instantly to the head of the genre on the empathy of Mick Jones's vocal. And so it goes. Complaints about "slick" production are absurd—Guy Stevens *slick?*—and insofar as the purity of the guitar attack is impinged upon by brass, pianner, and shuffle, this is an expansion, not a compromise. A gratifyingly loose Joe Strummer makes virtuoso use of his fournote range, and Paul Simonon has obviously been studying his reggae records. Warm, angry, and thoughtful, confident, melodic, and hard-rocking, this is the best double-LP since *Exile on Main Street.* And it's selling for about $7.50.   **A+**

The Clash: *Black Market Clash* (Epic Nu-Disk '80). CBS's transparent attempt to class up a dumb new line of ten-inch LPs that some marketeer thinks will make collectors of us all, this hodgepodge makes more sense than Elvis the C's long-awaited full-sized hodgepodge nevertheless. First side combines B's and a U.K.-only album cut from '77–'78, when everything they did was touched with the desperate euphoria of revolutionary holdouts, with two garageland covers, the Toots appropriate

and the Booker T. a stroke. Second is spacy Clash dub plus hooks, with the yearning "Bankrobber" more lyrical than anything else they've committed to plastic. Yet. [Later on twelve-inch.]   **A—**

The Clash: *Sandinista!* (Epic '81). At $9.99 discounted, figure sides five and six as a near-freebie sweetened by great cuts from Timon Dogg and a grade-school duo. Compare "Apple Jam" (you know, on George Harrison's *All Things Must Pass* triple, now there was a prophetic title) invidiously to the run of their dub ramble. Listen to *Sandinista Now!,* the promo-only one-disc digest Epic has thoughtfully provided busy radio personnel, and note that you miss (in my case) "Rebel Waltz" and "Let's Go Crazy" and "Something About England" (and who knows what in yours). Note that you also miss the filler and assorted weirdnesses which provide that heady pace and/or texture. Then note as well that the many good songs aren't as consistently compelling as on previous Clash albums, though God knows "The Sound of Sinners" is a long-overdue Christer spoof and words about reading are always apt and the romanticization of revolution is an inevitable theme. And conclude that if this is their worst—which it is, I think—they must be, er, the world's greatest rock and roll band.   **A—**

The Clash: *Combat Rock* (Epic '82). Those who (claim to) expect them to improve on Gramsci maintain that this is where they turn bozo once and for all. I counter that they're well ahead of a lot of respectable competition—the babble surrounding Robert De Niro on "Red Angel Dragnet," for instance, may well be the first evidence ever that *Taxi Driver* has something real to say about urban oppression. Neither their funk nor their tone-poem dub has gained much pizzazz since *Sandinista!,* where both were easier to avoid. But I guarantee that they're not sinking into the pop slime—they're evolving, and here's hoping that someday they write songs as terse and clear as "Janie Jones" at this higher level of verbal, musical, and political density.   **B+**

The Clash: *Cut the Crap* (Epic '85). Since I play the much-maligned *Combat Rock* as much as any Clash I own, the advance badmouth didn't faze me. The orchestral (synthesized?) horns on the lead cut did put me off, but most of this kicks in, stubborn and jolly and elegiac and together. In the aural fact, it isn't pathetic that Joe strums and chants as if there's no yesterday, it's brave. Convincer: "We Are the Clash."   **B+**

The Clash: *The Story of the Clash* (Epic '88). For as long as they hung in there, their compromises, false moves, and fuckups were their own. The U.S.-only shuffle of the incomparable U.K. debut, the ridiculous ten-inch compilation, the vagaries of *Sandinista!,* the disco remixes—all listened tough and made sense because all engaged the outside world the band never forgot was there. Though a few mediocrities are eliminated and there's a vague chronological rationale (start with the pop stuff kinda and then backtrack kinda), this two-disc repackage could have been programmed by a random-play button. It tells only one "story"—they fought the corporation and the corporation won.   **C+**

Otis Clay: *Soul Man—Live in Japan* (Rooster Blues '85). Clay is obviously no Al Green. He's no Syl Johnson either. He's not even O. V. Wright. He's not James Carr or Howard Tate or Jimmy Lewis or Benny Latimore or McKinley Mitchell or Z. Z. Hill. Having never cracked the r&b top twenty, he made one halfway decent album for Hi in 1973, and his broad delivery has gained no discernible acuity since. In short, he's a journeyman, and no matter what adoring Japanese innocents think, he's dull and overstated both. I know he's got Hi Rhythm behind him, but would you buy an Eddie Floyd album for Booker T. & the M.G.s—especially with Teenie Hodges taking an endless organ solo? Those whose answer to the above question is a proud yes are making this an exhibit in their Soul Forever campaign. I say it's evidence for the opposition.   **C+**

The Clean: *The Clean Compilation* (Homestead '88). These Maureen Tucker fans recorded their entire output six or seven years ago in a New Zealand that considered Split Enz the cat's pyjamas, so no wonder they went for simplicity. Give them credit for some funny moments, like the doc who takes his shot before he gives you yours, but don't expect much in the way of words, because there aren't many. What they care about is droning guitar jams. Allotted a concept notch for knowing they were a groove band. Entire Lyric of Very Nice Farfisa Theme: "Tally ho, tally ho."   **B+**

Johnny Clegg & Savuka: *Shadow Man* (Capitol '88). No matter what the British Musicians' Union says, I don't doubt that he's progressive in the ANC sense. I just wish he wasn't progressive in the Peter Gabriel sense, or at least had Gabriel's talent and taste—his keybs and drums left one innocent byhearer wondering why I was checking out the new Yes. This is the kind of college man who thinks rock is art and "human rainbow" and "ache that has no name" are turns of phrase. Even when he sticks to the facts that are all the metaphor any South African poet needs, his vocal melodrama empties the words of poignancy. Progress deserves better. So does a multiracial society.   **C**

Jimmy Cliff: *The Power and the Glory* (Columbia '83). He never gives up, and he never learns from his mistakes, exemplified by the stupefying professionalism with which his authentic JA band negotiates the U.S. pop-funk beats and changes on side one. Nor does he ever take full advantage of his gifts, exemplified by the gracefully sung and adaquately conceived international pop-reggae protest on side two.   **C+**

Patsy Cline: *Live at the Opry* (MCA '88). As someone who's always bought Cline's myth and never much enjoyed her recorded music, I can hardly express what a relief it is to hear her free of the glop that half-drowns the supposedly definitive *Patsy Cline Story.* The rockabilly raunch and uncanny phrasing her official work just hints at are the heart of these superbly remastered radio transcriptions—try the feral "Lovesick Blues" and the heart-stopping full-beat hesitations on "She's Got You," respectively. My only objection is that the compilers couldn't resist turning out a document, and thus include her debut flop and suchlike. There has to be a complete live best-of out there. And the world needs it. **A—**

Patsy Cline: *Live Volume Two* (MCA '89). Not really live, just cut for subsequent broadcast in the studio with small band rather than countrypolitan arsenal. But that's not really the problem—the problem is what and to a lesser extent when. None of these songs were hits for Patsy even though some of them were released as singles, and though career trajectory is no doubt part of the reason, so is quality of material. And though she was good in 1956, she did get better. **B**

George Clinton: *Computer Games* (Capitol '82). Nothing on this mature work of art will tear the roof off any mothersucker—Dr. Funkenstein's earthshaking jams are past. But that's hardly to suggest that he's lost his sense of rhythm or hermeneutics. In other words, if your ears say you've heard some of these grooves before, don't tell your ass about it and your mind'll never be the wiser. Clinton has deepened in the wake of his failure to turn the planet upside-down, and this is his most flawless album, paced and orchestrated without a dead spot and thought through like a mothersucker. Even the earthshaking jams of the past are accounted for, and in two or three different ways. Man's best friend spelled backwards is? And why would anyone want to spell it backwards? **A**

George Clinton: *You Shouldn't-Nuf Bit Fish* (Capitol '83). This isn't as smart as *Computer Games,* or as soulful either—success will always go to George's head. So be thankful the head is a capacious one, and connected to his rump. Side one leads off with his version of *The African King* and quickly proves his most irresistible since *Motor-Booty Affair,* with "Quickie" a riff/groove that gleams like "Flash Light" and "Last Dance" a big fat fart in David Bowie's face. Even the talkover filler on the title track is worth listening to, and Philippe Wynne's lowdown oinks make "Stingy" a worthy heir to none other than the Coasters' "I'm a Hog for You." **A**

George Clinton: *Some of My Best Jokes Are Friends* (Capitol '85). Some of his best jokes are rhythm parts, too, which isn't going to help the Thomas Dolby fans pick up on them. Oh well, they got their chance on *Computer Games* and *Bit Fish* and who bought those? The same tackheads who've always passed George their grift. So here he pulls Dolby in for real computer games, thus convincing Capitol that he's reached the proper pitch of commercial desperation, and then makes an antiwar record with dirty parts just like always—except that this time the antiwar stuff is very explicit. I wish it included something as ingratiating as "Atomic Dog" or "Quickie" or "Last Dance." But when he augments the drum machine with a flute solo and a middle-aged man gasping in the throes of sexual excitation, this tackhead-by-association can't resist. **A—**

George Clinton: *R&B Skeletons in the Closet* (Capitol '86). Conceptually, featured vocalist Vanessa Williams and Pedro Bell's Neegrow cover are the only coups. Lyrically you'll have to settle for pidgin pygmy here, title credo there, some fast-food jokes, and the cautionary "Cool Joe." Groovewise it's Clonesville. In short, George's flattest in a decade. And you'd still settle for it in Boise. **B+**

George Clinton / Parliament-Funkadelic: *The Mothership Connection (Live from Houston)* (Capitol '86). Listening to their long-gone live double is like sitting midway back in the Garden because the fun is atmospheric: familiar epiphanies rise up out of the smoke, leaving the roof intact. This budget-priced one-sided video soundtrack offers a healthy serving of '70s raunch from about Row H of a hot '80s show—*intense* bottom, vocals loud and clear. Second side's a compilation, leading from "Atomic Dog" to two rereleases that'll make friends for *Some of My Best Jokes.* For fans, obviously. But if you're not some kind of fan by now, I've failed in my life's mission. **B+**

George Clinton: *The Best of George Clinton* (Capitol '86). The best-of has always been a dubious consumer service: even when it's a genuine bargain, it allows bizzers to make money off the same music twice, and don't think they don't love every dollar of it. In this case one of the bizzers is the artiste, who already stuck two of these cuts onto that strange half-live, half-compilation "mini-album" earlier this year. There's not much arguing with the individual selections. Since it reshuffles the entire first side of *You Shouldn't-Nuf Bit Fish,* the most playable Clinton of the '80s if not all time, it's stronger cut for cut than that one, and it's a better dance record than *Atomic Dog.* But it's totally lacking in epistemological integrity, and if you think that's a ridiculous thing to say about a funk album, you've got placebo syndrome—George knows what I'm talking about, and without a dictionary.   **B+**

George Clinton: *The Cinderella Theory* (Paisley Park/Warner Bros. '89). Except for the ballad (George, how could you), there isn't a track here that doesn't stick out its tongue at the merely clichéd. The first side isn't vintage, it's kinda fresh: guitar find and/or Rogers Nelson clone Tracey Lewis contributes a lite opener about getting down by never coming down, Chuck and Flav climb into bed with George's paisley hosts, "Why Should I Dog You Out?" rallies canines everywhere. Later, "French Kiss" sticks out its tongue for real. As happened so often when he ruled the world, the luck of the funk isn't always with him. But give Rogers credit for asking him back.   **A—**

Club Nouveau: *Life, Love and Pain* (Warner Bros. '87). In the unlikely event that you both don't know and care, I'll note that this is the follow-up cum answer record to 1986's biggest one-shot, Club Vieux's "Rumors." The auteur is rejected Club Vieux svengali Jay King, who proves which half of the one-shot had the professionalism by turning in a listenable as opposed to barely competent album. Why it's a hit album I couldn't tell you—"Lean on Me" cries out for a weathered voice, not fresh beats.   **B—**

Club Ska '67 (Mango '80). *Intensified! Vol. 3* is a little later, hence a little slicker. Like some would-be early reggae sampler, side two begins with four full-fledged songs in a row; the early reggae standard "Shanty Town" blocks side one's all-instrumental flow. But if you've developed a weakness for the style's random inspiration, you won't say no to one more hodgepodge of found masterstrokes and delightful accidents. Strange to think this was all happening simultaneously with *Sgt. Pepper.*   **A—**

The Coachmen: *Failure To Thrive* (New Alliance EP '88). Shit-rock iconographer J. D. King's NYC art band included a guitarist named Thurston Moore, and the halting melodicism of their circa-'79 demos will surprise pioneering Sonic Youth fans, though Thurston was only the guitarist, after all. It also surprises me, because I never heard or heard of them at a time when I was clubbing three-four times weekly. They sure deserved some word-of-mouth. On the other hand, they weren't deeply special, not on this evidence. This is why critics get a little jaded.   **B**

Bruce Cockburn: *Humans* (Millennium '80). Occasionally he hits a phrase that merits its aura of heightened significance: coming at the climax (not end) of "Guerrilla Betrayed," the line "I'd like to put a bullet through the world" says it all. More often he wrecks an acceptably literate description with the likes of "across the straight [really 'strait,' but spelling doesn't count] a volcano flew a white smoke flag of surrender." Vocals that work a nice synthesis of conversation and declamation cover his ass.   **B—**

Bruce Cockburn: *Resume* (Millennium '81). Cockburn is like a smart, nice, but not especially hip/cool English prof—if he caps "Mama Just Wants to Barrelhouse All Night Long" with "Lord of the Starfields," just how raunchy is his barrelhouse likely to be? I'll take smart and nice over hip/cool anytime, and this best-of showcases his conventional wisdom at its most eloquent—you'll never catch the Devil taunting John Denver with an ecstatic "Why don't we celebrate?" But I skipped grad school because tragic-sense-of-life ironies weren't enough for me, and they still ain't.   **B+**

Bruce Cockburn: *Stealing Fire* (Gold Mountain '84). The songs about life and love fade into the usual high-IQ lyricism, but the ones about politics bite and hold. Not just because they're more violent (guns and copters galore) or virtuous (folk-rock *Sandinista!*)—because they're more specific. It isn't just ideology that makes "Who put that bullet hole in Peggy's kitchen wall?" a better lyric than "Pay attention to the poet / You need him and you know it." Me, I pay attention to rocket launchers. **B**

Bruce Cockburn: *World of Wonders* (MCA '86). Cockburn's a very smart guy with as tough and articulate a line on imperialism as any white person with a label deal. Few singer-songwriters play meaner guitar, and as befits an anti-imperialist he knows the international sonic palette. Unfortunately, his records never project musical necessity. The melodies and/or lyrics carry the first side anyway, but though I'm sure Cockburn has some idea what the synthesized pans are doing on the cry of politico-romantic angst and the vaguely Andean fretboards on the Wasp dub poem, what the world will hear is the oppressive boom-boom of four-four drums. **B**

Bruce Cockburn: *Waiting for a Miracle* (Gold Castle '87). After listening to two LPs worth of "Singles 1970–1987" three times, I'm convinced the miracle he's waiting for is one that transmutes a single into a hit. I'm waiting for his benefit compilation for the Committee in Solidarity With the People of El Salvador. **B**

Bruce Cockburn: *Big Circumstance* (Gold Castle '89). Where other singers have soul, Cockburn has dudgeon, more fierce and bitter with every record. Delivering lines like "don't breathe when the cars go by" and "may their gene pool increase" as if his life depended on them, which before he's dead it could, he reveals rules about the ineluctable bad faith of the political for the know-nothing shibboleths they are. Too bad he still cultivates his "personal" side. **B**

Joe Cocker: *Sheffield Steel* (Island '82). No, his voice isn't shot, though it's certainly lost a lot of soft edges and warm crannies—a lot of phlegm. Partial compensation provided by the decline of L.A.: there are more good songs lying around than at any time since Cocker and Three Dog Night invented interpretive rock way back when. And Sly & Robbie's loud, fast Memphis beat is the toughest backup of his life. Original grade: B plus. **B**

Cockney Rejects: *Greatest Hits Volume One* (EMI import '80). Anybody who doubts the artiness of L.A. punk purism should check out the London version— where *NME*-subscribing suburbanites speed up the Pistols, East End oi boys slow them down (just slightly, to about the tempo of a fast football march). Sure the songs blur too much anyway, especially on side two, but the 'tween-rave-ups are rousing throughout, "I'm Not a Fool" is worthy of 1977, the line after "Join the Rejects" is "And get yourself killed," and the toaster-introed "Where the Hell Is Babylon?" ("I wanna go") is an overdue answer song whatever its racial subtext— my only regret is that they didn't slip a dig at the Dolls into it. **B**

The Coconuts: *Don't Take My Coconuts* (EMI America '83). I can forgive August Darnell the filler on side one because he's a gifted disco producer, which means his throwaway jingles and premature remakes and cynical trifles add up to dance music that's more listenable than most. But the failures on side two are as unfocused as anything he's ever committed to vinyl— excepting only "If I Only Had a Brain," an all too apt cover for these would-be bimbos. **B**

Cocteau Twins: *Blue Bell Knoll* (Capitol '88). Harold Budd records in their studio. The Bulgarian State Radio and Television Female Vocal Choir records on their label. I understand that they're more foolish than either (not naive, not after six years), and that they've been known to milk momentary momentum out of electric guitars, but the affinities are there—these faeries are in the aura business. So what are they doing on the alternative rock charts? Ever hear the one about being so open-minded that when you lay down to sleep your brains fall out? **C+**

Code Blue: *Code Blue* (Warner Bros. '80). OK, they're a bit more proficient than most "tight" "new wave" bands. But Lee Abrams himself couldn't hear a hit here. So how'd they get their blue vinyl and blue-ribbon executive producers—both Lenny Waronker and Russ Titelman? Well, Dean Chamberlain works a&r for Warners, and real producer Michael Ostin's dad Mo is an even bigger wig at Warners than the aforementioned. I'd never call this process deplorable per se—like pols' kids Vietnamizing their dads in the '60s, somebody has to punk up the biz's sires, and tandem tyro Paul Wexler did Tin Huey a solid that way. In this particular case, however, the outcome isn't even cute or catchy enough to dismiss as skinny-tie music—although the drummer does wear one, just in case.   **C—**

Leonard Cohen: *Various Positions* (PVC '85). With a new crop of beautiful losers arising out of the latest bohemia as inexorably as ailanthus out of a vacant lot, the man who wrote the book is worth attending, because he's not bitter. After all, righteous anger has never been his long suit, and what does he have to be bitter about? At fifty, he's still living comfortably off the fruits of his spiritual torment. Of course, not every loser is so talented, or resilient. The hymn "If It Be Your Will" and the fable "The Captain" are as rich and twisted as anything in his career, and "The Law" does justice to his patented romantic irony, which by now has a soothing glow. If you're sick of hearing him whisper in your ear that to be a roue is a religious calling, so be it—me, I think this is a better advertisement for middle-aged sex than *Dynasty.*   **B+**

Leonard Cohen: *I'm Your Man* (Columbia '88). A European best-seller from the Francophone capital of the Western Hemisphere, Cohen isn't the grizzled folk-rock parvenu we take him for. He works a far older and more honorable tradition, that of the French *chansonnier,* the singing poet who'll cheerfully appropriate any simple music that fits his meter without giving a second thought to how authentic or commercialized it might be. Because words are his stock in trade, Cohen's

music rarely obtrudes no matter how classy or schlocky its usages. So despite what some consider a misguided attempt to yoke stark instrumentation and femme chorus, his latest recording seems no more or less natural/unnatural than his previous offerings, and the poems are his most consistent in a decade. Envoi: "But you'll be hearing from me, baby, long after I'm gone / I'll be speaking to you sweetly from a window in the Tower of Song."   **A—**

Coldcut: *What's That Noise?* (Tommy Boy/Reprise '89). Things work out all too predictably for this smart young studio duo. Eclectically danceable and righteously segued though their samples are, they're too bare-bones in themselves to move the crowd—the world beyond the dance floor. When a real vocalist climbs aboard—Lisa Stansfield, Queen Latifah, Junior Reid (though not, righteous eclecticism aside, Mark E. Smith)—everything is swinging. And when the music is all beat and concept, it's all beat and concept—though "Party and party and party and bullshit" is certainly in the great tradition of postmod self-criticism.   **B**

Lloyd Cole and the Commotions: *Rattlesnakes* (Geffen '85). A Glaswegian whose romanticism mixes the mundane and the pretentious in nice lyrical proportions, Cole is like a middle-class Roddy Frame escaped to university instead of the bohemian fringe. Born just before the Beatles made it respectable for college kids to like beat music, he claims student life as the rock and roll subject it so obviously is, and I say about time. So what if he can't stop talking about books and movies and gathers his material on day trips from his walkup flat? Does that make him so different from you?   **B+**

Lloyd Cole and the Commotions: *1984–1989* (Capitol '89). As an exemplary undergraduate he had his place in the great chain of being, but as a perpetual grad student he needs ID. (Maybe also a better rhythm section.) On this compilation, with two B sides for bait (and four accredited *Rattlesnakes* tracks for quality), he applies for his card. I wouldn't put it past college radio to give it to him. (The card, I mean—

college radio wouldn't know a good rhythm section if one played live in the studio.)   **B—**

Ornette Coleman: *Of Human Feelings* (Antilles '82). Ornette's pioneering *Dancing in Your Head* was completely unrelenting, his ancillary *Body Meta* somewhat amorphous; Blood Ulmer's records are jagged, Shannon Jackson's uneven. Which makes this album, cut three years ago with five young musicians who have gotten even better since, a breakthrough if not a miracle: warm, listenable harmolodic funk. Most great lyric artists shore up their effusions with irony, but the way this music confounds mind-body dualism should provide all the release from tension anyone needs. The teeming intellectual interplay of the rhythms is no less humane than the childlike bits of melody. And the way the players break into ripples of song only to ebb back into the tideway is participatory democracy at its most practical and utopian.   **A+**

Ornette Coleman and Prime Time: *Opening the Caravan of Dreams* (Caravan of Dreams '86). Only the second LP by the harmolodic funk originators, this was recorded live at the well-appointed Fort Worth avant-garde emporium in 1985, and it's a live album for sure—it lacks the studio-engendered beginning-middle-end that focuses *Of Human Feelings* and for that matter Metheny/Coleman's *Song X.* When it threatens to break altogether "free," its risks seem more like entropy than thrills and chills. But it's a live album showcasing one of the great improvisers, as well as musicians who never sound more authoritative than when following his orders.   **A—**

Ornette Coleman: *In All Languages* (Caravan of Dreams '87). Packed by their eternal leader into ten cuts averaging 3:22, Cherry-Haden-Higgins surge hotter at fifty than they ever dreamed old or new, as if harmolodic funk is an essentially structural principle, inhering more in the constraints of song conception than in the electric pulse. It's the Quartet disc that evokes the dense flow of *Of Human Feelings,* which leaves Prime Time room for patches of free cacophony as daunting as the Quartet in its youth. Defining both bands is the natural iconoclasm and indefatigable lyricism of the fifty-seven-year-old rebel who's probably the most widely respected musician in the world, and who somehow doesn't get any less amazing as a result.   **A**

Ornette Coleman and Prime Time: *Virgin Beauty* (Portrait '88). If the quietest of the Prime Time records—lyrical, sublimely reflective, autumnal at times, even Milesish when Ornette picks up his trumpet—ain't rock and roll, that doesn't mean it isn't "rock." The pulse pulses, and Jerry Garcia, never King Kickass, fits right in. The tuneful themes show off Ornette's pop feel, and while Garcia has rarely comped or noodled more purposefully, it's the unsung Charlee Ellerbee or the equally unsung Bern Nix who does the tighten-up beneath "Bourgeois Boogie." In and around the themes Ornette improvises a whole lot of saxophone without once showing off. He's beyond that now.   **A**

Ornette Coleman: See also Pat Metheny/Ornette Coleman

Steve Coleman and Five Elements: *Sine Die* (Pangaea '88). Between their groove-busting tempo shifts and putative profundities, Coleman's two earlier records were enough to make you wonder whether smart fusion was any better than the dumb kind. This is definitely an improvement—at its best, it combines the modern tonalities of schooled bebop with the snap and kick of professional funk. Not the bump and thump, though. And while Cassandra Wilson sings more and intones less, she still has to deal with Coleman's lyrics. Which must be why Sting likes the guy.   **B**

Albert Collins: *Frostbite* (Alligator '80). In its way, this is as formulaic as a Linda Ronstadt album—pick good tunes, gather good musicians, identify good takes. But in blues the Good is simpler, more satisfying, and harder to come by than it is in super-pop, and while I wouldn't say Albert plays better than Linda sings, I wouldn't argue if you did. Albert sings OK, too.   **B+**

Albert Collins: *Frozen Alive!* (Alligator '81). Simply by putting him in a studio with songs and sidemen worthy of the genre, Bruce Iglauer got the best album this Texas legend ever cut, 1978's *Ice Pickin'*, but faced with the blues producer's eternal what-next he settled for a record on which a full horn section jostled uncomfortably against Collins's down-home wit. Fortunately, the next next goes for the bare live bones, with the classic "Frosty" establishing a bite and authority that are never relinquished. I miss that down-home wit, though—giving your bass player room for a hornpipe is the kind of dumb joke that's afflicted live albums for years. **B+**

Albert Collins: *Don't Lose Your Cool* (Alligator '83). Kicking off with a blistering boogie, borrowing wisdom from Percy Mayfield and wit from Oscar Brown Jr., and played with an edge throughout, this is everything you could ask of a blues album except—except that it isn't quite not just another good blues album. A must for aficionados and a fine introduction for novices, but inbetweeners can live rich and meaningful lives without it. **B+**

Albert Collins: *Cold Snap* (Alligator '86). In which Bruce Iglauer shoots for a Grammy by setting up his big man with a big band—Jimmy McGriff, Mel Brown, Uptown Horns, the works. They do work, too. But nobody ever mistook Albert for Jimmy Witherspoon, much less Jimmy Rushing—he doesn't have the kind of built-in bullhorn essential to that big effect. As if NARAS will care. **B**

Albert Collins/Robert Cray/Johnny Copeland: *Showdown!* (Alligator '85). Collins gets top billing not just because he's Alligator's man but because this is his album. He takes a solo on all nine cuts where Cray and Copeland are vouchsafed a total of seven, and shares vocals about equally with his costars, both of whom cut him. Not that they're trying—if they were, this would live up to its title. As it is, whether the problem's will or conception or ability, you'll get more fireworks from Lonnie Mack w/ Stevie Ray Vaughan. **B**

Bootsy: *Ultra Wave* (Warner Bros. '80). Though the Rubber Band was the only P-Funk spinoff to sell through, distin- guishing it from the parent organization quickly became problematic. Conceived partly as bait for Warner Bros., it did serve the special interests of subteen Geepies for a while, not to mention the special interests of Bootsy, certainly the most charismatic Funkateer save the Dr. himself, but before long Parliament was making kiddie moves and the Starman was fizzling. So on the one hand this is a welcome return to form, and on the other it's interim P-Funk— from the "Shortnin' Bread" intro through the "unenjoyment line" protest through the jump blues tribute all the way to the climactic "Sound Crack," which after several dead-end tangents returns all space travelers to the ineluctable One. Original grade: A minus. **B+**

William "Bootsy" Collins: *The One Giveth, the Count Taketh Away* (Warner Bros. '82). Not the one to give, but who's counting? **B+**

Bootsy Collins: *What's Bootsy Doin'?* (Columbia '88). I always suspected he was hemmed in by his P-Funk kiddie show, and after six years of figuring shit out he proves it. The old mob is on hand, but the most Clintonish turn this vaudeville takes, "Shock-It-to-Me" 's superimposition of electrocutes and Alabama gals, was produced by Bill Laswell, and elsewhere Bootzilla working alone constructs a sweet persona a grown-up can love. Still a loyal brother of the P, he may not want to hear that "(I Wannabee) Kissin' You" and "Yo Moma Loves You" are prime Steve Arrington, but I intend a compliment. And though it's wishful to claim we're all winners because our sperm got to the egg first, it's nice of him to see it that way. **A—**

Phil Collins: *No Jacket Required* (Atlantic '85). Between his self-deprecating videos and his good taste in business associates (better Philip Bailey than, say, Steve Perry), Collins isn't as hateful as an art-rock leader-by-default turned best- selling - solo - artist - in - the - world - this - month might be. In fact, he's not hateful at all. But it takes more than that to make me want to hear a stupid love song again. Never mind the absolutely unsurprising lyrics and arrangements and just tell me why this is the great mean of Britpop voices? Is it because no one ever wonders what it sounds like unfiltered?   **C**

Colors (Warner Bros. '88). From Ice-T's horrorshow credo to Eric B.'s mastermix fantasia, the originals and rarities on side one constitute an uncommonly solid rap compilation. Side two's iffier, with a transcendently irritating Roxanne Shanté cut, punctuated by whooping JB gasps uncannily similar to the ones D.J. E-Z Rock stole from house's house, deflated by a crime-does-not-pay ending from M.C. Shan and soulmate Rick James. Bargain-hunters won't pass this chance up, but I still want Roxanne on a twelve-inch—keep pretentious people out of the house.   **B+**

The Commercials: *Compare and Decide* (Eat '80). In the tradition of Jon Tiven, another bad rock critic turned good bandleader, Loyd Grossman doesn't let details like not being able to carry a tune get in the way of his small-minded, hooky little songs. So why should we? Only an ex-crit would put out an album with titles that damn near write the review: "Ramona" and "She Said She Said" and an Abba cover for influences, "I'm So Heavy Metal" and "El Disco Es Cultura" for satiric breadth. Best song: "X-Girlfriend" (serves him right). Message (from "Bongo Party"): "Don't bring a bottle / Don't bring a friend / Don't bring your favorite tape."   **B+**

Commodores: *Heroes* (Motown '80). With Lionel Richie turning his attentions to inspirational numbers varying the theme "Got To Be Together," with "Jesus" joining William King's "Mighty Spirit" for the finale, this is an improvement. For one thing, most of the brotherhood anthems—which avoid the gender-specific, actually, with lots of "people," "folks," and "y'all"—have a somewhat more rousing beat than "Three Times a Lady." And on the fond "Old-Fashion Love" and the cold-hearted "Sorry To Say," the brothers remind Lionel that this is still supposed to be a funk band.   **B**

Commodores: *In the Pocket* (Motown '81). With Lionel readying his farewells, they'd better take care of tunecraft, but only on "Lady (You Bring Me Up)," where William King shares the credit with someone I presume is his wife and someone else I presume is a song doctor, do they give off the signals. Lionel antes up two slow ones, both of which cut the funky competition.   **B−**

The Commodores: *Anthology* (Motown '83). As this summation makes clear, they never quite connected as a pioneering funk band because their secret weapon was Lionel Richie, who does not number funk among his natural gifts. Beyond him they're a cut above the Johnson Brothers. Richie will be better off without them. And they'll be worse off yet without him.   **B**

Commodores: *Nightshift* (Motown '85). Title tune's pretty slick as rock and roll heaven songs go, but ever since Lionel—who they could have used on "The Woman in My Life"—they've been too tame for their own good. A new singer from Heatwave obviously isn't going to change that. When they thank Dennis Lambert "for being so good at what you do," you should remember that what he does is schlock.   **C+**

Conjure (American Clavé '84). Ishmael Reed or no Ishmael Reed, to hear Taj Mahal, David Murray, and Allen Toussaint playing not alongside but with one another is really something. Thank Murray for his virtuosic atavism on the smartly paced blues side, and Mahal for his progressive heart on the more desultory jazz side. Thank Steve Swallow and Billy Hart for their humble shuffles. And then hail Ishmael Reed, whose pan-Afro-American modernism was the occasion of these miracles. Nothing like an oral tradition to make written words sing.   **A−**

John Conlee: *Greatest Hits* (MCA '84). Conlee sounds the way Merle Haggard would if Merle sang through his nose and didn't like jazz. He may even deserve his billing, "The Common Man"—apparently he still works a farm and drives to Nashville in a pickup. The sole romantic ballad here drips with contrition—like most country artists he's more at home with sin than with grace. And like 'most everybody he's better off when he gets away from such polarities—on the thematic "Backside of Thirty" and "Common Man," and especially on "Friday Night Blues," about a guy who's too bushed to go out with his wife. Time: 29:43.   **A—**

Ry Cooder: *Borderline* (Warner Bros. '80). Cooder's current soul/r&b interests inhibit his songfinding—"634-5789" and "Speedo" may enlighten his esoteric faithful, but to a dumb old rock-and-roller like me they're just lame covers. "Down in the Boondocks" ain't so functional either. "The Girls From Texas" I can use—one more communiqué on the battle of the sexes from a combatant who's been minoring in the subject from jump street. In this one she blows his head off, and that ain't all.   **B—**

Ry Cooder: *The Slide Area* (Warner Bros. '82). From racially suspect novelty number to *Street-Legal* tribute to immodest claims on "Gypsy Woman" and "Blue Suede Shoes," side one is weird old Ry at his most misguided. Despite a topical update on Willie Dixon's "Which Came First," side two is Ry the company folkrocker trying to squeeze his weird old self into a formula that wasn't really commercial when the company devised it.   **C+**

Ry Cooder: *Get Rhythm* (Warner Bros. '87). With his desire to please and his lust for lucre both slaked by his renown as a soundtrack composer, he's free to follow his ugly voice where it leads—he's never been louder, and it suits him. Somebody else's blues, "I Can Tell by the Way You Smell," articulates his raw sense of dirty; somebody else's calypso, "Women Will Rule the World," does the same for his postfeminist blues sexism. And "Going Back to Okinawa" is an original only a folklorist could distinguish from the found weirdness that's always been his redeeming social value.   **B+**

Sam Cooke: *Live at the Harlem Square Club, 1963* (RCA Victor '85). Some people think live albums capture the essence of rock and roll; I don't even think live shows do. That may be why this record, which yea verily doth document a little-noted aspect of Cooke's amazing career, leaves me mostly tepid. But I blame it on headlong show-band arrangements so single-minded they soon undermine what conceptual interest inheres in the transformation of this seminal crossover teen dream into fit fare for the over-twenty-ones in a Miami r&b club. I like grit as much as the next postprimitivist, but good grit admits interpretive flair just like any other mode—more than Cooke puts into these hits, originally designed to downplay his gritty side.   **B**

Cookie Crew: *Born This Way* (FFRR '89). The Wee Papa Girls sound more English, but the Cooks have the spunk; dissed sisters and boys-do-it-better notwithstanding, this is the first U.K. rap album worth bragging about. Davy D's stutterstep "From the South" is the only departure, but Daddy-O oversees the music with his usual pride of craft, getting a long overdue hook out of Edwin Starr and one more grunt out of the ever-bountiful JB. Conclusion: boys don't do it better, but Americans still do.   **B+**

The Coolies: *Dig . . ?* (DB '86). Lame as the assembled Simon & Garfunkel songs were in the original, they're lamer still in these speedy, occasionally funny-voiced takeoffs. Though the band might have gotten away with an EP featuring "Having My Baby," the only satire here with any teeth and the only one that doesn't target Paul Simon, I find it bewildering that anyone can hate *Graceland* enough to pay them for turning their stoned fantasy into an album. A glaring example of the postmodernist dictum that art about art is boring but junk about kitsch isn't.   **C**

Cool It Reba: *Money Fall Out the Sky* (Hannibal EP '82). They're hardly the first art band with a great rhythm section, but just like Pylon and the B-52's, they're fronted by a singer you remember—the slightly demented David Hanson, who does a beefcake variation on Fred Schneider's sharply campy attack. The four songs on their candid bid for wealth, fame, drugs, and wealth sort themselves out nicely. But except on a title number in which Hanson envies Sammy Davis Jr., Leroy Nieman, and Colonel Tom Parker—in which he longs to "live like

Elvis"—they do slide back to their primordial white-funk bottom when you leave them alone.   **B+**

Greg Copeland: *Revenge Will Come* (Geffen '82). Producer Jackson Browne has gone after absolutely predictable mid-tempo studio rock, but with a tough edge that's augmented by Copeland, who sounds like (of all things) Jackson Browne with a tough edge. Propitious—if Copeland can move his mentor's personalist millenarianism far enough left to write protest lyrics that surrender neither psychological dimension nor American mythos, I bet other young rock mainstreamers are thinking the same way. Original grade: B plus.   **B−**

Johnny Copeland: *Copeland Special* (Rounder '81). It's the stellar horn section (led by George Adams, Byard Lancaster, and Arthur Blythe) that calls attention to this album, but anybody who buys blues albums for horn sections has missed the point. Copeland boasts better-than-average chops as both singer and guitarist, not such a common parlay (especially among debuting 44-year-olds), but anybody who buys blues albums for chops has really missed the point. The point is conviction, more palpable here than on any new blues to come my way since Johnny Shines's 1977 *Too Wet To Plow*. Put across by those chops, of course. And quite probably inspired by that stellar horn section. **A−**

Johnny Copeland: *Make My Home Where I Hang My Hat* (Rounder '82). At the outset Copeland identifies himself as a "Natural Born Believer," then applies himself to the bluesman's dilemma of making that belief come just as naturally to us. On his debut album, an all-star horn section and a quarter century of pent-up ambition put him over, but here he opts for the homey (and perhaps overfamiliar) spontaneity of his road band and instead gets horns and songs that sound half-dead until he mixes in some covers overdisc.   **B**

Johnny Copeland: *Bringin' It All Back Home* (Rounder '85). "It's the same music, the same old beat," Copeland reports on this largely instrumental blues album, the first ever recorded where it all sort of began. Fortunately, that's not what his guitar says, nor his continentally integrated band, which finds a groove somewhere between an airborne Congolese rumba and a Gulf Coast shuffle with some tricky dance figures thrown in. And who knows, maybe all concerned were capacitated by the illusion of unity. When wise guys like Yusef Lateef and Stewart Copeland visit Africa in search of *la différance,* they come back with albums that are neither here nor there.   **B+**

Johnny Copeland: See also Albert Collins/ Johnny Copeland/Robert Cray

Elvis Costello and the Attractions: *Get Happy!!* (Columbia '80). This Stax-based twenty-song loss leader establishes not his fecundity but his fallibility—lotsa duds. I count maybe eight originals I'll remember half as well as the Sam & Dave obscurity, and n.b.: the Sam & Dave obscurity was the hit (U.K. hit, of course I mean). His rueful disavowal of "Knock on Wood" (in a dud) is no less impressive than his proud claim on "Time Is Tight" (in a keeper), and tropes and hooks abound—why deny lines like "You lack lust you're so lackluster" or "I speak double dutch to a real double duchess"? On the other hand, why bother digging them out?   **B**

Elvis Costello: *Taking Liberties* (Columbia '80). OK, twenty more songs, all B sides etc., how could it hold together, but some sentimental part of me is taken with its reflexive passion and half-finished serendipity—this detritus was the work of a punk fellow-traveler, and he'll be missed. "Girls Talk" and "Stranger in the House" and "I Don't Want To Go to Chelsea" are more indelible than *Get Happy!!* at its happiest, and let me put in a word for all 1:43 of the previously unreleased "Hoover Factory," a punless piece of melancholy throwaway sarcasm that reminds us that he's in this because he's pissed, not because he's glib.   **B**

Elvis Costello and the Attractions: *Trust* (Columbia '81). Who ever said he wasn't much of a singer? Was that me? No, I said he wasn't much of a poet—all wordplay as swordplay and puns for punters (one of which means something, one of which doesn't, and both of which took me ten seconds). But here he makes the music make the words as he hasn't since *This Year's Model.* This is rock and roll as eloquent, hard-hitting pop, and Elvis has turned into such a soul man that I no longer wish he'd change his name to George and go country.   **A**

Elvis Costello & the Attractions: *Almost Blue* (Columbia '81). Put this on the shelf behind Bowie's *Pin Ups* and Lennon's *Rock 'n' Roll,* which also seemed "important" when they appeared. Take it from me, EC fans: start with the Flying Burrito Brothers' *Gilded Palace of Sin,* then try *24 of Hank Williams' Greatest Hits,* then George Jones's *All-Time Greatest Hits: Volume 1,* and Merle Haggard's *Songs I'll Always Sing.* Then start exploring.   **B−**

Elvis Costello and the Attractions: *Imperial Bedroom* (Columbia '82). I admit it—I love the lyric sheet. Helps me pay attention, though not always, and persuades me absolutely that "The Long Honeymoon" and "Kid About It" are as great as songwriting ever gets. But it also shores up my impression that he can be precious lyrically, vocally, and musically, and gnomic for no reason at all—in short, pretentious. And while I'm glad he's got soul, too often he invests emotion in turns of phrase he should play cool.   **B+**

Elvis Costello and the Attractions: *Punch the Clock* (Columbia '83). Without the sustained melodicism of *Imperial Bedroom* (first side, anyway) to impart the illusion of meaningful wholeness, this is adjudged a major letdown by Elvis's acolytes. But "Boxing Day" is hardly the first time one of his punderous constructions has failed not just to signify but to communicate. Most of this disparate collection (first side, anyway) does what he's always done—convey an elusive feeling that's half pinned down by the words because that's all the grasp he's got on it. And though the alternate versions of "Shipbuilding" (Robert Wyatt) and "Pills and Soap" (the Imposter) are indeed more gripping, their literalness does place his personal contortions in useful perspective.   **B+**

Elvis Costello and the Attractions: *Goodbye Cruel World* (Columbia '84). In these changing times it's good to know there are things we can rely on, so here's another solid if unspectacular effort from this thoughtful, hard-hitting, surprisingly tender singer-songwriter. Highlights include the lilting country cover "I Wanna Be Loved," the straight-to-the-point "Inch by Inch," and—who says there are no great protest songs any more?—"Peace in Our Time," which almost got him booed off Carson.   **B+**

Elvis Costello and the Attractions: *The Best of Elvis Costello and the Attractions* (Columbia '85). From "Alison" and "Watching the Detectives" to "Everyday I Write the Book" and "The Only Flame in Town," this would seem the solution to anybody's Elvis C. problem—it consists entirely of songs you like so much you think you understand them. But from there to there is a long way. As Columbia knows, writing catchy doesn't make him a singles artist—for better or worse his LPs have gestalt. Including this one, I guess—it's programmed to flow, sowing confusion around your recollection of how past gestalts flowed. But never expect a perfect compilation from somebody who essays a perfect album every time out.   **A−**

The Costello Show (Featuring Elvis Costello): *King of America* (Columbia '86). The Attractions always betokened Elvis's punk integrity—his commitment to collective creation, his rejection of the International Pop Music Community's expedient playing around. And the last time they were fully equal to his music was on *This Year's Model* in 1978. So finally he ditches them for T-Bone Burnett and a bunch of studio pros Steve Stills himself could get behind, one set anchored by Elvis I–approved L.A. rockabillies James Burton and Ron Tutt, the other by New Orleans–gone-L.A. drummer Earl Palmer and Modern Jazz–gone-L.A. bassist Ray Brown. And they all collaborate with their paymaster on that incommensurable token of collective creation, a groove. The wordplay is still too private, but the music has opened up: the careworn relaxation of Elvis's live vocals fits the uncompromised careerism of this groove as simply as 1978's raging tension did the angry young speed-rock of *This Year's Model.* Good show. Original grade: A.   **A−**

Elvis Costello and the Attractions: *Blood and Chocolate* (Columbia '86). To pigeonhole this as just another Elvis C. (and the Attractions) record is to ignore the plain fact that he (they) hasn't (haven't) sounded so tough- or single-minded since *This Year's Model.* Like *Little Creatures,* it's a return to basics with a decade of growth in it, and until midway through side two, when the songs start portending more than they can deliver, it's so straightforward you think he must be putting you on. But he's just voicing his pain and the world's, in that order, as usual. When the two strongest songs on a pop record run over six minutes apiece, we're talking sustained vision. **A—**

Out of Our Idiot (Demon import '87). Credited to "Various Artists" who include Elvis Costello & the Attractions, Elvis Costello & the Confederates, the Coward Brothers, and the Emotional Toothpaste, all of them the musical workaholic who didn't release an LP under any of his own names this year. In other words, *Taking Liberties Vol. II.* EC and T-Bone's "People's Limousine" has a rep, and well-crafted it is—meaningful, too, I think. But the compelling contemporaneity of our genius's current one-offs (not to mention his current taste in companions) is best conveyed by my own personal favorite: a cover of the Shirelles' "Baby It's You" featuring none other than the Jesus of Cool, Mr. Nick Lowe. **B—**

Elvis Costello: *Spike* (Warner Bros. '89). Paul Whiteman was a bigger star, and though my jazz friends may cringe, I doubt he was as good. But like Elvis C., he made the mistake of applying his refined taste to what he knew was the music of the future—hiring fine players, commissioning Ellington and Copland, emphasizing the danceability of an orchestra too grand to be called a band, he honored the classics. Who knows which of Costello's virtues will seem equally irrelevant forty or ten years hence—his obsessive wit? his precise arrangements? his respect for musical history? Unless I'm mistaken, though, he's doomed to be remembered as fatally self-conscious. And doomed as well never to convert the unconverted again. **B**

John Cougar: See John Cougar Mellencamp

Mary Coughlan: *Tired and Emotional* (Green Linnet/Mystery '87). Irish blues, or should I say more Irish blues? These are cabaret-style, murmured and crooned in a smoky hillbilly brogue by a Galway folkie who took it from the bathtub to the stage five years ago. Thank producer Erik Visser for suggesting the move. And ask him to please keep his songs to himself. **B+**

The Cover Girls: *Show Me* (Fever '87). Set on pulling a marketable girl group out of a Latin hip hop concept, their svengalis channel the mix toward wall-of-sound, fuzzing beats and harmonies with a nostalgic soupçon of Spectorian grandeur. The damage is minor but, for me, decisive—I prefer Exposé's hooks to these (superior) songs, can't get with Angel Sabater even though she makes Lisa Lisa sound like a hussy. It's a game of inches out there. **B**

Cowboy Junkies: *The Trinity Session* (RCA '88). One consequence of the rootsy two-track recording is that despite her austere-to-impoverished arrangements and bell-like murmur, it's often hard to understand what Margo Timmins is saying—is she driving to "Nashville" or on "ashfault"? The tempos don't help either—takes her many seconds to get from subject to predicate. Leaving us with the usual oxymorons—histrionic understatement and vague specificity. Why is she so sad? She just is, that's all. **C+**

The Cramps: *Songs the Lord Taught Us* (Illegal '80). From the time they stormed a jaded—hence novelty-hungry—CBGB two or three years ago, they've been a joke that wears thin before it's over. "TV Set" and "Garbage Man" and a couple of others are everything they're supposed to be—archetypally rockin', outrageously funny. But when the songs are neither or even only one, the band's inability to sing, play, produce, or prance around your living room detracts significantly from your pleasure. Then you stop listening altogether. **B—**

The Cramps: *Psychedelic Jungle* (I.R.S. '81). After setting the mood with two obscure sureshots from the *Pebbles* anthology (why wasn't "Green Fuz" a hit?), En Why's own mock rockabillies come up with an actual novelty album instead of a theoretical one. If only there weren't these jokes about rape, voodoo, and jungle folk (at least they're not called "bunnies," although they do "hop"), I might still be chuckling. **B**

The Cramps: *Bad Music for Bad People* (I.R.S. '84). One hears loose talk of minimalism from their demented admirers, but except for a few realists, which these artistes ain't, cartoonists are minimalists by definition. So how do they draw? Crudely, but with an undeniable flair. And are they good for a few laughs? Boiled down to greatest jokes they are. My favorite is "She Said" 's slavering geezer. **B+**

The Robert Cray Band: *Who's Been Talkin'* (Tomato '80). Hailed by the ever tightening knot of blues loyalists as the next . . . Son Seals?, Cray can recite his catechism without kowtowing to orthodoxy—guitar like Albert Collins only chillier and more staccato, voice like B.B. King only cleaner and, well, thinner. Willie Dixon and Howlin' Wolf songs lead for good reason, but both artist and producers write with uncommon acidity (try "Nice as a Fool Can Be" and "The Score" respectively), and country-soul cult hero O. V. Wright adds the right kind of historical perspective. A little more vocal muscle and he might compete with . . . Son Seals. [Later on Atlantic.] **B**

The Robert Cray Band: *Bad Influence* (Hightone '83). Finally he sounds like the comer they rave about: side one is as engaging a 17:04 of new blues as I've heard in a decade. Ranging from down-and-out *aab* to lounge-tinged soul cry on the first two cuts, the songwriting had me caring less about the singing, especially given the chop-and-roll guitar. But whenever the material fails to provide its own highs, Crays's inability to reach for extra power or sweetness makes a difference. **B+**

The Robert Cray Band: *False Accusations* (Hightone '85). After several metastases worth of bar smoke, Cray's voice has finally changed: his singing is strong and unashamed, adorned only by his waste-free guitar. But what makes Cray a major artist in an obsolescent style is the songs, the sharpest often written by his producers. Dennis Walker is the obsessed sinner ("Porch Light" 's guilt-as-pleasure, "I've Slipped Her Mind" 's month after), Bruce Bromberg a/k/a D. Amy more the all-purpose pro, though "Playin' in the Dirt" certainly feels lived in. And Cray, who has a credit on that one, gets all of "The Last Time (I Get Burned Like This)." Not since Moe Bandy was an honest man has anyone laid out the wages of fucking around with such unflagging precision. **A−**

The Robert Cray Band: *Strong Persuader* (Mercury '86). At thirty-three, Cray is a mature multithreat talent: fearless formal innovator, brainy bandleader, terse yet fluent guitarist, and—amazingly, given where he started—the most authoritative singer to emerge from blues since Bland and King. Add an array of gems as perfectly realized as Randy Newman's *12 Songs* and you have not just a great blues album but a great album. Cray's sexual roles range from the good-time man of "Nothing but a Woman" to the cuckold-turned-predator of "New Blood" to the suspicious schmuck of Dennis Walker's outrageous "I Guess I Showed Her," who bests the woman he caught "having lunch with some new guy" by abandoning her to the house, the car, and no him. But it's the remorseful lust of the title character, who sits listening impassively through thin apartment walls as the woman he's just chalked up breaks with her husband, that dominates a cold-eyed, country-influenced record occupying uncharted territory on the blues side of soul—full of feeling, yet chary of soul's redemptive promise. Original grade: A. **A+**

The Robert Cray Band: *Don't Be Afraid of the Dark* (Mercury '88). Yeah, I could live without David Sanborn myself, but if you leave it at that you're refusing to hear a major artist who bends blues tradition to his own artistic ends as surely as Jimi Hendrix or Jimmy Page, a suave cool motherfucker obsessed with the male sex roles blues defined for rock and roll. No shit—his determination to bring his tradition into the pop present equals his determination to escape the cultural residue and/or primal urge that compels him to pitch woo, talk murder, and make obscene phone calls. Because this life-project can never end, a continuing tension stretches and strengthens his music. The songs here aren't as consistently amazing as *Strong Persuader*'s, but all that means is that Cray and his writers are mortal. Summing up is Bruce Bromberg's "Night Patrol," in which a laid-off streetstalker, tortured quote unquote by his bad habits quote unquote, joins the homeless legions whose ways he knows so well. **A—**

Robert Cray: See also Albert Collins/Johnny Copeland/Robert Cray

Crazy Backwards Alphabet: *Crazy Backwards Alphabet* (SST '87). Though Beefheart-FFKT drummer John French, Dixie Dregs bassist Andy West, and hockey-mad Swedish avant-rocker Michael Maksymenko get equal billing, this is Henry Kaiser's pickup project—you can tell because he's on every cut. Concept is Beefheart as Dixie Dregs, kind of, with intermittent lyrics, not always in English. You'll go for Maksymenko singing ZZ Top in Russian, and Kaiser-West-Maksymenko rocking Albert Ayler. Both covers, you notice. I never did get Dixie Dregs. **B**

Creedence Clearwater Revival: *The Royal Albert Hall Concert* (Fantasy '80). No devotee of live albums by anybody, much less by guys who come out and recreate their studio renditions of songs and choogles conceived in Lodi, I do hereby certify that this one, said to be a newly discovered 1970 tape, is tighter and more explosive than the flaccid *Live in Europe* double of their breakup's afterglow. I also acknowledge that after three or four years with bands who want nothing so much as to finance studio renditions of songs and explosions conceived in lower Manhattan, I've learned to enjoy the form. Just make sure you get the studio renditions first. [Later retitled *The Concert.*] **B**

Marshall Crenshaw: *Marshall Crenshaw* (Warner Bros. '82). This album seems simple because it is simple, yet it continues to unfold long after you believe its byways played out—not by exploiting the snazzy bridges and key changes of the traditional pop arsenal, but with lines repeated at odd junctures, choruses reentering when you anticipate another verse. Brushing by the everyday phrases that are the stuff of pop songwriting—cynical girl, she can't dance, the usual thing—to add a twist or make an oblique point, Crenshaw captures a magic ur-adolescent innocence without acting the simp. It's as sly and well-meaning as his love of girls. Original grade: A minus. **A**

Marshall Crenshaw: *Field Day* (Warner Bros. '83). With Steve Lillywhite doctoring Crenshaw's efficient trio until it booms and echoes like cannons in a cathedral, the production doesn't prove Marshall isn't retro, though he isn't. It proves that no matter how genuine your commitment to the present, you can look pretty stupid adjusting to fashion—as usual, production brouhaha is a smokescreen for the betrayal of impossibly ecstatic expectation. Think of *Talking Heads 77, New York Dolls, Exile on Main Street,* or (for you oldsters) *Moby Grape,* all in fact a little botched aurally, all classics. Since the problem here isn't mess but overdefinition, a more precise comparison might be *Give 'Em Enough Rope,* but with a crucial difference: *The Clash* had better songs than its follow-up, while this follow-up has better songs than the debut. The man has grown up with a bang—though his relationships are suddenly touched with disaster, he vows to try till he dies. And you know what? Lillywhite's drum sound reinforces Crenshaw's surprising new depth—both his sense of doom and his will to overcome it. Original grade: A. **A+**

Marshall Crenshaw: *U.S. Remix* (Warner Bros. import EP '83). That's right, *import*—the long-rumored non-Lillywhite unhyped-drums version of three songs from *Field Day* plus a live Elvis (Presley) cover and a DOR remix of "One Day With You." In addition to balancing the instruments, the remixes add a few decorative flourishes, and as a Crenshaw fanatic I've already put them on a special tape. Did I get it free? You bet. What do you take me for—a collector?   **B+**

Marshall Crenshaw: *Downtown* (Warner Bros. '85). One reason his debunkers can't decide whether he's ripping off Buddy Holly (nice boy, wears glasses) or John Lennon (played him in *Beatlemania*, wears glasses) is that he loves the music of the '50s just the way '60s rockers did before they fell victim to hippie condescension—not as living tradition but as living music. With its played-not-produced intimation of process, *Downtown* gets this unpretentious message across—this is the kind of album whose negligible songs can open your set. It's well-crafted, fully imagined. The commitment and understated sexual urgency of Crenshaw's singing make it real. But it's filled with the quality retropop his debunkers always thought he wrote. Even the pointedly mature "The Distance Between" has a fairly arbitrary happy ending, which you'd figure from the way it stresses "When it gets right down to the bottom line." Two years ago, Crenshaw would have glanced right off that tired trope.   **A—**

Marshall Crenshaw: *Mary Jean & Nine Others* (Warner Bros. '87). Work too long toward a future that never arrives and you lose your hold on what comes naturally. Where once he soared, now he drags, and don't blame Don Dixon, whose hitbound modesty and popful soul match Marshall's fine. When your strongest song is about how nobody understands you, you're crying out for a spiritual lift no producer can provide.   **B**

Marshall Crenshaw: *Good Evening* (Warner Bros. '89). With three covers, two written-to-orders, three collaborations, and just two songs by Crenshaw working alone, it looks like his muse got bored waiting and departed for greener climes. But not since the debut has he sounded so at ease, so himself. The way he sings them, Richard Thompson's choleric "Valerie" and John Hiatt's lost "Someplace Where Love Can't Find Me" are kind, and Bobby Fuller's "Let Her Dance" turns into an I-love-music song no less awestruck (or womanstruck) than Crenshaw-Llanas-Neumann's "Radio Girl." Maybe his ex-

pectations have diminished so far that he's in that Zen zone where all effort is grace. Simple because he's simple—the second time around.   **A—**

Crosby, Stills, Nash & Young: *American Dream* (Atlantic '88). Forget the careerist compromise, dazed ennui, and soggy despair, and take this hustle for what it pretends to be and at some level is: four diehard hippies expressing themselves. Poor old guys can't leave politics alone—there's more ecology and militarism here than when they were figureheads of pop revolution, and though the rhetoric is predictable, the impulse has a woozy nobility. Not that that's ever been reason to pay Graham's ditties any mind, or that Stephen's steady-state egotism is redeemed by stray references to judges and changing the world. But while David's cocaine confessional makes "Almost Cut My Hair" seem self-abnegating, his "Nighttime for the Generals" sure beats Sting. And Neil lends musical muscle and gets commercial muscle back. So, not as horrible as you expected—nor good enough to give a third thought.   **C+**

Crossover Dreams (Elektra '86). Good flick or no, Rubén Blades is subject to the iron law of soundtracks just like crasser mortals, and though salsa atmospherics beat Dave Grusin by me, this one bogs down in reprises, living-room music, and the song Blades's character sells out with. Nor does featured vocalist Virgilio Marti prove legendary enough to compensate.   **B**

Crowded House: *Crowded House* (Capitol '86). Art-pop is like the dB's and XTC, when a fascination with craft spirals up and in until it turns into an aestheticist obsession. Split Enz was an art-rock band gone pop—sillier, crasser, more full of itself—and Neil Finn's California-based trio dispenses only with the silly. Hooks you can buy anywhere these days, and for directness you might as well apply straight to Bruce Hornsby—beyond the occasional hint of guitar anarchy, this is product for sure.   **C+**

Crowded House: *Temple of Low Men* (Capitol '88). Problem's not that philistine tastemakers are quashing Neil Finn's hit-debut blues, but that Finn has neglected the only thing he has to offer the world: perky hooks. Programmers don't care what he's brooding about because nobody else does. Plenty of popsters have managed to stir up interest in their petty anxieties. Be thankful there isn't one more.   **C**

Crucial Reggae Driven by Sly & Robbie (Mango '82). The second Taxi compilation broadens its base by including other producers' JA hits—with Dunbar & Shakespeare on groove, of course. But it's not enough. Great pop is a tricky commodity, and this isn't quite tricky enough to make up for received melodies and competent-plus vocals—not even in the groove.   **B+**

Julee Cruise: *Floating Into the Night* (Warner Bros. '89). This new age chantoozy is no mushmelon: her sentimental schlock and quasi-classical quietude are at the forefront of the latest hip convolutions. And when admirers claim she sounds best in a dark room at three in the morning, I wonder whether she puts them to sleep too.   **B−**

The Cucumbers: *The Cucumbers* (Fake Doom EP '83). "My Boyfriend" is a girl-group masterstroke for a feminist age. It revitalizes the notion of cute, and might actually hit if there were actual top forty anymore. In its way, so's "Susy's Getting Married," in which Deena Shoshkes panics at the thought of her girlfriend's desertion, defeat, or coming of age. In their way, so are the self-explanatory "Go Ahead and Do It" and "Snap Out of It."   **A−**

The Cucumbers: *Who Betrays Me . . . And Other Happier Songs* (Fake Doom '85). I used to assume they were just a good little band who'd latched onto a great little song, but while their new white-funk rhythms are superfluous and none of the tunes is "My Boyfriend," I'm beginning to think they could go national. Depends on how the world takes to Deena Shoshkes. She makes some sophisticates cringe, but the more I hear of her vivid sweetness the more sexy and unprecedented it seems. Time: 26:04.   **B+**

The Cucumbers: *The Cucumbers* (Profile '87). Shit-rockers will find this arch, flimsy, even (if they have the guts to come out with it) commercial, and in fact it's all three, and all three are virtues. Say the music's subtext is the vigor, intensity, even (thank you Horatio Alger) pluck that co-exist with what few have the guts to label feminine weakness any more—that ingratiating flirtatiousness some women get over on. As for the texts, try holding babies, sharing showers, you don't own me, I love you madly anyway, and the best song ever written about gentrification or Hoboken.   **A−**

The Cult: *Electric* (Sire '87). Rick Rubin meets the doom fops of the former Southern Death Cult and concocts the metal dreams are made of—Zep for our time, supposedly. One reason it's a great joke is that in 2087 almost nobody will be able to tell it from the real thing. The other reason it's a great joke is that right now almost anybody can. Direct comparison reveals that Jimmy Page's thunderclap riffs, Robert Plant's banshee yowls, and John Bonham's ka-boom ka-boom are just as hard to replicate as you thought they were. I hear Steppenwolf (an unconvincing "Born To Be Wild"), Cream ("Tales of Brave Ulysses" as "Aphrodisiac Jacket"), and Aerosmith—fop but no fool, Ian Astbury apes Steve Tyler rather than the unapproachable Plant. I also hear lots of Zep simplified—no sagas, no tempo shifts, no blues. Inspirational Verse: "Zany antics of a beat generation / In their wild search for kicks."   **B+**

The Cult: *Sonic Temple* (Sire '89). Having risen from cultdom as a joke metal band metal fans were too dumb to get, they transmute into a dumb metal band. Dumb was the easy part.   **B−**

Culture: *Two Sevens Clash* (Shanachie '87). Previously U.S.-available only as an import if at all, this even more than early Spear is the wellspring of the roots apocalypse that detonated the lion's share of great late reggae. Imagine a man from the hills sitting on a bus in Kingston and possessed by a vision: 1977, the year of the beast, the two sevens come down in all their numerological fury. No wonder every catchphrase sounds like God's word: this is where the Black Starliner and calling Rastafari became the moon-June-spoon of a music industry. The melodies are indelible, the rhythms early Drumbar, the ululations Winston Rodney gone all childlike and lyrical, at least seven tracks absolute classics. One of the ten best reggae albums ever made, says Shanachie's Randall Grass, but he has to watch his credibility. Bob Marley aside, it's the best, and I've been putting Bob Marley aside for it since 1977.   **A+**

Culture: *Culture at Work* (Shanachie '87). No simple purist, Joseph Hill rings generic changes on the roots he defined a decade ago; only "Worried" is touched immutably by Jah. They are changes, though, and they do ring. He may rework conventions from "Money Girl" to "Dance Hall Style," but he's full of unexpected pleasures as both singer and lyricist—amused grunts, intuitive tropes. And if JA's finest studio rats aren't touched by Jah here, they must be touched by Joseph Hill.   **A—**

Culture: *Cumbolo* (Shanachie '89). A decade after it was revealed to Jah's chosen, this one takes a while to connect. It's less archetypal than *Two Sevens Clash*— more general in folk hymns like "Poor Jah People" and "Natty Never Get Weary," more specific in conversational complaints like "Pay Day" and "Innocent Blood" ("One year after slavery / The people were all suffering from smallpox"). Once you have ears to hear, though, you got roots rockers paradise, all strictures sundered by studio musicians who angle into the formula more or less at will—chattering underneath "Poor Jah People," or adding the trombone glissando that sometimes hooks the chorus of "Natty Dread Naw Run" and sometimes doesn't.   **A—**

Culture: *Good Things* (RAS '89). After a ten-year layoff they have a right to simultaneous albums, but not simultaneous genre exercises. The overriding theme befits the layoff—they feel beset by all these *kids* who have strayed from the right path. "Cousin Rude Boy" and "Youthman Move" are fearful and imploring, so alienated that they're a tad less ordinary than you'd figure, while the title tune is posi-

tively avuncular—in one of the most unmillenarian sentiments ever uttered by a Rasta, it urges youth to enjoy electric lights and fax machines while they're still around. "Psalm of Bob Marley" has a great tune.   **B**

Culture: *Nuff Crisis!* (Shanachie '89). Even more generic because it's less obsessive, this tour of reggae cliches (titles include "Peace, Love and Harmony" and "Jah Rastafari") makes up for it—with folkloric tropes (titles also include "Frying Pan" and "Bang Belly Baby"), the Roots Radics, and an edge of intensity. "Crack in New York," about Manley's war on ganja, almost gloats. Inspirational Cackle: "Even professionals get spoiled by it too (hah!)."   **B+**

Culture Club: *Kissing To Be Clever* (Epic/Virgin '82). A lot of new English bands I wish were even worse than they are—every time Haircut 100 or Depeche Mode finds a riff or a groove it means they may last longer than the fifteen months allotted by the march of fashion. This new English band I wish were better, because for all their fashionability I think their hearts are in the right place—they look so weird because that's the way they feel. They do come up with catchy tunes, too. But their bland Caribbean rhythms move no muscles, and their confrontations with racial issues are rarely more than a phrase deep.   **B**

Culture Club: *Colour by Numbers* (Epic '83). Boy George really doesn't sound like Smokey Robinson, you know—not the way Frankie Miller sounds like Otis Redding, not even the way John Cougar sounds like Bruce Springsteen. If he did, he could probably put this tuneful collection all the way over—Smokey's spiritual gravity has redeemed some pretty lightweight lyrics, so his sensual specificity might just salvage some vague ones. As it is, George's warm, well-meaning, slightly clumsy croon signifies most effectively when it has the least to say—when it's most purely a medium for his warm, well-meaning, slightly clumsy self. Just like Helen Terry, who packs the voice of Merry Clayton into the body of Gertrude Stein, his real aim in life is to reenact the story of the ugly duckling—and to radiate the kind of extreme tolerance that's so often engendered by extreme sexual ambiguity. **B+**

Culture Club: *Waking Up With the House on Fire* (Epic '84). Since I had even less use for the dismissive because-he-wears-dresses theory than for the ridiculous new-Smokey analysis, I could never figure out this cutie-pie's means of commercial propulsion, but I know why he's having trouble staying up there: because he wears dresses. Given the discernible leftward shift in his soft focus, led by a catchy, censored single, this calls for concerted protest—which might be easier to whip up if the latest album weren't part three of more-of-the-same. **B**

Culture Club: *From Luxury to Heartache* (Virgin/Epic '86). For once the title trip sounds like tragedy rather than just desserts. Not a musical tragedy, though suddenly the music bores both dispirited artiste and disaffected audience. As always, it's the artiste himself I care about—which is why I have no doubt he was a true star. **C**

Culture Club: *This Time: The First Four Years—Twelve Worldwide Hits* (Epic/Virgin '87). Stephen Holden thinks kids liked Boy George's singing more than I did because he evoked not a soul man but a synthesizer. Right: a synthesizer who wants to be your friend. His music is too nice to withstand much critical scrutiny, which means he's best when he puts a vaguely dishy edge on his female-identified pansexual humanitarianism: "Karma Chameleon," "Church of the Poison Mind," "Black Money." And the topper is "The War Song," which contributed more conspicuously to his U.S. downfall than mere heroin abuse. "War is stupid / And people are stupid"—now is that nice? **B+**

The Cure: *Boys Don't Cry* (PVC '80). The sound is dry postpunk, with touches of Wire's spare, arty melodicism, more *Pink Flag* than *154*. Never pretty, it's treated with a properly mnemonic pop overlay—scan the titles and you'll recall a phrase from all but a few of these thirteen songs. Intelligent phrases they are, too. Yet what are we to think of a band whose best song

is based on Albert Camus's *The Stranger,* a book that was holy writ for collegiate existentialists before Robert Smith was even born? The last thing we need is collegiate existentialism nostalgia. **B+**

The Cure: *Pornography* (A&M '82). "In books / And films / And in life / And in heaven / The sound of slaughter / As your body turns . . ."—no, I can't go on. I mean, why so glum, chum? Cheer up; look on the bright side. You got your contract, right? And your synthesizers, bet you'll have fun with them. Believe me, kid, it will pass. **C**

The Cure: *The Head on the Door* (Elektra '85). In the wiggy abstraction of his self-regard, Robert Smith has evolved into a Brit art-pop archetype. Eccentric though his songs are, they offer nothing arresting in the way of imagery ("like a baby screams" and "it's so smooth it even feels like skin," which latter is admittedly pretty good, are as meaty as it gets), much less character or incident. They're not really observed—it's more like they're experienced at a distance. Yet they're not dreamlike, though while he's at it he does report on his dreams—it's more like he doesn't know the difference between loneliness, solipsism, and satori, with lots of stuff about loved ones (girlfriends, I mean) who one way or another aren't there, or real, or something. His characteristic vocal technique is the unacknowledged sob. Yet his music, which on this album runs from New Order rip and electrodisco pseudo-strings to guitar sounds of many lands, isn't rendered any more normal by its exceedingly skillful deployment. And his originality is winning—he's clearly not just intelligent but hyperaware, at home in his alienation, and hence hero, even sex symbol, to a generation. Or at least its arty, collegiate market share. **B**

The Cure: *Standing on a Beach: The Singles* (Elektra '86). Caught in his least lugubrious moments, Robert Smith stands revealed as a guy who gets a lot of skin because he believes he can live without it. He just won't play the "stupid game" that hooks the definitive "Let's Go to Bed," with its rotating I-don't-if-you-don't challenges—care, feel, want it, say it, and of course play it (and now let's go to bed, it's getting late). Guys who don't make passes because they wear glasses hate him for this, as do guys who don't get laid despite their muscular bods and heads. Above the fray, I think he's kind of amusing myself—a real cool type.   **B+**

The Cure: *Kiss Me Kiss Me Kiss Me* (Elektra '87). Samey samey samey is the strategy—repeat repeat repeat repeat the same four-bar theme for sixteen, twenty-four, forty-eight, sixty-four bars before Robert Smith starts to whine, wail, warble, work. Because Smith hasn't veered this far pop since he was a boy, most of the themes stick with you, and in a few cases—my pick is "Just Like Heaven," which gets off to a relatively quick start—his romantic vagaries have universal potential. But especially over a double album, the strategy gets pretty tedious unless Smith happens to be whining, wailing, warbling, or working to you.   **B**

The Cure: *Disintegration* (Elektra '89). With the transmutation of junk a species of junk itself, an evasion available to any charlatan or nincompoop, it's tempting to ignore this patent arena move altogether. But by pumping his bad faith and bad relationship into depressing moderato playloud keyb anthems far more tedious than his endless vamps, Robert Smith does actually confront a life contradiction. Not the splintered relationship, needless to say, although the title tune is a suitably grotesque breakup song among unsuitably grotesque breakup songs. As with so many stars, even "private" ones who make a big deal of their "integrity," Smith's demon lover is his audience, now somehow swollen well beyond his ability to comprehend, much less control. Hence the huge scale of these gothic cliches. And watch out, you mass, 'cause if you don't accept this propitiation he just may start contemplating suicide again. Or take his money and go home.   **C+**

Cutting Crew: *Broadcast* (Virgin '87). Hip punky look, hip-hop name, superhip label (and airline), pop dreck. The only good Brit is a good Brit.   **C−**

Dag Nasty: *Field Day* (Giant '88). D.C. posthardcore postboys with an ex-Descendent on bass, their apostate pop is like *Milo Goes to College* only more expansive. Concise and propulsive the way hardcore's supposed to be, the music could carry any old lyrics half the time, but that's not necessary—these descriptions and accounts of their growing store of experience are no less metaphoric for their factual aura, and remind us that most postboys understand their own troubles better than they do the world's. Vide "Typical (Typical Youth)": "Now that it's gone, just admit it to yourself / It was nothing special, no more special than yourself." **A—**

Dancehall Stylee: The Best of Reggae Dancehall Music Vol. 1 (Profile '89). As JA post-toasting evolves from change-of-pace to staple, as disco habitues learn to perceive its marginal distinctions, tolerate its generic repetitions, and crave its pulse, the style becomes less accessible to simple curiosity-seekers like yours truly. I'm sure every song on this assiduous compilation was a special favorite in context, and I appreciate all the little touches—the late-breaking piano hook on "This Feeling Inside," the lilting Sunday School promise of "Prophecy," the multiple interjections of "Nah Go Switch," the aggressively incredulous "Wha-at's" of "Bun and Cheese" and then "Life," the squeaky echo of "Life." But even at that the closing "Watch a Them" and for that matter

"Nah Go Switch" seem too damn marginal in their distinction. And excepting three or four—Tiger's "Ram Dance Hall" (he roars), Gregory Peck's "Oversized Mumpie" (blue patois), and Derrick Parker's "Cool It Off" (sounds like "coup d'etat"), with Shelly Thunder's "Kuff" a dark horse—none stand much chance of becoming special favorites of mine. Ordinary favorites, maybe. **A—**

Dance Traxx (Atlantic '86). Disco not only lives but goes pop, just like all those bizzers who blew their collateral on it years ago dreamed it would. Not C-Bank or Mantronix—hardcore dance acts today are cult gods just like Barabbas and Don Ray last time. But here on these two discs, cunningly remixed and segued as is only mete, you get the only Phil Collins Isleys rip you need own, the only Laura Branigan Donna Summer rip you need own, and the only Yes Art of Noise rip you need own. Plus the compleat Shannon in two parts. And now that I've clued you in just promise me this—if you like the Steve Arrington you'll take a flier on the album. **A—**

Dana Dane: *Dana Dane With Fame* (Profile '87). Dissing women is nothing. Any fool can dis women, educated fools included. Where you have to hand it to the New York City school system is the way it took a moderately talented kid from the projects and taught him to be this snide this fast. Serves him well in the business world, of course—nothing threatening about snide, goes with Hurby Luv Bug's beats. But there are less retrograde (and funnier) ways for rap to go pop. I'll take the Fat Boys' vaudeville over Dane's in a minute. Also Salt-n-Pepa's.   **C+**

The Charlie Daniels Band: *A Decade of Hits* (Epic '84). "Uneasy Rider" is still perfect—a tall tale of a new outlaw, peace-loving but not a damn fool about it, grabbing a redneck by the symbolic short hair. But a year later "The South's Gonna Do It" sang the praises of long-haired rednecks, and he never looked back. A safer tall tale, the predictable "Devil Went Down to Georgia," put him back on the singles charts in 1979, and in 1980 the Russkie-baiting "America" proved what the self-reliant individualism of a "Long Haired Country Boy" was good for. Already pushing fifty, he's just a Southerner of a certain generation. Sometimes he's a lot of fun. If he sang as good as Merle Haggard we might even forgive his jingoism.   **B**

Danny and Dusty: *The Lost Weekend* (A&M '85). Danny is Green on Red's Dan Stuart, a likable fool, Dusty the Dream Syndicate's Steve Wynn, a pretentious wise guy, and with the help of some L.A. drinking buddies they've come up with an album less ambitious and more satisfying than any either band has produced on its own. It makes a concept of the loser mythology that's such a big deal in L.A., and I was prepared to hate it—I've never believed that "we've all gotta go down." But the songs are relaxed, unassuming, and funny. I guess if the Heartbreakers could make heroin addiction sound like a good time, these guys have a right to do the same for alcoholism—they certainly have tradition behind them.   **B+**

Terence Trent D'Arby: *Introducing the Hardline According to Terence Trent D'Arby* (Columbia '87). He can sing sweet or gritty, write sweet, gritty, or pretentious. His rhythms and arrangements show a sense of roots and a sense of style. He's got black consciousness and pop ambition. Which sums up why everybody

wants this record to achieve what it promises. Summing up what it does achieve is the best cut, a Smokey Robinson song—which you'll think is his own until you check the fine print.   **B+**

Terence Trent D'Arby: *Neither Fish Nor Flesh* (Columbia '89). The tortured imagery and spacy affectations of the first five minutes had me regretting my professional obligation to listen to it again. So believe me, I don't love this record for its ambition—I love it for its achievement, which turns out to include the first five minutes. D'Arby's worst lines are so bad they tempt you to believe he'll never straighten out, but in fact there are three or four superb lyrics here, led by "Billy Don't Fall," humbly literal in the face of difference and death. And even at its most forced the music proves D'Arby a master of the black spectrum from the trad r&b of "I'll Be Alright" to the reconstructed Prince-funk of "This Side of Love"—even though psychedelic pop is just as much the album's category. Let his pretensions put you off, and believe me, you'll be missing something.   **A−**

David & David: *Boomtown* (A&M '86). The upscale mixes and faux-soul exaggerations of generic AOR are such a turnoff that I wouldn't have played this twice if it hadn't been produced by Davitt Sigerson, who's made a career of justifying such mannerisms as critic and artist. Turns out it's got the goods technically—songs, hooks, subtle little touches. And not only do these two studio rats know the follies of their chosen profession, they don't romanticize them much—or else they romanticize them effectively, which is even rarer. Put it all together and maybe you end up with another piece of beautiful-loser mythology. But somehow this fallacy is acceptable in two guys you've actually never heard of, especially two guys with the guts (and interest) to apply their craft to at least one revolutionary fantasy. Sometimes winners are beautiful, too.   **A−**

Morris Day: *Color of Success* (Warner Bros. '86). Now that he's a movie star, Morris proposes to cover his flank and go straight. After all, the Time's comically cocksure overstatement was just a way to get the music noticed, and now that he's a household name his sidelong synthbeats will pull in the customers all by themselves. He thinks. I think people will demand beats and comedy both. We shall see.   **B**−

Peter Dayton: *Love at 1st Sight* (Shoo-Bop EP '81). On the B, former La Peste vocalist Dayton and aspiring producer Ric Ocasek combine for an OK title tune and a sub-OK instrumental. On the A, they concoct the Cars-sexy "Skintite" and the Velvets-catchy "Stuck on the Same Refrain." Which I'm stuck on. Original grade: B plus.   **B**

The dB's: *Stands for Decibels* (Albion import '81). En Why's own Southern Anglophiles keep their potential for Beatley let-loose and Box Topsy get-down in such close check that their compulsive studiocraft radiates a mad joy all its own. This is pop at its tensest—the precise harmonies, broken rhythms, and Byrdsy zoom effects are drawn so tight they make the expertly rendered romantic ups and downs of the songs sound intense and earned. [Later on I.R.S.]   **A**−
The dB's: *Repercussion* (Albion import '81). A man of simple tastes, I'm thrown into a tizzy when I find myself uninterested in playing an album comprising twelve tunes I can hum after a dozen plays. I think it's because they're so prepossessing they short-circuit my simple aesthetic sense. I was thrown off for weeks, to take one example, by the soul horns that open the lead cut. They sounded fussy. Soul horns. On a pop record. Overreaching. [Later on I.R.S.]   **B**+
The dB's: *Like This* (Bearsville '84). This is a different, less ambitious band without Chris Stamey, whose taste for the uncanny is missed when the lyrics wind down into the enigmatic (nice word for vague, unrealized, etc.) stuff on side two. But Chris Butler's eight-cylinder production suits the straightforward thrust of Peter Holsapple's young-adult love songs, and melodies have never been their problem. A piece of Inspirational Verse, then: "I can understand / Why you want a better man / But

why do you wanna make him out of me?" And one request: How about a whole album that kicks like "A Spy in the House of Love"?   **A**−
The dB's: *The Sound of Music* (I.R.S. '87). Yeah it rocks, but when a pop group leaves it at that they're no better than their latest song, and when their sole remaining songwriter is still dissecting serial monogamy as he says bye to thirty, chances are his latest song doesn't even interest him all that much. With Chris Stamey they really had a sound. And with Chris Butler they really had a groove.   **B**

Fats Deacon: *Buzzardhead* (Ames Griffin EP '83). Proving that not all black rock-and-rollers have forgotten Chuck Berry, or maybe that not all black musicians have forgotten rock and roll, young Fats shouts out his claim. Maybe "Stagger Lee" is the only completely convincing song on the record, but how many rock-and-rollers can do Stack convincingly any more?   **B**

Dead Kennedys: *Fresh Fruit for Rotting Vegetables* (I.R.S. '80). I do want there to be more punk rock—I do, I do. I do want there to be more left-wing new wave—really. By Americans—I swear it. But not by a would-be out-of-work actor with Tiny Tim vibrato who spent the first half of the '70s concocting "rock cabaret." Admittedly, I'm guessing, but I'm also being kind—it sounds like Jello Biafra discovered the Stooges in 1977.   **C**+
Dead Kennedys: *In God We Trust, Inc.* (Faulty Products EP '81). "Moral Majority," which proceeds directly from the Mickey Mouse club theme to a rousing verse prominently featuring the words "Blow it out your ass," and the long-awaited "Nazi Punks Fuck Off" ("you'll be the first to go") are their best songs or whatever since they attacked California and Cambodia. Both are available on a single. Forgo the documentary value of "Kepone Factory" 's false start ("Itstooslow") and the intensely appropriate "Hyperactive Child." Think small.   **B**−

The Dead Milkmen: *Big Lizard in My Backyard* (Fever '85). Their jokes can be obvious ("Tiny Town") or tasteless

("Takin' Retards to the Zoo") or backbitingly sophomoric ("Bitchin' Camaro") as well as wildly unexpected—up with swordfish, down with sole, fuck Charles Nelson Riley. Either way, they're the young snots of the year hands down, and either way they'll make you laugh. Also, when you don't feel like listening to the words, their smart fringe hardcore will keep those nineteen tracks coming.   **A—**

The Dead Milkmen: *Eat Your Paisley* (Restless '86). I was delighted that these hostile but not asocial fellows hadn't taken to agonizing over their girlfriends, assuming they have any—they were playing the songs for laffs just like on the debut. Then I noticed that except for "Beach Party Vietnam" I wasn't laffing (or even chuckling), only smiling encouragingly now and then. Between the right attitude and the right stuff falls the lead balloon.   **B—**

The Dead Milkmen: *Bucky Fellini* (Enigma '87). Just like Howard Stern says, it's tough being funny every time out, but at least they're in there pitching, hurling sophomoric knuckleballs at every freshman in sight. Though they've picked up some sarcasm at the feet of Camper Van, pop gothic remains their thing, from the '60s to Graceland to exploitation flicks to Anglodisco "art fags," an epithet I'm sure Mark Knopfler will find hilarious.   **B+**

The Dead Milkmen: *Beelzebubba* (Enigma '88). For a while there I thought they'd scored a comedy album worthy of their IQs—its forward motion makes them sound like kids again. But they're such shallow little doofuses that the jokes only stick when they're aimed at the right targets, always a subjective call. My special favorites blast punk rock and PBS—in a clever, whiny little way.   **B+**

The DeBarges: *The DeBarges* (Gordy '81). Four harmonizing siblings, and if you think Berry's been here before, you're a lot less than 80 percent right. For one thing, Berry's not calling the shots—they produce, they write, they even play (supposedly). Not too long on substance in those departments, I admit, but young adults who sing with the grace of children don't just get away with flight fantastic—when they fly as high and free as Bunny

(who's a girl) and Eldra (who isn't), it's their destiny.   **A—**

DeBarge: *All This Love* (Gordy '82). They came from nowhere with an airy debut that never touched ground or stopped coming, and nowhere is where it went. So this time they go against their own best instincts, bearing down on individual compositions rather than immersing themselves in sound. When they hit one—slow stuff like "All This Love" and "I Like It" is why the Lord blessed them—you can hear it breaking through and crossing over, always the Motown ideal. When they don't, all you hear is exquisitely cautious product. [Later with *In a Special Way* on one CD.]   **B+**

DeBarge: *In a Special Way* (Gordy '83). When first I fell in love with the austere lilt and and falsetto fantasy they've pinned to plastic here, I thought it was just that I'd finally outgrown the high-energy fixation that's always blocked my emotional access to falsetto ballads. So I went back to *Spinners* and *Blue Magic,* Philip Bailey and my man Russell Thompkins Jr., and indeed, they all struck a little deeper—but only, I soon realized, because the superior skill of these kids had opened me up. I know of no pop music more shameless in its pursuit of pure beauty—not emotional (much less intellectual) expression, just voices joining for their own sweet sake, with the subtle Latinized rhythms (like the close harmonies themselves) working to soften odd melodic shapes and strengthen the music's weave. High energy doesn't always manifest itself as speed and volume—sometimes it gets winnowed down to its essence. Original grade: A.   **A+**

DeBarge: *Rhythm of the Night* (Gordy '85). Eldra DeBarge's genius isn't especially with-it—uptempo arrangements do nothing for his outstretched melodies and chilly harmonies. But he and his countless siblings scored one hit after another off *In a Special Way,* which led to a traumatic tour with the unsinkable Luther Vandross when Eldra might have been working up new product. Hence this mishmash—a Richard Perry–produced soundtrack one-off, a Giorgio Moroder–produced soundtrack one-off, a 1981 ballad featuring Eldra and sister Bunny in their classic falsetto mode, four standard medium-fasts from C-list funk-popper Jay Graydon, and two uptempo numbers from Eldra, who seems to be getting a handle on the stuff. Pray the paranoia underlying his all-too-interesting "The Walls (Come Tumbling Down)" dissipates when he settles into the studio again.   **B+**

El DeBarge: *El DeBarge* (Gordy '86). Especially since Eldra, to honor the name his mama gave him, has shown something like genius as both writer and producer, the plethora of outside help is a double down. But though you can be sure this projected crossover is expected to produce a run of peppy crossover singles, starting with El's second straight meaningless movie theme, it has the flow of an album, even the personal stamp. This is provided not by what they're selling, the boyish clarity and indomitable sweetness of a voice a just God would have bestowed on a braver guy, but by the outside help, most of it sufficiently skillful and second-rate to mimic his rhythmic and melodic quirks. With lyrics adding hints of maturity to his customary show of naiveté and hooky beats fattened with the plush keybs of big-league pop, he almost passes as one more ingratiating opportunist. Original grade: B plus.   **B**

El DeBarge: *Gemini* (Motown '89). With his solo debut an old stiff, several lesser siblings convicted cocaine traffickers, and Uncle Berry passed on to his corporate reward, this is black pop on a beeline for the cutout bins, which I guess means it isn't really black *pop* at all. Just good black music, ancient to the future, all jumping rhythms and space-case melody, less catchy song than gorgeous sound. Can't say maturity's done him any good. But at least it hasn't killed him.   **B+**

The Decline of Western Civilization (Slash '81). Every big-name L.A. punk this side of Samoa gets soundtracked here. X are the great ones (buy their albums), Black Flag the good ones (keep an ear out for Greg Ginn's axe). After that come Fear, L.A.'s version of the Sic Fucks, tighter musically (big Van Halen fans) but less, er, subtle (spokesperson Lee Ving could be Don Rickles with a botched facelift). Then the

Circle Jerks, L.A.'s other version of the Sic Fucks (bet there's more). And in the pits three critics' bands: Catholic Discipline (somebody tell Claude Bessy zat zere is no such thing as French rock and roll), Alice Bag (Craig Lee, call your office), and the Germs (L. Bangs: "Bye, schmuck"). Not bad, but no fun. For docudrama I'll take *An Evening With Wild Man Fischer,* for social theory I'll take *Psychotic Reaction,* or even *Carburetor Dung,* and maybe you'd better just see the movie.   **B—**

Deep Purple: *Deep Purple: The Very Best of Deep Purple* (Warner Bros. '80). Cut the shit, keep them away from large auditoria, and what you end up with is surprisingly kick-ass: lifting one or two songs from half a dozen albums that have only pushy organist Jon Lord and dum-dum drummer Ian Paice in common, this rocks. With the predictable exceptions—solo here, bridge there, Lord's conservatory application "Child in Time" throughout—it's barely even pretentious. "Black Night" and "Woman From Tokyo" and of course "Highway Star" are as worthy of *Nuggets* as anything the Strangeloves ever recorded.   **B**

Def Jef: *Just a Poet With Soul* (Delicious Vinyl '89). Bronx-raised and moved to Cali, he rhymes hard and fast over pop-r&b samples and the straight JB funk they're rendering passe. Just ordinary enough to get overlooked, just good enough to deserve better, he leads the beat like it comes naturally, and writes so persuasively about loving to write that you know he'll be around.   **B+**

Def Leppard: *Pyromania* (Mercury '83). Fuckin' right there's a difference between new heavy metal and old heavy metal. The new stuff is about five silly beats-per-minute faster. And the new lead singers sound not only "free" and white, but also more or less twenty-one.   **C**

Def Leppard: *Hysteria* (Mercury '87). You know about the music, and if you don't think you'll like it you won't: impeccable pop metal of no discernible content, it will inspire active interest only in AOR programmers and the several million addicts of the genre. In short, it's product—but as product, significant, because it's product for the CD age. Stuck with over an hour of material after four years (after all, could twelve songs be any shorter?), they elected to put it all on one disc because as technocrats they instinctively conceive for formats that can accommodate an hour of music: cassettes, which now outsell vinyl discs, and CDs, which outdollar them. The cassette sound is a little too dim, as commercial cassette sound usually is, and though I sometimes find myself preferring the depth of the vinyl once I've turned my amp up to six or seven, the clarity of the CD gets more and more decisive as the needle approaches the outgroove. I mean, I have trouble perceiving these guys as human beings under ideal circumstances. Not docked a notch because at least they didn't pad it into a double.   **C**

Carmaig de Forest: *I Shall Be Released* (Good Foot '87). He's an acerbic miniaturist who knows words—just like one of his romantic antagonists, he's forever sharpening his clauses. He's got Alex Chilton on his side. A lot of smart guys will love him every time out. I think he proves that these days smart songwriters consider politics rather than romance the fun challenge, reserving my love for the shaggy-dog "Judas" and the self-explanatory "Crack's No Worse Than the Fascist Threat."   **B+**

Defunkt: *Thermonuclear Sweat* (Hannibal '82). At twenty-eight, Joseph Bowie comes on as spoiled and stunted as the most solipsistic hardcore teen, so it says worlds for the power of his rhythm section and the imagination of his guitarists that he can't ruin his own music. More Ornette than Contortions this time, he even shows off his good breeding by funkifying a Charlie Parker tune. On the other hand, his "For the Love of Money" sounds like slumming, especially from a guy who couldn't outsing Kenny Gamble in the shower.   **B+**

De La Soul: *3 Feet High and Rising* (Tommy Boy '89). An inevitable development in the class history of rap, they're new wave to Public Enemy's punk, and also "pop" rather than pop, as self-consciously cute and intricate as Shoes or Let's Active. Their music is maddeningly disjunct, and a few of the twenty-four-cuts-in-sixty-seven-minutes (too long for vinyl) are self-indulgent, arch. But their music is also radically unlike any rap you or anybody else has ever heard—inspirations include the Jarmels and a learn-it-yourself French record. And for all their kiddie consciousness, junk-culture arcana, and suburban in-jokes, they're in the new tradition—you can dance to them, which counts for plenty when disjunction is your problem.   **A—**

The Del Fuegos: *The Longest Day* (Slash '84). You want unpretentious? Will these boys give you unpretentious! And their *debut album* has more good songs on it than *The Best of the Standells*!   **B**

The Del Fuegos: *Boston, Mass.* (Slash '85). This is the story of Dan Zanes—his passion, his pain, his steadfast refusal to hire a synth player. Its real location is Anywhere, U.S.A. "I Still Want You" would make some garage band a nice slow one.   **B—**

The Del Fuegos: *Smoking in the Fields* (RCA '89). Bless my stars if it isn't clubland nostalgia—these gumsuckers have hung in long enough to pose as avatars of a great tradition that never was. "I've got the strangest feeling we can do it again," they announce, alluding to the halcyon days when real men danced to the Real Kids. Will teenaged radio programmers fall for it? If not, there's always the romantic "I'm Inside You."   **C+**

The Del-Lords: *Frontier Days* (EMI America '84). Unless you see a band week after week, you have to wait till the album to gauge the depth of their songwriting, and these nice guys do all right by the sounding. The melodies are pretty basic, but that was to be expected; what's important is that they stick. The lyrics go for Blasters-style populism and achieve it with fewer downhome details and more international perspective. And if there's less singing and playing here than four or five gigs made me hope, that just makes me hope that next time they'll go commercial enough to hire a real producer instead of nice guy Lou Whitney.   **A**–

The Del-Lords: *Johnny Comes Marching Home* (EMI America '86). By saving "Heaven" for Pat Benatar's producer they assure its standing as an unmatched distillation of rock and roll's utopian thrust. Elsewhere their politics are sentimental and misconceived, with the Pete Seeger reference the giveaway and the bad TV movie "Against My Will" the nadir. Despairing or hopeful, the love songs are more tough-minded. That's the way it is with rock and roll's utopian thrust. **B**+

The Del-Lords: *Based on a True Story* (Enigma '88). Their populist Americana expressed rather than subsumed by Neil Geraldo's hard-rock production, they can come on like the old Lower East Siders they are without sounding irrelevant. The most convincing songs show the populi the "beatnik world" of "The Cool and the Crazy"; the prettiest one allows as how they still dream of "Cheyenne" while they sit and watch TV. Last time the love songs were tough and the political statements soggy; this time the fast ones are tough-and-a-half and the slow ones soggy. Which adds up to progress, right?   **B**+

Depeche Mode: *Speak and Spell* (Sire '81). "New Life" is worthy of Eno at his most rhapsodically technopastoral, but most of this tuneful pap crosses Meco (without the humble functionalism), Gary Numan (without the devotion to surface), and Kraftwerk (without the humor—oh, definitely without the humor). You'd think after seventy-five years people would have seen through the futurist fallacy—an infatuation with machinery is the ultimate one-sided love affair. But then, this isn't futurism—they call it pop.   **C**+

Depeche Mode: *Catching Up With Depeche Mode* (Sire '85). Their second half-assed compilation in a year and a half finally gets it half right, putting a single sleeve around their most tuneful technotopia and death-fluff. Granted, it omits their only actual U.S. hit, "People Are People," already reprised to bait the dire *Some Great Reward,* baiting instead with the previously un-American *Everything*

Counts EP, which holds up indifferently in such select company, though the squishy "Fly on the Windscreen" bookends the blasphemous "Blasphemous Rumors" neatly enough. But the collection has a structure, proceeding chronologically from young technotopian romance to slightly older technodystopian despair. First they "Just Can't Get Enough," then they ponder "The Meaning of Love," then they doubt "Love in Itself," then they play "Master and Servant." The little girls understand.   **B**+

Depeche Mode: *Music for the Masses* (Sire '87). When Vince Clarke departed Yazward in 1982, Fashion-in-a-Hurry's commercial doom was presumed sealed, whereupon Martin Gore went ahead and proved how easy it is to write ditties once you're in a position to exploit them. It's not as if anybody can, but at this point in pop's progress potential supply far exceeds potential demand. Yet only rarely is the production process altogether mechanical. Gore can't create without venting his shallow morbidity, which happens to mesh with a historically inevitable strain of adolescent angst, and he takes himself seriously enough to have burdened albums with concepts and such. This time, however, the title announces his determination to give it up to his even shallower singer, David Gahan, who likes Gore's message because it's a good way to impress girls. Dark themes combine with light tunes until the very end of side two. Anybody with an interest in adolescent angst (adolescents included) can sob or giggle along as the case may be.   **B**+

The Descendents: *Milo Goes to College* (New Alliance '82). These fishermen don't kid around about what powers hardcore hyperdrive—not simply an unjust society, but also a battered psyche. When they're feeling bad, any kind of power—money, age, ass-man cool, the possession of a vagina—can set off their anarchic, patricidal, "homo"-baiting, gynephobic rage. But their bad feelings add poignant weight to the doomed vulnerability of the last four songs, which happen to be their hookiest— "Marriage" ("I want you to marry me"), "Hope" ("I'm not giving up"), "Bikeage"

("Don't be afraid, it's not too late") and—chillingly—"Jean Is Dead." And you thought there were no more concept albums. Time: 24:15. [Later on SST.]   **A—**

Descendents: *I Don't Want To Grow Up* (New Alliance '85). They "don't even know how to sing," they excoriate themselves as perverts for wanting sex, and when they fall in love they try to write Beatles songs. Chances are you'll find them awkward, but I'm tremendously encouraged that they can fall in love at all. Anyway, their Beatles songs are pretty catchy. Time: 28:56 [Later on SST.]   **B+**

The Descendents: *Bonus Fat* (New Alliance EP '85). Adding two forgettable, surprisingly poppish pre-Milo songs and the notable post-Milo "Global Probing" to their punk classic, the 1981 seven-inch *Fat E.P.* Which consists of the gluttonous fifteen-second "I Like Food" ("Juicy burgers, greasy fries / Turkey legs and raw fish eyes / Teenage girls with ketchup too"), the contemptuous thirty-six-second "My Dad Sucks" ("It's value judgment time again"), the pugnacious 1:35-minute "Hey Hey" ("If you think that everything's OK / Then go home and lock your brains away"), and my second fave, a virtual miniopera at 2:09, "Mr. Bass," pronounced to rhyme with "ass," because it's about a scaly creature, not a musical instrument, as befits rock-and-rollers who work as fishermen. And topping it all off is their masterpiece, "Weinerschnitzel," eleven seconds of dialogue augmented by two guitar blams. All of the fifty or so listeners I've subjected to it have had the same basic response: "Play it again, willya?" So buy it again, willya? The sound's better. [Later on SST.]   **A—**

Desperate Teenage Lovedolls (Gasatanka '84). Wish I could report that these thirteen posthardcore toons for amateur Super-8 rock and roll flick constitute a stronger soundtrack than anything the youth marketers over in the pricier part of Hollywood have commissioned. Unfortunately, it sounds like another Rodney Bingenheimer anthology.   **C+**

Jimmy Destri: *Heart on a Wall* (Chrysalis '82). Blondie's keyb man has always been a more adaptable songwriter than Bill Wyman or John Entwistle, but like Jerry Harrison he's a less engaging singer than either, which is going some, and in addition he lacks Harrison's flair as an arranger. Top track: quasi-instrumental starring Chris Stein.   **C**

Detox: *Detox* (Flipside '85). Imagine a hardcore band who open with a cretin hoedown entitled "No Reggae in Russia" and you'll get some idea of their satiric range. And limitations. Inspirational Dialogue, from "I Hate the French": "Can you translate th-this?"   **B+**

William DeVaughn: *Figures Can't Calculate* (TEC '80). This singing (and writing) sewer designer scored three anachronistically soulish hits in 1974, then dropped from sight. Here he resurfaces with an anachronistically soulish (and anachronistically disco-ish) "new version" of his biggie, "Be Thankful for What You've Got." And covers "You Send Me" as Curtis Mayfield might were Curtis still so deep. And writes some more.   **B**

Devo: *Freedom of Choice* (Warner Bros. '80). Hey now, don't blame me—I insulted them every chance I got back when your roommate still thought they might be Important. But now that that's taken care of itself we can all afford to giggle. Robot satire indeed—if they ever teach a rhythm box to get funky, a Mothersbaugh will be there to plug it in.   **B+**

Devo: *Devo Live* (Warner Bros. EP '81). Just what you've always wanted—live robots, and overpriced ones at that. Who prove their vitality by slopping around a little. Me, I think their precision is the joke and the joke is their all.   **C—**

Devo: *New Traditionalists* (Warner Bros. '81). Filler plus three major songs, each of which gets an explanatory video in concert, which with these art-school ciphers is a comfort. In "Through Being Cool," a sexually and racially integrated platoon of "young alien types" do in fact "eliminate the ninnies and the twits," though rather than the bone-crunching tactics the lyric prescribes they utilize a ray gun that reduces two discoids to a Clyfford Still blur, transforms three joggers into old people, and blows two old people away. In "Love Without Anger" two humans in chicken suits bill and coo after fighting over pecking order. And in "Beautiful World" the mild closing disclaimer "But not for me" is amplified by a panoply of newsreel horrors. None of which will satisfy the ninnies and twits who think war toys and visual aids are evil by definition. So zap'em.   **B**

Devo: *Oh, No! It's Devo* (Warner Bros. '82). Because their secret contempt for their cult receded once the cult gathered mass, moral impassivity that once seemed like a misanthropic cop-out (or worse) now has the feel of Brechtian strategy. They've never sounded wimpier, but they've never sounded catchier either, and with this band wimpiness has a comic purpose. "Time Out for Fun" is recommended as both text and music to leisure theorists who reject electropop as a matter of humanistic principle. Original grade: A minus.   **B+**

Devo: *Shout* (Warner Bros. '84). Marking time (actually, a computer marks it for them), they create the rock—no, new wave—equivalent of baseball's "Play me or trade me." I played it. Now I'm trading it.   **C**

Devo: *Total Devo* (Enigma '88). This package of "11 digital cartoons" is improved by the balloons, which distract momentarily from its retro-electro sheen. In case you were wondering (hadn't given it much thought lately myself), the Devo Philosophy has a lot in common with the Playboy Philosophy—as the Bard put it, to thine own self be true. Note quotes from John Lennon, Elvis Presley, and T.S. Eliot—quick, before the retro-electro comes round again.   **C+**

Howard Devoto: *Jerky Versions of the Dream* (I.R.S. '83). In which the nastiest wimp since Ron Mael makes his pop move, sometimes diverting and never positively offensive. That includes the title—Howard knows his audience. Granted, *Dreamy Versions of the Jerk* would have been more to the point, but accuracy has never been Howard's forte.   **C+**

Dexy's Midnight Runners: See Kevin Rowland.

DFX2: *Emotion* (MCA EP '83). From a label that has never before issued an EP, a San Diego quartet who sound like the Stones—despite hints of Lou and Ig, the *Some Girls* Stones, irreverently bluesy as personal style and personal commitment, an odd and apt effect in a teenaged band for whom *Now!* and even *Exile* are artifacts. Less ironic, and funnier, than the originals, so that titles like "Emotion" and "No Dough" mean what they say, they're rock-is-lifers—not immune to sexism, with all the usual retrograde attitudes. And believe it or not they do it do it do it do it, which makes the attitudes seem somehow worthwhile, just like always. Let's hope they grow up right.   **A**

Sona Diabate & M'mah Sylla: *Sahel* (Triple Earth import '88). Two singers from the storied policewomen's band Les Amazones de Guinée join a guitarist-marimbist and a flutist-saxophonist in Paris, where everybody plays folk music once removed. Falsetto intensifies the high-end voices and the flute is very prominent, so that the intrusions of saxophone and sometimes even guitar have the effect of male voices demanding confidently to be heard. Secure in their realm, the women continue to muse or chatter or make a joyful noise.   **B+**

Zani Diabate & the Super Djata Band: *Zani Diabate & the Super Djata Band* (Mango '88). What jumps out of the speakers isn't the Malian Jimi of the jacket copy but a groove harsher than Zaire's and more ferocious than Senegal's. There's lots of cheesy keyb in the mix; full-repeat call-and-response and mullah harangues stir up the hectic mood. It's on top of all this that you get the guitar, which sings and declaims and shouts out loud instead of just chiming or chattering. I find the hottest soukous relaxing. I put this on to wake up.   **A—**

A Diamond Hidden in the Mouth of a Corpse (Giorno Poetry Systems '85). I've always felt guilty about ignoring Giorno's self-promotions, which combine name avant-rockers with name artist-artists, so when this one led off with Hüsker Dü and David Jo I listened forthwith. And found myself returning—to hear Giorno and his buddy Bill Burroughs. The bait is perfectly okay. But compilations are usually less than the sum of their parts anyway, and I don't get the feeling Giorno's rock allies save their best songs for him. Giorno himself, on the other hand, is making a pop move. And Burroughs knows he's the star of both shows.   **B**

Diblo: Super Soukous (Shanachie '89). Melding what's finest about the original into a conceptual variant—like *Sweetheart of the Rodeo* turned *Gilded Palace of Sin,* say, or the Time turned Jam & Lewis—this solo debut (later albums are available under the band name Loketo) is the best kind of spin-off. Though it's fronted by soft-sung Aurlus Mabele, Kanda Bongo's man Diblo Dibala dominates—rolling out sweetly, sheerly, endlessly, piling signature riff on signature riff, his guitar lines and interludes lift and lyricize the boss's stripped-down Afrodisco. Thematically, he's traditional Afropop. Spiritually, he has more going for him.   **A—**

Hazel Dickens: Hard Hitting Songs for Hard Hit People (Rounder '80). Dickens's brother died of black lung, an irrefutable reason to turn protest singer, and her vocals evoke Appalachia with a twangy, unadorned directness that must be the envy of Si Kahn, whom she covers. A natural feminist, too—try "Crumbs From Your Table" or the agonizing "Lost Patterns." But unlike Kahn she has trouble coming up with touches like Buddy Spicher's fiddle on "Busted" or the refrain of her own "West Virginia My Home"—music that makes you want to commit the message to memory.   **B+**

The Dickies: Great Dictations: The Definitive Dickies Collection (A&M '89). Parody punks long dismissed as no-laff ninnies even in L.A., they're rehabilitating their reputations as their accounting careers fall through, with this '78–'80 compilation (in tandem with current product to remain nameless) the spearhead. So OK, sometimes they actually were funny—I like their Simon & Garfunkel knockoff better than the Coolies'. I promise I'll play them on request if they promise I never have to think about them again.   **B—**

The Dictators: The Dictators Live: Fuck 'Em if They Can't Take a Joke (ROIR cassette '81). Twelve toons, which because they include three new originals and two new covers don't even constitute a half-assed best-of. As annotator Borneo Jimmy points out, "Rock and Roll Made a Man Out of Me" is for these boys an admission of defeat. To dig their stoopid smarts you'll have to seek out *Go Girl Crazy,* cut before they turned into grown-up buffoons with pro-am chops, and funnier without stage patter than this is with.   **B—**

Dinosaur Jr.:   You're Living All Over Me (SST '87). The singer implores in a childish whining drawl while dramatic paradiddles and sculpted streams of molten garage guitar enact one more nostalgic reconciliation with AOR metal. But this one isn't on metal's terms (too winsome), or AOR's either (what they arrange is sloppiness). All these growing malcontents want is a little structure and meaning in their lives. Is that so much to ask?   **B+**

Dire Straits: Making Movies (Warner Bros. '80). If any up-and-coming rock-and-roller aspires to auteur status it's Mark Knopfler, and among those with a taste for his rather corny plots (Romeo and Juliet, fancy that) this establishes his claim. Me, I note that his third album closes with his second gay-baiting song, and that I wasn't surprised. Better he should work on somebody else's stories—his guitar has emerged from Eric Clapton's shadow into a jazzy rock that muscles right past Larry Carlton and ilk. Steely Straits, anyone? Or would that be Dire Dan? Original grade: B minus.   **C+**

Dire Straits: Love Over Gold (Warner Bros. '82). I admit that Mark Knopfler is a classy enough guitarist and producer to entice me into his nostalgic obsessions: at its best "Telegraph Road" sounds like supernal Mark-Almond, and the cheesy organ on "Industrial Disease" betrays a sense of humor. But the portentous arrangements on the other three cuts (right, that makes five, mean length 8:24) suggest nothing so much as ELP with blues roots. And Knopfler's sarcastic impression of a Harley Street M.D. on the very same "Industrial Disease" leaves no doubt that even his sense of humor is pompous.   **C+**

Dire Straits: *Brothers in Arms* (Warner Bros. '85). "Money for Nothing" is a catchy sumbitch, no getting around it, and the first side moves with simple generosity, not a virtue one associates with this studio guitarist's ego trip. But it's too late for the old bluesboy to suck us into his ruminations on the perfidy of woman and the futility of political struggle, and "Money for Nothing" is also a benchmark of pop hypocrisy. We know Mark Knopfler's working-class antihero is a thicky because he talks like Randy Newman and uses the same word for homosexual that old bluesboys use, a word Knopfler has somehow gotten on the radio with no static from the PMRC. I mean, why not "little nigger with the spitcurl" instead of "little faggot with the earring," Mark? And while we're at it, how the hell did you end up on MTV? By spelling its name right?   **B−**

Dire Straits: *Money for Nothing* (Warner Bros. '88). An active member of the Fraternal Order of Old Farts since birth, Mark Knopfler has always identified simply, spontaneously, and soddenly with anybody who's bitter because life has passed him by—no, not "him or her," that's just the kind of pussyfooting a man's man won't abide. He's most convincing when directing his empathy at musicians—cf. "Sultans of Swing," in which glam types reject trad tsk-tsk, and "The Walk of Life," in which our hero dances as best he can. Skillfully accompanied on guitar, his supposedly unfashionable ressentiment has made him a rich man. How could such a thing happen?   **B−**

Dirty Dancing (RCA Victor '87). Five pre-Beatle classics plus six postmodern horrors equals the soundtrack to the world's longest rock video, a brutally depressing top-forty apotheosis. The comparisons are torture—revolting as the contempo material is, it sounds even worse in among the Five Satins and Mickey & Sylvia, who are in turn rendered unlistenable by the commercial manipulations that bring them back to commercial life. Even accessory before the fact Phil Spector sounds not just innocent but simple up against the technocratic ardors of Medley & Warnes's Grammy/Oscar-validated "(I've Had) The Time of My Life" or Eric Carmen's merely radio-validated "Hungry Eyes." The new songs epitomize AOR as CHR, turning everything rock and roll taught us about rhythm and emotion into the melodrama that prerock schlock left behind when it abandoned operetta and the drawing-room ballad. They're almost as good a reason to hate mass culture as Ronald Reagan.   **D**

The Dirty Dozen Brass Band: *My Feet Can't Fail Me Now* (George Wein Collection '84). I may never get over early reports describing this New Orleans neotrad octet as "funky," which I took to mean that in addition to integrating Monk and Bird tunes into marching-band polyphony they had a bottom like James Brown or at least the Meters. After one listen, I realized what I already knew—that to get a funk beat out of tuba, bass drum, and snares isn't difficult, it's impossible. Maybe the big deal is that they're not only fun in a mild, neotrad way, but also what Dr. John used to call "fonky"—that even though they play jazz, people dance to it. A not inconsiderable conceptual triumph, but those who dance a lot anyway are unlikely to appreciate it. Upped a notch for integrating Monk and Bird tunes into marching-band polyphony.   **B**

The Dirty Dozen Brass Band: *Mardi Gras in Montreux: Live* (Rounder '86). No longer bummed out by false promises of funk, we can settle for fun. Even if it's right to suspect that their synthesis is less than historic, their lively, unsentimental update of New Orleans jazz heritage proves once again that the best way to honor the dead is with a party. But not that the guest of honor should get up in his best suit and sing "Stormy Monday."   **B+**

The Dirty Dozen Brass Band: *Voodoo* (Columbia '89). The cameos—by Dr. John, Dizzy Gillespie, and Branford Marsalis—are the giveaways, because this jaunty concept needs those guys, to sing or solo as the case may be. The headliners are the lounge band of a tourist's dreams, and that's all they are. Why in the world cover Stevie Wonder's message-laden "Don't Drive Drunk" as an instrumental (polyphonic, mais oui)? Because it's a deathless piece of music? To prove how up-to-date you are? Or to stump the clientele in a game of name-that-tune? **B**

Dirty Looks: *Dirty Looks* (Stiff/Epic '80). Clear, tuneful, hard-driving, this is one of those records that jumps you so good you may never think to wonder why they bothered. I did, however—occupational hazard, you know. Except for "Take Your Life," boyishly power-pop yet precisely as murderous as its title, I figure it must have something to do with the love of rock and roll. **B**

Divinyls: *Desperate* (Chrysalis '83). The voracious readymade chords of this Australian quintet aspire more to rock than to rock and roll, but when you think about it, so do Joan Jett's. Christina Amphlett plays a town slut who's moving up in the world of sexual—and emotional—obsession, like Iggy Pop with a heart as big—and needful—as his dick. And on the Easybeats' "Make You Happy" she gets to the infantile root. **A—**

Divinyls: *What a Life!* (Chrysalis '85). With Mike Chapman the hooker, Christina Amphlett enters the race for Miss Bad Girl of 1986 and is fairly depressing for side one. After dumping a bucket of water on her head, she starts to play rough overdisc, but it's too late. Having once interrupted coitus by throwing my back out, I've never been convinced that the line between pleasure and pain was as thin as Mike and Christina claim. **B**

Divinyls: *Temperamental* (Chrysalis '88). This is the genderfucked Sweet that Mike Chapman should have gotten out of Christina Amphlett last time, before Vic Maile and Girlschool beat them to it, but as with

straight Sweet, the tunes pound by a little too evenly to change the world. "Dirty Love" will never besmirch CHR, and unless she gets lucky with "Hey Little Boy," a genderfucked cover the world's been waiting for since 1966, it could be three-strikes-she's-out for a dirt-eater who deserves better. **B**

Don Dixon: *Most of the Girls Like To Dance but Only Some of the Boys Like To* (Enigma '86). The R.E.M. etc. producer's semilegendary status as leader of Arrogance got even less credence from me than from everybody who'd never heard of them, because I'd heard them: arena-rock as club sandwich. But it's his band experience that powers his good little Southern pop record. Not only does he write hooky songs with a twist—my two favorites involve a bisexual and a one-night stand, half a dozen stand out, and most of the rest plus two covers are fun at least—but he sings them with the kind of ersatz soul that floors houses and counterbalances his Farfisa riffs with compressed guitar spectacles. In short, he ain't cute. **A—**

D.J. Jazzy Jeff & the Fresh Prince: *He's the D.J., I'm the Rapper* (Jive '88). From Fabian and Chubby Checker to Cosby and this crew, Philadelphia has always produced too many unthreatening teen dreams—it's enough to make you stop worrying and love Schoolly-D. Though I grant the Fresh Prince's acting ability and find myself touched when he tells the crowd he's seventeen, he makes the mistake of coming on smug in a genre whose staple is confidence. In life, maybe the wheedle is more socially advanced than the demand; in art, it's a turnoff. **B—**

D.J. Jazzy Jeff and the Fresh Prince: *And in This Corner . . .* (Jive '89). The Prince is already planning for life after rap. Will settle for standup, but wants his own series. Does creditable Richard Pryor-style impressions—rev, grandma, barber, wino. Writes good situations, too—"Who Stole My Car?," "I Think I Can Beat Mike Tyson," "The Men of Your Dreams." Then there's the gold digger (calls her a '49er, a new one on me), and the cannibal yarn no white artist would dare anymore.   **B+**

DNA: *A Taste of DNA* (American Clavé EP '81). Five "songs" lasting nine minutes in which Arto Lindsay, who refuses to corrupt his talent by learning chords, beats his guitar about the neck and body while yelping and ululating and just plain screaming the incomprehensible urban blues. Lester Bangs calls it horrible noise, I call it skronk and I say it's funny as hell and just as gut-wrenching—chaos neither celebrated nor succumbed to, just shaped into, well, postchaos. Ikue Mori's postceremonial drums and Tim Wright's post-Ubu bass complete the picture.   **A−**

D.O.A.:   *War on 45* (Alternative Tentacles EP '82). Hearty, no-bullshit songs for Canadian hardcore to march by, and that they hail from verdant Vancouver sure doesn't hurt the charity of their politics, or of their tempos either. Best originals: "Liar for Hire" and "Let's Fuck" (multilingual so it gets on Francophone radio, right?). Best covers: "War in the East," "Class War," and "War."   **A−**

D.O.A.:   *Bloodied but Unbowed* (CD '83). Subtitled "The Damage to Date: 1978–83," this six-buck special selects nineteen tracks from the three-single, four-EP, two-LP output of the hardest working band in hardcore. Though they're never as scintillatingly sophisticated as the Dead Kennedys at their rare best, these Vancouver boys are much more consistent, getting over on the momentum that defeats so many similar bands for the first side and writing real songs by the second. Old Clash fans will stand up and cheer their chanted oi-together-now hooks—and their state-smashing politics, too, I hope. **B+**

D.O.A.:   *Let's Wreck the Party* (Alternative Tentacles '85). Decking their cover with quotes from Durutti and Chagall and slogans like "Bring Back the Future" and "We Don't Need Unity . . . We Need Co-Operation," these Vancouver lifers have obviously made something of their hardcore anarchism. If only the music had as much spirit. Amid the slightly Britified metal-mania so many professional punks drift into, the great moments are stolen—a

speed-anthem cover of "Singin' in the Rain" and a "Hot Blooded" rip calling for a "General Strike." But since property is theft, maybe that's as it should be. **B−**

D.O.A.:   *True (North) Strong and Free* (Profile '87). These permanent punks not only had the discernment to cover "War" in 1982 but the breadth to link it up with the Dils' "Class War" and Ranking Trevor's "War in the East." Here they have the candor to join ranks with fellow clod and countryman Randy Bachman on an inspiring and sarcastic "Takin' Care of Business," and perhaps by osmosis, the roar into which the originals sink isn't as dull as usual. The protagonist of "Lumberjack City" takes care of business while drinking anything that comes in a barrel. "Bullet Catcher" is a policewoman who shouldn't have got shot. And fifteen years from now, some enterprising enemy of the star-spangled banner can make a roots medley out of their "51st State" and New Model Army's. Time: 28:37.   **B+**

The D.O.C.:   *No One Can Do It Better* (Ruthless '89). For three cuts it doesn't matter that he says nothing fast—not only is the music funky (his favorite word), it's clever, multileveled, gut-wrenching, ear-opening. Add the raucous Michel'le cameo "Comm. Blues" and you begin to think he deserves his best-seller, message or no message. And then, zip. Except on the tongue-twisting "Portrait of a Master Piece," the funk straightens out so abruptly you soon wonder what he's got to say. The less the better, as it turns out—guess who's "Beautiful but Deadly."   **B**

Dr. Buzzard's Savannah Band: *Calling All Beatniks!* (Passport '84). Disinclined though I am to blame music on engineering, I reluctantly decided that what ailed this five-years-awaited fourth album wasn't just uncharacteristically inelegant arrangements and lyrics unworthy of Stony Browder but a fuzzy, cavernous mix that at times turned Cory Daye into another background element. Then I remembered that I'd gotten an advance last spring, and when I compared the two I was shocked. Remix engineers Gary Hellman and Rob Paustian—abetted I'm sure by schlock svengali Sandy Linzer and possibly Browder, credited with coproducing the new version—have ruined a crisp, spare, inelegant-on-purpose rock and roll album, smothering a great singer in artificial fog along the way. They've also deleted two songs, each strong enough to lead a side of the advance, neither (hmm) produced by Linzer. And you know what else? The little subhead that says "featuring Cory Daye" on the original cover is gone as well. Docked a notch or two to encourage boycott. Time: 33:29.   **C+**

Dr. John: *The Brightest Smile in Town* (Clean Cuts '83). By playing the preserver of New Orleans piano tradition, the Dr. does an injustice to his equally fertile heritage as a music-biz sharpie, and too often on his second unaccompanied mostly-instrumental album he's as pleasant and boring as any other session man doing his thing. The new Pomus-Rebennack tune that kicks off side two raises hopes of a half save—until he stops singing again.   **B−**

The Doctor's Children: *King Buffalo* (Restless '87). Like so many Brits (and Yanks), they think they've got a new wrinkle on "American rock," and with bespectacled Peter Perrett soundalike Paul Smith writing and singing and playing, they manage one: chaotic feedback and organ murk subsumed in the soaring Byrdsy-Velvetsy ebb and flow. But I wouldn't say they "return it ['American rock'] with a looping back-spin," which is hardly a momentous claim. And so it goes in the realm of better-than-average guitar bands.   **B**

Swamp Dogg: *I'm Not Selling Out/I'm Buying In* (Takoma '81). One problem with pinning your hopes on eccentrics is that they're hard to tell from cranks. He's right about El Salvador and baby formula, wrong about abortion and loud dance music, boring about natural foods, the media, etc. And only when Esther Phillips pitches in does his beloved soul music get over.   **B−**

Swamp Dogg: *The Best of* (War Bride '82). This is oldish stuff, I think—nothing from 1975's Island swandive or 1981's Takoma sunklikeastone, six of the nine

originals from 1969's legendary *Total Destruction to Your Mind,* a couple from 1973's deep-fried *Gag a Maggott,* and there my research must end (except to note that "Please Let Me Kiss You Goodbye" 's velvet bell-bottoms are definitive early-'70s), because the only person I'm sure (pretty sure) owns every Swamp Dogg album is Jerry Williams himself. But oldish doesn't mean dated. These days, the man claims he composes twenty or thirty songs a day while driving his cab, and you can bet they're very much like these—more political, not as prime. You know he's still detailing the marriage wars with embarrassing pungency, still hearing a Stax-Volt-cum-Malaco four-four with blues obbligatos, still dreaming of the glory he deserves. Always will, I bet—dream about it, and deserve it.   **A−**

Swamp Dogg: *I Asked for a Rope and They Threw Me a Rock* (S.D.E.G. '89). Worth finding for his liner notes alone ("Why does jury duty pay more than my job and why is it the only Joy I know is a dishwashing detergent?"), an unvanquished professional and hopeless eccentric goes sane. His voice won't fend off nuclear attack anymore, but from Shirley & Lee to the Bellamy Brothers, from black history to rap, his vision of soul remains unique, and also remains a vision of soul. Sure "We Need a Revolution" is wordslinging—but not the wordslinging of a simp or a phony.   **B+**

Dogmatics: *Everybody Does It* (Homestead EP '86). A punk joke that sustains its burlesque of teen angst—hope nobody tells Dion about "Why must I be a teenager on drugs?"—for a whole side before slipping into mere "Saturday Nite Again." And even there the line about sticking latecomers with the Old Milwaukee bears the mark of a lived life.   **B+**

Thomas Dolby: *The Flat Earth* (Capitol '83). Dolby is a bright and honest fellow by no means in thrall to his synthesizers. "She Blinded Me With Science" proved he knows his way around a good beat, and the lyric sheet bespeaks a level of literacy rarely achieved by songwriters. But as with so many artists fascinated by synthesizers (and more than a few beguiled by their own literacy), his passion for texture subsumes what small knack he has for cruder, more linear devices. If there's an objective correlative for boring, that's it.   **C+**

Anna Domino: *East and West* (Les Disques du Crépuscule import EP '84). Fans of femme folk–new wave—Raincoats, Young Marble Giants, etc.—should check out this EP even though the artist floats her lyricism in a gentle electronic wash and doesn't appear to hail from Britannia. Me, I'm a fan of early Tom Tom Club, Velvets-era Nico, and Maureen Tucker singing "Afterhours." Hypnotic with no cosmic aspirations, she could be labeled spaced out, but in a dreamy, nicely sophisticated way. Composer of best song: Aretha Franklin.   **A−**

Anna Domino: *"Rythm"* (Les Disques du Crépuscule import EP '85). "Behind the myth lies the effort of the rhythm [rythm?]," she muses in re racial relations. But the effort of the rhythm is in the preparation and production, not necessarily the final product. I prefer the debut's dreamy melancholy, and note that the best tune is once again a cover: "Sixteen Tons."   **B**

Anna Domino: *Colouring in the Edge and the Outline* (Giant EP '89). Neither of her albums has gotten to second base with me, and not because I'm unwilling—all three EPs score. Here she croons about metaphysical-sounding stuff like luck and joy over the snaky electrorhythms that in her past work were all too metaphysical themselves. And never sounds like stamina's her long suit.   **B+**

The Donner Party: *The Donner Party* (Cryptovision '87). R.E.M. as punks. Feelies as folkies. Horseflies without horseshit. "John Wilkes Booth." "When You Die Your Eyes Pop Out." "Surfin to the Moon." "Jeez Louise."   **B+**

Donner Party: *Donner Party* (Pitch-a-Tent '88). Like Camper Van Beethoven, who started the label in their DIY days, they're sardonic ethnic/folk-rock postpunks, just as Kaleidoscope and the Cleanliness and Godliness Skiffle Band were sardonic e./f.-r. hippies two decades ago. I don't know why northern California does

this to its bohemians, but rootlessness must contribute; rootlessness fertilizes popular culture, forces it to reach out. As in their fabulous folk-punk name, these postteenagers are fascinated by mortality—their most striking songs are about infancy, ingestion, illness, fucking yourself up, and various commonplace-to-horrible vicissitudes. They're postteenage psychologically as well as chronologically because they don't romanticize death—just joke about it a lot.   **A−**

The Doobie Brothers: *One Step Closer* (Warner Bros. '80). The absence of musthums brings into stark relief the magnitude of their debt to Steely Dan. Michael McDonald, of course, but more significantly Skunk Baxter, now departed and you can't even tell, so sedulously do the other guitarists emulate his virtuoso harmonies. The Doobies are now socially responsible artists, stopping at nothing in their battle to let the radio audience taste musical quality in the breaks. If the songs themselves had any content, well then obviously there'd be no chance to enlighten the masses. Don't dare ask them to abandon this mission.   **B−**

The Doobie Brothers: *Best of the Doobies Volume II* (Warner Bros. '81). Though this sums up their brush with greatness, a/k/a Michael McDonald, McDonald has grasped greatness but once: on the eternally recurrent apothegm "What a Fool Believes," here isolated overdisc from such grazes, whisks, and sweeps as "Here To Love You," "Real Love," and "Minute by Minute." Vanity, vanity—usefulness rather than greatness is the purview of a record like this, and thus the first volume stands as a more fetching collection of ephemera. Better than *Minute by Minute* and *One Step Closer* on the sociological ground that it got more total airplay.   **B**

The Doors: *Alive, She Cried* (Elektra '83). The concert and sound-check tapes they've unearthed for the revival are of some quality, with Robbie Krieger a white blues twister on "Little Red Rooster" and Jim Morrison an effective focus as long as he just sings. But when he emits his poetry or deigns to lay his narcissistic come-on on an imaginary teeny-bopper, it is to duck. If kids today feel cheated by history because they never experienced the fabled Jimbo charisma first hand, that's one more reason to be glad there are no new rock heroes.   **B**−

The Doors: *Live at the Hollywood Bowl* (Elektra EP '87). Teaser "soundtrack" to the MCA video of the same name. Bad rockpoets never die—never.   **C**−

Gail Ann Dorsey: *The Corporate World* (Reprise '89). Conventional exercises on side one: liberal protests ("Wasted Country") and reflective love songs ("If Only You"). But from the literal title tune to the Beethoven-drenched romantic climax, side two is the yuppie blues, its killer the literal "No Time," about how busy she is. Pet Shop Boys, this is how it sounds with soul.   **B**

Do the Right Thing (Motown '89). Though Spike Lee may romanticize blackness, neo-reactionaries are bullshitting when they claim he romanticizes black rage. On his most coherently contemporary piece of aural upward mobility, he centers Afro-America's great tradition in soul, with Stevie Wonder a key influence; the rage begins and ends with "Fight the Power" and is countered by Take 6's postgospel "Don't Shoot Me" ("I didn't mean to step on your sneakers"). Guy and EU give Spike primo new stuff for the rhythmic-wonderland side, but only Rubén Blades fully transcends the songwriting problems on the vocal-riches side—problems that begin and maybe end with de facto producer Raymond Jones.   **B**+

Double Dee & Steinski: *The Payoff Mix/Lesson Two/Lesson 3* (Tommy Boy promo EP '85). Securing copyright waivers on the bits and pieces from which voluble media nut Steve Stein and hands-on groove technician Doug DeFranco construct their postindustrial dance collages proved such a nightmare that this isn't officially for sale. Bootlegs are showing up, though, which given the information barons' arbitrary usufruct is just. Mixing witty, knowledgeable mastermixes (comprising, say, "Apache," "I'll Tumble 4

Ya," and "Starski Live at the Disco Fever") with spoken-word interjections from the likes of Humphrey Bogart and Fiorello LaGuardia, it's speculative art in which question and answer are complementary functions of a very contemporary quasi-parodic tone—a tone you could call postmodernist if it wasn't so unpretentious and optimistic, so pop and maybe populist. Steinski provides cognitive dissonance, Double Dee a rhythmic logic as ineluctable as a whole greater than the sum of its parts. Half deconstruction and half celebration, this is a message of brotherhood for the age of media overload, disarming late capitalism with humor, know-how, access, and leftfield panculturalism. No wonder CBS wants to censor it.   **A**+

Dramarama: *Cinéma Verité* (New Rose import '85). In these days of acoustic punks and live Paul Revere elpees, six guys who salute their roots with Reed and Bowie covers are like unto a breath of springtime—and so unfashionable that though they reside in Wayne, New Jersey, they had to put out their album in Paris, France. One John Easdale would seem to be the auteur, if you'll pardon my French. Sounds a little like Richard Butler without the delusions of Vaughan Monroe, and the main things he has going for him are an acerbic but not self-serving way of describing his woman problems and a band that rocks without hyphens—in other words, plenty.   **A**−

Dramarama: *Box Office Bomb* (Questionmark '87). They'd rather stay home and make records than go out and play bars, which gives them less of a shot at a jealous following and more of a shot at you and me. Album two's songs don't leap out quite so fast, but everything has more kick—John Easdale's deeper, edgier vocals, Mr E Boy's articulated guitar, and especially Jesse's drums. And soon what you play for just one more post-Pistols taste shakes down into articulated tracks of surprising emotional range. [Later available with better half of *Cinéma Verité* on CD.]   **A**−

Dramarama: *Stuck in Wonderamaland* (Chameleon '89). Imagine a Richard Butler who's not ashamed he watches television—who feels free to color his dolor with junk detail. That's American guy John Easdale, and it's too bad that like Butler he's slowing down as he grows older. The music's lickwise and the writing's fine, but only "Last Cigarette" is possessed by the runaway verve that drove them before they hied away to Wonderamaland. I do appreciate the Ian Hunter cover, though—the good ole '70s.   **B+**

The Dream Syndicate: *The Dream Syndicate* (Down There EP '82). Karl Precoda has the feedback down, and Dennis Duck simulates Mo's style while intensifying her groove and doubling her drive, but Steve Wynn needs to work on his Lou—he projects too much. Denying the Velvets ever cross his mind is a nice conceited Loulike touch, though. [Later on Enigma.]   **B+**

The Dream Syndicate: *The Days of Wine and Roses* (Ruby '82). Punctuated as well as buoyed by drummer Dennis Duck, Karl Precoda shapes a guitar master's trick bag of basic chords and ungodly electric accidents into drones that won't quit, so abrasively tuneful I get off on this album strictly as a groove—the way I get off on perfectly mindless funk like, say, the Gap Band singles. But Steve Wynn's take on the usual world-weary table topics is gratifyingly matter-of-fact and no more, and music like this—music where the fun is in the no-fun—feels incomplete when it stops there.   **B+**

The Dream Syndicate: *Medicine Show* (A&M '84). Very subtle—the sharper you listen the duller it sounds. Those desperate for Tom Verlaine's next one might conceivably settle for Sandy Pearlman's ampliclarification of Karl Precoda's guitar, but now that Steve Wynn is flexing his literary imagination we know where the interpersonal vignettes on the debut came from: when he grows up, Steve wants to write new journalism about adolescent anomie for *California* magazine.   **B−**

"D" Train: *"D" Train* (Prelude '82). Their burgeoning street rep reflects the burly appeal of James Williams, who sings lead like the president of the Teddy Pen-

dergrass Fan Club, Boys and Girls High chapter. More power to him. But their chart success reflects the complete control of keyboard pro Hubert Eaves III. Hooks don't grow on streets.   **B+**

"D" Train: *The Best of "D" Train* (Prelude '86). Dwarfing pretenders as estimable as Colonel Abrams. James Williams has owned the ranking Pendergrass shout since he surfaced barely out of high school five years ago, but he hasn't grown—hasn't broadened and deepened into the booming power of a world-class hunk. And although the filler here is a lot stronger than the filler on the debut, the debut provides the three lead and best cuts. And "You're the One for Me" keeps sneaking back on its recycled synth hook. Their first shot was their truest.   **B+**

Lucky Dube: *Slave* (Shanachie '89). A South African who's studied his Bunny Wailer, Dube thinks reggae is "the one and only type of music that will bring black people back to their roots (where they belong)." I don't. But he earns his stylistic fundamentalism: the shared r&b affinities of JA and S.A. deepen his groove, "I'm just a slave, a legal slave" overtaxes no metaphor, and the transcendent falsetto of "How Will I Know" conquers all. **B+**

The Dukes of Stratosfear: *Psonic Psunspot* (Geffen '87). If this is XTC's real psychedelic album, what the hell was *Skylarking?* So call it their real psychedelic parody—a concept album about acid damage, which I guess they read about somewhere. I was going to complain that the word "precious" isn't in their vocabulary and ought to be when I noticed that the last song is called "Pale and Precious." Then I realized that for all its kaleidoscopic byplay the parody is a little pale as well. But with every other hook intact, "Pale and Precious" is the only track you might miss without the credits.   **B+**

Dumptruck: *D Is for Dumptruck* (Incas '84). These smart young depressives not only work their variation on the garage-guitar Amerindie vernacular, they make it signify: the sludgy stasis of the rhythms and offhand density of the textures reinforce ruminative, overheard lyrical commonplaces. Their commitment and concentration are the best argument for pop formalism since the Shoes, and if one key difference is that they never try to be tuneful, another is that they never try to be cute. Instead, they get so into being down they convince you it's interesting. [Later on Big Time.]   **A—**

Kevin Dunn: *Tanzfeld* (Press import '86). First a Fan, then sole leader (and member) of a Regiment of Women, this Atlantan has been making art damage seem like fun ever since he put "Nadine" on sideways seven years ago. Not exactly a font of creativity, he sticks "Nadine" on this album along with three more covers, a postmodernistically kitschy instrumental, art-maimed instrumental, and three "original" songs: one called "Nam," one beginning "Mommy, I don't want to be a fascist," and one consisting of movie titles that begin with "I." Inspirational Verse, from his lyrics-provided cover of "Louie, Louie": "A fine little girl a-wait for me— / Ah cotch a chill: ah! certainly. / Peel the *linga:* Aranda cone / (we never divine how Ah make it home)."   **B+**

Duran Duran: *Rio* (Capitol '82). With music drily electronic enough to pass for new wave and moistly textural enough to go over as pop, lyrics that rearrange received language from several levels of discourse into a noncommital private doggerel, and a limitless supply of Bowie clones to handle the vocal chores, this is Anglodisco at its most solemnly expedient. It lacks even the forced cheerfulness of (whatever happened to?) Haircut 100 (wait, I don't really want to know), and if it had as many hooks as *A Flock of Seagulls* (not bloody likely) it still wouldn't be silly enough to be any fun.   **C—**

Duran Duran: *Seven and the Ragged Tiger* (Capitol '84). As public figures and maybe as people, these imperialist wimps are the most deplorable pop stars of the postpunk if not post-Presley era. Their lyrics are obtuse at best, and if you'd sooner listen to a machine sing than Simon Le

Bon, what are you going to do with both? Yet the hit singles which lead off each side are twice as pleasurable as anything Thomas Dolby is synthesizing these days. Which had better teach you something about imperialism.   **C+**

Duran Duran: *Decade* (Capitol '89). Liars till the end, they pretend their decade didn't end around 1984–'85, when U.K. new pop conquered the world and went phfft. But the best-of proves it. First side's all anyone needs of the brightly tuneful meaninglessness that made them video stars, and after side two cut one, "The Reflex," they sink into an anonymity relieved only by the greatest record they never made, Nile Rodgers's "Notorious," and the softcore closer "All She Wants." Sometimes I think the little girls don't understand a damn thing.   **B—**

Bobby Durham: *Where I Grew Up* (Hightone '87). In the Nashville pattern, Durham provides the twang, and his producers provide the material. Only this is California, where Durham's been a mainstay of Bakersfield honky tonk since the '60s and his producers feed gritty, well-turned country lyrics to their label's bluesmen. So, no neotraditionalist bullshit—just traditionalism pure and simple.   **B+**

Ian Dury & the Blockheads: *Laughter* (Stiff/Epic '80). I feel like a stick-in-the-mud pointing this out, but he could do with more tunes and less talkover. Honorable as it is to devote an entire album to crackpots and the vulgar tongue—only a prig could complain about a lyric like "You call me a ninny / You're a stupid twat"—the invective does tend to blur into itself. "Superman's Big Sister" having somehow failed to storm the charts Stateside, I don't have much hope for its only competition melodywise, string section notwithstanding. "Fucking Ada," it's called.   **B+**

Ian Dury: *Lord Upminster* (Polydor '81). "Spasticus Autisticus" is every bit as startling as Dury must have hoped after *Laughter* got lost in the hustle, but on the rest of his major-label move he sounds like a retired ad man. I suppose the idea is to let the riddims of Steven Stanley, Chaz Jankel, and Sly & Robbie turn jingles into rallying cries, but how much human kindness can you sell with slogans like "escape is a jape"?   **B**—

Ian Dury & the Blockheads: *Juke Box Dury* (Stiff '81). Dury has had great taste in musicians since pub-rock, and he's bent to dance-music convention without betraying sweet Gene Vincent. But this compilation of singles proves quite definitively that his genius is for lyrics. His literacy seems as natural as his command of slang, and he rhymes like some cross between Chaucer and Ogden Nash. What's more, he has something to say—his slightly salacious humanism is the perfect match for his diction.   **A**

Ian Dury and the Music Students: *4000 Weeks' Holiday* (Polydor import '84). Bowie does a song about international pop star Andy Warhol; more deeply cultured and deeply Brit, Dury does one for London pop visionary Peter Blake. His culture broad, informed, and utterly unhierarchical, his Britness rooted rather than snobbish or xenophobic, Dury has tended toward rock and roll music hall, but with the U.S. audience out of reach his music is drifting toward Europop cabaret, and sometimes his determination to ennoble the cliché seems a bit arch: "I like you very much" is preceded by a series of tropes that could have come out of a bad children's book and probably did. But on the B he toughens up, from "Percy the Poet" who's smarter than Pinter to "The Man With No Face" and his life's supply of dope. Internationalists will want to hear it.   **B**+

Ian Dury: *Sex & Drugs & Rock & Roll* (Demon import '87). Presumably, this substitutes "Superman's Big Sister" and "You're More Than Fair" for *Juke Box Dury*'s "Wake Up and Make Love With Me" and "Sweet Gene Vincent" because the latter are available on *New Boots and Panties!!,* his second-best LP, while the former are rare items as well as genuine singles. They ain't as good, though, and if they're why Demon reprogrammed a perfect record, it is to weep. I even prefer the earlier title—if a change was required, give me *Reasons To Be Cheerful,* not a slogan

more misused than born-in-the-U.S.A. But you can't buy *Juke Box Dury* any more, and that's not Demon's fault. The millions who foolishly passed it by should lay down their inflation-wracked dollars or pounds for this reasonable facsimile.   **A**

Bob Dylan: *Saved* (Columbia '80). In case you were wondering, *Slow Train Coming* wasn't Jerry Wexler's album, or the former R. Zimmerman's, or Jesus Christ's. It was Mark Knopfler's. Anyway, the first flush of faith is the deepest. May Bobby never indenture soul sisters again.   **C**+

Bob Dylan: *Shot of Love* (Columbia '81). Dylan's abandonment of Muscle Shoals for the fleshpots of El Lay—Benmont Tench! Ron Wood! Ringo Starr on tom tom!—has a reassuring aura of apostasy, which may be why I think this year's born-again boilerplate "sounds better" than last year's. But two songs that belong in the lower reaches of his canon don't hurt. "Property of Jesus," about how bad it is to mock born-againers, has Staple Singers written all over it. "Lenny Bruce" is apostasy down to its reverent setting.   **B**—

Bob Dylan: *Infidels* (Columbia '83). All the wonted care Dylan has put into this album shows—musically, "License To Kill" is the only dud. His distaste for the daughters of Satan has gained complexity of tone—neither dismissive nor vituperative, he addresses women with a solicitousness that's strangely chilling, as if he knows what a self-serving hypocrite he's being, but only subliminally. At times I even feel sorry for him, just as he intends. Nevertheless, this man has turned into a hateful crackpot. Worse than his equation of Jews with Zionists with the Likud or his utterly muddled disquisition on international labor is the ital Hasidism that inspires no less than three superstitious attacks on space travel. God knows (and I use that phrase advisedly) how far off the deep end he'll go if John Glenn becomes president.   **B**—

Bob Dylan: *Real Live* (Columbia '84). Hitch Mick Taylor to a locomotive, make sure the songs are twenty years old, and you could get shit. But you could also get a decent live album if the auteur happened to be interested that night. "Maggie's

Farm" and "Tombstone Blues" are the keepers, "License To Kill" and the ludicrous white reggae "I and I" are the ringers, and "Tangled Up in Blue" gets some new lyrics—or maybe they're really old ones.   **B**

Bob Dylan: *Empire Burlesque* (Columbia '85). The absurd contention that by utilizing electronic horns and soul girls and big bam boom he's finally mastered pop fashion and state-of-the-craft production—I've actually heard this referred to as "Disco Dylan"—proves only that his diehard fans are even more alienated from current music than he is. At best he's achieved the professionalism he's always claimed as his goal. No longer "relevant" enough to make "statements" that mean shit to any discernible audience—vide *Infidels* or, on this record, "Trust Yourself" (only if you say so, Bob)—he's certainly talented enough to come up with a good bunch of songs. Hence, his best album since *Blood on the Tracks*. I wish that was a bigger compliment, but debunking comparisons to *Street-Legal* are also way off—the arrangements and especially the singing are, yes, tasteful enough to support material that puts Elton John to shame. I mean, how did he *get* that ominous calm, that soupcon of prophecy? And how did he come up with the toughest Vietnam-vet song yet?   **B+**

Bob Dylan: *Knocked Out Loaded* (Columbia '86). Automatic horns and Dylanettes echoing every chorus, covers and collaborations—sounds like something he threw together in a week and away forever. But throwing it away is how he gets that off-the-cuff feel, and side two is great fun. Tough rocker with Tom Petty, lissome popper with Carole Bayer Sager, and with Sam Shepard one of the greatest and most ridiculous of his great ridiculous epics. Doesn't matter who came up with such lines as "She said even the swap meets around here are getting corrupt" and "I didn't know whether to duck or run, so I ran"—they're classic Dylan. And on side one we have automatic horns and Dylanettes echoing every chorus, covers and songs he wrote all by himself.   **B**

Bob Dylan: *Down in the Groove* (Columbia '88). Where *Self-Portrait* was at least weird, splitting the difference between horrible and hilarious, now he's forever professional—not a single remake honors or desecrates the original. All he can do to a song is Dylanize it, and thus his Danny Kortchmar band and his Steve Jones–Paul Simonon band are indistinguishable, immersed in that patented and by now meaningless one-take sound. And yet, and yet, there's a glimmer—the Dylan-Hunter throwaway "Ugliest Girl in the World," guaranteed to remind the faithful how much fun the one-take ethos used to be.   **C+**

Bob Dylan: *Oh Mercy* (Columbia '89). His seventh studio job of the decade is the third he didn't just churn out and thus the third to get hyped as a turnaround, but really, there is a difference. Daniel Lanois's understated care and easy beat suit his casual ways, and three or four songs might sound like something late at night on the radio, or after the great flood. All are modest and tuneful enough to make you forgive "Disease of Conceit," which is neither. So I forgive him.   **B**

Dylan & the Dead: *Dylan & the Dead* (Columbia '89). Dylan is Bob, the influential singer-songwriter who's resurfaced as the brains of the Traveling Wilburys; the Dead are Grateful, and not just because charismatic guitarist-antileader Jerry Garcia survived an offstage coma—they're rich men, and they sound it. Like Dylan, Garcia plays hardest and works most playfully when somebody pokes him a little—Ornette Coleman, say. But unlike Ornette Coleman, Dylan's not forever young, and what he makes of his catalogue here is exactly what he's been making of it for years—money.   **C−**

Sheila E: *The Glamorous Life* (Warner Bros. '84). With its breathy singsong, dancy hooks, electrotreated steals, pseudo-random white dissonance, and generally thrown-away air, this gyroscopic Prince spinoff reminds me more than a little of the first Tom Tom Club. Definitely not for kiddies, though. Teenyboppers maybe. **B+**

Sheila E.: *Sheila E. in Romance 1600* (Warner Bros. '85). Joining her playmates' games of can-you-top-this with a ringleader's enthusiasm, she gives full rein to her imagination, such as it is. And comes up with several intelligent enigmas and two almost-orgies deeply influenced by Hollywood costume drama. It's got some arty passages, and you can dance to it. **B**

Sheila E.: *Sheila E.* (Paisley Park '87). Without fear of humiliation or venereal disease, and without chumping for either, the real Janet Jackson shows the age of abstinence her underwear. Though it's all a show even if she fucks as much as she lets on, which I doubt, she has a sexy way of standing smack between the centerfold fantasies of Vanity/Apollonia and little sister's wishful bravado while kicking the grooves hitbound. **B+**

Eagles: *Eagles Live* (Asylum '80). New originals: O*. New covers: 1**. Rerecording quotient: −.2***. Spontaneity quotient: −.5***. *"Life's Been Good" doesn't count. **Washed-out "Seven Bridges Road." ***On a scale of +1 to −1. **C−**

Eagles: *Greatest Hits Volume 2* (Asylum '82). I admit it—this made my A shelves after the Bellamy Brothers softened me up. But that was unjust to the Bellamy Brothers. The Eagles are slimy not smarmy, pulchritudinous not purty, multiplatinum titans not singles artists, pretentious cynics not small-time con men, Topanga Canyon not San Fernando Valley. Sure their tunesmanship, zeitgeistheit, and guitar goodies were fun on the radio. But the next time I weeded my shelves, they were tracked to the reference collection. Original grade: B plus. **B−**

Steve Earle: *Guitar Town* (MCA '86). "I was born in the land of plenty now there ain't enough." "I gotta two pack habit and a motel tan." "I admit I fall in love a lot." In other words, he's like ten thousand footloose rock-and-rollers before him, only he's got new ways to say it. Even makes the road seem like a hardship worthy of *Scarecrow,* if not *Born in the U.S.A.* An American yes, a fool no, and Phil Alvin could do worse than give him a call. **A−**

Steve Earle: *Early Tracks* (Epic '87). Though they're nowhere near as lame as the artist claims (what do artists know? and why should they tell us about it?), these occasionally surprising studies in neotraditionalist rockabilly do lack that crucial aura of authority—the walking bass sounds more committed than the callow abandon when it should be the other way round. Still, side one won't disillusion, and two strokes shouldn't get lost on the B: the supernal male narcissism of "My Baby Worships Me," and "Devil's Right Hand," a ban-handguns parable you'd swear is as old as the Louvin Brothers. Time: 24:52.   **B**

Steve Earle & the Dukes: *Exit O* (MCA '87). Last time you knew he was a rock-and-roller because he was a soulful wiseass, full of piss, vinegar, and super unleaded. This time you know he's a rock-and-roller because he puts his band's name on the slug line. Whether Nashville has a contract out on him or he harbors a secret desire to become a folksinger, his will to boogie gets mired down in the lugubrious fatalism that so often passes for seriousness among self-conscious Americans. Maybe the problem with country boys who are smart enough to write their own lyrics is that they're also smart enough to read their own reviews.   **B**

Steve Earle: *Copperhead Road* (Uni '88). This time, it isn't only the heavy beat, loud guitars, and wild-ass vocal mannerisms that make it rock—the giveaway's the melodrama that rock set-pieces substitute for the flat inevitability of the country variety. So my prescription is simple: more Tom T., less Bruce. Meanwhile, just say his vision of history is more convincing than his vision of personal relations. Which these days is another giveaway.   **B**

Earth, Wind & Fire: *Faces* (ARC/Columbia '80). Leaping from mediocrity to wretched excess, they throw two discs on the market when they don't have the material for one. The lead cut/single, "Let Me Talk," is too political in its fluffy way to break down the racism of today's top 40, and after that they never top the Doobies rip side three—certainly not with the title number, which I blame on the fools who think they abandoned their principles when they gave up ersatz jazz.   **C+**

Earth, Wind & Fire: *Raise!* (Columbia '81). As long as they hew to a few simple rules—up on the tempos, down on the bullshit, etc.—there's no reason why these fellows can't turn their sparkling harmonies and powerful groove into a pure, contentless celebration of virtuosity. I mean once a year—at least in theory. But this is the first time the possibility's ever even occurred to me, which must mean they felt a show of strength was due. Original grade: A minus.   **B+**

Earth, Wind & Fire: *Powerlight* (Columbia '83). Since classic EW&F succeeds in spite of Maurice White's universalist hoohah, the paucity of inspirational numbers is a blessing. The one that celebrates voting is gratifyingly practical, the one that celebrates children's eyes one too many, and otherwise we're free to gape at this band's spectacular popcraft. Their sonic affluence and showtime groove encompass whispering strings no less perfect than their JB guitarbeats, Funkafunnies harmonies no less schmaltzy than their Lionel Richie homages, and when the synthesis is this catchy it's the best argument for universalism they'll ever make.   **A−**

Earth, Wind & Fire: *Electric Universe* (Columbia '83). Careerist ebb-and-flow notwithstanding, I'm tempted to blame the letdown on the return of Philip Bailey, whose falsetto spirituality might well have disoriented what's turned into a great pop show band. Especially if his own attempted breakthrough as a pop solo is any example.   **B**

Earth, Wind & Fire: *Touch the World* (Columbia '87). Though supposedly they've reconstituted as a lean quintet, the credits credit Maurice White and hired guns, notably Philip Bailey who sings lead on two cuts, shares lead on three, and backs up wherever. White gets only two compositions, which may explain why such a fabrication seems more in touch with the world than his solo album, where he made the mistake of expressing himself. Canceling out El Lay buy-a-song like "Every Now and Then" are the side-openers, the strongest protests this seminal pop transcendentalist has ever gotten down. Both focus on money, something he obviously has a feel for.   **B+**

Earth, Wind & Fire: *The Best of Earth, Wind & Fire Vol. II* (Columbia '88). Vol. I was 1978 and there are still only two '80s cuts, with 1980's "Let Me Talk," all that's worth salvaging from *Faces,* and 1987's "System of Survival," the closest they've ever come to actual protest, both missing.

And you know what? At one nullity and one dubiety a side, it's every bit as solid as Vol. I, which happens to be the best album they ever released. I should mention that because I prefer their slick early-'80s decline to their soulful late-'70s ascendancy (not to mention their fusoid early-'70s launch), my tastes in this matter are unorthodox if not crackpot. But if you could scarcely give a shit, which at this late date is sane enough, here's some slick, soulful fun. **A—**

Easterhouse: *Contenders* (Columbia '86). Like so many leftist ideologues before them, they make promises they can't keep. "Out on Your Own" opens side one by calling the Red Wedge's bluff, "Get Back to Russia" opens side two with praise of Leningrad in spring, and then it's mostly uniform arena-jangle. **B**

Clint Eastwood & General Saint: *Two Bad D.J.* (Greensleeves '82). I've always had reservations about the avant-garde rep of Jamaican engineering—a lot of those whooshes, zooms, and sprongs strike me as the aural equivalent of a light show. So I get off when these two clowns play it as vaudeville. Trading chants over a fine array of twisted dials and session-man offbeats, they make sex & apocalypse & rockers' roles seem like such a cosmic joke that their rhythmic life can sneak up on you. Rub a dub and what do you get? You get the answer to one of life's stubbornest mysteries—how to come and laugh at the same time. **A—**

Clint Eastwood & General Saint: *Stop That Train* (Greensleeves '83). If this album's enjoyably joky yarns and stoned satire seem to come from backstage while the debut's came from outer space, it's not just because the surprise factor is gone. It's also the settings, devised by Kingston's most dubwise studio astronauts on the first album but assigned here to rude Inity Rockers with ska accents and music hall tempos. **B+**

Eazy-E: *Easy-Duz-It* (Ruthless '88). "I might be a woman-beater but I'm not a pussy-eater," boasts this man's man, and that sums up his wit and wisdom right down to the way he hides behind Richard Pryor when he says it. There's sure not much music to hide behind—Eazy the label owner doesn't get the real good shit out of his boys. Only the video. **C+**

Echo and the Bunnymen: *Crocodiles* (Sire '80). If anything might convince me that the term "psychedelic revival" means something it's "Villiers Terrace," a real good terror-of-drugs song. And the music flows tunefully, in a vacant, hard-rock sort of way. But oh, Jimbo, can this really be the end—to be stuck inside of Frisco with the Liverpool blues again? **B**

Echo and the Bunnymen: *Heaven Up Here* (Sire '81). Word was these erstwhile-and-futurist popsters had transcended songform, so I gritted my teeth and tried to dig the texture, flow, etc. Took the enamel clean off. I hold no brief against tuneless caterwaul, but tuneless psychedelic caterwaul has always been another matter. Ditto for existential sophomores. And, need I add, Jim Morrison worship. **C**

Echo and the Bunnymen: *Echo and the Bunnymen* (Sire EP '83). In a desperate attempt to market Ian McCulloch's crumpled shirts and skin problems (two of the most likable things about him, I'd say), Warners pulls two top cuts off *Porcupine,* counted by some a step in the right direction. Revealingly, they're the two worst things here, though where "The Cutter" is a pretentious dog (quills sticking out all over the little bugger), "Back of Love" is merely more histrionic than the competition. Suggested motto: "Do It Clean," which here builds to a casual vocal rave-up in a seven-minute concert version that could almost make you believe these spaced-out student existentialists were rock-and-rollers. **B+**

Echo and the Bunnymen: *Songs To Learn and Sing* (Sire '85). Their best-of includes all five songs ("Do It Clean" in an inferior studio version) from their eponymous 1983 bread-upon-the-waters EP. Which provide its four best tracks. It also includes a lyric sheet. Which taught me nothing I wanted to know. **C+**

Ed Gein's Car: *Making Dick Dance* (EGC '85). Like any hardcore band with the money, they include a lyric sheet. Unlike most, they don't need one—their work is admirably recognizable, words and music both. Which doesn't make it admirable. You can be sure these guys don't shoot "screwdriver boys"—that's Bernie Goetz. And they don't "beat up gays"—that's their dog. They're not steamed because they're "feeding legions of wogs"—that's some middle-aged protofascist. They wouldn't rape anybody—that's the "sick fucker" who's on the street because "the courts don't care." But they do "want to fuck a girl like you." Funny fellows. Docked a notch for their taste in personas. **B**

Dave Edmunds: *Twangin* (Swan Song '81). With Nick Lowe butting out, Edmunds wheels into his leather-boy fantasy with all the delicacy of a Harley 1000 on diesel fuel. He digs a thirteen-year-old version of "Baby Let's Play House" out of the basement, ignores Guy Mitchell's whistled hook on "Singing the Blues," and acts as if George Jones left something out of "The Race Is On." Topper: Lowe-Carter-Edmunds's "Living Again If It Kills Me," which happens to be a slow one. **B**

Dave Edmunds: *The Best of Dave Edmunds* (Swan Song '81). Ignoring his slower and more eccentric moments for the nonstop energy punks misprise from rockabilly, with bullheaded recent covers of "The Race Is On" and "Singing the Blues" decelerating into upper midtempo for respite, this compilation defines Edmunds as a trouble boy. Actually, if you'll listen to "Trouble Boys" for two minutes you'll learn that Edmunds is scared shitless of trouble boys—as were, I'll bet, Gene Vincent, Eddie Cochran, the Everly Brothers, and Elvis himself. But if you'd rather leave his quirks to critics and his mama, you can just, well, rock on. **A—**

Dave Edmunds: *D.E. 7th* (Columbia '82). It's a measure of my respect for Edmunds that at this point his meticulous collections of oldies and newies impress me much the way good new Chicago blues albums do, and I vouch for number seven, especially the newies on side one. When was the last time you were more than mildly excited by a good new Chicago blues album? **B+**

Dave Edmunds: *Information* (Columbia '83). Not since the onset of a career always marked by consistent taste and uncertain utility has Edmunds strayed so far from the trad, and though his perfidy/courage is characteristically marginal, it's still a mistake. The two Jeff Lynne–produced tracks have given him the hit he needs, but where 1971's echoey "I Hear You Knockin' " was a departure, 1983's teched-up "Slipping Away" is an accommodation to market trends the Edmunds of Rockpile bucked. And as a symptom of his faltering commitment, the songs he's selected for side two are quite humdrum, which isn't characteristic at all. **B—**

Bernard Edwards: *Glad To Be Here* (Atlantic '83). Edwards's career training as a bass player doesn't suit him for lead roles, which means that what is basically a rather subtle Chic album may never sneak up on you the way it did on this fan. For what it's worth, the two Chic-est grooves on the album feature Nard as vocalist but not bassist, leaving that role to synth whiz Ray Chew. Could this be magic? **B+**

Eek-A-Mouse: *The Mouse and the Man* (Greensleeves '83). Neither of this JA original's previous albums evinced much poetry, but the material here is as eccentric, matter-of-fact, and casually associative as his dub-minimalist music and calmly wacko vocal mannerisms. Beginning with an account of Hitler—"This is history and remember this ain't no joke"—and moving on to mix lesser horrors (death occurs in three of the remaining nine songs) with happier reflections, he comes across deeply compassionate, deeply bemused, and perhaps not as modest as you'd first think. Inspirational Verse: "Some of the them may call you a turkey / Some look on you and say you flaky." **A—**

Eek-A-Mouse: *Assassinator* (RAS '83). What kind of artist interprets the legend of Tarzan to the tune of "Wimoweh" immediately after outlining his "Triple Love" life just so he can revel in "en" rhymes ("ten," "den," "lend," "bend," "them," "Ardenne," "Hughenden," "Gwen," "Jen," "Karen," "they even make love with my best friend Ken," and of course the literal nonsense "lah-den")? A major eccentric who makes most of those who cultivate that image look like self-serving twits, that's who. Also an eccentric whose first three songs here start with death by gunfire.   **B+**

Eek-A-Mouse / Michigan & Smiley: *Live at Reggae Sunsplash* (Sunsplash '84). Michigan & Smiley are the Statler Brothers of toasting, but this 1982 performance is where the mighty Mouse transcended the novelty pigeonhole. His delight in the comic highs and lows of his range and the syllabic adaptability of his tongue and palate are even more vivid live than in the studio, and two of the songs here, including the quietly devastating "Neutron Bomb," aren't on any of his five other U.S.-release albums.   **B**

Eek-A-Mouse: *Mouseketeer* (Greensleeves '84). Prolific and then some, he's a little less consistent on this album than on its immediate competitor, and since there are no printed lyrics I'll probably never know what the anorexic was doing at Reggae Sunsplash. But the hot pressing and dubbed-up Henry Junjo Lawes production do compensate for his tendency to set all his songpoems to the same melody, leading off with his account of Queen Elizabeth's unscheduled audience and climaxing with an explanation (?) of how he got his name betting the horses.   **B+**

8 Eyed Spy: *Live* (ROIR cassette '81). I've always had my doubts about Lydia Lunch, but this Chris Stamey–recorded tape establishes her beyond doubt as the most promising female novelty artist in the American underground. Unlike Debora Iyall, she makes no apparent distinction between sex and eros, which is why she's a novelty artist, but Iyall should follow her lead in the giving-it-what-you-got department. Pat Irwin's dissenting sax and George Scott's pushy bass are what they got, and where they got it was James Chance.   **B+**

Elbow Bones and the Racketeers: *New York at Dawn* (EMI America '84). With a new Dr. Buzzard in the works and Kid Creole still August Darnell's principal outlet, it's amazing that he's found time and songs for yet another project—or so I thought until I heard the project. Only the declaration of infidelity "Other Guys" is more than a skillful black-music genre exercise, and though other singers might pull it out, Gichy Dan and Stephanie Fuller don't.   **B−**

Eleventh Dream Day: *Beet* (Atlantic '89). Only in a world where major labels have publicity departments and the Pixies are rock and roll future could this tuneless guitar band be a hot rumor. The major attraction is a girl drummer who chimes in on backup and should write more. Plus, of course, a raunchy, energetic guitar sound. No solos or anything—that would be corny (and hard). Just a sound.   **C+**

The Elvis Brothers: *Movin' Up* (Portrait '83). If you're really committed to the "fun" only unpretentious pop can provide, you might as well go directly to these proud posers, who generate hooks in an abundance that will shame whatever "authentic" locals you retain a sentimental yen for. Connoisseurs of pop plasticity will get an additional kick out of how affectlessly they shift from the usual ersatz teen romance to equally meaningless and equally commercial outlaw and rebel themes. Plus an uncanny Beatle impression on "It's So Hard."   **B−**

Joe Ely: *Musta Notta Gotta Lotta* (South Coast '81). Hanging out with the Clash hasn't been so great for Ely's music—he's rocking harder than ever, but with a forced urgency that detracts from the songs. Only "I Keep Getting Paid the Same" is heightened by his breakneck boogie, and both Roy Brown's "Good Rockin' Tonight" and Shorty Long's "Rock Me My Baby" would come across better if they rolled a little. Best in show: Butch Hancock's Spanish-tinged "Wishin' for You."   **B+**

Joe Ely: *Live Shots* (MCA '81). Like a thousand blues and jazz guys before him,

Ely is an American whose live album should have seen America first—not a year, a charting studio record, and a major endorsement after touring the U.K. The claim that this injustice was a corporate blunder is boogie bullshit: even prime material acutely performed sounds a little redundant in an artist whose fundamental is songs. Still, this is prime and acute. Let's hope he rides the Clash's tailwind right into downtown Lubbock.   **B+**

Joe Ely: *Hi-Res* (MCA '84). I have no theoretical objection to the man's hard rock move—it's the dumb-ass conventionality of the actual hard rock in question that gives me a pain. Where Lloyd Maines and Ponty Bone were aces on their country-identified instruments, Ely's new guys are arena dorks in their dreams. You remember the tunes and licks after a while only because they're so similar to thousands of others you soon forgot. And where Ely's own songs have always worked best as change-of-pace, here they're expected to carry the shebang. Except for the febrile "Imagine Houston," buried on side two, and maybe "Cool Rockin' Loretta," a find of a throwaway but no more, they sink it instead.   **C+**

Joe Ely: *Lord of the Highway* (Hightone '87). A decade of being told what a hot shit he is has Ely oversinging to signify his intensity, which is too bad: he might have snuck in "Silver City" if he'd talked the song instead of howling it. But when he keeps it light—pissed off at Billy the Kid or his girlfriend's karate lessons or that s.o.b. Lucky, who gets the lowdown on the honey he left behind—Ely rebounds like he's made of silicone. He's an honest man—when Steve Earle and Dwight Yoakam meet women who take self-defense courses, they're too fucking pure to admit it.   **B+**

Joe Ely: *Dig All Night* (Hightone '88). Not one track runs under four minutes. Not one arrangement reveals why he was ever mistaken for country. Not one song was written by Butch Hancock, by anybody but Joe—though he did get help on the title tune, which suggests a self-knowledge otherwise in retreat.   **B−**

The Embarrassment: *The Embarrassment EP* (Cynykyl EP '81). From exotic Wichita, with a gift for hookily hypnotic guitar lines that need a haircut. The big name at "Celebrity Art Party" is Art Carney, so they also have a gift for the off-rhyme. The rest is harder to remember.   **B**

The Embarrassment: *Death Travels West* (Fresh Sounds EP '82). Eight droning, astringent, strangely catchy songs about everything from the Lewis and Clark Expedition to "There's no doubt about it my old friend's a monster." The horror—the horror.   **B+**

The Embarrassment: *Retrospective* (Fresh Sounds cassette '84). Now that I've finally gotten the message, a year and a half after this great lost American band dispersed into the wilds of Wichita, I still can't repeat it back to you. Which may help explain how the band got lost. Even garage-rock isn't a broad enough genre description—the song shapes here are just too ungainly. Their lyrics are too wide-ranging and elusive for modern romance, yet too down-to-earth and just plain funny to get lumped in with the neotrippies. And while the voice of John Nichols, described by annotator Drew Wheeler as belonging to "an All-American adolescent in a state of psycho-sexual confusion," provides a convenient way in, I know that what makes me sit up and say yeah is the kick of Bill Goffrier's rather grungy guitar. You figure it out.   **A−**

The English Beat: *I Just Can't Stop It* (Sire '80). Known simply as the Beat in England, and rightly so—their ska is deep and driven. Thank drummer Everett Martin, born St. Kitt's 1951, with roots from reggae to Armatrading, and bassist David Steele, born Isle of Wight 1960, who's parlayed the usual classical training into a rhythm kid's twist and crawl. That's a title, of course, naming a bass line that moved more feet than anything Bernard Edwards came up with in 1980. Riding atop the full frontal velocity are two lean, warm, modest voices, almost indistinguishable until Ranking Roger turns up the accent. Hidden below it are songs, most of them by covocalist David Wakeling. Lyric of the electoral year: "Stand Down Margaret." [Later on I.R.S.]   **A—**

The English Beat: *Wha'ppen?* (Sire '81). David Wakeling shows more character (and timbre) than Terry Hall, Ranking Roger could rub his dub in a pedigreed reggae band, and the rhythms aren't solely riddims. So as two-tone grays out, the Beat follow their chops into the world-beat sweepstakes, where snaky grooves are worth their weight in yen. The Afrobeats and studio spaces and steel drums are as seamlessly colloquial as the depression politics and depressed romances, so it would be a shame if its sinuous midtempos dismay fans of its predecessor's hectic pace. I hear not resignation or compromise but a stubborn, animated adaptability. Unity rocker: "Doors to My Heart," in which love means eros and agape simultaneously, and Wakeling finds that dread blocks the way to both, and Roger advises him to stop his fighting. [Later on I.R.S.] Original grade: A minus.   **A**

The English Beat: *Special Beat Service* (I.R.S. '82). Careerwise, a conservative move—never has their four-four come on plainer, and when David Wakeling claims it's harder to write about the personal than the political, you're right to figure the songs will prove it. But David Steele can't resist a slight skank, and Everett Martin, who's such a pro he'd do Ringo imitations if they asked him, is also such a pro he can make any groove move. Anyway, Wakeling is always thoughtful about the irrational fear and real danger of letting go. The troubled decency of his modern romance, spilling over now and then into a barely discernible self-disgust, is the exact left-liberal equivalent of his social concern, of use to the great audience as well as the seekers after young lust and high infidelity he's aiming at. Original grade: A.   **A—**

The English Beat: *What Is Beat?* (I.R.S. '83). With its remixes, live versions, and non-LP U.K. singles, this Jamaican farewell portends the consumer confusion of compilations to come. Strictly speaking, eight of its thirteen offerings are new to LP, but in general I prefer the original cuts (and sequencing), and I can't understand why the hot disco remix of "Twist and Crawl" was left out of the grab bag. Col-

lectors might as well go for the cassette, which though it's slightly inferior audiowise does exploit the biz's sanest tactic in the noble campaign to scourge home taping by adding four tracks, two live and two U.K.-only, including the secret classic "Wrong Side of the Bed."   **B+**

Brian Eno: *On Land* (Editions EG '82). In pulse, movement, and textural detail, this falls somewhere between the static *Music for Airports* (a bore) and the exotic Jon Hassell collaboration (a trip). Whenever I play it (usually late at night) I experience an undeniable pleasure so mild I'm not sure anyone would want to pay for it. Caveat emptor.   **B+**

Brian Eno: *Apollo: Atmospheres & Soundtracks* (Editions EG '83). Designed to help a moonshot documentary "present a set of moods," this is ambient Eno at its most accessible—often very pretty, and not without guitar. Still, I expect mood music to sustain a mood, and while as you might expect none of this is unlistenable, some of it is very nearly inaudible, which can be almost as annoying. Left to itself, "Drift" does just that, and "Stars" and "Under Stars" sound like sleep sequences. Original grade: B plus.   **B**

Brian Eno: *More Blank Than Frank* (EG '86). With this forcebeat pioneer now ensconced as new age paterfamilias, his selection ("biased towards my taste") of "songs from the period 1973–1977" is rather more quiet than a rock-and-roller would hope. And the three *Another Green World* tracks stick out like paradoxes if you happen to be intimate with that complete work. But never think the man doesn't know how to put a record together. Except for the forebodingly atmospheric "Taking Tiger Mountain," these very individual songs stand up as units and unit—certainly a stronger unit than *Before and After Science,* former home of the forcebeat classic "King's Lead Hat." Young people who consider him a mood-music maestro might as well learn their lesson here.   **A—**

Brian Eno–David Byrne: *My Life in the Bush of Ghosts* (Sire '81). Something fishy's going on when unassuming swellheads like these dabblers start releasing their worktapes. As cluttered and undistinguished as the MOR fusion and prog-rock it brings to the mind's ear, this album has none of the songful sweep of *Remain in Light* or the austere weirdness of Jon Hassell, and the vocal overlays only inten-sify its feckless aura.   **C+**

Enya: *Watermark* (Geffen '88). A new name with a pedigree—she brought her family's upmarket Irish folk concept Clan-nad into the synthesizer age before leaving to pursue her own economic interests. Whilst humanizing technology, perpetrat-ing banal verse in three languages (I'm guessing about the Gaelic after reading the English and figuring out the Latin), and mentioning Africa, the Orinoco, and other deep dark faraway places, her top-ten CD makes hay of pop's old reliable women-are-angels scam. At least the Cocteau Twins are eccentric. At least ELP were vulgarians.   **D+**

EPMD: *Strictly Business* (Fresh '88). Out of nowhere to the top of the charts, these frosty freezers are one more proof of the supposedly subliterate-to-subcriminal rap audience's exacting prerogatives—what's snapped up as freshest often is. The beats are disco hooks sampled full effect, two or three to the track; the attack is traditional-ist, formalist, minimalist. Rapping almost exclusively about rap, E Double EE and Pee MD don't emote or pander or yuck it up. In their one sex boast, the skeezer gets the last word.   **A—**

EPMD: *Unfinished Business* (Fresh '89). The full-sized hooks and understated groove still mesh, but fame has rendered this self-made duo less brazen and more arrogant simultaneously. The real money (and pussy) they now boast doesn't suit them any better than the increasing sub-tlety of their steals—they need tunes, not just beats. But beyond the humble origins described in "Please Listen to My Demo" and the dramatized public service an-nouncement "You Had Too Much To Drink," the overriding idea seems to be that stars can do it themselves. Which is the usual half-truth.   **B+**

The Equators: *Hot* (Stiff '81). An all-black ska band from Britain—they posed for the

cover photo in a greenhouse. Unencum-bered by message, concept, or apparent neurosis, the groove has more vim, muscle, get-up-and-go than the 2-Tone competi-tion. Less interest, though. That's the thing about neurosis—it can really be in-teresting.   **B**

Eramus Hall: *Gohead* (Capitol '84). The best Clinton spinoff since the Brides (not including Bootsy, who's on board as well) makes the funk album of the year (not in-cluding rap, which I guess is where funk went). Of course, to hear Capitol tell it, George discovered these Detroit pros long after they had their own thing. In the nick of time, I'd say.   **B+**

Roky Erickson and the Aliens: *The Evil One* (415 '82). Never a big Satanism fan, I've resisted this crazed and-you-thought-acid-was-bad testament from the long-wasted leader of the long-departed 13th Floor Elevators. But not one of the West Coast's new psychedelic rockboys has come up with half this many dirty guitar riffs, or anything that holds a candle to "Don't Shake Me Lucifer." And unlike the Flesh Eaters' Chris D., for instance, he seems to mean it, whatever exactly "it" might be.   **B+**

Roky Erickson: *Don't Slander Me* (Pink Dust '86). A garage rant about blues theol-ogy that built from blues readymades and accelerated on the kind of mad thrust you don't hear much from revivalists or any-body else, the now rerecorded title single was all natural timing and spirit posses-sion, a paradise regained of rock and roll cliche. The album exploits this miracle—sounds like a bunch of would-be old farts (with genuine article Jack Casady lending a touch of authenticity) latching onto the old wildman for the kind of magic carpet ride other music lovers only collect. It's too precise, too forceful, too showy. And if you can bear the protracted tributes to Erickson's private gods, it'll rock you out anyway. Try "You Drive Me Crazy." Or "Crazy Crazy Mama." Or "Bermuda," about the triangle.   **B+**

Roky Erickson: *Gremlins Have Pictures* (Pink Dust '86). Live-and-studio outtakes for curiosity-seekers who believe maniacs are best appreciated in their natural surroundings. I say it proves maniacs need engineers, backup bands, and other accoutrements of civilization even more than the rest of us.   **C**+

Gloria Estefan and Miami Sound Machine: *Let It Loose* (Epic '87). She's compelling when the rhythm gets her, annoying when she pledges slow-motion devotion, just like uncounted party girls before her—and also like uncounted rock pros before her, which is more the point. Don't deny her her gimmick—received or stolen though this suburban salsa may be, it can getcha.   **B**+

Gloria Estefan: *Cuts Both Ways* (Epic '89). I was perplexed to catch myself enjoying parts of this until I recognized the feels-so-good-when-it-stops   syndrome— who wouldn't perk up at a sleek salsa montuno or tap-dancing synperc break when the alternative is Karen Carpenter with an unlocked pelvis?   **C**

Gloria Estefan: See also Miami Sound Machine

Ethel and the Shameless Hussies: *Born To Burn* (MCA '88). The music is standard-issue neohonkytonk, but at least this red hot mama who smokes in bed writes her own lines. Good for a change and sometimes a hoot, and more progressive than Janie Frickie for damn sure.   **B**

E.U.:   *2 Places at the Same Time* (Island '86). Like disco DJs, go go bands get high on contingency—all the interactive variables that pertain when you try to turn a crowd of dancers into a pulsating mass. So in theory I approve of these live, side-long jams of grooveful quotes and fragments. Except for the ultimately untheoretical fact that once they're recorded, they're not so damn contingent any more.   **B**

E.U.:   *Livin' Large* (Virgin '89). In which the winners of D.C.'s five-year elimination tournament come to terms with a truth of the recorded medium: unless you're James Brown, and not always then, even a Möbius groove benefits from some variety. With Mother Africa, doowop, Spike Lee/ Marcus Miller, Salt-n-Pepa, and white girls adding assorted spice, fundamental

romps like "Buck Wild" and "Livin' Large" have somewhere to go go.   **A**−

Eurythmics: *Sweet Dreams (Are Made of This)* (RCA Victor '83). In theory, synth duos have always been okey-doke with me, especially when the resulting pop is as starkly hooky as what Dave Stewart comes up with here. And you might say Annie Lennox has a bono vox. But like so many with comparable gifts, both these people are fools, and pretentious fools at that. Remember, folks—when they tell you everybody's out to use or get used, make certain you go along for the ride you paid for. Original grade: B minus.   **B**

Eurythmics: *Touch* (RCA Victor '84). Physical gifts and technical accomplishments tempt a singer to overdramatize— Annie Lenox makes altogether too big a deal of punching the sofa. But even if she isn't, well, "cooler than ice cream" (really), I'm glad she's normal enough to want to be. If it's high-grade schlock you seek, this'll do as well as early Quarterflash. And Lennox has better hair.   **B**

Eurythmics: *Be Yourself Tonight* (RCA Victor '85). New wave's answer to Shirley Bassey is finally connecting with those of us who won't settle for voice-plus-hooks not because she shows signs of having a soul, but because she shows signs of having a brain. Of course, the two go together— her lush, brassy emotionalism is more coherent partly because it's grounded, less taken with alienation as a way of life. Dave Stewart's guitar doesn't hurt either. And neither do Aretha, Stevie, or Elvis. **B**+

Eurythmics: *Revenge* (RCA Victor '86). Annie Lennox's rich, lustrous range and diction   threaten   to   overwhelm   these stripped-down   arrangements,   bringing such odious Annies as Haslam and Wilson to mind. But while you'd never call her enthusiasm natural, it's not forced or foolish either—this is rock and roll as sheer performance, its basics paraded with pride and a glint of humor. If only it was all side-openers like "Missionary Man," recommended to Pat Robertson, and the V-8 airmobile "Let's Go."   **B**+

Eurythmics: *Savage* (RCA Victor '87). Beethoven-lover as Neiman-Marcus girl, trans-Asiatic jilt, real live pseudoferal yowl announcing the cock-crazy "I Need a Man," synthesized pseudorathskeller clink-and-chatter punctuating the sarcasm-crazy "I Need You"—this record peaks so high that I tried to ignore all the in-between. It's there, though—medium-tempo romantic-as-in-movement psuedoschlock, edgier than their worst but not so's it cuts much ice. **B+**

Eurythmics: *We Too Are One* (Arista '89). "A bold new beginning," proclaims the sticker, and given their late-'80s sales it had better be, so essentially they go pop—rather than "ironic" new-wave metapop, a distinction that escaped every Tom Petty type who made Dave Stewart his new-waver of choice. Despite a few fabulous Elvis similes, this bold stroke is sorely lacking in je-ne-sais-quoi. Bet that within three years Annie lets her hair grow out and stops wearing makeup —makeup visible to the naked eye, anyway. **C+**

The Everly Brothers: *Reunion Concert* (Passport '84). They were a vital team right up to *Roots* in 1968, but then they lost it, which was perhaps a cause of their estrangement, perhaps a result, or perhaps mere entropy. This 1983 gig was their first in ten years, and they sure didn't slough it off. But it's nostalgia anyway, adding nothing but a pushy drummer and a slight slackening of the voices to a superb body of work available in better record stores everywhere. **B−**

The Everly Brothers: *EB 84* (Mercury '84). They're singing as good as ever, but not the same as ever—with the harmonies more luxurious and soulful, they can finally pass for grown men as they approach fifty. Unfortunately, maturity doesn't suit them any better than Dave Edmunds's lacquered, interpretation-enhancing production, because mature interpretation will never be their forte. They may sound like grown men and they may sound soulful, but that doesn't mean they sound like soulful grown men—a certain emotional complexity eludes them. Of all these hand-tailored comeback-special songs, only Paul Kennerly's "The First in Line"

and Don's own "Asleep" are simple enough to fit. **C+**

Every Man Has a Woman (Polydor '84). Like most multiple-artist compilations, this lacks the sense of identity that gives good albums their momentum, which means that while it does vindicate Yoko Ono's songwriting—there's not a clinker in the dozen—it's far from establishing her as the compelling popular artist she'd like to be. Pick hit: Rosanne Cash's penetrating, soulful "Nobody Sees Me Like You Do." And let us not forget: John Lennon's "Every Man Has a Woman Who Loves Him." **B**

Everything New Is Old . . . Everything Old Is New (Ambient Sound '82). Like all formalist art, doowop is a cultist's calling. Not only is its view of romance willfully adolescent, its view of adolescence is willfully romantic, inspired in the face of irrefutable evidence by a few freak singles, most of them slow (which is a snap to duplicate) and preternaturally beautiful (which isn't). Even its oft-heralded vocalism serves this vision—doowop tenors are supposed to be mild, as moony as "a teenager in love." But by unerringly selecting the two best cuts from five brand new doowop albums, this sampler escapes cultdom. In the great indie-label tradition, it concentrates on the catchy and programmable, including five ingenious covers, so that most of the slow songs sound beautiful, though rarely preternatural. **A−**

Explainer: *The Awakening* (B's '84). It's a little disorienting to encounter a dance music that lives or dies aesthetically by its lyrics—partying's not supposed to be that way. Yet here it is. Back when Winston Henry was a struggling young soca man, he came by his sobriquet honestly; these days he doesn't miss a chance to kiss Reagan's ass or make like "our skin color not get in our way." As a result (?), his groove gets nowhere. Interesting that back when he was a struggling young soca man his "Lorraine" sported as ferocious a hook as the style has known, while now his pop moves are reduced to a certain slackening of the tempo and the occasional keyb texture. **C+**

Exposé: *Exposure* (Arista '87). This paints its frontwomen a blank beige so as not to distract from the electrobeats, which it mixes high and clear enough to deliver three dancy hits and set up the platinum-plated schlockaballad "Seasons Change." Smart shoppers will note that the "Seasons Change" twelve-inch features a ten-minute megamix of said hits, then learn that the megamix isn't quite long enough—the thrill of a great electrobeat is having it ravish you again after you thought you'd had your fill. Smart bizzers have already noted that the concept leaves room for the Cover Girls' knockoff. **B—**

The Fabulous Thunderbirds: *T-Bird Rhythm* (Chrysalis '82). In theory I always appreciated this Texas party band's penchant for understatement—most white bluesboys demean themselves and the music they love by playing it strictly for raunch. But in practice their albums were, if you'll pardon my jargon, boring. So new producer Nick Lowe, who could find a pop hook in a field holler, makes a difference. Both sides open with fetchingly offhand ravers, Kim Wilson works his shoo-fly drawl for gumbo lilt, and the mysterious J. Miller contributes the irresistible "You're Humbuggin' Me," which had me tearing through my Jimmy Reed records in a fruitless search for the original. **B+**

The Fabulous Thunderbirds: *Tuff Enuff* (CBS Associated '86). The groove's tough enough, but like their fellow retroists the Bangles they don't write 'em as good as they pick 'em. This is the wages of retro—trying to replicate the musical spirit of a time that's passed means going against history and sacrificing the authenticity retroists live for. Can't blame Dave Edmunds for that. Or for the video, either. **B−**

Chaba Fadela: *You Are Mine* (Mango '89). I was on this from the day I played the import because, like *Rai Rebels*, it kicks off with her 1985 comeback with her husband Cheb Sahraoui—"N'Sel Fik," rai's most incandescent and universal moment, one of the greatest singles of the decade. But it took me months to sort it out clearly in my uneducated recollection from Middle Eastern product as distinct as Ouardia's Berber songpoems, or Ofra Haza's Barbra-Streisand-gone-ethnic and song-contest-with-hip-beats. Now I hear shades of emotion I don't ordinarily get from foreign-language pop—something as elementary as the way "Ateni Bniti" ("Give Me Back My Daughter") moves from affliction to angry resolve, say. I also notice Oran superproducer Rachid outdoing rather than compromising himself as he aims for the bigger time. And reflect that if now it's for bad boys, rai was originally the domain of women who knew better. Fadela sounds like a sister. **A−**

Fad Gadget: See Frank Tovey

Donald Fagen: *The Nightfly* (Warner Bros. '82). Apparently, what Walter Becker brought to Steely Dan was an obscurantism that lost its relevance after the posthippie era. With words that always mean everything they want to say and aural pleasures that signify, these songs are among Fagen's finest, and if their circa-1960 vantage returns us to the student memories of *Countdown to Ecstasy* and *Pretzel Logic*, their tenderness is never nostalgic and their satire never sophomoric. Fagen's acutely shaded lyrics put the jazziest music he's ever committed to vinyl into a context that like everything here is loving but very clear-eyed, leaving no doubt that this is a man who knows the limits of cool swing and doesn't believe the world was a decisively better place before John Kennedy died.   **A**

Marianne Faithfull: *Dangerous Acquaintances* (Island '81). More conventional than *Broken English,* which isn't to say it's less feminist. On the contrary, Faithfull is even writing her own lyrics instead of letting some man do it, and coming up with universal truths like "where did it go to my youth" and "looking to find my identity" in the process. And singing in such palpably broken English that she almost gets away with it. This time.   **B+**

Marianne Faithfull: *A Child's Adventure* (Island '83). Skilled work, hookful and lithely arranged and sung with a racked grace far more accomplished than the harrowing croaks of *Broken English.* If I were a woman in search of rock and roll models, I might well dote on it. But model rock and roll it's not—*Broken English* still got the power.   **B+**

Marianne Faithfull: *Strange Weather* (Island '87). Scornful of the notion that realism entered pop music with rock and roll (a/k/a "the blues"), Hal Willner introduces Faithfull to a world-weary band of Lou Reed/Tom Waits sessioneers and hopes everybody'll like the same songs he does—by Leadbelly and Henry Glover, by Dylan and Jagger-Richard, but also by Kern and Dubin-Warren. The result can rightfully be called rock Billie Holiday. Faithfull's nicotine-cured voice serves the material instead of triumphing over it; its musicality equals its interpretive intelligence. Just because she's jaded doesn't mean she can't be a little wise.   **A—**

The Fall: *Totale's Turns* (Rough Trade import '80). "The difference between you and us is that we have brains," Mark Smith announces to what the written notes call an "80% disco weekend mating audience" at the top of forty-three minutes of rant. The difference I notice is that the band is getting paid, but never mind—I'm so hungry for punk these days that I'm a sucker for the overall sound, maybe even the attitude. Yet though the minutes are divided officially into ten song titles, I con-

fess I have trouble telling one from another except to point out that "Roche Rumble" is pretty fierce momentumwise. I also enjoy "Choc-Stock" (sounds like "pop star") and "That Man" (sounds like "Batman"). And almost any time Smith revs his delivery up toward squeal.   **B**

The Fall: *Grotesque (After the Gramme)* (Rough Trade '81). As postpunk splinters into a thousand shafts of shadow, these arty lefties are definitely going for poetry readings with two-chord backing. My favorite is the first punk song ever to mention Herb Alpert, who appears not as a musical icon but as a record executive—at the company that distributed them back when they were trying to sell out.   **B**

The Fall: *Slates* (Rough Trade EP '81). There's no denying it—taken as a whole, the six songs do exude punk-style intelligence. Titles like "Middle Mass," "An Older Lover Etc.," and "Prole Art Threat" don't disappoint—Mark Smith is interested in the kind of stuff you want intelligent-style punks to be interested in, and gives evidence of understanding it, too. But only "Fit and Working Again," marked by an exploding two-note guitar riff, makes itself felt as an individual entity. And in the end it's hard to know exactly what Smith does think about all that stuff he's interested in—except that it's interesting. Inspirational Instruction: "Don't start improvising, for God's sake."   **B**

The Fall: *A Part of America Therein, 1981* (Cottage '82). They're as consistent as the Isley Brothers: no notable rise in quality or interest, and also no falloff. This one's a U.S.-recorded live double divided into north and south discs (San Francisco counts as south, they claim). I prefer the north, especially "The N.W.R.A."—stands for North (of England?) Will Rise Again—and "Totally Wired," which has the boys singing backup and something that will pass for a hook.   **B**

The Fall: *Perverted by Language* (Rough Trade import '83). New members, even female ones, aren't news with this group, but Mark E.'s guitarist wife Brixe Smith does lend his poetry readings apparent direction. The appearance is created by side-openers that go on so long you don't really notice your attention flagging as their momentum gives way to, well, po-etry readings—roughly accompanied, as usual.   **B—**

The Fall: *This Nation's Saving Grace* (Beggars Banquet '85). If the sentimental fallacy of good American rock and roll is roots, the sentimental fallacy of good Brit-ish rock and roll is amateurism. Not that these veterans distinguished themselves from themselves before Yank guitarist Brix E. Smith righted husband Mark E.'s feckless avant-gardishness. Still, what they've arrived at now is cunningly sloppy, minimally catchy Hawkwind/Stooges, with each three-chord drone long enough to make an avant-gardish statement but stopping short of actual boredom. And yeah, it beats roots by me.   **B+**

The Fall: *The Frenz Experiment* (Beggars Banquet '88). If Brix is so busy leading Mark into the valley of the shadow of sell-out, how'd she let him get away with an album of vamps with recitation? Lyrics center around a title catchphrase—"Get a Hotel," "The Steak Place," and "Oswald Defence Lawyer" are the cutest—and al-lude to crime. Vamps are mostly—shame on you, Brix—catchy.   **B+**

The Fall: *I Am Kurious Oranj* (Beggars Banquet '88). Vamps, drones, laid-back forcebeats, and a steady stream of allusive satire add up to the enjoyable postpunk pattern of countless other Fall albums. Yet from the opening nag—"Check the record, check the record, check the guy's track [later 'rock'] record"—small strokes keep me turning this one up. First side's got the nag and Brix's drolly tinny AOR "over-ture" and William Blake. Second's more patternlike, though who could resist the OMD-Stooges combo? Besides radio, I mean.   **A—**

The Fall: *Seminal Live* (Beggars Banquet '89). Back before they were musicians—before they played riffs requiring digital articulation and sang the occasional backup or even response—they tossed off live product all the time. The formula was simple—Mark E. harangued and the band crashed and droned. No atmo-spheric gunk like "Mollusc in Tyrol" or incompetent covers like "Pinball Ma-chine" and, yes, "Victoria," which in the great tradition of bad live albums betrays

its studio version. "Mollusc in Tyrol" and "Pinball Machine," God help us, *are* stu-dio versions.   **C+**

The Family: *The Family* (Warner Bros. '85). Paisley Park's attempt to pick up where the Time left off, this has the beats to prove it, but the best of them is cursed with a witlessly glamorous ersatz-Morris vocal and lyric and two others are instru-mentals. Then there's the slow stuff, most of it cursed with damply purple ersatz-Prince vocal and lyric. Maybe some enter-prising rapper will rip off the tracks. Till then, rest content with this Inspirational Verse: "Your body it covers my tower / Ecstasy is ours."   **C+**

The Fastbacks: *. . . and His Orchestra* (Popllama '87). Ace junk guitarist Kurt Bloch is the orchestra leader, off-key hero-ine Lulu Garguilo his girl singer, and they care so much that if the mixes were cleaner they'd strike fear in the heart of the sainted Joan Jett. As it is, even the lyrics are pretty garage. Maybe next time they'll abandon their principles a little.   **B+**

Faster Pussycat: *Faster Pussycat* (Elektra '87). Supposedly, these glammers are the plastic (isn't that the term?) Aerosmith rip, as opposed to the authentically (right?) nasty boys in Guns N' Roses. They sure do mow down their allotted share of dynamite riffs on side one, though—fit right onto *Toys in the Attic.* And if side two is pretty generic, it's only a rip, its meaner impulses undercut by Russ Meyer camp.   **B**

Fat Boys: *Fat Boys* (Sutra '84). These prize porkers parody insatiability—long after the break of dawn (long after you're limp, Dick), they'll still be stuffing it. They won't ever be great rappers technically, though Prince Markie Dee has the poise and clarity to get close and the bass-kazoo hums and belchlike aspirations of the Human Beat Box show rhythmic instinct and sonic imagination. But their sham-bling, cheerful fat-boy dance is a party for kids of all ages. I love the hooks on "Fat Boys" and the barks on "Don't You Dog Me," and if "Jail House Rap" is no "Mes-sage" or "Hustler's Convention," neither is it a trivialization—at least as silly and serious as Lee Dorsey in the coal mine or Sam Cooke on the chain gang.   **A—**

Fat Boys: *The Fat Boys Are Back* (Sutra '85). Novelty moves never stay fresh for long, but the Run-D.M.C. rip here is pretty extreme—"Don't Be Stupid" is a gimpy copy of the stalwart "You're Blind," "Hard Core Reggae" a lame copy of the gimpy "Roots, Rap, Reggae," "Rock-n-Roll" a paraplegic copy of the powerhouse "Rock Box." The only sparks come off their surviving novelty moves—Human Beat Box and gluttony boasts.   **C+**

Fat Boys: *Big and Beautiful* (Sutra '86). Just by announcing a "stupid def side," they reaffirm their timeless message: stupid is def, def is stupid, all is one. Former sideman Dave Ogrin updates their beats without trying to tackle Rick Rubin head on. Their run-in with the Russkies is as meaningful a cultural exchange as "Rapp Symphony (In C-Minor)." And even more than their moving rendition of "Sex Machine," the title track sits all over rap's serious macho heavies. It may even get these jumbo gigolos something good to eat.   **B+**

Fat Boys: *The Best Part of the Fat Boys* (Sutra '87). A label-changing ceremony that cannibalizes half their debut, it also spices up leftovers from their depressing gold follow-up—who would have thunk their ersatz reggae would outlast Run-D.M.C.'s? A musical commodity in which personality pokes through packaging as much as it does in good Ray Parker or Go-Go's, say—and more than it does in good Thompson Twins or Kool and the Gang.   **A—**

Fat Boys: *Crushin'* (Tin Pan Apple/Polydor '87). Rap's longest-running cartoon has all the street credibility of a DONT WALK sign, but that doesn't mean the anticrack and procondom messages won't make an impression with the home viewing audience. Doesn't mean the boys don't crush, either. Once a homemade music starts fulfilling its fantasies in the studio, it can also be manufactured there.   **B**

Fat Boys: *Coming Back Hard Again* (Tin Pan Apple '88). Where's the fat? "Big Man" says they're bigshots. They eat "Jel-lyroll" only in the Bessie Smith sense. So when they start going on about "ain't no joke," you know the junk food has finally gone to their heads.   **C+**

Fear: *The Record* (Slash '82). I know why Belushi liked this band—Lee Ving sings like a Punk Brother. And in the tradition of Belushi, who was such a great actor he convinced me he really was a childish glutton, Ving convinces me that he really does hate (and fear) "queers," "sluts," etc. As a moralistic square, I protest—especially given music that at its most original echoes either Mars or the Dead Kennedys. Time: 26:36.   **C+**

Feedtime: *Shovel* (Rough Trade '88). One Melbourne fan says they're like standing too close to a moving freight train with a six-pack in you, and that's corny-to-classic enough to evoke their size and inexorability—a little slower and more old-fashioned than the IRT the Ramones/Dolls came in on, which definitely doesn't mean they're slow or old-fashioned. Just an art band cum power trio that's spent nine years perfecting its sonic wisdom. Jesus and Mary Chain are wimps by comparison, Motorhead sellouts, yet in the end all three (all five) provide the same minimalist thrill—the one that's forever convincing us rock and roll will never die. You think maybe it won't?   **A—**

Feedtime: *Cooper-S* (Rough Trade '88). Most cover albums trip over their own roots—self-conscious simplicity is too neat a trick to bring off a dozen times running. These guys are adepts of self-conscious simplicity, so naturally they have trouble negotiating the radio classics that got them started. I mean, "Paint It Black" and "Street Fighting Man" have *tempo shifts, man.*   **B**

The Feelies: *Crazy Rhythms* (Stiff '80). They're suburban lads from New Jersey every bit as normal and unspoiled as, oh, Brian Wilson, only this ain't 1961: why shouldn't they know about Coltrane and "Sister Ray"? Beneficiaries of local privilege note that the magnitude of their raveups—and in essence all they do is rave up—doesn't come fully alive on record, but their freshness and purity of conception does. Exciting in a disturbingly abstract way, or maybe disturbing in an excitingly abstract way, and either way is just the way these so-straight-they're-cool weirdos want it. **A−**

The Feelies: *The Good Earth* (Coyote '86). Coproducer Peter Buck is occasioning harrumphs about how suddenly they sound like R.E.M., but if anything R.E.M. sounds like them with excess baggage: aching lyricism, gorgeous hooks, mumbled poetry—in a word, corn. The Feelies, in turn, sound a lot like a classic band called the Velvet Underground. And like themselves, unmistakably, even though six years and Peter Buck have rounded off their gawky corners and filled out their sound. **A−**

The Feelies: *No One Knows* (Coyote EP '86). Adds the slightly arcane Beatles song "She Said She Said" to the slightly arcane Neil Young song "Sedan Delivery" before it resorts to two *Good Earth* cuts that seem doubly otiose after Jonathan Demme has proven them capable of an all-cover EP. Or LP. **B**

The Feelies: *Only Life* (A&M '88). With rock and roll—music—as mystico-cerebral as the Feelies', analysis takes you only so far. In the end, you get it or you don't. Me, I find album three their most accomplished and least effective, and suspect that both its accomplishment and its (relative) ineffectiveness reflect the same crisis of growth. After all, this is rock and roll, not music; rock and roll has always had trouble with the mature perspective signaled by a couplet like "Got a ways to go / So much to know." Just because the perpetual nervousness of *Crazy Rhythms* and the pastoral lyricism of *The Good Earth* are callower, they fit the musical concept better. Either that or the concept is fading for me. Or for them. **B+**

Fela: *Black President* (Arista import '81). Building steadily off unpolyrhythmic traps, underpinning/undermining the beat with multiple drums, stating and embellishing horn phrases and then stating and embellishing them again, repeating verbal taglines countless times again or varying them by a few words to strengthen his

points, Fela has constructed Afrobeat, which to my ear is as like and unlike any competing African pop style as it is like and unlike any American pop style. It's just Fela, instantly recognizable, although not always instantly distinguishable from other Fela. Distinguishing themselves here are "I.T.T." ("international thief thief") and "Sorrow Tears and Blood" ("dem regular trademark"). That's three-quarters of the record. [Later on Capitol.] **B+**

Fela Anikulapo-Kuti: *Original Sufferhead* (Capitol '84). The musical definition is so sharp it's hooky, with arresting commentary from a backup chorus that includes many of the leader's wives. And the lyrics help, especially "Power Show"'s bitter observations in re bureaucratic status-tripping. The title (and other) track, in his geopolitical mode, makes its point less cleanly. **B+**

Fela Anikulapo-Kuti & Egypt 80: *Live in Amsterdam* (Capitol '84). There are obviously significant political differences between Fela and the musician he most resembles, James Brown—JB has never been imprisoned for his egomania, which is the least inflammatory construction that can be put on why Fela is in jail at this moment. More likely it's the ingrained defiance of the Nigerian government voiced (though my pidgin isn't so advanced that I get all the details) by the three songs he squeezes onto this live double. That's right, three songs—like JB, Fela is a true son of vamp-till-ready. Unfortunately, since he's not a world-class saxophonist or singer, and since this touring unit is long on brass and short on things to hit (one conga total), eighty minutes of steady but not quite uplifting groove punctuated by interesting horn arrangements is what you get. **B−**

Fela Anikulapo Kuti: *Army Arrangement* (Celluloid '85). I've never had complete confidence in Fela's myth. By both African and Euro-American standards, his arrangements are repetitive, his singing and playing nothing special, and his political ideas ill-informed and grandiose. But as pop pros of any culture go, he's an original and a radical, and even if he weren't his music would deserve our attention and his imprisonment our abhorrence. Let's hope this Bill Laswell remix proves propitious. Rather than bedizening it with aural gee-gaws, Laswell imports sympatico cousins to beef up the groove—Bernie Worrell (on Hammond B-3!), Aiyb Dieng (on five different percussion devices), and, most spectacularly, Sly Dunbar, whose Simmons pulse could make a skinhead dance one foot at a time. Fela's best album—wonder if they'll let him hear it.   **A—**

Fela: *Shuffering and Shmiling* (Celluloid '85). Circa 1977, shortly after the Army torched his compound, an incorrigible troublemaker raps about the limits of God, sometimes in outrageous mock Arabic. Only one drawback: label's marketing the 12:21-minute song plus 9:47-minute version as an $8.98-list LP. As a single, this makes my top twenty-five. As an album, it's docked two notches for forced format.   **B**

Fela Anikulapo Kuti: *No Agreement* (Celluloid '85). Like all groove artists, Fela benefits mightily from marginal differentiation, which on this 1977 outing with Afrika 70 is provided by the blats, splats, and tuneful snatches of Lester Bowie's trumpet. The 15:36 title side is distinguished from its 15:48 companion by a few minutes of Fela mouthing off and a catchier keystone ostinato.   **B+**

Fela Anikulapo Kuti: *Teacher Don't Teach Me No Nonsense* (Mercury '87). Fears that imprisonment has turned him into a shell can be put aside, and by tacking twelve- and fourteen-minute instrumentals in front of fourteen- and eighteen-minute songs Wally Badarou goes a long way toward solving the man's record-making problem. At half an hour apiece, his grooves have time to prove themselves, and the vinyl sound is bright enough if you pump up the volume a little. As for message, the lyrics are certainly touched by his incarceration, but his pan-Africanism seems unchanged: it's as limited, as scathing, and as justifiable as ever.   **B+**

Fela Ransome-Kuti & the Africa 70: *Greatest Hits* (EMI import '84). Read the fine print: "Recorded in Lagos Nigeria [sic] and EMI, London 1971–1973." In other words, in the early days of Afrobeat,

while Fela was *(a)* in the throes of inspiration or *(b)* getting his shit together. Or, as you'd figure, some combination. Familiar riffs and beats are already in place on these four-minute songs, and harsh rhetoric, too. At times the singing goes for a feral power abandoned later. But the sonority and build and staying power of great Fela are missing, and missed.   **B**

Ferron: *Testimony* (Philo '82). It sure isn't her male backup that gives this Canadian the edge on her pastoral-lesbian sisters in the U.S.A.—the Olivia collective could duplicate these modestly imaginative folk-rock arrangements and maybe even think them up. But Ferron's natural musicianship is something special: the light, grainy, "halfway pretty" mezzo glances off sweet-and-sour words and melodies with a fetching ease that's never laid-back. And given the utopian burden of so much "women's music," an old sinner like me is reassured by all the grief she cops to.   **A—**

Ferron: *Shadows on a Dime* (Lucy import '84). She knows two or three melodies, she sings flat, she phrases every line the same, she can get pretty gauche lyrically, and in most of this she reminds me more than a little of, I'm sorry, the young Bob Dylan. The repetitious insistence of her most powerful songs drives home her commitment to folkie usages that in other women's-music practitioners sound pat, purist, and out of it, and a shifting pool of (male and female) backup players provides the variety. From her smokily confessional introspection to her habitual occultism to her eight-minute, eight-stanza "It Won't Take Long" ("it" being the Revolution or something similar), her bullshit is her own. And she'll make you like it.   **A—**

Bryan Ferry: *Boys and Girls* (Warner Bros. '85). Sure "Make believing is the real thing." When Ferry is grooving, though, the emphasis is on the make-believe, not the real. Here there's heavy slippage, especially on side one. His voice thicker and more mucous, his tempos dragging despite all the fancy beats he's bought, he runs an ever steeper risk of turning into the romantic obsessive he's always played so zealously.   **B—**

Bryan Ferry: *Bete Noir* (Reprise/EG '87). As with Mick Jagger, of all people, the signal that self-imitation has sunk into self-parody is enunciatory ennui—vocal mannerisms that were once ur-posh are now just complacent. Except for the Parisian title tune the second side is unlistenable. The first side is faster. **C+**

Bryan Ferry/Roxy Music: *Street Life: 20 Greatest Hits* (Reprise '89). Their third compilation in twelve years is the third to include "Love Is the Drug," but I won't quibble. "These Foolish Things" was always better as title than as rendition, but I won't quibble. The number in the subtitle follows the formula twenty = CD, and I'm quibbling. A great gift idea—for yourself you can buy less or more. **B+**

Richard "Dimples" Fields: *Dimples* (Boardwalk '81). Except for Betty Wright's backtalking one-upwomanship, the prime originals here—"I Like Your Lovin" and "She's Got Papers on Me"—are standard-issue love-man come-ons, but "Dimples"'s appropriation of the two greatest doowop oldies is self-aggrandizing sentimentality at its most audacious. And "I've Got To Learn To Say No!" leaves no doubt as to just what he gets from his earth angel in the still of the night. **B+**

Richard "Dimples" Fields: *Mr. Look So Good* (Boardwalk '82). Aware that Fields brought something quite his own to the soul/r&b heritage, I wondered why his buttery come-on never moved me. Reason's simple—he's as egoistic and ultimately lightweight as James Taylor, another traditionalist original. Dissecting women with a butcher's eye one minute and quoting Biblical prophecy the next, he persuades me of neither his essential goodness nor his essential badness. I've got nothing against the combination, either—just ask Marvin Gaye, who works at least as hard at it as Fields, or Al Green, who doesn't. **B−**

Fiends: *We've Come for Your Beer* (Bemisbrain '84). This hardcore comedy highlight includes tributes to the MC-5, the Brady Bunch, John Belushi, and Bob Hope ("Die Bob Die") among its twelve tunes or tracks or whatever. Not counting

the perfectly timed "Ramblin' Rose," my favorite is "No More Drugs," an idea that's always good for a cheap laugh. Just wish more of them had as much tune or whatever. Time: 23:36. **B+**

Fihlamahlazo Nabochwepheshe: *Ziphansi Izintsizwa* (Vulindlela import '88). On several of the mbaqanga albums now available from New Music Distribution Service, the shock of the simple is neutralized by the dull ache of the monotonous. Here the beats remain pretty basic, and damned if I can hear the rude-bowed fiddle depicted on the cover, but the bass is active, there's constant squeezebox byplay, and the leader never shuts up, following song with harangue on almost every cut. Wish I had some idea what he was talking about. **B+**

Fine Art: *Scan* (Good EP '82). Leading off with a deliberate, hypnotically bass-hooked existentialist ditty called "You Tell Me" that's the catchiest piece of white-woman art-funk since "Too Many Creeps," they roll calmly downhill until the anticlimactic "Scheduled Interruption," when they fall off a cliff that students of band names will have anticipated. Original grade: B plus. **B**

Fine Young Cannibals: *Fine Young Cannibals* (I.R.S. '85). Andy Cox and David Steele aren't quite up to Beat-quality tunes or the post-Caribbean funk that might compensate, and some will find Roland Gift's Brit-soul strain affected. Me, I knew he was singing about something real long before I checked out the lyrics, which testify as does all too little black crossover these days to an ordinary life of hard choices—a lot harder than whether to believe that woman, which rest assured does enter into it. **B+**

Fine Young Cannibals: *The Raw and the Cooked* (I.R.S. '89). All I can tell you about the content of these songs is that they seem to concern romantic love. That makes them pop. I can also tell you that I don't much care if I know what they're about or not. That makes them good pop. And add that since this is 1989, good pop doesn't mean melodies and hooks, though neither matter is overlooked. It means beats (most admittedly quite hooky) and vocal ID tag.   **A**—

Firehose: *"Ragin', Full-On"* (SST '86). Maybe Ed Crawford appeared to Mike Watt and George Hurley as in a vision, but he appears to us as their new frontman, and the courage they showed starting fresh after D. Boon took the Minutemen with him resists auralization almost as obdurately as that vision does. In short, this sounds pretty good insofar as it postpunks like the old band and pretty bad insofar as it makes room for Crawford, a moderately hot guitarist whose vocal instincts are as sappy as his lyrics.   **C**+

Firehose: *If'n* (SST '87). They sound more like a regular rock band and also more like the Minutemen, which isn't a contradiction because the Minutemen were evolving into a regular rock band when D. Boon died—one that resembled this fluidly funky outfit a lot more than it did the weird and wimpy hippies of the debut. This time Ed Crawford provides enough garage hooks to get by, meaning Mike Watt doesn't disappear amid the new guy's mannerisms. I only wish Watt's Central American mention held like his Richard Hell mention and his Michael Stipe tribute.   **B**

Fire Town: *In the Heart of the Heart Country* (Beat '86). No oblique harmonies or tricky meters or underhanded lyrics to prove how arty they are, just a blunt collection of pop songs that hauls out the hooks and hits you over the head with them thump-thump-thump. Which could and does get annoying when you're not feeling complaisant, but for the most part has its unfashionable charm. If you think the Smithereens are something, I dare you to play "Rain on You" three times. And if you don't, I double-dare you. [Later on Atlantic.]   **B**+

Fishbone: *Fishbone* (Columbia EP '85). Looking like postmodern vaudevillians who've just signed themselves in at the mental hospital, with sartorial details appropriated from the Specials, Dizzy Gillespie, Jimi Hendrix, Stepin Fetchit, and whoever, these six black L.A. teenagers show a flair for visual outrage worthy of George Clinton himself, though funk is far down on an equally eclectic list of musical influences that subsumes metal, new wave, and cool-jazz finger-pop into a ska Prince Buster never dreamed of. It's all too scattered, without much songwriting focus beyond the Devo-meets-Clinton "? (Modern Industry)," but in a world of Prince clones and ugly presidents these guys are cause for hope.   **B**+

Fishbone: *In Your Face* (Columbia '86). Last time they looked like sons of P-Funk and sounded like sons of Frank Yankovic's dotage, which suggested their stock in trade was cognitive dissonance. This time they look like 2-Tone fashion plates and sound like big-time new wave satirists, which suggests their stock in trade is haircuts. Uniting the two phases is their sense of rhythm or lack of same.   **B**—

Fishbone: *It's a Wonderful Life (We Gonna Have a Good Time)* (Columbia EP '87). Songwriting on this Xmas novelty was so noticeable I thought maybe they'd reconstructed some obscurity from the flick of the same name, but the pissed-off title track's an original, as are Saint Nick as debbil-cum-wino, Christ as comsymp, and Uncle Scrooge as Uncle Jam. All are well-served by the band's feckless eclecticism, too. Call it a gift from God and hope it presages a brighter day.   **B**+

Fishbone: *Truth and Soul* (Epic '88). They're better at truth than soul, always a harder sell, and harder to push beyond interesting, too. Taken one at a time, about half these experiments would change any radio station's pace quite satisfactorily. Taken in sequence, they don't follow. **B**

Edi Fitzroy: *Youthman Penitentiary* (Alligator '82). "With the Roots Radics Band," announces a subtitle, and that's the usual good sign. "Featuring his three 1982 top 10 Jamaican hits!" crows a sticker, and I wish I were sure that the third one (after the title track and "First Class Citizen," which gives itself away with a dub) were "Dread Locks Party" and its borrowed sax, not "African Queen" and its stolen Sedaka. "The only new vocal star to emerge this year," inform the notes, and I hope 1983's has more than one trick in his or her gullet.   **B**

The Fixx: *Reach the Beach* (MCA '83). As with most Anglodisco, this record's success isn't totally bewildering—it assembles an acceptable complement of catchy secondhand riffs and beats. Only I suspect that what sells it is the very thing that makes me hope I never hear those riffs and beats again—Cy Curnin's agonized can-this-be-adulthood? vocal style, influenced by everyone from Bryan Ferry to Lou Gramm but oh so much more doubt-ridden than any old fart.   **C**

Roberta Flack: *The Best of Roberta Flack* (Atlantic '81). On the evidence of these hits (the early albums were marginally livelier), she has nothing whatsoever to do with rock and roll or rhythm and blues and almost nothing to do with soul. The analogy isn't Donny Hathaway (who lives on in duet after duet), much less Stevie Wonder (also represented)—it's Barry Manilow. She made "The First Time Ever I Saw Your Face" and "Killing Me Softly With His Song," he made "Mandy" and "I Write the Songs," and who is to say which achievement will prove more durable? Flack has much better taste, I agree—that's the point. In the long run, pop lies are improved by vulgarity.   **C**

Flashdance (Casablanca '83). Ten different singers collaborate with half a dozen producers to collapse a myriad of pop polarities onto one all-inclusive rock-disco concept soundtrack. Tenors and contraltos, guitars and synthesizers, lust and love, ballads and DOR—all are equal as these mostly undistinguished, mostly quite functional artistes proceed through their mostly undistinguished, mostly quite functional material. Concept: the overinsistent beat, which signifies how compulsively they seek a good time that retains shreds of both meaning and ecstatic release.   **B—**

Fleetwood Mac: *Live* (Warner Bros. '80). The name of the leader is Lindsey Buckingham. His milieu is the studio, his metier pop. So the lax arrangements on this two-LP profit-sharing plan must have pained him almost as much as trying to fill solo space better suited to the likes of Peter Green and Jeremy Spencer. I wonder whether any of the five songs not on their three big LPs will see daylight again after this sorry beginning. And not counting the Brian Wilson chorale—just the composer to do live, right?—I wonder whether Lindsey will mourn any of them.   **C+**

Fleetwood Mac: *Mirage* (Warner Bros. '82). This is the safe follow-up *Rumours* wasn't, and I find myself alternately charmed by its craft and offended by its banality. After seven years, you'd think they'd weary of romantic tension-and-release. But despite the occasional I'm-scareds and can't-go-backs, you'd never know how much passion they've already put behind them—they write about infatuation and its aftermaths like twenty-year-olds. This is obviously a commercial advantage, and I wouldn't want to be immune to its truth. But pop music offers endless variations on that truth, and since only the most graceful are worth pondering I have to say that there isn't another "Hold Me" here.   **B+**

Fleetwood Mac: *Tango in the Night* (Warner Bros. '87). Fifteen years ago, when their secret weapon was someone named Bob Welch, they made slick, spacy, steady-bottomed pop that was a little ahead of the times commercially. Now, when their secret weapon is their public, they make slick, spacy, steady-bottomed pop that's a little behind the times commercially. This is pleasant stuff, nothing to get exercised about either way—no *Rumours* or *Fleetwood Mac*, but better than *Bare Trees* or *Mystery to Me*, not to mention *Mirage*. Marginally better, anyway. In a style where margins are all. And all ain't all that much any more.   **B+**

Fleetwood Mac: *Greatest Hits* (Warner Bros. '88). To my surprise, I had more fun replaying side two of *Mirage,* which turns out to have some weird and pleasant shit on it. Reminding me that what distinguished them from your average great pop band was that their hits were improved by their putative filler. So with some obvious—in fact, all too familiar—exceptions, the radio-ready format makes them seem blander than they actually are.   **B**

The Flesh Eaters: *A Minute To Pray a Second To Die* (Ruby '81). Brainchild of sometime *Slash* editor Chris D. and featuring a saxophone and an X-rated rhythm section, this eschews the no-speed-limit egoism of El Lay punk convention for a more matoor view of the world, based on the idea that horror movies are worth taking seriously. Not bad for a laff.   **B+**

The Flesh Eaters: *Forever Came Today* (Ruby '82). I've always taken Chris D.'s horror-movie imagery as a joke that went with his singing, aptly described by one admirer as a "strangling werewolf commercial." Here it's no joke, but rather a wellspring of metaphor with which to evoke the horrors of modern love, so to speak. This reflects poorly on the moral and intellectual resources of young people today. It also sounds like a strangling werewolf commercial.   **C+**

Fleshtones: *Up-Front* (I.R.S. EP '80). I didn't believe they were nothing but a party until I witnessed them leap out on the NYU stage tossing packs of Camels to the mob, then demolish Nervus Rex in a battle of the bands. And from these five songs you still won't believe it. Best but not great is "The Girl From Baltimore"—real party city, cross between Philly and D.C., none of which the song implies. Nervus Rex album's pretty nice.   **B−**

Fleshtones: *Roman Gods* (I.R.S. '81). This is where they get the junk-rock down—reckless enthusiasm plus the less stylish strains of late-'60s dance music add up to their own groove. But though it's hooky and endearing, it's short on what one might call nuggets, which is why a whole side of unexceptionably jet-propelled tracks tends to lose momentum. In fact, whenever I try to concentrate for even an entire cut, my mind starts to wander, just like with Jackson Browne.   **B+**

Fleshtones: *Blast Off!* (ROIR cassette '82). As a student of history I'm glad these mythic 1978 sessions are finally for sale; as a connoisseur of inspired amateurism I must remind fun-seekers that magic is hard to mass-produce. The cruddy sound doesn't make it any more like being there, and after the wacko "Soul Struttin' " and the anthemic "American Beat" I start daydreaming about the next garage.   **B**

The Fleshtones: *Hexbreaker* (I.R.S. '83). Fun is a fine principle, but it works better when you start with the fun than when you start with the principle, which is why so much theoretically unpretentious rock and roll sounds forced anyway. Gets harder with every album, too. This is number three.   **B−**

Flipper: *The Generic Album* (Subterranean '82). I love 'em, you may hate 'em, and that's the way Flipper planned it. Live, they play the same two chords until everybody who doesn't want to have fun goes home, then reward those delighted/mesmerized by their synthesis of the Stooges and the Grateful Dead by throwing in an extra chord and revving up half a step. The record somehow manages to achieve the same effect about eight times in forty minutes. For this they're classified as hardcore, but Jim Fouratt (leaning toward hate-'em as their set passed the two-hour mark) calls the band art-damaged and that's more the idea. The playing is crude ("Everybody start at the same time, ready"), unremitting ("Sex Bomb" has seven words and lasts close to eight minutes), and immensely charitable and good-humored (Iggy with Jerry's soul, I'm not kidding). The lyrics are existential resignation at its most enthusiastic. Inspirational Verse: "It's Life! Life! Life is the only thing worth living for."   **A**

Flipper: *Gone Fishin'* (Subterranean '84). I must have listened to *Generic* Flipper fifty times without fully registering the dark and more or less unceasing roil of Ted Falconi's guitar. On this album it was the first thing I noticed. Watch out for bands who get heavily into texture. And stop making jokes.   **B**

Flipper: *Public Flipper Limited* (Subterranean '86). A live double recorded mostly in '80 and '82, when their fuck-it wasn't yet a defeat, this has the spirit. But though they were anarchists they were no fools, so they put their best material on their first and forever best album, leaving the profusion of originals finally available here to bring up the rear.   **B+**

Flipper: *Sex Bomb Baby!* (Subterranean '88). They had another classic in them after all, or call it a semiclassic—all the stuff from their moment that didn't make the classic. On twelve inches of vinyl (three extras make the cassette/CD too much of a bad thing), the six sides of single (including the power-drone black-comic bohemian-realist paranoid-commonsensical "Old Lady Who Swallowed a Fly") and three compilation cuts (including a live "Ever" that climaxes with Woodstock warnings for hardcore brats) sound made for each other. And the fanzine flexidisc adds that soupcon of shit.   **A—**

A Flock of Seagulls: *A Flock of Seagulls* (Jive '82). This is very silly, and I know why earnest new-wavers resent it. But I think it's a hoot—so transparently, guilelessly expedient that it actually provides the hook-chocked fun most current pop bands only advertise. The human drummer and all-too-human guitarist provide reassuring links with a past these boys have no more intention of giving up than you, me, or Rod Stewart. And if the cheerfully mechanical voices and cheerfully mechanical melodies do once or twice venture toward cheerfully mechanical lyrics about the direly mechanical end of the world, well, that's just the shape of bubblegum to come.   **A—**

A Flock of Seagulls: *Listen* (Jive '83). If you think I enjoy enjoying this epitome of new-wave commercialism, this pap beloved of no one but MTV-addled suburbanites (not even *NME,* ever!)—well, you're right. I'm not just being campy, either, except insofar as camp means the luxury of surrender to stupidity—in this case to sheer, sensationalistic aural pleasure, whooshes and zooms and sustains and computerized ostinatos and English boys whining about their spaced-out, financially secure lot, all held aloft on tunes Mr. Spock could hum and a beat a veejay could dance to. There are too many slow ones on number two, so I don't play both sides indiscriminately like I do with the debut. But hell, "What Am I Supposed To Do" even has a decent lyric.   **B+**

A Flock of Seagulls: *The Best of a Flock of Seagulls* (Jive '87). If they were never as sublime as "Chewy Chewy," they were never as icky as "1, 2, 3, Red Light," and unlike the Ohio Express or the 1910 Fruitgum Co., they-wrote-all-the-songs-themselves. I might even claim that this was where the idiots took over the studio if I hadn't noticed that their weakest cut by far—1985's terminal "Who's That Girl (She's Got It)," designed to convince us that they're human beings—is the-one-they-produced-themselves.   **A—**

Rosie Flores: *Rosie Flores* (Reprise '87). From the person or persons responsible for Dwight Yoakam comes this former Screamin' Siren and unheralded neonothingist. Her slightly husky voice one-third promise and two-thirds self-respect, she doesn't even know how to put on airs about not putting on airs. All she does is deliver ten songs that are worth her while, which from Reba McEntire or George Jones these days would qualify as a miracle. And once in a while bassist and occasional songwriter James Intveld contributes a harmony. Gram and Emmylou in reverse—a touch I like.   **A—**

The Flying Burrito Brothers: *Farther Along: The Best of the Flying Burrito Brothers* (A&M cassette/CD '88). "I don't think I ever really appreciated Gram until these last few years," allows Chris Hillman, whose 1970 arrival catalyzed the Burritos' decline into one-dimensional "country-rock," a term Hillman disdains, probably because "folk-rock" is more his speed. "This collection represents the best and worst of the 'Parsons-era Burritos,'" he clucks, and since Parsons's worst was brainier and more soulful than the folk/country-rock norm, that's why even the outtakes—four songs and one version never available on any U.S. album, including a Bee Gees cover I bet Chris vetoed—have more bite than most anything they recorded after their genius moved farther along. I miss "My Uncle" and even "Hippie Boy" from *Gilded Palace of Sin,* and "Older Guys," their least Hillmanesque effort thereafter. But any reissue that respects even the cut order of a timeless LP that it reproduces almost in full deserves its digital remix. Which doesn't overdo the drums, by the way.   **A**

John Fogerty: *Centerfield* (Warner Bros. '85). The hosannas and precious metal showered on this slight, self-centered reentry tempt one to overlook its slight, self-centered virtues. Fogerty's drumming has definitely sharpened, though he doesn't hold up the break on "Zanz Can't Dance" any better than Doug Clifford would have, and cut for cut *Centerfield* is catchier than his previous effort—he had nine years to come up with the tunes, after all. But the material just isn't Creedence-quality. The mythopoeic genre piece "The Old Man Down the Road" was the keynote single not out of commercial caution but because it's the strongest thing on the record, yet does anyone claim it's the equal of "Proud Mary" or "Green River" or even "Rockin' All Over the World"? And is anyone foolish enough to believe that the generalized "Mr. Greed" (not to mention the simpy "I Saw It on T.V.") has the teeth of "Don't Look Now" or "Fortunate Son," or that his first-ever career resumé "Centerfield" is a personal statement to compare with "Lookin' Out My Back Door"—in short, that the genre pieces are illuminated by visionary flashes, which is what made Creedence a great band to begin with?   **B+**

John Fogerty: *Eye of the Zombie* (Warner Bros. '86). With his compact songs and workingman's aura, Fogerty was an outsider in the '60s. In the '80s, with his San Fran contemporaries either cozying up to MTV or peddling nostalgia on the bar circuit, it's clear that he took the visionary fallacies of the time as deeply to heart as Jerry Garcia himself, and good for him. Then as now he had no interest in fashion, which is why his music retains an undeniable modicum of interest. But like they say, the '60s are over.   **B**

Ellen Foley: *Spirit of St. Louis* (Epic/Cleveland International '81). This well-intentioned side trip from punk postpurism to Weimar-manqué artsong might be less embarrassing if Foley and all her voice les-

sons weren't such typical backup stuff, but as it is she really bollixes such conceits as "Priests married themselves, using Bibles and mirrors / In China all the bicycle chains snapped at once." Which Joe Strummer, here reduced to strummer and backerupper, might actually spit out with some authority. Producer Mick Jones, dubbed "My Boyfriend," acts as if too many chops are Peter Asher's problem, but it's just the opposite—in studio-rock, every note has to be perfect and then some, which leaves Paul, Topper, Mickey etc. two steps short much of the time.   **C**

Folkways: *A Vision Shared—A Tribute to Woody Guthrie and Leadbelly* (Columbia '88). Half a century after the fact, Popular Front song achieves the industrial credibility of Popular Front flick. It isn't just Uncle Pete and Li'l Arlo and Taj Mahal and Sweet Honey in the Rock pitching in on these Woody and Huddie covers, proceeds earmarked to help purchase the leftwing Folkways catalogue for the august Smithsonian Institution. It's magnates like Bruce and Mellencamp and U2, legends like Little Richard and Brian Wilson and Bob Dylan, even Willie and Emmylou defying country's rightwing line. And wherever they come from they put out. Dylan hasn't sung this fresh or Taj this tough in years, Arlo picks a lethal obscurity from his father's vast book, Mellencamp's folky pretensions seem natural, Springsteen escapes momentarily from his slough of significance, and Sweet Honey earn their leadoff spot. Every example I've cited threatens to surpass its model. Elsewhere, the material holds up.   **A—**

Fool Proof: *No Friction* (Gramavision '88). "Jazzmen Play the Blues," says the cover sticker, a claim that has excited me unreasonably ever since I witnessed Henry Threadgill and friends back Left-Hand Frank lo these many years ago, and what could live up to that? Not this, if only because no real bluesman (as opposed to rocker) anchors it. After progressing from Delta to New Orleans to bebop to lounge-organ, it settles into jazzmen's r&b, with Pheeroan akLaff staying in Al Jackson's pocket on "Love and Happiness" but favoring a more swinging groove. Ronnie Drayton and Bernie Worrell make some lounge act, and "August Wilson's Urban Blue Blues" is what a young Ornette Coleman might have come up with if he'd tried to write a "Now's the Time"—bent bebop, blues mostly by association.   **B+**

Footloose (Columbia '84). Since the idea of this deeply cynical movie is to assure teen-agers not only that AOR equals youth rebellion but also that they can dance to it, and given AOR's enduring commitment to racial segregation, it seems appropriate to note that the two first-rate songs on this offensively glitzy, offensively hyper soundtrack are by black people. Deniece Williams and Shalamar, in case you didn't know, both available as singles and a good thing too.   **C**

The Force M.D.'s: *Love Letters* (Tommy Boy '84). If only there was a little something to the songwriting, the cute idea of anchoring a falsetto group to a rap rhythm section might have produced more than an exceedingly cute album. Certainly the fivesome sing sweet and rap sharp, and the LeBlanc-Wimbish-McDonald bottom is almost lithe enough for a top, even on the reggae. But not quite.   **B**

Force M.D.'s: *Chillin'* (Tommy Boy '86). What scattered grown-ups seem to like about these teen goody-goodies is the touch of authenticity the sweet burr on the edge of T.C.D.'s tenor injects into the New Edition formula—a promise of, what else, soul. But the more I listen the more irrelevant that seems—when you crave a little authenticity, you don't go to a cute factory for it. What they need is more stringent quality controls than they're likely to get from chief producer Robin Halpin—not to mention the bozos who captain the ill-conceived Fat Boys excursion, or even "Tender Love" 's Jimmy Jam and Terry Lewis, who've never made balladry their long suit. I know, the kids'll buy it anyway. But it won't keep any of them in school, I guarantee you.   **C+**

Franco & Rochereau: *Omona Wapi* (Shanachie '85). Individually, they're the great rivals and grand old men of Zairean "rumba" and all that's followed—very roughly (and I mean very), think of them as James Brown and Frank Sinatra. Frankly fat Franco is a guitar-wielding rhythm-master with a sweet, high voice, Rochereau (a/k/a Tabu Ley) a supernal tenor who favors cummerbunds. They've released well over two hundred LPs between them, but fine as the eight or ten I've managed to hear are, not one comes close to this Paris-recorded collaboration (their third, or sixth, or some such number)—one of the few African records in which the singing outshines the rhythms, and the rhythms are gorgeous. Its effortless propulsion and shameless beauty are so unmistakable that two acquaintances, neither a professional, have asked the title after hearing it over the telephone. That's O-M-O-N-A W-A-P-I.   **A+**

Frankie Goes to Hollywood: *Welcome to the Pleasure Dome* (Island '84). Hype is a word I try to use no more normatively than I do guitar—one's almost as intrinsic to rock and roll as the other. And this is a truly great hype. We're not just talking spectacularly entertaining, like the dripping labia of Mom's Apple Pie, or spectacularly profitable, like the Monkees, or both, like the "Thriller" video. We're talking hype as primary signifier, as a carrier of rich, profound, and potentially subversive meanings. I love the hype right down to the album package, and will even grant that the appalling quality of the band's music enriches the meaning further. But that doesn't mean I'm going to be caught dead telling anybody to listen to it. The singles side is okay—"Relax" has proven itself a fetching fuck-mantra, "Two Tribes" is fair-to-middling political art. But on the whole Frankie are a marginally competent arena-rock band who don't know how to distinguish between effeminacy and pretension, like an English Grand Funk gone disco. Follow the ads by all means. Watch the videos. And steal these inner sleeves.   **C**

Aretha Franklin: *Aretha* (Arista '80). Yes, there are bright spots—a funk trifle with Re on piano, an autobiographical reminiscence speeded up Vegas-style, her voice. But the guidance she gets from new corporate mentor Clive Davis is typified by the vamp she adds to "What a Fool Believes." "Get the funk, get it now," she murmurs valiantly over a rhythm section anchored, as they say, by Louis Johnson and Jeff Porcaro. And who do you think plays the sax outro? If you guessed David Sanborn you get the picture. [Catalogue number: AL 9358.]   **B**−

Aretha Franklin: *Love All the Hurt Away* (Arista '81). This is her best pop album since *Young, Gifted and Black* because it's her best groove album since *Spirit in the Dark.* The swinging, streaming, Quincy Jonesish dance pulse of (no getting around it) Toto (though Arif Mardin did have the smarts to add Jacksons vet Greg Philinganes) even helps her through jivy remakes of "Hold On I'm Coming" and "You Can't Always Get What You Want" on side one. But side two is, as Aretha puts it in her candid "Whole Lot of Me," the "cream de la cream": for once her voice is as rich and confident as it always has every right to be, and Aretha asserts her needs and prerogatives as if they go with the flow. Which they do.   **A**−

Aretha Franklin: *Jump to It* (Arista '82). Luther Vandross is a great singer, and he's gotten a great singer's album out of Aretha. But he's not a great songwriter, and great singers do their greatest work with great songs. Sometimes great singers don't even know what a great song is, which is why we get to hear Aretha perform artificial respiration on Sam Dee's "If She Don't Want Your Lovin' " and the Isleys' hoary "It's Your Thing." And sometimes great singers are also great songwriters, which is why Aretha and Luther thank their stars for Smokey's "Just My Daydream."   **B**+

Aretha Franklin: *Get It Right* (Arista '83). As long as Luther Vandross produces her she'll never do anything awful, but she might do something bland. Vandross's problem, obviously, is songs—he does his job on the title track, but even the one by Aretha's son outclasses his other four, which I blame in part on collaborator Marcus Miller, whose bass anchors the suavely pervasive groove. His virtue, just as obviously, is that he lets Aretha sing—

there's a hoarse velvet grain to her voice here that turns Michael Lovesmith's "Better Friends Than Lovers" into a major statement and Ann Peebles's "I Wish It Would Rain" into an Aretha song. **B**+

Aretha Franklin: *Who's Zoomin' Who?* (Arista '85). It seems so simple now that it's happened, but let's face it—she's been trying to sell out this big for at least ten years. And take my word for it—she hasn't done anything near this good in over a dozen. It couldn't have happened without the top-forty revival, and it couldn't have happened without Narada Michael Walden, who unhesitatingly plugged his first legend into one pop format after another and came up with classics almost every time. From lead rocker to hooked ballad to Caribe Richie carnivalesque, these songs go no deeper than Franklin can make them by breathing, but their instant inevitability could keep this album alive for years. And when somebody like Aretha Franklin goes multiplatinum, the world rejoices.   **A**

Aretha Franklin: *Aretha* (Arista '86). In which Narada Michael Walden returns to the land of weenies whence he came, and on some underling's steam—not up to composing these turkeys himself, he hired the songs out and then laid them on Re, who managed to sing as if she still cared. Duet attraction George Michael can't touch Annie Lennox; duet attraction Larry Graham can't even touch Peter Wolf. For this Clive didn't milk *Who's Zoomin' Who?* till it bled? [Catalogue number: AL 8442.]   **B**−

Aretha Franklin: *One Lord, One Faith, One Baptism* (Arista '88). This artist-produced special-price live double comes from somewhere inside her—her soul, say—that doesn't distinguish between the personal, the political, and the religious. Structured to evoke a real church service, every side interrupted by a lengthy patch of prayer/ invocation/sermon, it offers scant beat and lots of vocal glory, with much laying on of harmony. Guests include Mavis Staples, the Mighty Clouds of Joy, Jaspar Williams, and (on three sides for fourteen minutes total) Jesse Jackson. At times it seems like a self-indulgence, but more often its refusal of commercial compromise triumphs. Call it her tribute to her daddy. And never complain about her taste in clothes again.   **B+**

Aretha Franklin: *Through the Storm* (Arista '89). Of the five count-'em five producers who labored over these eight tracks, only Narada Michael Walden— who claims four, including three of the four count-'em four celebrity cameos—can assure a very modern pop album. But only in spite of Walden is it a moderately seductive modern pop album. Delegating the JB duet to dodos who don't have the sense to sample him, buying noncommital generalizations even Whitney can't resist twisting, asking Elton in on the title number, the man epitomizes pop as market research. Singing her ass off on some halfway decent tunes, the artist epitomizes genius.   **B+**

French Frith Kaiser Thompson: *Live, Love, Larf and Loaf* (Rhino '87). First side's got the skewed songcraft you'd hope, second the avant-folk excursions you'd fear, and both outdo anything you'd dare expect. Despite the prolonged "Drowned Dog Black Night," first side's also the strongest Thompson since he elected to pursue his solo dick. Good that he doesn't have to do it all—from French's wacky "Wings à la Mode" to the collective demolition of "Surfin' USA," it's an ad hoc collaboration that sounds as good as it reads. As for the excursions, well, renowned guitarist Thompson exercises a restraining influence on wealthy plectrum enthusiast Kaiser. Maybe next time they'll persuade Frith to put down his fiddle and join them in a fifteen-minute "Free Bird."   **A—**

Doug E. Fresh and the Get Fresh Crew: *Oh, My God!* (Reality '86). With the outrageous anticrime message of "Nuthin' " and the star-time joyride of "Lovin' Every Minute of It" surrounding his Big Hit, I'd call this a one-sided album if I wanted to be kind. But I don't, not when he dedicates it to G-O-D in the absence of Slick Rick and informs the ladies in the house that abortion (rhymes with mind distortion) is of "the devil." Buy the single, which doesn't put the Supreme Being so high in the mix. Inspirational Verse: "Cause I'm like Moses, no one knows this / The way I dress and my lifestyle shows this."   **B—**

Fresh Reggae Hits (Pow Wow '89). Here's where a novelty-hungry dance audience demands variations on moves so subtle that novelty-hungry outsiders can't even hear them. Though somatic judgments are more subjective than most, Half Pint's "Level the Vibes" leads off, suggesting that a lot of bodies feel it the way mine does— as a dance track from God, not quite "Word Up" or "You Dropped a Bomb on Me," but close. Next two cuts are winningly songful. But it's only on side two, with Sophia George's "Tenement Yard," that I find anything else for my tape.   **B**

Fresh Reggae Hits—Vol. 2 (Pow Wow '89). And just for the record, there are two things on this compilation—J.C. Lodge's elsewhere-available "Telephone Love" and Shelly Thunder's elsewhere-available "Kuff"—that might have made volume one almost as useful as Profile's prestige job. No doubt Profile figured prestige was the road to modest profit, while Pow Wow, which also has a King Jammy compilation on the market, went for quantity. Haven't we been here before? Many times?   **B—**

Glenn Frey: *The Allnighter* (MCA '84). If there's a new way to go Hollywood, Glenn'll find it. His latest solo album had died a just and speedy death when the *Beverly Hills Cop* blitz reached "The Heat Is On," a more Eagle-worthy song, than anything on this smarmy piece of sexist pseudosoul, and who ever thought Eagle-worthy would someday be a compliment? Then *Miami Vice* keyed an episode to "Smuggler's Blues," the album's only non-DMSR track—the anti-Soviet "Better in the U.S.A." doesn't count, because the main thing that's better seems to be making out. Bingo, certified gold.   **C**

Robert Fripp: *The League of Gentlemen* (Polydor '81). Much as I admire Karen Durbin, Chip Stern, Terre Roche, Richard Goldstein, and Ellen Willis, to list only those commentators whose spoken overlays I recognize from personal conversation, I'm just as glad none of them was theorizing in my ear during last year's

League of Gentlemen gigs at Irving Plaza, where Fripp's "dance band" sounded somewhat less dinky. And that goes double for J.G. Bennett.   **B**

Robert Fripp: *Let the Power Fall (An Album of Frippertronics)* (Editions E.G. '81). I admit to having sat mesmerized as Fripp spun out his austerely lyrical guitar loops, but having examined a set at my leisure I can only assume that the fine distinction between the trance and the nod took me in again. Always have trouble with that mystical stuff.   **B—**

Bill Frisell: *Before We Were Born* (Elektra/Musician '89). He can get too abstract in both jagged and atmospheric modes, and the eclecticism signals a sideman's record: it's more impressive than meaningful to pass from hoedown to skronk in a second and then switch to harmolodic hymn next cut. But it is impressive—also fun. And unlike his predecessor Pat Metheny, Frisell needn't turn to Ornette for urban grit or deep content—which isn't to say Julius Hemphill doesn't sound right at home.   **B+**

David Frishberg: *Can't Take You Nowhere* (Fantasy '87). "You knock back the schnapps / You talk back to cops / You walk in the room and conversation stops," begins the album and title tune; "I owe it all to you," he tells his "attorney Bernie" to kick off side two. These are the things this jazzbo songwriter knows, and he knows them well enough to delight nonjazzbos with an interest in exotic subcultures. Nor will they turn down the jazzbo pianist's Ellington or Berlin. But that doesn't mean they'll buy his beliefs that Frank Loesser is a great American hero, Zoot Sims the essence of swing, and, (L.A. trumpeter) Jack Sheldon "one of the most gifted of all jazz musicians," presumably because he gets work as an actor. Or forgive the ecology song he produces to demonstrate he's not a cafe-society cynic. [Two excellent extra cuts on CD.]   **B+**

Front 242: *Official Version* (Wax Trax '87). This Belgian bund's bad reputation isn't a simple function of safe-and-saners' deplorable tendency to brand powerful art

they don't like fascist (viz. Albert Goldman on the Rolling Stones, 1969). In a time that demands consciousness, mobilization, taking sides, apolitical objectivism is objectively, comme on dit, reactionary. But with their stated aim of transforming received information into powerful aural images, they're aggressive-passive as opposed to passive-aggressive. The worst you could say of them is that they'd try to make their way no matter who took over— and become antifascist six months too late. As far as they're concerned, of course, the worst you could say of them is that their club and cult hits "Masterhit" and "Quite Unusual" don't exactly carpet-bomb the sensorium. But they don't. You've heard of preaching to the converted? These guys shoot the executed.   **B—**

Front 242: *Front by Front* (Wax Trax '88). Could it be that these impassive disco powermongers are the latest in the long line of European rockers who have symphonic grandeur so deep in their bones that they believe they can reach the, er, masses with it? Well, let's hope they're wrong—if they got popular we might have to take them seriously.   **B—**

Front 242: *Never Stop* (Wax Trax EP '89). It's hard. Hard synthbeats that sound suspiciously danceable despite virtuous protestations that this isn't a mere dance band. *Mit* samples—including, gasp, some guy intoning "242" *in German!*   **C+**

The Fugs: *Refuse To Be Burnt-Out* (New Rose import '85). Rarely has an aging hippie lost his sense of humor with more grace than Ed Sanders, who could be wild-ass and even a little nasty on what looked like the brink of cultural triumph but turned careful and considerate once he realized the struggle might never end. Instead of degenerating into a "bitterly bickering bitter-shitter," he's put his youthful idealism front and center. His laughs are gentle, word choices rather than jokes; with special help from Steve Taylor, latest in the proud line of folkie-Fugs, his lyricism is resilient, reedlike; and he preaches with sounder grounding in moral philosophy than Holly Near and Johnny Rotten combined. As for Tuli Kupferberg, who was in his forties when it all began, praise the

Lord—he hasn't lost a bit of his youthful sarcasm.   **B+**

Full Force: *Full Force* (Columbia '85). Beats being what they are to street music, these guys were the brains as well as the muscle behind the two most unstoppable street records of the year, and a major-label debut is their reward. Good beats abound, of course, and with the help of major muscle one of the great ones—if not "Alice, I Want You Just for Me!" maybe "Half a Chance"—might make it down to the streets. But like the seduction manuals say, brains and muscle combined have nothing on personality.   **B−**

Full Time Men: *Full Time Men* (Coyote EP '85). Three pleasantly unkempt songs by a concept comprising Fleshtones guitarist Keith Streng, who plays almost everything, and R.E.M. guitarist Peter Buck, who plays guitar. The best is about owning a car. The second-best is what they like about the South.   **B+**

Full Time Men: *Your Face My Fist* (Coyote '88). "Members of the Fleshtones and lots more famous people," screams a sticker in more garish typography, and thus does a one-off turn into new-wave die-hard nostalgia. It even remakes two tracks from what should have been their only record—rowdier, natch, and not as good. Great lost Fleshtones song: "High on Drugs."   **C+**

The Fun Boy Three: *The Fun Boy Three* (Chrysalis '82). This spinoff stretches the Specials even thinner—so thin it's like a minimalist statement, as if chants and jingles were the music of the people. And though "The Lunatics" is the only track I'm hooked on (I sing it for anyone within earshot and sound like Robert Goulet by comparison), it might be novelty album of the year if all the others achieved the rudimentary, skeptical charm of "Faith, Hope and Charity" and "The Telephone Always Rings."   **B**

Fun Boy Three: *Waiting* (Chrysalis '83). From "Our Lips Are Sealed," proof that a "definitive AOR version" (as the sticker calls it) can negotiate between cheery veneer and breast-beating bullshit, to "Well

Fancy That!," proof that not everyone who has problems with "boy love" (as men call it) is as self-serving as Howard Smith, David Byrne's production suits songwriting that has advanced beyond the undernourishment of their breakaway debut. "Farmyard Connection" lays out the class inequities of herb production. Elsewhere they're not in love with love. Original grade: B.   **B+**

Funkadelic: *Connections and Disconnections* (LAX '80). "This album does not include any performances or creations by George Clinton," disclaim Fuzzy Haskins and his band of claim-jumpers, but they sure try to simulate same, with generally pathetic results (except when they make "P-Funk" sound like "hee haw"). Where Jerome Brailey's mutiny on the mamaship deepened the funk, these renegades aspire to fuzak—pleasant only if you forget who they say they are.   **C**

Funkadelic: *The Electric Spanking of War Babies* (Warner Bros. '81). His embattled empire/utopia in pieces around if not against him, George Clinton reaches into the disgusting depths of his drug-addled mind and comes up with the solidest, weirdest chunk of P-Funk since one nation gathered under a groove. Featuring icky sex, Sly getting stronger, and an on-the-one reggae about digging "the first world" that should make his brethren and sistren (way) down south splank their spliffs. In short, chock-a-block, for which we can thank the baddies at Warner Brethren, who forced him to reduce a projected double-LP down to this supersaturated single. Original grade: A.   **A−**

The Furies: *Fun Around the World* (Infrasonic '87). Sticking their art-pop in your face, they write cute rock and roll tunes about their band, a famous band, an opera singer, a private museum, "arts and crafts." "There is no difference between art and life," they warble; violence and pollution and Russia they know about from the San Fran *Chronicle*. Their best songs are about a female friendship (they "talk about art") and a lousy lover (the opera singer). Their candor is refreshing, their triviality not quite clever enough.   **B**

Jimmy G. and the Tackheads: *Federation of Tackheads* (Capitol '85). Those who bewail George Clinton's drum-program conversion should get a load of the rhythm chip he has working on this collaboration with former Slave laborer and master of his own Aurra Steve Washington—not to mention Mr. G., a kid brother George hopes to save from a life of petty crime and presidential aspiration. The industrial-strength whomp of these willfully simple-minded tracks makes the big beat of the notorious "Hydraulic Pump" sound like something Trick James might cross over on. One nice thing about simple-minded—when it hits you you feel all right. **B+**

Peter Gabriel: *Peter Gabriel* (Mercury '80). After hitting a sophomore jinx with *Peter Gabriel,* on Atlantic, the first man of Genesis fulfills the promise of *Peter Gabriel,* on Atco—with pessimistic postprog art-rock minidrama rather than DIY DOR. "Games Without Frontiers," a different kind of internationalism, and "Biko," a different kind of Africanism, lead and finish side two rather than side one. Either he doesn't know his own strengths or he underestimates his audience—or both. **B−**

Peter Gabriel: *Security* (Geffen '82). If Gabriel can't resist orchestrating his rock and roll, better he should lay on third-world rhythms than simulate first-world themes. But self-conscious primitivism hasn't cured his grandiosity—lyrical protestations notwithstanding, the only time those rhythms are around him and inside him, in control and in his soul, is on "Shock the Monkey," which has a good old first-world hook. Only Gabriel probably doesn't want to be cured—bet he admires African music not because it flows like a stream but because it taps the divine, and while he may know in his head that animists can't have one without the other, he's not about to become a believer. **C+**

Peter Gabriel: *So* (Geffen '86). Gabriel's so smart he knows rhythm is what makes music go, which relieves him of humdrum melodic responsibilities but doesn't get him up on the one—smart guys do go for texture in a pinch. Like his smart predecessor James Taylor, who used to climax concerts with the clever macho parody "Steamroller," this supporter of good causes reaches the masses with "Sledgehammer," which is no parody. Where is "Biko" now that we need it more than ever? **B−**

Galaxie 500: *Today* (Aurora '88). With their strained, murmuring sprechgesang, half-speed rave-ups, and sobbing guitar, they evoke circa-"Pale Blue Eyes" Velvets so beautifully you think they're an imitation until you recheck the original. Instead it's like *Today*'s supposed to be as soft and gawky compared to *The Velvet Underground* as that album was up against *The Velvet Underground and Nico.* Like Jonathan Richman, source of the sole cover, they're sweet young aesthetes who love the Velvets without making them role models. "I'd rather stay in bed with you / Until it's time to get a drink"—what kind of decadent is that?   **B+**

Galaxie 500: *On Fire* (Rough Trade '89). Who needs world beat when indie darlings might as well be singing in Tagalog? I don't mean the words are physically or even semantically incomprehensible, either. Twinkies and decomposing trees and staring at the wall do break through the fog; motivated, I could probably construct a lyric sheet. But just like Lisandro Meza or Chaba Fadela, only not as well, what they produce for the curious outsider is a sound—halting, folk-psychedelic guitar signatures that establish each song's atmosphere. With George Harrison's "Isn't It a Pity" the measure of their wisdom, verbal motivation isn't on the agenda. **B**

Dee Dee Sharp Gamble: *Dee Dee* (Philadelphia International '81). After "Breaking and Entering" and "Let's Get This Party Started" get the party started, Dee Dee torches into "I Love You Anyway," written to a disaffected hub by none other than ex-hub Kenny G. This she brings off with such heartbrokenly matter-of-fact determination—all for show, I hope—that I felt ready for a whole side of slow ones. Which unfortunately I got. **B**

Gang of Four: *Entertainment!* (Warner Bros. '80). Though the stressful zigzag rhythms sound thinner on record than from the stage where their chanted lyrics/nonmelodies become visible, the progressive atavism of these university Marxists is a formal accomplishment worth attending. By propelling punk's amateur ethos into uncharted musical territory, they pull the kind of trick that's eluded avant-garde primitives since the dawn of romanticism. And if you want to complain that their leftism is received, so's your common sense. No matter how merely liberal their merely critical verbal content, the tension/release dynamics are praxis at its most dialectical. Don't let's boogie—let's flop like fish escaping a line. **A**

Gang of Four: *Gang of Four* (Warner Bros. EP '80). Whatever your reservations

about quickie twelve-inches, the wide grooves here power a bassy hi-fi that does justice to an ace club band. Two forward-looking new songs, two forward-looking old ones, all eminently consumable. **A−**

Gang of Four: *Solid Gold* (Warner Bros. '81). Only when a jazz critic uttered the word "harmolodic" in conjunction with this music did I realize why I admired it so. Not for its politics, which unlike some of my more ideological comrades I find suspiciously lacking in charity. And not for its funk, which like some of my more funky comrades I find suspiciously lacking in on-the-one. And certainly not for its melodies. I admire it, and dig it to the nth, for its tensile contradictions, which are mostly a function of sprung harmony, a perfect model for the asynchronous union at the heart of their political (and rhythmic) message. Here Jimmy Douglass's production strategy is to cram everything together. Compare the more spacious versions of the two rerecorded songs on their 1980 EP, and dig those to the nth as well. Original grade: A minus.   **A**

Gang of Four: *Another Day/Another Dollar* (Warner Bros. EP '81). Caveats about live-version/album-available EP ripoffs don't apply to this product, which adds the militantly dialectical "History's Bunk!" and the U.K.-only outside-agitating "Capital (It Fails Us Now)" to the endlessly repeatable "To Hell With Poverty" on the all-studio A and debuts concert versions of the undeniable "What We All Want" and the ineffable "Cheeseburger" on the B. Hungry Americans who find *Solid Gold* dry should taste-test these juicy, nutritious remakes.   **A**

Gang of Four: *Songs of the Free* (Warner Bros. '82). What I love about their records is the very thing that keeps me from playing them much—the guitars are so harsh, the rhythms so skewed, the voices so hectoring, the lyrics so programmatic that they function as a critique of casual hedonism. Their pleasure is like Barthes or forward bends—good for you, in a limited way. So while it's all right in theory for "I Love a Man in a Uniform" to make me think I've been underrating the Human League every time its intro makes me want to get up and dance, I don't find such amenities formally appropriate. And never fear—there are almost as few here as they think they can get away with.   **A**—

Gang of Four: *Hard* (Warner Bros. '83). This record is damn near dead on its feet, but I don't think the missing ingredient is Hugo Burnham's human chops so much as his humane spirit. The sick-soul-of-success lyrics are part of it—even their most received new-left truisms always had a sloganeering hookiness about them. What really makes the difference, though, is the detachment of Jon King's delivery. If I didn't know better, I'd wonder whether now he really wants to turn into Phil Oakey. And actually, I don't know better.   **B**

Gap Band: *Gap Band IV* (Total Experience '82). Although women may disagree, I don't think the cartoon sincerity of Bootsy and the Ohio Players will ever evolve into romantic credibility. So while I'm not saying these total entertainers sound like Huey, Louie & Dewey on the slow ones, I insist that they don't sound like the Temptations either—vocally, they're mere professionals singing merely professional love songs. Which isn't to deny that the funk tunes burn rubber and the funktoons drop the bomb.   **B+**

Gap Band: *Gap Band V: Jammin'* (Total Experience '83). Like Cameo and Rick James before them, these old pros blew their sure shots on the breakthrough—this drops no bombs. But once again the follow-up album compensates for never getting up by never letting up—the uptempo stuff steadfastly maintains their hand-stamped party groove, and like Cameo (forget Rick James), they've figured out what to do with the slow ones. That Stevie Wonder move is a no-fail—just ask George Benson, or Eddie Murphy.   **B+**

Gap Band: *Gap Gold: Best of the Gap Band* (Total Experience '84). What a waste. If ever a band cried out for that corny old fast side/slow side split, it's the creators of "Burn Rubber," "You Dropped a Bomb on Me," "Early in the Morning," and, God spare you, "Season's No Reason To Change." Taken in a single rush, the uptempo classics (augmented by a few expert imitations, including "Party Trains" 's imitation Gap Band) would stand as twenty-five minutes of rock and roll so spectacular you'd never think to turn the damn thing over.   **B+**

Gap Band: *The 12" Collection* (Mercury '86). Tsk-tsk—"Party Train," which leads off side two, repeats the formula of "You Dropped a Bomb on Me" and "Burn Rubber" and for that matter "Early in the Morning," which begin-middle-and-end side two. I mean—wotta formula: stratoliner funk that leaves their more than passable P-Funk rip in the dust. In fact, *Party Train* is what they should have called the only Gap Band anybody need own. And anybody includes you.   **A**

Marvin Gaye: *In Our Lifetime* (Tamla '81). Personal to David and Brian: For techno-Afro atmospherics, try this. Pay attention to Nigel Martinez's drumming on "Far Cry" or Frank Blair's bass on "Funk Me" and you might even try to hire them. And though the words are confused, at least they're sincere, which in an age of irony has its advantages. Just like on your record, not one cut announces itself, but that's only because these days Gaye aspires to a line (by which I mean a con or a come-on as well as a musical schema) more sinuous and insinuating than the peculiar hooks and JB elementals of yore. And though not one cut announces itself, every one gets through the door.   **A**—

Marvin Gaye: *Midnight Love* (Columbia '82). Gaye's always had more feel for sexual healing than for wholly-holy or inner city blues, and this album's concentration on the carnal is one reason it's his best ever: after a week of grumping about his coke-snorting super freaks, dick-brained Bob Marley tribute, and jive ooh-la-la, I realized I was in bed with the man anyway and decided to lie back enjoy it. His wet croon makes up for the lost grit of *Let's Get It On,* and never before has this rhythm master layered the tracks with such deftness and power. King Sunny Adé, meet Dr. Feelgood. Original grade: A.   **A**—

Marvin Gaye: *Dream of a Lifetime* (Columbia '85). Like a lot of rock and roll geniuses, Gaye was also a nut (or jerk, if you prefer). One reason he worked so assiduously in the studio was that he was loath to let us see all the way inside him, which means that these posthumously consummated outtakes and private jokes are by his own best standard too unmediated to carry much aesthetic weight. By my own best standards, too. On "Ain't It Funny (How Things Turn Around)," the only track that bears Gaye's rhythmic and harmonic signature rather than Gordon Banks's or Harvey Fuqua's schlock-it-to-'em, and "Savage in the Sack," a joke he knew enough to find funny, his wit and charm shine through. Elsewhere he's just letting off guilt in heavenly visions or sexual fantasies out of control. Maybe bondage freaks will find "Masochistic Beauty" a turn-on—what do I know? I know what I infer from "Sanctified Lady" (formerly "Sanctified Pussy")—that this man found himself despising women for doing the kinky things he forced them to do. And there's no way that's a turn-on.   **C+**

Marvin Gaye: *Motown Remembers Marvin Gaye* (Tamla '86). These "never before released masters" were rejected for good reason—they lacked both the hooky spark that spelled hit to Mr. Gordy and the show-tune gentility he thought appropriate to the upscale LP market. The result is a groove album Motown wouldn't have risked back in 1965, by which time seven of these twelve tracks had been laid down, though not so sparklingly engineered. As much a showcase for the Funk Brothers band as for the jazz-tinged pop-gospel phrasing of the label's pet matinee idol, it's a chance to hear Motown's music unalloyed, without the distraction of sweet memory. And damned if I can tell what flaw Gordy descried in Smokey's "Just Like a Man," Ashford & Simpson's "Dark Side of the World," or Cosby & Stevenson's "That's the Way It Goes."   **A—**

Marvin Gaye: *Romantically Yours* (Columbia '86). The sad testament of a tortured weirdo who longed to redeem himself in the world of middle-class convention. On side one he covers "standards" that are beneath him ("More"), beyond him ("Fly Me to the Moon"), or beside the point ("Maria"). On side two he attempts to write his own. The singing isn't bad—was it ever? The strings are godawful.   **C+**

Spoonie Gee: *The Godfather of Rap* (Tuff City '87). Spoonie is so unreconstructed he talks the same old shit without even pretending he made it up—a little romantic vulnerability (not much) is as venturesome as he gets thematically. His rhymes'll sneak up on you, though, and his groove is so old it's new. Surprising a Mike Tyson fan is such a counterpuncher; Lee Dorsey as JB, he doesn't float like a butterfly—more like a waterbug on a shore current. Marley Marl is his match, deploying riff and dub and dissonance with a laggardly subtlety that'll pass hotbloods right by. So let me put it this way—Spoonie probably thinks Bob Marley stole his handle from Marl, and he's still the first rapper to come by his reggae naturally.   **B+**

The J. Geils Band: *Love Stinks* (EMI America '80). So it's broad—nothing wrong with broad. Just ask the uproarious single and title tune. But really, the rest is more overbearing white r&b—Seth Justman's organ blams, not to mention his furbelows on the endless-at-3:35 "Desire," are the work of a man who thinks "No Anchovies, Please" is funny.   **C+**

The J. Geils Band: *Freeze-Frame* (EMI America '81). For me, their best since *Monkey Island* if not the debut divides neatly into three groups of three: slick get-me-off trash (hit single plus two music-as-escape songs), slick get-'em-off trash (opener, closer, and "Angel in Blue," a whore with a heart of brass that I'm just a sucker for), and slick get-offa-me trash (two throwaways at the end of side one plus "River Blindness," a more pretentious try at "Monkey Island," that album's sole bumout). If you're discovering the great audience these days it might even change your life for a month. But I guarantee you it didn't change the band's.   **B+**

The J. Geils Band: *You're Gettin' Even While I'm Gettin' Odd* (EMI America '84). This has always been an unnecessarily obvious pop group, and while fill-in vocalists Seth Justman and Stephen Bladd eschew illusions of grandeur, they're neither gifted nor skilled enough to dance that nuance. And so the hooks pound on, making the wordplay in the sex lyrics seem unnecessarily salacious and the poetry in the political lyrics seem unnecessarily overwrought.   **B—**

Bob Geldof: *Deep in the Heart of Nowhere* (Atlantic '86). As a struggling front man he had a weakness for bathos; as a disappointed Nobel laureate he makes me miss Harry Chapin. On and on he blathers, a Bowie clone with glossomania, rolling out additional songs and verses for cassette and CD because they can't be squeezed onto twelve inches of vinyl. Though he knows far more about world suffering than you or I, he's almost incapable of writing about it. All he proves is that when you dwell on suffering you get pompous, something all too many rock-and-rollers have already noticed.   **C**

General Public: *All the Rage* (I.R.S. '84). Songcraft notwithstanding, I find that the (English) Beat's (debut) ska and (followup) panafrobeat albums wear better than their (farewell) pop album, and I'm sorry to report that Dave Wakeling's and Ranking Roger's new group turn a tendency into an avalanche. Although they've managed a unique sound within current English pop fashion, which makes do with unintrusive dance grooves instead of beat and melody, they don't break out of its rut. Their new rhythm section is no more an improvement on David Steele and Everett Martin than Wesley Magoogan was on Saxa. They place too much weight on lyrics that even when they escape modern romance simply don't deconstruct cliches the way they propose to (viz. "As a Matter of Fact"). And the breathy expressionism of their vocals is fast evolving into affectation.   **B—**

Genesis: *Invisible Touch* (Atlantic '86). For a while I was tempted to buzz Phil Collins over his former fearless leader. He's a warmer singer, God help them both, and the formerly useless Tony Banks proves adept with the keyb hooks. But in the end I couldn't tolerate the generalization density—not just of the lyrics (where Peter Gabriel's personal and geopolitical

details offer some evidence that he's been there) but of the hooks, which end up feeling coercive, an effect unmitigated by Collins's whomping instrumental technique. And just to prove they're still Genesis, we get solos.   **C+**

Georgia Satellites: *Georgia Satellites* (Elektra '86). If you love "Keep Your Hands to Yourself" for its own raunchy self rather than appreciating the alternative it affords to Bon Jovi and Cyndi Lauper, you want this album. Opening the B is a bottleneck rocker that slides as hard as "Happy," and while nothing else matches the inspiration of hit and followup, these guys do know how to put out those two-guitar basics. They just don't know why—except to provide an alternative to Bon Jovi and Cyndi Lauper. "Happy," after all, never pretends to be anything more than a change of pace, and because Keith Richards understands its limits, he's lining up a new front man right now.   **B**

The Georgia Satellites: *Open All Night* (Elektra '88). Forget bars 'n' barbecue—the twenty-four-hour eatery of the title tune belongs to Dan Baird's new sweetie ("I just got to know if that thing is open all night"), who shouldn't be confused with "Mon Cheri" ("Her skirt rolled up and I could see she was French"). I know, I know, but trust me when I say their appetite makes up for their boogie recidivism. Sure they'd like to be the the the Stones, but they're smart enough to know they won't make it and young enough to take their fun where they can get it.   **B+**

The Georgia Satellites: *In the Land of Salvation and Sin* (Elektra '89). No longer content to be known as a boogie animal, Dan Baird shares with us his pain, his songcraft, his abiding respect for Lowell George. Just what we needed—a pretentious boogie animal.   **C+**

Mark Germino: *London Moon and Backyard Remedies* (RCA Victor '86). These days singer-songwriters are as likely to start out in Nashville as end up there, and though this literary thirty-five-year-old loves words too much to keep it simple and celebrated his big break by recording in London, he's a country boy at heart. When he falls in love he hears crickets and jackrabbits, when he tunes a diesel it sings like Patsy Cline, and when he gets to thinking about barn burnings and "suicide amortization" he writes one called "Political." Even his Dylanesque turns have their poetry, and if he betrays both his muse and his immigrant forebears with "God Ain't No Stained Glass Window," just remember—country boys always sink into bathos when they approach the Almighty. **B+**

Get Crazy (Morocco '83). This soundtrack to a barely existent Alan Arkush movie may look tempting in the cheapo bins, so Ramones and Marshall Crenshaw fans should know that these tracks are for completists only. Music fans should know that Lou Reed's "Little Sister" could turn into a forgotten masterpiece if somebody isn't smart enough to put it on a compilation soon—or later, if necessary.   **C+**

Gettovetts: *Missionaries Moving* (Island '88). "Intellectual terrorism" by "Rock Box" out of Sly and Robbie's *Rhythm Killers,* this Rammellzee-Laswell metal-rap is heaviest when it's funkiest and can move the crowd just by moving its ass. Slows down on the rhythm dirge "Go Down! Now Take Your Balls!," which is Laswell's indulgence, and comes to a virtual halt on the wacko lecture "Lecture," which is Rammellzee's.   **B+**

Ghostbusters II (MCA '89). My daughter having commandeered the thing a hundred times in the past six months, I've come to admire (nay, love) the candor and restraint of Ray Parker's original "Ghostbusters"—making no bones about its own silliness, it does its job with efficient good humor, where Bobby Brown's "On Our Own" bogs down in plot-hyping talk of proton packs and children's parties. Though not all the entries here are equally egregious, the movie dominates the cross-promotion. It's almost like ten different versions of "Ben," albeit with better music—and also worse.   **B−**

Debbie Gibson: *Out of the Blue* (Atlantic '87). People think there's something cute about this schemer, but I ask you—is it really possible to be a self-made millionaire and the girl next door simultaneously? I'll take a Harvard M.B.A. any day. Paul Anka wrote his own songs too, and he had more of a flair for language. As for beats, well, I'm not going to argue with "Only in My Dreams" or "Shake Your Love." But the one she *produced* by herself is a flat-out dog.   **C+**

Debbie Gibson: *Electric Youth* (Atlantic '89). Casting about for a clue to a cipher, I found a gem in the bio: "My mom and dad took me to literally thousands of auditions, lessons, and performances." Making her a showbiz kid manqué who immersed her perfect pitch and competitive Chopin in disco and Billy Joel, with every pop dream supported by doting parents who didn't want to raise a rebel and got their wish—so far. Unable to mine an alienated childhood for inspiration, her music is synthesis without thesis or antithesis. A mimic and nothing more, she emits banalities about relationships and life choices that are no doubt deeper than anything she's actually experienced—so far.   **C+**

Gilberto Gil: *Um Banda Um* (Warner Bros. import '82). I'm not naive—I know importers love stupid haircuts and Japanese vinyl. But it still disturbs me that no one has worked this Brazilian item in the U.S. Already a dozen albums to the good, Gil converted me utterly at a recent Beacon concert with tunes I'd never heard before yet will know by heart when he brings them back, and most of these are the same way. Usually I play side one, the perfect upful morning groove, but when I turned it over to make sure I hadn't been kidding myself, old friends sashayed out of the speaker and shook my hand. We'll meet again.   **A−**

Gilberto Gil: *Human Race/Raça Humana* (WEA International '85). How readily songs breach the language barrier varies inversely with how verbal they are. As engaging as Gil's vocabulary of trills, growls, whoops, keens, and discretionary phonemes may be, he's also a careful wordsmith, and listeners who don't know Portuguese feel an absence unallayed by universalist title or Jamaican rhythm section (though a printed translation might help). Which makes the relative legibility of *Um Banda Um* all the more miraculous—though it's worth noting that that title sounds like discretionary phonemes to this English speaker.   **B+**

Gilberto Gil: *Soy Loco Por Ti America* (Braziloid '88). Milton Nascimento and Caetano Veloso are aesthetes like, to be kind, Joni Mitchell; Gil is a pop adept like Stevie Wonder, which I'd probably think was kind to Stevie if I understood Gil's lyrics. A warm-voiced natural melodist at home with Afro-American rhythms of every latitude, he's tried to break here with tours and Anglophone flops and reggae albums. Only Brazil fans have taken much notice—Nascimento and Veloso get much snazzier institutional support—and this effortlessly funky tour de force won't do the trick either, but go for it. I find most Brazilian music genteel myself. Gil ain't, and this definitely ain't.   **A—**

Jimmie Dale Gilmore: *Jimmie Dale Gilmore* (Hightone '89). Cut in Joe Ely's basement, Gilmore's 1988 debut sank or swam with his rather pinched delivery, so if it contained anything as gorgeous as Gilmore-Hancock's "See the Way" and "When the Nights Are Cold," there was no way to know it. Cut in Nashville, this one beefs up both voice and settings. The imagistic honky tonk of Gilmore's "Dallas" and Hancock's "Red Chevrolet" are why poets would-be like steel guitars. Mel Tillis is tapped for a sneakily oblique opener. And the rest is the kind of principled professionalism that's made Randy Travis a heartthrob.   **A—**

Gipsy Kings: *Gipsy Kings* (Elektra '88). If it wasn't for "My Way," maybe the one-worlder in me would adjust his horizons to embrace flamenco guitar and let the rest pass. But there it is, and don't riposte indignantly that "My Way" is a French song—that's the point. Their florid Andalusian emotionalism is Europop's cornball showbiz alternative to soul. I'll take Al Jolson, who invented something.   **B—**

Girlschool: *Nightmare at Maple Cross* (GWR/Profile '87). Since these five

females or others of the same name have been doing the old forced march since 1980, I assume the crucial exuberance of their recycled Sweet-metal is something of a simulation. But second-hand cock-rock it ain't—no rape threatened or implied. Just show business.   **B+**

The Gladiators: See Albert Griffiths.

Philip Glass: *The Photographer* (CBS '83). With its intrusive melodies and who-needs-a-cannon? climax, this is Glass's most obvious record, and I like it that way. After all, which is more likely to touch a rock-and-roller's heart—an opera about an Asian saint, or a multigenre piece about an American artist-gadgeteer who shoots his wife's lover and lives with the consequences?   **A—**

Philip Glass: *Songs From Liquid Days* (FM '86). From *Satyagraha* to *Mishima,* much of Glass's recent work has invoked the mood if not the methods of nineteenth-century classical music, a realm of discourse where I'm reluctant to pass judgment, though I will mention that this hardly makes him unique among soundtrack composers. When it comes to vocal production, though, I have my proud prejudices. Without passing judgment on *Satyagraha*'s Douglas Perry, who applies his tenor to one song here, I'll insist without fear of ignorance that he's a less than apt model for the Roches and Bernard Fowler (Linda Ronstadt can do what she wants). Even Suzanne Vega's lyrics read better than they sound. Which may just mean Glass is too spiritually enlightened to set meaningful texts to music.   **C+**

The Go-Betweens: *Before Hollywood* (Rough Trade import '83). "I've got a feeling, sounds like a fact / It's been around as long as that," goes my favorite hook of the past few months, which is something of an aberration: in the great tradition of post-modern pop these folky-arty Aussies abjure melody much of the time, though the second side does begin to sing after a few plays, and after much longer the textures on the first assume a mnemonic aura as well. A little static for rock and roll, but as poetry reading goes, quite kinetic.   **B+**

The Go-Betweens: *Metal and Shells* (PVC '85). When what the Brits call pop isn't popular, it's usually rock and roll chamber music if it's any good at all. This U.S. debut, a best-of that highlights the soulful ache in the vocals and the quirky opacities in the lyrics and does what it can for a modest tune sense, honors that suspect notion. It's not stylized, and not static either, but it's pretty subtle, and its half-finished edges and kinetic lyricism are best appreciated in tranquility if not repose. Where it can be expected to unfold for quite a while.   **A—**

The Go-Betweens: *Liberty Belle and the Black Diamond Express* (Big Time '86). The lyrics, which set oblique but never opaque romantic vicissitudes against a diffidently implied existential world-historic, aren't the secret of their lyricism, and why should they be? These Aussies make music, with Robert Forster's intensely sincere vocals and Grant McLennan's assertive but never pushy hooks pinning down the melodies. Granting all reservations about the form itself and with apologies to skillful romantics from R.E.M. to XTC, there are no popsters writing stronger personal love songs. I doubt there are any page poets envisioning more plangently, either.   **A—**

Go-Betweens: *Tallulah* (Big Time '87). They stick to what they know, and their knowledge increases. The quartet's a quintet now, up one violin, which may not seem like much but does serve to reinforce the hooks that have never been a strength of their understated, ever more explicit tales from the bourgeois fringe. So though I was pulled in by "The Clarke Sisters"— "They sleep in the back of a feminist bookstore"—I soon got involved with every song on the album, with a special rush for "Right Here," where Robert Forster or Grant McLennan, I still have trouble telling them apart, stands by his woman. Original grade: A minus.   **A**

The Go-Betweens: *16 Lovers Lane* (Capitol '88). The title may portend the worst kind of major-label move, but their worst is pretty good. On the straightest and catchiest bunch of love songs they've ever produced, the likes of "Quiet Heart" and "Love Is a Sign" admittedly cry out for a little tension. But so does "Streets of Your Town" until you notice the battered wives and butcher knives. To put it simply: they ain't the Smithereens. They're smarter, they're nicer, they're tougher. And they're still the romantic poets good popsters ought to be.   **A—**

God and the State: *Ruins: The Complete Works of God and the State* (Happy Squid '85). They played a typical minimalist grunge-funk in L.A. in 1983. The guitarist now studies philosophy in Toronto, the bassist architecture in Italy; the drummer has sold his kit. And on the cover they're considerate enough to provide their own review: "The record was produced in ten hours, for $200 (US). There are a lot of jokes in the songs; but some listeners don't think they're funny, and others don't even think they're jokes, rather symptoms of spiritual decay. There is an intended message of hope, of finding power in yourself against domination and power's corruption; but some find the songs cynical and as glib as the clever people they occasionally denounce."   **B+**

Scott Goddard: *Your Fool* (Enigma EP '84). Though the former Surf Punk is in it strictly for laughs, "I know it's been done before / All my songs about boring stuff" is as close as these six tracks come to a quotable joke. Though he varies his singing comedian's monotone with the occasional inflection or preverbalism, delivery isn't his secret either. And though the generically catchy, vaguely apt arrangements can make me smile all by themselves, I couldn't tell you why. Maybe there's just something intrinsically funny about Southern California.   **B+**

Go Go Crankin' (4th & B'way '85). If one measure of George Clinton is that he's spun off the finest franchises since Colonel Sanders, another is that he's inspired such staunch nonimitators: New York's rappers and the happy feet mob of Chocolate City. This D.C. dance compilaton evokes the endless party groove of a P-Funk concert better than any Clinton vinyl, yet it's definitely a go go record—maybe even *the* go go record, given the style's all-the-way-live commitments. The cowbells and timbales share one rhythmic language, and by gleaning prime cuts from five bands who make a habit of spacing out their peaks, the collection achieves a concentration suitable for the medium—these aren't singles, they're album tracks.   **A**—

Go Go Live at the Capital Centre (I Hear Ya EP '88). Visuals don't make it a mythic live music—certainly not visuals the much longer accompanying video has the chops to convey. Spirit does, a spirit the harmonica-synth version of E.U.'s signature "Go Ju Ju Go" captures more boisterously than most crowd recordings. So does a groove that translates with ingratiating naturalness to the sonic limitations of live recording.   **B+**

The Go Go Posse (I Hear Ya '88). Three-four years after not becoming the next big thing, the groove is as indomitable as ever—a groove more steeped in black history, in swing and jump blues and Afro-Cuban, than any dance rhythm of the past three decades. But the optimism has lost spritz—what passes for crazee on this multiartist compilation is an anticrack rap with D.C. Scorpio as Captain Kirk and a reminder that D.C. doesn't stand for Dodge City. Not becoming the next big thing can take its toll. So can black history.   **B+**

The Go-Go's: *Beauty and the Beat* (I.R.S. '81). Unlike so many groups who live and die by the hook, this one's got hooks, and when you pay attention to the lyrics it seems possible that they don't live and die by the hook after all—"Tonite" and "Skidmarks on My Heart," to choose but two unprepossessing examples, work subtle twists on teen fatalism and obsession, respectively. When you don't pay attention to the lyrics, which isn't hard, you begin to think they live and die by the hook after all. And you're probably right.   **B+**

Go-Go's: *Vacation* (I.R.S. '82). Bizzers will no doubt rend their overpriced garments when this fails to follow *Beauty and the Beat* into Platinum City, but all its failure will prove is that you can't build a wall of sound (much less an empire) out of tissue paper. The uniform thinness of the non–Kathy Valentine songs here does clear up the mystery of why virtual nonwriter Belinda Carlisle gets to play frontwoman—her voice fits the image.   **B**—

Go-Go's: *Talk Show* (I.R.S. '84). Pop is such a plastic concept that to call this a pop comeback just confuses things—with its clean, bold, Martin Rushent sound and confident basic chopswomanship, it shares less with *Beauty and the Beat* than with, oh, *Sports* (and less than *Bananarama* does, too). In other words, it's an AOR move (with top-forty goals assumed). Lyrically, it represents a retreat—no place for sly subcultural anthems among these straightforward love songs (really relationship songs), which while sensible enough are never acute or visionary (or thematically consistent/complementary). And having peeled away several layers of resistance, I find the record thrilling. Its expressive enthusiasm gives me the same good feeling I used to get from their musical godmothers in Fanny—a sense of possibility that might touch women who are turned off by more explicit politics, and that these women are strong enough to put into practice.   **A**—

The Golden Palominos: *The Golden Palominos* (Celluloid/OAO '83). This cacophonous avant-funk expedition was masterminded by master drummer Anton Fier for Bill Laswell's label (and basses, and on one cut scratching), and it's their pulse that keeps it going. But as an incorrigible content freak, I regard it as an excellent source of Arto Lindsay, who sings or plays on six out of seven cuts and helped compose five. It's not as funny or demented as the best DNA, but it's funny and demented enough that unless you liked DNA you probably won't consider Lindsay much of a singer or player. I never put it on at bedtime myself.   **A**—

The Golden Palominos: *Visions of Excess* (Celluloid '85). As formal experiments go, this packs quite a wallop, and not just because a drummer supervised the mix—Anton Fier clearly loves and understands that much-mocked arena-rock megawattage. But a formal experiment it remains, because neither guitars nor voices carry meaning of their own. Jody Harris has always had a weakness for the genre exercise (as has Mike Hampton, for that matter), and the five stellar singer-lyricists sound like they were brought in to finish the tracks. Even in arena-rock that's not how it's done.   **B+**

The Golden Palominos: *Blast of Silence* (Celluloid '87). It was thankless enough conceptualizing arena-rock, so what gave Anton Fier the bright idea of adding country to the synthesis, as he probably calls it in the privacy of his own cerebration? Did he meet T-Bone Burnett at a party? Fight with Syd Straw about her roots? Or just think it would sell? Anton, get this straight: especially as you approach country, sincerity sells. Sincerity soulful, sincerity stupid, sincerity ironic, sincerity faked if necessary. Not this cold shit.   **B−**

Steve Goodman: *Affordable Art* (Red Pajamas '83). Finally free of the spend-money-to-make-money fallacy, a likable cult folkie puts together his most modest and most likable album. True, he's too sentimental when he's serious; even when he's funny he's too sentimental. His natural lyricism is a palliative, though, and when he's funny (about half the time) he's funny. "Vegematic" and "Talk Backward" and the cruelly antinuke "Watchin' Joey Glow" may be easy jokes, but I ask you, why did the chicken cross the road? Hope he sells at least ten thousand.   **B+**

Steve Goodman: *Santa Ana Winds* (Red Pajamas '84). Recorded shortly before Goodman died in October, this is a fitting testament to a likable artist who often went soft around the edges. Goodman's intelligence never quelled his appetite for bathos, be it honest ("I Just Keep Falling in Love"), parodic ("Fourteen Days"), or stupid ("The Face on the Cutting Room Floor"). He liked to laugh ("The Big Rock Candy Mountain"), but though he was a clever satirist ("Hot Tub Refugee"), his targets were rarely original ("Telephone Answering Tape"). And oh yeah—he did love music ("You Better Get It While You Can (The Ballad of Carl Martin)"). Since he never made an altogether convincing album, now would be the ideal time for the indie label he founded when the majors said bye to put together a big fat compilation. Wanna help out, Asylum? Buddah? Yeah sure.   **B**

Good To Go (Island '86). Live albums are one way to finesse go go's refusal to organize itself into discrete, hooky, recordable compositions. Anthologies are the other, and despite soundtrack illustrations of the synthy adaptability of the D.C. groove from Sly & Robbie and Wally Badarou, this one may even steal a beat on *Go Go Crankin'*. But do you love "Good To Go," "We Need Money," "Drop the Bomb," and "Movin' and Groovin'" enough to buy 'em twice, no matter how hot the remake? For James Brown completists and other rhythm connoisseurs.   **B+**

The Goonies (Epic '85). As I hope you've figured out, the New Soundtrack is no such thing: it's a cross-promotional concept that permits record bizzers and movie bizzers to exploit each other's distribution. But because the film comes first, the music pros work to order whether or not their songs function thematically or appear in the movie at all. So even when the resulting albums don't suffer from the hodgepodge effect that afflicts all compilations and goes double when music is slotted into vastly disparate moods and locales, they still breed hackwork. Which is why this one is such a relief. First of all, it's no hodgepodge: high-register vocals predominate, dance beats mesh. And not only do Teena Marie, Luther Vandross, and Philip Bailey come in at peak form, but REO Fucking Speedwagon produces an actual anthem, John Williams's scion Joseph contributes a nifty pop-funk tune, and Dave Grusin himself strolls sweetly under the closing credits. Bless music consultant Cyndi Lauper, whose two good-to-excellent tracks almost get lost by comparison. Original grade: A minus.   **B+**

Peter Gordon: *Innocent* (FM '86). Gordon's affectless downtown tone sticks in my craw even though I've learned to have fun with it in other versions. But at least his new mewzick isn't deliberately cheesy. It's kitsch, but it's not cheap kitsch, not factitious so-bad-it's-good; in another time, snobs might have branded it middle-brow, meaning dolts like you and me think it has substance. As a here-disco there-jazz everywhere-semiavant soundtrack to life in media central, kind of fun—though more resistant than fun, or mood music, should ever be.   **B+**

Peter Gordon: *Brooklyn* (FM '87). On side two he's up to his usual tricks if not regressing a bit—first three cuts no better than the schlocky instrumental disco-rock they postmodernize, last cut no better than the pretty kora exotica it exploits (which if you're following means it's literally pretty—very, in fact). But side one, how about that, has real words—which are, it took me months to accept this, evocative ("Brooklyn"), romantic (" 'Til We Drop"), and funny ("Red Meat"). In an oblique way, but Gordon's problem isn't that he's oblique, it's that he's too oblique. The right dose of oblique can be tonic in this crash-boom world.   **B+**

Robert Gordon: *Bad Boy* (RCA Victor '80). As our increased familiarity and his increased facility reduce his dependence on ironic context, he becomes unnecessary—totally unnecessary, I mean. Sure he uses his excellent voice better than genre loyalists give him credit for. But that makes him either a "real" rockabilly or an interpreter with moldy-fig tastes—competition for either Ray Campi or Roomful of Blues. I mean, like wow. He was more interesting, and more emotionally effective, as a joke with no punch line.   **C+**

Robert Gordon: *Too Fast To Live, Too Young To Die* (RCA Victor '82). A shame Brian Setzer beat him to it, I suppose. But given his by-now veteran status and RCA's failure to beef things up with the rockabilly ballads that have always set him apart from the other cats, this compilation has four too many words in its title.   **B−**

The Gospel at Colonus (Warner Bros. '84). Gospel music without Jesus? Sounds like heaven on earth, doesn't it? Well, though I feel like a sorehead saying so, the formalization of ritual in both Greek drama and choral gospel can be a little distancing in its grandeur, or maybe grand in its distanc-

ing. That's probably just what Lee Breuer and Bob Telson want, but I'm greedy enough to prefer my pleasures and my truths a little more direct, as in the Thom Bell rip, or every time Clarence Fountain steps up front—especially on "Stop Do Not Go On," which has a hook.   **B+**

Grandmaster Flash and the Furious Five: *The Message* (Sugarhill '82). Their belated first album tries to be commercial, to touch a lot of bases with a broad demographic, but it's anything but formulaic. On the contrary, it's an act of self-expression—they do consider Rick James a hero—and thus experimental like albums used to be. The only instant killer is the opener, a borrowed funk showpiece featuring calisthenic bassist Doug Wimbish and three-handed drummer Keith LeBlanc. But in the end every experiment justifies itself, from the one Rahiem wrote for and performs like Stevie Wonder (he can actually sing, thus distinguishing himself from Kurtis Blow, Joseph Bowie, and the entire population of the United Kingdom) to the vocoder number to the idealistic Spinners-cum-Edwin-Starr impression to the one Rahiem wrote for God and performs like a believer.   **A−**

Grandmaster Flash and the Furious Five: *Greatest Messages* (Sugarhill '83). Establishing vocal individuality without entering the cartoon territory that is rap's comic blessing and romantic/realistic curse, they locate rap somewhere to the left of the hardest hard funk tradition, James Brown circa "Sex Machine" and "Mother Popcorn," rocking the body by pushing the beat (like Trouble Funk or the Treacherous Three) rather than teasing it (like Spoonie Gee or Soul Sonic Force). This almost athletic physical excitement, this willed and urgent hope, has been the core of their real message no matter what party slogan or all-night boast they've set it to. It's a disgrace that Sylvia Robinson's latest attempt to cash in their rep fades away to the forty-five edits that never did a thing for them—even "The Message," which doesn't lose a word except its coda, surrenders an unbearable tension along with its instrumental breaks. Culturally depriveds who don't own such twelve-inches as "Birthday Party," "It's Nasty," and "The Message" itself are advised to settle if they have no choice. **B+**

Grandmaster Flash: *They Said It Couldn't Be Done* (Elektra '85). I was and am rooting for Flash, Creole, and Rahiem—they have good hearts, and from the Fats Waller cover and the way "Iko Iko" sneaks scratch-style into the lead cut, you can tell they're trying. But Creole isn't powerful enough for a lead rapper, Rahiem's crooning is wimp ordinaire without bombast for ballast, and sometime Herbie Hancock vocalist Gavin Christopher not only isn't anywhere near as funky as the Sugarhill gang (which I assume everyone knows) but has none of the pop production flair that might move them into Rick James territory, assuming that's even a desirable destination any more. And the words! "Sign of the Times" is the kind of confused protest you could hear on sucker twelve-inches a year ago, "Jailbait" isn't so fucking good-hearted, and "Girls Love the Way He Spins" is the claim that's supposed to make the competition hang up their mikes and go home. Why do groups break up? It's enough to make you lose your faith in capitalism. **C+**

Grandmaster Flash: *The Source* (Elektra '86). Their original-is-still-the-greatest message might seem more original if they weren't still using some of the rhymes they introduced back when they and their brother Mel were number one. Imagine Wings getting back at John for "How Do You Sleep?" with a concept album and you'll have some idea of how thoroughly they waste these beats. **C**

Grandmaster Flash and the Furious Five: *On the Strength* (Elektra '88). Like a big band that costs too much to put on the road, their fluid five-man rat-a-tat-tat is a throwback to a more innocent era; their attempts to keep up—their "boyee"s, their samples, their Steppenwolf cameo—are depressingly flat. And despite an amazing "I have a dream" cover, Mele-Mel's return doesn't do all that much for their moral fervor. A "Gold" worthy of the subject wouldn't slip past miners and murders on its way to the IDs, and to hear onetime love man Rahiem make pimp jokes is to

wonder just how he'll get by after their next label drops them. **C+**

Grandmaster Melle Mel and the Furious Five: *Grandmaster Melle Mel and the Furious Five* (Sugarhill '84). When he's most original, Melle Mel's political chops are startling: "Hustler's Convention" closes with a right-on analysis, "World War III" resists thanatos and reminds Vietnam vets that they were dumb to go. But with Rahiem and Creole and Flash gone, idealism and romance are totally perfunctory, and original clearly ain't where they're heading: from the Prince rip to the Run-D.M.C. rip—both expert, enjoyable, even a little innovative—they come off as 1984's answer to the Sugarhill Gang, pros whose aim in life is to make more than chump change off whatever's on the street. Also, they can't sing. **B+**

Eddy Grant: *Killer on the Rampage* (Portrait '83). There's an expediency to Grant's songwriting—try "Latin Love Affair," or the equally routine "Funky Rock 'n' Roll," or a rhyme like "My heart does a tango / I love you like a mango"—that makes it hard to believe he's a hero. Instead of drawing some Caribbean analogy, I'd compare him to the Isley Brothers—artist-entrepreneurs with good intentions and a good assembly line. Of course, there's a ramshackle quality to the assembly line that saves even its most expedient product from slickness, and this is far from that—except on the hard-to-find *Live at Notting Hill* import, his good intentions have never been more out front. **B+**

Eddy Grant: *Going for Broke* (Portrait '84). Though it pains me to put it in black and white, Grant is half hack, and pop gambles are by their very nature never as all-or-nothing as his brave title pretends. The dance cuts don't walk on sunshine, the rockers show no special feel for that beat, and as a ballad singer he's such a born belter it's amazing he brings off even the charming "Blue Wave." **C+**

Grateful Dead: *Go to Heaven* (Arista '80). Not counting the lovely revamped "Don't Ease Me In," the best song here is a Garcia-Hunter trifle called "Alabama

Getaway." It grieves me to report that it isn't about dope dealers fleeing the troopers. 'Cause without hippiedom, they're lost. Utter wimp: new keybist Brent Mydland.   **C**

Grateful Dead: *Reckoning* (Arista '81). I know you're not going to care, but I've played all of this live-acoustic twofer many times and felt no pain. Sure it's a mite leisurely, sure Jerry's voice creaks like an old floorboard, sure there are remakes if not reremakes. But the songs are great, the commitment palpable, and they always were my favorite folk group.   **B+**

Grateful Dead: *In the Dark* (Arista '87). Despite the hooks, highlighted unnaturally by do-or-die production, this is definitely the Dead, not Journey or Starship. But only "When Push Comes to Shove," a ruminative catalogue of paranoid images that add up to one middle-aged man's fear of love, shows up the young ignorami and old fools who've lambasted them as symbols of hippie complacency since the '60s were over. One problem with the cosmic is that it doesn't last forever.   **C+**

Grateful Dead: *Built To Last* (Arista '89). Though the hookwise production values are even more obtrusive, this *still* sounds like the good old Grateful Dead. Except for newish guy Brett Mydland, who sounds like Don Henley. Survivors have to stick together.   **C+**

Great Plains: *Born in a Barn* (Homestead '84). Even though Ron House's whiny monotone gravitates toward the same melody no matter the song, each folk-punk arrangement stands out, and the lyrics show a sense of Americana worthy of a band from Columbus, Ohio—college town, state capital, boondock. Ever since high school I've been waiting for a rock and roll song about Mark Hanna, and I didn't even know it.   **B+**

Great Plains: *Great Plains Naked at the Buy, Sell, and Trade* (Homestead '86). If they don't quite live up to titles like "Chuck Berry's Orphan," "Dick Clark," and "Fertile Crescent," who could? If their organ-drenched four-four jams are objectively boring, they'll make you hum and pat anyway. If the organ-hooked "Letter to a Fanzine" is the sole masterstroke,

hard-to-resists are almost legion. And if "Why do punk rock guys go out with new wave girls" is part of the parody, I bet these punk-wavers know the answer from experience.   **B+**

Great Plains: *Sum Things Up* (Homestead '87). Here Ron House follows through on his titles, sum of them bigger and better than the one on the cover—the projected J.C. Mellencamp cover "Alfalfa Omega" and definitely "Martin Luther King and Martin Luther Drinking," both of whom Ron counts as heroes. Fact is, this English major is bidding to become a Tom Waits or August Darnell of the garage, which could use some lit. Since his thrift-shop finds are purchased to cover rather than adorn his nakedness, his adenoids will never follow Frank's frog to Broadway or Creole's tails to Carnegie Hall. So you'd better catch him at his practice space. Watch out for oil stains. [Two good extra tracks on cassette and CD.]   **A−**

The Great Rap Hits (Sugarhill '80). Well, not exactly. This expedient collection is why Sugarhill changed over from fabrications like Sequence and the Sugarhill Gang itself to street-dance kids like the Funky Four Plus One, half of whose Enjoy debut, "Rappin and Rocking the House," brings up side one. The slight shift of gears is almost startling—the real party people stay a split second ahead of the beat, while such creatures of the sixteen-track as Super Wolf and Lady B. lag cunningly or uncomprehendingly behind. Still, not a one of these six cuts is without charm—by mining the dozens and God knows what else for boasts, insults, and vernacular imagery, Sylvia Inc. could convince anybody but party people that rap is really about words.   **A−**

Greatest Rap Hits Vol. 2 (Sugarhill '81). The first volume was a charming concatenation of oddities foreshortened for long-player; this melds six terrific full-length twelve-inches, including two of the greatest singles of this or any year ("Wheels of Steel" with a boisterous new coda), into one all-time classic funk album, unified by the superb Sugarhill house band (Doug

Wimbish! Doug Wimbish!) and the pervasive smarts of Grandmaster Flash & Co. In its way, rap's up-and-at-'em sex-and-money optimism is as misleading as the willful down-and-outism of L.A. punk—joke-boast tradition or no, kids who find they can't go at it till the break of dawn may not need a Darby Crash to inspire thoughts of ending it all. But the way these fast talkers put their stamp on a cultural heritage both folk and mass is the most masterful pop move to hit Communications Central since the Ramones.   **A**

Great White: *Twice Shy* (Capitol '89). Sucked into the business when their girlfriends took them to see *This Is Spinal Tap,* they're the most physically unprepossessing glam boys in history except Kiss, and beneath the red satin and airbrushed navels are workaday attitudes, riffs, and yowls. The Ian Hunter–penned hit puts their artistic achievement in perspective—closest they come to a detail like "And the heater don't work" is "Hiway lights / Freeway sights," closest they come to a metaphor like "Before he got his hands / Across your state line" is "Let the small head rock her." No smaller than the one on your shoulders, dude.   **C**

Boris Grebenshikov: *Radio Silence* (Columbia '89). Closely akin to the early-'70s progressive rock that evolved into AOR, this sort of Romantic claptrap made Grebenshikov an underground hero in the U.S.S.R., which proves only that totalitarianism forces you to take risks for the most toothless banalities. Granted, some of the fast ones are vaguely visionary in a rockpoety kind of way, and the eclecticism is total—this is a guy who listened with bated breath to every silly piece of contraband he could get his ears on. Probably he writes better in Russian; possibly Dave Stewart's highly unironic production gloss creates the wrong impression. But his art-folk filigrees and art-rock ostinatos, not to mention the Aching Lyricism of his voice itself, are more deja vu than anybody with access to media should be asked to stomach.   **C**

Al Green: *The Lord Will Make a Way* (Myrrh '80). Think of it this way: he knew that sex was running out of inspiration for him, so he moved on to God as his source of ecstasy—an ecstasy he approaches most readily in what he really lives for, music. I might end up praising God myself if He or She gave me the most beautiful voice in creation and then let me keep it when I descended into purgatory. As it is, I'll praise Al for his lead guitar, which lends such a down-by-the-riverside feel to these rolling gospel tunes that you hardly notice the violins.   **B+**

Al Green: *Tokyo . . . Live!* (Cream import '81). You can tell when Green is bad live because he doesn't sing, often deserting mike or even stage for emphasis, which would be hard to render on disc. So his in-concert double had to be pretty strong. Like Otis's *Live in Europe,* it captures a sensitive soul man at his toughest and most outgoing. But unlike *Live in Europe* it offers no ecstatic epiphanies to make up for the forced crescendos—"I Feel Good" is louder in this version but wilder on *The Belle Album.* And speaking of loud, somebody fucked up the drum mix.   **B+**

Al Green: *Higher Plane* (Myrrh '81). Meek and mild, *The Lord Will Make a Way* was Green's sincere attempt to bend to gospel tradition, but on this record it's tradition that bends. He exerts himself with such fervor that I don't even mind when he and Margie Joseph (a lame pop singer anyway) desecularize "People Get Ready." I've always believed angels should sing like they still have something going down below. And if there are rhythm sections like this in Heaven (praises be to new drummer Aaron Purdie), the place may be worth a stopover after all.   **A**

Al Green: *Precious Lord* (Hi/Myrrh '82). Couldn't figure out why I found myself basically unmoved by this exquisitely sung collection of hymns, four of them familiar to me since my days in the First Presbyterian Church of Flushing. Then I realized that the Memphis groove of Al's first two Myrrh albums had somehow turned into rote tent-gospel timekeeping. Then I read the back of the album and learned that it was cut in Nashville, with all that implies. Which may also be why I know the material from First Pres. Going "sacred" on us, Al? Crossing over to the other side?   **B**

Al Green: *I'll Rise Again* (Myrrh '83). This isn't great Al—it doesn't come through with the spiritual charge of a *Call Me* (secular) or *Higher Plane* (religious). But it is good Al, and after much soul-searching I've stopped worrying about what kind of gospel music it might be. If Green wants to attribute his positivity to Jesus, well, I never took him literally when he attributed his positivity to romantic bliss, either, though I did find it easier to suspend disbelief. And while Christ and Eros are both more rewarding objects of faith than music, my guess is that at this point music is Al's bottom line—his very personal road to religious and secular glory glory.   **A—**

Al Green: *Trust in God* (Myrrh '85). Al shouldn't let his originals out of Sunday school these days, but he's always had a way with the covers. "Lean on Me" and the rushed, simplistic "Ain't No Mountain High Enough" are too obvious, but elsewhere he's his usual catholic self (that's a small C, Al—look it up); here he takes over "No Not One," which he found in an old church, and there "Up the Ladder to the Roof," which he found on an old Supremes album. And the uptempo country rollick he makes out of Joe South's "Don't It Make You Want To Go Home" is up there with the downcast urban plaint he made out of the Bee Gees' "How Can You Mend a Broken Heart."   **B**

Al Green: *He Is the Light* (A&M '86). It's not that Al's reunion with Willie Mitchell makes no difference—the difference is fairly striking when you listen for it. What's striking when you think about it, though, is that you have to listen for it. Leroy Hodges's famous bottom keeps the record flowing like none of Green's other Jesus LPs, but it's still songs that make or break—and in this case do neither.   **B+**

Al Green: *Soul Survivor* (A&M '87). His boyish delicacy and mellow insouciance have roughened slightly with the years, but he can still muster that high moan, and here he bids to connect with unbelievers once again. The key's the covers, and those who consider "He Ain't Heavy" bad company for "You've Got a Friend" and vice versa should pause to recall "How Can You Mend a Broken Heart": just as the shameless yet muted poignancy of that homage dramatized the poignancy of Al's crossover dreams, the low-down show of agape he makes of these two universalist-humanist war-horses transports his Jesus fixation into the realm of schlock, where it fits in real nice.   **A—**

Al Green: *I Get Joy* (A&M '89). By now he's B.B. King or Ray Charles—his genre exercises are more joyful than lesser mortals' great leaps forward. Only Al is more consistent, and he shares his genre with Amy Grant: pop songs addressed to God. What distinguishes this exercise is unflinching formal exposition—no Supremes or James Taylor ringers. Even the electrofunk belongs.   **B+**

Al Green: *Love Ritual: Rare and Previously Unreleased 1968–1976* (MCA '89). Cut one wild night in early 1975, the polyrhythmic title track was hot enough to lead *Al Green Is Love* and lend its name to a misbegotten 1978 compilation before Colin Escott ever dreamed of remixing it, but that's not to say it isn't even wilder with strings censored and voice and percussion up front. *Livin' for You*'s "So Good To Be Here" also thrives, and the rest is as advertised—singles and outtakes originally deemed too eccentric for general consumption, many of them unadorned uptempo jams with the eternal Hi Rhythm Section. Willie Mitchell was no fool—"Strong as Death (Sweet as Love)" and "I Want To Hold Your Hand," which were released, top "Mimi" and "Ride Sally Ride," which weren't. But Escott is no fool either, and in retrospect these songs of mysterious origin cohere into a phonogram as desirable as *Greatest Hits Volume II*.   **A—**

Green on Red: *Green on Red* (Down There EP '82). Dan Stuart and friends are as hooky as the L.A. trash aesthetic gets, with Chris Cacavas's organ the nugget. But though lots of New York bands ought to wish they'd thought of "Aspirin" first, Stuart would be easier to take straight if he didn't favor the B-movie imagery so prevalent in the film capital of the world. [Later on Enigma.] Original grade: B plus.   **B**

Green on Red: *Gravity Talks* (Slash '83). Static on stage, its records diverting but ephemeral, L.A. neopsychedelica is yet another nostalgic, romantic, "commercial" extension of/reaction to an uncompromising rock and roll vanguard; it bears the same relation to slam-pit hard core as New York neopop did to CBGB punk. Since psychedelica was fairly silly even in the '60s, I'm agin it, at least in theory. I must admit, though, that the dumb tunes on this album not only stick with me but grow on me, in their gauche way. Just wish I knew whether I was laughing with them or at them. And when the verse about the dead dad follows the verse about the dead dog, I suspect the worst.   **B+**

Green on Red: *Gas Food Lodging* (Enigma '85). They used to be fun, partly because you couldn't tell whether they knew how risibly their wacked-out post-adolescent angst came across. So now they unveil their road/roots/maturity album, which extols heroic dreams and revives "We Shall Overcome" around the usual Americana—drunks, murderers, husbands who've "passed away." Fun it's not. And in addition to the melodies thinning out, as melodies will, the playing's somehow gotten sloppier.   **B−**

Green on Red: *No Free Lunch* (Mercury EP '85). Dan Stuart's not so much an acquired taste as an arbitrary one—though I find his phony drawl kind of cute, I understand those who find it kind of hopeless better than those who consider it the essence of populist substance abuse. But his booze roots aren't ready for the mulch pile quite yet, and after too many plays I was surprised to conclude that his second Americana move was far catchier and more good-humored than number one. If you think it's hopeless, though, I won't argue.   **B+**

Green on Red: *The Killer Inside Me* (Mercury '87). In which yet another pseudoauthentic unlocks the cellar door of the American psyche, revealing—gasp! horror!—the violence that dwells within each and every one of us. What horse manure.   **C+**

Green on Red: *Here Come the Snakes* (Restless '89). Just when you thought he'd wandered off into dipsomania, Dan Stuart reemerges on Jim Dickinson's shoulder as Neil Young and Mick Jagger fried into one bar singer. With Chuck Prophet playing the blues and Dan wailing about careless what-have-you, this is the Crazy Horse album Neil hasn't had the jam to toss off since Somoza.   **B+**

Green on Red: See also Danny and Dusty

Nanci Griffith: *The Last of the True Believers* (Philo '86). Among the signifiers jammed into the back-cover portrait are an acoustic guitar and a Larry McMurtry novel—not just a folkie, a *literary* folkie, from *Texas,* get it? Yes, we see. We see auburn hair in a French roll, white shawl thrown casually over antique flower-print dress, eyes demurely downcast. A mite precious, all told, with songs to match. Bet she reads Bobbie Ann Mason, too, but there's just no prose in her. What's amazing is that she almost gets away with it. On "Looking' for the Time (Workin' Girl)," about a prostitute who can't afford a heart of gold, she does get away with it. I think it's the melody.   **B−**

Nanci Griffith: *Lone Star State of Mind* (MCA '87). Band's the same, and there's not a whole hell of a lot of distance between Jim Rooney, a marketwise old folk pro, and Tony Brown, a principled neo country pro. Yet Brown's production provides the soupcon of schlock that turns the raucous "Ford Econoline" into a landmark of country feminism as well as saving "Trouble in the Fields," about noble victims selling the new John Deere to till their family farm with their own sweat and sinew. Too often, though, she's still a folkie playing just folks.   **B**

Nanci Griffith: *Little Love Affairs* (MCA '88). For Griffith, the notion that the past was better than the present isn't just a bias, it's a worldview—consider "I Knew Love" ("when it was more than just a word") or "Love Wore a Halo Back Before the War" (WWII, she means). And with Tony Brown pushing her ever more firmly toward such marketable cliches as the raunchy growl and the pedal-steel whine, she's one neotraditionalist with a future. If you can forgive "I Knew Love" 's purism, first side doesn't quit—the regrets of

"Anybody Can Be Somebody's Fool" and "So Long Ago" are as permanent as they come. Second side's got John Stewart as Waylon Jennings and real country songs by the auteur.   **B+**

Nanci Griffith: *Storms* (MCA '89). Having gained her precious country credibility, she promptly released a live acoustic best-of. Now she asks the never-say-die Glyn Johns to . . . what? Turn her into Suzanne Vega? I don't know. But I bet she thinks it has to do with art.   **C+**

The Gladiators: *Symbol of Reality* (Nighthawk '82). Albert Griffiths has never been a musical fundamentalist—1979's *Sweet So Till,* the group's first self-produced LP and only previous U.S. release, placed too much faith in synths, and when that didn't go over they went in with Eddy Grant, which didn't go over either—so maybe he's joined the Itals on this roots-conscious label because he's got nowhere else to go. But the same sense of pithy conviction that made *Proverbial Reggae* a classic album makes this a good one. The revival of the anthemic "Dreadlocks the Time Is Now" is no more impressive than the proverbial "Mister Goose," which unfortunately is the only song about women here that bespeaks as much loving wisdom as the songs about Jah.   **B+**

Albert Griffiths and the Gladiators: *Country Living* (Heartbeat '85). There's nothing progressive and plenty idiosyncratic about Griffiths's quest for naturality, which is fine—in reggae, idiosyncrasy makes all the marginal difference. The interested will thrill to the sweetness of the gutturals, the placement of the harmonies, the shifting center of the groove. The bored will remain so. [Later on *A Whole Heap* CD with subsequent *In Store for You.*]   **B+**

Albert Griffiths and the Gladiators: *On the Right Track* (Heartbeat '89). More than any other rootsman I'm hearing, Griffiths keeps his spirits up. Though it's no longer in JA's cultural mainstream, there's tremendous life and variety to this music—falsetto play and jazzy interactions and catchy dubs, even an Elvis cover. "It's Now or Never," in case you were wondering. And if you're still interested, it may just be definitive.   **B+**

The Gun Club: *Fire of Love* (Ruby '81). Mix slide guitar with loose talk about sex, death, and, er, Negroes, and pass yourselves off as the Rolling Stones of the nuevo wavo. Wish I could claim absence of merit, but in fact it has its tunelessly hooky allure. No matter how seriously Jeffrey Lee Pierce pretends not to take it, though, I'll take it less seriously than that—and more.   **B**

Guns N' Roses: *Appetite for Destruction* (Geffen '87). It's a mug's game to deny the technical facility claimed by one-upping crits and young victims of testosterone poisoning—not only does Axl cruise where other "hard rock" singers strive, but he has a knack for believability, which in this genre is the most technical matter of all. When he melds scream and croon on the big-beat ballad, you understand why some confused young thing in an uplift bra is sure it's love sweet love. But Axl is a sucker for dark romantic abstractions—he doesn't love Night Train, he loves alcoholism. And once that sweet child o' his proves her devotion by sucking his cock for the portacam, the evil slut is ready for "See me hit you you fall down."   **B−**

Guns N' Roses: *G N' R Lies* (Geffen '88). Axl's voice is a power tool with attachments, Slash's guitar a hype, the groove potent "hard rock," and the songwriting not without its virtues. So figure musical quality at around C plus and take the grade as a call to boycott, a reminder to clean livers who yearn for the wild side that the *necessary* link between sex-and-drugs and rock-and-roll is a Hollywood fantasy. Anyway, this band isn't even sex and drugs—it's dicking her ass before you smack up with her hatpin. (No wonder they want to do an AIDS benefit.) "One in a Million"—"Immigrants and faggots / They make no sense to me / They come to our country / And think they'll do as they please / Like start some mini-Iran / Or spread some fucking disease / They talk so many goddamn ways / It's all Greek to me"—is disgusting because it's heartfelt and disgusting again because it's a grandstand play. It gives away the "joke" (to quote the chickenshit "apologies" on the cover) about the offed girlfriend the way "Turn around bitch I've got a use for you" gives away "Sweet Child o' Mine." Back when they hit the racks, these posers talked a lot of guff about suicide. I'm still betting they don't have it in them to jump. **E**

Gwen Guthrie: *Good To Go Lover* (Polydor '86). "No romance without finance," she announced on the song that made her self-produced album possible. And on the seven others she compensates for this pride and avarice by making herself available sexually and emotionally, no credit check necessary if you'll just give her that johnson. **C+**

Guy: *Guy* (Uptown/MCA '88). Until you absorb the beats and focus in on Aaron Hall, Teddy Riley's main band sound like almost arrogantly anonymous light funksters. Riley would always rather insinuate than overwhelm, and Hall lacks the chops and the inclination to soul anybody out—

learned his main shit from the Gap Band and Stevie Wonder. He often sounds like he's winging it. But where Bobby Brown and Al B. Sure! play the love-man falsetto straight, Hall adds depth by straying toward the manly emotionalism of the church. And unlike most light funksters, Riley doesn't aspire to slow ones. **A—**

Buddy Guy: *Stone Crazy!* (Alligator '81). With or without Junior Wells, Guy hasn't put so much guitar on an album since *A Man and the Blues* in 1967, and if anything this is wilder and more jagged. Which is great if you like your blues straight, without Otis Spann stitching a groove. I prefer mine on the rock. **B+**

Buddy Guy & Junior Wells: *Drinkin' TNT and Smokin' Dynamite* (Blind Pig '82). I assume this 1974 live-at-Montreux was finally released because it features Bill Wyman, who does seem to know the parts, but saints be praised, he's not the star. Saints be criticized, neither is Wells, who was once a sharper, tighter singer. He's plenty soulful, though, especially on harp, and Guy picks up the slack—listen to him think on "Ten Years Ago." **B+**

Charlie Haden: *The Ballad of the Fallen* (ECM '83). Voicing the great Spanish and Latin American revolutionary themes that Carla Bley has arranged for a norteamericano liberation orchestra, this testifies to the inestimable beauty and value of cultural autonomy, and by extension cultural cross-fertilization. It's assured but never immodest, elegiac but never maudlin, and Haden's two originals partake of the spirit. Bley's seem inconsequential, though, and the freestyle improvisations (kept in check until side two) generate little pleasure or meaning—except unintended questions about the ultimate relevance of late-capitalist avant-gardism to anti-imperialist struggle, not to mention disparate meanings of freedom in vastly disparate economic situations. **A—**

Hagar, Schon, Aaronson, Shrieve: *Through the Fire* (Geffen '84). I know, no point complaining about these grizzled dildos—it's only corporate metal. But shouldn't their merger at least produce a decent name for a law firm? **D+**

Nina Hagen: *Nunsexmonkrock* (Columbia '82). Hagen is one of those Yurrupean artists who consent to perform "rock" because it's vunderful theater. Big of her with her operatic training and all, dontcha think? And she does have a new-wave sense of humor—instead of taking on Maria Callas with her umpteen-octave range she does impressions of Linda Blair and Mercedes McCambridge. Unfortunately for those of us who believe rock is vunderful songs, her drama transcends the form. The exception is the scary antiheroin minidrama "Smack Jack." **C+**

Merle Haggard: *The Way I Am* (MCA '80). "Wake Up," a devastating final-night plea that's one of Haggard's few great love songs, is the only original that transcends his usual poses, with "Sky-Bo"—"That's a new kind of hobo for planes"—the most cloying offender. But Haggard's chief value has been vocal ever since "Okie From Muskogee" saddled him with an image, and here his resonant, reflective baritone transforms three Ernest Tubb tunes from standards into timeless pieces of Americana. If Willie Nelson is Bing Crosby, Haggard's Sinatra. **B+**

Merle Haggard: *Big City* (Epic '81). Having charged CBS considerable to slide into that notch on Billy Sherrill's gun, Merle signifies his seriousness by saving the flaky stuff for next year and clearing his throat before he sings. This isn't just for his cult— it's for the whole damn country audience. "My Favorite Memory" and "I Always Get Lucky With You" are love songs that may cloy eventually but at least stick for now. "Big City" and "Are the Good Times Really Over" are by the Merle who wrote that song about hippies. And just like on a real Nashville album, you can only tell how much filler there is by listening till you're sick of it. **B**

Merle Haggard and George Jones: *A Taste of Yesterday's Wine* (Epic '82). What might have been a historic get-to-gether overplays both the good-old-boy camaraderie and the cry-in-your-beer sentimentality of country's male-bonding mode. Willie Nelson's keynote tune becomes completely bathetic, and that the nostalgia and mutual self-congratulation it presages are even bearable is one more proof of Jones's genius.   **B−**

Merle Haggard: *Going Where the Lonely Go* (Epic '82). Country legend or no, Haggard has no more business doing an album about broken relationships than Public Image Ltd. As a result, material that might be touching from a more austere singer is barely credible, and the three songs that open side two—one by Merle and Jimmy Dickens, one by Merle's off-and-on wife Leona Williams, and one by the austere Willie Nelson—ooze with the kind of moist self-pity ordinarily encountered only in leaders of the men's liberation movement.   **C+**

Merle Haggard/Willie Nelson: *Poncho and Lefty* (Epic '82). Haggard hasn't sung with so much care in years, which is obviously Nelson's doing—the difference between this "Half a Man" and the one on *Going Where the Lonely Go* is the difference between a husband who doesn't deserve to be cut down and a shit who does. But if Waylon brings out Willie's self-righteousness, Merle brings out his self-pity—Leona Williams doesn't want you to know it, but both of these boys have had more soft places to fall than any good man needs.   **B+**

Merle Haggard: *His Epic Hits—The First Eleven—To Be Continued . . .* (Epic '84). Though at first this just seems sad, an objective person will admit that actually the songs are kind of memorable—in other words, not filler. He wrote most of them himself, too. But an objective person will also note that the two side-openers (and the two best tracks by a mile) both feature Willie Nelson. And wish he hadn't ruined a great stanza in "My Favorite Memory" with that stupid line about how she made their vacation a ball. And get kind of sick at the reactionary nostalgia of "Are the Good Times Really Over." And wonder whether Mrs. Hag really ended up in George Jones's bed like he claims in "C.C. Waterback," and whether Hag minded, and if not why not. And get sad all over again.   **B−**

Merle Haggard: *His Best* (MCA '85). Though occasional jingoisms like last year's *Amber Waves of Grain* encourage citified ignoramuses to believe he can't see beyond Muskogee, over the years his musical sophistication has surpassed even Willie Nelson's. His Strangers are a stripped-down version of Bob Wills's Playboys, his soft timbre and lazy swing marks of a singer who'll never get old, and unlike Nelson he keeps writing. This compilation is overdue—he deserted the label in '81—and not all it should be. It draws too heavily on the all too conceptual 1980 *Back to the Barrooms*. Its two best songs may steer you away from the minor pleasures of the all-encompassingly unconceptual 1980 *The Way I Am*. And it's recommended to ignoramuses nevertheless.   **B+**

Merle Haggard: *Songwriter* (MCA '85). The best cuts here would make *His Best* better. But the real reason Haggard has never chalked up the great compilations a great country artist has in him is the reason MCA is perfectly justified in repackaging duff stuff like "Red Bandana" and "From Graceland to the Promised Land." On the country charts, those were hits—that's the way the country audience can be with great country artists. Best cut: the dangerously self-referential "Footlights," which was never released as a single.   **B**

Merle Haggard: *A Friend in California* (Epic '85). Just when I decide he's gonna lay back forever he ambles into this. No Nippophobia, minimal love pap, a touch of Mexico, and lots of swing—except for one Freddy Powers pledge it keeps going till the obligatory sentimentality of the last two cuts. But though Merle's writing is rolling the prize is Floyd Tillman's "This Cold War With You." I vote for a tribute follow-up.   **B+**

Merle Haggard: *Chill Factor* (Epic '87). Supposedly a good one, and since it features an illustrated inner sleeve and six songs on one side that must be the intent. But by peaking with "Thirty Again," all it proves is that his great theme is age rather than love, which of course dominates. Further proof includes the overtaxed title metaphor and a Hank Cochran copyright so bitter and direct it makes you think his women get sick of him for the simple reason that he's full of shit. **B—**

Merle Haggard: *5:01 Blues* (Epic '89). It wouldn't be strictly accurate to claim Haggard has pissed his talent away, but the temptation to say so anyhow beckons. His laid-back vocal signature is the lazy man's friend. His originals suggest that he has no reject pile—just entunes any old piece of verse for the annual session. And again and again his famous ecumenicism camouflages lame genre excursions—on this album, the Bellamy-reggae "Sea of Heartbreak." A slight improvement over 1988's feckless *Out Among the Stars,* due mostly to a formulaic title tune Hag didn't write. But if he thinks he isn't getting away with shit, he needs a shrink. **C+**

Haircut One Hundred: *Pelican West* (Arista '82). "The important thing to keep in mind is that anywhere else in the world, besides the US, this is not considered a 'New Wave' record. It is as mainstream and as accessible as you can get."—*Rockpool Newsletter.* (Editor's note: cf. Doobie Brothers.) *"Britons can't sing"*—Simon Frith, *New York Rocker.* (Editor's note: italics in original.) **C+**

1/2 Japanese: *1/2 Gentlemen/Not Beasts* (Armageddon import '80). Beloved of their art therapist, their parents, Lester Bangs, and whoever owns Armageddon, Jad and David Fair's boxed three-record set is enriched with a poster, a (truncated) lyric sheet, and a one-pic-per-thick-red-page comic entitled "Becky the Monkey." Most of the budget went into the display—the sound suits the one-take learning-our-chords musicianship and vocals that make Jonathan Richman sound like Vaughan Monroe. Originals usually concern girls and sometimes mention artists; covers include "Funky Broadway," "Tenth Avenue Freeze-Out," and "She Cracked." Also included are several lengthy instrumental experiments and a live disc. Won't these superstars ever learn to boil their self-indulgences down into one tight, well-selected album? **C+**

1/2 Japanese: *Loud* (Armageddon import '81). Art moves get a lot more half-assed these days than this musically illiterate atonal jazz-punk. The noise becomes wearing, and (ask DNA) professional recording would do wonders for the textures, but front man Jad Fair is hysterical in more ways than one, and both are appropriate. My favorite moments are his plans to trash his high school, his squalling baby routine, and his mysteriously sexy Doors cover. **B**

Half Japanese: *Horrible* (Press EP '83). A concept EP about horror movies by a band given to simulating the nightmares of a teenaged boy whose voice is changing. Star of the show is "Thing With a Hook," who ruins makeout sessions by decapitating teenaged boys' girlfriends. Boo! **B**

Half Japanese: *Our Solar System* (Iridescence '84). This is the band cultists love, give or take a few tokens of encroaching maturity—the tantrums are shorter and more entertaining, the musical forms marginally recognizable. Lots to laugh at, including an instrumental: "Hall of the Mountain King"/"Louie Louie." They don't have the chops for "European Son," though. **B**

Half Japanese: *Sing No Evil* (Iridescence '84). As the postpunk Modern Lovers gain musicianship (accrue musicians?), they're beginning to sound vaguely like Beefheart, and these days I prefer them—better nerd primitives-turning-primitivists than hippie primitivists-turning-pretenders. Any of their thousand faithful who fear this latest album represents some accommodation with commerce shouldn't have nightmares about *Unconditionally Guaranteed*—it's more along the lines of *Shiny Beast (Bat Chain Puller).* Meanwhile, their target market, which must number at least ten thousand, can sing along to nearly everything here and recollect most of it in moments of unwonted tranquility. I love all the songs about Jad Fair's pathetically normal sexual obsessions, but my favorites are his nerd "Secret Sharer" ("There's a man who looks like me / And talks like me / And acts like me / But that's where the similarities end") and his nerd "Ball and Chain" ("It's not fair!").   **A—**

Half Japanese: *Music To Strip By* (50 Skadillion Watts '87). What was still authentic cacophony last time has evolved inexorably into avant-gardism, its jazz/r&b elements articulated by ever classier sidemen. All twenty-two cuts are entertaining at least, and the musicianship adds listenability, which has its uses even with a singer who models himself on a wiseass nine-year-old—"Silver and Katherine" is almost "beautiful." But the crude, breakneck, sui generis primitivism has slipped away somehow, and for all his protean whatsis (he's definitely a *maturing* nine-year-old, a contradiction I come to praise not to bury), Jad Fair is less himself without it. As of now, anyway.   **B+**

Half Japanese: *Charmed Life* (50 Skadillion Watts '88). How can you not love a band who label the cassette version: "Added Bonus!—10 Extra Songs Not Found on the LP"? Even if four of them are alternate takes and two or three others concern wrestling. Even if "Madonna Nude" (its coda a wrestling-style challenge to Sean Penn) really belongs on a twenty-one-song vinyl version devoted to the love fantasies of a geek with glasses.   **B+**

Half Japanese: *The Band That Would Be King* (50 Skadillion Watts '89). Just because Jad Fair is some kind of genius doesn't mean he benefits from the genius treatment—he needs a real producer forcing him to develop his material, not Kramer letting 'er rip. Most of these songlets—twenty-seven on vinyl, thirty on CD—go by so fast you don't notice them end, so that slow ones like "Daytona Beach" and "Deadly Alien Spawn" stand out. I bet if somebody made him sit down and work out extra verses, we'd know what the best fast ones were. Suggested pep talk: "Think funny, Jad."   **B—**

Daryl Hall: *Three Hearts in the Happy Ending Machine* (RCA Victor '86). Bloated by endless codas, superfluous instrumentation, hall upon hall of vocal mirrors, and the artist's unshakable confidence that his talent makes him significant, these ten songs average almost five minutes apiece. Cut down to the trifles they are by a lightweight collaborator, they might qualify as likable pap. We'll never know.   **C**

Daryl Hall & John Oates: *Voices* (RCA Victor '80). It wasn't inevitable that the return to form heralded in the trades should accompany the waning of whatever made them mildly interesting to the so-called consumer press, but the coincidence is worth noting. Except for "Kiss on My List" (number-one singles are laws unto themselves), the mildly interesting stuff is commercial filler: gently clever like "Big Kids," secretly dark like "Diddy Doo Wop (I Hear the Voices)." And for all the hoo-hah surrounding Daryl and his "repressed" solo album, his singing is as pallid as his partner's: "You've Lost That Loving Feeling" is the greatest thing to happen to oldies stations since *Grease*.   **C+**

Daryl Hall & John Oates: *H2O* (RCA Victor '82). The bristling hookcraft and fussy funk of their crossover has never been more unmistakable, and neither has its small-mindedness. Only "One on One," the album's sole seduction song, breaks the waspish music into something bigger, and while their dispatches from the sex wars might gain heart if gender-reversed (women get partial lyric credit on no less than five of them) I just don't believe "Maneater" was conceived with Nona Hendryx in mind.   **B—**

Daryl Hall John Oates: *Rock 'n Soul Part 1* (RCA Victor '83). This best-of is where to get to know them, but I wouldn't sit around waiting for that marriage proposal if I were you. There's no denying the instant pleasure of such slick tricks as the seductive "One on One," the bitchy "Rich Girl," the inevitable "She's Gone," and for that matter the sexist "Maneater." But in this pop era, instant pleasure never carries a lifetime guarantee.   **B+**

Daryl Hall/John Oates: *Big Bam Boom* (RCA Victor '84). What makes these guys so depressing is their definitive proof that instinctive musicality insures no other human virtue. Rival popsters, Bruce and Cyndi included, don't do nearly as much for Arthur Baker's hip-hop dub, which in this context is sly and graceful and goofy and catchy and thrilling, and they even have the good taste to like, you know, soul. Yet if in the end you think the music doesn't connect, you get a gold star—the affluent anomie I wish were only a pop-sociology cliché pervades not just the lyrics but the mix itself. And you want to know something even more depressing? Millions of record buyers either don't notice or like it like that.   **B**

Daryl Hall John Oates: *Ooh Yeah!* (Arista '88). Break up? Them? Nah, that was just a sabbatical, and to prove it here they are justifying their brand new advance, crafting that platinum as craftily as they know how. Daryl's stiff had nothing to do with it. Of course not. 'Cept that both records do overdo the overdubs, less fulsomely on this very model of second-hand black than when Daryl calls all the shots, but fatally nevertheless. I dare you to make out hitbounds like "Missed Opportunity" and "Rockability" or talismans like "Downtown Life" and "Keep On Pushin' Love" in the time it takes a music director to push reject. The album came out in May. It's dropping out of the top two hundred. It's not platinum. Justice abides in the world.   **C+**

Tom T. Hall: *Everything from Jesus to Jack Daniels* (Mercury '83). Returning from five misspent years at RCA, with his 1982 Earl Scruggs collaboration for CBS a halfway house, Hall delivers his strongest album in a decade and bitterest ever, chock full of death, decrepitude, and disillusion. In fact, T. sounds so down on himself you'd think he was an aging rock star—real truth-sayers rarely get this cynical. "The Adventures of Linda Bohannon," the only yarn in his classic mold, is also the only song here to end with his patented shrug-and-chuckle. Life does go on, just like he's always said, and now that he's decided to give honest music another try he should get out and talk to folks again. Time: 29:00.   **B+**

Tom T. Hall: *The Essential Tom T. Hall: Twentieth Anniversary Collection/The Story Songs* (Mercury '88). He makes his stories seem easy, like he jots them down on coffee break, and nobody in music can touch them—damn few in fiction, either. I'd call him a cross between Chekhov and O. Henry, but that would date him, because next to what the lit crowd calls sentimentality, sometimes played as a capper and sometimes as an offhand theme, the self-conscious narrator is his most characteristic device—one he never seems self-conscious about, fancy that. He also sings and picks, of course; his sometimes pensive, sometimes rowdy monotone puts across variations on a tiny, well-polished store of classic melodies. Except maybe for "Old Dogs, Children and Watermelon Wine," in which a janitor feeds Hall one of the sentimental truisms that are his nonnarrative downfall, there's not a clinker in this twenty-item carload. Nobody who owns fewer than eighteen of them should do without it.   **A**

Billy Hancock & the Tennessee Rockets: *Shakin' That Rockabilly Fever* (Solid Smoke '82). Don't misunderstand—he wants to shake "it," as it's called, not the fever, and sometimes he actually sounds hot. A Virginia boy whose career began in 1959, the year the singer turned thirteen and the music died, Billy gets off one classic rocker ("Please Don't Touch") and one inspired medium-fast ballad ("Lonely Blue Boy"), venturing closer to the EP grail than such fellow semiauthentics as Ray Campi and Sleepy LaBeef, not to mention the current crop of hair sculptors. But he does it more with his will than his voice, and even though he comes by his affection for echo and hiccup naturally, they're still mannerisms that can't sound any more spontaneous after twenty-three years of adolescence.   **B**

Herbie Hancock: *Future Shock* (Columbia '83). As a guy who likes his funk obvious, I think those who esteem "Rockit" as highly as *Head Hunters* are too kind to *Head Hunters.* Small thanks to Herbie, lots to Material and Grand Mixer D.St., it's the best novelty instrumental in years and the best pop of Hancock's life. Elsewhere various bright ideas, such as Pete Cosey, are obscured by the usual aura of set-piece dink—jumpy enough and often fun, but fusoid nevertheless.   **B+**

Herbie Hancock: *Sound-System* (Columbia '84). *Future Shock* was a pretty good album despite its dink quotient; this is a better album despite its schlock quotient. Where's-the-melody is beside the point, because even when they're just hooks the melodies seem a little obvious, without the physical or intellectual bite of the rhythm tracks (nowhere mightier than on the amazing "Metal Beat," recommended to those who think Trevor Horn is into something heavy). And me, I doubt Herbie should be playing more "jazz"—several of the false moments here are provided by Saint Wayne Shorter himself. The African exotica of Foday Musa Suso and Aiyb Dieng, on the other hand, sounds right at home. As does the South Bronx exotica of D.St.   **A—**

Herbie Hancock: *Perfect Machine* (Columbia '88). Unlike Kraftwerk's, definitely a reference and rip, Laswell/Bootsy's beats bite, but not so as to tear anybody limb from limb. Sometime vocalist Sugarfoot should stick with the Ohio Players. As for Herbie's contributions, I know fusion when I hear it, and so does he. Guess he actually likes the stuff. Original grade: B minus.   **C+**

Hanoi Rocks: *Back to Mystery City* (PVC '84). This Finnish fivesome is led by glam guys named Monroe and McCoy who yowl English-language lyrics that must impress Finns more than native speakers like myself. The quintet's patina of two-guitar anarchy is cute if overcalculated, but they seem to have spent more time contemplating their Dolls photos than their Dolls records. Maybe in Helsinki a look is supposed to beat a hook. That's certainly the trend in London.   **C+**

Pearl Harbour: *Don't Follow Me, I'm Lost Too* (Warner Bros. '81). The rockabilly that Clash/Dury factotum Mickey Gallagher gets out of Pearl's anonymous sidepeople is crude and often a little leaden. But beyond the rare genius singer (Elvis, Jerry Lee) or player (Charlie Burton, Jerry Lee), rockabilly was always more attitude than fillip anyway, and for all their slap-bass oomph and sly guitar modernisms, I think the main reason the oft-praised Stray Cats like the style is that it lets them cover the borderline-racist "Ubangi Stomp." It's a little different when this half-Filipino woman—that's g-u-r-l, boys—resurrects "Filipino Baby" and "Fujiyama Mama" and then adds her own songs about sex manuals, fear of dentists, and "Everybody's Boring but My Baby." I mean, I do believe that's a *punk* chip on her shoulder, which in 1981 is the kind of wood I want to knock on.   **B+**

The Harptones: *Love Needs* (Ambient Sound '82). With their serious tempos and platonic quest, the Harptones are archetypal doowop purists: even 1953's "A Sunday Kind of Love," an acknowledged classic, failed to crease the national r&b (or pop) charts. On this uncompromising album they almost get away with it because Willie Winfield, now fifty-three and a professional funeral director, retains the virtually characterless sapling tenor of a half-formed youth. Absolutely lovely—too absolute, in fact. Only on Jackson Browne's "Love Needs a Heart," its lyric, melody, and vocal harmonies all touched with an uncharacteristically complex pain, do they achieve the transcendence they long for. Inspirational Verse: "Take this for what it's worth / I am yours, you are mine."   **B**

George Harrison: *Somewhere in England* (Dark Horse '81). Twice Warners sent these sappy plaints back for seasoning. Then a former associate of Harrison met with an accident, and Harrison wrote his catchiest tune in years, based thematically on this epigraph from Sri Krishna: "There never was a time when I did not exist, nor you. Nor will there be any future when we cease to be." His associate has not commented.   **C—**

George Harrison: *Cloud Nine* (Dark Horse '87). "Gettin' old as my mother," right on and why not. "Feel more like Big Bill Broonzy," not so fast. For one thing, the Other Beatle should know better than to risk comparison with his betters. For another, he's not ready to settle for Broonzy's audience share.   **B—**

George Harrison: *The Best of Dark Horse 1976–1989* (Dark Horse/Warner

Bros. '89). A simpleton, but also a genuine weirdo. Voice doubles wah-wah as surely as Robert Plant's Jimmy Page impression, and he seems genuinely troubled by evil doings here on the wrong side of the veil of maya. Not that there's anything a mere star-in-spite-of-himself can do about it, except write the occasional ditty about playing in a rock and roll band.   **B**−

Jerry Harrison: *The Red and the Black* (Sire '81). Though the polyrhythms degenerate at times into steamy clutter, Harrison comes up with keyboard hooks I'd like to hear elsewhere; I recommend "Slink" to G. Clinton Assoc. But Jerry should keep his teeth clenched at all times. Bright enough not to try and carry a tune or anything, he apparently hasn't figured out that the talky voiceovers he essays instead are the worst fad of the year—it's as hard to avoid making them pompous or nagging or twerpy as it is, well, to sing.   **C**+

Debbie Harry: *KooKoo* (Chrysalis '81). Blondie plus Chic sounded like a natural— charming klutz confronts the meaning of grace. But in the world of surfaces that both inhabit so intensely there are no naturals, and the kind of spiritual heat that might have made the bond take is rare at any depth. Lots of sharp little moments are intermittently arresting, and if both artists establish themselves as classic the strain may sound noble eventually. Right now it sounds klutzy.   **B**−

Debbie Harry: *Rockbird* (Geffen '86). It's her achievement and her curse that just listening to the record you'd think she never went away. Vocal technique and vocal identity are sharper than when she withdrew from the fray five years ago, and the songs are brasher and more insouciant than on *The Hunter* or *KooKoo* or *Autoamerican*. If the sound could be a mite fresher, that's because the world is now overrun with the dance-rock Harry made possible—just as it's overrun with cartoon sexpots carrying tunes, whose collective existence give her a larger identity problem she refuses to confront. But it's also because the late '70s were Harry's heyday. Not too many pop icons get more than one of those. Original grade: B plus.   **B**

Debbie Harry/Blondie: *Once More Into the Bleach* (Chrysalis '88). She's known since "Rapture" where the dance action was, which is why Nile Rodgers produced *KooKoo*. So this last-ditch two-LP disco-targeted repackage, half of it totally extraneous 1988 remixes of group and solo titles by Jellybean, Coldcut, and lesser mortals, proves that knowing it ain't doing it. The spare-to-wimpy electrotrack of the original "Rapture," for instance, is decisively more graceful than Teddy Riley's newbeats. DOR was her destiny. And new jack is a new generation.   **C**+

Deborah Harry: *Def, Dumb and Blonde* (Sire '89). Though she only approaches the daffy, wryly detached tone of past glories on maybe four songs (including a couple by the Thompson Twins), she's got the right idea and some nice touches—little recitatives, unassuming rap and house, Ian Astbury chiming in like Fred Schneider on Chris's occult number. The opener eagerly awaits the 21st century: "I'll keep the money / You can have the fame"; the closer goes on elegiacally about the pastness of past glories: "I knew it then / It won't be back again." And in the end she's worth the trip if you can go CD, thus securing a lyric sheet and four add-ons, three of them punky.   **B**+

Grant Hart: *2541* (SST EP '88). Hart played drums and wrote catchy tunes for a trio called Hüsker Dü. On this three-song breakaway, he reminds us that Hüsker Dü was a guitar band.   **B**−

Grant Hart: *Intolerance* (SST '89). Playing all the instruments (notably a Hammond C-3), he sounds more spontaneous than his former bandmate's fully interactive new-wave supergroup. After all, Hart was the hummable Hüsker—nothing like a simple tune to create that off-the-cuff feel. Also, he generally says what he means. But for all his drug-drenched vicissitudes, he doesn't know quite enough to go it alone.   **B**

Jon Hassell/Brian Eno: *Fourth World Vol. 1: Possible Musics* (Editions EG '80). For anybody but an expert (in what, though—anthropological minimalism?), preferences regarding, shall we say, ambient esoteric kitsch are pretty, shall we say, subjective. But I find this piece of cheese the most seductive (and best) thing Eno's put his name on since *Another Green World.* In addition to trumpeter, auteur, and ethnomusicological gadabout Hassell, the crucial voices belong to Brazilian percussionist Naná Vasconcelos and Senegalese percussionist Aiyb Dieng, but the overall effect is Arab—heard casually at medium distance in Dakar, maybe. You could also call it head music.   **A**

Jon Hassell: *Dream Theory in Malaya* (Editions EG '81). "Fourth world music: classical by structure, popular by textural appeal, global-minded," explain the notes. The goal is worthy enough, the result basically friendly and weird, just like the year's Eno collaboration. But with Eno ancillary, the textural appeal is artier than necessary, from the muted trumpet stutter of the irritating opening cut to the sequenced field-tape fragment of the centerpiece to the dust on the needle that conquers all before the finale is finalized.   **B**

Jon Hassell: *Aka/Darbari/Java* (Editions EG '83). With much help from Senegalese drummer Abdou Mboup, Hassell fabricates ambient groove music. The rhythms lull rather than motivate, their goal contemplation rather than unconsciousness. On *Fourth World Vol. 1,* the goal was more like transcendence. Original grade: A minus.   **B+**

Jon Hassell: *Power Spot* (ECM import '86). With the same drummer and keyb man on all seven cuts, this is the composer-trumpeter's strongest and harshest music to date. The trio is basically a rhythm band (keybs play "facsimile bass, percussion, strings, etc."); more than ever, Hassell is a colorist rather than a melodist (much less a soloist). If there's a problem it's that the music's ambient anonymity is compromised by its astringency. But us city folk are so steeped in the shit that we take pleasure in putting background dissonance under quiet control.   **A—**

Jon Hassell: *The Surgeon of the Nightsky Restores Dead Things by the Power of Sound* (Intuition/Capitol '88). Minimalist trumpeter discovers keyboard textures while abandoning quasi-traditionalist surface, just like Miles Davis before him. But though it's also true that both men have done their schlockiest work while tickling the microchips, Hassell's impulses are so esoteric that a little schlock becomes them. I doubt he'll ever equal his first Eno project, and *Power Spot* is tougher. But if you're looking for ambient music that eschews new-age sweetener, this'll calm your nerves real nice. Original grade: A minus.   **B+**

Jon Hassell/Farafina: *Flash of the Spirit* (Capitol/Intuition '89). The idea was for the exoticist to collaborate with flesh-and-blood "traditional musicians," whatever that can mean in such a context. The result was to reduce Yurrup and Burkina Faso to a lowest common denominator—background music. Worse still, the aural environment neither flashes nor fuses—rather than a "forced collision of cultures," it sounds like they just barely missed each other.   **B—**

Ted Hawkins: *Watch Your Step* (Rounder '82). Cut ten years ago by a street musician and jailbird who sings like Sam Cooke and strums acoustic guitar like Bob Dylan, these fourteen songs—especially the four backed by Phillip Walker's humdrum blues band—wouldn't have seemed so remarkable had they been released back then, in the late soul era. But they are remarkable, because Hawkins is a true folkie hero, by which I mean that his lyrics are his own. These little dramas of passion, tenderness and betrayal are stamped with the sin-and-redemption of a lived life. And if the musical conception is excessively elementary, the singing is distinctive—derivative or not, the voice is expressive and earned.   **A—**

Ted Hawkins: *Happy Hour* (Rounder '87). This L.A.-based folk bluesman can bring you up short by latching onto homely details or just telling the embarrassing truth. I'll never forget "Bad Dog" ("What's the reason your dog don't bark at that man?") or "You Pushed My Head Away" ("Baby that sucker had to learn too"). But the unaffected can also be naive, and the unsophisticated can also be received. To ignore how often he falls into both traps is to condescend to an artist who deserves our respect.   **B**

Bonnie Hayes With the Wild Combo: *Good Clean Fun* (Slash '82). "They got a word for girls like me," she begins, and don't go guessing "pop-tart" just because she never lets on what it is. Though she hides her "penchant for the printed" page behind arrangements that are "dum fun" and a guitarist who digs Larry Carlton, she comes off smarter, surer, and more sisterly than just about any new rock and roll woman I can think of. After all, a girl who can seduce Larry Carlton into dum fun is working on a lotta levels.   **A—**

Bonnie Hayes and the Wild Combo: *Brave New Girl* (Bondage EP '84). Her climactic love song is called "Night Baseball," so obviously her tomboy credentials are in excellent order. Which come to think of it could be why the compassionate, catchy cool of her debut album has succumbed to the schlocky pop her (male, natch) musicians have a yen for.   **B—**

Heart: *Bebe Le Strange* (Epic '80). So Nancy Wilson breaks up with her fella, soundman Mike Fisher, who naturally departs the band, along with his brother Roger, who happens to be the guitarist. And whether it's the absence of pomprockish Roger, stripping to a five-piece, or what hell hath no fury like, suddenly they're lean and mean and playing to the sisters—title cut's a fan letter to the female Johnny B. Goode, who I guess is Nancy, now playing a lot of lead. Take note, fellas—as Zep rips go, this one is something special, and not just for its sexual politics. Unfortunately, things go gushy at the end with an Ann-penned love song. Men—who needs 'em?   **B+**

Heart: *Greatest Hits/Live* (Epic '80). Even their hits were never all that great beyond *Bebe Le Strange* and the usual coupla others—without "Barracuda" and "Crazy on You," they would never have gotten to wear stupid expensive clothes on the back cover or joke around in the studio for a couple hours and boil the results down into a tape collage called "Hit Single" ha ha ha. And with most of the hits all the way studio, the live stuff is long on covers, permitting Ann to run her suboperatic chops smack into "Unchained Melody" and "Tell It Like It Is." But the live "Bebe Le Strange" and the distaff "Rock and Roll" make them sound like contenders we need nevertheless.   **C+**

Heart: *Bad Animals* (Capitol '87). You'd never know Ann Wilson was riding the catchy intricacies of hired songwriting unless you listened more carefully than the resulting trifles deserve or her relentless overkill permits. And although the camp follower in me is sometimes tickled by the mismatch, it was the professional in me who noticed it. Only in the title cut, where a failed opera singer throws down the gauntlet for the heavy metal boors she's sworn to defend, does the end justify the means.   **C**

The Heartbeat of Soweto (Shanachie '88). Earthworks having cast in with Virgin, Shanachie goes to the well and tests Zulu hegemony with its own mbaqanga compilation. There are big advantages to the wider range of tribal melodies and beats—in Western pop terms, sharper hooks and a less monolithic groove. Seven artists divide up the twelve tracks, and while the hottest stuff is still Zulu—Usuthu's eternally recurrent tunelet, Amaswazi Emvelo's supertipico forward grind—this album has its urban heart in the bush. From the simple Tsonga drumbeats of Thomas Chauke's opener to the Shangaan family chorale of M.D. Shiranda's closer, unprofessionalism in no way diminishes the music's skill or complexity. Folkies may well prefer it to *Indestructible*. Rock-and-rollers with ears won't settle for one or the other.   **A**

Heartbeat Soukous (Earthworks/Virgin '88). Think of this Zaire-goes-to-Paris sampler as a best-of from a faceless disco supersession like Change or Kleeer, with interlocking musical directorates and a not all that different voice heading every track. The sectional structures—from femme chorus to synth cheese to unison horns, say—recall late disco as well. There are also distinctions, natch, especially in the beats, which interlock with an intricacy undreamed of in Giorgio Moroder's philosophy, and the sweet guitar figures that underlie every weave. The one on "Zouke-Zouke" is some kind of spiritual experience.   **A—**

Heaven 17: *Heaven 17* (Arista '82). As communiques—in Britain, where this group speaks directly to a general youth public—these cool-to-gnomic commentaries on a modernity in which jobs aren't roles, dreams aren't ideals, and the personal isn't quite the political undoubtedly earn some anthemic aura. As artifacts—in the U.S., where this group is sometimes confused with Duran Duran—they're dance music, albeit with generally thought-provoking hooks.   **B+**

Heaven 17: *The Luxury Gap* (Arista '83). Although their second U.S. album lacks the surface appeal of the debut compilation, it runs deeper, and politics makes the difference—not because their conscience impels them to come up with likable protest novelties like "Fascist Groove Thing" and "Let's All Make a Bomb," but because their compassion induces them to explore a subject to which they have privileged access. Nowhere else in music or sociology will you learn so much about the would-be hedonists who live the technopop/Anglodisco life. Obsessed with an upward mobility that fails to produce the advertised highs, their protagonists suffer the weariness known only to those who habitually overtax their wills. And Glen Gregory's cultivated, well-meaning vocals combine concerned observation with hard experience just soulfully enough. Original grade: A minus.   **B+**

Heavy D. & the Boyz: *Big Tyme* (MCA '89). He's got a smooth, rhythmic delivery. He knows his beats and cliches, assigning Teddy and Marley to set the bait and his own DJ to pull in the lines. Although he doesn't always use his vocabulary very precisely and isn't above "happy like a faggot in jail," he rarely pumps the boasts or the sexism all the way to wack. He even samples Martin Luther King. In short, he knows the right people and does the right things. Which is never enough.   **B—**

Richard Hell: *Destiny Street* (Red Star '82). With Material's Fred Maher replacing Voidoid-turned-Ramone Marky Bell and engineer-bandleader Naux augmenting Robert Quine on guitar, this is no lowest-common-denominator job: it's fuller and jazzier than *Blank Generation* without any loss of concision. Or toon appeal—the dissonantly dissident fun includes the antiscene "Lowest Common Denominator" and the antiscag "Ignore That Door." These days the *poéte maudit manqué* who once equated private sex with Faustian sin is looking for love that doesn't come in spurts. The key is "Staring in Her Eyes," where he explicitly surrenders his narcissistic nihilism to achieve the bliss described in the title. The song is affecting, its lyricism intensified as usual by the yearning inexactitude with which Hell pursues its melody, and I sympathize in principle with his new head. I'm just not convinced he has his heart in it yet.   **A—**

Richard Hell: *R.I.P.* (ROIR cassette '85). Supposedly the farewell of annotator Lester Meyers to his alter ego Hell, this fourteen-song all-previously-unreleased compilation begins with Johnny Thunders in New York, ends with Ziggy Modeliste in New Orleans, and preserves seven new songs and eight new Robert Quine cuts. What could be bad? you ask perspicaciously, and yet I'm a little disappointed. Only Fats Domino's "I Live My Life" and a painful lament for a masochist groupie called "Hurt Me" would improve *Blank Generation* or even *Destiny Street,* and the alternate versions alter nothing. Recommended to Walkpeople.   **B+**

Jimi Hendrix: *Nine to the Universe* (Reprise '80). With posthumous Hendrix it's always best to concentrate on the improvisations as if he were a jazz musician, and these relaxed jams are his jazziest contexts to date. Unfortunately, at least in theory, the only jazz player on hand is organist Larry Young, who got pretty far out with Miles and McLaughlin but sounds like Jimmy Smith over the Billy Cox–Mitch Mitchell beat. The result is bracing progressive r&b with Jimi stretching out, and the question is whether tighter structures wouldn't have made him think harder and faster.   **B+**

Jimi Hendrix: *The Jimi Hendrix Concerts* (Warner Bros. '82). Limited by Noel Redding and Mitch Mitchell, never the world's greatest living rhythm section, this barrel-bottom houses Hendrix the heavy metal paterfamilias rather than Hendrix the nonpareil rock improviser (not that the two weren't sometimes the same). There've been more exciting versions of such highlights as "Hear My Train a Comin' " (on *Rainbow Bridge*), "Little Wing," and especially "Red House" (both on the criminally deleted *Hendrix in the West*). But "Are You Experienced" has never been noisier.   **B+**

Jimi Hendrix: *Jimi at Monterey* (Reprise '86). Since I've oft been chastised for suggesting that the JHE's U.S. splashdown was less than extraterrestrial, I'm surprised at the yes-we-have-no-hosannas greeting this verbatim version. Maybe it's because only three of the ten tracks are previously unreleased. Maybe it's because after years of repackaging only suckers and acolytes get hot for another live Hendrix album. Or maybe it's because Jimi speeds alarmingly, Mitch Mitchell keeps tripping over his sticks, and "Like a Rolling Stone" is patently hokey. Nevertheless, such extramusical factors as historical verisimilitude and tinless audio incline me to charity. Peace-and-love-and-egomania at its most far out.   **B+**

Jimi Hendrix: *Johnny B. Goode* (Capitol '86). Like Hendrix's other 1986 releases, this budget-priced mini-LP (time: 26:08) is vivid testimony to the uses of digital mastering for archival music, especially music recorded direct to two-track. "The Star Spangled Banner" and "Machine Gun" occupy the B, and while there's no need to own either twice, the powerful sound is at least a reason. On the A, a compressed, guitar-heavy "Voodoo Chile" and an intense "Watchtower" surround the disc's only previously released (though long unavailable) track, which provides the album title for good reason—it's the definitive version of the definitive guitar anthem. Roll over Chuck Berry and tell Keith Richards the news.   **A−**

Jimi Hendrix: *Band of Gypsys 2* (Capitol '86). I suppose side one of this belated sequel wasn't side two of the original because Jimi had a personal or Capitol a financial stake in such brotherhood bromides as "Power of Soul" and "We Gotta Live Together." But for better or worse he's a lot more impassioned working apolitical traditions—debuting "Hear My Train a Comin' " or reprising "Foxy Lady" or letting Buddy Miles cover Howard Tate's "Stop." What's more, the Hendrix classics by the Mitch Mitchell edition of Band of Gypsys on side two sound a lot fresher now than they would have fifteen years ago, and not just because pressing techniques have taken such a leap. Which makes the second first by me.   **A−**

The Jimi Hendrix Experience: *Live at Winterland* (Rykodisc CD '87). This reconstructed hour-plus, drawn from the same three-night October '68 engagement that showed up on the 1982 *Jimi Hendrix Concerts,* is what the format is for. The sound is bigger and better in every way for an artist whose sound was his music—a vast improvement on live analog remixes, a meaningful improvement on the digitals that redefined live Hendrix last year. The uninterrupted length makes sense, conveying a concert's pace and logic into your audio-only living room. Also, the performances are splendid. [Later in all formats.]   **A**

The Jimi Hendrix Experience: *Radio One* (Rykodisc '88). If it's getting like Coltrane, crazies examining umpteen versions of the same tune, Hendrix's versions do bear scrutiny like no other rock and roll. Noncrazies aren't obliged or even advised to make the effort, yet newcomers could just as well start with these BBC sessions as with *Are You Experienced?,* also cut when he still led kind of a pop band. Ace new stuff includes Curtis Knight's "Drivin' South" and Elvis Presley's "Hound Dog."   **A−**

Nona Hendryx: *Nona* (RCA Victor '83). Charged with curbing Nona's insatiable desire to make rock records, Bill Laswell and Michael Beinhorn were abstemious enough not to make a Material record instead—just a slightly cerebral who-*is*-that-singing? funk record, with the cerebration mostly Nona's. As you might deduce, it could be smarter, but you can dance to it without losing your mind.   **B+**

Nona Hendryx: *The Art of Defense* (RCA Victor '84). Nona earns her loyal insider support. She's honest; she cares about the right music and the right issues in the right way. But she just isn't as talented as you wish she was, and on this follow-up her undifferentiated melodies come back to haunt her. Her singing is surprisingly careful, Material's groove surprisingly straight-ahead, and I can guess why—everybody involved knew how thin the ice was.   **C+**

Don Henley: *I Can't Stand Still* (Asylum '82). Makes sense that Henley's candid self-involvement should prove of more intrinsic interest than Glenn Frey's covert self-pity, but nobody capable of the distinction figured it would get as interesting as this. If there were anything to actually like about the guy, his complaints and revelations might even be moving. As it is, let's call them strong—like primo tequila, or the smell of an old jockstrap.   **B+**

Don Henley: *Building the Perfect Beast* (Geffen '84). This one makes you listen— its abrupt shapes and electro/symphonic textures never whisper Eagles remake. So thank cocomposer, multi-instrumentalist, and occasional arranger Danny Kortchmar, whose "You're Not Drinking Enough" (Merle Haggard, call your agent) and "All She Wants To Do Is Dance" (T-Bone Burnett, ditto) are at once the simplest and most effective songs on the record. Then blame the turgid lengths, tough-guy sensitivity, and "women are the only works of art" on the auteur, who still thinks perfect love is when you're crazy and she screams.   **B**

Don Henley: *The End of the Innocence* (Geffen '89). Bitch bitch bitch, bloat bloat bloat. Six of ten tracks run over five minutes, and not 'cause he's building a groove, although the antiripoff "Gimme What You Got" does appropriate a JB riff, which I guess is ironic, or totally unconscious. Nope, Don wants drama and plenty of it—seven of ten instrumental in-

tros are thirty seconds plus, with three up around an L.A. minute (as distinguished from a "New York Minute," 'cause Don says your life can change in one of those). Theme: "This brave new world / Gone bad again." (Again?) Solution: love—only don't blame him if it falls through.   **C+**

Henry Cow: *Western Culture* (Interzone '80). Right, it's not "rock"—it's modern chamber music utilizing "rock" instruments, namely guitar-organ-drums, as well as brass and woodwinds of varying couth. It's jarring without valorizing the random, the way this group always is at its best, and it eschews the highbrow vocalizing favored by this group at its worst. I don't know much about chamber music, but I know what I like—"rock" instruments.   **A−**

The John Herald Band: *The Real Thing* (Rooster '84). Fallible though he may be, I'll take this bluegrass-based traditionalist over Ricky Skaggs any day. Maybe his transported singing honors George Jones and Jerry Lee Lewis along with Red Allen and Bill Monroe because his long experience in folkiedom taught him something new about authenticity. Or maybe it's just that he's not above sinning.   **B+**

John Hiatt: *Two Bit Monsters* (MCA '80). Stupid that they're comparing this perennial future cult hero to Elvis C.—Hiatt beat Costello to his voice, such as it is, by four years. Still, a lyric like "Back to the War," which sounds bitterly political and was probably inspired by an errant lover or business associate, makes me think twice, as does the impenetrable "New Numbers." When Costello is impenetrable, which is usually, he makes it look clever. And when Hiatt is penetrable, which is also usually, his cleverness varies.   **B**

John Hiatt: *All of a Sudden* (Geffen '82). Carpers have always claimed there was nothing underneath his gift for the hook, and now that Hiatt's finally gotten his big shot, on David G.'s label with David B.'s producer, he seems intent on proving it. Median cut length is up from 2:55 (on 1979's *Slug Line*) to 3:31, Tony Visconti has dehumanized Hiatt's uncommercial voice with filters that make him sound like a Hoosier Steve Strange, and even his cover photo has been reduced to benday dots. The veteran up-and-comer as overblown cynic. **B−**

John Hiatt: *Riding with the King* (Geffen '83). With well-respected albums on three major labels and boosters from Three Dog Night to Ry Cooder, Hiatt must be doing something wrong. Singing is my guess—just like Ry, he's immersed himself in the mannerisms of soul without enjoying access to its physical substance. But in the end this is his best album because the songs are so much his catchiest and pithiest. Most of them reflect smashed hopes. The tenderest is called "She Loves the Jerk." And of course the jerk ain't John. **A−**

John Hiatt: *Warming Up to the Ice Age* (Geffen '85). Commercial failure hasn't touched Hiatt's devotion to craft, but it's been hell on his sense of humor. He still cracks wise while rolling out the hooks, but the sprightly feel of *Riding With the King* has given way to a soulish hard rock that suggests he's satirizing all these bitter macho men in the first person because satire isn't the main idea. **B**

John Hiatt: *Bring the Family* (A&M '87). "I don't think Ronnie Milsap's gonna ever / Record this song," moans the wandering pro on the lead cut, which announces his intention to go get "good and greasy" in Memphis before subjecting himself to "one more heartfelt steel guitar chord" in the Music City he calls home. But now more than ever he seems to derive his idea of good and greasy from, I don't know, Joe Cocker, which only works when he makes nasty. Well-written though it may be, most of this is Ronnie Milsap's kind of thing. **B−**

John Hiatt: *Slow Turning* (A&M '88). Cut with his road band rather than a select cast of studio heavies, which probably took some pressure off a perpetual comer who turns the juice up too high when he gets nervous. Anyway, the high-grade country fodder—"Is Anybody There?" to a woman who loves him, "Georgia Rae" to a newborn daughter, and so forth—goes down easier. And the mean stuff he's always been best at—a roving couple who

shoot up an automatic teller for laundromat change, a roving couple who steal one of Elvis's Cadillacs, a guy who cheats the world just like his daddy did—has a properly rowdy edge. **B+**

John Hiatt: *Y'All Caught?: The Ones That Got Away 1979–1985* (Geffen '89). "She Said the Same Things to Me" and "It Hasn't Happened Yet" are winning answers to the wimmin question, and every time they come up I feel like I love this male chauvinist victim. But not so's I pull out *Warming Up to the Ice Age* or *Two Bit Monsters*. The rest of his greatest misses are catchy, clever, even compassionate when you listen hard. Three are from *Riding With the King,* which I did go find—and still prefer. **B+**

Hicks From the Sticks (Antilles '81). I don't think I'm familiar with any of the tunes on this 16-cut compilation, originally released Brit in 1980 by Rockburgh Records. But I might as well be. Here on one convenient A side is everything that has made the Anglophile dance-rock scene so deadly—the synth grooves, the minimelodies, the robot vocals, the confusion of late industrial anomie with the zeitgeist. In short, the new art-rock and the new disco in one conflation, with the boring rhythms of today replacing the boring solos of yesteryear. I mean, when a pop admixture provides the rock and roll, I go home. **C+**

Joe Higgs: *Triumph* (Alligator '85). The ska pioneer and fourth Wailer is one of reggae's most respected writers of songs and singers of harmonies. He's been around too long to have much use for millenarian cant, and he's too honest to play the romantic stud—he sings about love because he needs it soul and body in the ghetto where he figures to spend the rest of his days, and at forty-five he feels like he's got a lot of days ahead of him. His weathered voice and reassuringly deep and unpredictable backup also articulate the way he understands the world. I know of no Jamaican whose sensibility is more accessible to ordinary American music lovers of a certain age. **A−**

Joe Higgs: *Family* (Shanachie '88). In a chronically undifferentiated music, subtlety can be a curse, and though I've gotten to know every song here and have no trouble admiring most, I wish Higgs had rehired the musicians who backed *Triumph* three years ago. It's my guess—and with subtlety you have to guess some—that the likes of Chinna Smith, Wire Lindo, and Augustus Pablo made the difference between an acknowledged classic and an obscure near thing.   **B+**

Hilary: *Kinetic* (Backstreet EP '83). "Goose Step Two Step"'s Hitlerism-as-horror-movie is such an exploitation I may never hear "I Live" again, but I'll always get off on the A. Title tune's the catchiest Gary Numan number since "Cars" and the most affirmative Depeche Mode number since "New Life." "Drop Your Pants" is nothing more but nothing less than what the title says, as "ironic" as a Playmate's as-told-to. Make no excuses, boys and girls—this is DOR softcore. If it doesn't titillate you, you don't get it.   **A−**

Hi-Life International: *Music To Wake the Dead!* (Rounder '84). With Ghana's big-band dance style now regarded as overpolite in its country of origin, highlife's virtues are ripe for exploitation elsewhere—namely, London, where these expatriates perceived an opening and moved in. The melodies are so fetching they camouflage the overcasual vocals, but the three attempts to cash in on Zaire's big-band dance style don't kick home. Soukous isn't supposed to be polite.   **B+**

Z.Z. Hill: *Down Home* (Malaco '81). No relation to Top, Hill is an old pro who's never been able to decide whether he's a soulful blues man or a bluesy soul man and has never found the material to make anyone care for more than a single or two. Now that the question is commercially moot, he's somehow scored eight out of ten pungent, basic songs on an LP cut in and for Jackson, Mississippi. A bluesy soul man, in case you were wondering.   **A−**

Z.Z. Hill: *I'm a Blues Man* (Malaco '83). The title boast is inauspicious. If Hill's 1981 *Down Home* turned into a phenomenal 450,000-sold-and-counting sleeper on mere stylistic integrity, then why didn't his

1982 *The Rhythm and the Blues* do almost as well? You guessed it—song quality went way down. But after the bad start it rebounds considerably here. Personal to Tommy Couch: is Jimmy Lewis ready for another album of his own, or is he a stay-at-home?   **B+**

Z.Z. Hill: *Greatest Hits* (Malaco '86). Don't romanticize him. A bluesy veteran whose plentiful earlier music is for loyalists and specialists (cf. his U.K. compilation on Stateside), he turned a Bobby Bland rasp into a trademark at Malaco, which couldn't promote the original anywhere near as profitably. Maybe his secret is that he had less voice to shoot, or that deep down he was more country. Anyway, in the last three years of his life a predominantly black songwriting stable obsessed with the perils of monogamy joined forces with white producers good for soul bottom and dollops of sweetening to make him a regional star. In short, he was a hack who finally hit the jackpot, and this best-of—not the *In Memoriam* comp Malaco put together right after he died at forty-eight in 1984, not even his breakthrough *Down Home*—is his testament. It has no secrets, this record, just one great song after another: George Jackson's embittered "Cheatin in the Next Room," Jimmy Lewis's generous "Get a Little, Give a Little," Jimmy Lewis's calculating "Three Into Two Won't Go," Dave Clark's unrepentant "Friday Is My Day," and I could go on. Residual culture, my man Raymond Williams calls this sort of throwback. Hope he'd love it.   **A**

Justin Hinds and the Dominoes: *Travel With Love* (Nighthawk '85). Conservative rhythmically and conventional lyrically, this is the reggae equivalent of Otis Clay–style soul, yet it'll come this close to getting you: the style is so modest that the singer has no trouble burnishing up the requisite patina of sweet belief.   **B**

Hip House (DJ International '89). "A rap on a House record does not make Hip House"; an unassuming rap punctuated by simple sung hooks over house piano, pumped bass, and the occasional Brown-whoop does. As per house rules, the breaks are too abstract to justify their length. But party music that would be escapist at this hip-hop moment is a hard move on these kids' scene, so they sound proud of themselves, and they ought to be. Put your hands in the air, and wave 'em like you just don't care.   **B+**

Peter Hofmann: *Rock Classics* (CBS '83). If all ten selections were as hilariously wrong as "The House of the Rising Sun," which kicks off this chenu-wine Cherman heldentenor's bid for the unwashed market, it might qualify as a camp masterpiece. Instead it's merely dreadful, an object lesson in how poorly the technical paraphernalia of European good-and-beautiful serve American pop. You can hear why the effortless purity of Hofmann's three-octave range gets over with opera enthusiasts—Judy Collins would kill a whale for it. But "Bridge Over Troubled Water" has never sounded lovelier than in Simon & Garfunkel's original because their fragile harmonies underscore the modesty that makes the melody soar. And if not even Ray Charles could make much of "The Long and Winding Road," he also had the good sense to avoid "MacArthur Park" and "Nights in White Satin" altogether. What is it they're supposed to have over in Europe? Oh, I remember—taste.   **D**

Buddy Holly: *For the First Time Anywhere* (MCA '83). If like me you were crying, waiting, hoping, or just wishing for new songs, dream on—other versions of the five originals and five covers are already familiar to owners of the six-disc *Complete Buddy Holly* import, most of whom bought this the week it was released. Those who've settled for *20 Golden Greats* will greatly enjoy meeting the originals, especially since they sound much stronger in these recordings. And now here's wishing I could say the same for the covers—Holly rejected "That's My Desire" because it was a dog, and if the new "Brown-Eyed Handsome Man" is competitive with the one you know, the new "Bo Diddley" isn't. Time: 21:03.   **B+**

Homeland (Rounder '87). Nine of these twelve tracks, all produced by Rounder's man in Azania Clive Risko, clock in within two seconds of 3:00. They all seem to use the same efficiently uninspired rhythm section. So the initial effect is wearing, especially on the hour-long CD version. And in the end the vocal variety up top shines through like a new day coming.   **B+**

The Honest Cartwrights: *The Honest Cartwrights* (Honest Cartwrights EP '83). As craft enjoys its inevitable comeback, here are four guys who don't make it sound like a strain—over-thirties, I'll bet, big Steely Feat fans, only fresher because they've got something to prove, to themselves if no one else. And if you think alcoholism, masturbation, and nuclear war sound punky, tell me what punk band would cap their bomb song with a mournful "There goes my career"?   **B+**

The Honeydrippers: *Volume One* (Es Paranza EP '84). This meeting of the immortals—I refer of course to R. Plant, J. Page, and A. Ertegun, not the less than obvious r&b classics they, to borrow one of the quaint titles, "rock at midnight"—looks like the largest selling EP in history. It's not unlistenable, but I'll tell you who to buy first: Ray Charles, Roy Brown, even Phil Phillips. And Led Zeppelin—definitely Led Zeppelin.   **B−**

Hoodoo Gurus: *Stoneage Romeos* (A&M '84). "Tojo" and "Leilani" and "Zanzibar." "Death Ship" and "I Was a Kamikaze Pilot." Hiccups from Lux Interior and counterpoint from the Pink Panther and attitude from Mental as Anything and rhymes from Danny & the Ramones. Those with no use for trivial pursuits can ignore this one, but if you enjoy the game when the fun isn't forced, these cheerfully maladjusted Aussies certainly beat what's been coming out of the bat-garages of L.A. and London these past two–three years. And if you want to read meaning and feeling into "Arthur" (who dies) or "I Want You Back" (which like "My Girl" isn't a cover) or even "Zanzibar" (a secret masterpiece, sez I), they—by which I mean the songs, not the band—won't spit in your eye.   **B+**

Hoodoo Gurus: *Mars Needs Guitars!* (Big Time '85). This is tuneful enough if you give it more of a chance than it deserves, but it's no fun because it's not funny. Without a few sly laughs they're just a macho pop band, which is less than you can say of the Fleshtones, the Nomads, presplit Squeeze, or prime Mental as Anything, to name just four.   **B—**

Hoodoo Gurus: *Magnum Cum Louder* (RCA '89). One of the enduring kicks of college radio's minor-league "underground" is young believers and venerable adepts extracting something fresh from the same old fours. One of its nagging annoyances is headstrong faithful and professional guitarists claiming that competent variations on the truths they hold to be self-evident are brand new fun.   **B—**

John Lee Hooker: *The Healer* (Chameleon '89). Pushing one hundred thirty now, Hook will still walk anybody into the studio for cash up front. Though the pickings have been getting leaner, here anybody includes Carlos Santana, George Thorogood, Bonnie Raitt, Robert Cray, Canned Heat, and Los Lobos, most of whom commit crimes against his ageless essence that tone up the product considerably. And for the purist market, the product ends with four solo stomps.   **B+**

Hooters: *Nervous Night* (Columbia '85). Just when you thought there was no more AOR, this overwrought Philadelphia-brand hookarama goes gold on MTV—Love cover, revolutionary propaganda, and all. And about that blond—he may be Finnish (-American), but I bet he dyes his hair.   **C+**

Bruce Hornsby and the Range: *The Way It Is* (RCA Victor '86). Schlock has roots, too, which is why sentimental bizzers hail this mildly surprising platinum-plus debut as the second coming. Hornsby roughs up a piano that's more Elton John than Floyd Domino with a voice on the boogie side of country-rock and adds sometime folkie David Mansfield to songs that divide the same way—they sound like pop and read like something closer to the source. Title tune was my guilty pleasure of 1986 because what makes me feel guilty is succumbing to the blandishments of liberalism. The rest I don't have much trouble fighting off.   **B—**

Bruce Hornsby & the Range: *Scenes From the Southside* (RCA Victor '88). This unassuming platinum mine is compassionate, serious, literate. He plays a "real" piano. And he's a menace. I mean, in the privacy of your own mind, try crossing vague Bruce with '80s Elton. Then run it through Firefall. Finally—this is important—*slow down those tempos.* No no no, leave the drum sound up. See?   **C**

The Horseflies: *Human Fly* (Rounder '87). You can tell these sardonic folkies have big plans because they've come up with a slogan: "neoprimitive bug music," which definitely beats "the Ithaca sound." Overimpressed with Philip Glass, bluegrass, or both, they utilize lots of repetition. Very hypnotic, or strophic, or static. Also kind of tedious, like the grim lifecycle they so often evoke—a little goes a long way, which I guess beats nowhere. Check out the Cramps cover.   **B**

Hot Chocolate: *Mystery* (EMI America '82). Maybe the reason Errol Brown's never broken through Stateside is the inscrutability that's always made him such a provocative pop figure—he gives you nothing to hold on to but the hook. And though his hooks have never been more abundant, I'm beginning to wish I knew why he took so much trouble. Original grade: B plus.   **B**

Housecoat Project: *Wide Eye Doo Dat* (Subterranean '88). Played this because I liked the band's name, played it some more because I liked the singer, played it a lot more because I'm in the market for bohos to believe in. Meri St. Mary may not be the cross between Lou and Patti her label claims, but she's at least a female Bob Pfeifer, with nice sharp words—"Wild wimmin don't die / They just dye their hair / And get on out of town," or

"Doesn't he know that we'd still like him / Even if he was one of the Rolling Stones?"—to go with the nice sharp Lou/ Patti arrangements. And why anybody but Bay Area barflies should care I couldn't tell you.   **B**

House Hallucinates: Pump Up the World Volume One (Vendetta '89). Take it from your Uncle Bob—even at the time, no one thought hallucinogens enhanced gross motor function. Self-expression, utopian possibility, all that good stuff with insufficient material base—maybe. But as the hippie girls (not to mention boys) freaking through *Woodstock* and *Monterey Pop* remind us, acid didn't go with dance crazes. And with their hooks vanishing into the mix, the trickily rhythmic, subtly incremental, frustratingly one-dimensional synth doodles that dominate this two-disc acid house compilation are about as engrossing as a Greg Elmore drum solo. I observe admiringly that the music is kind of avant-garde. I note that the lyrics are mantralike. And I concede that all of it must connect better in context. But I doubt I'd take a shine to the context even if I didn't have to get up in the morning. So I advise the curious to check out the context first.   **C**

The Housemartins: *London 0, Hull 4* (Elektra '86). Fashion leaders in their cardigans and baggy pants, these unpretentious soul-boys-in-a-pop-band are so perky you think they're about to break into a cereal commercial, but in fact they have a different product in mind: socialist revolution. I'd leave it at something vaguer (Marxist Christianity, say) if their disdain for fence-sitters and other sheep wasn't so fervent, so bitter, and—rarest of all—so just. And if their catchiest hook didn't go (hum along, now) "Don't shoot someone tomorrow / That you can shoot today." Very nice.   **A—**

The Housemartins: *The People Who Grinned Themselves to Death* (Elektra '87). Pop this venomous constitutes a formal leap way beyond the reach of spewing "postmodernists" who can't distinguish between their own ugliness and the world's. Telling the farmer that Jesus hates

him or begging Johannesburg not to make any fuss on their account, they're Christians after my own heart: they nurture a righteous rage, and aim it at the right targets. Couching their invective in choirboy cute or lacing their quiet melodies with sulphuric acid, they're subversives after my own heart as well: oppression hasn't sapped their lyricism. They're telling us they're indomitable. Wouldn't it be amazing if they turned out to be right? **A—**

Whitney Houston: *Whitney Houston* (Arista '84). I'd never claim that this sweet, statuesque woman and her sweet, statuesque voice are victims of exploitation. She obviously believes in this schlock. But not counting the Jermaine Jackson duet from his own Arista debut, only one of the four producers puts any zip in— Narada Michael Walden, who goes one for one. And it could have been worse—they could have sicked Barry Manilow on her the way they did with cousin Dionne. Then the credits could also have read: "To Barry Manilow, It was a privilege to work with a talented professional who's made so many millions of dollars for Clive Davis. Together, we can make many millions more."   **C**

Whitney Houston: *Whitney* (Arista '87). It takes more than unsullied venality and the will to power to reign as the most revolting pop singer in Christendom. It takes active aesthetic miscalculation and, truth be told, more than a little luck. Like falling into the lame dance grooves of Jermaine Jackson and the odious megaschlock of Michael Masser, with Narada Michael Walden limited to "How Will I Know"— which becomes your breakthrough song as well as the only critically forgivable thing on your best-selling debut album in history. So this time Walden gets seven shots, with Masser down to two and Jermaine returned to the bosom of his family, and the results are forgivable—she does have a good voice, you know.   **C+**

Hugo Largo: *Drum* (Opal '88). Former hardcore advocate and MTV copywriter Tim Sommer claims his latest fantasy reformulates "the 30-year-old concept of what a rock band sounds like." Right—

and so do the Kronos Quartet, the Bulgarian State Radio and Television Female Vocal Choir, and George Winston. With stringed/bowed instruments (no drums, get it?) under the sway of inaccurata soprano Mimi Goese—to say she sounds like Natalie Merchant mourning a lost orgasm understates her commitment to her affectations—this is the definition of arty twaddle. Inspirational Verse: "Balancing glasses on your nose / By the crystal ball / Purified of vulgar things / Planted feet along the hall."   **D+**

The Human League: *Dare* (A&M '81). It's not flesh-and-blood chauvinism that puts me off Britannia's hookiest dance-synth monster. I'll boogie to the right machine; I can even imagine fucking a cyborg. But while the cyborg of my dreams would keep it light, not act too impressed with all the tricks stored in his/her memory, League spokesman Philip Oakey comes on like three kinds of pompous jerk. The only time I light up is when Susan Solley takes her verse on "Don't You Want Me," which I recommend to Quarterflash.   **B−**

The Human League: *Hysteria* (A&M '84). It's clear enough that despite aural appearances Phil Oakey does have feelings, but so do BBC news readers, and nobody expects them to lead popular singing groups. If these Yoo Kay yuppies are really hysterical, they're also dangerously repressed. Polite hooks feh.   **C**

Human League: *Greatest Hits* (A&M '88). I still don't believe humans bought these songs because they liked them. As the leader says, or intones, or even sings if you want to be polite: "(Keep Feeling) [dig those parentheses] Fascination." At their best, they're fascinating—masters of body-snatcher music, articulate simulated emotion fortified with the coldest hooks ever manufactured. Which is why their Jam-Lewis move was such a fraud. "I'm only human / Of flesh and blood I'm made"— yeah sure.   **B+**

Human Switchboard: *Who's Landing in My Hangar?* (Faulty Products '81). Have rock-and-rollers ever reflected more matter-of-factly on the travails of sexual commitment? Bet both Pfeifer and Marcarian were raised up in the First Church of Humanity (Secular), because unlike Elvis II and the X kids, for instance, they don't find much thrill in confessional—just get annoyed, pissed off, very pissed off, and insane with rage. Also unlike the aforementioned, they get lyrical, quite light and playful in fact, which adds charm to their organ-based garage style. Not many cool guys boasting about their girlfriends' "looks" these days.   **A**

Hungry for What: *The Shattered Dream* (Better Youth '86). Black up the leader's cuspids and change their name to Garageland or London Calling and they could play any tribute bar between Boston and D.C. Only difference is they write their own anthems and don't fake any Cockney—when you start out in German, singing English is tribute enough. And though they won't make you love it, I bet they could make you like it—there's more spirit in their frank, admiring imitation than in the ersatz originality of whichever hybrid is tearing out the alternative playlists this week.   **B**

Alberta Hunter: *Amtrak Blues* (Columbia '80). After the bland *Remember My Name* soundtrack, John Hammond's gem is a blessing—it would have been tragic if the rebirth of this eighty-five-year-old wonder of nature and history, easily the most authoritative classic blues singer alive, had been documented only in print. A hot rhythm section, anchored by pianist Gerald Cook and jazzed up by hornmen Vic Dickenson, Doc Cheatham, and Frank Wess, pitch in with undeniable verve on material from "The Darktown Strutters' Ball" to "Always" to several worthy Hunter originals. Timing and intonation are as savvy as you'd figure, and though the voice isn't quite as full as it must have been, it packs an amazing wallop—when Hunter gloats about getting her butter churned, the memory sounds quite fresh, like maybe the dairy man poked his head in that morning. More good news—she'll be back in the studio with Hammond soon.   **A**

Alberta Hunter: *The Glory of Alberta Hunter* (Columbia '82). It's a given that octogenarians like Sam Chatmon, Eubie Blake, even George Burns have more vitality than just about any singing war baby you care to name—they prove that by breathing. But life-begins-at-eighty isn't really Hunter's secret, except insofar as it deepens her wisdom, which isn't a given at all. It's not like Bessie Smith raising her voice among us, because Hunter is less titanic. But she spins her blues and gospel and pop with the spontaneous affection not just of somebody who never knew there was a difference between art and entertainment but of somebody who had the heart to leave show business and work as a nurse for twenty-three years. Her raunch ("You Can't Tell the Difference After Dark") is as unforced as her love of God ("Ezekiel Saw the Wheel") and her female indomitability ("I've Had Enough"), and her band plays even better than she sings.   **A—**

Alberta Hunter: *Look for the Silver Lining* (Columbia '83). Since wonders of nature make bad records just like anyone else, what's amazing is that the flat writing, corny sentiment, and automatic mannerisms that bring this down barely touched the two before it. And don't be surprised if she celebrates her nintieth by coming back yet again next time.   **B—**

Michael Hurley: *Snockgrass* (Rounder '80). More songs about dying and food—and rambling, mustn't forget rambling—from the old-timy existentialist, whose oblique wail recalls both Jerry Garcia and John Prine because all three are more obsessed with mountain vocal styles than most mountain vocal stylists. "Jole' Blon," "Tia Marie," and a few others are more or less what you'd expect, but if you ever expected "You Gonna Look Like a Monkey" or "I Heard the Voice of a Porkchop," you're two up on me.   **A—**

Michael Hurley: *Blue Navigator* (Rooster '84). Us snockgrass fans didn't await this long-awaited album quite long enough—sounds as if Hurley padded over to the studio before he was done with his nap. I know it's always sleepy time up north in Wolfville, and Hurley obviously spent part of his four-year vacation thinking about seven new originals. But except for the . . . climactic "Open Up (Eternal Lips)," even the best of them get lost on their way to the outhouse. Inspirational Insert: "Feel free to tape this album: *Blue Navigator* is not soley [sic] a commercial venture but is intended for a spiritual life far out traveling the destination of one arrow."   **B**

Michael Hurley: *Watertower* (Fundamental '89). His core audience couldn't be much over two thousand, and since I'm on its fringe, I don't much care that this typically unheralded, offhand, and tardy acoustic collection will make no converts. He still writes more calmly and curiously about the great beyond than anyone. What's more, "Broadcasting the Blues" and "I Paint a Design" break thematic ground—television and professionalism, respectively.   **B+**

Hurricane Zouk (Earthworks/Virgin '88). Slickly high-tech like no other African or Caribbean style, Antillean zouk is Afro-Caribbean plus vive-la-France. On these prize cuts the singers—most strikingly Francky Vincent, a/k/a Dr. Porn—are joky, sly, lascivious. There's something comic and triumphant about the eclecticism of old Kassav' hand G. H. Guamaguy, who favors horn and fiddle frills, and new champion Servais Liso, who goes for glitzier electronic effects. Name me another twentieth-century pop that's thrived so exuberantly under the depredations of Gallic wit. Original grade: A.   **A—**

Hüsker Dü: *Land Speed Record* (New Alliance '81). Like a good Eno ambient, this raving nonstop live one provides just enough surface detail—recombinant noise guitar, voices tailing off like skyrockets, slogans such as "data control," "do the bee," and "ultracore"—to function as mood rather than trance music, though admittedly not for the same kind of mood. Guaranteed to assuage the nervous tension of co-op conversion, labor strife, bad orgasm, World War III, and other modern urban annoyances. In other words: *aarrghhh!* Time: 26:16.   **B+**

Hüsker Dü: *Everything Falls Apart* (Reflex '82). Documenting their power-trio approach to hardcore, with each instrument distinctly virtuosic and each instrumentalist an accomplished yowler, here's proof that these shaggy dogs from Minneapolis are the musical equal of Black Flag and Minor Threat and more sensible than either (though not a *lot* more). Like any self-respecting hardcore band, they spend more time criticizing their subculture than criticizing their society, which they assume you know isn't worth the trouble. Inspirational Verse, from "Obnoxious": "You say we play too fast / Music's not gonna last / Well I think you're wrong." Cover: "Sunshine Superman."   **A—**

Hüsker Dü: *Metal Circus* (SST EP '83). While Bob Mould isn't quite Ian MacKaye's equal as a front man or Greg Ginn's as a guitarist, Hüsker Dü's reenactments of hardcore's hyperdrive ritual have always matched Minor Threat's and Black Flag's on sheer collective enthusiasm, and this EP translates their heart into song. With Mould molding molten metal into whopper hooks and drummer Grant Hart contributing emotional vocals on two key cuts, they take Minor Threat's trust-yourselves-not-us message seriously. And while I'm a little uneasy with the high-powered fatalism of "Real World" and "Deadly Skies," somehow it doesn't seem final with a band that cares this much.   **A**

Hüsker Dü: *Zen Arcade* (SST '84). I'll swear on a stack of singles that "Turn on the News" could rouse as much rabble as "London Calling" or "Anarchy in the U.K." I play side three for pleasure and side two for catharsis. And I get a kick out of the whole fucking thing, right down to the fourteen-minute guitar showcase/mantra that finishes it off. But though I hate to sound priggish, I do think it could have used a producer. I mean, it was certainly groovy (not to mention manly) to record first takes and then mix down for forty hours straight, but sometimes the imperfections this economical method so proudly incorporates could actually be improved upon. It wouldn't be too much of a compromise to make sure everyone sings into the mike, for instance, and it's downright depressing to hear Bob Mould's axe gather dust on its way from vinyl to speak-

ers. Who knows, put them in the studio with some hands-off technician—Richard Gottehrer, Tony Bongiovi, like that—and side two might even qualify as cathartic music rather than cathartic noise.   **A—**

Hüsker Dü: *New Day Rising* (SST '85). With its dawn-over-the-lake cover, guitar chimes, and discernible melodies—on as many as ten of the fifteen songs!—this is the Hüskers' pastoral. I suppose a few hardcore urbanists will think it's wimpy or something, but by any vaguely normal standard it's clearly their finest record even if they have turned off the news in pursuit of a maturity I trust they'll outgrow. Not that they haven't matured. Bob Mould's ambivalence gets him two places instead of none, and I love Grant Hart's love objects—one with a big messy room and "a worn out smile that she'll wear some more," another who's heavily into UFOs. Play loud—this is one band that deserves it.   **A**

Hüsker Dü: *Flip Your Wig* (SST '85). They've never sounded so good. Spot's gone, as are most of the cobwebs that obscured their clamor, so without kow-towing to Michael Wagener we really get to hear Bob Mould's guitar. Thing is, what's made them major isn't Mould's guitar, their mainstay from the first—it's songcraft. And now Grant Hart has gotten so crafty (or happy) that he's turned conventional—"Green Eyes," about beauty never jealousy, and "Flexible Flyer," which advises that we keep our hearts "burning brightly," are attractive in their way, but they betray a pop simplemindedness unworthy of the hard-driving oddball love songs that make *New Day Rising* such an up. As for mainstay Mould, he's still honestly confused and mad as hell. May his heart burn this bright forever.   **A—**

Hüsker Dü: *Candy Apple Grey* (Warner Bros. '86). Grant Hart breaks up with the love of his life, Bob Mould can't shake off a bad trip, and hand in hand they sell out to the big bad major with the most disconsolate record of their never exactly cheerful career. Of course, between the swelling melodies that are supposed to give them pop accessibility and an attention to recorded sound that does some justice to their humongous musical details, the overall effect is more inspirational than depressing—this is the album that combines the supersonic soar of *Flip Your Wig* with the full-grown vision of *New Day Rising*. As for pop accessibility, we shall see.   **A**

Hüsker Dü: *Warehouse: Songs and Stories* (Warner Bros. '87). They invented this barrage, and they've perfected it: for close to seventy minutes, songs rise out of the roiling seas like elephant seals, bellow their hooks, and sink sleekly away. But there's a downside to the overwhelming consistency of what those who take the title literally assume is a hodgepodge. Now that they've mastered the feat of yoking elemental noise and elemental melody, their power of musical expression has apparently rendered irrelevant the meaning of individual songs. So that almost as soon as you notice one—Grant Hart's "You're a Soldier," with its sermon to the enemy, or Bob Mould's "It's Not Peculiar," with its stuttered refrain—you're not sure you trust it.   **A—**

Winston Hussey: *The Girl I Adore* (Live & Learn '83). This is the kind of reggae most Americans dismiss as impossibly monotonous: the melodies are simple and often repetitive, the singing plaintive and crude, the words barely literate. I'm not claiming any of these qualities are virtues in themselves, but they can be. Working a shameless variation on Gregory Isaacs, Hussey projects intense innocence of a sort increasingly rare in English-language music; replete with homy references to liniment and parlors and pajamas, his sexual musings and militant pacifism must seem a little uncool even in Kingston. And for those with ears to hear, he's backed by the Roots Radics, who are far from succumbing to the subtler monotony that eventually afflicts great studio bands.   **A—**

J. B. Hutto & the New Hawks: *Slippin' and Slidin'* (Varrick '84). Good new Chicago-style blues albums are rare occurrences that fall into two categories. On last year's, A. C. Reed enlivened an ordinary-plus groove with hilarious-minus material. On this year's, the now deceased slide guitar king makes his tightest and most raucous recorded music since 1968's definitive *Hawk Squat!* He gets telling (and tellingly understated) help from the Roomful of Blues horns. Telling-minus material would have helped even more.   **B+**

Lucia Hwong: *House of Sleeping Beauties* (Private Music '86). This intelligent if hyper-romantic new-age prestige item would make a nifty soundtrack for *Lost Horizon* and comes with the blessing of new-age titan (and sometimes soundtrack composer) Philip Glass, who identifies Hwong as one of those select young composers who are equally conversant with Eastern and Western music. Unfortunately, not many Western listeners will hear it as more than high-class chinoiserie—maybe those sopranos derive from Chinese opera, but they sound like Hollywood angels anyway. I trust the artist's decolletage derives from Chinese opera as well.   **B+**

Abdullah Ibrahim: *Water From an Ancient Well* (BlackHawk '86). Pining for his South African home, where American jazz has long symbolized black possibility, Ibrahim syncretizes. Relinquishing neither the modernist idiosyncrasy that underpins his exile nor the big-band entertainment values that have shored up the townships for close to half a century, he roots himself in the shared melodies and rhythms that give South African jazz its sound. Except maybe for tenor man Ricky Ford, the all-Americans who complete his Ekaya octet aren't great improvisors, but Ibrahim writes to their strengths and adds plenty of his own. *Ekaya* was more exuberant, but as inspiriting as I find the lilt of "Mandela" and "Manenberg Revisited," it's the brooding spiritual reserves of side two that convince me of Ibrahim's power. Not only does this artist have something to be serious about, he's found a way to make it breathe. **A—**

Ice-T: *Rhyme Pays* (Sire '87). With heavy help from DJ Afrika Islam, this reformed criminal is the rap equivalent of pimp-turned-paperback-writer Iceberg Slim. Can't know whether his streetwise jabs at Reagan and recidivism will make a permanent impression on his core audience, but his sexploitations and true crime tales are detailed and harrowing enough to convince anybody he was there. Wish I was sure he'll never go back. **B**

Ice-T: *Power* (Sire '88). I don't know about his role-modeling: for anyone who thinks real men defy danger, dealing is a surer, easier route to the gold than rapping. But he's got his own sound—flat, clipped, quick-lipped. And when he sticks to his subject, his narrative style is as gripping and understated as Islam's samples. **B+**

Ice-T: *The Iceberg: Freedom of Speech . . . Just Watch What You Say* (Sire '89). Realer than Luke Skyywalker, glibber than Frank Zappa, able to scare small radio programmers with a single sound, his new artistic vocation is talking shit to the PMRC. Gratuitous F-words, obscene street rhymes, hilarious metal s&m, Jello Biafra recitations, the joke about boring into a motherfucker's skull with a cordless drill—all are designed to enrage censors while talking to the people live and direct. And as always, the gangster tales bite harder than fact. Fierce. Funny. **A—**

Icicle Works: *Icicle Works* (Arista '84). Of course they know how to play—art-rockers usually do. And in correct contemporary art-rock fashion they've modeled their Byrds and Bootsy studies into a densely rhythmic synthesis that might even signify something interesting were it attached to different vocals and lyrics. But all it means at the moment is that Young Love is Important and Poetic in this Doomed World. I already believed that. I'm less sure of it now. **C+**

Billy Idol: *Don't Stop* (Chrysalis EP '81). Don't stop for "Don't Stop" or touch "The Untouchables," but "Dancing With Myself" is DOR's theme song, and "Mony Mony" works almost as well as it did for his great preceptor Tommy James. Would Billy were as principled, but these are cynical times, and they like Billy just the way he is.   **B**

Billy Idol: *Billy Idol* (Chrysalis '82). Even in punk's heyday he obviously wanted to be a teen idol, but back then he couldn't very well admit that his hero was Elton John. Yet here he is with Kiss's manager and an album that rocks as hard as the first side of *Caribou*—for three cuts, including a hit single and "White Wedding," a call to innocence regained as desperate and persuasive as "Start Me Up." If he could keep it going I'd be happy to buy my pop from a phony, but neither Burundi beats nor overzealous voice practice do anything but accentuate the jaded professionalism that takes over.   **B**

Billy Idol: *Rebel Yell* (Chrysalis '84). Videos have been the making of this born poser's career and the unmaking of his music. Not that they've changed how hard and hooky it is, much less turned off the unwitting many who find sexism sexy. But if you've got no taste for the sound of the sneer, the visuals definitely aren't fantasy enough.   **C**

Billy Idol: *Whiplash Smile* (Chrysalis '86). A year and a half in the making, and don't think he didn't pour heart and soul into it. It's just that he's . . . well, I hate to put it this way, but the guy is cursed: emoting love poetry from under enough Keith Forsey echo to fill Carlsbad Caverns, he still can't sing without sneering. That he gets off the occasional good one even so only reveals his *essence d'Elvis* for the plastic pop franchise it is, and don't blame him for the bullwhip on the sleeve—the devil made him do it.   **C+**

Billy Idol: *Vital Idol* (Chrysalis '87). In which the con artist who convinced the majors the EP was a profit-taker makes something of an even more useless and cost-effective marketing ploy, the remix. The more he pixilates his pseudosex with studio sensationalism—reverb, big beat, every synthesized redundancy known to applied science—the more closely he approaches his cartoon essence. Second side's just macho disco nevertheless, but the first is macho disco at its . . . well, let's use a technical term here: hottest.   **B+**

The Iguanas: *Reptiles, Lust and Dogs* (Midnight '87). The voice is more bullfrog than lizard, like Iggy or Buster in deep blooze mode only more generic, fraternal twin to the single-minded guitar drones that keep this Topeka trio raving. Both emanate from one Alan Wilson, who succumbs to the style's bad cliches on "Hot Rod" (to h--1) and defeats them only on "Coffee O.D.," recommended to morning jocks everywhere.   **B**

Ignition: *Machination* (Dischord '88). It's a mild up to run into the old hardcore idealism, and somehow no surprise that the singer is brother to the producer, too-idealistic-for-this-world straight-edge avatar Ian MacKaye. The lyrics avoid the excesses of hardcore rant and posthardcore doubt without rejecting the truth of either—or equalling the evolutionary smarts of the guitar. Attack's tough, minimal, fast but no longer speedy. High points are slow side-closers: "Strain" with its honest struggle and pain, "Lucky Thirteen" with its Flipper refrain.   **B**

I-Level: *I-Level* (Epic '83). New music, if you insist—relaxed white technofunk under Sam Jones's sepia vocals. As product, though, it's an utter throwback. The two first-rate songs, "Minefield" (about dancing in one) and "Give Me" ("What you can't get back"), were both singles. Each leads off a side that passes from the mind before it vacates the ear. Only the surrounding confusion of configurations indicates that the year isn't 1962—the B side of the "Minefield" twelve-inch features a "Give Me" remix plus the very mildly interesting "No. 4." Buy the EP, or twelve-inch, or whatever it is.   **C+**

Imagination: *Body Talk* (MCA '82). Possessed of a sweet, undemanding falsetto not unlike those of second-string Miracle Billy Griffin and second-string Temptation Damon Harris, black Englishman Leee

John knows better than to be expressionistic—this music is just as sweet and just as undemanding, anchored by simple keyboard hooks and drum patterns and never venturing beyond a croon in tempo, volume, or message. Even those entranced by his trio's current dance hit, "Just an Illusion," might as well buy the album—the formula actually gathers charm over a whole side.   **B+**

Imagination: *In the Heat of the Night* (MCA '82). Most English disco albums project the music into a chrome-plated video-game "future"; this one conjoins it to a flesh-and-blood rock and roll "past." Sweeter and simpler—but no dumber—than their alienated-adolescent counterparts across the color line, Leee John and friends depict themselves on the cover as Flash Gordon–style gladiator-cosmonauts on an endless keyboard into space, but they're love men and almost soul men nevertheless, and one more hook as hypnotic as "Just an Illusion" 's would have every android from here to Triton making out on the couch.   **B+**

Imagination: *New Dimension* (Elektra '84). This sensuous trio still enjoy their work, but though they get off some insinuating touches, it's hard to remember any single one when the act is through. I don't believe that's how sex should be.   **C+**

Incorporated Thang Band: *Lifestyles of the Roach and Famous* (Warner Bros. '88). After laying low for a couple of years, George Clinton enlists a new bunch of unsuspecting young people into P-Funk Mark VIII (Plus or Minus III), so say ho. His mid-'80s electrowhomp is in place, and the catchy lounge-rocker wasn't stolen from the Main Ingredient or somebody. But with "jack" the keyword and "chiropracter" and "androgynous" the polysyllables, he never comes up with the catchphrase that reestablishes his street connection—not even a "Do fries go with that shake?" Which may be why the electrowhomp shows its technics.   **B**

Indeep: *Last Night a D.J. Saved My Life* (Sound of New York '83). With its nonelectronic JB rhythms and outlandish sound effects (percussion includes a flushing toilet), this terse little sleeper of a novelty-hit spinoff bridges predisco and postdisco funk cannily and unassumingly. Reggi Magloire is a nasty girl who's not just trying to impress the boys, Rose Marie Ramsey's her more romantic counterpart, and with help from writer-producer-arranger-band Michael Cleveland they make street music together. Time: 29:05.   **A−**

Indeep: *Pajama Party Time* (Becket '84). I took a deep breath when I noticed that the raunchy vocal duo who'd fronted the greatest sleeper album in disco history was down to Rose Marie Ramsey, not the raunchier of the two. And you know, I never did exhale. No DJ will save this one.   **C+**

The Indestructible Beat of Soweto (Shanachie '86). At once more hectically urban-upbeat and more respectfully tribal-melodic than its jazzy and folky predecessors, marabi and kwela, the mbaqanga this compilation celebrates is an awesome cultural achievement. It confronts rural-urban contradictions far more painful and politically fraught than any Memphis or Chicago migration, and thwarts apartheid's determination to deny blacks not just a reasonable living but a meaningful identity. Like all South African music it emphasizes voices, notably that of the seminal "goat-voiced" "groaner" Mahlathini, who in 1983 took his deep, penetrating sung roar, which seems to filter sound that begins in his diaphragm through a special resonator in his larynx, back to the studio with the original Mahotella Queens and the reconstituted Makgona Tsohle Band. But with Marks Mankwane's sourcebook of guitar riffs hooking each number and Joseph Makwela's unshakable bass leading the groove rather than stirring it up reggae-style, it's also about a beat forthright enough to grab Americans yet more elaborate than the r&b it evokes. The defiantly resilient and unsentimental exuberance of these musicians has to be fully absorbed before it can be believed, much less understood. They couldn't be more into it if they were inventing rock and roll. And as a final benison, there's a hymn from Ladysmith Black Mambazo. Original grade: A.   **A+**

Indigo Girls: *Indigo Girls* (Epic '89). "I am intense, I am in need, I am in pain, I am in love": from the state that couldn't sell Oh-OK, two folkies whose big declamatory voices convince people to take their verse seriously, which is the only way they want it. As with Tracy Chapman, the strategy is to hire extra instruments and still sound like folkies, though when Jay Dee Daugherty adds a climactic fill to "How much further, if you are smooth" (a stone-skipping reference), rock dreams clearly beckon. Docked a notch for dropping the name of the Jeu de Paume.   **C−**

The Individuals: *Fields* (Plexus '82). They're easily the best of En Why's Pop Three on stage, scruffy and forceful and lithe, but as with most postteen modernists their lyrics lack that universal touch, and their records have none of the dB's' lapidary virtuosity or the Bongos' seductive drone.   **B**

Inner City: *Big Fun* (Virgin '89). Kevin Saunders and Paris Grey want to be Chic ten years after, and they have the jumpy club hits to prove it—"Good Life," "Big Fun," yum. Computer literacy notwithstanding, what they don't have is Nile or 'Nard.   **B−**

Insect Surfers: *Wavelength* (Wasp '80). Ah, suburbia, synthesizing information overload into unheard-of pop combos native to everywhere and nowhere. Take these presumptive civil service brats, for instance. Why, they cram Commie propaganda, a Wire cover, Europop, electro-DOR, and of course surf music onto one eight-song, twenty-five-minute, $5.98-list "EP." But the only cut that'll be heard of again in my house is the revealingly entitled "Fascination With the Neon."   **B−**

Inti-Illimani: *Palimpsesto* (Redwood '84). Exiled in Italy since the 1972 coup, these Andean traditionalists from Chile have softened their conception just like so many other folk professionals—compare this to the austere 1971 *Canto Para una Semilla*.

So it's not surprising that the lead cut here is an original composition that sounds like French soundtrack music played on exotic flutes and strings. What is surprising is that it makes you want to see the movie—and that except perhaps during "Danza," the instrumental which opens side two, the group's romanticism is somewhat less winning when expressed more "authentically."   **B+**

Iron City Houserockers: *Have a Good Time (but Get Out Alive)* (MCA '80). Although Springsteen has his imitators—take a bow and pose for the trades, Johnny Cougar—you'd expect there'd be more. Maybe would-be up-and-comers have figured out that his sales don't match his status, or maybe integrity on that scale seems too much like work. Integrity doesn't scare Joe Grushecky, or work either, but the scale escapes him—he's less a competitor than a slightly self-conscious soul brother, shorter on talent and longer on roots. His best songs are about bars. His most revealing song is an honest if off-kilter disco-sucks anthem—called "Blondie," it's about how he and Angela can't get in where they're playing her song any more, as if this is somehow her fault, and as if they're not still playing her song in places he can get in. Original grade: B.   **B−**

I.R.S. Greatest Hits Vols. 2 & 3 (I.R.S. '81). Miles Copeland's philosophy of new wave is simple—sign it cheap and gimme gimmick. So it's no surprise that the hooky (and not so hooky) samplings on this well-chosen twofer tend toward faddish one-liners. A lot of good ones, though—rule-provers from the Cramps, the Damned, and the Stranglers, one-offs by Fashion and Alternative TV, all you need of the Humans, Skafish, and Patrick D. Martin, good bait for the Fall, the Buzzcocks, and (get hooked) Sector 27, and crowning it all Brian James's "Ain't That a Shame," which may not be heard again until the pop archaeologists get to work.   **B+**

Gregory Isaacs: *Best of Gregory Issacs Volume 2* (GG '81). Jamaica's reigning crooner is what people mean when they say reggae all sounds the same. Like most great popsters, he has a genius for the disarmingly memorable ditty, but initially he makes Shoes or the Ramones sound like a veritable smorgasbord. And while James Brown is an apter analogy, Brown's rhythmic attack is just that—vocally and instrumentally, he aims to get you up on one leg doing splits, while Isaacs and his band favor the skank, that metasexual trance best described as trucking in place. Me, I think he's kind of great. Prolonged exposure to this collection of mostly recut hits reveals his hooks at their semiglossiest, his usually romantic lyrics at their dreadest, his rhythm players at their trickiest, and his cool, droning baritone at its most plaintive and hypnotic. **A−**

Gregory Isaacs: *More Gregory* (Mango '81). All Gregory Isaacs songs sound the same, but some of them sound more the same than others, and for a long time I was ready to relegate his best-distributed LP to the Land of Nod. Turns out there isn't a bad track on side one, though I don't guarantee any great ones. And don't forget side two. **B+**

Gregory Isaacs: *Mr. Isaacs* (Shanachie '82). From "Sacrifice," in which spirituality and even beauty itself follow inevitably from the comprehension of oppression, to "Slavemaster," in which revolt follows inevitably from the comprehension of oppression, side one establishes the subtle power and grace of Isaacs' rather urban reggae, not least because it stops off at Billy Vera & Judy Clay's "Storybook Children." Side two establishes his willingness to settle for product, not least because it leads off with Smokey Robinson's "Get Ready." **B+**

Gregory Isaacs: *Night Nurse* (Mango '82). Cumulatively, Isaacs's resourcefulness is very impressive—he almost always manages to vary his sad, soothing midtempo formula not just riddimically but with enduring bits of melody and observation. But because the formula is sometimes too soothing he needs more than bits to go over the top. Rastafarian marginal differentiation fans will love this record. **B+**

Gregory Isaacs: *Out Deh!* (Mango '83). At least once the great lover takes his formulaic bent too far—"Private Secretary" is a remake of the sex fantasy "Night Nurse" in which he plays a boss instead of a patient, no advance. And on "Sheila" and elsewhere the melodies are banal rather than simple. But the rest of the time they're not only simple, but less simple than they seem, enhanced as usual by the Roots Radics' profound angularity and Isaacs's smooth concentration and subtle hooks. **B+**

Gregory Isaacs: *Private Beach Party* (RAS '85). After sinking into ever more unctuous hits-plus-filler formula for most of the decade, JA's love king hied to producer Gussie Clarke, who put contract songwriter Carleton Hines on the case. Despite some icky moments, notably a duet about feeling irie, the move is for the good: there's a light touch to this music—Isaacs whispering and murmuring around diffident horn-section filigrees—that I'd call sexy. Maybe even irie, who knows. **B+**

Gregory Isaacs: *I.O.U.* (RAS '89). Isaacs evolves so slowly that he'll still be catching up with pop history when he's seventy, which makes keeping up with him less fun than quality music ought to be. Like Smokey, he's given up on songwriting and production, yet musically he's deeper now than five years ago: when Gussie Clarke tells him to lead with an unskanking soul-ballad groove, he gets into it no questions asked—like he owns it. Politically, however, he's disappeared, and since one of his charms was how naturally he yoked resistance and romance, he falls on just the wrong side of the almost imperceptible margin between the crafty and the generic. Though if Clarke had come up with more sound effects like the warbling electronic cricket hiding in the underbrush of "Report to Me," I'd never think to mention it. **B**

Chris Isaak: *Silvertone* (Warner Bros. '85). Like his East Coast counterpart Marshall Crenshaw, Isaak comes to his sources as a professional musician, not a bohemian dabbler. This is attractive, only his sources aren't as rich as Crenshaw's, and neither is his talent. Reflective modernized rockabilly played for echoing atmosphere. **B**

Chris Isaak: *Chris Isaak* (Warner Bros. '87). For me, the almost genteel formalism and romanticism of this dreamy foray into rockabilly's dark, hurtful, sensitive side is epitomized by the fiddle-as-violin that adds its sad color deep behind "Fade Away." Don't get me wrong, it *sounds good.* Whole damn thing *sounds good.* **B**

Iscathamiya: Zulu Worker Choirs in South Africa (Heritage import '86). Put off by its ethnographic audio, I shelved this as a field reference until my boundless thirst for knowledge induced me to take it out and turn it up. Whereupon it exploded. Although everything I read says all contemporary South African choruses derive from the "soft" style Joseph Shabalala developed in the '60s, this stuff doesn't come off as *cathama* ("to walk softly")—sounds like *ibombing* ("bombing"). It's aggressive where Ladysmith is spiritual, which seems fitting, since its commercial purpose is triumph in all-night hostel competitions. Also worth noting are lyrics that both zero in on broken families, the most galling symptom and symbol of apartheid to black South Africans, and defy the tribalism that's one of its nastiest strategies. **A—**

Ism: *A Diet for the Worms* (Original Sin '83). Liberal plaints about hardcore protofascism are so ignorant that it's a little surprising to find a band who fit the bill. Oh, they do an anti-Moonie number and probably couldn't hack it in the KKK, but "Put on Your Warpaint" ("They send us spies / We send them grain") is galloping anti-Russkie paranoia and "White, Straight and Male" ("I'm a victim of the quota system") middle-class backlash at its most vicious. Relatively oblique about race ("no speak-a English") and women ("I don't wanna catch your herpes"), they make it up on gays; though homophobia is only to be expected in sexually insecure young men whose brains are up their asses, and though pedophilia is hardly beyond criticism, I do think "Man/Boy Love Sickie"—"You've got no human rights / We have to protect"—goes a bit far. Worst of all, sometimes they make it stick: "White Castle at 3 A.M." and "Dance Club Meat Market" are riotously memorable, two more scary reminders that lots of straight white males are feeling more squeeze than their talents deserve these days. **C+**

Ism: *Constantinople* (Broken Box EP '84). These posthardcore miscreants cop to their boho dreams: a Residents cover and a Fugs cover surround a goosy pseudo-'60s psychechoogle and some sexist-agist puritan-in-reverse yah-yah yuh-yah-yah about fucking old ladies (bet some of 'em are *at least* fifty). Bet one thing that gets them all *enragé* is that back when the Fugs (not to mention fifty-year-old ladies) were coming up, bohos didn't have to choose between getting a job and living with Mom and Dad. **B+**

Ism: *Nightmare at Noon* (Raw Power EP '87). Years later, two strong but unmomentous pieces of power pop and an instrumental snippet. As Handsome Dick Manitoba put it long ago: "This is just a hobby for me." **B**

The Itals: *Brutal Out Deh* (Nighthawk '82). Took this for yet another of JA's hookless wonders until Bob Palmer advised me to concentrate on the singing, at which point I realized that the precise harmonies framing Keith Porter's Marleyesque tenor were fine gospel music. Except for a perfunctory nod to lovers rock and a "thou shalt not steal" for ganja pirates, every one of these dauntless outcries of tribulation and deliverance could be sung comfortably (with a few modifications of terminology) by African Methodists on a Sunday morning, and in a few cases I bet they'd know the tunes. **A—**

The Itals: *Give Me Power* (Nighthawk '83). Same harmonies for sure, same devotion to Jah one assumes. But a touch softer here, a touch popper there, a touch slower (or more not-fast) somewhere else. It's a music of margins out there. **B+**

Freddie Jackson: *Rock Me Tonight* (Capitol '85). To compare the latest platinum love man to Marvin Gaye is to ignore his voice. If Luther Vandross relaxed more and (what may be the same thing) sold himself love man first and singer second, this is how he'd sound. A pure make-out record—mellow groove, mellow sound, just lie back and enjoy it. **B**

Janet Jackson: *Control* (A&M '86). I scoffed at Janet's claims of autonomy—figured Jam & Lewis wrote her in as collaborator for a price she could afford. But she must have had some input—otherwise what would be not to like? Great beats here, their deepest ever. If her voice ever changes, she may even live up to them—and convince the world she's her own woman. Till then she's just playing, which does have its entertainment value. Original grade: B minus. **B**

Janet Jackson: *Rhythm Nation 1814* (A&M '89). She's still Janet Jam-Lewis to me—Quincy Jones's natural bodily rhythms are nothing like *Thriller*'s, but every Flyte Tyme production has showed off these angular beats. Not so smashingly is all—if the P-Funk pretensions of "nation" are a little much from somebody whose knowledge of the world is based on the 6 o'clock news, the "rhythm" is real, and I give her credit for it. Her voice is as unequal to her vaguely admonitory politics as it was to her declaration of sexual availability, but the music

is the message: never before have Jam & Lewis rocked so hard for so long. Best slow stuff: the murmured moans and irregular breathing of the sexually available "Someday Is Tonight." **A—**

Jermaine Jackson: *Let's Get Serious* (Motown '80). For a while, the jumpy drive and axiomatic simplicity of the Stevie Wonder–composed and –produced title track got me into the skittish banality of the others (including the two Stevie ballads). Now I recommend the single, seriously. **B—**

Jermaine Jackson: *Jermaine Jackson* (Arista '84). An educational contrast for those who scorn the synthetic sheen of *Thriller* and *Victory,* this label debut by the Jackson who's a Gordy is so generic it seems cloned. Not that the fast poppers aren't fun in their mechanical way. But Jermaine's singing is devoid of idiosyncrasy. His short-lived "new-wave" bent surfaces as the nagging predictability of the catchy-catchy-catchy hooks/beats/riffs. And the songwriting is farmed out to such El Lay stalwarts as Michael Omartian and Andy Goldmark except on two cuts, one of them the utterly sincere, utterly bathetic "Oh Mother." Oh brother. Original grade: B. **B—**

Jermaine Jackson: *Don't Take It Personal* (Arista '89). As he turns 35, the 5's original teenthrob undertakes to fill little brother's shoes. Having dominated songwriting as well as lead vocals on the family's *2300 Jackson Street,* a perky piece of disposable pop-funk that failed to go gold, he's forced to handpick black-crossover hacks from Surface to David Z on his (huxtry, huxtry) "first solo album in over three years." A mild-voiced journeyman whose heyday is ten if not twenty years behind him, he's equally bland as love man (title hit promises they can still be friends) and stud (though he does thank six foals on the back cover). Docked a notch not just for muttering, "Hey baby, I'd like to buck you," but for having some hired B-boy chime in with the requisite "Word."   **C**−

Joe Jackson Band: *Beat Crazy* (A&M '80). Just in case Jackson is about to turn into last year's model for good, I thought I'd mention that I kind of like his poorest-selling album. The melodies escape me as usual, but the beat is getting tougher and more resilient and the lyrics are at their best. Granted, the social comment and romantic reflections still sound smug at times, but anybody who can justify a dedication to Linton Kwesi Johnson ("Battleground") and say something new about fooling-around-on-the-road   ("Biology") hasn't thrown it in yet.   **B**

Joe Jackson: *Joe Jackson's Jumpin' Jive* (A&M '81). Put this on the shelf in front of Bowie's *Pin Ups,* Lennon's *Rock 'n' Roll,* and Costello's *Almost Blue.* Granted, Jackson doesn't sing as well as any of them, not to mention Cab Calloway or Louis Jordan, who originated most of the '40s r&b novelties here revived. But he obviously gets a kick out of this stuff, and that counts for something. What counts for much much more is that MCA has slipped three budget Louis Jordan compilations into better record stores.   **B**

Joe Jackson: *Night and Day* (A&M '82). Every musical era generates its Paul Simon, I suppose, and though this one does avoid that literary patina, his sudden (and no doubt sincere) attraction to salsa has the same secondhand aura. Decent, intelligent sentiments decently and intelligently expressed. Original grade: B.   **B**−

Joe Jackson: *Mike's Murder Soundtrack* (A&M '83). What a pro. The song side spices up his patented mild satire with more Latin rhythms, a Booker T. Winwood organ part, and the semiclassic "Laundromat Monday." And on the instrumental side, watch out Dave Grusin—Joe was once musical director of the Portsmouth Playboy Club. Original grade: B minus.   **C**+

Joe Jackson: *Body and Soul* (A&M '84). Jackson's done it again—fabricated a creditable facsimile of somebody else's music, not jump blues this time but a brassy, Broadway pan-Gotham pastiche, sort of like *West Side Story* if you correct for talent differential and years elapsed. And because the new-wave Billy Joel is a sweeter guy than his unacknowledged role model, it's likable enough. But I prefer *West Side Story,* and I prefer jump blues more.   **B**−

Joe Jackson: *Small World* (A&M '86). He's even more adenoidal than his worthy forebears Graham P. and Elvis C., so how come he's the one with the gold records? Must have something to do with keeping it simple, don't you think? Not that he sticks to simple subjects—the guy actually has a sense of history—but that he makes their ironies seem straightforward. And maybe he's got something—I'm not going to tell you there's any inherent truth value in bitterness or paradox. I just wish he weren't so adenoidal.   **B**−

Joe Jackson: *Will Power* (A&M '87). An *orchestral* album? By *Joe Jackson*? Sounded like the quickest reject in history, but I should have known better than to expect something so distinctive from this perpetually well-meaning guy. Not terrible by any means.   **C**+

Michael Jackson: *Thriller* (Epic '82). The best-selling album of the millennium was clearly a hits-plus-filler job from the beginning—what we couldn't know is how brilliantly every hit but "P.Y.T" would thrive on mass exposure and public pleasure. The inexhaustible "Beat It" broadcasts Eddie Van Halen wielding his might in the service of the antimacho that is his secret vice. "The Girl Is Mine" got interracial love on the radio and proved cuter than "Michelle." "Wanna Be Startin' Something" starts something every time an air or floor jock starts it up. "Billie

Jean" is Michael's clearest statement to date on sexuality and stardom. And "Thriller" is the rare song that's improved by its video, which fleshes out the not-quite-a-joke scariness of "the funk of 40,-000 years" for (Michael and) his (white) fans. Original grade: A minus.   **A**

Michael Jackson: *Bad* (Epic '87). Anybody who charges studio hackery is too narrow-minded to be able to hear pros outdoing themselves. Studio mastery is more like it, the strongest and most consistent black pop album in years, defining Jam & Lewis's revamp of Baby Sis as the mainstream and then inundating it in rhythmic and vocal power. But what made *Thriller* a miracle wasn't consistency—it was genius like "Beat It" and "Billie Jean" and the unknowable allure of the pure star. The closest thing to genius here is the CD-only "Leave Me Alone," which isn't all that close and also suggests what's happened to his allure—the more knowable he gets, the more fucked up he seems. This is a record that damn near wrecks perfectly good dancin' and singin' with subtext. He's against burglary, speeding, and sex ("Dirty Diana" is as misogynistic as any piece of metal suck-my-cock), in favor of harmonic convergence and changing the world by changing the man in the mirror. His ideal African comes from Liberia. And he claims moonwalking makes him a righteous brother. Like shit.   **B+**

Michael Jackson: *The Original Soul of Michael Jackson* (Motown '87). Once you get past the slipshod cynicism of Motown's catalogue exploitation, you have to admit that this mostly remixed, sometimes synthed-up mishmash has its charms and even uses—that in fact it's superior to the "real" 1975 best-of the label long ago deleted. I love the previously unreleased "Twenty-Five Miles" and the preteen-sings-the-blues "Doggin' Around," could live without the two J5 nonhits, and will no doubt pull this down when I want to remember "Dancing Machine" and "Rockin' Robin."   **B+**

Millie Jackson: *For Men Only* (Spring '80). This starts with a bang—Millie's unemployed husband hits her. And for a while she runs with it, giving no quarter to either side in the sexual war. But then the plot blurs over into an ill-conceived affair that only heats up when Millie says no. She's very good at saying no. She's not such a hot ballad singer.   **B**

Millie Jackson: *I Had To Say It* (Spring '80). Who better to do a rap parody—a damn funny one first few times through, closes with MJ invited into the KKK. I like the infidelity-on-the-road piece, too, and note that much of side two—"I Ain't No Glory Story," the Phillip Mitchell duet, "Ladies First" (and you'd better last)—tops *For Men Only.* But either Millie's growing weary of her shtick or we are—she sounds bone tired.   **B**

Millie Jackson: *Live and Outrageous* (Spring '82). Because her dirty mouth is more purely a shock effect than most pop concepts, it's sure to lose its zing for the audience even if Millie stays interested, which according to her last few studio albums she hasn't. But this one-volume follow-up to 1979's live double is also a de facto best-of, claiming the pop classic "This Is It" from Kenny Loggins and the pop throwaway "Passion" from Rod Stewart as well as preserving for posterity at least one rap that makes me squirm, and I don't squirm easy.   **B+**

Millie Jackson: *E.S.P.* (Spring '84). It stands for extra-sexual persuasion, but that's not what it means—it means he knows where her hot spots are. This is doubly inappropriate because Millie seems sick of sex. She's still convincing when she parodies sexercise or does her on-the-make impression or pleads a generic headache, but the preposterous "Slow Tongue" is obviously just the faked orgasm that follows the faked foreplay of the title cut. And since South Africa, she's somehow lost her feeling for the slow sermons that used to save her bleep.   **B−**

Ronald Shannon Jackson and the Decoding Society: *Eye on You* (About Time '81). There may be drummers who can cut Jackson, but nobody else moves so fluidly from free time to on-the-one. I only wish he'd indulge himself with a drummer's record. The music is never less than dense and jumpy, and he's keeping things compact—eleven cuts total. But handing your themes over to (guitarist) Bern Nix and (violinist) Billy Bang is no way to show off your composing. Stanley Crouch has a word for this kind of thing: eso, as in eso-teric. Pretty good eso, sure. But even in my head I don't dance to it. **B+**

Shannon Jackson & the Decoding Society: *Nasty* (Moers Music import '81). "Small World," featuring the unison horns of Lee Rozie, Charles Brackeen, and Byard Lan-caster, is the most fiercely swinging track in all avant-fusion. After that Jackson car-ries rhythm and melody on his kit for ten minutes as the vibes swirl around him, and then there's a haunting harmolodic blues. But overdisc it's back to eso. The title piece is OK if you can't get enough Ornette homages, but "When We Return," which takes up almost a third of the record, is your basic freebie-jeebie noisemaking ses-sion, more accomplished than "Radio Ethiopia" but less endearing conceptually. By now, Jackson's supposed to know bet-ter. **A—**

Ronald Shannon Jackson and the Decoding Society: *Mandance* (Antilles '82). De-spite Jackson's Blood pedigree and predi-lection for electric plectrists, I'm hard-pressed to describe this as "rock" or even harmolodic funk, because while Jack-son is the master of every drum rhythm from march to free time, the feel of the record is more swinging than funky, with heavy doses of Tony Williams force-beat. What it really adds up to is a fusion album on which the soloists are forced to think concisely by compositional structures that are more than cute riffs. Guitar hero: Ver-non Reid, who also gets to play banjo. Original grade: A. **A—**

Ronald Shannon Jackson and the Decoding Society: *Barbecue Dog* (Antilles '83). He wouldn't connect without Shannon writing the tunes and swinging the funk, but the star is Vernon Reid, especially on straight Les Paul—he articulates with so much more delicacy and incisiveness than the perfectly suitable horn players, who often serve as his scrim. On Stratocaster he's power-packed. On guitar synth he's fusion or wah-wah. On banjo he sets down and thinks for a spell. On steel guitar he sounds like he's playing something else. And on "Say What You Will" he writes the tune himself, reminding us who's the leader. **A—**

Ronald Shannon Jackson: *Decode Your-self* (Island '85). Believing correctly that what distinguishes Jackson's harmolodic fusion from Coleman's and Ulmer's isn't less musicality so much as no fun, Bill Las-well persuades him to beef up the themes and steady the beat. The upshot is the swinging "Software Shuffle" and other fun stuff. But it's also a record that tends to blare like regular old fusion, and it's not fun enough. **B+**

Ronald Shannon Jackson With Twins Seven Seven: *Live at the Caravan of Dreams* (Caravan of Dreams '86). For the first time, harmolodia's master drummer requires no decoding; sparked by a Nigerian chantmaster, he vamps along without ever risking implosion. But a vamp isn't always the deepest of grooves, and though the synthesis should engage devotees from both sides, only "Iré," in which various sidemen shadow the chanter a note and a harmony behind, will give agnostics a joyride. **B+**

Ronald Shannon Jackson and the Decoding Society: *When Colors Play* (Caravan of Dreams '87). It's good that Jackson's avant-fusion sounds like no one else's and a little confusing that it always sounds ex-actly like itself, presenting the average con-sumer with the jazz-rock equivalent of the choice among Ricky Skaggs albums. As always, this studio-tight live set is domi-nated by andante unison statements of me-dium-complex themes that sometimes break down into vamps for counterpoint. It leans more than usual toward both small-group jazz ("Blue Midnight" 's blue saxophones) and hard fusion ("Good Omen" 's raving guitars). Skaggs's live album is one of his best, too. **A—**

Ronald Shannon Jackson: *Texas* (Cara-van of Dreams '88). It hasn't been funk for years and it's rarely fusion any more—just memorable themes, serious mood pieces, solo room for players who deserve the op-portunity but not our undivided attention. In other words, jazz. **B+**

The Jacksons: *Triumph* (Epic '80). More cluttered than *Off the Wall,* partly because Michael's brothers are butting in, partly because Quincy Jones isn't. But most of the clutter is sheer, joyous muscle-flexing—hated the chorale that opens "Can You Feel It" at first, but now I chuckle at their audacity every time it comes on. Anyway, you know about solo albums—the songs do improve when the group butts in. Original grade: A. **A—**

The Jacksons: *Live* (Epic '81). Quincy Jones marshals subtler dynamics, and the only classic (?) that gets full treatment is "Ben," still a song that could make you hate rats. But both material and singer(s) are live-er than you'll ever be. **B+**

Jacksons: *Victory* (Epic '84). Victim of a truly perverse heightened-expectation syndrome, this expert pop record is certainly in a league with *Destiny* and *Triumph,* now remembered as unjustly ignored black-music milestones by many of those who unjustly ignored them. What it lacks is Michael at the pitch of gulping syncopation we've learned to love so well, although I do think his two turns suffer the worst backlash of all—better a Stones throwaway than a Wings throwaway, and better the high-strung delicacy of "Be Not Always" than the mundane sensitivity of, say, "If You're Ever in My Arms Again." As for the Other Bros., this showcases them more vividly than the tour of the same name—there can never be too many crafty tunes about wanting a body or saving the world. **B+**

Mick Jagger: *She's the Boss* (Columbia '85). History may absolve him. Jeff Beck earns his fucked-up legend here, and Bill Laswell puts together several bands—like Beck - Martinez - Hancock - Shakespeare-Dunbar-Ponce on "Running Out of Luck"—that should only tour. So maybe a hundred years from now folks who've never read *People* will admire the timbral virtuosity and breath control of the man atop the tracks. But Jagger has become such an overbearing public presence that I for one find it impossible to care about his romantic vagaries no matter how hard he leather-lungs. It would be going too far, unfortunately, to say he's a joke. But the only thing left for him to do with his persona is burlesque it, which is why the title track is the only one that's any fun. And

as my wife complains, he probably thinks it describes the way things are with him and Jerry. **C**

Mick Jagger: *Primitive Cool* (Columbia '87). He grooves his overpaid pickup band, he tells Jeff Beck what to do, he writes love songs for every occasion, he doesn't even over-sing much—in short, he realizes his solo move, which beats botching it if only because the sound of a plutocrat's desperation is such an awful thing. But when I realized that "Let's Work" was no metaphor—that it was the plutocrat importuning his lessers to "kill poverty" from the bootstraps up—somehow I stopped worrying whether his "life is trivialized." Your choice, mister—you live with it. **B—**

The Jam: *Setting Sons* (Polydor '80). Likable lads, as always, and improving themselves, too. The music has gained density and power, and they do OK with the social commentary—nice to see some empathy for doomed middle-class plodders like "Smithers-Jones" instead of the usual contempt, and "The Eton Rifles" and "Little Boy Soldiers" place them firmly on the left. On the other hand, some of this is pretty dumb ("Wasteland," ugh), and overarrangement (not so much extra instruments as dramatic vocal shifts) is no way to disguise thin melody. **B+**

The Jam: *The Jam* (Polydor EP '81). There are two theories about these guys—one that they're getting better, the other that they're getting worse. As you might fear, this interim product ("5 British Hit Singles," boasts the sticker, so imagine how excited they are in Britain) proves both—songwriting up, punk excitement gone forever. **B**

The Jam: *The Gift* (Polydor '82). It's easy to understand why this is Britannia's favorite band—their dedication is very winning. Nobody plays ex-punk quasifunk with less ostentation or more skill, and Paul Weller goes Springsteen one better—not only is he working-class, he's young. As usual, his good-heartedness is palpable here. He takes on suburban racism, nine-to-five fatigue, even general strike without talking down or claiming exemption from sin. And if he's written half a dozen good melodies since he stopped settling for Who hand-me-downs, three of them have passed me by.   **B**

The Jam: *The Bitterest Pill* (Polydor EP '82). Fan fodder there, where Paul Weller is a god; cult fodder here, where he's an artist. It made sense for him to revive a Pete Townshend obscurity on his previous EP-in-waiting, and the arty horn and bass-line touches on the evergreen "War" are not without interest. But only worshippers want his "Fever." In fact, agnostics aren't sure about the title tune either.   **B**

The Jam: *Snap!* (Polydor '83). They never got past second base here for the same reason cricket didn't. What's made Paul Weller such a hero in England is his Eng-lishness—ever since he outgrew the pure punk urbanism of *In the City,* his closely observed lyrics have worked to reflect a national culture exactly as universal as dozens of others. Given his charming but nonetheless limiting musical limitations, he's no more a world musician than Win-ston Rodney or Sunny Adé, and probably less. Because he doesn't share a gift for the riff with his mod hero Pete Townshend, even his hits get across more on tension and tenderness than on such body-balms as melody or his proudly proffered beat. This is where you'll find the hits, and where to begin. If he hits you where you live, or where you wished you live, *All Mod Cons* is the one his admirers love. I prefer *In the City* myself.   **B+**

James: *Stutter* (Sire '86). These Lancashire lads have staked out their own kitchen garden on guitar-bass-and-drums' densely cultivated common. Folkedelic with hints of postpunk-pop, it's a place pleasant, un-kempt, and all their own, but not private enough to suit them—hence their wry, well-meaning, angst-ridden, and ulti-mately impenetrable lyrics.   **B**

The Colorblind James Experience: *The Colorblind James Experience* (Earring '87). Speaking of bands that won't change the world—do we have anything better to do?—here's a dry good-timy outfit who ob-viously feel something's amiss out there but can't quite articulate what it is. Or rather, won't—they cultivate a subtlety that will piss some off and pass most by.

Me, I think "Dance Critters" is a mean antiboogie and "A Different Bob" a diffe-rent cheatin' song, and direct your atten-tion to "Considering a Move to Memphis," where Colorblind expects to bowl, speak in tongues, visit Graceland, eat piroshkis, and (most important) get to know Gus Cannon.   **B+**

Etta James/Eddie "Cleanhead" Vinson: *The Late Show* (Fantasy '88). *Volume One: The Early Show* showcased Clean-head well past his prime and Etta at her most dispensable, mixing lax remakes of signature tunes with blues standards resist-ant to revitalization. This one's just fun, as Etta diddles blues tradition with stock re-frains and off-color jokes. Plus a nice "Teach Me Tonight" duet. Too bad about "He's Got the Whole World in His Hands."   **B+**

Etta James: *Seven Year Itch* (Island '88). Unbeknownst to white people, she was Soul Sister Number Two—more and bet-ter top-twenty r&b back when than Dionne Warwick, Martha Reeves, Tina Turner, Carla Thomas, Irma Thomas, any black woman besides Soul Sister Number One and Diana Ross, who belongs to pop. She's been a cult heroine since around the time she kicked heroin in 1974—albums with Wexler and Toussaint, tour with the Stones, etc. But her many post-'60s record-ings have disappointed: often out of touch with herself (didn't kick alcohol till much later), she could coast on savvy and a fabu-lously down-and-dirty voice. So I expected not much from what turns out to be her best album since she met Barry Beckett at the *Tell Mama* sessions in 1968. Part of the difference is Beckett, the producer who's constructed the solidest bottom and sharpest top of her career, but mostly it's the something extra she invests in these half-remembered Memphis-type stan-dards. Not all the way there—all the way there is *hard* after thirty-five years in the biz. But not cult-only either.   **B+**

Rick James: *Garden of Love* (Gordy '80). Slick James, the P-Funk propaganda min-istry calls him, but on his getting-laid album Slick Lame is more like it. After limping onto the set with the quasi-uptempo "Big Time" ("And I know success is all mine"), he makes with the free-love smarm, returning to what he calls funk only on the climactic "Mary-Go-Round," which takes a utilitarian view of a woman who lives the free-love life.   **C**—

Rick James: *Street Songs* (Gordy '81). There's never been any doubt that James was commercial, as they say, but this time that's a plus—when he's not rocking, which is mostly, he even comes up with some dynamite love-man bullshit. And the street simulations are convincing enough. But I still want to know whether "The kind of girl you read about / In new-wave magazines" is "kinky" after the manner of the one in "Ghetto Life" who has "pigtails down to her shoulders." 'Cause with her, it may just be the hair. Original grade: B plus.   **A**—

Rick James: *Throwin' Down* (Gordy '82). James is such a pro I'm sure he didn't even want to top *Street Songs.* Might give his fans the wrong idea, and soon he'd actually have to work. So there's nothing as visionary as "Give It to Me Baby" or the epochal "Super Freak" here, and no protest numbers either. But all of the fast ones are such bad fun. Stealing his licks from G. Clinton & Co. (or maybe himself, who cares anymore?), he's the nearest thing to a pop musician in the rock and roll sense that today's black charts—not to mention today's white charts—can offer. And in that great tradition he should never sing a ballad again.   **B**+

Rick James: *Cold Blooded* (Gordy '83). As his head continues to expand, tricks that once seemed honorably functional begin to smack of expediency, with upwardly mobile cameos throwing his shortcomings into heavy relief. Teena Marie and the latter-day Tempts he could keep up with, but on this album Smokey Robinson shows up Rick's rank sentimentality, Billy Dee Williams his cornball cool, and Grandmaster Flash his roots of clay. And the redeeming social value of "P.I.M.P. the S.I.M.P." trips over his fashion sense—this is not a man who should criticize his peers for dressing funny.   **B**—

Rick James: *Glow* (Gordy '85). Rick has never been Mr. IQ, but this record is so stupid—not stoopid, just plain stupid—that his continuing failure to conquer MTV seems more disgraceful than ever. I mean, with his monotonous hooks, one-dimensional beat, fop coiffure, and relentless sexual self-aggrandizement, that's clearly where he belongs—he may be smarmier than Billy Idol, but what's a little grease among professionals?   **C**

Rick James: *The Flag* (Gordy '86). I generally ignore charges that political content is commercially motivated, but with James I buy 'em. The Real Rick was the moist romantic fop of *Glow,* and when his self-expression didn't get over he churned out some lines on the Bomb, honing his craft by the by.   **C**+

Rick James: *Wonderful* (Reprise '88). Free at last from Mr. Gordy's plantation, James gives up that begged, borrowed, or stolen funk. "Loosey's Rap" casts Roxanne Shanté as skeezer and proud (kudos in the Special Thanks list but not the credits to Big Daddy Kane and Marley Marl); "So Tight" is expert Larry Blackmon (ditto to "Cameo for inspiration"); James himself could have sired "Judy" and "Wonderful" and "Love's Fire." But he still can't resist ballads, a big mistake for a man who spells l-u-v like c-u-m. Docked a notch for first peeping as "the girls go down," then suggesting that a devil lesbian get straight by dropping to her knees and fishing his dick out.   **C**+

Chas Jankel: *Questionnaire* (A&M '82). Eight cuts designed for dancing by Ian Dury's departed keyboard genie, with Dury-penned rhymes that beat Lord Upminster's and sweetly anonymous treated vocals by the auteur. If only I was dancing more these days. Original grade: B plus.   **B**

Jason & the Scorchers: *Fervor* (EMI America EP '84). Crossing Gram Parsons's knowledge of sin with Joe Ely's hell-bent determination to get away with it, Jason Ringenberg leads a band no one can accuse of fecklessness, dabbling, revivalism, or undue irony. The lyrics strain against their biblical poetry at times, but anyone who hopes to take a popsicle into a disco is in no immediate danger of expiring of pretentiousness. And to spice this repackage of the Praxis original, somebody came up with the perfect perfervid gesture—*Blonde on Blonde*–era Dylan at 180 miles per hour.   **A—**

Jason & the Scorchers: *Lost and Found* (EMI America '85). It's the punk side of country punk that takes imagination for a Nashville boy, so unlike his bicoastal brethren he throws himself into rocking out and doesn't think awful hard about words or tunes. This is rarely the most effective way to rock out. He gets by this time, but he's running on attitude, and attitude has a way of running thin.   **B+**

Jali Musa Jawara: *Soubindoor* (Mango '89). The emotional tenor of Mory Kante's multi-instrumentalist brother soars over interwoven balafon (a big, deeply resonant xylophone) and kora (an intricately harp-like guitar) while his guitar talks underneath and harmonies from women surnamed Diabate and Keita add commentary and color. In Guinea, it's reconceived Mandinka folk music; in the U.S., it's world beat as world music, exotically pleasurable education for the ears.   **B+**

The Jayhawks: *Blue Earth* (Twin/Tone '89). Gram Parsons comparisons get you nowhere, but I'm not kidding—this is the obliquely songful followup the Burritos never made. Mark Olson is spared Parson's obsessions and probably his genius. When he sings about death—there are three angels in the first four songs, two grievous though not identified as such—you suspect Gram rather than Thanatos got him thinking on the subject. But his "Commonplace Streets" are his own.   **A—**

Garland Jeffreys: *Escape Artist* (Epic '81). After four years of having been, Jeffreys makes like a macher. With Roy Bittan playing the colorist, Garland's affinities with Uncle Bruce are suddenly obvious, and with Big Youth and Linton Kwesi Johnson on counterpoint his reggae ties have never been firmer. "Modern Lovers," his basic theme, is one he knows more intimately than, let us say, Hall & Oates, but my two faves break the mood: "Jump

Jump," his greatest name-dropping song and an anthem for rock critics everywhere, and "Miami Beach," Dennis Bovell–produced American dub that's too strong musically and politically to relegate to a bonus EP. Jeffrey's weakness for doggerel sticks out when he's writing this well, and the Springsteen connection reminds me that *Ghost Writer*'s static rhythms cut into its durability. But this man should be given the keys to every city whose streets he walks—ours first.   **B+**

Garland Jeffreys: *Rock & Roll Adult* (Epic '81). Jeffreys and his band (four cheers for the Rumour) are on top of this live material. But such concert faves as "Matador" and "35 Millimeter Dreams" were too stagy on record to begin with, and now, returned to plastic, they're even stagier—without the stage. Shticked to death: "Cool Down Boy."   **B**

Garland Jeffreys: *Guts for Love* (Epic '83). Jeffreys's odd weakness for rock without roll is the ruination of this overproduced, undercomposed anachronism—even the reggae grooves are tinged with synthesized AOR melodrama, and the dance numbers do not jump jump.   **C+**

The Jesus and Mary Chain: *Psychocandy* (Reprise '86). Pistols comparisons are Anglocentrism—from fuzzy vocals to minimalist tunes, from hard-and-fast surface to sweet-and-chewy center, the formal coups that have made this such a sensation are pure Ramones. My favorite parts are the cheapest; when the feedback wells up over the chords in perfect pseudomelodic formation I feel as if I've been waiting to hear this music all my life. And when the fuzzy lyrics hint half-decipherably at a luxuriant doom impervious to democratic device, I worry that maybe Ian Curtis knew more than I gave him credit for.   **A—**

The Jesus and Mary Chain: *Darklands* (Warner Bros. '87). "I'm going to the darklands / To talk in rhyme / With my chaotic soul." Right—they know damn well their putatively erotic-existential despair speaks to thrill-seeking normals by making chaos rhyme. Seems inevitable for them to take their folk-simple hook-ditties in an acoustic direction, too. Yet as a normal I miss the feedback—without all that chaos, the trick just doesn't come off death-defying enough.   **B+**

The Jesus and Mary Chain: *Barbed Wire Kisses* (Warner Bros. '88). Not collectors-only—collectors already have this shit. The singles, the CD come-ons, the EP experiments, etc.—some every bit as good as the boys' less memorable album tracks, a few even better than that. Prize: the Jan & Dean cover. Oh those phony brother acts.   **B−**

The Jesus and Mary Chain: *Automatic* (Warner Bros. '89). Success didn't lighten them up, but failure straightened them out—this is the hard-driving stuff preferred by all but the true gloom addicts in their target audience, with the gloom taken care of by lyrics about drugs, death, or both. It's as if they live in the glam-metal netherworld, only ever so much more tastefully—they flaunt no groupies, solos, or stupid fashion statements. If you've always had your doubts about their shtick, chances are you'll find the loss of aural mystery fatal.   **B−**

Joan Jett: *Bad Reputation* (Boardwalk '81). Fans of *Slayed?,* Fanny, "Rock and Roll Part Two," and Arthur Kane before he hurt his thumb should give thanks that nostalgia has finally come this far and then check for lines around the eyes. Producers Kenny Laguna and Ritchie Cordell make the old glitter formula of readymade riffs 'n' blare sound suitable for albums, and they get plenty of help from reformed Runaway Jeff, who has writing credit on four of these twelve tunes and comes on tuffer than any gurl in history.   **A−**

Joan Jett and the Blackhearts: *I Love Rock 'n Roll* (Boardwalk '81). Covering the Dave Clark Five and "Little Drummer Boy" on the same side is a great schlock yea-saying move, but a move is all it is—makes me want to hear the originals rather than play the side again. Maybe if I knew the real "Nag" I'd feel the same about that. As it is, "Nag" has a spark that's lacking in all of Jett's originals except the complementary "You're Too Possessive." And I love rock 'n roll for its spark.   **B+**

Joan Jett and the Blackhearts: *Album* (MCA '83). It's one of Jett's virtues that unlike so many rock traditionalists she doesn't let her sense of humor undercut her commitment—"Fake Friends" (cf. "Back Stabbers") and "The French Song" (cf. "Triad") are the real stuff. It's also one of her virtues that unlike so many other rock traditionalists she does have a sense of humor. Even makes fun of the Stones—they called "Starfucker" "Star Star," she covers it as "Star Star" (cassette-only until retailers pressured MCA into taking it off, still available as twelve-inch B-side), then dubs her own "Scumbag" "Coney Island Whitefish." And if you don't see what's so funny about her tuneless "Everyday People" (the twelve-inch in question), I guarantee Sylvester Stewart is laughing all the way to his next label. No joke: her nagging love-is-pain cliches.   **B+**

Joan Jett and the Blackhearts: *Glorious Results of a Misspent Youth* (MCA '84). Seekers after the unvarnished rock and roll truth needn't haunt used record stores and postbohemian beer joints—here it is in all its generic glory, with an independent woman on top providing a preideological political kicker. The problem for those of us who still care about "art" is that it's all a little too generic—in 1984 they may be better than the Stones, but they'll never be as good. I don't miss Mick—if Joan's lyrics are rarely clever, they're always pithy, and these days she's the smarter singer—but I do miss Keith, some musician whose writing/playing might make the songs sound like models rather than examples of the genre.   **B+**

Joan Jett and the Blackhearts: *Good Music* (Blackheart '86). The title signifies something cruder than coverees Hendrix, Richman, and Beach Boys, who aren't likely to show up on WNCN or WPAT themselves, and its moral certitude is what you have to love about her. She's a bit simple, our Joan, but so undoubting she can get away with transporting Route 128 to the West Side Highway. And even though only three or so of these selections—"Good Music," "Black Leather," maybe "Just Lust" or "This Means War," none of the covers—will be on her song list in 1990, it's heartening to know she'll be there in 1990, and that she'll sound like she did in 1982. **B+**

Joan Jett and the Blackhearts: *Up Your Alley* (Epic '88). Jesus I wish she was just a little bit better than she actually is, and by closing side one with the cover exacta "Tulane" and "I Wanna Be Your Dog," she comes this close to convincing me she's made the leap. But though nobody else male or female puts out such a reliable brand of hard rock, lean and mean and pretension-free, and though being female gives her an edge in a quintessentially male subgenre, not since her start-up has she made something special of her populist instincts. It's as if that's the idea. **B+**

Flaco Jimenez: *Arriba El Norte* (Rounder '89). Comparison to Santiago Jr.'s more generic-sounding *Familia y Tradicion* leaves no doubt as to why Flaco has been the hep Chicano box-squeezer since Doug Sahm brought him to New York in 1972. For this brother, traditionalism doesn't mean straight and square— he's sprightly and flexible, "pop" only because he's not allergic to change. So a 1969–1980 compilation from his San Antonio label, complete with translations and knowledgeable notes, ought to be the Flaco for me. But though a similar collection by his rock-oriented compadre Steve Jordan did the trick, I find that I'm still on the outside after ten plays, which ought to be enough. I'm a New Yorker who doesn't know Spanish, and folk music isn't my thing. So be it. **B+**

Jive Bunny and the Mastermixers: *The Album* (Atco/Music Factory '89). These evildoers sample as if enacting a worst-case scenario for the copyright mafia—except that they pay for the privilege, which means the copyright mafia doesn't even suffer as a result. And they trivialize every stupefyingly obvious piece of music they touch. Little Richard to Everlys to Cochran to Elvis to Haley—it's like being stuck on a tight-playlist oldies station that's afraid you may get a new idea about one of its touchstones if you hear it all the way through. So for perversity's sake I got one anyway: the big-band components of these syndrummed pastiches demonstrate that the great rupture wasn't as precipitous as we thought—that '50s teens lindied to rock and roll because the music swung. Which is fine with the evildoers, who mean to convince the '50s generation (and anybody else who'll buy it) that Chuck and Elvis have advanced on the nostalgia scale—that they're now as safe as the music our parents liked. This is the opposite of recontextualization, which suggests new meanings in familiar (and not so familiar) music, thus recharging it. Somebody sue the motherfuckers for crimes against history. **D**

The Jive Five Featuring Eugene Pitt: *Here We Are!* (Ambient Sound '82). Won over by their yearning cover of Steely Dan's "Hey Nineteen," which for once encompasses all the ironies of middle-aged acolytes singing teen music in a world whose teens are beguiled by almost-middle-aged pop pros, I developed an addiction to side one, then checked out their Relic/Beltone best-of. A find, that one, not only unpretentious but fun (oh those pop impurities), and the beauty part is that on their mature album they've bettered themselves. Pitt's doowop has absorbed soul usages without getting soggy, and he writes (and rewrites) originals which neither abandon the style's romanticism nor turn it into a silly lie. Also, somebody up there knows how to pace and program an album. And isn't above fishing for hooks. **A—**

Billy Joel: *Glass Houses* (Columbia '80). From the straight-up hubba-hubba of "You May Be Right" to the Rick Wakeman ostinatos of "Sometimes a Fantasy" to the McCartneyesque melodicism of "Don't Ask Me Why" to the what-it-is of "It's Still Rock and Roll to Me," it's all rock and roll to him, but to me it's closer to what pop meant before ironists and aesthetes, including yours truly, appropriated the term. Closer than any skinny-tie bands, that's for sure: gregarious, shameless, and above all profitable. Of course, if it doesn't make up in reach what it lacks in edge, ironists and aesthetes needn't notice it's there. And beyond "Sleeping With the Television On," I couldn't tell you thing one about side two, which I just played three times.   **B—**

Billy Joel: *The Nylon Curtain* (Columbia '82). "People my age, 25 to 40, who grew up as Cold War babies, we don't have anybody writing music for us. There's a lot of formula rock aimed at the 11-year-old market, and there's a lot of MOR for people over 50. But this is an album dealing with *us,* and our American experience—guilt, pressures, relationships, and the whole Vietnam syndrome." Imagine—in a world where formula rock, MOR, and most of the in between is guilty of association with Billy's (and my) demographic, he talked that shit. OK, you say, so he's no sociologist, and though sociological aptitude does tend to clarify "experience," I'll let it pass. What shocks me is the realization that this consummate rock professional is working on instinct. The basic belief of Cold War babies is that anything less than everything is a cheat, and their piano man agrees. Sure, "Allentown" digs into the rust belt. Right, "Goodnight Saigon" ain't *Rambo*. And in the relationship songs, sexual politics rads like me were fretting about a decade ago come home to haunt guys who thought they were a crock. But always this music feeds off a sense of deprivation that transcends specifics—it's built into the psyche of the singer and his audience. Does it help that the John Lennon impression (signifying seriousness) vies with the Paul McCartney impression (signifying entertainment value)? You bet. But he's no less deluded than his audience.   **B**

Billy Joel: *An Innocent Man* (Columbia '83). His art album having gone platinum and failed to clear bottom line, Joel comes at his poor neglected generation direct, peddling a nostalgia no one will mistake for philosophy. And although he's still a wordy bastard who can't leave a simple piece of music alone, the pre-Beatle "concept"—unmistakable references to the Four Seasons and Otis Redding (as if Otis entered Billy's world before the Beatles, but never mind) marking a selfconsciously simplified musical orientation—does rein in his showbiz ornateness. A good half of these songs have the timeless melodic appeal of the greatest pop (the greatest pre-

rock pop, but never mind)—the chorus he stole from "L. v. Beethoven" is by no means the most pleasing thing here. And though his Stax horns are way too ornate, that doesn't mean they're no fun.   **B+**

Billy Joel: *Greatest Hits: Volume I & Volume II* (Columbia '85). I give up—it would be as perverse to resist his razzle-dazzle as to pretend Led Zep doesn't knock your socks off. Songpoetry, rock and roll, the showtunes to come—such categories just get in his way. He's pure Tin Pan Alley, George M. Cohan if not Irving Berlin for a self-conscious, neo-primitive age, and in this high-quality context his soft early successes—"New York State of Mind," "She's Always a Woman" may the Lord forgive me, the image-making "Piano Man"—sound like the consumer durables there can be no doubt they'll be. It's unfortunate that the confessional codes of contemporary pop put his eternal insecurity around independent females up front, but his woman problems are no worse than Bob Dylan's—or for that matter John Lennon's or Bruce Springsteen's, although he's less pious, hence stupider, about them. He's pretentious, but never pious—going for the pop jugular is all he knows. The worst you can say about him is that half the time his aim isn't perfect. And the worst you can say about this album is that he baited it with two new misses.   **A—**

Billy Joel: *The Bridge* (Columbia '86). Maybe his youthful lyricism, meaning his knack for the tearjerker, is abandoning him. On *Greatest Hits* "Just the Way You Are" and "She's Always a Woman" are every bit as alive as "Movin' Out" and "Allentown," but here he's best when he's brassy and literal: failed wise guy in "Big Man on Mulberry Street," Ray Charles's coequal on "Baby Grand." And even at his most rockin' he's seventy-five years retro whether he likes it or not—whenever he doesn't hit it just right you want to quarantine him for life in Atlantic City. Original grade: B minus.   **B**

Billy Joel: *Storm Front* (Columbia '89). Instead of going Broadway with his cautionary tales and cornball confessionals, he hires the man from Foreigner. And it makes no difference—even in arena mode he's a force of nature and bad taste. Granted, the best songs are the ones that least suit the mold—the tributes to Montauk and Leningrad, the lament for the working couple, the quiz from *Junior Scholastic*. And even the worst maintain a level of craft arenas know nothing of.   **B**

David Johansen: *Here Comes the Night* (Blue Sky '81). With the help of sideperson extraordinaire Blondie Chaplin, the paterfamilias has finally mastered his own fast, vulgar studio-rock style, and this is his best solo, though only we who truly love him will hear it that way. True, the words aren't what they were in the Dolldays— "Marquesa de Sade," which rhymes "girl," "world," "pearls," and "social whirl" with an insistence that makes me wince, is typical. But like almost every other song here, "Marquesa de Sade" is also hooky and hearty. If *In Style* sounded desperate, this one sounds past caring, and carelessness was always the Dolls' secret. Inspirational Cliché: "You think I'm a whore / But I got a heart of gold."   **A**—

David Johansen: *Live It Up* (Blue Sky '82). The inspired deployment of taste, always Johansen's specialty, is why his solo career has flourished live even when it's floundered on record. By kidding around with such florid models as Eric Burdon and Levi Stubbs, he can make a populist commitment that never seems cowardly, condescending, or corny—and bring off an in-concert LP (featuring six cuts he's never recorded in his present incarnation) that conveys all his good humor, deep feeling, and entertainment value.   **A**—

David Johansen: *Sweet Revenge* (Passport '84). The synbeats and keyboard colors on his first studio LP since 1980 don't flush away the corn that is his destiny, but after years of records geared to grandiose AOR-cum-band-bar guitarism, they update its context. Just in time, because—ignoring a few easy rhymes and possibly excepting "N.Y. Doll"—his best solo album ever showcases his best songwriting since the N.Y. Dolls, including but not limited to the hedonist "I Ain't Workin' Anymore" (he got money), the hostile "The Stinkin' Rich" (they got too much money), the fast-talking "King of Babylon" (baby he was born to rap), and the explicit "Heard the News" (in solidarity with the people of El Salvador). As for the corn, I believe every word.   **A**—

Elton John: *Jump Up!* (Geffen '82). You say you don't *care* that it's his best album in seven years? I swear, you young people have no respect. This little guy was a giant, helped keep us sane back then, and though it's true he hasn't come up with a "Honky Cats" or "Bennie and the Jets" ("I Am Your Robot" might qualify if there were still AM radio), it's gratifying enough that after all these faithful years he's started to get good songs out of Gary Osborne (gunning for a Frank Sinatra cover on "Blue Eyes") as well as Bernie Taupin (who really shouldn't ever write about politics). Original grade: B plus.   **B**

Elton John: *Elton John's Greatest Hits, Volume III, 1979–1987* (Geffen '87). The bitch is gone, presumably forever. Never an artist you looked to for aesthetic principle, John provided a nice ersatz hard rock before punk and metal split that alternative down the middle. So he sunk to the depths and then resurfaced as an '80s pop singer. No point comparing him to Springsteen or Costello when he's competing with Barry Manilow, to whom he is infinitely preferable, and Billy Joel, who gets the decision on aesthetic principle. His only classic of the period is "Sad Songs (Say So Much)," which is much faster than most of these hits. It's not especially sad, either—and "I Guess That's Why They Call It the Blues" isn't a blues.   **B**

The Johnnys: *Highlights of a Dangerous Life* (Enigma '87). After doing their impression of an Australian cowpunk band who want to be the Rolling Stones covering the New York Dolls' version of Archie Bell's "Showdown," they turn back into an Australian cowpunk band. And with that lead-in, get away with it for a side.   **B**

Evan Johns and the H-Bombs: *Evan Johns and the H-Bombs* (Jungle '87). Johns is a local hero, a rock and roll crazy who lives for the music and whose undeniable gift doesn't do justice to the magnitude of his devotion. After years of fringe rockabilly in D.C., relocating to Austin has brought out the Doug Sahm in him. On "guitars, vox organ, lap steel, upright and electric bass, slide, harmonica, and lead vocals," he rolls out tune after generically catchy tune in his somewhat raspy drawl. Most of them are about purty girls and hellacious wimmin, but I can't even claim he deserves the latter, because the specifics just aren't there—the words are unfailingly good-humored and never anything more, including funny. My favorite cut is an instrumental named after its entire lyric, "Hey Whew!," but those so enamored of authenticity that they fake it can fool their collector fans by covering "Life Sentence in Love" or "Love Is Murder" or "Moonshine Runner" or "My Baby, She Left Me."   **B**

Don Johnson: *Heartbeat* (Epic '86). Is the news that a competent singer has emulated his best buddies' music enough to get him on the cover of *Rolling Stone?* Formally, after all, it's the 1986 equivalent of a fifteen-minute extravaganza about Atlantis—bizzers at their most empty and self-congratulatory. What redeems it up to a point is *Miami Vice*'s garish vision of El Lay rock as the epitome of high-rolling sleaze, hyping jaded emotions into some semblance of recognizability. And what does it in is Johnson's competence. Tina Turner can make such stuff signify, but Johnson, who rasps through his TV lines, goes clear when he sings. Isn't knowing Don Henley good for anything?   **C+**

Jesse Johnson's Revue: *Jesse Johnson's Revue* (A&M '85). "I had to do something different," the former Time guitarist revealed to his press agent sometime after the Time broke up. At around the same time he fired off a warning to rival Prince/Time imitators: "If you don't know the formula, you should leave it alone." Different? Formula? You figure it out.   **B−**

Jesse Johnson: *Shockadelica* (A&M '86). I don't know what it means to you that he managed to spike this album with a classic fake-Prince single featuring the barely functional Sly Stone. To me it means he needs help—any help he can get.   **C+**

Linton Kwesi Johnson: *Bass Culture* (Mango '80). As if to dispel suspicions that he's an interloper, the poet emphasizes music—sometimes dubwise, sometimes jazzy, with guitarist John Kpiaye cutting the difference in a satisfying show of state-of-the-art support. But Johnson's command of the tonalities and rhythms of Jamaican English is the most musical thing about an artist whose musicality isn't in question, and the more room he gives his players, the less that leaves him.   **B+**

Linton Kwesi Johnson: *Making History* (Island '84). For a while I thought the light-handed fills, tricky horn parts, and swinging rhythms went against the artist's hard-hitting message, not to mention my own hard-hitting tastes. Only after seeing him live did I recognize those embellishments for what they were—hooks. Dennis Bovell's arrangements take the natural lilt of LKJ's self-conscious patois to a new level of musicality. He may not be quite the man of the people he wants to be, but he comes a damn sight closer than most leftists (not to mention most semipopular musicians), which is why he puts so much care into the pleasure of his propaganda. And he's as smart as anyone could want to be, which is why he puts so much care into his analysis.   **A**

Linton Kwesi Johnson: *Reggae Greats: Linton Kwesi Johnson* (Mango '84). Thrown together to fill out a reissue series, its excellent tracks not programmed but shuffled, this is useless unless it's the only LKJ you can find. So look harder—for *Making History, Forces of Victory.*   **B**

Linton Kwesi Johnson: *In Concert With the Dub Band* (Shanachie '85). If Island's best-of was a superfluity, this live double is sweet excess, adding the beat, heat, and high spirits of reggae's most cosmopolitan backup to Johnson's calm, reasoned fury. No new material, but the five titles from back when the billing was Poet and the Roots might as well be. Even *Making History,* which is where Dennis Bovell started fancying up the horns, has gotten more extreme on tour.   **A−**

Syl Johnson: *Ms. Fine Brown Frame* (Boardwalk '82). Johnson has the rep and pedigree of a down-home treasure, but like so many of his fellow workers both re-nowned (Johnnie Taylor) and obscure (O.V. Wright), he's rarely better than his material if almost never worse. Having re-leased bluesy soul records out of sweet home Chicago since the dissolution of his '70s label, where his final album was a dis-mal piece of out-of-it disco, Johnson here constructs his best collection since 1975's *Total Explosion* and his best side ever on the firm foundation of the title track, a superb piece of out-of-it disco. And may well have something equally interesting to show us in another seven years.   **B+**

The Jolly Boys: *Pop 'N' Mento* (First Warning '89). No matter what it says on the back, mento isn't roots' roots—it's se-condhand calypso that's been tourist music since Harry Belafonte was a folkie. It's also good dirty fun. Tourist Jules Shear couldn't resist Allan Swymmer's noncha-lant vocals or Moses Deans's laggardly banjo, and did the world a turn by getting them down.   **B+**

George Jones: *I Am What I Am* (Epic '80). Smiling corpse or committed cuckold or drunk peering over the edge of the wagon, a sinner is what he am, and he's never sounded so abject or unregenerate—the twenty-years-in-five thickness of his Epic voice only intensifies the effect. If Billy Sherrill's chorales signify his help-lessness, their unobtrusiveness-in-spite-of-themselves prove his triumph. And remember, it was Sherrill who found him these songs.   **A—**

George Jones: *Still the Same Ole Me* (Epic '81). Dumb title, appropriately enough, and every word true—just like his lies about lifetime troth in the title number, one of those inane stick-to-the-medulla-oblongata tunes no one will ever do better. And side-openers, the man has side-open-ers—a brand-new honky-tonk classic and a brand-new wages-of-honky-tonk classic. Nothing else stands out except for the in-trusion of young Georgette Jones (Wy-nette?) (surely not Richey?) on "Daddy Come Home," which even George can't get away with. But it all stands up.   **B+**

George Jones: *Anniversary—Ten Years of Hits* (Epic '82). Sure he's inconsistent

and self-destructive, but he's such a natu-ral that all his insanity goes into the mix, and such a pro that the greatest perform-ance on all four sides, "He Stopped Loving Her Today," was recorded with a year be-tween the first verse and the bridge. Note also that it was completed in 1980—the strictly chronological sequencing clarifies how he and Billy Sherrill grew into their collaboration. As countrypolitan evolves into country-pop, yielding a standard country best-of on the first two sides, Sher-rill gives up on forcing Jones into the mold, instead encouraging his prize to be what he is, the greatest country singer in history—not so much with arrangements, though they do get sparer, as with increasingly hyperbolic and goofy material. Jones's Starday and Musicor best-ofs are as essen-tial as Jimmie Rodgers or Robert Johnson. Side four—ruminative, mannered, drip-ping with pain—cuts them.   **A—**

George Jones: *Shine On* (Epic '83). Char-ley Pride couldn't get away with the lucky songs Billy Sherrill's stuck George with this time, and though the unlucky songs are better, superstar guilt and second-con-volution cheating just don't suit him. Granted, "Ol' George Stopped Drinkin' Today" is a near-perfect fit. But when it comes to "Almost Persuaded," I'll take the original—by David Houston, Tammy's first singing partner.   **C+**

George Jones: *You've Still Got a Place in My Heart* (Epic '84). This not-great George Jones record should reassure any-body who was worried he'd never make another decent one without hitting the bot-tle again. First side leads off with messages to wives of various periods, second with a Jones-penned chestnut that happens to be the title of his new bio, a great pseudofolk-song (or maybe it's real, which is what makes it great), and a *very* cheerful expla-nation of why he'll never hit the bottle again. We believe you, George.   **B**

George Jones: *By Request* (Epic '84). At least there's a rudimentary honesty to the title—this compiles the legend at his most broad-based, and while I'd request half of it myself, only the Ray Charles duet can't be found in more exciting company.   **B—**

George Jones: *First Time Live* (Epic '85). If it's amazing that this inexhaustible record machine has never resorted to a live quickie, it's doubly amazing that he's never dared one. Less amazing is the career moment it captures, the period of sobriety that's turned his never-ending stage fright into shtick. "No Show Jones" opens the show, naturally, and this being country music it kicks off with his guitarist's Merle Haggard imitation. Elsewhere there's a set-down-a-spell band feature, a get-it-over-with medley, and the usual quota of you-had-to-be-there cornball, which Jones, whose stage fright isn't altogether irrational, delivers pretty clumsily for a thirty-year-man. And on top of it all there's irrefutable proof of how instinctive his tricks and mannerisms are—you've heard these vocal grimaces and bursts of prose poetry before, but never in just these heart-stopping places. Definitive: "He Stopped Loving Her Today." **B**

George Jones: *Too Wild Too Long* (Epic '87). As per recent habit, "I'm a Survivor," "One Hell of a Song," and "Too Wild Too Long" adduce his legend without justifying it. "The Old Man No One Loved" is as pointless as anything he's ever walked through, "The U.S.A. Today" not as bad as you'd fear. But "The Bird" is gloriously silly, and he hits "I'm a Long Gone Daddy" on the noggin. As for "Moments of Brilliance"—well, "Moments of Brilliance" is the whole truth and nothing but the truth. **B−**

George Jones: *Super Hits* (Epic '87). Four of these undeniably super tracks are on Epic's essential *Anniversary—Ten Years of Hits,* two more on Epic's near-essential *All-Time Greatest Hits: Volume 1.* Included is the mawkishly obvious "Who's Gonna Fill Their Shoes." Omitted is the tragically obscure "Don't Leave Without Taking Your Silver." Time: 28:43. **B−**

George Jones: *One Woman Man* (Epic '88). Less than no way to tell this is his best album since *I Am What I Am* nine years ago—Billy Sherrill himself doesn't know, not with two cuts previously released and one of those nothing special. The other, however, is the homicidal "Radio Lover," which I first heard on the makeshift *By Request.* Points of interest include veteran honky-tonk, shameless tearjerk, and the impossible "Ya Ba Da Ba Do (So Are

You)," about three icons sitting around talking—Elvis Presley, Fred Flintstone, and George Jones. **B+**

Grace Jones: *Warm Leatherette* (Island '80). When Jean-Paul Goude's chocolate-covered s&m fantasy hit the discos in 1977, she seemed more "Pretty Vacant" than "Send in the Clowns," and with DOR taking over the dance floors she admits it, moving in on the unoccupied title tune and taking it from there. With Smokey Robinson and Chrissie Hynde scripting adventures in dominance and fellow Jamaicans Shakespeare and Dunbar adding cyborgian oomph, the theoretical allure of her persona is finally made flesh. I just want to know why Barry Reynolds didn't give "Bullshit" to Marianne Faithfull. **B+**

Grace Jones: *Nightclubbing* (Island '81). For as long as "Love Is the Drug" and "Private Life" last, Jones makes you forget the Pretenders and Bryan Ferry by sheer weird force of personality, but Bill and Iggy never relinquish "Use Me" and "Nightclubbing." And then there are the ones she wrote herself. **B−**

Grace Jones: *Living My Life* (Island '82). I still don't know why people get hot and bothered about Jones's statuesque if not motionless voice, but that sure is one great disco band, and each album edges her a little closer to her material. "Everybody Hold Still," about getting mugged, moves the New Yorker in me almost as much as Melvin Van Peebles's unblinking urban matin "The Apple Stretching," and three of the five remaining cuts convince me Jean-Paul Goude doesn't know the half of her. **B+**

Grace Jones: *Island Life* (Island '85). Is she rock or disco? Disco, ripostes this farewell label sampler, right up to the Trevor Horn–ghosted aubobiography "Slave to the Rhythm." A lot of her best material is simply ignored, and the likes of "Love Is a Drug" and "My Jamaican Guy" succumb to the concept. "Pull Up to the Bumper," it turns out, *is* the concept. **B−**

Grace Jones: *Inside Story* (Manhattan '86). This isn't the weirdest album this weirdo has ever made, not with last year's stupid Trevor Horn cut-up in the running. Sometimes it goes too far, as on the religious title cut: "How great thou art / How great is art." And beyond the perfect "I'm Not Perfect (But I'm Perfect for You)," Bruce Woolley's tunes aren't up to Nile Rodgers's beats or Grace's lyrics. But the beats strike the perfect balance between David Bowie and Diana Ross, and the lyrics—well. "Chan Hitchhikes to Shanghai," "White Collar Crime," "Barefoot in Beverly Hills"—what kind of disco diva sings about such things? You got it—a weirdo.   **B+**

Grace Jones: *Bulletproof Heart* (Capitol '89). The title means nothing, because without giving up her stentorian tendencies, the dominatrix is here reborn as love bunny. "Seduction Surrender," "Amado Mio," "Love on Top of Love," "Someone To Love," "Paper Plan" with its "marriage of the heart," even "Kicked Around"—all proclaim her vulnerability and/or softness of orifice. The effect is so incongruous that when she quotes Nancy Reagan on crack (never say she has no social conscience), there's only one answer. No, Grace—no!   **C**

Howard Jones: *Human's Lib* (Elektra '84). "The cynical few," by which Howard appears to mean people who can think, will detect in the very title of this revolving self-help manual a hint of what the German cynic Nietzsche called ressentiment. No special interests here, folks, because all of us—male and female, rich and poor, white and other, top of the pops and glued to the telly—are in the same human boat. You think you have problems, even enemies? Think again: "And if they were not meant to be / Well don't you think they wouldn't be"? Howard's music, up-to-date synthpopbeat featuring a human voice that may well belong to Howard himself, reflects his acceptance of the known world by adding not a thing to it. Here's hoping he changes his head sometime soon—he sure could use a new one.   **C−**

Howard Jones: *Dream Into Action* (Elektra '85). Smarter than Cat Stevens. Sexier than Norman Vincent Peale. But not vice versa. And less soulful than either.   **D**

Marti Jones: *Unsophisticated   Time* (A&M '85). Suggesting both Dusty Springfield's breathy yearning and Karen Carpenter's AM plainstyle, Jones is a Bonnie Ronstadt for the local-band era—a nonwriter ready to raid the enormous store of good songs only pop cultists have ever heard. Of course, in the CHR era her audience may never get beyond pop cultists, which would be doubly unjust: it's bad enough when a dB's album leads off with two Peter Holsapple sure shots and stiffs, but this record leads off with two Peter Holsapple sure shots and then goes on to mine Richard Barone, Elvis Costello, even producer-svengali Don Dixon. And topping them all is a loony vow of romantic devotion called "Follow You All Over the World," by one B. Simpson. Wonder how many more B. Simpsons have hidden such stuff away on their demo cassettes. (Please do not mail tapes to *The Voice;* Donald Dixon, c/o A&M Records, 595 Madison Avenue, will do fine.)   **A−**

Marti Jones: *Match Game* (A&M '86). Seeking airplay worthy of Bonnie Raitt if not Linda Ronstadt, Don Dixon slows Jones down a little, to less than no avail—the airplay has failed to materialize (or whatever airplay does), and the tempos reveal the reluctance of perfectly hooky modern songwriters to say something and/or the inability of a perfectly attentive modern interpreter to make you ignore it. I know the world is confusing enough to warrant indirection. But when you're going nowhere, do so either fast or in fine style.   **B**

Marti Jones: *Used Guitars* (A&M '88). She satisfies that familiar hankering for self-expression, a disquiet known to any female interpreter worth her salt, by doing her lesser songwriting buddies some favors—at least their material will be identified solely with her. Best track is the outright cover, written and originally performed by well-known feminist Graham Parker.   **C+**

Oran "Juice" Jones: *Oran   "Juice" Jones* (Def Jam '86). Supposedly, this is the lowdown on love men: when his lady ventures off her pedestal, Juice drops the sensitive act and treats her like a gangster. And love him or hate him, he's about talking, not singing. I mean, personally I find his brand loyalties and "y'unnerstand?"'s kinda revolting, but he talks 'em like he walks 'em, so I can understand why hipper folks think they're hilarious parodies of the player's life and line. What I don't get is why any lady should be fooled by his sensitive act—he's got the falsetto to negotiate the second-rate Chi-Lites songs his raps are buried in, but not to put them across. Which makes the concept a cheat and the album a bore.   C+

Oran "Juice" Jones: *To Be Immortal* (OBR/Columbia '89). The push here is an anticrack message that's not as fresh or convincing as he pretends, but whatever the man's relationship to cocaine, he's finally confronted his demon—he can't sing. Not a stupid guy, he hits upon a model more within his means than Blue Magic, generating the best Ray Parker Jr. record since "Ghostbusters" obviated the original's need for same. Not a nice guy either, he goes for a harder tone, with real live insight into the "Gangster Attitude" he knows so well. But the angular studio funk and talky vocals ring the right bells, and the slow ones you can ignore.   B+

Quincy Jones: *Back on the Block* (Qwest '89). Q's ecumenicism stands as a beacon to the narrow-minded. Jazz, pop, rap, schlock, anonymous divas he's got a piece of, choruses going doo-doo-doo—they're all black music to him. The superrap with Zulu chant is a crossover worthy (also reminiscent) of Michael J., and Kool Moe Dee and Big Daddy Kane's "Birdland" lets Joe Zawinul into the canon while setting up a scat connection that further twists the eternal is-rap-bop-or-dozens? debate. As for Barry White, he's done worse. But he's also done better.   B+

Rickie Lee Jones: *Pirates* (Warner Bros. '81). Crossing Springsteen and Waits from a male-identified female point of view, Jones doesn't let on whether she's narrating or evoking. She slurs like a convinced lush. Her impressionistically structured, jazz-tinged studio arrangements are the El Lay equivalent of art-rock. In short, she writes and sings and composes as if she has something to hide. From herself, most likely.   C+

Rickie Lee Jones: *The Magazine* (Warner Bros. '84). I'm glad for her sake that she's taken the beatnik indulgences out of her life, but they're not gone from her work. A mediocre poet is one whose imagery doesn't tempt you to figure out what he or she is saying. Even when he or she is backed up by studio musicians who hang upon his or her every word. Real song: "The Real Thing."   B−

Rickie Lee Jones: *Flying Cowboys* (Geffen '89). She's got her feet on the ground, with a warm simple song about motherhood and a cracked blues about addiction the signposts, but everywhere there are images of flight—as something heroes do, as something she used to do, as something she still can do in her mind. For anyone who never bought her effusions, the music is an advance—grounded as well, from studio-rock four to white-reggae depth charge to the guitars and synths of that blues. Problem is, it rarely flies—which with her more effusive lyrics leaves her not adrift, just nowhere.   B

Jonzun Crew: *Lost in Space* (Tommy Boy '83). I love "Space Cowboy," in which hooks from Tom Tom Club and Clint Eastwood converge on the ghost of Gary Numan. Elsewhere, however, Numan's shade has all too much space to him/itself. Sure the cross-rhythms are niftier, and I know Bambaataa has given this kind of silliness his blessing. But not everybody can be blessed—or silly.   C+

Janis Joplin: *Farewell Song* (Columbia '82). The title tune, the last she recorded with Big Brother and the best original here, is tamer than the dullest cut on *Cheap Thrills,* which like all her Big Brother music thrived on sheer hippie farout get-down weirdness. Four of the five other Big Brother tracks are *Cheap Thrills* rejects, while "One Night Stand" and the rap that interrupts a quite decent "Tell Mama" are predictable crows of sexual pragmatism. Verdict: deceased.   B−

Steve Jordan: *The Return of El Parche* (Rounder '88). In a decade that's rediscovered the accordion's heritage as portable people's orchestra, this fifty-year-old is as timely as Astor Piazzolla. Influenced by both Afro-Latin rhythms and the border polkas he played as a kid, he's every bit as original and a lot raunchier. It's the usual overstatement to call him the Jimi Hendrix of Tex-Mex—though I don't doubt he's the finest improviser in his idiom, Jimi cuts him deeper than the assailant who took two years out of Jordan's career in a New Mexico bar in 1973. But if on casual hearing Carl Finch's loving compilation sounds insularly subcultural, the briefest check against Finch's two multiartist Rounder ¡Conjunto! collections puts Jordan's all-American swing and sonic range into relief—even Flaco Jimenez is folkloric (though equally wondrous) by comparison. Far from generic, Jordan's distinctive sound can connect furriners like me to the genre. I'm sure I can't feel it the way someone who lives among Chicanos can, but I'll call it rock and roll if he will.   **A—**

Journey: *Frontiers* (Columbia '83). Just a reminder, for all who believe the jig is really up this time, of how much worse things might be: this top ten album could be outselling *Pyromania,* or *Flashdance,* or even *Thriller.* Worse still, Steve Perry could run for the Senate as a moderate Republican from, say, Nebraska, where his oratory would garner excellent press—and then, having shed his video-game interests, ram the tape tax through.   **D+**

Joy Division: *Unknown Pleasures* (Factory '80). With Ian Curtis having hanged himself from the apex of a love triangle well before this 1979 U.K. debut came out in the States, it's hard to pass off his depressiveness as affectation even though critiques of his sincere feelings are definitely in order: the man is idolizing as fast as he oxidizes, a role model as dubious as Sid or Jimbo for the inner-directed set. Nevertheless, it's his passionate gravity that makes the clumsy, disquieting music so convincing—not just a songwriting stroke like "She's Lost Control" but gothic atmosphere like "Candidate" and "I Remember Nothing." Do what he does, not what he did. [Later on Qwest.]   **A—**

Joy Division: *Closer* (Factory '81). Another anticlimactically after-the-fact American release for these purveyors of melancholy and autohypnosis, and enough to make you understand why whole writing seminars haunt the import shops awaiting their next twelve-inch. Ian Curtis's torment is less oppressive here because it's less dominant—the dark, roiling, off-center rhythms have a life of their own. And if last time the dancier material had hooks, this time even the dirges have something closely resembling tunes. [Later on Qwest.]   **A—**

Joy Division: *Substance* (Qwest '88). Where New Order's *Substance* showcases the trajectory of secret singles specialists, Joy Division's recollects the byways of a natural album band. Starting out as unhysterical punks, they follow their pessimism where it leads, into slower tempos and machinelike rhythms, getting excited only at the end of side one, where enveloped by the dark of night they find their beat and shout out "Dance, dance, dance, dance to the radio." They follow that beat where it leads, back down into a pessimism that's now frankly romantic and personal if you've got the sense to hear it that way. And then love tears them apart.   **B+**

The Judds: *Wynonna and Naomi* (RCA Victor EP '84). They've got a gimmick—not only are they a mother-and-daughter act, you can't tell who's who. But the music's simply solid—three fine ones plus three pretty good ones equals the most actively pleasurable Nashville of the year. I especially like the way "Isn't He a Strange One" and "Mama He's Crazy" tweak the same trope twice.   **A—**

The Judds: *Why Not Me* (RCA Victor '84). They harmonize with uncanny consanguinity. Their six-piece production is neotraditionalist (which in Nashville means liberal, right?), totally violinless (fiddleless, even). But after defying convention by indulging not a single soppy song on their tryout EP, they've flabbed the follow-up several times. And I bet they get even more complacent. Original grade: B plus.   **B**

The Judds: *Heart Land* (RCA Victor '87). This which-one-had-the-baby mother-and-daughter act was cute for about fifteen minutes. They've long since revealed themselves as neotraditionalism's most shameless nostalgia pimps, and the only way their sexual politics could get more disgusting is if their songwriters slipped them wife-swapping jokes. To honor this achievement, their label herewith institutes a nine-track limit for country LPs. I remember when twelve down to eleven was a scandal, and submit that in this case like so many others zero might be a more socially responsible target.   **C**

The Judds: *Greatest Hits* (RCA Victor '88). Although it recycles a full one third of their only worthwhile long player (their debut mini) and returns to life both "Love Is Alive" (". . . at the breakfast table" vomit) and "Grandpa (Tell Me 'Bout the Good Old Days)" ("Did families really bow their heads to pray?" fuck goddamn), this is pretty close to a worthwhile long player itself. Even at their most neocon they sound confidently prog-trad, and they have a knack for finding tunes that transcend their titles.   **B+**

Juluka: *Scatterlings* (Warner Bros. '83). The musical and political strengths and weaknesses of apartheid-fighters Johnny Clegg and Sipho Mchuna are best understood if you think of them as folkies. Beginning as a biracial guitar-and-voice duo committed to Zulu traditionalism, which many apartheid-fighters consider objectively counterrevolutionary, they've become a rock band out of commercial happenstance. Like most folkies, they're often corny—"Simple things are all we have left to trust" and so forth. But being a folkie in South Africa takes a lot more guts than it does in liberal societies, and that's audible all over this album—as are the melodic resources of the Zulu tradition, which happens to be vocal rather than percussive. Original grade: B plus.   **B**

Jungle Brothers: *Straight Out the Jungle* (Idlers '88). Like an early Bambaataa jam with comic timing, it starts out looser and more comradely than most rap dares any more. Then it stays that way. Crew name turns an insult around while permitting some light pan-Africanism, a Melle Mel hook, and the simple point that anywhere

people get killed for the color of their skin is a jungle for sure. Samples come every which way—here Mingus, there Farfisa-cum-Hammond-B3, and over there drumbeats so offhand you'd swear they were live. And reinforcing their professions of solidarity is the fact that they hardly boast at all—unless you're afraid claims that their jimbrowskis are seven feet tall will be taken literally by their tragically ill-informed audience.   **A—**

Jungle Brothers: *Done by the Forces of Nature* (Warner Bros. '89). Somehow these young Afro-New Yorkers have evolved a rap version of urban African pop at its most life-affirming: the boasts low-key, the propaganda beyond hostility, the samples evoking everything tolerant and humane in recent black-music memory, this is music designed to comfort and sustain. Between DJ AfriKa's casual drawl and sidetalk that ebbs and flows under the main track like an inner-city *McCabe and Mrs. Miller,* the sound is as original as De La Soul's, and the dreams of pleasure are straight out the urban jungle—in my favorite, a smooth brother muses to the Coasters' "Shopping for Clothes" as a tropical stream washes over his family jewels. And though I can live without promises that the final judgment is at hand, the JB's do wonders for one's sense of doom just by sounding merciful.   **A**

Junie: See Junie Morrison

Junior: *Ji* (Mercury '82). The Stevie Wonder surrogate that vocalist-songwriter Junior Giscombe and keyboardist-producer Bob Carter have synthesized in their London studio is certainly England's most impressive recent export, but it does lack the effervescence and spacy lyricism of the real thing. Only on the two hits is its gift for the ordinary bewitching. Original grade: B plus.   **B**

Just Desserts: *Sentimental War* (Earhorn '87). Seventeen songs, hopefully airplay-ID'd "blues-rock," "country-soul," "ballad," "nightclub," "eclectic," performed (and composed, you bet) by two virtually indistinguishable blues-country-soul-rock-nightclub groaners whose dolor seems as much fated as principled. Pretty uninviting, yet the best of the writing—notably a detox diptych and an acrid call to arms and alms—kept me listening for the sprawling masterpiece I had somehow missed. It wasn't there. But I never got tired of the good stuff. **B**

The Justified Ancients of Mu Mu: *The History of the JAMS* (TVT '88). Though the results are more interesting than compelling—not to mention postsignificant, prerevolutionary, better than hip hop, and whatever else Britcrits claim—the drum-machine cut-and-paste of these white rappers cum dance-music guerrillas definitely deserves its footnote in the annals of sampling. Announcing themselves with "All You Need Is Love" as AIDS protest, they rob the BBC, rip off hunks of Sly, kidnap Whitney Houston, construct the ultimate Eurodisco homage, and do whatever else they can to give copyright lawyers apoplexy. Of enduring artistic originality and importance for sure, judge. **B+**

Si Kahn: *Doing My Job* (Flying Fish '82). Not one of these fifteen skillful pieces of work is narrowly ideological, and several sound like exceptionally useful organizing tools—the three funny ones plus "Detroit December" ("Eight hours a day to draw my pay / And overtime to see me through") and "Go to Work on Monday" (with Old King Brown Lung). But *Home*'s subtlety, originality, and sheer conceptual elegance are missed—only "Five Days a Week" and "Doing My Job" do more than the job. **B+**

Si Kahn: *Unfinished Portraits* (Flying Fish '84). At his best, Kahn writes like the gifted local organizer he still is sometimes: his political commitment is bound up in the incidents that precede issues. But his modest folkie renown seems to have cut him off from his sources in much the way that superstardom starves pop genius at the root. With one exception (El Salvador as seen by a farmboy-turned-soldier), the best songs here are the most personal: two for the new love of his life, one for a gay coworker. The political stuff is often generalized, conceived to serve an idea, and while he gets away with it sometimes (an antiharassment song that kicks off from the turn-of-the-century "It's the Same the Whole World Over"—smart), he does seem to think that "It's not how large your share is / But how much you can share" is an inspirational couplet. **B**

Kajagoogoo: *White Feathers* (EMI America '83). Anglophile album buyers are nothing if not fickle, and this well-named bit of fluff is just forgettable enough to get caught in the backlash. No, it's not entirely fair—the single's cute, as are the little fuguey bits. Boo hoo. **C+**

Ini Kamoze: *Pirate* (Mango '86). If reggae all sounds the same, this is something else. Kamoze's vocals match Richard Dunn's sheets of synth, which are more art-rock than lover's rock. "Betty Brown's Mother" is a long overdue answer to Ernie K-Doe and sequel to Herman's Hermits. And Robbie Shakespeare's riddim guitar leads the sliding headlong groove of "Rough." **B+**

The Kampala Sound (Original Music '89). Though some may find it too mild, here is the most plainly irresistible John Storm Roberts compilation since *Africa Dances*. Roberts credits mission-school melodies and natural Bagandan rhythms for the simple, striking, singsong charm of this Nairobi-recorded, Kinshasa-dominated "1960s Ugandan dance music"; note also the r&b-derived basslines of Charles Sonko underpinning whoever has his or her name on the label, and his sister Frida's modest vocals. Created for commercial gain in a Ugandan market that pre-Amin enjoyed the ultimate gift, existence, the music floats in on an innocence of intent that escapes today's self-consciously folkloric African culture preservers. Imminent brutalization lends its lyricism a poignancy I hope no one involved had any inkling of at the time—unless, of course, foresight helped save their lives.   **A**

Kanda Bongo Man: *Amour Fou/Crazy Love* (Carthage '87). Paris-based soukous keyed less to sweet Congo patois than to supernaturally light-fingered guitar. Quick enough to raise the dead, I swear. Only problem is, it goes by so fast you forget it was ever there—now you hear it, now you don't.   **B+**

Kanda Bongo Man: *Kwassa Kwassa* (Hannibal '89). Vocals mild, tempos unvaryingly moderate-plus, named for an African dance craze that's only a wonderful name to me or you *("Quoi ça? Quoi ça?"),* this one-hour serving of modern soukous cynosure is what vulgar poppophiles call samey. The first two cuts played back-to-back will certainly delight whoever you play them for. Any two cuts played back-to-back will probably delight whoever you play them for. All ten cuts played back to back will fade into the background as surely as Brian Eno or the washing machine.   **B+**

Big Daddy Kane: *Long Live the Kane* (Cold Chillin' '88). Faking a stutter or crooning a chorus or rat-a-tat-tatting a salvo of "ill" rhymes, he can rap that rap, and he's so prolific he spins off lyrics for labelmates in his spare time. But too often Marley Marl lets all this facility carry the music instead of adding the right sample, and when Biz Markie comes on the set you suddenly realize what vocal presence means. Of course, Markie's clown can wear as thin as Big Daddy's big man. What a duo they'd make.   **B**

Big Daddy Kane: *It's a Big Daddy Thing* (Cold Chillin' '89). Mr. Asiatic gets respect for his virtuosity and his upright character—though the self-reliance dis of "Calling Mr. Welfare" seems harsh to a bleeding heart like yours truly, the whole first side raps up to the unity message of "Another Victory," with tough, generous music to match. Turn it over and pig on

"pimp shit" designed to weed out dilettantes like yours truly.   **B**

Raymond Kane: *Master of the Slack Key Guitar* (Rounder '88). Never having heard a Gabby Pahinui record, I'm obliged to enjoy this relaxed, talky music-doc soundtrack as exotica. Couldn't tell you whether Kane's strange gutturals are a product of his tradition or his emphysema. Can tell you that his story of how Hawaiian guitar came over with the vaqueros and then got changed utterly is a trip as both music and musicology.   **B+**

Mory Kante: *Akwaba Beach* (Polydor '88). Maybe those who find Afropop too ethnic will appreciate the confident compromises of this Guinean griot turned Malian pop star turned Parisian bandleader. Unlike his rival Salif Keita, he considers dance music his mission—even the title song, a romantic showcase for his flawless tenor, maintains a groove. Not out of hopes for world peace did his hyped-up arrangement of the traditional "Yé Ké Yé Ké" become a giant single in Europe—his mix of brass, synths, polyrhythm, and kora is a typically hokey Eurodisco alignment. And it sure beats house by me.   **A—**

Paul Kantner: *Planet Earth Rock and Roll Orchestra* (RCA Victor '83). A concept album about "a San Francisco band that, in the near future, develops a computer assisted telepathic amplification technology" which enables it to flee first to Australia and then to outer space? Godspeed, sez I.   **D+**

Kaoma: *World Beat* (Epic '89). I find it impossible to work up the fine pitch of loathing this piece of product arouses among the right-thinking. It's only *(a)* hit-plus-filler and *(b)* Europop, lame two ways by definition, which is no reason to listen to it but also no reason to be dismayed by its lameness; the lameness of the Brazilian dance-pop it rips off is more dismaying, because it's more misguided. In a time when Third World musicians dream of First World rich-and-famous, when Parisian sensibility deracinates the rhythms of the African diaspora one day and adds muscle to them the next, when France seeks to regain world cultural preeminence by embracing an essentially spurious multiracialism, this version of lambada fits an inevitable market niche. It's Europop with a café au lait face and a bouncy bottom, and on the hit and the two cuts that follow it has the vulgar vitality of all great pop commerce. After that it's filler.   **C+**

Kashif: *Kashif* (Arista '83). As if he were Dick Griffey or somebody, admirers cite the radio appeal of this Brooklyn pheenom's smooth concoctions and recall the heroic deeds of Berry Gordy. Whether that rings true with you depends on whether you value the radio of the '80s as much as that of the '60s.   **C+**

Kassav':   *Kassav' #5* (Celluloid '87). Like Senegalese mbalax and Zairean rumba, Antillean zouk has its schlocky tendencies—singing in Creole doesn't get all the French out of your system. So Celluloid's two U.S. Kassav' LPs, both from the early '80s, feature synthesizers and fancy horns and ladies going duh-do-do-do as well as hot polyrhythms and soul/calypso/rumba horns and the occasional catchy theme. *Georges Decimus* is pretty tuneless, closing one side with a drum piece that won't signify to anyone who doesn't know the difference between ti bwa and Saint Jean (they're both rhythms), and while *Kassav' #5* is a lot catchier, I bet greatest hits plucked from the two dozen albums recorded by the band and its many offshoots would be a lot catchier than that. Saved by the schlock-like-it-oughta-be of "Anki Nou"—a quiet storm that crosses "A Whiter Shade of Pale" with "Maggot Brain."   **B+**

Kassav':   *Vini Pou* (Columbia '88). It's no more filler-proof than any other disco album, and though the production has gained depth, zouk didn't develop its studio rep because the brothers Decimus laid off the special effects. Nevertheless, this major-label debut is the latest, the longest, and the easiest to find LP from the guys who invented world dance music. Probably the cheapest, too. But if you run across *Kassav' #5* at a discount, go for it. Original grade: B plus.   **B**

Kassav':   *Majestik Zouk* (Columbia '89). What this accomplished display of pop production values proves is that they're big in France because they speak French. With keyb hooks and basslines mixed way up, most of the tracks jump you like the radio. But the pretty-to-gritty voices have nothing intelligible to say to Anglos—nothing to grab the market share they have such designs on. And with average track length under four minutes, the groove ejaculates prematurely almost every time.   **B**

Katrina and the Waves: *Katrina and the Waves* (Capitol '85). For a while I thought the only thing Capitol had done right was sign them, but between the exuberant Katrina Leskanich and the surefire Kimberley Rew this band would be hard for any label to fuck up: not one of the twenty songs on the band's two Attic LPs—*Walking on Sunshine* and *2*, both recommended as Canadian imports—is a loser. U.S. producer Scott Litt's tricky new version of "Machine Gun Smith" makes up for the Motown horns he adds to "Walking on Sunshine." The hyped-up drums of his rather glaring remix don't really hurt anything. And if his selections favor Rew's conventional side, well, after earning his art badge with the Soft Boys the composer is working fulltime for Katrina, and hence making a specialty of direct expression in any case. Believe me, direct expression is something I don't scoff at these days.   **A−**

Katrina and the Waves: *Waves* (Capitol '86). Especially with Kimberley Rew down to two tracks, songwriting isn't the point and shouldn't be. Anything more meaningful than the received, catchy tunes and themes of readymade pop vehicles—the country affectations of Lone Justice, say—would interfere with the pleasure of the singing. Katrina doesn't illuminate these small-time universals with her lusty contralto, she subjects them to her own purposes, which come down to lighting up the world.   **A−**

Katrina and the Waves: *Break of Hearts* (SBK '89). When it's bad it sounds like

Taylor Dayne and/or Heart. When it's good it sounds like Katrina and the Waves wishing they could be as big as Taylor Dayne and/or Heart. And they produced it themselves.   **B—**

Lenny Kaye Connection: *I've Got a Right* (Giorno Poetry Systems '84). "I've Got a Right" is an anti-Falwell anthem that ought to ring from every corner of this great land, and the next four songs hold up. But they aren't concise enough to justify such flat production, and Lenny doesn't sing powerfully or credulously enough to put their slightly overwrought emotions across. Then there's "Record Collector" and "As I Make Love," which Patti herself couldn't put across—I don't think.   **B**

KC and the Sunshine Band: *Greatest Hits* (T.K. '80). Bubblegum funk, kvetch some. Right, bubblegum funk, kvell I—beats cocktail funk, avocado-and-sprouts-sandwich funk. TV-dinner funk. Thank God there's nothing suave or healthy or mass-produced about it—just sweet and silly. I need say no more because anybody reading this already knows what they sound like: except maybe for their brothers in crime the Bee Gees, nobody since the Beatles has concocted a sound more broadly familiar. They didn't sustain, and they could have been chewier, but if you've always thought they might be fun to play at parties, or feared that nothing so ebullient could escape oblivion, this is the investment you've been waiting for. [Later available as *Best of KC and the Sunshine Band* on Sunnyview import CD.]   **A—**

Tommy Keene: *Places That Are Gone* (Dolphin '84). Though I'm sure I wouldn't be niggling if every composition on this EP had the electric lyricism and admonitory dolor of "Back to Zero Now," Keene's keen Beatle extrapolation falls just on the other side of what a modern man must hope for. He always seems either sad or resentful, which does spell nostalgia to me.   **B+**

Salif Keita: *Soro* (Mango '87). As he showed those few who heard the sole U.S. release by his Ivory Coast–based Ambassadeurs (on Rounder in 1984), this albino Mali nobleman is one of Africa's great singers. Like his Senegalese neighbor Youssou N'Dour, he's Francophone with Islamic projection, and like anybody this side of Jackie Wilson he falls short of N'Dour's purity and range. But he's old enough to compensate with experience, by which I mean not savvy but feeling and authority. And now, his ambassadorial ambitions largely thwarted, he's making his world pop move solo, recording in Paris with French musicians black and white. Though there's nothing as awkward as the "Rubberband Man" N'Dour committed with similar intentions, the arrangements sacrifice a quantum of groove for dramatic effects that wouldn't sound out of place on an Elton John record, and wouldn't wash there either. The way the choral work calls up the musical interludes of a Hollywood safari movie is one of the record's attractions. Needless to say, an attraction ain't all it is.   **B**

Salif Keita: *Ko-Yan* (Mango '89). Even as an avowed enemy of his nation's caste system, Keita hasn't abandoned his royal responsibilities—he's exhorting Malians, or maybe West Africans, and hoping others will listen. Thus the lack of a lyric sheet is no great loss for world peace. The lead cut on the A, keyed to a Bambara word that means "at one and the same time life, fortune, power, reputation and the devil," and the lead cut on the B, keyed to a Bambara word that "refers at one and the same time to the King, power, alcohol and drugs," would be hard to translate into English not just linguistically but culturally, and except for the bitterly cryptic black protest "Nou Pas Bouger," everything else seems curious international fare. But in compensation, *Ko-Yan* corrects *Soro*'s melodrama for groove. The music is still very much composed rather than created or spun out. But the production goes lighter on the atmospheric kora colors, the abrupt bursts of horn, the synth-simulated whistles and pans and balafon, with Keita's voice—often in tandem with a strong female chorus that sounds a lot less Hollywood this time—riding the rhythm in a nice compromise with the dance music

Keita mastered leading the Ambassadeurs. And in the end this fusion may teach non-Malians as much about the complexities of modernization as his lyrics ever could. Anyway, isn't it pretty to think so? **B+**

Paul Kelly & the Messengers: *Under the Sun* (A&M '88). Disinclined though I am to believe that styles just wear out, I note that when this inspired wordsmith doesn't get it right he sounds corny—not just on a gaffe like "Desdemona," but on the sex tropes of "Happy Slave" or the frontier boogie of "Forty Miles to Saturday Night." Problem's those four-square Messengers, the rock and roll band of a wordsmith's dreams—never threaten his suzerainty for a second. Granted, when he's outlining a young fool's marriage in "To Her Door" or the story of his life in "Dumb Things," it's just as well they don't. But you know his admirers feel all warm inside when they hear that moderate four-four, never suspecting that "Forty Miles to Saturday Night" would sound corny from Hüsker Dü.   **B**

The Kendalls: *The Best of the Kendalls* (Ovation '80). Moral Majority take note: The Kendalls are a father-daughter duo who sing about adultery. With each other. Granted, they do invoke all the Calvinist cheatin'-song antinomies—heaven or hell, devil or angel, etc. But ultimately they're soft on sin—their upbeat melodies and perky arrangements make infidelity seem about as heavy as a very successful Tupperware party. I'd be lying if I said I wasn't fascinated, but I'd also be lying if I said I wasn't put off. And so are Moe, Willie, and George & Tammy.   **B+**

Cheb Khaled/Safy Boutella: *Kutché* (Capitol/Intuition '89). Maybe he is Elvis for Arabs, but the analogy wouldn't ring true here even if we understood the words—even if we understood their tradition. The culture he rebels against is just too different from ours, especially in re sex and gender. So though Khaled's urgently masculine melody lines are a necessary condition, the explosive made-for-CD glory of Boutella's settings is what sells this variation on the rai hypnogroove. Supposedly Algeria's top composer, the German-born, Berkeley-educated Boutella relates to Debussy and Davis, it sez here—and to flamenco and house, it sounds there—but at this distance his influences only enrich his Maghreb identity. What texture, what backtalk, what interpolations, what sound effects. What beats.   **A—**

Chaka Khan: *Naughty* (Warner Bros. '80). Although she's grown into her jazzy pretensions in a distinctively pop way, replete with borderline banality and wretched excess, her distinctive pleasures aren't available on the pop surface. You have to concentrate to hear her outcomp Leon Pendarvis on "Clouds" or remold the melody of "So Naughty" or bop the funk on "All Night's All Right." But what you're concentrating on isn't the song per se—it's transcendence of the song. Like I said, she's grown into her jazzy pretensions.   **B+**

Chaka Khan: *What Cha' Gonna Do for Me* (Warner Bros. '81). Between the self-affirmative signals—writing more, steady band, you know—and the "Night in Tunisia" cover, this is where she's supposed to come into her own, but the real clue is the leadoff "We Can Work It Out," a great song she does nothing for because what she's really after is pop credibility. Although I've never thought of her as a crucial funk artist, without her usual quota of popping bass and mother-popcorn guitar her pop is soft. Nancy Wilson herself could have covered "Night in Tunisia."   **B—**

Chaka Khan: *Chaka Khan* (Warner Bros. '82). Her fans, who like everything she does, really like this one. It's never dumb, and achieves the oft-promised funk-bebop fusion with some spritz. But her fans don't care that not a single song catches like, for instance, "Tell Me Something Good" or "Once You Get Started" or even "I'm Every Woman." Nonfans will. Or rather, they won't.   **B+**

Chaka Khan: *I Feel for You* (Warner Bros. '84). Physically, her voice is as splendid as the rest of her, and as usual she's coasting on it. A classic single for the second year in a row and almost all the musical interest (as opposed to attraction) on the album-of-the-same-name is provided by John Robie, Melle Mel, etc. Feel for her? **C+**

Chaka Khan: *Destiny* (Warner Bros. '86). Though supervising producer Arif Mardin lends an appearance of unity to the credits, the eight-count-'em-eight coproducers take it away, leaving yet another candid concatenation of crossover wannabees. Those who treasure Chaka's quirkiness will object—the Coltrane snippet's an obvious sop. Those who've always found her unfocused will admire the professional standard of Osborne, LaBelle, etc. while dreaming of a whole album with Scritti Politti. **B**

Chaka Khan: *Life Is a Dance: The Remix Project* (Warner Bros. '89). This peculiar compilation of newly commissioned remixes makes two artistic assumptions. First, that Chaka's voice and expressive reach render her the Aretha of the '80s. Second, that for various house-identified producers to fiddle with eleven of her solo titles is both an homage to and a reinterpretation of her oeuvre—even when, as does happen, her voice and expressive reach are reduced to icing and florets in the process. I accept neither. And I discern a commercial assumption underneath it all—here's a low-cost way to milk Chaka's cult. **C+**

Chaka Khan: See also Rufus and Chaka Khan.

Kid Creole and the Coconuts: *Off the Coast of Me* (Antilles '80). Reformed high school teacher August Darnell having split with black-sheep bro Stoney Browder, the music thins out—Dr. Buzzard's progressive retro is hard to top, Darnell's naturally sarcastic voice short on bottom. So the not exactly all-embracing "Calypso Pan-American" and "Off the Coast of Me" neither justify nor transcend their distanced tone (typically, the title tune affects a megaphone filter), while comedy numbers like "Bogota Affair" (the effete Creole as cuckold), "Mr. Softee" (the effete Creole as limp-dick), and "Darrio . . ." (the effete Creole as new-waver) are simple and strong. When clever means this clever, maybe we should settle. **B+**

Kid Creole and the Coconuts: *Fresh Fruit in Foreign Places* (ZE/Sire '81). When August Darnell kicks off his Caribbean extravaganza with a Foreigner power chord, or the Coconuts sing the I-Threes behind Andy Hernandez, or a JB riff sneaks into a tune called "Table Manners," I'm convinced that both words and music are witty enough to stand. But overwhelmed I'm not. Darnell's pastiche just isn't Stoney Browder's synthesis, and his campy sprechgesang just isn't Cory Daye's babes-on-Broadway razzmatazz. In short, his polyglot musical conception never gets the kind of translation that delves below the signifier. **A—**

Kid Creole and the Coconuts: *Wise Guy* (Sire/ZE '82). August Darnell has synthesized his polyglot influences so thoroughly you'd think all show music is written over a fast funk bottom. Two of the eight tunes—"Imitation," a sorta-star's complaint in disguise, and the mum "Stool Pigeon"—could use some narrative context, but usually it doesn't even matter much that Augie is singing. The end pieces are the wickedest: "Annie, I'm Not Your Daddy," in which he breaks it to her traumatically, and "No Fish Today," the nastiest song about class since "Career Opportunities." Original grade: A minus. **A**

Kid Creole and the Coconuts: *Doppelganger* (Sire '83). Counting his previous (and best) album some kind of sellout because it's held together by a dance groove, the Kid here returns to the musical comedy stage for yet another original-cast recording. As usual, the book exists only in his head, and the putative plot precis does little to clarify just what these songs are about. And I really want to know—the more closely I analyze the apparently surface wit of the Kid's lyrical-musical synthesis-pastiche, the more I wish I could see the show. **A—**

Kid Creole and the Coconuts: *In Praise of Older Women and Other Crimes* (Sire '85). Though personally I don't much care whether Cole Porter comes again, I must point out that August Darnell suits the part better than Stephen Sondheim or Paul Simon or Elvis Costello. Certainly no one in rock or musical comedy maintains such a consistent level of lyrical sophistication, even if he does overdo the brittle satire at times like these (which may be because brother Stoney is helping out again). And those who would bewail his relationship to the great European harmonic tradition should remember that Cole Porter was a rhumba man and ponder the title of Andy Hernandez's attack on white-collar crime: "Dowopsalsaboprock."   **A**—

Kid Creole and the Coconuts: *I, Too, Have Seen the Woods* (Sire '87). Mr. Softee isn't the type, but somehow August Darnell has turned into Old Faithful. Mortality impinges attractively on this typically elegant and literate dance album, which few will dance to and enough buy—especially in Europe, where they think he's Josephine Baker. If you've never gotten him, chances are you're stuck with your deaf spot. Otherwise, get it.   **A**—

Kiddo: *Kiddo* (A&M '83). Michael Hampton's band—Donnie Sterling's, really—is caught midway between P-Funk, where it's coming from, and Zapp, where it wants to go. P-Funk teaches that more is more only when you can carry that weight. Zapp teaches that when you strip down you'd better go all the way.   **B**—

Kid 'n Play: *2 Hype* (Select '88). If professional rap can get tired, it can also get busy. Joyous safari-movie go go, Billy Crystal rip, James Brown rip, James Brown rip, above all the bust-this "Gittin' Funky"—every one gits funky. And when they stick in some sexist shit, the joke's on them.   **B+**

Killing Joke: *What's This For . . . !* (Editions EG '81). Not so strange that these heavy-metal mutants should turn up on the ambient-music label. In fact, their all-over sound is a plus—better echoey vocals and flash-free guitar than the stupid doomsday strut of their forefathers. But I rarely crave ambient technohorror, even when it has lead drum parts—prefer my immolation with lines around it. Which is why I bought "Change" as a single, and hope to do the same with "Tension." DNA goes to a par-tee.   **B**

Carole King: *Pearls—Songs of Goffin and King* (Capitol '80). Forget Jerry Garcia, Robin Williamson; hell, forget Laura Nyro and Melanie. Pop's ultimate hippie isn't some sagaciously addled bohemian-for-life. It's this Brill Building alumna—she can afford it. A fireman's daughter who married her lyricist before she was one-and-twenty and divorced him before she was too old to trust herself anymore, she proved she wasn't born to follow by producing an enduring monument to you-do-your-thing-and-I'll-do-mine   and then sank into the quicksand of live-and-let-live. I had hopes she'd pull out by returning to her ex-husband's lyrics, which combined commercial pith with a foretaste of the benevolent-to-cosmic truisms to come. Unfortunately hippie simplicity demands a bad faith foreign to the Shirelles, who always knew they were in show biz. While her versions of Goffin-King's late hits for the Byrds and Blood, Sweat & Tears come naturally enough, she can't do "Chains" or "The Loco-Motion" straight. At her best, she condescends kindly like the Bowie of *Pin Ups.* At her worst, she half-swings 'em, like a folkie gone jazzie, or Bobby Rydell at an oldies show.   **B**—

Dee Dee King: *Standing in the Spotlight* (Sire '89). He does have his own style—not even Deborah Harry would dare rap over such one-dimensional beats—and I like "Too Much To Drink," the latest in the surprising spate of rock temperance anthems. But Dee Dee, we German-Americans believe in grammar. You're not "the baddest rapper in Whitestone, Queens"—you're "the *worst* rapper in Whitestone, Queens."   **C**

Earl King and Roomful of Blues: *Glazed* (Black Top '86). Like B.B., Albert, and even Freddie before him, New Orleans's finest juices a horny blues record with prime guitar. Helps as well that he's been pulling in songwriting royalties for thirty years—nobody ever mistook him for a singer.   **B+**

Evelyn King: *Get Loose* (RCA Victor '82). Examining this for more timeless trifles after rediscovering "Love Come Down" on Capital Radio, I got to like side two's opener as well. Unfortunately, the other tracks were just pleasant enough to keep me trying until I rediscovered how few trifles are timeless.   **B**—

King Crimson: *Discipline* (Warner Bros./ E.G. '81). It's amazing how somebody who gabs as much as Robert Fripp gets fucked up by words. Maybe he's afraid to take on a real singer because he knows singers take over bands. So he hires Adrian Belew, who between his David Byrne impressions and his John Wetton impressions and his man-in-the-studio candid-microphone shtick damn near takes over anyway. Musically, not bad—the Heads meet the League of Gentlemen, although I wish the valiant Bill Bruford knew as much about rhythm as John Chernoff. But throw away that thesaurus.   **B**

King Crimson: *Three of a Perfect Pair* (Warner Bros. '84). Unburdened by any natural predisposition to play it again, I'm an unusually unbiased judge: side two again demonstrates Robert Fripp's rare if impractical gift for sustained instrumental composition in a rock context. Having expended many fruitless hours trying to appreciate Adrian Belew's two solo albums, I'm an unusually qualified judge: side one again demonstrates that the guy neither sings nor writes like a frontman.   **B**—

Kingdom Come: *Kingdom Come* (Polydor '88). Lenny Wolf's brainchildren share a selling point with the guys they rip so shamelessly: shamelessness. I'm not curious enough to ascertain which Zep songs provide which hook riffs, but that doesn't mean I can't lay back and enjoy a musical force as musical form—a humongous abstraction perfect for flattening the medulla oblongata.   **B**

The "King" Kong Compilation (Mango '81). Greil Marcus compares the late Leslie Kong to Sam Phillips, and as the man who turned ska into reggae he deserves the accolade, but it was already 1969 in the global village by then, so it's no surprise that there's a Jerry Wexler (not Berry Gordy) sophistication to his sound. An Impressions/Temptations/Cooke soulfulness pervades these sixteen tunes as well, although their fervor is more innocent and their sheer chops are less brilliant. None of the less familiar tracks is up to those you know (and perhaps own) by the Maytals, Desmond Dekker, and the Melodians, but Tyrone Evans's newly uncanned "Let Them Talk" and the Pioneers' "Samfie Man" come close.   **A**—

Redhead Kingpin and the F.B.I.: *A Shade of Red* (Virgin '89). Proud Jeffersons fan, casual abortion foe, his stupid fresh showing the occasional expiration date, this Englewood eclectic stores his brains somewhere near his ass, where his beats do his thinking for him—first couple of cuts'll have you bopping so happy all you'll care is that he doesn't stammer or sass your mama. Both were mixed and arranged by Teddy Riley, whose salutary effect on Red's mind-body continuum is evinced by his alternating presence and absence throughout.   **B**

King Tee: *Act a Fool* (Capitol '88). Looking for Biz Markie Compton-style, I got a gold abuser whose idea of a fool is my idea of a punk motherfucker—somebody who smokes cheeb and drinks forties, then assaults women. D.J. Pooh (and James Brown) carry him until the anticlimactic "I Got a Cold," which records for posterity the funkiest snurfling you've ever heard in your life.   **C**+

The Kinks: *Come Dancing With the Kinks/The Best of the Kinks 1977–1986* (Arista '86). I didn't attend the seven-album output reduced here to two discs with the care due a legendary songwriter— the "survivor" in him swallowed the songwriter years ago. His anomalously autumnal U.S. ascendancy was a disaster—attitudes forgivably eccentric in one of the great dotty Englishmen turned ugly and mean, and tunecraft so delicate it threatened to waft away on the next zephyr assumed an unbecoming swagger. The title tune was his biggest hit since 1964 because it's a perfect pop sentiment. Second-best is by Dave Davies, not Ray: "There's no England now," he opines, which explains a lot.   **B**—

Kino: *Groupa Kroovy (Blood Type)* (Gold Castle '89). Just Russian new-wavers, their translated lyrics unobtrusively poetic, alienated by habit, politically aware, resigned. But Victor Tsoi's solidly constructed tunes have a droll charm that's fresh if not new, and to an English speaker, the physical peculiarities of his talky voice, which saunters along as if a low baritone is the natural human pitch, seem made for the offhand gutturals and sardonic rhythms of his native tongue. When his boys ooh-ooh high behind "It's Our Time, Our Turn!," it's as if someone has finally concocted an answer record to "Back in the U.S.S.R." **B+**

The Kinshasa Sound (Original Music '83). Much more than his Kenyan and Swahili anthologies, this John Storm Roberts collection makes immediate impact on American ears, first of all because its quarter century of Zairean singles carry a heavy Cuban influence. I prefer the modestly melodic Lingala vocals to their romantic-virtuosic salsa counterparts, and am more than content to follow the music's rhythmic journey across the Atlantic and back again as re-Africanization takes hold in the '70s. But I suspect the main reason I keep listening is that every one of these thirteen cuts began life as a pop dance hit. **A−**

Kleeer: *License To Dream* (Atlantic '81). I started with side two, where the light funk of "Get Tough" got lost (soulful John Wayne impression and all) between the inspirational title cut ("Speculate positivity don't turn around") and the smarmy slow one. Turns out there's a light funk tour de force on the A—a mild one, but that's the only way they come. Highlights: "Running Back to You"'s congas-and-timbales interweave, "Hypnotized" 's Latin accent, and the sexy slow one. **B+**

Klymaxx: *Meeting in the Ladies Room* (Constellation '85). In theory, these ladies are my favorite Prince rip because the attitude they give off all over the room is their own. But though they and their men friends do nice stuff with those layered robot rhythms, their attitude thins out fierce once they've had their say at the top of each side. **B−**

KMFDM: *UAIOE* (Wax Trax '89). In both reggae and rock modes, this twisted Belgian dance band is groovier than the noise norm—positively sinuous sometimes, especially on the pick-to-click "Murder." Guest vocalists—metal heldentenor, spliffed-up toaster—add personality, risking the verboten corn. Yet the product emerges unscathed. Dare to struggle, dare to win. **B+**

The Knack: *. . . But the Little Girls Understand* (Capitol '80). When last seen they were onstage at Carnegie Hall, reading that stanza about writers and critics from "The Times They Are A-Changin'," and despite the title this is obviously their stab at artistic respectability, less *The Knack's Second Album* than *Commander Chapman's Nasty Mouths Club Band.* Or maybe they understand what critics don't: that little girls think it's cute and sexy to write songs about Mexican guys pimping their wives to Jewish guys. What critics understand and they don't—or maybe they're just so close to satori that they accept their limitations—is that whatever the subject, little girls prefer catchy, punchy secondhand songs to varied, indecisive thirdhand ones. In fact, so do critics. **C−**

Gladys Knight and the Pips: *Visions* (Columbia '84). Accurately acclaimed as her finest work in a decade, this is amazingly uniform for an album featuring eight different bassists and eight different drummers recorded in eight different studios in L.A., Nashville, and Vegas. To an extent that's a tribute to Leon Sylvers's consistent vocal and rhythm arrangements. To an extent it's a tribute to the authority this great pop singer still commands when she's in the mood. And to an extent it's attributable to flat material. **B**

Gladys Knight & the Pips: *Life* (Columbia '85). The reflectiveness of her interpretations has never extended to her choice of material—the honest journeywoman in her must prefer contract songwriting. So she does what she's always done over "contemporary" settings that don't clash or mesh or otherwise call attention to themselves. Amid the various shades of schlock and dancy compromise, the best songs are those she wrote with her coproducers, Sam Dees and Bubba Knight, and the only notable one is "Strivin'," the most straight-up bourgie boogie since "Bon Bon Vie." Even at its most committed, professionalism can get pretty boring.   **B−**

Gladys Knight and the Pips: *All Our Love* (MCA '87). The CD-era duration does indulge Knight's middle-class vices. At twenty-eight minutes for six songs that are longer on melodrama than break beats, the second side is like a suburban living room that seems overfurnished even though all the pieces are in the best contemporary taste. But Knight has one of those burgundy voices, designed to age, and since her albums have rarely done it justice, the edgy writing and overall strength of this multiproducer soul-dance-pop-whatever comeback is a gift.   **B+**

Gladys Knight & the Pips: *The Best of Gladys Knight & the Pips: The Columbia Years* (Columbia '88). Five essentially identical Vegas funk grooves on the A, five essentially anonymous pop-soul ballads on the B. You recall all ten as they come on, two or three as you reread the titles. What does it take to jolt this woman out of her own competence?   **B**

The Knitters: *Poor Little Critter on the Road* (Slash '85). With Dave Alvin and John Doe getting a chance to pick and Exene getting a chance to sing purty, this ad hoc roots excursion is often tuneful and appealing, sometimes much more. I have my silly faves, but the convincer isn't silly at all—"Cryin' but My Tears Are Far Away," in which Doe not only writes and sings (and how) a classic country ballad, but creates a paradigm of urban alienation at the same time. Unfortunately, the bad stuff can be revoltingly cute, beatnik romanticism's soft folkie underbelly, as in the Old MacDonald intro to "Rock Island Line" or the speeded-up tag to "Walkin' Cane," which seems designed to convince alienated urbans that you can get rock and roll out of this hick stuff.   **B**

Knotty Vision (Nighthawk '83). Though at first I tagged this as one more choppy multiple-artist compilation, in fact it's as integral and inevitable as death and glory. Beginning with a wailing Burning Spear chant and finishing with a burning Wailing Souls admonition, it's where fundamentalist reggae will convert you if you're destined to feel the spirit at all. Give the first side three or four tries with some time between and you should be able to get to the lyric intensity of six voices possessed by a single song. And eventually the tunes on the B surrender the conviction at their root.   **A−**

Konbit!: Burning Rhythms of Haiti (A&M '89). Because Caribbean musicians use horns the way African farmers use cattle—not just as resources, but as measures of wealth—it took me six months to hear through the sonic givens on this inspired potpourri. The basic style is an unsurprising relative of zouk, which saxman Nemours Jean-Baptiste anticipated by decades in what he called *compas* (French) or *konpa* (Creole, or rather Kreyol). And by insisting on the same kind of variety and politics that have undone other world-beat compilations, conceptmaster Jonathan Demme and hands-on producer Fred Paul rescue theirs from UNESCO disco. Buoyant Jean-Baptiste songs from 1960 and 1957 lead and close, and in between we find not the usual indigenous hits but three specially commissioned songs, some agit-prop, the Nevilles, and Haitian bands working out of New York, where their displaced countrymen have enough money to support bootstraps recording. Some tracks go for the congas, others build a tension that repays concentration, and it's a tribute to all concerned that you can't tell the new stuff without a scorecard—though not that the bilingual lyrics are cassette/CD only.   **A−**

Kool and the Gang: *Celebrate* (De-Lite '80). It says something for these funk pioneers that unlike James Brown, George Clinton, and the Ohio Players they've adapted painlessly, nay profitably, to disco: a number-one single leads their Deodato-produced album into the top ten.

What it says is that their funk was as bland as you suspected. Even the number-one single is disco as transformed not by funkateers (cf. "(not just) Knee Deep" or even "The Original Disco Man") but by bizzers (cf. "Fame" or even "Guilty")—disco without a cult, which means without a loyal audience either.   **C−**

Kool & the Gang: *Emergency* (De-Lite '84). Funk pioneers in the early '70s, crossover pioneers in the early '80s, and don't blame yourself if this impressive double play missed you coming and going—anonymity is their signature. When I undertook a professional reexamination of their latest piece of platinum, I was surprised to recognize all their hits on side one from the radio. Quite liked "Misled," sort of liked "Fresh," rather disliked "Cherish"— and had never wondered who did any of them.   **B−**

Kool and the Gang: *Forever* (Mercury '86). If in 1973 I'd been told that thirteen years hence Casey Kasem would name a then ghettoized funk group as the top singles act of the '80s, my heart would have swelled until my head interjected that the top singles act of the '70s was the Osmond family. In this I would have been wise, and if I'd then been told that the secret of Kool's success would be a bland black singer named James Taylor, I would have observed that he couldn't possibly be worse than our white one. In this I could have been unduly optimistic.   **C−**

Kool & the Gang: *Everything's Kool & the Gang: Greatest Hits and More* (Mercury '88). If the glitzy, vaguely hip-hop electro-disco "club remixes" of such barebones funk milestones as "Jungle Boogie" and "Hollywood Swinging" are a little disorienting, they're far from sacrilegious. Together with the hits (plus the well-earned "Rags to Riches," companion piece to the well-earned "Money and Power"), they put this undependable band in its place, a step ahead of the Commodores. Maybe two steps.   **B**

Kool G Rap & D.J. Polo: *Road to the Riches* (Cold Chillin' '89). From nasty piano steal to harp hook to bicycle horn to layered ear-scrape to Gary Numan cover to Memphis blues again, this is Marley

Marl at his most encyclopedic, and G's fast, harsh lisp is straight outta Queensbridge. But there's too much boast, too much money, too much gay-dissing no matter how ridiculous. I don't think G is obliged to transcend a spiritual trap he never made. But until he does he'll have to be a genius, not just the new hard on the block, to escape his ghetto.   **B+**

Kool Moe Dee: *Kool Moe Dee* (Jive '87). Sex is this Treacherous Third's only great subject, and before you tell him to grow up already, check out the dumb hyperbole of "Monster Crack" and bite your tongue. His braggadocio and jibes at the fair sex also won't mollify liberals, but that's even less the point than it usually is. This man boasts for the sheer joy and truth value of it. He loves words more than any thesaurus or rhyming dictionary can teach, and though I'm sure he owns several, they're not where he got "I'm a rap warrior / Elite Astoria / I'll take on a hundred and four-aya," not to mention "Drip-drip-drippin' and pus-pus-pussin'." Which latter isn't even the raunchiest moment on "Go See the Doctor," a safe-sex song followed hard on by yet another monitory tribute to the dumbness of dick. Knowing sex is both dangerous and funny is unadolescent enough for me, his offbeats are def, and Harlem computer whiz Teddy Riley keeps him on the one-and.   **A−**

Kool Moe Dee: *How Ya Like Me Now?* (Jive '87). As a solitary rapper of the old school, locked into praising his own dick, mouth, and brain, Moe Dee doesn't have much room to stretch, but does he make the most of it. He never lets the jaunty, out-of-kilter swing generated by his electronic percussion lie there—trick rhymes, variable lengths, filters, double tracks, sung refrains, and the occasional extra instrument all work to shift the beat without undercutting its dominance. He never throws a song away, and makes a virtue of "sticking to themes"—last time sex, this time rap itself. The story of "Wild Wild West" and the sound of "Way Way Back" establish his back-in-the-day credentials. "Don't Dance" is the boast to end all boasts. And lest you think he's hung his jock out to dry, "I'm a Player" features the most realistic assessment of male chauvinism yet attempted in a music that makes a fetish of the disorder. He will, he will rock you.   **A—**

Kool Moe Dee: *Knowledge Is King* (Jive '89). His beats grander, his samples funkier, his cadences harder, Moe Dee not only ain't no joke, he's lost his sense of humor. He's feeling his age with something to prove: all that gladiatorial imagery sounds pretty defensive. With help from Teddy Riley, his natural swing puts the first set of boasts across anyway, but on the B, only the magnificent "Pump Your Fist" (attention, JDO: he has the chutzpah to call the Middle Passage a "Holocaust") shows the kind of knowledge that is power or vice versa.   **B+**

Kraftwerk: *Computer World* (Warner Bros. '81). I once convinced myself to enjoy this band—if there had to be synthesizer rock, I thought, better it should be candidly dinky. And this is their funniest to date—every time I hear that machine intone "I program my home computer / Bring myself into the future," I want to make a tape for all those zealots who claim a word processor will change my life. But fun plus dinky doesn't make funky no matter who's dancing to what program. Funk has blood in it.   **B**

Bernie Krause & Human Remains: *Gorillas in the Mix* (Rykodisc '89). "Every sound on this record has been created from the voices of animals except as noted in the credits," claims the credits intro, which goes on to list six different keybmen and no other players. And sure enough, the coyotes, dolphins, whales, walruses, and (yes) turkeys who carry the electrofunky tunes all sound like synthesizers. Now is that sick or what? Hi-hat chores go to the snapping shrimp, kick drum to the ruffed grouse, and so forth, with the key cop-out *"from* the voices," for rarely are the voices *of* animals heard on this disc; whenever a horse or crow or pig or otter is allowed an untreated interjection it comes as a moment of grace. You don't have to be an animal rightser to believe that only a hairless biped could conceive anything so cosmically cutesy. **C+**

Kraut: *An Adjustment to Society* (Cabbage '82). New York's most likely hardcore boys keep the hooks coming for a whole side of enlightened rant—not twenty yet and they've figured out that past and future are real categories, always a tough lesson for rock-and-rollers. Overdisc, despite a terrific antiwar closer, they settle for blurred distinctions.   **B**

Lenny Kravitz: *Let Love Rule* (Virgin '89). For a black Jewish Christian married to Lisa Bonet who overoveroverdubbed his Hendrix-Beatles hybrid himself, not bad. But that's a lot of marketing to live down.   **B—**

Kris Kristofferson, Willie Nelson, Dolly Parton, Brenda Lee: *The Winning Hand* (Monument '82). This twenty-song mix-and-match isn't even monumental in theory, because two of these "kings and queens of country music" haven't earned their crowns—BL is a rock and roll princess who never really graduated, KK a frog ditto. But BL is also a pleasing bedroom-voiced journeywoman who turns in half of a surprisingly definitive "You're Gonna Love Yourself in the Morning." The other half comes from WN, who's on nine cuts and sounds like he's thinking even when he also sounds like he's asleep. DP teams with WN on a surprisingly definitive "Everything's Beautiful in Its Own Way," but sounds more at home on the album's two utter unlistenables— "Ping Pong," in which DP at her cutesiest is outdone by KK at his klutziest, and "Put It Off Until Tomorrow," in which DP kisses KK's warty little head and he croaks back. Time: 59:45.   **B—**

Krush Groove (Warner Bros. '85). Whether the ecumenicism is a musical leap forward or a commercial hedge, it does integrate the strong voices of Sheila E., Chaka Khan, and too-long-gone Debbie Harry into Russell Simmons's very male roster, and unlike the Gap Band and the Force M.D.'s, the ladies keep things moving. The krush grooves are two Rick Rubin metal-rap steamrollers. And for some reason the stars of the show only make the credit medley.   **B+**

Tuli Kupferberg: *Tuli & Friends* (Shimmy-Disc '89). At sixty-five, the guy "who jumped off the Brooklyn Bridge this actually happened and walked away unknown and forgotten into the ghostly daze of Chinatown soup alleyways & firetrucks, not even one free beer" (that's from "Howl," kids) survives as the great American bohemian. Yeah, he was in a rock and roll band (the Fugs, kids), but pure bohos rarely gravitate toward such large-scale forms. Tuli prefers found photographs, newspaper clippings, stick figures, new lyrics for famous tunes—the best stuff on his legendary 1968 ESP-Disk spoken-word was want ads. So I grant that this excessively long-awaited follow-up is of specialized interest. Still, music-lovers should hear "Evolution," dictated from the other side by John himself; "Swami" ("How I love you how I love you / Swami Everykinanda"); "Way Down South in Greenwich Village," an updated '20s classic with ukulele impression; and, no joke, "Morning, Morning," a song about life and death and their fleeting beauty that deserves eternal salvation.   **B+**

Fela Anikulapo Kuti: See Fela

La Bamba (Slash '87). To covet Ritchie Valens's rebel rock for your cultural heritage is neither sentimental self-deception nor desecration of capitalism. It's an inevitable impulse that exploits defiant gestures—which in this case showed small animus against either sentimentality or capitalism—for their enduring value, for the historical connections and intrinsic beauty sure to inhere in any defiant gesture worth remembering. Face it—at his wildest Valens is no longer much of a threat, even as an example. That Los Lobos didn't attempt to reconstitute that threat is unfortunate and no sin. Take the connections and the beauty for what they're worth.   **B+**

Patti LaBelle: *Winner in You* (MCA '86). No previous crossover diva has purveyed such an out-and-out fabrication. Tina's weathered sexpot, Whitney's soulful yuppie—these are credible plays on credible personas. But though Patti is managed by her longtime husband and advised by her longtime son, she nevertheless keynotes her multiplatinum bid with a tribute to the loneliness of the soulful yuppie, written by yet another successfully married couple but inspired I'm sure by one-cut-stand Michael McDonald (cf. Tina meets Bryan, Aretha meets George, and I bet Whitney trades Jermaine in on Phil Collins or somebody next time). Then again, Patti doesn't start out with such surefire goods—her abrasive nasality has always kept her reputation cult. Which is

why it's just as well for Patti that Richard Perry overwhelms the eight other producers: beats and tunes kick in till you could care less what organ she's singing through.   **B**

Lady Pank: *Drop Everything* (MCA '85). An impossible cross between the Vibrators and Men at Work is brought off by a Polish quintet who got their name misspelling punk and sing in English translation for their capitalist debut. They sound fresh without even trying, which is probably the only way.   **B+**

Ladysmith Black Mambazo: *Induku Zethu* (Shanachie '84). This immensely successful South African vocal ensemble isn't my kind of thing. Their lyrics are in Zulu, which may be just as well, since they probably serve culturally conservative values. They employ no instruments, drums most certainly included, and generate almost no pulse; they sound like a glee club. And since I've never heard them before, I can't tell you how their umpteenth album stacks up. All I know is it's amazing—serious, intricate, droll, eerie, precisely rehearsed, and very beautiful. It's too thoughtful to fade into the background, but like so much good African music it possesses calmative properties. Anyone who thinks he or she might like it probably will.   **A—**

Ladysmith Black Mambazo: *Ulwandle Oluncgwele* (Shanachie '85). How does one distinguish between this album of a cappella Zulu gospel music and the other album of a cappella Zulu gospel music available in discriminating record stores? Well, this one came out first back home, which may mean it's purer and may mean it's less advanced and probably means nothing. On this one, they wear choir robes instead of tribal garb and say amen and hallelujah, which may be why it's not as much fun. The easiest way to tell them apart, though, is that the other one is called *Induku Zethu.* Write it down. They're both pretty good, believe me.   **A**—

Ladysmith Black Mambazo: *Inala* (Shanachie '86). Unless I learn Zulu (long shot) or someone starts providing trots (great idea), chances are my favorite Ladysmith album will always be the first one I listened to, 1984's *Induku Zethu.* But your favorite will probably be the first one *you* listen to, and if you were busy in 1984 you might help Paul Simon do a good deed and start here. By now you should know what you'll get: a male a cappella chorus comprising two families of brothers and cousins in which Joseph Shabalala's cunning tenor darts in and out of the harmonic brush. Though they can dance to it, you probably can't, but unless you're hopelessly culture-bound you'll soon hear how beautiful it is. As a crossover gesture there's one song in English, full of sly domestic observations that provide welcome insight into how they deploy both words and sounds.   **A**—

Ladysmith Black Mambazo: *Shaka Zulu* (Warner Bros. '87). Though I continue to prefer the curlicued sound effects of *Induku Zethu,* the lyric sheet alone (with four songs in English!) makes this the Ladysmith album of choice for any normal U.S. dabbler. Roy Halee separates the harmonic elements just enough to enhance their fit and shows off Joseph Shabalala's grainy tenor, which anybody but a devoted family man would go solo with tomorrow. The politics settle in around a generalized gospel yearning, but the sheer sound is gorgeous enough to embarrass most Americans. Let's just hope they last longer on Warners than Urubamba did on CBS, so we get a chance to listen deeper.   **A**—

Ladysmith Black Mambazo: *Umthombo Wamanzi* (Shanachie '88). Though it's worse than ridiculous for Grammy taste-mongers to classify these slick professionals as folk musicians, they are exotics, subject to foreign pop's law of diminishing returns—after you get past how different it is, you're stuck with differentiating it from itself. So, a couple of hints. One, this is a harmony album; Joseph Shabalala isn't submerged, but he isn't showcased either. That makes for a nice little change. Two, it's a religious album, replete with full translations and twelve ways to sing amen. That I'm not so sure about.   **B**+

Ladysmith Black Mambazo: *Journey of Dreams* (Warner Bros. '88). Transcriptions from the Zulu help the student trace the intricate structures in forty-eight-track detail. Lyric summaries reveal three songs about God, three about their career, two that mention oppression in South Africa, two that mention Paul Simon. Simon takes the lead on "Amazing Grace," the "Send in the Clowns" of roots music.   **B**+

Laid Back: *Keep Smiling* (Sire '84). The Danes in this duo are to disco what the Germans in Trio are to rock and roll—just as deliberately minimalist but, in the tradition of the genre, a lot smarmier. If you wanna be rich, scratch 'em where they itch.   **C**+

Lakeside: *Fantastic Voyage* (Solar '80). Surprise—the fast ones are fun, the slow ones aren't. Fast ones might be even more fun if this weren't a band that praises Toto (the dog, but I think they're funning) in the same stanza with James Brown. Slow ones might be some fun if the singers had the style (skill's not the problem) to convey why they bother.   **B**

Lakeside: *The Best of Lakeside* (Solar '89). Never long on personality, these cogs in Dick Griffey's machine can at least muster a consistent compilation (unlike such rival pros as Atlantic Starr, say). Among their eleven years' worth of occasional hits, only one post-'84, are their signature dress-up number "Fantastic Voyage," "It's All the Way Live" 's primitive forerunner of the "Good Times" bassline, and "I Want

To Hold Your Hand" as a moderately personable slow one.   **B+**

Robin Lane & the Chartbusters: *Robin Lane & the Chartbusters* (Warner Bros. '80). Formally, this is reactionary, from Lane's chesty melismas to the band's fake-book licks, and the songs go on too long. But every one catches, and despite Lane's lady-macho stage moves, her lyrics seem felt in what I can only call a progressive way—autonomous but not anomic or selfish, compassionate but not infinitely long-suffering.   **B+**

Robin Lane and the Chartbusters: *5 Live* (Warner Bros. EP '80). A new wave demands new gimmicks, and bizzers have been working overtime to create them. For the big guys they long ago came up with the redundant live double. So for the little guys they've devised the redundant live half.   **C**

K.D. Lang: *Shadowland* (Sire '88). Whether claiming Nashville for torch song, joining Tracy Chapman's New Dignity movement, or embalming country the way lead tunesmith Chris Isaak embalms rockabilly, Lang resembles Patsy Cline (or whomever) less than the Pet Shop Boys—impossible to suss out her relationship to music she presumably loves.   **B**

K.D. Lang and the Reclines: *Absolute Torch and Twang* (Sire '89). Finally she swells with the contained enthusiasm of *Tracy Nelson Country* twenty years ago, back when authenticity wasn't such a vexed concept. Willie Nelson's "Three Days" and Wynn Stewart's "Big Big Love" do stand out, but not so's they embarrass Lang's originals, most of which are pretty metaphysical for country music. They're just highlights, like her own lusty "Big Boned Gal" and her own metaphysical "Luck in My Eyes." And "Nowhere To Stand" is an even smarter (and more abstract, fancy that) battered-child song than Suzanne Vega's or Natalie Merchant's. Maybe it's out of place on a quasi-authentic country record, though you have to like the way she sneaks in the phrase "family tradition." But vexed concepts cut two ways.   **B+**

Daniel Lanois: *Acadie* (Opal/Warner Bros. '89). In which Lanois adapts the all-embracing New Orleans groove to new-age—not soft or lite or adult-contemporary—rock. It has that intellectual aura, you know? Contemplating the human condition in sound as well as folkish words and melody, the mild-voiced Eno crony pieces together compositions that are half song, half "atmosphere" (as in "The atmosphere for this goes back a few years"). And tops them off with just you guess—"Amazing Grace," dummy.   **B–**

Denise LaSalle and Satisfaction: *Guaranteed* (MCA '81). Leading off with the irritating "I'm Tripping on You" (he's also "a contact high"), side one is more of the utterly ordinary dance music this self-starting singer and songwriter has been wasting herself on for years. But side two puts three of her sexual autonomy specials around the best hook on the record, which is connected to something called "E.R.A. (Equal Rights Amendment)." The subtitle's to let you know she's not singing about earned run averages or the Economic Recovery Administration—she's singing about the Amendment, the piece of paper itself, and she knows it spells more than sexual autonomy. Ideal for dance-party fund-raisers.   **B**

Denise LaSalle: *Rain and Fire* (Malaco '86). LaSalle earns enough in Malaco's songwriting stable to limit her recording career to a humdrum album every year or two, and since that's all she managed as a perpetual also-ran, there was no reason to hope for serendipity. But here she learns her revenge from the soaps and her tune from George Jackson, throws role model Sylvia Robinson a cover, name-drops all over a toot-toot follow-up, and demonstrates what Millie Jackson might be today if she hadn't put on airs—a teller of truths too raunchy for the country moralists who prime but fail to satisfy her market. High points include the eight-minute saga "It Be's That Way Sometime" and dovetailing critiques of the hard-on, "Dip, Bam, Thank You Ma'am" and "It Takes You All Night" ("To do what you used to do all night"). Plus this Inspirational Verse:

"They can't eat no more, no sir / They got anorexia nervosa."   **B+**

David Lasley: *Missin' Twenty Grand* (EMI America '82). Great falsettos like Smokey Robinson and Clyde McPhatter flow uphill, while lesser ones like Maurice Gibb and Russell Thompkins settle for the formal panache and expressive limitation of acknowledged artifice. Lasley certainly doesn't flow, but he doesn't settle, either—his struggle toward full emotional range sounds forced at first, but then willed, which is different. Playing head voice for homosexual angst rather than love-man tenderness or androgynous affect, he sets his colloquial confessions to pristine studio soul backup completely appropriate in a concept album about a white guy in love with black music. But at times it does seem forced.   **B+**

David Lasley: *Raindance* (EMI America '84). The artiest love man since Eugene Record wasn't the next Dylan, Lasley adds a wonderful rap for "queers" and a terrible street-talk verité playlet called "Euripides Meets the Shangri-Las" to his straightforward sha-la-la lyrics and Brill Building grooves, with fellow Detroiter Don Was throwing in Linn drums and such. His falsetto has gained color and heft, too.   **B+**

Last Exit: *The Noise of Trouble (Live in Tokyo)* (Enemy '87). The return of free jazz was inevitable in this time of '60s nostalgia, and believe me, it could be a lot worse. At least Bill Laswell and Ronald Shannon Jackson revert to rhythm when the path of pure inspiration peters out, and Sonny Sharrock is without sonic peer. Somewhat less imposing is the group's unacknowledged center, West German saxophone legend Peter Brötzmann, but Ornette himself couldn't make consistent music out of a concept that eschews not only heads but rehearsal, and he probably wouldn't want to. Consistency's not the idea—becoming is, and those who'd rather watch childbirth movies may have a point. All three of the group's albums are live. *Last Exit* documents the blinding headache of their first gig and is often played by Lester Bangs to keep angels and rock critics away. My sentimental favorite is *Cassette Recordings 87*—because its Jimmy Reed cover is "Big Boss Man," because its "Ma Rainey" mentions Alexander Pope, and because half of it was recorded in Allentown. But this is the one that actually comes together. The so-called suite kind of is, "Panzer Be-Bop" is pure atonal convergence, and Herbie Hancock sticks in his two cents like he knows what for.   **B+**

Bill Laswell: *Baselines* (Musician '83). One thing's sure—this is shitty background music. That's intentional, of course, but if Laswell's/Material's avant-fusion experiments are to prove useful to avant-pop listeners, they'd better reward attention more brilliantly than they do. Pulse or no pulse (and it can be either), the all-star textures here are too often the usual interesting-to-inventive, and even though I prefer Laswell's urban, conflict-ridden taste in noise to the ecological romanticism of the ethnojazz school, I don't hear the street or the subway (or my stereo) any better than before I put this on.   **B**

Bill Laswell: *Hear No Evil* (Venture '88). Only such a cold bastard could conceive new age so undisgusting. Some hear *Another Green World* in the thing, and there's that. Also r&b readymades and George Harrison's *Wonderwall* and packages of free noodles. I swear I can hear him laughing; sometimes I laugh myself. I swear he thinks it's good of its kind, too. So do I.   **B+**

Latimore: *I'll Do Anything for You* (Malaco '83). As T.K. was folding in 1980, this after-the-fact soul hero resorted to L.A. session men to define his seriousness, which proved no less schlocky than most pop seriousness. But his 1982 return to his roots on Malaco was only slightly less schlocky, because at least temporarily the man has lost his knack as a composer. Here the title tune and the first three cuts on side one are the hottest soul tracks of a year that saw as many new soul albums as the previous three or four put together, but it isn't just the Mississippi rhythm section that's catapulted him back into the action. It's also the Memphis songwriting stable. Say thank you to George Jackson and Denise LaSalle.   **B+**

Stacy Lattisaw: *With You* (Cotillion '81). As I hope his guru tells him, Narada Michael Walden is always better off Helping Others, and who better than this going-on-fourteen cross between Teena Marie and Michael Jackson, whose natural cuteness absorbs the sickly-sweet aftertaste of Walden's jumpy little tunes? But she can't do much more with dumb ballads than sing her heart out on them, always a misuse of good young flesh. **B+**

Peter Laughner: *Peter Laughner* (Koolie EP '82). These club dubs and worktapes aren't for audiophiles, but should convince mere rock-and-rollers that the Cleveland rock critic, a founding and former member of Pere Ubu before he excessed himself to death in 1977, deserves his musical legend. The songwriting is Dylanesque ("Baudelaire") or better ("Sylvia Plath"), the early-Dylan impression uncanny ("Rag Mama"). His guitar moves aren't so undeniable—when I'm feeling world-historic they sound prophetic, but soon the mood passes and they revert to the untutored one-offs and amateur sketches they were. Original grade: B plus. **B**

Cyndi Lauper: *She's So Unusual* (Portrait '83). Initially, this blue angel won my heart by covering the two most profound pop songs of the past five years, "Money Changes Everything" and "When You Were Mine." Now, with "Girls Just Want To Have Fun" the official pep song of the daughters of *Ms.* and Pepsi-Cola and "Time After Time" throbbing hearts by the millions, I've softened my strictures about her Betty Boop bimboism—if a kook who's loved, respected, and taken seriously by her sisters fools boys into believing she can be fooled with, more power to her. First side's an eternal classic. Second sneaks by on the one where she kisses me and the one where she diddles herself. Original grade: B plus. **A**

Cyndi Lauper: *True Colors* (Portrait '86). Cheap sentiment plus star-budget video make the first side so disheartening that the second isn't much more than a relief. Just as the sensitive relationship songs retreat from the perils of triads and the pleasures of jerking off, "What's Going On" is a nostalgic generalization after the first album's confrontation with capital. Girls just want to have money—and no fun changes everything. **B−**

Cyndi Lauper: *A Night To Remember* (Epic '89). Can you believe she's talking this one up as a triumph of self-expression (meaning "personal" songs, like that Kodak ad) over spiritual adversity (meaning commercial shortfall)? How embarrassing to have placed hope in this woman. And how sad to compare the bold finds and off-the-wall vulgarity of the only good album she'll ever make to this big-time pop—a parameter stretched not an iota by songs about one's very own breakup, not to mention strokes as prudently defiant as the lyric about not being a pet, which was probably Christina Amphlett's idea anyway. **C+**

Eddy Lawrence: *Walker County* (Snow Plow '86). A folkie who works in NYC, Lawrence cultivates a pastoral gift for vernacular narrative, as in the Alabama locale of his title and most of his material—lots of red dirt gone to asphalt, farmland gone to housing tract, homes gone to trailers. Sure he veers into sentiment, but only the instrumental is without its turn of phrase. **B+**

Eddy Lawrence: *Whiskers and Scales and Other Tall Tales* (Snowplow '89). You know the routine—local folkie sets down with a couple of stringed instruments and lets fly. It works or it doesn't; usually it doesn't. But Lawrence is showing off so much eye, ear, and imagination that his stories barely require the appearance of music. Try the catfish farmer. Or the Marine's big-talking little brother. Or the bigamous lady trucker with the girlfriend in Wisconsin. Or Tommy's mommy's swami playing hide the salami. He's even moderately funny about fishing. **B+**

The Leaving Trains: *Well Down Blue Highway* (Enigma '84). Side one does honor to the straight (nonhippie/nonhardcore/nonbiz) bohemianism of X, the Gun Club, and Chris D. Cruder and sloppier than X, as you'd guess if not hope, and a lot less pretentious than the other two, with songs that stay with you long enough to make you ponder Falling James's unhistrionic take on impending doom. That's side one. Side two is neopsychedelic drone. **B**

The Leaving Trains: *Kill Tunes* (SST '86). Where once Falling James Moreland inclined his raggedy band toward blues, here he rediscovers his roots: punk. If the whole album were punchy put-downs it wouldn't be the answer to our problems. But it'd give Falling James's poetry a break. **B+**

Led Zeppelin: *Coda* (Swan Song '82). They really were pretty great, and these eight outtakes—three from their elephantine blues phase, three from their unintentional swan song—aren't where to start discovering why. But despite the calculated clumsiness of the beginnings and the incomplete orchestrations of the end, everything here but the John Bonham Drum Orchestra would convince a disinterested party—a Martian, say. Jimmy Page provides a protean solo on "I Can't Quit You Baby" and jumbo riffs throughout. **B+**

Legal Weapon: *Death of Innocence* (Arsenal '82). Since like so much L.A. gothic this punk metal cultivates melodrama with an enthusiasm that could be campier, I don't quite know how to take Kat Arthur's tales of young woe. If she really did get sodomized by daddy on the floor, the hooky crudity of her response is guts ball. But if she just thought incest a fitting hook for such a crude grabber of a riff, she should have thought some more. And the strain of such distinctions renders the crudity less satisfying than its hooks warrant. **B+**

Legal Weapon: *Your Weapon* (Arsenal '82). The follow-up is less unrelenting, but it's also subtler in crucial little ways—tempo change here, Byrdsy decoration there, burr in the throat all over the place. Kat Arthur may well be turning into Joan Jett with something to say and something else to say it with. She's still young and she

still means it, but she's gained perspective on her bombed-out blues. **B+**

Legal Weapon: *Interior Hearts* (Arsenal '85). You look at Kat Arthur's mascara and chains and listen to the band's simple hard rock and wonder whether they're HM or punk. If Arthur were a guy, this would bode ill, but a guy she definitely ain't, so she still has Joan Jett to look up to. And like Joan Jett she's got more instinct than brains, which is why her third indie album isn't quite what her cult and well-wishers have been long awaiting. **B−**

Legal Weapon: *Life Sentence To Love* (MCA '88). Kat Arthur makes her belated major-label debut too damn late, carrying the eternal Joan Jett comparison far into love-is-pain cliché. The tunes are even further from Jett's best than Jett's latest, and the dark undertow that once colored Brian Hansen's music has given way to upbeat hooks that rise out of the locomotion like bluebirds fluttering hopefully around Kat's erotic doom. **B−**

Ray Lema: *Nangadeef* (Mango '89). Lema knows too much keyboard. Orchestrating for drama and structure, he ends up with a music of brilliant passages—now Ellingtonian, now almost Brazilian. If you equate Zaire with the eternal groove you'll find him irritating. But if you get your kicks contemplating rhythms as well as consuming them, try this rooted fusion of soukous, funk, reggae, mbaqanga, rock, fusion, and whatever—complete with shrewd, languid vocals of equal intelligence, or wisdom. **B+**

John Lennon/Yoko Ono: *Double Fantasy* (Geffen '80). In a special message for all the ignorami who think he never should have married the pretentious bitch, John turns the professional rock he hacked his way through when they were separated to the specifics of his life (and genius) as it's now constituted. In a special message for all the ignorami who think pretentious bipeds should stay out of recording studios, Yoko keeps up with him. This is an unfashionable piece of music—only Poly Styrene, of all people, has gotten away with anything remotely similar all year. But you don't have to be married to hear its commitment and command. I hope.   **A**

John Lennon: *The John Lennon Collection* (Geffen '82). I grant that it's superfluous—basically an Apple best-of plus John's songs from *Double Fantasy.* It goes on my A shelf because John was John, not just half of John & Yoko. Also because it omits the half-cocked "Cold Turkey" and ragtag "Happy Xmas (War Is Over)" from the official Apple best-of and doesn't medley "Give Peace a Chance."   **A—**

John Lennon/Yoko Ono: *Milk and Honey* (Polydor '84). Those too numbed by tragedy or hope to connect with *Double Fantasy* aren't likely to hear this one either—it's definitely more of the same, in John's case outtakes. But these were clearly rejected on conceptual rather than musical grounds, as just too quirky to suit the careful househusband image John wanted for his return to the arena. Which is why I like them better, especially spiced with asides he would have erased before final release. Yoko's songs are more recent and that's another plus, because her pop only began to jell with *Double Fantasy;* the horny querulousness of "Sleepless Night" and the cricket synthesizers on "You're the One" are confident personal elaborations of a tradition she comes to secondhand. Only the two middle cuts on the B get soupy. What a farewell.   **A**

John Lennon: *Live in New York City* (Capitol '86). Just by putting his all into such unsung great songs as "Well, Well, Well" and "It's So Hard," the great singer comes a lot closer to justifying this ad hoc document than Jagger did with *Ya-Ya's* or Daltrey did with *Leeds.* The alternate "Instant Karma" and "Cold Turkey" and "Mother" are also welcome. But his accidental romance with Elephant's Memory never did him any good musically. And for all his encouragement Yoko wasn't yet a rock-and-roller, so "Hound Dog" remains a concept.   **B**

John Lennon: *Menlove Ave.* (Capitol '86). The late-night session-band workups of songs later embalmed on *Walls and Bridges* are startlingly stark and clear, making side two the finest music of the hiatus between *Imagine* and *Double Fantasy,* whose precisely felt studio-rock they prefigure. Phil Spector produced the commercial versions. He also produced *Rock 'n' Roll,* source of the outtakes of side one, which were rejected because they're even stiffer than the intakes. John never could figure out what to do about loving Rosie & the Originals. And Phil wasn't the guy to tell him.   **B+**

John Lennon: *Imagine: John Lennon: Music From the Original Motion Picture* (Capitol '88). Nothing wrong with the music, though you can do without the bait—"Imagine" work tape, carefully hoarded *new song* work tape. But the useless configuration, foreshortening the Yokoless first half of his career and romanticizing the de-Beatled second, wouldn't exist without the tireless promotional efforts of Albert Goldman.   **C+**

Julian Lennon: *Valotte* (Atlantic '84). I'd hoped to let this one die in dignified silence—figured you couldn't blame the boy for trying. But as it's now sold over 500,-000 RIAA-certified copies, discretion is useless. Anyway, I do blame him for trying. Aside from the eerie vocal resemblance, this is bland professional pop of little distinction and less necessity—tuneful at times, tastefully produced of course, and with no discernible reason for being, more Frank Sinatra Jr. than (even) Hank Williams Jr. Julian seems well brought up, a credit to his long-suffering mom. I suggest he invest his royalties in medical school—or else, if he's so keen on not wasting his genetic heritage, launch a career in the visual arts.   **C**

LeRoi Brothers: *Check This Action* (Amazing '83). With Texophiles buzzing these guys up as the roadhouse band of a college cowboy's dreams, I was put off some—that big, brawling sound has never been this honorary pencilneck's idea of Saturday night. More listens later than I would have thought tolerable, while Steve Doerr romped all over "Ballad of a Juvenile Delinquent," I finally got the joke. Remember, the Dictators knocked them dead in Dallas too.   **B+**

The Leroi Brothers: *Forget About the Danger Think of the Fun* (Columbia EP '84). Gyrating second vocalist Joe Doerr joins the Texas quartet whose neoroadhouse album went cult last year. The kid sings like he only masturbates twice a day because his boner makes it impossible for him to walk to his car, adding a memorable rockabilly urgency to "Treat Her Right" that puts the manly confessional boasts "Ain't I'm a Dog" and "D.W.I." in suitably adolescent perspective. **B+**

Less Than Zero (Def Jam '87). Despite the execrable title song and Poison's attempted "Rock and Roll All Nite," this is one tough and imaginative soundtrack. I love the way the Bangles schlock up "Hazy Shade of Winter" (sounds like the Grass Roots song it should have been) and Slayer revs up "In-A-Gadda-Da-Vida" (a great tune cut down to size). Even better are a debut by the Black Flames, a def and jamming answer to the Force M.D.'s, and a Public Enemy track that finally lives up to their fierce political rep (they like Farrakhan and dis critics, but nobody said you had to agree with them). "Are You My Woman"/"Bring the Noise," the resulting twelve-inch is called. Those who never trust a soundtrack should buy one. **B+**

Let's Active: *Cypress* (I.R.S. '84). If only they'd had twenty-four-track consoles in the '60s, maybe Byrds albums would sound as great as their legend. And if only Mitch Easter had something to say, maybe Let's Active albums would sound as great as Byrds albums—although even Michael Clarke provided more forward motion than this. **C+**

Let Them Eat Jellybeans! (Virus import '81). This anthology of seventeen U.S. indie singles isn't all hardcore, but with Jello Biafra doing the compiling side one will pass, from Flipper's classic-if-a-bit-slow "Ha Ha Ha" to the Subhumans' at-last-it-can-be-told "Slave to My Dick." Postliberal racism from the Offs and "faggot"-baiting from the Feederz is balanced by surprising L.A. anthems from the Circle Jerks (anti-war), Geza X (antinuke), and Christian Lunch (anti). And even San Fran arties

like Wounds and (especially) Voice Farm come up with engaging stuff. Plus lyrics, addresses, band lists, and much, much more! [Later on Alternative Tentacles] **A—**

Huey Lewis and the News: *Picture This* (Chrysalis '82). The onetime Marin country-rocker and Elvis C. backer-upper is now working a working-guy variation on Rindy Ross (Quarterflash, dummy), cutting his macho strut with pop moues and knowing nods at women's lib. Though he has none of Springsteen's feeling for narrative and sings from the diaphragm rather than the gut, he's canny enough to pick good covers and writes his share of reasonable facsimiles: "Workin for a Livin" could be primo Bob Seger and "The Only One" is worthy of Geldof or Lynott if not the master. But Chris Hayes's metal furbelows soon remind you how much Huey sounds like Louie (Gramm) (Foreigner, dummy). I mean, Dewey really need one more rock pro bulling his way through options that just aren't as limited as he makes his livin pretending? **B—**

Huey Lewis and the News: *Sports* (Chrysalis '83). You said it, the man's an utter cornball, but on this album I simply succumb to the stupid pleasures of his big fat rockcraft. Even though I know it isn't the "same old back beat" that keeps rock and roll alive, but rather musicians brave or bored enough to fuck with it, something same-old has me grunting with pleasure at that song every time I let down my guard. No guard required: "I Want a New Drug" (recreational), "Bad Is Bad" (bad), and "Walking on a Thin Line" (when are Vietnam Veterans Against the War putting together their compilation album?). **B+**

Huey Lewis and the News: *Fore!* (Chrysalis '86). Last time he said bad is bad, this time he says hip is square, and there you have the difference between a straight-shooting album and a conventional one, between one that catches your elbow and one they ram down your throat. **B—**

Huey Lewis and the News: *Small World* (Chrysalis '88). Miffed when the Dems rejected the title tune as a campaign song—"It just doesn't rock hard enough," an unidentified Harvard pol complained—

Huey offered it to George, who found it bland and worried that its call for a kinder, gentler planet wasn't specific enough. So then Huey took it to the radio.   **C**−

Jerry Lee Lewis: *Killer Country* (Elektra '80). First time he was trying, second time he wasn't, third time he gets lucky, from a "Folsom Prison Blues" that far outgrooves groove numbers like last time's "Rockin' Jerry Lee" to the magnificently over-the-hill "Thirty-Nine and Holding" to various generic throwaways about his mama and his pianner and his tomcat ways. Even "Over the Rainbow" ain't bad.   **B**+

Jerry Lee Lewis: *When Two Worlds Collide* (Elektra '80). The title weeper's a cut above the rest, but new producer Eddie Kilroy doesn't push Jerry Lee the way Bones Howe did on *Jerry Lee Lewis.* In fact, all that rescues this record from boredom and arrogant excess are two ancient throwaways—"Alabama Jubilee" (1915) and "Toot, Toot, Tootsie Goodbye" (1922)—plus an obscure BMI copyright called "I Only Want a Buddy Not a Sweetheart" that also evokes prerock tradition. His voice is on its way out and he's lucky if his spirit shows up on alternate Thursdays, but if he wants to tell us he's a classic I'll nod my head. And pat my foot. **B**−

Jerry Lee Lewis: *The Best of Jerry Lee Lewis Featuring 39 and Holding* (Elektra '82). Though like most country best-ofs this isolates some strong songs, it also courts the middle-aged crazy market by picking titles old farts will recognize, like his lame-ass "Who Will Buy the Wine" and "Good Time Charlie's Got the Blues." We don't get his loose-as-a-goose "Toot, Toot, Tootsie Goodbye." We also don't get his rockin' "Rita Mae," his rockin' "Don't Let Go," his rockin' "Folsom Prison Blues," and I could go on. Lewis made three albums for Elektra. Two of them beat the best-of.   **B**

Jerry Lee Lewis: *Rockin' My Life Away* (Tomato '89). Last time I saw this fugitive from Madame Tussaud's was a 1984 performance video that convinced me Mr. Scratch had collected his half of the bargain in advance. So I expected nothing from this live-at-the-Palomino rehash, James Burton or no James Burton. And

was immediately confronted with a "You Win Again" so bitter, so resigned, so defeated, so above-it-all, so miserable that for a few songs I suspected the monkey-gland shots had worked—except that he sounds old, old and lecherous, old and lecherous and determined to enjoy it. Things do wear down in the middle, and the voice can get weird. But James Burton is hot. And when and if he finally dies, Jerry Lee's gonna challenge Mr. Scratch to a piano-playing contest. Then he's gonna show Cousin Swaggart his ass.   **A**−

Liliput: *Liliput* (Rough Trade import '82). Formerly Kleenex has kept the faith even though only the lead cuts pack the goofy punch of "Split" 's massed whistles and saxophones, or the chaotic rallying cry "Eisiger Wind"—not to mention "U," or "You," or "Ain't You." Where the Slits aspire to Mango and the Raincoats to ECM and the Au Pairs to Grunt, these women clearly belong with the rest of Rough Trade's amateur anarchohumanists; they're the best thing to happen to Switzerland since John Berger. In another context I might disapprove of the clumsy white funk toward which their instrumental atmosphere has evolved, or fret about just what their references to ichor, stilts, and kicking heels mean. But this music combines the spirit of a kindergarten rhythm band with the sophistication of a wartime art school, just like the real Cabaret Voltaire.   **B**+

David Lindley: *El Rayo-X* (Asylum '81). Jackson Browne's sideperson extraordinaire (plays eight instruments and actually sings in French) is an El Lay weirdo like you thought they didn't make anymore (until you remembered Lindsey Buckingham), with a folk-rocking tree surgeon's sense of root systems (country-reggae, as in country-rock) and irony (cf. Ry Cooder). Does only passably by the golden oldies (compare ye golde Everlys, Tempts, Isleys/Beatles), comes up with middling-to-good "originals" (by one Bob "Frizz" Fuller except for the aptly titled "Pay the Man"), and knocks you dead with the obscure covers (cf. Ry Cooder).   **B**+

Linx: *Intuition* (Chrysalis '81). The funk of these two black Brits is so light you could mistake it for 3-in-One oil at thirty yards and Pablo Cruise at fifteen. Well, don't. They're sly devils from the door-slam drums of "Throw Away the Key" to the slick antiliberal militance of "Don't Get in My Way," and that's only side two. On side one they make clear that they've thought more about love than Pablo Cruise, who wouldn't know what to do with a steel drum if they got shipped home in one. **A—**

Lipps, Inc.: *Mouth to Mouth* (Casablanca '80). How can bizzers moan about the downfall of disco with this Silver Convention homage bigger than the Royal Guardsmen? Auteur named Steven Greenberg, medium named Cynthia Johnson, funky town named Minneapolis, thirty long minutes, one great hook. An accountant's dream. **C**

Lisa Lisa & Cult Jam With Full Force: *Lisa Lisa & Cult Jam With Full Force* (Columbia '85). Lisa got to sing "I Wonder If I Take You Home" because she sounded like the kind of amateur who might put words to the tune of yah-yah yah-yah-yah. At album length her musical comedy training comes to the fore. A Rosie & the Originals for our more pretentious time. **C+**

Lisa Lisa and Cult Jam: *Spanish Fly* (Columbia '87). Aphrodisiac they ain't— just Hispanic and, supposedly, fly. Hell's Kitchen scullions who've made good in typical one-part-talent-to-ten-parts-application *Fame* fashion, they're just street-smart enough to want nothing so much as to escape to the suburbs. Their kids will either carry on the family business or join hardcore bands. **C+**

Little Girls: *Thank Heaven!* (PVC EP '83). As pure a girl group as retro has washed up on the shores of commerce— unabashedly catchy, slight, and received white pop-rock with cute, clever, prefab lyrics. Funny thing is, the teenaged sisters up front wrote the stuff. I recommend "The Earthquake Song." And no matter what they say I wouldn't be sure the earthquake wasn't their fault. **B+**

Little Steven and the Disciples of Soul: *Men Without Women* (EMI America '82). The lyric sheet makes good reading— the confessions of a working-class teenager who got what he wanted and lost what he had (though he would have lost it anyway by now, and had less money besides). Unfortunately, Little Miami Steve sounds like arena-period Dylan doing the *Born To Run* songbook, and the E-Streeters in his band blare like Silver Bullets. If the Boss really is driving around El Lay wondering what happened, as one rumor has it, he could do worse than rescue "Men Without Women" and "Princess of Little Italy." Only don't pronounce it "Lily," okay, Bruce? **B—**

Little Steven: *Voice of America* (EMI America '84). I deeply respect Steven Van Zandt's brave translation of rock and roll libertarianism into internationalist antiwar propaganda, and I don't think he's done badly by the songwriting—somebody cover "Fear," or "Justice," or "Among the Believers." But please, please, please don't make me listen to him sing them anymore. His voice is devoid of dynamic or dramatic zip. When he's not bellowing, he's plodding. And he's got a band to match. **C+**

Little Steven: *Freedom No Compromise* (Manhattan '87). There are good singers who moan and good singers who whine, but this doomed soul is neither. He's just a guy who longs to let all the love and pain and ambition inside him out, and who isn't even any good at imitating those who know how. Civic virtue, rhythmic responsibility, sartorial overkill—none of them will gain him an ounce more popular credibility than he's already gained on the coattails of this icon or that issue. As usual, it's only as a writer of protest songs that he shows any knack—Rubén Blades could probably lift "Bitter Fruit" the way Black Uhuru did "Solidarity," and without Steven's phony accent. One hell of an expensive demo. **C**

Living Colour: *Vivid* (Epic '88). A few songs — the just-minding-my-own-business-sucker "Funny Vibe," the Mick

Jagger production/tribute "Glamour Boys," and "Middle Man" if it's as un-ironic as I hope—are smart enough, but while it's momentarily exhilarating to hear this all-black band come power-chording out of the box, after a while the fancy arrangements and strained soul remind me of, I don't know, Megadeth. Like any New Hendrix, Vernon Reid is only as good as his last context, and I'm not positive crossover metal is a good idea even in theory.   **B**

L.L. Cool J: *Radio* (Def Jam '85). Rick Rubin's thwonging minimalism and Cool J's proud polysyllables are fresh, def, and so forth. From the daring little piano hook of "I Can Give You More" to Russell Simmons's motormouth prevarications on "That's a Lie" to the humble love-man details of "I Want You," this is the most engaging and original rap album of the year. But the post-Run-D.M.C. school does betray a penchant for what you might call bourgeois individualism. Laying off messages is one thing, but the Hollis crew rarely projects much community or solidarity either. Which sometimes leaves a solo artist alone with his DJ and his fine self.   **B+**

L.L. Cool J: *Bigger and Deffer* (Def Jam '87). Like the pop-metal egotists he resembles every which way but white, J proves that there's something worse than a middle-class adolescent who's gotta be a big shot this instant—the same adolescent the instant he becomes a big shot. Overrated though it was, the debut had guts, spritz, musical integrity, and Rick Rubin. Breakthrough though it may be, the follow-up has a swelled head, a swollen dick, received beats, and quotes from Berry, Brown, and the Moonglows that confuse me. Could it be that the planet existed before he brought it to fruition?   **C+**

L.L. Cool J: *Walking With a Panther* (Def Jam '89). From self-centered teenager to man with a mission: "I hope to prove to the world that I can reach all materialistic goals and be young, black and legal." On the cover he and his panther wear gold while his three women sport tight dresses and Moet, with not an Africa medallion in sight, but call it part of a larger strategy:

justifying conspicuous consumption with conspicuous production. His output totals sixteen tracks for sixty-eight minutes on a single vinyl LP, with three extra on CD and the superhard B side "Jack the Ripper" completing an eighty-five-minute, twenty-track cassette. Though one of the ballads is a killer, the other two are, well, changes of pace; the (vinyl) side-closers make "Jack the Ripper" sound slow; the arrogant sense of humor comes with a snide, irritating, completely original laugh. My standard response to such overkill is to wish someone had boiled it down to the great album it contains, but with this egocentric, hedonistic, workaholic materialist, I'll take it all—definitely including the nonvinyl "Change Your Ways," which preaches compassion to the young, black, and legal competition.   **A—**

Richard Lloyd: *Field of Fire* (Mistiur import '85). In crucial ways he predates punk, and formally this is more Warren Zevon or Tom Petty than Tom Verlaine. What makes it go isn't songwriting—please, kids, never *ever* rhyme "fire" and "funeral pyre." It's Lloyd's concentration, plus of course his guitar, which I'll take over Mike Campbell's or even Waddy Wachtel's nine tries out of ten. [Later on Moving Target.]   **B+**

Local Boys: *Moments of Madness* (Island '83). A studio group fabricated by superproducer Glyn Johns around the unbankable Andy Fairweather Low, they're really international men, but the conceit suits Andy somehow. His aphoristic colloquialism and cracked, unassumingly intense vocals carry everything on the record except the lovely, Lofgrenish "Angels Falls," which belongs entirely to second banana (and sometime Who keyb man) Tim Gorman, and the overblown, Springsteenish "Shoot Out on the Highway," which must be somebody's idea of AOR.   **A—**

Robert Jr. Lockwood & Johnny Shines: *Hangin' On* (Rounder '80). The formal double-bind of the Delta blues these two students and near-contemporaries of Robert Johnson pursue so loyally isn't as constricting as that of the more recent

Chicago style—there's no dated "commercial" formula, so attempts at progress aren't as likely to sound like awkward compromises. The acoustic duets, alternated (never shared) lead vocals, relaxed two-man horn arrangements, and funk-influenced drumming of their recording debut may read like a mishmash, but Shines's singing and songwriting fills in the holes for Lockwood, who has made unpretentious eclecticism a specialty for years. **A—**

Nils Lofgren: *Flip* (Columbia '85). The wuntime wunderkind is "talkin' 'bout survival," which he at least points out beats "self denial," and I guess it's a small miracle that he's no longer the blustering never-was of the late '70s. But 1983's *Wonderland* testified more gracefully to his eternal youth, and even there it was hard to tell what he'd learned since 1971. To seek eternal youth in the absence of temporal wisdom is one of the great American vices, and most Americans aren't even wise enough to know it. **C+**

Kenny Loggins: *Vox Humana* (Columbia '85). "My goal was to transform my music into a more and more personal medium," says this harmless case study in contemporary pop of his first self-produced album, so he must think a lot about "love," a word which appears in seven of the nine songs. The subject is all-important for sure, but tricky to make new, as they say. Loggins succeeded in 1979 with the put-up-or-shut-up epiphany "This Is It." Here he hopes his rhythmic savvy and supple falsetto prove epiphany enough for Contemporary Hits Radio. Which given the promotional budget and catchy arrangement of the confidently entitled title tune, they already have. **C+**

Lone Justice: *Lone Justice* (Geffen '85). Although Maria McKee sure does have a big voice for such a young thing, sometimes I get the feeling she's playing grown-up with it—"After the Flood," about staying put on the family farm come hell or high water, doesn't exactly reflect the personal experience of someone who met her guitarist in a parking lot in the San Fer-

nando Valley. Not that I doubt her passionate sincerity. Just that I find it generates more credibility when she worries about her man working late or warns him not to insult her in front of her friends. Original grade: B plus. **B**

The Long Ryders: *10-5-60* (PVC EP '83). What Jason and the Scorchers are to punk these guys are to new wave, with a soul Gram Parsons fans will recognize. But though Sid Griffin has assimilated the right songwriting skills, there's something tentative if not theoretical about the way he puts them to use—like he feels a little unworthy. Which means he probably is a little unworthy. Original grade: B plus. **B**

The Long Ryders: *Native Sons* (Frontier '84). The down-to-earth poor-boy stance is an improvement on the boho excesses of the new L.A., though sometimes it's hard to pin down why these impressively particular songs go with this impressively seamless country-rock synthesis. Put it this way—they don't soft-pedal life's big fat downside, but they're good-humored about it. If you don't pay attention, you think Mel Tillis's "(Sweet) Mental Revenge" is one of theirs. **B+**

The Long Ryders: *State of Our Union* (Island '85). "Looking for Lewis and Clark" is some anthem, but like "Start Me Up" it may reveal more than it intends. These guys seek the explorers rather than the wilderness for the same reason they name Gram Parsons and Tim Hardin as forefathers, rather than Hank and Lefty. The self-conscious distance may be healthy—whatever drove Parsons and Hardin to their roots also turned them into dead junkies. But it's got to cut into the immediacy of the music, and for all the informed intelligence of songs like their tribute to black Memphis superstation WDIA, the album does come to a point at "State of My Union," which aggravates the honest chauvinism of Ronnie Van Zant's reflections on the same subject with the gratuitous self-righteousness of Neil Young's. **B+**

Loose Ends: *The Real Chuckeeboo* (MCA '88). Conceived in London and cut in Philadelphia, their funk is so suave and supple that on previous albums it slipped into the background without anyone noticing, including them—and until now, me. Here the ballads have more energy and the groove has more thwock, with the result that the whole first side moves like a living thing. This is fitting—despite a modicum of drum/keyb programming and a plethora of overdubs, the two instrumentalists constitute a band almost neotraditional in its liveness, its discreet spontaneity and sinuous swing. And the three voices are deployed with sensuality and effervescence.   **B+**

The Lords of the New Church: *The Lords of the New Church* (I.R.S. '82). Add the soul of the Damned to the heart of the Dead Boys and you get new-wave Black Sabbath, complete with technoprofessional arena echo guaranteed to attract music-lovers who will either take the band's superstitious yet not altogether worthless political doomsaying as gospel or else ignore it altogether.   **C**

Los Lobos: *". . . And a Time To Dance"* (Slash EP '83). At first I suspected tokenism or worse, but that's because the solid craftsmanship of a committed club band only gathers full impact at LP length. Once I saw them—felt them, really, in my bones more than my soul—the suspicion that maybe hip white Angelenos were working off Chicano guilt never entered my mind again. I just wondered whether there weren't more where they came from, and decided that finding competitors of equal chops, breadth, and reach would be pretty tough, especially with young Mexican-Americans so heavily into metal. Good old rock and roll East L.A. style, with a lope Doug Sahm fans will recognize long before Joe "King" Carrasco fans.   **A−**

Los Lobos: *How Will the Wolf Survive?* (Slash '84). This takes generic to a whole different level. Where their EP was a straightforward account of a world-class bar band in command of what we'll call Chicano r&b, a relatively specialized indigenous style with unexploited mass potential, their debut LP makes it sound as if

they invented the style. Who did the original of that one, you wonder, only to discover that you're listening to the original. Listen a little more and you figure out that these slices of dance music have lyrics, lyrics rooted in an oppression the artists really know about—the love songs return incessantly to the separation that defines migrant laborers' lives. And from the moment you hear "I Got Loaded" you'll know that while Cesar Rosas is merely a generic singer in the best sense, David Hidalgo is some kind of tenor.   **A**

Los Lobos: *By the Light of the Moon* (Slash '87). These guys are a world-class band. If they want to go Motown, who wouldn't? If they want to downplay the accordion, they have the guitars to compensate. But if they think pop means compassionate generalizations after the manner of John Cougar Mellencamp, they're selling themselves short. Though they're less confused for sure, with a gift for snapshot images that suggest the dimensions of suffering in this troubled land of ours, only on "The Hardest Time" do they drive that suffering all the way home. Leaving us with world-class jukebox grooves and vocals and some affecting protest songs.   **A−**

Los Lobos: *La Pistola y El Corazón* (Slash '88). This tastefully modernized tour of their Mexican roots is admirably uncommercial and more than pleasant, but without imputing "reverence" or some other backhand insult, I'll mention that I prefer Rounder's *¡Conjunto!* albums because they're faster. Or put it this way: usually, strange music is most efficiently conveyed by strangers.   **B**

Lost in the Stars: The Music of Kurt Weill (A&M '85). First time I heard this I started muttering, "Kurt Weill invented rock and roll," which I report only to indicate how turned on I was, because it's ridiculous—Weill really only invented rock. Milking abrasive pop for outreach and meaning, he had more in common with Dylan and Newman than with Porter and Berlin, and the rock artistes who take their turns on this sequel to Hal Willner's 1983 Monk tribute sound completely at home. You can imagine improvements on some of Willner's choices—David Jo rather than Sting on "Mack the Knife," the Clash rather than Stanard Ridgeway on "Cannon Song," etc.—but that's a parlor game. With Lou Reed's "September Song" and Marianne Faithfull's "Ballad of a Soldier's Wife" the unmitigated triumphs, every track on this hour-long disc holds its own. Introduce yourself to one of the century's greatest songwriters and composers. Or augment your Weill collection and be glad you did.   **A**

Los Van Van: *Songo* (Mango '89). This Paris-rerecorded compilation of top tunes by Cuba's top band is tasteful like *Sesame Street* rather than *Masterpiece Theatre,* stealing wittily from commercial culture rather than embalming good ideas in respectability. Electronics, double-hook song structures, sly vocal switchovers—all fit smoothly into a simple, expandable groove that's mellower and more polyrhythmic than Nuyorican salsa. Making it an ad for subsidized pop whether you like it or not.   **A−**

The Lounge Lizards: *The Lounge Lizards* (Editions E.G. '81). John Lurie has a real gift for night-crawling high-kitsch themes, but to hear him improvise alongside Arto Lindsay is to learn how hard it is to make music out of noise. After all, it's the precisely timed cut-'em-up verve with which Arto skronks and gweezes into the themes that gives the Lizards their edge. But for some reason—weak takes? rushed mix? Lurie's sense of posterity? vanity, perhaps?—he's all but inaudible on many cuts here. Result: *Slaughter on Tenth Avenue* Goes to the Mudd Club—fun, but not the real fake.   **B+**

The Lounge Lizards: *Live From the Drunken Boat* (Europa '83). Divested not only of fifth columnist Arto Lindsay but of all the guitar's vulgar "rock"-tinged associations, the Lizards get beau ideal Teo Macero to produce a studio album in live drag. They sound like an arty jazz combo who've landed a month at a pretentious cocktail lounge in Minneapolis, or Brussels. Sometimes they gear their originals to what they deem the declasse ambience of the place, other times they say fuck it and

lay down the simplified Cecil Taylor dearest to their hearts. They're better when they lower themselves. And they don't make it past Saturday night.   **B**

Lounge Lizards: *Live 79–81* (ROIR cassette '85). Before they were a mediocre jazz group or a hot fusion band they were a mordant postpunk concept, the avant-Raybeats. More than their antiseptic Editions EG album, this captures their raw sleaze, not to mention John Lurie's reptilian embouchure and (on three cuts) Arto Lindsay's cool-defying guitar.   **B+**

The Lounge Lizards: *Live in Tokyo/Big Heart* (Island '86). Initially, John Lurie's fake jazz was so conceptual it needed the chordless wonder of Arto Lindsay to knock the stuffing out of it every bar or two, but after trying to play the real thing he's settled for composing a full-fledged counterfeit. Blaringly dissonant and tunefully noir at the same time, Lurie's ensemble writing is Mancini boheme rather than Thelonious manqué—sometimes almost danceable, sometimes theme music for a movie too slick to star him, and always something else besides. Only brother Evan's "Punch and Judy Tango" tempts you to take the solos literally.   **A−**

The Lounge Lizards: *No Pain for Cakes* (Island '87). The record ends with John Lurie grousing about the way his minions skip practice. Disgusted, he says the hell with it himself and checks out a party, soon revealed as the source of the greasy, swinging groove underpinning his voiceover. Lurie likes the music so much that he goes into the next room to peep the band, and oops, it's the Lizards. On none of the garish set pieces preceding this capper do they sound so at ease with themselves. But on every one they sound as sardonic as the guy who thought it up. Which is how he wants it.   **B+**

The Lounge Lizards: *Voice of Chunk* (1-800-44CHUNK cassette/CD '89). Determined to become the thinking man's David Sanborn by hook or by crook, John Lurie swallows his indignation and elects to market himself—you achieve retail access by dialing the label name on your home telephone. And dial you might. His tone is as rich as his tunes, his solos are lifelike, his musicians thrive as individuals, his musicians function as a unit, and his arty moves kick in with a satisfying thwock. As usual, free jazz meets Henry Mancini meets Kurt Weill meets Peter Gordon meets the Ramada Inn. But the pomo patina has worn away—he's lyrical and catchy rather than "lyrical" and "catchy." Biting and funny he never put quotes around.   **A—**

Love of Life Orchestra: *Extended Niceties* (Infidelity EP '80). Concertmeister Peter Gordon doesn't deploy Arto Lindsay's untuned guitar as wickedly as lizard-leader John Lurie does, but how can you not love the way he punctuates and punctures the girlies crooning "Don't, don't please don't leave me" to close things off? It's enough to make you believe Gordon's otherwise unsung rock parody is funny.   **B**

Love of Life Orchestra: *Geneva* (Infidelity '80). With David Byrne and Arto Lindsay replaced by the Soho equivalent of studio musicians, Peter Gordon turns to self-consciously chickenshit disco/soundtrack mewzick, kitsch he posits as punk and/or no wave and/or minimalism's next convolution. No no no, "posits" is wrong, bring that back to "parodies." How about "exploits"? Whatever, the important thing is that their friends think it's cool and people they meet at parties don't. Think about it. Don't listen, just think about it.   **C+**

Loverboy: *Get Lucky* (Columbia '81). Wish I could work up the fine pitch of loathing this received, synthesized, male chauvinist pop metal theoretically deserves, but in fact it's not completely awful: "Working for the Weekend" articulates a real class dilemma, "Get Lucky" puns on the band's careerist fortunes, and "Emotional" is a better Stones rip than "It's Only Rock 'n Roll."   **C+**

Lyle Lovett: *Lyle Lovett* (Curb/MCA '86). Writes like Guy Clark only plainer, sings like Jesse Winchester only countrier, and if you've got a clear idea who both guys are you'll probably like him fine.   **B+**

Lyle Lovett: *Pontiac* (Curb/MCA '87). He's another Nashville neotraditionalist who's trying his damnedest to surpass a not-bad debut, a rounder who's better off playing the husband (as in the unembittered "Give Back My Heart" and "She's No Lady"), with something of Merle's jazz feel and a weakness for songpoetry ("If I Had a Boat," help). And he's something of a hit as he joins such success d'estime as pure Ricky Skaggs, clean Dwight Yoakam, clear-eyed Ricky Van Shelton, straight George Strait, reborn Reba McEntire, King Shit Randy Travis, and the great Rosanne Cash in a critical-commercial conflux that recalls the chart-topping days of Beatles, Stones, and, er, Jefferson Airplane. Why isn't this more of an up? Because all it means is that the folkies have taken over the establishment again, and a piss-poor one at that—these artists often spend the better part of a year going gold. Granted, the new trend does lend credence to the old folkie claim of proximity to the hearts of the people. But it also lends credence to the old antifolkie charge of middle-class romanticism in disguise.   **B—**

Lyle Lovett: *Lyle Lovett and His Large Band* (Curb '89). After kicking off with a sharp r&b instrumental, the lapsed grad student dispenses with pretension and boils country down to the basics. Singing: well-schooled. Songcraft: canny, humorous. Concept: women, you can't live with 'em and you can't live without 'em—and it's their fault. Lest anyone mistake his intentions, he also covers "Stand by Your Man." Very humorous.   **B**

Lene Lovich: *Flex* (Stiff/Epic '80). In the absence of a lucky hook or three, this universal expatriate is better off unhinged and pretentious (side two) than headed straight down the pop pipe (side one). Of course, in the absence of a lucky hook or three, so's Neil Diamond. Just wish I was sure the song about Joan of Arc was tongue-in-cheek.   **B—**

Lene Lovich: *New Toy* (Stiff/Epic EP '81). Songwise three for four and to those who carp that the track total is six, I say Les Chappell swings like Jerry Dammers himself on filler instrumental. Forget it, Jake—it's an EP.   **B+**

Lene Lovich: *No-Man's Land* (Stiff/Epic '82). Lovich hasn't so much gone Anglodisco as vice versa: she was swooping through postpunk well before the coming of the synthesizers, and she's no less goofy today. Nevertheless, she does *sound* less goofy, because she's surrounded by swoopers. Which doesn't make her secret privatism any easier to get to. **B**

Andy Fairweather Low: *Mega-Shebang* (Warner Bros. '80). When I heard the funky force-beat of "Night Time DJukeing" I was delighted—sounded like the man had invented DOR all on his own, and in Wales yet. But as I perused the lyrics I began to suspect that his heart—a concept that in Low always includes the mind—wasn't entirely committed. Good fun from an artist who's capable of the best. **B+**

Nick Lowe: *Nick the Knife* (Columbia '82). He's shed one guitar player and no hooks and as a man he's probably better for it: his cool seems more casual, his lust more committed. But the music is tossed off with what sounds like indolence rather than charm, and since Billy Bremner and Terry Williams are still on hand it would be too pat to claim he needs a real band. Hard to make that casual commitment sing, I guess. **B+**

Nick Lowe: *The Abominable Showman* (Columbia '83). Pretends he only goes for bad puns, yeti trails "Time Wounds All Heels" with "(For Every Woman Who Ever Made a Fool of a Man There's a Woman Who Made a) Man of a Fool." No tour de force, just unlabored love songs, and my best to the Lowe-Carters. **B+**

Nick Lowe: *Nick Lowe and His Cowboy Outfit* (Columbia '84). Marital strife seems to have transformed Lowe from a power popper with brownout problems into the genre artist of roots eclectic he's always wanted to be. Slighter than ever lyrically and yet stronger overall than its two predecessors, this leads with a Tex-Mex something called "Half a Boy and Half a Man," and that's where it means to stay. **B+**

Nick Lowe and His Cowboy Outfit: *The Rose of England* (Columbia '85). For five years Lowe has marked time without ever quite losing the beat, and his most mild-mannered album of the decade is also his most consistent. I admit I missed the trademark sarcasm at first—until I realized that the most remarkable cut was a straightforward band-composed instrumental best described as mild-mannered Duane Eddy. Then I decided that the wimpy "I Knew the Bride" remake was deliberate—old beau Nick in the throes of fond regret—and went on from there. Will anybody notice this stirringly minor achievement? Probably not. Will I remember it myself a year from now? I wouldn't stake my job on it. **B+**

Nick Lowe: *Pinker and Prouder Than Previous* (Columbia '88). Another small victory in his longstanding battle against the irony that made him famous, and he sure ain't the only one. As they get older, guys who were smart enough to keep their distance as callow authenticity fans can't resist playing their hard-earned experience straight—even Mick Jagger wants to be soulful these days. At least Nick is smart enough to take himself seriously with a smile. **B+**

Nick Lowe: *Basher: The Best of Nick Lowe* (Columbia '89). Fourteen tracks recap the two great albums of 1978 and 1979, when he declared himself pure pop and spelled out the sound of breaking glass—roadie with arm torn off, actress eaten by dog. The remaining thirteen cull from the six good albums of the subsequent decade, when the fringe professional proclaimed a "Lovers Jamboree." The rowdy songs know whereof they kick, "Stick It Where the Sun Don't Shine" wounds all heels, and every decent halfboy/half-man has a couple of good love songs in him—"Heart" pure pop, "Raging Eyes" true romance. **A−**

L'Trimm: *Drop That Bottom* (Atlantic '89). I know, these girls are a male fantasy—if Jesse Helms had any idea how sexy-cute they are he'd tack them onto a kiddie-porn law. The music's a fantasy too—simple rap beats, simple house hooks. And I get a buzz off 'most every track. So I'm weak. So sue me. **B+**

Lucinda: See Lucinda Williams

Lydia Lunch: *Queen of Siam* (ZE '80). Having walked out on three different bands led by this dame, I have the credentials to certify this funny, sexy, accidental little record. Half the time she exaggerates her flat Cleveland accent into a hickish, dumb-and-dirty come-on or parody of same, and half the rest of the time she plays her foolish nihilist poetry for laughs, which leaves a quarter of the time when she's the nihilist fool I'll walk out on till the day she dies. Pat Irwin's big-band atonalisms suit her city-of-night shtick perfectly. And "Spooky" is the cover of the year. Original grade: A minus.   **B+**

Luxury: *#1 EP* (Angry Young EP '81). Six slightly disorienting pop songs from one Rick Swan of Des Moines, who on the evidence of side two, where the choicer and more dangerous ones are located, related to Bible school the way Jerry Lee did to Bible college. As the unchurched may not know, Bible school is tamer—kid stuff complete with cookies and Kool-Aid.   **B+**

Lynyrd Skynyrd: *Legend* (MCA '87). What made them a great boogie band was that Ronnie Van Zant had a mean, sly edge on him. What made them a damn fine boo-gie band was that they knew how to relax. Except maybe for a bit about "Hollyweird," there's no special edge on these B sides, outtakes, reconstituted demos, and live one. But a decade after the fact, they sound damn fine.   **B+**

Lyres: *AHS-1005* (Ace of Hearts EP '81). Are these four rather Dollsish (Johansenish, really) tracks hard-rocking, or are they the platonic ideal of hard-rocking? A close call. Which is why I'm not convinced DMZ veteran Jeff Conolly makes up for his bad rep with inspired madness—either he's not inspired enough or he's not mad enough.   **B+**

Lyres: *On Fyre* (Ace of Hearts '84). Just like their fellow neotraditionalists in rockabilly and r&b, these pillars of garage principle set themselves the nearly impossible task of substituting magic for the real thing every track out. As the best of such bands so often do, they get off to a rousing start, in this case by marshaling their two best originals, which they keep going with the help of a couple of covers through all of side one. On side two they slow down a little, and not only isn't the result magical, it's barely rhythmic.   **B**

Baaba Maal et Dande Lenöl: *Wango* (Syllart import '88). The talking drummer dominates three other percussionists on Maal's attempt to forge forward-looking pop from the rhythms of Senegal's Tukulor minority. Tricky, sometimes busy, with Maal's tenor cutting confidently through the crowd, it's closer to rock than soukous—funky sax here, lead guitar there, horn charts everywhere. It's also very much itself. Which gives you some idea of where one tradition-conscious African thinks the future must lie. **B+**

Baaba Maal and Mansour Seck: *Djam Leelii* (Mango '89). The most compelling and beautiful of West Africa's ever-increasing stock of folkloric preservations is a 1984 collaboration between two Tukulors, an ex-law student and a blind griot. Brit reviews suggest a cult record on the order of *Mystère des Voix Bulgares*: "timeless, resilient and dignified," "mesmeric, stately and gently stirring," "gentle, cyclical," "transfix and hypnotise," and oh yes, "on permanent repeat." For postindustrialized listeners, the interplay of recurring guitar patterns and penetrating Afro-Islamic voices adds up to background music with soul, nearly an hour of it on CD—in a quiet mood, we can still the world's sorrow by immersing in it. There's no point denying that it's valid as such. But my pleasure is dimmed slightly by the knowledge that the title track, for instance, is about young Tukulors forced by colonial borders and encroaching drought to seek work far from the roots the music celebrates. Seems a tad exploitative to bend such specifics to my needs. At the very least I'd welcome a trot. **A−**

Lonnie Mack: *Strike Like Lightning* (Alligator '85). Never much shook by the wham of that Memphis man, I was surprised as hell when this started motorvating me around the living room. Were those overdubs, or had he found himself a young hotshot? Turns out every 'bout-a-mover on the thing features coproducer Stevie Ray Vaughan, who in the famous Derek Effect benefits from Mack's company. What's more, every non-Vaughan cut benefits from Vaughan's proximity. **B+**

Madhouse: *8* (Paisley Park '87). This isn't "fusion jazz"—it's both more and less, which with "fusion jazz" are both good things. In the tradition of Rogers Nelson Dance Music Inc., it not only digs into rhythms jazzbos would dub mechanical, it also makes up new ones—while permitting the drums what sound like snatches of improvisation. Augmented by snatches of eavesdropped dialogue and one faked orgasm, the rhythms impose an ironic distance designed to discourage us from taking the assorted mood-to-avant clichés up top too seriously. And clichés they remain. **B**

Madness: *One Step Beyond* (Sire '80). We have entered the era of the white drummer—suddenly every young rock and roll band that touches vinyl can generate a moderately exciting pulse. Of course, Madness's pulse is exotic as well, and if at first I compared them to the Kingsmen, seeking fame and fortune by adding local color stories from the Portland bars to their repertoire of borrowed licks and melodies, that was mostly because it wasn't rock and roll enough. But after I heard more ska, lots more, the exoticism faded, and not just from exposure—I realized that a big problem with Afro-polka was that it didn't sound hip enough, and resisted. Anyway, Madness do it more rock and roll than anybody. Homy and bumptious, they're more purely fun than the most giddily self-conscious power pop. Original grade: B. **B+**

Madness: *Absolutely* (Sire '80). Just like the Specials and the Selecter, they have second album problems, with the cockneys soft-pedaling the same subject that confounds the two-toners: "Embarrassment," which saxophonist Lee Thompson says was inspired by his sister's mixed-race pregnancy, sounds like it's about an arrest, or the wrong haircut. And though close attention reveals the same class contretemps and irrational fears that haunt Jerry Dammers, no American will suss these songs unaided. This may be localism and it may be songcraft, but it's probably both. **B−**

Madness: *Complete Madness* (Stiff import '82). These Anglo lads have failed to click Stateside because they offer nothing to snobs and because they're so Anglo they only connect when they hit a song on the nose. Though I doubt they'll ever approach the jaunty excitement of their debut again, the hits here compiled come as close as an open-minded American could ask to solving the second problem. Their compassion and common sense are as jolly and traditional and working-class as their ska, which edges ever closer to polka and music hall. And jolly though they may be, they see a lot of pain. Original grade: B plus. **A−**

Madonna: *Madonna* (Sire '83). In case you bought the con, disco never died—just reverted to the crazies who thought it was worth living for. This shamelessly ersatz blonde is one of them, and with the craftily orchestrated help of a fine selection of producers, remixers, and DJs, she's come up with a shamelessly ersatz sound that's tighter than her tummy—essence of electro, the D in DOR. At first I thought the electroporn twelve-inch that pairs "Burning Up" with "Physical Attraction" was the way to go, but that was before she'd parlayed the don't-let-me-down vagueness of "Borderline" into a video about interracial love (sex, I mean) and a sneaky pop hook simultaneously. At one stiff per four-song side, smarter than Elvis Costello. Original grade: B. **A−**

Madonna: *Like a Virgin* (Sire '84). If a woman wants to sell herself as a sex fantasy I'll take a free ride—as long as the fantasy of it remains out front, so I don't start confusing image with everyday life. But already she's so sure of herself she's asking men and women both to get the hots for the calculating bitch who sells the fantasy even while she bids for the sincerity market where long-term superstars ply their trade. And to make the music less mechanical (just like Bowie, right?), she's hired Nile Rodgers, who I won't blame for making it less catchy. Original grade: C plus. **B**

Madonna: *True Blue* (Sire '86). Critics flock to her uneven product the way liberal arts magnas flock to investment banking—so desperate are they to connect to a zeitgeist that has nothing to do with them that they decide a little glamour and the right numbers add up to meaningful work, or at least "fun." I'm not saying her flair is pleasureless—the generosity she demands in the inexhaustible "Open Your Heart" is a two-way street and then some. But she doesn't speak for the ordinary teenaged stiff any more than Reagan speaks for union members (that's called "selling to," folks). And while the antiabortion content of "Papa Don't Preach" isn't unequivocal, and wouldn't make the song bad by definition if it were, the ambiguity is a copout rather than an open door (or heart), which *is* bad. In a time of collective self-deception, we don't need another snow job. Original grade: B minus. **B**

Madonna: *You Can Dance* (Sire '87). Only two of the seven songs on her best LP haven't surfaced on an earlier album, but it's no best-of, and not just because she's saving her radio hits for yet another compilation. The effects, repeats, breaks, and segues added by a star crew of remixers headed by Jellybean Benitez and Shep Pettibone amount to new music—this time the songs don't surface, they reach out and grab you. Reminding us that her first and probably truest calling was disco dolly—before she stormed MTV, she had an audience that loved the way she *sounded.* **A—**

Madonna: *Like a Prayer* (Sire '89). Three times I've mistaken her polymorphic promo and gross ambition for standard-issue lowest-common-denominator pandering, and three times her audience has disabused me in the months and years that followed. But though I swear I won't get fooled again, it's hard to hear an icon in the privacy of your own home, especially if you don't believe in her, and I won't sink that low or fly that high—I can't. So say the kiddie psychedelia is ick, the side-closers are over when they're over, and everything else sports some little touch to remember it by, Prince or musique concrete or broken quote from the Association. The cocksucker's prayer is anybody's classic, but coming from, I don't know, Suzanne Vega, the declaration of filial independence and the recommendation of romantic independence would be uncharacteristically catchy clichés. Coming from an icon they're challenging, thrilling—and they'll get more thrilling. **B+**

Magazine: *After the Fact* (I.R.S. '82). Everything you need and more from ex-Buzzcock Harold Devoto's pioneering foray into postpunk pretension. "Shot by Both Sides" was all too paranoid, "I Love You You Big Dummy" a prescient tribute, "Goldfinger" not as good as Blondie's or Peter Stampfel's but at least Howard recorded his. After that, you get the definitive art-twit. We hate you you little smarty. **C+**

Magic Slim and the Teardrops: *Raw Magic* (Alligator '82). It ain't magic be-cause it ain't raw enough—Slim conscientiously approximates the licks and grooves of his betters without adding a thing. In contrast, his Rooster EP is a lot cruder and considerably more exciting. Which is not to suggest he could keep it up for forty minutes anywhere but a South Side bar. **B—**

Mahlathini: *The Lion of Soweto* (Earthworks/Virgin '88). Recorded in the late '70s, with tough mgqashiyo mbaqanga out of favor among cultural as well as as-similationist blacks, this proves Mahlathini's staunch loyalty to the style he originated, his total lack of alternatives, or both. The notes say its "refusal to compromise" delivers "Mahlathini at his very peak"; I say that without Makgona Tsohle and the Mahotella Queens it sounds almost as generic as late Toots, even though (and probably because) the man carries the lion's share of the music himself. But I'll add that the glosses make me wish I could follow along more closely. A city "where women have got no mothers," a challenge to witch doctors, and a greeting to the spirit of his own youth all seem to transgress ever so slightly against the traditionalism that is mbaqanga's chief strength and most daunting limitation. Good. **B+**

Mahlathini and the Mahotella Queens: *Thokozile* (Virgin '88). The great groaner's 1983 reunion with his greatest backup groups—not just the Queens, returned to the life after a decade of domesticity, but Makgona Tsohle, featuring nonpareil guitarist Marks Mankwane and ubiquitous saxophonist-producer West Nkosi—culminates for the nonce in this 1986 showcase. Not counting "I Wanna Dance," exactly the sort of "disco" that's supposed to be against his principles, it's unexceptionably indestructible, bottomless baritone flexed inexorably against stout sopranos, with Mankwane's licks and Nkosi's pennywhistle darting like traffic up top. Professional dance music at its finest and roughest. **A—**

Mahlathini & Mahotella Queens: *Paris-Soweto* (Celluloid import '88). He no longer sings as goatishly or as much, which is a loss, but until someone compiles his best-of, this will be proof he deserves one. The songs are new, many with far from embarrassing English verses and hooks you swear you've heard before, but it's production values that make it his first export album to soar. Soukous audio gives the beat bite. Strong support—not just Makgona Tsohle and the Queens, but West Nkosi second-stringers Amaswazi Emvelo—helps carry that weight. And I bet they took the time to get it right, too—blessed by the relief of a European tour, they waited till the spirit was more than willing. Original grade: A minus. [Later available as Polydor cassette/CD.]   **A**

Mahotella Queens: *Izibani Zomgqashiyo* (Shanachie '86). Associated in an earlier incarnation with Mahlathini, a woman-group trademark gets the billing on this 1977 album, but various kings get the good parts, groaning or just singing lead calls or embellished responses on every one of these reported hits. This is mbaqanga at its catchiest. The structures are varied just enough to keep you on your toes, and the beat is indomitably alive.   **A—**

Miriam Makeba: *Sangoma* (Warner Bros. '88). It's disorienting at first to hear women singing what sounds like mbube, and though the weave would be richer (and more competitive) if most of them weren't this fifty-five-year-old matriarch, whose still-powerful voice has definitely thickened, the disorientation is salutary—South African pop is very male. Half the tunes are gorgeous and all of them are traditional, drawn from a cross-section of tribal cultures dominated by Makeba's clicking Xhosa. But they're not recreated, which usually means embalmed at best—they're interpreted for the studio, which permits Makeba her overdubs and enables Russ Titelman to lock in the spare accompaniment. There's even a synthesizer, and damned if I can tell exactly where.   **A—**
Miriam Makeba: *Welela* (Mercury '89). Too bad for Americans that this smart singer-songwriter collection—the voice sure and soulful without bearing down on the dignity, every tune greeting you like an old friend as its arrangement kicks in—is mostly in Xhosa. Also too bad that the

songs in English are nothing special—makes you wonder whether the rest are as smart as they sound.   **B+**

Malopoets: *Malopoets* (EMI America '85). Urban music from South Africa, with tunes and beat compact enough to squeeze into an American time slot, and what could be bad? Well, though their corn quota's a lot lower than Juluka's, we have heard guttier mbaqanga—on Rough Trade's *Soweto,* Earthworks's *Zulu Jive.* Can't help wondering whether impresario Martin Meissonnier doesn't consider the mysterioso aura generated so inevitably by his aristocratic Nigerian friends essential to every Afro-American connection.   **B+**

Cheb Mami: *Prince of Rai* (Shanachie '89). 'Tis said this tux-clad pretender has a sweeter voice than the goat-king Khaled, but is a green olive sweeter than a lamb chop? He's just higher, more adenoidal, more adolescent. Recorded recently enough to get the groove-bending bass and violin right, this is less monotonous than the competition. Standout cut features a synthesizer echoing the melody line in tribute to "the style 'L'Oranais,' a form that predates 'Rai.'" Nothing like a touch of tradition to add pop novelty to the world-beat norm.   **B**

Mandingo: *Watto Sitta* (Celluloid '84). On his recent *Hand Power* and his two Mandingo Griot Society albums, all cut for the folk specialists at Flying Fish, Foday Musa Suso went right past me. Was he playing his kora like a poser or a master, watering his tradition down or raising it to a new level? Because I was too ignorant to tell, I soon stopped caring. This Bill Laswell–produced dance record is audibly cruder—just gives the groove its head, with help from Herbie Hancock and even a drum machine as well as Suso's usual sidemen. And thus it makes the most convincing case this side of Sunny Adé for Afro-American fusion without apologies.   **B+**

Louise Mandrell & R. C. Bannon: *The Best of Louise Mandrell & R. C. Bannon* (RCA Victor EP '83). In "From 18 to 33," they spend fifteen years not getting divorced and live to enjoy it. The rest of their conjugal hogwash is distinguished primarily by two timeless puns—"Just Married" (from bumper sticker to state of being) and "Our Wedding Band" (barroom buddies)—and, can it be, a syndrum. **B**—

Sam Mangwana: *Aladji* (Syllart import '88). A notoriously footloose and political Angola-born Zairean, Mangwana shocked loyal followers of both Rochereau and Franco by working first with one titan and then the other before his African All-Stars brought kick-drum kick and Brownian nonstop to soukous. Long since single again, he here joins up with the hot Guinean-Parisian producer Ibrahim Sylla for an album said to stand with such landmarks as *Maria Tebbo, Canta Moçambique,* and the legendary Franco collaboration *Cooperation.* International technofuturist variety is the idea. But much as I enjoy the sustained midtempo lyricism of "Aladji" and the chunky mbaqanga subtext of "Soweto," only the jet-launched "Trans-Beros," which leads French Celluloid's *Zaire Choc* compilation as well, leaps my language barrier. [Later on Shanachie.] **B+**

Manhattans: *Greatest Hits* (Columbia '80). Dedicated journeymen, true sons of the street corner, they ended up outlasting even the Chi-Lites, making their mark and their living adding greaseless Barry White moves to old-fashioned slow stuff, and they deserved the fluke crossover "Shining Star," which made this album possible. It's baited and/or larded with two "hits" that were only projected, shall we say, when the album was released, and how about that—one's a memorable almost-uptempo that eventually went top-twenty r&b, and the other's inspired doowop manqué that sounds just fine leading side two even though it's out of time as far as the charts are concerned. My favorite tune here braved the year of our disco 1977: "We Never Danced to a Love Song." Bet you they did—even in 1977. Original grade: B plus. **A—**

Karen Mantler: *My Cat Arnold* (Xtrawatt '89). You'd best believe her mom's her best friend—her bangs, her pout, and her drily comic, jazz-informed tone all owe Carla Bley. But where Carla's a jazz composer with pop instincts, Karen's vice versa and sui generis enough, her personal unconfessions, educated chords, and meaty obbligatos a relief from standard singer-songwriterese. And where the competition oozes feeling, Karen's weakness is detachment—she seems settled into her existential anxiety. Male lead: Eric Mingus. **B+**

Mantronix: *Music Madness* (Sleeping Bag '86). The first rap act since Flash to be named after its DJ will make a believer out of you maybe half the time—Mantronik's beats have that much groove, variety, and (damn right) human touch. "Listen to the Bass of Get Stupid Fresh Part II," which features a harmonica, is a minimalist tour de force. M. C. Tee, poor soul, needs boasting lessons. **B—**

Thomas Mapfumo: *Ndangariro* (Carthage '84). No crib sheets accompany these six circa-1983 tracks, but I gather they're less propagandistic than the wartime output of this rock-influenced Zimbabwean singer turned Mugabe partisan, which given his main man's Shona chauvinism is probably a good thing. What I'm sure is that they generate a ferocious groove—the rhythm guitar attack of Mapfumo's Blacks Unlimited band never slacks off, maintaining the indomitable uprush of great African pop well past its usual fading point. You think music "transcends" politics? Then get this sucker. **A**

Thomas Mapfumo: *The Chimurenga Singles 1976–1980* (Meadowlark '86). If you want to know what revolutionary music might sound like, put aside the translations and just listen. Sounds like regular music, doesn't it? In plain English, Mapfumo's expressive and rhythmic authority are all the meaning you need. And the translations from the Shona suggest other virtues. He has sufficient respect for his listeners' intelligence (and his own life, though he was jailed for a while anyway) to couch his messages in innuendo. And unlike so many African pop stars, he's not afraid to take on traditional wisdom when traditional wisdom is impeding history. **A—**

Thomas Mapfumo: *Corruption* (Mango '89). Though there's nothing here as compelling as the Bristol-stomping "All my life" wail of "Hupenyu Wangu," this is looser and more indigenous than such renowned mid-'80s albums by the father of Zimbabwean pop as *Chimurenaga for Justice*. Never have his guitars sounded more like mbiras; never have his rhythms better evoked their own intricate selves. The vocals are also relaxed, giving off an aura of ruminative wisdom that may even have some truth to it. What can it be like to sing the poor against the rich in the language of your tribally divided country's ruling culture? Helps that, on a global scale, Shona is still a have-not tongue. **A—**

Teena Marie: *Lady T* (Gordy '80). This young white hope isn't breaking "r&b" because she sounds so "black"—she's not a whole heck of a lot funkier than the Doobie Brothers. She's breaking r&b because that's what Motown knows how to do. The hit, "Behind the Groove," is funky enough (the Doobies would give up golf for it), but then again, the more typical "You're All the Boogie I Need" is boogie enough. On the fast ones she sounds like Suzi Quatro blessed with a boyfriend smart enough to take it slow. On the slow ones she sounds dumb. **B**

Teena Marie: *Irons in the Fire* (Gordy '80). The self-production sounds more like license than liberation to me—she was better off with Richard Rudolph telling her what not to do. Maybe she could sing the telephone book and make me like it, but compared to the telephone book, "You make love like springtime and I can't control my passion / You make love like springtime even when love's not in fashion" lacks serendipity—especially after five minutes, with seasonal changes for variety and a jazzy 3:20 reprise for excess measure. **C+**

Teena Marie: *It Must Be Magic* (Gordy '81). I have my usual slow-fast problems with this pheenom, and I admit that all four (out of nine) slow ones give her overripeness time to turn. But no matter how rotten you think the liner poem is (and cf.

Bob Dylan, etc.), you gotta dig that flowers-and-butterflies dress. It's her thing, you know? The fast ones are colorful and juicy, too—squooshy with funk slides and compulsive puns, so unguarded in their emotionality you'd fear for her sanity if she weren't so tough. And on one of the slow ones she quotes that liner poem and makes you like it. **A—**

Teena Marie: *Starchild* (Epic '84). Ballads aren't Teena's problem—self-expression is. Marvin and Aretha are so abundantly endowed they can afford to meander occasionally, but neither would dare stretch "Out on a Limb" to 6:38. Better Teena should make like Maya Angelou and design her slow ones for the page. On the other hand, Teena's fast ones need no apology, which she may finally have learned doesn't mean they need no hooks. And when she's riding a hit she can take Marvin and Aretha to the bank. **B**

Bob Marley & the Wailers: *Uprising* (Island '80). With Tosh and Bunny departed, he rose to power as a bandleader rather than a songster, writing well enough while he mastered groove and sound and interplay. Except for "Jamming," a title that sums up the period perfectly, nothing since his solo-with-band debut *Natty Dread* has had the instant-classic immediacy of two very different offerings here: the dancy pop shot "Could You Be Loved" and the spirit anthem "Redemption Song." "Real Situation" ("It seems like total destruction / The only solution") and "We and Dem" (need dey say more?) are apocalyptic enough to scare the bejezus out of Babylonian well-wishers, "Coming in From the Cold" and "Forever Loving Jah" mellow enough to hold out hope. Pray for him. Pray for all of us. **A—**

Bob Marley: *Chances Are* (Cotillion '81). Compiled from what executive producer Danny Sims claims are unreleased 1968–1972 tracks and Sims's adversaries claim are overdubbed 1968–1972 demos, this is grave-robbing either way. Neither songs nor singing are what you'd call exquisite, and while the production shares certain of its awkwardnesses with the Marley-penned reggae that Sims's old partner Johnny Nash laid down after "I Can See

Clearly Now," it's busier and rougher—busier and rougher than pre-*Catch a Fire* Wailers, too. Musically, there's often not much difference between unreleased tracks and overdubbed demos.   **C**

Bob Marley & the Wailers: *Confrontation* (Island '83). There are no major songs among these lovingly selected outtakes, and on side two the material drags as low as the forced, synth-drenched "I Know." But even that one has a bridge typical of the songcraft that set Marley apart from his brethren, and on every track his vivacious attention to detail jumps out when you listen up. Inspirational Verse: "Oh Lord, give me a session not another version."   **B+**

Bob Marley and the Wailers: *Legend* (Island '84). This painstaking package captures everything that made Marley an international hero—his mystical militance, his sex appeal, his lithe, transported singing and sharp, surprising rhythms. And oh yes, his popcraft, which places him in the pantheon between James Brown and Stevie Wonder. Though he had a genius for fashioning uncommon little themes out of everyday chords, he was no tunesmith—"No Woman No Cry" and "Redemption Song" could be said to have full-fledged melody lines, but from "Is This Love" to "Jamming" most of these gems are hooky chants. Which given his sharp, surprising rhythms only makes them catchier—play either seven-cut side twice before bedtime and you won't know where to start humming next morning.   **A**

Rita Marley: *Who Feels It Knows It* (Shanachie '82). The first analogy is Alice Coltrane, who also trivializes a faith her husband brought miraculously and paradoxically alive with simple-minded music, but though it's just as well Rita doesn't play the harp, Merry Clayton and Patti Austin are more to the point: beware of backup singers' solo albums, no matter how surefire the single or committed the session men.   **C+**

Ziggy Marley and the Melody Makers: *Conscious Party* (Virgin '88). Neither his arty producers nor his Ethiopian band force the kind of cheer that wimped out his earlier crossovers, and his sharp, gritty singing replicates his old man's lower half even if the spiritual-romantic flights are beyond him. He's gotten less platitudinous, too, though as a prophet's scion he never invests Rasta doctrine with the authority of ideas struggled for—a black Jamaican cosmopolitan enough to voice sympathy for a "white guy in love with black beauty" sounds as priggish as any other puritan when he goes on about alcohol and processed foods.   **B+**

Ziggy Marley and the Melody Makers: *"Time Has Come . . .": The Best of Ziggy Marley and the Melody Makers* (EMI-Manhattan '88). First time around, I was willing to give this stuff a break—might connect once we heard what he really had to say, and keep your fingers crossed. Now that we've heard what he really has to say, I'm filing it away as juvenilia.   **C+**

Ziggy Marley and the Melody Makers: *Bright Day* (Virgin '89). He's a confident international entertainer where his dad was a driven third-world artist, which is a loss, but disgruntled accusations that he's betraying his heritage, his confreres, and the great reggae diaspora would disappear if he could take his songs where he wants them to go. Until that if-ever, the synthesis will be more impressive both macro (reggae-rock headed Afrofunk) and micro (this guitar break, that piano comp) than in the middle distance where life is lived and music heard.   **B**

Marley Marl: *In Control, Volume 1* (Cold Chillin' '88). Best sample: the horny blast that introduced Grandmaster Flash on "Freedom" and honors him on M.C. Shan's show rip of the same name. Lean JBeats, nasty scratches, and stolen dialogue keep the likes of Craig G. and Heavy D. moving—who knows, maybe someday they'll outdo themselves too. But like any ace producer, Marl is no better than his talent—certainly no better than Master Ace, who stands out from the crowd on the party-starting "Simon Says" (not a 1910 Fruitgum tribute) and speed-rapped "Keep Your Eye on the Prize" (and you were too cool for Channel 13). N.b.: Roxanne Shanté's "Wack Itt" is her fourth straight great one. Where the hell's her album?   **B+**

Maroon: *The Funky Record* (Arb Recordings '88). College wiseasses is all they are, biting the Beasties as if they'd made the shit up, stealing hooks from operas and disco records I never even heard of (or heard, anyway). Their gimmick is that they're not stupid (or stoopid, whatever)—mention Icarus, dis guys who don't know their mikes from their dicks ("should be castrated," very funny). Also dis Reagan and Koch, for that "political" touch. Pure opportunism. Must admit I get off on their skinny little beats, though. Beats count for a lot with this shit.   **A—**

Mars: *The Mars EP* (Infidelity EP '80). Major-label flunky that he was, Eno sold them out—one of their *No New York* tunes could be "I Wanna Be Your Dog" told by an imbecile, signifying nothing. Arto Lindsay is more steadfast—at this Christmas 1978 session he reveals his eternal CBGB billmates as the skronk nightmare of DNA's dreams. The voices are mixed-back exclamations and yowls. The guitars are all sludge, bang, and buzz—no chords, no timing, no articulation, maybe an upsurge occasionally. The drummer's job is to destroy any rudiment of a beat. Noise won't get much purer than this—I don't think.   **C+**

Wynton Marsalis: *J Mood* (Columbia '86). As the first young jazz musician ever to enjoy true major-label promotion, Marsalis is trapped into selling an image whether he likes it (or admits it) or not. On the one hand, he inevitably attracts admirers who respond not to the substance he hawks so assiduously but to the idea of it, which makes me wonder whether they really thrill to the shadings and dynamics that up till now have constituted his genius. And on the other hand, those of us who can't stand his expensive tailoring and neoconservative pronunciamentos are tempted to dismiss the pleasures they insure. Listen hard enough and pleasures reveal themselves in profusion, but despite what Marsalis believes even their profusion isn't quite reason enough to bother,

because in his wrongheaded determination to adjure the trendy and the obvious, he never lets loose. Most of us would say that inventing meaning while letting loose is the essence and promise of jazz. Neoconservatives wouldn't—maybe because they're not up to it.   **B+**

Martha and the Muffins: *Metro Music* (Virgin '80). The subhook on "Echo Beach," the club hit that brought this Canadian skinny-tie music to our attention, is perfect: "My job is very boring I'm an office clerk." The worst bore in the world wouldn't say "office" in that sentence; it's there to scan. Yet there's something endearingly gawky in the obviousness of the device. See also this confessional: "I wish that I could be decisive / Then I'd understand where life is going for me."   **B—**

Moon Martin: *Street Fever* (Capitol '80). Nick Lowe graduated from Brinsley Schwarz; Moon graduated from Southwind. As an authentic Texahoma native, he does up his hooks neorockabilly style, affecting a country-punk toughness that comes complete with the formal distance that's caught on in France and other distant places. He is to Nick Lowe as Southwind was to Brinsley Schwarz. There is no substance to reports that he'll join Jules Shear in a cult supergroup called Pop Pile.   **B—**

Moon Martin: *Mystery Ticket* (Capitol '82). Martin seems intent on fulfilling his formal promise: the hooks keep getting bigger and the beat keeps getting edgier. In fact, for a thirtyish wimp who frequently threatens to murder his girlfriend, he's quite an attractive fellow.   **B—**

Hugh Masekela: *Techno Bush* (Jive Afrika '84). Like Malcolm McLaren with a birthright, Masekela has given up the dull demijazz of his U.S. period and returned to Africa, where he cops riffs and rhythms, calypso raps and organ jive and of course trumpet parts, as cannily as the cleverest imperialist, then serves them up in a highly palatable English-language fusion. Beyond a few leftover dull spots my only cavil is the lyric of the demihit, "Don't Go Lose It Baby"—shouldn't crow so about being a "winner" in a country where the deck is stacked like it is in Botswana. Original grade: A minus. **B+**

Hugh Masekela with Kalahari: *Tomorrow* (Warner Bros. '87). The words document his losses, his struggle, his oppression as a South African exile. I learned from them, and that's high praise for any lyric. The music documents the life he wants to lead, which is as corny as any other dance-fusion jazz played by musicians overimpressed with their own chops. He has a right to that life, obviously. Just as obviously, I have a right to pursue my own life elsewhere.   **B−**

Massacre: *Killing Time* (Celluloid/OAO '83). This Fred Frith thang is given to the same deconstructive clichés that undermine so many of the others. But the no-bullshit powerdrive of Bill Laswell and Fred Maher provokes some of his sharpest compositions since Henry Cow—and some fairly sharp improvisations, too. It pains me to report, however, that the blistering, acerbic pace I've heard them build live never materializes.   **B+**

Material: *Temporary Music* (Celluloid import '81). The two EPs here repackaged document not the no-wave-meets-newthing experimenters but the art-rock band that likes its minimalism funky. At Material's best gigs Sonny Sharrock's aural grimaces challenge the impassively abrasive rhythm section; here Cliff Cultreri marches to bassist and drummer while Michael Beinhorn flatters Philip Glass. Still, both guys could choose stupider models—probably will someday. And there's something winningly perverse about ambient music that means to destroy its enemies.   **B+**

Material: *Memory Serves* (Elektra/Musician '82). Although his angular, slightly hyped-up groove on the instrument is distinctly his own, Bill Laswell is a typical bass player in the most important way: what he expresses depends on who he works with. Beyond drummer Fred Maher and synth threat Michael Beinhorn, his collaborators here include Fred Frith, Sonny Sharrock, and Henry Threadgill augmented by lesser avant-jazzmen. All

obviously love the harsh, expansive intelligence of preschlock jazz- (and art-) rock. But their great ideas are rewarding rather than tempting, and they're not exalting either. Nor are they supposed to be.   **B+**

Material: *One Down* (Elektra '82). Laswell, Beinhorn & Co. have obviously been listening to the radio instead of complaining about the end of the world. The result is a protean disco album that sounds like real New York rock and roll. Chic guitar and planet-rocking vocoders are only the beginning—several of these experiments seem designed to cross over right behind "Eye of the Tiger," and never have electronically processed rhythms throbbed with such life. All that's missing is a deeper feeling for singers and songs, an old problem that the finest and most atypical track suggests is remediable—Soft Machinist Hugh Hopper's "Memories," which guest stars Whitney Houston and Archie Shepp, transfers into one of the most gorgeous ballads you've ever heard.   **A−**

Curtis Mayfield: *Love Is the Place* (Boardwalk '82). With help from Dino Fekaris, Mayfield's best album in years includes his first hit in years, but neither has created much stir, which is fair enough— the single is catchy and nothing more, the album honest and nothing more. Except, except. "Just Ease My Mind," a Mayfield-composed ballad, is a gentle plea for succor so purely country I think I've happened upon some disciple of Stoney Edwards or Jesse Winchester every time it catches me unawares. It shouldn't be lost.   **B**

Prince Nico Mbarga and Rocafil Jazz: *Sweet Mother* (Rounder '81). Wish the praises of God etc. weren't half in English, though I suppose the Prince's upwardly mobile platitudes go with his need to venture beyond his tribal tongue. Anyway, from this Nigerian popster the blandest platitude sounds blissfully gentle and upward mobility has a good sense of rhythm.   **B+**

Mbube!: Zulu Men's Singing Competition (Rounder '87). In which the judge at a Durban singing meet whittles nineteen choirs and six hours down to nine choirs and forty-eight minutes. It's the kind of record that appeals to the converted; I wouldn't have paid so much attention to a similar document from Bahia or the Caucasus or a Pentecostal church in North Carolina. But I swear the notes and song summaries are lively enough to hook the curious, and anybody whose knowledge of Zulu chorale stops at Ladysmith should check out these hymnful shouts, stomps, whistles, yodels, and ululations. The deep, muscular harmonies of the Easy Walkers get my blue ribbon, but every rock-and-roller ought to hear the Greytown Evening Birds, who sing about their hunger like the Beach Boys.   **B+**

Paul McCartney: *McCartney II* (Columbia '80). Paulie's 1970 DIY sounded homemade—its unfinished musings intimated an appealingly modest freedom. This one was recorded on a sixteen-track with an engineer in attendance. The instrumentals are doodles, the songs demos by a man who scores the occasional hit only to prove he's a genius. Which he isn't.   **C**

Paul McCartney: *Tug of War* (Columbia '82). Most rock-and-rollers look like simps or cynics by the time they hit thirty-five. Others retain the irrepressible exuberance of a Stevie Wonder, or grasp it again in magic moments the way Carl Perkins does on this album's most affecting cut. A few rare ones age gracefully into fresh-eyed wisdom, like Neil Young and John Lennon. But no matter how serious and sensible he gets, McCartney's perpetual boyishness conveys the perpetual callowness of a musical Troy Donahue. I don't think this is intentional—in his personal life he seems at least as adult as anyone I've named, and he's put his hard-earned craft to mature use on this LP. But it might almost be dumb love songs. Original grade: B plus.   **B**

Paul McCartney: *Pipes of Peace* (Columbia '83). I've finally figured out what people mean when they call Paulie pop—they mean he's not rock. But to me pop implies a strict sense of received form whether crafted by the dB's or Billy Joel. McCartney's in his own world entirely, which is the charm of his music. And of

course, a reliance on charm has always been his weakness. This is quite pleasant except when Britain's number-one earner preaches against violence as if self-interest wasn't an issue, which is also the only time it comes into firm contact with the great outside.   **B−**

Paul McCartney: *All the Best* (Capitol '87). Of the seven cuts this doesn't share with 1978's twelve-cut, fifty-four-minute *Wings Greatest,* only the lost 1972 B side "C Moon" and the 1983 M. Jackson duet "Say Say Say" (in its flimsy non-Jellybean mix) are worth anyone's trouble. And "My Love" is among the survivors. Somebody call . . . the Better Business Bureau?   **C+**

Mary McCaslin: *A Life and Time* (Flying Fish '81). When I fail for a fourth time to listen to a title song all the way through, I stop blaming myself and start blaming the singer-songwriter. Whose best original here, a passionately reserved exploration of the limits of gotta-move-on-babe, was written in 1969, and whose best cover, a passionately tender lesson in the limits of I-can't-trust-babe, copies an arrangement by the Dirt Band. Side-openers both, which is why I bothered with the title song.   **B−**

Dick McCormack: *Live at the 1983 Vermont Midsummer Festival* (Rooster cassette '83). His most recent offering doesn't show off this Vermonter's durable songwriting (and collecting) like 1981's acerbically folkloric *"Who Ever Said It Would Be Easy?"* disc—something in a live crowd must bring out the easy wisdom in him. But he almost compensates with jokes, one of which is a drawn-out tale of Jack & Allen & Neil & Clams that's irresistible the first three or four times through and another of which will give you an idea of his style of state chauvinism: "How many Vermonters does it take to screw in a lightbulb? It takes five—one to screw it in and four to complain how much better the old one was."   **B**

Mel McDaniel With Oklahoma Wind: *Mel McDaniel With Oklahoma Wind* (Capitol '84). A rugged old pro who's hewed a path between outlaw grease and countrypolitan silicone, McDaniel here enters a Nashville studio with his road band, a mild act of defiance that produces an album sensible folks can listen to clean through without Bromo-Seltzer—though the overly tough-minded may want to keep a Tum or two at hand.   **B**

Mel McDaniel: *Just Can't Sit Down Music* (Capitol '87). With his best material—not commercially but critically, a concept that doesn't cut much vinyl down in Nashville—slotted three and four on each side, McDaniel remains a notably decent artist caught between his druthers and his a&r man. So be glad the album's gem, "Stand on It" (composer credit: "B. Springsteen"), did eventually make some noise as a single—albeit not enough to qualify for the best-of that followed it into the racks.   **B**

Mel McDaniel: *Greatest Hits* (Capitol '87). McDaniel's marginal distinction doesn't depend on the marginal cleverness of songsmiths, but if his hits don't equal his high points, they're not his low points either. "Hello Daddy, Good Morning Darling" is a heart-tugger that would work for anybody from Ronnie Milsap to George Strait, but his commercial specialty is the mild raunch of "Louisiana Saturday Night," "Baby's Got Her Blue Jeans On," and "Stand Up," where he invites all the mild raunch fans to testify and tempts nonbelievers to forgive "Do You Want To Say Goodbye."   **B+**

Michael McDonald: *If That's What It Takes* (Warner Bros. '82). On his solo bid the El Lay soul man sounds like he should leave his therapist, not his group. He's feeling so hard the sense of strain is constant, as if ordinary romantic travails are driving him to the edge of existential patience. Yet despite it all not one of these commonsense homilies has the common wisdom of "This Is It" or "What a Fool Believes"—there's a smugness about his determination to go with the serially monogamous flow. And I sure hope the next single is "Love Lies" or "No Such Luck"—I'm sick of the rest already.   **C+**

Reba McEntire: *My Kind of Country* (MCA '84). Though it enabled her to waltz off with the Country Music Association's artist-of-the-year award in her gender division, this longtime up-and-comer's second MCA album may pass outsiders right by. Its vaunted neotraditionalism is long on detail work—a thick hillbilly accent so soft-spoken it never intrudes, songcraft so steeped in the canon it splits the difference between evocation (side one) and cliché (side two). Those who miss the good old days are advised to think of her as Tammy Wynette with a natural and take what breakthrough they can get. Time: 25:37.   **B+**

Reba McEntire: *The Best of Reba McEntire* (Mercury '85). I'll take this benighted distillation over what we've heard of her kind of country, mostly because it's a distillation (from 1980–1983, when she was on her way to neoclassicism). Donna Fargo at her cheeriest couldn't get away with the keynoting "(You Lift Me) Up to Heaven," the Platters cover would be useless even without the strings, and "My Turn" is sexy-gal at its most repulsive ("You have reached the woman in me through the man in you," she notes as she offers the guy a blow job). But songs like "I Don't Think Love Ought To Be That Way," "I'm Not That Lonely Yet," and "You're the First Time I've Ever Thought About Leaving" group around the same sexually self-possessed persona and would stand out on any album she has in mind. Jerry Kennedy rarely overdoes the schlock. And though the voice has less character, it's also less sedate. Time: 27:53.   **B+**

Reba McEntire: *Have I Got a Deal for You* (MCA '85). Finally her own award-winning, best-selling woman, she assumes coproducer status and sheds Harold Shedd, whom some would say got her this far. And indeed, with a little help from Jimmy Bowen she refines the formula—no backup choruses, no newfangled keyboards, no bedroom lyrics. She's a lot more her own woman than hot-to-trot centerfold candidates like Janie Frickie. But though occasionally her music defeats country's sex-role divisions—the self-composed I-never-actually-cheated song "Only in My Mind" is so proud and virtuous and deeply regretful it could give a fella bad dreams—she suggests that female country singers are going to have trouble rebelling neotraditionally. Especially with men providing the material.   **B**

Reba McEntire: *Whoever's in New England* (MCA '86). Winning though her directness may be, McEntire is neither as clear as George Strait nor as lavish as John Anderson. In fact, the basics she gets back to recall Rosanne Cash more than anyone else, and no matter how she tries, she just can't rock out (or sing) like Nashville's crossover queen. Most convincing are the jauntily defiant cheating-on song "Little Rock," where she plays a rich man's wife, and the dolefully forgiving cheated-on song "Whoever's in New England," where she plays a young executive's wife. Elsewhere she's mostly just direct.   **B**

Reba McEntire: *The Best of Reba McEntire* (MCA '87). How great you think she is depends on how great you think her voice is. I say that for all her reach and technique she's too contained and too generic; direct comparison with Wells or Cline or Lynn or Wynette or Parton leaves her in the dust. Which means that like other mortal country artists she's made for the best-of, where every song counts. This one marches them past chronologically, two by two from each of her first five MCA albums (omitting the current *Last One To Know*). Significantly, the only dud is the only violin showcase, from her label debut—pseudopurism does suit her. Also significantly, the greats are from albums two, three, and four, not five (or six). And the centerpiece is "Whoever's in New England," where pseudopurism lets on how far its thoughts sometimes stray from home.   **A—**

Bobby McFerrin: *The Voice* (Musician '84). He's an innovator, he's a virtuoso, he even has a sense of humor, but he's also a mite precious, not to say arty, and this unaccompanied scat demonstration encourages his formalistic proclivities. As with so many solo recitals, technical display is emphasized; fact is I've heard numerous saxophonists do more with "Donna Lee" and numerous drummers do more with "I Feel Good." One reason the voice is such a sublime instrument is that it can pronounce words, and give or take a catchphrase or two the only ones he bothers with here are his own lyrics for "I'm My Own Walkman." Wonder when some creative type is finally going to stick up for those of us who'd rather consume music than manufacture it.   **B—**

Bobby McFerrin: *Simple Pleasures* (EMI-Manhattan '88). No matter how much aid and comfort it gives the enemy, there's no point denying "Don't Worry, Be Happy" unless you're tin-eared enough to think it doesn't capture a feeling or deluded enough to think poor people never share it. Title tune's the real Republican lie—McFerrin's celebration of 6 A.M. wake-up neglects to mention that his morning is unencumbered by a j-o-b—and even that's probably a tragic consequence of some fundamental mindlessness. Passing as an Artist on skill and fluidity alone, he's a vocal Keith Jarrett come down with the cutes—or maybe a musical Marcel Marceau.   **B—**

MC 5:   *Babes in Arms* (ROIR cassette '83). Despite all the rare mixes and original versions adduced in the notes, the only great track totally unfamiliar to this proud (and lucky) owner of the 5's three albums is a cover of Them's "I Can Only Give You Everything." The rest of the obscure stuff merely augments a superbly paced compilation. The raw songcraft and new-thing chaos of Detroit's other great protopunk band were further ahead of their time than it seemed five years ago. And drummer Dennis Thompson was a motherfucker.   **A—**

Kate & Anna McGarrigle: *Love Over and Over* (Polydor '83). Having reclaimed their equilibrium and resigned themselves to making their own music in their own place, the sisters come up with the rockingest album of their reluctant career, with Andrew Cowan's guitar a pervasive presence and Mark Knopfler himself sitting in on one track. The effect is gratifyingly smart, tasty, and unforced, with every song perfectly articulated. But the equilibrium extends all too comfortably to the material itself—there's none of the wrenching luminosity of a "Mendocino" or a "Walking Song" or a "Bundle of Sorrow, Bundle of Joy." Which reminds us once again that careerism does have its artistic advantages.   **A—**

The McGuires: *Start Breathing* (Righteous '87). With hundreds of other bands working out imperceptible variations on songform, usually by admixing noise or roots or exoticism, the McGuires aim to do nothing new, and since they have the gift of song to begin with, that's a plus. Oh, they do call their friendly sound "barbecue-beat," but there's no petty territoriality here, no minute formalism expressing selves that are barely worth the trouble. Just middle-class rock-and-rollers voicing their middle-class disaffection with a measure of lyric grace. I'm fond of "T.V. Party" (they're not going), "Let You Down" (and apologize in advance), and "She's a Lawyer" ("Sorry, sister, she's not gay"). You may like the one about the prophet Elijah.   **B+**

M.C. Hammer: *Let's Get It Started* (Capitol '88). If EPMD's surprise rise was a revelation, the unheralded progress of this Bay Area rapper up the black album chart is a story in the trades. With his stolid boasts, heavy beats, and circumspect samples, he sounds like D.M.C. gone solo, but he's also got a local base, some new-jack steps, and a video. In short, he's a pro as in product—already.   **C+**

M C Lyte: *Lyte as a Rock* (First Priority Music '88). Unlike so many of her femme-metal counterparts, she knows how to talk tough without yielding to the stupid temptations of macho. But as nobody's girl, she spreads ten tracks among four producer-DJs, who chill too close to the max as she attempts to carry the music with her bare rap. Even their weirdest hooks are understated by half, and Lyte's quotes (not samples) from "I'm in the Mood for Love," "Big Girls Don't Cry," "I Am Woman," and "Hit the Road Jack" aren't loud enough to compensate. Minimal isn't the only way she can go, as Sinéad O'Connor

fans know. Are they in for an unpleasant surprise.   **B**

MC Lyte: *Eyes on This* (Atlantic/First Priority Music '89). No longer a minimalist, she layers samples ("Rockin' It"! Millie Jackson!) and backtalk like a pro, sometimes like an original—the rhythmic obscenities on the spectacularly unsisterly "Shut the Eff Up! (Hoe)" are mind-boggling. Her tales of the drug wars are tough and prowoman, and the narrative tone of "Cappucino"—part fable, part metaphor, part confessional revery, part dumb it-was-only-a-dream—is avant-garde. Elsewhere she's a pro.   **B+**

James McMurtry: *Too Long in the Wasteland* (Columbia '89). He's gonna be a prestige item, just you wait—quality singer-songwriter from the heartland-wasteland. He's been there, he's still there, has his own RFD box on the back cover lest you doubt his authenticity. Also an eye for detail, perhaps from his novelist dad, and John Mellencamp showing him around the studio. I enjoy his sketches, particularly their weary women. But like so many singer-songwriters and so many local-colorists, he tends to a soft fatalism, especially on big statements: the metametaphorical "Painting by Numbers," or "I'm Not From Here," which notes that we've been picking up and leaving "since the stone age." No way a simple quality singer-songwriter can change that, now is there?   **B+**

Christine McVie: *Christine McVie* (Warner Bros. '84). Both sides are unimpeachably sensible and unfailingly pleasant; except for the closer, each of the ten tunes paces proudly by in full confidence that it will set you humming. Yet as reported, the proceedings are a little, shall we say, somnolent, which I blame not just on a voice whose deep satisfactions are best appreciated in the company of brighter and flightier ones but on a drummer who isn't Mick and a bassist who isn't John.   **B+**

The Meadows: *The Meadows* (Radio '81). This vocal trio from Chattanooga was recorded by Brad Shapiro in Miami and Muscle Shoals for a Fort Lauderdale–based Atlantic subsidiary. Brother Wilson sings lead and writes most of the funky music (and lyrics). Brother Eugene keeps a low if handsome profile. Brother Wallace wears a shirt that says Las Vegas on it. Soul music lives.   **B+**

Meat Beat Manifesto: *Storm the Studio* (Wax Trax '89). Bill Burroughs having given the word, Brit art-schoolers shape two years of twelve-inches into four sides of industrial-strength samples and "annihilating rhythm." And though they do sometimes settle for electrodance, the laughs and abrasions keep on coming.   **B+**

Meat Puppets: *Meat Puppets* (SST EP '81). These Phoenix boys not only realize L.A. punk's no-wave proclivities in brief, doomy noise songs that sound like DNA meeting the Marx Brothers, they cover "Tumblin' Tumbleweeds." And include a dandy lyric sheet featuring lines like "You are like children in the marketplace / Shouting to your playmates" and "We get stones like it's going out of style." None of which they go so far as to pronounce over or under the hardcore roar. Original grade: B plus.   **B**

Meat Puppets: *Meat Puppets II* (SST '84). Alone with various strange gods (is there another kind?) in the wide open spaces of his psyche, Arizonan Curt Kirkwood has stumbled upon a calmly demented country music that does more to revitalize the dubious concept of "psychedelic" than California suburbia's whole silly infatuation with the late '60s. He conflates the amateur and the avant-garde with a homely appeal bicoastalists would give up their nonexistent roots for. Rarely if ever has incipient schizophrenia sounded like such a natural way to go.   **A—**

Meat Puppets: *Up on the Sun* (SST '85). Furious negativist then, goofy nature mystic now, Curt Kirkwood is the David Thomas of endearing sloppiness. The tunes unfold loosely and sweetly, with Curt's guitars not so much chiming as chattering in a nonchalantly unstylish take on neofolk lyricism. But the music's charms are a little too flaccid to hold up

the most unabashedly lysergic worldview yet to emerge from postpunk.   **B+**

Meat Puppets: *Out Our Way* (SST EP '86). In a time when EPs register microdistinctions among white bohemians, not to mention professionals, this is one piece of product that's more than a holding action in musical strength and commercial strategy. It's a departure, toward a less spacy, more bottomy hardcore-gone-folkloric. It covers "Good Golly Miss Molly" at a speed approximating that of the original—which was considered fast in its time, believe me.   **B+**

Meat Puppets: *Mirage* (SST '87). At their most unhinged these space potatoes always had the charm of true seekers. Who cared if they were soft in the head—their tentative lyricism conveyed the sense of endless discovery that's the great blessing of softheadedness. This time, they've found what they were looking for, and it's hard to believe it took them so long.   **C+**

Meat Puppets: *Huevos* (SST '87). The rebound from the almost meaningless *Mirage* is right there in the title. This one not only means "balls" in Spanish, which translates "punch" in the intractably sexist dialect of rock and roll. It also means "eggs"—in fact, it mainly means eggs. And while the lyrics do tend to glimmer away like heat rising off asphalt, they start from an everyday place anyone can see. Sometimes it's funny: "Whoa, crazy, got myself a job." Sometimes it's pissed: "You said you'd make it grow / You said you'd make it green." Sometimes it's cheerful: "I got a shirt that cost a dollar twenty-five / I know I'm the best-dressed man alive." And sometimes it's goddamn euphoric: "This is paradise."   **A—**

Meat Puppets: *Monsters* (SST '89). Supposedly a combination of their two 1988 albums (a mirage omelet, thanks a lot), this is really the guitar-god record Curt Kirkwood always had in him—on all but a couple of cuts the arena-rock bottom that's only an interview fantasy for those who haven't caught them on a ZZ Top night powers his chunky riffs and psychedelic axemanship. What'll keep them from turning into plutonium is the utterly unmacho vocals, brother harmonies making even "Party Till the World Obeys" and the one that begins "Tie me up/Get it right" seem like critiques of power, which is what they are—psychedelic in the nicest way yet again.   **A**—

The Meditations: *Greatest Hits* (Shanachie '84). Usually I have to let reggae albums grow on me, but the sweet tunes and sweeter harmonies on this devoted overview made themselves felt immediately. Problem is, they never reached any deeper—instead I began to notice the low homily level and nonexistent signature lead. How greatest?   **B**+

Medium Medium: *The Glitterhouse* (Cachalot '81). "Hungry So Angry" is so much their greatest moment—the dropdead riff that's their entree to the Funk Club—I'm tempted to recommend the EP, which offers two versions of the thing. But in the context "Hungry So Angry" sets up, the more abstract music they prefer comes across not only raw and spatial but also danceable, and you hardly notice their arty vocal dementia. Which isn't to say you shouldn't go for the EP. Original grade: B plus.   **B**

Megadeth: *So Far, So Good . . . So What!* (Capitol '87). Dave Mustaine is earnest about his rage—at nuclear holocaust and the PMRC and lying scumbags and his own self-destructive tendencies. He covers the Sex Pistols like a champ. He doesn't boast, he doesn't preen, he allows himself but a single "bitch" on an entire long-playing record (she sounds very irresponsible and probably deserves it). And thus the latest well-regarded metal band gains its modest portions of profit and respect. But where's the monster guitar? Where's the angel singing like a bat out of hell? Where's the big deal? Upped a notch for meaning well.   **B**—

The Mekons: *The Mekons* (Red Rhino import '80). Must be a confusing time in the old country, what with Eurodisco coming back postpunk and the no-wave imperative advancing on no future. Where the Gang of Four respond by constructing a herky-jerk funk from their own inexpertise, their Leeds comrades—who were on

that one last year already—yoke an amateur anarchism less obstreperous than Wire's or the Fall's to vaguely traditional songs almost domestic in their attention to modest detail. They also rewrite "Lipstick on Your Collar" I think it is. You figure it out.   **B**

Mekons: *The Mekons Story* (CNT import '82). Over sixty minutes of previously unreleased tunes or worktapes have been crammed onto twelve inches of vinyl by this since disbanded band or collective, so play it loud or it'll sound like a tree falling in the forest with no one there to hear. Which is actually the idea. As rock *épater les bourgeois* goes, it's humane, imaginative—none of the malignant contempt of *Metal Machine Music* or *Flowers of Romance*. A few of the tracks forge form from the refusal of technique, with the thirty-four-second hotel-room punk of "Letter's in the Post" and Mark White's mad-busker voice-and-footstomp revery "The Building" more convincing candidates than any of the rough postpunk or folk-rock or Anglodisco numbers. But unless you're heavily into the byways of anarchist negation, most of it demands more consideration than there's any reason to expect from the ordinary harassed citizen, social worker, journalist, or record executive.   **B**—

Mekons: *Fear and Whiskey* (Sin import '85). Just when I never wanted to hear a roots-rock record again, along come these British anarchists with a sort of concept album sort of about life during wartime. The Americans are clearing a sector down south, but that doesn't stop the good guys from playing their anarchic country-rock and doing their anarchic Morris stomp and fucking up their anarchic love lives and drinking to keep from shitting their pants and rolling down a highway that may finally be lost for real. Yes, amateurism is still a sentimental fallacy, and if you want to know why it's such a powerful one, listen up. Original grade: A.   **A**+

Mekons: *Crime and Punishment* (Sin import EP '86). Four stories that don't quite make sense about waking up with your friend's wife, going to hospital, failing, drinking. Actually the drinking one, a Merle Haggard song, makes sense on its own terms, but in the Mekons' world nothing makes sense, which in the least pessimistic construction is because all these songs are about drinking one way or another. In fact, all seem written from a permanent hangover. But it's fair to say that they've been driven to drink—by life, which is hard and then you die. Original grade: B plus.   **A—**

Mekons: *The Edge of the World* (Sin import '86). If the continuing existence of their music doesn't place these anti-American country-rockers squarely among the undefeated for you, the continuing eloquence of their lyrics ought to—whether it's Sally Timms trying to talk to the drunk she's stuck with or Jon Langford downing cat food because he doesn't feel human tonight, they haven't given up on saying their piece. Thing is, the listener has to concentrate to be sure, which despite the lyric sheet isn't so easy this time. That's the problem with making fatigue your great theme—it sounds tired awfully fast.   **A—**

Mekons: *Slightly South of the Border* (Sin import EP '86). Marking time and maybe taking a small, honorable profit in the bargain, they heat up the remixed title tune to accompany (surprise) a Gram Parsons cover and two originals: a typically realistic, typically depressive response to the miners' strike, and a typically commonplace, typically grim letter from a woman who should have blown the whistle on her dad.   **B+**

The Mekons: *Honky Tonkin'* (Twin/Tone '87). Nobody would take them for amateurs or anarchists on this evidence. Just a catchy, rocking Brit country band with more enthusiasm than skill in the vocal department and lyrics-included that don't seem to have much to do with honky-tonks—that tend overmuch to the metaphysical, metaphorical, and obscure for all their show of specificity. I await the next phase.   **B+**

Mekons: *New York* (ROIR cassette '87). Finally given their megashot at us "American vermin" by the giant Twin/Tone conglomerate, they labored harder than the huddled masses they champion and flubbed it like the born-to-losers they are. So this offhand hour of U.S. live from their self-employed days is doubly welcome. Interspersed with tour-bus patter, soused ad libs, and other memorabilia, its selected honky-tonk retatters the reputation of a band that's made something friendly of the slop aesthetic without being jerks or airheads about it. Dim ROIR sound adds to the aura by subtracting from same. **A—**

Mekons: *So Good It Hurts* (Twin/Tone '88). Reports that they've "gone reggae" are grossly exaggerated and no big deal—the Bellamy Brothers beat them to that crossover by a country mile, and the skank that kicks things off is as lovable as anything they've ever done (bumbling semipros they may be, but their drummer used to work for the Rumour). If only they were hip enough to cover "Old Hippie" (that's a Bellamys song, kids), all would be well. As it is they cover (some would claim redefine) "Heart of Stone" and write bookish lyrics I don't understand even when I've read the authors in question.   **B+**

The Mekons: *The Mekons Rock 'n' Roll* (A&M '89). If you love rock and roll (which is possible even if you slum the spelling with apostrophes), but don't think *Rock and Roll* (much less *Rock 'n' Roll*) a propitious title hook right now, you could love this album, which takes their love-hate relationship with America to the bank. Musically, it's rock and roll despite the fiddles sawing louder than ever, almost as Clashlike as the promo claims, with Steve Goulding bashing away louder than ever too. Lyrically, in great song after great song, rock and roll is devil's-breath perfume, capitalism's "favourite boy child," a commodity like sex, a log to throw on the fire, a "shining path back to reconquer Americay." Are they implicated? Of course. Do they love it? Yes and no.   **A**

Mekons: *Original Sin* (Twin/Tone CD '89). *Fear and Whiskey* was a triumph in search of a war, and even their fans lost the two EPs that followed in the shuffle. Minus a Merle Haggard cover and plus two other cuts, one of which stinks just in case you mistook them for great artists, all this product comes together on this remastered repackage, and it coheres wonderfully—the EPs resonate off an album that doesn't leave you hungering for something completely different when its thirty-five minutes are through. If you're among the millions who missed *Fear and Whiskey,* this is a golden opportunity. These guys know how to make the most of failure. That's the kind of anarchist revolutionaries I like.   **A**

John Cougar: *American Fool* (Riva '82). The breakthrough fluke of the year has it all over his predecessors in REO Speedwagon—Bob Seger, Cougar's current role model, has been dreaming of riffs with this much melodic crunch ever since *Night Moves,* and when I don't think about whys and wherefores they satisfy my mainstream cravings. But the guy is a phony on the face of it, and not in a fun way—anybody with the gall to tell teen America that once you pass sixteen "the thrill of living is gone" has been slogging toward stardom for so long he never noticed what happened to Shaun Cassidy.   **B**

John Cougar Mellencamp: *Uh-Huh* (Riva '83). The changed billing indicates John's eagerness to talk straight after years of filtering himself through an inconclusive image, and I wish every AOR hero put his triple platinum to such honest use. Only thing is, the depth of John's populist intentions far outstrips the depth of his populist perceptions—he was just as interesting telling little white lies.   **B**

John Cougar Mellencamp: *Scarecrow* (Riva '85). Having long wondered what gave this longtime Bowie stablemate the right to speak for the average guy, I've decided it's his talent, which is pretty damn average. That's okay, because the success ration here, a nice average fifty-fifty or so, just goes to show you what sincerity, hard work, and modest ambitions can do. Mellencamp has half outgrown the fatalism that always underlined the predictability of his Stonesish bandmates, who've gotten tougher with age, an encouraging sign in rich musicians. I wish I knew (I wish *he* knew) exactly what "Justice and Independence '85" is trying to say. But I'll take "You've Got To Stand for Something" at face value.   **B+**

John Cougar Mellencamp: *The Lonesome Jubilee* (Mercury '87). In which Mellencamp's confused conscience and self-serving defeatism become so single-minded they take on the force of truth. His protagonists don't expect all that much and get less, but they're not beautiful losers—they're too ordinary, too miserable. Riding a spare, tough groove I don't hear *Scarecrow* matching, they convince you (but not themselves) that they're the heroes America deserves.   **A—**

John Cougar Mellencamp: *Big Daddy* (Mercury '89). He's miserable because his half-earned success gets him more love than his hard-fought principles, because he still isn't sure what justice is, because his bones creak, because he's an American fool. He wrote the eleven originals sans band for a Woody Guthrie feel, as if structure were the secret, and as rendered by said band they sound so loose-limbed that at first you may blame yourself for not loving the shit out of them. But every one bogs down in his bitter pretensions, as Mellencamp must suspect. Why else would he sneak in the devastating unannounced cover (nonvinyl-only, principle fans) of the 1967 one-shot "Let It All Hang Out," where four loose-limbed fools who never heard of Woody Guthrie achieved the feel he's striving for without even trying—in hopes of becoming pop singers, yet. The loss of grace it signifies could make anybody miserable.   **B—**

Melody Makers: See Ziggy Marley and the Melody Makers

Men at Work: *Business as Usual* (Columbia '82). They call Australia Oz because it's about as exotic as Kansas upside down, and these five sturdy-sounding, fragile-down-under blokes make the most of it. Ten thousand miles from the heart of darkness they're free to project honest, ordinary, low-level Anglo-Saxon anxiety, with enough transpositions of key and meter to establish that they've thought about it some. Call the music auxiliary Police, with more players and fewer dynamics. The words aspire to a bland compassion that sings its origins in the vaguely rebellious "Be Good Johnny," about a schoolboy who "only like[s] dreaming," and justifies its universalism by finding Australians everywhere from Brussels to Bombay. Original grade: B minus. **B+**

Men at Work: *Cargo* (Columbia '83). A touch dour, two touches bemused, and probably way too passive, they're so smashingly unambitious that they're forgettable when they don't strike just the right note. But I've always considered democracy more radical than misanthropy. And I appreciate their sniping at the military-industrial establishment. Original grade: B plus. **B**

Mental as Anything: *Creatures of Leisure* (A&M '83). As benign an evolutionary mishap as the koala bear, this displaced pub-rock band does its level best to act friendly and crazy despite disheartening life experiences. Along the way, keybman Greedy Smith sings Roy Orbison's "Workin' for the Man" like Dave Edmunds couldn't dream it, and headman Martin Plaza enlists his mates in the impossible task of closing the Nick Lowe gap. **B+**

Men Without Hats: *Rhythm of Youth* (Backstreet '83). "Who are you listening to—Jethro Tull?" someone asked over the phone, and that's new music for you. What makes it new is how ruthlessly it goes for the one-shot, which sometimes means the good song—"The Safety Dance," available as a twelve-inch. As for the rest, well, Ivan Doroschuk seems smarter than anybody in A Flock of Seagulls. And Ian Anderson seemed smarter than anybody in the Ohio Express. **C+**

Metallica: *Master of Puppets* (Elektra '86). I feel at a generational disadvantage with this music not because my weary bones can't take its power and speed but because I was born too soon to have my dendrites rerouted by progressive radio. This band's momentum can be pretty impressive, and as with a lot of fast metal (as well as some sludge) they seem to have acceptable political motivations—antiwar, anticonformity, even anticoke, fine. But the revolutionary heroes I envisage aren't male chauvinists too inexperienced to know better; they don't have hair like Samson and pecs like Arnold Schwarzenegger.

That's the image Metallica calls up, and I'm no more likely to invoke their strength of my own free will than I am *The 1812 Overture*'s. **B−**

Metallica: *. . . And Justice for All* (Elektra '88). Problem isn't that it's more self-conscious than its predecessor, which is inevitable when your stock in trade is compositions not songs. Problem is that it goes on longer—which is also inevitable when your stock in trade is compositions not songs. Just ask Yes. **C+**

Pat Metheny/Ornette Coleman: *Song X* (Geffen '86). I've always regarded Metheny as a harmless, well-meaning talent whose interests are as far from mine as, I don't know, Nino Rota's. It was nice that he admired Ornette, but his jazz was still way too tame. Well, never mind—this collaboration is the best pure jazz album Coleman's made since I started keeping track in the early '70s. No rock moves, and no funk, harmolodic or otherwise—it's all sweet lyricism, sonic comedy, and headlong invention. Metheny obviously doesn't deserve top billing, but he holds his own, especially on guitar synth, where his duet responses, ensemble parts, and choo-choo noises all fit in. And while rhythm stalwarts Charlie Haden and Jack DeJohnette make everything swinging, it's Metheny's taming effect that keeps the music in trim. **A**

Augie Meyers: *My Main Squeeze* (Atlantic America '88). History having advanced backwards, the eternal Tex-Mex sideman picks up an accordion. Ronda's on his Honda, and if Velma from Selma's dad doesn't turn him into enchiladas, all will be well. **B**

Miami Sound Machine: *Primitive Love* (Epic '85). CBS's preemptive strike at MCA's TV-soundtrack capability casts Gloria Estefan, in real life the daughter of a Batista bodyguard, and her hub Emilio, "Percussion, Manager," as minstrels to Viceland's cocaine trade in crossover mode. Real criminals like their music tougher (also live-er), but before you tsk-tsk the perfidy of cops you should heed your body and note that these prefab grooves move—not least the one called "Mucho Money." **B**

Miami Sound Machine: See also Gloria Estefan and Miami Sound Machine

George Michael: *Faith* (Columbia '87). As everybody but avant-bigots knew from hearing Wham! on the radio, Michael can prove that photogenic and popwise aren't mutually exclusive while combing his hair with his left hand. Substance, depth, simple human decency—that kind of stuff is more problematic. So the show of soul, in the grain of the lyrics as well as the voice, makes a difference. But let no one forget that the vulnerability and compassion here purveyed are staple commodities of the truly popwise, and that the album's only conceptual coup, "I Want Your Sex," stands as an ambiguous publicity stunt worthy of Madonna herself. **B+**

Michel'le: *Michel'le* (Ruthless '89). "People say I sound like a baby, but I'm a hundred per cent woman," she chirps on "Special Thanks," most of them tendered to the usual sexist suspects surrounding her producer and guest rapper, N.W.A.'s Dr. Dre. A rapper she's not—like Bobby Brown or Al B. Sure, she's a singer in a rap world, and though her voice is less surprising when she doesn't talk, she gets the decibels up there even with her warble set on squeal. She can liquefy like Chaka or Teena, too, which is impressive even though neither songstress could get away with these slow ones. The fast ones hint at what an L.A. woman has to do to get the sexist suspects to stop calling her a bitch with the tape running—act half-nice, half-nasty (in a word, "Nicety"), and assume real love is her prerogative. **B+**

The Micronotz: *The Beast That Devoured Itself* (Fresh Sounds '85). Haven't heard an indie album with this kind of unaffected formal integrity since Hüsker Dü's *Land Speed Record*. Lots of garage bands craft their songs more cannily, but these kids have the spirit. They believe their basic guitar riffs will provide all the melody their rush-and-roar needs, and they're right. **B+**

Bette Midler: *Divine Madness* (Atlantic '80). From anybody else, the second live album in under four years would have me charging unfair trade practice. From Bette it has me begging for intros—which rarely forthcome on a concert-flick "soundtrack" that plays better on screen than turntable. Streisand's claque is right—she's a sloppy singer, which without the diversionary shtick of *Live at Last* sometimes matters. On anything she's perfected in the studio, for instance. Or when she expresses herself all over "Stay With Me" or "Fire Down Below," good notions that suggest cabaret may be her musical calling after all. "E Street Shuffle" she can handle—maybe because it has a plot. **C+**

Bette Midler: *No Frills* (Atlantic '83). Although it helps that she gets stronger material than usual from yet another phalanx of International Pop Music Community pros, what makes this Bette's best studio album in a decade is a Habana production number set in Miami, a newly written Sophie Tucker song about a driving wheel, and not-quite-comic readings of Marshall Crenshaw and Jagger-Richard. What makes it not good enough is the curse of Broadway rock and roll—the beat is conceived as decoration or signal rather than the meaning of life, or even music. **B−**

Midnight Oil: *10,9,8,7,6,5,4,3,2,1* (Columbia '83). Figures that a major-label, major-management band expressly obsessed with nuclear holocaust and man's inhumanity to man should smell slightly progressive, which I do not use in the lefty sense. The multiplex structures, emphatic mix, and sardonically melodramatic vocals all add a pompous air to music that comes on as uptempo rock and roll. Message: everything would be quite all right if human beings weren't such stupid fools—and major power brokers have nothing to do with it. **C+**

Midnight Oil: *Diesel and Dust* (Columbia '88). After not figuring out who Peter Garrett sounded like (sotto voce Roger Waters slightly, Peter Gabriel not at all, Peter Hammill not really, David Bowie what else is new), I decided his animadversions were in fact generic, and not in a bad way—he hectors like a crank politician would hector if the politician were a rock singer. Since this rock singer is in fact a crank politician, his authenticity requirement is thus satisfied. Nor is it a bad thing that his band is hooking it up these days. Garrett remains irritating even as you start singing along in spite of yourself, which is all anyone can ask of a crank.   **B+**

The Mighty Diamonds: *Reggae Street* (Shanachie '81). As on so many reggae albums, songs that sound flat at first sink in if given the chance. But reggae's simple melodic devices are wearing so thin that this isn't always a plus—I resisted the title cut even more stubbornly once I remembered how it went, and the old political messages remind me more and more of Sunday school. Nevertheless, I remain basically interested until the middle of side two, with special curiosity as to the current whereabouts of "King Kong."   **B+**

The Mighty Diamonds: *Indestructible* (Alligator '82). There hasn't been a Diamonds album as tuneful as this lovingly pieced-together collection since *Right Time* in 1976, and Sly & Robbie certainly have elaborated their legerdemain in the meantime. But with most of the three-part unisons giving way to Tabby Shaw's lissome but somewhat reserved tenor and the tunes themselves accommodating the dubious "sincerity" of lovers rock, the new classics number only three: one about prison, one about revolution, and one about passing the pipe.   **A—**

The Mighty Diamonds: *The Roots Is There* (Shanachie '82). The amazing thing about reggae of a certain quality—in which an affecting singer like Donald Shaw joins ace session players—is that no matter how sedulously it restates platitudes about roots and girls and Jah, its small graces eventually get its equally sedulous melodies across. But why should anyone who doesn't credit the platitudes give them that long?   **B**

The Mighty Lemon Drops: *Happy Head* (Sire '86). These shamblers do sometimes twist the clichés gently in an attempt to bring them back to life—the gurl who's "Like an Angel" is stuck up, for instance.

But mostly they rely on guitars somewhat more punkish in attack than those of the countless American bands who've been working the same garage-pop angle since long before the Brits invented it.   **C+**

Frankie Miller: *Standing on the Edge* (Capitol '82). People used to complain that Miller sounded like Otis Redding. Now, inspired by the Muscle Shoals boys and countless dangerous wimmin, he sounds like Bob Seger. This is not an improvement.   **C+**

The Steve Miller Band: *Circle of Love* (Capitol '81). You whippersnappers want catchy pop tunes, this high-tech cornball's got 'em with blues changes—four nifties on side one. You want hypnotic electrogroove, he's got that with blues changes too—eighteen minutes of it, complete with muddled attack on the military-industrial establishment. Both sides offer sound effects at no additional charge, and Steve would like everyone to know that he's been doing this shit since 1968.   **B**

The Steve Miller Band: *Abracadabra* (Capitol '82). With longtime bandbuddy Gary Mallaber making like Jeff Barry, Miller fulfills his hippie destiny and turns into the Archies, or really the Monkees, since he did write the title hit himself, and it will probably stand as the biggest pop tune of 1982, by which I definitely don't mean the most quintessential, because this one is blissfully catchy and blissfully simple and blissfully schlocky and blissfully tricky, like the rest of the album only more so. Original grade: B plus.   **B**

The Million Dollar Quartet: *The Million Dollar Quartet* (S import '87). This isn't a phonograph album, it's a documentary—audio verité proof that the great rockabillies called black men "colored guys" and each other "boy." Also that they knew and loved all kinds of music, which always bears repeating. But I guess the immemorial working title of this legendary event misled me. Fine as the three voices overheard by the Sun tape recorder were, I keep waiting for Elvis, Carl, and Jerry Lee to coalesce into a group. And spontaneous as the family sing is, I keep waiting for the session. [Later on RCA, with artist's credit to Elvis Presley.] **B**+

Milli Vanilli: *Girl You Know It's True* (Arista '89). Frank Farian's great Eurodisco experiment Boney M didn't go over Stateside for the simple reason that it was too Euro. His Eurorap is hipper, sexier, even a teensy bit soulful—in short, indistinguishable from the highest quality Amerischlock give or take some snazzy sound effects. The title cut is the best cut. The remix of the title cut is the second-best cut. **C**

Ministry: *Twitch* (Sire '86). Chicago's Anglodisco clones meet Anglodisco renegade Adrian Sherwood and promptly improve themselves by trading in wimpy on arty. Fleetingly gothic, marginally industrial, unrelenting in a vaguely threatening way, they shout "The world is ending" on a crowded dancefloor. No one panics, but some do drift off—they're getting a little bored. **B**−

Ministry: *The Land of Rape and Honey* (Sire '88). Alain Jourgenson is said to hate Steve Albini, and why not, but I still think Big Black changed his life. Whomp whomp whomp whomp, these huge ugly slabs of beat are like the metal of dreams, all urban din and therapeutic brain damage, only done with synthesizers. Though I wish I knew what they were bellowing about down in the abyss, this will tone up your innards a lot more efficiently than whatever's hep in garage grunge these days. And you can dance to it—supposedly. **B**+

Ministry: *A Mind Is a Terrible Thing To Taste* (Sire '89). Industrial's edge on metal is anonymity—unlike major-brand sonic barrage, it presents itself as a resultant rather than an expression, music/noise emanating from a society/culture. It's objective; it doesn't imply a subject. This illusion boosts the music/noise's impact and authority while rendering it virtually indistinguishable from itself (as well as difficult to access from what's human/humanist in our aesthetic sense). The bestselling Chicago version gets faster and purer with every release. Even when Alain Jourgenson raps, or apes (hires?) John Lydon, I could give a fuck who he is or what he thinks. Which is essential to the intended sensation. **B**+

Mink DeVille: *Le Chat Bleu* (Capitol '80). Goils—they break your heart, run off with your coke, mess up your drug deals, and take your count when you go to the blood bank. Rhythm and blues was never like this, so maybe he's a punk after all. But more likely he's one more struggling professional musician. **B**−

Sugar Minott: *Sufferer's Choice* (Heartbeat '83). Play this back-to-back with Minott's 1979 *Black Roots* and then tell me reggae never changes. The progress is subtle, but I promise you'll hear it plenty clear enough. It begins as usual in the rhythms, which Sly & Robbie take over from lesser lights, but that doesn't explain why Minott, a creamy lovers rocker of no special distinction, not only keeps up but adds fillips of his own, fillips that would have been buried in the 1979 recording even if he'd been capable of them then. Sure the songwriting's improved too, but in this kind of music meaning inheres in responsive interaction. If formalism it must be, let it be formalism of the body. **B**+

Sugar Minott: *Inna Reggae Dance Hall* (Heartbeat '86). A mild-mannered pro who "Nah Follow Nuh Fashion" because he never lets it get ahead of him trades in the Roots Radics on a computer-compatible rhythm machine, upping the tempo slightly and shifting his croon toward chant. Product, sure, but useful product, which even in Jamaica is an achievement these days. Original grade: B plus. **B**

Minuteflag: *Minuteflag* (SST EP '86). This 'tween-band instrumental jam wasn't supposed to be released until they'd both broken up. As if we needed another reason to mourn D. Boon. **D**

Minutemen: *The Punch Line* (SST EP '81). They're politniks who love punk, with a name that mocks hardcore's right-wing rep and their own aesthetic—these eighteen "songs" average under fifty seconds apiece. The lyrics don't rhyme or even scan, less poems than the jottings of young men given to cultural bullshit. "History Lesson"—"hundred thousand years ago homosapiens stood erect mind empty fresh created love and hate created god and antigod human slaughtered human for power"—gets the flavor: not Fredric Jameson, but better-informed than the skinheads they play for. And where last year's seven-inch *Paranoid Time* could pass for speed-rock, the funky dissonance here has no parallel in the genre or anywhere else: not Ornette Coleman, but better-informed than the Circle Jerks they play with.   **B**

Minutemen: *What Makes a Man Start Fires?* (SST '82). The lyrics are richer, bleaker, and smarter than the hardcore rant that softened the world up for this art band in disguise, but I prefer their music. The more you listen the less fragmentary these eighteen tense little guess-you-have-to-call-them tunes sound—each transforms its own riff into an identity that meshes with the album's guess-you-have-to-call-it gestalt. Since they're not purist (or unpop) enough to resist putting the strongest material first, their steady-state kineticism does lose a notch or two of stress as each side proceeds, but that's the only way they could work it—any kind of climax would be too romantic for these guys. Time: 27:39.   **A—**

Minutemen: *Buzz or Howl Under the Influence of Heat* (SST EP '83). These guys define the future of atavism if anybody does. Subtle structures and sharp musicianship—rhythm-slasher D. Boon is as much a guitar antihero as labelmates Bob Mould and Greg Ginn—serves music that continues to seem primitive, even crudely offhand; lyrics articulate, elaborate, and, that's right, criticize the fucked-up despair of the world where they make their living and preach their uncoercive gospel—the fucked-up despair that in true hardcore makes such a great excuse for not thinking.   **A—**

Minutemen: *The Politics of Time* (New Alliance '84). They sound smart and there and committed to change, and as with most mortals their outtakes is outtakes and their live shit is live shit: couple-three good songs out of twenty-seven total (this is when they were pure).   **B—**

Minutemen: *Double Nickels on the Dime* (SST '84). Maybe by designating a "side chaff" and aiming a boast at their four-sided labelmates ("take that, hüskers!"), the L.A. (really San Pedro) punk-fusion (really "chump rock"?) trio mean to acknowledge that a forty-six-song double-LP is overdoing things. But I have my faves throughout, topped by a Steely Dan cover that wouldn't have survived first weed, and I'm not sure I'd like them so much at a different pace. Eleven of the titles are over 2:00 and thirteen more over 1:40, but structures are still so abbreviated that the way one riff-song segues into the next changes both. This is poetry-with-jazz as it always should have been, and while D. Boon may be a somewhat limited singer, he's a hell of a reader, with a guitar that rhymes.   **A—**

Minutemen: *Project: Mersh* (SST EP '85). Where at first this seemed to prove that irrepressibly avant-garde bands are catchier when they don't set out to "write hit songs," now it's obvious that the commershal concept is total rather than part joke—only the trumpet parts (horns symbolize sellout to punks, maybe because they're so hard to play) mark a significant departure. Songs are catchy enough, too, with the catchiest lasting eight minutes including six-minute outro. Very mersh.   **B+**

Minutemen: *3-Way Tie (for Last)* (SST '85). Since their uncompromising reach always exceeded their fairly amazing grasp, I tried to cut myself a little critical distance in the wake of a rock death that for wasted potential has Lennon and Hendrix for company. Sure they never sounded better, I said, but they're still a little naive here and conceptual there. Only that wasn't distance—it was denial. D. Boon's singing, writing, and playing here are all infused with a new lyrical lift that adds unexpected buoyancy to a band that was generous at its most cynical and confused, and as a result their zigzag rhythms and interesting conceptualisms get the songful relief they need. After seven fairly amazing years he was just getting started. Shit, shit, shit.   **A**

Minutemen: *Ballot Result* (SST '87). As someone who's never had much patience with the mystique of the ill-recorded moment, music overheard just before it slips into the historical void its creators figure it for, I'll make a partial exception for the Minutemen, because I miss them so much. I know most of the songs on this mostly live double in versions I prefer, but better than any studio distillation it underlines the crucial point: they lived. And given the modesty so intrinsic to their world-historical public ambitions, its muffled, take-a-flier intimacy speaks. Also, I like the covers.   **A—**

The Miracle Legion: *The Backyard* (Incas EP '84). Mark hooks his evocations of dazzled childhood and yearning adolescence on Ray's insistent guitar figures and sings like Loudon Wainwright III's kid cousin the Shoes fan. Joel and Jeff cultivate a discreet anonymity that suggests they may not like R.E.M. as much as Mark and Ray do. [Later on Rough Trade.]   **B+**

The Miracle Legion: *Surprise Surprise Surprise* (Rough Trade '87). As with so many middle-class suburban Amerindies whose music starts hazy, they're making atmosphere their vocation. Problem's less tunes than lyrics, and less the way the lyrics make evocation their vocation than what they evoke—*New Yorker* poems about mowing the lawn, rather than just mowing the lawn.   **B—**

The Miracle Legion: *Glad* (Rough Trade EP '88). Second side's live remakes are already overdue—amazing how a little loud can tone up the sensibility. From "A Heart Disease Called Love," a John Cooper Clarke setting that might have been plucked from the bowels of Nashville, through "Glad" and "Hey, Lucky," first side's new studio songs aren't what you'd call glad—more like mournful, angry, and depressive. Also strong.   **B+**

Miracle Legion: *Me and Mr. Ray* (Rough Trade '89). Me is Mark, Mr. Ray is Ray, rhythm section is gone. Unidentified toilers back the pleasant tracks; the unpleas-

ant ones are all voice, bad poetry, and instrumental accompaniment. It gets worse than ". . . you could be my Venus / I'll close my eyes and hold my ears and walk up to a broken heart," but only rarely does it wuss out in your face like that—usually Mark's more obscure. Sure he's also bright, sensitive, and honest (probably). But so are you (probably). So go sing in the shower.   **C**

Daniel Owino Misiani and Shirati Band: *Benga Blast!* (Virgin '89). Not all that easy to tell this Kenya-recorded '80s-spanning compilation from Shirati Jazz's London-recorded 2/11/87 *Benga Beat* even though Misiani is missing from the earlier release, which consists entirely of material penned and cut/recut by members of the band he continued to lead twenty-five years after he invented it. Quality does emerge: Misiani's writing is catchier, and he's good for an extra measure of vocal and instrumental authority despite the U.K. production's superior audio. But what defines both is the still-delicate benga sound, uncommonly folkish for modern Afropop even though the soukous competition has prodded it toward what passes in Kenya for revisionist HI-NRG. Sweet and beaty.   **A—**

Missing Persons: *Spring Session M* (Capitol '82). By combining me-first ideology with kewpie-doll vocals, spokesperson Dale Bozzio makes it sound as if she caught on to the autonomy fad kind of late. By combining cold studio gloss-and-kick with surefire electronic hooks, music-meister Terry Bozzio makes it sound as if he caught on to the new-wave fad kind of late. Another perfect marriage.   **C+**

Mission of Burma: *Signals, Calls and Marches* (Ace of Hearts EP '81). "That's When I Reach for My Revolver"/"This Is Not a Photograph" would be some follow-up to this power trio's 1980 one-hook wonder "Academy Fight Song." Maybe you could even stretch it to two singles, b/w "Fame and Fortune" and the instrumental "All World Cowboy Romance." The rest is overtones. Original grade: B.   **B+**

Mission of Burma: *Vs.* (Ace of Hearts '82). Is it merely the cornball in me who wishes these stiff, snarling, abrasive rave-ups would break into anthem a little more often? After all, how much of a cornball can I be if I believe stiff, snarling, abrasive rave-ups would be just peachy if only they did—maybe even if the words connected for more than a line at a time. N.b.: departing guitarist Roger Miller wrote more than half the songs, and anthemic he ain't. What next?   **B+**

Mission of Burma: *The Horrible Truth About Burma* (Ace of Hearts '85). One of the two most impressive tracks on this live all-new-material farewell from the seminal Boston indie band is a Stooges cover. The other is an Ubu cover. The rest—eight songs—is entirely original. I'm sure this isn't the horrible truth their label has in mind, but rock historians should jot it down somewhere.   **B**

Mission of Burma: *Mission of Burma* (Rykodisc CD '88). More even than most postpunk they were also prenoise, harbingers of a rock and roll (or rock) far more traditional than no wave both formally and sonically except that it eschewed (or failed to achieve) melody (or tune). Not indefensible, but less sonically compelling than the defense would have you believe—or so it seems from my generational vantage. Comprising all of *Signals, Calls and Marches* and *Vs.* plus the great "Academy Fight Song" and lesser arcana, this compilation boasts a new world-record CD length of 80 minutes, which under the sonic/melodic circumstances isn't something to boast about—it goes on for fucking ever. Adepts of the select button need own nothing else. Everybody else should go for what they know.   **B**

Mr. Magic's Rap Attack Volume 2 (Profile '86). Run-D.M.C. doth not a rap label make, and that ain't all, 'cause these days rap has a serious one-better problem. Playing the dozens live leaves you some slack, but enter the age of mechanical reproduction and they can check you out against history every time. Inevitably, shock deliquesces into outrage. So Pebblee-Poo's half of the Masterdon Committee's "Get Off My Tip!"—"You're a twenty-dollar

nigger in a fifty-dollar world with a hundred-dollar hat and I'm a million-dollar girl"—fails to justify Dana Dane's compulsion to top macho with gynephobia. Nor do junk-culture excavations by the Kartoon Krew, the Showboys, Word of Mouth, and other off-target one-shots yield actual novelty hooks.   **B−**

Mr. Magic's Rap Attack Volume 4 (Profile '88). For the first time since the series began, he corrals the most undeniable singles of the year—"It Takes Two," "Don't Believe the Hype," "Strictly Business," "Push It," "Wild Wild West." Only the Cold Chillin' posse, led by his sometime mixer Marley Marl, declined the honor. Except for "It Takes Two," every aforementioned title is on an album worthy of the name, but those who are still resisting the only collectively vital American subgenre will find this compilation educational. Even the filler's high-grade.   **A−**

Joni Mitchell: *Wild Things Run Fast* (Geffen '82). This is good Joni, for the first time since the mid-'70s, and I suspect it comes too late, because good Joni simply means old Joni, and old Joni is better. I mean, if she'd put "Solid Love" at the very end I still wouldn't believe her, but at least I'd think she'd learned something. Instead she proves her maturity with a climactic hymn to St. Paul's kind of love which is much the worst of the three covers—because to be honest the Al Hibbler and Elvis Presley songs are what kept me listening.   **B**

Joni Mitchell: *Dog Eat Dog* (Geffen '85). When you peruse the lyrics, which are of course provided, the rage she directs at evangelists, racketeers, financiers, and so forth seems like the usual none-too-deep left-liberal modernism—a "culture in decline" enthralled by hedonism and rapacity and the image, tsk-tsk. But by taking her mind off her ever-loving self she's broken a long drought. There's no what-shall-I-do ennui in her singing; she isn't musing, she's telling us something, and her interest in these well-expressed middlebrow clichés comes through. Damned if I can tell just what Thomas Dolby has done for her jazzbo sound, but I suspect he helps as well. Maybe he convinced her it was pop music. Original grade: A minus. **B+**

Joni Mitchell: *Chalk Mark in a Rain Storm* (Geffen '88). Dreaming, fabulizing, playing the ingenue, speaking for the displaced Native American, preaching about materialism and ecocatastrophe and the engines of war (and abortion, though not so's you can tell where she stands), she's matured into a sententious liberal. Give me the Poet of the Me Decade. At least Joan Baez is a sententious radical. **C**

Mofungo: *End of the World* (unlabeled cassette '81). These aging no-wave stalwarts have outgrown the blinding-headache approach without giving up their stubbornly untrendy belief that you play music for love, with some well-aimed hate thrown in. "End of the World" could pass for early Television, and "El Salvador"—the title is half of the lyric—is the political song of the year (and available even more clear and tortured as a Rough Trade single). Perhaps because the final ten tracks weren't mixed by Chris Stamey, this fourteen-song, thirty-minute tape does cry out for aspirin as it proceeds. But I play it for love. Original grade: A minus. **B+**

Mofungo: *Out of Line* (Zoar '83). Where hardcore kids rail against empty leisure and media images, these working bohemians ground an analysis in the dismal daily grind. Their politics more or less match thick, uningratiating music that is dissonant but not quite amelodic, industrial but not at all mechanical. The match isn't exact because their lyrics are sometimes so simplistic they deserve a single dumb folkie guitar, while the music gets thin in a more unavoidable way, reflecting their blocked access to the means of production. And though I doubt anything would render their "We're gonna change the world" literal, my analysis is that a few extra tunes wouldn't hurt. **B**

Mofungo: *Frederick Douglass* (Twin/Tone/Coyote '85). What would a stranger make of this friendly but apparently overwrought and tuneless cacophony? Wish I were sure s/he'd find it as winning as I do. Not counting "El Salvador," this is the only time in eight years they've treated themselves to a mix forceful enough to clarify the apparently casual musicianship that goes into what are actually canny, complex, and suggestive structures. Even when you have no idea just what words they're hanging from titles like "Migrant Assembly Line Workers" and "Our Days of Weakness Are Over," you know they like grunge, a good joke, and other people. You know they're pissed off, too. Time: 29:51. Original grade: B plus. **A—**

Mofungo: *Messenger Dogs of the Gods* (Lost '86). Things fall apart—that we know. The question is what to do about it. Pop craftsmen combat this truth, or lie about it, by fashioning antientropic modules within which a salutary dose of abandon can do its work, while keepers of the avant-garde tradition walk into a collapsing building and plug in their amps. An infinity of further choices awaits both camps, and most of them are wrong. Mofungo's are right: pride rather than self-congratulation, anger rather than loathing, struggle rather than despair. Both funny and witty, unassumingly compassionate, glancing fondly off the folk musics they look to and the rock they play, they sound less weird and inchoate the more you listen. Some avant-gardists would tell you that's their problem. What do you think? **A—**

Mofungo: *End of the World, Part 2* (Lost '87). In its weary postfolk delicacy and righteous politics, "Ku Klux Klan" is definitive despite a clumsy Willie Klein add-on about Rehnquist, who deserves worse. A bow to Apollinaire, kiss-offs to Reagan and Baby Doc, and three Elliott Sharpened remakes do the job as well, but the remakes also suggest shortfall. As does the useless militancy of "Science Song #1" (ozone lesson), "SR-71 Blackbird" (even Bruce Cockburn could blow it out of the sky), and "Lemmings" (guess who). **B+**

Mofungo: *Bugged* (SST '88). In an evolution that now seems inevitable if exceedingly slow, they jam hot, and this is how they'll prove it in Alaska, California, Buffalo, and other distant locales. Helps that they've learned their own instruments and each other's moves after ten years. Helps even more that they've integrated a real live misguided virtuoso into the concept. Elliott Sharp's fills and solos are the making of "#1 for Take-Off" and "The Pope Is a Potato" and "The Wit and Wisdom of Judge Bork." Which latter I trust SST's dance department will start promoting immediately. **A—**

Mofungo: *Work* (SST '89). Despairing, cynical, basically unlistenable unless you grant it your full attention, this is far more pessimistic than anything disco doomsters purvey—it's literal, articulate, no fun. I don't necessarily agree that "voting is for suckers" or "the oceans are dead," but I know why they do, and their most inaccessible yowls in years aided my understanding. Alternate title: *End of the World: The Final Chapter.* **A—**

The Moments: *Collector's Addition Vol. I* (Victory '82). Lifting everything worth lifting off their 1977 double-best-of and adding four recent hits, this is Subsequently Ray, Goodman & Brown's legacy despite the French "Look at Me I'm in Love" and a shrill pressing that narrows their falsettos. Among the additions is "I Could Have Loved You," a second chance at a one-night stand worthy of Smokey Robinson (with a writing credit for Bette Midler). Among the keepers is "Love on a Two Way Street." Remember that one? You will. **B+**

More Intensified! Volume 2 Original Ska 1963–67 (Mango '80). Brit postpunks prefer Jamaican r&b to American r&b for the simple reason that it's punker—despite the horns (nobody comes near a fast tune on trumpet or trombone without years of experience), this stuff is so crude it gets across solely on DIY enthusiasm and the loping pelvis polka of its homegrown groove. Since I wasn't there, I can report without fear of nostalgia that Volume 1's material is no better or worse than this selection. Garveyite special: "Congo War," which makes fun of Kasavubu's name rather than solemnizing his tragedy. By Lord Brynner and the Shieks, spelling in original, wonder if he shaved his head, how punk. **A—**

Junie: *Bread Alone* (Columbia '80). J. Morrison's funk is pleasingly plump, replete with pear-shaped tenor, well-rounded rhythms, and thick do-it-yourself mix. He has a sensuous way with a melody, and his romanticism is winningly sincere. But not even the lead cut's tricky be-my-baby hook has that get-up-and-dance kick. **B+**

Junie Morrison: *Evacuate Your Seats* (Island '84). Not just guitarless but wholly synthesized, with Junie's all too childish falsetto playing daddy to a smurf club, this is as half-assed as most P-Funk spinoffs even if it wastes a few more ideas. I'd like to hear a bigger artist take over. Think maybe George would mastermind a total remix of "Break 6"? **B—**

Van Morrison: *Common One* (Warner Bros. '80). Sententious, torpid, abandoned by God, this six-song, fifty-five-minute meander is Morrison's worst since *Hard Nose the Highway*—*Astral Weeks* fans even think so. He does have a direct line to certain souls, though, and they still hear him talkin'. As in fact do I, twice—on the only vaguely fast one, which goes "I'm satisfied / With my world," and on the truly nutball "Summer in England," which goes "Did you ever hear about / Wordsworth and Coleridge, baby?" **B—**

Van Morrison: *Beautiful Vision* (Warner Bros. '82). After a period of transition, Van has finally achieved the eternal Kansas City—this music is purely gorgeous (or at times lovely), its pleasure all formal grace and aptness of invention. Only "Cleaning Windows," a cheerful, visionary, deeply eccentric song about class and faith and culture, stands among his great tunes. But every one of these songs makes itself felt as an individual piece of music. And every one fits into the whole. Original grade: A. **A—**

Van Morrison: *Inarticulate Speech of the Heart* (Warner Bros. '83). In this troubled time, rock-and-rollers have every right to place their faith in the Jehovah's Witnesses or even Scientology when they discover that Jackie Wilson didn't say it all. But to follow one with the other appears weak-minded, like praising Omar Khayyam in tandem with Kahlil Gibran. A hypothesis which the static romanticism of these reels-for-Hollywood-orchestra and other slow songs bears out. **B—**

Van Morrison: *A Sense of Wonder* (Mercury '85). By marrying r&b usages to Celtic mysticism in an art that honors both and then some, Morrison proved there was more to r&b than even Ray Charles had dreamed. But when inspiration fails him, he's left with uninspired art. At his most automatic, Charles still has r&b.   **C+**

Van Morrison: *Live at the Grand Opera House Belfast* (Mercury '85). Where you file this de facto best-of from Van's slackest and most spiritual period depends on whether you mourn *Astral Weeks* or *Moondance.* I'm putting it in the reference library.   **B**

Van Morrison: *No Guru, No Method, No Teacher* (Mercury '86). No soap radio, no particular place to go, no man is an island. No spring chicken, No-Doz, no can do.   **B−**

Van Morrison: *Poetic Champions Compose* (Mercury '87). His first interesting album in five years sounds best as a CD for the same reason it isn't all that interesting—in his current spiritual state, which could last until he rages against the dying of the light, he doesn't much care about interesting. He just wants to roll on, undulating from rhythmic hill to melodic dale. If only he'd resequenced the third-stream instrumental "Celtic Excavation" so that it closed the full-length digital work instead of opening its nonexistent second side, he'd have framed his dinner music perfectly. Yeah, dinner music—I figure if it doesn't make me want to vomit, it must have something going for it.   **B+**

Van Morrison & the Chieftains: *Irish Heartbeat* (Mercury '88). Having finally met up with the jet-setting Irish traditionalists, known the world over for sitting down with anybody who'll look good on their resumé, the blocked poet essays a few jigs in a misguided attempt to prove he hasn't lost his rebop. Instead he should take another cue from the bluesmen who taught him his shit—once you settle into other people's songs, the secret of an honorable senescence is your own sense of rhythm.   **C+**

Van Morrison: *Avalon Sunset* (Mercury '89). Like it or not, Morrison's genre exercises are kind of boring. Having long since sold his soul to his Muse, he's her slave for life, and though he keeps importuning various gods to loose his chains, the best they can offer is extra inspiration once in a while—now, for instance. Cliff Richard's support on his liveliest tune since "Cleaning Windows" suggests that Christ the Redeemer is lending a hand, but on the first side Van prefers to find the divine in the blessed present—folk lyric, poem about bird-watching, song called "I'd Like To Write Another Song." Side two comes out more today - is - the - first - day - of - the - rest - of - Van's-life—that is, his own genre exercise. And for a side he gets away with it.   **A−**

Morrissey: *Viva Hate* (Sire '88). From my pinnacle of disinterest I can attest that this solo move is neither here nor there. Vini Reilly doesn't have a unique sound like Johnny Marr, and autonomy does encourage the camp grandiosity of a guy who tries to make "I love you more than life" live: though he may think it's funny for "Late Night, Maudlin Street" to go on for 7:40, in fact it's as boring as you'd expect despite the great line about his revolting nakedness. But the Smiths rarely if ever came up with a hook as must-hear as "Everyday Is Like Sunday" 's and in general the monotony factor has decreased. The artiste is no longer a kid, and he likes it that way. Essential for acolytes, educational for the rest of us, just like always.   **B**

Bill Morrissey: *Bill Morrissey* (Reckless '84). There's ten years of rough jobs and bumming around in these trenchant, unassuming songs, with no aura of folkie slumming to stink things up. Morrissey took those jobs to make money, not to gather material, and he went on the road to get away from home. Of course, industrial New England leaves its stamp on everything he writes anyway—his lyrics are so local, so devoid of pop universals, that even if he wanted more than finger-picking on his LP I doubt anyone would give him the budget for it. Which sad to say leaves only a stylized is-that-John-Prine? drawl to carry his familiar little tunes.   **B+**

Bill Morrissey: *North* (Philo '86). His deep voice sheds affectation as his music approaches the delicacy of pure folkie accompaniment, all the better to show off what he's here for: "idiot verse." Which is laconic, not idiotic, and damn near definitive on his great theme—how much men need to work and how much they'd rather be doing something else. Never before have so many protagonists been snowbound and liked it.   **B+**

The Morwells: *The Best of the Morwells* (Nighthawk '81). These half-legendary reggae veterans deserve a U.S. compilation, but not every hitmaker on an island of two million is guaranteed to lead us into Zion. Bingy Bunny moans guilelessly, a laid-back Winston Rodney, while Flabba Holt and Style Scott keep the riddims so close to earth you have to figure they don't command any chancier options.   **B**

Pablo Moses: *A Song* (Mango '80). Definitively unprepossessing, Moses lays his murmured chants amid standard reggae instruments that sound like they were placed in different studios so as not to gang up on his voice so mild. At first you don't believe anything this simple can also be this cunning, but unlike the Fall, say, Moses is nothing like an amateur, and neither, Jah knows, are his instrumentalists. He's also kind and hopeful, not vain enough to dream his music could tear Babylon down: just wants to grant us a glimpse of paradise before it goes.   **A−**

Pablo Moses: *Pave the Way* (Mango '81). It's the same for Sly & Robbie as for Stax-Volt, Gamble & Huff, or for that matter Richard Perry—if a great studio style is going to break out of its formula and zap the listener, the record had better offer identification, inspiration, or hooks. But me, I'm no Rasta, or any other kind of theist or cultural nationalist; are you? And the gain in vocal competence strikes me as a dangerous thing—because Moses always "projects" now, he deprives his basic singsong of the nursery-rhyme lucidity that makes his best work so winning.   **B**

Pablo Moses: *In the Future* (Alligator '83). With his precise, delicate, discreetly dubwise production—sly horn part there, elegantly understated percussion effect here, bass and drums measured into the groove—and quiet, even timid vocal manner, this poet-turned-rootsman sounds like the most live-and-let-live of ital mystics. In fact he's not only urban but interested in subways and Bellevue, not only militant but smart about it—which is to say among other things that he doesn't seem to think his natural is the only natural.   **A**

Pablo Moses: *Reggae Greats* (Mango '84). The first three cuts of this "compilation" are the first three cuts of *A Song,* which everyone knows is the better of the two albums he cut for Island. The fourth appears later, as does one from side two; "Each Is a Servant," *A Song*'s purest cut, does not. The fine-as-can-be *Pave the Way* selections represent an aural break just like always. Sure, buy the sampler if you can get it cheap. And if *A Song* gets sent to the bins to make room, steal 'em both.   **B+**

Pablo Moses: *Tension* (Alligator '85). Moses's singsong melodies have always been simplistic even by reggae standards, but on these cautionary ditties neither lyrics nor groove manage the sly, subtle grace of the best of them. Catchy, yes, and righteous too, but as annoying at times as a Sugar Crisps commercial.   **B**

The Motels: *All Four One* (Capitol '82). "Take the 'L' out of Lover and it's over"? "Apocalypso"? "Tragic Surf," for Christ's sake? They've got to be kidding. But Martha Davis torches so enthusiastically that the result is about as funny as Meat Loaf—so "subtle" that nobody naive enough to buy the record will catch on. She has better taste in music then Jim Steinman, though.   **C+**

Motley Crue: *Shout at the Devil* (Elektra '84). It's hardly news that this platinum product is utter dogshit even by heavy metal standards; under direct orders from editors who don't know Iron Maiden from Wynton Marsalis, my beleaguered colleagues on the dailies have been saying so all year, and every insult goes into the press kit. Still, I must mention Mick Mars's dork-fingered guitar before getting to the one truly remarkable thing about this record: a track called "Ten Seconds

To Love" in which Vince Neil *actually seems to boast about how fast he can ejaculate* (or as the lyric sheet puts it, "cum"). And therein, I believe, lies the secret of their commercial appeal—if you don't got it, flaunt it. Follow-up: "Pinkie Prick."   **D**

Motorhead: *Ace of Spades* (Mercury '80). Punks have never bought his leather jacket and indie connections because Lemmy Kilminster's grizzled-biker-born-to-rock is metal without the heavy—no preening solos or blow-dried bullshit. I recommend the bit where he promises to get fast and loose with his latest receptacle as soon as he finishes the song about it (not *her,* of course not), and note that his writing is more one-note than need be, wit and all—fucking for the hell of it can drive anybody into a rage, and tuneless fucking for the hell of it is really pointless. Anthem: "(We Are) The Road Crew."   **B**

Motorhead: *No Sleep 'Til Hammersmith* (Mercury '81). Vic Maile's power-packed definition obliterates my bias against live recording. Remakes of white lies like "No Class" and "Stay Clean" and calling cards like "Bomber" and "Motorhead" save valuable shelf space. So what if it gives me a headache? Sometimes a headache comes as a relief.   **B+**

Motorhead: *No Remorse* (Bronze '84). The critics who used to call Motorhead the worst band in the world had a point, which may be why Lemmy's high-speed metal has now turned into the thinking person's headbang. The stuff is so pure it's almost rarefied: no operatic declamations, no schlocky guitaristics, no satanism or medievalism or sci-fi or sexist s&m. Just aggression, violence, noise. Lemmy doesn't even bellow—his voice is more a hoarse, loud, one-note roar. This tasteful two-disc best-of-plus-four (new and definitive: "Killed by Death") is the first Motorhead product praised by Headheads since *No Sleep 'Til Hammersmith,* eight of whose eleven songs it includes (the eight best, too). Unless you've got an extra Y chromosome or beat your meat till it bleeds, you likely don't need it on a regular basis. But it'll sure come in handy at those precious moments when you want nothing so much

as to smash somebody's face. Original grade: B plus.   **A—**

Motorhead: *Orgasmatron* (GWR/Profile '86). I admire metal's integrity, brutality, and obsessiveness, but I can't stand its delusions of grandeur—the way it apes and misapprehends reactionary notions of nobility. One thing I like about Lemmy is that he's proud to be a clod, common as muck and dogged in his will to make himself felt as just that. Add that rarest of metal virtues, a sense of humor, which definitely extends to the music's own conventions, as on the lead cut of his first album in three litigation-packed years: yclept "Deaf Forever," a good enough joke right there (especially for Sabbaf fans), it turns out to be a battlefield anthem—about a corpse. And then add Bill Laswell, who was born to make megalomania signify: where most metal production gravitates toward a dull thud that highlights the shriek of the singer and the comforting reverberation of the signature guitar, Laswell's fierce clarity cracks like a whip, inspiring Lemmy, never a slowpoke in this league, to bellow one called "Built for Speed." Result: work of art.   **A—**

Motorhead: *Rock 'n' Roll* (GWR/Profile '87). Though he's shed Bill Laswell's sonic entourage and rehired the lovable Philthy Animal Taylor to beat skins, Lemmy's brush with perfectionism seems to have transformed his recording philosophy. That layer of grunge is just gone, excised by the sharp vocal and percussive attack that made *Orgasmatron* the onslaught they'd promised for so long. Songwriting's still there, too, though "Eat the Rich," which ends up with Lemmy's rig on the menu, is the closest it comes to transmuting metal the way "Deaf Forever" did. Guest divine: Michael Palin, who prays for trousers.   **A—**

Motorhead: *No Sleep at All* (Enigma/GWR '88). Ten hunks of meat tossed to a horde of ravening Finns, and if six of them surfaced all too recently on Nuevo Motorhead's two studio albums, that doesn't stop me from scarfing down this live one the way Old Motorhead's cult devoured *No Sleep 'Til Hammersmith.* No remorse, and no excuses, except to remark that Nuevo Motorhead has songwriting down. Further evidence: the very underground smash "Killed by Death" (if you want one, Lemmy says he has ten thousand in his house) and the never-before-recorded "Just Because You Got the Power," which rages against the moneyheads without kidding anybody about capitalist hegemony.   **A—**

Bob Mould: *Workbook* (Virgin '89). Mould-Maimone-Fier are some kind of supersession, but they're no band, and between the cello and the acoustic guitar and the moderato and the lyric sheet that ought to have a little typeface note like at the end of a Borzoi book, I find myself disliking their record intensely. Until the raving finale, it's so respectable, so cautious, as if honest thought were a suitable substitute for wisdom, sarcasm, a good joke, or a suicide run for the next intro.   **C+**

Judy Mowatt: *Black Woman* (Shanachie '83). Mowatt seems like an exceptionally decent person. Her avowals of sisterhood are a welcome corrective to Rasta sexism. But as a frontwoman she's a backup singer. The straightforward decorum of her timbre suits her fine, but her lack of inborn dramatic grace and soul technique make her modest tunes more tedious than they have to be. And I don't hear the boys in the band putting their backs into it.   **B—**
Judy Mowatt: *Working Wonders* (Shanachie '85). The positivity of reggae's most autonomous woman isn't rendered any more credible by her brightly idealistic delivery—sounds like she's leading the community sing at Camp Nyabinghi. Her genteel Rastafarianism partakes of the usual fundamentalist delusions—she ignores Babylonian propaganda about Ethiopia, and she's sufficiently protective of her wonder worker's masculinity to insist that unlike those other women she's "not up to any tricks"—without the saving grace of fundamentalist conviction. If you're going to be unreasonable, you might as well get all possessed and transported about it.   **C+**

Alison Moyet: *Alf* (Columbia '85). Hooking up with Imagination's Swain & Jolley for hologram soul that takes advantage of her giant voice as well as their cushiony electrodance, she gives off all the right signs, romantic victimization prominent among them. I don't believe a word, even though I know it could all be "true." Maybe an aura of artificiality is the point— do I take Leee Johns literally?   **C+**

Mtume: *Juicy Fruit* (Epic '83). How deeply these clever funk lifts and comehither ululations penetrate your mindbody continuum depends on how deeply you're into big-league fucking, which for these folks seems to involve a confusion between candy and fruit. I like both, prefer the latter, and wouldn't advise going to bed with anyone who doesn't know which is which.   **B**

Maria Muldaur: *Gospel Nights* (Takoma '81). In the end I'm not won over by this Rock and Roll for Christ, but I do want to note that Muldaur has never sung with more confidence. Maybe she was of two minds about that sexy w-o-m-a-n stuff.   **B**

Hugh Mundell: *Africa Must Be Free by 1983* (Rockers '85). Mundell was all of sixteen when he cut this record in 1976; in 1983 he was shot to death. He brings to the naivete that can be so annoying in Rasta homilies a sweet, clear, militant innocence rendered even more delicate by Augustus Pablo's piano-tinged production. He believes in life everlasting, and he probably deserved it.   **B+**

Eddie Murphy: *How Could It Be* (Columbia '85). "Singers get all the pussy," the fledgling songwriter and vocalist observed on his last album, devoted to the comedy for which he is best known. "You sing, women go crazy." Poor guy, is he that hard up? Or is it just that like all comedians he longs to prove that he's not as nasty as we know him to be in his finest moments? Well, women aren't gonna take him on down because he sings like this—his voice is so thin that in the end Rick James

("Comedians get all the pussy. You crack a joke, women fall into bed with you") wastes his best track in years on it. And though Stevie Wonder donates two songs, Murphy doesn't bring out his Stevie impression except on his own "I, Me, Us, We," which as a result is the strongest piece of music here. It also typifies the one-worlder cheerleading of a lyricist who can't be as bright as we'd hoped him to be in his finest moments—he's got politics like Jerry Lewis, only with less soul.   **C−**

Eddie Murphy: *So Happy* (Columbia '89). The failure of this wicked Prince rip to scale the charts reminds us once again how difficult it is for defiant outsiders to break new pop ground. Murphy will never be El DeBarge, but he's perfect for cartoon funk, and over the years his wheedling croon has gotten serious. Maybe the problem is that his sexual urges still don't emanate from very deep inside. Often, in fact, they're inspired by his bathroom reading—he's big on locations, spends an entire song convincing her to do it in a chair. Inspirational Dialogue: She: "Are you close?" He: "If I get any closer I be behind you."   **B+**

Anne Murray: *Greatest Hits* (Capitol '80). Following "Snow Bird" with "Danny's Song" with "A Love Song" with "You Won't See Me," the first side is all any curiosity-seeker need own or even know of the singing gym teacher from Nova Scotia. Only a boho bigot could deny these middle-American apotheoses; they bridge cultures as resolutely as C.P. Snow. They also show off Brian Ahern's Nashville country-rock, with Jim Ed Norman's side-closing "You Needed Me" improved by the association. Second side's all Norman, and though most of it is equally tuneful and confident, its complacent calculation is why we need boho bigotry. All told, as neat a demonstration of aesthetic principle as *Metal Machine Music*.   **B+**

Musical Youth: *The Youth of Today* (MCA '82). The miraculous "Pass the Dutchie" was originally a fine Mighty Diamonds song called "Pass the Koochie," so even though the arrangement is pure genius and the switch from ganja (a koochie

is a pipe) to food (a dutchie is a cookpot) pure social responsibility, they've yet to write their first hit. And with reggae bands, not to mention kid bands (even English bands), one-shots are an old story. So I regret to report that the album evinces neither pop songcraft nor the signature groove with which seasoned reggae artists compensate. And am surprised to add that between young Kelvin's biddle-biddle toasts and the reggae songcraft they do command—check out "Youth of Today" and "Young Generation"—they almost get by and then some. Original grade: B plus.   **B**

Music Revelation Ensemble: *No Wave* (Moers Music import '80). I know, Blood Ulmer and his boys probably spent more time plugging in their amps than knocking off the music. Too much of it is free-jazz fucking around, even less faithful to their nuclear fusion in its carelessness than the Rough Trade album in its care. Still, when David Murray starts to blow on the one they call "Baby Talk," and not even over one of Jackson-Ali's funkier beats, it's fun, and a revelation. Buy the official version first. But up this one a notch for erring in the right wrong direction.   **B+**

Mutabaruka: *Check It* (Alligator '83). Is it okay to be impressed by this reggae poet's decidedly unmystical humanist Rastafarianism and still wish his presentation had more of that old-time religion? Though he camouflages his intellectual distance better than Linton Kwesi Johnson, his compassion is less self-effacing, and his dub modernism plays a little too loose with the riddims to suit me. But he has plenty to teach anyone who values reggae strictly for its straightforward charm.   **B+**

Mutabaruka: *Outcry* (Shanachie '84). The man has his merits: "Rememberance" rallies consciousness around the grim history of black oppression, and "Sisters Poem" goes a healthy halfway toward opposing Rastafarian sexism. But too often he's just smart enough to be dumb. What he has in mind for the sisters is the pious pedestal of "Black Queen." Those pondering the Palestinian conundrum may be surprised to learn that "Canaan Lan" will revert to the sons of Ham come millennium time. And any well-meaning white lefty who wonders why U.S.-born blacks don't always rush into common cause with West Indians, not to mention well-meaning white lefties, should check out "Blacks in 'Merika," yet another vague, patronizing, moralistic, ignorant tract imposed from yet another outside.   **B**−

Mutabaruka: *The Mystery Unfolds* (Shanachie '86). "Dis poem is like all the rest / dis poem will not be amongst great literary works." That's what I call attitude, especially since even the first line is true in its unique way, and both are matters of pride. For the first time, this back-to-nature Rasta is showing some of LKJ's sophistication, and on his own terms—he doesn't inveigh against ice cream or trip over his own hapless sexism, but he declines the blandishments of reason in re technocratic conspiracy and revolutionary entertainment, and his political statement is stronger for it. "Dis poem will not change things / dis poem need to be changed." He insists on calling his songs poems, and he doesn't throw one of them away on the riddim. But he has started letting his words hear the music, which capitalizes on reggae's variety, from dub to jazz to anthem to the unaccompanied "Dis Poem." "Dis poem shall be called / borin / stupid / senseless / dis poem is watchin u / tryin to make sense of dis poem."   **A**−

Mutabaruka: *Any Which Way . . . Freedom* (Shanachie '89). I wouldn't give back rock and roll if it were mine to relinquish and Africa's to claim. But for all his ital hit-and-miss, I hope this Afrocentrist is taken seriously—especially when it comes to such crucial matters as God in the sky ("a universal lie") and when-is-a-revolution-not-a revolution? (when it's a revolt). Let it also be noted that he breaks into Afrobeat and pop-funk and chamber-synth more meaningfully than universalists do.   **B**+

Mzwakhe: *Change Is Pain* (Rounder '88). Child of a Zulu father, a Xhosa mother, and the Soweto uprising, he lives on the run, reciting his poetry unannounced and unaccompanied at weddings, funerals, union meetings: an authentic art hero, and as committed a revolutionary as ever cut an album. Which doesn't mean he can be comprehended out of context. So what's amazing about his first stab at music isn't the incompleteness of the translation, but the power. Before he utters a word there's some halting guitar that could make you weep, and despite the disorderly percussion favored by Black Consciousness bands he powers a South African dub poetry—with intimations of an apocalypse that's lived every day and agape so hard-earned only a Boersymp would doubt it.   **B**+

The Nairobi Beat *(Kenyan Pop Music Today)* (Rounder '89). Again and again, tintinnabulating guitar lines lift this carefully annotated compilation of ten dance-length indie singles. When the vocals are something special—a couple of sister acts and the trailing harmonies of two guys who don't want to mind the baby—the lift is all the way to heaven. When they aren't it clears the treetops. **B+**

The Nairobi Sound (Original Music '82). It's not "primitivism" or "simplicity" that makes African pop so exciting—it's the doubly complex interaction of two sophisticated demotic languages, polyrhythm and technomedia, each with its own style of self-consciousness. Unlike his *Africa Dances,* however, this John Storm Roberts anthology has a folkloric feel. Very local in origin and outreach and not really intended for dancing, these Kenyan tunes, especially those in the acoustic (and rural) "dry guitar" style, have enormous charm and not much impact, except for those always special moments of inspiration that propel folk music out into the great world—like the soprano duo "Chemirocha," which technomedia fans will be pleased to learn is a tribute to Jimmie Rodgers. **B+**

Najma: *Qareeb* (Shanachie '88). With no aesthetic judgment implied, the reality encompassed by mass-produced soundtrack schlock and sitar masters fills me with dis-interest, and although I find ragas inoffensive accompaniment to chana vazi and shag panir, I've never voluntarily played one. So I put this on out of professional responsibility (not even curiosity), and fell. Najma is a British Pakistani who popularizes an ancient Urdu lyric form called the ghazal. The words are traditional, with translations that read like abstract love poetry provided. The melodies and vocal harmonies are hers, with soprano sax or fretless bass or guitarlike santoor adding just a touch of Western exoticism. The overall effect is twofold: gentle culture clash and sheer physical beauty. Either one of which would do. **A—**

Naked Raygun: *All Rise* (Homestead '86). Great white hopes they ain't—just anthemic punks with no discernible protofascist undertow, and pretty good at it, too. Which is more than you can say of a lot of white hopes these days. **B**

Roy Nathanson, Curtis Fowlkes and the Jazz Passengers: *Broken Night/Red Light* (Les Disques du Crépuscule import '87). Sax man Nathanson is the second-best composer and best improviser (though not player) in the Lounge Lizards, trombonist Fowlkes his fellow traveler. Here they indulge their fondness for jazz of the real variety without sacrificing their sense of humor or taste in packaging. The tunes are warm but never corny, a distinction lost on the brothers Lurie. The free passages are kept to a modest minimum. The covers include a health-food "Rascal You" and Yiddish "Speedo." **B+**

Native Tongue: *Yowl* (Modern Method '83). What can it mean when all I'm sure of after playing an album a dozen times is that the band likes Wire a lot? But in the end I give them considerable credit for keeping their taut drone on my turntable long past the point when I've sent umpteen similar bands to the warehouse. Which reminds me that in today's permeable musical atmosphere it's conceivable they've never even heard Wire, just Wire's ideas. And actually, I'm also sure they feel "Hoodwinked," the lead cut that kept me coming back after six or seven spins. I bet I even know why they feel hoodwinked. But not because they helped me figure it out. Recommended to rabid formalists and rabid *Pink Flag* fans. **B**

Youssou N'Dour: *Nelson Mandela* (Polydor '86). One *NME* raver cites Einstürzende Neubauten, which may not turn everybody on but does imply Eurocentrism subjected to underdevelopment and its discontents. I hear a gifted singer making a choppy crossover move. The horns recall the pretentious big-band clutter Dave Crawford and Brad Shapiro worked up for a fading Wilson Pickett, and the tama drum is so far up in the mix it tapdances on the groove. N'Dour's high Islamo-Cuban cry and crack Afro-Gallic byplay generate plenty of intrinsic interest, but only on the simple little "Maginnde" do they avoid fragmented overconceptualization. If you say it's ethnographic condescension to prefer the more organic effects of *Immigrés* (Celluloid import), I say it's reflexive progressivism to claim that nobody ever trips going forward—or that every African pop star is a moral force. **B**

Youssou N'Dour: *Immigrés* (Virgin '88). Cut in Paris in 1984 and now wisely remixed, this isn't as epochal as N'Dour thought it was when he wrote the title tune to his displaced Afro-Gallic brothers and sisters. Just a sample of what happens to soukous when West Africans mix in their own beats (and, especially in the horn

lines, their Islamic melodies). And of how beautiful his voice is when he isn't trying too hard. **B+**

Youssou N'Dour: *The Lion* (Virgin '89). Produced by Peter Gabriel henchman George Acogny, this is no more a rhythm album than whatever Gabriel opus you care to recall. It's just a very good Peter Gabriel record. Gabriel's m.o. is to pump up rock and "third-world" sonorities with grandiose settings and structures, then put them across with a big beat; N'Dour's arrangements are less forced, his beats indigenous enough, and his lyrics better. Sure there are old saws ("Truth will always win against deceit," "You should help those with less than you"), and "Macoy," a compassionate vignette of lost virginity concealed, is overwhelmed by its portentous synth-wash-and-percussion accompaniment. But when N'Dour, who's put down as a "ladies" singer by some Senegalese (men, presumably), advises his four-year-old daughter to follow her "destiny," or collaborates with Gabriel on a feminist anthem you can believe in, I think his quest for fame could be as humanitarian as corporate one-worlders claim. And when he's inspired to write a song about a slavery museum in Africa, the NASA museum in Washington, and his favorite, "the museum town of Old Tucson," his ambition—to grasp the past, change the future, and master the very media to which he's been subject by accident of national origin for most of his young life—suddenly seems heroic. **B+**

Negativland: *Escape From Noise* (SST '87). Like so many performance artists of the computerized tape recorder, they would have been called comedians or just wise guys in prepostmodern times, so it's nice that they know something about both music and yucks. Rather than elucidating the title theme, I'll name favorite bits: real-estate ad atop handgun ad, J5 cartoon, four-year-old singing "Over the Rainbow," lecture on the Autonomous Commie Republic, orgasm on the Playboy Channel. And mention that I listen with interest/pleasure to every one. **B+**

Negativland: *Helter Stupid* (SST '89). These Bay Area naysayers have made a conceptual leap—they're like Double Dee & Steinski refracted through the Firesign Theatre, manipulating found (and sought) spoken-word segments over ironic musical segues and backgrounds. Each side-long satire flows and coheres, suitelike on the seven-part "The Perfect Cut," motif-style on the disinformation symphony "Helter Stupid." Dominated by '70s audio promotions and trade ads, "The Perfect Cut" makes a more telling case against commercial radio than any smug media theory (or "alternative" programming). And "Helter Stupid," the fallout from a phony press release implicating one of their songs in a teen ax murder, orchestrates a hash of socially conscious clichés—sensationalism, rock censorship, random violence, gun control, assassination, even that rotten horse the broadcast evangelist—into a funny, slightly scary, dumbfoundingly surreal demonstration of why those clichés so excite rock-culture left-liberals. Because they're all scary, that's why.   **A**—

Bill Nelson: *Vistamix* (Portrait '84). Snazzy guitarist turned decent-enough synth guy, the Spirit of Bebop Deluxe comes up with more dance hooks than Dolby—more even than Duran, at least on this U.S. compilation. And sings like Bowie doing a Jon Anderson impression or vice versa.   **C+**

Willie Nelson & Ray Price: *San Antonio Rose* (Columbia '80). Nelson's groove has resembled a rut since he hit paydirt with *Stardust,* so give a cheer—maybe he's out of it. Country standards gone vaguely Western swing (in Nashville, without horns), this is nothing startling, but the false steps and lackadaisical jams of the live doubles and the Leon Russell job are gone. Price, who tends to posture in countrypolitan settings, thrives on the relaxed atmosphere. People who don't know the originals are going to fall in love.   **B+**

Willie Nelson: *Somewhere Over the Rainbow* (Columbia '81). Nelson's best since *Stardust* isn't quite the rehash it seems to be. The often uptempo music is suffused with Western swing, the standards not all that standard. Which would

be great if only Nelson's ecumenicism didn't run in the direction of "My Mother's Eyes," the aforementioned "Over the Rainbow," and a jazzed-up "Twinkle, Twinkle Little Star."   **B+**

Willie Nelson: *Willie Nelson's Greatest Hits (and Some That Will Be)* (Columbia '81). Nelson's strength is hitting a song on the button while glancing off in the other direction, and a compilation is no way to highlight it—the necessarily haphazard structure makes him seem not so much casual as indolent. He needs a little album structure—standards, collaboration, half-assed narrative—to tone things up. Song for song, relaxing; on the whole, mushy.   **B+**

Willie Nelson & Webb Pierce: *In the Jailhouse Now* (Columbia '82). The strained nasality of Pierce's endless string of '50s honky-tonk hits hasn't aged especially well, but his voice sure has—any suggestion of the callow or awkward is long since gone, which means that for somebody who wasn't there (like me and probably you), some of these remakes sound tougher and more vibrant than the originals. And the originals are honky-tonk standards for a reason. Time: 25:19.   **A**—

Willie Nelson & Roger Miller: *Old Friends* (Columbia '82). As a staunch admirer of "You Can't Roller Skate in a Buffalo Herd" who's had less than no use for Miller since he got serious, I'm almost persuaded by this tribute-to-the-composer cum duo quickie. In fact, one more standout like "Old Friends" (including Ray Price), "Sorry Willie" (didn't know you thought she was your darlin'), and "When a House Is Not a Home" (one of Nelson's patented dry-eyed weepers) would make the difference. Time: 29:42.   **B**

Willie Nelson: *Tougher Than Leather* (Columbia '83). In the end, I don't know what the fuck this supposed concept album is trying to say, and if Nelson does he should continue to keep it to himself—something about murder and honor and other romantic clichés. But since he felt duty-bound to *write* the thing, it does of necessity include a number of those modern rarities, *new Willie Nelson songs!* Including two that *somebody else* might actually want to cover: the throwaway coda "Nobody Slides, My Friend" and the new-cowboy advisory "Little Old-Fashioned Karma." Plus, for (symbolic) life, a rousing new version of "Beer Barrel Polka"! **C+**

Willie Nelson: *Without a Song* (Columbia '83). With music as subtle as Nelson's you wonder whether you're imagining things. Maybe we've just had it with his shtick—maybe a Martian couldn't tell the difference between this and *Stardust.* Then again, what do Martians know? Not only is Nelson choosing cornier material—self-serving schlock like the title song, awkward fripperies like "A Dreamer's Holiday"—but the relaxed, let's-wing-it delicacy has simply disappeared. When he tries at all, he usually oversings, and he's finally hitting the wrong clinkers. If you don't believe me, compare this "Autumn Leaves" to *Stardust*'s timeless "September Song." Or ask yourself whether Julio Iglesias doesn't sound right at home on "As Time Goes By." **C+**

Willie Nelson & Hank Snow: *Brand on My Heart* (Columbia '85). If you're tempted by Willie and Double K's *Songwriter* soundtrack, go on to the next graf. Best thing about his mucho pusho duet compilation with Hank Williams, Julio Iglesias, Lacy J. Dalton, and so forth is its title: *Half Nelson. Highwaymen,* featuring Johnny Cash on every track plus Waylon and Double K on many, is *Outlaws III* (or *V,* who's counting?), with Cash's "Committed to Parkview" providing a therapeutic shot of contemporary realism. *Angel Eyes,* backed by the Nashville-gone-jazzer guitar of Jackie King, is Nashville-gone-jazzy. The Faron Young collaboration *Funny How Time Slips Away* is almost on a level with Willie's Ray Price album, but Young's timbre has thickened so moistly you'd swear the Hank Williams he's now imitating is Jr. And so. I've always been put off by Snow's up-north propriety, more Vernon Dalhart than Jimmie Rodgers, but after 70 years his baritone is finally beginning to crack, providing Willie just the opening he needs to loosen the old pro up: without sacrificing a diphthong of his famous enunciation, Snow sounds completely relaxed. The tossed-off serendipity of so many Nelson records translates here into a casually engaging, deftly eclectic bunch of classics and obscurities, Willie's best album since he and Webb Pierce cut *In the Jailhouse Now* on a long coffee break in 1982. Original grade: A minus. **A**

Willie Nelson: *Me and Paul* (Columbia '85). Nothing like a concept to nudge an interpreter's near misses closer to direct hits, but not any concept will do. On 1984's *City of New Orleans,* Willie added less than nothing to the self-consciously distanced sentimentality of country songs manqué that had their own integrity coming from Arlo Guthrie, Danny O'Keefe, even Dave Loggins. Here the album is dedicated to his hellraising longtime drummer Paul English and the self-conscious distance is from himself. Backed by his road band and singing three Billy Joe Shaver sure shots and nine mostly pre-CBS songs of his own, many of which you'll be certain you know but fail to locate in your record collection, he comes up with his most unassuming and inevitable album since the ten 1961 demos of 1978's *Face of a Fighter.* **A—**

Willie Nelson: *A Horse Called Music* (Columbia '89). Over the four or five albums of a commercial decline that's probably permanent, he's proven more George Jones than Merle Haggard. That is, he's a genius interpreter who always stands a chance of hitting you where you live—even though, like Merle, he still occasionally writes his own, and because of rather than despite the show of laziness the two share. Assuming you can stomach many strings and two pretentious clinkers (the title trope plus one called "If I Were a Painting"), this is his best of the period, maybe because he put the least effort into it—it's when he tries to sing powerfully, or traffics in concepts like the '50s standards of *What a Wonderful World,* that he flounders. Sometimes, of course, his modest efforts come across flat; sometimes, no doubt, they really are lazy. But most of these murmured tributes to good love getting better and gone bad are touching and apt. **B**

Willie Nelson: See also Merle Haggard & Willie Nelson

Nervus Rex: *Nervus Rex* (Dreamland '80). Lauren Agnelli has gotten noticed ever since she was Trixie A. Balm, but Shaun Brighton is the secret: no matter how much you object to his fruity singing, don't miss his songs. Imagine the Left Banke with Mike Chapman, a sense of humor, and the wherewithal to hold up their own legend. Imagine "Don't Look" following up "Walk Away Renee." **B+**

Aaron Neville: *Orchid in the Storm* (Passport EP '85). In which Joel Dorn lets the eerie, quavering shimmer and imperturbable naturalness of Aaron's falsetto run, drift, float, or soar with six '50s covers. The singer avoids the overstated Russell Thompkins mode more wanly than necessary, but with teen dreams from Johnny Ace and the Penguins turned into the essence of timeless romance, the sublimely silly "Ten Commandments of Love" sounds like dictation from Mount Sinai. [Later on Rhino.]   **B+**

Aaron Neville: *Make Me Strong* (Charly import '86). Produced between 1968 and 1975 by Allen Toussaint, every song here stiffed if it got released at all, yet taken together they constitute a classic singer's album as well as the ideal testament to Toussaint's spacey romanticism. The unhurried tempos often do without Toussaint's piano, but Neville's buttery tenor captures the spirituality that Lee Dorsey's waggishness obscured and Toussaint's bare vocal competence doomed to limbo.   **A−**

The Neville Brothers: *Fiyo on the Bayou* (A&M '81). Unlike their Jack Nitzsche–produced flop, this one sounds like gumbo—the spirit is willing and the flesh can't resist. Unfortunately, the tunes are so surefire that I long ago memorized the way other Nworlins stalwarts (and Jimmy Cliff) do 'em—in a word, better. An enjoyable way for neophytes to get into the most universal rock and roll style—and a lazy way for oldtimers to convince themselves that the world isn't changing.   **B+**

The Neville Brothers: *Neville-ization* (Black Top '84). Every once in a while an album comes up from New Orleans that captures the seemingly timeless spirit of the place as if by magic. But it's fun to figure out the tricks. The novelty of the Mardi Gras Indians made the Meters doubly infectious on *The Wild Tchoupitoulas.* Subtly hyped-up arrangements nudged Professor Longhair on Atlantic's live double. And here the secret isn't just the ever more exquisitely articulated harmonies of the city's definitive band, but also the unpressured live setting that instead of positing pop potential (the Capitol album) or archival integrity (the A&M) presents them as the lounge-act-gone-to-heaven they are. How often does an improvisation improve a classic original like Aaron's "Tell It Like It Is"? How many bands can get away with both "Caravan" and an antinuke ditty? If only they thought it was okay for women to wear pants.   **A−**

The Neville Brothers: *Treacherous* (Rhino '86). Except for Aaron, they're journeymen rather than geniuses, neither as major nor as pure as they're made out to be. Art and Cyril have never sung better than their material, often rendering it soulfully generic, and Art's keyboards were less integral to the ass-busting complexities the Meters worked on New Orleans's Latin tinge than Leo Nocentelli's guitar, George Porter's bass, or, God knows, Ziggy Modeliste's drums. This two-disc career summation is less essential than the Meters' *Sophisticated Cissy,* not to mention *The Wild Tchoupitoulas,* which it cribs from. But it does isolate four thoroughly enjoyable Art tracks (two more than you'll find on his own *Mardi Gras Rock 'n' Roll*), and sum up in two sides everything that's most winning about the slightly showy, uniquely unoriginal New Orleans rhythm synthesis their cult craves.   **A−**

The Neville Brothers: *Uptown* (EMI America '87). Contrary to rumor, the drums are almost all live, but they so rarely venture an offbeat that it's a solecism to call the result commercial funk. It's not crossover because the Nevilles have no black/"urban" base to cross over from, and no one's claiming it's New Orleans. Nope—between adult themes, solidly insinuating tunes, uncommonly grizzled vocals, and faint indigenous lilt, what we have here is a pretty damn good CHR album. Too bad "Whatever It Takes" and "Midnight Key" will never prove the durability of their old-love-rekindled and night-lust-unloosed in the crucible of high rotation; too bad "Shak-a-Na-Na" 's second-linish Brit imagism and "Old Habits Die Hard" 's Tops-Tempts-Tavares homage aren't gimmicky enough to push some gatekeeper's everything-old-is-new button. Because this risks the unknown just the way the crass dance-fad novelty "Mardi Gras Mambo" did in 1954. There's aesthetic tension in its craft and blind ambition, and reason to think it'll sound quirkier and realer than *Fiyo on the Bayou* another 23 years down the line.   **B+**

The Neville Brothers: *Yellow Moon* (A&M '89). Daniel Lanois's production is so subtle that at first this seems like a return to mighty-kootie-fiyo, but in fact it's the modernization they've been chasing since the Meters were history. Whether isolating rhythm-makers, adding electronic atmosphere, or recontextualizing "natural"-seeming instrumental effects (the un–New Orleans bottleneck that grounds "The Ballad of Hollis Brown," the Dirty Dozen horns that rescue "Wild Injuns" from generic throwaway), Lanois isn't afraid to go for drama, and while drama does have a way of palling eventually, the songs are worth the risk. The expansive "My Blood" and the educational "Sister Rosa" are their finest millennial-political originals ever, and though "Hollis Brown," "With God on Our Side," "A Change Is Gonna Come," and "Will the Circle Be Unbroken" may seem like an obvious bunch of covers, their total effect is audacious instead (one '64 Dylan OK, but two?). Add Art's singing lessons (from Aaron) and Charles's horn lessons (from Lee Allen, say) and you have their masterpiece. Even the languors of "Healing Chant" seem apt and premeditated.   **A**

The New Dylans: *The New Dylans* (Caveat Emptor EP '86). Backed by bass and drums from 10,000 Maniacs of Jamestown, New York, James Scott Reilly and Reese Edward Campbell Jr. of Warren, Pennsylvania, make songs out of the shopping malls and bad marriages of their shitty little town (well, that's what they seem to think). Their Byrdsy hooks (out of R.E.M., by 10,000 Maniacs) decorate dense yet literal lyrics—lyrics whose specifics sour as you listen. Their name may not be as ironic as they hope—like Bobby, they read too much poetry. And love 'em or hate 'em, they don't say much for shitty little towns. Original grade: B plus.   **B**

New Edition: *Candy Girl* (Streetwise '83). In which amassed svengalis manage an album that won't leave those captivated by the big hit feeling ripped off—the rap is cute, the recitative is cute, and "Popcorn Love" is a neat kiddiephile conceit. But the kiddies don't sing that good. And they're not even related.   **B**

New Edition: *New Edition* (MCA '84). Though a confusion of production teams—five in all, none associated with the ousted Arthur Baker except by ripoff (from Freeez's "I.O.U.," very clever)—gives these kids' major-label hit a misbegotten look, in the end the album achieves the winning commercial variety Baker didn't get out of them. But I admit it—for me the biggest winner is "My Secret," which does sound an awful lot like the Jackson 5.   **B+**

New Edition: *All for Love* (MCA '86). Bright and shiny as a new cliché, Ralph Tresvant is equal to any J5 (or MJ) fantasy the group's multifarious writers and producers throw at him, and for most of the first side so are they. Second side's more like, you guessed it, the Force M.D.'s, and won't keep anybody in school either.   **B–**

New Kids on the Block: *Hangin' Tough* (Columbia '88). At six million and counting, this isn't the rank offense its demographic tilt would lead you to expect—auteur Maurice Starr has positioned two exceedingly cute uptempo hits atop two overly balladic sides. Really, why shouldn't a black svengali mastermind the safe white r&b ripoff for once? Funkier than the Osmonds *or* Milli Vanilli. As hip as New Edition.   **C+**

Colin Newman: *A-Z* (Beggars Banquet import '80). Projected and rejected as the fourth Wire album, it would have been the right step backwards—regressive only if you consider noise uncouth. Producer Mike Thorne's keyboards are indeed all over the place, but rather than laying down the trancy gloss of 154, they do what they can to rub a body the wrong way, just like Newman's guitar. Leading me to suspect that the absent Graham Lewis is Wire's new-waving fifth columnist. Of course, Lewis also probably contributes the catchy stuff—where on *Pink Flag* you remember every allusively desperate little song, here you recognize the oblique, abrasive gestalt. And remember "B," which has no lyrics at all, every time its rousing climax comes around.   **B+**

Randy Newman: *Trouble in Paradise* (Warner Bros. '83). The reason 1979's *Born Again* took three years to sink in for me was that Newman never pinned down the distance between himself and the creeps he wrote his first-person songs about. Because he's gained control as a singer, his oafish drawl here turns into a unifying voice, and the accompaniments are as eloquently integral as the American-colloquial pastiche of his *Ragtime* sound-track. So this time the baffled racist of "Christmas in Capetown" and the happy-go-lucky Disney hero of "I'm Different" and the sentimental pimp of "Same Girl" and the mournfully manipulative patriot of "Song for the Dead" and the unflappa-bly egoistic rock star of the outrageous "My Life Is Good" all seem to be the same guy. And while that guy isn't Newman, Newman does go out of his way to under-stand his point of view.   **A—**

Randy Newman: *Land of Dreams* (Re-prise '88). He who lives by the putdown shall die by the putdown, so Newman's first nonsoundtrack album in almost six years is unlikely to increase his renown or his financial holdings. And indeed, it's half mishmash, replete with compulsive irony, rap parody, and spare, hooked love songs that are equally unbelievable happy or sad. But there's a new pitch of displacement to the pseudo-autobiographical triptych at the outset, and a new pitch of bitterness to the scabrous putdowns that highlight the close. The airplay hit "It's Money That Matters" and the "We Are the World"

answer song "I Want You To Hurt Like I Do" are the attention-getters. The cruelly laid-back supply-side boogie-woogie "Roll With the Punches" and the symphonically overstated going-to-school reminiscence "Four Eyes" are the strokes. Inspirational Verse: "Here's your little brown shoes, *can you tie them yourself?*"   **B+**

New Model Army: *No Rest for the Wicked* (Capitol '85). The State Depart-ment says they can't tour the U.S.—"no artistic merit." You can understand why they think this reflects on their politics, which are in the old English tradition of left chauvinism—they hate consumer blandishments with a passion that springs not from their readings in Hans Magnus Enzensberger but from a natural militance that deplores softness in class allies. Such an ideology would exclude artistic merit in the minds of most bureaucrats (as indeed would many other ideologies, not to mention the presence of electric guitars), and that's abhorrent. I'd be hard-pressed to argue compelling positive distinction on an often plodding football-punk sort of album, its words sharper in tone and spirit than content. But I'd give it a try.   **B**

New Model Army: *The Mark of Cain* (Capitol '86). If Tom Robinson had been young and proletarian enough to want the TRB to sound like the Clash, this oi band gone pop is how it might have come out. After three albums their gift for the an-them far exceeds, for instance, Easter-house's, as in the anti-American "51st State" and the anti-'76 "Heroes." And though their vigilante rhetoric and doubts about terrorism have some young reds thinking fascist dupe, they're just working-class guys whose left instincts are ahead of their ideology—which I hope never shrugs off street crime or package bombs.   **A—**

New Model Army: *New Model Army* (Capitol EP '87). Although the object of Slade the Leveller's fury isn't hard to fig-ure out—"She'll dance on our graves" doesn't refer to his mum—the analysis on the three new studio songs is a bit meta-phorical for such a populist band. What white coats? What Valley of Death? What Chinese whispers? The live best-of on the

B is a live best-of plus half an unannounced sea chantey. **B**−

New Model Army: *Thunder and Consolation* (Capitol '89). The alienation most bands traffic in is a byproduct of moderate privilege—with sustenance a given, they rant or joke or whine or bellow about meaning. This band sings for the true losers. Given their subject/audience, it's no wonder they've been known to make Britcrits fret—crippled and scattered by Thatcherism, deprived of the belonging the family isn't good for anymore, these ordinary ungifted people could turn into reaction's foot soldiers. Of course, give up on them and that's what you leave them. Identify, empathize, observe, remember, and they've got that much margin. **B**+

New Order: *Movement* (Factory '81). For months I've sworn to concentrate on the lyrics and be done with this goddamn record, but it ain't gonna happen. The singing isn't literally inaudible, but it is literally unprojected, much less noticeable than the surrounding drum, guitar, and synthesizer rhythms/effects. Very atmospheric—the spaceship as sepulcher, with a beat. And as long as I literally don't have to hear their doomy doggerel, not a bad way to go. **B**+

New Order: *1981–1982* (Factus '82). Bargain hunters shouldn't pass up this chance to own "Temptation" plus-four for close to the price of the twelve-inch. But I don't call the twelve-inch "Temptation"/ "Hurt" for the same reason I can't remember which of the four is which after playing them all fifteen times. "Temptation" is where Manchester's finest stop hearing ghosts and stake their claim to a danceable pop of unprecedented grimness and power. If it isn't the definition of romantic obsession, it's even richer than I think it is. But it's also the first real song this sharp-cornered sound-and-groove band has ever come up with. **B**+

New Order: *Power, Corruption and Lies* (Factus '83). The second or third Joy Division II album has occasioned disputation among the faithful. Some claim that it cynically recycles their riffs, while others think it raises that old new music to transcendent summits. Me, I find it relatively

gentle and melodic in its ambient postindustrial polyrhythms, their nicest record ever. I also think it sounds pretty much like the others. **B**+

New Order: *Low-Life* (Qwest '85). Where once they determined to keep all affect out of their music, now they determine to put some in. Any dance-trance outfit that can lead off its Quincy Jones debut with an oblique "Love Me Do" quote has its heart (or a reasonable facsimile thereof) in the right place, so one doesn't want to quibble. But inserting affect isn't the same as actually feeling something, and it isn't the same as expressing (or even simulating) a feeling, either. **B**+

New Order: *Brotherhood* (Qwest '86). I never knew why their definitive electrodisco impressed me more than it moved me, and now I don't know why it has me rocking out of my chair or grinning foolishly as I forage for dinner at the supermarket. The tempos are a touch less stately, the hooks a touch less subliminal. Bernard Albrecht's vocals have taken on so much affect they're humane. And the joke closer softens up a skeptic like me to the pure, physically exalting sensation of the music. **A**

New Order: *Substance* (Qwest '87). Twelve cuts, eleven previously released some way or other, five available some way or other on U.S. albums, only one in this form. The emphasis is on twelve-inch mixes, with a new vocal patched into the hallowed "Temptation." The double-CD includes a whole extra disc of collectorama, but the double vinyl has no fat: it does nothing less than show off the greatest disco band of the '80s except Chic, and these guys outlasted Chic. Of course, not until Chic was gone did their disco dwell fully among us. The secret of Bernard Albrecht's elementary vocals, Gillian Gilbert's two-finger exercises, Peter Hook's strummed bass, and the compressed physicality of Steve Morris's drums was never virtuosity—it was conception, timing, rapport, devotional concentration. Originally attracted to disco because it was trancelike, they broke through when they devised a system of kinetic percussion and hypnotic chants to keep themselves awake. Cultists miss the murk of the early mixes, but I prefer them hyped and speeded up. Pure rhythm machine with an ironically mysterious overlay of schlocky melody to help it go down, this album is a case study in sensationalist art, and I say the world is better for it.   **A**

New Order: *Technique* (Qwest '89). The catchy Anglodisco that gloom fans have complained about ever since the band lightened up finally arrives, and it's a lot franker and happier (hence smarter) than Depeche Mode. But now that Bernard is a full-fledged human being, we find out he's a slightly boring human being. Is this why he was always in the dumps?   **B+**

Olivia Newton-John: *Olivia's Greatest Hits Vol. 2* (MCA '82). With a kick in her pert little butt from John Travolta, the Melbourne chameleon has abandoned her conquest of Nashville for a funkier brand of perky, with seven more top-ten singles her reward, and she's sexier than Barbara Mandrell for damn sure. Any heterosexual man who can deny "Physical," with its detonating blonde bombshell switching off from "physical" to "animal" for the grand finale, needs his monkey-gland shot—to dismiss it as an aerobics song is brunette chauvinism, period. The rest you can pass on to your exercise teacher without permission from the Board of Health.   **B−**

New York Dolls: *Lipstick Killers* (ROIR cassette '81). Nine great songs, three of them covers, including the previously unavailable "Don't Mess With Cupid." If I knew no other versions, I'd recommend these 1972 demos, but as it is Johnny sounds tame, doomed drummer Billy Murcia halting, Arthur out of tune (shocking!), and David perhaps halfway to the wit and assurance that brought this great band together.   **C+**

New York Dolls: *Red Patent Leather* (Fan Club import '84). Featuring the original lineup plus a tactful second bass and full of unavailable originals and covers, this live recording from their 1975 fling with Malcolm McLaren looks like a gem and sounds like shit. Literally: audio is maybe a notch above Velvets-at-Max's or Beatles-at-Star-Club, with David undermiked and the guitars buried behind Ar-

thur & Friend. What's more, the originals are all Syl's, highlighted by "Teenage News," which he improved on his generally forgettable solo album four years later. For documentarians only.   **C+**

Mbongeni Ngema: *Time To Unite* (Mango '88). Once you get past the underwhelming Jo'burg-goes-B'way rhythm section and the overpowering Jo'burg-takes-B'way chorus, Ngema's background as a township guitarist makes itself heard. The man projects so powerfully that you begin to think his political commitment, theatrical gifts, and way with South African English could make mbaqanga a truly international style. Then you notice that while in *Sarafina!* the girls take over, the villains of these pieces—a golddigger, an aborter, and an informer—are all women. Ain't contradiction the shits?   **B**

Yaa-Lengi Ngemi: *Oh, Miziki* (MiyeMi '86). Spare and delicate where most West Africans layer on the rhythms, this Harlem-based Zairean doesn't have much choice—except for two backup vocalists and a guy who chips in the occasional horns and auxiliary guitar, he plays everything himself. Ngemi's conversational tenor lifts off into falsetto whoops, his pulse is cleaner if less awesome than its homegrown counterparts, and the high, sweet, minimal guitar obbligatos never let you down. Four titles, an hour of beguiling groove.   **A−**

Obed Ngobeni: *My Wife Bought a Taxi* (Shanachie '88). Unable to contain his pride in his wife's nursing diploma or his homeland's bus service, Ngobeni shouts roughly and excitedly at the three Kurhula Sisters, who shout boisterously and joyously right back at him, with the "social commentary" promised in the notes limited to the usual warnings against gossips and ne'er-do-wells. As so often with South African pop, I wonder how much good (and bad) such lyrics can do. But I have no doubts about Ngobeni's Shangaan beat, which lopes through the grass and pounds along with its nose in the dust simultaneously, and I love the way the synthesizer evokes now a mbira, now an accordion, now a Farfisa, now a Hammond B-3.   **A**—

Nightmare Alley: *Victim Turns Blue/*
Bop Ramboe and the Ratbags: *Ratbags on Parade* (Weatherproof Stew '85). Ramboe used to be Nightmare Alley's rhythm guitarist, and since his Ratbags comprise bass and drums from his old band, I suggest he return to that position with expanded responsibilities. His postliterate wit ("When you got 'em by the balls you got their hearts and minds") and referential rock and roll ("Give My Regards to Broadway"?) are cut from the same cloth, and maybe if he and Frank Ruscitti traded vocals, making this an album instead of a double EP, they'd achieve that mysterious simulation of musicality that induces radio's overseers to program wise guys. Then again, maybe they wouldn't—Ramboe is pretty tuneless, Ruscitti pretty tense.   **B**+

The Nitecaps: *Go to the Line* (Sire '82). Things get gritty like clockwork on this little bit of soul, which John Xavier signifies—rather inappropriately, I feel—by gargling. The Uptown Horns keep themselves busy up top.   **C**

Mojo Nixon and Skid Roper: *Mojo Nixon and Skid Roper* (RBI '85). Folkies, I guess—front man Mojo on acoustic guitar, Skid on harp, washboard, etc. But with strange roots: the blues rant that leads off quotes both "Road Runner" and "I'm Waiting for the Man" as it rambles insanely from inspiration to inspiration. Mojo is definitely touched by something—he preaches like Jimmy Lee Swaggart in the devil's hands, gobbles mushrooms and sniffs turds, sleeps on your couch. But he also fucks your mama and your girlfriend from behind, solicits head from "art fag hags," and for his last trick beats up some gal who must have had it coming. Some white boys just can't handle the blues.   **C**+

Mojo Nixon & Skid Roper: *Frenzy* (Restless '86). Though it pulls up lame midway through side two and resorts to rape jokes that piss on the memory of Howlin' Wolf and for that matter Wolfman Jack, this album is as rude as it wants to be. Where competing raunch hands end at obscenity, Mojo starts there and moves on, saving his most raucous loathing for songs like "I Hate Banks" (and he don't mean Ernie or the Mississippi) and "Ain't Got No Boss" ("This *is* a personal phone call").   **B**+

Mojo Nixon and Skid Roper: *Get Out of My Way* (Enigma EP '86). Pop anarchobeatnikism has its political attractions—hard to argue when a college band calls for mall-burning even if the moment isn't historically propitious. But if Mojo thinks freedom's just another word for passing me on the shoulder in a traffic jam, let him try it—I'll veer right and proceed at exactly the same speed as our fellow citizen-sufferers, which I know from experience will make their day as much as it'll piss Mojo off. And if Mojo rams me in extended adolescent frustration, I'll sue his ass for the rights to "Stuffin' Martha's Muffin." Always did think those royalties should redound to National Rape Crisis Headquarters. [Also included on CD version of *Frenzy.*]   **B**+

Mojo Nixon & Skid Roper: *Bo-Day Shus!!!* (Enigma '87). Art statements like "Wash No Dishes No More" and "I Ain't Gonna Piss in No Jar" can't be laughed off these days, "Elvis Is Everywhere" is for Phil Ochs in heaven, and by laying down cassette-and-CD-only tracks worth hearing they face up to their formal problem—making irresponsibility new. Not only would the agape-riven "Don't Want No Foo-Foo Haircut on My Head" and the primordial "Story of One Chord" fit quite audibly onto twelve inches of vinyl, they'd enlighten Mojo's collegiate followers. This cannot be said of the Americana-mongering "We Gotta Have More Soul!" and "B.B.Q. U.S.A.," much less Skid's "Lincoln Logs," in which the poor folkie misses his boyhood toys boo hoo.   **B**+

Mojo Nixon and Skid Roper: *Root Hog or Die* (Enigma '89). With Jim Dickenson's sparely applied sidemen adding the funky feel that Mojo previously sought to provide with Howlin' Wolf and Jimmy Lee Swaggart impressions, this is his finest artistic achievement. Skid's cut is the usual yawn, but everything else cooks with gas.

"Pirate Radio" turns out to be a Shane-MacGowan-as-Captain-Hook chantey, "Chicken Drop" gets rid of his four-letter-word and junk-Americana obligations in the same song, "I'm a Wreck" warns against excess without moralizing. "She's Vibrator Dependent" is laced with a self-deprecation rare in his previous gyne-phobic forays. "Burn Your Money!," "Legalize It," and a "This Land Is Your Land" that features the Mojoland amusement park all voice a gonzo-leftist anarcho-populism that I trust has rubbed off on his MTV following. And the keynoting "Debbie Gibson Is Pregnant With My Two Headed Love Child," written in the supermarket-tabloid style that exerts such a strong influence on Mojo's poesy, is the humane version of "Stuffin' Martha's Muffin."   **A**−

The Nomads: *Outburst* (What Goes On import '84). Why is this neogarage band better than all other neogarage bands? Admittedly, it could just be taste in covers—Alex Chilton and Sleepy John Estes as well as the Kinks and the eternal Standells. And it could be appetite for covers—eight all told leave room for only four overly generic originals. But it certainly helps that they're from Sweden—means their preference for American music is democratic rather than chauvinistic and adventurous rather than sentimental. Original grade: A minus.   **B+**

NRBQ: *Grooves in Orbit* (Bearsville '83). They really are virtuosos of fun, a major accomplishment that makes for minor records. They're so dedicated to the perpetual adolescence of pure (or purist) rock and roll that they imitate youth—Joey Spampinato is the most egregious coy-boy in this band of players first and singers second—rather than redefining youthfulness, a more appropriate task for artists of their advancing years. I know they're only kidding (har har), but at some level these are guys who still believe a real girl (not woman, please) sews your shirt and shines your shoes.   **B**

NRBQ: *Tapdancin' Bats* (Rounder/Red Rooster '83). Here's the fun record these fabled funsters have had in them for fif-teen years. Concentrating on original novelty tunes, all big requests at parties, it neutralizes their fatal cuteness by making a virtue of it, with highlights that include tributes to their manager and their sweeties, a throwaway rockabilly raver, and yuck-it-ups about hard times. Even the three sloppy-cum-experimental chops-and-noodles instrumentals fit in, although I could do without the climactic title number, which seems to feature a saxophone reed.   **A**−

NRBQ: *God Bless Us All* (Rounder '87). The first live album by the Northeast's finest road band stands a chance of showing the rest of the world what it's been missing. It also runs the risk of revealing how the rest of the world managed to stay away. Face it, fans—expecting the same old unexpected can deaden the synapses too, and 20 years can put the snazziest key changes and time signatures in a rut. One set, no song list, audience all unawares, hot-cha-cha.   **B**

NRBQ: *Wild Weekend* (Virgin '89). First cute, then peculiar, then annoying, their callow act is turning positively perverse as they twinkle-toe past forty. "Boy's Life" and "Immortal for a While" are only where they state their interest in so many words—everywhere Joey Spampinato's eager eternal-adolescent whine rubs up against Terry Adams's sly grown-up changes. They may be smart enough to consider this a creative tension, but it isn't. It's an evasion—a fib as opposed to a lie, kiddies—and it isn't funny anymore.   **B**−

N.T.U. Small Tigers: *Mususkungibulala Wethu* (Kaya import '87). Anybody with a taste for mbube's droll complexities, especially those who find Ladysmith too sweet (the pleasures some people deny themselves for tough-mindedness's sake), will get a kick out of this alternative. Without a great voice up top, the Small Tigers emphasize quirk and interplay, cutting whistles and clicks and animal noises and nasalities through the harmonies. Sing in English, too—but sound more at home in Zulu.   **B+**

The Nuclear Regulatory Commission: *Reactor* (Official '80). Music: Jefferson

Starship meets Foghat meets Devo, completely unoriginal except in the guileless enthusiasm of its unoriginality. Bonnie Bonnickson: Lydia Pense meets Lene Lovich, ditto. Social nexus: The Farm, Stephen Gaskin's dubious venture in counterculture communalism. Rationale: No more nukes. Message: Hippie lives! And protests! And still has a sense of humor about it! Pix to click: "White Sugar," which is pro, and "Fax," ditto. Original grade: B plus.   **B**

Nuestras Mejores Cumbias (Globo '89). Where the competing *Fiesta Vallenata* has the imprimatur of the world-music good guys at GlobeStyle and Shanachie, this Colombian compilation comes from an RCA subsidiary—two stocking-clad gams stretch ceilingward through a field of balloons on the cover. But I swear it wasn't antiliberal tendencies that induced me to put *Fiesta Vallenata's* raggedy-ass polkas in the hall while carrying this jaunty, chintzy subsalsa to friends' birthday parties. It was spontaneous attraction. I've since learned that accordion-based vallenata is cowboy music turned cocaine-lord music, while clarinet-hooked cumbia is a mulatto urban style with a longer pop history, and I'm glad I chose the right side. But if the cocaine lords seize cumbia (and for all I know they already have), I bet what makes it jaunty, though maybe not what makes it chintzy, will still liven up a party.   **A—**

Ted Nugent: *Great Gonzos—The Best of Ted Nugent* (Epic '81). Anybody who gets misty-eyed about the MC-5 owes it to himself (or herself, believe it or not) to ponder this Detroit boy's, well, let's call it his sexual rhetoric, which was virtually invented by the White Panthers. Maybe the when-in-doubt-whip-it-out of "Stranglehold" and "Wang Dang Sweet Poontang" and "Free for All" are only metaphors, but as metaphors, well, let's just say they suck. And having done so, let's add with only slightly guilty pleasure that his musclebound gooniness is a hoot. It's an evasion to pass him off as a harmless joke, but it's a distortion to pretend that he or anyone in his audience takes his bullshit more

than half seriously. From flash guitar to locomotive beat to secret tunes, he's an unreconstructed '60s survivor—the hippie-biker as feral sex fiend, terror of countless timid ninnies and nice people. One way or another, well, let's just say I get off on everything here, with the slobbering "Wango Tango" a special favorite. Rock and roll!   **B+**

Gary Numan: *The Pleasure Principle* (Atco '80). Once again, metal machine music goes easy-listening. But last time the commander-in-chief of the tubeway army was singing about furtive sex, policemen, and isolation, while this time he's singing about robots, engineers, and isolation. In such a slight artist, these things make all the difference.   **B**

N.W.A.: *Straight Outta Compton* (Ruthless '88). "It's not about a salary / It's all about reality" they chant as they talk shit about how bad they are. Right, it's not about salary—it's about royalties, about brandishing scarewords like "street" and "crazy" and "fuck" and "reality" until suckers black and white cough up the cash. "Fuck tha Police" is a fantasy, "Fuck with me I'll put my foot in your ass" an exaggeration, "Life ain't nothin' but bitches and money" a home truth, and I bet Ice Cube gets more pussy now than when he copped the line. Somehow DJs Dr. Dre and Yella, who's also got the brainiest rap on the Charles Wright rip that busts out of their ghetto, drive the three MCs past their own lies half the time. It would be poetic justice if both of them departed for greener pastures.   **B**

Nyboma: *Doublé Doublé* (Rounder '84). Four eight-minute dance tracks plunked down into a standard African (also disco) album format, this features the almost feminine tenor of the leader of Zaire's Orchestre les Kamalé, but it's made by the guitar parts. The one that hooks the title track resolves a familiar African contradiction—it's both the trickiest and the most propulsive thing on the record, and well worth owning. The rest is at least worth hearing.   **B+**

N.Y.C. Peech Boys: *Life Is Something Special* (Island '83). This is virtually an encyclopedia of N.Y.C. dance music—no microchips anywhere carry so much verve, sex, or grit. Only in N.Y.C., however, do people dance a whole lot to encyclopedias, and I fear that if "Don't Make Me Wait" didn't convert the great out-there then the rest of this is doomed to a life of obscurity.   **B+**

Laura Nyro: *Mother's Spiritual* (Columbia '84). Though for a long time Nyro's heartfelt commitment to solipsism blocked her access to the greater truth, the romantic generalizations of matrifocal ecofeminism prove as ideally suited to her moody style of gush as the pat improvisations of "women's" folk-jazz do to her once unique and still arresting swoops and changes. Now that she's not only a refugee from the city but a mom herself, she's created an album "dedicated to the trees." Of course, earth motherhood can be a bummer sometimes, so if she can get hold of "a ship from space" she'll take her leave of this "world that cannot give." Then we'll be sorry. Inspirational Footnote (to the line "while hawks* destroy"): "*This word is being used in its traditional sense of war consciousness and not in reference to the spirit of the soaring bird."   **C+**

Ebnezer Obey: *Juju Jubilee* (Shanachie '85). I didn't pay much heed to complaints that this album cheated Nigeria's other big juju star by fading his hot tracks early. After all, juju isn't supposed to begin and end the way mbaqanga or Europop does—songs are designed to segue together for nonstop dancing. And there are notable themes and spectacular sounds throughout. But since they never assert a collective identity, cheating Americans of the wholeness they look for in African music, I have to assume the fades are at least partly at fault. **B+**

The Obvious: *Home* (I Wanna EP '87). When neopunks do the slowun twice, once with "shitty" changed to "pretty" for (college) radio, you can be fairly sure the slowun's a goodun, and very sure that just like most neopunks they haven't managed to imbue their formal skill with the urgency that once made the form compelling. **B**

Ric Ocasek: *Beatitude* (Geffen '83). They say Ocasek forces it with the Cars, but *Shake It Up* sounded too relaxed, while this solo effort is tense throughout. And if instrumentally the effect is bracing, vocally it's constipated: only on the avuncular "Jimmy Jimmy" do his affections (not to mention his pretensions) have any roughage to them. **B−**

Billy Ocean: *Suddenly* (Jive '84). Jimmy Cliff he ain't, and Jimmy Cliff ain't all that much. But platinum-plus he is, and it's my considered guess that we'll be hearing more lilting, faintly West Indian tenors, the closest England comes to soul. **C+**

Billy Ocean: *Greatest Hits* (Arista '89). All second-rate soul singers are creatures of their arrangements; what makes it harder to pin Billy down is that these days a lot of first-rate soul singers are also creatures of their arrangements. "When the Going Gets Tough, the Tough Get Going" and "Get Outta My Dreams Get Into My Car" not only hold the record for the most uses of a verb other than "love" in a great hit and its de facto follow-up, they're also a great hit and its de facto followup. Many other fast ones are quite OK. One of the "newly recorded hit singles" utilizes the Fresh Prince. Second-rate soul singers have to keep up with the times. **B**

Sinéad O'Connor: *The Lion and the Cobra* (Chrysalis '87). Lots of Peter Gabriel and Kate Bush, goodly helpings of Irish folk and European art, touches of Laurie Anderson and Diamanda Galas and Patti Smith. Some U2, probably; Jesus, maybe some Horslips. Titles like "Troy" and "Jerusalem" and (what?) "Just Like U Said It Would B." Gaelic recitation. Loads of melodrama—loads. Yet let me tell you, there's something really riveting about the way she wails and screams and piles on the percussion effects, and "I Want Your (Hands on Me)" is as sexually obsessive as Kim Gordon at her most slatternly. Squeaky Fromme isn't the only one who can shave her head and make something of it. Original grade: B plus. **A—**

The Official Music of the XXIIIrd Olympiad Los Angeles 1984 (Columbia '84). Though Olympic ideology valorizes what Philip Glass vacuously designates "shared humanity," you'd never guess it from the unprecedented procession of pompous asses (more than 200 Oscar and Grammy nominations among them) Lee Guber and Jon Peters have gathered together for this unprecedented display of El Lay hegemony. Only Herbie Hancock suggests by choice of players or style that the concept of international might extend beyond Giorgio Moroder and Foreigner. And only Hancock-Laswell-Susu-Dieng's "Junku" suggests that games involve play as well as the striving egomania summed up so eloquently in this classic Moroder-Zito-Engemann couplet: "Reach out for the medal / Reach out for the goal" (or is it gold?). The Russians were right, folks, and not just because Guber/Peters don't like balalaikas. **D+**

Oh-OK: Furthermore What (DB EP '83). Last year's seven-inch *Wow Mini Album* comprised four toy songs totalling 6:42 in which two girls—definitely the word—with tiny little voices and sharp little minds dissected such subjects as sibling narcissism, personhood, and the impermanence of waves. This is a slight letdown, threatening to cross the line from unflappably fey to oneirically arty. But the Linda Hopper–Linda Stipe tunes allude to half-remembered melodies in much the same way the lyrical catchphrases do, and Georgia boys contribute Georgia guitar and Georgia drums. So in the end it's as charming and sexy as it intends, which is plenty. **A—**

Oingo Boingo: Only a Lad (A&M '81). Ahh, El Lay. With hysterically catchy vocals and spoiled overarrangements shoring up Ayn Rand–style lyrics that glorify the "Nasty Habits" they pretend to satirize, these guys combine the worst of Sparks with the worst of the Circle Jerks. Inspirational Verse: "You don't believe what you write." Would it were true. **C**

Oi!—The Album (EMI import '80). This precedes and outstrips the notorious *Strength Thru Oi!*, suspected by cultural determinists of helping to spark the Southall riots. Both albums have been hastily deleted, but a search might be worth it. Though the style tends toward tuneless football-cheer monotony and undiscriminating bully-boy dynamics, the best oi songs (by the Cockney Rejects and the Angelic Upstarts especially) recall the anthemic power of good Slade and early Clash. And though the skinheads who are oi's core audience have always been associated with random racial brutality, the politics of these lyrics is strictly pro-working-class and anti-authoritarian. What's more, the misogyny of El Lay punk is all but absent, if only because these boys hardly sing about girls at all. **A—**

Sonny Okosun: Liberation (Shanachie '84). If I were more conversant with the infinite shadings of African pop, I might get a sharper buzz off Okosun's panstylistic Afro-reggae, and I might be ready to settle for reassuring uplift if the two chants on Heartbeat's *Black Star Liner* sampler had been reserved for his U.S. debut. But as things stand, this sounds a little soft to me, just like the universalist-influenced politics that go with it. The curse of not-Marley strikes again. **B+**

Sonny Okosun: Which Way Nigeria? (Jive Afrika '84). For an African groove to buoy those of us who haven't been swimming in it since childhood, it has to be articulated in distinct detail, which is why I thank the engineers who popped each element out this time. Agile horn arrangements from a man called Dave also stir it up. As on Okosuns's Shanachie compilation, the lyrics (all but "My Ancestors" in English) are kind-hearted, militantly progressive, and a little simple—maybe too much so when he's following Nigeria's new leaders.   **B+**

Old Skull: *Get Outta School* (Restless '89). With their shrill tantrums and chaotic coherence, these three nine-yes-nine-year-olds win a hardcore novelty prize on aptness of sound alone. Shit does stand out, too: "Hot Dog Hell" ("Whoever works here doesn't know how to cook a hot dog"), "Kill a Dead Eagle" ("You can't kill a dead eagle / Just like you can't kill a devil with a bomb"), "Homeless" ("I hate you, Ronald Reagan"), and especially "AIDS." "We don't know that much about AIDS," they sing, for all of us. "How does it make you feel? / I feel afraid."   **B**

Alexander O'Neal: *Alexander O'Neal* (Tabu '85). From the Timexes who gave the world the new improved S.O.S. Band, a new improved black matinee idol. They start one side with a can't-miss postvulnerable ballad, the other with a can't-miss dance song deceptively entitled "Innocent." The rest they leave to craft. Is this any way to serve a new improved matinee idol? Probably.   **B**

Alexander O'Neal: *Hearsay* (Tabu '87). This took a lot longer to break through in the living room than it would have on the dance floor, so homebodies be patient. What makes the difference in the end is that Jam & Lewis are letting their love man play the nasty guy—"Fake" and "Criticize" take the offensive after "Hearsay" puts it sweetly. And unlike Jam & Lewis's nasty girl, O'Neal has the vocal muscle (and biceps) to back his nasty up. What's more, the same muscle turns "Sunshine" into a confection you could take home to mother.   **B+**

Alexander O'Neal: *All Mixed Up* (Tabu '89). Duty dictates that I detail my discographical cavils, to wit: the original versions of six of the eight songs remixed here (one of them in two permutations) were all on *Hearsay,* the better of the two albums (oops, three: forgot the Xmas collection) he's managed since 1985. Four (five counting the extra permutation) are on side one—everything but "Hearsay" itself. So if like me you own *Hearsay,* if like me you

convinced yourself to enjoy the ballads, you lose: the usual arguments for concision just don't wash here. Maybe these remixes are no better than the originals, but they're also no worse: at seven minutes or so apiece, nothing wears. If you're not tired of that familiar canted bass line climbing those familiar canted steps by now, for all practical purposes you never will be. Get your fast ones here.   **A−**

100 Flowers: *Drawing Fire* (Happy Squid EP '84). As the Urinals, they were a joke the world missed. Then they grew up, into symbolic Maoists-manqué, and on this live farewell they finally bloom. Very Mission of Burma in their atmospherically tough attack and undogmatically postpunk attitude—so much so that if they worked Boston instead of L.A. they might still be looking for a pot to piss in.   **B+**

Remmy Ongala and Orchestre Super Matimila: *Songs for the Poor Man* (Real world '89). Isolated culturally and economically by socialist underdevelopment, Tanzanian pop nurtures national treasures more diligently than neighboring Zairean and Kenyan styles—though since soukous is hegemonic from Accra to Harare, you can bet both compete mightily. Ongala's unbrassy lineup—three guitarists, three percussionists, a bassist, and a sax player or two—doesn't strive the way Afro-Parisian often does, which is a relief. Rather than relentless Afrodance upmanship, he cultivates a variety that suits Tanzania's folk-friendly cultural policy. And whatever their actual rhythmic origins, the up-front conga parts that double the guitar lines convey an esteem for both tribal difference and East African ways that complements the caring precision of Ongala's singing and the undulating buoyancy of his groove. Sweet. Strong. Maybe even self-sufficient.   **A**

The Only Ones: *Baby's Got a Gun* (Epic '80). Prepunk and for that matter prepub, Peter Perrett may well have been an only one, and he fits in now only because this is such a tolerant and/or commercially desperate time. He's not "power pop," of course—on record, at least, power's got nothing to do with it. With his lazy drawl tightrope-walking on the cusp of the love-death continuum, he's just a perversely if not insincerely wistful rock and roll balladeer who hopes you'll sleep with him and will get peeved if you don't—vulnerably seductive now, but don't be surprised if he quickly starts demanding specialties. **B+**

Yoko Ono: *Season of Glass* (Geffen '81). The little voice "chokes" and "crackles" (her words), the production relies on the usual sessioneers (Newmark, McCracken, yawn), and the composition is elementary (not primal). Yet damn near every song is affecting, and the segue from "Extension 33"'s retrospective irony to "No, No, No"'s cut-off vulnerability positively gut-wrenching. After all, we've never heard a forty-eight-year-old learn to rock (not rock and roll) before. Or a widow's concept album, either. **A—**

Yoko Ono: *It's Alright* (Polydor '82). Supposedly a big shrewdie, Yoko is transcendently simplistic at the core, which in many ways worked better when she was an avant-gardist than it does in her belated pop phase. This somewhat presumptuous message of hope to the world is cunningly devised around the edges—she exploits the studio with fifty years' and countless dollars' worth of childlike delight. But back at the core, the singing and the songs are more one-dimensional than good pop ever is. **B—**

Yoko Ono: *Starpeace* (Polydor '85). Bill Laswell looked like the perfect choice to assist Yoko's rebound from *It's Alright,* especially given his commitment to non-Western music and his penchant for avant-gardists, mostly jazzmen but a few of Yoko's ilk. But despite unfailingly humorless lyrics and the skillful input of Laswell regulars from Aiyb Dieng to Anton Fier, the result is insistently, self-consciously, and rather clumsily light in the head. Often it tries to be cute, which is difficult for anyone and utterly impossibly for Laswell, who isn't exactly a froth specialist. Sure he helps with the hooks and beats, that's his job, but the overall effect is as joyless as the kind of record Toto might cut for a girlfriend of their man-

ager's—the soulless studio-rock anti-intellectuals have always accused him of making. Great exception: "You and I," a silly love song for Sean. **B—**

Roy Orbison: *In Dreams: The Greatest Hits* (Virgin '87). From Chuck Berry on Mercury to the reunited Everlys, rerecorded best-ofs like this one rarely deliver magic or chops. The youthful buoyancy that kept the melodrama from getting soggy is in short supply, and without much trade-off in the standard interpretive nuance. A quarter-century later, his voice still socks and soars, and if on some songs—"Pretty Woman" of course, "Blue Bayou," "Candy Man"—it's clear that only the original artyfact will do, nobody who wasn't there would swear to the general inferiority of this marginally more tasteful recreation. After all, just exactly how great were his hits? Crowning him rock's first neurotic is as overwrought as damning Donald Duck for a protofascist—pop-rock (cum countrypolitan) self-pity has its own conventions just like slapstick did, and he is their slave. So as a heretic who isn't positive Phil Spector was good for rock and roll, and also as a heretic who was there, I'll stick with the artyfacts after all. They're certainly no worse. And versions you don't need. **B**

Roy Orbison: *Mystery Girl* (Virgin '88). If you're guessing once-in-a-lifetime opportunity squandered by the assembled bigshots, guess again. They've done their man's tradition proud. Problem's the tradition—just listen to the latest Rhino retrospective, which celebrates its inevitable schlockification at MGM, and you'll know why Orbison's comeback was made for this corporate era. When he gets a great tune produced just right—Wilbury-penned lead hit, Bono-Edge title ballad, Waylon's "In Dreams" sequel—his unassuming seriousness can make you think twice about opera. But with his mythic voice no longer distinguishing surely between tenderness and sentimentality, "A Love So Beautiful" and "Windsurfer" are bathos. And when Elvis C. leaves him stranded atop a ferris wheel and he just sits there contemplating his tragedy in song, the only thing mythic is the scale of the self-parody.   **B**

Orchestral Manoeuvres in the Dark: *Junk Culture* (A&M '84). Now that they've come down a little I can take their sad tales of hard days seriously. Even on "Junk Culture" proper, which stirs up memories of their direct atmospherics, they do their best to cheese things up, and elsewhere hurdy-gurdy synths and android girlies emitting no-no-nos do right by the title, a title anybody who once dubbed an album *Architecture and Morality* had damn well better earn. Original grade: B plus.   **B**

Orchestral Manoeuvres in the Dark: *The Best of OMD* (A&M '88). Oh so functionally, it renders *Junk Culture* obsolete by relieving it of "Tesla Girls," technocratic dance-kitsch as amusing as "Electricity" and "Enola Gay," and "Talking Loud and Clear," their cutest and catchiest romantic medium-tempo—though the many others here included will certainly entertain the hookily inclined.   **B+**

Orchestra Makassy: *Agwaya* (Virgin import '82). Four sweet male vocalists dominate this clear, buoyant fifteen-man group from Tanzania, who like all Tanzanian musicians have to travel to Kenya to record their pioneering East African variation on ur-Cuban Congolese styles. Salsa-shaped (a mere three drums) and calypso-inflected, their song forms will relieve or perplex listeners whose contact with Afropop begins and ends with Sunny Adé—they're much simpler. Those who find Adé too damn pleasant will be relieved to learn that Makassy occasionally cut the lovely flow with soulful grit in a lead vocal or sax solo. Me, I love them because they're lovely.   **A—**

Original Concept: *Straight From the Basement of Kooley High!* (Def Jam '88). A couple of years ago these guys released two mysterious singles with almost nothing on them but bass, buzz, beats, and offhand joshing. One of those singles is lost among the protests, admonitions, sexism, camaraderie, laugh lines, true stories, and samples of this professional rap album. It's

the old rock and roll story—a lot of knowledge can also be a dangerous thing. **B—**

Jeffrey Osborne: *Don't Stop* (A&M '85). Osborne proves that the secularization of black pop needn't mean the end of a great vocal tradition, only of its church roots, and he doesn't sing as if he learned how at Performing Arts, either. Instead he sounds like what he is—a son of the most uncompromised black secular music, funk. The slightly herky-jerk bent of his phrasing and pronunciation is geared to the rhythm, and when he bears down into a ballad he sounds fresher than more conventionally soulful singers. Of course, he also sounds stranger if you're not prepared, which is why the uninitiated will take more readily to the somewhat stronger material on *Stay With Me Tonight*. Me, I just got the message, and I've been playing both.   **B+**

Jeffrey Osborne: *Emotional* (A&M '86). I'm trying to figure out what it means to say I kind of like this record, a big-budget multiproducer job of the sort suddenly standard in crossoverland. It's not just that I'm impressed with all the heavy equipment, from Osborne's dolomite voice to the usual phalanx of hitmen turning out materiel. I respond—that's one thing kind of liking it means. And though the response feels synthetic, it's not unreal. Which is just what I'd say of the emotions on display, from be-mine to Soweto-must-be-free.   **B**

K. T. Oslin: *80's Ladies* (RCA Victor '87). After "Do Ya'," side two is dreck, squeezing its sob stories down to the last overripe chord change, but when she asserts herself this countrypolitan career woman can tell you more about the vagaries of erotic love than two male neotraditionalists half her age combined. Not surprisingly, she asserts herself only when she writes a song all by her lonesome—on "80's Ladies," "Younger Men," and "Do Ya' " too. And the only tune she didn't have a hand in is a sob story that should convert anyone who thinks lady songwriters shouldn't launch singing careers in the prime of life. A voice she's got.   **B**

K.T. Oslin: *This Woman* (RCA '88). The songwriting may never kick in full time, though it sure has its moments—when a girl with a new used car invites a cute young thing out for a spin, or a single begins her status report with a quiet "I'm overworked and I'm overweight." But there are other reasons to root for this full-timbred New York–based outsider—not only does she challenge Nashville's hidebound gender roles, but she doesn't cotton to neotraditionalist canons. In fact, her music hints at pop, and if you think that has to mean schlock or rock, don't tell the guitarists.   **B**

Donny Osmond: *Donny Osmond* (Capitol '89). Donny listened to the radio for a couple of days and said to himself, "Why should all these professional no-talents make the money? I'm a professional no-talent myself, and I've got a name and connections." And in Donny's life the ability to create standard-issue pop-funk is a genuine liberation—he's Hollywood hip at last, and what a long hard road it must have been. But he sounds anonymous anyway, standard-issue, and corporate. After all, the best pop functions as a liberation

even when it's formally received—celebrates a formula in ways that are audible, and infectious. The last time this bozo managed that trick was "One Bad Apple."   **D**

Out of Our Idiot: See also Elvis Costello

Buck Owens: *Hot Dog!* (Capitol '88). The two rock and roll covers are unbelievably clumsy coming from country's great lost missing link, and not just rhythmwise—did he choose the teen protest "Summertime Blues" because his gerontologist thought it would do wonders for him? Nor are many of the originals worthy of the career-capping compilation I hope is on the way. But he has a lesson to teach both his cocky epigones (emotion and commitment) and his exhausted contemporaries (emotion and commitment '88). Sounds like he's learned some things, too—from premier contemporary George Jones, whose late work had the same phlegmy maturity and every-syllable-counts concentration until the emotion and commitment went out of him.   **B+**

Jimmy Page: *Outrider* (Geffen '88). With the heretofore useless John Miles doing Plant (you barely notice when the man himself sneaks in for a song) and the heretofore unproven Jason Bonham doing Daddy (assuming Page isn't sampling Boom-Boom like everybody else, flesh and blood being no substitute for the real simulacrum in today's studio), side one is easily the best Zep rip ever recorded. Zep blooze, not Zep mythopoeia, with titles like "Wasting My Time" and "Wanna Make Love"; Page's riffs are classic, which isn't to say anybody has or hasn't played them before, and the momentum is fierce and enormous. On side two the mostly ridiculous Chris Farlowe takes over, his unlistenable "Hummingbird" inspiring fond thoughts of Leon Russell. Jimmy and Jason should form a band, invite Plant as a courtesy, and hope he turns them down. If Miles won't do what he's told, Lenny Wolf will be happy to step in. **B+**

Pajama Slave Dancers: *Cheap Is Real* (Pajamarama '85). Like most collegiate humor, this isn't as funny as it thinks it is, and like most collegiate humor it holds up against competing professional product. "Farm Rap" is recommended to the Red Hot Chili Peppers, "No Dick" to the Meatmen. And from nerd-macho proem through lyric-sheet verses to the climactically yearning chorus of "I want to play hide-the-salami with you," the magnificent "I Want To Make Love to You" is on a level with Spinal Tap itself. **B**

Robert Palmer: *Riptide* (Island '85). If we're to take the old fashion plate at his word (yeah sure), his pop breakthrough (finally! after all those good reviews!) was inspired by an affair with a high roller—holdings in Singapore and IBM, great dancer, like that. Sounds daunting, I must say. And as usual, what makes him barely listenable is his holdings in r&b. **C+**

Robert Palmer: *"Addictions" Volume 1* (Island '89). Is this fraud really the Dorian Gray wannabee of jacket photos? I don't know, and unless the women he beds are a lot more interesting than the models who populate his videos, I don't even want you to tell me. Rather than a tax-exiled roue, I prefer to imagine him as a secret straight who takes the fast train to his modest Surrey estate after a hard day's posing in London, arriving in time for a civilized dinner with wife and children before plopping in front of the VCR with a bottle of cognac. Honesty compels me to acknowledge, however, that my wife doesn't think he's a fraud—once spied him buying groceries just around the corner, and liked what she saw. In a world where male rock critics get Sheena Easton and Kim Gordon—who owns Palmer's only great song, "Addicted to Love," the way Junior Tucker owns "Some Guys Get All the Luck"—she's got a right. But I still give the grades around here. **B−**

Graham Parker: *Another Grey Area* (Arista '82). Mixed success isn't becoming to Parker, who can no longer blame his bad personality on unemployment. By replacing the Rumour with studio regulars, he's lost the edgy drive that used to help his bitterness cut through, and his revitalized melodic craft only takes him so far—if hooks don't justify kneejerk sentimentality, they don't justify jerkoff paranoia either. **B**

Graham Parker: *The Real Macaw* (Arista '83). In which Parker finally justifies his abandonment of rock and roll outcry for self-referential studiocraft by more or less acknowledging the private sources of his bitterest protests. The male chauvinism he mocks in the opener is almost certainly his own, and the love he can't take for granted right afterwards is probably his wife's, which in the end proves more durable than he's afraid it will. That's why he's glad to have a glass jaw, why he's advised to ignore everything that sounds like chains, and why except for one misplaced complaint side two is a happy-to-ironic-to-credibly-sappy paean to a marriage that has lasted—talk about your miracle a minute—one whole year. Original grade: A minus. **B+**

Graham Parker and the Shot: *Steady Nerves* (Elektra '85). "I'm not exactly into humor," he observes in "Canned Laughter," and truer words were never spoken—unless you count "Mercury Poisoning," I don't think he's cracked a joke in ten years. So maybe he should give it a try. I know sensitivity didn't work. But squeezing out one more round of angry hooks doesn't work either. **B−**

Graham Parker: *The Mona Lisa's Sister* (RCA Victor '88). No rocker this sarcastic has any right (I didn't say business, though who knows what bizzers see in him at this late date) coming on so relaxed, and no rocker this relaxed has any right coming on so sarcastic. Add 'em up and you got smug. Cover: "Cupid." Auxiliary art reference: Bosch. Now are you impressed? **C+**

Graham Parker: *Human Soul* (RCA '89). Latest objects of his bottomless rancor: sugar, hamburgers, mailman (black). But not his lost youth—his lost youth makes him feel all gushy inside. **C**

Ray Parker Jr. and Raydio: *Two Places at the Same Time* (Arista '80). Leading off with one polite Chic rip and closing out with another, this well-named piece of product is the kind of hither-and-yon effort that signals commercial alarm. Sometimes fawningly pop, othertimes hyperbolically party-hearty, it scores in neither mode. And with this guy, scoring is all. **C+**

Ray Parker Jr. & Raydio: *A Woman Needs Love* (Arista '81). Parker's mild-mannered description of what happens to those stingy with, er, respect—"You might come home early and get your feelings hurt"—typifies his understated autofunk. Playing guitar, synthesizer, piano, and drums as well as his home bass, which doesn't sound like a lead instrument either, he serves up eight tunes that bump and/or swoon into ear and/or ass with undeniable and virtually unrecallable effectiveness. I like every one, really. But don't ask me which is which—or why it matters. **B+**

Ray Parker Jr.: *The Other Woman* (Arista '82). Blessed with a one-track mind in a twenty-four-track world, he provides all the basic vocal and instrumental parts on an unannounced concept album about "romance," i.e. sex with all the fixings. Sometimes he's merely raunchy—"The Other Woman" and "Streetlove" are male and female versions of sex-for-its-own-sweet-obsessive-sake, and in "Let's Get Off" they come together. But at other times he gets serious, which is to say raunchy and romantic, upping the ante with leave-him-for-me speeches and patient propositions ("anyplace you like" refers to body parts, not apartments). Even when he proposes marriage it's only because the lady's stuff is so good he wants his name on it. Couldn't say how many positions he knows—in "It's Our Own Affair," he swears his partner to secrecy. But I'm sure he's got them all written down for the follow-up. Original grade: B plus. **A−**

Ray Parker Jr.: *Greatest Hits* (Arista '82). Parker is that ever rarer prize, an *inspired* journeyman. His music is eloquently unobtrusive, and while he doesn't talk his songs, he has no need for vocal pyrotechnics he couldn't muster—his stylishly textured conversational timbre, halfway between a murmur and a purr when he's turning it on, is a cunning interpretive device. In a subgenre whose practitioners hone their sexual personas as sharp as Cole Porter rhyme schemes, he can't be said to have come up with something new—the secure, sincere superstud is a role Teddy Pendergrass exploited less cleverly for years. So this collection is just the thing for those benighted who can't believe they need more than one piece of long-playing ass-man jive. Well, actually they don't—necessity has nothing to do with it.   **A−**

Ray Parker Jr.:   *Woman Out of Control* (Arista '83). "I Still Can't Get Over Loving You," his sweetest, sexiest hit ballad ever, rips Brit synth-pop as shamelessly as "The Other Woman" ripped the Stones, but his grip becomes less definitive on the very next tune, which barely loosens the hem of Prince's garment. And side two holds on strictly to Ray's tried and true.   **B**

Ray Parker Jr.:   *Chartbusters* (Arista '84). Greatest Hits is definitive, "Ghostbusters" a contemporary classic available in seven- and twelve-inch formats, and this a redundancy from an artist whose contract is coming up.   **B−**

Ray Parker Jr.:   *Sex and the Single Man* (Arista '85). Maybe Ray is getting jaded—pussy comes so easy now that he no longer bothers to hone his come-on. Whether he's scoring on sensitivity (oh really, "Men Have Feelings Too"?) or studsmanship (though I do enjoy the bone and puddy-tat lines in "I'm a Dog"), he's putting out just enough to get her into the car. The sole exception is "I'm in Love," in which a workaholic falls for "an interesting girl" who doesn't have a job. Workaholic—now that sounds like the real Ray to me.   **B−**

Ray Parker Jr.:   *After Dark* (Geffen '87). No no no, Ray—"Let you play with my tool after dark" isn't really a double entendre. It's a little, you know, obvious. And forget Alexander O'Neal—he can *sing*. That's why he doesn't need double entendres.   **C+**

Van Dyke Parks: *Jump!* (Warner Bros. '84). Parks is a naughty choirboy and Kathy Dalton is auditioning for the Broadway lead, but theatrical preciosity is all you can expect from a musical comedy

concept album anyway. What you don't expect from musical comedy is exotic Americana like Parks's irrepressible arty-vernacular verbal and musical puns, which combined with his rich melodies compensate for the annoyances.   **B+**

Parlet: *Play Me or Trade Me* (Casablanca '80). Even though P-Funk's second-string auxiliary has no Dawn Silva or Jeanette McGruder, this comes on as strong as *Never Buy Texas From a Cowboy,* because it doesn't take much for funk to come on strong. Just a few dance-phrases is all—"help from my friends," "play me or trade me," "now button it up, I'll put it away." Endurance is something else. Watch them do their thang indeed.   **B**

Parliament: *Trombipulation* (Casablanca '80). Reports of George Clinton's demise are premature, but there's reason to worry about his body tone. Although the transcendent silliness of "Agony of Defeet" recalls past glories, the quotes from Bach, Brylcreem, and Mother Goose are dim echoes of the sharp confidence games of yore, and on occasion this sounds kind of like Fuzzy Haskins & Co. Hmm.   **B−**

Parliament: *Parliament's Greatest Hits* (Casablanca '84). Clinton, Collins, Worrell & Co. always saved their funnest riffs (and scored their smashest hits) for P-Funk's kiddie half, which means that these radio-length condensations of the peaks toward which their concerts unwound (and around which their albums cohered) constitute their most tuneful and atypical LP. In a band that made a point of prolonging foreplay, it's like a serial climax, and the effect can be exhausting and even disorienting. But as you might imagine, it's also very exciting, an opportunity to concentrate on the deep vertical pleasures of music that makes forward motion a first principle. And as you ought to know, it was always the dense layering of whomever's guitar, Worrell's keyboards, Collins's bass, and Clinton's crafty vocal arrangements that made their forward motion stick.   **A**

Gram Parsons and the Fallen Angels: *Live 1973* (Sierra '82). I don't know why it took eight years, but after several botches on A&M here it is, a satisfying live-posthumous from the inventor of country-rock, for which he is not to blame. All five A-songs are more forceful on *GP,* but these versions (recorded in downhome Hempstead, Long Island) have a grace and lightness that for once show off the advantages of folkie roots, as does the new stuff on side two. Emmylou fills her appointed role, N.D. Smart II keeps things moving smartly, and a good time is had by all.   **B+**

Dolly Parton: *9 to 5 and Odd Jobs* (RCA Victor '81). How you respond to this quasi-concept album about (of all things) work, which offers exquisitely sung standards from Mel Tillis, Merle Travis, and (I swear it) Woody Guthrie as well as Parton originals almost as militant as the title hit, depends on your tolerance for fame-game schlock. I'd never claim Johnny Carson's damaged her pipes or her brains, but that doesn't mean I have to like Music City banjos and Las Vegas r&b.   **B+**

Dolly Parton: *Heartbreak Express* (RCA '82). If Willie and Merle, her equals as country artists, can turn into premier pop singers, why can't Dolly? Maybe because she's justifiably smitten with her physical gifts. Just as she can't resist pushup bras, she can't resist oversinging, showing off every curve of a gorgeous voice that's still developing new ones. On the other hand, maybe it has to do with why she wears wigs, which if I'm not mistaken is because she doesn't really like her hair.   **B−**

Dolly Parton: *White Limozeen* (Columbia '89). The crossover that marked her move to Columbia never got to the other side, so she lets Ricky Skaggs call the shots—these days he's commercial. Except for the Easter song, he cans the production numbers, and since she can still sing like a genius anytime opportunity knocks, her most country album in years is also her best. Of course, even genius country singers are dragged by ordinary country songs. And though the borrowings are better-than-average, she no longer writes like a pro without help—here provided by, such is life, Mac Davis.   **B**

Dolly Parton, Linda Ronstadt, Emmylou Harris: *Trio* (Warner Bros. '87). By devoting herself to Nelson Riddle and operetta, Sun City scab Linda Ronstadt has made boycotting painless, but her long-promised hookup with Dolly Parton and Emmylou Harris will be hard to resist if the vocal luxuries of the mainstream biz make you swoon. Acoustic country delving from "Farther Along" and Jimmie Rodgers to Kate McGarrigle and Linda Thompson, it's a slightly scholarly yet sometimes thrilling apotheosis of harmony—three voices that have triumphed in the winner-take-all of the marketplace making a go of cooperation. Free of tits, glitz, and syndrums for the first time in a decade, Parton's penetrating purity dominates the one-off as it once did country music history. The only one of the three who's had the courage of her roots recently, Harris sounds as thoughtful up front as she does in the backup roles that are her forte. And while Linda's plump soprano will always hint of creamed corn, she's a luscious side dish in this company. Original grade: A minus.   **B+**

Party Party (A&M '82). A soundtrack where new-wavers young and old sing rock and roll tunes young and old for dancing pleasure at your party party. Sting covers Little Richard as if he has to and Little Willie John as if he wants to, Modern Romance resuscitates Freda Payne, Dave Edmunds bravely tackles Chuck Berry—why, it's a *Moondog Matinee* for our time. Pauline Black's "No Woman, No Cry" radiates feeling, Banarama's "No Feelings" radiates smarts, and Madness's "Driving in My Car" is a worthy "Janie Jones" joke. And oh yeah, the title song is by Elvis Costello.   **B+**

Passage: *Passage* (A&M '81). Though I wish he wouldn't dedicate this venture (or his life) to "Our Savior, Lord Jesus Christ of Nazareth," that's not why (Brother) Louis Johnson pisses me off (cf. Al Green, Maria Muldaur). He pisses me off because he's as sterile and chickenshit as the polite elevator funk he uses to sell his message—too chickenshit to mention, for instance, that he believes "Mr. Jewish

Man" and "Mr. Muslim Man" are doomed to burn in hellfire. Heed my advice, people. When somebody tells you to "say good-bye to the reasoning / That's standing in your way," think some more. And when somebody tells you that without Jesus "you can't be livin'," take a deep breath. **D**−

Teddy Pendergrass: *TP* (Philadelphia International '80). With the Futures doing backup and Stephanie Mills doing duet and Ashford & Simpson doing their number and Cecil Womack doing himself proud, this may well be the definitive Teddy. Only once does he break into a fast tempo, which is fine with me, because schmaltz is the man's meat. He needs, he demands, he comes on hard, he comes on subtle, he goodtimes, he longtimes—in short, he inspires heavy petting, and we all know what that can lead to. **A**−

Teddy Pendergrass: *Greatest Hits* (Philadelphia International '84). Heard in retrospect, Teddy's solo ascendancy seems a quantum more relaxed than his indenture with Harold Melvin—the aural equivalent of Tom Selleck, though Teddy isn't quite so coy about how much pussy he gets. It also seems more seminal than I would have figured, the inspiration for midtempo come-ons by everybody from Jeffrey Osborne and Al Jarreau to the creaky old O'Jays and Isleys. Teddy even induces a normal guy like me to enjoy this deplorable trend. Slick-talking greaseballs like Eddie Levert and Ronnie Isley are a social menace, but hunks like Teddy are just wonders of nature. And thank God there aren't too many of them. **A**−

Teddy Pendergrass: *Workin' It Back* (Asylum '86). Forget platonic love—this is platonic sex. I mean, the man is the best-known paraplegic in America; when he sings songs called "Never Felt Like Dancin'" or utters lines like "The thought of your body has got me erect," their status as mere collections of signs is understood literally by his fans. And thus their status as fantasy can be approached literally as well. Helps that while only "Love 4/2" is up to, let us say, vintage Jerry Butler, just about every cut at least maintains the atmosphere. Also helps that he's transferred his vocal savvy to however much of his body he's got left. **B**+

Penguin Cafe Orchestra: *Penguin Cafe Orchestra* (Editions E.G. '81). Not since *Another Green World* has ambient music sounded this rich. The big difference is that the instruments are mostly acoustic—Simon Jeffes does count electronic organ and ring modulator among his fourteen, but he runs more toward ukelele and pennywhistle, and the ensemble includes violin, cello, and oboe. The tempos are poky, the playing tender, impulsive, and a bit ragged, and the mood nostalgic—although it's my bet that melodies this minimal were unheard of in fin-de-siècle pop. **A**−

Penguin Cafe Orchestra: *The Penguin Cafe Orchestra Mini Album* (Editions E.G. EP '83). Simon Jeffes outlines a music from everywhere that could easily turn into a music for nowhere: "music which is influenced by the above [classical, rock, jazz, folk] but also by African, Japanese, Venezuelan, Celtic (Scottish and Irish), Cajun, Reggae, and other sources." But where Paul Winter, whose program isn't all that dissimilar, is half pundit and half mooncalf, Jeffes's gentle wit, unmystical posture, and fondness for urban life combat vague-out. Whether he also reaches the "heart of our own time and culture," however, is another matter. His eccentric postfolk orchestrations seem more like escapes to me—into fantasy, into a future with reassuring connections to the past. Which makes this an odd piece of product. "The Penguin Cafe Single" is more useful here than on the premature *Music From the Penguin Cafe.* The two new pieces are simple, charming, and very slight. And the three finest tunes, two in new but hardly definitive live versions, are also available on the nonmini album they put out in 1981, the length of which better suits the leisurely pace of Jeffes's panpop impressionism. **B**

Penguin Cafe Orchestra: *Broadcasting From Home* (Editions EG '84). Marginal differences count for plenty with these subtlety specialists. More emphatic production bespeaks sharper conception—sometimes dramatic, sometimes representational, sometimes self-consciously atmospheric. The music is "better"—and therefore relatively (marginally) conventional. It's lost its incidental aura, and despite the instant appeal of compositions like "Heartwind" and "Music for a Found Harmonium," an edge of charm.   **B+**

Pere Ubu: *New Picnic Time* (Chrysalis import '80). Recitative, animal noises, and industrial waste for the ear threaten their precarious (by definition) art-rock balance. "A Small Dark Cloud" is mostly voice and sound effects, "The Voice of the Sand" mostly whisper and sound effects, "All the Dogs Are Barking" barely more. Then again "Jehovah's Kingdom Comes!" rocks, and "Goodbye" is as quietly hypnotic as it's supposed to be. When David Thomas starts off crowing "It's me again!" he's not really boasting—he's hitting us with the very best he has to offer.   **A−**

Pere Ubu: *The Art of Walking* (Rough Trade '80). It's impossible to wish these utopian singers of the industrial pastorale anything but the best. But between the passages of synthesizer buzz and the fond talk of birdies, fishies, and horsies (pace Patti, they do call it "Horses"), you have to figure that neither Red Crayola's Mayo Thompson (in for Tom Herman) nor the one true God (David is now a Jehovah's Witness) is counseling anybody to rock out. Undestructive violence is a hard act to continue. Original grade: A minus.   **B+**

Pere Ubu: *Ubu Live: Volume 1: 390 Degrees of Simulated Stereo* (Rough Trade '81). Recapping the Hearthan and Blank Records period that a born-again Crocus Behemoth will never look in the eye again, this is a find for fans who missed the early singles and the *Datapanik* EP (source of four songs, with another previously unreleased and seven more from *The Modern Dance*). Material and performance are fine, with variant lyrics and new guitar and synthesizer bits mitigating (though not eliminating) the redundancy factor. But most of these recordings were intended for reference only, and that's how they sound—devoid of aural presence. For demo addicts, tape traders, and incorrigible cultists like me.   **B+**

Pere Ubu: *Song of the Bailing Man* (Rough Trade '82). In his Jehovah's Witness phase—which could last the rest of his life—David Thomas is just like any other eccentric "progressive." With Mayo Thompson and Anton Fier replacing Ubu's two committed rockers on guitar and drums, the group can't carry him along on populist pulse anymore, which means that although Thomas's compositional ideas may be "original" and "interesting"—and unlike most art-rock, this music deserves both adjectives—how compelling you find the gestalt depends on the power of Thomas's private obsessions. Once again the man outdoes himself—some of these lyrics actually read as poetry. But it's minor poetry for sure—his musings on the ineluctable wonder of the natural order go deeper than, say, Peter Hammill's damn fool doomsaying, but they're long on whimsy and short on tension. As Christian rock goes, it's smart stuff, but as Christian art goes I'll take Graham Greene.   **B+**

Pere Ubu: *Terminal Tower: An Archival Collection* (Twin/Tone '86). Side one is the long unavailable *Datapanik in the Year Zero* EP, itself comprising two indie singles and a compilation cut and as powerful a sequence as side one of *Dub Housing* nevertheless. Side two collects the kind of oddments that rarely cohere on LP, yet here the outtakes and B sides and stray singles come together as a record of David Thomas's slide or progress from willed optimism to blessed whimsy. In short, this is a gift from God—a third Ubu album from the former Crocus Behemoth's pre-God period.   **A−**

Pere Ubu: *The Tenement Year* (Enigma '88). Yes, this is Ubu—four of the seven players were on *Dub Housing*. But before Scott Krauss was brought in—can't expect much backbeat with Chris Cutler hogging the drums—it was also the most recent edition of David Thomas's Pedestrians/Wooden Birds making a rock move. So what's astonishing isn't just the high spirits and good faith, both rare enough on reunions, but the singleness of purpose. It's not as if Thomas's crotchety nature-boy mysticism has been blown away—one of these songs is an attack on zoos. But the momentum of the backbeat and the electric clamor of the whole move straighten him out and toughen him up, while at the same time his loving, surrealistic sarcasm dominates the music, with Allen Ravenstine reaching untold heights of kooky reintegration. This record proves not only that good-hearted eccentrics can live in the world, but that they can change it for the better. Every song stays with you, but the one for the ages is "We Have the Technology," which leaves you thinking that we just may and we just may not. Thank you, Scott Krauss. **A**

Pere Ubu: *Cloudland* (Fontana '89). "We'd never been asked to write a pop record before," David Thomas says. "I guess it never occurred to anyone." Thomas was happy to oblige. No private visions of decaying cityscape, just equally obscure (and evocative) love songs, down on their knees to rhyme with please. Produced mostly out of Ubu's old Ohio home, then smoothed down and hooked up in London, their signature avant-garage survives with its stop-and-go effects and unsalable recitative in fine fettle. If you're a fan, the six Stephen Hague–produced or Daniel Miller–remixed cuts will sound misbegotten at first. But if you're really a fan, you'll come to recognize them as the urban pastoral of Thomas's whimsical period adapted for the cheap seats, which deserves the attention. **A−**

Peripheral Vision (Zoar '82). Ah, these boho compilations. As a belated and partial convert to *No New York,* I still don't get Mars, and I bet in 1986 I won't get the Hi-Sheriffs of Blue or the State or I/S/M or (Gawd) Crazy Hearts, certainly not all four, even if I do like Mars by then. Unless they've all improved as much as Mofungo has since 1978, of course. I hope the album V-Effect deserves is better recorded than these two cuts, which are the best-sounding things here in more ways than one nevertheless. Which leaves the Scene Is Now, whose "Finding Someone" should be the single, and the Ordinaries, who combine the nicest parts of Glenn Branca and the Moody Blues and more power to them. Ah, these boho documents. **B**

Lee "Scratch" Perry and the Majestics: *Mystic Miracle Star* (Heartbeat '82). Found the hypnogroove a little flat even for a Clash producer's reggae record until I discovered that the Majestics' bottom was two guys named LaVilla and Schwartz. But if they're more rock than rockers, they're perfect for the legendary Perry, who does a mean Dylan on harp and whose crazed rhyming puns and mystagogical patter sound like Marcus Garvey on Highway 61. Move over Jesu, here come Jah. **B+**

Steve Perry: *Street Talk* (Columbia '85). The head Journeyman's USA for Africa cameos were so discreetly intense and discreetly tossed off they made me wonder what I'd been missing. Now I know—musical gastroenteritis. Pat Boone didn't understand, so why should Steve Perry—oversinging signifies not soul and inspiration but will and desperation. Upped a notch for good intentions, and just in case Sam Cooke has finally taught him a lesson. **C**

Persian Gulf: *Changing the Weather* (Raven EP '84). Except maybe for Rank and File (who are bitterer) and Springsteen & Co. (who are grander), I can't think of an American band whose account of the world is more unflinchingly on. Conscious rather than correct, without a hint of hardcore's parricidal/misogynistic hysteria, these eight songs are constricted and expansive, sour and ebullient all at once. Hal Shows understands his own anarchic/apocalyptic impulses, and his Lennonesque rhythm guitar provides the extra momentum he needs to stay on top of things. **A**

Persian Gulf: *The Movie* (Raven '86). Barking out lyrics loud and clear over an uncommonly forthright groove, Hal Shows led this band to a left-field EP debut two years back, and I wish he'd tried to repeat, because at album length his forthrightness gets out of hand. The world his best lyrics create isn't what the band's music makes it seem—it's an untrustworthy place where being a little crazy can help you get by, full of implicit regrets and sidelong insults and allusions that mean more than they add up to. But when he tries to spell things out in protest or satire, or boil them down into haiku, he seems less than a little crazy.   **B+**

Peter and the Test Tube Babies: *Peter and the Test Tube Babies* (Profile '87). In this time of micromargins and cults subdividing like paramecia, we gravitate toward bands that hark to whatever obscure titans we picked up on when obscurism was a harmless sideline. For me it was the Vibrators, the wildest and tightest of Britain's trad rockers in punk disguise, and I bet these guys were there. Despite the chiming expansiveness of the hooks and song lengths, they're the same nasty group, driven to drink by their microcultish prospects.   **B+**

Pet Shop Boys: *Please* (EMI America '86). The music's blandness is part of the quite well-executed concept: articulating the ambivalent romanticism, immodest hopes, and not-so-quiet desperation behind the suburban facade of the people who create *Smash Hits* pop, and maybe consume it, too. I hum most of the catchily namby-pamby tunes and ponder most of the yearningly cynical lyrics, but the moments I really love are provided by sound effects—sirens and breaking glass so skillfully integrated into the synthesized textures that at first I didn't notice they were there. Original grade: B plus.   **A−**

Pet Shop Boys: *Disco* (EMI Manhattan '86). Serious about not being taken seriously, they set Shep Pettibone (or is that Pet Sheppibone?) to remixing their greatest hit, then ask Pet/Shep, Arthur Baker, and the Latin Rascals to remix three other fairly nifty songs from the only album they've ever released. Just for variety, the lead cuts are the B sides from their great hit and their lesser hit, and I confess I'm glad to own both, brand names and all. Also, "West End Girls" does hold up quite nicely for 9:03. Still . . .   **B**

Pet Shop Boys: *Pet Shop Boys, Actually* ((EMI-Manhattan '87). Calling Neil Tennant a bored wimp is like accusing Jackson Pollock of making a mess. Since the bored wimp is his subject and his medium, whether he actually is one matters only insofar as the music sounds bored and/or wimpy—and only insofar as that's without its rewards and revelations. From Dusty Springfield to hit Fairlight to heart beats and from insider shopping to kept icon to Bowiesque futurism, this is actual pop music with something actual to say—pure commodity, and proud of it.   **A−**

Pet Shop Boys: *Introspective* (EMI-Manhattan '88). What a cerebral band—if they keep on at this rate, they'll inspire more deep thinking than David Bowie and Henry Cow combined. The textures on their bubble-salsa statement are so cheesy that it takes forever to penetrate to its intellectual essence, which lends the cheese its savor. And as a pop aesthete I'm offended by the pace—average cut length on this six-song disco mix is a languorous 8:20. Guess I'm just a sucker for lyrics that give Ché Guevara his due.   **A−**

Tom Petty and the Heartbreakers: *Hard Promises* (Backstreet '81). Hard to gainsay the class solidarity of a rich rock star who sues his record company to keep his list price down to $8.98. And glancing at the lyric sheet, I was pleased to note that the antiboho number—"Kings Road," in which a Pakistani tries to sell Tom funny-looking English underwear—had a lighter touch than usual. The reason I hadn't noticed, unfortunately, is that Petty clobbers the thing like he's singing about how much he hates the road. Elsewhere he's more understated, fortunately, but it just goes to show you—no matter how much they respect the working fan, rich rock stars tend to fill up on themselves.   **B**

Tom Petty and the Heartbreakers: *Long After Dark* (Backstreet '82). Petty's been complaining that he's tired, and this holding action—from a guy not noted for vanguard engagements when he's fit to fight—shows all the signs. In case you were wondering, he can't live with them and he can't live without them.   **C+**

Tom Petty and the Heartbreakers: *Southern Accents* (MCA '85). Petty's problem isn't that he's dumb, or even that people think he's dumb, although they have reason to. It's that he feels so sorry for himself he can't think straight. Defending the South made sense back when Ronnie Van Zant was writing "Sweet Home Alabama," but in the Sun Belt era it's just pique. The modernizations of sometime coproducer Dave Stewart mitigate the neo-conservative aura somewhat, but unmitigating it right back is Petty's singing, its descent from stylization into affectation most painful on side one's concept songs. Side two is less consequential, and better. Note, however, that its show-stopper is "Spike," in which a bunch of rednecks, I mean good old boys, prepare to whup a punk. It's satire. Yeah sure.   **B**−

Tom Petty and the Heartbreakers: *Let Me Up (I've Had Enough)* (MCA '87). For such a downhome guy, Petty has a major instinct for the news hook. Here, after defying premium pricing, reconstructing the South, and touring with somebody famous, he exploits the Dylan connection once again. In the tradition of his new hero, Petty's plan was no plan—he and the guys just went into the studio and these *songs* came out. And whaddaya know? Stick the thing in your playback mechanism of choice and these *songs* come out—for the first time in his career, the man sounds like the natural he's worked so hard at being.   **B**+

Tom Petty: *Full Moon Fever* (MCA '89). He wanted something off-the-cuff and got lucky: except for the punk putdown and the pseudo-Dylan throwaway, both nice on their own terms, nary a lyric nor tune clashes with the terrific early-Byrds cover. If guys made roots-rock albums anymore, anything here would spruce one up. **B**+

Bob Pfeiffer: *After Words* (PVC '87). When half of the greatest couple band this side of X makes a solo album that broods obsessively about a broken relationship, we're entitled to our biographical assumptions. Damn right it's more fun to fuss and fight than to sit home feeling sorry for yourself, but the idea is to illuminate this truth, not prove it. **B**−

P-Funk All-Stars: *Urban Dancefloor Guerillas* (Uncle Jam/CBS Associated '83). Though side one shows off songs so tuneful and witty they'd have me doing handstands if they showed up on a Cameo or Gap Band album, their raggedy-ass elan doesn't quite suit the spritz they generate. Anyway, songs aren't George Clinton's gift to the world. Side two is George Clinton's gift to the world. You pump up and down, you pump up and down, you pump up and down, and then you break it down. **A**−

Phases of the Moon: Traditional Chinese Music (Columbia '81). Blessed with neither roots nor technical insight, I come to this 58-minute collection of 11 subtle, surprising instrumental pieces—most of folk origin, though three are postrevolutionary and one "a treasure of Chinese classical music"—as a sublime novelty record. That is, I get off on its strangeness, and why not? Though the mood is quiet the total effect is far from ambient, not just because things do get loud at times but because most of these melodies are instantly arresting. They don't repeat as insistently as Western folk tunes do, either. At times I wonder if I'm back in sixth grade memorizing "Minuet in G" and "Hall of the Mountain King" for Mrs. Tully, and I find that the thing can grate if I start playing it two or three times a day. But why do I keep putting it on? What a trip.   **A**

The Pheromones: *Yuppie Drone* (PVC EP '86). Two folkie "brothers" with cheap electronic instruments as well as acoustic guitars. Also with half-decent day jobs, I bet—they know the texture of selling out. Their jabs at the international monetary system and the world leader they dub the Great Rondini are simple and telling, and there can never be too many of them.   **B**+

Phezulu Eqhudeni (Carthage '85). There's nothing folkloric about the firm yet intricately catchy bass-and-guitar rhythms of the Makgona Tshohle Band—like so many rock-and-rollers before them, these are country people permanently displaced to the city. And if Boer culture has produced a singer with half the intrinsic humor and spirit of Mahlathini, I assume he or she is thinking seriously about exile.   **A**−

Esther Phillips: *Good Black Is Hard To Crack* (Mercury '81). No longer the blueswoman slipping into a more fashionable rhythm, Phillips has made that light, guitar-accented dance beat her own, and here she pursues it without compromises—no violins or fancy horns, just the groove. Only occasionally is the material more than adequate, but to hear her twist a song's natural shape against the smooth pulse and background harmonies is to wonder which is going to crack first.   **B+**

Willie Phoenix: *Willie Phoenix* (A&M '82). Phoenix knocked me out on sheer pizazz fronting a raw, Beatley band called Romantic Noise at Max's three or four years ago; here he surfaces as a Springsteen convert and almost does it again, although after a dozen plays I wonder whether Romantic Noise's songs matched its pizazz. God knows Phoenix doesn't go for ersatz John Cougar epics—his tribute is all musical style, which since his voice outrings Springsteen's can be pretty impressive until the drama calls your attention to the words. Original grade: B.   **B−**

Phranc: *Folksinger* (Rhino '85). You don't come back to a singer-songwriter w/ guitar-and-harmonica for music no matter how winning her "Lonesome Death of Hattie Carroll." You come back because you really like her. As a "life-loving" jock who can do without female mud wrestling and people who crash handicapped parking spaces, Phranc is familiar enough as a general type. But little things like her name and her flattop set her off from the Olivia separatists, and so do big things, like her sweet sense of humor and her two-newspapers-a-day habit. After all, you can do without female mud wrestling and people who crash handicapped parking spaces yourself.   **A−**

Phranc: *I Enjoy Being a Girl* (Island '89). The first uncloseted lesbian to bed down with a major label since Isis, and what does she come up with? The cover art of the year and an album so arch it crumbles without a proscenium. Not that she never gets away with it—the chamber-styled Toys R Us tribute and the praisesong to Martina that spells out her nation of origin are worth hearing even after you know the jokes. But any record that makes its most effective political statement on behalf of child-eating polar bears is resorting to weirdness as a protective device.   **B**

Astor Piazzolla: *Tango: Zero Hour* (American Clavé '86). Until Piazzolla, I never gave a thought to tango, which I conceived vaguely as the music of displaced Europeans slumming their way through an American limbo, compounding angst and self-regard into ridiculous sexual melodrama. But now that I put all that down on paper, it seems both kind of interesting and ripe for destabilization. Piazzolla has been exploring both possibilities since 1946 and claims this is the best of his 40 albums. True semipop, dance music for the cerebellum, with the aesthetic tone of a jazz-classical fusion Gunther Schuller never dreamed.   **A−**

Astor Piazzolla: *The Rough Dancer and the Cyclical Night* (American Clavé '88). Suddenly hot in Dollarland at age 67, Piazzolla is flooding the bins, with his earlier American Clavé albums reissued by Pangaea (structure and sustained intensity make *Tango: Zero Hour* an unusually unsoporific CD), a Montreux concert with Gary Burton available from Atlantic Jazz, and a collaboration with Lalo Schifrin out on Nonesuch. Piazzolla has even less to do with jazz than Gary Burton; he's closer to Bartok the composer than to Ellington the orchestrator, and tends to limit improvisatory space. But the symphonic accompaniment of Schifrin, an Argentinian who straddles pop and classical himself, rarely obtrudes and sometimes even amplifies, so those who prefer their exotica with cushions should opt for *Concerto Para Bandoneon/Tres Tangos*. Me, I don't find Piazzolla's music so alien that it can't be absorbed full force, in the acerbically melodramatic compositions he creates for his quintet. Conceived for a theater piece, this collection is episodic even given the composer's penchant for abrupt mood shifts. But its historical overview, beginning with the "primitive" tango that shook a younger pop world, is just the thing to provide the hint of roots rockers prefer in their exotica. Oh those crazy urban folk.   **A−**

Astor Piazzolla: *La Camorra: La Soledad de la Provacación Apasionada (La Camorra: The Solitude of Passionate Provocation)* (American Clavé '89). Maybe I'm getting sated—how many jazz-classical-tango suites does a Yank rock-and-roller need? Still, as someone who never had much use for *Red Headed Stranger*, I note that the historical metaphor this time is the *guapo*—a "hero or hoodlum," hold the hero. Also, the ruminative interludes suggest that Piazzolla's gift is for passion rather than romanticism. **B+**

Pinhead: *Where Are You?* (BSharp EP '83). Six unhurried songs from a Vermont band given to satire (and music) whose hale, unsmartalecky tone could never happen in the city. Inspirational Verse: "There were these birds called butterflies / They used to fly inside of the sea / We had this stuff called oxygen / It used to hang from all of the trees." **B+**

Pink Floyd: *A Collection of Great Dance Songs* (Columbia '81). With the rerecorded "Money" sporting a livelier bottom to protect them from truth-in-titling and felonious irony charges, this gathers up their tuneful moments, which have always been far between—so far between, in fact, that even the unconverted may miss the ersatz symphonic structures in which they're properly embedded. **B+**

Pink Floyd: *The Final Cut* (Columbia '83). Though I wish this rewarded close listening like John Williams, Fripp & Eno, or the Archies, it's a comfort to encounter antiwar rock that has the weight of years of self-pity behind it—tends to add both literary and political resonance. With this band, aural resonance is a given. **C+**

Pink Floyd: *A Momentary Lapse of Reason* (Columbia '87). "One Slip," which provides the title at just the moment the singer is so "decadent" as to copulate with a woman, is no less sexist than the rape-fantasy cover of Roger Waters's *Pros and Cons of Hitchhiking*. "The Dogs of War," ID'd with blues bottom, could almost be the tin soldiers of Waters-as-Floyd's *The Final Cut*. In short, you'd hardly know the group's conceptmaster

was gone—except that they put out noticeably fewer ideas. **C**

Pink Floyd: *Delicate Sound of Thunder* (Columbia '88). Like the tour it documents, this is supposed to show that Floyd doesn't need "Another Brick in the Wall." Like *A Momentary Lapse of Reason,* which contributes five songs to a disastrously dreary opening, it proves instead that no matter who's the nice guy, Roger Waters is the writer. **C**

The Pistons: *Flight 581* (Twin/Tone '81). There's nothing especially forbidding or avant about these six Minneapolis boys, but chances are they'll never get to Milwaukee, and not for lack of talent, though they could use a singer. It's just that they're obviously in it for the art. This is generic rock and roll for the sheer formal pleasure of it—now pop, now punk, now Stones, now nice, now nasty, usually nasty. **B+**

The Pixies: *Surfer Rosa* (4AD/Rough Trade '88). By general consensus the Amerindie find of the year, and I'll say this for them: they're OK. Aurally articulate but certainly not clean, much less neat, with guitar riffs you actually notice and a strong beat that doesn't owe any subgenre. Feature a woman as equal partner—no separatism or blatant gender aggression. If I was on the lookout for contemporaries who proved my world wasn't coming to an end, I might overrate them too. In fact, maybe I still do. **B**

Pixies: *Doolittle* (4AD/Elektra '89). They're in love and they don't know why—with rock and roll, which is heartening in a time when so many college dropouts have lost touch with the verities. You can tell from the bruising riffs, the rousing choruses, the cute little bass melodies, the solid if changeable beat. But not from any words they sing. They'll improve in direct relation to their improved contact with the outside world. Getting famous too fast could ruin them. **B+**

Robert Plant: *Pictures at 11* (Swan Song '82). Plant's recreation of Led Zep's sonic feel with more mundane musicians is quite impressive, always the operative superlative with him. It's also more insinuatingly hooky than Led Zep ever was. But the insinuation makes one wonder what's being insinuated, which brings one to the question of meaning, which brings one full circle back to almost nowhere. Original grade: B plus. **B**

Robert Plant: *Now and Zen* (Es Paranza '88). Plant's two earlier solo albums were striking and forgettable—bankable self-indulgences that turned a profit on brand loyalty alone. Because they had the virtue of existing, they inspired loose talk about who "really" led his former band, probably from people who secretly believed pomp made the band artistic. This time he looks to solidify his future by imitating his past—even sampling it, an idea he says he got from Rick Rubin (what a card), or hiring his former band's guitarist for a solo. At its best, it's far from forgettable. Overall effect is a cross between his former band and the Cars. **B**

Plasmatics: *Coup D'Etat* (Capitol '82). Now that they've copped to heavy metal tempos, they could last as long as Judas Priest, although since the HM hordes do demand chops, Wendy O. might be well advised to try singing with her nether lips. Not only can't she carry a tune (ha), she can't even yell. Inspirational Thing She Says Backward on Outgroove: "The brainwashed do not know they are brainwashed." Inspirational Message Scratched on Outgroove: "You were not made for this." **D—**

Plasticland: *Plasticland* (Enigma '85). The fairyland psychedelica and many-hued outfits on the cover led me to dismiss the music as camp satire or idiot nostalgia. But "Euphoric Trapdoor Shoes" and "Rattail Comb" work for their laughs, and other songs achieve an even greater complexity of tone. The group's Anglophile diction can be prissy or sarcastic or acid-wild; their music is gimmicky and even silly sometimes, but like "She's a Rainbow" or "Itchycoo Park" it's also melodic and pleasurable and strong. Almost alone among the neopsychedelics, they actually have something to say about the '60s: they understand that to write lines like "Loneliness

is a sad companion / Loveliness is all she feels" may well mean you're foolish but doesn't necessarily make you a fool. **B+**

The Plastic People of the Universe: *Passion Play* (Bozi Mlyn import '80). In its heretical return to a time-honored people's form, its appropriation of available spiritual values as an antidote to materialist oppression, and its embrace of the Christ who "blasphemed against the order of the world," this smuggled religious message from the long-suffering Czech anarchists makes perfect sense. Out of context, however, it's a little hard to take—happy though I am to have a trot, I don't find myself personally enriched when I read along with the Biblical texts and stories. And despite the obsessive bass lines and ostinatos, the only "rock" it brings to mind is Henry Cow, which on a strictly compositional level seems purer to me. But that's not to say that this whatever-it-is music, masterminded by free saxophonist Vratislav Brabanec, isn't satisfying on its own terms—or to mention that side two, especially the long, painful "Father, Father," makes my stomach churn every time I concentrate. **B+**

The Plastic People of the Universe: *Leading Horses* (Bozi Mlyn import '83). Though it was the grim everyday comedy of *Egon Bondy's Happy Hearts Club Banned* that made it not just a stirring document but the ultimate bootleg album, somehow they've gone and lost their sense of humor. Must have to do with their leaders going to jail and their concert sites getting torched. Yet through it all their sound has remained their own, just about the only "European"-"rock" synthesis that never stinks of sentimentality, of pretentiousness. And the aura of dour mockery around Vratislav Brabanec's saxophone on side one gives the odd turns of the lyrics (printed in Czech with translations on the inner sleeve) a significance they couldn't generate on their own. Unfortunately, side two is so dirgelike it'll attract only those with an established appetite for stirring documents. Upped a notch for staying alive anyway. **A—**

The Plimsouls: *Everywhere at Once* (Geffen '83). I explain the "underground" rep of these L.A. power-poppers by asking myself whether I wouldn't be mystified by the Fleshtones if I lived in L.A. As befits an L.A. band, they make more of a show of hitcraft, martialing coherent lyrics to actual emotional effect on a couple of slower ones, and less of a show of party-mania. And I don't like the Fleshtones' records a whole lot either.   **B—**

The Pogues: *Red Roses for Me* (Stiff import '84). Having been left tepid by Irish music from the Chieftains to Clannad, I filed this after a token try. Drumbeats or no drumbeats, I figured it was just beyond me. And some of it is—reels that aren't rockin', accents further garbled in the speedfolk rush. But in general this bunch of disaffected limeys, not all of them from the site of the troubles, yoke the indelible bitterness of the Irish horror to a more adaptable punk rage. Tepid it ain't. [Later on Enigma.] Original grade: B.   **B+**

The Pogues: *Rum Sodomy and the Lash* (Stiff import '85). "And the Band Played Waltzing Matilda" comes from Australian folkie Eric Bogle, one of the least commanding singers in any hemisphere you care to name, but its tale of Gallipoli is long as life and wicked as sin and Shane MacGowan never lets go of it for a second: he tests the flavor of each word before spitting it out. I associate this technique with producer Elvis Costello, who probably deserves credit as well for the album's clear, simple musical shape. But none of it would mean much without the songs—some borrowed, some traditional, and some proof that MacGowan can roll out bitter blarney with the best of his role models. Try "The Old Main Drag," about Irish lads tricking, or "The Sick Bed of Cuchulain," about Irish heroes dying. [Later on MCA]   **A**

The Pogues: *Poguetry in Motion* (MCA EP '86). Though I could skip the reel and fear this got released Stateside for its upbeat mood, any of the three new Shane MacGowan songs would add something to *Rum Sodomy and the Lash*. It's not as if upbeat has to mean escapist, or even happy. Just somewhere this side of desperate.   **A—**

The Pogues: *If I Should Fall From Grace With God* (Island '88). With Steve Lillywhite out to prove he's both a true punk and a true son of Eire, neither pop nor rock nor disco crossover stays these groghounds from the swift accomplishment of their appointed rounds. Lillywhite is so permissive he lets Shane MacGowan slur the words Elvis Costello forced him to enunciate, and at tempos like these you can be sure there are plenty of them. Politics, down-and-outers, New York, the broad majestic Shannon—just don't lose your lyric sheet.   **B+**

The Pogues: *Peace and Love* (Island '89). After I secured a CD, with both digital definition and the lyric sheet Island pulled from the vinyl correcting their chronic incomprehensibility, this phonogram finally began to make sense to me. But the horns still betoken folk-rockers moving on rather than the brass bands I bet they're supposed to evoke. And the trot convinces me that Shane MacGowan will remain the only Pogue in the down-and-out hall of fame.   **B**

Poi Dog Pondering: *Poi Dog Pondering* (Columbia '89). Their psychedelic world-music rep won't prepare you for what they actually sound like, which is a circa-'86 Brit shambling band that knows how loose is too loose. Imagine the Mighty Lemon Drops with extra percussion singing about breakfast, sex, and wonder in a place where central heating just isn't an issue. Honolulu, Austin, what's the dif? They're Sun Belt hippies either way, glad to be alive where the living is easy.   **B+**

Buster Poindexter: *Buster Poindexter* (RCA Victor '87). Entranced by the commercial potential of this novelty act, I forgot how novelty acts translate to plastic. The Upfront Horns overstep themselves by half, the inflections are too Jolson for their own good, and even if the television audience is never the wiser, the material is pretty obvious. I want more "Screwy Music" and "Hot Hot Hot," less "Smack Dab in the Middle" and "Good Morning, Judge." And while it's kinda hip to pick up on songs that Al and Aretha were covering back when you favored fishnet hose, it's also foolhardy, especially when you're hard pressed to beat Eric Burdon at "House of the Rising Sun." **B+**

Buster Poindexter: ***Buster Goes Berserk*** (RCA '89). Be kind and call it Bette Midler's Disease. Or remember what they used to say (stupidly, but why quibble) about the Dolls: you had to be there. Even then the flat-on-its-face overstatement of recorded Buster is pretty appalling. Intimations of minstrelsy he's always subsumed live become all too Negroid with the melon-chomping bass man of "Who Threw the Whiskey in the Well?," even the *Sarafina*-backed "All Night Party." And Buster's no better at big-time schmaltz than David was. I begrudge him nothing. But I don't want to say thanks for the memories yet. **B−**

Pointer Sisters: ***Pointer Sisters' Greatest Hits*** (Planet '82). In the four years since Richard Perry aimed these former eccentrics (see MCA's reretro *Retrospect,* 1981) at the middle of the radio, they've had three top-ten hits, three top-five hits, three you remember: "Fire," "Slow Hand," "He's So Shy." With a couple of minor exceptions, which are also the two remaining top-thirty entries (would markets were always so efficient), everything else has been El Lay assembly-line crapola. Everything Perry included on this kiss-off to Elektra distribution, anyway. **B−**

Pointer Sisters: ***Break Out*** (Planet '84). It's supposed to be tragic that these long-running pros have walked away from America's rich musical heritage in pursuit of the pop buck, but as someone who's always had his doubts about their historical depth, I think the electrodance they settle on here suits them fine. Certainly Richard Perry has assigned songs that throw the new style in your face—titles like "Automatic" and "Neutron Dance" and "Dance Electric" may offend those who wish they still dressed like the Savoy. All jobs well done, I say. **B+**

Pointer Sisters: ***Greatest Hits*** (RCA '89). What a strange story. First they abandon retro chic for the Richard Perry mainstream, with three gems and much dreck to show for it—only the gems save the premature best-of that marked the depar-

ture of Perry's Elektra-distributed Planet label for RCA. After one ground-breaking hit, the only decent regular-release album of their lengthy career adds three more classics to their oeuvre, all in the perfervid robot-disco style of "I'm So Excited." And then—and here's the really weird part—it's over. Five years after *Break Out,* with scads of failed group and solo projects behind and a Motown contract ahead, this postmature best-of lives and dies with the same four robot-disco classics (remixed, though at least not newly remixed) and the same three mainstream gems. I hate to think what they spent their money on. **A−**

Poison: ***Open Up and Say . . . Ahh!*** (Enigma/Capitol '88). Hard rock trash as radio readymades, these cheerful young phonies earn their Gene Simmons cover art. A residue of metal principle spoiled the top forty on their debut, but here they sell out like they know this stuff is only good when it's really shitty. "Nothing but a Good Time" and "Back to the Rocking Horse" are clubby arena anthems, "Look but You Can't Touch" mocks cock-rock with a self-deprecating gesture, and the Loggins & Messina remake has been waiting to happen for fifteen years. **B+**

Polecats: ***Make a Circuit With Me*** (Mercury EP '83). From their colorized art-school quiffs to their synthesized Dave Edmunds production values, these guys aren't rockabilly, they're technopopabilly. T. Rex cover, Bowie cover, "Juvenile Delinquents From a Planet Near Mars," even "Rockabilly Dub"—effervescent muzik built from the solidest chords mankind has known. **B+**

The Police: ***Zenyatta Mondatta*** (A&M '80). Not to be confused with *Reggatta de Blanc,* I don't think, this is where the latest vanguard of musicianly postminimalists abandons all pretense of pop (or reggae) mindlessness. Stewart Copeland's rhythms skank plenty while looting the whole wide world. Andy Summers's guitar harmonies are blatantly off-color, his melodic effects blatantly exotic. And Sting's words are about stuff—itchy general, teacher not petting with teacher's pet, plus, ahem, the perils of stardom. Summing it all up is their first true hit and only true masterpiece: "De Do Do Do, De Da Da Da."   **B**

The Police: *Ghost in the Machine* (A&M '81). It's pointless to deny that they make the chops work for the common good—both their trickiness and their simplicity provide consistent pleasure here. But with drummer, manager, and booking agent all scions of a CIA honcho, I have my doubts about their standing as a progressive force. Whether you're following in the old man's footsteps, offing the motherfucker, or striving for a livable compromise, roots like that leave you twisted, if only to the tune of a middlebrow cliché like Sting's "There is no political solution." In the kindest construction, say their politics are as astute, liberal, and well-meaning as those of Pete "Won't Get Fooled Again" Townshend, who also needs reminding that we're not just spirits in the material world—we're also matter in the material world, which is why things get sticky.   **B+**

The Police: *Synchronicity* (A&M '83). I prefer my musical watersheds juicier than this latest installment in their snazzy pop saga, and my rock middlebrows zanier, or at least *nicer*. If only the single of the summer was a little more ambiguous, so we could hear it as a poem of mistrust to the Pope or the Secretary of State; instead, Sting wears his sexual resentment on his chord changes like a closet "American Woman" fan, reserving the ambiguity for his Jungian conundrums, which I'm sure deserve no better. Best lyrics: Stew's "Miss Gradenko" and Andy's "Mother." Juiciest chord changes: the single of the summer.   **B+**

The Police: *Every Breath You Take: The Singles* (A&M '86). Though they're thought of as slick, no putative pop band of this era has aired more pretensions. The new-agish textural excursions (not the chords and structures that flesh out their tunes) are excised here, but Sting is scarcely less pompous when servicing the marketplace than when expressing himself in the privacy of his own throwaways. From the love object with the dress of red

to the dreams of imaginary energy sources, from sexist condescension to Sufi twaddle he's one step up the evolutionary ladder from Billy Joel. He's got loads of musical gifts. He's even got verbal gifts. But he's tried to convert the sharpest couplet he'll ever write—"De do do do, de da da da / They're meaningless and all that's true"—into a philosophy of life. He's just lucky it was possible musically.   **A—**

Polyrock: *Polyrock* (RCA Victor '80). The same sopranos who sound so right choraling through coproducer Philip Glass's rockish hypnorhythm pieces make this arty dance-rock band sound like, dare I say it, disco. At other points the music whispers, I feel constrained to add, Philip Glass. The strangulated vocals I blame on, who else, David Byrne. That it almost gets over anyway is a credit to crescendo techniques developed by, that's right, the Feelies—who could have used some coproduction themselves.   **B**

The Pontiac Brothers: *Fiesta en la Biblioteca* (Frontier '86). Their dense mix is twixt-punk-and-pop Replacements with plenty of Huskers thrown in, their idea of cover tribute the Dead's "Brown Eyed Woman." So say they're a roots band the way the *Exile* Stones were, shading their guitar barrage into bottleneck and fingerpick. The songs are mostly on it, too. But Hunter & Garcia had tuffer attitude—beyond the occasional one-line hook, medium equals message here. Again.   **B+**

The Pontiac Brothers: *Johnson* (Frontier '88). First they were Stones clones, then replacement Replacements, their roughhewn ways a joy to those who find the former too slick and/or the latter too clever. Me, I take pleasure in how closely they resemble their superiors without surrendering their independence—you never get the feeling they're trying to be anybody but themselves. Also enjoy their sonics, lyrics, hooks, etc.   **B+**

Iggy Pop: *Soldier* (Arista '80). This is sheer product—hard uptempo sessions with the pickup band that featured Glen Matlock and Ivan Kral. But the formula serves him well; he can apparently generate satirical energy over a clean rock bottom at will. Play this a few times and in two years you'll still recall five songs when you put it on again: "Dog Food," "I Snub You," "Loco Mosquito," "I'm a Conservative," "Play It Safe." And all the others will sound pretty good.   **B+**

Iggy Pop: *Party* (Arista '81). Although the music's "tight," and sometimes kinda hip rhythmically too, I guarantee it took him longer to get the Uptown Horns on the telephone than to write these lyrics. Iggy: "Ivan, what rhymes with 'touches my feet'?" Ivan: "How about something with 'creep'—about how you're not a creep, you know?" "But Ivan, I am a creep." "No one will ever know."   **C+**

Iggy Pop: *Zombie Birdhouse* (Animal '82). Granted artistic freedom by idealist entrepreneur Chris Stein after three albums of hard-rock self-formulization for bad old Clive Davis, the Ig comes up with the most experimental record of his career. Which sucks. Don't blame music-meister Rob duPrey, whose settings maintain stylistic continuity yet generate a certain theoretical interest of their own. Blame the slogans, social theory, in-jokes, bad poetry, and vocal dramaturgy he had to work with.   **B−**

Iggy Pop: *Choice Cuts* (RCA Victor '84). Give or take some song-shuffling and a minor substitution, side one of this strange piece of product comprises side one of Ig's 1977 Bowie-produced *The Idiot* and side two comprises side one of Ig's 1977 Bowie-produced *Lust for Life*. Makes you think Bowie knew what he was doing—"Jimmy, please, what do you say we put the, ah, less accessible things on the B?" Though I would have subbed with "Success," that's a quibble on such a consistent album, and though I find that the less accessible things retain their narrow interest, I admit that this is the first time in the '80s it's occurred to me to listen to them. Obviously, no one who owns the originals needs this record, but dollarwise students of that long-ago time should be grateful. Too bad they'll never hear "Dum Dum Boys."   **A−**

Iggy Pop: *Blah-Blah-Blah* (A&M '86). You could point out that *The Idiot* and *Lust for Life* were cut with the Bowie of *Low* and "Heroes" while *Blah-Blah-Blah* was cut with the Bowie of *Let's Dance* and "Dancing in the Streets." Or you could surmise that copping to conscience did even less for Ig than finding true love did for Chrissie Hynde.   **C+**

Iggy Pop: *Instinct* (A&M '88). Twixt the thematic if hardly definitive "Cold Metal" and the humorous if hardly hilarious "Squarehead," Mr. Big Dick makes like the gargoyle he is, crooning in his ghastly Vaughan Monroe baritone when he isn't asserting his tenuous connection with HM, which whatever its offenses is at least popular, and punk, which whatever its offenses is at least arty. If Bowie can't save him and Laswell can't save him, maybe he gone.   **C+**

Popeye (Boardwalk '80). The orchestrations are Kurt Weill meeting Lionel Newman at the Firesign Theatre, and the actor-vocals are as overheard as a Robert Altman soundtrack. Composer Harry Nilsson hasn't worked this hard since Schmilsson; arranger Van Dyke Parks hasn't worked this wisely since *Song Cycle*. So although nothing will appease my hunger for the glorious and inexplicably omitted "Everything Is Food," which I trust Neil Bogart will release as the B side of a disco disc, this beats *Xanadu, Flash Gordon,* and *Urban Cowboy* combined—as a movie, and as a piece of vinyl.   **A−**

The Pop-O-Pies: *White EP* (415 EP '82). New wave's first Grateful Dead tribute band (Minor Threat don't count, they're not new wave) feature hardcore and rap versions of "Truckin' " as well as the real thing. Also "Timothy Leary Lives" (which they regret) and "The Catholics Are Attacking" (which they also regret). They'd obviously better be as funny as they think they are. I think they are.   **A−**

The Power Station: *The Power Station* (Capitol '85). Problem's not Bernard Edwards's textures or Tony Thompson's pulse. It's not the condescending concept that united them with young posers John and Andy Taylor. (How To Tell Them Apart: Andy's guitar has six strings, John's only four!) It's not even the Taylors' songs, though I'll take the T. Rex and Isleys covers and so will you. Problem's old poser Robert Palmer, whom the Taylors thought a suitable Simon Le Bon substitute. Ask any Duranie: he's got wrinkles, and they're not as cute as Bruce's. And even when he didn't the little girls understood.   **C+**

Power Tools: *Strange Meeting* (Antilles New Directions '87). Obliging fellows that they are, Ronald Shannon Jackson and Melvin Gibbs cede this trio to guitar taste-master Bill Frisell, yielding his strongest music and their nicest. Somehow the effect is basically atmospheric whether they're new-aging "Wadmalaw Island" or covering "Unchained Melody" or wrecking "The President's Nap" or pulling out the rage on "Howard Beach Memoirs." Yet somehow they're always funky as well. Nice and strong—especially nice.   **B+**

Prefab Sprout: *Two Wheels Good* (Epic '85). Paddy McAloon is a type we've met many times before—the well-meaning cad. Expressing himself with a grace befitting an intimate of Faron Young and "Georgie" Gershwin, he's sweet enough to come out on the losing side sometimes, but in the end he'll probably "let that lovely creature down," because he can't resist a piece of ass. J.D. Considine calls this music "Steely Dan Lite," which suggests the crucial contribution of producer-sideman Thomas Dolby but misses its pop-folk roots. Reminds me more of the justly obscure, unjustly forgotten Jo Mama—or of Aztec Camera if Roddy Frame were a cad.   **B+**

Prelude's Greatest Hits (Prelude '83). "Beat the Street," "I Hear Music in the Streets," "Must Be the Music," "Body Music," "Shake It Up (Do the Boogaloo)." Get it? From salad days to dog days, this is bootstraps disco. There's an unplayable Euro side that gets even worse than the bland Quebecois ingenue France Joli, and in general the programming is frustrating—just like dancing in discos, if you're not an adept. But New York dance music has always been rawer than the movie version. These one-shots were made for each other.   **B+**

Elvis Presley: *This Is Elvis* (RCA Victor '81). Almost half of this two-record soundtrack comprises previously unreleased live tapes, usually of songs we have in studio versions—some forgettable (the two Chuck Berrys on side three), some historic (the Dorsey-show Joe Turner medley). In any case, the point is documentation, and for once I approve. Even trivia like "Viva Las Vegas" and "G.I. Blues" work in this context—in fact, it makes the context, just like the interviews (try Hy Gardner's) and intros (Ed Sullivan's). In short, buy *The Sun Sessions* (now midline-priced) and *Gold(en) Records* first, but this is the overview.   **A−**

Elvis Presley: *Elvis: The First Live Recordings* (The Music Works EP '82). In which the pre-RCA tyro finds a groove while making nice for squealing young country fans. What's amazing about the groove is that it's drumless, loose if not at all improvised, far more like blues and/or folk music than even his earliest studio work. What's amazing about the nice is how lascivious it is—when he invites his gal to "do what we done before" in "Baby Let's Play House," you can just about see her legs sticking over the back of the couch. Both features are more amazing on side one's relatively obscure covers than one side two's documented classics. **B+**

Elvis Presley: *Elvis—A Legendary Performer: Volume 4* (RCA Victor '83). Deemed a worthy addition to the canon by hagiographers who label the *First Live Recordings* EP a rip, this apocrypha—dominated by bent unreleased versions (and songs) that include a genuinely embarrassing duet with Ann-Margret and a priceless live "Are You Lonesome Tonight?" in which the King collapses into giggles before he's done with the first chorus—marks the unchallenged ascension of Elvis Unmasked among the faithful. It's a fascinating document. I'd rather listen to the EP.   **B**

Pretenders: *Extended Play* (Sire EP '81). The medium-priced four-to-six-track twelve-inch is introductory product suited to young bands who are getting their songwriting shit together (or have already shot their songwriting wad). For this young band, however, it's interim product—two singles that went nowhere on the charts, one B side that goes nowhere period, one B side that goes to Cuba with Bo Diddley, and a live version of a single that already went somewhere (though live it goes even further). All of it you've heard before, and some of it you'll hear again, when they get their follow-up album shit together. **B+**

Pretenders: *Pretenders II* (Sire '81). Even though "The Adultress" comes off as an empty boast, I find Chrissie Hynde more memorable when she's dishing than when she's wishing—her tough surface has more depth than her heart of gold. Anyway, it's always the words I remember, not the melodies. I mean, I never thought they were such hookmeisters to begin with, but at times this relies so much on texture and flow it sounds like a punk *Hissing of Summer Lawns.* Which is kind of an achievement, actually. Original grade: B. **B+**

The Pretenders: *Learning To Crawl* (Sire '84). "I'm not the kind I used to be / I've got a kid, I'm thirty-three" is certainly a quotable quote, and whether rock-and-rolling her baby or growling at fat cats Chrissie Hynde backs it up. It's as if two deaths in the family plus her fruitful union with Ray Davies have convinced her beyond any lingering adolescent doubt that other people are there; Chrissie the fuck-off queen always had these humanistic attitudes in her, and it's good to hear her make the thin line between love and hate explicit. Unfortunately, they're still only attitudes, which is to say that like her mate she hasn't thought them through all that much, and as a result the impressive songcraft here doesn't bear hard scrutiny. But since unlike her mate she keeps her nostalgia under control, she gets her comeback anyway. **A—**

The Pretenders: *Get Close* (Sire '86). She's in a mature relationship, she loves motherhood, and she earns her keep fronting a band. The new guys are funkier than the old guys, the tunes are up to par, and despite "How Much Did You Get for Your Soul?"—it's offensive to dis black pop when your idea of on-the-one is "Fame" cops—her lyrics are pretty mature, with a sisterly offering I'd like to hear some soul

man put across. But let's face it—it's hard to make exciting music out of a mature relationship even when fronting a band is the meaning of your life. **B**

Pretenders: *The Singles* (Sire '87). In a pop environment where even honest artists make a virtue of fabrication, Chrissie Hynde expresses herself. Her fierce, instinctive independence makes even Joan Jett's aggressiveness seem like a pose; unlike Patti Smith, she doesn't append an avant-garde escape clause to her deal with the rock and roll verities. Accessible though they are, her song structures follow no formula anyone else could copy, growing spontaneously (she tells us) out of a personal rhythmic relationship to beats and riffs much too powerful and uncute to be called hooks, which is what they are. Since she has the sense of humor of your average ayatollah, her self-righteousness can be a drag—this is her best album because the radio audience keeps her in line. But she's so tough that there's no reason to think it's her testament. **A**

Prince: *Dirty Mind* (Warner Bros. '80). After going gold in 1979 as an utterly uncrossedover falsetto love man, he takes care of the songwriting, transmutes the persona, revs up the guitar, muscles into the vocals, leans down hard on a rocksteady, funk-tinged four-four, and conceptualizes—about sex, mostly. Thus he becomes the first commercially viable artist in a decade to claim the visionary high ground of Lennon and Dylan and Hendrix (and Jim Morrison), whose rebel turf has been ceded to such marginal heroes-by-fiat as Patti Smith and John Rotten-Lydon. Brashly lubricious where the typical love man plays the lead in "He's So Shy," he specializes here in full-fledged fuckbook fantasies—the kid sleeps with his sister and digs it, sleeps with his girlfriend's boyfriend and doesn't, stops a wedding by gamahuching the bride on her way to church. Mick Jagger should fold up his penis and go home. **A**

Prince: *Controversy* (Warner Bros. '81). Maybe *Dirty Mind* wasn't a tour de force after all; maybe it was dumb luck. The socially conscious songs are catchy enough, but they spring from the mind of a rather confused young fellow, and while his politics get better when he sticks to his favorite subject, which is s-e-x, nothing here is as far-out and on-the-money as "Head" or "Sister" or the magnificent "When You Were Mine." In fact, for a while I thought the best new song was "Jack U Off," an utter throwaway. But that was before the confused young fellow climbed onto the sofa with me and my sweetie during "Do Me, Baby."   **A—**

Prince: *1999* (Warner Bros. '82). Like every black pop auteur, Prince commands his own personal groove, and by stretching his flat funk forcebeat onto two discs worth of deeply useful dance tracks he makes his most convincing political statement to date—about race, the one subject where his instincts always serve him reliably. I mean, you don't hang on his every word in re sex or the end of the world, now do you?   **A—**

Prince and the Revolution: *Purple Rain* (Paisley Park '84). Like the cocky high speed of the brazenly redundant "Baby I'm a Star," the demurely complaisant "Thank you" that answers "You're sheer perfection" signals an artist in full formal flower, and he's got something to say. Maybe even a structure: the frantic self-indulgence of "Let's Go Crazy" gives way to a bitter on-again-off-again affair that climaxes in the loving resignation of the title song—from in-this-life-you're-on-your-own to in-this-life-heaven-is-other-people(and-you're-still-on-your-own). But insofar as his messages are the same old outrageous ones, they've lost steam: "1999" is a more irresistible dance lesson for the edge of the apocalyse than "Let's Go Crazy," "Head" and "Jack U Off" more salacious than the ground-out "Darling Nikki." He may have gained maturity, but like many grown-ups before him, he gets a little blocked making rebel-rock out of it.   **A—**

Prince and the Revolution: *Around the World in a Day* (Warner Bros. '85). It's pretty strange, given that he looked like a visionary not long ago. But this arrested adolescent obviously don't know nuthin about nuthin—except maybe his own life, which for all practical purposes ended in his adolescence, since even for a pop star he does his damnedest to keep the world out. So while his sexual fantasies are outrageous only in their callous predictability and his ballads compelling only as shows of technique, they sure beat his reflexive antinomianism and dim politics. Which suggests why the solid if decidedly unpsychedelic musical pleasures our young craftsman makes available here don't wash. Only the crass "Raspberry Beret" and maybe the crooning "Condition of the Heart" are worth your time.   **B—**

Prince and the Revolution: *Parade* (Paisley Park '86). Musically, this anything but retro fusion of *Fresh*'s foundation and *Sgt. Pepper*'s filigrees is nothing short of amazing. Only the tin-eared will overlook the unkiltered wit of its pop-baroque inventions, only the lead-assed deny its lean, quirky grooves, both of which are so arresting that at first you don't take in the equally spectacular assurance with which the singer skips from mood to mood and register to register. I just wish the thing weren't such a damn kaleidoscope: far from unifying its multifarious parts, its soundtrack function destroys what little chance the lyrics have of bringing it together. Christopher is Prince, I guess, but nothing here tempts me to make sure. I'd much rather find out whether the former Rogers Nelson really takes all this trouble just so he can die and/or make love underneath whatever kind of moon, or if he has something less banal in mind.   **A—**

Prince: *Sign 'o' the Times* (Paisley Park '87). No formal breakthrough, and despite the title/lead/debut single, no social relevance move either, which given the message of "The Cross" (guess, just guess) suits me fine. Merely the most gifted pop musician of his generation proving what a motherfucker he is for two discs start to finish. With helpmate turns from Camille, Susannah, Sheila E., Sheena Easton, he's back to his one-man-band tricks, so collective creation fans should be grateful that at least the second-hottest groove here, after the galvanic "U Got the Look," is Revolution live. Elsewhere Prince-the-rhythm-section works on his r&b so Prince-the-harmony-group can show off vocal chops that make Stevie Wonder sound like a struggling ventriloquist. Yet the voices put over real emotions—studio solitude hasn't reactivated his solipsism. The objects of his desire are also objects of interest, affection, and respect. Some of them he may not even fuck. Original grade: A.   **A+**

Prince: *The Black Album* (unlabeled cassette '88). Uncle Jam's sonic wallop and communal craziness are the project's obvious starting point, though Prince will never be as funny. Even better, they're also its finish line. Except for "When 2 R in Love," easily the lamest thing on two otherwise distinct records, the bassy murk never lets up, and at its weirdest—an unpleasant impersonation of a dumbfuck B-boy that's no lost masterpiece and far more arresting than anything on the official product—it's as dark as "Cosmic Slop." With retail sources drying up (I have a fourth-generation dub from a relatively inside source myself), those who pine for heavy funk should nag their local dealers. This is capitalism, so supply'll meet demand, right? [Available on CD in Japan, rumor has it.]   **A−**

Prince: *Lovesexy* (Paisley Park '88). He's a talented little guy, and this has plenty of pizzazz. But I'll take *The Black Album*'s fat-bottomed whomp over its attention-grabbing beats and halfway decent tunes any day, and despite appearances it sure ain't where he explains why sexiness is next to godliness—lyrically it's sloppy if not pseudo if not stupid. This is doubly bothersome because added religious content is what it's supposed to have over its not terribly shocking alternative. Leading one to the obvious conclusion that the real reason the little guy made the switch was that he was scared to reveal how, shall we say, unpop he could be.   **B+**

John Prine: *Storm Windows* (Asylum '80). Finally Prine has fun in the studio without falling bang on his face like he did at Sun. Unless you count the spy at the House of Pies, the closest the lyrics come to existential absurdity is "Living in the Future"—"We're all driving rocket ships /And talking with our minds /And wearing turquoise jewelry /And standing

in soup lines." But he's not throwing them away; you can tell because he's no longer slurring like 8 A.M. on the Tuesday of a lost weekend. And with Barry Beckett in control, his latest band negotiates the changes between happy and sad like 11:30 on a Friday night. Not stunning, but real smart, real relaxed—one to play.   **A−**

John Prine: *Aimless Love* (Oh Boy '84). Prine's reappearance on his own label suggests that the reasons for his absence were more corporate than personal. The songs suggest that he's not reading *True Love* on the back cover for solace or satire. Only "The Bottomless Lake," copyrighted in 1977, falls into his wild-ass whimsy mode, and only the musically retiring "Maureen, Maureen" gets any more acerbic than that.   **B+**

John Prine: *German Afternoons* (Oh Boy '86). Just in case you were wondering, this relaxed, confident album is where Prine comes out and admits he's a folkie, opening with an A.P. Carter tune he's been performing for a quarter century and commandeering sidemen from New Grass Revival and suchlike. The songs are straightforward and homemade, their great theme the varied love life of a man whose wife Rachel plays bass and sings harmony here and there, though not on the extended beer commercial "Out of Love," nor on "Bad Boy," about "how to be guilty without being Catholic."   **B+**

Professor Longhair: *Crawfish Fiesta* (Alligator '80). Why is this record better than all other Professor Longhair records? Well, the backup is more sympathetic (sweet and sour horns) and the songs well-chosen (rhumbafied blues from Muddy Waters and Jay McNeely and Walter Horton) and Fess's tendency to waver off pitch in the vocals is turned to advantage (cf. Dr. John). Also, there aren't that many Professor Longhair records—two U.S. LPs total for the man who invented modern New Orleans piano. And now he's dead.   **A**

Professor Longhair: *The Last Mardi Gras* (Atlantic/Deluxe '82). Recorded live in two nights in 1978 by the odious Albert Goldman, this full-price double-album has a look of crass class—how many "Tipitina"s does the world need?

And indeed, a few of the new tunes are genre exercises and many of Fess's vocal deviations fail to qualify as the jazzy fantasias Goldman palms them off as. Nevertheless, his Longhair is better performed (as well as much better recorded) than Nighthawk's *Mardi Gras in New Orleans* oldies and a lot steadier than Harvest's *Live on the Queen Mary.* And though the hard, punchy drive of Alligator's *Crawfish Fiesta* makes for a more consistently exciting record, the lazy insouciance of the tempos and horn parts here sure feels like New Orleans to me. Original grade: A minus.   **A**

Professor Longhair: *Rock 'n' Roll Gumbo* (Dancing Cat '85). Everybody should own a Longhair album, and this exceptionally consistent 1974 session—which adds two tracks and a hotter piano mix to the sporadically available French version—won't disappoint. It's got Gatemouth Brown on guitar and fiddle and makes an excellent companion piece to Alligator's peakier *Crawfish Fiesta,* with which it shares a tough uptempo edge and zero songs, not even "Bald Head" or "Tipitina." It does, however, duplicate a lot of the material on Atlantic's endlessly seductive double live *Last Mardi Gras.* So cogitat emptor, and kudos to none other than George Winston for making such reflection possible in the good old U.S.A.   **A—**

Professor Longhair: *Houseparty New Orleans Style* (Rounder '87). If you don't know why Fess is a national treasure of obstinate localism—not rock and roll or blues or even r&b, just Nworlins—these lost recordings from just after his 1971 revival will teach you a lesson. Fess's wobbly vocals and careening piano apotheosized the city's crazy independence the way Allen Toussaint's did (if not does) its pop affability. With eight of fifteen songs otherwise available, novices can skip it if they promise to start somewhere else. Treasure hunters need only be apprized that Snooks Eaglin is on every track and Ziggy Modeliste behind four.   **A—**

The Proletariat: *Soma Holiday* (Non-U/Radiobeat '83). The hardcore debut of 1983 doesn't sound very hardcore, which may not bode well for the movement—this is like a more rigorous, less cosmic PIL. There's a touch too much Geddy Lee in Richard Brown's vocals, but he sure doesn't think like Geddy Lee—avoiding tantrum and who-am-I?, these spare slogans are underpinned by actual left theory, though not much practice. Entire stanza: "Lines form / Stretch for blocks / City blocks / Many wait / Benefits / Stigmatized / Sit and wait / Benefits / Bread."   **B+**

Propeller Propeller cassette '81). This cooperatively produced eighteen-song tape hangs together for a simple reason—none of these ten Boston bands was born to rock. Not that they don't try; not that they don't often succeed. But they come to their (often punk-funked) popsongs self-consciously, with an awkwardness that is consistently charming. Only the Neats (healthy minimalists) and CCCP-TV (nervous about sex) come up with two sureshot bounce-alongs, but only V: is totally unengaging. Theme songs: Art Yard's "The Law" ("Language must go on and on and on") and Chinese Girlfriends' "Let's Be Creative" (alternate title: "Let's Be Ironic"). Assured of its grade because it costs only $4 from 21 Parkvale Avenue #1, Allston, Massachusetts 02134.   **B+**

The Psychedelic Furs: *The Psychedelic Furs* (Columbia '80). They're a posthippie band who satirize hippie fatuousness as well as a punk-era band who send up antihippie orthodoxy, but I love them for simpler reasons: they're great junk and they sound like the Sex Pistols. Richard Butler's phrasing and intonation owe so much to Johnny Rotten's scabrous caterwaul that he's got to be kidding and ripping him off simultaneously, and the calculated rave-ups recall the overall effect sought by the punk godfathers, who were always somewhat grander than their speedy, compulsively crude epigones. That's what makes the Furs great junk—it can't be great unless the possibility remains that it's really pretentious.   **A—**

Psychedelic Furs: *Talk Talk Talk* (Columbia '81). Don't let Richard Butler's heartfelt snarl and Vince Ely's pounding pulse stun you into thinking that this merely recapitulates a great formula. It's richer melodically, texturally, and emotionally; Butler's '70s-'60s mind games have evolved into the bitter double nostalgia of a reluctant romantic who half-believed in 1967 and then half-believed again in 1976. And if commitment gives him problems, at least he's passionate about sex. I loved the first Furs album because it seemed so disposable; I love this one because it doesn't.   **A**

The Psychedelic Furs: *Forever Now* (Columbia '82). It's not band breakdown (Duncan Kilburn's sax replaced, John Ashton's guitar gone) nor pop sellout (Todd Rundgren in for Steve Lillywhite at the board) nor tired songcraft (hookier than the junk-punk debut if more ornate than the powerhouse follow-up) that makes this quite entertaining album less than credible. It's the half-life of cynicism as a public stance. Last time Richard Butler's surprising new emotionality made for a winning world-weariness, but this time it sounds just slightly pat, more or less what you'd expect from a quite likable phony.   **A—**

The Psychedelic Furs: *Mirror Moves* (Columbia '84). Tired of the sardonic fake Pistolese, Richard Butler turns his heartfelt dispassion to an approach that bears the same relation to Bowieism as the earlier Furs did to punk. His seducerama is in the manner of an aging matinee idol who isn't quite as famous as he thinks he is; he sings as if he's known you for years even though you're both perfectly aware that so far your relationship goes no further than his offer of a lift back to your place. And if you're feeling detached enough yourself, you just may take him up on it.   **B+**

Psychedelic Furs: *Midnight to Midnight* (Columbia '87). As his pose proves ever more profitable and baroque—dig that silken-haired punk déshabille—Richard Butler reminds me more and more of Glenn Miller, who in his time also provided a lush, enthralling, perfectly intelligent alternative to the real thing. Butler's snarl is a croon, his harsh guitar sound a grand echo, his selfish rage a soothing reminder that some things never change.   **B**

The Psychedelic Furs: *All of This and Nothing* (Columbia '88). This best-of sounded tired last summer, but when I returned it to the turntable around Election Day "President Gas" presented itself as prophecy and Richard Butler's existential fatigue as the decade's great romantic stance. Pitting his penchant for beautiful melody against his penchant for ugly guitar and wrapping it all up in the mournful ennui of his carcinomic baritone, Butler is an unapologetic poser, but the pose takes on unexpected dignity when you hear how faithfully he's explored it over what is now a full-length career. He rages against the dying of the light, and refuses to play the cornball in the process.   **A**

The Psychedelic Furs: *Book of Days* (Columbia '89). Because this was unmistakably the P-Furs and unmistakably a stone bore, I figured we must have overrated this band. No one ever accused them of having the funk, after all. Comparison with *Talk Talk Talk* and even *Forever Now* soon set me straight, however. Before slipping into chronic depression, Richard Butler intoned amid chaos—the dissonant drones that here parade by in formation detonate all over the earlier records, which makes most of the difference. And although this isn't as lugubrious as you first fear, speed also matters. Usually folks who quit drinking stop sounding sorry for themselves afterwards.   **C+**

Public Enemy: *Yo! Bum Rush the Show* (Def Jam '87). It may seem redundant to accuse a rapper of arrogance, like accusing a politician of seeking power, but Chuck D takes the bully-boy orotundity of his school of rap elocution into a realm of vocal self-involvement worthy of Pavarotti, Steve Perry, or the preacher at a Richard Pryor funeral. And while I know the idea is to play him off the wheedling motor-mouth of his boy Flavor-Flav, why should I like the great man's fan any more than I like the great man? They've got literary chops—amid puns more Elvis Costello than Peter Tosh, their "Megablast" is cutting anticrack narrative-propaganda—and they make something personal of rap's ranking minimalist groove. But there's no fun in these guys, which given the intrinsic austerity of the groove means not much generosity either. Original grade: B. **B+**

Public Enemy: *It Takes a Nation of Millions To Hold Us Back* (Def Jam '88). Chuck D is so full of shit Chuck E can dis him: "You know Public Enemy are punk rockers, 'cause they bitch about rock crits and airwaves so much." To which I'll add: "And make art about conflicts with the law that as a scion of the middle class (albeit an Afro-American and a second-generation leftist) D's been able to avoid in real life." That said, the leader gets points for oratory, political chutzpah, and concealing his own asininity. If I'd never encountered him and Professor Griff in the public prints, I'd still figure them for reverse racists—last cut boasts that "Black-Asiatic man" got here first as if he should therefore inherit the earth. But their "freedom is a road seldom traveled by the multitude" wouldn't in itself have clued me to their contempt for the black audience, because these dense, hard grooves are powered by respect: musically, no pop in years has reached so far while compromising so little. Bill Stephney, Hank Shocklee, and Terminator X juice post-Coleman/Coltrane ear-wrench with the kind of furious momentum harmolodic funk has never dared: the shit never stops abrading and exploding. Yet it holds fast, a revolutionary message D's raps have yet to live up to—which isn't to say that isn't a lot to ask or that they don't sometimes come close. I mean, me and Chuck E like punks— D's not the first talented asshole to front a great band. In fact, he's in a grand rock and roll tradition. Original grade: A. **A+**

Public Image Ltd.: *Second Edition* (Island '80). In which former three-chord savage J. Lydon turns self-conscious primitivist, quite sophisticated in his rotten way. PIL complements Lydon's civilized bestiality by reorganizing the punk basics—ineluctable pulse, impermeable bass, attack guitar—into a full-bodied, superaware white dub with disorienting European echoes. Much of the music on this double-LP version of the exorbitant three-disc, forty-five r.p.m. *Metal Box* is difficult; some of it fails. But the lyrics are both listenable and readable, and thanks to the bass parts even the artiest instrumentals have a leg up on, to choose a telling comparison, Brian Eno's. Don't say I didn't warn you, though—it may portend some really appalling bullshit. No matter what J. Lydon says, rock and roll doesn't deserve to die just because it's twenty-five years old. J. Lydon will be twenty-five years old himself before he knows it. **A—**

Image Publique S.A.: *Paris au Printemps* (Virgin import '80). Supposedly let out of the pen to head a bootleg off at the specialty shops, this live album has a suitably cynical look, but mostly it just sharpens the drums and guitar of songs from 1978's flat and hasty *First Issue,* "Public Image" unfortunately not among them. It cuts deepest on the previously unrecorded (I think) "Psalmodie," which could almost make you think John Lydon liked rock and roll. **B+**

Public Image Ltd.: *The Flowers of Romance* (Warner Bros. '81). J. Lydon's right—rock and roll is boring. And needless to say, so's rock criticism—in a multimedia age I should be able to write my reviews in scratch-'n-sniff. If I could, this one would smell like an old fart. I mean, rock and roll may be boring, but at least it's boring in an engaging way. Bassless Araboiserie is interesting in a boring way. Original grade: B. **C+**

Public Image Ltd.: *PiL* (Virgin import EP '83). Comprising the "Public Image" theme song that made us believe Johnny was forever back in innocent 1978, the magnificent recent A side "This Is Not a Love Song" in two versions, and the self-indulgent recent B side "Blue Water" in one, this is obviously some kind of rip-off. But since it's possible that he'll never record anything else you want to own, you might rip him off back by scarfing it up while you've got the chance, thus avoiding messy compilations later. Original grade: B plus. **A—**

Public Image Ltd.: *This Is What You Want . . . This Is What You Get* (Elektra '84). The howls of outrage greeting this album come from smart optimists who just realized they'd been had. In fact it's no more cynical than *The Flowers of Ro-*

mance, and since it does maintain a groove as well as glinting sardonically on occasion, it's also more fun to listen to. But that's not to say it's fun to listen to. Where *Second Edition* throbs and *The Flowers of Romance* thuds, this shrieks, with some of history's ugliest and most useless horn parts—including the one that ruins "This Is Not a Love Song"—leading the way.   **C+**

Public Image Ltd.:   *Album* (Elektra '86). John Lydon's name on the sticker, combined with his sudden eagerness to shoot the shit with representatives of the press, has everybody confused. This isn't a Lydon record that (the conveniently uncredited) Bill Laswell happened to produce, it's a Laswell record custom-designed for Lydon, with whom the auteur shares a disappointed revolutionary's professional interest in power. Just abstract the production style Laswell's adapted to artists as diverse as Mick Jagger and Herbie Hancock, think Sex Pistols, and you'll get something like this, as clinical as brain surgery and as impersonal as a battering ram, with unlikely virtuosos playing the Cook and Jones parts. It kicks in because they're both cold bastards; it feels out of whack anyway because Lydon can't match Laswell's commitment and still has too much integrity to fake it (and maybe also because he has never been in the same room with most of the musicians in this "band").   **B+**

Public Image Ltd.:   *Live in Tokyo* (Elektra '86). This 1983 U.K. release was PIL's second live album in three years. It documents the lost work of a pickup band that toured for money. It was brokered in the U.S. as part of the price of their commercial album ha-ha. For a new label ho-ho. Bizzers—they never learn.   **C**

Public Image Limited: *Happy?* (Virgin '87). As sheer aural sensation, this may be PIL's best, synthesizing the deep dubwise pessimism of *The Metal Box* with the sharp studiowise pessimism of *Album.* But as total experience, it's product. My favorite line was "We want your money" until I realized it really went "We want your body"—another antisex rant, jeeze. Transcending John's unwavering self-regard is "Fat Chance Motel," a definitive

piece of aural sensation apparently conceived during a desert vacation he apparently didn't enjoy.   **B**

Public Image Ltd.:   *9* (Virgin '89). Johnny's gotten so tired and cynical he can't cut to anywhere new: no matter how hard he tries (and as a working professional he does try), he's stuck with his own ideas. Stephen Hague is a tabula rasa—when he does the Pet Shop Boys he seems smart, when he does Spigue Spigue Sputnik he seems false, when he does Erasure he seems blank. So when he does PIL he seems blank with a few harsh cross-rhythms. And if you consider it corny of me to pick on Johnny's electrodance record, let me observe that if he'd gone to Iggy Pop or George Clinton things would be just as bad. Maybe worse.   **C+**

Pussy Galore: *Right Now!* (Caroline '87). All these postdadaists want is to provide the forbidden visceral thrill of rock and roll at the moment they snatch it away as an impossible fake—to be the-thing and not-the-thing simultaneously. How much more could they ask of life? They have fair success, too, commanding an impressive palette of horrible noises and effectuating a pretty good beat for art-rock. But what you remember in the end is the snatch; you're left to mull over a concept that will thrill only those whose lived experience verifies it. Me, I don't find Route 66 has run out of kicks quite yet.   **B**

Pylon: *Gyrate* (DB '80). Vanessa Ellison's bellowed admonitions, Randy Bewley's guitar gradients, Michael Lachowski's peripatetic bass, and Curtis Crowe's prodigious roundhouse drumming add up to an unmistakable sound. I'm impressed. But I wish they'd come up with a few more riffs/melodies as deliberate and haunting as those of "Volume" and "Stop It" and the foolishly omitted "Cool." And while I admire their bare-boned lyrical concept, often the unpretentiousness seems mannered, like some comp-lit cross between Robbe-Grillet and Ted Berrigan.   **B+**

Pylon: *Chomp* (DB '83). The only band named after a Faulkner novel, and that's what I like about the South. Though I honor their collective front, and believe in my heart that Curtis Crowe is the great musician here, I know for damn sure that the one who makes me murmur "Oh yeah, that one" five seconds into each of these twelve tracks is Randall Bewley. And suspect the reason I can say no more is Vanessa Briscoe, who looks a lot earthier than she turns out to be.   **A—**

Pylon: *Hits* (DB CD '89). From the cradle of Southern civilization, all of *Gyrate* and half of *Chomp,* and I'd still do it the other way round. Also all four sides of two su-

perb seven-inches. "Cool" booms out like the art-DOR sleeper of all time, its only rival "Never Say Never," while "Crazy" and "M-Train" leave the LP stuff wondering what to do. Plus lyrics, which answer many nagging questions and inspire others. How does one grade this pricy embarrassment of riches? I guess one gives it the benefit of the doubt for the singles, which merit digital technology, and the band's big yet spare and spacy sound, which suits it.   **A—**

Quarterflash: *Quarterflash* (Geffen '81). This Seattle sextet makes music for stewardesses if ever there was such a thing, and if you think I'm being condescending that's your problem—I'm awed. What a complex artifact! The lyrics Marv Ross writes for wife Rindy, who sings like a cross between Stevie Nicks and Olivia Newton-John and does clarinet impersonations on the saxophone, are all about how love doesn't last, especially with "Valerie," Rindy's benefactor and then some during an ill-advised stint in art school. And the band, which boasts chops beyond tight, steals only from the masters—Steely Dan chords and guitars, Steve Stills and Joni Mitchell vocalisms, Fleetwood Mac ambience, and of course that soupçon of "Baker Street." Inspirational Verse, I swear: "Hallelujah, Friday's here / The week is long for the insincere." **B**

Queen Ida & the Bon Temps Zydeco Band: *On Tour* (GNP Crescendo '82). Since these Grammy winners have bagged a rep on the folk circuit, where drumming is still regarded as one of the arcane arts, I feel obliged to point out that their exploration of groove is pro forma, their singing uninspired, their material trite, and their bonhomie strictly show business. Even Clifton Chenier has never made great records, and when this battle is over, it won't be Queen Ida wearing his crown. **C+**

Queen Latifah: *All Hail the Queen* (Tommy Boy '89). "And when I say I'm 'Queen' Latifah, it has nothing to do with rank. It has to do with how I feel spiritually." That's her claim, and I'm a believer. It's a relief to hear a woman grab onto the mother-worship that's an unhonored subtext of male rap Afrocentrism—the feminist instincts of "Ladies First," a duet with Brit sister Monie Love, and "Evil That Men Do," with KRS-One's music underpinning the budding matriarch's message, are years over due. Her Afrocentrism is beatwise, too—eager reggae, deep house, "Chicken Scratch." De La Soul, Daddy-O, and her steady mixer Mark the 45 King prove they're good enough for her by playing consort for a track apiece. **A—**

Queensryche: *Queensryche* (EMI America '84). Heavy metal's excuse for existing is its status as the generic expression of a white-male-adolescent underclass, but these five devotees of "the American work ethic" from an affluent Seattle suburb buy none of that—they're into selling. They woodshedded for two years, avoiding the seamy bar circuit in their pursuit of the rock and roll dream, which is of course a big contract. And when they got it they gave two weeks notice on their day jobs like the second-generation managers they are. What EMI paid for was the operatic tenor of Geoff Tate emoting "fantasy" lyrics over hyped-up new-metal tempos, and if you think the brand name panders to sexism and fascism, you're free to set up picket lines for as long as the First Amendment remains in force. **D+**

Robert Quine/Fred Maher: *Basic* (Editions EG '84). Though he does like to play as well as think, Quine's solo work reminds me of somebody. His two-guitar experiment with Jody Harris had the spiraling arty-rocky trippiness of Eno's ill-fated LPs with Cluster, but this time he's chosen to write tunes and add a drummer, and the result is as tough and weird as Eno's classic Jon Hassell collaboration. Just because it's more specific, changing mood and color decisively from track to track, it doesn't exert the same kind of generalized ambient hold, but it sure does have its own gestalt: the avant-garde equivalent of the great album Duane Eddy never made. **A—**

Raheem: *The Vigilante* (A&M '88). For all his disco suck-ups and rock samples, this Houston rapper has gone nowhere, which I'm afraid reflects inept promotion or raw regional prejudice rather than the political consciousness of the market. His handle I tolerate—up against the but-then-you'll-get-caught glamourizations of an Ice-T, anticrime outside the law has its ethical attractions in a time of unpoliced drug war. But even in rap his contempt for women is something special—whether freak or whore or crackhead, the human detritus he means to blow away is almost always female. And first, if she's lucky, he will test his theories of natural lubrication, summed up in a rhyme whose accidental acuity shouldn't get lost in the cutout bins: "I got the tool that she needs / To make her insides bleed." **C+**

The Raincoats: *The Raincoats* (Rough Trade import '80). In their dubious pro-am musicianship and unavoidably spacy ambience, both of Rough Trade's very modern girl groups recall late-'60s art-rock of the Cantabrigian school—Kevin Ayers, Soft Machine, that ilk. But where Essential Logic also recalls art-rock of the Juilliard school, the Raincoats' punk-goes-folk-rock feels friendly even in its arty hostility. If the tentativeness of the rhythms and vocals is accentuated by the medium tempos they prefer, the unevenness of their songwriting means some of it is very good. Sure the multiple genderfuck "Lola" is what

sucks you in, but you may end up preferring the other side. As with Lora Logic's sax, the signature and hook is Vicky Aspinall's violin, which she saws rather than plays. **B+**

The Rainmakers: *The Rainmakers* (Mercury '86). Imagine an unironic Stanard Ridgway with the volume up to eight and you'll have a bead on the innate charms of Bob Walkenhorst's vocals. Seductive he ain't, and too bad, because he mostly outwrites Ridgway in his unironic way, counseling healthy excess in the battle against repression: "Let My People Go-Go." For better and worse, the band's as straight-up as the leader, who's got so much preacher in him that you wonder whether he believes anyone should get their government cheese. **B**

The Rain Parade: *Emergency Third Rail Power Trip* (Enigma '84). I guess what's supposed to make the psychedelic revival cool is that it's postpunk; secondhand purism like this suggests that in our negative age it's a positive statement to replicate the wimpy singing, wispy tunes, unsure drumming, repetitive guitar effects, and naive world view of, oh, Kaleidoscope, Morning Glory, Aum. It ain't. Smart hippies knew how dumb a lot of that music was even then. It's twice as dumb now. **C+**

Rainy Day (Llama '83). Four L.A. neogarage bands collaborate on nine of their '60s faves, and guess what—no Strawberry Alarm Clock. They actually meld the Velvets and Big Star (a ringer, I admit) with the Beach Boys and Buffalo Springfield, picking fine songs that are rarely obvious—most impressively, the Who's "Soon Be Home." Will Glenn's violin hook on "I'll Keep It With Mine" is the only don't-miss, but with two exceptions everything is flowing. Not surprisingly, the Three O'Clock's insufferable Michael Quercio sings lead on both losers—alone among these otherwise well-meaning young people, he clearly thinks the music calls for condescension, with his coyly inept parody of a Keith Moon drum take-out presaging the meandering eleven-minute pseudo-Hendrix jam that closes things on a flubbed note. [Later on Rough Trade.]   **B+**

Rai Rebels (Virgin '88). Lewd bellydancer music rocked by angry young men semi-improvising to a click track for producers who add the accompaniment afterwards—how could it not be great? Lots of ways, especially if you don't feel Algerian culture or speak Arabic (though any rock-and-roller will dig those gutturals). With its mad intensity and funkadelic guitar, "N'Sel Fik" may stand forever as rai's (and multi-instrumentalist Rachid's) one transcendent moment. Take the rest as a visit to exotic modern-day Oran, poised between old and new . . .   **B+**

The Raisins: *The Raisins* (Strugglebaby '83). All but the schlockiest variants of what must still be called mainstream rock are listing toward marginality so fast that soon the whole genre will be a purist specialty like white blues. Overlooking a few organ arpeggios and obvious guitar solos, these four Adrian Belew–produced Ohioans do their passion proud, with Rob Fetters's funny but not parodic (or slavish) Springsteen impression on "Miserable World" a typical high point. The songs stick, too, though the lyrics are matter-of-fact enough about bent sex to make me wonder what the really kinky people in Cincinnati are like. Then again, in Cincinnati a purist mainstream rock band may well define really kinky.   **B+**

Bonnie Raitt: *Green Light* (Warner Bros. '82). On *The Glow* the present-day female interpreter refused to die, and now she does even better by the suspect notion of good ol' you-know-what. The strength of this album runs too deep to rise up and grab you all at once, so you might begin with "Me and the Boys," arch as usual from NRBQ but formally advanced pull-out-the-stops (with all postfeminist peculiarities accounted for) when Bonnie and the boys get down on it. Other starting points: "I Can't Help Myself," in which she takes more helpings than she can count, and "River of Tears," in which Eric Kaz rocks one more once.   **A–**

Bonnie Raitt: *Nine Lives* (Warner Bros. '86). Sometimes selling out takes courage, and it's heartening in a way that Raitt, who's hardly immune to moldy fig, is willing to adapt her blues-rock to hookarama convention. But her laidback grit doesn't quite mesh with the style, which likes its singers shiny and up-up-up. Either that or she couldn't put her heart into a depressingly conventional set of theoretical singles.   **C+**

Bonnie Raitt: *Nick of Time* (Capitol '89). "A lot of people were probably wondering when they heard about the pairing whether I was going to make a funk record like Was (Not Was)," Bonnie surmises. Right—loyalists were shaking in their boots, I was licking my lips, and now the suspense is over, unfortunately. She deserves respect, not the obeisance she gets from career sicko Don Was, who fashions an amazing simulation of the El Lay aesthetic she helped perfect and we all thought he hated. Bonnie being Bonnie, it sounds perfectly OK, but most of the songs are so subtly crafted they disappear under her tender loving ministrations, and though Was lets her play guitar for the whole first side, his studio pros could just as well be Peter Asher's.   **B**

Bop Ramboe and the Ratbags: See Nightmare Alley

Ram Dancehall (Mango '89). I expected more of our former finest reggae label, though Jamaica hasn't been its strength since it turned into one of our three finest

African labels. Anyway, these selections are just a little too subtle (the way Johnny P.'s "Ring a Roses" finally gets you going, the synthpan intro on Cocotea's "Bad Love Affair" that doesn't return often enough to act as a hook) or second-drawer (Tiger's "Never Let Go" rather than his supposed title cut, Brian and Tony Gold's "Maniac" rather than Michael Sembello's). Manhattan Special: Admiral Tibet's "Mad Man."   **B**

Ramones: *End of the Century* (Sire '80). Sad. The best cut is "I'm Affected" (note double-edged title); the second best is a Ronettes remake (Joey outsings Andy Kim); the third best is a ballad about their manager (now departed). They also remake two of their own songs—"Judy Is a Punk" (good sequel) and "Rock 'n' Roll High School" (unnecessary Spectorization)—and one of the Heartbreakers' (inferior). And take on the Sports and Joe Jackson with a song about the radio that would be the worst they'd ever written were it not for "This Ain't Havana" and "High Risk Insurance," in which the group's reactionary political instincts finally escape that invisible ironic shield (bet Johnny provided worse-than-Barry-McGuire rhymes like "on your way to life's promotion / You hinder it with emotion"). Phil Spector doesn't make that much difference; his guitar overdubs are worse than his orchestrations, and they're not uncute. But this band sounds tired.   **B+**

Ramones: *Pleasant Dreams* (Sire '81). I know number six comes off corny compared to the aural rush and conceptual punch of their first (or third) (fourth, even). But song for song it sure beats the fifth, and in future centuries it's not gonna sound all that different from *Ramones Leave Home*—less focused, maybe, but fun anyway. And I want to know what future centuries will make of American rock having left its first anti-KKK song to an announced Reaganite.   **A−**

Ramones: *Subterranean Jungle* (Sire '83). "I'm just a guy who likes to get drunk / I'm just a guy who likes to dress punk," Joey chants as side one fades away, incisively and affectionately locating the real

audience he's brought into being after all these years of mythos and stabs in the dark. And despite one hopeless lyric (Dee Dee on Disneyland) and one dubious cover (token pure pop to balance off double-O-soul remembrances of the Chambers Brothers and the Music Explosion), this is more worthy of an audience than anything they've done in the '80s. Not a mass audience, certainly not a great audience, maybe not even a cool one—just guys who have finally discovered a taste for the raw roar the Ramones invented (bigger now but no less tuneful) and are smart enough to know that when Joey goofs his way through the five syllables of "psy-che-del-i-cized" he's some singer.   **A−**

Ramones: *Too Tough To Die* (Sire '84). Who would have thunk it? With Tommy producing again after five years, these teen-identified professionals (mean age: thirty-three) make a great album, with the cleansing minimalism of their original conception evoked and honestly augmented rather than recycled—just like their unjudgmental fondness for their fellow teen-identifieds. This time the commercial direction is more metal than pop, but satanists they ain't: just as Joey came up with punk's most useful anti-KKK song, here Dee Dee comes up with punk's most useful anti-Reagan song. Dee Dee also imitates Bugs Bunny on steroids on two well-placed hardcore parodies and provides the first single's salutory lyrical hook: "I want to steal from the rich and give to the poor."   **A**

Ramones: *Animal Boy* (Sire '86). Even if "Animal Boy" and "Ape Man Hop" were code for B-boy, which they're not, this wouldn't keep the promise of the remixed and retitled "My Head Is Hanging Upside Down (Bonzo Goes to Bitburg)," because these days code is too fucking subtle. And what we get instead is jungle bunnies, two (pretty good) songs about Joey's drinking, another (not so good) one about his misery, Dee Dee one-for-three, the defensive-sounding "She Belongs to Me," the defensive-sounding "Crummy Stuff," and an anthem I believe called "Something To Believe In." If only they could stop squandering their compassion on cartoons and believe in something.   **B+**

Ramones: *Halfway to Sanity* (Sire '87). It kills me to say this, but with Richie or whoever on the lam, Dee Dee moonlighting as a punk-rapper, Joey frequenting all-acoustic showcases, and Johnny Johnny, a great band has finally worn down into a day job for night people.   **C+**

Ramones: *Ramonesmania* (Sire '88). Begins with "I Wanna Be Sedated" instead of "Blitzkrieg Bop," eh? Odd choice, though it sounds fine, just like everything else they recorded in the '70s, which is why I was hot to lap up the surfeit of this best-of twofer all the way to the third cut, 1980's lamer-than-ever "Do You Remember Rock 'n' Roll Radio?" Lessee—forty-five-only mixes, archival 1910 Fruitgum cover, hmm. Look, kids, let me boil it down for you. First *Ramones*. Then *Rocket to Russia*. Then *Too Tough To Die*, which was 1984. After that you're on your own. Have fun.   **B**

Ramones: *Brain Drain* (Sire '89). Laswellization neither saves their souls for rock and roll nor turns them into a metal band. First side's basically Dee Dee, period-hopping from the pleasantly dreamy "I Believe in Miracles" to the East Coast surf cover "Palisades Park." Second side's basically Joey, pushing the envelope on "Ignorance Is Bliss," going flat on "Come Back, Baby." For professionalism, not bad.   **B**

R&B Cadets: *Top Happy* (Twin/Tone '86). Who out there remembers Stoneground, a buncha hippies who also made quite pleasant, quite forgettable albums rooted in an outmoded black-music groove? And who were also a gas live.   **B**

Rank and File: *Sundown* (Slash '82). As rock concepts go these days, the idea of making like the fourth-best bar band in Wichita Falls is plenty warm-blooded, so that even though I disapprove in theory of the loud, klutzy dynamics of this ex-punk country-rock, its zeal wins me over every time. Helps that they leave "Wabash Cannonball" etc. off the album and explain their excellent motives in their own words, fleshed out with a few of the guitar licks they found lying around that bar.   **A—**

Rank and File: *Long Gone Dead* (Slash '84). There's definitely something off about these country punks, and I think it's that they're serious. Where the Scorchers, Meat Puppets, and Replacements come on crazy, the good times here give off an aura of formal discipline and military rhythm that isn't much like fun. But in a disquietingly cerebral way the music is very moving, with the Kinman brothers' wide-spaced close harmonies adding a unique sweet-and-sour lift to their defiantly doomy tunes. At a moment when the word "rain" has become rockese for all human suffering, I can't help but like folks with enough sense to pay attention to the way it falls.   **A—**

Rap's Greatest Hits (Priority '86). It sure ain't "the biggest sellers of all time!" because there ain't no Sugarhill on it. But if you appreciate rap as *among other things* a novelty music, you'll love these titles: "The Show," "Rumors," "Roxanne, Roxanne," "Pee-Wee's Dance," "Friends," "A Fly Girl." Furthermore, not a single one is on an album worthy of the name, and were I not a tasteless fool I could add "Fat Boys" to the list. So buy "King of Rock" twice. Give them "The Roof Is on Fire" by Rockmaster Scott & the Dynamic Three, which I never heard of either. This is that greatest of rap rarities, a bargain.   **A—**

Ras Michael & the Sons of Negus: *Rally Round* (Shanachie '85). Lifelong Rastafarian Michael Henry does Jah's work by reclaiming pop music for the folk, slipping a line from Wilson Pickett here and Bob Marley there into hymns and chants whose elemental melodies invoke the most high on rivers of funde drums. Not that the beat is more sinuous than mainstream reggae. If anything it's more direct—Michael is a primitivist's primitivist, and thus he overpowers reggae's all-sounds-the-same dilemma. Some feel that this brightened and clarified compilation foreshortens his hypnotic scope. I say it renders him suitable for outside consumption.   **A—**

The Rattlers: *Rattled* (PVC '85). Led by Joey's little brother Mitch (Leigh), this is the terrific little pop band the Ramones never convinced anybody they wanted to be. The Ramones' conceptual smarts earned them an aura of significance even when they made like sellouts. The Rattlers are neater—sharp formally and technically, terse and tuff. The KKK didn't take their baby away, just some radioactive mutant, and they cover "I'm in Love With My Walls" as if Lester Bangs wrote it just for them, which he half did.   **A—**

The Rave-Ups: *Town and Country* (Fun Stuff '85). Near as I can tell, the main thing country-rock does for Jimmy Podrasky is let him sing his songs in a drawl. The drawl doesn't pass—when it comes to Appalachia, Podrasky's native Pittsburgh is close but no corncob pipe. The songs, however, are pretty hip, a credit to Podrasky's lit-major fondness for Dylan and Twain. This being country-rock, they generally take a chugging freight-train rhythm. And Podrasky being a closet popster, they generally have hooks.   **A—**

The Rave-Ups: *The Book of Your Regrets* (Epic '88). As a somewhat skeptical admirer of Jim Podrasky's country-rock pop-craft—how much can so static a commodity be worth in these careening times?—I was irritated at first by the big drum sound, tacked on to this pop product as it is to all others in these conformist times. Only when startled from a revery induced by a competing commodity did I realize that cowriter Terry Wilson's indubitable guitar-banjo-lapsteel-keybs-etc. demanded the percussive kinetics. The boy can't be stopped, his virtuosity serving a song-form rock and roll that's implosive rather than onrocking, pyrotechnic rather than jet-propelled. Even when Podrasky's romantic headaches and American tragedies aren't at a peak of observation, you listen. When they are, you learn. Original grade: A minus.   **B+**

Ready for the World: *Ready for the World* (MCA '85). "I want your lips / I even want your tongue, love": Melvin Riley Jr. puts into words the erotic aspirations that have motivated love men since the first falsetto seduction. From wet ballad to videogame beat, the Prince influence is so palpable it's almost comic and so brazen it could take your breath away. But where Prince thinks sex is nasty, Melvin makes nice-nice. La-la means he'll fuck you.   **B+**

Ready for the World: *Long Time Coming* (MCA '86). How long, oh Lord, how long? An official 47:28, which comes (as they say) to 4:45 per cut, almost every one a slow if not sluggish grind. And with "Mary Goes Round" insisting that sluts need not apply, 6:29 of "Love You Down" is all a good girl needs.   **C+**

The Real Roxanne: *The Real Roxanne* (Select '88). Roxanne Shanté's the real Roxanne. This one's the real Lisa Lisa—smart, fast-talking, Puerto Rican and proud, up on the get down. By working her fine brown frame off without ever taking chance one, she verifies rap's pop scope, from Hurby Luv Bug's cute stuff to Howie Tee's dense samples. Also scores two out of three half-sung slow ones, including a day - in - the - life - of - a - rapper - and - aren't - you - jealous? that can only be described as a modest boast. Would I like all this as much if a guy did it? Of course not. And of course, no guy has.   **A—**

Leon Redbone: *Christmas Island* (August '88). Beyond sacred schlock-by-association and rock and roll gifts, Christmas is a pop holiday that plays best in the background, which suits Redbone's forgettable old-timy lassitude. Who needs a major stylist interpreting "White Christmas" and "Frosty the Snowman"? Both material and occasion call for a pleasantly anonymous medium, and if he sticks in a pleasantly distinctive obscurity like the hula-tinged title tune, don't look it in the chord changes. [Later on Private Music.]   **B+**

Red Crayola With Art & Language: *Kangaroo?* (Rough Trade '81). What the hell is it with radio anyway? A great concept album elucidating Marxist aesthetics and does AOR give it a shot? Nah—all we get is Stevie Nicks and AC/DC. So take my word for it. Not only could John Berger have written "A Portrait of V. I. Lenin in the Style of Jackson Pollock"—"They say it's art killed Pollock /As if that could be / In fact he missed a bend /And drove his Ford into a tree"—but he'd approve of the triumphant pseudo-operatic warble with which Lora Logic stretches out that last word (and no, Berger doesn't like the Essential Logic album either). Also instructive are "The Milkmaid" and "The Tractor Driver," twin parodies of capitalist idealism and socialist realism. And the Au Paris and the Gang of Four are directed to the side-closers, both of which are dubious about romantic love and one of which is entitled "The Principles of Party Organisation." Does it rock? Not much. Does it work? You bet. **A—**

The Red Crayola With Art & Language: *Black Snakes* (Recommended import '83). Here they extend themselves thematically, and while it ain't bad for what it is, what it is is arty satire—"Sloths" is smarter than "The Devil Lives in My Husband's Body," but if it were really smart I couldn't make the comparison. Lora Logic has flown, as is her wont, leaving Mayo Thompson to vocalize, with the result that the same song which nails Jackson Pollock on the first album leaves me feeling sympathetic in this version. To paraphrase Pollock: "An Englishman's an Englishman in thought and act /And you'd expect his analysis to be qualified by that fact." **B**

Otis Redding: *Recorded Live: Previously Unreleased Performances* (Atlantic '82). Eight cuts from the engagement that produced *In Person at the Whiskey-a-Go-Go*, recorded in April 1966, twenty months before he died, and unreleased until late 1978. Only two of three new titles are attached to new songs, including an "A Hard Day's Night" that's apparently a warm-up for the "Day Tripper" on *Live in Europe*. Sounds good anyway, atonal horns and all, but it's docked a notch for making one wonder why almost all the classic studio stuff is currently unavailable. **B—**

The Reddings: *The Awakening* (Believe in a Dream '80). Of the core group—Otis III on guitar, brother Dexter on bass, and cousin Mark Lockett on keyboards—only Lockett does much writing, and he had nothing to do with the hit, "Remote Control," as apt a radio song as Elvis C. or Van M. has ever come up with (well, almost).

But it's 1980, and this ain't no soul group, and for better or worse, writing (not to mention singing) isn't what funk groups are about, as three slow ones that would have stymied even Otis III's dad demonstrate. Playing is what funk groups are about, and if you don't believe me, listen to Otis III on "Doin' It" and "Funkin' on the One" or Dexter anywhere. **B**

Redd Kross: *Teen Babes From Monsanto* (Gasatanka EP '84). At a moment when heavy metal's theoretical attractions—stubborn grass-roots loyalty and low-class aggression—are more potent than at any time since punk did it better, this junk miner's delight performs a real public service. Obscure *tunes* from Kiss, Bowie, even the Stones, that'll blast the cobwebs clean out of your brainpan. Now if only the boring parts of the concept didn't exude them right back. **B+**

Redd Kross: *Neurotica* (Big Time '87). Convinced that a life is a wonderful thing to waste, the McDonald brothers devote theirs to writing better songs than Blue Cheer and the Barbarians—and rocking out harder, too! References to Gandhi, George Harrison, and Buffy Sainte-Marie establish their historical breadth, insults to their girlfriends their punk roots. And only their new drummer's hippie-dippy love throwaway holds a candle to any of the '70s schlock-metal covers they came up on. **B—**

The Red Hot Chili Peppers (EMI America '84). As minstrelsy goes, this is good-hearted stuff (and as minstrelsy, it had better be). The reason it doesn't quite come off isn't that it's good-hearted, either: the band is outrageous enough, though probably not the way it thinks it is. Perhaps there's a clue in this mysterious observation from spokesperson Flea: "Grandmaster Flash and Kurtis Blow have great raps, but not that great music with it." In a bassist, that's serious delusion. **B—**

Red Hot Chili Peppers: *Mother's Milk* (EMI '89). Punks who loved Hendrix and P-Funk way way back, they're finally cashing in on their good taste, and though unbelievers dis their sincerity, execution's the problem. They didn't have the chops to bring it off then, and by pushing the guitar up front they sound even cruder now. But they're perfectly nice fellas, really—mention "compassion" in the very first verse.   **C+**

Red Lorry Yellow Lorry: *Paint Your Wagon* (Red Rhino import '86). Poised provocatively between revolutionary powerhouse and droning bore, the Lorries are yet another sign that music in Britain may yet again get as tough as life in Britain. The sound is New Order meets Test Dept., with singer Chris Reed having it both ways. Always a skeptic in re dirges, I wish they'd picked up the pace with a single like "Spinning Round." And will spin their next around posthaste in the vain hope that they've taken my advice.   **B**

Red Rockers: *Condition Red* (415 '81). After starting out as a tribute band called first Garageland and then White Riot (just a joke fellas, put those guns away please), these heavy New Orleans postpunks set themselves to writing anthems for the next American revolution, anthems I'm sure would be more rousing if the next American revolution were as simple and inevitable as they pretend. Sure there's a "teenage underground," but only "Grow Up" and maybe "Peer Pressure" dig beneath its surface. Time: 27:39.   **B−**

The Reducers: *The Reducers* (Rave On '84). A glorified demo, so the sound could be crisper, but Tom Trombley compensates by sending out a flat, tough beat as pure if not as magical as Charlie Watts himself. And the material is there: "Out of Step" and (in a less theoretical vein) "Black Plastic Shoes" might qualify as theme songs for a band given to voicing the discontents of fairly ordinary nonmetropolitan under-twenty-fives who don't want to buy into the system if they can help it.   **B+**

The Reducers: *Let's Go!* (Rave On '84). Suspiciously generic though they may seem, nobody can name the genre—the attack of speed boys like the Vibrators yoked to a Stonesish but very American "honky imitation of the blues." You know, rock and roll like you dream about it. Their

cross-class sniping isn't as sharp as their what-the-fuck-are-we-doing-in-New-London? because no matter how you strip them down and speed them up, blues and country sources still put a premium on personal expressiveness. Thus the Reducers' satire is straightforward rather than deadpan, their anger their own. For cartoony affectlessness they substitute contained, rapid-fire soul; for chordal roar, licks and even quick, clipped, vaguely Claptonesque solos; for ur-pop hooks, a honky imitation of the blues.   **A−**

The Reducers: *Cruise to Nowhere* (Rave On '85). Less bracing than the nonstop *Let's Go!*, with only a few tunes—the miniature ("Fistfight at the Beach") even more than the metaphor ("Cruise to Nowhere") or the final statement ("Sound of Breaking Down")—that bite hard enough to break the skin. But on "Pub Rockin' " they cop to their roots' roots, and you have to be amazed at how good punk was for these guys. They're devoid of Ameriphilia—of Dr. Feelgood's raunchy role-playing or Ducks Deluxe's mud-bottom romanticism. And if they don't write with the panache of Nick Lowe, they sure get to the point faster than Sean Tyla.   **B+**

Red Wave: 4 Underground Bands From the USSR (Big Time '86). With glasnost glimmering, four officially unrecognized bands smuggle their tapes out to get them heard here, one side per band. Though their benighted countrymen think they're newwavers, by Western standards all are pretty tame—the legendary Aquarium play art-rock, Aquarium protégés Kino play pop, Alisa play boogie, and Strange Games play, well, ska. The Russian gutturals are suitably aggressive, and here and there—the first two Aquarium tracks, the guitar (synth?) that cuts against the magic words "rock and roll" repeated again and again in Alisa's "Bad Boy"—you'll hear acerbic harmonies that I assume are Slavic. But the most convincing set overall comes from the ska guys, and I know why—the polka connection.   **B−**

A. C. Reed & His Spark Plugs: *Take These Blues and Shove 'Em* (Ice Cube '82). The crudest blues album anybody's made on purpose since Hound Dog Taylor died allows this saxophone player to sing—about needing a day job. Unlike his sometime leader Albert Collins, Reed doesn't stand a chance of knocking you over with his chops, which he knows. Unlike his noncousin Jimmy (whose tunes and harp parts he's wont to lift), he's far from certain to win you over with his slurs, either. This he may not know. But his earthiness is down-and-dirty enough to ensure that he'll come close.   **B+**

A. C. Reed: *I'm in the Wrong Business!* (Alligator '87). Title boast to the contrary, Reed has a commercial knack—he knows how to distinguish himself from competing bluesmen, more gifted ones included. His specialty is novelty lyrics like the title boast, here augmented by "Fast Food Annie" and "Don't Drive Drunk." Reparations from Stevie Ray Vaughan don't hurt either.   **B+**

Lou Reed: *Growing Up in Public* (Arista '80). This unabashedly literate album isn't pretentious on paper—Lou's just an educated guy for whom middlebrow names like Poe and Vidal and Shakespeare and Escher mix as naturally into the conversation as dictionary words like "harridan" and "lucid" and "ore" and "encroachment." But musically he's trying too hard with no place to go—projects the opener from midway down the esophagus as if *Street Hassle* leads to *Street-Legal,* then doesn't even stick with that. Mostly these are intelligent songs that misfire slightly. The two gems are two of the simplest both verbally and vocally. In one Lou's father gives him shit while his mother dies. In the other he proposes.   **B**

Lou Reed: *Rock and Roll Diary 1967–1980* (Arista '80). In which Mr. Heroin promotes the '60s. Really. Just compare the studio-Velvets first side with the hodgepodge-Arista closer and tell me he wasn't more confidently himself—I mean *happier*—negating optimism than fumbling through its aftermath. Admittedly, beyond the inescapable "Street Hassle" the Arista song choices are perverse even for Lou—three from his album of six months ago, neither great one among them. And beyond the inescapable "Walk on the Wild Side" the RCA choices aren't much more coherent (cf. RCA's own *Walk on the Wild Side*). So Clive's minions hire Ellen Willis to make sense of it all—which, striving almost too mightily, she almost does.   **B**

Lou Reed: *The Blue Mask* (RCA Victor '82). After this becomes a cult classic, in a week or so, noncultists are gonna start complaining. "My Dedalus to your Bloom / Was such a perfect wit"? And then bringing in "perfect" again for a rhyme? What kind of "spirit of pure poetry" is that? One that honors the way people really talk. Never has Lou sounded more Ginsbergian, more let-it-all-hang-out than on this, his most controlled, plainspoken, deeply felt, and uninhibited album. Even his unnecessarily ideological heterosexuality is more an expression of mood than a statement of policy; he sounds glad to be alive, so that horror and pain become occasions for courage and eloquence as well as bitterness and sarcasm. Every song comes at the world from a slightly different angle, and every one makes the others stronger. Reed's voice—precise, conversational, stirring whether offhand or inspirational—sings his love of language itself, with Fernando Saunders's bass articulating his tenderness and the guitars of Robert Quine and Reed himself slashing out with an anger he understands better all the time. Original grade: A plus.   **A**

Lou Reed: *Legendary Hearts* (RCA Victor '83). If *The Blue Mask* was a tonic, the follow-up's a long drink of water, trading impact and intensity for the stated goal of this (final?) phase of Reed's music: continuity, making do, the long haul. The greatest songs on *The Blue Mask* honored the extremes he was learning to live without while "My House" and the like copped to the implicit sentimentality of his resolution. Here both ends approach the middle. "Legendary Hearts" and "Betrayed" clarify Reed's commitment by laying out the down side of romantic marriage; "Bottoming Out" and "The Last Shot" and the elegiac "Home of the Brave" excise melodrama from his waves of fear. Equally important, "Martial Law" and "Don't Talk to Me About Work" and the almost, well, *liberal* "Powwow" prove that sometimes his great new band is just a way for him to write great new songs, which is what his endurance had better be about in the end.   **A**

Lou Reed: *Live in Italy* (RCA import '84). Unlike *1969 Velvet Underground Live,* this isn't a song album, which is no surprise—a guitar album is what I was hoping for. But unlike *Rock n Roll Animal* it isn't a showoff showcase, either—it's a guitar ensemble album, which is subtler than I was hoping for. Reed and Robert Quine get their moments, but the matter at hand is the interaction of a crack rock and roll band. One of the things that makes Quine a great guitarist is his formal tact, and just as Fernando Saunders's bass defines Reed's recent music on record, the modulated anarchy of Quine's acerbic fills and background commentary defines the live stuff. Even so, I wish they'd arrived at a way for him to cut loose more within the structure, especially since Lou doesn't seem deeply interested in the well-worn classics that dominate the show. The function of crack rock and roll bands, after all, is to set songs.   **B+**

Lou Reed: *New Sensations* (RCA Victor '84). This wonderful record feels like product at first—a solid but expedient bunch of songs like *The Bells* or *Coney Island Baby* or even *Sally Can't Dance.* Although the title cut is definitely the centerpiece, and thematic at that, there are no grand statements like "Women" or "Legendary Hearts" and no tours de force like "The Gun" or "Betrayed." And boy, does it sneak up on you. Instead of straining fruitlessly to top himself, Reed has settled into a pattern as satisfying as what he had going with the Velvets, though by definition it isn't as epochal. The music is simple and inevitable, and even the sarcastic songs are good sarcastic songs, with many of the others avoiding type altogether. Think he can keep doing this till he's fifty? Hope so.   **A**

Lou Reed: *City Lights* (Arista '85). His second Arista mix-and-match is said to unveil Lou the evolving romantic, though the voice is more compassionate than the songs it sings. The theme is "Gimmie Some Good Times," much more at home here than on the aimless *Rock and Roll Heart.* Who ever said a romantic couldn't crack jokes whilst baring his heart—his lust and anger casual, his passion no more deeply felt than his cool? Reinforcing the impression: all the sides you need of *Take No Prisoners*—one.   **B+**

Lou Reed: *Mistrial* (RCA Victor '86). Young modern Lou makes his electronic move, dispensing with live drums on six tracks and leaving the programming to newly anointed computer whiz Fernando Saunders. Old fart Lou works up a pretty fair head of current decrying "Video Violence" and bows to the '80s by situating evil "Outside." His most expedient album since *The Bells* and his worst since *Rock and Roll Heart.*   **B**

Lou Reed: *New York* (Sire '89). Protesting, elegizing, carping, waxing sarcastic, forcing jokes, stating facts, garbling what he just read in the *Times,* free-associating to doomsday, Lou carries on a New York conversation—all that's missing is a disquisition on real estate. I don't always find his politics especially smart—though I have no problem with his grousing about Jesse's Jewish problem, I wish he'd called the man on Hymietown rather than Arafat. But that's not really the point, is it? As usual, the pleasure of the lyrics is mostly tone and delivery—plus the impulse they validate, their affirmation that you can write songs about this stuff. Plus, right, the music. Which is, right, the most Velvets of his entire solo career. And which doesn't, wrong, sound like the Velvets. Just bass, drums, and two (simple) guitars.   **A−**

Re-Flex: *The Politics of Dancing* (Capitol '83). If you want to explore "the politics of feeling good," a correct enough program, then make people feel good first. Avoid "carbon copies of the same old lines." And return to beauty school any front man whose guitar simulates a second synth and whose Bowie rip might just as well be Bryan Ferry and Ric Ocasek harmonizing in a sewage pipe.   **C−**

Reggae Dance Hall Classics (Sleeping Bag '87). Near as I can tell, dance hall represents a hedonistic rebellion against Rasta religiosity not unlike disco's rejection of rock pomposity, and a lot of it is as forgettable outside its context as disco was. What's crucial about these eight tracks is that they all made themselves in Manhattan discos—downtown, natch, but that's the point. All are naggingly uptempo, most one-shots and/or novelties, many hooked with universal melodies that somehow slipped the collective mind—"5000 Miles," "Frere Jacques," "Dem Bones," "For the Love of Money." You can just imagine how weird they must have sounded twixt Madonna and Fad Gadget. Even up against one another they sound pretty weird.   **A−**

Reggae Dance Party (RAS '87). Not the promo sampler you might expect from the foremost U.S. reggae label. Only four of the eleven artists have RAS albums, and only Black Uhuru's Arthur Baker remix boosts LP product with any oomph. That's because the foremost U.S. reggae label had damn well better know its twelve-inches. The side-openers are Natural Beauty's "Nice Up Dancee," cravenly omitted from the *Something Wild* soundtrack, and Paul Blake & Bloodfire Posse's ten-minute dub-included "Get Flat," custom-designed for JA's gun wars. Oldtimer Horace Andy's venture into computerese is also worth committing to memory. The rest will OK up dancee.   **B+**

Reggae Greats: Strictly for Lovers (Mango '84). Unlike the useful but scattered and redundant toasts on *D.J.'s,* these eleven lovers' rock tracks, only one pre-1982, play as an album while expanding the genre. The must-hears are Winston Reedy's seductively seductive "Dim the Lights" and sixteen-year-old Junior Tucker's sweetly devastated "Some Guys Have All the Luck." Prereggae stalwarts Ken Boothe and Jimmy Riley prove more timeless than usual. And Aswad and Struggle have the good sense to identify romantic spirituality with the "Roots Rockin'" and "Rocky Music" they're so militant about.   **B+**

Steve Reich: *Octet/Music for a Large Ensemble/Violin Phase* (ECM '80). I get shy when I write about putatively avant-garde composers like Reich—who am I to judge their compositional acuity? Some-

body who knows great kitsch when he hears it, that's who. *Music for 18 Musicians* is damn near transcendent kitsch— what seems suspiciously lightweight at first reveals itself over countless hearings as durably ethereal. In contrast, these pieces sound dinky over the long haul— listenably dinky, but dinky. My favorite is "Violin Phase," written for a solitary instrument back in 1967, before Reich got unpretentious.   **B+**

R.E.M.: *Chronic Town* (I.R.S. EP '82). This headlong tumble proves them the wittiest and most joyful of the postgarage sound-over-sense bands, probably because they make so little sense that their sound has to be articulate indeed. Physically incomprehensible lyrics make them harder to parse than somebody else's mystical experience, but every so often a chaotic undertow suggests there's more to their romanticism than Spanish moss.   **A−**

R.E.M.: *Murmur* (I.R.S. '83). They aren't a pop band or even an art-pop band— they're an art band, nothing less or more, and a damn smart one. If they weren't so smart they wouldn't be so emotional; in fact, if they weren't so smart no one would mistake them for a pop band. By obscuring their lyrics so artfully they insist that their ("pop") music is good for meaning as well as pleasure, but I guarantee that when they start enunciating—an almost inevitable move if they stick around—the lyrics will still be obscure. That's because their meaning and their emotion almost certainly describe the waking dream that captivates so many art and pop bands. Which leaves me wondering just how much their pleasure means. Quite a lot, I think.   **A−**

R.E.M.: *Reckoning* (I.R.S. '84). This charming band makes honestly reassuring music—those guitar chords ring out with a confidence in the underlying beauty of the world that's all but disappeared among rock-and-rollers who know what else is happening. As befits good Southerners, their sense of necessity resides in their drummer, which is why the Byrds analogies don't wash (who ever noticed Michael Clarke?) and why they shouldn't get carried away with the country moves (slow ones really are supposed to have words). **B+**

R.E.M.: *Fables of the Reconstruction* (I.R.S. '85). If you had any doubts, new producer Joe Boyd clinches it: their formal frame of reference is folk-rock, nothing less and nothing more. Because they're Southerners, they've always defeated folk-rock's crippling stasis: they have a good beat, and you can boogie to them. But as formalists they valorize the past by definition, and if their latest title means anything it's that they're slipping inexorably into the vague comforts of regret, mythos, and nostalgia. Trading energy for ever richer textures, their impressionism sacrifices its paradoxical edginess: it's doleful, slower, solidly grounded but harder to boogie to nevertheless. **B+**

R.E.M.: *Lifes Rich Pageant* (I.R.S. '86). Musically, this talented minor band's fastest-breaking album represents no significant departure from the past, though just how many recapitulations of their lyricism one needs is clearly beginning to trouble those who took it too seriously in the first place. The players still make them and the singer-lyricist still refuses to define them, and while his projection has improved, it's hardly crystalline and wouldn't tell you anything you didn't know if it was. I mean, this is music for mushheads, and that it retains an undeniable if rather abstract charm only proves that there's a little mushhead in all of us. I give album four the nod over number three for its compelling snare sound and dynamite cover version. And insist that any normal person can make do with number one, when all this was a tad more spontaneous. **B+**

R.E.M.: *Dead Letter Office* (I.R.S. '87). Peter Buck describes these B sides and outtakes as "a junkshop." Dumpster would be more like it. You can throw away a Velvets cover or three without anybody getting hurt, but bad Pylon gives unsuspecting young people the wrong idea. **C+**

R.E.M.: *Document* (I.R.S. '87). Their commercial breakthrough eschews escapism without surrendering structural obliqueness, and after six years of mushmouth I wouldn't have thought it possible either. Maybe they finally figured out that intelligibility doesn't equal closure (can't,

actually). Or maybe they just wanted to make sure everyone knew how pissed off they were. In any case, these dreamsongs are nightmares of a world in flames, the kind you remember in all their scary inconsistency because you woke up sweating in the middle. How it will all end I couldn't say, but it's a healthy sign that their discovery of the outside world has sharpened their sense of humor along with everything else. Inspirational Title: "It's the End of the World as We Know It (And I Feel Fine)." Original grade: A minus. **A**

R.E.M.: *Eponymous* (I.R.S. '88). Though the cruder original "Radio Free Europe" and clearer original "Gardening at Night" obscure the evolution slightly, you can hear them change. At first, with Peter Buck pouring out cunning hooks and sweet rondels, Bill Berry locomotivating past any hint of wimp, Mike Mills forthrightly tuneful, and Michael Stipe moaning and mumbling and emoting as if he knows exactly what he's singing about, rock and roll is all they need—it's poetry, it's energy, it's beauty, it's meaning enow. Yet only as they decide that maybe rock and roll isn't enough after all does their music embrace the brains and muscle of the real thing. Divided into "early" and "late" sides that acknowledge this dichotomy, with a train song from their fuzziest regular-release album kicking off side two, this compilation does nicely by the lyricism and depends too heavily on Document for the rock and roll, but their longstanding avant-singles commitment justifies the package. **A−**

R.E.M.: *Green* (Warner Bros. '88). The "air" side combines the bite of their realest rock and roll with the shameless beauty their cult once lived for—it's funny and/or serious and/or rousing and/or elegiac right up to "The Wrong Child," a title that speaks for itself and heralds the shit to follow. Which they dub the "metal" side, with heavy tempos and dubious poetry that make good on their intermittent moments only during the funny, serious, elegiac "I Remember California." **B+**

Remember Soweto 76–86: Bullets Won't Stop Us Now (Mordam '86). Outsiders seeking politically specific antiapartheid music won't get much satisfaction out of repressed South Africa itself: neither the brave, impotent folk-rock of the End Conscription Campaign's *Forces Favourites* nor the ANC's docuprop *Radio Freedom,* both on Rounder, will connect away from home. And Mordam's San Francisco–based *Viva Umkhonto!* is as subculture-bound as most hardcore comps. But this earlier collection from the Afrikaners' Netherlands fatherland speaks the language of international postfolk protest with a Eurorad accent, war before peace. Pop Afrobeat and avant Afrobeat and reggae and dub poetry and hardcore and plastic-people art-rock, by exiles black and white from South Africa and elsewhere, it puts secondhand talent to firsthand use. Includes propaganda booklet and comic, with all proceeds to Umkhonto We Sizwe, the ANC's military wing.   **B**

René & Angela: *Street Called Desire* (Mercury '85). Their youth and street aura are as much Peaches & Herb as Womack & Womack or Ashford & Simpson, but maturity is what they're after—the determined bliss and hot friction of a union beset like most unions by temptations, intrusions, distractions, and the need to eat. Though they sing better than they write, they also sing better than the competition, and as it happens this is the strongest set of songs in the tradition since W&W's *Love Wars*—nothing classic or groundbreaking, but sometimes the truest hearts aren't legendary ones.   **B+**

REO Speedwagon: *Hi Infidelity* (Epic '80). I'm not saying they deserve the biggest seller of their crummy era. But however meaningless the results, they do know something about the hook and the readymade. My favorite is "Tough Guys," which will never go top forty because it features this Inspirational Verse: "They think they're full of fire / She thinks they're full of shit."   **B−**

REO Speedwagon: *The Hits* (Epic '88). Let history record that they got better—pioneers of AOR schlock-rock schlock-pop, they were honoring Fleetwood Mac and the Doobie Brothers by the time of *Hi*

Infidelity. Let history also record that they then got worse.   **C**

The Replacements: *Sorry Ma, Forgot To Take Out the Trash* (Twin/Tone '81). A not-quite-hardcore Twin Cities quartet who sound like the Heartbreakers might have if they'd started young and never seen Union Square: noisy, disgruntled, lovable. I mean, with liner notes like "this could have come close to rock-a-billy if we had taken the time," "stole a mess of these words from a guy who's never gonna listen to this record," and "written 20 mins after we recorded it," how bad could they be? Yeah, I know, pretty bad, and anyway, how good could they be? Hearing is believing. Inspirational Verse: "I hate music / It's got too many notes."   **B+**

The Replacements: *Stink* (Twin/Tone EP '82). They're young and they're snotty. They think fast and short but play it too loose for hardcore. And they make getting pissed off sound both funny and fun, which is always the idea. Tunes emerge from the locomotion, sometimes attached to titles like "Fuck School," "God Damn Job," "White and Lazy," and "Dope Smokin Moron," sometimes not—usually it doesn't matter all that much. They even have their lyrical moments.   **A−**

The Replacements: *Hootenanny* (Twin/Tone '83). Thrashing their guitars or shambling like bumpkins or reading the personals w/ musical accompaniment, this young band has a loose, freewheeling craziness that remains miraculously unaffected after three records. They'll try anything—there's even synthesized percussion on one cut. If the rock and roll spirit is your bottom line, you'll love 'em. But because they play it so loose they do gravitate toward sloppy noise, which means that too often they're more conceptual than a loose, freewheeling rock and roll band ought to be.   **B+**

The Replacements: *Let It Be* (Twin/Tone '84). Those still looking for the perfect garage may misconstrue this band's belated access to melody as proof they've surrendered their principles. Me, I'm delighted they've matured beyond their strange discovery of country music. Bands like this don't have roots, or principles either, they just have stuff they like. Which in this case includes androgyny (no antitrendie reaction here) and Kiss (forgotten protopunks). Things they don't like include tonsillectomies and answering machines, both of which they make something of. Original grade: A.   **A+**

The Replacements: *Tim* (Sire '85). No songwriter in memory matches Paul Westerberg's artful artlessness, the impression he creates of plumbing his heart as he goes along. Statements like "Hold My Life" and "Bastards of Young" are pretty grand when you think about it, but you don't notice in the offhand context of the tastelessly amorous "Kiss Me on the Bus" or the tastelessly resentful "Waitress in the Sky." So far Westerberg hasn't been touched by the pretension and mere craft that seem to be inevitable side effects of such a gift, and I see no reason to anticipate that he will be. With a band this there, presence is all. Original grade: A.   **A−**

The Replacements: *The Shit Hits the Fans* (Twin/Tone cassette '85). This slop bucket of shit-aesthetic covers from Lloyd Price to X with lotsa BTO/Foreigner/Skynyrd in between was "recorded live at the Bowery, Oklahoma City, Oklahoma, 11.11.84" without the band's knowledge: "Our roadie pulled it out of some enterprising young gent's tape recorder toward the end of the night." Sound is more than adequate considering, songs mostly good-to-great, overall effect a little unrealized for my taste. I might want to hear them do "Misty Mountain Hop" twixt "God Damn Job" and "I Will Dare," but twixt "Iron Man" and "Heartbreaker" I'll take Led Zep's.   **B**

The Replacements: *Pleased To Meet Me* (Sire '87). It's no different for Paul Westerberg than for less talented mortals—sooner or later he had to grow up or fall apart. That's why he got rid of Bob Stinson, who threatened to destroy the band along with himself and anybody else within range. But that doesn't mean Westerberg's guitar can extend Stinson's perpetually broken promise to harness the power of naked anarchy. Or that he can altogether avoid the sentimentality inher-

ent in subjects like teen suicide and red red wine. Of course, with almost any other band those two songs would be airplay cuts, but compared to "I.O.U," "Alex Chilton," "I Don't Know," "Valentine," they're product and filler. For the third straight album Westerberg delivers the goods—grimy, uplifting, in the tradition and shocking like new. No competing rock and roll mortal can make such a claim. If by some stroke he learns to handle maturity, Valhalla awaits him.   **A−**

The Replacements: *Don't Tell a Soul* (Sire '89). Circa *Let It Be,* Bob Stinson's guitar was a loud, unkempt match for Paul Westerberg's vocal, only he'd juice the notes with a little something extra and probably wrong, defining a band whose idea of inspiration was crashing into a snowbank and coming out with a six-pack. Especially on side two, the basic guitar move here is much classier: new guy Slim Dunlap plays hooks. On "Back to Back" Westerberg sings "Back to back" and Dunlap doubles a four-note cadence, on "Achin' to Be" Westerberg sings "She's achin' . . ." and Dunlap chimes in two-one two-three—like that. They aren't always so simplistic, but a decade-plus after the dawning of power pop the device reeks of the mechanical—except in country music, where formula is part of the charm, it's tough to bring off without sounding corny or manipulative. At its worst—I vote for "Achin' To Be," which starts off "She's kinda like an artist" and never once slaps itself upside the head—*Don't Tell a Soul* is both. At its best—the Who homage "I Won't" ("I w-w-w-w-w-won't"), the Tommy Stinson anthem "Anywhere's Better Than Here," or even "I'll Be You," with Dunlap reaching bell-like through serious clamor—it sounds like old times.   **B+**

Repo Man (San Andreas '84). Because the movie is zero per cent promotional device, most of the music that goes with it is free to function as barely heard background noise. But separated out as songs on this "soundtrack" disc it complements the film's dryly spaced-out take on L.A. punk. Not until K-Tel goes hardcore will you find Black Flag's "TV Party," Suicidal Tendencies' "Institutionalized," and Fear's "Let Have a War" on the same LP. Iggy Pop's title song is powered by the best of Chequered Past. And Sy Richardson's Shaft parody goes his film bit one better.   **B+**

Keith Richards: *Talk Is Cheap* (Virgin '88). State-of-the-art rock and roll traditionalism. Steve Jordan and Ivan Neville aren't just schooled in the verities, they're cocky enough to teach the verities new tricks, and the songs really do have a near-classic, half-remembered feel. It isn't just the late date that prevents them from going that extra mile, though—it's that Keith is singing, and Keith wrote the words. He's the soul of the Stones, fine. But as the Stones defined it, neotraditionalism takes concept, and no matter how fucked Mick is, concept would seem to be his department.   **B+**

Lionel Richie: *Lionel Richie* (Motown '82). At least Jeffrey Osborne wants to sing like Peabo Bryson or somebody; no sooner does Richie split off from his unnecessarily successful funk group than he starts making like Andy Williams. Not that this comes as a surprise to those who know the funk group. But there are better ways to integrate this great nation of ours. Original grade: C.   **C+**

Lionel Richie: *Can't Slow Down* (Motown '83). Given Richie's well-established appeal to white people, this surprisingly solid album bids fair to turn into a mini-*Thriller,* and good for him—it's a real advance. In the years since he became a ballad writer he's learned how to sing them—"Hello" is nowhere near as magical a song as "Easy," but the grain of Richie's delivery gives you something to sink your ears into. And where the Commodores' funk often sounded a little forced, his jumpy international dance-pop comes to him naturally even when he's putting on that stupid West Indian accent.   **B+**

Lionel Richie: *Dancing on the Ceiling* (Motown '86). Though it's customary to situate Richie square in the middle of the pop mainstream, in fact he's more austere than that, and more distinctive—his pla-

cidity and simplicity yield a lulling, almost mantralike entertainment that recalls Sade or J.J. Cale. Granted, his clichéd verse isn't always as transparent as he hopes—mawk like "Ballerina Girl" is all too noticeable. And sometimes he doesn't put his heart into the semi-fast ones. But he compensates with a knack for tune that puts him over the fine line between lulling and boring—a knack that Sade or Cale would go metal for.   **B+**

Jonathan Richman & the Modern Lovers: *Jonathan Sings!* (Sire '83). Like a lot of great modern rock and roll only more so, Richman's surprising return to his senses plays havoc with all notions of artistic maturity. It couldn't have happened if he hadn't finally grown up, but it wouldn't have been half as striking if he'd relinquished his kiddie lyricism in the bargain. "Not Yet Three," "The Neighbors," and the admonitory campfire anthem "That Summer Feeling" have the magical complexity of masterworks without the reassuringly forbidding aura of mastery, generating just enough authority to shore up lesser songs that might have seemed merely eccentric on their own. Granted, without the disarmingly precise backup of Ellie Marshall and Beth Harrington, Jonathan's singing might have seemed merely eccentric as well. It doesn't.   **A**

Jonathan Richman and the Modern Lovers: *Rockin' and Romance* (Twin/Tone '85). It's a thin line between ooh and ick, and when he starts saying bum for ass (butt, buns, behind, backside, rear end, tush, I'll even settle for bottom) you can figure the feybirds have flitted off with another album. I like Walter Johnson myself, but Jonathan should realize that maybe Vincent van Gogh deserved to be called an asshole.   **B−**

Jonathan Richman and the Modern Lovers: *It's Time for . . .* (Upside '86). I think eternal youth is the secret of rock and roll myself. But if anybody really and truly believes that feeling "Just About Seventeen" is the way to achieve it, the arch nostalgia of this moderately gifted neoprimitive egomaniac should send them running for the Geritol.   **B−**

Stan Ridgway: *The Big Heat* (I.R.S. '86). Greil Marcus argues that the former Wall of Voodoo frontman is "playing with" the American voice Raymond Chandler once described: "flat, toneless and tiresome." Pretty clever, only I don't hear much play. That voice is no creation—it's Ridgway, who shares with Chandler the literary sins of cynicism and literariness. Like a city reporter with a drinking problem or a novelist turned night clerk, Ridgway is a wise guy who isn't as wise as he thinks he is, and while a fair number of these songs have the sleaze-infatuated atmosphere L.A. artists from West to Waits have gone for, only a couple—"Walkin' Home Alone," a song of lost love any asshole would be proud of, and "Pick It Up (And Put It in Your Pocket)," the dirt on Reaganomics—belong in the same paragraph as Raymond Chandler. **B**

Stan Ridgway: *Mosquitos* (Geffen '89). The voice of the American antihero deepens—Ridgway invests his tall tales of the end of the line with lazy, crazy conviction. He thanks Samuel Beckett for "Dogs," rings James M. Cain for "Peg and Pete and Me," and isn't altogether stupid about "Newspapers." But it's a lead-pipe cinch that if he says he can't find "The Last Honest Man," he's a liar. **B**

Ritual Tension: *I Live Here* (Sacrifice '86). "Here" is the Lower East Side, and they're talking to (or yelling at) you, Ms. "Social Climber"—or, more generally, Person Who Doesn't Live on the Lower East Side. Surprisingly, this parochial approach is good for music more intense and universal than, to choose the relevant example, the Bush Tetras' "Too Many Creeps." Unsurprisingly, it's also good for doomy drivel. **B−**

Roachford: *Roachford* (Epic '89). Between Brit trendies and American neocons, you'd think this strong-voiced black Free fan was the next Terence Trent. But TT gets over on formal spark and a sense of manifest destiny. Absent both, quality here is a function of the songwriting, which while it hits the occasional phrase isn't any more revealing in its clarity than TT's in its opacity. **B−**

Margaret Roadknight: *Living in the Land of Oz* (Redwood '84). In Australia she's been dubbed "queen of jazz," which says more about Australia than it does about jazz. As does she—what's most appealing on this U.S. compilation is topical (and usually humorous) material about her native continent that's recommended to Nick Cave and Olivia Newton-John. But though she musters an impressively gruff blues timbre and on occasion some rudimentary swing, I'm not convinced she always goes flat on purpose, and when she emotes she may strain the credulity even of those who set their standards by Nick Cave and Olivia Newton-John. **B+**

Robbie Robertson: *Robbie Robertson* (Geffen '87). Once established as an icon of quality, he always took himself too seriously, and age has neither mellowed him nor wised him up. So now, casting about for a contemporary context, he hooks up with the two most sententious young artists of quality on the charts. Took some guts for such an unrepentant Americana-monger to risk Anglophobe wrath, but unfortunately, the mesh didn't take. Because whatever you think of Peter Gabriel and Bono Vox, you have to admit that unlike the old man they're a) idealists, b) singers, and c) at no loss for context. **C+**

Fenton Robinson: *Nightflight* (Alligator '84). Is he the real thing? Yes. Does he play better than Michael Bloomfield? Yes. Does he play better than Elvin Bishop? Yes. Does he play better than Michael Bloomfield and Elvin Bishop put together? Depends on what you mean by better. Does he sing better than Paul Butterfield? Probably not. Not even Paul Butterfield? Right. Is it 1965? No. Is he the real thing? Depends on what you mean by real. Doesn't it always? **B**

Smokey Robinson: *Warm Thoughts* (Tamla '80). The tardy top-forty success of "Cruisin' "—plus maybe, who knows, an evocative title à la *A Quiet Storm*—has created the impression that the follow-up album's the comeback, but commercially and artistically that was last year's *Where There's Smoke . . .* Smokey's songwriting has sharpened, but not so's it isn't enhanced by a nice ersatz medium dance tempo. Granted, you'd probably enjoy these songs just as much if all you did was make out to them, which seems to be the idea. But that's expecting a lot of the old marrieds he plays to these days. Original grade: A minus.   **B+**

Smokey Robinson: *Being With You* (Tamla '81). Aspiring popsters should welcome this proof that our greatest living poet is able to make do (and then some) with sneaky-fast melodies and rhythms and a vocal style of irreproachably guileless sophistication. Lets them off the, er, hook. Wordwise, that is. Not melodywise, rhythmwise, or voicewise. Original grade: A minus.   **B+**

Smokey Robinson: *Yes It's You Lady* (Tamla '82). He's lost purity on the high end, but the rich grain of his mature midrange more than compensates, and he's never sung with more care, intelligence, or yearning. Unfortunately, he hasn't settled for such ordinary material in years; his equation of love and "irresistible merchandise," for instance, dishonors his penchant for the prepossessing polysyllable, and that's on the title cut. Does he almost get away with it anyway? Yes, he almost gets away with it anyway.   **B**

Smokey Robinson: *Touch the Sky* (Tamla '83). Since his turn-of-the-decade renaissance, Smokey's been slipping back among the marginalia, where qualitative distinctions (better than *Yes It's You Lady* but not *Being With You*) get fine if not strictly personal. This one's recommended especially to cheating-song fans—"Gimme What You Want" is defiant enough for Millie Jackson, "All My Life's a Lie" defeated enough for George Jones—though I'll admit that what pushed me over the line was the way the positivity of the title cut fades out on a pleading "touch it, touch it" that I'd swear aims lower than the sky.   **B+**

Smokey Robinson: *Blame It on Love and All the Great Hits* (Tamla '83). Not only does it follow dubious recent biz practice by baiting/larding the compilation with three previously unreleased "hits"-by-association, it leads with them. Not only do all three follow dubious recent Smokey

practice by farming out his songwriting, all three are stiffs. So this is hardly the reintroduction those who deserted him in 1968 or 1975 could use. And the corporate vice-president in him approved the whole deal.   **B−**

Smokey Robinson: *Essar* (Tamla '84). The one about how much he wants to get next to a young thing who's been almost family since she was a baby is as convincing as "Shop Around." But with Smokey convincing doesn't necessarily have anything to do with factual. Which is the only reason "And I Don't Love You" (who else would begin a song "The whippoorwill—whippoor won't"?), "Gone Forever," and the agonizing "I Can't Find" don't have me worried (much) about him and Claudette. Sure there's filler, some of it written by Essar himself—he would try and get away with "Close Encounters of the First Kind" in 1984. But one thing you can say about Smokey's filler that you can't say about anybody else's—Smokey's singing it.   **B+**

Smokey Robinson: *One Heartbeat* (Motown '87). With executive producer Berry Gordy very hands-on, the man who named the quiet storm goes for his own—middle-aged platinum, just like Tina and Aretha and Dionne and Marvin, God rest his soul. After entrusting the lead single to outsiders who've made pop-funk their metier, he inputs some songwriting, with superpro results that carry the A. But only side two's "Love Don't Give No Reason," one of those shocking domestic melodramas that have dotted his maturity, packs the slightest surprise. Moreover, I doubt he'll get his own. Being perpetually underrated ain't about talent—it's about glamour. As is middle-aged platinum.   **B**

Tom Robinson: *Sector 27* (I.R.S. '80). This attempt to fuse TRB's music-hall cheer with postpunk postfunk isn't as innovative as its sources, but it comes across better on record. Robinson has always flattened his flair for melody under one-dimensional rhythms and vocal attack, but here the arty touches—that is, Stevie B.'s perverse little guitar parts—serve what I'd call a "commercial" function if only the record were selling better. And who ever said politics and propaganda were the same thing? **A**

Tom Robinson: *North by Northwest* (I.R.S. '82). Robinson's bonhomie is rarely seductive—he picks such stiff, strident, perhaps even rigid drummers that his records require effort or at least concentration. But this is where I stop wondering whether he's a fluke. Just about every one of these songs synthesizes his protest-oriented TRB phase with the more cryptic and personal musicality of *Sector 27*. And though Richard Mazda isn't the collaborator Stevie B. was, after five plays or so nearly every track sinks in deep. **A−**

Tom Robinson: *Hope and Glory* (Geffen '84). With its saxophone parts and enriched vocals, this reaffirms Robinson's affinities with cabaret after two albums of straight rock and roll and two inspired compromises with postmodernism. "War Baby" is a wrenching triumph and "Rikki Don't Lose That Number" a great moment in gay liberation, but though it's nice that he sings "Looking for a Bonfire" and "Listen to the Radio" more affectingly than he did on *North by Northwest,* I'd rather he'd written more affectingly. **B+**

Tom Robinson: *The Collection 1977–87* (EMI import '87). First side's a seven-song Tom Robinson Band best-of more useful than 1982's full-length job, second a chronicle of his non-oi phase that omits anything from the intimate, underrated *Sector 27,* why I know not but convenient for anyone who can locate the thing. Fans will appreciate the U.K.-only highlights. And those who've always been put off by his tuneless sincerity will learn firsthand that gay rock and roll needn't be arch or confrontational to establish its identity. **A−**

Rochereau: *Tabu Ley* (Shanachie '84). Comprising six recent full-length dance tracks by the bandleader whose clarion baritone has made him the biggest singer in Zaire for twenty-five years, this is a well-designed compilation documenting Africa's dominant pop style. Most of the cuts have real tunes, with French lyrics accessible to a wide range of high school graduates, and two feature his female protegee M'bilia Bel. But Rochereau is a showbiz pro because he always goes for what he knows works, and outsiders may well find his up-up-up propulsion steady-state if not a little wearing. **B+**

Tabu Ley: *Babeti Soukous* (Realworld '89). More showbiz if not Vegas than his great rival/collaborator Franco, soukous's surviving coinventor is a cornball so seigneurial that I've walked out on him twice, and at first I found this hectically eclectic live-in-the-studio best-of hard to listen to. But when I gave it a chance its constituent parts snuck up on me—the procession of dance beats and guitar styles, the female vocal cameos, even the Smokey-styled/stolen ballad. Take it as the Zairean equivalent of Sunny Adé's *Juju Music*—an unguided tour through a long, deep pop tradition. **B+**

Rochereau: See also Franco & Rochereau

The Roches: *Nurds* (Warner Bros. '80). They're trying too hard. The title cut's all moue and double-take, you can hear Suzzy upstaging her big sisters, and Maggie's side-closers are so intense and compressed it's impossible to know what they mean, though for sure a more experienced poet wouldn't put so much weight on her metaphors (chocolate versus soybeans somehow getting us to boat people living—and no doubt sufferin'—in Suffern, whew). Nor does Paul Simon henchman Roy Halee channel them the way Robert Fripp might have. Even so these songs have an almost magical esprit; Maggie's "One Season" will be in their act when they're fifty. Nobody in pop music equals their intelligence or delight. But I hope they calm down some. **B**

The Roches: *Keep On Doing* (Warner Bros. '82). This sounds so good I'm beginning to believe Robert Fripp was put on earth to produce the Roches (each of us has a place in the cosmic plan, after all). It's not just the honest depth and sweet bite of the voices that make it richer musically than the debut—the songs ring with acoustic guitar ostinatos hookier than any Byrds rip you fancy. The writing has rebounded, too, though because the narrative punch and sense of overarching purpose still lags they no longer seem like protofeminist avatars—just pros who set out to prove themselves with a good album and damn right succeeded. **A−**

The Roches: *Another World* (Warner Bros. '85). "Love Radiates Around" has a once-in-a-lifetime melody and was written by a pal of theirs, but its blissful sentiments don't suit this depressing compromise of a "rock" record any better than it would one of their Robert Fripp jobs. Even turning out songs on deadline they're sardonic weirdos, and though the material could be stronger, the monkey wrench is the received irrelevancy of the synthbeats and guitar solos furnished by three strangely indistinguishable production teams. "Gimme a slice" is one thing, "with everything on it" another.   **B+**

The Roches: *No Trespassing* (SOS EP '86). I'd like to blame this depressing reading of the marketplace on coproducer, cocomposer, synth player, and man Andy Bloch. But the possibility that they've been listening to Jane Siberry cannot be discounted.   **B−**

The Roches: *Speak* (MCA '89). It took them ten years to make a second record as unmediated by market anxiety as their first, and that's probably not how people who think they're too smart for their own britches will hear it. They make no special effort to curb their "arty" "New York" tendencies—that's who they are. So despite moderate tempos and a unified production style (electronic folk-rock, say), the album is beautiful but not irresistibly listenable—you have to listen to the words beneath the harmonies. Fourteen honest, intelligent songs about anxious, difficult love, and if there was any justice they'd bury the Indigo Girls. But there isn't.   **A−**

Rockers (Mango '80). Fine flick—the good guys wear black, and they win—and like the film, the soundtrack follows up *The Harder They Come* more honorably than is rumored without performing a miracle. First side's a smart reggae compilation, with Jacob Miller, Peter Tosh, Junior Murvin, and the Heptones all living up to the impossible memory of "Pressure Drop" and "Johnny Too Bad," but since their tracks are U.S.-available on good if less than essential albums, there's no shock of revelation. From Bunny Wailer's theme song to Rockers All Stars and Kiddus I to Winston Rodney by the sea to third-world label promo, side two's just honorable soundtrack, with revelation irrelevant. Original grade: A minus.   **B+**

Rockin' Sidney: *My Zydeco Shoes Got the Zydeco Blues* (Maison de Soul '85). All over America eccentrics match doggerel to jingle and then importune song publishers for their pot of gold. Sidney Simien commits his creations to vinyl, but with his big talk of "Sidney's hits" and "Takin' over," his world is no less wishful, except for one thing—he made his breakthrough. A small one, to be sure, but however you spell it "My Toot-Toot" shows off his sporadic lyrical flair and is already a New Orleans standard. Not that there's any compelling reason to hear the way Sidney does it, especially since he plays all the instruments himself (drums last, sounds like). His album is of value primarily as a specimen of guileless folk ambition, of a man struggling to adapt a local tradition to what he understands of the great outside.   **B−**

Rockpile: *Seconds of Pleasure* (Columbia '80). Though Lowe & Edmunds's touring vehicle piledrives too much, if you just stand there and get run over you'll enjoy it. Aurally, Edmunds prevails: this hits the ear as a collection of good neoclassicist rock 'n' roll songs, less mindless than prog nitpickers claim and less meaningful than rock 'n' roll loyalists wish. Conceptually, Lowe gets the last word, last song first side: "Play That Fast Thing (One More Time)" not only sums up their limitations, it sums up their knowledge of their limitations—which will separate them forever from the run of good neoclassicist rock 'n' rollers, Dave Edmunds included.   **A−**

Rockwell: *Somebody's Watching Me* (Motown '84). Berry Gordy III sounds like he learned his accent from British Airways ads rather than Boy George or George Harrison, which would be bad enough. Worse still, the cartoon only begins there. Never trust a rich man's son, even a prodigal, when his misgivings about government focus on the IRS, and don't be sure he's so damned concerned about runaways either.   **C**

Nile Rodgers: *Adventures in the Land of the Good Groove* (Mirage '83). Because the basic bass parts are Nile's and not Bernard's and the basic drum patterns Nile's and not Tony's and the basic vocals Nile's and not Alfa's, this groove is stiffer, sharper, tougher, weirder, and less pleasant than Chic's. It's also good if not better, colored with Rodgers's trenchant, voluble guitar talk and rendered meaningful by his willingness to experience lust as an unsentimental need that can turn into unsentimental love.   **A—**

Nile Rodgers: *B-Movie Matinee* (Warner Bros. '85). Since it's all, or mostly, in the groove, I can only guess at an explanation. New producer Tommy Jymi? New drummer Jimmy Bralower? Nile's hot romance with the Synclavier? Luck? Whatever, Rodgers hasn't made such a jumping record since the underrated *Take It Off,* or such a substantial one since the underrated *Real People.* Some may miss that reassuring Bernard Edwards substratum, but I'll take my rhythms rising to the top.   **A—**

The Rolling Stones: *Emotional Rescue* (Rolling Stones '80). No one will ever mistake this for a great Stones album, but I bet it sounds more interesting than *It's Only Rock 'n Roll* should we take the time to compare and contrast in our respective retirement communities. The mid-'60s charm of such tossed-off tropes as "Where the Boys Are" and "She's So Cold" goes with music that's far more allusive and irregular and knowing: for better and worse its drive isn't so monolithic, and the bass comes front and center like Bill was James Jamerson. Looser than you'll ever be.   **B+**

Rolling Stones: *Sucking in the Seventies* (Rolling Stones '81). C'mon, fellas, it's not that bad—you didn't really *suck* in the '70s. Made a number of, er, classic albums, in fact. Sucking them dry for this hodgepodge is what sucks. As I'm sure you know as your lackeys laugh all the way to your Bahamian tax shelters.   **C+**

Rolling Stones: *Tattoo You* (Rolling Stones '81). There's no denying it, unfortunately—this is a damn good record, a great band showing off its mastery, like Muddy Waters (just as a for instance) getting it up

one more once. But where *Some Girls* had impact as a Rolling Stones record, a major statement by artists with something to state, the satisfactions here are stylistic—harmonies, fills, momentum. And the lead singer isn't getting any less mean-spirited as he pushes forty.   **A—**

The Rolling Stones: *"Still Life" (American Tour 1981)* (Rolling Stones '82). They sound very professional, they also sound big and rough and raunchy, and with Charlie driving and Keith making dirty noises they transform "Let Me Go" from an emotional vacuum to a ready-made classic. But "Twenty Flight Rock" has been done better by Robert Gordon (also Eddie Cochran) and the two Motown covers are disgraceful, primarily because of Mick, who has progressed from aging self-parody to old roué—"Satisfaction" sounded more worldly-wise in 1965 (also fresher), and the same goes for every other remake here.   **B—**

The Rolling Stones: *Undercover* (Rolling Stones '84). What do people *hear* in this murky, overblown, incoherent piece of shit? True, they still slip naturally into the kind of vernacular specificity other bands strive for; despite the wind-tunnel mix Keith still sounds like the incorrigible genius-by-accident he is, nothing stops Charlie, and Mick's Texas chainsaw monologue is a scream. Also, two of the songs have political themes, which I guess is supposed to fill me with gratitude. But I'm such a churl I'm only grateful for good songs, and these are as tired and witless and nasty as the rest. Their worst studio album.   **C+**

Rolling Stones: *Rewind (1971–1984)* (Rolling Stones '84). Disinclined though I am to increase their wealth or validate what is at bottom their corporate farewell to WEA distribution, I can't deny the songwriting on this compilation. By now the Jagger-Richards book is deeper than Johnny Mercer's, Willie Dixon's, like that—the first-ever lyric sheet, at one level a token of their utter loss of principle, is pure pleasure (and convinces me "Tumbling Dice" is forever Linda's, too). Surrounded by three of their all-time best ("Miss You," "Brown Sugar," "Start Me Up"), even the political profit-taking of

"Undercover (of the Night)" accrues artistic dignity. Song for song, a stronger album than anything they released in the period, and while for concept I'll take not just the eternal *Exile* but the casual *Some Girls,* it flows and maybe coheres.   **A—**

The Rolling Stones: *Dirty Work* (Rolling Stones '86). Dreaming of solo glory, Mick doesn't have much time for his band these days—just plugged into his Stones mode and spewed whatever he had to spew, adding lyrics and a few key musical ideas to tracks Ron and Keith completed before the star sullied his consciousness with them. And I say let him express himself elsewhere. For once his lyrics are impulsive and confused, two-faced by habit rather than design, the straightest reports he can offer from the top he's so lonely at, about oppressing and being oppressed rather than geopolitical contradiction. In the three that lead side two, always playing dirty is getting to him, as is his misuse of the jerks and greaseballs and fuckers and dumb-asses who clean up after him, yet for all his privilege he's another nuclear subject who's got no say over whether he rots or pops even though he'd much prefer the former. Especially together with the hard advice of "Hold Back," these are songs of conscience well-known sons of bitches can get away with. Coproducer Steve Lillywhite combines high-detail arena-rock with back-to-basics commitment and limits the melismatic affectations that have turned so much of Mick's late work in on itself. Let him have his own life and career, I don't care. What I want is the Stones as an idea that belongs to history, that's mine as much as theirs. This is it.   **A**

Rolling Stones: *Steel Wheels* (Rolling Stones '89). All rancor and bad vibes, *Dirty Work* was the Stones; all impartiality and bad boys grown up, the reunion is an amazing simulation. Charlie's groove enlivens—and IDs—the mature sentiments while gibes at "conscience" and "reason" hint obliquely at self-awareness. But for Mick, self-awareness means above all accepting one's status as a pop star. Maybe he thinks "So get off the fence / It's creasing your butt" saves "Mixed Emotions" from its own conventionality. Probably he thinks giving Keith two vocals is democracy and roots. Certainly he thinks he needs the money. Wrong, wrong, and wrong again.   **B—**

Sonny Rollins: *G-Man* (Milestone '87). The live soundtrack to Robert Mugge's *Saxophone Colossus* is jazz for rock-and-rollers to cut their teeth on. It's exciting, fun, a gas, all that stuff great rock and roll is supposed to be and so rarely is these days. Title track is fifteen minutes of Rollins at a peak—a showman who never shows off, a virtuoso who's never pretentious or (in this situation) even difficult. It's like what some teenager might imagine both "free jazz" and "a honking session" sound like from reading LeRoi Jones or John Sinclair—riffs jumping and giving long past their breaking points, notes held so long it's a wonder Rollins hasn't passed out. Elsewhere are ten-minute workouts on two proven flag-wavers, "Don't Stop the Carnival" and "Tenor Madness" (the latter CD-only although the vinyl runs under thirty-five minutes, my only objection to the package). Everyone else in a quintet accelerated by the amazing Marvin Smith feels the spirit, although their inventions are more strictly harmonic and rhythmic where Rollins's are always sonic as well. Free jazz and honking sessions rarely get this good. I haven't enjoyed a record so much all year.   **A+**

The Romantics: *In Heat* (Nemporer '83). I was annoyed at first by the loud drums and big echo, which tend to dwarf their simple pop-rock, but daily doses of "Talking in Your Sleep" destroyed my resistance. Really, fellas, anything you say, I'll stop thinking altogether if that's the ticket. Just give me another *HOOK!*   **B+**

Max Romeo: *Holding Out My Love to You* (Shanachie '81). You get a reggae pro who's always shown good pop sense, you get producer Keith Richards doubling on gittar, you get Sly & Robbie &c., and what do you get? You get the Kingston equivalent of an ordinary Philly International album, which is better than ordinary Motown, not as good as ordinary Stax.   **B**−

Romeo Void: *It's a Condition* (415 '81). Those who find sex and love in the new bohemia a theme that hits home admire this for its literary value, but only one cut kicks it on back: the opener, "Myself to Myself." Until the likes of "Charred Remains" and "Confrontation" attain an equally hypnotic self-absorption, I'll relegate Debora Iyall's alienation tales to my sociology shelves.   **B**

Romeo Void: *Never Say Never* (415 EP '81). This is no EP, it's a dance twelve-inch with three B sides nobody will remember. And nobody will remember anything about its reason for being except Debora Iyall lashing out with one "I might like you better if we slept together" after another. But that's not the reason they'll remember. They'll remember because of the beat, big drum doubling big guitar, and the sax breaks marking time. Which is quite enough.   **B**+

Rose Royce: *The Best of Rose Royce* (Omni '87). If Norman Whitfield had been content to concoct a disco trademark, they could have been greater than, I don't know, the Undisputed Truth. Instead he fed them, you know, ballads, exactly one of which is good enough for, let's say, Jennifer Holliday at the Holiday Inn. Leaving three nice dance grooves and the eternal "Car Wash."   **C**+

Diana Ross: *Diana* (Motown '80). The right-every-which-way "Upside Down" and all-purpose gay lib pep song "I'm Coming Out" are only the highlights: not since *Lady Sings the Blues* has Ms. R. been forced into such a becoming straitjacket. Her perky angularity and fit-to-burst verve could have been designed for Rodgers & Edwards's synergy—you'd swear she was as great a singer as Alfa Anderson herself. And Nile is showing off more axemanship than any rhythm guitarist in history. Original grade: B plus.   **A**−

Diana Ross: *All the Great Hits* (Motown '81). First time through this double I said fine, perfect in fact—only aficionados will

remember anything else. Even ascertained that the fifteen-minute Supremes medley, segued together from the originals rather than recorded live with her show band, wasn't offensive. But it is useless, and it's also true filler—imagine, her entire solo decade has been good for less than four sides of compilable material. This woman is nothing without a context, and beyond the obvious, Rodgers & Edwards are the only one she was ever made for—Ashford & Simpson's domesticity still sounds awkward on her after years of familiarity, and her movie themes are no better than Shirley Bassey's. The great exception is "Love Hangover," produced in 1976 by true hack Hal Davis, who with that song and that track could probably have gotten a disco classic out of June Pointer, Sarah Dash, Cindy Birdsong—though not Shirley Bassey.   **B**

Diana Ross: *Workin' Overtime* (Motown '89). How 'bout that—"an equity partner" "returns to the foundation of kids' street music," with well-known former expert Nile Rodgers guiding her every note. Which song means the most to her personally? Is it the well-named "Workin' Overtime"? The even better-named "Bottom Line"? Perhaps the revealing "Going Through the Motions"? The answer is "Take the Bitter With the Sweet." Comments Ross: "Every person and every moment is a combination of bitter and sweet, and that is what makes life so rich and surprising." Thanks for letting us in on this secret, equity partner.   **C**+

Rossington Collins Band: *Anytime, Anyplace, Anywhere* (MCA '80). Not a rerun. Skynyrd without Ronnie Van Zant isn't Skynyrd, so four survivors regroup under a more accurate name, and even more impressive, honor Van Zant's irreplaceability absolutely—by installing a woman up front. In the happy ending, the woman's singing and writing would be as singular as Van Zant's, but this is real life and real death, and instead Dale Krantz is merely strong and competent in a generalized "rock" way—here boogie, there almost art-metal. It's a surprise and a pleasure to hear her timbre on top of those guitars.

But only the over-the-top cheating song "Three Times as Bad" rises out of the sound. **B—**

David Lee Roth: *Crazy From the Heat* (Warner Bros. EP '85). Since I'm a person of broader culture than the average Van Halen fan, it didn't smash my preconceptions to hear him cover the Beach Boys and the Spoonful and Dan Hartman and "Just a Gigolo"—just irritated me, reconfirming my instinctive belief that he chose metal over Vegas because Vegas wouldn't have him. Way back when, that is—it's clearly where he'll end up if his movie career should fall through. And as it turns out, his movie career has softened me up—the panoply of grotesquely stereotyped caricatures who populate his videos grosses me out a little, but its capacity to shock is tonic in this bland musical moment. This is an adequate soundtrack. **B**

David Lee Roth: *Eat 'Em and Smile* (Warner Bros. '86). With everybody from Patti to Belinda to Peter to Eldra kissing pop's ass, Roth gives it a pinch and keeps on trucking. Maybe because he lived out his wimpier fantasies on last year's EP, here he's free to mastermind his own piece of multiplatinum potential. Sure he covers "That's Life," but he also assembles a metal band that'll cut old buddies: Maynard Ferguson drummer, cult heaven bassist, and on guitar former Zappa and Lydon sideman Steve Vai, who splits the difference between parody and virtuosity. I mean, Vai is funny without opening his mouth. And of course, so is our voluble auteur, who makes Miss Liberty a burlesque queen and neither lady a whore. **B+**

David Lee Roth: *Skyscraper* (Warner Bros. '88). In which the Van Halen parody of his debut LP gives way to the Vegas parody yeah-sure of his predebut EP. Instead of speed-metal, speed-Sinatra: while Steve Vai and Brent Tuggle make noises that once employed whole phalanxes of AFM members (brass and strings, respectively), Dave shares with us the wit and weary wisdom gained in his career at stud. **C+**

Dexy's Midnight Runners: *Looking for the Young Soul Rebels* (EMI import '80). Perhaps it will clear something up to specify that this is not a soul record. It is a weird record. Never have soul horns sounded remotely as sour, and Kevin Rowland can't carry a tune to the next note. There are horn interjections that make me laugh out loud at their perfectly timed wrong rightness, and with Kevin Rowland quavering through his deeply felt poesy and everybody else blaring away, I enjoy it in much the same way I enjoy a no-wave band on a good night—DNA, say. But DNA I understand. **B**

Kevin Rowland and Dexys Midnight Runners: *Too-Rye-Ay* (Mercury '82). Rowland's arrangements are impossibly busy and his vocals impossibly mannered, but on this record he does the impossible— makes me believe he's found some young soul rebels. The unison horn voicings and post-Stax fiddles impart an underlying simplicity that'll pass for Celtic, and if Rowland swoops and swerves where a real soul singer would just emote, his earnestness prevails anyway. **B+**

Roxy Music: *Flesh & Blood* (Atco '80). Except maybe on "My Only Love"— imagine a song of that title written for (no, rejected by) Perry Como—this never sinks to their Liebschmerz-drenched nadir. But the secondhand funk is getting too easy to take. Much as I enjoy the languorous "Midnight Hour" and above-it-all "Eight Miles High," I always get suspicious when covers overwhelm originals. **B**

Roxy Music: *Avalon* (Warner Bros. '82). At its juiciest Bryan Ferry's romanticism has always seemed too arch and too sour, not to mention too juicy, which is why this minor triumph sounds mild or even dull at first: after all these years its sweet simplicity is unexpected. We've always known he recorded "These Foolish Things" in the fond hope that someday he'd believe it, and while I never will, I can enjoy his pleasure in the accomplishment. **A—**

Roxy Music: *The High Road* (Warner Bros. EP '83). At 26:28, a generous live mini. Limber amplifications of the putatively impassioned "Can't Let Go" and the formerly unbearable "My Only Love" grace the A. "Like a Hurricane" and "Jealous Guy" redefine the parameters of rocksy retro on the B. Next time you want to hear Bryan croon or Phil wail, take a flier.   **B+**

Roxy Music: *The Atlantic Years 1973–1980* (Atco '83). Borrows "Do the Strand" from *For Your Pleasure* (originally on Reprise, fellas) and "Love Is the Drug" from *Siren* and *Greatest Hits,* the better to showcase Roxy Music the creamy dance band. I wouldn't swear it's a better album than *Manifesto,* from which it appropriates four cuts. But I would swear it's a better album than *Flesh + Blood,* from which it also appropriates four cuts.   **B+**

Roxy Music: See also Bryan Ferry/Roxy Music

Royal Crescent Mob: *Land of Sugar* (No Other EP '86). White funk that by some alchemy generates not only a groove, which is rare enough, but also the irrepressible fun every garage band pretends to think it's having. Two of the originals are up to the two covers, Slick James's wasn't-that-by-Kiss? "Love Gun" and the Ohio Players' long-time-no-hear "Love Rollercoaster." Couldn't have hurt their karma that lead singer David Ellison cut an Ohio Player's lawn when he was a kid, and somehow seems fitting that first pressing they got mixed up at the plant with a Christian heavy metal record.   **A−**

Royal Crescent Mob: *Omerta* (Moving Target '87). Although those who think all funk sounds the same might confuse them with, er, Cameo, unlike other umpteenth-generation new-wavers they have identity to burn. Say they're '60s types hip enough to have learned their wacked-out anarchy from Pedro Bell's mid-'70s psychedelic cartoons. Partly because funk gets over on a groove more muscular than they can cut and partly because they put their all into a self-manufactured EP, only "Get Off the Bus," which also led the EP, and "Mob's Revenge," for an ass-grabbing asshole and featuring a rousing "You're fucked" refrain, belong on their best-of. But their

identity comes this close to carrying them over the top anyway.   **B+**

Royal Crescent Mob: *Something Old, New and Borrowed* (Moving Target '88). The borrowed is the largely legendary *Land of Sugar,* now available only as a Play It Again Sam import. The new is a Richard Gottehrer–produced single, half generic white funk, half sui generis garage pop. The old is five cuts "live at the fair," though just exactly which fair is left unspecified. I smell a ringer right down to the wild cheers for the James Brown cover and the cries of "You suck," though the Led Zep cover and the vamp-with-intro about corn dogs and heat-vs.-humidity certainly do the concept proud.   **B+**

Royal Crescent Mob: *Spin the World* (Sire '89). Bridging the modest distance between Ohio Players fans and Aerosmith-for-the-fun-of-it, they lock into their groove and don't give a single song away. Even the hardcore tribute "Stock Car Race" shows off their somehow unsurprising new command of the everyday detail: home for supper, love at a red light, five more minutes with a face you'd had enough of. One protagonist wants to design men's clothes and is on his way to Paris with EU in the Walkman. Another hates doing overtime and eagerly awaits the corporate apocalypse: "I'm on the bottom and I'm not afraid."   **A−**

The Royal Philharmonic Orchestra: *Hooked on Classics* (RCA Victor '82). I always knew English art-rock would be good for something eventually, and *voilà*—on one disc the Phils have woven together (well, maybe "strung" would be more accurate) no fewer than one hundred three melodies that have stood the test of time, every one a milestone of European culture. At long last the three Bs get to roll back over on Chuck Berry—there are more catchy tunes here than on a Beatle Weekend. And though I admit that the segue from "Stranger in Paradise" to "Hello Muddah, Hello Faddah!" is a little abrupt for my tastes, I figure that's the kind of avant-garde *épatement* that's always made modern art so exciting. Who's in that rhythm section?! And are you listening, Glenn Branca?! **B**

Rubber City Rebels: *Rubber City Rebels* (Capitol '80). When it comes to El Lay punk, you take the sun-addled Germs and Circle Jerks and Dickies and leave me these stagestruck outlanders, Doug Fieger production and all. At least they understand what being phony *means.* "Young and Dumb" doesn't replace *From Akron's* definitive "Brain Job" because it's not about the Rebs. But anybody who can link the hallowed anomie of (the Pistols') "No Feelings" to the cartoon cannibalism of (the Rebs') "Child Eaters" deserves to tour with the Psychedelic Furs. Original grade: B plus. **B**

Rubber Rodeo: *Scenic Views* (Mercury '84). Shooting straighter than I'd expect of the Tubes or Orchestra Luna, these art-schoolers look at the Wild West and see laundromats, tourist attractions, and hand-tooled footwear. And shooting even lower than I'd hoped, they hear synth-pop with dobros and steel guitars. Commerciality—it's so campy. **C**

Rufus and Chaka Khan: *Live—Stompin' at the Savoy* (Warner Bros. '83). Especially since "Ain't Nobody," the killer hit her last album cried out for, comes courtesy of Rufus's main man Hawk Wolinski, this reunion is like a gift—for three sides live and one studio she's finally free of her freedom. It's not the '70s best-of a cynical admirer like myself might wish, but the material is stronger than anything she's compiled with Arif Mardin for sure, and "Ain't That Peculiar" is a complete natural. But beyond "Ain't Nobody," Wolinski contributes nothing special songwise. Which I guess is one reason she wanted her freedom. **B+**

The Runaways: *The Best of the Runaways* (Mercury '82). Ignore the sticker—if Kim Fowley had known how to make a Joan Jett album, he would have done the deed in 1976. **C+**

Run-D.M.C.: *Run-D.M.C.* (Profile '84). Though a bit upwardly mobile for the highbrow-lowbrows who regard money lust and the death throes of capitalism as two sides of rap's only fit subject—D.J. Run boasted about attending St. John's, of all things—the competitive fatalism of the spare, brutal "It's Like That"/"Sucker M.C.s" was unforced and dead on, and Eddie Martinez's Hendrix-Funkadelic metal on the expansive "Rock Box" proves that even street minimalists can love guitars. But this does more than fill in around two of the finest singles of the past couple of years. It's easily the canniest and most formally sustained rap album ever, a tour de force I trust will be studied by all manner of creative downtowners and racially enlightened Englishmen. While their heavy staccato and proud disdain for melody may prove too avant-garde for some, the style has been in the New York air long enough that you may understand it better than you think. Do you have zero tolerance for namby-pamby bullshit? Do you believe in yourself above all? Then chances are you share Run-D.M.C.'s values. **A—**

Run-D.M.C.: *King of Rock* (Profile '85). You can tell these guys are real rock-and-rollers because they sounded so much fresher before they got what they wanted, and you can tell they didn't get it all because their rhymes still make a lot of sense sometimes—especially "You're Blind," a protest for and at the ghetto rather than about it. But their well-timed "You Talk Too Much" routine runs aground on stupid insults ("nagging wife," gosh) and old jokes ("Why don't you find a short pier / And take a long walk," groan). "It's Not Funny" is either a perverse albeit well-named joke or a complete washout. Even the boasts run thin. "Take airplane flights / At huge heights"? I mean, what do sucker MCs do? Just taxi around the runway? **B+**

Run-D.M.C.: *Raising Hell* (Profile '86). Like the Rolling Stones twenty years ago, they're middle-class lads who are into music that's hard above all—they're street because they want to be. Granted, the analogy is less than exact. Where the Stones dramatized their streetness by becoming bohemians, Run-D.M.C. remain defiantly and even paradigmatically middle-class, a much tougher trick. Run-

D.M.C. project less respect for women than the Stones, and less interest in them, too. They commit more lyrical gaffes. And their music is a lot further out. Without benefit of a "Rock Box" or "King of Rock," this is their most uncompromising and compelling album, all hard beats and declaiming voices. They're proud to be black all right, but I don't think it has much to do with George Washington Carver. They're proud to be black because it means they can do this.   **A**—

Run-D.M.C.:   *Tougher Than Leather* (Profile '88). Coming off their sophomore jinx and out to prove their mastery, they ended up celebrating it as well; coming off their triumph and feeling too damn big for their minor label, they merely demonstrate it. Technically, the kings are

nonpareils—not a duff beat or a forced rhyme. But for the moment they lack desire. I'll enjoy the genre-busting side-closers anywhere, the original-metal title tune and anticrime message on the radio, and the rest later.   **B**+ .

Patrice Rushen: *Straight from the Heart* (Elektra '82). Hard to believe this nouveau ingenue was once a full-time jazz pianist—forgetting "Forget Me Nots," the whole first side could be one dancy vamp, and since in pop you're supposed to write the tunes before hand you have to wonder how she fared when she had to make them up on the spot. Did a lot of vamping, I suspect. Granted, there's real songcraft on side two, if nouveau ingenues are your idea of real. I prefer side one.   **C**+

Sade: *Diamond Life* (Portrait '85). Though there's not much range to her grainy voice or well-meaning songwriting, she and her associates put their project over, and with a fashion model's virtues—taste, concept, sound (cf. "look"). There's no superfluity, no reveling in *la luxe,* not even an excessive tempo. Which is no doubt why I find myself crediting her humanitarian sentiments, even preferring her "Why Can't We Live Together" to Timmy Thomas's equally spare but naive original. And why those who find "Hang On to Your Love" and "Smooth Operator" seductive (instead of just warming, like me) will think they carry the whole album. **B**

Sade: *Promise* (Portrait '86). Even when it's this sumptuous, there's a problem with aural wallpaper—once you start paying attention to it, it's not wallpaper anymore, it's pictures on the wall. And while as a wallpaper these pictures may be something, they can't compete with the ones you've hung up special. That's why I prefer my aural wallpaper either so richly patterned you can't see past the whole (Steve Reich's *Music for 18 Musicians*) or so intricately worked you can gaze at the details forever (Eno's *Another Green World*). In between I'll take Julie London. **B**

Sade: *Stronger Than Pride* (Epic '88). I'm glad this self-made aristocrat has a human side, but I prefer her image: now that she's singing billets-doux, she's even further from rewarding the concentration she demands than she used to be. Touching your beloved with a few true clichés is hard enough. For an audience you have to come up with something that doesn't fade into the background like the new-age jazz she went pop with. **B−**

Doug Sahm: *Juke Box Music* (Antone's '89). Alive and well well well—I've never heard him in better voice than on this unexpected r&b record. Not a cleaning-up song in the carload, either. But there's also only one original after an eight-year dry spell, and though I'm happy to hear from him again, I hope the follow-up isn't more Tex-Mex for the white blues circuit. I also hope there's a follow-up. **B+**

Doug Sahm: See also Sir Douglas Quintet

Dédé Saint Prix: *Mi Sé Sa* (Mango '88). Saint Prix's chouval bwa rhythm is an uncle of zouk, much less high-tech even in this modernized version and a little light for my tastes—the leader counts the flute among his accomplishments, and rarely does his keyboardist rev up high enough to drown one out. Yet the sense of give comes as a relief when you're braced for Antillean NRG. You can actually parse the patois. **B+**

Sakhile: *Sakhile* (Arista/Jive-Afrika '84). When a black Johannesburg crossover band split up so they can "grow musically" and the bassist and sax player come up with a slack Crusaders homage, I understand—in South Africa that'll pass for progress. Here too, actually. But here I expect people to know better—especially record executives. **C+**

Walter Salas-Humara: *Lagartija* (Record Collect '88). If this were really an ace songwriter doing his own thing, rather than a long-suffering semipro wondering why his group is short a label deal, he'd showcase songwriting. Instead he concentrates on riff-tunes—pretty good ones that aren't what you'd call propelled by the auteur's overdubbed guitar and drums. Which must mean he's saving the ace stuff for the Silos. Good. **B−**

Salt-n-Pepa: *Hot, Cool and Vicious* (Next Plateau '86). In the updated "Tramp" (former A side of "Push It," bargain hunters), two gals dis an easy lay cum slave to his dick, but elsewhere the raps are only the gender change you'd hope, not the one you couldn't have imagined—feisty, not too reverse-macho, yet fairly predictable. What I love is how the sampled hooks and not-so-predictable scratches pounce out of the mix, always good for a shiver of recognition/dissociation. And the change is certainly due. **A−**
Salt-n-Pepa: *A Salt With a Deadly Pepa* (Next Plateau '88). "Shake Your Thang" is a stroke because as a duo they can come out for two opposing sexual prerogatives at once—one does, the other doesn't, and it's nobody's thang but hers either way. Nor does E.U. hurt their soul. Elsewhere, the confusion signaled by the "See label for Sequencing" is reflected in ordinary rhymes, scattershot beats, and a second Isleys cover, this one masquerading as a Beatles cover. **B**

Sarafina! (Shanachie '88). Maybe I should lighten up and let this album do what an original-cast album is supposed to—evoke the theatrical experience, which as it happened surpassed any phonographic one to come my way in 1987. But I've always believed evocation should be a side effect, and as a thing-in-itself, this is no *South Pacific* or *West Side Story,* not to mention *Threepenny Opera* or *Indestructible Beat.* Mbube rubs shoulders with mbaqanga sitting atop Jo'burg jazz giving way to musi-

cal-comedy declamation; the guitarist is great, the drummer isn't, and the young singers do what they're told. If you want to know what the show is like, go into hock and check it out. A complete killer. **B**
Sarafina! The Music of Liberation—Broadway Cast Recording (RCA Victor/Novus '88). Though the music isn't much changed, the full original-cast-album treatment points up the virtues of Shanachie's smaller-scale approach. The dialogue and array of extra material do make for a superior document. But not a superior phonograph record. **B−**

Joe Satriani: *Surfing With the Alien* (Relativity '87). The latest guitar god calls up keywords like "taste" and "musicality" rather than "flash" and "heavy"—not only does he write melodies (and countermelodies), he fuckin edits them. Thus he delivers both the prowess cultists demand and the comfort they secretly crave. That it surprises him to hear the result behind insurance commercials only goes to show how little guitar gods know of the world. **C+**

Savage Republic: *Tragic Figures* (Independent Project '83). First side is somehow sui generis and foreordained at the same time, and how to describe it? Flipper doing Afropop originals? Maturing hardcore boys who like Talking Heads more than the Doors? Unwired Wire? How about auteurist noise guitar played for one-dimensional melody over recently learned but not quite clumsy drum syncopations? Unfortunately, there are also vocals, your basic self-important postadolescent whine and yowl. On side two, the vocals take over. **B**

Boz Scaggs: *Middle Man* (Columbia '80). A decade ago now, Boz joined a struggle—the struggle to prove a white man could sing not merely the blues, but their pop equivalent. Between his hippie pipes and his tendency to take things easy, it was hard, but determination shone through his most laid-back music—he stood out partly because few white guys were trying anything so contemporary, and partly because he had to go that extra inch lyrically to make his point. Since *Silk Degrees,* however, his only struggle has been to stay on top of the new white pop hegemony he helped create. Though he writes better material than Michael McDonald, the difference isn't degree, just taste. And though he's learned a lot about singing—maybe too much—McDonald has better pipes. **B−**

Boz Scaggs: *Hits* (Columbia '80). His renown as the man who brought black-tie New Year's to Bay Area haute bohemia seems a fitting climax to a career that's transformed Marin County languor into the hippest in pop cool. Listening back to his biggest tunes, the best of which (except for the mean, jaunty pimp-song "Jojo") seem to have been recorded in the mid-'70s, you can hear everything from old compatriot Sly Stone to more recent compatriot Elton John. But many of his "hits," in case you didn't notice, were recorded right here in 1980, and so this collection includes three from *Middle Man,* one from *Urban Cowboy,* and one brand new fabrication. *Silk Degrees* isn't as tuneful. But when I want to remember how Marin County languor converted the masses, that's what I'll play.   **B+**

Scandal Featuring Patty Smyth: *Warrior* (Columbia '84). The ryffs keep the treadmyll moving with nary a twytch, not once does a lyric offer a detail of behavior or decor, or even a real metaphor—the sexist twaddle of Nyck Gylder's "stereo jungle child" in the title chartbuster, now transmogrified into lyberated twaddle because a woman is singing, is as hot as it gets.   **C**

Scandal Ska (Mango '89). The excuse for the label's very belated fourth ska compilation is the Christine Keeler movie that lends it a title and a rather generic lead Don Drummond instrumental. Cut in '60 and '61—and thus predating rather than duplicating *Intensified!, More Intensified!,* and *Club Ska '67*—these sixteen cuts are ska as imitation r&b, their chugalong a kissing cousin to a New Orleans shuffle, and sometimes they really don't require an excuse. In addition to early Cliff and Marley and Dekker, there are songs here that

feel as impossible as any obscurely wondrous '50s novelty—Skitter's "Mr. Kruschev," or Lloyd Clark's "Japanese Girl." But sometimes unknown r&b songs are curiosities, nothing more.   **B+**

The Scene Is Now: *Burn All Your Records* (Lost '85). Admirers of Red Crayola's *Kangaroo?,* the only album in history based on Marxist art criticism, will find this hauntingly familiar, not just in its often arcane leftism but in its apparent indifference to musical niceties like vocal pitch. Its pleasures are manifold, and its variety not of the obvious sort you might expect from four guys who play twenty-eight instruments. They combine awkwardness and grace, comedy and admonition, intellect and grunge in politically enlightened proportions. And borrow their pithiest lyric from Mao Tse-Tung.   **B+**

The Scene Is Now: *Total Jive* (Lost '86). The rhythms and harmonies are properly knotty, the ideology grounded, the prosy, dissociated lyrics never corny. The singing is more tuneless than the tunes can afford, the politics more situationist than the sense of detail requires, the poetry insufficiently suggestive/evocative. Bohemia strikes again.   **B**

The Scene Is Now: *Tonight We Ride* (Lost '88). My skepticism in re "good" voices is well-documented, and I admittedly find it impossible to hear the alternative I pine for in my mind's ear—something sweeter, softer, more murmured. (Paul Simon half an octave lower and cleansed of the cutes? Never mind.) But I know damn well I'd enjoy their pomo chamber-rock more if the singer could carry a tune. There—I said it and I'm glad.   **B+**

Fred Schneider & the Shake Society: *Fred Schneider & the Shake Society* (Warner Bros. '84). "Summer in Hell," about the ultimate in endless parties, and "Monster," about Fred's penis, might have made the next B-52's album a great one. "It's Time To Kiss," with Patti LaBelle raring to go, probably wouldn't fit, but that doesn't go for such lesser tracks as "Orbit" and "This Planet's a Mess," both of which could use a shot of Cindy & Kate. Ahh, self-expression.   **B**

School Daze (EMI-Manhattan '88). A filmmaker who hopes his soundtrack "encompasses the many different idioms of Black music" had better forget de movies and go into record production full time. Even if he can get soundtrack-plus out of E.U. and Stevie Wonder. Even if his daddy can concoct amazing simulations of torch and revue and spiritual at reasonable rates.   **B**

Schoolly-D: *Schoolly-D* (Schoolly-D '86). From the beginning, rap has been a music of aggressive, expansive possibility, claiming the world on beat and boast alone. This Philadelphia street tough claims only his turf. His powerful scratch rhythms are as oppressive and constricted as his neighborhood, and his sullen slur conveys no more hope or humor than the hostile egotism of his raps themselves. I'm not saying he isn't realer than all the cheerful liars the biz has thrown back to the projects, or that his integrity doesn't pack a mean punch. But he's still an ignorant thug, and he's cheating both his audience and himself by choosing to remain that way.   **B+**

Schoolly-D: *Saturday Night* (Jive '87). Maybe two of the three new cuts on this fattened major-label reissue are weak, but liberals will certainly be heartened by "Housing the Joint"'s explicit denial of those "racism" rumors. Me, I don't give a shit one way or the other, because even though the subtlety would be lost on me if he held a .357 to my head or gangbanged my bitch in the back room, I'm certain that the secret fascination this professional B-boy holds for white critics isn't just his exotic brutality, which he certainly makes the most of—"motherfucker" is such a rhythmic word. It's his intimations of vulnerability—not L.L. Cool J's romantic shit, but something wryer and stupider. What other rapper would write a rhyme about the night his mother pulled a gun on him—or make it so clear that, just like in *West Side Story*, he's depraved on account of he's deprived. This doesn't speak too well of

white critics, obviously, but it also doesn't take away his raps, his rips, or his muscleman groove. Docked a notch for gang-banging a bitch in the back room.   **B**

Schoolly-D: *The Further Adventures of Schoolly-D* (Rykodisc CD '87). Still getting paid, Schoolly offers another consumer option: one pricy little phonogram comprising *Schoolly-D* and the unfattened, premajor *Saturday Night*. Very street—the beats are real realistic.   **B**

Schoolly-D: *Smoke Some Kill* (Jive '88). Anybody as smart as Schoolly, who on his own testimony turned down a scholarship from Georgia Tech because he only wanted to study art, must be held responsible for his own bullshit, especially if he makes a large part of his living selling black fantasy to white thrill-seekers. Are B-boys really like this? How the fuck am I supposed to know? What I do know is that between his cheeba and his malt liquor and his foldaway dick and his casual "faggot"'s and his eagerness to blame an unspecified cocaine habit on a nameless and maybe even figurative "white bitch," he's the white audience's paranoid-to-masochistic fantasy of a B-boy. He deserves credit for realizing the fantasy so scarily, and for commanding his own tough-guy sound. But that doesn't mean you have to like him.   **B–**

Schoolly D: *Am I Black Enough for You?* (Jive '89). Some call Schoolly's show of racial solidarity a career move, but I find Sly and P-Funk and Malcolm and James I-Am-Somebody and Richard Pryor's coke routines a productive use of his sound. Almost believe "Pussy Ain't Nothin'" is designed to convince the womenfolk that he wants their brains.   **B**

Gil Scott-Heron/Brian Jackson: *1980* (Arista '80). Having already written more good antinuke songs than the rest of MUSE put together, they add a third on their best album ever. The melodies are only functional but the rhythms are seductive and the singing is warm. And then there's the words. Subjects include compromise (necessary), "surviving" (cop-out), aliens (surviving), the shah (dead), the road (long), and the future (here).   **A–**

Gil Scott-Heron: *Real Eyes* (Arista '80). Never would have believed it, but the switch from Brian Jackson's supportive groove to Carl Cornwell's elliptical horn charts adds intellectual and historical weight to the songs that merely say good things as well as those that put them pungently. The two that constitute the latter category kick this off like the great album he's got in him. The two that say sentimental things slowly are unredeemed by Jackson's groove and Cornwell's flute, respectively. **B+**

Gil Scott-Heron: *Reflections* (Arista '81). " 'B' Movie," his smartest political rap ever, is also his first airplay hit since "Angel Dust," maybe because black radio cherishes no expectation of crossing over to Ray-Gun. Hooray. But no less than four cuts—the jazz and reggae tributes as well as the Bill Withers and Marvin Gaye covers—are diminished by the mere serviceability of Scott-Heron's post-Brian Jackson musical conception (execution?), because each invokes the power of music that only becomes truly powerful when it's more than serviceable. That's not to say each of them isn't of service, though. **B+**

Gil Scott-Heron: *Moving Target* (Arista '83). With Malcolm Cecil coproducing, Scott-Heron's music comes back strong— the horns and rhythm are progressive funk as it was meant to be, Tower of Power without Vegas, dissonant and intricate and talky and natural. But the Caribbean inflections are compromised enough to suit a lyric that sounds commissioned by the Jamaican Tourist Board if not Edward Seaga himself, and while this album has plenty of good parts, they come together only on the side-openers: two on side one, one on side two. **B**

Gil Scott-Heron: *The Best of Gil Scott-Heron* (Arista '84). Good that he refuses to shy away from explicit revolutionary reference, but *1980*'s "Third World Revolution" would have spared us the "hairy-armed women's liberationists" Scott-Heron's been smearing ever since he recorded "The Revolution Will Not Be Televised" in his angry immaturity fifteen years ago. Besides, it's catchier. From "The Bottle" to "Re-Ron," though, this should convince doubting sympathizers that effective political art— aesthetically effective political art, I mean—isn't tantamount to avant-garde polarization. It's got a good line, and you can dance to it. **A−**

Scrawl: *Plus, Also, Too*— (No Other '87). As female-identified garage-rock, this never attempts to glorify its ineptitude with swagger or poetry—it has the guts to make plain that ineptitude isn't so damn far from vulnerability. Too often, right, it's merely inept—tuneless and quiet instead of tuneless and loud. But when S. Hershe worries that she's turning into "a slut," or wonders if she should "decide not to worry," or simply sings "I'm sad, I'm sad, I'm so fucking sad," her brains could break your heart. [Rough Trade CD includes subsequent *He's Drunk.*] **B**

The Screaming Blue Messiahs: *Gun-Shy* (Elektra '86). Last year's *Good and Gone* import EP was too perfect for neogarage, too formally aware to get rough enough, but here (with two of the EP's best reprised) these pros seem like a different kind of tribute band—not Garageland Calling but the London Sandinistas, strictly roots punks who can really play their axes. I don't mean ex-punks, either. They bury those roots except when they need a hook, and age has not withered nor custom staled their compulsion to snarl at the military-industrial complex and the girl next door. **B+**

The Screaming Blue Messiahs: *Bikini Red* (Elektra '87). Slot "I Wanna Be a Flintstone" as a college-radio novelty that insults their cockney roots in Clash 'n' blues if you wanna. I say it's definitive, situating their Americana, their apocalypse, and their primitivism amidst the illustrated literature whence they came. **B+**

Scritti Politti: *Songs To Remember* (Rough Trade import '82). With the force of religious conversion, abrasive anarchist Green Gartside emerges as a pop-funk sweety-pie. Though he'd sing like Al Green if could, he settles for a gentle conversational tenor but tries too hard. The lyrics always bespeak literacy and sometimes deliver wit ("I was like an industry / Depressed and in decline"), as does the music, which shores up the out-of-pocket rhythms with tunes rather less often it undercuts them with dissonance. He's still in the deconstruction business, after all. The one that goes "My sincerity, my penicillin, my window, and my drudgery" is called "Jacques Derrida."   **B**

Scritti Politti: *Cupid & Psyche 85* (Warner Bros. '85). Green's Gallic allusion of choice—the name of his pubbery, in fact—is "jouissance," but although he's playful and verbal enough to make it his own, he falls short in the climax department. I'd suggest a less gushy conceit: esprit. The high-relief production and birdlike tunes and spry little keyb arrangements and hippety-hoppety beat and archly ethereal falsetto add up to a music of amazing lightness and wit that's saved from any hint of triviality by wordplay whose delight in its own turns is hard to resist. Usually I suspect lyricists who refuse to be clear of never having figured out what they mean, but here the puns are so clever and incessant that they become an end in themselves. I wouldn't be surprised to learn that Green knows what he wants to say.   **A—**

Scritti Politti: *Provision* (Warner Bros. '88). Wonder how much Green knows about Immanuel Kant, who rhymes with "Gaultier pants"—more than you or me, probably, and less than he should before he starts name-dropping. But thereafter he strives to right his arty rep. The ones that begin "Gonna get that girl," "I wanna get 'em girl," and "Get you girl" proceed as you'd expect, into a flighty funk of positively offensive banality. I always thought his pretensions were kind of fun myself.   **C+**

Son Seals: *Bad Axe* (Alligator '84). Seals will never be a Muddy Waters or B. B. King, and his fifth LP lacks the edge of *Midnight Son* or *Live and Burning*. But he's such an impassioned craftsman he makes the distinction problematic, and he doesn't stand still—this time he's singing tenderly enough to bring off the self-servingly sentimental "I Can Count on My Blues." Which I guess he can.   **B+**

The Searchers: *Love's Melodies* (Sire '81). I kept listening to this record at the behest of two dear friends—Tom Smucker, known Beach Boys fanatic, and Greil Marcus, all-purpose self-starter. Eventually I got it, too. It's bigger and glossier and rockinger than anything they managed as the second-best group in Liverpool, and not only that it's more tuneful. They even cover Big Star's "September Gurls," which shows true power-pop hip. But for me it's a big, glossy, rocking, tuneful bore, because except on "Radio Romance" ("I love the radio / But the radio don't love me"), their only discernible motive is to take what they did well back in the '60s and do it even better, i.e., more professionally. Back in the '60s they had more motive than that.   **B**

Marvin Sease: *Marvin Sease* (London '87). The ten-minute "Candy Licker" isn't so much audacious as preposterous, which isn't going to stop collectors and others from craving their own cache of "I want to lick you till you come." Elsewhere Sease is an ingratiating soul man who's totally unconscious of how anachronistic he is, probably because he thinks licking women till they come is the essence of modernity.   **B**

Seduction: *Nothing Matters Without Love* (A&M '89). If I harbored the slightest weakness for disco ballads—sit-down harmony numbers with side-opening titles like "Give My Love to You" and (the hit) "(You're My One and Only) True Love"—I could go all the way with these girls. They sing, they rap, they sex it up; they honor Rob Base and Taana Gardner with subtle samples and proud savoir-faire. I say the murmured "a mountain of spices in the arms of the desired" could almost be Coleridge (all right, Rossetti). My wife says it sounds like Sidney Sheldon. And therein lies their charm.   **B+**

Bob Seger & the Silver Bullet Band: *Against the Wind* (Capitol '80). Slow songs about sex and medium-rocking songs about sex contend with slow songs about love and medium-rocking songs about love. Title, concept, and follow-up single: slow song about the futility of life. Just in case you think he's "sold out" or some such.   **C+**

Bob Seger & the Silver Bullet Band: *Nine Tonight* (Capitol '81). I know they've been hit-filled—deservedly so, I once thought. But five years is a hell of a short time between live doubles. He speeds up the schlock and, it still sounds like schlock. He speeds up the deservings and they deserve yet again.   **C+**

Bob Seger & the Silver Bullet Band: *The Distance* (Capitol '83). I had filed this as unlistenable until the amazing tuneout power of "Roll Me Away" piqued me into determining why. The songs aren't half bad—adequate melodically and with moments of good writing. But Seger's romantic individualism is a little simpleminded, more late-outlaw than Bruce, and it's suffocated by overstatement. Almost any country singer could show him how to approach a cliché kinda easy like. In fact, with his connections Seger could probably get lessons from Willie himself. But with his taste he'd probably choose Waylon instead.   **C+**

Bob Seger & the Silver Bullet Band: *Like a Rock* (Capitol '86). The songwriting's sharper, but he's not. Whether their focus is personal ("Like a Rock"), social ("Miami"), or personal-as-social ("Tightrope"), all his evocations of this rock and that hard place add up to is high-grade soap opera. Between John Robinson's measured arena beat and Craig Frost's Bittanesque semiclassicisms, Seger comes on as a world-weary elder statesman, which is to say an incurable cornball. Transcending all this is "The Ring," the tale of a good marriage that didn't get it all, and too bad Bruce won't cover it.   **B**

The Selecter: *Too Much Pressure* (Chrysalis '80). Except for songwriter-guitarist Neol Davies, these two-toners are black, reassuring in a movement that calls up fears of folkie patronization. Lead singer's a woman, too, a refreshing piece of progress no matter how self-consciously progressive its motives. Taking a folkie risk like their confreres the Specials, they honor their undercapitalized roots by emulating the two-track sound of the cult hits

they love. Fortunately, Davies has an amazing ability to recapture the ska spirit without pretending it's 1965—impossible to tell whether "Time Hard" or "Too Much Pressure" is the new one without external clues—and it saves them, just barely. Play loud.   **A—**

The Selecter: *Celebrate the Bullet* (Chrysalis '81). With Pauline Black fallen under the influence of Lene Lovich and the groove wavering along with her, it's up to the songwriting. Which features more dreams, water, reflections, stormy weather, and "jagged imagery" than is healthy for bomb scare victims or ska bands.   **B—**

The Sequence: *The Sequence* (Sugarhill '81). In which the la-dees cover P-Funk, recite the Big Mac formula, and advise knocked-up fans to keep doing that body rock after the daddy gets gone—in short, rap wisdom, down-to-earth but not what you'd call an alternative (Medicaid abortions, anyone?). And I probably wouldn't complain if Sugarhill's studio gang gave them as good as they give the boys. **B—**

The Sex Pistols: *The Great Rock 'n' Roll Swindle* (Virgin import '80). The soundtrack to the mythical *Who Killed Bambi* is a joke, a rip-off, a piece of conceptual art, etc. But it's also a lovely memento, and you can listen to it—every one of its four sides will bring a smile to your lips. These notes, then. A) The symphonic "EMI" tops the disco medley tops the symphonic "Anarchy." B) Ronnie Biggs singing "Belsen Vos a Gassa" is at least as entertaining as Johnny Rotten singing "Belsen Was a Gas." C) Johnny Rotten forgetting Chuck Berry lyrics is more entertaining than Sid Vicious remembering Eddie Cochran lyrics. D) Sid Vicious singing "My Way" is more entertaining than Frank Sinatra singing "My Way." E) Frank Sinatra does not appear on this record.   **B+**

Shalamar: *Three for Love* (Solar '80). In which these *Soul Train*-trained prettyboy/girl teen-throbs make good every which way on the commercial breakthrough of 1979's *Big Fun*. Including commercially, of course—more hits than Dick Griffey could fit into a release schedule here. Hits subclassification "soul," I mean—as in "black," or "r&b," or should we just say "race music"? Or "not pop"? Which is pretty weird, since the album's theme song ought to be the finale, "Pop Along Kid"—pop as in the kind of music it is, and also as in what their funk does. It pops, as in "popping bass" and "finger-pop." Griffey, who understands the marketplace far better than I, hasn't put it on his release schedule.   **A—**

Shalamar: *Go for It* (Solar '81). What they're going for is the gold. Especially when headstrong dandy Jeffrey Daniel displaces shifty houseservant Leon Sylvers III in the driver's seat, the rhythms mean to stomp out funk rumors—"Rocker," this finale is called, as if that should settle those nagging airplay questions once and for all. It won't, but amazingly, the damage is minimal; because their lissome interplay runs deeper than groove, this is as creamy and sensual as ever. Those with a taste for postpretentious epiphany should keep an ear out for the very pretty slow one that goes "In the final analysis [long pause] I love you."   **A—**

Shalamar: *Friends* (Solar '82). Their first album since WEA started distributing Solar is also their first album since the one they wrote themselves failed to go top one-hundred. And it's also safe and sorry: Leon Sylvers and cohorts in complete control. Sure they'll score their ghettoized best-sellers, maybe even sell their allotted five hundred thou. But there'll be no reason to cry foul when that's all they do.   **B—**

Shalamar: *Greatest Hits* (Solar '82). Five of ten cuts began life on *Three for Love,* which nevertheless has better to offer—amid corporate machinations too tawdry to detail, this profit-taker goes with what went, and so ends up a little soft. On the other hand, it's silly to seek sharp edges from the Solar production signature—anonymity is its strategy. Tuneful love songs feature the warm, mildly acrid tenor of Howard Hewett and the perky, slightly insinuating soprano of Jody Watley. Say Ray Parker and Prince are rockers in disguise and call it the most consistent black pop of the postdisco era.   **A—**

Shalamar: *The Look* (Solar '83). I prefer *Go for It*'s soft-spoken groove, but the brilliant vocals and processed high-end percussion of their latest crossover move are an up. Added group participation probably helps, though contract players continue to dominate. And it definitely helps that the contract players have written some hits with punch, both certified—the percussive "Dead Giveaway"—and honorary—the Jeffrey Daniel vehicle "No Limits (The Now Club)."   **˙B+**

Shalamar: *Heart Break* (Solar '85). There's no denying the vivacity of Howard Hewett's reconstituted trio—the harmonies and rhythms pop out of the speakers with a brightness of definition that's good for a real lift. But if Hewett has any other interests, he doesn't make them plain—always look again when the standout track comes from contract songwriters. And if Hewett's new sidekicks have other interests, their solo turns make me hope they keep them out of earshot.   **B**

Shanghai Dog: *Clanging Bell* (SDEP import EP '84). Imagine Mission of Burma's military beat played for militance, post-punk with a rod up its ass: four tight, angry, judgmental songs about work, madness, the intransigence of the world. Not the kind of thing you'd expect from Vancouver, I know. Neither is D.O.A.   **B+**

Shango: *Shango Funk Theology* (Celluloid '84). With its positive party line, international beats, ensemble vocals, and tributes to P-Funk, Sun Ra, and Sly, this may well be the first rap album that fully expresses the ideals and ideas of the group with its name on the cover—or at least of its esteemed leader, who happens to be Afrika Bambaataa. But because not one member of the ensemble (or all of them together) qualifies as any kind of grandmaster, and because Material's best rap track is still by Tribe II, the cuts that open each side (functionally enough, too) never even broke through as twelve-inches. And whatever they express, "Thank You" and "Let's Party Down" are filler.   **B—**

Shannon: *Let the Music Play* (Mirage '84). Reports that this product makes it as an album are probably due to the addictive novelty of its rhythmic colors, in which one-man synth army Rob Kilgore surrounds a sweet, yearningly anonymous disco woman with a medium-b.p.m. carillon. But "Give Me Tonight" is a surprisingly essential follow-up, and the rest is crafted proportionately. Which is why some let the filler play too.   **B**

Shannon: *Do You Wanna Get Away* (Mirage '85). Her pleasantly expressive voice free of inconvenient conviction, she slips unassumingly from stance to stance—fantasy lover to wronged Cosmo Girl to horny wildcat to committed lifemate. Thus she never gets in the way of true stars Chris Barbosa and Mark Liggett, whose production is consistently engaging but less peaky than back when they were earning the right to develop their property.   **B−**

Roxanne Shanté: *Bad Sister* (Cold Chillin' '89). I'd loved everything else she'd ever done, and at first this album irritated me, but now I hear it as a self-conscious return to the street appeal of 14-year-old Lolita Gooden's "Roxanne's Revenge." Even the remixed "Wack Itt," heavy with the housed bass fuzz that's the record's aural signature, and "Go On Girl," vocals phased and speeded over hyped congas, suit music intended to sound crude and overheard in an era of packed mixes and clean hooks. So do the casually nasty rhymes, most of which Roxanne didn't write, and almost every one of which—the exception is "Fatal Attraction," a carefully plotted tale that ends with a jimmy in a pickle jar—could have been made up on the spot by the unassuming owner of the most natural voice in rap. Spunky, sexy, conversational, full of fun, with a burr turning quaver that radiates hesitation and delight, she's still in contact with her happy, lucky fourteen-year-old self. In other words, a true rock-and-roller. **A−**

Sonny Sharrock: *Guitar* (Enemy '86). New thing's answer to Hendrix and McLaughlin circa 1970 and Material's embodiment of creative chaos circa 1980 sits in a studio and plays some tunes—sometimes more than one at a time, either counterpointed or strung together in a suite. Like so many jazz avant-gardists, Sharrock got his start in r&b, and you can tell—with the bullshit cut away he's both funky and beautiful. Tempos are slow to moderate, melodies simple and even lyrical, structures clear, and still he generates enough sonic danger to drive that roommate you can't stand right up the wall. Original grade: A minus.   **A**

The Sonny Sharrock Band: *Seize the Rainbow* (Enemy '87). Despite a patch or two of signature chaos, this is as accessible as good jazz-rock gets. The beat is assured by stalwart bassist Melvin Gibbs and two drummers, jack-of-all-avant Pheeroan ak-Laff and sometime Benatar-Earland henchman Abe Spellman, and as he approaches fifty the most fearsome noise guitarist of the '60s is nurturing not only a taste for melody but a gift for it. Like his solo album, his group's debut is uncommonly beautiful and direct without flirting with the saccharine or the simplistic. And like his solo album, it gets even better after you put it away for a while.   **A**

Pete Shelley: *Homosapien* (Arista '82). By replacing the three heaviest losers on the English LP with three catchy little numbers, American Arista has come up with what might be the most interesting case of great-song-plus since Billy Swan's *I Can Help*. Shelley's voice is definitely harder to take wobbling around this discofied electropop than outshrieking the Buzzcocks' guitars, but the one-man groove suits his marginally solipsistic homophile romanticism quite neatly.   **B+**

Ricky Van Shelton: *Wild-Eyed Dream* (Columbia '87). In his white cowboy hat and sleeveless undershirt, he's as honest as George Strait with a day job—except maybe when picking an album title, because like most neotraditionalists he's too damned tasteful to stay wild-eyed long. As I hope he's noticed, the outlandish "Crime of Passion" is his ticket to ride. Guarantee you it will be remembered when all the small perfect moments surrounding it have passed into good-taste limbo.   **B**

Sheshwe: The Sound of the Mines (Rounder '88). Those who get a kick from accordion-heavy gumboots mbaqanga might be lured to this Sotho compilation—with one producer overseeing and one bassist underpinning, unity wouldn't seem a big problem. Unfortunately, what unifies it is how tuneless and static all four groups are—despite Sebata Sebata's rudimentary hooks and the whistles and rude percussion deployed by the others, these songs about snakes and kings and magic bones are more folkloric than most non–South African fans need. Also than some South African fans need. Cf. Tau Ea Lesotho's *Nyatsi Tloha Pela'ka* (Kaya 1984), which drives stronger shouting with a livelier rhythm section (is that a syndrum?), or the vocal esprit of Puseletso Seema & Tau Ea Linare's *He O Oe Oe!* (GlobeStyle 1985) (is that a woman?). Harder to find, but believe me, both will satisfy your minimum daily grit requirement.   **B**−

Shirati Jazz: *Benga Beat* (Carthage '87). Benga is a vaguer term than the notes suggest, indicating any modern Kenyan dance-pop, not just Luo but Kamba or Luhya or Kikuyu, that moves the light and rather folkish Kenyan guitar sound toward the big-time West African competition as it explores tribal rhythms of more meaning to Kenyans than to us. Without their guitarist-leader, self-crowned "King of Benga," Owino Misiani, Shirati Jazz recut some hits in London for this collection, a good thing in what is largely an ill-recorded singles music. They do sound light and rather folkish to me—delicate without juju's cosmopolitan intricacy, rhythmic without mbaqanga's urban drive. But in exotics, charm counts for plenty.   **B**+

Michelle Shocked: *The Texas Campfire Tapes* (Mercury '86). "Recorded on a Sony Walkman at Kerrville Folk Festival, Kerrville, USA," announces this U.K.-first debut—rather coyly, but you know those alternative Brits. And you have to hand it to those Japanese—without much depth to account for, the audio ain't bad. And maybe you should hand it to Shocked

too. She's got more vocal personality than is common among solo folk, her guitar accomps her wherever she goes, and though she may be a little long on folkie mythos (sleeping in the park, guys with tattoos, etc.), she has a reporter's eye and a talespinner's ear. Beyond mythos: "The Secret Admirer," about a good-looking woman's looks.   **B**+

Michelle Shocked: *Short Sharp Shocked* (Mercury '88). "Anchorage" is the fondest friend-from-a-former-life song you've ever heard. The East Texas barn burning, driving lesson, and beer run evoke the bored fun of a rural adolescence like nothing you could imagine. Shocked understands the tougher formal challenges of protest and metaphor flight, too, especially on the unclassifiable "When I Grow Up." The Jean Ritchie cover seems unsuitably traditional until you realize it's Jean Ritchie. And the uncredited punk-rock extra reminds us that this singer-songwriter puts music second, just like they all do.   **A**−

Michelle Shocked: *Captain Swing* (Mercury '89). First line of the last one was "When I grow up I want to be an old woman," first line of this one is "God is a real estate developer." Last time she stuck to received country/folk-rock, this time she essays horn arrangements that got lost in the mail. I appreciate the genderfucks (she's hetero here, homo there, and male when you mess with her sister) and could go for a few of the love songs (the long-suffering "Silent Ways" in its current incarnation, the long-suffering "Sleep Keeps Me Awake" and roving "On the Greener Side" gone to heaven). But on the whole this is too arch, too busy, too artistic, too political, succumbing to the overreach that always beckons when you have greatness thrust upon you.   **B**

Shoes: *Tongue Twister* (Elektra '81). For three straight albums I've started out resenting the pure pop-rock blandishments of these Ramones of the heartland, and for three straight albums I've ended up clucking appreciatively at every fill. As befits heartlanders, they wear theirs on their sleeves, not just for decoration but because that's where they belong; their formula serves a supple expressionism in which sincerity is a given. Inspirational Liner Note: "No keyboards." **A—**

Shoes: *Boomerang* (Elektra '82). These aging, insulated teen romantics haven't lost their skill at hook construction, but added studio muscle does nothing for their fragile allure. Striving to preserve their male-adolescent prerogatives—"Does he keep you amused between the covers?" is hardly a teen question—they fail to conquer the distinction between girl trouble, a forgivable adolescent malady, and woman trouble, an offensive adult affliction. Maybe they should try out this Inspirational Verse in the first-person plural: "She's losing her tested charms / Any little thing seems hard." **B**

Shoes: *Best* (Black Vinyl CD '87). Starting with the most ironic label name ever entered in the digital sweepstakes (Coated Aluminum just wouldn't sound as homy), this compilation is quintessentially problematic. Fine bit-by-bit, with worthwhile bonus goodies (especially the four from the import-only *Silhouette*) and unexceptionable sequencing and selection, its generous length places an impossible burden on these quintessentially slight popsters, reducing them to the light background entertainment those with no tolerance for fragility thought they were to begin with. Who but their moms and their girlfriends (especially their girlfriends, some of whom I hope are wives by now) want to concentrate on such fragile virtues for an hour and a quarter? **B+**

Shoes: *Stolen Wishes* (Black Vinyl '89). Still hooky after all these years, the three principals divide up fifteen more love songs: John Murphy makes up to break up, Jeff Murphy starts happy-happy and gets blown away, Gary Klebe obsesses and suffers and obsesses some more. All over Zion, Illinois, bedrooms quake at the mere mention of these thirtysomething lotharios' names. **B**

Shop Assistants: *Shop Assistants* (53rd & 3rd import EP '86). Four gals and one guy—who plays guitar, darn it—spend two days in Edinburgh doing the impossible: recreating punk. They're everything I wanted the Slits to be: fast, tuneful, primitive, hard, tender, a little mysterious, and not altogether averse to slow ones. Speedy one's called "Safety Net" (they don't have one, "you" do), fast one's called "Almost Made It" (and if it wasn't for "you" we would have), slow one's called "Somewhere in China" (searching for a better life). Speedy one's the A. **A—**

Jane Siberry: *No Borders Here* (Open Air '85). "Canada's most critically acclaimed new artist" says the sticker, but you know Canadians—they lose their heads when a native evinces the merest soupcon of originality. She's even been compared to Laurie Anderson, I guess because she's abstract sometimes. I'll say. How thoroughly she's transcended what I'm sure was a careful upbringing is summed up in a statement of aesthetic principle that I swear is unsullied by the tiniest smudge of irony: "Symmetry is the way things have to be." **B—**

Davitt Sigerson: *Falling in Love Again* (Island '84). Essentially a producer-composer rather than a performer, Sigerson pursues AORish rockcraft and studio-guaranteed aesthetic distance in the manner of such paradigmatic early-'70s ironists as Randy Newman and Fagen-Becker—but also, before you get your hopes too high, John Simon and Terry Melcher. His theme song is "My True Feelings" ("are whatever you think you see"); his themes are both hooky (musically) and kinky (verbally). At his best ("Over and Over"), he proves how life-affirming the hookily kinky can be; at his worst ("Danish Modern"), he proves how weak-minded irony can be. **B+**

The Silos: *About Her Steps* (Record Collect '85). Nobody would have thought twice if this unknown band had debuted with an EP, especially the complete winner they had in them. Imagine *The Velvet Underground* as country-rock, fragile lyricism colored with fiddle (or viola) and pedal steel and toughened by a commitment to the everyday. The five (out of eight) songs I'd have chosen are the five longest—since sharp and tight aren't where their gifts are, they don't do anything special with terse little rockers.

Though they might yet. Original grade: B plus.   **A**—

Silos: *Cuba* (Record Collect '87). A marriage of heaven and earth, a divorced father, and a Green Mountain wedding close out side one, stretching rather than subverting or sentimentalizing country parameters. As rock-and-rollers, however, they're still just in there kicking.   **B+**

Paul Simon: *One-Trick Pony* (Warner Bros. '80). The soundtrack to a going-nowhere flick about an over-the-hill rocker that he scripted, starred in, and of course scored is also his first true album in five years, and while it's literate, tasteful, etc., it's also—self-evidently—the work of a man who thinks he's too big for music (at five-foot-two, gosh). So if individual songs don't stand out the way they have ever since "The Sound of Silence," maybe he doesn't work as hard at them anymore. Like so many aging folkies he's devolved into a vaguely jazzy pop, and except for the lead cut and the one with Ray Charles on it everything serves the excuse for a groove.   **B**—

Paul Simon: *Hearts and Bones* (Warner Bros. '83). In his deliberately slight way, this fellow could be a comer. Rarely have the quiddities of pushing forty with more brain than heart or bone (or muscle) been explored with such obsessive attention to detail—acute musical touches match involuted lyrics small surprise for small surprise.   **B+**

Paul Simon: *Graceland* (Warner Bros. '86). Opposed though I am to universalist humanism, this is a pretty damn universal record. Within the democratic bounds of pop accessibility, its biculturalism is striking, engaging, unprecedented—sprightly yet spunky, fresh yet friendly, so strange, so sweet, so willful, so radically incongruous and plainly beautiful. For Simon, the r&b-derived mbaqanga he and his South African sidemen—guitarist Ray Phiri, fretless bassist Baghiti Kumalo, and drummer Isaac Mtshali, all players of conspicuous responsiveness and imagination—put through their Tin Pan Alley paces seems to represent a renewed sense of faith and connectedness after the finely wrought dead end of *Hearts and Bones.* The singing has

lost none of its studied wimpiness, and he still writes like an English major, but this is the first album he's ever recorded rhythm tracks first, and it gives up a groove so buoyant you could float a loan to Zimbabwe on it. Despite the personalized cameo for Sun City scab Linda Ronstadt (a slap in the face to the ANC whether he admits it or not) and the avoidance of political lyrics elsewhere, he's found his "shot of redemption," escaping alienation without denying its continuing truth. It's the rare English major who can make such a claim.   **A**

Paul Simon: *Negotiations and Love Songs 1971–1986* (Warner Bros. '88). As vinyl, a gyp: $12.98-list double-LP (albeit single CD or cassette) with just three more songs than CBS's superb and now out-of-print one-disc 1977 best-of, nine of which it includes, though not in such fetching order. The best Warners stuff is all from *Graceland* and wants to go home, and though the music is fine if you like such stuff, this is the kind of consumer manipulation that merits a boycott.   **B**

Simon and Garfunkel: *The Concert in Central Park* (Warner Bros. '82). In the great Woodstock tradition, this gift from a flower (or two) to a generation (or two) is also a corporate boondoggle—a classy way for Warner Bros. artist Simon to rerecord, rerelease, and resell the catalogue CBS is sitting on. Paul has forgotten Art enough to relax as a singer, which means that much of the S&G material has improved since 1971. But live doubles are live doubles, nostalgia is nostalgia, wimps are wimps, and who needs any of 'em? **C+**

Simple Minds: *Themes for Great Cities* (Stiff '82). Dance sources assure me that I heard all or most of this "Definitive Collection 79–81" in clubs during the years indicated, and it must be, since even today it makes me want to sit down on the spot. English DOR at its intricately ambient Eurodisco-cum-art-rock nadir, replete with steps for subtle metronomes and computerized sound effects that avoid vulgar sensationalism at all costs. Somebody take a good look at that singer's eyes and ask him whether he loves his mother.   **C**—

Simple Minds: *New Gold Dreams (81–82–83–84)* (A&M '83). With more effort than hedonism should ever require, I make out three or maybe four full-fledged melodies on this self-important, mysteriously prestigious essay in romantic escape. Though the textures are richer than in ordinary Anglodisco, they arouse nary a spiritual frisson in your faithful synesthetician. Auteur Jim Kerr is Bowie sans stance, Ferry sans pop, Morrison sans rock and roll. He says simple, I say empty and we both go home.   **C+**

Simple Minds: *Once Upon a Time* (A&M '85). Pittsburgh DJ in *Billboard:* "The term 'superstar' is used too loosely. Simple Minds are a superstar to [A&M's] Charlie Minor, but a lot of my listeners have never heard of them." That's how bad things are, and that's not the half of it. Because you know damn well Charlie Minor thinks Simple Minds are "artists," too.   **B–**

Simply Red: *Picture Book* (Elektra '86). I like Mick Hucknall enough to not want to mention that there are only two songs on this album—one by David Byrne, one by the Valentine Brothers, both of which he runs away with. And until the last two tracks—the finale is "Picture Book" itself, which wanders worst of all—he and his Brit soulsters carry it off on mood and groove alone, and with hardly a love song, either.   **B+**

Simply Red: *Men and Women* (Elektra '87). Where the two covers carried the debut, they drag the follow-up. But Mick Hucknall's originals are improving, and their guileless self-interest has its advantages—"I Won't Feel Bad," about his right to make pots of money because he's not the power elite, and "Infidelity," about his right to fuck around because it's his right, are more convincing for their refusal to shilly-shally. They're also more convincing because Hucknall's an inherently convincing singer. All this is relative to the Anglopop norm, however. Better hot narcissism than cool narcissism, and better soul acolytes than Bowie clones. But not that much better.   **B**

Simply Red: *A New Flame* (Elektra '89). First album never mentioned his roving third eye and got him noticed. Second told the unvarnished truth about his fast way with the ladies and didn't make him a star. So the third comes on as smarmy as Tom Jones, and not so he'll get laid more—it's rack jobbers who have been his great romantic disappointment. What else can a poor boy do, 'cept try to be the white Teddy Pendergrass?   **C+**

Singles: The Great New York Singles Scene (ROIR cassette '82). I'd include Lester Bangs's "Let It Blurt" and Stumblebunny's "Tonight," both in a league with "Piss Factory," "Little Johnny Jewel," and "Blank Generation," which open this tape with a bang it never follows up on. But since neither was by a scene-making band, I understand why compiler Tom Goodkind didn't. And since Goodkind led U.S. Ape, I understand why he chose that one, which in truth sounds better than the Mumps, Speedies, and Student Teachers songs that close the thing. In between we get what sounds in retrospect like a lot of primitive art-rock (Theoretical Girls the savviest) and a lot of primitive pop (Nervus Rex the most polished). Although scenes are often better seen than heard, down beneath the greats this one just about earns its document. But it doesn't make you bewail its wasted genius. And where's "No More Nukes"?   **B+**

The Sir Douglas Quintet: *The Best of the Sir Douglas Quintet* (Takoma '80). With five of its twelve cuts lifted from Doug's 1969 Mercury debut *Mendocino,* which I replaced for 97 cents not long ago, and none of the rest from his mid-'70s star shots for Atlantic and ABC, this best-of is pretty archival—a good deed, modest promo for a deserving genre artist. John Fahey's indie is proud to claim now that no one expects to turn his genius into gold. Of course, given the specifics of Doug Sahm's genius, it would have sounded pretty archival in 1973, too. Riding in on Augie Meyer's organ, Tex-Mex like "Nuevo Laredo," "Dynamite Woman," and "She's About a Mover" sounds as inevitable as "Honky Tonk Woman" or "Louie Louie." "Mendocino" and "Stoned Faces Don't Lie" say more about hippiedom than "Woodstock" and "Eight Miles

High." And "Song of Everything" is a dog.   **A—**

Sir Douglas Quintet: *Border   Wave* (Takoma '81). He handles horns better than most, but the quintet is Doug's home concept, and this reunion could be his best LP ever. It's loose, it's tight, it's got great Kinks and Butch Hancock and 13th Floor Elevators covers, it's got Alvin Crow playing guitar and taking a song, it's got Johnny Perez on drums, and it's got Augie Meyers doing what he was born to do. It also has Doug making you believe he just thought up classic titles like "Old Habits Die Hard" and "Revolutionary Ways," because he just did. Making "simple" rock and roll this late in the game ain't easy. But simplicity has always been his gift.   **A—**

Sister Breeze: *Riddym Ravings* (ROIR cassette '87). Prey to moralizing condescension like all self-appointed spokespersons for the downtrodden, Jamaica's female dub poets do enjoy one advantage over their brethren—they see through the male supremacism that suffuses the island's alternative culture as well as its official ideology. This former schoolmarm leads both sides of Heartbeat's 1986 *Woman Talk* anthology on conceptual reach alone, and here she gets to put her theatrical experience to work, impersonating both a big-talking petty criminal and a girl from the hills gone paranoid schizophrenic in NYC. The riddyms and the eco-African rhetoric could be deeper, but this is one propagandist who isn't afraid to admit how fucked up struggle can get.   **B+**

Sister Carol: *Jah Disciple* (RAS '89). Like so many rappers, this dancehall queen gets over on music—irrepressible Augustus Pablo, live and computer drums out of nowhere, the explosive spunk of a delivery rich in interjection, admonition, whoop, holler, and sound effect. Lyrically, she loves Africa and "intelligence" but thinks the space invaders on the Challenger had it coming.   **B+**

The Sisters of Mercy: *Floodland* (Elektra '87). There's dumber gothic—cf. *Melody Maker* poll winners Fields of the Nephilim for something totally ridiculous. At least these guys cut their doldrums with crass—they go disco and drop proper nouns. But Andrew Eldritch's sepulchrally stentorian stylings could arise only in a nation where David Bowie is a voice for the ages.   **C+**

Ricky Skaggs: *Waitin' for the Sun To Shine* (Epic '81). Skagg's taste and technique are impeccable; not one of these ten songs, many of them classics I'd never heard before, falters melodically or lyrically, and the arrangements, snazzy though they are, are so steeped in country tradition they could be from decades ago. Which I guess is my beef, because the only way you'd guess it isn't decades ago is from the faint folk-wimp whine in Skaggs's mountain tenor. Time: 29:10.   **B+**

Ricky Skaggs: *Highways and Heartaches* (Epic '82). If Skaggs has come up with the best country album of the year, as he probably has, it's because despite his abandonment of bluegrass purism he's still a bluegrass purist at heart. Which means his commitment is more to the style than to the songs. Which means that above all his success is proof positive of the pusillanimity of the competition.   **B+**

Ricky Skaggs: *Don't Cheat in Our Hometown* (Sugar Hill/Epic '83). Nothing if not an astute traditionalist, Skaggs understands that what makes country music go is the tension between heaven and hell. But where most great country singers come off mealy-mouthed in the virtuous mode, Skaggs makes it sound as if he only sins because he knows he's supposed to. This may mean he's not a great country singer.   **B+**

Ricky Skaggs: *Country Boy* (Epic '84). Act authentic for too long and it begins to sound like an act even if it isn't. I mean, didn't John Denver preempt the title of this thing? Oh right, his went "Thank God I'm a Country Boy." God, I bet Ricky wishes he could get away with that one.   **B**

Ricky Skaggs: *Love's Gonna Get Ya!* (Epic '86). Technical brilliance and conceptual integrity put Skaggs on top of Nashville's neotraditionalist totem pole and make his albums run together like bluegrass. But this one has an edge. Maybe it's the moments of calculated grace—blues intro to "Walkin' in Jerusalem," Everlys cover that could break them up all over again, duets with James Taylor and Sharon White. Or maybe it's just the drum sound.   **B+**

Skatalites: *Stretching Out* (ROIR cassette '86). Recorded live in 1983 on a two-track TEAC and God knows what else by a reconstituted bunch of originators, some of whom hadn't seen one another in a decade and wished it was longer, this forty-eight-minutes-a-side retrospective sounds better than the '60s studio rarities Top Deck compiled a few years ago and is a lot of fun to boot. We're talking party soundtrack for lazybones, the universal polka hop-and-shuffle of a thousand folk dances. Bump bottoms to "Confucius," "Fidel Castro," "Lee Harvey Oswald."   **B+**

Skeleton Crew: *Learn To Talk* (Rift '84). Fred Frith and Tom Cora's fractured songforms on "Side Free" make their seditious point more sharply than I'd feared, but I'm glad I had the sense to play "Side Dirt" first—I do prefer songs to song forms. The post-Weill sound and critique will strike a minor chord with admirers of Henry Cow and the Art Bears, though especially given Frith's rough, sardonic vocals, the presentation's less formal—which I also prefer.   **B+**

Skid Row: *Skid Row* (Atlantic '89). Bio plays up their anti-"formula" "bad-itude," leaving open the question of whether any of these double-platinum Jerseyoid bar boys has recorded professionally before. Sounds like *someone* knows the formula: metal guitar plus amped-to-ten frontman times pop structure equals East Coast G N' R. Class animus is their excuse, the 9-to-5 dead end rejected for salvation by sleaze. Female characters include three hookers, a junkie, a classy bitch, a shotgun bride, a cheater who catches the back of her man's hand and the next train to Kalamazoo, and a crybaby craving "more, more, more." And at least they're characters rather than objects—by the standards

of the subgenre, this is not an offensively sexist band. Sheesh.   **C+**

Skyy: *Skyyline* (Salsoul '81). Catchy and functional, but the funny voices don't know any jokes and the lady who sings the hit is about to fuck her girlfriend over. In short beyond the reggae and the kazoos it's neither adventurous nor ingratiating—just catchy and functional.   **B−**

Slave: *Stone Jam* (Cotillion '80). "No no no," an A&R man to remain nameless exclaimed to Steve Washington last year. "Not funk. Funk's not the future. It's disco, disco." Whereupon Washington, unaware that by the time his album appeared the same a&r man would either have declared disco dead or been declared dead himself, bought some string programs, taught the boys to sing those backups high, and made room for Starleana Young. Sure there's still a fair amount of thump and wah-wah-wah. But with Starleana singing over their shoulders, they're embarrassed to get too dirty about it.   **B−**

Slave: *Show Time* (Cotillion '81). For those as can take their funk straight, this is the brawny beast in all its callipygean glory, complete with jokes (could use more) and slow one (could use fewer). The "Snap Shot"/"Funken Town" twelve-inch does boil it down conveniently to kickoff and touchdown, but the ball keeps moving throughout. Leading ground-gainer: Mark L. Adams, who in real life plays . . . (starts with B, ends with S, and ain't bongos).   **A−**

Slave: *Visions of the Lite* (Cotillion '82). Each side kicks off with a small bang and proceeds pleasantly enough, but Mark L. Adams's half of the band spells it like the beer for a reason—not enough body to make you rub your belly after the brew has gone down.   **B−**

Slave: *Best of Slave* (Cotillion '85). If pop best-ofs showcase hooks, funk best-ofs showcase beats—cowbell grace note here, JB-plus guitar there—and side one is Slave's movingest ever. But assuming Mark Adams's bass and ignoring the disco hook of "Just a Touch of Love," what makes side two listenable is two tracks from their movingest album ever, *Show Time,* which also contributes "Wait for Me" to side one. One of these LPs you could probably use.   **B+**

Slayer: *Reign of Blood* (Def Jam '86). I'm not about to check out the complete works of Venom to make sure you can't do better, but anyone who wants to know what gets Washington ladies hot should steal, tape, or purchase this piece of speed satanism quote unquote. Rick Rubin focused, CBS passed, guitar's quicker than a theremin on reverb, and "Jesus Saves" mauls the enemy. Who ain't Jesus—or, damn right, Satan either. Time: 27:58.   **B+**

Slayer: *South of Heaven* (Def Jam '88). The slower tempos will please their target audience and diminish their joke appeal for outsiders. The lyric sheet will please their target audience and make outsiders laugh at them. (Two consecutive lines: "Impulsive habitat. / Bastard sons begat your cunting daughters.") For guitarniks, antiabortionists, and target audience only.   **B−**

Grace Slick: *Software* (RCA Victor '84). Gracie keeps up with the times: in 1974 she called her sludge-rock *Manhole,* and if her silicon-pop title doesn't have quite as sharp a reverse-sexist twist it's because the ensuing decade has done more for her amour-propre than for her IQ. She demonstrates her usual staunchness of principle with an amazingly dumb piece of satire or something which takes on EKGs and electric blankets but not Linn drums. And is that Gracie singing "Through the window through the window / I could almost touch the pane"? Rhymes with "I was in the pouring rain," doesn't it?   **C−**

Slick Rick: *The Great Adventures of Slick Rick* (Def Jam '88). Like that other girly-voiced rapper Dana Dane, Rick masks insecurities about his masculinity by dissing the opposite sex even uglier than the ugly competition. From the clarion "Treat Her Like a Prostitute" through this bitch and that cocaine dolly and the fake virgin "with a yay-wide gash" and the one who meant yes when she said no and ended

up marching a tribe of Indians out her cunt, this man hates women. His ballad is keyed around the refrain "Don't hurt me again" and is directed at all treacherous females, not just one. His anticrime warning closes with a convincing imitation of how bad you groan the first time you get cornholed.   **C+**

Sly and Robbie Present Taxi (Mango '81). These catchy (the Wailing Souls' "Sweet Sugar Plum") to groovy (Sheila Hylton's "Bed's Too Big Without You") love songs are why Jah made syndrums: reggae as pure pop, with only Junior Delgado's haunted "Fort Augustus" and General Echo's droll "Drunken Master" presenting any political distraction from the polypercussive hooks of Jamaica's greatest production team if not citizens.   **A−**

Sly and Robbie: *Rhythm Killers* (Island '87). *Language Barrier* was a world-music mishmash. *Taxi Connection Live in London* and *The Sting* are show and schlock reggae respectively. This is nonstop funk—powered by world pop's greatest rhythm section, which happens to be Jamaican, and filled out by a chauvinistic variation on Bill Laswell's usual international brigade—Daniel Ponce and Aiyb Dieng are the only furriners, although Henry Threadgill, Nicky Skopelitis, and D.S.T. aren't exactly from the same neighborhood. Art-rapper Rammelzee, Brooklyn toaster Shinehead, and studio mouthpiece Bernard Fowler add their lyrical signatures to those of P-Funk satellites Bootsy and Mudbone, but S&R's sensationalism combines with Laswell's imperiousness to rock each side from its Ohio Players or Allen Toussaint intro. Word.   **A**

Sly & Robbie: *Silent Assassin* (Island '89). The BDP raps are as strong as the S&R riddims, but despite their wealth of narrative detail they're more predictable, flattening this attempt to formalize a reggae–hip hop synthesis already in progress. Attributes not present: wit, joy, jokes, hooks.   **B+**

Sly and the Family Stone: *Ain't but the One Way* (Warner Bros. '82). I called

Back on the Right Track his best since *Fresh* in 1979, and for what that's worth it was, and this may even be a little better—the aphoristic snap of the songwriting recalls better days, and the mix generates some heat. But where in 1979 it seemed theoretically possible that Sly was on some track or other, there's no way this'll pull him through—often sounds as if he's not even there. Which he wasn't when Stewart Levine finally converted the tracks he'd laid down in 1980 into 1983 product. What a waste.   **B**

Sly Fox: *Let's Go All the Way* (Capitol '86). From thumping stop-and-go bottom to gleeful Beatle allusions, the title track is the most far-out piece of music to break pop all year, and you keep waiting for the rest to go . . . somewhere, if not all the way. I'm not saying the filler isn't as meaningful as Bootsy gone romantic or Levi's gone doowop. But it sure doesn't convey the same sense of adventure.   **B—**

Smashed Gladys: *Social Intercourse* (Elektra '88). Idealism in the young is always to be encouraged, which is why I can't resist a band so straightforward about its values: "Not for the money / Not for the fame / We do it . . ."—for the love of rock and roll, right, Unca Bob? sorry, Tipper, not this time—". . . TO GET LAID!" So it grieves me to report that only rarely do Bart Lewis's glam-metal riffs live up to such Sally Cato lines as "You play the fool and I play the tart" or "It's a filthy lie but someone's gotta live it." Not even the cock-rock riposte "Lick It into Shape" is hard enough. Get down, guys, or your hot mama's gonna go bye-bye.   **B**

Frankie Smith: *Children of Tomorrow* (WMOT '81). "Double Dutch Bus" having mixed Wolfman Jack, ghetto pig Latin, kiddie chorus, and a critique of Philadelphia's municipal transportation system into a long overdue great-grandchild of Shirley Ellis's "The Name Game," the title announces Smith's reluctance to jump rope for an entire album. But the recurring little synthesizer part makes you doubt his strenth of purpose, and the title tune makes you regret it. Despite a welcome slizang lesson and other modest diversions, buy the twelve-inch.   **B—**

Patti Smith: *Dream of Life* (Arista '88). At first I took this for that most painful of embarrassments, a failed sellout. Was she unwilling to waste her hard-won politics on weirdos? Proving herself a fit mother by going AOR, only she hadn't heard any AOR in about five years? Sad, sad. But soon I was humming, then I was paying attention, and now I think of this as the latest Patti Smith record. If she doesn't sound as unhinged as last time, she probably isn't, but as matrons go she's still out there. Her prophetic rhetoric is biblical just like always, with a personal feel for the mother tongue I wish more metal Jeremiahs knew enough to envy. The music is a little old-fashioned and quite simple, controlled but not machined, and the guitars sing. Her *Double Fantasy,* suggests a Detroit Smith named RJ. Only we don't formalize our equality by doling out turns, adds a Detroit Smith named Fred Sonic.   **A—**

Chris Smither: *It Ain't Easy* (Adelphi '84). Unless you're a genius on the order of John Hurt, who's remembered in a medley here, it's damn hard to make a consistently interesting album out of your voice and an acoustic guitar. Smither comes within a dud original and a few extraneous covers of bringing it off, and they're all on side one. Overdisc the two originals are for real and the way he wraps his voice and fingers around "Maybelline" and "Glory of Love" makes them sound not brand new but old as truth.   **B+**

The Smithereens: *Especially for You* (Enigma '86). All pop propaganda to the contrary, Pat DiNizio's no surefire songwriter—he's only moderately hooky, and even the lyrics he hits encapsulate romantic situations you already know the ins and outs of. Takes some singer to score consistently with such songs, and no pop propagandists are palming off that lie.   **B—**

The Smithereens: *Green Thoughts* (Capitol '88). I know Pat DiNizio is Beatlesque, but is that why he writes cheerful-sounding love songs that turn out to be kind of mean when you pay attention? Or allows as how he's a jealous guy? I suspect he would have discovered these creative avenues on his own, spurred by deep expressive need.   **C+**

The Smiths: *The Smiths* (Sire '84). Morrissey's slightly skewed relationship to time and pitch codes his faint melodies at least as much as Johnny Marr's much-heralded real guitar. What's turned him into an instant cult hero, though, is his slightly unskewed relationship to transitory sex—the boy really seems to take it hard. If you'll pardon my long memory, it's the James Taylor effect all over again—hypersensitivity seen as a spiritual achievement rather than an affliction by young would-be idealists who have had it to here with the cold cruel world.   **B−**

The Smiths: *Meat Is Murder* (Sire '85). It makes a certain kind of sense to impose teen-macho aggression on your audience—for better or worse, macho teens are expected to make a thing of their unwonted hostility. These guys impose their post-adolescent sensitivity, thus inspiring the sneaking suspicion that they're less sensitive than they come on—passive-aggressive, the pathology is called, and it begs for a belt in the chops. Only the guitar hook of "How Soon Is Now," stuck on by their meddling U.S. label, spoils the otherwise pristine fecklessness of this prize-winning U.K. LP. Remember what the Residents say: "Hitler was a vegetarian." Original grade: C.   **C+**

The Smiths: *The Queen Is Dead* (Sire '86). After disliking their other albums instantly, I was confused enough by my instant attraction to table this one, especially since I had no stomach for the comparisons I knew an investigation would entail. And indeed, I still can't stand the others. But here Morrissey wears his wit on his sleeve, dishing the queen like Johnny Rotten never did and kissing off a day-job boss who's no Mr. Sellack. This makes it easier to go along on his moonier escapades, like when he reveals that looks and fame don't guarantee a good social life. Which gives you time to notice the tunes, the guitars, the backup munchkins.   **B+**

The Smiths: *Louder Than Bombs* (Sire '87). Supposedly, Johnny Marr's unobtrusive virtuosity and subtle hooks saved Morrissey from drowning in his own self-involved wit, but on this U.S.-only retrospective of twenty-four previously uncollected songs I hear Marr and Morrissey gliding along on the crest of the same conversational cadence. Morrissey's nattering volubility can get annoying, but the cadence itself always has its charms, and just when you think you've had it he gets off a good line. One of my favorites goes "Et cetera, et cetera, et cetera."   **B+**

The Smiths: *Strangeways, Here We Come* (Sire '87). Having conquered my wimpophobia to where I reflexively enjoy the supple smarts of their sound, I bore down anticipating even tastier goodies, and now I must face facts. In three of these songs somebody's dead or dying, in three more somebody contemplates murder, and in the rest somebody's in a selfish pet of the sort that led to the aforementioned threats. So the liveliest tracks are where somebody's dead or dying: AIDS song, biz song, song about how selfish and petty you feel when somebody you've raged at actually dies.   **B**

The Smiths: *Rank* (Sire '88). Morrissey and Marr were nearing the end of the trail by the October '86 concert where this de facto retrospective was recorded. The songs are choice in that live best-of-way and the performances are spirited enough, but the chemistry is by formula, if you know what I mean. Those who thought them too delicate will get something out of it. But they weren't.   **B**

Patty Smyth: *Never Enough* (Columbia '87). I'm probably overrating this record a little. Certainly there are times when its big, every-hair-in-place production makes the big, barely controllable emotions she's going for sound hopelessly false, and from rejected partner Billy Steinberg to new producer Rick Chertoff, the songcraft is manufactured Springsteen. Yet something just slightly bruised in Smyth's big voice recalls the pop axiom that manufacture and integrity aren't mutually exclusive. Kind of like with Katrina Leskanich, only not so's you'd play the album of your own free will. And most would say I overrate Katrina Leskanich. **B—**

Phoebe Snow: *The Best of Phoebe Snow* (Columbia '81). Most New Yorkers know a woman like this: from a liberal background, with loads of artistic interests, she's insecure about her weight and hence her looks (which are OK at least) and hence her talent (which there's no questioning), and after plenty of therapy her emotions are still all over the place. Only none of her sisters can sing the postblues like Snow—neurotically, that's what she's about, but with incisive power. She's erratic, so given to bad poetry and intermittently eager to please that her albums are off-putting unless you have a weakness for the type. But this compilation—four originals, six covers, including "Shakey Ground," which she owns because it's her all over—is smart, quirky, deeply felt. It proves the type deserves more credit than it usually gets. **A—**

Soft Cell: *Non-Stop Erotic Cabaret* (Sire '81). I've always found "Tainted Love" catchy-annoying rather than catchy-seductive, but these takeoffs on Clubland "decadence" get at the emotion underneath with just the right admixture of camp cynicism. Now you feel it, now you don't. **B+**

Soft Cell: *The Art of Falling Apart* (Sire '83). Marc Almond's compassionately bitchy exposés of bedsitter hedonism and suburban futility risk bathos when they eschew burlesque. I'm sure his faithless U.S. audience would find the non-LP B side "It's a Mugs Game," in which Marc pukes on his shoes, more edifying than the mock?-tragic "Baby Doll" or a bedhopper's lament like "Numbers." And David Ball's synthesized Hendrix on the bonus twelve-inch isn't funny enough to compensate. **B—**

Something Wild (MCA '86). From the oppressive *Top Gun* to the not unattractive *Pretty in Pink,* the predictability-in-diversity of the soundtrack album typifies promo's novelty fetishism, and if this one's no different, at least it's better. Not only does Jonathan Demme do right by found

exotica like Sonny Okossun, he knows how to special-order it, from a David Byrne-Celia Cruz duet to Sister Carol's saucy reggae "Wild Thing." He even gets songs that don't need pictures from eternal sidemen Steve Jones and Jerry Harrison—though not from Oingo Boingo's indefatigable Danny Elfman, or from eternal once-was Jimmy Cliff. **B+**

Sonic Youth: *Sonic Youth* (Neutral EP '82). You may not think Glenn Branca's proteges are a rock and roll band, but after all, why else would they essay a lyric like "Fucking youth / Working youth"? At their worst they sound like Polyrock mainlining metronome, at their best like one of Branca's early drafts. The best never last long enough. Not for nothing is the sonic grown-up so attached to phony grandeur. [Later on SST.] **C**

Sonic Youth: *Confusion Is Sex* (Neutral '83). Back in 1970 I played Max Kozloff, a Cal Arts colleague of distinctly Yurrupean musical tastes, some singles I thought instructive—"Brown Eyed Girl," "California Earthquake," "Neanderthal Man," like that. The one he flipped for was "I Wanna Be Your Dog." So if you think the sonic cover here proves they're rockers at heart, you have a fine art critic on your side. The dull rock critic wants to mention that the cover doesn't rock too good. Of course, neither did King Crimson a lot of the time. [Later on SST.] **C+**

Sonic Youth: *Kill Yr. Idols* (Zensor import EP '83). Idolization is for rock stars, even rock stars manqué like these impotent bohos—critics just want a little respect. So if it's not too hypersensitive of me, I wasn't flattered to hear my name pronounced right, not on this particular title track— nor pleased to note that, though "Brother James" is a dandy Glenn Branca tribute and one of the tracks lifted directly from *Confusion Is Sex* is a lot niftier than the other track lifted directly from *Confusion Is Sex,* the title cut's most likely to appeal to suckers for rock and roll as opposed to suckers for boho posers. Boho posers just shoot off their mouths a lot. With rock-and-rollers you never know. **B—**

Sonic Youth: *Bad Moon Rising* (Homestead '85). They're sure to disagree—what else are they good for?—but despite all their apocalyptic integrity and unmediated whoziwhatsis, the achievement of their first halfway decent record is strictly formal: simple, rhythmic songs that neither disappear beneath nor get the better of the clanging and grinding of their brutal late-industrial guitars. Whatever credibility the guitars lend to their no doubt painful but nonetheless hackneyed manic depression is undermined by their usual sociopathic fantasies, and in the end the music isn't ugly or ominous or bombs bursting midair. It's just interesting. **B**

Sonic Youth: *Death Valley '69* (Homestead EP '85). Lydia Lunch feature from current LP b/w best-of sorta from their three previous releases—all of them, as is noted once you've paid yer money and zipped yer shrink-wrap, still available in the kind of shoppes that stock such arcana—plus pieceashit outtake from current LP. Suck their dicks or pussy as the case may be. **D**

Sonic Youth: *Evol* (SST '86). By deigning to play a few tunes and eschewing both dirge and breakdown for minutes at a time, these media heroes work up a credible representation of the avant-porn clichés that mean so much to them—you know, passion as self-immolation, life redeemed on the edge of death, and (last but not least) it was only a dream. The deliberately stoopid title, misspelled frontwards and misapprehended backwards, captures the loopy tone they've achieved. In fact, the good parts are so good that for a while there I thought I was enjoying the bad parts. Guess I must have been woolgathering. **B+**

Sonic Youth: *Starpower* (SST EP '86). Yet another reshuffled ripoff from these master packagers, and while those who eat their Lower East Side bullshit for breakfast will want something messier, I must admit I love it: superior, edited remixes of the two baddest songs on *Evol* plus Kim Gordon's Kim Fowley cover—done in a monotone far catchier than the old rip-off artist deserves or could manage himself. Glad they've finally acknowledged this key influence. **A—**

Sonic Youth: *Sister* (SST '87). Finally, an album worthy of their tuning system, and

no, it's not like they've suddenly started to write tight or see a shrink. All they cop to is making their bullshit signify, which means keeping a distance from the insanity they find so sexy and not letting their slack-jawed musings drone on too long. Hence, those with more moderate tastes have space to feel the buzz and a chance to go on to something else before boredom sets in. With the California punk cover acknowledging their debts and the bow to coherent content safeguarding against that empty feeling, their chief pleasure, as always, is formal—a guitar sound almost unique in its capacity to evoke rock and roll without implicating them in a history few youngish bands can bear up under these days. **A**

Sonic Youth: *Master-Dik Beat on the Brat* (SST EP '88). If you believe their revolutionary potential is realized only in confusion, this, how you say it, bricolage of white rap, Ramones cover, Swiss interview, and studio fuckaround will turn your world topsy turvy (again!). It's pretty long, too, which doesn't make it a bargain. Nothing revolutionary about bargains. **C+**

Sonic Youth: *Daydream Nation* (Enigma/Blast First '88). At a historical juncture we can only hope isn't a fissure, a time when no sentient rock-and-roller could mistake extremism in the defense of liberty for a vice, the anarchic doomshows of Our Antiheroes' static youth look moderately prophetic and sound better than they used to. But they don't sound anywhere near as good as the happy-go-lucky careerism and four-on-the-floor maturity Our Heroes are indulging now. Whatever exactly their lyrics are saying—not that I can't make them out, just that catchphrases like "You've got it" and "Just say yes" and "It's total trash" and "You're so soft you make me hard" are all I need to know—their discordant never-let-up is a philosophical triumph. They're not peering into the fissure, they're barreling down the turnpike like the fissure ain't there. And maybe they're right—they were the first time. **A**

Sonic Youth: See also Ciccone Youth.

The S.O.S. Band: *Sands of Time* (Tabu '86). The all but anonymous creatures of the hottest rhythm team in the universe, they could almost pass as the new Chic, getting whole albums over on groove alone. But though there's frisson in the way Jam & Lewis put their slow drag through its paces, what got Chic over was Rodgers & Edwards saving their trickiest beats for their love child.   **B**

Soul Asylum: *Made To Be Broken* (Twin/Tone '86). Unless the meaning of life is passing me by, Bob Mould's proteges are the latest concept band, admired more for their correct aesthetics than for how they actually sound (or what they actually say). Fast turmoil rools, with hints of metal anthem and country warmth sunk deep enough in the mix that nobody'll cry corny. As a concept, pretty admirable.   **B**

Soul Asylum: *While You Were Out* (Twin/Tone '87). Dave Pirner's songs and Chris Osgood's sound do focus their barrage-band intensity, but once again the most striking track is a slow country-folk rip, this one cribbed more or less direct from "On Top of Old Smokey." Which isn't to put down Pirner's better-than-average tunes, but to suggest that barrage meanings may not be his calling.   **B+**

Soul Asylum: *Hang Time* (A&M '88). Somewhere in here they warn of "a mountain made of sand," which gets at their problems neatly—their shared sense of Sisyphean impotence and their big music no one can get a grip on.   **B−**

Soul Brothers: *Jive Explosion* (Virgin '88). An '80s best-of from Azanian pros who come as close as mbaqanga ever does to Ladysmith—and also to what Americans consider pop music. The saxes are smooth, the deep bass is fluid, a Fairlight fills out five tracks, and the vocals honor old Zulu harmonies while showcasing David Masondo's aching tenor. No matter what they're singing about—as much as they think they can get away with, say—their elegance is something they had to win.   **A−**

Soul II Soul: *Keep On Movin'* (Virgin '89). The vapidity of "A happy face, a thumping bass, for a loving race" wouldn't bother anybody if these Londoners didn't take dread in vain—with hair like that you're supposed to be more, you know, cultural. But for a disco band they're quite all right, really—very tuneful, with a nice loping groove and vocals out of Chic and Eddy Grant. And though I wish they liked saxophones, the flute is them.   **B+**

Sound d'Afrique (Mango '81). This unannotated compilation of six hit (I assume) dance (though "Jalo" gets pretty meditative) tracks out of Francophone Africa is a sampler rather than a true album, jumping and skipping style-to-style. From Senegal, Muslim soul; from Côte d'Ivoire, sound-effects guitar; from Upper Volta, underdeveloped structure and rich feeling. From Cameroun, Zaire, and Congo, the continent's dominant beat: Afrorumba over sweetly chattering rhythm guitar, hooked on the opening cut by a refrain so unforgettable Pete Seeger would shit cobalt in the Hudson for it. Original grade: B plus.   **A−**

Sound d'Afrique II: Soukous (Mango '82). "Soukous is a word understood throughout French-speaking Africa (the source of this album). It simply means: going out, checking the music, dancing and, cool or passionate, having the Best Time." As in juking, say. But also as in the slang term for the Congolese style that dominates the continent's pop—which this features, thus avoiding the eclectic distractions of Mango's first Afropop collection. Salsafied stuff with vocals that sometimes float sweet and high and sometimes twist and shout, none of it by big-name stars. In short, an African disco compilation. Nice.   **A−**

Soundgarden: *Louder Than Love* (A&M '89). This AOR reclamation job isn't retro because so many of their culturally deprived boho contemporaries have pretty much the same idea. It isn't Led Zep because they're interested in (good at?) noise, not riffs. Covertly conceptual, arty in spite of itself, and I bet metal fans don't bite.   **C+**

Sounds of Soweto (Capitol '87). If mbaqanga admirers find this contemporary compilation techno, that's their prejudice. At any acceptable level of economic development, electronic instruments are people-friendly, and music that mediates between South African blacks and the cities apartheid bars them from has its progressive function. Of course, quality can still vary. Condry Ziqubu and Lumumba burn; Lionel Petersen and the Winners kowtow. Some lyrics avoid the censors while sticking to the grit—corn, coal, crime in the streets. Others lie—if Petersen feels so damn "free to sing a song," that's another reason to suspect it doesn't mean shit. First side never lets that upwardly suave beat quit, and none of the others gets so smarmy you'll push reject. **B+**

Soup for One (Mirage '82). Hoped this soundtrack might double as a Rodgers & Edwards sampler, but they don't quite mesh with Carly or Teddy, and Sister Sledge's track is a pleasant throwaway. They do better by Fonzi Thornton, who's one of their own, and better still by Chic, on the title tune and a folkish etude called "Tavern on the Green." Original grade: B plus. **B**

South African Trade Union Worker Choirs (Rounder '87). These groups have an aura of officialdom, as if organized at the workplace by wily fomenters of solidarity. Women make themselves heard in a traditionally male domain; the style is relatively declamatory, confident of its platform and its captive audience; American jubilee and mass-choir voicings abound; the acronym for "Federation of South African Trade Unions" bedecks six of the twenty-five titles. But for agitprop, it's long on highjinks, with stomps and whistles erupting frequently around the exhortations. If South African pop makes the struggle of the South African people doubly immediate, this does the same for South African politicos—while apprising skeptics of how close to the people they are. **B+**

Soweto (Rough Trade import '82). It's fair to assume that these fourteen crude, tuneful little singles, released six or seven years ago out of a Johannesburg record shop and featuring a writer-producer named Wilbur Dlamini and a backing band of Jo'burg Zulus called the Bamalangabis, are typical of nothing. They're apolitical except by their sheer existence, mostly small-group instrumental, with guitar, sax, and organ leads. Not too clearly recorded, either. And they're delightful. It's possible Dlamini is a lost genius. It's also possible that when I've heard more music from South Africa's hellish black urban work zones I'll find him minor or derivative. But what's certain is that a lot of very talented people are getting lost in black South Africa. Ain't capitalism grand? Original grade: A minus. **B+**

Soweto Never Sleeps (Shanachie '87). For all but a tiny minority of its U.S. cult, mbaqanga is a fantasy of resilience and resistance—we hear in it the defiant strength we believe must lurk beneath its surface whatever its ostensible subject. Reflecting its earlier date of origin, the latest collection is less sure-footed than *The Indestructible Beat* (compare "Wozani Mahipi," a/k/a "Hippies Come to Soweto," to its source, the Meters' "Chicken Strut"). It's also less catchy, with what I assume to be the traditional chant of the midtempo title tune the prize melody. But I suspect the major reason it doesn't connect as powerfully is that it compiles "classic female jive." Even though the idiom's male and female singers both adhere to the conventions of tribal syncretism gone showbiz, those conventions format women more tightly than men. As a result, the men sound more assertive. Which suits our fantasy. **A−**

Spandau Ballet: *Journeys to Glory* (Chrysalis '81). Thoughts while hearing "To Cut a Long Story Short" at Hurrah the week before it closed: (1) Eighteen months ago, any "rock" DJ who spun a disco disc replete with kick-drum, synwash, and voice-pomp would have risked a lynching. (2) "Question," the title of the Moody Blues' best (only good) song, is the catchword of Spandau's best song. What is the answer? **C**

Sparrow: *King of the World* (B's '84). Though one distinction between calypso and soca is that the earlier style wasn't geared to phonographic reproduction, I much prefer the two hard-to-find calypso compilations I've recently gotten to know (*More Sparrow More!!* on Recording Artists, *Hot and Sweet* on Warner Bros.). And though the greatest of the modern calypsonians claims right here that he's not a "Soca Man," the album's dance groove is compulsive enough for disco. But Sparrow remains a supremely resonant singer with a taste for resonant lyrics: "Grenada" lays into Cuban accommodations without letting Reagan off the hook, "Marahjin Cousin" satirizes racial complexities unimaginable in our polarized land. The reason he works variations on the same few melodies is that they're all classics. And his groove is worth a go.   **A—**

Special Ed: *Youngest in Charge* (Profile '89). With the sixteen-year-old rhyming quick as he can think over Howie Tee's tenacious samples, this starts off flying—nine "ax"es in thirteen seconds clim"ax" "Taxing," with sense no barrier. But thematically it's the usual, and as Howie downshifts and Ed pulls out his skeezer number ("I hate cheap sex," he warns us, neglecting to add "after it's over" and "unless I'm selling it"), you wish he'd grow up, fresh or no fresh.   **B**

The Specials: *The Specials* (Chrysalis '80). If it takes longer than you'd figure for these jingles to get across, that's partly because the ska they don't quite reinvent tends to skip where the reggae that succeeded it dug in, but also partly because their sound, especially their vocal sound, is just too thin to make an immediate impression (compare their "Monkey Man" to Toots's if you dare). In the end, though, there's a jaunty confidence to this music that's a lot less forced than power pop's. And there's no gainsaying their commercial messages—promote racial harmony, use contraceptives. Original grade: B plus.   **A—**
The Specials: *More Specials* (Chrysalis '80). This time they make the ska sound their own by synthesizing its trippy beat and their own inborn vocal attenuation into a single formal principle—a platonic ideal of fun. Especially on side two, the result is so light it's almost ethereal, political consciousness and all.   **B**
The Specials: *Ghost Town/Why?/Friday Night Saturday Morning* (Chrysalis EP '81). Boom gone bust, everyone restless, no live music cos there's fighting on the dance floor, and the recorded music all ghostly. "Did you really want to kill me?" a victim who's proud of his black skin asks an assailant who's proud of his white. "You make me an angry man." A mild-sounding weekend reveler wishes for lipstick on his shirt instead of piss on his shoes. In short, a recipe for a riot—just in time for the end of the world. Original grade: A minus.   **A**
The Special AKA: *In the Studio* (Chrysalis). There's miraculous rhythmic progress from the polkafied chug-along of the Specials' ska to the suave Caribbean lilt here, which makes Jerry Dammers's most reclusive flights functional. But Dammers (together with mouthpiece Stan Campbell) never convinces me that the anomie he evokes so stubbornly has the public dimension that its proximity to "Bright Lights," "Racist Friend," and "Free Nelson Mandela" implies. Not often that the political songs on an album seem most down-to-earth.   **B+**

The Speedboys: *That's What I Like* (I Like Mike '82). Harking back to a time when pop and boogie weren't mutually exclusive, Robert Bobby recalls such unlikely influences as Dino Valenti, Roy A. Loney, Marty Balin, and George Gerdes on tunes that are neither speedy nor boyish enough for '80s cool. Cheerfully regressive in more ways than one, his gift for the pungent phrase is inspired mostly by the Colorado resident celebrated in "Little Bit Nasty, Little Bit Nice." "My baby's mean as she can be / But she's only mean to me," he exults; "I knew something was cooking / When you took your matte knife to my back," he realizes; "Come on home and / Treat me wrong again," he pleads. Guitarist Bobby Blue Blake adds off-color chords.   **A—**
The Speedboys: *Look What Love's Done to Me Now* (I Like Mike '83). I don't often wonder what the world is coming to be-

cause someone can't get a record contract—after all, life is unfair—but here I'm tempted. A sharp, witty bar-band–blues LP like the first is one thing, but the mid-tempo stuff on this entry could fit in right next to Tom Petty and Bob Seger if only some hotshot producer would oil Robert Bobby's voice up a little. That's no advantage as far as I'm concerned, but uncommercial it ain't. What could be the problem? Surely not the antinuke overtones of "Hearts Like Atoms Split." Maybe somebody noticed the chorus of "Anna": "Anna, anabolic steroid / Oh Anna, you made a man outta me."   **B+**

Spinal Tap (Polydor '84). Sonically, these long-suffering limeys don't pack the priapic overkill that might make their compilation as convincing as the "rockumentary" which finally won them critical acclaim. The problem is physical—neither vocalist David St. Hubbins nor guitarist Nigel Tufnel possesses equipment of HM's gargantuan proportions, although they might have faked it if producers Guest-McKean-Shearer knew recording studios like they do movie sets. Nevertheless, Tap were ahead of their time in 1965 ("Cups and Cakes" is very late '66) and 1973 (that synth on the classic "Big Bottom"), and they're pathfinders today as well—funnier than the Dictators ever were.   **B+**

Split Enz: *Waiata* (A&M '81). They're still hyped as "avant-garde." Probably because they mix their twitty, intermittently tuneful art-pop with Nino Rota homages and stereo effects that go back to the house of Gary Usher.   **C+**

Split Enz: *History Never Repeats (The Best of Split Enz)* (A&M '87). From Down Under, where Vanda-Young are Goffin-King if not Lennon-McCartney, pretenders who made Squeeze, their pop compatriots across the Tasman Sea, seem like heavyweights on spritz and detail alone. Tunes and metaphors are brought skillfully to completion like an A student's notebook exercise—you'll remember every song. But you'll never know why you bothered.   **B−**

A Split-Second: *. . . From the Inside* (Wax Trax '88). Avatars of a slightly slowed-down Belgian industrial-disco style (subculture?) that I suspect is called "new beat" because buyers will know what the phrase means anywhere in the EEC, they don't overdo the wimp and doom factors that ruin so much synth-based dance music—just play them for tune and discord respectively. A taste for sex and the occasional funny bit facilitate this achievement.   **B+**

Spot 1019: *Spot 1019* (Pitch-a-Tent '87). Some Camper Van fans will suck up the only other band on their heroes' indie vanity label, but the true faithful won't believe. All together now, children, in your best Valley-boy-turned-surf-punk accents: "They're just an imi-*tay*-shun." Actually, without the (tongue-in-cheek) psychedelic utopianism and (closet) one-worlder rhythms, they're much more the college dropout humor magazine. Get off their share of snotty-to-spacy jokes, too.   **B**

Bruce Springsteen: *The River* (Columbia '80). All the standard objections apply. His beat is still clunky, his singing overwrought, his sense of significance shot through with Mazola Oil. He's too white and too male, though he's decent enough to wish he weren't; too unanalytic and fatalistic, though his eye is sharp as can be. Yet by continuing to root his writing in the small victories and large compromises of ordinary joes and janies whose need to understand as well as celebrate is as restless as his own, he's grown into a bitter empathy. These are the wages of young romantic love among those who get paid by the hour, and even if he's only giving forth with so many short fast ones because the circles of frustration and escape seem tighter now, the condensed songcraft makes this double album a model of condensation—upbeat enough for the radio here, delicate enough for a revery there, he elaborates a myth about the fate of the guys he grew up with that hits a lot of people where they live.   **A−**

Bruce Springsteen: *Nebraska* (Columbia '82). Literary worth is established with the title tune, in which Springsteen's Charlie Starkweather becomes the first mass murderer in the history of socially relevant singer-songwriting to entertain a revealing thought—wants his pretty baby to sit in his lap when he gets the chair. Good thing he didn't turn that one into a rousing rocker, wouldn't you say, though (Hüsker Dü please note) I grant that some hardcore atonality might also produce the appropriate alienation effect. But the music is a problem here—unlike, er, Dylan, or Robert Johnson, or Johnny Shines or Si Kahn or Kevin Coyne, Springsteen isn't imaginative enough vocally or melodically to enrich these bitter tales of late capitalism with nothing but a guitar, a harmonica, and a few brave arrangements. Still, this is a conceptual coup, especially since it's selling. What better way to set right the misleading premise that rock and roll equals liberation?   **A—**

Bruce Springsteen: Born in the U.S.A. (Columbia '84). Imperceptible though the movement has been to many sensitive young people, Springsteen has evolved. In fact, this apparent retrenchment is his most rhythmically propulsive, vocally incisive, lyrically balanced, and commercially undeniable album. Even his compulsive studio habits work for him: the aural vibrancy of the thing reminds me like nothing in years that what teenagers loved about rock and roll wasn't that it was catchy or even vibrant but that it just plain sounded good. And while *Nebraska*'s onenote vision may be more left-correct, my instincts (not to mention my leftism) tell me that this uptempo worldview is truer. Hardly ride-off-into-the-sunset stuff, at the same time it's low on nostalgia and beautiful losers. Not counting the title powerhouse, the best songs slip by at first because their tone is so lifelike: the fast-stepping "Working on the Highway," which turns out to be about a country road gang; "Darlington County," which pins down the futility of a macho spree without undercutting its exuberance; and "Glory Days," which finally acknowledges that, among other things, getting old is a good joke. Original grade: A.   **A+**

Bruce Springsteen & the E Street Band: *Live/1975–1985* (Columbia '86). Any

event this public will provoke backlash, and any album this monumental is sure to arouse unreasonable expectations and unlikely to satisfy the reasonable ones. So if not one of the eight songs from *Born in the U.S.A.* improves on the studio version, how bad does that make them? If what little remains of the mid-'70s shows that turned him into a legend is overblown enough to make you wonder if you got taken, trust yourself. If the three new originals and four covers don't leap out, figure they weren't supposed to. This album is about continuity and honest reassurance, a job very well done. Although it takes some smart chances (e.g., "War"), it wasn't meant to shock or enlighten or redefine—it was meant to sum up, and it does. There isn't one of its ten sides that excites me end to end, and there isn't one I couldn't play with active pleasure now or five years from now. If anything, it isn't long enough.   **A—**

Bruce Springsteen: Tunnel of Love (Columbia '87). Where *Nebraska* was plunged in a social despair he never quite made his own, this companion piece comes out of personal compulsion. By depicting the fear of commitment as sheer terror, he does the impossible: renews L-O-V-E as pop subject. First side's got distance, bravado, optimism, even a joke, but then comes one long deep look inside, so well-observed that he seems neither self-pitying nor self-important, just a decent guy with a realistic understanding of his major but not insoluble emotional problems. And although the format is almost as spare as *Nebraska*'s, the man has worked on his sense of rhythm the way he's worked on his marriage, which means he's pleasing to hear with just a drummer or alone. Next thing you know he'll learn to dance.   **A**

Bruce Springsteen: Chimes of Freedom (Columbia EP '88). If the title cut on this live charity record invests Dylan's protest with an aura of sacred majesty, the other three invest honorable Springsteen copyrights with an aura of sacred cow. Supposedly, his "reinterpretations" of his own "classics"—acoustic "Born To Run," E Street "Tougher Than the Rest"—have a demythologizing effect, but years of enormous rooms have finally taken their spiritual toll; the self-importance he's always accused of drips from his all-American drawl like Vitalis off a DA. He's staved off this fate for as long as he has with modest strokes like *Nebraska,* and it's conceivable he'll come up with another one. Then again, this was probably supposed to be another one.   **B—**

Squeeze: *Argybargy* (A&M '80). Popophiles Chris Difford and Glenn Tilbrook don't settle for have-fun fall-in-love feargirls. They pen short stories worthy of early Rupert Holmes, and with a beat (alternate title: *Herkyjerky*). 'Tis said McCartneyesque tunefulness is the ticket here, but to me Tilbrook sounds more like Ray Davies after est—at peace with himself and out for big bucks, pounds being a foregone conclusion.   **B—**

Squeeze: *East Side Story* (A&M '81). They're finally beginning to show the consistency that's the only excuse for obsessive popcraft. The songs are imaginative, compassionate, and of course hooky—the warped organ on "Heaven" bespeaks divine intervention. And with Elvis Costello coproducing, the music is quite punchy, though I wouldn't go so far as to say it rocks.   **B+**

Squeeze: *Sweets From a Stranger* (A&M '82). In a classic rock and roll success story, Tilbrook & Difford are getting laid more and enjoying it less. Not that enjoyment in the usual sense is the point—flesh is hardly their *specialité.* But the ever more disconcerting hookcraft signifies a "maturing" emotional grasp in which a scheduled album seems like as good a reason as any to think up nine new ways to leave your lover.   **B+**

Squeeze: *Singles—45's and Under* (A&M '82). They're so principled in their unpretension, so obsessed with the telling detail, that their lesser moments are positively minuscule—not unfine when you squint at them, but all too easy to overlook. And as self-conscious craftsmen, they know their own strengths—no blowing the compilation they're made for with pet failures. Pop connoisseurs will of course crave the entire oeuvre—all the albums, all the picture sleeves, and now the previously unreleased "Annie Get Your Gun." Nonminiaturists will wonder why so few of their working-class protagonists call up the compassion of "Up the Junction" and save shelf space.   **A—**

Squeeze: *Babylon and On* (A&M '87). The most noticeable of Difford & Tilbrook Mark II's three LPs is a case study in pop-star devolution, suffused with the regrets of successful young professionals who drink too much liquor, smoke too many cigarettes, and don't want to be alone any more. Their best song is about how they really don't understand Americans, most of the rest leech off love lives that comprise long successions of small failures, and where once they were storytellers, now they've withdrawn into metaphor—surprisingly murky metaphor for such detail specialists, with lots of time references.   **B—**

Chris Stamey: *It's Alright* (A&M '87). After two excessively eccentric solo LPs, Stamey's new wave supersession is excessively conventional, subsuming his mad pop perfectionism and repressed inner turmoil in mere well-madeness. Under the leader's iron thumb, Fier, Lloyd, Easter, Worrell, and the pack push all the right buttons, even the one marked Liftoff, thus transporting those who've been waiting five years for their hero to take them for a ride.   **B**

Stampfel & Weber: *Going Nowhere Fast* (Rounder '81). Seventeen years after the original Holy Modal Rounders first recorded for Prestige, the same two voices and three stringed instruments actually sound better. Well, Weber doesn't—check out "Junker's Blues." But I've never heard anyone—anyone—sing with the sheer enthusiasm for singing that Stampfel puts out here, and where he once channeled his passion for song into folk material, now he'll take on anything from Shakespeare, with Antonia collaborating, to Phil Phillips's newly atonal "Sea of Love."   **A—**

Peter Stampfel and the Bottle Caps: *Peter Stampfel and the Bottle Caps* (Rounder '86). At his best, Stampfel does a kind of slack-wire act, striking his own crazy folkie balance between soul and satire and his own crazy rock and roll balance between hell-bent enthusiasm and musicianly effect. Here he plays it closer to solid ground, falling less often but relying a hair-and-a-half too much on satire and effect. Which doesn't hold down the mind-expanding covers, including a protectionist drinking song and an obscure Lloyd Price ditty featuring a spoken coda in which a smitten, pimply-sounding Stampfel explains the orbit of the moon to his date ("Hey, you wanna talk about something else?"). Nor harm his own "Surfer Angel," which crushes "Wipe Out" and "Endless Sleep" down into a surf death song, a subgenre I'm surprised no one got to in the '60s, or the actively uncompassionate "Lonely Junkie." Inspirational Verse: "My bowels are in stasis / My atrophied ass / Is heavy and leaded / And loaded with gas." **A−**

Peter Stampfel and the Bottle Caps: *The People's Republic of Rock n' Roll* (Homestead '89). The title and no doubt the intermittently "commercial" sound are about band democracy, or maybe dictatorship of the proletariat—Stampfel gives up three lead vocals and five songs and gets the most uneven record of a career that's never confused consistency with virtue. The division is almost too neat—only one Stampfel loser, and also only one non-Stampfel winner, the John-Lee-Hooker ad absurdum "Mindless Boogie," which together with Stampfel's democratically romantic "Bridge and Tunnel Girls" may actually earn the college-novelty rotation he's always deserved. Which I hope doesn't prevent all concerned from learning their lesson. **B+**

Chuck Stanley: *The Finer Things in Life* (Columbia '87). The tender heart palpitating beneath Public Enemy's hard-boiled exterior, Stanley is out of Oran Jones's league. His juicy baritone rises easily to a rich falsetto, and Luther or Freddie would pay cold money for either. But the range of his instrument becomes an end in itself—he never projects Luther's personal intensity or even Freddie's personal style. And while he's not yet a big enough love man to bore the world by controlling his own publishing, the soft fantasies of the hard-boiled do have their runny tendencies. **B**

Mavis Staples: *Time Waits for No One* (Paisley Park '89). This dream meeting between the criminally underexploited black singer and the black-pop capo doesn't flop altogether—both principals can generate a certain minimum interest sleepwalking. The two songs composed by old Stax hands are slightly embarrassing, but they sound like Mavis, who's made meaningful schlock her lifework. The six by Prince sound like a top-of-the-line disco producer who can't say no to a great voice or a deep ballad. **B**

The Staple Singers: *Turning Point* (Private I '84). This is indeed a spiritual return to their commercial heyday on Stax a decade-plus ago, which for those who don't remember was sometimes clumsily (sometimes even comically) uneven in tone and achievement. "That's What Friends Are For" is a sermon that'll keep you awake, but "Bridges Instead of Walls" would tempt the marginally pious to play pocket pool or peruse the weekly bulletin. And Mavis is more convincing as David Byrne than as Millie Jackson. **B**

The Staple Singers: *Are You Ready* (Private I, '85). Mike Piccirillo and Gary Goetzman, who brainstormed not only the Heads cover that brought the Staples back last year but also the bedroom-eyes embarrassment that was supposed to cement their chart status, here discover that the great pop subject of this reformed gospel group is public morality. And lead off with two covers—the first from, are you ready, Pacific Gas & Electric, topped by "Life During Wartime"—so incandescent they lend a glow to the producer-penned protest sentiments that follow. Of course, Mavis's commitment to these sentiments doesn't hurt. **B+**

Edwin Starr: *The Best of Edwin Starr* (20th Century-Fox '81). He's more exciting at his best—check out his five tracks on Volume 3 of the *Motown's Preferred Stock* series, if you can find it and don't wear a pacemaker—but one reason he suits the disco format better than, for instance, Johnnie Taylor, is that he isn't as good as Johnnie Taylor. That is, his excitement inheres mostly in his formula. Just as you expected, the formula here isn't up to full-speed Motown like "Agent Double-O Soul," "War," or (the here reprised) "25 Miles," though "Accident" comes close. Not only that—to salve his conscience they let him have some full-length ballads.   **B**

Ringo Starr: *Starr Struck: The Best of Ringo Starr, Vol. 2* (Rhino '89). I played this in the spirit of one more once, just in case I'd missed something—for instance the Joe Walsh-produced *Old Wave,* released 1983 Canada-only, how sad. But whatever his charms as an ex-Beatle, he's been El Lay for most of his adult life, and even on rock and roll ditties drummed up by ex-Beatles George Harrison and Paul McCartney (not exactly surefire hitmakers, I know, though John Lennon's isn't much better), his dogged directness can't cut it. Better than Telly Savalas, but no match for George Harrison, or Joe Walsh.   **C**

Starstruck (A&M '83). Performed mostly by ingenue Jo Kennedy and Split Enz split-off the Swingers and tailored mostly to cinematic concept, these eleven-plus songs not only constitute an unusually disc-effective soundtrack but sound fresher than just about any collection of rock and roll ditties to come off the wall this year. In a moment when spontaneity can be prepared to order, you wonder why authenticity hounds get so exercised about the "real" thing. Original grade: A minus.   **B+**

Stay Awake (A&M '88). Packed the tape but forgot the notes, and after three bewildered plays I was wondering whether Hal Willner's Disney tribute featured not the usual smart rocksters but lounge-jazz singers Whitney Balliett himself wouldn't profile. Then Willner acting alone would have perpetrated the feckless equation of fantasy and whimsy that wrecks this pastiche. Instead, his accomplices include Los Lobos, the Replacements, the Roches, NRBQ, Nilsson, Garth Hudson, and Ringo Starr. The arty, the miniature, and the atmospheric give way to "straight" interpretations that provide relief only until you realize how slight the song is. For me, the big exceptions are Sun Ra's jolly "Pink Elephants" and Aaron Neville's supernal "Mickey Mouse Theme," the small ones Buster Poindexter's villainous "Castle in Spain" and, yup, James Taylor's sleepy "Second Star to the Right." In none of them are the personal and the literal mutually exclusive—none of them goes flat or makes high-flown excuses for itself. Each takes pleasure in Disney's reality without hypostasizing it. Isn't that the idea?   **C+**

Steel Pulse: *Reggae Fever* (Mango '80). Geoffrey Chung's crystalline production, David Hinds's catchy melodies, and Selwyn Brown's straight-ahead vocals may offend those infatuated with reggae's steamy aura of ambiguity: once you get used to the abrasions of their English Jamaican, you notice that neither bass lines nor lead vocals have the tropical thickness of Jamaican Jamaican. Roots, culture, the presence of Jah—who can gainsay them? But over Rastafarianism's deep quietism I'll take the aggressive ideological edge of Hinds's politico-inspirational mode. Also the aggressive pop edge of his romantic mode. And attribute both to urban industrialism, thank you.   **A−**

Steel Pulse: *True Democracy* (Elektra '82). One reason I've liked them is that they've always steered clear of Rasta misogyny, but not now—would they call out a *man* who "says carnal love is a must"? Other reasons have included groove, politics, and hooks—groove alone won't do. Best politics: "A Who's Responsible?" and "Worth His Weight in Gold." Best hooks: "A Who's Responsible?" and "Worth His Weight in Gold."   **B**

Steel Pulse: *Earth Crisis* (Elektra '84). David Hinds has always signed his music by swinging the beat a little more than is normally advisable, and this time, subtly but tellingly, his jazzbo tendencies catch up with him. Where in the past he'd add a subliminal tension to the groove by extending syllables slightly, here his phrasing sometimes goes slack—at one point he even adds a "now" that would do Joe Piscopo proud to the line "As long as Babylon is my foe." So despite strong material, this lacks the requisite steely edge. And whether the confusion of "laboratory" with "lavatory" is simple ignorance or one of those deep Rasta puns, it sums up his wit and wisdom on "these times of science and technology" all too neatly.   **B+**

Steel Pulse: *Reggae Greats: Steel Pulse* (Mango '84). Lifting five cuts from the overrated *Handsworth Revolution* and only two from the underrated *Reggae Fever,* retrieving two detachable songs-as-songs from the basically conceptual *Tribute to the Martyrs,* and adding a great lost single, this is as economical an introduction as you could reasonably expect to the English reggae pioneers, who've never surpassed their early peak. You say it all seems a little too "rock-influenced" to you? You were expecting maybe Gregory Isaacs? English—they're English.   **A−**

Steel Pulse: *State of Emergency* (MCA '88). Imperialism, harassment, dead-end economy—haven't they wailed about these things *firsthand* within living memory? You know their roots are shot when they aim their most heartfelt protests at disco bouncers and the perils of air travel. Inspirational Verse: "Hijacking I need some fun / You got me on the run."   **C+**

Steely Dan: *Gaucho* (MCA '80). With Walter Becker down to composer credits and very occasional bass, Donald Fagen progresses toward the intellectual cocktail rock he's sought for almost a decade—followed, of course, by a cadre of top-drawer El Lay studio hacks, the only musicians in the world smart enough to play his shit. Even the song with Aretha in it lends credence to rumors that the LP was originally entitled *Countdown to Lethargy.* After half a dozen hearings, the most arcane harmonies and unlikely hooks sound comforting, like one of those electromassagers that relax the muscles with a low-voltage shock. Craftsmen this obsessive don't want to rule the world—they just want to make sure it doesn't get them.   **B−**

Steely Dan: *Gold* (MCA '82). Pure contract fulfillment—Donald Fagen's solo debut is due on Warners in a few months—and nowhere near as consistent

as the useless 1978 *Greatest Hits,* with only *Gaucho* to show in between. Yet as product this one makes a certain sense, rescuing "Hey Nineteen" and "FM" and in a way "Deacon Blue" and even "Green Earrings," livelier in this livelier company than on *The Royal Scam.* Though not as lively as "Chain Lightning" or "King of the World," from back when they masqueraded as a rock and roll band rather than a "sophisticated pop/jazz group."   **B+**

Stetsasonic: *In Full Effect* (Tommy Boy '88). A dream of raised consciousness, "the world's only hip hop band" has teamed with Jesse Jackson on an "edu-taining" twelve-inch about the frontline states, and when Wise dreams of "a woman with a realistic imagination, a woman who thinks for herself, whose thoughts are bold and free," I swear he's not euphemizing freaky sex techniques, and that he wouldn't be grossed out by them either. Problem is the mere competence that afflicts so many well-meaning bands: it's versatile of them to generate as well as sample beats, but "A.F.R.I.C.A." went nowhere musically, and Wise's smart talk is buried in a "Float On" remake even ickier than the original. Album two gets across not on ace cuts like the revolutionary credo "Freedom or Death" (Professor Griff please copy) or the sampling credo "Talking All That Jazz" (James Brown please copy), but on a camaraderie that reaches deeper than the usual homeboy bonding. How much further it can go remains to be seen.   **B+**

Ray Stevens: *Greatest Hits Vol. 2* (MCA '87). Not only does he lay off the "Everything Is Beautiful," his funny stuff is funny, presumably because he now buys from professionals—the three lamest cuts are the three oldest are the three he wrote himself. If you appreciate a fella who can imitate a chicken singing Glenn Miller and thinks his sweetie should love him because he can fart with his armpits, this'll make you laugh even after you know the jokes. Other selling points include the timely "Would Jesus Wear a Rolex," the timeless "Mama's in the Sky with Elvis," and "I

Need Your Help Barry Manilow," homage from the man who wrote "Everything Is Beautiful."   **A—**

Gary Stewart: *Cactus and a Rose* (RCA '80). Getting treatment for writer's block, in for commercial retooling, whatever— the man in the black hat has been shuffled off to affably self-aggrandizing Memphis country/soul/rock/biz legend Chips Moman, who put him together with a couple of Allmans and a whole side of Chips Moman songs. The title tune has something to do with a New York penthouse, and what the hell this hard-drinking redneck is doing there nobody can figure out. Overdisc the country-rock is more billy and more swamp and sounds almost like old times on the only Stewart song included, the title of which encapsulates his poetic gifts: "How Could We Come to This After That." How indeed.   **B—**

Gary Stewart: *Greatest Hits* (RCA '81). Half of these ten tracks are on *Out of Hand* or *Your Place or Mine,* both worth owning, only let's face it—you don't. Sounded pretty good for country music, but since he wasn't Hank Williams, you passed. This was dumb. I'm not gonna claim he's Hank, though he's a damn sight closer than Waylon or Hank Jr., because Hank preceded Jerry Lee Lewis, not to mention Eddie Rabbitt, while Gary lives in a world that includes both—no matter what they think at RCA, he's no stranger to concepts like "rock" and "commercial." Which is not to suggest that boogie or schlock dilutes these vibrato-laden outcries of desperate abandon—they're the pure hard country of a honky-tonk piano man. No matter how justly Jerry Lee suffers, he always seems affronted that this should be happening to him. Though he hasn't thought about going to church two successive Sundays since he was twelve, Gary knows that what the Bible says is true—that sin and hell are the same place. And he lives there.   **A**

Gary Stewart & Dean Dillon: *Brotherly Love* (RCA Victor '82). They have two good reasons to try to make buddyful music together—Gary's goin' down and Dean's comin' up—and they work at it manfully enough. But the disappointments begin

with the jacket, where Gary sports a medallion (wore hippie beads in the good old days), and are symbolized by a slickly lascivious title hit that sums up the honky tonk as singles bar. Original grade: B.   **B—**

Gary Stewart: *Brand New* (Hightone '88). Hard living deepens great voices, but it's hell on the smaller ones, and so naturally Stewart compensates by oversinging, burying the songs in a mannered misery and wild-ass desperation that for all you can tell he may actually be feeling. Wordplay's half-there at best: "I was born the life of the party / And honey I'm dyin' tryin' to get one started," which is terrific, is preceded by "I was born the son of a honkytonk woman / My daddy was a natural-born gamblin' man," which is terrible. And which provides the song's title.   **B**

Jermaine Stewart: *Frantic Romantic* (Arista '86). Here's one princeling who's smart enough to know that the only way to bring off simpering high-life bullshit is flamboyantly, and that's exactly as far as his smarts go: "I'm not a piece of meat / Stimulate my brain," very funny, so buy the single, because he didn't write it. Without Aretha, meanwhile, Narada Michael Walden is just another Sri Chinmoy disciple, albeit one who dabbles in s&m jokes.   **C+**

Rod Stewart: *Foolish Behaviour* (Warner Bros. '80). It's not fair for punks to pick on him—rock Hollywood has spawned worse corruption, and his band is tougher and cooler than the Stranglers ever were. But he doesn't do himself many favors. He might have provided real songs after cut one side two, might have helped us believe in his ordinary blokehood by not putting the hotels he's trashed on a poster. Didn't really have to repeat the phrase "kill my wife" umpteen times (tell Britt it was only a "very nasty dream") or invoke "Passion" as universal solvent (like an asshole at a bar where the women are taken). And he didn't have to bury "Oh God, I Wish I Was Home Tonight" on an album no one will remember two years after it goes platinum. Vulnerable, waggish, rude, he begs his sweetie to save the best parts on her pornographic postcard for him. "I haven't a cent," he adds; he's calling long distance on somebody else's phone. We know he's making it up. But we remember the young stud who was good enough for Maggie May.   **C+**

Rod Stewart: *Tonight I'm Yours* (Warner Bros. '81). This is not only a comeback but a speedup—comes on like he thinks Depeche Mode is the next Vanilla Fudge. These days the "Mandolin Wind" man only sounds genuinely sensitive when his ego's threatened—on the cuckolded "How Long," not the icky-inspirational "Never Give Up on a Dream." And he's most convincing when he sounds really mad, on the cuckolded "Jealous." Original grade: B plus.   **B**

Rod Stewart: *Out of Order* (Warner Bros. '88). You know what "Produced by Rod Stewart, Andy Taylor & Bernard Edwards" means? It means he's elected to replace Robert Palmer in Power Station. And you know why Jim Cregan, David Lindley, and Lenny Pickett are on the record? Because he didn't have the guts to go all the way.   **C**

Sting: *The Dream of the Blue Turtles* (A&M '85). Not since Paul Simon's dangling conversations has a pop hero made such a beeline for the middlebrow cliché. Romantically he runs the gamut from if-you-love-somebody-set-them-free to each-man-kills-the-thing-he-loves, and of course he doesn't ignore the cosmic side of things—"There is a deeper world than this / That you don't understand." Speaking of deeper worlds we don't understand, I'm pleased by his pro-miner sentiments, but wonder why he has to (my italics) "*hope* the Russians love their children too," since I've always assumed they do. And displacing the Police's sere dynamics we have bathtubs full of demijazz, drenching this self-aggrandizing and no doubt hitbound project in a whole new dimension of phony class.   **C+**

Sting: *". . . Nothing Like the Sun"* (A&M '87). He's more relaxed this time, because he's gotten to know his band or maybe just because he's got to less to prove, but except

on the lovingly funky "We'll Be Together," no doubt a sop to the market, you're not going to catch him having fun. That would entail his getting out of himself, and from the jazzy insouciance of his Noah sendup to the aching compassion of his tribute to the mothers of the Chilean slain, the focus is always on the man singing. Pretentious, this is called, and no matter how humane your intentions it buries your subject matter in ego.   **B**

The Stone Roses: *The Stone Roses* (Silvertone '89). These Britindie pheenoms are overhyped for sure, so there's a temptation to blow them off. What do they do that the Byrds and the Buffalo Springfield weren't doing better in 1967? And that a hundred Amerindie bands don't do just as well now? But they aren't all press clips—they're postmodern English, filtering folk-rock romanticism through Joy Division and Jesus and Mary Chain hyperromanticism. Though they have their moments as songwriters—"Bye Bye Badman" always stops me, and "I Want To Be Adored" sums them up—their music is about sound, fingers lingering over the strings and so forth. And in the end they're surprisingly "eclectic." Not all that good at it, but eclectic.   **B−**

George Strait: *Strait Country* (MCA '81). This isn't so much hard country as quiet honky tonk, which I don't hold against Strait, a handsome and discerning fellow whose pleasant baritone, though not designed to swallow whole cans of corn (cf. John Anderson, Ricky Skaggs), boasts a subtle, built-in catch. But he's so unassuming I'm afraid he's destined to remain a minor pleasure—one more lonely tiller in fields left fallow by Billy Sherrill.   **B+**

George Strait: *Does Fort Worth Ever Cross Your Mind* (MCA '84). As an unreconstructed rock-and-roller, I prefer my country music out on the edge—if not zany or wild-ass then at least (and often at best: Jones, Frizzell, Wynette) deeply soulful. Despite his regard for the zany, wild-ass, and deeply soulful verities, what I get from Strait is a convincing show of honesty. And what I get from his best album and song selection to date is a convincing, tuneful show of honesty.   **B**+

George Strait: *Greatest Hits* (MCA '85). Strait isn't a phony, and that isn't faint praise. With holdout authentics like Willie Nelson and Ricky Skaggs choking on their own auras, those who still look to country for the simple things treasure the matter-of-fact commitment of the man, who could have been named by a press agent but wasn't. And in the great country tradition, the best-of reduces cliché density by a crucial quantum: no surprises, just catchier and cleverer ways of dealing with the endless contradictions of sexual fidelity. Inspirational Titles: "Let's Fall to Pieces Together" and "If You're Thinking You Want a Stranger (There's One Coming Home)."   **A**−

George Strait: *Something Special* (MCA '85). Heretofore the man in the white hat has been a little too bland to open up the honky tonks or bring off any but the most perfect extended metaphors. This time he sings with such an ache that it was five plays before I noticed that one song equated "redneck" and "hillbilly" and the next was lifted from *How To Pick Up Girls*. No such peccadilloes sully the tearjerking glory of "Haven't You Heard" or "I've Seen That Look on Me (A Thousand Times)." And thus George earns "Lefty's Gone."   **A**−

George Strait: *#7* (MCA '86). Nothing if not modest, less interpreter than pure medium, Strait lives and dies with his material. On this album "Nobody in His Right Mind Would've Left Her" passes for a witticism, and while I know it's not saying much to observe that the Western swing "White Christmas" on his brand-new *Merry Christmas Strait to You* cuts anything here, would you believe "Frosty the Snowman"?   **C**+

George Strait: *Greatest Hits Volume Two* (MCA '87). The lackluster professionalism seems like the fulfillment of his always modest gifts and ambitions, with *Something Special* a blip. Not counting "The Chair," which is on both records, there are five songs on that album that top anything besides "All My Ex's Live in Texas" on this one. "You're Something Special to Me," which is also on both records, isn't

among them. Instead it exemplifies the factory-certified hookiness of his current singles strategy, though its plain sentimentality is a little extreme—better the mild overstatement of "Ocean Front Property" or even the mild whoop-de-do of "The Fireman." No tuneouts, that's the ticket. Just blandouts.   **B**

Syd Straw: *Surprise* (Virgin '89). Fitting roots tastes to theatrical background, she connects song by song, eventually—lost dB's hit, riddle-me-rhyme, futurist nostalgia. But nowadays the smoothest singer-songwriter effort sounds mannered, and smooth this ain't: recorded in NYC, Woodstock, London, L.A., Austin, San Marcos, and Brian Eno's house with thirty-seven musicians (no horns, no strings, thirteen fairly famous guitarists), the album creaks with intelligence. Don't judge her by her claque. But don't believe her claque either.   **B**

Stray Cats: *Built for Speed* (EMI America '82). Though the soft, shuffling bottom makes up in volume what it lacks in angle of attack and Brian Setzer integrates quite an array of modernistic exotica into his pickin', the mild vocals just ain't rockabilly. You know how it is when white boys strive for authenticity—'57 V-8 my ass.   **B**−

Stray Cats: *Rant n' Rave with the Stray Cats* (EMI America '83). I love the sound of this record—it's much bigger and rawer, as if *Built for Speed*'s prettification was just to get over. Only an ideologue would deny that these unlikely pop stars tear into rockabilly readymades with twice the gusto of any purists or authentics now recording. And Brian Setzer is the snazziest guitarist to mine the style since James Burton. But he's also a preening panderer, mythologizing his rockin' '50s with all the ignorant cynicism of a punk poser. He's no singer, no actor, no master of persona. And if he can write songs he didn't bother.   **B**−

Barbra Streisand: *Guilty* (Columbia '80). Produced by Gibb-Galuten-Richardson, and Barbra Goes Disco ain't all. Somewhere in their success-addled minds Barry and Robin saw a chance to return to heart-throb ballads like "To Love Somebody" and "How Can You Mend a Broken Heart?" But after years of writing fluff—great fluff, occasionally, but fluff—they can't match that standard. Lucky for them Streisand doesn't oversing every time out, even floats some of the uptempo stuff—music of the spheres if you consider her voice a platonic ideal, polyurethane disco if you don't. But most of the time she oversings. And when she dramatizes a soap like "Life Story," the mismatch is ridiculous. **C+**

Barbra Streisand: *The Broadway Album* (Columbia '86). I had hopes for this record, honest. I certainly prefer the show tunes of her flowering to the "rock" (and schlock) of her Hollywood phase, and I enjoy discovering musical-comedy gems my normal interests would never steer me to. But unearthing gems is not Barbra's purpose. There are only three lyricists here—Ira Gershwin, Oscar Hammerstein II, and the album's real reason for being, Stephen Sondheim, who sums up his aesthetic philosophy by rewriting a song about Seurat so it applies instead to that other great artiste, la Streisand. I've enjoyed all the non-Sondheim songs in less precisely wrought versions and am also familiar with a little something called "Send in the Clowns." I admire the cattiness of "The Ladies Who Lunch." The others I'll live the rest of my life without. **C**

Joe Strummer: *Earthquake Weather* (Epic '89). A man without a context, Joe digs into Americana up to his elbows, up to bebop, up to Marvin Gaye, cramming obsessions and casual interests into songs as wordy and pointless as Ellen Foley's. Foley's absence is a relief, but with Joe emulating Gaye and Bird—crooning and murmuring instead of screaming and spitting, cramming in the syllables—not that much of a relief. New guitar sidekick Zander Schloss does what he can to make things worse. **C**

The Style Council: *Introducing the Style Council* (Polydor '83). A rather lengthy "mini-LP" continues the strange and touching saga of Paul Weller, who gave up the Jam because fronting Britain's best-loved band had turned into a superstar routine. Here he records relaxed lounge-soul tunes with a keyb-playing partner, and as with the Jam's rock tunes it's unclear to a mere Yank what the big deal is. Weller's unabashed working-class leftism is a treasure, and his charm is undeniable at any distance. But there has to be undeniable music in here somewhere as well. Doesn't there? **B**

The Style Council: *Internationalists* (Geffen '85). One reason Paul Weller's rock and roll never convinced non-Brits was his reedy voice, which he has no trouble bending to the needs of the fussy phonographic cabaret he undertook so quixotically and affectedly after retiring the Jam. I'm sure the move has cost him audience, but the new format suits the specifics of his socialism. A self-made Fabian rather than a would-be demagogue, he hopes to inspire militance with description and analysis. *My Ever Changing Moods* was so moody it flirted with incoherence, but here the politics are concealed on the surface of a fluent if not seamless Europop that goes down easy. **B+**

The Style Council: *The Singular Adventures of the Style Council* (Polydor '89). Because I thought it was my problem that I'd never listened hard after *Internationalists,* I put heavy time into these hits, if that's what they really were. And slowly it began to dawn on me that maybe Paul Weller's motives for disbanding the Jam weren't all that pure—that he knew damn well pop smoothies were taking over from guitar bands. Tuneful, sometimes memorable, and often far from stupid, this Euro-wise white funk comes from the same place musically as Culture Club and George Michael. Only it's not quite as good. **B**

Poly Styrene: *Translucence* (United Artists import '80). If the retarded tempos and professional musicians mean this isn't rock and roll, then what the fuck do you call the Shirelles? Speed and crudity aside, the pleasures here recall *Germ Free Adolescents*—nursery-rhyme melodicism and tongue-in-cheek versifying superimposed on an image of provocative, charming plasticity. And if you believe that means she's "plastic," just what exactly is your beef? Are you a hippie or something?   **A—**

The Suburbs: *In Combo* (Twin/Tone '80). I know it's endearing amateurism that makes middle America's new wave tick, but these Minnesotans think clockwork is fun—their music is glibly witty, even decelerating into a mournful country-rock triad to make a joke. Their scattershot, nasty-to-nutball humor is oblique or tongue-in-cheek enough to convey an undercurrent of empathy most of the time. And when they're comparing cows' feet to those of sheep, little empathy is required.   **A—**

The Suburbs: *Credit in Heaven* (Twin/Tone '82). A band takes a chance when they follow up an offbeat but well-received debut with a double-LP and a lyric sheet—gives strangers the chance to get to know them. My considered conclusion is that for all his presence Blaire John Chaney is rather more affected than his quota of mother wit makes altogether seemly. His arch cynicism looks gratuitous up close, as arch cynicism usually does. Talented? Mais oui. Not talented enough to fill a double album and a lyric sheet, though.   **B—**

The Sugarcubes: *Life's Too Good* (Elektra '88). Their sense of mischief isn't just playful—it's experimental and a little wicked. It's also so imperfectly realized that you have to infer it out from underneath their breathy swoops, willful shifts and starts, and translated lyrics—so imperfectly realized that most of their fans, critics included, barely notice it. Which means that on the level of attention they deserve (and get), they're either a cult band to the max or vaguely irritating pop exotics.   **B**

The Sugarcubes: *Here Today, Tomorrow Next Week!* (Elektra '89). They're as quirky as you thought they were, but no longer are their quirks strictly personal, which may help their disjointed musical effects impact on the rest of us. Björk's Freudian fantasies are subsumed in a not unfantastic adult sexuality, and she shares more of the stage with Einar, who plays madness to her empathic concern even when she's abandoning him to the encroaching ice. The end of the world interests them now that they've got a place in it: they face or face down their doom with a humor and affection that's sometimes fatalistic but never passive. In short, they're beginning to sound like a band with at least as much future as the rest of us.   **B+**

Sugarhill Gang: *8th Wonder* (Sugarhill '81). Although the Gang harmonize professionally enough to make you wonder what their gig was before they discovered talking, professional is as good as they get, and in the absence of vaguely interesting words the singing tracks are funktional dance music at best. The rap words aren't any more meaningful (this group never had better material than on its first, worst, and biggest single), but their rhythmic significance makes that irrelevant. You've heard of talking drums? Rappers are walking talking drums. Original grade: B plus.   **B**

Donna Summer: *The Wanderer* (Geffen '80). If you can't abide her unnaturalness—her plastic, opportunistic willingness to belt out any well-fabricated sentiment—then this rock move will turn your stomach. Personally, I delight in the synthetic perfection of the thing, from pop sin to schlock redemption. Here a night predator, there a card-carrying Christian, she epitomizes the fervor people invest in received emotions. She loves a good hook the way she loves her own child. And you can (still) dance to her.   **A—**

Donna Summer: *Donna Summer* (Geffen '82). Turkeys this humongous will soon go the way of the dodo, and for the same excellent reason—they defy all aerodynamic principles. Misshapen and useless despite a not-bad hit single and a not-bad Springsteen song, it's an object lesson in record-biz malfeasance from the Horatio Alger lies of "Livin' in America" to the lumpish desecration of "Lush Life," and Summer thanks God so often it's surprising she couldn't talk Him into joining Dyan Cannon, Kenny Loggins, Stevie

Wonder, and Peggy Lipton Jones in the All Star Choir that chants this Inspirational Verse from Jon Anderson and Vangelis: "Shablamidi, shablamida / Shablamidi / Shablamidi, shablamida."   **C**

Donna Summer: *She Works Hard for the Money* (Mercury '83). In which schlocky Michael Omartian replaces magic man Quincy Jones and Summer is born again. You know why? Because Omartian believes in Jesus, that's why. The result is the best Christian rock this side of T-Bone Burnett, and not just because it's suitable for Danceteria, although that helps. After all, can T-Bone claim to have introduced the concept of agape to the secular audience? Original grade: A minus.   **B+**

Donna Summer: *Cats Without Claws* (Geffen '84). The mildly compelling steady-hooks-all-in-a-row construction suggests that Michael Omartian knows his Ric Ocasek, and it will do just fine for those who get a glow just hearing her rare back and sing. But what made the last album was two undeniably singular singles. This time she leads with a cover. Which Ben E. King rared back and sang better a quarter-century ago.   **B**

Donna Summer: *Another Place and Time* (Atlantic '89). I tried to credit her comebacks, giving up only when that song about fucking Einstein cracked WBLS. But though Stock Aitken Waterman are no Einsteins, they're smart enough to know a voice when they hear one, which usually happens when they listen to other people's records—they've invented a pop machine that enables singers as adenoidal as the average British teenager to pass for Motown Mark XC after one or two treatments. Since Summer's great gift has always been her ability to emote inconsistent banalities as if her life depended on them, which after all those failed comebacks it kind of does, she lights into these retooled tunes with a phony enthusiasm that must have scared the shit out of Bananarama. Ever up, ever danceable, ever *there*, she's once again a believer, or rather "believer." And hidden over on the second side is a succinct new cliché about why women leave their men.   **B+**

Al B. Sure!:   *In Effect Mode* (Warner Bros. '88). Winner of a Sony talent contest at nineteen, he uses amateur technology to define a private dreamworld rather than a public space, and he cracked black radio almost instantly, going pop with the DIY cockiness of his rapper homeboys. This is electronic cocktail soul as thrill-a-minute mood music, and as usual the secret is rhythm—playful riffs and echoes and synthetic percussion setting off a hopelessly slight, totally supple voice.   **B+**

Billy Swan: *I'm Into Lovin' You* (Epic '81). Chagrined with Billy's tendency to cope with maturity by hitting himself over the head with violins, I almost didn't give this a chance, which would have been a shame—it's simple and gentle and steadfastly tuneful, mostly domestic with a few winsome courtship songs to prove he's a Nashville pro. Theme: "Not Far From 40." Still loves rock and roll, he says, and I know just what he means. Time: 28:26.   **B+**

Swans: *Filth* (Neutral '83). With percussion techniques borrowed from the scrap industry and a guitar bottom that lows like mechanical cattle and howls like the wind in a zombie movie, this is no wave with five years of practice, too messy for mysticism and too funny for suicide. In the great tradition of their live sets, it gets wearing, and lyrics are available to suckers on request. Not only isn't it for everybody, it isn't for hardly nobody. I think it's a hoot.   **B+**

Keith Sweat: *Make It Last Forever* (Elektra/Vintertainment '87). For credentials the next big love man proffers beats on the slow ones and lyrics whose seduction strategy is never to offend. The lyrics don't define either, which is no surprise, just the usual disappointment; the beats prove Teddy Riley New York's answer to Jam & Lewis. So the fast ones are fine. They're also outnumbered.   **B**

Sweat Band: *Sweat Band* (Uncle Jam '80). The all-instrumental intro is the P-Funk horns as the Mar-Keys introducing Otis, and since Bootsy claims this light funk as his own concept quote unquote, don't blame George if Otis never shows. Influences include Herbie Hancock, the 5th Dimension, and a mambo of unknown origin. Best moments are a second-drawer riff-tune called "We Do It All Day Long" and Bootsy's Ian Dury impression.   **C+**

Sweet: *Sweet 16: It's It's . . . Sweet's Hits* (Angram import '84). Side one is pure pop for then people, eight pieces of punchy Chapman-Chinn bubblegum from the mid-'70s glam band whose cross between T. Rex and Slade made the competition look both authentic and inefficient. Songs like "Poppa Joe" and "Wig Wam Bam" will take on the spiritual resonance of "Chewy Chewy" only if you happened to reside in Britain when they were dominating the airwaves, but give them a few spins and they'll push your fun button. Side two is more problematic, summing up as it does the period after they parted with Chapman-Chinn to write their own songs and earn their own royalties, or so they thought.   **B+**

Rachel Sweet: *Protect the Innocent* (Stiff-Columbia '80). Breasts barely budding beneath her rugby shirt on the back cover of *Fool Around,* she was a young sweet sixteen, but two years later she's no innocent—black leather jacket half unzipped, gauntleted hands over the face of her younger charge, she's seen one too many photos of Siouxsie Sioux. Only Siouxsie Sioux has a lousy voice—and Siouxsie Sioux knows what to do with it. A longtime pro if the truth be known, Sweet never quite connected as a new-wave ingenue, but there were nice tensions in the gaps. As a new-wave Linda Ronstadt—she covers Graham Parker, she covers Lou Reed, she covers the goddamn Damned—her only interesting song is one she wrote herself: "Tonight Ricky," about how they're finally going all the way. It seems like an old memory.   **C+**

Swingrass '83:   *Swingrass '83* (Antilles '83). "Progressive" folk/country/bluegrass guys and gals are always watering down Western swing that could use some

beefing up, and from there their jazzy moves go downhill to various mood enhancers and cocktails for carrot-juicers. But here supereclectic jazz bassist Buell Neidlinger mixes with fiddler Richard Greene and mandolin whiz Andy Statman, both of whom do astute work whenever they're given the chance, and together they play three of the sprightliest Ellington tunes you'll ever hear, as well as three of the drollest Monks. Drummer Peter Erskine is too heavy-handed for the gig, but at least he's a jazzman of sorts, and though tenor player Marty Krystall's solo space impinges on the mood a little, he's got the spirit too. Even Peter Ivers's slightly klutzy harmonica fits in. Left-field instrumental of the year.   **A—**

Swollen Monkeys: *Afterbirth of the Cool* (Cachalot '82). I've been a fan of the irrepressible Ralph Carney since Tin Huey, but he doesn't have a bandleader's sense of purpose. Moderately entertaining on stage with its four or five horns and almost as many clever lyrics, his polka-to-salsa "world rhythms" outfit comes perilously close to mess on record, where you can't see how unpretentious their highjinks are. If sidemen are gonna goof around, better they should be smart, nice sidemen. But not that much better.   **B—**

Sylvain Sylvain: *Sylvain Sylvain* (RCA Victor '80). "Teenage News" has been a great one ever since Syl introduced it with the Dolls. "What's That Got To Do With Rock 'n Roll?" is a pretty good one. And that's as many songs as this born sideman should ever sing in half an hour—though since he was born a sideman, it's more than he ever got before. Time: 29:57.   **C**

The System: *Sweat* (Mirage '83). Funk's answer to the Thompson Twins conflate the organic and the electronic more blatantly than Prince. If silent partner David Frank can't quite induce his computerized rhythms to grunt and moan and postsoulful Mic Murphy has the same problem with his guitars and vocals, they more than compensate by making the synthesis grab and hook. Nick Lowe Title Pun Trophy:

"You Are in My System." Original grade: A minus.   **B+**

The System: *X-Periment* (Mirage '84). Titles announce concepts with this bareboned synth-and-voice pop/funk duo. In the x-periment here, they dispense with hooks/riffs not to mention sweat. Only Depeche Mode devotees will fail to anticipate the result.   **C+**

Tabu Ley: See Rochereau, Franco & Rochereau

Jamaaladeen Tacuma: *Show Stopper* (Gramavision '83). There's more to harmolodics than funk, and Prime Time's bassist knows it. Hence the Colemanesque lyricism of a second side any old-and-new dreamer would boast about and many couldn't put together, with the master contributing the theme of an atmospheric solo showpiece and Hemphill, Dara, and Ulmer sitting in. And don't worry, side one has the funk covered—with surprising help from reed player James R. Watkins, who damn near has the master covered. **A—**

Jamaaladeen Tacuma: *Music World* (Gramavision '87). First side's my kind of new age, a kitschy travelogue laid down with local fusioneers in Tokyo, Paris, Istanbul. Second side journeys from New York to Philadelphia, and let me tell you—both "The Creator Has a Master Plan" and "One More Night" have sounded more at home elsewhere. **B**

Take Cover (Shanachie '87). The buzzy sound that has me skipping the first side is no mbira, so I assume it's a tragedy of underdevelopment—a recording lapse serious enough to annoy even a lo-fi schmo like me. Though perhaps I'd reconsider if its two best-sounding tracks weren't a folk song and a call to Christian vigilance. Side two is Zimbabwe like it oughta be, softsung popchants hooked on clear, dancing treble guitar figures, with a second guitar echoing on the beat or embellishing lightly around it. You think maybe Stevie Wonder could donate a predigital console to a bright young engineer in Harare? **B+**

Talking Heads: *Remain in Light* (Sire '80). In which David Byrne conquers his fear of music in a visionary Afrofunk synthesis—clear-eyed, detached, almost mystically optimistic. First side's a long dance-groove more sinuous than any known DOR that climaxes in the middle with the uncontorted "Crosseyed and Painless" but begins at the beginning: when Byrne shouts out that "the world moves on a woman's hips"—not exactly a new idea in rock and roll—it sounds as if he's just discovered the secret of life for himself, which he probably has. Second side celebrates a young terrorist and recalls John Cale in his spookiest pregeopolitical mode but also begins at the beginning: with "Once in a Lifetime," the greatest song Byrne will ever write. It's about the secret of life, which even a woman's hips can't encompass. **A**

Talking Heads: *The Name of This Band Is Talking Heads* (Sire '82). Live albums by essentially nonimprovisatory artists who do definitive work in the studio are always slightly extraneous, but the choice songs and prime performances compiled on this twofer (one disc 1977–79, the other 1980–81) may turn out to be definitive themselves. David Byrne seems more outgoing and somehow normal in this context, yet also more eccentric—his collection of animal cries is recommended to Van Morrison. Five years and not a misstep—think maybe they're gunning for world's greatest rock and roll band?   **A—**

Talking Heads: *Speaking in Tongues* (Sire '83). With Eno departed, the polyrhythms no longer seem so portentous—this funk is quirkily comfortable, like the Byrne-produced B-52's or the three-piece of Byrne's earlier primitivist period. Unfortunately, the polyrhythms no longer seem so meaningful, either. Though God knows there's no rock and roll rule that says playfulness can't signify all by itself, the disjoint opacity of the lyrics fails to conceal Byrne's confusion about what it all means. Yet side two lights me up nevertheless, sandwiching the purest anticapitalist song he's ever written and the purest pro-love song he's ever written around two pieces of typically ironic-optimistic futurism.   **A—**

Talking Heads: *Stop Making Sense* (Sire '84). Always skeptical of live albums, I note that this is their second in a four-year period that has netted only one studio job while establishing them as a world-class live band. Number one was a useful overview; number two is a soundtrack, albeit for the finest concert film I've ever seen, that repeats three songs from the overview and four from the studio job. Buy the video.   **B+**

Talking Heads: *Little Creatures* (Sire '85). As I assume you've figured out, this return to basics isn't exactly *Talking Heads '77*. What the relatively straight and spare approach signifies is that their expansive '80s humanism doesn't necessarily require pluralistic backup or polyrhythmic underpinnings. It affirms that compassionate grown-ups can rock and roll. The music is rich in hidden treasures the way their punk-era stuff never was, and though the lyrics aren't always crystalline, their mysteries seem more like poetry than obscurantism this time out. Anyway, most of the time their resolute happiness and honest anger are right there, and in "Stay Up Late" they come up with a baby song that surpasses "Willie and the Hand Jive" itself.   **A**

Talking Heads: *True Stories* (Sire '86). These songs were conceived for a movie, rarely an efficient way to initiate an aural experience. Yet they're real songs, not detached avant-garde atmospherics, and honest though David Byrne's sympathy may (I said may) be, they leach their vitality from traditions that demand more heart than he ordinarily coughs up. Interesting they remain. But no way the rhetorical gris-gris of "Papa Legba" or the evangelical paranoia of "Puzzlin' Evidence" or (God knows) the escapist solace of "Dream Operator" is gonna fascinate like "Crosseyed and Painless" or "Slippery People"—for one thing, Byrne lets us know what the new songs mean, which ain't much. Do they rock, you want to know? Oh yes they do.   **B**

Talking Heads: *Naked* (Sire '88). Where Paul Simon appropriated African musicians, David Byrne just hires them, for better and worse—this is T. Heads funk heavy on the horns, which aren't fussy or obtrusive because Byrne knew where to get fresh ones. What's African about it from an American perspective is that the words don't matter—it signifies sonically. The big exception is the glorious "(Nothing But) Flowers," a gibe at ecology fetishism that's very reassuring in this context. Original grade: A minus.   **B+**

Tango Argentino (Atlantic '86). Nurtured by pimps in the teeming suburbs of immigrant Buenos Aires, the tango symbolized salaciousness early in this century—just like the waltz early in the last, I know, but listen to the painstakingly authentic (which sure doesn't mean untheatrical) recreations on this original-cast album and you begin to understand how melodrama can go to the gonads. You can almost see the ebony-haired temptress snake her tongue down her partner's throat as he grinds his thigh into her pubis, both of them hating each other's guts all the while.   **A—**

Tantra: *The Double Album* (Importe/12 '81). Alternate title: *The Last Eurodisco Album*. Travelogue esoterica, Africanisms to shame Brian Eno, guitarisms to shame Earl Slick, and a chorus of Grace Jones clones singing "Don't really know what to do / I think I'll kill myself." Plus a whole side (or maybe two) of meaningless, enervating throb, the kind of stuff that makes people believe the real Grace Jones is a "peak." Graded leniently for conceptual perversity.   **B+**

The Tanzania Sound (Original Music '87). These fourteen tracks were cut mostly in neighboring Kenya circa 1960, back when the British colony of Tanganyika was turning into Julius Nyerere's socialist proving ground. Congo rumbas that sing their East African provenance in lithe Arab-tinged melodies and Kinshasa rhythms, they have the same urban-folk directness you hear on John Storm Roberts's *Africa Dances* anthology. These days Dar Es Salaam's renowned live music scene is documented only in state radio's tape library; Tanzanians have made virtually no records since the early '70s, which wasn't how Nyerere planned it when he closed off the Kenyan border. The socialist in me hopes Tanzania's pressing plant starts up soon—and also hopes the music remains as distinctive and unforced as it used to be.   **A−**

Hound Dog Taylor and the HouseRockers: *Genuine Houserocking Music* (Alligator '82). The HouseRockers were the Ramones of Chicago blues, cutting three wonderful, virtually indistinguishable albums before Taylor left this self-composed epitaph in 1975: "He couldn't play shit, but he sure made it sound good!" His secrets were cheap equipment, a slide fashioned from the leg of a kitchen table, and the most enthusiastic reliance on "Dust My Broom" since Elmore James. It's completely fitting that this all-new album should be almost as fine as the two that came out of the twenty-cuts-a-night 1971 and 1973 sessions from which it's culled, yet somehow reassuring that it doesn't quite match up: Taylor slurs too much, quite a claim in this context, and "What'd I Say" and "Kansas City" are bar-band throwaways, by which I mean that George Thorogood, Taylor's chief epigone, could do them better.   **B+**

Koko Taylor: *Queen of the Blues* (Alligator '85). This is definitive only in the sense that any good Chicago blues album is. But she does sink her chops into some exceptionally well-conceived songs on the A, and on the B she's got Albert Collins, Son Seals, and Lonnie Brooks sprucing things up guitarwise. Also, not a slow one anywhere.   **B+**

The Teardrop Explodes: *Kilimanjaro* (Mercury '80). If Bunnyman Ian McCulloch favors the schlock mysterioso Jim Morrison, Droplet Julian Cope prefers the schlock heartthrob, complete with romantic authoritarianism ("Well I don't think this is real / To criticize our love" is prime hippie bullshit, no?), "Touch Me" horns, and AM potential. No, really, "Sleeping Gas" was once a very poppy indie single, and some of this stuff would probably sound pretty neat on the, er, radio is what we used to call it I guess. But why anyone who didn't acquire an addiction that way would prefer this to Blondie or the Box Tops is beyond me. I mean, Cope is a little smarter than Jay Black or Gary Lewis, but that just makes him harder to take.   **B**

Tears for Fears: *Songs From the Big Chair* (Mercury '85). Never one to pay much mind to the plaints of English lads with synthesizers, I got duly annoyed at the surface and let it go at that. Imagine my surprise when I discerned substance underneath—uncommon command of guitar and piano, Baker Street sax, synthesizers more jagged than is deemed mete by the arbiters of dance-pop accessibility. Even found a lyric that went "We are paid by those who live by our mistakes," not bad at all. Yet in the end the surface is still annoying—not so much pretentious as portentous, promising a depth and drama English lads have been falling short on since the dawn of progressive rock.   **B**

Technotronic: *Pump Up the Jam: The Album* (SBK '89). Fitting that true house's first true smash should prove a fountainhead of formal innovation, albumizing the genre's natural configuration, the twelve-inch, with follow-ups that suggest remixes—alternate versions of Ya Kid K's unjustly maligned punk-house songtalk and the technogroove underpinning the smash. There's also a male rapper who rhymes "posse" and "bossy" (ho!). If you love the single as much as you should, the album will keep you going. And if you're in thrall to moribund aesthetics, there are other songs on it.   **A—**

Television: *The Blow Up* (ROIR cassette '82). John Piccarella and I annotated this eighty-five-minute tape because guitar heroes like Tom Verlaine and Richard Lloyd deserve a heroic live album. While the more word-heavy songs worked better in the studio, on the likes of "Foxhole," "Prove It," and "Marquee Moon," ahem, "Verlaine takes off in directions that even he probably didn't anticipate, indulging a lyrical wanderlust he never permitted himself when he had time to think about it. And Lloyd, always constrained by the necessity of getting his solos and rhythm riffs just right in the studio, goes nuts here—what he wanted to express on 'Satisfaction' was so beyond his chops that he would regularly unwind his bottom E string, twist it behind the neck, and tense the guitar like an archer's bow, producing the unearthly noises preserved for posterity on this cassette." You also get two other key covers and a definitive "Little Johnny Jewel." But the sound could have been brighter—cf. *Arrow,* the bootleg disc where I first encountered the finest of these performances. And so, as with so many ROIR cassettes (and commercial tapes in general), audio makes the difference between a laudable document and living history.   **B+**

Television's Greatest Hits (TVT '85). Ignorant of (not altogether uninterested in) television and resistant to (not dead set against) camp, I didn't think this collection of sixty-five TV-show themes would get to me, and I'm happy to report I was wrong. I mean, total immunity to such a document would be counterproductive, like total immunity to Ronald Reagan; you fight the power better if you feel it sometimes. Not that anything so grave is involved here—just corn and cuteness so concentrated they make your teeth hurt.

You get plot summaries and program music, jingle singers and cartoon characters, pseudocountry and pseudoclassical. Also great tunes (dja know Gounod wrote the Hitchcock theme?), memories you didn't know you had, memories you didn't have, and Don Pardo for continuity. Love it or leave it.   **B+**

Telex: *Looney Tunes* (Atlantic '88). These disco-mad Belgian technopoppers take off like a computer run amok. By the time they're through with the lovable "I Don't Like Music" and the ducky "Temporary Chicken," they could be the Art of Noise doing a comedy album, or Tom Tom Club on a roll—they've earned the right to call one "Spike Jones." But despite the "Frere Jacques" and "Jingle Bells" rips to follow, "Spike Jones" is as crazy as side one gets. And despite "I Want Your Brain," side two is technodisco.   **B**

The Temptations: *Reunion* (Gordy '82). Motown has put a lot into this event, with Berry, Smokey, and even Rick pitching in on new songs, but since most of the leads remain with Dennis Edwards, who led the Tempts into the nightclubs, it's possible to forget that David Ruffin and Eddie Kendricks are back. Edwards demonstrates his professionalism by not breaking into giggles during "I've Never Been to Me," but when he proclaims loyalty to the "punk funk" on James's entry, the best-sung George Clinton rip ever, I simply don't believe him.   **B—**

Ten City: *Foundation* (Atlantic '89). The Sylvester homages of house-circuit fame are attractively soulful if a mite specialized—slower than us old-timers like our dance music, especially when we're not dancing. But from the first scrapes of its pseudosynth violin vamp, "That's the Way Love Is" shouts H-I-T—a classic pain-of-love cliché, all hooks and harmonies and going to the bridge. That it never broke pop is why old-timers get mad at Paula Abdul. The follow-up is a touch slower. I'm rooting for it anyway.   **B+**

10,000 Maniacs: *Secrets of the I Ching* (Christian Burial '84). True enough, these new-wave art-folkies don't sound like anybody else, including their kissing cousins in R.E.M. Reason one is Robert Buck on "principal guitars devices," all delightful space effects and airily elliptical hooks. But reason two is Natalie Merchant and her equally airy "voice." Not only does Natalie inflect the English language as if she grew up speaking some Polynesian tongue, but she writes lyrics to match, lyrics which from the crib sheet I'd adjudge the most sophomoric poetry-of-pretension to hit pop music since lysergic acid was in flower. Random stanza: "Patrons in attendance / To disarm a common myth / Homage paid to the victor of immortality / Cloaked in bold tones." Jesus.   **B**–

10,000 Maniacs: *In My Tribe* (Elektra '87). Natalie Merchant's nasal art-folk drawl isn't altogether intolerable, and her "Peace Train" cover sets up dippier expectations than her new lyrics deserve. Signaling her professionalism by deprivatizing her metaphors, she actually says something about illiteracy, today's army, and cruelty to children. In private, however, she remains a Cat Stevens fan with a nasal art-folk drawl.   **B**–

10,000 Maniacs: *Blind Man's Zoo* (Elektra '89). Natalie Merchant has her own prosaic prosody, with off-kilter guitar accentuating its eccentric undertow. The whole second side makes politics not love, and sometimes—like when the lottery-playing mom of "Dust Bowl" rubs her fevered youngest down with rubbing alcohol—she brings you there. But somehow I knew that when she got down to cases she'd still be a fuzzy-wuzzy. This is a woman whose song about Africa (called "Hateful Hate," now there's a resonant phrase) brushes by slavery on its way to elephanticide and ends up condemning "curiosity"—again and again. No wonder she won't listen to "common sense firm arguments."   **B**–

The Textones: *Midnight Mission* (Gold Mountain '84). I've tried to work up some enthusiasm for this well-meaning, well-reviewed quintet. I've tried to hear the commitment and imagination I know it took for a woman from Texas to infuse the tiredest straight-ahead rock with politics

and personality. But except for "Clean Cut Kid"—written by the new Dylan, sounds like the old Stones—what I mostly hear is committed straight-ahead rock that's tired by formal definition.   **B**–

That Petrol Emotion: *Manic Pop Thrill* (Demon import '86). With shrieking guitar racing thumpity bass racing headlong drums to the blessed dreamy interludes, this professional Irish garage band exploits an American mode too often neglected over there—they're psychedelic punks who don't know one's supposed to preclude the other. Which doesn't mean they emulate the Count Five, or the Fleshtones either. Having absorbed and assumed twenty more years of noise, they define a sizable new piece of aural turf both conceptually and technically. And through the haze of desperate imagery you sense that their sound and fury signify.   **A**–

That Petrol Emotion: *Babble* (Mercury '87). Although I'm a known sucker for fast guitar bands, I've turned down hundreds that shall remain nameless. So why do I love these guys? Specifying comes as hard to me as their originality comes easy to them. Except in snatches I can't understand the words, which apparently only add up to snatches anyway. From the press packet I gather that their politics are no more than you'd expect from Northern Ireland, not enough to win me over. And however I shuffle perfectly applicable terms like "punk" and "pop," they just won't form a suitable pigeonhole. One thing I notice: in addition to tunes, which can't put bored music over any more, they're given to scalar guitar hooks that remind me of nothing so much as art-rock ostinatos. In theory, I hate this device. But here it's just another token of smart, untrammeled enthusiasm.   **A**–

That Petrol Emotion: *End of the Millennium Psychosis Blues* (Virgin '88). So what happened to these guys? I know, they depunkified, but just because they seem to think funk has something to do with Tower of Power is no reason to take them off the guest list. Read the lyric sheet—if anything, they've grown in wisdom. If you didn't read the lyric sheet you'd never notice. That's what happened.   **B**

That's the Way I Feel Now: A Tribute to Thelonious Monk (A&M '84). At first this ambitious two-disc multiple-artist memorial to the greatest composer of the post–World War II era left me cold—be nice if a few kids got pulled in by Joe Jackson or Todd Rundgren, but I'd been a Monk fan since the '50s. And indeed, I still prefer Monk's Monk to anybody else's, so much so that the discography here has me expanding my collection. But only Donald Fagen's synthesizers and John Zorn's weirdnesses approach the level of desecration jazzbos discern, and more often the extravagantly good-humored (NRBQ) or carnivalesque (Dr. John) or obvious (Chris Spedding) rock interpretations are instructive alongside the subtler, more reverential readings of Steve Lacy, Barry Harris, Sharon Freeman. In short, when I feel like Monk, occasionally I may play this.   **A—**

Thelonious Monster: *Next Saturday Afternoon* (Relativity '87). It's an old trick, this articulateness-in-inarticulateness, but in the words, the singing, the drumming, even the guitar (though you can tell the guitarist wants to be good real bad), this joke hardcore band that got lost on its way to college definitely has a bead on it. Start with side two, which rises from the singer as jollied-along asshole into smart and almost straight dope on Pleasant Valley teens, then quickly devolves into won't somebody come over, unhousetrained dog, demented half-audible vamp, and "Tree 'n Sven Orbit the Planet," which is an instrumental, as it damn well better be.   **B+**

Thelonious Monster: *Stormy Weather* (Relativity '89). Bob Forrest wasn't taking Monk's name in vain after all—any Orange County punk who gives it up to Lena Horne and Tracy Chapman has a healthy yen for the Aryan Nation shitlist. Best song's about the Forrests' white flight ("They said it wasn't a question of race / It's just property values"), and the relationship stuff beats Paul Westerberg's—"So What if I Did" with its John Doe guitars, the hopeless "Real Kinda Hatred." Laff at "Sammy Hagar Weekend" all you want, but Forrest feels sorry for those guys. He'll never lead a joke band

again. [CD version includes *Next Saturday Afternoon*.]   **A—**

They Might Be Giants: *They Might Be Giants* (Bar/None '86). Two catchy weirdos, eighteen songs, and the hits just keep on coming in an exuberantly annoying show of creative superabundance. Their secret is that as unmediated pop postmodernists they can be themselves stealing from anywhere, modulating without strain or personal commitment from hick to nut to nerd. Like the cross-eyed bear in the regretful but not altogether kind "Hide Away Folk Family," their "shoes are laced with irony," but that doesn't doom them to art-school cleverness or never meaning what they say. Their great subject is the information overload that lends these songs their form. They live in a world where "Everything Right Is Wrong Again" and "Youth Culture Killed My Dog."   **A**

They Might Be Giants: *Lincoln* (Restless/Bar/None '88). XTC as computer nerds rather than studio wimps—change for chord change and beat for irrelevant beat, they're actively annoying even if intelligence is all you ask of your art-pop. Except maybe on the antiboomer "Purple Toupee," side one's hooks begin and end with "Ana Ng," a beyond-perfect tour de force about a Vietnamese woman they never got to meet; until "Kiss Me, Son of God," which closes the album and could be anti-Castro if they let it, side two's are cleverness for cleverness's sake. And damned clever they are.   **B+**

3rd Bass: *The Cactus Album* (Def Jam '89). The music will have to connect like the spoken-word samples before these two get as large as they want to be. But that's not to say it's close to lame, and even without the multileveled "Spinning Wheel" loop they throw around the Beastie Boys or the cool groove of "Monte Hall," they'd be sizable on lyrics and attitude alone. Their pussy song is "The Oval Office," a metaphor so elaborate it may be the first rap inspired by John Donne, and it's not their style to forget that they're white guys moving on a militantly Afrocentric subculture. They equate white racism with leprosy, but irrelevant slanders about monkeys in the Caucasus disgust them as well—"third stage knowledge" is their program. And in case you think they take themselves too seriously, a Satchmo-voiced interlude assures them, "You got soul / Comin' out your asshole," and notes, "You're gonna work with a lot of white people think they're black." Their sexual politics are less hip, unfortunately, though dense and oblique enough to get by. Inspirational dis: "We're Professor Griff—that means we're outta here."   **A—**

38 Special: *Tour de Force* (A&M '83). The function of the catchy nothing-but-love-songs on this skillful but otherwise derivative slice of boogie is to enable Don Barnes to show the would-be hellions in his audience, all of whom have to betray their rowdy principles if they're to keep their jobs and get on with their lives, just exactly how a good old boy acts sincere. Gauge its potential usefulness in your own life accordingly.   **C+**

38 Special: *Flashback* (A&M '87). Those who claim them as a pop band in disguise get ten songs on twelve inches. Vinyl lovers who cling to the boogie band of their thwarted dreams get four live ones on a thirty-three-r.p.m. seven-inch. Those who realize they're the band Molly Hatchet only wished they could be buy something else.   **C+**

This Are Two Tone (Chrysalis '83). I recommend this knowledgeably programmed six-artist sampler as a longtime ska skeptic—although I grew to like the best albums of every band here, all of them are a bit narrow, which is one reason the style converts so smoothly to compilation. The other reason is that it was more than a style—it was a true movement, the most likable of all Britain's postpunk stabs in the dark. Only the Specials—six tracks, three from the debut—are overrepresented. And after all, it was their idea—and their label.   **A—**

David Thomas & the Pedestrians: *The Sound of the Sand and Other Songs of the Pedestrian* (Rough Trade '81). It's not

as if the last two Ubu albums didn't hint at such a consummation, but it's still a shock to hear Thomas dive like a fat swan into the art-rock he's accused of by prole ideologues. Smarter and funnier—more talented—than all but a few of the (mostly English) eccentrics who write oddly textured pancultural songs with drums but no beat about birds, shoes, hairpins, and other "simple things," he ain't winging it. But he is more eccentric than one might hope. Interesting Note (to "The New Atom Mine"): "This song does not toast The Physicist as an individual or a class. Rather, it's an expression of appreciation for the publishing of exciting information."   **B**

David Thomas and the Pedestrians: *Variations on a Theme* (Sixth International '83). David Thomas leader-member was willing to have his ideas fucked with; David Thomas solo isn't. Maybe that's because the ideas have gotten narrower; they've certainly gotten slighter. His whimsies can be charming, his jokes are often worth a chuckle, and he couldn't ask for more sensitive accompanists than Richard Thompson and Anton Fier. Maybe someday he'll write a *Peter and the Wolf* for our time.   **B**

David Thomas & the Pedestrians: *More Places Forever* (Twin/Tone '85). How about that—it's *Peter and the Wolf.* Thomas is a cabaret artist now, more at home for better or worse with arty Euroswingers like Chris Cutler and Lindsay Cooper than he ever was with roots-rockers deep down like Richard Thompson and Anton Fier. For a while there, his whimsy seemed arid and forced. Here, once again, he's palpably "Enthusiastic."   **B+**

David Thomas and the Wooden Birds: *Monster Walks the Winter Lake* (Twin/ Tone '86). David's in fine talk-show form on side one, peddling metaphysics and quoting dictionaries and wending his way through the associative title tale. The music follows along just right, and his monster postscripts are also fun. But side two is associative enough to make one wonder just how interesting one fellow's fantasy life can be.   **B**

David Thomas and the Wooden Birds: *Blame the Messenger* (Twin/Tone '87).

The nadir of Thomas's art-song mode, which reduces music to a setting for words and voice, both exceedingly eccentric for better and mostly worse, and also—ironically, as they say—encourages the autonomy of musicians who like most musicians are wise to follow orders. Even the humorous Velikovsky debunk goes nowhere, which is too bad—might teach David's fans something.   **C+**

Linda Thompson: *One Clear Moment* (Warner Bros. '85). Nothing like a busted marriage to bring out the latent feminism in a woman, and this one has a mouth on her—"Hell, High Water and Heartache" makes me wonder whether she got cheated out of some publishing on "Hard Luck Stories." So lyrics, while not always brilliant, aren't the problem. Problem's musical conception, which between producer Hugh Murphy and collaborator Betsy Cook turns this into the best Carly Simon record I've heard in a while.   **B**

Marc Anthony Thompson: *Watts and Paris* (Reprise '89). Over a jumpy synth-funk concrete that's kin to Scritti Politti and the Ambitious Lovers, a prodigy ten years past his clubland heyday and five years past his one-man debut has the world surrounded—not pinned, just surrounded. He wants to "sleep with a precedent," slips into the wrong hole, remembers Ricky Ricardo and Ezra Pound. He dreams he's Paul Simon and wakes up Bruce Springsteen: "My lips were gone my weenie shrunk / I tried to dance but I moved like a drunk." Hope we find out how he dances when he's himself.   **B+**

Richard Thompson: *Hand of Kindness* (Hannibal '83). Divested of Linda, RT stands tall as just another first-rate singer-songwriter. Near as I can tell, divides his first solo album since 1972's passing strange *Henry the Human Fly* between the four songs on side one that bid a poisoned farewell to his tear-stained wife and the four songs on side two that praise her replacement for saving his life before warning her not to toy with his affections and criticizing her dancing. Rocking in that blocky Morris-dance manner, but distinctly contemporary, these could be passing stranger. They're of such uniformly excellent quality, however, that even Warren Zevon, say, will be hard-pressed to top them in 1983. Gosh.   **A−**

Richard Thompson: *Strict Tempo!* (Carthage '83). Cut in 1981, these "traditional and modern tunes for all occasions" are strictly instrumental, with Dave Mattacks holding the tempo. They're recommended to folkies, ex-folkies, guitar adepts, and students of European song. The Duke Ellington cover excepted, I just wish they swung as much as the rest of Thompson's catalogue.   **B**

Richard Thompson: *Small Town Romance* (Hannibal '84). What can it mean that the five best cuts on this live-and-unaccompanied-in-1982 cult item are the five he's never recorded before. It means that as a singer he has real trouble carrying slow songs that were designed for Linda and/or a band, preferably both, and that his solo versions of the fast ones can't compete with a memory. Granted, his new songs are so winning cultists won't care. What this half-cultist wonders is how much he knew when he wrote the oh-so-true "Love Is Bad for Business."   **B**

Richard Thompson: *Across a Crowded Room* (Polydor '85). Moderate fame and/or extreme divorce has rendered Thompson predictable. He writes well-crafted songs about his love life, and while most of them are pretty good, only "Fire in the Engine Room" packs the old metaphorical wallop and only "You Don't Say" sneaks in the old emotional double-take. He does take leave of himself on "Walking in a Wasted Land," the generalization level of which betrays yet another pop pro who should get out more, and whose guitar isn't going to save him forever. Original grade: A minus.   **B+**

Richard Thompson: *(Guitar, Vocal)* (Carthage '85). Thompson was once the most scandalously unavailable English artist in America. Now he not only has a cult that sells compilation cassettes to fanzine subscribers, he has a cult that includes a small record company. Which in addition to compiling this not unpleasing two-record set of outtakes and live stuff keeps all his real albums in print. That's a hint. **B**

Richard Thompson: *Daring Adventures* (Polydor '86). I don't think it's the material and I hope it's not Thompson—with nuevo roots hack Mitchell Froom introducing his charge to the band and then saying go, there's no way to be sure. Somebody put those guitar breaks in an emulator right now. **B**

Richard Thompson: *Amnesia* (Capitol '88). Often impressed and rarely interested by his solo years, I sat up for "Don't Tempt Me," which opens side two in a persona-fied outburst of uproarious jealousy: "That's not a dance, that's S-E-X / Ban that couple, certificate X!" Followed by "Yankee Go Home," summing up forty-three years of Anglo-American relations in one mixed metaphor. Whereupon I could contemplate subtler innovations— lead cut with a hook, political lyric with a point. Plus the usual twisted love songs and shitload of guitar. **A—**

Richard & Linda Thompson: *Sunnyvista* (Chrysalis import '80). Back to Fairport conventions after their El Lay lies vanished into the ether, and of course it's a disgrace that an "independent" label won't let Americans hear the stomp and clang and clamor of real folk-rock—Richard's storehouse of strange licks, tunes, and styles just add to his axemanship, and Linda's acid contralto is a lead instrument. But though only the heavy-handed title satire lacks surface charm, the songwriting is thin—too many ordinary ideas aren't twisted the way his most striking phrases would have you believe. Also, are "Justice in the Streets" and its praise-Allah chorus about Teheran? Or am I just being paranoid? [Later on Carthage.] **B+**

Richard & Linda Thompson: *Shoot Out the Lights* (Hannibal '82). News of the wife's solitary return to England brings this relationship-in-crisis album home— including the husband's "bearded lady" warning in "The Wall of Death," ostensibly a synthesis of his thanatotic urge and lowlife tic. If poor Richard's merely "A Man in Need," I'm an ayatollah, but I have to give him credit—these are power-

fully double-edged metaphors for the marriage struggle, and "Did She Jump or Was She Pushed?" is as damning an answer song as Linda could wish. **A**

Thompson Twins: *Into the Gap* (Arista '84). No longer saddled with one of the most vacant art reputations in the history of hype, this decidedly unavant unfunk trio are free to pursue the airhead pop they were born to, and first try they've scored a natural: "Hold Me Now" is a classic on chord changes alone, i.e., even though Tom Bailey sings it. Nothing else here approaches its heart-tugging mastery, but the album remains lightly creditable through the title-cut chinoiserie which opens side two. After that, as Alannah Currie herself puts it, who can stop the rain? Original grade: B. **B—**

Thompson Twins: *Here's to Future Days* (Arista '85). Tired of complaining about the problems of the world (not that anyone else noticed him doing it), Tom Bailey elects to add to them instead, with an English positivity album that's a case study in the limits of catchy—I'd pay money *not* to hum these tunes. Love is great stuff, but beware of rich pop stars telling you it's all you need, especially in so many words— and in 1985. **C+**

Thompson Twins: *Greatest Mixes/The Best of Thompson Twins* (Arista '88). Their star power was so evanescent that they commemorate themselves as a dance act rather than a pop act, which is fine as far as song selection goes—this is most of what you'll want to remember before you forget. But from a pop perspective the Thompsons are why DOR turned into a dirty acronym: their tepid beats will drift anyone who isn't an acolyte of cool off the floor, and their pop is so wispy it fades before their dance mixes are over. **B**

Thompson Twins: *Big Trash* (Warner Bros. '89). No one cares, but this is their best by miles. Though their singing is as characterless as ever, at last their brains show, and when their well-named homage to Blondie and the B-52's adduces Salvador Dali, it leaves no doubt that they admire him as a charlatan, not an artist—or at least that they regard the two callings as closely related. So maybe the B-52's should hire Bailey/Currie when they need something catchy and meaningless, as they do. Deborah Harry did just that and wound up with a side-opener.   **B+**

Fonzi Thornton: *The Leader* (RCA Victor '83). As a fan of this second banana, I'd hoped he'd earn his title. Unfortunately, no quantity of returned favors from such class pop-funkers as Kashif, Ray Chew, and Nile & Bernard will do the trick for a man who not only doesn't sing as indelibly as pathfinder Luther Vandross, which is understandable, but doesn't write as indelibly either. Best Chic song: the perky "Perfect Lover."   **C+**

George Thorogood and the Destroyers: *Bad to the Bone* (EMI America '82). Thorogood has added true boogie power to his blues, so his Diddley and Hooker no longer sound like three-quarter-size juke-joint facsimiles. And in a predictable trade-off, he's added true boogie macho to his persona, so he gets his rocks off complaining about the Mann Act.   **B−**

The Three Johns: *Atom Drum Bop* (Abstract import '84). I know I have a weakness for demented three-chord rant, but so should you. Don't you wish you knew some Americans who could cop snatches of Jimmie Rodgers and the Golden Gate Singers and "Don't You Start Me Talking" and "The Night Has a Thousand Eyes" without imitating any of them? These are guys who not only consider it their mission to keep rock and roll "The Devil's Music" for as long as the world goes to hell, but who also don't want the world to go to hell. They're my favorite new Brits in years. Their album was manufactured in France.   **B+**

The Three Johns: *Brainbox (He's a Brainbox)* (Abstract import EP '85). With its DOR beat and football-disco chorale, the title track of their sixth EP since 1983 is a deceptively catchy antiyuppie rallying cry, and all three tunes on the B—especially "Crazytown," the theme song of a hundred more forgettable bands—are worth hearing twice. This is more than can be said of the B fodder on EP num-

ber five, *Death of a European,* soon to be rendered altogether extraneous by the appearance of *its* title track on their second album. Anarchism in action? Something like that.   **B+**

The Three Johns: *Crime Pays . . . Rock and Roll in the Demonocracy: The Singles '82–'86* (Abstract import '86). The Johns' maiden release, 1982's "English White Boy Engineer," exports the U.K. equivalent of Timbuk 3's nuclear science major to South Africa, where he blames the bad stuff on the Afrikaners. Great. But in general this reminds us that a single is what a cult band puts out when it doesn't have enough songs for an album. Some of it is upstanding rant, like "AWOL." Some of it, wouldn't you know, is EP-tested, like "Brainbox" and (that again?) "Death of a European." And some of it is pure B-side, like the beatbox showcase "Two Minute Ape."   **B+**

The Three Johns: *The World by Storm* (Abstract import '86). Doomy politics, detached declamations, Leeds connection—they're the Gang of Three, obviously, and if they're not as smart, so be it. No funk crossovers for them—the drums are sure to pick up pattern and accent, but their genius is for basic (and unnostalgic) rock and roll of a purity rarely heard outside punk, if indeed that's where it's located. This time the songs are there, even though the analysis isn't terribly smart either. (That ain't America, lads, it's Capital.) And, considering how much good smarts did the Go4, maybe we should be grateful it's rancor and sarcasm that make them go.   **A−**

The Three Johns: *Live in Chicago* (Last Time Round '86). Indies cater to collectors, and collectors will buy any old shit. Yet this verbatim show isn't just specialist product. The impolite patter includes a clarion call for international socialism, and the cover versions are droll if a tad conceptual—T. Rex as the Eagles, "Like a Virgin." There's half a carload of new songs from a writing machine that's already filled two LPs and two EPs since 1985. And if the remakes aren't revelations, most of them are copped from album one, which is now third in line at the checkout counter.   **B+**

The Three Johns: *The Death of Everything* (Caroline '88). Descrying the "gothic" tattoo that ID's a cartoon Jon Langford on the inner sleeve, I was reminded, invidiously, of his fondness for the Sisters of Mercy. The Johns are political jokers, hence not gothic two ways. But there isn't a track here as high-powered (or funny, or politically efficient) as "This Corrosion," and from the sound Adrian Sherwood gets out of "Never and Always," I just know Langford wishes there was.   **B**

The Three Johns: *Deathrocker Scrapbook* (ROIR cassette '88). Sloppy on principle, prolific to the point of automatism, they too have outtakes—and how. "Fun and games," maybe. "Some great fun and games," not bloody likely.   **C+**

The Three O'clock: *Sixteen Tambourines* (Frontier '83). I keep trying to find an analogy for the precious falsettos affected by this baroquely tuneful little band. But except maybe for that prepsychedelic Dreamer Freddie Garrity, none of the obvious influences—early Bee Gees, early Floyd, Strawberry Alarm Clock, Lemon Pipers—is insufferable enough. Really, fellows, the first time around this stuff might (I said might) have been fun. In 1983 it's like to make a grown man puke.   **C+**

Throwing Muses: *Throwing Muses* (4AD import '86). When friends turn psychotic, I withdraw. I haven't found black leotards sexy since I broke up with Sheila in 1962. I'm rarely persuaded that verbal dissociation reflects any social problems but the poet's own. So while I'm happy to grant the originality and even craft of Kristen Hersh's quavery free-form folk-punk, I'd do the same for the art of H.P. Lovecraft, Anaïs Nin, or Diamanda Galas. Fans of whom will pay more mind to Hersh's buzz than I do.   **C**

Throwing Muses: *House Tornado* (Sire '88). That collegians fall for this conflation of women's music and bad poetry proves how desperately both sexes yearn for anything that abrogates the male chauvinism of guitar-bass-and-drums tradition. Its virtues are all in the guitar, bass, and drums, which play off the melody line instead of mimicking or augmenting it and are only accompaniment anyway—meaningless without Kristen Hersh's personalized verbiage, meaningless with it.   **C**

Throwing Muses: *Hunkpapa* (Sire '89). Whether the more down-to-earth (hardly "pop") tunes and grooves here signal a Kristin Hersh head-change or simply create the right impression, the result's an evolution from bad poetry to obscure poetry—an improvement, definitely, but not the difference that will make the difference.   **B—**

Thunder Before Dawn—The Indestructible Beat of Soweto Volume Two (Earthworks/Virgin '88). This compelling version of mbaqanga is preeminently a music of professional rhythm sections—the legendary Makgona Tsohle Band driving Mahlathini's cuts, the guitar-organ motor behind Amaswazi Emvelo. Unlike such urban roots musics as Chicago blues or Memphis soul, it doesn't mess much with laid-back—as deep into street action as punk, its forward motion is almost frantic with joy, which may mean it's less joyful than we assume (and it pretends). It's no shock that the level of inspiration doesn't match Volume One's—how many miracles do we get in a lifetime?—but the falloff in warmth is a little disappointing. Only Jozi's "Phumani Endlini" has much pastorale in it, and only the three instrumentals cut life much slack. My favorite comes from Malombo, a "black consciousness" band who've always seemed pretentious to read about, but whose haunting understatement bears the same relationship to this nonstop anthology as Ladysmith's pop spirituality did to its vigorously secular predecessor.   **A—**

Johnny Thunders: *Too Much Junkie Business* (ROIR cassette '83). Forced to choose between this Jimmy Miller–coproduced miscellany and the French live-LP-plus-studio-EP *In Cold Blood*—not to mention PVC's French-EP-plus-bait *Diary of a Lover*—I'd dig out *So Alone* or *Live at Max's* and ponder his spent youth. The tape costs less and has more new songs than the French package, which sounds better and runs a little longer. But neither sustains for more than five minutes at a stretch. Even from JT I expect consistency some of the time. **B**

Tiffany: *Tiffany* (MCA '87). As a commercial strategy, following a merely schlocky cover of a schlock-rock classic with the better of two schlock ballads was aces—number-one singles, double-platinum LP, what more could a svengali ask? But she's got better in her. This is a fantasy about the growing pains of a wholesome California teen, flexing her sexuality slightly as she moons over that soulful Mexican boy, with two schlock classics of its own: "Should've Been Me," jealously obsessing on an ex-boyfriend's jacket, and "I Saw Him Standing There," which drags a rock and roll classic through the mud by its cheesy Prince-schlock synth riff. Beatlemaniacs who aren't even dead yet will roll over in their graves. I can't wait. **B**

Tiffany: *Hold an Old Friend's Hand* (MCA '88). Maturity doesn't become her—exchanging remakes for still more Hollywood readymades, she's hellbent for biz divahood and may well get there. But she hasn't shed that husky Valley-girl drawl quite yet. **B—**

Tanita Tikaram: *Ancient Heart* (Reprise '88). Figure on some ethereal escapist or new-age poseur and the dark, throaty contralto will bring you up short—it recalls much uglier people, like Marianne Faithfull, Leonard Cohen, Joni Mitchell. The voice retains its interest, too—which is not repaid by promising lyrics that don't benefit from a crib sheet or ingratiating tunes that deserve more help than Rod Argent can provide. **B**

'Til Tuesday: *Voices Carry* (Epic '85). In the great tradition of Kansas and Starcastle (and also, let's be real, Berlin and Scandal), these social climbers infuse a Brit idea of dubious truth value with a shot of marketable American vulgarity—not only do they roll out synth-pop hooks like vintage A Flock of Seagulls, but Aimee Mann's throaty warble sounds almost human. And while the generalization level of her aggressively banal lyrics signals product, not expression, every one lands square on a recognizable romantic cliché. **B—**

Timbuk 3: *Welcome to Timbuk 3* (I.R.S. '86). Pat Macdonald and his wife Barbara K. are outsiders who don't make a big thing of it—not weirdos, really, just observers. Like most satirists they're strongest when they get inside their targets, as with the going-places nuclear science major who sings the hit, but they're capable of a certain sidelong lyricism, and Pat's way with words stays with him even when he's indulging in invective: "Just another jerk takin pride in his work," pretty nasty. The music is basically traditional, not averse to partying r&b licks, but appropriately detached. Also appropriately, Pat and Barbara play and sing every note on the thing. **A—**

Timbuk 3: *Eden Alley* (I.R.S. '88). True folkies, the MacDonalds evolve toward lyric sincerity—or on the debut single, an obvious stiff (which doesn't mean a terrible song), straight sarcasm. Occasionally they get away clean—"A Sinful Life" tugs at my heartstrings for sure. But crooked sarcasm remains their special gift. I'm happy not to know whether they consider the disco champs of "Dance Fever" winners or losers in the end. And I wonder whether their latest foray into tape technology, "Sample the Dog," couldn't break from further out in left field than "Future's So Bright" did. **B+**

Timbuk 3: *Edge of Alliance* (I.R.S. '89). "Dirty Dirty Rice" is the single, and before you say, "Just what we need, another song about soul food," give them credit—that would be "Dirty Rice." Dirty dirty rice is a street delicacy available in the dumpster of your local Popeye's, and releasing singles about such stuff could keep them on "the B side of life" for the rest of their natural days. Since they not only cop to the prospect but can live with it—"I like my free time and I love my wife"—I predict that their songs will remain winsome and wise for as long as the record company puts them out. And that they could hit the jackpot again without trying. **B+**

The Time: *The Time* (Warner Bros. '81). The Bugs-Bunny-gets-down voice that's been a funk staple since the Ohio Players is death on ballads—cf. Slave, Rick James. These Princeoid punks are slyer—"Oh Baby" can pass as a mock seduction in the manner of "Cool," which is a mock boast, though I wouldn't be sure about "Big Stick" (mock metaphor?). And that's only side two. But it's also half the tracks, and while the others are fun, I wouldn't call them funny—especially the ballad. **B+**

The Time: *What Time Is It?* (Warner Bros. '82). "Wild and Loose" pops wilder and looser than anything they've cut, and their dogging-around jive is wilder and looser still—on "The Walk," Morris Day does an outrageous burlesque of Prince as pussy-stalking youngblood, an inside version of one of the cutesy-pie jokes the little boss plays on himself to prove he's human. The slow "Gigolos Get Lonely Too" is Princelike, too—Morris doesn't approach that patented love-man croon, but he does induce you to take a ridiculous conceit literally. And then there are three great grooves. Original grade: B **A—**

The Time: *Ice Cream Castle* (Warner Bros. '84). This is certainly the most "conceptual" of the three Morris Day showcases, but "Jungle Rock" certainly digs as deep a pocket as "Cool" or "The Walk," and the two spoken-word tracks are outrageous, weird, and waggish enough to hold up against Morris's dubious (mock?) confessional ballads on *What Time Is It?*. They may well devolve into a comedy act, but for now it's just as well that the holes in the player Day plays (is?) gape as wide as possible. **B+**

Sally Timms and the Drifting Cowgirls: *The Butcher's Boy Extended Player* (T.I.M.S. International import EP '86). The most seriously country (or maybe just the most serious) Mekon exercises her pipes and her sensibility. "Long Black Veil," a folk song that isn't a folk song, and "Dover," a Dolly Parton cover that could just as well be, are up in Gram Parsons's neck of the stratosphere. One of the Langford-Timms originals comes close. **A—**

Tin Machine: *Tin Machine* (EMI America '89). The hard-rock version of *Let's Dance:* in his corporate, iconic way, D. Bowie is sincerely trying to impress consumers. Before it's too late. Guitars range from imitation Thurston Moore to imitation Frank Marino, songs are as pissed off as a millionaire can be. But he isn't the supersponge he used to be, and as he already knew in 1983, the inescapable groove lends itself to skillful manufacture better than the righteous onslaught. **B—**

T La Rock: *Lyrical King* (Fresh '87). Without making a novelty of themselves, these three guys—not just the king, who's no special wit, but beatmaster Louie Lou and beatbox Greg Nice—are f-u-n fun. Electronic noises, vocal noises, good-natured ethnic caricatures, and a country boy with hair on his butt who keeps on and on till the record's gone. **B+**

Tom Tom Club: *Tom Tom Club* (Sire '81). Vaguely annoyed by "Wordy Rappinghood"'s arch, prolix postverbalism, I resisted this record until the "Genius of Love" signature, already the basis of two rap covers, caught up with me in a club in Queens. Now I enjoy every cut, even the one with the radio transmission, a device I ordinarily regard as the worst permutation of the worst fad of the year. Between Tina Weymouth's childish vocals and the consistently playful pulse, the best kiddie funk since *Motor-Booty Affair*. **A—**

Tom Tom Club: *Close to the Bone* (Sire '83). As a one-off, this band was a delight, with a big push from the riff of the '80s and the help of consistently sly and kooky lyrics. But in rock and roll, delight is a fragile thing, and this codification flirts with the insufferable. The simplistic tunes and singsong delivery do no service to the coy credos of freedom, equality, and happiness they accompany, and there are times when all this praise of jitney drivers and four-way hips suggests the kind of irresponsible exoticism cynics always suspect when rich white people find the meaning of life in the tropics. **C+**

Tom Tom Club: *Boom Boom Chi Boom Boom* (Sire '89). This spin-off seemed like a good idea at the time because a good idea was all it was. As a career alternative that lets them feel useful when David goes off on a tangent, it's product. The Arthur Baker–coproduced late-'88 stuff is arch, subfunctional dance music that transmutes "Wild Wild West" into "Wa Wa Dance" without the writing credit Sugarhill ceded "Genius of Love" way back when. The late-'87 is minimalist Europop, and in that it's not charmless.   **C+**

Tone-Loc: *Loc-ed After Dark* (Delicious Vinyl '89). If you suspect he's a no-talent, the reason's his lowdown instrument with groove to match—neither fits the accepted rap categories. If his boasts don't convince, the reason's his good humor—instead of blowing the genitalia off the ho or drag queen who leads him on, the sucker just grins and says hasta la vista. Payback: history's biggest rap single, and a better album than you suspect.   **B+**

Too Much Joy: *Son of Sam I Am* (Alias '88). Best thing about their debut was the title, *Green Eggs and Crack,* and even now their music is a strictly functional medium for smart-ass words. But there's melody, there's some sock, and you can hear Jay Blumenfeld's guitar ("Not lead guitar, not rhythm guitar. Just guitar."). Where formerly Tim Quirk spoke his lyrics in tune, now he mocks, expostulates, kid-drawls, projects, so that sometimes they sound smarter (and assier) than they read. And though sometimes they read fine—the scary suburban fairy tale "Connecticut," or "Kicking," which may be about cancer and is definitely about turning twenty-three—listeners may prefer "Making Fun of Bums." Or "I didn't like being Edgar Allen Poe, I was sick a lot when I was Rimbaud."   **A−**

Too Short: *Life Is . . . Too Short* (Dangerous Music '89). Musically, Oakland's finest is a throwback, his repetitive monotone trailing midtempo drum-machine beats embellished by low-tech scratches, simple bass and guitar lines, and other synthesized band noises. Not exactly uplifting, either—though he extols the hard haul that got him his Benz, he accepts "freaks" and "rock cocaine" as viable career alternatives, and in general is as matter-of-factly despairing as anyone who opposes suicide can be. Thing is, despair suits the "City of Dope," the generic urban dystopia that the hards down south half-wittingly glamorize with their fancy samples and staged defiance. And though his dirty mind is in effect, Short's not so cock-proud he'll refuse a blow job from Nancy Reagan or stop the chorus from dissing his dick.   **B+**

Toots: *Toots in Memphis* (Mango '88). From Sam or Dave or Wilson Pickett these oldies would be the latest nostalgia move, but Otis's greatest student has always been shy of the soul songbook: for him, a new batch of reggae is the past he can't escape and Stax-Hi the chance of a lifetime. Like all aging soul men, he can no longer flush out the gravel at will, but the vocalese is incorrigibly exuberant, the material ranges within the concept, and Sly & Robbie synthesize the unimaginable groove you'd expect.   **B+**

Toots and the Maytals: *Just Like That* (Mango '80). "Turn It Over" is an instrumental. So's "Turn It Up." "Chatty Chatty" is a charming throwaway. So's "Dilly Dally." "Let's Get It Together" is a message number. So's "Israel Children." "Journeyman" is about just who you'd hope, for better and worse.   **B**

Toots and the Maytals: *Toots Live* (Mango '80). Toots's spirit and improvisatory verve merit a concert LP, and for a while I thought this one might double as a best-of—I was even ready to hold my fire on the inevitable remake of "Funky Kingston" when offered the first U.S.-album version of his magnificent "5446 Was My Number." But the exigencies of crowd control induce Toots to work that bittersweet ex-con's victory cry as a shoutalong, and when something similar happens to the climactic "Time Tough" I give up. Toots's ability to exult in suffering (cf. the unfortunately omitted "Famine") may be a miracle, but loaves and fishes it ain't. So why should a multitude join in?   **B+**

Toots and the Maytals: *Reggae Greats: Toots and the Maytals* (Mango '84).

Jumping all over the place chronologically and indulging his recent crooning ventures, this still isn't the ideal Toots Hibbert record. But it'll do. Leading off with "54-46 That's My Number," as unbowed and compassionate a prison song as any in the Afro-American tradition, it includes the two *Harder They Come* standards as well as a remake of the primeval "Bam Bam" that proves he doesn't have to croon if he doesn't want to. Because he's never cultivated a deep reggae pocket, tumbling naturally into a rocksteady groove even with Sly & Robbie, the programming doesn't jar as it skips from 1969 to 1976 to 1980. And 1983's "Spiritual Healing" proves he can croon if he really wants to.   **A**—

Yomo Toro: *Funky Jibaro* (Antilles New Directions '88). Since there's more "world music" than anybody can hear, not to mention enjoy, often preferences are arbitrary. No aficionado of Spanish romanticism, I've never gotten into salsa, but I happened to go see Toro at S.O.B.'s, where I was won over by his unassuming fingerpicked mastery of the cuatro (kind of a large ten-string mandolin), as well as the unassuming cornball showmanship of his group. Maybe that's why I like his sweet mountain record better than, say, Daniel Ponce's hot city record or Naná Vasconcelos's big ethnomusicological record on the same label, or maybe it's because I've always resisted horny bands while favoring the simple charanga this vaguely recalls. A sometime salsa trumpeter I know says he likes it too—sound reminds him of Penguin Cafe Orchestra.   **B**+

Peter Tosh: *Wanted Dread and Alive* (EMI America '81). Tosh is more worldly-wise than the average reggae singer—maybe even smarter. Darryl Thompson's guitar gets rock-style solo space on several tracks here, but not rock-style aural prominence, a nice synthesis, and in general the music's subtlety is impressive. Especially if you're impressed by musical subtlety, if you know what I mean. I'm impressed by the Gwen Guthrie duet with the session-name horns pasted on. It stinks.   **B**

Peter Tosh: *Mama Africa* (EMI America '83). A surprisingly good album from a man who's been acting the fool for years, but the quality's in the groove, not the man—and in the Afrogroove rather than the reggae groove at that. Best songs: "Stop That Train," which he almost ruins with lounge-roots phrasing, and "Maga Dog," which has never sounded better. Both were written in the '60s.   **B**

Peter Tosh: *The Toughest* (Capitol '88). Who knows what got him—some combination of ganja and the screws beating him half to death just when his music took its definitive downturn in the late '70s. Anyway, by finessing his recent past—only four tracks less than seven years old—compiler Neil Spencer camouflages the sad deterioration of one Jamaican artist whose hazy alienation always had a political edge. Sly & Robbie, great Mick Jagger cameo—it's enough to make a charitable person forgive the insufferable "Mystic Man," which is of course included. **B**+

Toto: *Toto IV* (Columbia '82). Wish I could claim this millionaire Grammy-rock was totally pleasureless, but professionalism is rarely that neat. The fattest of all studio bands is almost as hooky as Shoes or the Ramones, and their production excesses at times betray verve, delight, even (though I must be mistaken) a sense of humor. But the lyrics are utterly forgettable, and the tone and spirit have nothing to do with rock and roll—unlike Thom Bell, to whom they've been rapturously compared in *Billboard,* they don't know the difference between slick and smooth, between hedonism and conspicuous consumption. At least Michael McDonald learned his shit from the real thing; Bobby Kimball and Steve Lukather learned theirs from McDonald. Still, for a band that crosses Chicago, Asia, and the Doobie Brothers, they have their glitzy moments.   **B**—

Ali Farka Toure: *Ali Farka Toure* (Mango '89). A Malian whose guitar owes onetime employer John Lee Hooker, Toure fascinates students of the Africa-blues connection, and his side-openers and foot-stomping Hook tribute are good to hear. Nevertheless, I prefer my blues with a rhythm section. I also prefer Hook. **B**

The Tourists: *Reality Effect* (Epic '80). Great band name for a bunch of style-copping eclectics if only their distance from home wasn't so offputting. Great album name for a bunch of attitude-copping pastiches if only the effect was realer. Naive believers in Annie Lennox's "great voice" are directed to the collected works of Dusty Springfield, who owns the only memorable song on this U.S. combo of two Brit releases I presume were even sorrier. **C**

Frank Tovey: *The Fad Gadget Singles* (Sire '87). A robot baritone so fascinated with bodily functions he's just lucky his native land has synthesizers and the avant-disco that goes with them—otherwise he'd have to emigrate and start scripting horror comics. Pretty committed for avant-disco, but only the phantom veins and excess scar tissue of "Collapsing New People" will make normals properly queasy. **C+**

Peter Townshend: *Empty Glass* (Atco '80). Townshend has said the only reason this isn't a Who record is that it wasn't time for a Who record, which must be his oblique way of apologizing for not being able to sing like Roger Daltrey. On his earlier solo excursions, the casually reflective mood suited his light timbre. Here he's coming to terms with love, frustration, punk, and other subjects that overtax his capacity for urgency and anger (and understanding). Who fans find the gap between aspiration and achievement touching, even thematic. Nonbelievers find it whiny. And they hate those ostinatos. **B−**

Pete Townshend: *All the Best Cowboys Have Chinese Eyes* (Atco '82). What intelligence must have gone into this album! What craft! What personal suffering! What tax-deductible business expenditure! In 1982, at 37, Townshend has somehow managed to conceive, record, and release a confessional song suite the pretentiousness of which could barely be imagined by an acid-damaged Bard drama major. That is, it's pretentious at

an unprecedented level of difficulty—you have to pay years of dues before you can twist such long words into such unlikely rhymes and images and marshal arrangements of such intricate meaninglessness. A stupendous achievement. **D+**

Translator: *Everywhere That I'm Not—A Retrospective* (Columbia '86). Always wondered why random tastefuls stuck with this ahistorical folk-rock melange, and if I don't figure it out now I never will, so here goes: wry title tune, catchy antimunitions tune, Jefferson Airplane impressions, name-brand guitars that jingle-jangle-jingle. And jingle-jangle-jingle some more. **C+**

Transvision Vamp: *Pop Art* (Uni '88). By Sigue Sigue Sputnik out of Blondie and T. Rex, and some suspect them of being—oh, the shame of it—posers; G. Cosloy claims they are as McDonald's is to a home-cooked meal. Which is what they get for wearing their inauthenticity on their sleeves in a rock and roll nation riven by identity crisis. My complaint is their inadequate command of trash—better riffs are available for hijacking. As things stand, their Holly and the Italians cover cuts not only "Revolution Baby" but "Andy Warhol's Dead." **B**

Transvision Vamp: *Velveteen* (Uni '89). Unlike the Sex Pistols, whom they resemble in so many ways, these cheesy media sluts want to Grow Musically. So they cop "Louie Louie" whole for their lead cut, and once they've scored that automatic bullseye, the shit just keeps on coming. Wendy James does love-versus-sex and tragedy-of-fame almost as good as Patti now, and with "Dust My Broom" and "Bo Diddley" ahead of her, she should create enduring art for the next two-three years or as long as her attitude holds, whichever comes first. **B+**

Traveling Wilburys: *Volume One* (Wilbury '88). The clumsy conceit—has-been supersession masquerading as family road band—produces more or less the mishmash you'd expect. Roy Orbison and Bob Dylan have never sung like brothers to anyone, much less each other, leaving Tom

Petty's chameleon, Jeff Lynne's teddy boy, and George Harrison's dork to blend as best they can. Harrison's the only lead guitarist; Lynne plays not piano or Hammond B-3 but a marooned synthesizer; Orbison and Harrison take solo turns on songs that belong on their own albums. Yet from Harrison's "Margarita" hook to the ridiculous ride-your-automobile metaphors of "Dirty World," this is the fun get-together it's billed as—somebody was letting his hair down, that's for sure. My bet is Dylan, who dominates half the tracks and is the only man here capable of writing a clever lyric on call. Maybe he's a genius after all. Original grade: B plus.   **A—**

Randy Travis: *Storms of Life* (Warner Bros. '86). With his rotogravure cover and spare instrumentation, Nashville's hot new thing cultivates an aura of neo-traditionalist quality, as is the fashion these days. Fortunately, the quality at least is real. He sounds like an unspoiled John Anderson singing the material of a lucky George Strait. The two hits are the two side-openers are the two best, and neither could have been written by anybody who didn't work nine-to-five thinking up puns and angles.   **B+**

Randy Travis: *Always and Forever* (Warner Bros. '87). Nashville's latest sure-shot is exactly as strong as his material. How this distinguishes him from Tammy Wynette or Carl Smith I don't get.   **B**

Randy Travis: *Old 8×10* (Warner Bros. '88). One of the two duds counts "at least a million love songs / That people love to sing," so now these are at least a million and eight, and like the man says, they're all a piece even though themes and titles vary. This being country, he means love as in relationship—only "Honky Tonk Moon" is flushed with romance. Sometimes he's steadfast, usually he fucks up, always he sings like the neotrad master he's content to be. Original grade: B plus.   **A—**

Randy Travis: *No Holdin' Back* (Warner Bros. '89). Travis doesn't get lucky on this one, which is dragged like most country albums by its quota of ordinary—"Singing the Blues" should be ceded permanently to Guy Mitchell. But after kicking off with a Richard Perry–produced "It's Just a Mat-

ter of Time" that apes and aces Brook Benton's original, side two reminds us why Travis is currently the genre's ranking pro—the tunes and turns just keep on coming.   **B+**

Tribute to Steve Goodman (Red Pajamas '85). Although his friends and coreligionists associate Goodman with all the songs on this live double wake, we don't, which is why it isn't much like the posthumous two-LP summation I still expect from him. But as an unsanctimonious evocation of why Goodman was such a catalyst in folkiedom, it's got more than its share of songs and picking and jokes (and bathos and missed opportunities).   **B+**

Trio: *Trio and Error* (Mercury '83). Though their wit is rather dry, it doesn't lack warmth or fun, and their idiot melodies have real charm. But if the joke is economy of means, do they ever tell it deadpan: more than any rock-and-roller, *der Sänger*'s middle-aged monotone recalls Leonard Cohen. Jokes this subtle have to hit dead on if they're to be enjoyable at all.   **B+**

Tripod Jimmie: *Long Walk Off a Short Pier* (Do Speak '82). Those who mourn the industrial-strength Pere Ubu find understandable solace in this harsh, hard-driving one-off featuring former Ubu guitarist Tom Herman. But it gets across mainly on its rough-cut spirit, and it could use a convincing front man, something the simpiest Ubu has never lacked.   **B—**

Trotsky Icepick: *Poison Summer* (Old Scratch '86). Not a hardcore band (name's too educated) or an art band either (too politically charged). A pop band if anything, firming up a lyricism that wouldn't have sounded out of place at the Fillmore in 1967 with compact structures, foreshortened solos, and a drummer from the (metaphorical) East Bay. A pop band that regards acts of sectarian vengeance as emblematic, an inescapable environment if not topic.   **B+**

Trotsky Icepick: *Baby* (SST '88). Thanks be to Kjehl Johansen's riffbook and Vitus Matare's cool-to-be-kind sarcasm, they're catchier than "Don't Buy It" 's "Don't buy anything rancid / Don't buy gifts for Christmas / Don't buy what plays on the radio" or "Bury Manilow" 's "I love all the latest popsongs / Those hooks really mess my mind" suggest they want to be. Evoke their real-life needs and anxieties quite cunningly, in fact. And are at their most interesting (and catchiest) dissing consumerism and Barry Manilow. **B+**

Trotsky Icepick: *El Kabong* (SST '89). In which a noisy rather than grungy garage band works to resolve its attraction-repulsion to pop—in the direction of something like ugly pop, maybe they think. They probably also think it's better, and technically they're right. But as their intentions and ideas become clearer, one realizes that it was unresolved attraction-repulsion as much as their surprising pop gifts that rescued them from the garage. **B−**

Trouble Funk: *Drop the Bomb* (Sugarhill '82). Title track's the baddest antinuke music yet, not least because it'll offend the pious even before the rhythms put them out of joint—which is not to suggest that "Let's Get Hot" is Trouble Funk's version of the nuclear freeze, although in a way it is. Actually, "Drop the Bomb," "Hey Fellas" (which—oh that direct, unironic street culture—uses "backstabbers" as a compliment), and the primal "Pump Me Up" are all hotter (or maybe cooler) than the overarranged "Let's Get Hot"—which is to suggest that when it's pumping, this rapid Chocolate City street funk is the death. **A−**

Trouble Funk: *In Times of Trouble* (D.E.T.T. '83). MacCarey's timbales and Dyke Reed's synths give these loyal D.C. homeboys more instrumental distinction than most of their major-label competition, but on the studio half of this double-LP you'd almost forget what sharp rappers they can be. The crowd on the live disc reminds you. **B+**

Trouble Funk: *Saturday Night Live! From Washington D.C.* (Island '85). The better half of D.E.T.T.'s *In Times of Trouble* kicks it live, as the saying goes—though 4th & B'way's "Still Smokin' " twelve-inch is even kickinger, and also more current, if

that concept meshes with the go-go ideal of eternal recurrence. **B+**

Trouble Funk: *Trouble Over Here/Trouble Over There* (Island '87). Rather than solving this party band's problems, lead and background vocals from guest producers Kurtis Blow and Bootsy Collins underline it—ain't a one of the four vocalist-percussionist-keybist/bassists up front who's trouble enough. **B**

True Sounds of Liberty: *Beneath the Shadows* (Alternative Tentacles '82). Musically and verbally, TSOL stand between the high-school protest of L.A. neopunk and the collegiate lyricism of L.A. neopsychedelia. Wordwise this is half a disaster—their colors running into the sand are even less interesting than Black Flag's antiauthoritarian rant or the Dream Syndicate's postnarcissistic angst. It's only because of the lyric sheet that you notice, though—Jack Delauge yawps out catchphrases as passable as anybody's and pretty much garbles the rest. And while the musical synthesis isn't as formally sophisticated as that of the more fashionable new American sound bands, it's more direct, so robust and determined it blows all suspicions of nostalgia away. Original grade: B plus. **B**

True West: *True West* (Bring Out Your Dead EP '83). The roughest, toughest band of the West Coast psychedelic whozis sound like caffeine is their drug of choice (or maybe speed) (and/or alcohol). On "I'm Not Here," with Frank French's diddleybeats exploding as big as Russ Tolman's guitar, the chaos approaches hardcore intensity with nothing left to speed. Even at their most songful—that's right, songful—the shit's pretty loud. Songful about what, you wonder. Displacement, more or less. And playing so loud you don't care. Original grade: B plus. **A−**

True West: *Drifters* (PVC '84). They're still loud, they're still songful, but the balance is now so cautious that their elegiac, hard-driving Television-goes-country-rock wins this month's *Trouser Press* Memorial What-Does-It-All-Mean Award for Formalism, an eye-catching statuette of gilded virgin vinyl that looks kind of like an ear and kind of like a question mark. Blame it on the new drummer if you want. My guess is attrition, a/k/a maturity.   **B**

Tru Fax and the Insaniacs: *Mental Decay* (Wasp '82). So many indie LPs are as useless as the slimiest megacorp product that this near-miss from D.C. is worth remembering. Diana Quinn's fey feminism and David Wells's broken buzzsaw ride the flat garage rhythms as far as they'll go, which means their half-absurdist ditties work best when they're purely satirical: "Up in the Air" is the funniest (and archest) anti-Reagan song to date and "Washington" hits suburbia where it lives (for once).   **B**

Bibi Den's Tshibaya: *"The Best" Ambiance* (Rounder '84). From Africa via la France, another four-cut disco ("soukous") album from the authenticity-mongers in Somerville. Because it's disco, it's more useful than most authenticity; because it's authentic, it's more engaging than most disco. Next.   **B**

T.S. Monk: *House of Music* (Mirage '80). Sandy Linzer's Chic move in the sense that Odyssey was his Dr. Buzzard move, with Thelonious Jr. playing drums and sister Boo Boo singing. But the world-historic irresistibility of the band's counterpart to the urbane "Native New Yorker"—the c'est-si "Bon Bon Vie," a rich song about aspiring to the rich life that's ebullient on top and this far from desperation underneath—inheres as much in Thelonious Jr.'s unslick, high-humored vocal and explosive percussion as in an arrangement that keeps revealing new pleasures. Maybe next time Linzer will produce a follow-up. This time you might consider purchasing a single worth the price of an LP.   **B–**

Ernest Tubb: *Live, 1965* (Rhino cassette/CD '89). You may never love his amazingly resonant baritone—he *always* sings flat, and by his own admission can't hold a note for longer than a beat. After nearly fifty years on the road, though, his two "live" albums were applause-added phonies, so this posthumous find is something new. Cut by an engineer friend when Tubb was fifty-one (not so bad when you consider that he rerecorded his compilations for stereo and full rhythm section in his midforties), it documents a show that evolved but never really changed—unhurried, genial, skipping from Tubb standards to chart fare to honky-tonk classics to band features to climax with his first and greatest hit, "Walkin' the Floor Over You." Reliable, reassuring, the man who invented honky-tonk belies truisms about how great pop music is always passionate or urgent or necessary. And sounds weird as hell.   **A–**

The Tubes: *Outside Inside* (Capitol '83). Encouraged by "a black friend" (Uncle Remus?) to "let this r&b music out," these soulful California cats did their professional best to simulate a Journey album. Well, all right, not quite—Journey's never sublimated misogyny into a hit single about sex emporiums, nor induced Maurice White to advocate cunt-lapping, nor essayed a Captain Beefheart imitation, nor risked an all-percussion extravaganza "inspired by Sandy Nelson," nor closed off with an ambiguous comment from a black friend that I hope will make Tubes fans wonder who's got the inside track in any racial crossover.   **C+**

Moe Tucker: *Moejadkatebarry* (50 Skadillion Watts EP '87). EPs are still supposed to showcase emerging bands, but many of the best are true ends in themselves if not totally sui generis, like this impossible answer record, which proves who was the body and maybe soul although not brains of the Velvet Underground. With forever-young Jad Fair playing front man, they run through three joyous VU obscurities, a Jimmy Reed blues, and a throwaway instrumental just the way the original guys might have if jaded hadn't been their thing. What does it answer? Not *VU*, I guess—*VU*'s too alive. But definitely *Another View*—any VU that sounds like a last gasp. Original grade: A minus.   **B+**

Moe Tucker: *Life in Exile After Abdication* (50 Skadillion Watts '89). The illusion of commercial potential that induced the Velvets to tighten up without squelching their experimental impulses can't be sustained by any Moe smart enough to have come this far, and so, encouraged by her loony Half Japanese bandmates, she wastes valuable minutes fucking around. Songs meander, her third "Bo Diddley" in three albums still doesn't get it, the endless instrumental is Sonic Youth in runny jam mode. But except for the jam, it's all nice enough—Tucker's modest middle-aged housewife is an innovation in much the way her drumming once was. And "Work," "Spam Again," and "Hey Mersh!" are Amerindie knockouts, lived postpunk takes on the grind and release of lower-middle class adulthood, a subject rock-and-rollers usually leave to Nashville company men. Somebody try and make a hit out of this woman.   **B+**

Tina Turner: *Private Dancer* (Capitol '84). Her voice was shot even before she split with Ike, ten years ago now, and videotaped evidence belied the dazzled reports that filtered in from the faithful when she began her comeback, two and a half years ago now. Less than converted by her reverent reading of the Reverend Green's "Let's Stay Together," I noted cynically that the album lists four different production teams, always a sign of desperation. Which makes its seamless authority all the more impressive. The auteur is Tina, who's learned to sing around and through the cracks rather than shrieking helplessly over them, and who's just sophisticated (or unsophisticated) enough to take the middlebrow angst of contemporary professional songwriting literally. Also personally—check out how she adapts the printed lyrics of Paul Brady's "Steel Claw" to her own spoken idiom. Original grade: B plus.   **A−**

Tina Turner: *Break Every Rule* (Capitol '86). Charges that Tina has betrayed her precious heritage come twenty years too late—not since she and Ike reeled off five straight r&b top-tens between 1960 and 1962 has she pursued the black audience with any notable passion. Her benefactors of the late '60s were Phil Spector, Bob Krasnow, the Rolling Stones, and the Las Vegas International Hotel, where she and Ike were fixtures at the time of Elvis's comeback; their big numbers of the early '70s were the totemic rock anthems "Come Together" and "Proud Mary." That she should now realize the pop fabrications of white svengalis is just a couple more steps down the same appointed path, and she's damned good at it, even an innovator—*Private Dancer* remains the archetypal all-singles all-hits multiproducer crossover, and Whitney Houston should be so soulful. Unfortunately, the follow-up musters no archetypal crossover singles, and no totemic rock anthems either (Bryan Adams induces her to go metal, which is more than Bowie or Knopfler can claim). Fortunately, ranking svengali Terry Britten gets his own state-of-the-pop-art side. If he and Tina can't convince you that rich people have feelings too, you're some kind of bigot for sure.   **B+**

Tina Turner: *Tina Live in Europe* (Capitol '88). Almost two hours of double-LP, with an extra half of covers on cassette and CD, and not as pointless as you think. It's interesting to hear songs originally crafted for sixty-four-track crossover streamlined or steamrollered by the gruffly inexorable forward motion of a crack road show, and sometimes—a "Break Every Rule" with that live elle-sait-quoi followed by a sharply funky "I Can't Stand the Rain," or most of side three, from Pickett parlay to Cray and Clapton cameos to the inevitable "Proud Mary"—there are transformations or revelations. Then there's the Bryan Adams cameo. And before that there are the David Bowie cameos—two of the ugly things.   **B**

Tina Turner: *Foreign Affair* (Capitol '89). Crossing Josephine Baker and Grace Jones in a magisterially self-possessed style of "blackness," Tina's a full-fledged superstar in Europe. In the U.S. she's more like Ray Charles or Tony Bennett—her iconic clout is heaviest when she's selling products other than her own expertly sultry recordings. And since chances are Plymouths make her just as hot as romantic sensuality, maybe this is as it should be.   **B−**

The Twinkle Brothers: *Country Men* (Virgin Front Line import '80). They're ten-year pros from Jamaica's north coast—rather than Kingston, hence the title—whose hotel gigs have taught them the ins and outs of soul (and doowop?), and though this isn't as upbeat as their signature "Rasta P'on Top," it shows a range no competing harmony group approaches. Jahwise lyrics and plangent tunes are overfamiliar. Dub-tinged arrangements and deep, intimate vocal interplay have the spirit.   **B+**

The 2 Live Crew: *As Nasty as They Wanna Be* (Skyywalker '89). The ACLU may not want it advertised, but this record is pornographic; that's one of the few good things about it. Hooked by two Hispanic/ Asian working girls uttering rhythmic fuckwords, the number-one rap single "Me So Horny" packs the gross eroticism of a good hardcore loop. The rest is just gross. Romance isn't an issue; liking women isn't even an issue. Thus there are few distracting rationalizations about how this or that bitch did them wrong—these Miami knuckleheads are just normal red-blooded American misogynists. They like it "rough and painful"; they tell men how to "give her more than she wants"; they never touch a woman anywhere but between her legs. And since their raw samples rarely generate the heat of the single, in the long run they're almost as unlikely to inspire good sex as a sermon by Daniel Wildmon. They don't belong in jail. But remember John Holmes: he who lives by the dick shall die by the dick.   **C**

Two Nice Girls: *2 Nice Girls* (Rough Trade '89). With Nice Girl number three helping them do the Roches, their hook is "Sweet Jane" with a Joan Armatrading tag, tart and pretty enough to show up the Cowboy Junkies' suicidal tendencies. Ex– Meat Joy Gretchen Phillips's salty attitude permeates the discreetly physical lesbian love song "Goons" and the regretfully rowdy lesbian love anthem "I Spent My Last $10.00 (On Birth Control and Beer)." Laurie Freelove counts Cat Stevens among her influences.   **B**

UB40: *Signing Off* (Graduate import '80). Eight black-and-whites from Birmingham who named themselves after the dole card they know so well, they don't play no ska—they're songsmiths in a deep reggae groove. Like good reggaeheads (and unlike punk/mod ska speeders), they take their time instead of pressing on to the next one, and more than one instrumental outwears its welcome. But when they're singing "Tyler pleads guilty" or "King where are your people now?" or "I'm a British subject and I'm proud of it" or—guess who—"Madame Medusa," patience is rewarded. **B+**

UB40: *Present Arms* (DEP International import '81). They're not about to revolutionize JA—not by carpentering the bass lines, horn charts, and dub effects of the reggae of yesteryear (1975, say) into an indigenous pop r&b. And though they have their own DIY label, they're not about to revolutionize their native U.K. either. But their conscience is catching—I know, because I fell for "One in Ten" on Radio Luxembourg despite my objections to its merely liberal message. Their toasting is pretty infectious too. And they relegate the instrumentals to a bonus twelve-inch. Still, I doubt they'll break the DOR barrier here—what passes for mild protest in England these days might sound dangerous Stateside. It might even *be* dangerous. Original grade: A. **A—**

UB40: *The Singles Album* (DEP International import '82). As satisfying as their albums are once you surrender to their steady state, certain characteristic devices—the sax obbligatos, the calm ache of Ali Campbell's vocals—do eventually cry out for some kind of change. Hits are designed to meet the need for some kind of change, and since unlike so many Brit bands this one isn't above putting hits on LPs, their compilation is a best-of in the American sense. I miss "Madame Medusa," I miss "Sardonicus." But the Randy Newman cover is here, and "King" and "Tyler." The other albums won't disappoint. But this is a worthy consumer service. **A—**

UB40: *1980–1983* (A&M '83). Only Bunny Wailer's inventions have anything on the deep consistency of this integrated English world-class reggae. And if Ali Campbell's sufferating vocal leads are tamer than the outcries of such rootsmen as Winston Rodney and Keith Porter, they certainly don't lack for soul or expressive reach, except perhaps on the upful side, where the fast-talking Astro comes to the rescue before any serious tedium is done. Repeating only three tunes from their U.K. best-of, eschewing long-winded dub, this overdue U.S.-debut compilation is where to get hooked. **A—**

UB40: *Labour of Love* (A&M '83). Slightly annoyed at Ali Campbell's low pain threshold, I was about to dismiss these classic covers as a reggae *Pin Ups* when I noticed Astro's toasts and the U-Threes' backups saving the two *Harder*

They Come remakes. A week or two thereafter it hit me once again that reggae tunes can take a long, long time to hook in. And by then, guess who I was suffering along with.   **A—**

UB40: *Geffery Morgan* (A&M '84). Seemed dull even for reggae first time through, and even for the soulfully monochromatic Ali Campbell well after that. I persevered only because an Afrosax instrumental kept taking me by surprise. Then the lilting "Seasons" won my heart. And then—presto!, or at least lento . . . —I was focusing in on almost every cut, and admiring the jumpy depth of the production throughout. Could be their strongest ever, I swear. Still, there's reason to worry about how long the first impression will last.   **A—**

UB40: *Little Baggariddim* (A&M EP '85). The speeded-up "One in Ten" is just like "I Got You Babe" with Chrissie Hynde as Cher—an unabashed and possibly unprincipled bid for the red wine audience from reggae men who've always been political by choice rather than racial destiny. And the statistical metaphor it draws does seem a little less grim now. But good politics are rarely grim, and though I've loved "One in Ten" since the first time I heard it, this is the version I'll put on, if only because Chrissie makes such a soulful Cher. Also, two of the five tracks are toasts, which seems about the right proportion to me.   **A—**

UB40: *Rat in the Kitchen* (A&M '86). One way you know they're a real reggae band is that you always think they've run out of songs until you play the album one last time. But they're a pop band, too—you don't perfect such seamless effects on a reggae budget. It would be puritanical to refuse the salves and ointments of this kind of intelligent political product. But it would be utopian to claim it cures anybody's ills.   **B+**

UB40: *UB40 CCCP—Live in Moscow* (A&M '87). To the usual concert-album flaws of redundancy (*Labour of Love* and *Rat in the Kitchen* revisited) and speedup (what do Russians know of deep grooves?), UB40 adds a presumably well-intentioned attempt to cram an hour of music onto one vinyl disc. As a result, the

vocals are even hollower and duller than you'd expect—on vinyl. The CD, wouldn't you know, is markedly richer and clearer. But for sheer audio I still prefer *Little Baggariddim.*   **B**

UB40: *UB40* (A&M '88). This is such an uncommonly steadfast band—the same eight musicians pursuing the same reggae-protest since 1978—that I'm willing to believe the love songs signify a break not in dedication but in "macho bravado," as they claim. And as usual, everything hooks in after a long eventually. What'll get to you eventually is a neoclassic instrumental, a Chrissie Hynde oldie duet, and one of the protest numbers.   **B+**

UB40: *Labour of Love II* (Virgin '89). The differences are subtle, like everything with this band—rather then being dashed, your high hopes for the sequel succumb to a lingering illness. The beat glides a little too much, the synth washes a little too much, Ali Campbell sings the prize covers a little less and runs them through his voice a little more. And maybe, just maybe, the covers themselves aren't quite as prize.   **B**

Tracey Ullman: *You Broke My Heart in 17 Places* (MCA '84). Unlike most of her cocharting cofemales, Ullman has undertaken a conscious genre exercise—she plays girl-group tradition for naive if not dumb passivity. The songs new and old are tuneful and right, the production exquisitely not-quite-schlocky, but just compare her "Bobby's Girl" to Marcie Blaine's original—Ullman sings with too much force and skill to make the conceit convincing. On the other hand, it's probably her musical conscience that saves the project from unmitigated "ironic" condescension. "They Don't Know" did hit at face value, after all.   **B+**

James Blood Ulmer: *Are You Glad To Be in America* (Artists House '81). After a year of fix-it-in-the-mix, the gutsier audio of this long-awaited U.S. version just doesn't transform the harmolodic guitarmaster's Rough Trade debut into a sow's ear. It's still too stiff, too composed, too contained, not (primarily) because the sound is too thin, but because at a mean

4:20 the tracks are too damn short. The compositions are so brilliant they never relax or rock out, and Olu Dara and Oliver Lake get in David Murray's way. Hemmed in by crossfire, the sextet never finds room to wail with the ecstatic power of the classic Tin Palace quartet, which always did justice to what Ulmer loves about his three favorite local rock bands—not just the arrant Colemanism of the Contortions, but the the surprising harsh angularity of the Voidoids and the climactic dynamics of the Feelies. Though they implode with more brains and soul than any fusion mucksters, they never bust loose. Which is half the concept, right?.   **B+**

James Blood Ulmer: *Free Lancing* (Columbia '81). Ulmer's conception is so audacious, so singular, that he can't cut a bad record—his most pro forma moments would make you sit up and notice ordinary jazz-rock. But despite his uncanny one-take double-track drone and the polyrhythmic facility of Amin Ali and Calvin Weston, I find the trio format thin here, and the three lyrics are trivial compared to "Are You Glad To Be in America?" and "Jazz Is the Teacher." Recommended to unbelievers and George Clinton: the hard, horny funk of "High Time." Original grade: A minus.   **B+**

James Blood Ulmer: *Black Rock* (Columbia '82). You can tell this Next Hendrix stuff is getting serious when Ulmer, always more an improviser/composer than a singer/songwriter, makes like a romantic heavy and musical philosophizer. Yet despite his grizzled visage and mouthful of marbles, he's getting away with it. As with Hendrix, his singing and thinking both seem crude at first, as do the simplified bottom of Calvin Weston and Amin Ali. But in the end the force of the conception, and of the sound itself, turn all doubts around. Ulmer's pixilated leads are more nerve-wracking than Jimi's wail, and I still await the transcendent synthesis his earliest jazz-funk gigs promised. But this is my idea of Raw Power 82.   **A—**

James Blood Ulmer: *Odyssey* (Columbia '83). I always figured great Blood would sound like the climactic "Swing and Things"—pure virtuosic rave-up, Mahavishnu with soul and ideas. But of course, great Blood ended up sounding like nothing I could have predicted. With a new band comprising drummer Warren Benbow and violinist Charles Burnham—that's right, funk fans, no bass, though with Ulmer's strong fingers you can't always tell—he's created an ur-American synthesis that takes in jazz, rock, Delta blues (suddenly his mush-mouthed vocals kick home, especially on the heart-torn "Please Tell Her"), and even country music (though Burnham's fiddle also has a Middle Eastern effect). I don't mean he goes from one to the other, either—most of the time, you'd be hard-pressed to pin just one style on any of this painfully beautiful stuff. Great Blood, that's all.   **A**

James Blood Ulmer: *Part Time* (Rough Trade import '84). Cut at Montreux around the time of *Odyssey*, Ulmer's strongest LP, this repeats four titles and is close to his weakest. The live recording dulls his sonic concept, with only "Swings and Things," compacted into 3:27, providing compensation. Which isn't to say he doesn't still outrock Pat Metheny, or that "Encore," the most striking of the three new tunes, shouldn't get an encore. **B+**

James Blood Ulmer: *Live at the Caravan of Dreams* (Caravan of Dreams '86). Decked out like a rent-a-pasha on the colorized cover, bellowing/muttering lyrics he might as well be making up on the spot ("Gonna get me a cow and dick around"?—nah, can't be), Blood's too wild and woolly for his own good here. But if wild and woolly is the price of live and well, his admirers should be happy to pay up.   **B+**

James Blood Ulmer: *America—Do You Remember the Love?* (Blue Note '87). One danger of putting Bill Laswell in the studio with the likes of Blood is his respect for the avant-garde. From Nona Hendryx or Motorhead or even Sly and Robbie he'll brook no bullshit, but give him a committed innovator and he can turn into a humble servant of the muse, as in his worthy, inconsequential Celluloid LPs for Daniel Ponce, Billy Bang, etc. From Sonny Sharrock he got a definitive record that way; from Blood he gets a dud. The digital neatness may be Blue Note's fault, and the schematic instrumentals typify Laswell's compulsion to contain chaos. But the thinness of the guitar itself sounds like Blood's misplaced idea of a Wes Montgomery move. And I guarantee you Laswell didn't think any of the three vocal tracks were radio fare, no matter who he hired to sing backup.   **B**—

James Blood Ulmer: See also Music Revelation Ensemble

Ultravox: *Vienna* (Chrysalis '80). First they wanted to be machines, now they want to have roots—it's new, it's different. "A European legacy, a culture for today," sings former Rich Kid Midge Ure through a signifying synthesizer, and he's not being ironic—new Europeans may be jaded, but they avoid irony except in totally frivolous contexts. So they buy electronic instruments, rendezvous in Köln with Conny Plank, and manufacture dance music for the locked pelvis. One strange thing, though—sounds like "Western Promise" should be called "Algiers."   **C**

Ultravox: *Quartet* (Chrysalis '82). Art-school posers, working-class climbers, 'umble tunesmiths, or whatever—in a world where the eternal artistic truths of pop and disco are probably known to Maggie Thatcher herself by now, Midge Ure and associates can't hide behind catchy synthbeats. Ure sings from the top of his larynx like some sixth-form opera parody and acts as if humorless clichés gain demotic significance when you string them together, as in: "Give me an inch and I'll make the best of it." Take that as a warning.   **C**

The Undertones: *Hypnotized* (Sire '80). From the opening chorus—"Here's more songs about chocolate and girls / It's not so easy knowing they'll be heard"—the good-kids-of-the-year are as honest as power pop (remember power pop?) ever gets. They're also as powerful, which I bet has something to do with why they're so honest. The improved melodies have something to do with why it's not so easy any more.   **A**—

The Undertones: *Positive Touch* (Harvest '81). "Here's more songs about chocolate and girls / It's not so easy knowing they'll be heard"? No, that was last time.

Here's still more, and it's even harder—not being sure whether they'll be heard or not (at least in the land across the sea) is worst of all. Nevertheless, the boys are equal to the task—just about every one of the fourteen is catchy and felt. Almost inevitably, though, the arrangements are a little fancier, to no special avail, and the same goes for the subjects. Good luck, lads.   **B**+

The Unknowns: *Dream Sequence* (Sire EP '81). Near the top of the post–power pops, nasty and catchy instead of cute and same, is a Georgia-rooted L.A. quartet led by a guy who wields a mean-looking cane and suffers mean-looking tics, both of which he seems to need. Former Rachel Sweet svengali Liam Sternberg recommended the offbeats and echoed guitar that twist these loose-limbed tunes so neatly. Start with side two, which starts with "Suzzanne."   **B**+

The Urbations: *Urban Dance Party* (Metro-America cassette '82). "Goin' to Alpena, Cement Capital of the World," begins the twelve-bar blues that begins this tape, and I wish I could tell you it ever got that good again. Andy Boller and Mr. Dr. Blurt Sandblaster do enjoy their laughs—listen to the roller-rink organ Boller lays beneath the horny "I Need a Job"—but they don't write or sing with the difference that can raise neoclassicist white r&b to the level of necessity.   **B**

Urgh! A Music War (A&M '81). Yet another special-price double from new-wave compilation kings Herb Alpert and Jerry Moss. The gimmick is live (hence previously unreleased) versions of theoretical AOR and actual dance-floor faves by artists from all over, and despite the intrusion of a few A&M contractees the result is quite impressive, with the audience participation adding fire to pop-rock that lacked heat in the studio. For those who find that discos keep them up past their bedtime, here's an encouraging take on what's been happening—not world overthrow, that's for sure, but fun enough in the right doses. Original grade: B plus.   **B**

UTFO: *UTFO* (Select '85). For years rappers boasted that they were in it for the money, which given the amounts of money involved proved how close to the street they still were. These days you can't be so sure. After announcing their educated synthesis with a verse in pig Latin on their first single, the new guys on the block have proven street professionals—if they don't use a rhyming dictionary, then they'll probably market one. And Full Force comes up with the one great hook Roxanne Roxanne needs.   **B**

U.T.F.O.:   *Skeezer Pleezer* (Select '86). Some of their sketches and tall tales—especially the cheerfully amoral anticrime versifying of "Just Watch"—sound observed. But too often the gimmicks are received and the generalizations fabricated. And they can not "sing a little bit."   **B**

UTFO: *Lethal* (Select '87). They got no principles, so they head for the street, where rap albums sell—with its skeezer, its hard-on, and its dozens, even "Let's Get It On" isn't radio-ready. At their most B-boy, they tempt me to organize a boycott of my fellow "suckers" and "fags," but they do it with flair, and though the quotation marks around "Lethal" and "Diss" will be widely misconstrued, they satisfy my admittedly flexible irony requirement. Not only that, "The Ride" is a dick rap that burns rubber, and "Burning Bed" is a better half's revenge.   **B+**

Uthwalofu Namakentshane: See Amaphisi / Uthwalofu Namakentshane.

U2:   *Boy* (Island '80). Their youth, their serious air, and their guitar sound are setting a small world on fire, and I fear the worst. No matter where they're starting off—not as big as Zep, maybe, but not exactly on the grunge circuit either—their echoey vocals already teeter on the edge (in-joke) of grandiosity, so how are they going to sound by the time they reach the Garden? What kind of Christian idealists lift their best riff from PIL (or from anywhere at all)? As bubble-headed as the teen-telos lyrics at best. As dumb as Uriah Heep at worst.   **C+**

U2:   *October* (Island '81). As they push past twenty their ambitions are showing, and suddenly the hope-addicts whiff both commerce and pretension. Sure it's still all fresh-faced and puissant in that vaguely political way that so moves the concerned rock journalist (and fan)—just not altogether unspoiled, sniff sniff. Bono Vox gets poetic, Steve Lillywhite gets arty, and those of us who expect more than sonic essence of rock and roll get enough melody and construction to make the first side a bit of all right. What a stupid band to expect purity from.   **B−**

U2:   *War* (Island '83). The deadly European virus that's always tainted this band turns out to be their characteristic melodic device, a medieval-sounding unresolved fifth frequently utilized by monks in Hollywood movies. In other respects, however, their hot album is rock and roll indeed. The Edge becomes a tuneful guitarist by the simple expedient of not soloing, and if Bono has too many Gregorian moments his conviction still carries the music. Anyway, I'll take his militant if pacifist Christianity ("The real battle has begun / To claim the victory Jesus won") over most of the secular humanism and Jah love rockers are going in for these days.   **B+**

U2:   *Under a Blood Red Sky* (Island '83). They broke AOR rather than pop for the honorable reason that they get across on sound rather than songs, and this live "mini-LP" (34:28 of music listing at $5.99) should turn all but the diehards around. Only one of the two new titles would make a best-of, but the two-from-album-one, one-from-album-two, three-from-album-three oldies selection is the perfect introduction. And although I was right to warn that this was an arena-rock band in disguise, I never figured they'd turn into a great arena-rock band.   **A−**

U2:   *The Unforgettable Fire* (Island '84). Eno has shaped this record to accentuate Bono's wild romantic idealism, and while I prefer his moral force I have to admit that the two are equally beguiling to contemplate and dangerous to take literally. The romanticism gets out of hand with the precious expressionism of "Elvis Presley and America" (enough to make the King doubt this boy's virility), the moralism with the turn-somebody-else's-cheek glorification of Martin Luther King's martyrdom (death stings plenty where I live). But he gets away with it often enough to make a skeptic believe temporarily in miracles.   **B+**

U2: *Wide Awake in America* (Island EP '85). Especially after their unstinting live mini, this four-cut "special low priced collection of live recordings and out takes from the Unforgettable Fire tour and album" looks like the usual special low priced gyp. But though the outtakes wouldn't have been missed, they're OK to hear, and the opener, an eight-minute amplification of one of *Unforgettable Fire*'s more obscure titles, is why they could get away with superstar rip-offs if they wanted. Maybe Bono's charisma assumes special access to truth, but he doesn't act like that makes him more important than anyone else, and the Edge's elegiac guitar is self-effacing in much the same way—it exists to serve the awesome effect. Epic humility—take it or leave it.   **B**

U2: *The Joshua Tree* (Island '87). Let it build and ebb and wash and thunder in the background and you'll hear something special—mournful and passionate, stately and involved. Read the lyrics and you won't wince. Tune in Bono's vocals and you'll encounter one of the worst cases of significance ever to afflict a deserving candidate for superstardom.   **B**

U2: *Rattle and Hum* (Island '88). Pretentious? Eux? Naturellement, mais that ain't all. Over the years they've melded Americana into their Old World riffs, and while Bono's "Play the blues, Edge" overstates this accomplishment, their groove is some kind of rock and roll wrinkle. This partly live double-LP is looser and faster than anything they've recorded since their first live mini, with the remakes of "Pride" and "Silver and Gold" and "Still Haven't Found What I'm Looking For" improved by both practice and negligence. A good half of the new stuff could knock unsuspecting skeptics over, the B.B./Hendrix/Dylan cameos are surprising and generous, and as a token of self-knowledge Bono concludes a lecture on South Africa with a magisterially sarcastic "Don't mean to bug ya." Yet as usual things don't get any better when you decide to find out exactly what he's waxing so meaningful about.   **B+**

Luther Vandross: *Never Too Much* (Epic '81). In music as tactful as this, where so much of the meaning is carried on the skip and flow of rhythm and timbre, songwriting doesn't matter all that much. So Vandross can attach tropes like "sugar and spice" and "she's a super lady" to undistinguished melodies and make me like them. But when his touch is just a little off, the great hit single you've just heard (or at least the good one that's sure to follow) seems almost as forgettable as the loser he's singing. **B+**

Luther Vandross: *Forever, For Always, For Love* (Epic '82). Well, depends on what you mean by love—like any studio habitue Vandross is a sensualist at heart, an aural libertine who revels in sheer sound at the expense of any but the most received sense. His voice is so luxuriant I can understand why fans go all the way with him. But only on "She Loves Me Back" (set apart by the hard K at the end of the title phrase) do I really love him back myself. **B+**

Luther Vandross: *Busy Body* (Epic '83). Not counting "Superstar" and "Until You Come Back to Me," which perish in the tragic flood of feeling that finishes this album off, the only songs here that might conceivably survive without their support system are "I'll Let You Slide," which Luther lets slip, and the one that donates its title to the venture. Nor does Luther augment the support system's golden-voiced rep by sharing "How Many Times Can We Say Goodbye" with Dionne Warwick, who cuts him from here to Sunday. In short, he sounds like an ambitious backup singer. **C+**

Luther Vandross: *The Night I Fell in Love* (Epic '85). Though Vandross's devotion to pure singing will always be too pure to admit much content, his material has improved. Marcus Miller makes the fast ones hop to, and the ballads retain their shape no matter how far Luther stretches them—only dud's the ridiculously well-named "My Sensitivity (Gets in the Way)." On "It's Over Now" Mr. Nice Guy even orders his treat-him-bad woman to "hit the road"—although it is his femme backups who utter the actual words. **B+**

Luther Vandross: *Give Me the Reason* (Epic '86). If only Luther had a little less integrity he might sell out—he's such a great singer he could transform crossover twaddle into universal trivia without even breathing hard. Alas, he's also such a great singer he doesn't have to. But not such a great singer he can interest simple pop fans in his own songs. **B**

Luther Vandross: *Any Love* (Epic '88). Your grandma had a saying that applied to Luther, though he's so unstuckup she would have hesitated to use it on him: "That fellow's certainly in love with the sound of his own voice." **B−**

Luther Vandross: *The Best of Luther Vandross . . . the Best of Love* (Epic '89). Vandross is without question the decade's premier pop (forget "black" pop) singer, and this figured to be where he beat Marcus Miller's straitjacket beats and drummed not hummed past his own humdrum songwriting. It is, too—by about an inch and a half. I know it may only be me, but what do the ladies hear in his slow ones? The quiet sheen of his timbre is distinctive and luxurious, a cross between pewter and velvet—like male Dionne Warwick. But I swear his voice isn't as beautiful as El DeBarge's or Al Green's, and beyond his trademark niceness, all caring and credulous, he's emotionally unreadable. As a result, showstopping tours de feeling like "A House Is Not a Home" and "Superstar" are as incomprehensible to the uninitiated as his d.o.a. Gregory Hines duet. But on his catchiest dance songs, including every one here, he embodies the long-forgotten disco synthesis of comfort and energy. And the medium-tempo stuff is anonymous pop at its most personable.   **A—**

Van Halen: *Women and Children First* (Warner Bros. '80). Eddie VH's quicksilver whomp earns the Hendrix comparisons, and he's no clone—he's faster, colder, more structural. David Lee Roth adds a wild-ass sophistication to the usual macho—no mortal arena singer would even think of the goofy country blues takeoff that provides the title. But the message of the music isn't the exuberance of untrammeled skill, it's the arrogance of unchallenged mastery. Without being pompous about it, which is a plus, these guys show as little feeling for their zonked, hopelessly adoring fans as Queen. They're kings of the hill and we're not.   **B**

Van Halen: *Fair Warning* (Warner Bros. '81). Pretty impressive show-off stuff—not just Eddie's latest sound effects, but a few good jokes along with the mean ones and a rhythm section that can handle punk speed emotionally and technically. At times Eddie could even be said to play an expressive—lyrical?—role. Of course, what he's expressing is hard to say. Technocracy putting a patina on cynicism, a critic might say.   **B—**

Van Halen: *Diver Down* (Warner Bros. '82). Less impressive, if only because hangloose covers like "Big Bad Bill" and "Happy Trails" are for more attractive bands. More attractive, if only because the Ray Davies and Roy Orbison covers are so carefully conceived. Attractive sexist original, unattractive (hence unimpressive) sexist original, guitar as cathedral organ. And so it goes.   **B—**

Van Halen: *1984* (Warner Bros. '84). Side one is pure up, and not only that, it sticks to the ears: their pop move avoids fluff because they're heavy and schlock because they're built for speed, finally creating an all-purpose mise-en-scène for Brother Eddie's hair-raising, stomach-churning chops. Side two is consolation for their loyal fans—a little sexism, a lot of pyrotechnics, and a standard HM bass attack on something called "House of Pain."   **B+**

Van Halen: *5150* (Warner Bros. '86). Wonder how the guitar mavens who thought Eddie equalled Van Halen are going to like his fireworks displays and balls-to-the-wall hooks now that video star David Lee Roth has given way to one of the biggest schmucks in the known biz. No musician with something to say could stomach responding to Sammy Hagar's call, and this album proves it.   **C+**

Van Halen: *OU812* (Warner Bros. '88). Not that they give a shit, but trading Dave for Sammy sure wrecked their shot at Led Zep of the '80s—master guitarist, signature vocalist, underrated rhythm section. They wouldn't have made it anyway, of course. Eddie's obsessed with technique, Roth's contemptuous of technique, rhythm section's got enough technique and no klutz genius. But Sammy . . . like wow. If I can't claim the new boy owns them (property rights they protect), you can't deny he defines them. Not that they give a shit.   **C**

Vanity: *Wild Animal* (Motown '84). Anyone who dreamed (as I did) that Vanity 6 was in any significant way Vanity's idea should try to squeeze some pleasure out of this: where formerly she talked her way through bright, crisp, rocking high-end arrangements and kept the smut simple, here she "sings" verbose, amelodic fantasies rendered even duller by a dim, bassy mix. And anyone who dreamed that she'd liberated herself from pornographic role-playing should get a load of the electric dildos, come-stained frocks, and psychedelic sex slavery she flaunts as she strikes out on her own.   **C—**

Vanity 6:   *Vanity 6* (Warner Bros. '82). The latest Prince creation is a male fantasy even if the girls did write the lyrics themselves, and Vanity's insistence on seven-inch dicks would have made me feel insecure before I discovered hormone treatments. But all eight of these dumb, dancy little synth tunes get me off when I let my guard down, and most of them are funny, hooky, and raunchy at the same time.   **B+**

Stevie Ray Vaughan and Double Trouble: *Texas Flood* (Epic '83). People who think white guitarists with the blues are the essence of rock and roll never fully account for Alvin Lee, not to mention Robin Trower. I think rock and roll's essence inheres in momentum and song form, and find my attention wandering after the kick-off originals "Love Struck Baby" and "Pride and Joy."   **B**

Stevie Ray Vaughan and Double Trouble: *Couldn't Stand the Weather* (Epic '84). The problem with guitar virtuosos is that most of them wouldn't know a good musical concept if they tripped over it, which happens just often enough to keep everyone confused. The exception that proves not a damn thing is Jimi Hendrix, the finest guitarist in any idiom ever. Though he comes close sometimes, this Texan ain't Hendrix. But between earned Jimi cover and lyric refreshment, album two is almost everything a reasonable person might hope from him: a roadhouse album with gargantuan sonic imagination.   **B+**

Stevie Ray Vaughan and Double Trouble: *Soul to Soul* (Epic '85). All right, all right—he's a *great* guitarist, and an intermittently commanding vocalist. Unlike most Hendrixites he can step a sharp shuffle, and unlike most Texas boogiemen he's a great guitarist. But he's still not a great or even commanding artist, because the classic album he has in him, *Jimi Boogies,* keeps getting ruined by installments of *Stevie Ray Shows Off.* This moves along

right nice, especially on side two—until Vaughan elects to close with a long slow soulful one that only gets going with a Hendrix coda.   **B+**

Stevie Ray Vaughan and Double Trouble: *Live Alive* (Epic '86). Formally, this is generic live double: four prev unrec tunes, most of the ten remakes a minute or two looser. But Vaughan wasn't made for the studio—live is the only concept he has any feel for. His material blooms with a little weeding, his big throaty moan gathers heat under a spotlight, and the dumbfounding legato eloquence of his guitar rolls mightily down his band's expert arena-boogie groove. As a bonus, he ends by reminding his yahooing Texans about Africa: "I may be white, but I ain't stupid"—vamp, vamp—"and neither are you."   **A—**

Stevie Ray Vaughan and Double Trouble: *In Step* (Epic '89). Believe it or not he's writing blues for AA: "Wall of Denial" and "Tightrope" fall into ex-addict jargon like it was natural speech, which for ex-addicts it is. If the music was preachy or wimpy this would be a disaster, but not till I perused the lyric sheet did I even notice where his homilies got their start. Essential that the leadoff "House Is Rockin' " keeps on boogieing on—and that on the mood-jazz closer he escapes the blues undamaged for the first time in his career.   **A—**

Ben Vaughn Combo: *Beautiful Thing* (Restless '87). Unlike many comedians, this mild-mannered male chauvinist is funniest when he lets on how clever he is, as in "Jerry Lewis in France," "Growin' a Beard," and "I'm Sorry (But So Is Brenda Lee)," only one of which he was clever enough to put on his first U.S. album. He'll never be a Crenshaw (definitive "Brenda Lee"), but his rockabilly as whisper and idea has gained oomph—if he lets it all hang out he may eventually be as commercial as the Morells (definitive "Growin' a Beard").   **B**

V-Effect: *Stop Those Songs* (Rift import '83). Either Ann Rupel's vocals and David Zonzinsky's vocals and sax got squashed in the machinery somewhere or else their cheerful onstage chutzpah concealed chronic difficulties with breath production. Too bad—few bands anywhere make better rock and roll on the edge of artistic and political struggle. This may be because, as Zonzinsky likes to say, they're "leftist" rather than "political": their clarity of purpose helps them avoid the ingrown cacophony that their supposed comrades consider an improvement on programmatic oversimplification.   **B+**

Suzanne Vega: *Suzanne Vega* (A&M '85). If I walked into a folk club and came upon this woman strumming her songs, I'd be impressed too—she picks her words with evident care and conversationalizes her chosen vocal tradition with evident savvy. But that's not good enough: great lyricists either dazzle you utterly or sneak the imagery on by, and no folk-based vocal tradition ought to require conversationalizing. Despite her considerable talent, Vega is self-consciously Artistic like so many folkies before her, which means that while a rock and roll production might power her over her affectations, more likely it just wouldn't mesh—the slightly prissy precision of these arrangements is precisely what the songs demand. As for that ersatz medieval ballad (which ain't bad, actually)—it's no anomaly.   **B−**

Suzanne Vega: *Solitude Standing* (A&M '87). I bet "Luka" is a grand fluke like "You're So Vain" rather than a dawning of the light like "Mrs. Robinson." Better her closely observed recent songs than a tale of brave Ulysses or a lover with "hands of raining water" (wet yes, hot no). But close observation is still Creative Writing, and if Vega eventually graduates to, say, the flat command of Ann Beattie, she'll still be precisely nowhere. Real pop lyrics ignore such strictly literary alternatives altogether.   **C+**

The Vels: *Velocity* (Mercury '84). These three Steven Stanley–produced Philadelphians don't just dance in their heads. Not only do they command the spare formal pop eloquence that many popdance minimalists claim and few get next to, they have a generous regard for pop pleasure. Their simple hooks add up to full-fledged tunes, their basic-English lyrics are more than runes. And singer Alice DeSoto is unaffected and vivacious, a rare combination.   **B+**

The Velvet Underground: *VU* (Verve '85). Each of the Velvets' four official studio albums had a distinct personality, and so does this unofficial one, recorded mostly in mid-1969, right after *The Velvet Underground* appeared. It's goofy, relaxed, simultaneously conversational and obscure, an effect accentuated by the unfinished feel of takes the band never prepared for public consumption. As a result, especially given PolyGram's state-of-the-art remix, it's their most listenable record even if its friendliness is deceptive—the disarming straight-ahead rocker "Foggy Notion" has a lyric whose casual sadism beats any of *The Velvet Underground & Nico*'s shock-horror perversities. If you ever doubt the VU's rightness, just compare the flashy compromises of the solo "Lisa Says" and "I Can't Stand It" (itself the making of *Lou Reed*) to the flat rush of the Tucker/Morrison-powered versions here. A *Basement Tapes* for the '80s.   **A**

The Velvet Underground: *Another View* (Verve '86). One objective part of me knows that these barrel scrapings are for fanatics and archivists. But another objective part of me knows that the barrel scrapings of a seminal, protean, conceptually accomplished band are their own reward. From the raw power of the instrumental "Guess I'm Falling in Love" to the dry lyricism of the instrumental "I'm Gonna Move Right In," from the tight studio "We're Gonna Have a Real Good Time Together" to the intense early "Rock and Roll," you don't have to know jackshit about the band to enjoy the music—on the contrary, you have to put aside your preconceptions. Because nobody experimented more successfully than these folks.   **A−**

The Venanda Lovely Boys: *Bo-Tata* (Rounder '89). A taste for mbube, isichatamiya, ingoma ebusuku, or what these notes call cothoza will never come naturally to Americans, but if Ladysmith got you interested, try this. The sharp, nasal leads are dominated for the non-Zulu ear by waggish effects that are probably more sound than sense anyway—whoops, rattles, repartee, animal calls. In short, it's not especially beautiful, which is good. How many Joseph Shabalalas can there be? How many do you want?   **B+**

Tom Verlaine: *Dreamtime* (Warner Bros. '81). A pop boho and an ecstatic mensch, an exalted lead guitarist who loves to chunka-chunk that rhythm, Verlaine is a walking, cogitating rock and roll contradiction. Granted, the solo-with-backup hierarchy does constrict his wild gift a little. But Ritchie Fliegler's Richard Lloyd simulations get the job done, and anyway, this is Verlaine's best batch of songs since *Marquee Moon*—two years' worth, ten in all if you count the one that goes "Hi-Fi." Elsewhere, Verlaine evokes the touchy ironies of urban love—passion and detachment, adoration and despair—with deftness and soul. Original grade: A.   **A—**

Tom Verlaine: *Words From the Front* (Warner Bros. '82). Verlaine's ever-resourceful guitar has always been more richly endowed with mood and effect than with the hook riffs that make him a great rock-and-roller, and here for the first time things get too atmospheric. "Postcard From Waterloo" is a classic, but the strangulated vocals and expressionistic structures suggest that he really should get out more.   **B+**

Tom Verlaine: *Cover* (Warner Bros. '84). Anglophobes and wimpbashers won't hear it, but Verlaine's light touch constitutes a renewal and an achievement. Synthesized ostinatos and affected vocals are deplorable in themselves only when they're ends in themselves. Here they're put to the service of tuneful whimsy that has brains and heart, a sense of beauty and a sense of humor. Goofy romanticism at its driest and most charming.   **A—**

Tom Verlaine: *Flash Light* (I.R.S. '87). Supremely self-conscious, utterly unschooled, Verlaine writes like nobody else, sings like nobody else, plays like nobody else. His lyrics sound like his voice sounds like his guitar, laconic and extravagant at the same time. After three years off the boards, he's deemphasized keyboards in a quest for dynamite riffs, and he's found enough to thrill any fan. As usual, I'm not sure just what the songs mean. But that bothers me mostly because it may bother you.   **A—**

A Very Special Christmas (A&M '87). You get J.C. Mellencamp rocking "I Saw Mommy Kissing Santa Clause," Bon Jovi slavering "Back Door Santa," Madonna vamp-camping "Santa Baby," but you also get solemnity-and-a-half from Sting and Bob Seger and Whitney Houston (who in this context owes us some soul). No, what makes this the best Xmas album since Phil Spector got bored with Hanukkah is conceptual audacity: pop-rock sticks its schlock in your face, leaning on fourteen eternal hits only Scrooge and Steve Albini could hate on principle. And all for an utterly safe, indubitably worthy cause. This December I'm bringing it out to Queens for dinner.   **A—**

Via Afrika: *Via Afrika* (EMI America '85). That's as in Afrikaner—e.g. vocalist/bassist/drum programmer René Veldsman, who cut this strange little record with Michele Howe two years before they both emigrated and sang backup on "Sun City." It's all rhythm and soulful chants/shouts that with the help of the electronic drums come across distanced rather than passionate. This seems appropriate, somehow—I don't miss the cloying sincerity of such white Africans as Johnny Clegg and Tony Bird. And n.b.: beyond a plea to "Save Crocodiles" on the back cover, there are no politics here at all.   **B+**

Violent Femmes: *Violent Femmes* (Slash '83). If Jonathan Richman thought he was as sexy as Richard Hell, he'd come on like Gordon Gano. And if you believe Jonathan Richman damn well *is* as sexy as Richard Hell, which Gano is counting on, remember that what makes Jonathan's kiddie act so (shall we say) appealing is that he counts on nothing except his fingers and toes. Gano knows his stuff—the barely electric music is striking enough for rock and roll. But for all its undeniable humor and panache the effect is precious, wimp bohemianism so self-congratulatory it'll be sucking its own wee-wee next time we look.   **B+**

Violent Femmes: *Hallowed   Ground* (Slash '84). First time out they sounded so original musically that I made it a spiritual exercise to forgive Gordon Gano his bad personality. But everything you might hum along with on the sequel was invented generations ago by better men than he. And though "Black Girls" may not be racist (or "faggot"-baiting), it takes a great deal of petulant delight in daring you to call it a name. Then again, maybe it is racist.   **C+**

Virgin Prunes: *If I Die, I Die* (Rough Trade '82). If you can imagine mid-'70s Eno hung up on the Flesh Eaters (or a Gaelic counterpart that's somehow escaped my notice) and the Boomtown Rats, you'll get an idea of how these metronomic, exotophile Irishpeople sound, if not of why I enjoy them so thoroughly—which is probably because Eno abandoned the mid-'70s all too soon.   **B+**

Visage: *Visage* (Polydor '81). Oh of course they're not "fascistic"—that's what rockers always say about disco, and now it's what they always say about synth music, too, so what else do you expect? Granted, "boring" is another word that comes up, and that's a little harder to dismiss—impossible if the "Frequency 7"'s cute, paramilitary sheets of electronic sound weren't the Glass-pop downtowners have been bullshitting about for years. Not that it'll keep me on the floor. Or put me on the parade ground.   **B−**

Vision Quest (Geffen '85). This flick isn't an item on my particular grapevine, but between the sculpted pecs on the back cover and the "Only the Young" kickoff inside, I figure it's about Heroic Youth. They're "Hot Blooded," they're "Hungry for Heaven," they're gonna "Shout to the Top," and their idea of inspirational art is some amalgam of pop metal and dance-oriented schlock. Given the basic idea, these tracks are surprisingly okay, but only one fires my corpuscles: Don Henley's "She's on the Zoom," about a Dumb Chick.   **C+**

Viva Zimbabwe! (Earthworks import '83). For all the liner talk about electric dance music, what sets this apart is its roots in thumb piano. With that painfully mastered village instrument the melodic source, the guitar figures are the quickest in Africa—contrapuntal at their best, and always hooky. Vocals are likewise unassuming if not delicate, rhythms distinctly light. Takes a while to hear, will never hit you over the head, and you can dance to it. Call it folk-disco. [Later on Carthage]   **A−**

Voice of the Beehive: *Let It Bee* (London '88). California girls meet Brit rockers for fun and profit—in Britain, which explains how they chose one of the stupidest names in the history of fun and profit. They're not twee, I swear it. In fact, this could be the first Bangles album, back when the femme quartet took no shit and wrote like it did them good, except that it's brasher in rhythm and guitar—not so Anglophile, so twee. "The beat of love is a nasty one" sums up their worldview, and if unlike Joan Jett they don't relish it, they also don't deny its sick appeal. Stay single and keep your heart off your sleeve is their solution, and I hope for our sake they buy it for another album or two.   **A−**

Volcano Suns: *The Bright Orange Years* (Homestead '86). First side's got everything an insatiable Mission of Burma (or Hüsker Dü) fan could ask except Richard Harte's production, which might do justice to the band's command of detail. In fact, it makes me wish MOB had let drummer-vocalist Peter Prescott, who does most of the songwriting here, do most of the songwriting there as well. Second side's more clamorous, which these days is just another way of saying conventional.   **B+**

Volcano Suns: *Bumper Crop* (Homestead '87). The record's a little too dirgy-anthemic to review, but the press release is worth quoting: "The current lineup continues the mixture of surreal lunacy and singalong pop sludge that have already won them a spot in the hearts of many unemployed people on drugs."   **B−**

Volcano Suns: *Farced* (SST '88). Finally an album that captures the half of Mission of Burma who didn't turn to chamber music—the half that's half joke band—in all their half-assed glory. As in "Commune," about the hippies they never wert. Or "Can I Have the Key?," about the medicine cabinet. Or "Laff Riot," about a bassline.   **B+**

Jane Voss & Hoyle Osborne: *Get to the Heart* (Green Linnet '81). There's only one Irving Berlin song here, but it's Berlin's vulgar, magnanimous, democratic tunefulness that Voss claims for the folkie sensibility. And though her voice sure isn't as strong as Bessie Smith's, as she's good enough to point out in another tribute, she also wants to wail and moan. So where Joan Morris does Berlin by simulating the careful pitch and intonation of '20s pop singers, who still cowered in the shadow of operetta, Voss flats her melodies shamelessly, sounding half like a jazz improviser and half like Sister in her cups and/or parlor. Pianist Osborne is squarer than need be and composer Voss sometimes runs on at the mouth, but get to the heart they do. Original grade: A minus.   **B+**

The Vulgar Boatmen: *Me and Your Sister* (Record Collect '89). These guys make much more than you expect out of what sounds like almost nothing—just tuneful enough to warrant play two, their mild jangle gains sweetness and kick as your faith increases. But their lyrics come from an English prof who may be too much the formalist to say what he wants but more likely just doesn't know what he wants: hoping for more "Change the World All Around," what you get instead is six minutes of "Drive Somewhere." It's such a great riff you wouldn't care if it kept going, either. But an honorable, self-aware nowhere is where it'll end up.   **B+**

Bunny Wailer: *Bunny Wailer Sings the Wailers* (Mango '80). You'd think these remade rude-boy hits would hook in quick, since for most of us they're not haunted by the ghosts of the originals. Only they don't—the Third Wailer's somewhat ethereal vocal presence, as well as the intractably relaxed groove that rockers studio flash is heir to, assure that. But after too many plays hook in they do, especially on side one, where "Burial," "I Stand Predominate," and "Walk the Proud Land" form a gently triumphant triptych. **A—**

Bunny Wailer: *Tribute* (Solomonic import '81). In part because he understands so unmistakably that there'll be no new Marley, Bob's resolutely ital old bandmate is the one Jamaican artist who continues to exercise comparable vision, breadth, and authority. These versions of eight songs the leader sang first make clear that Marley was the more gifted vocalist, but they also make clear that Bunny's baritone added rough yearning to Bob's sweet sufferation. Better than *Bunny Sings the Wailers*. Maybe even as classic as *Lefty Frizzell Sings the Songs of Jimmie Rodgers.* **A—**

Bunny Wailer: *Hook Line 'n Sinker* (Solomonic import '82). The skanking Memphisbeat Sly & Robbie rolled out for Joe Cocker goes uptempo and downriver here, and Bunny rides it for the entirety of a delightful groove album. Imagine what a reggae-goes-Stax-Volt-second-line tune called "Soul Rocking Party" might sound like. No no no—imagine it *done well.* Now you've got it. **A—**

Bunny Wailer: *Roots Radics Rockers Reggae* (Shanachie '83). This expanded version of Solomonic's 1979 *In I Father's House* isn't primo Bunny. Even the nicely dubwise "Rockers" is flatter than side one of *Rock 'n' Groove;* what's more, the sacramental *Tribute* and the upful *Hook Line 'n Sinker* have me waiting on his soon-come live album. Nevertheless, this is a worthy sample of the unjudgmental preachments and reliable rhythms of Jamaica's solidest solo artist, and if you buy it maybe there'll be more. **B+**

Bunny Wailer: *Live* (Solomonic import '83). Though his voice echoes more hollowly than the most scientific dubmaster would ever intend, the only concert the man's given in seven years sounds like it was a natural thing. His best studio albums have more distinct identities, but this is where to sample his invincible spirit. **B+**

Bunny Wailer: *Marketplace* (Shanachie '85). From "Stay With the Reggae" to "Jump Jump" to "Dance Hall Music," Bunny strives to justify his less than propitious title. It's got a good beat and you can skank to it, but you'll have to slow down when you get to the love songs. **B—**

Bunny Wailer: *Rootsman Skanking* (Shanachie '87). Back in 1981, when Bunny's most unabashed sales bids ("Dance Rock" indeed) seemed swathed in an ital glow seven of these ten cuts surfaced as *Rock 'n' Groove,* on Bunny's JA-only Solomonic label. If they don't sound quite so unpremeditated now, they do cut a switch. Also a natural: the add-on ballad, "Cry to Me."   **A—**

Bunny Wailer: *Rule Dance Hall* (Shanachie '87). Bunny follows his failed bid for the marketplace by going to the people where his roots are. The results are definitely more ital, and more philosophically defensible as well. But the first side doesn't update his circa-1982 reggae&b quite nicely enough, and except for the "Stir It Up" remake, the songs on side two are a little too dubwise—abstractly dance-specific in the usual manner of disco turned in on itself.   **B**

Bunny Wailer: *Liberation* (Shanachie '89). He's studied his history, and the politics of his major statement are pretty smart. But ordinarily, only earnest organizer types who distribute lyrics at rallies ("To the tune of 'Down by the Riverside' ") think they can get a rousing song out of a line like "The OAU and the United Nations must stop all hypocritical sanctions." And Bunny should know better than to hire studio musicians to do what they're told.   **B**

The Wailing Ultimate (Homestead '87). As long as you don't take the hooks too literally—believe me, there aren't many more where they come from—this is a pretty fair introduction to garage postnihilism, a surprisingly palatable mix of musical and sociological interest. Just like the grooveful laborers on a reggae or hardcore compilation, Gerry's kids hold together for the kind of continuous listen most local/label samplers can't sustain. In fact, only their fans and their mothers could tell most of these fourteen bands apart without a scorecard, and I'm not so sure about their mothers. Mrs. Petkovic: "I liked that song you did about the well." John P.: "How could that be ours, mama? A girl sings it." Mrs. P.: "Isn't Samantha a girl?" John P.: "Ma, we're called Death of Samantha—*Death* of Samantha." Mrs. P.: "Oh Johnny, she's not really dead. That's just, what do you call it, poetic license, right?"   **B+**

Loudon Wainwright III: *A Live One* (Rounder '80). The cheap seats are the only seats at a Wainwright show, and too often he plays to them, but here the screwy faces and strangled diction and spastic phrasing and easy jokes are kept in check. It's not as if his albums are so ornately orchestrated that the man-and-his-guitar format is a breath of fresh air. But he's a singer-songwriter who deserves a best-of, and this will do till he gets it.   **B+**

Loudon Wainwright III: *Fame and Wealth* (Rounder '83). Loudon's most confident album since he split with CBS in 1975 is also his least ambitious, done folkie-style with two penetrating embellishments from Richard Thompson and two band cuts. For a while he walks his old tightrope, wild and nasty enough to make his chronic egoism seem of general interest. But the jokes and feelings are getting thinner, and soon you'll find yourself wishing he'd grow up, shut up, or both.   **B**

Loudon Wainwright III: *I'm Alright* (Rounder '85). Last time he was complacent in defeat, his irony all sarcasm and his permanent postadolescence an annoying bore. This time he's facing up—not to anything existential or absurd, that stuff comes too easy, but to what it might mean to make an alright career (and life) out of "unhappy love." The result is discernibly superior to the perfectly enjoyable oneliner miscellanies of the late '70s and not quite there even so. Just rooting for the Rangers and having his doubts about bellbottom pants once made him a (very minor) prophet; now they make him normal. My suggestion: a concept album about having kids.   **B+**

Loudon Wainwright III: *More Love Songs* (Rounder '87). With regret and trepidation, I'd venture that divorce has been good for his songwriting—after almost a decade of hit-and-miss, this is his second straight to lay down an attitude. The two tracks that tackle the split head-on aren't clever enough for Nashville, which with this clever bastard is a plus. On the other hand, the wit of "Man's World" is subsumed by its antifeminist rancor, so that after "Unhappy Anniversary" side two rides on attitude alone.   **B+**

Loudon Wainwright III: *Therapy* (Silvertone '89). He makes fun of it, and why not, but it's been good for him—the only time he revels in what a mean bastard he is you'd think he was describing somebody else. Not only has shrinkage sharpened his instinct for love's twists, it's gotten him musing about his great subject, parenthood. In "Thanksgiving" he rankles and dreams, in "Me and All the Other Mothers" he braves the playground, and in "Your Father's Car" he's insecure about his dad, his mom, his kids, an ex-wife, and the state—inside of 2:21.   **B+**

The Waitresses: *Wasn't Tomorrow Wonderful?* (Polydor '82). You know what kind of waitress Patty Donahue is—the kind who's waiting to break into the arts. A little scatterbrained, maybe, but she can use "alarmist" and "plotted" in declarative sentences. Not only is she believable, she's full of insight—only the Springsteenian "Heat Night" fails completely, and to make up there's the anti-Springsteenian "It's My Car." But only "No Guilt" is the tour de force that any man who sets out to create feminist rock and roll had better go for every time out, which may be because Chris Butler never asked all those women he interviewed what kind of music they liked.   **B+**

The Waitresses: *I Could Rule the World if I Could Only Get the Parts* (Polydor EP '82). The words still overcomplicate the music—the smartest person I know indeed. But even the title tune, written for Tin Huey, has pop momentum. Add the Xmas carol for singles (I say she was shopping at the Bleecker Street Gristedes') and the lucky TV theme (in which Chris Butler shows off his high school memories, or maybe his ethnographies), and the male-feminist Monkees reveal themselves as a cross between Blondie and the Bus Boys. And Tin Huey.   **A−**

Waitresses: *Bruiseology* (Polydor '83). Instead of cutting back on verbiage, Chris Butler solves his clutter problem by revving the music up so high it blares over its own complexity. The result isn't something you'll listen to all the time, but for most of us the same can be said of Ornette Coleman and the Sex Pistols. And if Butler's thematic concerns aren't universal enough to merit such heady company, his

grasp of specifics won't be denied. Original grade: A minus.   **B+**

Tom Waits: *Heartattack and Vine* (Asylum '80). Lurching from hip to bathetic in his doomed pursuit of the let's-get-wasted market, he needs an editor more than Jack Kerouac ever did. But Kerouac rarely came up with tropes as axiomatic as "I sold a quart of blood and bought a half a pint of Scotch" or "If you don't get my letter, then you'll know that I'm in jail," neither of which ought to spend their lives buried in overgrown verbiage and stentorian second-line. And sometimes he gets away with his shit, as in the tearfully tuneful "Jersey Girl" or the blisteringly bluesy "Mr. Siegal"—or "Heartattack and Vine," which could make you hope he's getting tired of getting wasted.   **B**

Tom Waits: *Swordfishtrombones* (Island '83). Though it never seemed likely that Waits had the intellect or self-discipline his talent deserved, after a full decade of half-cocked color he's put it together. He'll never sing pretty, but finally that's an unmitigated advantage. Taking a cue from his country cousin Captain Beefheart, he's making the music as singular as the stories, from the amplified Delta blues of "Gin Soaked Boy" to Victor Feldman's strange percussion devices (try the brake drum on "16 Shells From a 30-6"). And at the same time he's finding the tawdry naturalistic details he craves in less overtly bizarre locales—Australia, suburbia, his own head.   **A−**

Tom Waits: *Rain Dogs* (Island '85). By pigging out on a nineteen-track LP that goes on for fifty-four minutes without a bad cut, Waits demonstrates how fully he's outgrown the bleary self-indulgences—booze, bathos, beatnikism—that bogged down his '70s. He's in control of his excesses now, and although his backing musicians shift constantly, he's worked out a unique and identifiable lounge-lizard sound that suits his status as the poet of America's non–nine-to-fivers. But the sheer bulk of the thing does get wearing—it never peaks. I wish he'd figured out a way to throw "Union Square," "Cemetery Polka," and "Clap Hands" into sharper relief. And realize that those might not even be his high points, or yours.   **B+**

Tom Waits: *Franks Wild Years* (Island '87). Amid these fragments from a musical that wouldn't make all that much sense fully staged, you'll find five-six songs that stand on their own—coupla howlin' blues, coupla tuneful heart-tuggers, coupla Wayne Newton parodies. But if in the '20s Rudy Vallee sang through a megaphone because he wanted to sound modern, in the '80s Waits sings through a megaphone because he wants to sound old. This being the '80s, you're free to prefer Waits—as long as you don't kid yourself too much about his conceptual thrust.   **B**

Tom Waits: *Big Time* (Island '88). Sure he's an American original and all that. But from half-assed one-man original-cast album to soundtrack of filmed live show, Waits continues to confound the categories more aimlessly than seems necessary. Not counting one shaggy testicle story, the sharpest moments here subject overlooked songs to a crack cabaret-tinged band. From American originals I expect bigger surprises.   **B**

Collin Walcott/Don Cherry/Nana Vasconcelos: *Codona 2* (ECM '81). I don't trust music with bird noises in it, I don't trust concepts like "again," and I don't trust Oregon sitarist Collin Walcott, composer of the tweety "Again and Again, Again." I wonder why Walcott's "Walking on Eggs" sounds like an Ornette Coleman tune while "Drip-Dry," credited to Coleman, sounds like Walcott wrote it (sitars will out?). And when I really want recent Don Cherry I'll put on Johnny Dyani's *Song for Biko* and get Dudu Pukwana at the same time. But side one is the best UNESCO ad you'll ever hear. Starts with percussionist Vasconcelos's "Que Faser," which sustains itself without obvious melody or beat for 7:08, and continues through the traditional African "Godumaduma," a brief, elegant reminder of where Steve Reich learned his shit. And then there's Cherry's "Malinye," where he states an astonishingly lovely theme first on melodica and then on trumpet before allowing the music to break into crowd noises that somehow enrich the mood,

which is then picked up by none other than Collin Walcott—who by this time could sell me a used car, not to mention a brand-new day.   **B+**

Jerry Jeff Walker: *Greatest Hits* (MCA '80). After running his best-of against his live double one-on-one, I can only conclude that this longtime folkie and frequent drunk, a native New Yorker upstate division, turned himself into the archetypal Sun Belt hippie the natural way: interacting nice and easy with the lost gonzos in his band and the refugees from reality in his cult or audience or whatever. Cult, I guess. His audience comprises the far-flung "outlaw" fans who made small-scale country "hits" of a few of his singles—only one of which, the live "Mr. Bojangles," is even included here. Such interactions don't normally come through on plastic, especially in a factory-tooled genre like country music. This time, though, buy the live double.   **B−**

Joe Louis Walker: *Cold Is the Night* (Hightone '86). Producer-penned songs begin and fancy up each side, which is half the Hightone story—this would be one more piece of moderately sharp spit-and-shuffle blues without that spit-and-polish. The other half is label honchos Bruce Bromberg and Dennis Walker's insistence on artists determined to rise above—like Robert Cray, Ted Hawkins, and JLW, who must have started out emulating both Junior Wells and Buddy Guy and taken it from there.   **B+**

Joe Louis Walker: *The Gift* (Hightone '88). No house-band bar-rocker, no funkified keep-up-with-the-times hopeful, will never show up on a Tina Turner album. Like they say, he just plays the blues. Yet between sharp tempos and wordly-wise material, he overcomes the boredom factor built into that timeworn endeavor. Even when he lays back his beat has a forward tilt, and he's not proud about where he gets his songs—from producers or band members or fellow guildsmen. The sole throwaway is more than offset by the title tune, a bluesman's "Change Is Gonna Come"—twenty-five years later, for better and worse. It's not really a blues at all. The bluesman in question wrote it with no help from anybody except his father and his grandmother and the Lord above.   **A—**

Joe Louis Walker: *Blue Soul* (Hightone '89). I know, life is never this simple. But last time bass player Henry Oden had four songwriting credits, three of them winners. This time he's got none. Standout: the un-soullike, unaccompanied "I'll Get to Heaven on My Own."   **B**

Sippie Wallace: *Sippie Wallace* (Atlantic '82). This project scrapes by on taste and good intentions—the selection of songs by Wallace and contemporaries, Bonnie Raitt's unobtrusive voice and slide, and the impeccable swing of pianist Jim Dapogny and his Chicago Jazz Band. The problem is that where Alberta Hunter commands an almost regal strength in her eighties, Wallace sounds like a cartoon granny with denture problems. Her lyrics still sting after half a century, and her phrasing puts them across, but she doesn't even hint at the young Sippie's hard-won erotic composure. CBS and RCA: reissue.   **B**

Wall of Voodoo: *Call of the West* (I.R.S. '82). Those who believe synth-pop means that the end is near should cf. WoV's 1980 EP, which gave no hint they were capable of tunes as neat and witty as "Mexican Radio" or "Lost Weekend." Maybe soon vocalist-lyricist Standard Ridgway will fall in love with a human and start pretending he's a nice guy.   **B**

Joe Walsh: *You Bought It—You Name It* (Warner Bros. '83). *Joe Walsh's Comedy Album—Finally.* Featuring one pop standard gone studio-reggae, the ultimate (last?) video-game song, a cross between "Boobs a Lot" and "Dolly Parton's Hits," "Class of '65" for bathetic relief, and a song called "I Can Play That Rock & Roll" that *isn't stupid* (though it comes close).   **B+**

Wanna Buy a Bridge? (Rough Trade '80). Rough Trade has become the biggest British postpunk indie by (or at least while) brooking no compromise politically or aesthetically. Politically this has led to idiot rant like the Pop Group's "We Are All Prostitutes"; aesthetically it's meant rapprochements with incorrigible art-rockers like Mayo Thompson and Robert Wyatt as well as the diddle-prone experiments of Young Marble Giants, the Raincoats, Essential Logic, and Cabaret Voltaire. But it's also provided such classic punk protest as Spizz Energi's "Soldier Soldier" and Stiff Little Fingers' "Alternative Ulster," and none of the above-named diddlers would have been taken aboard without a surefire tune or two in their packet. Hence this superb fourteen-single compilation, Rough Trade's first U.S. LP. Kleenex's "Ain't You" and Delta 5's "Mind Your Own Business," two of the finest postpunk forty-fives anywhere, do help. As do Scritti Politti's arty, political, hypnotic "Skank Bloc Bologna" and "At Last I Am Free," by none other than Robert Wyatt.   **A**

War: *Outlaw* (RCA Victor '82). The pan–Afro-American groove is sharper and the tempos often approach medium fast, but the music sounds almost vintage anyway and that's the big surprise—why should they make their best album nearly a decade after their prime? Professionalism is its own reward—for once. Almost. Original grade: B plus.   **B**

Steve Wariner: *Greatest Hits* (MCA '87). "What I Didn't Do" puts sins of omission on country's conjugal hit list. "Small Town Girl" concentrates the whole of a genre's nostalgia on one overburdened woman from back home. "The Weekend" takes him off the deep end and he figures better that than nothing. After that, it's pretty generic—but likably generic, which in MOR country is an accomplishment these days.   **B**

Jennifer Warnes: *Famous Blue Raincoat* (Cypress '86). She's a background singer, a soundtrack diva, a Nashville-to-El-Lay pro. She loves Leonard Cohen's songs because she thinks they illuminate the dark side of the universe. Cohen thinks they are the universe. Which is why—Judy Collins be damned and Joe Cocker notwithstanding—they're all but inextricable from his tuneless, grave, infinitely self-mocking vocal presence.   **B—**

Was (Not Was): *Was (Not Was)* (Island '81). Brains galore, as both lyrics and horn charts trumpet. But if that ain't all, half the time it's too damn close—complementing the full complement of conceits is a grand total of three songs the way I count them. Which must make the omission of the rock-and-rolling "Wheel Me Out," and for that matter *A Christmas Record*'s "Christmas Time in the Motor City," the kind of hubris the brainy can't resist.   **B**—

Was (Not Was): *Born To Laugh at Tornadoes* (Geffen '83). "Nietzsche died a lonely madman—Jerry Lewis has his own telethon," concludes the back-cover "prologue." Not that their displacements achieve the depth of either artist, of course—that's the point, and the self-deflation is a relief after the hyperconscious waking nightmares of the debut. Won't get them a telethon, but it's worth five minutes on David Letterman, and they no longer sound as if they regard displacement as their own nutty-professor-turned-ubermensch joke on the world.   **B+**

Was (Not Was): *What Up, Dog?* (Chrysalis '88). Smooth has never been their forte—in fact, they've never given a shit about it. So this comes on as scattered as the literary art-funk you dimly remember. It's not, though—they relax a little, write real tunes, groove the overelaborate rhythmic attack, and add lyrical reach and purpose without soft-pedaling their ruefully cynical left-wing misanthropy. Which is their message to the world whether we (and they) like it or not. Since a little goes a long way, it's encouraging that two of the grotesque one-night stands have happy endings. As for the prodigal who tells his dad he wants to stay in jail and the good old goon who uses his pit bull as a credit card, they're just misanthropic fun.   **A**—

Muddy Waters: *King Bee* (Blue Sky '81). Can an old man rock the blues? Watch your mouth, punk. His toughest since *Hard Again,* and his softest. And it rocks like a mother.   **A**—

Roger Waters: *Radio KAOS* (Columbia '87). In which Waters's wheelchair-bound version of the deaf, dumb, and blind boy learns to control the world's computers with his cordless phone, then simulates impending nuclear holocaust just to scare the shit out of the powers that be. I have serious reservations about any record that can't be enjoyed unless you sit there reading the inner sleeve, but this is not without its aural rewards—a coverable song or two and some nice comping on shakuhachi as well as the deep engineering that made Floyd famous. As pretentious goes, not stupid.   **B**

Jody Watley: *Jody Watley* (MCA '87). Though Bernard Edwards has his name on three cuts out of nine, including the definitively cock-crazy "Love Injection," you know why former Prince lackey Andre Cymone wanted sole production credit. This is his revenge—a made-to-order dance-rock sex object with better credentials than Sheila E. herself. I have nothing against women pretending they want to go to bed with me. But I found it easier to pretend I wanted to go to bed with the disgruntled former Shalamar associate when she played the flirt.   **C+**

Jody Watley: *Larger Than Life* (MCA '89). Having cornered a new-artist Grammy by narrowcasting her lust for lust, the young black-pop veteran comes up against the perils of upward-mobility abuse—once you get hooked, you'll go to any length to keep rising to the top. Yet whatever she's like in "real" life, Jody's more credible servicing pop normals than disco nightcrawlers—demanding "Real Love," hanging onto her "L-O-V-E-R," dissing false "Friends" with a name rapper, etc. And for the first time, Andre Cymone's own grooves sound more original than his Prince imitations.   **B**—

Jody Watley: *You Wanna Dance With Me?* (MCA '89). An abstraction to begin with and a ripoff to boot, this woman suits her remix compilation. But it's still an abstraction. And a ripoff.   **B**—

The Weather Girls: *Success* (Columbia '84). Those who find "It's Raining Men" suspiciously campy will be doubly offended to hear producer-songwriter Paul Jabara steer his reformed gospel singers into praise of the Anvil and edible men.

Me, I think it's the ultimate gay disco song, four hefty-voiced black female survivors set loose on what is much more a gay than a female fantasy, and I love it—for its humor and for its uncompromising extravagance, from lyric to singing to orchestration to arrangement to beat. I tolerate the crass moments on this second long-playing contextualization because five of its six cuts make me laugh.   **B+**

The Weather Girls: *Big Girls Don't Cry* (Columbia '85). At a moment when soul is resurfacing as an ear-catching set of usages, a form basically independent of its original sources, these fat ladies—abetted by a new production team, and so it goes—take it one step further and make soul a cartoon, with the title cut the masterstroke. They'll cop material anywhere—debut single's from Jesse Winchester. And if at first their tricks seem inspired, by the time you get to Creedence and Neil Sedaka they're beginning to sound obvious.   **B**

Weather Report: *Night Passage* (ARC/Columbia '80). Finally it is revealed: they want to be Henry Mancini. The perky title cut could be a title theme for your local meteorologist, and after that they demonstrate their aptitude for mood music. Catchiest tune on side two was written by somebody named Ellington.   **C+**

Katie Webster: *Two-Fisted Mama!* (Alligator '89). Webster's legend has never connected on record, and by coming down heavy on the soul standards retro-rocking blues fans yammer for, her much-praised label debut *The Swamp Boogie Queen* sold her short. Boogie as in woogie, not as in bar band, is her gift—a rolling piano style she certainly didn't invent and just as certainly owns—and here the experts get it down. The quintessential tough-talking woman with sexual needs and a heart of gold.   **B+**

Jane Weidlin: *Jane Weidlin* (I.R.S. '85). All you cool folks who thought the Go-Go's were airheads, not to mention all you airheads who thought the Go-Go's were cool, will find these troubled relationships and geopolitical concerns very educational. I thought the Go-Go's were more

educational pretending to be airheads, not to mention sisters.   **C+**

Wham!: *Make It Big* (Columbia '84). Though George Michael seems more swellheaded than one would wish in a superstar (or a coworker), he does take care of business! His Isleys cover is less striking than his ersatz Motown! How many other pretty boys can make such a claim?!   **B**

Barry White, Love Unlimited, the Love Unlimited Orchestra: *The Best of Our Love* (Love Unlimited '80). I know you don't think he's good for anything but excess anyway, but if you'll allow me to get technical for a moment, there's good Barry White and bad Barry White. All the good Barry White any normal person needs is on his 1975 *Greatest Hits* for 20th Century, which this CBS-distributed two-disc compilation had better not displace in the racks. White's half begins with "I Love To Sing the Songs I Sing," its cannily repeated verb an excellent definition of bad Barry White, and ends with "Just the Way You Are," which he, well, sings. There's also a side of Love Unlimited that leaves their only good album untouched. And a side of the Love Unlimited Orchestra, Barry's Jackie Gleason tribute band.   **C**

Barry White: *Barry White's Greatest Hits, Volume 2* (20th Century-Fox '81). The moribund big man having bolted for CBS with the abysmal "I Love To Sing the Songs I Sing," the moribund minor has no recourse but to piece together a best-of. Which is of course the best album released under the big man's name since his last best-of for the minor. He doesn't rap enough, but at least he doesn't essay any true ballads—the tag line masquerading as a ballad he damn near invented, and he's surprisingly OK on the Hollywood-Latin of "Sha La La Means I Love You" and the uptempo masculinity of "I'm Qualified To Satisfy You." Sha la la means anything you want it to mean.   **B+**

White Animals: *Ecstasy* (Dread Beat '84). Despite the off name and kalimba intro, I figured these Nashvillians for an especially one-dimensional bunch of popsters after happy songs like "This Girl of Mine" and

"You Started Something" provided exactly what they promised. But eventually, wondering about the "Gloria" remake and the psychedelic blues, I realized that one-dimensionality is . . . not the point, because that would imply irony, but the payoff. Somehow these guys sincerely inhabit a very '60s-ish reality; their message isn't some kind of distanced commentary on their musical material, it's the material itself. They say they like soul, too, and I believe them. Original grade: B plus.   **B**

Whitesnake: *Whitesnake* (Geffen '87). The attraction of this veteran pop-metal has got to be total predictability. The glistening solos, the surging crescendos, the familiar macho love rhymes, the tunes you can hum before the verse is over—not one heard before, yet every one somehow known. Who cares if they're an obscure nine-year-old vehicle for the guy who took over Deep Purple's vocal chores five years before that? Rock and roll's ninth or tenth "generation" of terrified high-school boys can call them their own. And may they pass from the ether before the eleven-year-olds who are just now sprouting pubic hair claim their MTV.   **D+**

Whitesnake: *Slip of the Tongue* (Geffen '89). They got lucky, and they don't intend to let go. With fast-gun-for-hire Steve Vai operating all guitars and who knows what other geegaws, they've consolidated their sound into essence of arena: all pomp, flash, sentimentality, and male posturing, this is now the Worst Band in the World. So you just move over, Journey. (Hey—where *is* Journey?)   **D**

White Zombie: *Soul-Crusher* (Caroline '88). The lyric sheet that spruces up this rereleased-to-a-major-minor consumer-object-in-spite-of-itself makes a promise: "Out of the chaos comes a reason." But not out of the consumer object, an inedible noise-rock omelet distinguished from the competition by drawling voice-and-guitars. People consent to fascism because they think fascism will be more fun than this. They could be right.   **D+**

Barrence Whitfield and the Savages: *Barrence Whitfield and the Savages*

(Mamou '84). Though I really don't believe that Esquerita and the Seeds, say, loom larger in rock history than, say, Gamble & Huff and the Grateful Dead, this time I have to grant dumb-ass obscurantism its due. Whitfield isn't a genuine throwback, but he is a genuine historical oddity—an acceptable Little Richard substitute, with a band that doesn't fake it. He's not crazed or rubber-piped enough to go all the way with a frantic groove, though "Mama Get the Hammer" and "Ship Sails at Six" come close. But when everybody lets up a little, especially on semi-instrumentals like "Walking with Barrence" and "Cotton Pickin' " and the steady-spreading "Go Ahead and Burn," Art Rupe would be proud. Time for thirteen tunes: an authentic 27:52.   **B+**

Barrence Whitfield and the Savages: *Dig Yourself* (Rounder '85). No other r&b copy band has such an in at the chicken shack that transcends all knowing, and not just because they play and sing their asses off on covers remarkable, generic, and recondite enough to get born again as new classics. They're smart enough to play cool as well—so smart that only when the chicken shack disappears (as mysteriously as it has materialized, I'm sure) do you wonder just why they're so hot to spend all their time there.   **B+**

Barrence Whitfield and the Savages: *Ow! Ow! Ow!* (Rounder '87). Whitfield has yet to take a composition credit on three albums whose best originals are indistinguishable from the obscure old backbeat grooves and frantic novelties that are his trademark, but he's the auteur for damn sure—just replaced his entire band, with no trace of shift or slippage beyond the two overextended blues-soul showcases that lift him over the thirty-minute mark. These are merely generic because the boss has no special gift for expressive sincerity—not on the order of his gift for backbeat grooves and frantic novelties, here written mostly by his new helpers, and I dare you to pick out the "real" one without reading the label.   **B+**

Bill Withers: *Bill Withers' Greatest Hits* (Columbia '81). I don't know whether success ruined him or merely called forth his true nature, but despite my eternal affection for "Grandma's Hands" and my grudging admission that two of the three CBS-era tracks that here update his 1975 best-of are yeomanlike balladry, he sure does court the Roberta Flack market. The obsessively lustful "Use Me" and the obsessively jealous "Who Is He What Is He to You," both driven by hard rocklike beats, were what induced antisentimentalists to descry something tough beneath "Lean on Me" and "Ain't No Sunshine." They sound lost here. Which isn't to say "Lean on Me" and "Ain't No Sunshine" don't sound like nice songs.   **B+**

Keith Whitley: *I Wonder Do You Think of Me* (RCA '89). Already thirty-three, Whitley was just finding himself professionally when he died of acute alcohol poisoning while completing his fourth album last May, and where the hell he was hiding his voice beats me. Supple, resonant, deeply relaxed, he cuts Travis/Anderson/Haggard physically, and productionwise he's harder than any of them, ranging easily across all the purist subgenres except the bluegrass that gave him his start. With songs to match from the likes of Curly Putnam, Sanger Shafer, and Bill Rice, this could have been 1989's *Old 8×10,* with stringencies of formula serving only to keep the music on course. Instead it'll probably inspire another stupid suicide legend.   **A−**

Whodini: *Whodini* (Jive '83). With the secret of the great rap album still shrouded in mystery, you can't fault this attempt for starting with two intelligent if corny black youths from Brooklyn (cf. Wham! U.K.). But novelty hits do sometimes wear thin (cf. "The Haunted House of Rock: Vocoder Version"). And though you might get away with producing your album in London or even Cologne, going from one to the other is asking for trouble.   **B−**

Whodini: *Escape* (Jive '84). Like all aspiring popmeisters, producer Larry Smith and head rapper Jalil Hutchins turn out ingratiating variations on a formula. Fortunately, the formula isn't tired yet—it was a great singing synth riff that put "Haunted House of Rock" over, not the

novelty concept. Even the putative follow-up "Freaks Come Out at Night," dumber lyrically than "Escape" and "Friends" and dumber musically than the irresistible "Five Minutes of Funk," is five minutes of fun.   **B+**

Whodini: *Back in Black* (Jive '86). They're not just ladies' men, they're the big brothers every B-boy wishes he had. Or so they hope. Autobiographical examples make their stay-in-school and one-love advice more convincing than most, though just to cover all the bases they don't stint with the etiquette tips ("That's Dom Perignon, it's supposed to bubble"). But nowhere are they catchier than on the "tag team sex" of "I'm a Ho" or more realistic than on "The Good Part": "But I keep going for it and I won't stop / Because I don't believe there is a good part / Because I been searching and lurching and looking real good / Because if there is a good part it ain't in my neighborhood."   **B+**

Whodini: *Open Sesame* (Jive '87). I admit it, I get off on "Early Mother's Day Card," a rap achievement surpassing even a stay-in-school song capable of keeping somebody in school. But when it's all I notice beyond a def beat or two, I wonder whether they're still in the right business.   **B−**

Who's That Girl (Sire '87). From Scritti Politti and Coati Mundi you expect trickier spin, but they're outsiders, and outsiders times soundtrack equals contract work. For her own movie, though, the decade's purest pop icon should do better than sloppy seconds. Or *neat* seconds—worse still.   **C−**

Wide Boy Awake: *Wide Boy Awake* (RCA Victor EP '83). From the never-say-die twelve-inch "Slang Teacher" to the programmed gumbo of the contagious "Chicken Outlaw," these interracial veterans of the Antmusic scam sound unspoiled, casual, maybe even (Gawd) unambitious, capturing a little bit of a London nightlife that's destined to disappear faster than their youth. I mean, that is a song about going up to the roof to puke, now isn't it?   **B+**

Webb Wilder & the Beatnecks: *It Came From Nashville* (Landslide '87). Wilder is about as country as Olivia Newton-John. He's got one of those pencil-necked voices, like he not only went to college (which lots of real men and good old boys do these days) but maybe even prep school. His Steve Earle cover beats his Hank Williams cover, and his best song is about hanging out by a pool with a rule against dogs. And I almost don't care. Any Nashvillean who can honestly urge all his "patrons in the teen and sub-teen demographic to pursue happiness at every opportunity" gets slack from me.   **B**

Wild Seeds: *Mud, Lies and Shame* (Passport '88). A typical Amerindie story. Led by then-rockcrit Michael Hall, the Seeds took their Southwest-boho syncretism public in 1984 with a self-produced EP that hauled in heaps of hosannas, none so impolite as to note that not a single memorable song shored up the band's, what shall we call it, soulful Austin country-punk. *Brave, Clean and Reverent,* released in 1986 on the local Jungle label, failed to get them much further despite ace side-leaders: "Sharlene," about Hall's crush on a pretty boy, and "I Work Hard," about his compulsion to wage slavery. Now they've graduated to what's called a major indie, and the first three cuts are everything one could have hoped, especially the self-explanatory "I'm Sorry, I Can't Rock You All Night Long," a true classic as these things are measured. The rest continue their project of defeating male chauvinism in the male chauvinist roots-rock context, but not so's you'd notice. In a saner world, this would be their debut album. It would include "Sharlene" and "I Work Hard" (without horns, please), encouraging everylistener to bear down on their lesser material, the best of which is more than passable. How they would have made a living in the meantime I couldn't tell you. How they make a living now I couldn't tell you either.   **B**

Wild Style (Animal '83). Great rap records usually begin with killer riffs and add beats from live players, buttinski producer-engineers, scratchers, and rap attackers. On this soundtrack neither musical director Fab 5 Freddy nor big man Chris Stein do much to get things started, but the rhymes themselves, mostly folk-boast rather than commercial-protest and often captured live on the streets in a kind of simulated field recording, carry the music.   **B+**

Deniece Williams: *Niecy* (Columbia/ ARC '82). Williams's exquisite clarity and thrilling range have always slotted her among the perfect angels for me, but there's a lot more to her work with Thom Bell, who finally challenges Burt Bacharach on his own turf, applying strings and woodwinds and amplifiers with a deft economy that textures rather than sweetens. And Williams's lyrics, while never startling, become increasingly personal as her professional confidence grows—she's wrinkling her brow more and her nose less. Dionne Warwick fans: welcome to the '80s.   **B+**

Deniece Williams: *I'm So Proud* (Columbia '83). Minnie Riperton she's not— really. Cameos from Johnny Mathis (body) and Philip Bailey (spirit) bring out the character in her pure, intense soprano, and "Love, Peace and Unity" mentions the "arms race" in a welcome moment of negativity. But Williams has progressed, as they say, from Thom Bell's pop romanticism to George Duke's cosmic idealism, and these fusion guys have never understood about songs.   **B**

Hank Williams: *Just Me and My Guitar* (Country Music Foundation '85). Why do demos have such a mystique? Aren't they created solely to sell songs? And if Williams's prominence freed him of the need to compromise his expression, didn't it also free him of the need to put the song across at all? I mean, it wasn't evil bizzers who forced him to record with a band— the band was Hank's pride and joy. Listen to the static singsong rhythms of these strummed solo versions and you'll know why—when Vic McAlpin (?) provides a touch of vocal counterpoint on "You Better Keep It on My Mind," it's like somebody just pulled up the shades. Nor are all the obscurities as epochal as the side-openers, "Honky Tonk Blues" and "Jambalaya," both available and then some in livelier, more crisply recorded versions. Because Williams was a genius, his alternate takes are certainly of interest, and occasionally—the slow, stark "A House of Gold," for instance—they're riveting. But this is for serious collectors. Casual collectors should put their money into Polydor's complete-recordings twofers before evil bizzers kill the project.   **B+**

Hank Williams, Jr.: *Greatest Hits* (Elektra '82). He may be Rosa Luxemburg compared to the Nashville squares he's forever railing against, but he's also a self-indulgent, self-pitying, self-mythologizing MCP, and though this format maximizes the MCP's entertainment and truth value, he doesn't get away with "Kaw-Liga" or "Texas Women." Rosa inspires "The American Dream," which has truths to tell about a Hollywood square with the initials RR. The booster who made his debut on "The New South" tells two lies about New York.   **B**

Hank Williams Jr.: *Montana Cafe* (Warner Bros. '86). Having survived his brush with death, his defection to rock, and his obsession with his daddy, whom he now outsells, Williams rests on his laurels as professional braggart and secondhand showbiz legend. He's one of the few country artists who goes gold at least partly because he's not really country—like rock both '50s and post-Allmans, country's just grist for a macho vaudeville that on this album blows even harder than usual. The tip-off's "Bocephus," a return to unabashed me-me-me. But let us not overlook the ill-rhymed polka about cowboy hats, the Leon Redbone–styled "Harvest Moon," and the novelty rag about pretty girls whose "pig" friends interfere with the workings of Junior's dick.   **C**

Hank Williams, Jr.: *Wild Streak* (Warner/Curb '88). The age of AIDS hasn't left him untouched—he takes his women one at a time and indulges in telephone sex. But usually Junior comes on like such a wild-ass that you can only tell him from the average rapper by his primitive sense of rhythm and his failure to mention the size of his dick. Last album was called *Born To Boogie,* this one features

Gary Rossington in Skynyrd simulations that top Skynyrd's own, and the CMA is so desperate to stay up-to-dately in-the-tradition that it keeps kissing his ass. Not that "If the South Woulda Won" can be said to go against the Nashville grain—nobody really wants to go back to slavery, understand, but if that's the price of more hangings and no more foreign cars, we may have to bite the bullet. Anyway, Hank drops in a good word for Martin Luther King on the very next song. What do these people want?   **C+**

Hank Williams Jr.: *Greatest Hits III* (Warner Bros. '89). How embarrassing—when I let my guard down this flattering sampler catches me thinking that maybe the CMA has a point. The "Ain't Misbehavin' " isn't gratuitous, the miracle-of-science duet with his dad isn't dead, the star-studded "Mind Your Own Business" swings like a mother, the autobiography is good shtick, and the country songs are good country songs—"This Ain't Dallas" is a classic of the TV age. And though "Young Country" disses punks, I'll trade for r&b even up.   **B+**

Lucinda: *Happy Woman Blues* (Folkways '80). Having pledged allegiance with an album of traditional material that won't give anybody new insights into Robert Johnson, this guileless throwback to the days of the acoustic blues mamas follows through with an album of originals that won't give anybody new insights into men, solitude, or making music. But here's something to mull over—you'll love it. Partly because she means what she says and says what she means, and partly because she has a way of flatting key lines that's as fetching as the dimples on your bedmate's ass. But mostly because contemporary doesn't mean hip, cool, or fashionable—it means knowing what time it is.   **A−**

Lucinda Williams: *Lucinda Williams* (Rough Trade '88). The side-openers—"I Just Wanted To See You So Bad," which repeats the title nine times in twenty-one lines, and "Passionate Kisses," the last of a series of modest demands that begins with a bed that won't hurt her back (a good bed to sleep in, that means)—are winners as written, avid and sensible and all Lucinda. After that the songs are fine, but it's down to a big not enormous, handsome not beautiful voice that's every bit as strong as the will of this singer-by-nature and writer-by-nurture. So at home in blues and country that she won't abide a rock and roll pigeonhole, she fought seven years to do an album her way. She can make a winner out of any song that spurns the clichés she's too avid and sensible to resort to, and why any record man would want to order her around I can only guess. Maybe because she seems just an inch's compromise away from a hit. But that inch is why her rock and roll traditionalism still sounds fresh. Original grade: A minus.   **A**

Lucinda Williams: *Passionate Kisses* (Rough Trade EP '89). Pointing frantically at the title song, Rough Trade remixes it, adds an old version of another LP cut and three live country blues, and prays for airplay. Not the EP as interim product—the EP as promotional device.   **B+**

Victoria Williams: *Happy Come Home* (Geffen '87). Sui generis it may be, yet in a great semipopular tradition: oddball folkie meets El Lay, represented by her coproducers born-again Steven Soles and bicoastal Anton Fier, as well as venerable oddball Van Dyke Parks, whose string arrangements prove him her soul brother. Her roots are in Cajunland, so naturally she sings like a cross between Dolly Parton and Yoko Ono. If you fear art damage, I cannot tell a lie, so maybe you'll believe me when I add that it's tolerable. Shoes, Jesus, merry-go-rounds, and animals—lots of animals. Hirth Martinez would be proud.   **B+**

Cris Williamson: *Blue Rider* (Olivia '82). Proving that lesbians are normal folks with normal hopes, normal regrets, even normal string arrangements—just like you, me, and Nicolette Larson. Next question.   **C**

Wilma: *Wilma* (Subterranean '85). Some of their songs do well by such old staples as poststructuralism ("Life Without Adjectives") and fuck-men ("Love Vaccine");

others don't. Their idiot-avant instrumentals (cf. the Residents, Toiling Midgets) are never as oppressive as Frightwig's generic hardcore, Salem 66's slave-pop, Throwing Muses' muse, etc. And their cover of "Georgy Girl" blows away such monumental precedents as the Raincoats' "Lola" and Y Pants' "That's the Way Boys Are." A sarcastic rollick through a song you never knew meant so much or so little, it's interrupted by a futuristic dream sequence in which Georgy joins a punk band and utters the following Inspirational Verse: "I suppose you're thinking / We're a little queer / Well my boy I suggest you suck another beer / The bottle's warmyfru / It's got a foamy head / It doesn't cry it doesn't bleed it doesn't wet your bed."   **B**

Brian Wilson: *Brian Wilson* (Sire '88). What made Brian's utopian fantasy so believable was the guileless hypocrisy of the simpletons fate and family tied him to—his shy, sincere, goofy, subtly tortured lyrics were rooted in the cheerful hedonism of the Beach Boys' secular chorales and white-boy soul. Solo, the pain in his voice is all too unmediated, and he isn't deep enough to make something of it—he sounds like the sincere, talented, mildly pretentious nut he is. What's more, his multiproduced million-dollar return is weighed down by a collective Phil Spector obsession—comes off incredibly labored. Of course, *Smile* was probably kind of overwrought too.   **B−**

Pat Wilson: *Bop Girl* (Warner Bros. EP '84). Not related to Mari, though she does camp up her femininity, or Cindy, though this dinky-looking Australian mini wouldn't exist if the B-52's hadn't made trash-pop a joke worth hearing again. Presumably related to coproducer/cowriter Ross. I could go on (the name Ricky Fataar ring any bells?), but this kind of ephemera only endures when it's given the chance to sneak up on you.   **B+**

Jesse Winchester: *Talk Memphis* (Bearsville '81). For some reason I'd hoped that Jesse's meet-up with Willie Mitchell would inspire both of them to get funky—so much so that at first I mistook tuneful for a substitute. Then I recalled that these days tuneful demifunk is a working definition of pop. And realized that this isn't all that tuneful.   **B—**

The Wind: *Guest of the Staphs* (Cheft EP '84). From Bayside and/or Florida, they traveled south and/or north to record with the ubiquitous but stationary Mitch Easter, who never before has gotten so close to this kind of dense intensity—the extra drumbeats, the guitars that fall apart and then right themselves, the aggressive timing. It suffers the usual limitations of homage and formal exercise—you never really notice what the songs are about even though it's part of the game to write smart lyrics and sing medium clear. But especially on "Delaware 89763," which sounds like it could have been recorded at the Star Club long about 1966, they make you hear Carolina Beatlism for the romantic fantasy it is—from the *Beatlemania*-manqué of the Spongetones to the artsy-poo of Let's Active themselves.   **B+**

The Windbreakers: *Run* (DB '86). Enough bands fail to craft tuneful yet hard-rocking pop albums to make the success of this Mitch Easter project reviewable: it's tuneful, and it's hard-rocking. But there's nothing in music/vocals/lyrics/image to attract anybody specifically to the Windbreakers, nothing more than there is in Jeffrey Osborne, or Hall & Oates. In fact, they're less interesting than most stars, except maybe to young men who've devoted their lives to blurring the distinction between woman problems and girl trouble.   **B**

The Windbreakers: *A Different Sort* . . . (DB '87). With Bobby Sutliffe off following his muse like some junior Chris Stamey, Tim Lee remains as Peter Holsapple—sinewy soul, sandpaper cry, iron pyrite hooks, the works. No way is he as clever, but he compensates with an urgency that's his version of sound and groove both, and if a few of these jangle no-fail melodies went deeper than love hurts, he'd deserve better than he's likely to get.   **B+**

Johnny Winter: *Raisin' Cain* (Blue Sky '80). Up against the *Blues Brothers* soundtrack (a cousin, like it or not), the vocal gifts of this flashy white blues freak turned steadfast white r&b pro come clear—that drawling, high-pitched growl is his alone, and it's bluesier than Jake and Elwood for sure. On the other hand, Muddy Waters and Bobby Bland cut him. Unlike Jake or (especially) Elwood, and also unlike Muddy or Bobby, he doesn't seem to have a sense of humor. And he'll sing his bass player's songs.   **B—**

Steve Winwood: *Arc of a Diver* (Island '80). Winwood hasn't been a song artist since Dave Mason left Traffic, but at least here he takes responsibility for his own atmospherics. Instead of consorting with Ijahman or Stomu Yamashta, he's laid down this lulling British-international groove all by himself. Overdubbing, the technique is called. Very up-to-date.   **B—**

Steve Winwood: *Talking Back to the Night* (Island '82). Launched on a chart-certified comeback, he tries to consolidate his gains by writing songs instead of tripping over them the way he did with "While You See a Chance." Somebody throw a synthesizer at that man's ankles.   **C**

Steve Winwood: *Back in the High Life* (Island '86). This is the fate of a wunderkind with more talent than brains: after two decades of special treatment, he derives all the self-esteem he needs just from surviving, as they say. So he's confident that the veracity and unpretentiousness of his well-wrought banalities make them interesting, when in fact they're exactly as interesting as he is.   **C**

Steve Winwood: *Chronicles* (Island '87). What can you expect of a man who could have sung like Ray Charles and chose instead to follow in the voiceprints of Jack Bruce? Classy arena-rock, that's what, redolent at its best of his fellow studio obsessives in Steely Dan, only never as smart, and at its worst more like REO Speedwagon. His radio-ready arrangements, hired lyrics, and funk borrowings are all hallmarks of the most venal popular music of the age, and that his synthesizer moves were slightly ahead of their time doesn't make them an iota less annoying. In short, a worthy biz legend.   **C+**

Steve Winwood: *Roll With It* (Virgin '88). Wish I could claim the music's sapped by whatever moves him to submit material to his beer company before his record company even hears it, but that happened long ago. If anything, this is an improvement—his contempo soul has gained not only bite but speed, so you have less time to think about it. Give most of these meaningless songs to some open-throated journeyman white people have never heard of—Bert Robinson, say, any big-voiced belter who doesn't conflate strain and feeling—and they might even sound like Saturday night.   **B−**

Wire: *Document and Eyewitness* (Rough Trade import '81). At first I diagnosed the grungy sound and semipro execution of this live LP-plus-EP as the band's worst case of arty-farty yet. But for all the chatter and false starts and extended instrumental nothings, it packs real momentum—you could even say it gets wild. The new songs are worthy of the name, too. So when it comes to arty-farty, I'll take this over the neaty-beaty of *154*. By a hair and a half.   **B**

Wire: *And Here It Is . . . Again . . . Wire* (Sneaky Pete import '84). Documenting the evolution of punk's quintessential self-conscious aestheticians from semicompetent but never exactly crude thrashers to polished but never exactly slick art-poppers. The seven-title selection from the near-perfect *Pink Flag,* all 12:15 of it, leads off with the fuzzed-up live *Roxy London WC2* versions of "Lowdown" and "12XU" and has the effect of transforming that twenty-one-track marvel of seamless pacing into a string of sardonic punk blowouts. The succinct 1978 single "Dot Dash" and the all-out 1979 single "A Question of Degree" ease the transition in and out of the transitional *Chairs Missing.* And the three survivors from *154* sound like popular music—or at least popular art.   **A**

Wire: *Snakedrill* (Mute import EP '86). " 'A Serious of Snakes' " is *154* updated technologically, rhythmically, and spiritually, which is almost to say transformed utterly—dance-trance with a nasty surrealistic edge. "Drill" does the same for *Pink Flag.* "Advantage in Height" is less of both worlds. "Up to the Sun" is a cappella noodling. Welcome back. [Later on Enigma]   **B+**

Wire: *The Ideal Copy* (Enigma '86). The Wire of punk myth abraded like the smell of gunpowder, fucking in the sand, a scouring pad. This is more like digital sound turned up too loud, a cold shower, a dash of after-shave: chronic alienation converted into quality entertainment. Except on a terrible track that outdoes slow Roxy Music, it's pretty bracing in both rock and disco modes. It's also nothing more.   **B−**

Wire: *Kidney Bingos* (Restless EP '88). Live remake from their last EP and next CD, live remake from their last LP and next CD, studio preview of their next LP and next CD, studio preview of their next CD, remix of said preview not currently scheduled for rerelease. Talk about for vinyl junkies only.   **C+**

Wire: *A Bell Is a Cup Until It Is Struck* (Enigma '88). Waiting for my annoyance to articulate itself, I found appropriate contexts—subways, elevators, etc.—and stuck this into my personal portable. Where to my shock it proved fun fun fun. Maybe they are about to jump to Windham Hill, but only because Windham Hill wants to escape its suburban demographic. Mellifluous, deceitful background rock—but ugly, and with a kick.   **B+**

Wire: *Silk Skin Paws* (Restless EP '88). Sez the cover sticker on these three remixes and one previously-unavailable: "Specially Priced Mini-Album for the Wire Connoisseur." Sez the label: "45 RPM." Thus assuring that Wire connoisseurs will be the first to learn that Mighty Mouse has joined the group.   **C+**

Wire: *It's Beginning To and Back Again* (Enigma/Mute '89). In an arty variation on the remix best-ofs that pass for new dance product these days, they recorded some concerts and reworked them in the studio and then reworked that. I don't know whether the new versions are better art than the old ones. But formalists rarely can tell the difference between progress and attenuation. And as the ear candy once-removed that is Wire's current calling, this wanders.   **B—**

Wire: On Returning (1977–1979) (Restless Retro cassette/CD '89). With *Pink Flag, Chairs Missing,* and *154* all back in catalogue on the same label, there's a sense in which this compilation is de trop. Drawing heavily on all three, not as effective a unit as *Pink Flag* yet kicking off with thirteen of that masterpiece's twenty-one cuts, failing to convert this original skeptic to such *154* indulgences as "The Other Window" and the deadly "A Touching Display," mastermind Jon Savage presents a lovingly literal best-of rather than a half-collectorama half-intro like the 1984 Sneaky Pete anthology. But does it hold up, grabbing your collar with one brief, bitter tune after another for almost the entirety of a thirty-one-cut CD. They're not the only punks whose public protests eventually revealed their roots in personal frustration. But their plaints don't seem merely private. They seem emblematic of a time whose cruelties didn't begin and end with alienation, as sad art students sometimes believe, but for damn sure included it.   **A**

Peter Wolf: Lights Out (EMI America '84). Though the big deal is supposed to be the way collaborator Michael Jonzun brings Wolf's r&b into the space age, there's more electronic pizzazz in current Chaka or Ashford & Simpson. Such sweet sleepers as "I Need You Tonight" and "Baby Please Don't Go" and "Here Comes That Hurt Again," all of them originals, sound like obscure Motown covers. In short, a gratifyingly unassuming solo breakaway.   **B+**

Peter Wolf: Come as You Are (EMI America '87). Wolf's propensity to rev into high gear has always been his undoing. Only when he lightens up can he uncover what little nuance he has at his disposal. His solo debut was coproduced by space monkey Michael Jonzun. It was playful. This one's coproduced by his engineer. It's mechanical.   **B—**

Womack & Womack: Love Wars (Elektra '83). Though they're more purely soul music than either, this professional couple place closer to Ashford & Simpson than to Delaney & Bonnie on an urban-to-down-home axis, which may be why their soul music avoids not only nostalgia but conservatism: Al Jackson would have turned in his union card before permitting a drum floomph so loosely contemporary. Ace singers and songwriters (as opposed to singer-songwriters), their lyrics about loss and conflict are sharper than those about love and happiness. But "Express Myself" makes a passable "Is It Still Good to Ya" and their lyrics about loss and conflict—especially "Love Wars" and "A.P.B."—clearly come from lovers who wish they weren't fighters.   **A—**

Womack & Womack: Radio M.U.S.C. Man (Elektra '85). Just how low-profile the new songs are is made clear when a sweet cover of "Here Comes the Sun" snaps you from drugged semiconscious enjoyment to full attention. I love the relaxed groove and wavering back-porch harmonies that go into their unique sound—lazy, tender, patient, long-suffering, tired of fighting. But they don't have to get by on atmosphere.   **B+**

Womack & Womack: Conscience (Island '88). On stage, the shy sprite with the truth-telling voice seems way too good for the pompous baldhead she's saddled with, and his album notes don't dispel the impression: something about how a man trusts a woman and she does him wrong but he perseveres and in the end Love prevails, only not that clear. Thus what sounds at first like a great collection turns into a real good one larded with bullshit—its parts are most fruitfully enjoyed at face value, one at a time. Fortunately, Cecil sings a lot better than he talks or thinks; praise the Lord, Linda sings a lot better than Cecil.   **A—**

The Woman in Red (Motown '84). Since Stevie Wonder has become one of those pleasure artists I rarely enjoy of my own free will, I was dubious about this water-treading soundtrack, but after a while the rhythm parts—even the deja entendu synth patterns and bass lines—began to get me. Though Dionne Warwick's solo turn is more Manilow than Bacharach, the two duets are her most winning music since the Spinners. And "Don't Drive Drunk" soars high as a kite.   **B**+

Stevie Wonder: *Hotter Than July* (Tamla '80). Except for the all-embracingly Afro-pan-American "Master Blaster" and maybe the birthday greeting to Dr. King, there's no great Stevie here, but he does know how to have fun doing his job. Great advertisement for the political potential of oral culture, too. Between his free-floating melodicism and his rolling overdrive, his hope and his cynicism, he seems more and more like the best thing the '60s ever happened to. Sure outlasted Jerry Garcia, now didn't he?   **A**−

Stevie Wonder: *The Original Musiquarium I* (Tamla '82). Distilling an admirable but somewhat discursive album artist into one of rock and roll's most compelling songwriters (and rock-and-rollers), this would be an ideal best-of if the four (out of sixteen) new tracks matched up—only the ten-minute Dizzy Gillespie jam "Do I Do" belongs, though "Front Line" 's Vietnam-vet lyric tries. The political side—"Superstition"–"You Haven't Done Nothin' "–"Living for the City"–"Front Line"—makes you forget he's an institution, and the "Higher Ground"–"Sir Duke"–"Master Blaster"–"Boogie On Reggae Woman" groove parlay meshes like that's the way God planned it. On the other hand, the calm, condescending cruelty of "Superwoman" has worn so badly that it not only undercuts its own seductive melody but casts a pall on "You Are the Sunshine of My Life," the most beautiful song he'll ever write. Docked a notch for male chauvinism.   **A**−

Stevie Wonder: *In Square Circle* (Tamla '85). Compare this to the others in your head and you'll be hard-pressed to specify what's missing, but slap on *Talking Book* or *Hotter Than July* and you'll hear how cushy it is—polyrhythmic pop rather than polyrhythmic rock. Stevie's effervescence is so indomitable that it's a pleasure even so, but nothing rises far enough out of the stew—"Land of the La La" is no "Living for the City," "Part Time Lover" no "I Just Called To Say I Love You," etc. Then

there's the infectious "Spiritual Walkers," in which Stevie gives it up to Hare Krishna and witnesses for the Witnesses.   **B**+

Stevie Wonder: *Characters* (Motown '87). Nine lines in, he assumes the voice of God to assure sufferers that everything's gonna be all right, and instantly you lose heart. But then his chronic self-importance disappears—the worst it gets is spacy, and Stevie can make spacy a trip when he's on. Which he definitely is—melodically, rhythmically, emotionally, politically, sonically. Erupting in anti-Reagan rhymes or imagining a nasty joint or keying a love ballad to his own recorded bodily rhythms or whomping a groove with Michael Jackson or finding the balance between black-pride lyricism and antiapartheid militance, he sounds like he's got something to prove again. Ronald Reagan can do that to a black hero. So can Prince.   **A**−

The Woodentops: *Giant* (Columbia '86). With their "move away from cynicism" and airy touch, these Brits do bear a suspicious resemblance to Howard Jones if not Haircut 100, but at their best they're rootsy and rigorous. At their best, in fact, they ring one more change on the less-is-more magic you always think was exhausted the last time. The analogy is Feelies rather than R.E.M.—the lyrical uplift is a function of rave-up alone, with musical and verbal detail extraneous, as the perky/breathy/hooky/romantic distractions of this shot at the big time demonstrate all too well. "Shout" and "Get It On," even "Love Train" are their mission in life. "If we could always be together / It would be so sublime" is Lionel Richie's.   **B**

The Woodentops: *Well Well Well . . .* (Upside '86). Problem with this budget eight-song early-singles compilation is that at close to thirty-four minutes there isn't quite enough of it. The fast-faster-fastest sequence that leads into the slow, surprising obloquy on side one is excitement itself but doesn't put the anticlimactic Suicide homage across; "Special Friend" shoulda stayed a B side, and "Cold Inside" a dub remix. And given how often youth comes to full bloom these days, this is the Woodentops to buy nevertheless.   **B**+

The Woods: *It's Like This* (Twin/Tone '87). No way it can mean much at this late date, but for a first side that never quits Don Dixon's backup trio sound like relaxed late dB's remaking *Crazy Horse* as *Exile on Main Street*. Thus it's one of those off-the-cuff pleasures most Amerindies are too self-involved to provide any more, a busman's holiday rather than an artistic statement and/or a career move. On side two the songs run out, which could be why the career move is declined. Lucky thing— even with a dozen good ones they'd be riding for a fall. **B**

World Party: *Private Revolution* (Chrysalis '86). As a sourpuss who counsels self-improvement and jots down the occasional specific, Karl Wallinger is several steps up the evolutionary ladder from Howard Jones. But it's no less fatalistic to say humanity is defined by original sin than to say the world is good because God made it. Jones believes that war is over if you think it is, Wallinger that war is over if each and every one of you think it is; both prefer attitude to action, especially collective action. And if that's rock and roll, as I sometimes fear, it doesn't happen to be good rock and roll. **C**

Wreckless Eric: *Big Smash* (Stiff/Epic '80). A strange sort of double album, half of it the compilation indie Stiff stiffed with last year, the other a supposed commercialization. The theme is "Pop Song," which begins with a murmured "Put it in your mouth" before moving on to "Better write a pop record / With a money-spinning hook / If the muse don't hit you / You're off the books." 'Tis said the spunk has gone out of the lad, but though he does wax lyrical at times—I like the one where he admires the style of a girl handing in her tube ticket—he's as rude and scrawny as ever. Maybe the new stuff isn't altogether fabulous, but Stiff led with a compilation because he's mortal. If you count yourself among the millions who didn't purchase *The Wonderful World of Wreckless Eric*, do so now—you'll hardly notice the pop songs' rough sheen. If you count yourself among the thousands who did, ask yourself how much you love him and act ac-

cordingly. I love him moderately myself. Grade for new disc only. **B+**

Will Wright & Jim Reiman: *Childhood's Greatest Hits* (Rooster '86). Most kiddie musicians are, to be precise, yucky. These folkies are tart and spare as well as tuneful. They never force the cheer, never condescend, and never censor. If you want, they suggest you substitute "She tied up their tails, and played on her fife," but the lyric sheet for the all-instrumental sleepytime side has the original carving knife, and their dry vocals made me realize that the weasel pops the monkey in order to eat him. "Alabama Girls," "Skip to My Lou," "Row, Row, Row Your Boat," "Brahms' Lullabye," twenty-two sure shots in all, half wake-up sings, half instrumental lullabyes. I bet you don't own more than a few. And yes, the critic in the crib down the hall is almost as delighted to hear "Yankee Doodle" as she is "Ooh Poo Pah Doo" or anything by Madonna. **A—**

Robert Wyatt: *Nothing Can Stop Us* (Rough Trade import '81). In which the CPUK turns the unwary art-rocker into Pete Seeger. Long convinced that there's no percentage in soft-soaping the masses, Wyatt is more candidly propagandistic than, let us say, the Weavers—no "Kisses Sweeter Than Wine" (the Raincoats would never speak to him again), two tracks praising Stalin Foiler-of-the-Fascist-Foe. And his modernized concept of the folk enables him to transform a Chic song into a hymn. But internationalist sentiment still prevails—from Bangladeshi folk-rock to a stirring "Guantanamera"—and so does the shameless lust for killer melodies. In fact, if Wyatt had a freak voice as universal as Pete Seeger's he might move the left-wing masses quite nicely. [Later on Gramavision] **B+**

Robert Wyatt: *1982–1984* (Rough Trade '84). Wish there were English cribs for the two Spanish songs on this rather skimpy eight-cut compilation, because Wyatt's way with a lyric is one of the things that makes his hypnotic quaver so musical. But his arrangement of "Biko" for harmonium and percussion is so dumbfounding that I listen right through Victor Jara and Pedro

Milanos anyway, and the melodies are growing on me. Side one surrounds Thelonious Monk and Eubie Blake with two pieces of communist propaganda, one by Elvis Costello and one by Wyatt himself. Approximate time: 29:00.   **A—**

Robert Wyatt: *Old Rottenhat* (Rough Trade import '85). Set your political statements to unprepossessingly hypnotic music and you'd better be sure your politics are spot on—astute, clear, epigrammatic, correct. Don't deploy a slur like "aryan" anachronistically or attribute a phrase of Harold Rosenberg's to Noam Chomsky. Don't insult the genocide in East Timor with minimalist obscurantism. Don't preach to the converted until you've made more converts.   **B—**

Tammy Wynette: *Anniversary: Twenty Years of Hits* (Epic '87). Her corn pone all husk, her bouffant as sultry as Aretha's do, she sings like the heartbreaker who's about to best the long-suffering wife her lyrics put on a pedestal, but no matter how hypocritical her trademark equation between marriage, submission, and fulfillment, she remains the most soulful female country singer ever. And since she left George Jones (which no one in the world blames her for) and found fulfillment with George Richey a decade ago, her music has gone phfft. Twenty years my foot—the newest song here is a (professional) reunion with George (Jones) that's seven years old. In a world where *Greatest Hits, Greatest Hits Volume 4,* and *George & Tammy's Greatest Hits* still exist, this unexceptionable CD-length commemorative issue is about as useful as a kudzu seed. Consult your catalogue. Time: 55:18.   **B—**

X: *Los Angeles* (Slash '80). From poet-turned-chanteuse Exene to junk-guitar journeyman Billy Zoom, these aren't mohawked *NME*-reading truants who think Darby Crash is God or the Antichrist. They're sexy thrift-shopping bohos who think Charles Bukowski is Norman Mailer or Henry Miller. This may not be exactly the aura they crave, but combined with some great tunes it enables them to make a smart argument for a desperately stupid scene. Of course, when they're looking for a cover (or a producer), they go to the Doors, prompting L.A. critic Jay Mitchell to observe: "Their death and gloom aura is closer to the Eagles, which is to say it is all Hollywood." But only in L.A. is that an insult, elsewhere the distinction between a city and its industrial hub is more like a clever apercu. [Later on CD with *Wild Gift*.] **A—**

X: *Wild Gift* (Slash '81). Hippies couldn't understand jealousy because they believed in universal love; punks can't understand it because they believe sex is a doomed reflex of existentially discrete monads. As X-Catholics obsessed with a guilt they can't accept and committed to a subculture that gives them no peace, Exene and John Doe are prey to both misconceptions, and their struggle with them is thrilling and edifying—would the Ramones could cop to such wisdom. Who knows whether the insightful ministrations of their guitarist will prove as therapeutic for them as for you and me, but I say trust a bohemian bearing gifts. How often do we get a great love album and a great punk album in the same package? Original grade: A. [Later on CD with *Los Angeles.*] **A+**

X: *Under the Big Black Sun* (Elektra '82). John and Exene attribute "The Hungry Wolf's" rather feral view of marriage, in which lifelong mates roam the urban wastes with dripping jaws, to the Sioux, but I think they got the idea from Ted Nugent; they should check out Farley Mowat, who describes wolves as lifelong mates who live on mice and never fuck around. These are good songs bracingly played, but the words hint at a certain familiar down-and-out romanticism. They do it with more style and concision than Bukowski, Waits, or Rickie Lee Jones. They do it almost as well as Richard Thompson, in fact. But this time it's Billy Zoom and D.J. Bonebrake who are putting the songs over. Best lyric: "Dancing With Tears in My Eyes," written in Tin Pan Alley before any of these young bohemians, Billy included, was born. **A—**

X: *More Fun in the New World* (Elektra '83). Aimed at the no-future generation, X's passionate reconstruction of musical (and marital) tradition is salutary, and this is their most accomplished album. Both the songwriting and Billy Zoom's guitar reach new heights of junk virtuosity, and "Breathless" is a stroke. But they're too complacent in their tumult. Their righteous anti-Brit chauvinism prevents them from seeing that in its way Culture Club, say, is at least as satisfying and generous-spirited as the Big Boys. And their un-abashed beatnik identification not only stinks slightly of retro but misses the point of rock bohemianism, which is that a proudly nonavant band like this ought to risk a little of its precious authenticity in an all-out effort to make converts.   **A—**

X: *Ain't Love Grand* (Elektra '85). After five years of wresting art from commerce and/or vice versa, John and Exene try to have it both ways. Satisfying their bohe-mian urges with the neofolk Knitters on the art label Slash, they appease their major mentors and keep Billy in the band by taking X to the same producer as Chris-tian heavy metal boys Stryper. Only just as you'd figure, Michael Wagener can't make John and Exene (or even Billy) sound com-mercial enough to convert anyone. On the first side he has trouble making them sound like anything at all.   **B**

X: *See How We Are* (Elektra '87). Even during the first four songs, when the sus-tained detail of the writing—with a boost from Dave Alvin's tormented yet unembit-tered "4th of July"—makes it seem they'll fight for every inch, you miss Billy Zoom's syncretic junk: fine though he is, Tony Gilkyson is too neoclassy for these con-vinced vulgarians. Then the material de-volves into complaints, throwaways, wasted stanzas, and utter clinkers.   **B**

X: *Live at the Whiskey A Go-Go on the Fabulous Sunset Strip* (Elektra '88). Twenty-four titles, the half dozen new ones less than essential, and as Tony Gilkyson zips through sixteen songs made flesh by Billy Zoom you begin to wonder whether the guitarist was the secret of the band after all. Maybe it was just the guitar.   **B+**

XTC: *Black Sea* (Virgin/RSO '80). Vir-tuosos shouldn't show off—it's bad man-ners and bad art. I'm suitably dazzled by the breathless pace of their shit—from folk croak to Beach Boys croon in the twin-kling of a track, with dissonant whatnot embellishing herkyjerk whozis through-out—but I find their refusal to flow grace-less two ways. On what do they predicate their smartypants rights? On words that rarely reclaim clichés about working-class futility, middle-class hypocrisy, militarist atrocity—not to mention love like rockets and girls who glow. They do, however, show real feeling for teen males on the make and, hmm, the recalcitrance of lan-guage. [Later on Geffen.]   **B+**

XTC: *English Settlement* (Virgin/Epic '82). With voices (filters, chants, wimp cool) and melodies (chants, modes, arts cool) ever more abstract, I figured Colin Moulding had finally conquered Andy Partridge and turned this putative pop band into Yes for the '80s. But it's more like good Argent, really, with the idealism less philosophical than political—melt the guns, urban renewal as bondage, o! that generation gap. And fortunately, the melo-dies aren't so much abstract as reserved, with the most outgoing stolen from Vivaldi or somebody by none other than Andy Partridge. [Later on Geffen.]   **B+**

XTC: *Mummer* (Geffen '83). Having retired full-time to the studio, the defini-tive English art-poppers sound more man-nered and arid than ever, which is no less bothersome just because it's one way they have of telling us something. By now, there are hints of guilt-tripping in Andy Par-tridge's awareness of what he isn't, and while "Human Alchemy" ("To turn their skins of black into the skins / Of brightest gold") and "Funk Pop a Roll" ("But please don't listen to me / I've already been poisoned by this industry") are nota-bly mordant takes on two essential rock and roll subjects, Partridge deliberately limits their reach. The eccentric disso-nances that sour his melodies and the fitful time shifts that undercut his groove may well bespeak his own sense of distance, but art-poppers who command both melody and groove are rare enough that I wish he'd find another way.   **B—**

XTC: *Waxworks: Some Singles 1977–1982* (Geffen '84). Proof, or at least evi-dence, that they're the pop band they claim to be: though most of these songs were also album cuts, not a one of them—not even the samples from *Drums and Wires,* their most hard-edged and least fussy long-player—sounds more at home on its respective album than it does here, in the company of its peers. In short, this is the essential collection, less compelling than the Buzzcocks' comparable *Singles Going Steady* only because they mean to stimulate rather than compel. More equal than others: "Statue of Liberty," "Senses Working Overtime."   **A**—

XTC: *The Big Express* (Geffen '84). Remember when Difford & Tilbrook were writing a musical? Sounds like a job for Partridge & Moulding. They could name it after "The Everyday Story of Smalltown." Which would keep them working at the proper scale and be the best thing for steam-powered trains since Ray Davies.   **B**

XTC: *Skylarking* (Geffen '86). Imagine *Sgt. Pepper* if McCartney hadn't needed Lennon—if he hadn't been such a wet—and you'll get an inkling of what these insular popsters have damn near pulled off. Granted, there's barely a hint of overarching significance, but after all, this isn't 1967. With Todd Rundgren sequencing and twiddling those knobs, they continue strong for the first nine or ten (out of fourteen) songs. Only when the topics become darker and more cosmic do they clutter things with sound and whimsy; as long as they content themselves with leisurely, Shelleyan evocations of summer love and the four seasons, they'll draw you into their world if you give them the chance—most enticingly on a song called "Grass," about something good to do there.   **A**—

XTC: *Oranges and Lemons* (Geffen '89). Compulsive formalists can't fabricate meaning—by which I mean nothing deeper than extrinsic interest—without a frame (cf. *Skylarking,* even the Dukes of Stratosphear). The only concept discernible on this hour-long double-LP is CD. Def Leppard got there first.   **B**—

XTC: See also Dukes of Stratosphear

"Weird Al" Yankovic: *In 3-D* (Rock 'n' Roll '84). I don't want to belabor the obvious (that's Al's job), but this is *Mad* for the ears. Still, *Mad* does hit dead on now and then, and with a lot of help from its target so does "Eat It." Palatable follow-ups: the free-swinging "Polkas on 45," which goes Joe Piscopo ten better, and "Mr. Popeil," which exploits Yankovic's otherwise fatal resemblance to Fred Schneider. **C+**

Yarbrough & Peoples: *The Two of Us* (Mercury '80). The problem with received tropes about love and music isn't that they're a turnoff in themselves—finally, I don't care what the words of "Don't Stop the Music" are, and the same goes for "Crazy" and "Third Degree," which continue side one. But when the settings are undistinguished, as on side two, only very great singers can attract one's interest the way a good lyric might. Y&P are very good singers. **B**

Yaz: *Upstairs at Eric's* (Sire '82). If Depeche Mode, the most bloodless synth-DOR unit this side of the German Federal Republic, can spin off such a soulful second generation, all is not lost. A tape-layered playlist does disfigure side one, but better godawful than bland, and before you complain about Vince Clarke's hackneyed take on modern romance you ought to remember that he only rejoined the human race a few months ago. I like to imagine that the agent of his salvation was new-age tough mama Alf Moyet, who can make any romantic cliché moderately credible. And I know for sure that the agent of her salvation is Clarke, whose spare, bright, intriguing, juicy electrocomp makes the credible compelling. **B+**

Yaz: *You and Me Both* (Sire '83). Alf Moyet may not have as "good" a voice as Annie Lenox, but she's more fun to spend half an hour with—cut her and she bleeds, etc. A bit of an old romantic, though which really isn't that much better than the new kind. **B**

Dwight Yoakam: *Guitars, Cadillacs, Etc. Etc.* (Reprise '86). As seems retrospectively inevitable in the neoclassicist era, a major finally gave this bluegrass-tinged hardshell a shot, expanding his generous indie EP of the same title (on Oak, if you care to look) into a skimpy album. Even first time around his twang-power purism was more retreat than reclamation. Add two superfluous covers, a duet with Maria McKee, and a title tune in which all those et ceteras turn out to be "hillbilly music" and you get Ricky Skaggs for sinners. **B**

Dwight Yoakam: *Hillbilly Deluxe* (Reprise '87). Buck Owens may be his hero, but if George Jones earns a ten for contained intensity and Ricky Skaggs a one, Owens gets an eight and Yoakam maybe a four—he never breaks out of the jams, fixes, and world-historical dilemmas that are country music's reason for being. Reminding us once again that in a genre that's always fetishized tradition, neotraditionalism means immersing yourself in limitation until you convince yourself it's the air you breathe.   **B—**

Dwight Yoakam: *Buenas Noches From a Lonely Room* (Reprise '88). With the clout to take chances, Yoakam is out to prove he's one mean cocksucker. On side one, hopeless jealousy metastasizes into a killing rage, and for damn sure he's more interesting that way—Jerry Lee worshippers may even get hard. Side two's Buck Owens cameo and lament for a boozer dad convince me the revamped persona is for the better. The inspirational number he wrote for his mom convinces me of nothing.   **B+**

Dwight Yoakam: *Just Lookin' for a Hit* (Reprise '89). Plotting his escape from country radio, an ambitious neorowdy calls up the two generations of L.A. country-rock summed up by the Burritos' "Sin City" and the Blasters' "Long White Cadillac," which redefine a judiciously slanted selection from his three albums. With the honky-tonk filler that spoiled the flavor of his debut EP-turned-LP recontextualized and the strong but mean-spirited first side of *Buenas Noches From a Lonely Room* undercut by two second-side highlights, you might almost think he was as smart as Gram or Dave Alvin. Well, don't overexcite yourself. Just thank the forces of commerce for a country best-of.   **A—**

Yo La Tengo: *President Yo La Tengo* (Coyote '89). Exceptionally well-connected in a very social scene, Ira Kaplan seemed even less likely than his fellow semipros to record music worth telling the world about, especially after his breathy debut thumbed its larynx at vocal projection and the well-illustrated *New Wave Hot Dogs* proved typically forgettable in its lilt-and-yell competence. Yet except maybe for Thelonious Monster, no Amerindie band all year has come off stronger openers than "Barnaby, Hardly Working" (mysterioso guitar hook) and "Drug Test" ("I wish I was high"). Nor can I recall a "Sister Ray" homage as felt as the live ten-minute "Evil That Men Do." They rock out, they wax poetic, they cover Dylan, they do their bit for the boho weal.   **A—**

Yolocamba Ita: *Revolutionary Songs of El Salvador* (Flying Fish '83). This exiled quintet can bring off their programmatic, translation-provided celebrations, tributes, parables, and calls to action for this English-only Yank because political folk music makes an urgent kind of sense in a country where a politicized peasantry can be banished or much worse for enjoying it. In my limited experience, the closest parallels to their Andean/Indian guitars and percussion and around-the-fire interaction would be the Chilean groups Quilapayun and Inti-Illimani. This is both more quirkishly indigenous and more predictably Iberian-romantic, complete with a string synthesizer that lends its cheesy grandeur to the elegiac-anyway melodies that climax side two.   **A—**

Yo! MTV Raps: The Album (Jive '89). For dilettantes and LP abusers, especially those open-minded enough to consider the Fresh Prince a Harold Teen for our times, a pop companion piece to Profile's fourth Mr. Magic comp. Only "Wild Wild West" and the inexhaustible "It Takes Two" are on both, and in many other cases—Stetsasonic's "Talkin' All That Jazz," Boogie Down's "My Philosophy," Salt-n-Pepa's "Shake Your Thang," Ice-T's "High Rollers"—MTV's notorious crossover lifts great tracks off good albums. This is not what I call homogenization.   **A—**

Yabby You: *One Love, One Heart* (Shanachie '83). Like many a serenely anonymous Rastafarian tuneweaver, the former Vivian Jackson could almost be a muezzin (or three) chanting nursery rhymes, most of which concern the end of the world as we know it, a prospect which cheers him considerably. With the help of many justly famous Rastafarian session-men he's produced a typical reggae sleeper—no surprises (the end of the world is hardly news), but considerable cheer.   **D+**

Yabby You: *Fleeing From the City* (Shanachie '85). Shanachie's 1983 collection of the "greatest works" of this crippled country man and religious recluse, whose unkiltered voice and gentle faith are eccentric even by Jamaican standards, proved him a gifted arranger of millenarian ditties. It also inspired him to record for the first time since 1977. Remarkably, he just got better during his long, impoverished layoff: without sacrificing roots harmonies or compact tunes, this music leaves room for embellishment and comment. What was once eccentric now sounds almost strong.   **A**−

You Can Tell the World About This: Classic Ethnic Recordings From the 1920s (Morning Star '86). I slapped this world music on the turntable like it was *Give 'Em Enough Rope* in 1978, and the Ukrainian side-openers kept me coming back to the Welsh hymn and the Jewish cantor and the Turkish itinerant's song and the "masterful Spanish piping." But I remain a savage beast. Even if music is the goddamn universal language, it'll take more than the "commanding dynamics and engaging warmth" adduced in the vague and skimpy notes to put its dialects in meaningful contact. As it happens, the relaxed Puerto Rican Jardineras do jibe with those fiery Ukrainians, and if you believe in expressiveness for its own artistic sake you may enjoy every cut. But universalist humanism to the contrary, what differentiates the secular from the sacred and the Asian from the European is more important and more fun than what unites them.   **B**

Neil Young: *Hawks and Doves* (Reprise '80). Only Neil would make a deliberately minor record about war and peace after three successive masterworks about himself. Its music fragile and sometimes partial, its length under 30 minutes despite throwaways, it divides less neatly into "dove" and "hawk" sides than the packaging advertises. Side one's haltingly lyrical "Little Wing" and shaggy head story "The Old Homestead" can be read as hippie paradigms, side two's rallying cries for old marrieds and union stalwarts as middle-American anthems. But Young's working men are from the American Federation of Musicians, and the confused "young mariner" who finishes off side one with a half-swallowed "I hope that I can

kill good" doesn't sound much like a hippie to me. So what I want to know is whether the DEW-line boys in "Comin' Apart at Every Nail" launched a missile or let one slip through. Some joke on the Pentagon either way.   **A**−

Neil Young & Crazy Horse: *Reactor* (Reprise '81). Got loads of feedback. Ain't got no takeoff.   **B**+

Neil Young: *Trans* (Geffen '82). Like almost everybody, I thought this was his dumbest gaffe since *Journey Through the Past* at first—his Devo buddies at least figured out that robots sound more lifelike if you program in some funkbeats. Granted, good old Joe Lala does add the occasional kerplunkety, but down beneath the vocodered quaver in which Young sings most of these silly sci-fi ditties they belong rhythmically to Billy Talbot, who could no more get on the one than lead a gamelan ensemble. Gradually, however, I figured out that robots also sound more lifelike if they're singing those grade-A elegiac folk melodies Young makes up when he's in the mood, because this is as tuneful as *Comes a Time*. Also realized that although Young's sci-fi may be simple, it's not silly—or maybe I realized that although it may be silly it's also charming. I'm sure you'll be pleased to learn that his unending search for romantic perfection is under study by an android company.   **A**−

Neil Young: *Neil Young and the Shocking Pinks/Everybody's Rockin'* (Geffen '83). If Ronnie and Nancy are the only everybodys rockin' by name on the less than rousing title finale, then maybe what Neil means to say is that basic rockabilly isn't worth too much all by its lonesome. I agree, but expect the argument would be more convincing if Neil plus Ben Keith could match Brian Setzer chop for chop. The covers are redundant or worse, as are all but two of the originals. I hope Robert Gordon or somebody rescues "Kinda Fonda Wanda." And I hope Neil realizes that for all the horrible truth of "Payola Blues," nobody's three thou's gonna get this on top forty. Time 24:36. List: $8.98.   **C**+

Neil Young: *Old Ways* (Geffen '85). In a pathetic attempt to convince the world he makes a difference in the record business,

Warners touts this as his country move, but he doesn't and it's not. He's been making country moves ever since "Oh Lonesome Me" without once showing any flair for the literal narrative and pungent sentimentality the country audience goes for, though his modestly engaging melodies are the equal of any Music Row tunesmith's. So what you get when he's on is a catchy ditty that starts off like an utter cliché but soon jogs a little to the left lyrically, almost of its own accord. "Old Ways" are divided into bad (substance abuse) and not so bad (workaholism). "Are There Any More Real Cowboys?" hails "workin' families" who resist encroaching developers. "Bound for Glory" 's trucker abandons wife and kids for a hard-lovin' hitchhiker with new ideas and a dog.   **B**

Neil Young: *Landing on Water* (Geffen '86). Hidden away on this rock bellyflop (which must be scandalizing 'em in Nashville) are hints that he may still be a crazed genius—the hook on the otherwise more-than-predictable "Drifter," the urban neurosis of "Pressure," and especially the broken yet still encouraging "Hippie Dream." But from straightforward confessional to brand-new drummer, it's the dullest record he's ever made.   **C+**

Neil Young & Crazy Horse: *Life* (Geffen '87). The autobiography of a loose cannon starts things off with a bang, proving once and for all that this furriner should volunteer his literary services to the Central Intelligence Agency, where surrealistic inconsistency and casual racism are hallmarks of every cover story. Then there are the reflections on liberty (war?) and fashion (terrorism?) and a heroine from that bygone epoch when dusky-skinned peoples had natural nobility going for them. After which he turns the record over to riff on "Too lonely to fall in love" and toss off some mournful tunes and get his garage band to caterwaul "That's why we don't want to be good." Make no mistake, there's plenty of life left in the son of a bitch. Which should surprise no one who believes it.   **B**

Neil Young & the Bluenotes: *This Note's for You* (Reprise '88). Those who detect surer songwriting and tougher guitar amid the eccentric horns are right, but the horns render such details irrelevant if not unlistenable—their sour blare mimics Young's crude guitar sound all too crudely, and the charts lack that spontaneous spark, as charts generally do. Grabber: solo blues, with solitary trumpet fluttering in the background.   **B−**

Neil Young: *Eldorado* (Reprise import CD '89). This is certain to become a legend on rarity alone, and if you believe mad guitar is all he's good for, you may even think it's worth a buck a minute at the $25 it cost me. I think it's versions and/or work tapes, with two otherwise unavailable songs and mad guitar that ends too soon. I'm glad to own it. But I get reimbursed.   **B+**

Neil Young: *Freedom* (Reprise '89). For years it seemed pointless to wait till he found his bearings—his bearings in relation to what? Maybe he still had terrific albums in him, but history had passed him by—his saving eccentricity was no longer an effective weapon against the industrialization of pop, which had to be ignored altogether or taken to the mat. So apropos of nothing he comes up with a classic Neil Young album, deploying not only the folk ditties and rock gallumph that made him famous, but the Nashvillisms and horn charts that made him infamous. In addition to sad male chauvinist love songs, it features a bunch of good stuff about a subject almost no rocker white or black has done much with—crack, which seems to have awakened his eccentric conscience (though I bet a Yalie—as opposed to cowboy—president helped). Does this terrific album mean he's found his bearings? I doubt it. But I no longer put it past him.   **A**

Paul Young: *No Parlez* (Columbia '84). Unlike the interpretive singers of an earlier generation, Young projects a concern with emotion rather than emotion itself—an idea or a value rather than a passion. Where Joe Cocker and Maggie Bell played it hot, Young's take on the slightly archaic black singing styles he admires so candidly is cool and synthetic. While this aligns him neatly with urban contemporaries in the Jeffrey Osborne mold and helps him steal away with "Love Will Tear Us Apart," it puts a heavier burden on his powers of analysis than any rock-and-roller should risk. Fortunately, his delight in state-of-the-art production and arrangement, as well as in his own vocal resources, provides the underpinnings of authenticity any second-hand man needs. **B+**

Paul Young: *The Secret of Association* (Columbia '85). His fat voice even more a sign of the times than Laurie Latham's baroque production, Young is Boz Scaggs for the '80s: an honorable soul fake. It's all too much at times, but Young writes as well as Boz ever did and is smart enough to go elsewhere for the meaty lyrics he loves, including two antiwar songs that could make more of an impression than Boy George's. Be nice to think music could still do that sometimes. **B+**

The Young Fresh Fellows: *Refreshments* (Frontier EP '87). Outtakes and oddments from a too-silly-to-begin-with band who deserve credit for offering to rename "Beer Money" "Pepsi-Cola Money" if MJ's corporate sponsor will, well, bribe them. In the meantime: "The beer is free and we're on MTV/And we're opening for the Del Fuegos." **B−**

The Young Fresh Fellows: *The Men Who Loved Music* (Frontier '87). Bands this funny have to be funnier than they ever are to be as good as bands this smart want to be. Which isn't to say I don't enjoy most of the jokes and treasure several, like "When the Girls Get Here" ("We'll talk about integrated circuits and things") and "Amy Grant" ("Barry / Barry White"). **B+**

Young Marble Giants: *Colossal Youth* (Rough Trade import '80). What a modern romance—two brothers, a girl, and a rhythm machine. I'd call it cult music of the year, only cults inspire evangelical enthusiasm, and what their fans like is not getting excited about something—finally, after too much noise and three-chord thrash. With Alison Statton's fragile leads unthreatened by guitar, bass, organ, or rhythm machine, and Stuart Moxham's lyrics your basic Mensa applications, they're nothing more and nothing less than robot folkies. So call it cult muzak of the year—quiet, tuneful, passing weird. **B**

Young M.C.: *Stone Cold Rhymin'* (Delicious Vinyl '89). From the bright, cute funk of "I Come Off" to the Q. Jones Jr.–cowritten "Just Say No," he's just too clean. His polysyllables and quick lips aren't as fresh as he thinks they are, either. Much more than his East Coast counterpart the Fresh Prince, though, he has his own sparely hooky musical style—courtesy Matt Dike, Michael Ross, and the usual panoply of pop-funk geniuses past. Has his own style as a writer, too, summed up pretty well in the title—he's not a storyteller, he's a wordslinger. Fun fun fun until daddy takes the contract away. **B+**

Y Pants: *Beat It Down* (Neutral '82). The notion that women's music should be cute has as little theoretical attraction as the notion that it should be organic, and the notion that it should be arty as well has less. But these three Soho gals get away with it, no doubt because at some level deep beneath the ukelele and toy piano they're willing to be ballbusters. The key is a sweet, a cappella version of "That's the Way Boys Are" that's, er, marred halfway through by the sound of a woman screaming in the middle distance. Every one of these (ersatz-Andean?) melodies will sneak up on you eventually, and just maybe paste you one. **B+**

Chaba Zahouania: *Nights Without Sleeping* (Mango '89). Maybe singers dominate rai where Arabic is spoken, but as an export it's producer's music. When Rachid and Fethi electrify conventional Algerian arrangements on the A, Zahouania remains a travelogue novelty for all her lowdown. Second side they go to town—the pulse and timbre and timing and juxtapositions of the indelibly Middle Eastern elements are all arrogantly eclectic in the great rock-disco tradition. Only this time these priceless cultural resources are misused, and transfigured, by insiders. **B+**

Zapp: *Zapp* (Warner Bros. '80). "More Bounce to the Ounce," exactly. Like Bootsy's other funk alternative, Roger Troutman is a bit light—even when he grooves rather than croons he bounces rather than whomps. What makes him a smash with the black audience where the Sweat Band is barely a swoosh is his drolly mechanical detachment—especially when he turns on the vocoder, he could be Gary Numan with ants in his pants, or Kraftwerk on the one. **C+**

Zapp: *Zapp II* (Warner Bros. '82). This idly functional, playfully mechanical six-cut dance LP tested my tolerance for innocent mindlessness, especially after I realized that my favorite tune appears on both sides. But unlike its predecessor it is a real dance LP—side one will function your ass off. And you'll want to play "Playin' Kinda Ruff" again. **B+**

Zazou Bikaye: *Mr. Manager* (Pow Wow '86). Zairean Bony Bikaye's Felaesque chants (sans agitprop, avec Afrobeat girls) provide the identity, but the substructure is all French-Algerian Hector Zazou, whose synth arrangements are praised for their orchestral density and distinguished by their propulsive linearity. Most of the Afrogallic music I've heard makes too much (Toure Kunda) or too little (Manu Dibango) of its Africanness. This strikes me as an original balance: minimalist Eurodisco that trades pseudosophistication for pseudoprimitivism. **A—**

Zeitgeist: *Translate Slowly* (DB '85). I don't want to alienate my target audience or anything, but I can't contain myself: from their offhandedly opalescent songpoetry to their hints of social commentary to their chiming pop polytechnique to their better-name-than-Angst-at-least-only-these-fools-try-and-live-up-to-it, this is one collegiate band. There's hope, though—if they get picked up by Elektra and break through on a fluke video, they may start writing about cocaine and Holiday Inns.
B—

Zetrospective: Dancing in the Face of Adversity (ZE cassette/CD '89). Resuscitating the four standout tracks from the 1981 nouveau-disco anthology *Seize the Beat* and twelve others besides, this is the soundtrack to a lost era—art-scene disco according to Michael Zilkha on one side, art-scene DOR ditto on the other. It's very Manhattan, even more dilettantishly cerebral after all these years, and I prefer the disco even though the beat does get repetitive (those handclaps): only Kid Creole's "I'm a Wonderful Thing Baby," which oddly enough is the compilation's only readily available cut, has much give to it. But good work by uneven or ultimately tedious artists abounds. From Cristina's satiric "Disco Clone" to Was (Not Was)'s literal "White People Can't Dance," from Coati Mundi's bad-rapping "Que Pasa / Me No Pop Eye" to Lydia Lunch's sweet-talking "Lady Scarface," from Don Armando's cheesy "Deputy of Love" to Breakfast Club's cheesy "Rico Mambo," this is the first postmodern dance music—dance music with a critical spirit. And it's funny as hell.   **A—**

Zetrospective: Hope Springs Eternal (ZE cassette/CD '89). Rock anthologies rarely cohere like dance-music anthologies, because they have no groove running down the middle—at whatever level of execution, they're about meaning more than pleasure. Anyway, Michael Zilkha's rock tastes were more received than his disco tastes, and while there are lost wonders here—three great songs by the Waitresses, two or three by Davitt Sigerson—John Cale and John Robie and Zilkha's wife Cristina are middling at best. Kid Creole and Was (Not Was) you probably know.   **B+**

Warren Zevon: *Bad Luck Streak in Dancing School* (Asylum '80). I don't know why the title tune's the title tune, except maybe to contextualize the classical interludes he composed all by himself, and Lord help us he's been hanging out with the Eagles, just like Randy Newman, who could teach him something about slandering the South—even Neil Young could do better than incest and Lynyrd Skynyrd, though the brucellosis is a nice touch. In fact, just about every song boasts a good line or three. But the only ones that score are the jokes: Ernie K-Doe's sly, shy "A Certain Girl," and "Gorilla, You're a Desperado," a satire on the Eagles, not to mention Warren

Zevon. Don Henley sings harmony. Linda Ronstadt will not cover.   **B—**

Warren Zevon: *Stand in the Fire* (Asylum '80). If your idea of rocking out is lots of bass drum on the two (even during "Bo Diddley's a Gunslinger"), then Warren at the Roxy will do you almost as good as the climax of *Live Rust.* The three best songs are all from *Excitable Boy,* and only one of the two new originals stands the fire, but any Zevon album that bypasses "Hasten Down the Wind" and "Accidentally Like a Martyr" is the one I'll play when I need my fix.   **A—**

Warren Zevon: *The Envoy* (Asylum '82). What convinces me isn't the deeply satisfying "Ain't That Pretty at All," in which Zevon announces his abiding desire to hurl himself at walls—he's always good for a headbanger. Nor, God knows, is it the modern-macho mythos of the title cut and the Tom McGuane song. It's a wise, charming, newly written going-to-the-chapel number that I would have sworn was lifted from some half-forgotten girl group. If "Never Too Late for Love" and "Looking for the Next Best Thing" announce that this overexcitable boy has finally learned to compromise, "Let Nothing Come Between You" is his promise not to take moderation too far.   **A—**

Warren Zevon: *A Quiet Normal Life: The Best of Warren Zevon* (Asylum '86). Unlike so many songpoets, Zevon's real writer, and as lyrics his ravers hold up better than his songpoems. So this is where Warren the Rocker kicks Warren the Poet's butt. Though the selection forgives more reveries than one might prefer, they function as a well-earned respite from dementia; only "Accidentally Like a Martyr" throws up the kind of tuneful fog Linda R. fell for on the tastefully omitted (again—maybe he knows something) "Hasten Down the Wind." Because he inhabits his tricksters, blackguards, and flat-out psychotics rather than reconstituting variations on a formula, he tops his boy Ross Macdonald any day. Thompson gunner, mercenary, NSC operative, werewolf, easy lay, he puts his head on the tracks for penance, and when the train doesn't come gets up and hurls himself against the wall of the Louvre museum. Really now, could Ross Macdonald imagine such a thing? **A—**

Warren Zevon: *Sentimental   Hygiene* (Virgin '87). The real question about Zevon isn't whether he's really a wimp. That's a setup. It's whether he's really a clod—whether his sense of rhythm is good enough to induce you to listen as frequently as his lyrics deserve. I'm not talking swing or funk or anything arcane, just straight propulsion of the sort punk made commonplace, and here his latest sessioneers, R.E.M. minus Michael Stipe, add a rhythmic lift to this album's sarcasm. All three songs about the travails of stardom are a hoot. "Even a Dog Can Shake Hands" updates "Under Assistant West Coast Promo Man," "Detox Mansion" sends up every pampered substance abuser turned therapy addict in Tinseltown, and "Trouble Waiting To Happen" establishes the right unrepentant distance from Warren's amply documented binges: "I read things I didn't know I'd done / It sounded like a lot of fun." Taking off even higher is "The Factory," which sings the collective ego of the working-class hero, dissenting with a touch of nasty from the tragic paeans of the best-known of Zevon's many hairy-chested collaborators, Bruce Springsteen himself.   **A—**

Warren Zevon: *Transverse City* (Virgin '89). With his eye on the fate of the earth, from malls and gridlock to entropy and deorbiting heavenly bodies, Zevon succumbs to the temptations of art-rock. This beats country-rock, at least as he defines it, and given his formal training it was decent of him to wait until his material demanded sci-fi keybs—arpeggios and ostinatos and swirling soundtracks. With Little Feat's Richie Hayward the timekeeper, the stasis is a little heavier than anyone concerned with the fate of the earth would hope, but you don't get the feeling Warren's hopes are high enough to warrant anything livelier. "Splendid Isolation," about solipsism as a life choice, "Turbulence," about perestroika and Afghanistan, and "Run Straight Down," about the fate of the earth on the 11 o'clock news, are exactly as grim as they ought to be.   **B+**

Zimbabwe Frontline (Virgin '88). Hot Thomas Mapfumo, hooked Four Brothers. Fervent call for unity in a non-Zimbabwean tongue, husky cry of independence from a natural feminist. Mbaqanga rumba with West Nkosi in the control booth. Tart pop sweetmeats from Devera Ngwena, who outsell the Bhundus in Harare. A generic or two. Except maybe for Mapfumo's *Ndangariro,* which gets over on groove rather than songs, mbira guitar's most convincing showcase.   **A—**

Zulu Jive/Umbaqanga (Earthworks import '83). There's an urban punch and pace here missing from most Afropop, although the singing and rhythms are less powerpacked than we're told they can be, and only Aaron Mbambo, whose urgent high shout lifts his two cuts well out of the mix, is well-known in the style. Selected stanzas on the back refer painfully to curfews and pass laws as well as the money worries and familial perfidies of the companion compilation *Viva Zimbabwe!,* and they gain emotional thrust behind astringent harmonies from South Africa and instrumental colors from assorted ports of call: squeezebox, electric organ, heavy electric bass, oudlike fiddle, everything but horns. Which aren't missed. Original grade: A minus.   **B+**

Zvuki Mu: *Zvuki Mu* (Opal '89). Described by an admirer as "a witty drunkard, wild dancer and failed poet," Peter Mamonov is also an old-fashioned beatnik, with woman problems to match: "Yesterday you gave yourself to me / And now you think I owe you," "just don't thrust yourself upon me with your endless meals." These he recreates in a wild and witty way, complete with hypnotic cabaret-rock (or something). Like a lot of glasnost   culture,   he   has   his   retro attractions—in his own language, the quarter-truths of his boho sexism give off a pleasant shock. But like a lot of beatniks, he can't resist experiments that aren't as avant-garde as he thinks they are.   **B**

ZZ Top: *El Loco* (Warner Bros. '81). Their boogie's gotten grander again, more nationwide than homegrown, which at its best—the euphemistically misprised "Tube Snake Boogie" (and did you know "Pearl Necklace" is Southwestern for blow job?)—means only that it packs a more powerful kick. That they're eccentrics nonetheless is proven not just by the harmonizer-processed voice of evil shaking the DT's while working street PR, but by the brown-eyed mama who guards their groovy little hippie pad with .44, jeep, and German shepherd. The easy life ain't what it used to be.   **B+**

ZZ Top: *Eliminator* (Warner Bros. '83). Arena-rockers who never forgot heavy metal was once white blues, they took a long vacation and resurfaced as a fine white blues band starring a guitarist who always sounds like himself. Now, with hi-test b.p.m.s speeding the groove, they've motorvated back toward metal again— boogie in overdrive, a funny car that's half platinum and half plutonium. The videos make you smile, the record runs you over. That's the pleasure of it. Original grade: B minus.   **B+**

ZZ Top: *Afterburner* (Warner Bros. '85). With sales on *Eliminator* over five mil almost by accident, this hard-boogieing market strategy is defined by conscious commercial ambition—by its all but announced intention of making ZZ the next Bruce/Madonna/Prince/Michael, with two beards and a Beard at every checkout counter. The Trevor Hornish synth touches and out-front hooks are clues, but the proof is "Rough Boy," an attempted top-five ballad that would sound like pure take-me-or-leave-me revved up. And in case you think they've lost their sense of humor, there's a new dance called the "Velcro Fly." I'm laughing, I'm laughing.   **B**

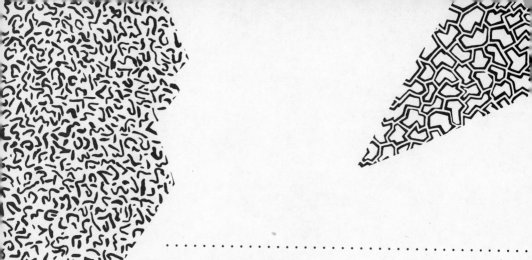

APPENDICES

APPENDICES

HOW TO USE THESE APPENDICES

Right, there's no way this book can be comprehensive. But you can't blame a guy for dreaming. So the first four appendices are attempts to cover up gaps I already know exist, as opposed to those I'm certain to discover later. Subjects for Further Research is an optimistic designation (borrowed from Andrew Sarris's *The American Cinema*) for artists who one way or another deserve more attention than the critic can give them. Genres I have no feel for, artists whose best work is hard to find on U.S. albums, oddities and oddballs with impressive critical or popular support, titans in decline or in holding patterns, and people I like but never found time to sort out are all included. (So are four artists on the U.N. Special Committee Against Apartheid's register of performers who have lent implicit support to Pretoria by working in South Africa. I have problems with cultural boycotts, but this is a case where solidarity is paramount, so I've relegated violators to '80s limbo.) Distinctions Not Cost-Effective dispatches artists unlikely to repay the time it would take me (or you) to cull their not-so-bad from their not-so-good. Meltdown lists artists unworthy of the time it would take to dispatch them. And New Wave names two hundred "alternative," "postpunk" artists that somebody out there likes—toward the top, maybe even me—but that after two or three (or five or ten) full plays I adjudged, well, unnewsworthy, just too minor to merit the space it would take to describe them. Unlike the first three appendices, this one is in roughly preferential rather than precisely alphabetical order.

After that there's a compilation index arranged by category that should prove especially useful in African music, where many of the finest U.S.-available albums are multiple-artist collections now strewn alphabetically by titles no one can remember throughout the text. Then there's a basic rock library with its own explanatory introduction. Next a long cross-index I've taken to calling "The A Lists": every A+, A, and A— I've found in the '80s, arranged by preference within each year. And finally there's a brief glossary of acronyms, biz and rockcrit jargon, and world-music terms.

So right, I'm a list freak. Go crazy.

SUBJECTS FOR FURTHER RESEARCH

Arrow I could be wrong, but I'm not physically attracted to soca; I find that unlike competing Caribbean grooves—from Cuba, Puerto Rico, the Antilles, Haiti, Jamaica for damn sure, though maybe not the Dominican, there's something in the up-up-up of merengue that hits me the same way—it has no give in it. That's why I never followed up the middecade foray into the style that taught me to love Sparrow, and also why the attempted U.S. breakthrough of this strong-voiced, weak-minded Trinidadian left me lukewarm lukewarm lukewarm.

Birdsongs of the Mesozoic Though Mission of Burma's answer to hearing damage slipped into bombast and soundtrack even on the ace *Magnetic Flip,* they were usually good for a nice postmodern version of the kick vintage fusion or art-rock used to provide occasionally. Debussy meets the electric guitar, sort of. Rykodisc's *Sonic Geology* collected their works. And of course there were offshoots, too.

Bobby Bland After MCA hung him out to dry he found a home at Biloxi-based Malaco, where Z.Z. Hill had become a belated hero by reproducing his mannerisms. He got good songs in a sympathetic environment, but with Bland the physical instrument was always crucial, and near as I could tell it had lost its edge. Hope I was wrong.

Brave Combo Carl Finch's conceptual conjunto starts with norteño's unlikely polkas and makes connections—to "pol-ska," which I guess is obvious, and to "Skokiaan," and to "O Holy Night Cha Cha Cha." And to "Rosemary's Baby" as a waltz. And to "People Are Strange" as a hora. In short, he interprets universalist humanism as the dance music of a thousand cruise ships. The idea is wonderful live—getting this silly in the company of a crowd that's half in on the world-music joke (and statement) can border on euphoria. But the records are too cute: not since 1982's *Urban Grown-Ups* EP have they made a serious stab at normal songwriting. The 1987 Rounder CD *Musical Varieties* is a representatively excessive selection for truly modern fun-seekers.

The Bulgarian State Radio and Television Female Vocal Choir Bulgaria used to be Thrace, a wellspring of Greek music in the Golden Age, and there are those who claim (with less historical logic than metaphorical flair) that the singers who dominate the unearthly cult hits dubbed *Mystère des Voix Bulgares* are as close as we'll ever get to that fabled, unheard stuff. When I'm in the mood I find the cutting calm of their concertized version far more vibrant and arresting than the nation's neoauthentic mountain styles. When I'm not I can be heard muttering, "Meet the new age, same as the old age."

Nick Cave I admit it, I have a problem with death freaks. And since I also have a problem with Americans who obsess on America's "dark side," I have more of a problem with non-Americans who follow suit. Death fans compare the Birthday Party to P.I.L. even though Cave's band was palpably cornier, which took some doing. They compare the Bad Seeds to, well, the Gun Club—only better, you know? Damn straight. There are strong songs on *Tender Prey,* and occasionally I think I might appreciate the covers album *Kicking Against the Pricks* when face to face with terminal illness. But somehow I suspect I'll have other priorities.

Ray Charles His abortive South African tour in 1981 defied the public outcry of both American and South African blacks, and he's been on the U.N. register ever since, which isn't as much of a loss as you'd think or maybe hope. For a long time now, the Genius has sounded best singing other people's songs or, better still, guesting on other people's records. He's a headstrong man who does as he pleases, so I'm sure it's just coincidence that his only strong album of the decade preceded the boycott: 1980's *Brother Ray Is at It Again.* Since signing to Columbia in 1983, he's pursued the country market. That's just coincidence, too, right? So was entertaining at the 1984 Republican convention. And getting that Kennedy medallion from Reagan in 1986.

The Crass As someone who listened to all of the boxed two-record *Christ—The Album,* I can report that the most politically hardline of all left-anarchist punk bands once hit it just right, with the furiously obscene single "Sheep Farming in the Falklands" ("Fucking sheep in the homelands," "Balls to you rocket cock," and so forth). The legend that they sent James Chance to the hospital when he put one of his audience-battering routines in their faces says something I like about their style of militance.

Hank Crawford Nobody records r&b instrumentals of more easeful mastery or deeper pocket than the former Ray Charles bandleader and Creed Taylor alto sax peon. Anchored by Crawford's drumming counterpart Bernard Purdie, Dr. John collaborations like *Roadhouse Symphony* (1985) and *Night Beat* (1989) will speak to any rock-and-roller. But as someone with zero tolerance for Hammond-organ funk, I'm opened wider by his Jimmy McGriff bands. "River's Invitation," on *Steppin' Up* (1987), actually taught me to appreciate Billy Preston, who guests on piano.

Miles Davis Miles came back in the '80s. No longer a recluse, he pursued a recognizable recording career, even changed labels, as he cashed in on the fusion movement his brilliantly unreadable post-*Bitches Brew* work transcended in advance. *Star People* reinvented blues cliches, and even schlock like *Tutu* and *Amandla* showed gratifying groove and class. But his best album of the decade was the serialist tribute *Aura,* in which Palle Mikkelborg wrote the themes, arranged the music, and picked the players, and Miles just soloed. It's at least as tasteful as anything Mikkelborg's mentor Gil Evans ever put his mind to. And I'll take 1976's chaotic, ad hoc, out-of-print *Agartha* in a minute.

Die Kreuzen Sympathizers cite a single-minded if not mad formal acuteness that never narrows into hardcore rant, and 1985's *October File* reveals an uncommonly riffy-hooky band with a standout sound. Also with the predictable metal tendencies, unfortunately, which seem just fine with Shriekin' Dan Kubinski, though he later denied it. Later, I should also mention, they sounded thrashier.

Michael Doucet   I love New Orleans rock and roll and all its African-diaspora cousins, but not for the French in them—maybe for the Latin, or for the seaport, the city. I've always had trouble with the bayou blues called zydeco, and I've always had trouble with Cajun, which I hear (ignorantly and perhaps absurdly) as country music with a lot of Normandy in it—dance music in a variety of meters, and still I find the rhythms wearing. Near as I can tell, this man is the class of a genre now hellbent on raking in the Yankee dollar. I prefer his more traditional group, Beausoleil (try Arhoolie's *Allons a Lafayette*), to Cajun Brew, which goes up against rock-oriented contenders like Wayne Toups. Either way he's a hell of a violinist, and he has a gentle touch.

Einstürzende Neubauten   Collapsing New Buildings, who in case you didn't guess are German, invented industrial, which by decade's end was an important strain of dance music, although they themselves were never disco-friendly. The rock-*concrète* experiments on *80–83 Strategies Against Architecture,* replete with banging radiators and other new-metal timbres, are certainly worth hearing once. The oft-praised *½ Mensch* intersperses arresting moments with seemly din. And though they never developed a pulse or a sense of humor, by the first side of 1989's *Haus der Lüge* they had achieved a symphonic grandeur that wasn't stupid or irrelevant, which in a rock context is always news.

Fearless Iranians From Hell   On their seven-inch EP they were an anti-American joke about racist paranoia, no less cathartic for the possibility that they would be taken literally by some racist somewhere—one of the Butthole Surfers in the band, say, or maybe the Iranian-American. The album wasn't so funny.

Franco   Dead of AIDS in late 1989, the Zairean instrumentalist-vocalist-bandleader will be remembered as a crucial 20th-century musician. He invented rumba guitar, which came to mean Afropop guitar, and always stayed on top of the changing rhythms of Zairean pop, which came to mean Afropop. The hot, sweet, soaring, exquisite *Omona Wapi,* a collaboration with his vocal counterpart and archrival Rochereau, is reviewed within. But though I own half a dozen of Franco's hundred-plus solo albums (as well as a tape of the renowned Sam Mangwana collaboration *Coopération*), sorting through them is like distinguishing among James Brown albums without knowing English. I do find the 1956 recordings on *Originalité* rather, well, primitive. Mélodie's *Ekaba-Kaba* definitely benefits from its Brussels production. Two on Makossa that both seem to be called *On Entre O.K. On Sort K.O.* (*Volume 1,* with a green cover, and *Volume 5,* with an orange cover) are gentle and sustaining.

Game Theory   Obsessed not just with the Beatles but with sometime Beatle obsessive Alex Chilton, rendering the ostensibly public essentially private, Scott Miller was a prototypical '80s rock artist—serious, playful, skillful, obscure, secondhand. His Mitch Easter–produced albums were like dreams of the early dB's, before their rhythm section began to cook, which isn't to say Miller and cohorts didn't also develop a groove as they got older. He was literary, too—loved Joyce. Adepts recommend 1987's *Lolita Nation,* which is said to make sense, though I don't know exactly what sense. At the level of attention I can afford, I kinda like 1988's excessive *Two Steps From the Middle Ages*, which sounded a little . . . funkier, I guess you'd call it.

Giant Sand   For years I couldn't tell his band from Naked Prey or Thin White Rope, though I confess I wasn't trying very hard, but both of Howie Gelb's 1989 releases on Homestead (his fifth label, and not his last), the collector's compilation *Giant Sandwich* and the eccentric's extravaganza *Long Stem Rant,* merited 1989's all-purpose kudo, the Neil Young comparison. He reminds me more of Green on Red's Dan Stuart, only without Stuart's sentimentality and mythopoeia. Also without his song sense, maybe. But unlike Howie (and Neil), Dan doesn't play guitar.

Emmylou Harris   In 1984 I wrote off her second best-of ("pristine neobluegrass, pristine rock oldies") even though I'd already put 1980's pristine neobluegrass *Roses in the Snow* on my A shelves. But 1986's rockish *Thirteen* impressed me almost as much as 1987's Parton-Ronstadt-Harris *Trio,* which Harris held together—this reformed folkie always sounds great on other people's records. She's genuinely at home in Nashville, and put into relief by competition like Nanci Griffiths, Kathy Mattea, and Lacy J. Dalton, she may well deserve to stand up there between Rosanne Cash and Reba McEntire. That best-of sounds better now.

Robyn Hitchcock   Hitchcock is the kind of English eccentric who becomes impossible to bear when he's taken up by American Anglophiles. I admired the Soft Boys' 1980 *Underwater Moonlight* and Robyn's own 1981 *Black Snake Diamond Role* from a distance, but my enthusiasm dimmed as he and his Egyptians became college-radio idols, and once I noticed the one about the guy who keeps his wife's corpse around for company, his considerable talent meant nothing to me. I have no doubt that scattered among his albums are songs strong enough to withstand his professional-oddball attentions, and if I were more spiritually advanced I might even swallow my prejudices and learn to enjoy him for what he is. Which is what? A rock and roll cross between H.P. Lovecraft and Kingsley Amis? Way too kind, but that's as much thought as I intend to give the matter.

Incredible Casuals   A wacko-retro club band who worked Cape Cod and environs as hard as NRBQ worked Woodstock and environs, they also recorded a bewildering profusion of obscure product, including cassettes they presumably peddled at gigs. Since Cape Cod is kinda near New York, permitting them to visit occasionally, they sent me a few, which were kinda good but not remarkable enough to get on. Ditto for their LP on Elvis Costello's Demon label. But "Yeah, a Little" and "No Fun at Parties," on their twenty-minute 1982 Eat EP *Let's Go!,* are song enough to persuade me there was at least an album's worth of material in all that roadwork. I wonder how many bands working closer to San Diego or Miami or Toronto and environs could say the same. Maybe none—maybe a dozen.

B.B. King   He's seldom been terrible, and when in 1978 he stopped trying for AM ballads and disco crossovers and moved on up to nightclub funk, he started making good albums again. *There Must Be a Better World Somewhere* (1981), anchored by Pretty Purdie with plenty of fine Hank Crawford sax and Dr. John piano, featured fine new songs from Dr. John and Doc Pomus. The voice was no longer exquisite and the licks might as well have been copyrighted, but for King, standard means classic. Then again, it also means predictable, and the only one of his well-made later albums I got into was Fantasy's *16 Original Big Hits,* a reissue of Galaxie's 1968 best-of. Now that's classic.

The Kinks   At around the time Steve Van Zandt was organizing Artists United Against Apartheid for "Sun City," the Kinks were playing there, not exactly a surprising move from cultural reactionaries long past their prime. The "survivor" in Ray Davies having swallowed the songwriter years before, his anomalously autumnal U.S. ascendancy was a disaster—attitudes forgivable in one of the great dotty Englishmen turned ugly and mean, and tunecraft so delicate it threatened to waft away on the next zephyr assumed an unbecoming swagger. The title tune on his depressing 1986 best-of *Come Dancing* was his biggest hit since 1964 because it expressed a perfect pop sentiment. Second-best is by Dave Davies, not Ray: "There's no England now," he opines, which explains a lot. Ray Davies—not the other Kinks—remains on the entertainers register of the U.N. Centre Against Apartheid. He's such a contrary chappy that he probably likes it there.

Love and Rockets   Three-fourths of Bauhaus atop the college charts—until "So Alive" in 1989 I refused even to listen to such a horrible idea. First play established that Bauhaus was Peter Murphy's baby (never listened to his college smash either). Closer study revealed that guitarist David Ash writes a good dumb ditty at fast or medium tempo (that means not slow, Dave—got it?). Maybe he could ditch the others (they're brothers, it's a natural) and form a macho Flock of Seagulls.

Maze Featuring Frankie Beverly   Nobody having told this long-running Oakland pro that soul music was dead, he racked up noncrossover hit after noncrossover hit, singing in a relaxed church-of-the-immaculate-cocktail-lounge tenor similar in general feel to whatever Isley brother you think you like. Totally uncountry and not even secondhand Southern, he cultivated a light funk bottom, a few years behind the times rather than proudly conservative; he sang about Africa and the pain of the ghetto without irrelevance or self-righteousness. All of which reads great but doesn't sound all that compelling unless you happen to be one of the middle-class black folk who turned him into gold. If you still think he reads great, try his 1986 live double, his 1989 greatest hits, or his 1989 Warners debut.

Malcolm McLaren   I always preferred *Fans* to *Duck Rock* myself—rap-mbaqanga big deal, but Puccini-disco was a marriage this old reprobate was born to broker. Still, when I discovered that his mbaqanga rips ("Song for Chango," said to date to "before Jesus Christ was born," is credited like almost all the other compositions to Malc and Trevor Horn) had landed him on the U.N. register as a violator of the cultural boycott, my only regret was "Algernon's Simply Awfully Good at Algebra." That's the one good song as opposed to idea on 1989's *Waltz Darling,* which romanticized the rich just like he's always romanticized the poor whilst pumping the only message he's ever cared about— teen sexuality as liberation, especially for old reprobates.

Minor Threat   In theory I agree that Ian MacKaye's D.C. crew was the definitive hardcore band. In theory I love "In My Eyes" and the Dead parody. But those tracks aren't altogether breakneck, and I'm afraid I'd rather theorize about Minor Threat than hear them—they were too fucking pure. Maybe this will change as I get older—or maybe I'll discover MacKaye's mature band, Fugazi.

Pamelo Mounk'a   In the fall of 1982 my friend Sue Steward took me to an African disco in Soho, London. The DJ played five or six songs that sounded real fine, then put on something by this Congo–Brazzaville soukous veteran, I know not what. I jumped, I raved, I gibbered. Six months later Sue brought me a copy of Mounk'a's *Propulsion!*, on French Sonics, thirty-plus minutes of soukous whose understated floodtide grew into my groove record of the year. Utilizing my scanty research facilities, I determined that Mounk'a's most famous song was the niftily entitled "L'Argent Appelle l'Argent," with an album of the same name attached. I never found it, to my knowledge never even heard it; never saw *Propulsion!* anywhere else either. I did eventually locate something called *20 ans de carrière,* and bought it against the advice of Ronnie Graham's *Da Capo Guide to Contemporary African Music.* Graham was right. If you run across *Propulsion!,* scarf it up. And if you find "L'Argent Appelle l'Argent," tape one for me.

Milton Nascimento   I don't understand Portuguese, and nothing in the way Nascimento sounds or translates makes me regret it. In pop, not to mention rock, there's often not much difference between those hailed as great artists and those remembered as pretentious artistes, and until he storms the pantheon, I'm pegging him as the Brazilian Peter Gabriel. If you like, you can believe Wayne Shorter, Paul Simon, and Spyro Gyra.

Ozzy Osbourne   I have no interest in his albums, but I've enjoyed and admired his travails. He mooned the PMRC every chance he got. And his egg-frying sequence in Penelope Spheeris's *Decline and Fall of Western Civilization Part II* should be a video.

Augustus Pablo   Before either route was more than a gleam in the zeitgeist's eye, the world's greatest melodica player set up house at the corner of "world music," with its vaguely folkie-futuristic aura, and "world-beat," a term favored by rockers dancing their way to the next big thing. By the middle '80s he was the greatest of all new-age musicians even though the new-age market didn't know he existed. It's entirely conceivable he'll prove reggae's most enduring artist a century from now, but I often feel he's a little beyond me, which I don't necessarily mean as a compliment, and would no more try to parse his oeuvre than I would, oh, Steve Reich's. When I'm in the mood for mood music, I think about him sometimes, only to put on *Another Green World* or something. *King Tubby's Meets Rockers Uptown,* which in 1976 made dub possible as a (highly specialized, I insist) subgenre, has the mark of greatness upon it. Also in my A shelves are 1980's *Original Rockers* (bracingly abrasive), 1987's *Rockers Comes East* (poppishly upbeat), and 1986's *Rebel Rock Reggae* (simply sui generis).

The Residents   Once I listened with respectful pleasure to the mechanical, displaced tunes of these anonymous San Francisco cutups, but when Ralph took me off the mailing list around 1981, presumably for lack of enthusiasm, I didn't complain. Later Rykodisc sent me *God in Three Persons,* an obscure or banal fable about pain 'n' pleasure narrated by an avant-garde cousin of Stanard Ridgway, and Enigma sent me *The King and I,* in which the same fella casts aspersions upon Elvis Presley in between covering his songs. Some will tell you these are great works. Which is why I myself am no longer dying to hear their much-praised Gershwin-Brown tribute *George & James.*

Linda Ronstadt   Since May 1983, Ronstadt has been on the U.N.'s register of entertainers who have supported apartheid by performing in South Africa—specifically Sun City, a showcase for the homeland policy at the heart of Pretoria's economic strategy. To get off the register she need only promise not to return until apartheid is ended, but she has steadfastly and self-righteously refused. So I stopped paying this stiff-necked middlebrow art singer much mind, which from her skinny-tie period to her Aaron Neville exploitation was no great sacrifice. I was especially revolted by the way she stifled pop standards beneath Nelson Riddle's arrangements and her moderately gorgeous voice. Genteel neoconservatives, knee-jerk pluralists, one-upping convolutionists, and out-and-out ignoramuses all got off on the idea of a "rock" performer validating the prerock values such songs signal. And with Linda singing, you'd never know they had anything else to say.

Santana   Though he'll never be as facile as Page or Clapton, Carlos Santana is a guitar god on sound alone, and in the '80s he probably did more honest work than any of them. As a bandleader, however, he's always had trouble distinguishing between the near-great (Armando Peraza, Coke Escovedo) and the abysmal (Neil Schon, Sri Chinmoy). I enjoyed his solo 1983 *Havana Moon* (the Willie Nelson cameo is the best vocal of Santana's career), admired his comradely *Blues for Salvador,* and listened all the way through 1988's smart three-disc coffee-table compilation, *Viva Santana!.* But even in 1968 he had too much dinosaur in him.

Adrian Sherwood   I enjoyed the African Head Charge album that came my way without ever seeking out another, mostly because everything else I heard from this mixmastering onetime Fall producer—by the Dub Syndicate, by Mark Stewart and Maffia, by Sugarhill permutations like Fats Comet and Tackhead—sounded better when I only heard *about* it. A possible exception is Tackhead's 1989 *Friendly as a Hand Grenade,* which may yet teach me to love the deconstructed groove—and to fully understand De La Soul.

Siouxsie and the Banshees   She has her cult—an army of black-clad college students eagerly waiting for the world to end. But though many Johnny Rotten fans proved smarter than Johnny Rotten, Siouxsie Pseud wasn't one of them. Since like Jim Morrison she disguises the banality of her exoticism with psychedelic gimmicks best consumed at their hookiest, the nightmare vignettes on her 1981 best-of were of a piece even though they spanned three years of putative artistic development. After that I kept waiting for Siouxsie to end. But she left a lot of product in her wake, and for all I know it conceals another best-of.

Sweet Honey in the Rock   Six politically correct black women, including one who signs (that is not a typo). The other five, er, vocalize, unaccompanied, except occasionally by yet other politically correct black women singers. Until they led and nearly stole Columbia's Folkways tribute, I found their congregation suspect and their lack of a backbeat fatal. But on 1988's *Live at Carnegie Hall,* and quite possibly elsewhere, they join as beautifully as vintage Persuasions or Miriam Makeba overdubbing *Sangoma.* And "Are My Hands Clean?," for instance, is ideologically stringent enough to make even a good lefty like myself wince a little.

The Treacherous Three   From Bobby Robinson's defunct Enjoy to Sylvia Robinson's defunct Sugarhill, from dance-party basics ("The Body Rock") to up-the-race traditionalism ("Yes We Can-Can"), their only rivals among the seminal rappers were Grandmaster Flash & the Furious Five. They spawned the record-holding Kool Moe Dee. Will some music-loving entrepreneur please buy the rights and release a compilation? Immortality awaits.

Caetano Veloso   The most credible explanation of why this soft-sung João Gilberto acolyte has more art-pop cachet than middlebrow icon Milton Nascimento or pop-r&b genius Gilberto Gil compares Veloso to Andy Warhol: supposedly he puts a lovingly ironic twist (you know, minor chords) on the sappy melodiousness of Brazilian music. No doubt it helps if you know the native language of this certified left-internationalist pop intellectual—the title song of 1989's Arto Lindsay–produced *Estrangeiro* (translations provided, and definitely where any American should begin) adduces Gauguin, Levi-Strauss, and Cole Porter in the first three lines. To me he just sounds soft-sung and sappily melodious. Guess I'm just wrong.

Papa Wemba   Wemba is probably the most famous and certainly the most flamboyant of the many graduates of Zaiko Langa Langa, the band that turned rumba into soukous with hard guitar and traditional rhythms and structures in the early '70s. Motto: "La ville et le village: deux visages que j'aime!" His high, harsh voice cuts like it's serrated, and the harmonies are almost acrid sometimes, just like Nguando Milos's lead guitar lines, which break away from the merely engaging competition both sonically and melodically. An admirer of the old discursive song forms, Wemba milks soukous's bipartite conventions for something very much like drama. Unfortunately, his easiest-to-find record—*Papa Wemba,* on Stern's Africa—synths up songs I prefer electric, having first heard them on Belgian Gitta's *L'Esclave,* which was findable as 1990 began. Two import albums on Disques Esperance, *Ekumani* and (thanks a lot) *Papa Wemba,* are also recommended.

The Who   The relatively stylish and passionate sex songs Peter Townshend wrote for 1981's *Face Dances* sounded forced from the aging pretty boy who mouthed them, and between the synths and the chorales and the writing in parts and the book-club poetry, 1982's *It's Hard* was the nearest thing to classic awful English art-rock since Genesis discovered funk. After that they broke up, thank God, but for me it was ruined—I could barely listen to the outtakes and arcana they continued to feed their fans, some of which I'd hoarded on tapes and U.K. pressings for decades, and their CD-market best-of made me sad. After that they staged a reunion.

Yellowman   Voice, timing, enunciation, and entertainment value made this unbleached blond the premier toaster of the '80s, but as his sexism and homophobia became more virulent, his rise to prominence with the reactionary Edward Seaga seemed less coincidental. At his best he's an unwitting amalgam of Eddie Cantor, Mae West, and Pigmeat Markham, but when his albums don't run together they distinguish themselves for the worst reasons. *Live at Reggae Sunsplash,* with its postclimactic "Sit Under Me," is suitably waggish and blue. Michael Manley should nationalize him and release a politically correct compilation.

John Zorn   Postmodernism done to a turn, Zorn's highbrow-lowbrow fragmentation made him the most broadly respected avant-garde composer of the '80s—a Philip Glass for our time, such as it is. He epitomized a generation of classical musicians who claim rock and roll as part of their heritage. But actually it's only a segment of a generation—nobody ever got smart underestimating the hermeticism of classical music. And perhaps because I epitomize a generation of rock and roll fans who don't know shit about classical music and don't especially care to find out, I find him highbrow. The only Zorn I respond to viscerally is the Ornette Coleman tribute *Spy Vs. Spy.* Ornette is hard to frag.

Buckwheat Zydeco I'm not a reliable judge of the style (cf. Michael Doucet), and without doubt the ranking blues accordionist qualifies as Clifton Chenier's great inheritor on modernized rhythms alone—I've seen him bring them all the way up to Stax-Volt live. But at various times I've found his records too flat, too cluttered, and too eager to please.

DISTINCTIONS NOT COST EFFECTIVE

Accept As I walked behind two teenaged boys with a boombox one hot vacation afternoon in 1983, these Swedish metalists knocked me out for at least thirty seconds. I must have been in a great mood.

Asleep at the Wheel Commander Cody with chops—which isn't what they (or Commander Cody) originally had in mind.

Adrian Belew A welcome addition to other people's music.

Regina Belle She raps, Anita Baker doesn't. That's called demographics.

Blue Oyster Cult Though the power-packed *Career of Evil* compilation stole great slabs of 1982's *Extraterrestrial Live,* only two of its songs were written in the '80s. They should know.

Laura Branigan Her big, anonymous voice and safe, Irish-American looks went debut gold in 1982, but dance-pop is fickle and Laura's not too talented. So she picked up a check in Sun City in 1988 and—unusually for such a "name"—returned in 1989. Guess she liked the culture.

Lonnie Brooks Back in the Depression, it made sense for bluesmen to choose Chicago over Mississippi. The ones from New Orleans didn't want to leave.

Jimmy Buffett His best title since *A White Sport Coat and a Pink Crustacean* told us what had become of him: *Last Mango in Paris.*

Cabaret Voltaire My taste in dadaist dance musicians runs to the Memphis Jug Band.

John Cale Provided more proof that he'd studied at Juilliard. Subcontracted his lyrics to a Dylanologist.

Cherelle I'll never forget the charcoal-gray number she wore on the cover of . . . what was it called again?

Alice Cooper Vitiated Ozzy's shtick by refusing to play down his 120 IQ.

Rodney Crowell Once this ace writer-producer vied for country-rock auteur, but soon his records sounded more like pop demos. And he was too much the pro to get anywhere on the neotrad gravy train.

The Damned Considered changing their name to the Darned.

Dissidenten So German pop-rock isn't your stein of beer? And Middle Eastern music still seems a little alien? Now imagine a fusion.

Sheena Easton Kim Basinger she wasn't—not without Prince, anyway.

The Four Tops I'll grant them this much—the same old song would have been even worse.

The Germs More valuable dead than alive.

Howard Hewett No matter how adorable Brits found Jeffrey Daniel, Howard was Shalamar. But that's all he was.

Hiroshima Those Japanese-American fusion musicians—what a sense of humor.

The Isley Brothers They started the decade with *Go All the Way, Inside You,* and *Between the Sheets.* Then they announced a two-for-one stock split.

Al Jarreau NARAS's idea of a jazz singer.

Waylon Jennings Once you loved him or hated him. No more.

The Jets Tongans transplanted to Minnesota, the black-pop Osmonds were discovered wearing native garb in a Holiday Inn. For their Apollo debut they dressed like African-American street kids. Clean-cut ones, of course.

Daniel Johnston R.D. Laing would be proud.

Greg Kihn Kihnformist.

Krokus Swiss metal—which doesn't even guarantee clockwork.

Laibach Not fascists—in fact, probably antifascists. That's something.

Love Tractor First they were Dixie Dregs for the New South. Then they started singing.

MDC Millions of Dumb Complaints.

Modern Romance Spearheaded Britain's 1982 salsa boom. You remember Britain's 1982 salsa boom, don't you?

Stevie Nicks Tolerable in a group that was vying for a Dorian Gray medallion by decade's end, she proved a menace solo, equally unhealthy as role model and sex object.

Kenny Rogers Reached out to Lionel Richie.

Todd Rundgren His Rhino/Bearsville best-of has an '80s side, including the unlistenable "Compassion." Stick him in a studio with Ted Nugent until he recants.

David Sanborn He wants to be Arsenio Hall, fine. King Curtis, forget it.

Spinners Philippe Wynne, 1941–1984. **R.I.P.**

Rick Springfield This was the '80s—the Partridge Family never did anything as carnal (or good) as the breakout jealousy anthem "Jessie's Girl." This was the '80s—they never went AOR crossover, either.

The The Uh-uh.

Third World The most profitable reggae band in the history of the first world.

Three Mustaphas Three Not really brothers. Not really from the Balkans. Now you know.

Toure Kunda They're said to have sold in France without diluting their Senegalese sources, so maybe the sources are the problem. Just listen to their rhythm section, the backbone of Kaoma.

Twisted Sister Dee Snider's congressional testimony remains unreleased. The rest you can watch on television.

Conway Twitty His polite courtly-macho speeches turned sheer pettifoggery whether he was running for stud or hubby.

John Waite Twixt fronting the well-named Babys and fronting the well-named Bad English, he produced one dynamite exploitation: 1984's "Missing You," an "Every Breath You Take" for nice guys. Later he claimed it created a backlash against his serious work.

Dionne Warwick She has no regrets—a *grande dame* is what she always wanted to be.

W.A.S.P. He who drinks like a fish shall fuck like a fish. And that's not the beast they had in mind.

Waterboys How could they be U2 imitators? They're from Scotland. Pompous as hell, too.

Bobby Womack He's no poet and he don't know it.

Yello Chickenshi.

Frank Zappa Oh shut up.

MELTDOWN

Hasil Adkins
Air Supply
Alabama
GG Allin
Basia
Bauhaus
Angela Bofill
Chicago
Christopher Cross
Dead or Alive
Dr. Jeckyl & Mr. Hyde
Dokken
The Fools
Kenny G
Amy Grant
Dave Grusin
The Human Sexual Response
Julio Iglesias
Iron Maiden
LaToya Jackson
Japan
Jefferson Airplane
Jefferson Starship
Kiss
Kitaro
Marillion
Richard Marx
The Meatmen
Menudo
Kylie Minogue
Ronnie Milsap
Mi-Sex
Mr. Mister

Eddie Money
Night Ranger
The Oak Ridge Boys
The Outfield
The Pandoras
Sue Saad & the Next
Sigue Sigue Sputnik
Frank Sinatra
Spyro Gyra
Starship
The Stranglers
Stryper
Vangelis
Andreas Vollenweider
George Winston

NEW WAVE

Men and Volts
Stiff Little Fingers
The Balancing Act
Charlie Pickett and the Eggs
The Tragically Hip
The Flies
Bad Checks
Masters of Reality
Ed Kuepper
American Music Club
The David Roter Method
The Ophelias
The Psychotics
The Bobs
The Godfathers
Opal
All
Konk
Blurt
Hex
Nena
Falco
Adolescents
Chain Gang
Michael Ward
Tête Noires
The Fartz
The Beat
Flamin' Oh's
Norman Salant
The Ordinaires
The Nobodys
Fish and Roses

The Neats
Wipers
Fetchin Bones
Toiling Midgets
K-Martians
Snatch
The Squalls
Lifeboat
Blue Orchids
Screaming Trees
The Plugz
Rockin' Shapes
Cristina
LESR
MDK
New Christs
Mudhoney
Texas Instruments
Death of Samantha
The Fibonaccis
Slickee Boys
Volume Unit
Ut
Gibson Bros.
Missing Foundation
Scruffy the Cat
Tim Lee
Treat Her Right
Holly and the Italians
God's Little Monkeys
The Verlaines
We Are Going To Eat You
Whooping Cranes
The Three-D Invisibles
The Cruzados
The Dance
The Proclaimers
Altered Images
Tall Dwarfs
Big Dipper
Flaming Lips
We've Got a Fuzzbox and We're Gonna Use It
Intensive Care
The Outnumbered
The Misfits
Shockabilly
Rip Rig and Panic
Pigbag
The Necessaries

The Lime Spiders
Swell Maps
Chrome
The Raybeats
The Wonder Stuff
Pop Will Eat Itself
The Pursuit of Happiness
China Crisis
A Certain Ratio
The Hard-Ons
Spanic Boys
Mary's Danish
Durutti Column
House of Freaks
The Christians
The Saints
The Nails
Liquid Liquid
Icehouse
The Primitives
Nip Drivers
JoBoxers
Eat
The Fire Engines
The Woolfe Gang
Bullet LaVolta
ESG
Bongo Bass and Bob
Henry Rollins
Alphaville
Live Skull
The Silencers
Peter Himmelman
Velvet Elvis
Died Pretty
Band of Susans
Vic Godard & the Subway Sect
Phantom Limbs
Hollywood Beyond
The Chameleons
Saccharine Trust
The Nils
Drivin' n' Cryin'
The Side Effects
Skinny Puppy
Velveteen
Christmas
Treva Spontaine
Gaye Bikers on Acid

Social Distortion
Talk Talk
The Blow Monkeys
Squirrel Bait
Felt
Voice Farm
A.R. Kane
Shriekback
The Milkshakes
The Neighborhoods
The Pop Group
The Men They Couldn't Hang
The Buck Pets
Delta 5
Guadalcanal Diary
Alfonia Tims and the Flying Tigers
Antietam
The Magnolias
Girls at Our Best
Everything but the Girl
The Lilac Time
Gene Loves Jezebel
Swing Out Sister
The True Believers
The Drongos
LMNOP
Method Actors
Salem 66
Das Damen
Josie Cotton
Big Pig
Deja Voodoo
Crime and the City Solution
Comateens
Tirez Tirez
Nitzer Ebb
Carmel
The Fuzztones
Adele Bertei
The Humans
Los Microwaves
Los Illegals
Hayzi Fantayzee
Malaria!
The Swimming Pool Q's
Face to Face
Danny Wilson
The Shaggs
Skafish

24-7 Spyz
Urban Verbs
Rifle Sport
Ruts DC
The Exploited
Frightwig
The Payola$
Wire Train
The Raunch Hands
Foetus
November Group
Modern English
Hunters and Collectors
Fashion
Personal Effects
Tav Falco's Panther Burns
Book of Love
Dead or Alive
Armand Schaubroeck
Oil Tasters

COMPILATIONS

POSTPUNK/NEW WAVE

Attack of the Killer B's (Warner Bros.)
The Bridge: A Tribute to Neil Young (Caroline)
Carry On Oi! (Secret import)
The Decline of Western Civilization (Slash)
Desperate Teenage Lovedolls (Gasatanka)
A Diamond Hidden in the Mouth of a Corpse (Giorno Poetry Systems)
Hicks From the Sticks (Antilles)
I.R.S. Greatest Hits Vols. 2 & 3 (I.R.S.)
Let Them Eat Jellybeans! (Virus import)
Oi!—The Album (EMI import)
Party Party (A&M)
Peripheral Vision (Zoar)
Propeller (Propeller)
Rainy Day (Llama)
Repo Man (San Andreas)
Singles: The Great New York Singles Scene (ROIR)
The Wailing Ultimate (Homestead)
Urgh! A Music War (A&M)
Wanna Buy a Bridge? (Rough Trade)
Zetrospective: Hope Springs Eternal (ZE)

RAP

Beat Street (Atlantic)
Beat Street Vol. 2 (Atlantic)
Christmas Rap (Profile)
Colors (Warner Bros.)
The Great Rap Hits (Sugarhill)
Greatest Rap Hits Vol. 2 (Sugarhill)
Hip House (DJ International)

Krush Groove (Warner Bros.)
Mr. Magic's Rap Attack Volume 2 (Profile)
Mr. Magic's Rap Attack Volume 4 (Profile)
Rap's Greatest Hits (Priority)
Wild Style (Animal)
Yo! MTV Raps: The Album (Jive)

DANCE

Best of House Music (Profile)
Black Havana (Capitol)
Breakin' (Polydor)
Dance Traxx (Atlantic)
Flashdance (Casablanca)
Go Go Crankin' (4th & B'way)
Go Go Live at the Capital Centre (I Hear Ya)
The Go Go Posse (I Hear Ya)
Good To Go (Island)
Hip House (DJ International)
House Hallucinates: Pump Up the World Volume One (Vendetta)
Prelude's Greatest Hits (Prelude)
Zetrospective: Dancing in the Face of Adversity (ZE)

AFRICAN

African Connection Vol. II: West Africa (Celluloid import)
African Connection Vol. I: Zaire Choc! (Celluloid import)
The African Typic Collection (Virgin)
Black Star Liner: Reggae From Africa (Heartbeat)
The Heartbeat of Soweto (Shanachie)
Heartbeat Soukous (Earthworks/Virgin)
Homeland (Rounder)
The Indestructible Beat of Soweto (Shanachie)
Iscathamiya: Zulu Worker Choirs in South Africa (Heritage import)
The Kampala Sound (Original Music)
The Kinshasa Sound (Original Music)
Mbube!: Zulu Men's Singing Competition (Rounder)
The Nairobi Beat: Kenyan Pop Music Today (Rounder)
The Nairobi Sound (Original Music)
Phezulu Eqhudeni (Carthage)
Sarafina! (Shanachie)
Sarafina! The Music of Liberation—Broadway Cast Recording (RCA Victor/Novus)
Sheshwe: The Sound of the Mines (Rounder)
Sound d'Afrique (Mango)
Sound d'Afrique II: Soukous (Mango)
Sounds of Soweto (Capitol)
South African Trade Union Worker Choirs (Rounder)

Soweto (Rough Trade import)
Soweto Never Sleeps (Shanachie)
Take Cover (Shanachie)
The Tanzania Sound (Original Music)
Thunder Before Dawn—The Indestructible Beat of Soweto Volume Two (Earthworks/
    Virgin)
Viva Zimbabwe! (Earthworks import)
Zimbabwe Frontline (Virgin)
Zulu Jive/Umbaqanga (Earthworks import)

REGGAE

Black Star Liner: Reggae From Africa (Heartbeat)
Calling Rastafari (Nighthawk)
Club Ska '67 (Mango)
Crucial Reggae Driven by Sly & Robbie (Mango)
Dancehall Style: The Best of Reggae Dancehall Music Vol. 1 (Profile)
Fresh Reggae Hits (Pow Wow)
Fresh Reggae Hits—Vol. 2 (Pow Wow)
The "King" Kong Compilation (Mango)
Knotty Vision (Nighthawk)
More Intensified! Volume 2 Original Ska 1963–67 (Mango)
Ram Dance Hall (Mango)
Reggae Dance Hall Classics (Sleeping Bag)
Reggae Dance Party (RAS)
Reggae Greats: Strictly for Lovers (Mango)
Rockers (Mango)
Scandal Ska (Mango)
This Are Two Tone (Chrysalis)

WORLD MUSIC

Brazil Classics 1: Beleza Tropical (Sire)
Crossover Dreams (Elektra)
Hurricane Zouk (Earthworks/Virgin)
Konbit!: Burning Rhythms of Haiti (A&M)
Nuestras Mejores Cumbias (Globo)
Phases of the Moon: Traditional Chinese Music (Columbia)
Rai Rebels (Virgin)
Red Wave: 4 Underground Bands From the USSR (Big Time)
Tango Argentino (Atlantic)
You Can Tell the World About This: Classic Ethnic Recordings From the 1920's (Morning
    Star)

ETC.

Attack of the Killer B's (Warner Bros.)
The Bridge: A Tribute to Neil Young (Caroline)
Christmas Rap (Profile)
A Christmas Record (ZE import)
Conjure (American Clavé)
A Diamond Hidden in the Mouth of a Corpse (Giorno Poetry Systems)
Every Man Has a Woman (Polydor)
Everything New Is Old . . . Everything Old Is New (Ambient Sound)
Folkways: A Vision Shared—A Tribute to Woody Guthrie and Leadbelly (Columbia)
The Gospel at Colonus (Warner Bros.)
Lost in the Stars: The Music of Kurt Weill (A&M)
The Official Music of the XXIIIrd Olympiad Los Angeles 1984 (Columbia)
Remember Soweto 76–86: Bullets Won't Stop Us Now (Mordam)
Sarafina! (Shanachie)
Sarafina! The Music of Liberation—Broadway Cast Recording (RCA Victor/Novus)
Stay Awake (A&M)
Tango Argentino (Atlantic)
Television's Greatest Hits (TVT)
That's the Way I Feel Now: A Tribute to Thelonious Monk (A&M)
Tribute to Steve Goodman (Red Pajamas)
A Very Special Christmas (A&M)
Zetrospective: Hope Springs Eternal (ZE)

SOUNDTRACKS

Back to the Beach (Epic)
Beat Street (Atlantic)
Beat Street Vol. 2 (Atlantic)
Beverly Hills Cop (MCA)
The Breakfast Club (A&M)
Breakin' (Polydor)
Colors (Warner Bros.)
Crossover Dreams (Elektra)
The Decline of Western Civilization (Slash)
Desperate Teenage Lovedolls (Gasatanka)
Dirty Dancing (RCA Victor)
Do the Right Thing (Motown)
Flashdance (Casablanca)
Footloose (Columbia)
Get Crazy (Morocco)
Ghostbusters II (MCA)
Good To Go (Island)
The Goonies (Epic)
Krush Groove (Warner Bros.)
La Bamba (Slash)
Less Than Zero (Def Jam)

Party Party (A&M)
Repo Man (San Andreas)
Rockers (Mango)
Scandal Ska (Mango)
School Daze (EMI-Manhattan)
Something Wild (MCA)
Soup for One (Mirage)
Spinal Tap (Polydor)
Starstruck (A&M)
Vision Quest (Geffen)
Who's That Girl (Sire)
Wild Style (Animal)
The Woman in Red (Motown)

ROCK LIBRARY: BEFORE 1980

This basic rock library reflects my belief that great records should sound pretty great when you play them. Occasionally I've stretched this standard a little—the Aerosmith and Ohio Players entries, for instance, aren't as perfect as I'd prefer. But I've bypassed such dubious milestones d'estime as the Beatles' White Album, Pink Floyd's *The Dark Side of the Moon,* and Marvin Gaye's *What's Going On?* despite all the smart people they've touched. I've pretty much skipped metal, too, though metal certainly deserves a bigger place in rock history than Kate & Anna McGarrigle, whose first two LPs make the cut. I wish Rhino would do a single *Nuggets* album as consistent as its doowop compilations, but the leading U.S. reissue label knows its market can't get enough garage-rock. I don't prefer Muddy Waters to Chuck Berry or Jerry Lee Lewis, but he happens to have at least three fine (though shortish) records on the market while their undeniable albums stop at one good-sized best-of apiece. And so it goes.

I've tried to assure that every title I recommend will be in print when the book appears, providing catalogue numbers when similar titles might cause confusion. In print doesn't always mean in the store or even the warehouse, however, and with catalogues disintegrating as vinyl phases out, even in print can't be guaranteed; in addition, a few selections are scheduled reissues that may get delayed. I've listed acceptable U.S. releases even in the rare cases when clearly superior imports were available, but if an import was my only option, I didn't hesitate. While almost every choice is CD-available, I've avoided CD-only product, and I've listed none of the coffee-table boxes record companies sell so dear—three-(vinyl)-disc compilations (Motown's *Anthology* best-ofs and Neil Young's *Decade*) are as massive as my choices get. (Laserheads might well go for the Beatles' CD-only *With the Beatles* and *Please Please Me,* original U.K. configurations longer than and at least as good as the early U.S. stuff. The only decent Loretta Lynn compilation is a twenty-hits CD. And the Chuck Berry and Otis Redding sets definitely tempted me.) I've also included a few crucial country collections, two compilations by jump-blues forerunner Louis Jordan, and a Woody Guthrie album. And after much going back and forth, I've listed Sun City boycott violators Ray Charles and Ray Davies, whose contributions to history far preceded the political pigheadedness that makes it so hard to get with them these days.

Initially, I planned to come up with 250 records; instead, I stopped where the great stuff ended. As a result, I can't imagine a rock and roll fan with ears to hear disliking more than a few cranky exceptions among the two hundred-plus records below. And for future reference and current used-record shopping I've listed forty-plus out-of-print albums that shouldn't be—in a few cases superior work (or just packaging and song selection) by artists on the main list, but mostly unjustly obscure classics and personal favorites. As rock history is boutiqued, I fully expect many of these to reappear. Happy hunting.

THE CORE COLLECTION

Aerosmith: *Rocks* (Columbia)
Africa Dances (Original Music)
Atlantic Rhythm & Blues, Vol. 3: 1955–1958 (Atlantic)
The Band: *The Band* (Capitol)
The Beach Boys: *Endless Summer* (Capitol)
The Beatles: *The Beatles at the Hollywood Bowl* (Capitol)
The Beatles: *The Beatles' Second Album* (Capitol)
The Beatles: *Meet the Beatles!* (Capitol)
The Beatles: *Rubber Soul* (Capitol)
The Beatles: *Sgt. Pepper's Lonely Hearts Club Band* (Capitol)
The Beatles: *Something New* (Capitol)
Chuck Berry: *The Great Twenty-Eight* (Chess)
The Best of Doo Wop Uptempo (Rhino)
The Best of the Doo Wop Ballads (Rhino)
The Best of the Girl Groups (Rhino)
The B-52's: *The B-52's* (Warner Bros.)
Big Star: *Radio City* (Big Beat import)
Bobby Bland: *The Best of Bobby Bland, Vol. 1* (MCA)
Blondie: *Parallel Lines* (Chrysalis)
David Bowie: *Changesbowie* (Rykodisc)
James Brown: *The James Brown Story: Ain't That a Groove 1967–1970* (Polydor)
James Brown: *The James Brown Story: Doin' It to Death 1970–1973* (Polydor)
James Brown: *Live at the Apollo (1962)* (Polydor)
James Brown: *Roots of a Revolution* (Polydor)
James Brown: *Solid Gold: 30 Golden Hits* (Polydor)
Buffalo Springfield: *Buffalo Springfield* (Atco SD2-806)
Burning Spear: *Marcus Garvey* (Mango)
Burning Spear: *Harder Than the Best* (Mango)
The Buzzcocks: *Singles Going Steady* (I.R.S./A&M)
The Byrds: *The Byrds' Greatest Hits* (Columbia)
The Birds: *Sweetheart of the Rodeo* (Columbia)
Captain Beefheart and the Magic Band: *Shiny Beast (Bat Chain Puller)* (Enigma Retro/ Straight)
Ray Charles: *Greatest Hits: Vol. 1* (Rhino)
Ray Charles: *Greatest Hits: Vol. 2* (Rhino)
Ray Charles: *Modern Sounds in Country and Western Music* (Rhino)
Eric Clapton: *461 Ocean Boulevard* (RSO)
The Clash: *The Clash* (CBS import)
The Clash: *Give 'Em Enough Rope* (Epic)
The Clovers: *5 Cool Cats* (Edsel import)

The Coasters: *Young Blood* (Atlantic)
Ornette Coleman: *Dancing in Your Head* (Horizon)
Sam Cooke: *The Man and His Music* (RCA Victor)
Elvis Costello and the Attractions: *This Year's Model* (Columbia)
Creedence Clearwater Revival: *Chronicle* (Fantasy)
Creedence Clearwater Revival: *Cosmo's Factory* (Fantasy)
Creedence Clearwater Revival: *Willy and the Poor Boys* (Fantasy)
Miles Davis: *Agharta* (Columbia)
Miles Davis: *Jack Johnson* (Columbia)
Derek and the Dominoes: *Layla* (RSO)
Bo Diddley: *His Greatest Sides, Vol. 1* (Chess)
Dr. Buzzard's Original Savannah Band: *Dr. Buzzard's Original Savannah Band* (RCA)
Fats Domino: *The Best of Fats Domino* (EMI import)
Donovan: *Greatest Hits/The Best of Times* (Epic)
The Drifters: *Golden Hits* (Atlantic)
The Drifters: *Their Greatest Recordings: The Early Years* (Atco)
Bob Dylan: *Blonde on Blonde* (Columbia)
Bob Dylan: *Blood on the Tracks* (Columbia)
Bob Dylan: *Bringing It All Back Home* (Columbia)
Bob Dylan: *The Freewheelin' Bob Dylan* (Columbia)
Bob Dylan: *Highway 61 Revisited* (Columbia)
Bob Dylan: *John Wesley Harding* (Columbia)
Bob Dylan: *Nashville Skyline* (Columbia)
Bob Dylan/The Band: *Before the Flood* (Columbia)
Eno: *Another Green World* (EG)
The Everly Brothers: *The Best of the Everly Brothers* (Rhino)
Fleetwood Mac: *Rumours* (Warner Bros.)
The Flying Burrito Bros.: *The Gilded Palace of Sin* (A&M)
Aretha Franklin: *30 Greatest Hits* (Atlantic)
Lefty Frizzell: *Lefty Frizzell's Greatest Hits/The Best of Times* (Columbia)
Funkadelic: *The Best of the Early Years Volume One* (Westbound import)
Marvin Gaye: *Anthology* (Motown)
Grateful Dead: *The Workingman's Dead* (Warner Bros.)
Al Green: *Al Green's Greatest Hits* (Motown)
Al Green: *The Belle Album* (Motown)
Al Green: *Call Me* (Motown)
Al Green: *Livin' for You* (Motown)
Woody Guthrie: *Dust Bowl Ballads* (Rounder)
Tom T. Hall: *The Essential Tom T. Hall: Twentieth Anniversary Collection/The Story
    Songs* (Mercury)
The Harder They Come (Mango)
Jimi Hendrix: *Are You Experienced?* (Reprise)
Jimi Hendrix: *The Cry of Love* (Reprise)
Jimi Hendrix: *Smash Hits* (Reprise)
Jimi Hendrix Experience: *Electric Ladyland* (Reprise)
A History of New Orleans Rhythm & Blues—Vol 1 (1950–1958) (Rhino)
A History of New Orleans Rhythm & Blues—Vol 2 (1959–1962) (Rhino)
Buddy Holly: *20 Golden Greats* (MCA)

Michael Hurley/The Unholy Modal Rounders/Jeffrey Fredericks & the Clamtones:
  Have Moicy! (Rounder)
The Impressions: *Greatest Hits* (MCA)
It Will Stand: Minit Records 1960–1963 (EMI America)
Michael Jackson: *Off the Wall* (Epic)
Etta James: *Her Greatest Sides, Vol. 1* (Chess)
George Jones: *The King of Country Music* (Liberty import)
Janis Joplin: *Janis Joplin's Greatest Hits* (Columbia)
Louis Jordan: *The Best of Louis Jordan* (MCA)
Louis Jordan: *Greatest Hits Vol. 2 (1941–1947)* (MCA)
B.B. King: *The Best of B.B. King Volume 1* (Ace import)
B.B. King: *Live at the Regal* (MCA)
The Kinks: *Greatest Hits* (Rhino)
The Kinks: *The Kinks Kronikles* (Reprise)
Led Zeppelin: *Led Zeppelin IV* (Atlantic)
John Lennon: *Imagine* (Capitol)
John Lennon: *Plastic Ono Band* (Capitol)
Jerry Lee Lewis: *18 Original Greatest Hits* (Rhino)
Little Richard: *18 Greatest Hits* (Rhino)
Love: *Forever Changes* (Elektra)
The Lovin' Spoonful: *Anthology* (Rhino)
Nick Lowe: *Labour of Lust* (Columbia)
Nick Lowe: *Pure Pop for Now People* (Columbia)
Frankie Lymon & the Teenagers: *The Best of Frankie Lymon & the Teenagers* (Rhino)
Lynyrd Skynyrd: *Gold and Platinum* (MCA)
Lynyrd Skynyrd: *Pronounced Leh-nerd Skeh-nerd* (MCA)
The Mamas and the Papas: *Farewell to the First Golden Era* (MCA)
Bob Marley & the Wailers: *Burnin'* (Island)
Bob Marley & the Wailers: *Catch a Fire* (Island)
Bob Marley & the Wailers: *Natty Dread* (Island)
The Marvelettes: *Greatest Hits* (Motown)
Kate & Anna McGarrigle: *Dancer With Bruised Knees* (Carthage)
Kate & Anna McGarrigle: *Kate & Anna McGarrigle* (Carthage)
Joni Mitchell: *Blue* (Reprise)
Joni Mitchell: *Court and Spark* (Elektra)
Joni Mitchell: *For the Roses* (Asylum)
The Modern Lovers: *The Modern Lovers* (Rhino/Beserkley)
Van Morrison: *It's Too Late To Stop Now* (Warner Bros.)
Van Morrison: *Moondance* (Warner Bros.)
Willie Nelson: *Stardust* (Columbia)
Randy Newman: *Good Old Boys* (Reprise)
Randy Newman: *12 Songs* (Reprise)
New York Dolls: *In Too Much Too Soon* (Mercury)
New York Dolls: *New York Dolls* (Mercury)
Ohio Players: *Gold* (Mercury)
Graham Parker and the Rumour: *Howlin Wind* (Mercury)
Parliament: *Funkentelechy vs. the Placebo Syndrome* (Casablanca)
Parliament: *Motor-Booty Affair* (Casablanca)

Gram Parsons: *Grievous Angel* (Reprise)
Dolly Parton: *Best of Dolly Parton* (RCA AYLI-5146)
Carl Perkins: *Original Sun Golden Hits (1955–1957)* (Rhino)
Wilson Pickett: *Wilson Pickett's Greatest Hits* (Atlantic)
The Platters: *Encore of Golden Hits* (Mercury)
Elvis Presley: *Elvis' Golden Records* (RCA)
Elvis Presley: *Elvis Presley* (RCA)
Elvis Presley: *The Sun Sessions* (RCA)
Elvis Presley: *A Valentine Gift for You* (RCA)
John Prine: *John Prine* (Atlantic)
John Prine: *Sweet Revenge* (Atlantic)
Bonnie Raitt: *Give It Up* (Warner Bros.)
Bonnie Raitt: *Home Plate* (Warner Bros.)
Ramones: *Ramones* (Sire)
Ramones: *Road to Ruin* (Sire)
Ramones: *Rocket to Russia* (Sire)
The Rascals: *Time Peace: The Rascals' Greatest Hits* (Atlantic)
Otis Redding: *The Best of Otis Redding* (Atlantic SD2-801)
Jimmy Reed: *Bright Lights, Big City* (Chameleon)
Smokey Robinson & the Miracles: *Anthology* (Motown)
The Roches: *The Roches* (Warner Bros.)
The Rolling Stones: *Aftermath* (Abkco)
The Rolling Stones: *Beggars Banquet* (Abkco)
Rolling Stones: *Exile on Main Street* (Rolling Stones)
The Rolling Stones: *Let It Bleed* (Abkco)
The Rolling Stones: *Out of Our Heads* (Abkco)
The Rolling Stones: *The Rolling Stones, Now!* (Abkco)
Rolling Stones: *Some Girls* (Rolling Stones)
The Rolling Stones: *Sticky Fingers* (Rolling Stones)
The Rolling Stones: *12 × 5* (Abkco)
Diana Ross & the Supremes: *Anthology* (Motown)
Sam & Dave: *The Best of Sam & Dave* (Atlantic)
Sex Pistols: *Never Mind the Bollocks: Here's the Sex Pistols* (Warner Bros.)
The Shirelles: *Anthology (1959–1964)* (Rhino)
Paul Simon: *Paul Simon* (Warner Bros.)
Sly & the Family Stone: *Fresh* (Epic)
Sly & the Family Stone: *Greatest Hits* (Epic)
Sly & the Family Stone: *There's a Riot Goin' On* (Epic)
Patti Smith: *Horses* (Arista)
Dusty Springfield: *Dusty in Memphis . . . Plus* (Philips import)
Bruce Springsteen: *Born To Run* (Columbia)
Steely Dan: *Can't Buy a Thrill* (MCA)
Steely Dan: *Countdown to Ecstasy* (MCA)
Steely Dan: *Katy Lied* (MCA)
Steely Dan: *Pretzel Logic* (MCA)
Rod Stewart: *Every Picture Tells a Story* (Mercury)
Donna Summer: *On the Radio: Greatest Hits, Volumes I & II* (Casablanca)
Talking Heads: *More Songs About Buildings and Food* (Sire)
Television: *Marquee Moon* (Elektra)

The Temptations: *The Temptations' Greatest Hits, Vol. 1* (Motown)
Joe Tex: *I Believe I'm Gonna Make It: The Best of Joe Tex* (Rhino)
Big Joe Turner: *Greatest Hits* (Atlantic)
The Velvet Underground: *The Velvet Underground* (Verve)
The Velvet Underground: *The Velvet Underground & Nico* (Verve)
Gene Vincent: *The Best of Gene Vincent* (EMI import)
Dionne Warwick: *Anthology 1962–1969* (Rhino)
Muddy Waters: *The Best of Muddy Waters* (Chess)
Muddy Waters: *The Real Folk Blues* (Chess)
Muddy Waters: *Trouble No More: Singles (1955–1959)* (Chess)
The Who: *A Quick One (Happy Jack)/The Who Sell Out* (MCA)
The Wild Tchoupitoulas: *The Wild Tchoupitoulas* (Antilles)
Hank Williams: *40 Greatest Hits* (Polydor)
Sonny Boy Williamson: *The Real Folk Blues* (Chess)
Jackie Wilson: *The Jackie Wilson Story* (Epic)
Jackie Wilson: *Reet Petite* (Ace import)
Wire: *Pink Flag* (Restless Retro)
Howlin' Wolf: *Howlin' Wolf* (Chess)
Howlin' Wolf: *Moanin' in the Moonlight* (Chess)
Stevie Wonder: *Fulfillingness' First Finale* (Tamla)
Stevie Wonder: *Greatest Hits, Vol. 1* (Tamla)
Stevie Wonder: *Greatest Hits, Vol. 2* (Tamla)
Stevie Wonder: *Innervisions* (Tamla)
Stevie Wonder: *Talking Book* (Tamla)
Tammy Wynette: *Tammy's Greatest Hits/The Best of Times* (Epic)
Neil Young: *After the Gold Rush* (Reprise)
Neil Young: *Comes a Time* (Reprise)
Neil Young: *Decade* (Reprise)
Neil Young & Crazy Horse: *Rust Never Sleeps* (Warner Bros.)
Neil Young: *Tonight's the Night* (Reprise)

GONE BUT NOT FORGOTTEN

The Beach Boys: *Wild Honey* (Capitol *or* Brother/Reprise)
David Bowie: *Station to Station* (RCA Victor)
James Brown: *Sex Machine* (Polydor)
Chic: *Risque* (Atlantic)
Dion & the Belmonts: *24 Original Classics* (Arista)
Fats Domino: *Fats Domino: The Legendary Masters Series* (United Artists)
Lee Dorsey: *Holy Cow!: The Best of Lee Dorsey* (Arista)
18 Original King Sized Hits (Columbia)
Joe Ely: *Honky Tonk Masquerade* (MCA)
The Everly Brothers: *Roots* (Warner Bros.)
The Five Royales: *The Five Royales* (King)
Aretha Franklin: *Spirit in the Dark* (Atlantic)
Aretha Franklin: *Young, Gifted and Black* (Atlantic)
Lefty Frizzell: *Columbia Historic Edition* (Columbia)
Funkadelic: *One Nation Under a Groove* (Warner Bros.)

Arlo Guthrie: *Amigo* (Warner Bros.)
Hot Chocolate: *10 Greatest Hits* (Big Tree)
The Insect Trust: *Hoboken Saturday Night* (Atco)
George Jones: *16 Greatest Hits* (Starday)
George Jones: *White Lightning* (Ace import)
It Will Stand: Minit Records 1960–1963 (EMI America)
B.B. King: *16 Greatest Hits* (Galaxy)
The Kinks: *Face to Face* (Reprise)
Jerry Lee Lewis & Linda Gail Lewis: *Together* (Smash)
Andy Fairweather Low: *Be Bop 'n' Holla* (A&M)
Andy Fairweather Low: *Spider Jiving* (A&M)
Loretta Lynn: *Loretta Lynn Writes 'Em and Sings 'Em* (MCA)
Manfred Mann's Earth Band: *Manfred Mann's Earth Band* (Polydor)
John McLaughlin: *Devotion* (Douglas)
Moby Grape: *Moby Grape* (Columbia)
Van Morrison: *Into the Music* (Warner Bros.)
Ricky Nelson: *Ricky Nelson: The Legendary Masters Series* (United Artists)
Pere Ubu: *Dub Housing* (Chrysalis)
Phil Spector's Greatest Hits (Warner/Spector)
Otis Redding: *Dictionary of Soul* (Volt)
Otis Redding: *The Immortal Otis Redding* (Atco)
The Spaniels: *16 Soulful Serenades* (Solid Smoke)
Otis Spann: *Walking the Blues* (Barnaby *or* Candid)
Dusty Springfield: *Dusty in Memphis* (Atlantic)
Howard Tate: *Howard Tate* (Verve)
The Vibrators: *Pure Mania* (Columbia)
Gene Vincent: *The Bop That Just Won't Stop (1956)* (Capitol)
War: *Greatest Hits* (United Artists)

THE A LISTS

The Clash: *Black Market Clash* (Epic)
Dollar Brand: *African Marketplace* (Elektra)
Steel Pulse: *Reggae Fever* (Mango)
The Undertones: *Hypnotized* (A&M)
T-Bone Burnett: *Truth Decay* (Takoma)
Henry Cow: *Western Culture* (Interzone)
Warren Zevon: *Stand in the Fire* (Asylum)
Bob Marley & the Wailers: *Uprising* (Island)
The Specials: *The Specials* (Chrysalis)
Ronnie Barron: *Blues Delicacies, Vol. One* (Vivid Sound import)
Aerosmith: *Greatest Hits* (Columbia)
George Jones: *I Am What I Am* (Epic)
Bunny Wailer: *Bunny Wailer Sings the Wailers* (Mango)
The Sir Douglas Quintet: *The Best of the Sir Douglas Quintet* (Takoma)
Joy Division: *Unknown Pleasures* (Factory)
Robert Jr. Lockwood & Johnny Shines: *Hangin' On* (Rounder)
The Jacksons: *Triumph* (Epic)
Pere Ubu: *New Picnic Time* (Chrysalis import)
The Psychedelic Furs: *The Psychedelic Furs* (Columbia)
Rockpile: *Seconds of Pleasure* (Columbia)
Gil Scott-Heron/Brian Jackson: *1980* (Arista)
Diana Ross: *Diana* (Motown)
Shalamar: *Three for Love* (Solar)
More Intensified! Volume 2 Original Ska 1963–67 (Mango)
Manhattans: *Greatest Hits* (Columbia)
Oi!—the Album (EMI import)
Big Youth: *Progress* (Negusa Nagast import)
Teddy Pendergrass: *TP* (Philadelphia International)
Donna Summer: *The Wanderer* (Geffen)
The Selecter: *Too Much Pressure* (Chrysalis)
The Suburbs: *In Combo* (Twin/Tone)
The Brains: *The Brains* (Mercury)
Club Ska '67 (Mango)
Gang of Four: *Gang of Four* (Warner Bros.)

1981 (64)

X: *Wild Gift* (Slash)
Ian Dury: *Juke Box Dury* (Stiff)
King Sunny Adé and His African Beats: *The Message* (Sunny Alade import)
Greatest Rap Hits Vol. 2 (Sugarhill)
Gang of Four: *Solid Gold* (Warner Bros.)
The English Beat: *Wha'ppen?* (Sire)
Elvis Costello and the Attractions: *Trust* (Columbia)
Gang of Four: *Another Day/Another Dollar* (Warner Bros.)
Phases of the Moon: Traditional Chinese Music (Columbia)
Human Switchboard: *Who's Landing in My Hangar?* (Faulty Products)
Al Green: *Higher Plane* (Myrrh)

Psychedelic Furs: *Talk Talk Talk* (Columbia)
The Specials: *Ghost Town/Why?/Friday Night Saturday Morning* (Chrysalis)
Black Uhuru: *Red* (Mango)
Black Flag: *Damaged* (SST)
Gary Stewart: *Greatest Hits* (RCA Victor)
Tom Verlaine: *Dreamtime* (Warner Bros.)
Chic: *Take It Off* (Atlantic)
Red Crayola With Art & Language: *Kangaroo?* (Rough Trade)
Funkadelic: *The Electric Spanking of War Babies* (Warner Bros.)
Penguin Cafe Orchestra: *Penguin Cafe Orchestra* (Editions EG)
Prince: *Controversy* (Warner Bros.)
Yoko Ono: *Season of Glass* (Geffen)
The Clash: *Sandinista!* (Epic)
Tom Tom Club: *Tom Tom Club* (Sire)
The Blasters: *The Blasters* (Slash)
Sly and Robbie Present Taxi (Mango)
The dB's: *Stands for Decibels* (Albion import)
Blondie: *The Best of Blondie* (Chrysalis)
James Booker: *New Orleans Piano Wizard: Live!* (Rounder)
Gregory Isaacs: *Best of Gregory Isaacs Volume 2* (GG)
Kid Creole and the Coconuts: *Fresh Fruit in Foreign Places* (ZE/Sire)
DNA: *A Taste of DNA* (American Clavé)
Joan Jett: *Bad Reputation* (Boardwalk)
The B-52's: *Party Mix* (Warner Bros.)
Shoes: *Tongue Twister* (Elektra)
Elvis Presley: *This Is Elvis* (RCA Victor)
Shalamar: *Go for It* (Solar)
Marvin Gaye: *In Our Lifetime* (Tamla)
Bunny Wailer: *Tribute* (Solomonic import)
UB40: *Present Arms* (DEP International import)
Rolling Stones: *Tattoo You* (Rolling Stones)
Teena Marie: *It Must Be Magic* (Gordy)
Z. Z. Hill: *Down Home* (Malaco)
Slave: *Show Time* (Cotillion)
Ramones: *Pleasant Dreams* (Sire)
Rick James: *Street Songs* (Gordy)
The DeBarges: *The DeBarges* (Gordy)
Johnny Copeland: *Copeland Special* (Rounder)
Joy Division: *Closer* (Factory)
Dave Edmunds: *The Best of Dave Edmunds* (Swan Song)
Phoebe Snow: *The Best of Phoebe Snow* (Columbia)
Sound d'Afrique (Mango)
Let Them Eat Jellybeans! (Virus import)
Shannon Jackson & the Decoding Society: *Nasty* (Moers Music import)
John Anderson: *2* (Warner Bros.)
The "King" Kong Compilation (Mango)
Aretha Franklin: *Love All the Hurt Away* (Arista)
Stampfel & Weber: *Going Nowhere Fast* (Rounder)
David Byrne: *Songs from the Broadway Production of "The Catherine Wheel"* (Sire)

Linx: *Intuition* (Chrysalis)
Sir Douglas Quintet: *Border Wave* (Takoma)
Muddy Waters: *King Bee* (Blue Sky)
David Johansen: *Here Comes the Night* (Blue Sky)

1982 (78)

Ornette Coleman: *Of Human Feelings* (Antilles)
Marshall Crenshaw: *Marshall Crenshaw* (Warner Bros.)
George Clinton: *Computer Games* (Capitol)
Flipper: *The Generic Album* (Subterranean)
Richard & Linda Thompson: *Shoot Out the Lights* (Hannibal)
Kid Creole and the Coconuts: *Wise Guy* (Sire/ZE)
Donald Fagen: *The Nightfly* (Warner Bros.)
Professor Longhair: *The Last Mardi Gras* (Atlantic/Deluxe)
Lou Reed: *The Blue Mask* (RCA Victor)
Michael Jackson: *Thriller* (Epic)
The Angry Samoans: *Back From Samoa* (Bad Trip)
Prince: *1999* (Warner Bros.)
George Jones: *Anniversary—Ten Years of Hits* (Epic)
Stevie Wonder: *The Original Musiquarium I* (Tamla)
The Itals: *Brutal Out Deh* (Nighthawk)
ABC: *The Lexicon of Love* (Mercury)
Gilberto Gil: *Um Banda Um* (Warner Bros. import)
Marvin Gaye: *Midnight Love* (Columbia)
Shalamar: *Greatest Hits* (Solar)
Clint Eastwood & General Saint: *Two Bad D.J.* (Greensleeves)
Ray Parker Jr.: *The Other Woman* (Arista)
Chic: *Tongue in Chic* (Atlantic)
King Sunny Adé and His African Beats: *Juju Music* (Mango)
Warren Zevon: *The Envoy* (Asylum)
Sound d'Afrique II: Soukous (Mango)
Ronald Shannon Jackson and the Decoding Society: *Mandance* (Antilles)
Ray Parker Jr.: *Greatest Hits* (Arista)
Bruce Springsteen: *Nebraska* (Columbia)
The Time: *What Time Is It?* (Warner Bros.)
The English Beat: *Special Beat Service* (I.R.S.)
Orchestra Makassy: *Agwaya* (Virgin import)
The B-52's: *Mesopotamia* (Warner Bros.)
The Roches: *Keep On Doing* (Warner Bros.)
Bonnie Raitt: *Green Light* (Warner Bros.)
Roxy Music: *Avalon* (Warner Bros.)
Van Morrison: *Beautiful Vision* (Warner Bros.)
Grandmaster Flash and the Furious Five: *The Message* (Sugarhill)
Ruby Braff: *Very Sinatra* (Finesse)
John Lennon: *The John Lennon Collection* (Geffen)
Madness: *Complete Madness* (Stiff import)
Gang of Four: *Songs of the Free* (Warner Bros.)

X: *Under the Big Black Sun* (Elektra)
Material: *One Down* (Elektra)
Neil Young: *Trans* (Geffen)
R.E.M.: *Chronic Town* (I.R.S.)
Ferron: *Testimony* (Philo)
Hüsker Dü: *Everything Falls Apart* (Reflex)
The Descendents: *Milo Goes to College* (New Alliance)
Minutemen: *What Makes a Man Start Fires?* (SST)
James Blood Ulmer: *Black Rock* (Columbia)
Bonnie Hayes With the Wild Choir: *Good Clean Fun* (Slash)
Trouble Funk: *Drop the Bomb* (Sugarhill)
Talking Heads: *The Name of This Band Is Talking Heads* (Sire)
Squeeze: *Singles—45's and Under* (A&M)
Rank and File: *Sundown* (Slash)
Willie Nelson & Webb Pierce: *In the Jailhouse Now* (Columbia)
Sweet Pea Atkinson: *Don't Walk Away* (Island)
Richard Hell: *Destiny Street* (Red Star)
D.O.A.: *War on 45* (Alternative Tentacles)
The Waitresses: *I Could Rule the World if I Could Only Get the Parts* (Polydor)
Calling Rastafari (Nighthawk)
A Flock of Seagulls: *A Flock of Seagulls* (Arista)
Ted Hawkins: *Watch Your Step* (Rounder)
UB40: *The Singles Album* (DEP International import)
Laurie Anderson: *Big Science* (Warner Bros.)
Everything New Is Old . . . Everything Old Is New (Ambient Sound)
The Psychedelic Furs: *Forever Now* (Columbia)
David Johansen: *Live It Up* (Blue Sky)
The Replacements: *Stink* (Twin/Tone)
Captain Beefheart and the Magic Band: *Ice Cream for Crow* (Virgin/Epic)
The Mighty Diamonds: *Indestructible* (Alligator)
The Jive Five Featuring Eugene Pitt: *Here We Are!* (Ambient Sound)
T-Bone Burnett: *Trap Door* (Warner Bros.)
Bunny Wailer: *Hook Line 'n Sinker* (Solomonic import)
Joe "King" Carrasco and the Crowns: *Synapse Gap (Mundo Total)* (MCA)
Swamp Dogg: *The Best of* (War Bride)
Tom Robinson: *North by Northwest* (Geffen)
Alberta Hunter: *The Glory of Alberta Hunter* (Columbia)

1983 (67)

DeBarge: *In a Special Way* (Gordy)
Marshall Crenshaw: *Field Day* (Warner Bros.)
African Music (Vertigo import)
The Blasters: *Non Fiction* (Slash)
James Blood Ulmer: *Odyssey* (Columbia)
DFX2: *Emotion* (MCA)
Lou Reed: *Legendary Hearts* (RCA Victor)
Hüsker Dü: *Metal Circus* (SST)

George Clinton: *You Shouldn't-Nuf Bit Fish* (Capitol)

Cyndi Lauper: *She's So Unusual* (Portrait)

Pablo Moses: *In the Future* (Alligator)

Jonathan Richman & the Modern Lovers: *Jonathan Sings!* (Sire)

Pamelo Mounk'a: *Propulsion!* (Sonics import)

UB40: *1980–1983* (A&M)

Talking Heads: *Speaking in Tongues* (Sire)

Womack & Womack: *Love Wars* (Elektra)

King Sunny Adé and His African Beats: *Synchro System* (Mango)

True West: *True West* (Bring Out Your Dead)

Oh-OK: *Furthermore What* (DB)

X: *More Fun in the New World* (Elektra)

UB40: *Labour of Love* (A&M)

Ronald Shannon Jackson and the Decoding Society: *Barbecue Dog* (Antilles)

The Cucumbers: *The Cucumbers* (Fake Doom)

Aztec Camera: *High Land, Hard Rain* (Sire)

The Kinshasa Sound (Original Music)

Kid Creole and the Coconuts: *Doppelganger* (Sire)

Joan Armatrading: *Track Record* (A&M)

Kate & Anna McGarrigle: *Love Over and Over* (Polydor)

The B-52's: *Whammy!* (Warner Bros.)

Divinyls: *Desperate* (Chrysalis)

R.E.M.: *Murmur* (I.R.S.)

U2: *Under a Blood Red Sky* (Island)

Local Boys: *Moments of Madness* (Island)

Eek-a-Mouse: *The Mouse and the Man* (Greensleeves)

ABC: *Beauty Stab* (Mercury)

This Are Two Tone (Chrysalis)

Tom Waits: *Swordfishtrombones* (Island)

P-Funk All-Stars: *Urban Dancefloor Guerillas* (Uncle Jam/CBS Associated)

MC 5: *Babes in Arms* (ROIR cassette)

Charlie Haden: *The Ballad of the Fallen* (ECM)

Richard Thompson: *Hand of Kindness* (Hannibal)

Pylon: *Chomp* (DB)

Ramones: *Subterranean Jungle* (Sire)

Los Lobos: *". . . And a Time To Dance"* (Slash)

Knotty Vision (Nighthawk)

Minutemen: *Buzz or Howl Under the Influence of Heat* (SST)

Viva Zimbabwe! (Earthworks import)

Yolocamba Ita: *Revolutionary Songs of El Salvador* (Flying Fish)

Madonna: *Madonna* (Sire)

Indeep: *Last Night a D.J. Saved My Life* (Sound of New York)

Butthole Surfers: *Butthole Surfers* (Alternative Tentacles)

Jamaaladeen Tacuma: *Show Stopper* (Gramavision)

Nile Rodgers: *Adventures in the Land of the Good Groove* (Mirage)

John Hiatt: *Riding With the King* (Geffen)

Philip Glass: *The Photographer* (CBS)

Al Green: *I'll Rise Again* (Myrrh)

Winston Hussey: *The Girl I Adore* (Live & Learn)

King Sunny Adé and His African Beats: *Ajoo* (Makossa)
Bad Religion: *Into the Future* (Epitaph)
Public Image Ltd.: *PiL* (Virgin import)
John Anderson: *All the People Are Talkin'* (Warner Bros.)
Hilary: *Kinetic* (Backstreet)
The Golden Palominos: *The Golden Palominos* (Celluloid/OAO)
Kurtis Blow: *Party Time?* (Mercury)
Earth, Wind & Fire: *Powerlight* (Columbia)
The Plastic People of the Universe: *Leading Horses* (Bozi Mlyn import)
Swingrass '83: *Swingrass '83* (Antilles)

1 9 8 4 (6 5)

Bruce Springsteen: *Born in the U.S.A.* (Columbia)
The Replacements: *Let It Be* (Twin/Tone)
Laurie Anderson: *United States Live* (Warner Bros.)
Parliament: *Parliament's Greatest Hits* (Casablanca)
Bob Marley and the Wailers: *Legend* (Island)
John Lennon/Yoko Ono: *Milk and Honey* (Polydor)
Black Uhuru: *Anthem* (Island)
King Sunny Adé and His African Beats: *Aura* (Mango)
Linton Kwesi Johnson: *Making History* (Island)
Lou Reed: *New Sensations* (RCA Victor)
Thomas Mapfumo: *Ndangariro* (Carthage)
Wire: *And Here It Is . . . Again . . . Wire* (Sneaky Pete import)
John Anderson: *Greatest Hits* (Warner Bros.)
Los Lobos: *How Will the Wolf Survive?* (Slash)
Arto Lindsay/Ambitious Lovers: *Envy* (Editions EG)
Ramones: *Too Tough To Die* (Sire)
Persian Gulf: *Changing the Weather* (Raven)
The dB's: *Like This* (Bearsville)
Ladysmith Black Mambazo: *Induku Zethu* (Shanachie)
Rubén Blades y Seis del Solar: *Buscando America* (Elektra)
Les Ambassadeurs: *Les Ambassadeurs* (Rounder)
Rolling Stones: *Rewind (1971–1984)* (Rolling Stones)
Hüsker Dü: *Zen Arcade* (SST)
Toots and the Maytals: *Reggae Greats: Toots and the Maytals* (Mango)
Minutemen: *Double Nickels on the Dime* (SST)
Joe "King" Carrasco and the Crowns: *Bordertown* (Big Beat import)
Run-D.M.C.: *Run-D.M.C.* (Profile)
XTC: *Waxworks: Some Singles 1977–1982* (Geffen)
Prince and the Revolution: *Purple Rain* (Paisley Park)
Laurie Anderson: *Mister Heartbreak* (Warner Bros.)
Gil Scott-Heron: *The Best of Gil Scott-Heron* (Arista)
David Johansen: *Sweet Revenge* (Passport)
Big Black: *Racer-X* (Homestead)
The Del-Lords: *Frontier Days* (EMI America)
The Pretenders: *Learning To Crawl* (Sire)

Anna Domino: *East and West* (Les Disques du Crèpuscule import)
Sparrow: *King of the World* (B's)
Bangles: *All Over the Place* (Columbia)
Half Japanese: *Sing No Evil* (Iridescence)
Burning Spear: *Reggae Greats: Burning Spear* (Mango)
Tom Verlaine: *Cover* (Warner Bros.)
Ferron: *Shadows on a Dime* (Lucy import)
Tina Turner: *Private Dancer* (Capitol)
Teddy Pendergrass: *Greatest Hits* (Philadelphia International)
Julie Brown: *Goddess in Progress* (Rhino)
That's the Way I Feel Now: A Tribute to Thelonious Monk (A&M)
Dumptruck: *D Is for Dumptruck* (Incas)
Motorhead: *No Remorse* (Bronze)
The Embarrassment: *Retrospective* (Fresh Sounds)
Robert Wyatt: *1982–1984* (Rough Trade)
Meat Puppets: *Meat Puppets II* (SST)
Herbie Hancock: *Sound-System* (Columbia)
The Reducers: *Let's Go!* (Rave On)
Conjure (American Clavé)
Rank and File: *Long Gone Dead* (Slash)
The Neville Brothers: *Neville-ization* (Black Top)
John Conlee: *Greatest Hits* (MCA)
Robert Quine/Fred Maher: *Basic* (Editions EG)
Blow-Up: *Easy Knowledge* (Polar)
Harold Budd/Brian Eno: *The Pearl* (Editions EG)
UB40: *Geffery Morgan* (A&M)
The Judds: *Wynonna and Naomi* (RCA Victor)
Iggy Pop: *Choice Cuts* (RCA Victor)
Fat Boys: *Fat Boys* (Sutra)
Go-Go's: *Talk Show* (I.R.S.)

1985 (57)

Franco & Rochereau: *Omona Wapi* (Shanachie)
Double Dee & Steinski: *The Payoff Mix/Lesson Two/Lesson 3* (Tommy Boy)
Mekons: *Fear and Whiskey* (Sin import)
The Pogues: *Rum Sodomy and the Lash* (Stiff import)
Aretha Franklin: *Who's Zoomin' Who?* (Arista)
Hüsker Dü: *New Day Rising* (SST)
Lost in the Stars: The Music of Kurt Weill (A&M)
The Velvet Underground: *VU* (Verve)
The Blasters: *Hard Line* (Slash)
Willie Nelson & Hank Snow: *Brand on My Heart* (Columbia)
Talking Heads: *Little Creatures* (Sire)
Minutemen: *3-Way Tie for Last* (SST)
Linton Kwesi Johnson: *In Concert With the Dub Band* (Shanachie)
The Replacements: *Tim* (Sire)
Go Go Crankin' (4th & B'way)

Dele Abiodun: *It's Time for Juju Music* (Super Adawa import)

Joe Higgs: *Triumph* (Alligator)

Scritti Politti: *Cupid & Psyche 85* (Warner Bros.)

Dele Abiodun: *Adawa Super Sound* (Shanachie)

Dramarama: *Cinéma Verité* (New Rose import)

Professor Longhair: *Rock 'n' Roll Gumbo* (Dancing Cat)

Yabby You: *Fleeing From the City* (Shanachie)

The Dead Milkmen: *Big Lizard in My Backyard* (Fever)

Rosanne Cash: *Rhythm and Romance* (Columbia)

Hüsker Dü: *Flip Your Wig* (SST)

George Clinton: *Some of My Best Jokes Are Friends* (Capitol)

The Descendents: *Bonus Fat* (SST)

The Go-Betweens: *Metal and Shells* (PVC)

The Robert Cray Band: *False Accusations* (Hightone)

Billy Joel: *Greatest Hits: Volumes I & II* (Columbia)

Marti Jones: *Unsophisticated Time* (A&M)

Katrina and the Waves: *Katrina and the Waves* (Capitol)

The Cars: *Greatest Hits* (Elektra)

UB40: *Little Baggariddim* (A&M)

Elvis Costello and the Attractions: *The Best of Elvis Costello and the Attractions* (Columbia)

George Strait: *Greatest Hits* (MCA)

Camper Van Beethoven: *Telephone Free Landslide Victory* (Independent Project)

Steve Arrington: *Dancin' in the Key of Life* (Atlantic)

Kid Creole and the Coconuts: *In Praise of Older Women and Other Crimes* (Sire)

Marshall Crenshaw: *Downtown* (Warner Bros.)

Phranc: *Folksinger* (Rhino)

Willie Nelson: *Me and Paul* (Columbia)

Fela Anikulapo Kuti: *Army Arrangement* (Celluloid)

John Anderson: *Tokyo, Oklahoma* (Warner Bros.)

Mofungo: *Frederick Douglass* (Coyote/Twin/Tone)

Nile Rodgers: *B-Movie Matinee* (Warner Bros.)

Alex Chilton: *Feudalist Tarts* (Big Time)

The Rattlers: *Rattled* (PVC)

Phezulu Eqhudeni (Carthage)

Artists United Against Apartheid: *Sun City* (Manhattan)

George Strait: *Something Special* (MCA)

Rubén Blades y Seis del Solar: *Escenas* (Elektra)

David Byrne: *Music for the Knee Plays* (ECM)

Ras Michael & the Sons of Negus: *Rally Round* (Shanachie)

The Silos: *About Her Steps* (Record Collect)

The Rave-Ups: *Town and Country* (Fun Stuff)

Ladysmith Black Mambazo: *Ulwandle Oluncgwele* (Shanachie)

1986 (79)

The Indestructible Beat of Soweto (Shanachie)
The Robert Cray Band: *Strong Persuader* (Mercury)
Beastie Boys: *Licensed To Ill* (Def Jam)
Hüsker Dü: *Candy Apple Grey* (Warner Bros.)
Papa Wemba: *L'Esclave* (Gitta import)
New Order: *Brotherhood* (Qwest)
Sonny Sharrock: *Guitar* (Enemy)
Rolling Stones: *Dirty Work* (Rolling Stones)
Pat Metheny/Ornette Coleman: *Song X* (Geffen)
Camper Van Beethoven: *Camper Van Beethoven* (Pitch-a-Tent)
Black Flag: *Wasted Again* (SST)
Gap Band: *The 12″ Collection* (Mercury)
Z.Z. Hill: *Greatest Hits* (Malaco)
Paul Simon: *Graceland* (Warner Bros.)
Motorhead: *Orgasmatron* (GWR/Profile)
Pere Ubu: *Terminal Tower: An Archival Collection* (Twin/Tone)
Sonic Youth: *Starpower* (SST)
Elvis Costello and the Attractions: *Blood and Chocolate* (Columbia)
Mekons: *The Edge of the World* (Sin import)
Mutabaruka: *The Mystery Unfolds* (Shanachie)
They Might Be Giants: *They Might Be Giants* (Bar/None)
The Jesus and Mary Chain: *Psychocandy* (Reprise)
The Costello Show (Featuring Elvis Costello): *King of America* (Columbia)
Royal Crescent Mob: *Land of Sugar* (No Other)
The Neville Brothers: *Treacherous* (Rhino)
Astor Piazzolla: *Tango: Zero Hour* (American Clavé)
Run-D.M.C.: *Raising Hell* (Profile)
The Housemartins: *London 0, Hull 4* (Elektra)
XTC: *Skylarking* (Geffen)
Steve Earle: *Guitar Town* (MCA)
Rap's Greatest Hits (Priority)
Will Wright & Jim Reiman: *Childhood's Greatest Hits* (Rooster)
The Lounge Lizards: *Live in Tokyo/Big Heart* (Island)
Kate Bush: *The Whole Story* (EMI Manhattan)
Ornette Coleman and Prime Time: *Opening the Caravan of Dreams* (Caravan of Dreams)
Mekons: *Crime and Punishment* (Sin import)
The Feelies: *The Good Earth* (Coyote)
Jimi Hendrix: *Band of Gypsys 2* (Capitol)
Brian Eno: *More Blank Than Frank* (EG)
Mofungo: *Messenger Dogs of the Gods* (Lost)
Salt-n-Pepa: *Hot, Cool and Vicious* (Next Plateau)
African Head Charge: *Off the Beaten Track* (On-U Sound import)
Phil Alvin: *Un "Sung" Stories* (Slash)
Abdullah Ibrahim: *Water From an Ancient Well* (Landmark)
Bruce Springsteen & the E Street Band: *Live 1975–1985* (Columbia)
Peter Stampfel and the Bottle Caps: *Peter Stampfel and the Bottle Caps* (Rounder)
Prince and the Revolution: *Parade* (Paisley Park)

Stevie Ray Vaughan and Double Trouble: *Live Alive* (Epic)
Afrika Bambaataa & Soulsonic Force: *Planet Rock—The Album* (Tommy Boy)
Tango Argentino (Atlantic)
Camper Van Beethoven: *II & III* (Pitch-a-Tent)
Jimi Hendrix: *Johnny B. Goode* (Capitol)
The Art of Noise: *In Visible Silence* (Chrysalis)
Thomas Mapfumo: *The Chimurenga Singles 1976–1980* (Meadowlark)
Warren Zevon: *A Quiet Normal Life: The Best of Warren Zevon* (Asylum)
Shop Assistants: *Shop Assistants* (53rd & 3rd import)
Jon Hassell: *Power Spot* (ECM import)
The Police: *Every Breath You Take: The Singles* (A&M)
Katrina and the Waves: *Waves* (Capitol)
That Petrol Emotion: *Manic Pop Thrill* (Demon import)
Black Flag: *Who's Got the 10½?* (SST)
Dance Traxx (Atlantic)
The Three Johns: *The World by Storm* (Abstract import)
The Go-Betweens: *Liberty Belle and the Black Diamond Express* (Big Time)
Aaron Neville: *Make Me Strong* (Charly import)
Timbuk 3: *Welcome to Timbuk 3* (I.R.S)
Don Dixon: *Most of the Girls Like To Dance but Only Some of the Boys Like To* (Enigma)
David & David: *Boomtown* (A&M)
New Model Army: *The Mark of Cain* (Capitol)
Laurie Anderson: *Home of the Brave* (Warner Bros.)
The Velvet Underground: *Another View* (Verve)
Marvin Gaye: *Motown Remembers Marvin Gaye* (Tamla)
Ladysmith Black Mambazo: *Inala* (Shanachie)
Mahotella Queens: *Izibani Zomgqashiyo* (Shanachie)
Yaa-Lengi Ngemi: *Oh, Miziki* (MiyeMi)
Pet Shop Boys: *Please* (EMI America)
Iscathamiya: Zulu Worker Choirs in South Africa (Heritage import)
Zazou Bikaye: *Mr. Manager* (Pow Wow)
Sally Timms and the Drifting Cowgirls: *The Butcher's Boy Extended Player* (T.I.M.S.
  International import)

1987 (63)

Sonny Rollins: *G-Man* (Milestone)
Prince: *Sign 'O' the Times* (Paisley Park)
Culture: *Two Sevens Clash* (Shanachie)
Ornette Coleman: *In All Languages* (Caravan of Dreams)
Sonic Youth: *Sister* (SST)
New Order: *Substance* (Qwest)
Pretenders: *The Singles* (Sire)
Sly & Robbie: *Rhythm Killers* (Mango)
The Sonny Sharrock Band: *Seize the Rainbow* (Enemy)
R.E.M.: *Document* (I.R.S.)
Bruce Springsteen: *Tunnel of Love* (Columbia)
Go-Betweens: *Tallulah* (Big Time)

The Jimi Hendrix Experience: *Live at Winterland* (Rykodisc)
Ian Dury: *Sex & Drugs & Rock & Roll* (Demon import)
The Angry Samoans: *Gimme Samoa: 31 Garbage-Pit Hits* (PVC)
Professor Longhair:. *Houseparty New Orleans Style* (Rounder)
Pet Shop Boys: *Pet Shop Boys, Actually* (EMI-Manhattan)
Dramarama: *Box Office Bomb* (Questionmark)
Stella Chiweshe: *Ambuya?* (GlobeStyle import)
The Replacements: *Pleased To Meet Me* (Sire)
The Tanzania Sound (Original Sound)
Kool Moe Dee: *How Ya Like Me Now?* (Jive)
Johnny Cash: *Columbia Records 1958–1986* (Columbia)
Marianne Faithfull: *Strange Weather* (Island)
Madonna: *You Can Dance* (Sire)
Kool Moe Dee: *Kool Moe Dee* (Jive)
Rosanne Cash: *King's Record Shop* (Columbia)
Reba McEntire: *The Best of Reba McEntire* (MCA)
Stevie Wonder: *Characters* (Motown)
John Cougar Mellencamp: *The Lonesome Jubilee* (Mercury)
The Housemartins: *The People Who Grinned Themselves to Death* (Elektra)
Tom Verlaine: *Flash Light* (I.R.S.)
Great Plains: *Sum Things Up* (Homestead)
French Frith Kaiser Thompson: *Live, Love, Larf and Loaf* (Rhino)
David Behrman: *Leapday Night* (Lovely Music)
That Petrol Emotion: *Babble* (Mercury)
Ray Stevens: *Greatest Hits Vol. 2* (MCA)
The Cucumbers: *The Cucumbers* (Profile)
Culture: *Culture at Work* (Shanachie)
A Flock of Seagulls: *The Best of a Flock of Seagulls* (Jive)
Ronald Shannon Jackson and the Decoding Society: *When Colors Play* (Caravan of
    Dreams)
Minutemen: *Ballot Result* (SST)
Rosie Flores: *Rosie Flores* (Reprise)
Motorhead: *Rock 'n' Roll* (Enigma/GWR)
A Very Special Christmas (A&M)
Bunny Wailer: *Rootsman Skanking* (Shanachie)
Kid Creole and the Coconuts: *I, Too, Have Seen the Woods* (Sire)
Mekons: *New York* (ROIR)
Warren Zevon: *Sentimental Hygiene* (Virgin)
Marshall Chapman: *Dirty Linen* (Tall Girl/Line import)
Black Uhuru: *Positive* (RAS)
Ladysmith Black Mambazo: *Shaka Zulu* (Warner Bros.)
Sinéad O'Connor: *The Lion and the Cobra* (Chrysalis)
Fat Boys: *The Best Part of the Fat Boys* (Sutra)
Meat Puppets: *Huevos* (SST)
Big Black: *Songs About Fucking* (Touch and Go)
Tom Robinson: *The Collection 1977–87* (EMI import)
Al Green: *Soul Survivor* (A&M)
Camper Van Beethoven: *Vampire Can Mating Oven* (Pitch-a-Tent)
Reggae Dance Hall Classics (Sleeping Bag)

Hüsker Dü: *Warehouse: Songs and Stories* (Warner Bros.)
Age of Chance: *Crush Collision* (Virgin))
Aztec Camera: *Love* (Sire)
Los Lobos: *By the Light of the Moon* (Slash)

1988 (64)

Public Enemy: *It Takes a Nation of Millions To Hold Us Back* (Def Jam)
African Connection Vol. I: Zaire Choc! (Celluloid import)
Tom T. Hall: *The Essential Tom T. Hall: Twentieth Anniversary Collection/The Story Songs* (Mercury)
Sonic Youth: *Daydream Nation* (Enigma/Blast First)
Mahlathini & Mahotella Queens: *Paris-Soweto* (Celluloid import)
The Heartbeat of Soweto (Shanachie)
Lucinda Williams: *Lucinda Williams* (Rough Trade)
Pere Ubu: *The Tenement Year* (Enigma)
The Psychedelic Furs: *All of This and Nothing* (Columbia)
Ambitious Lovers: *Greed* (Virgin)
Ornette Coleman and Prime Time: *Virgin Beauty* (Portrait)
The Flying Burrito Brothers: *Farther Along: The Best of the Flying Burrito Brothers* (A&M)
Pet Shop Boys: *Introspective* (EMI-Manhattan)
Zani Diabate & the Super Djata Band: *Zani Diabate & the Super Djata Band* (Mango)
Bhundu Boys: *Tsvimbodzemoto: Sticks of Fire* (Hannibal)
Patsy Cline: *Live at the Opry* (MCA)
The Robert Cray Band: *Don't Be Afraid of the Dark* (Mercury)
Folkways: A Vision Shared—A Tribute to Woody Guthrie and Leadbelly (Columbia)
EPMD: *Strictly Business* (Fresh)
Feedtime: *Shovel* (Rough Trade)
Zimbabwe Frontline (Virgin)
Michelle Shocked: *Short Sharp Shocked* (Mercury)
Najma: *Qareeb* (Shanachie)
Leonard Cohen: *I'm Your Man* (Columbia)
Eric B. & Rakim: *Follow the Leader* (Uni)
Traveling Wilburys: *Volume One* (Wilbury)
Guy: *Guy* (MCA)
Richard Thompson: *Amnesia* (Capitol)
Obed Ngobeni: *My Wife Bought a Taxi* (Shanachie)
Was (Not Was): *What Up, Dog?* (Chrysalis)
Jungle Brothers: *Straight Out the Jungle* (Idlers)
James Brown: *Motherlode* (Polydor)
Flipper: *Sex Bomb Baby!* (Subterranean)
Gilberto Gil: *Soy Loco Por Ti America* (Braziloid)
Earth, Wind & Fire: *The Best of Earth, Wind & Fire Vol. II* (Columbia)
R.E.M.: *Eponymous* (I.R.S.)
Miriam Makeba: *Sangoma* (Warner Bros.)
Womack & Womack: *Conscience* (Island)
Buzzcocks: *Lest We Forget* (ROIR)

Heartbeat Soukous (Earthworks/Virgin)

Motorhead: *No Sleep at All* (Enigma/GWR)

Mory Kante: *Akwaba Beach* (Polydor)

Thunder Before Dawn—The Indestructible Beat of Soweto Volume Two (Earthworks/Virgin)

Prince: *The Black Album* (unlabeled cassette)

Hurricane Zouk (Earthworks/Virgin)

The Go-Betweens: *16 Lovers Lane* (Capitol)

Patti Smith: *Dream of Life* (Arista)

The Chills: *Brave Words* (Homestead)

Too Much Joy: *Son of Sam I Am* (Alias)

The Jimi Hendrix Experience: *Radio One* (Rykodisc)

Steve Jordan: *The Return of El Parche* (Rounder)

Astor Piazzolla: *The Rough Dancer and the Cyclical Night* (American Clavé)

Joe Louis Walker: *The Gift* (Hightone)

Mahlathini and the Mahotella Queens: *Thokozile* (Virgin)

Dag Nasty: *Field Day* (Giant)

The Fall: *I Am Kurious Oranj* (Beggars Banquet)

The Real Roxanne: *The Real Roxanne* (Select)

Mr. Magic's Rap Attack Volume 4 (Profile)

Randy Travis: *Old 8×10* (Warner Bros.)

Voice of the Beehive: *Let It Bee* (London)

Bootsy Collins: *What's Bootsy Doin'?* (Columbia)

Soul Brothers: *Jive Explosion* (Virgin)

Maroon: *The Funky Record* (Arb Recordings)

Mofungo: *Bugged* (SST)

1989 (70)

The Mekons: *The Mekons Rock 'n' Roll* (A&M)

Neil Young: *Freedom* (Reprise)

Laurie Anderson: *Strange Angels* (Warner Bros.)

Beastie Boys: *Paul's Boutique* (Capitol)

Remmy Ongala and Orchestre Super Matimila: *Songs for the Poor Man* (Real World)

Jungle Brothers: *Done by the Forces of Nature* (Warner Bros.)

Mekons: *Original Sin* (Twin/Tone)

Pere Ubu: *Cloudland* (Fontana)

The Neville Brothers: *Yellow Moon* (A&M)

Wire: *On Returning (1977–1979)* (Restless Retro)

De La Soul: *3 Feet High and Rising* (Tommy Boy)

The Kampala Sound (Original Music)

George Clinton: *The Cinderella Theory* (Paisley Park/Warner Bros.)

Marshall Crenshaw: *Good Evening* (Warner Bros.)

Los Van Van: *Songo* (Mango)

Cheb Khaled/Safy Boutella: *Kutché* (Capitol/Intuition)

Boulevard of Broken Dreams: *It's the Talk of the Town and Other Sad Songs* (Hannibal)

Terence Trent D'Arby: *Neither Fish Nor Flesh* (Columbia)

Pylon: *Hits* (DB)

The Roches: *Speak* (MCA)

Neneh Cherry: *Raw Like Sushi* (Virgin)
Rosanne Cash: *Hits 1979–1989* (Columbia)
Negativland: *Helter Stupid* (SST)
The Lounge Lizards: *Voice of Chunk* (1-800-44CHUNK)
Alexander O'Neal: *All Mixed Up* (Tabu)
E.U.: *Livin' Large* (Virgin)
3rd Bass: *The Cactus Album* (Def Jam)
Van Morrison: *Avalon Sunset* (Mercury)
Chaba Fadela: *You Are Mine* (Mango)
Janet Jackson: *Rhythm Nation 1814* (A&M)
Yo! MTV Raps (Jive)
Fine Young Cannibals: *The Raw and the Cooked* (I.R.S.)
Diblo: *Super Soukous* (Shanachie)
Al Green: *Love Ritual: Rare and Previously Unreleased 1968–1976* (MCA)
Nick Lowe: *Basher: The Best of Nick Lowe* (Columbia)
Black Havana (Capitol)
Tabu Ley: *Babeti Soukous* (Real World)
Konbit!: Burning Rhythms of Haiti (A&M)
L.L. Cool J: *Walking With a Panther* (Def Jam)
Baaba Maal and Mansour Seck: *Djam Leelii* (Mango)
Nuestras Mejores Cumbias (Globo)
Roxanne Shanté: *Bad Sister* (Cold Chillin')
Royal Crescent Mob: *Spin the World* (Sire)
Culture: *Cumbolo* (Shanachie)
Technotronic: *Pump Up the Jam: The Album* (SBK)
Yo La Tengo: *President Yo La Tengo* (Coyote)
The African Typic Collection (Virgin)
Luther Vandross: *The Best of Luther Vandross . . . The Best of Love* (Epic)
Jimmie Dale Gilmore: *Jimmie Dale Gilmore* (Hightone)
Thomas Mapfumo: *Corruption* (Mango)
Thelonious Monster: *Stormy Weather* (Relativity)
Stevie Ray Vaughan and Double Trouble: *In Step* (Epic)
Dwight Yoakam: *Just Lookin' for a Hit* (Reprise)
Alpha Blondy: *Revolution* (Shanachie)
Daniel Owino Misiani and Shirati Band: *Benga Blast!* (Virgin)
Keith Whitley: *I Wonder Do You Think of Me* (RCA)
Queen Latifah: *All Hail the Queen* (Tommy Boy)
The Jayhawks: *Blue Earth* (Twin/Tone)
Pointer Sisters: *Greatest Hits* (RCA)
Ice-T: *The Iceberg: Freedom of Speech . . . Just Watch What You Say* (Sire)
Jerry Lee Lewis: *Rockin' My Life Away* (Tomato)
Meat Puppets: *Monsters* (SST)
Lou Reed: *New York* (Sire)
Zetrospective: Dancing in the Face of Adversity (ZE)
Mofungo: *Work* (SST)
Ernest Tubb: *Live, 1965* (Rhino)
Dancehall Stylee: The Best of Reggae Dancehall Music Vol 1 (Profile)
Clint Black: *Killin' Time* (RCA)
Mojo Nixon and Skid Roper: *Root Hog or Die* (Enigma)

GLOSSARY

A&R: literally, artists-and-repertoire; loosely, any record company–employed label-artist liaison

Afrobeat: specifically, Fela's jazz- and rock-influenced extension of Nigerian highlife; sometimes used to point vaguely in the direction of all rockish African pop

Amerindie: short for American independent, designating the network of "alternative" labels, clubs, stores, and radio outlets that developed in the U.S. postpunk

AOR: album-oriented rock, the culturally conservative, arena-rock-oriented radio format that happened to the "progressive" FM of the '60s after radio formatters got hold of it

b.p.m.: beats per minute, a measure of decisive significance to dance DJs since the rationalization of disco in the middle '70s

B-boy: the quintessential rap fan; though it originally designated a teenager adhering to a New York street style of sweatshirts and unlaced sneakers, it's now used to categorize any young black male thought to be of juvenile-delinquent mien

boite: *club intime*

CHR: Contemporary Hits Radio, a face-saving moniker devised for top 40 after top 40 was declared dead by radio savants

CMA: Nashville-based Country Music Association, which gives out awards of the same initials

comp: jazz slang for accompany, often with harmonically acute, rhythmically disquieting piano chords

countrypolitan: early Nashville crossover concept, usually distinguished by genteel diction, nonspecific subject matter, hosts of glee clubs, and lotsa strings

cover: newly recorded version of a known (or at least previously available) song

crossover: originally devised to describe movement from the black charts to the pop charts, it now designates any record that gets its start in a specialized market and then goes pop

cuatro: small Puerto Rican guitar with five double-stringed courses

dance hall: energetic, electronic, and escapist '80s reggae style

dis: hip hop slang for put down, insult (from "disrespect")

DIY: do-it-yourself (title of a 1978 Peter Gabriel song)

DMSR: Prince's abbreviation for dance-music-sex-romance

DOR: dance-oriented rock, a euphemistic acronym concocted to signify a nonlovydovy disco-punk fusion—disco white bohemians would dance to

dub: in reggae, a spare, spacy "version"; essentially a new piece of music derived from a few selected elements—bass lines, keyboard fragments, vocal phrases—of the original

forcebeat: John Piccarella coinage designating the ideal punk rhythm, which might be described as a flat four-four that moves faster than your body thinks it should

go go: D.C.-based funk-r&b fusion characterized by an unusually swinging dance rhythm and, sometimes, rap or rap-influenced vocals

hardcore: very fast, militantly antisocial punk variant that began in L.A. and D.C. in the late '70s

harmolodic: Ornette Coleman's name for his musical theory; some believe even he doesn't understand it; many believe they recognize it when they hear it regardless

highlife: Ghanaian pop style, vaguely big-bandish in its mature phase, that dominated Afropop before Zaire took over

hip hop: rap culture, especially rap dance culture

honky-tonk: hard, electrified country style that began in the Texas joints of the '30s and was disseminated by Ernest Tubb a decade later

hook: something that makes you remember a song, often inserted to just that end

ital: Rastafarian patois for healthy or natural (from "vital")

Jah: Rastafarian name for God

keyb: abbreviation for keyboard that became common in album credits at around the time keyboardists started deploying arsenals of synthesizers

kora: twenty-one-stringed West African harp-lute

kwassa kwassa: fast, simple soukous variant

legato: smooth and unbroken

lovers rock: romantic reggae of the early '80s

mbalax: Senegalese genre identified with Youssou N'Dour

mbaqanga: the r&b-ish urban-traditional hybrid that has been the South African townships' dominant indigenous pop since the '60s (literally, Zulu for cornbread)

mbira: Southern African thumb piano

mbube: South African choral singing style best-known via Ladysmith Black Mambazo's iscathamiya variant

MOR: literally, middle-of-the-road; applied to radio formats that shun or put stringent tempo and volume restrictions on rock, although "lite" and "adult contemporary" are now the preferred evasions

NARAS: National Academy of Recording Arts and Sciences, which has handed out Grammies since 1958

new age: vague catchall encompassing pretentious, lulling instrumental background music with roots in jazz, folk, or classical, even rock, or very commonly some combination of two or more—but not in so-called "beautiful music" pop

new jack: the slicker, more affluent and gangster-minded black street style that succeeded B-boy culture, associated with a more tuneful version of hip hop

new thing: '60s "free jazz"

new wave: a polite term devised to reassure people who were scared by punk, it enjoyed a two- or three-year run but was falling from favor as the '80s began

NME: *New Musical Express,* once the dominant and most intellectual British music weekly

norteño: very Hispanic, often ballad-based Tex-Mex style from Rio Grande country

obbligato: persistent background motif

oi: martial-sounding football-cheer punk favored by a subculture of working-class British males at the turn of the decade

ostinato: recurring melodic fragment, invariably on some sort of keyb—a device whose rhythmic potential was exploited by art-rockers into a humongous rock cliché

outgroove: the empty groove at the end of a record

outro: opposite of intro—sometimes faded, sometimes not

overdisc: on the other side of the record (my coinage, from "overleaf")

PMRC: Parents' Music Resource Center, which spearheaded the rock censorship drive of the late '80s

polyrhythm: rhythm laid on top of (or beneath) a related or contrasting rhythm (or rhythms)

positivity: jargon word that arose in the black pop of the '70s to designate what Bad Brains later dubbed PMA, for positive mental attitude; the usual combination of optimism and will

postpunk: literally, after punk (no shit, Sherlock); used as loosely as "postmodern" to indicate all the alternative musical directions that became possible after punk opened things up

power pop: term devised to encompass the fast, beaty, but tune-oriented bands who came to prominence in the wake of punk

pub-rock: a prepunk U.K. predecessor of roots-rock, it exploited rockabilly, r&b, and straight pre-Beatles rock and roll rather than blues or country

rai: Algerian pop-rock style usually featuring male singers improvising lyrics over electrified studio accompaniment

r&b: rhythm-and-blues; usually designates the black rock and roll preceding soul music, though it's sometimes extended to mean all post-'50s black pop

Rastafarian: adherent of antihierarchichal Jamaican religion emphasizing social separatism, African return, dreadlocks, and the divinity of Haile Selassie (a/k/a Ras Tafari)

rave-up: all the guitars making climactic noise at once, sometimes for an entire song

readymade: by Richard Meltzer out of Marcel Duchamp, a coinage designating any musical device ripe for transplant to another context

RIAA: the Recording Industry Association of America, which certifies gold and platinum albums and led the war against home taping

rumba: Cuban-influenced Zairean style that generated soukous

salsa: Afro-Cuban style developed in New York's Puerto Rican community in the '40s and then reinterpreted all over the Caribbean

salsero: male salsa singer (they're almost all male)

sanza: African thumb piano of many names, the most common of which is currently "mbira"

scratching: rap rhythmic effect achieved by pulling a spinning record manually back and forth under the needle

semipopular: my coinage for music that is popular in form but not fact—self-consciously arty music that plays off popular or formerly popular usages but isn't (supposedly) designed to sell; most postpunk is quintessentially semipopular

shakuhachi: Japanese bamboo flute of mellow, resonant tone

ska: the fast, jumpy, surprisingly polkalike Jamaican pop that preceded rocksteady and reggae

skank: move to ska or reggae; boogie, Jamaican-style

skronk: onomatopoiea for ugly no wave noise music

soukous: Zairean style generally regarded as roughening and simplifying the rumba that preceded it; polyrhythmic, with bipartite song structures and a distinctive chattering or billowing guitar sound, it has dominated popular music in black Africa for two decades

tipico: Spanish term somewhere between "traditional" and "characteristic of the culture"; echt

urban contemporary: euphemism devised for black music and especially radio to allay the fears of radio savants that white people (and for that matter upwardly mobile black people) wouldn't listen to it if you called it black

vamp: play the same simple succession of chords over and over, rhythmically if possible

vocoder: synthesizer that makes a voice sound like it's calling in from Venus

Western swing: country style melding swing usages into traditional fiddle-based dance music, identified with Bob Wills and His Texas Playboys

CREDITS

About a sixth of the reviews in this book are previously unpublished, as are all of the appendices. The introduction and the rest of the reviews are based (often verbatim, but sometimes very generally) on Consumer Guides and other pieces written for *The Village Voice* between 1980 and 1990, plus auxiliary material—in all but a few cases sentences or phrases—written for *Playboy* between 1985 and 1990 and (with my collaborator Carola Dibbell) for *Video Review* between 1982 and 1990. Citing the source or sources for each of approximately 3,000 reviews would obviously be impossibly unwieldy, but I would like to gratefully acknowledge permission from the *Voice, Playboy,* and *Video Review* to reprint writing that originally appeared in their pages.

Born in New York City in 1942, **Robert Christgau** began writing rock criticism for *Esquire* in 1967. He became a columnist for the *Village Voice* in 1969, and, after two years at *Newsday,* returned to the *Voice* as an editor and columnist in 1974. He has taught at the California Institute of the Arts, City University of New York, the Massachusettes Institute of Technology, and New York University and appears regularly in *Video Review* and *Playboy.* In 1987 he won a Guggenheim Fellowship to study the history of popular music. He lives in Manhattan with his wife and daughter.